Strong foundations

Early childhood care and education

Strong foundations

Early childhood care and education

UNESCO Publishing

The analysis and policy recommendations of this Report do not necessarily reflect the views of UNESCO. The Report is an independent publication commissioned by UNESCO on behalf of the international community. It is the product of a collaborative effort involving members of the Report Team and many other people, agencies, institutions and governments. Overall responsibility for the views and opinions expressed in the Report is taken by its Director.

The designations employed and the presentation of the material in this publication do not imply the expression of any opinion whatsoever on the part of UNESCO concerning the legal status of any country, territory, city or area, or of its authorities, or concerning the delimitation of its frontiers or boundaries.

Published in 2006 by the United Nations Educational, Scientific and Cultural Organization
7, Place de Fontenoy, 75352 Paris 07 SP, France

Graphic design by Sylvaine Baeyens
Iconographer: Delphine Gaillard
Layout: Sylvaine Baeyens and Hélène Borel
Printed by Graphoprint, Paris
ISBN 978-92-3-104041-2

Foreword

The Education for All goals focus on the need to provide learning opportunities at every stage in life, from infancy to adulthood. With only nine years remaining before 2015 – the target year for achieving these goals – we must not lose sight of this agenda's profoundly just and comprehensive perspective on education.

Tackling disadvantage and setting strong foundations for learning begins in the earliest years through adequate health, nutrition, care and stimulation. The 1989 United Nations Convention on the Rights of the Child, ratified by 192 nations, guarantees the rights of young children to survive, develop and be protected. However, many children are deprived of these rights.

This fifth edition of the *EFA Global Monitoring Report* assesses progress towards the first EFA goal, which calls upon countries to expand and improve comprehensive early childhood care and education, especially for the most disadvantaged children. Such interventions are crucial to improving children's present well-being and future development.

Yet the evidence suggests that young children in greatest need, who also stand to gain the most, are unlikely to have access to these programmes. Coverage remains very low in most of the developing world and few programmes exist for children under age 3. Even in the context of limited public resources, designing national policies for early childhood carries benefits for the country's entire education system. It is therefore vital that countries and the international community systematically make early childhood provision an integral component of their education and poverty alleviation strategies. This is essential for reducing extreme poverty and hunger, the overarching aim of the United Nations Millennium Development Goals.

A tone of urgency pervades this Report. While regions farthest from the goals are making impressive progress on enrolling new children into primary school, major challenges remain. Policies must address the barriers to education: household poverty, rural locations, poor quality, and lack of secondary schools and trained teachers, and not enough adult literacy programmes.

As the lead agency for coordinating EFA, UNESCO carries a particular responsibility for placing EFA at the forefront of national and international agendas. There are promising signs: aid to basic education is increasing and leaders at the G8 Summit in Saint Petersburg in 2006 affirmed the fundamental importance of Education for All as a contributor to national development and peace.

The findings of the 2007 *EFA Global Monitoring Report* remind us there is no place for complacency. We have a collective responsibility to ensure quality education for all, a responsibility that begins by providing strong foundations for children in the first years of life and continues through adulthood. Only by taking a comprehensive approach that encompasses all the EFA goals and society's most fragile and vulnerable members can this mission be honoured.

Koïchiro Matsuura

Acknowledgements

At UNESCO, we are indebted to Peter Smith, Assistant Director-General for Education, to Abhimanhyu Singh, former Director of the Division of International Coordination and Monitoring for Education for All, and Mark Richmond, Acting Director of the Division for the Coordination of UN Priorities in Education, and their colleagues for their support.

The Report's international Editorial Board and its chairman Ingemar Gustafsson provided much valuable advice and support. Consultations on the outline of the Report (online and among UNESCO colleagues) strengthened the thematic part of the report.

The EFA Report depends greatly on the work of the UNESCO Institute for Statistics. Director Hendrik van der Pol, former Director a.i. Michael Millward, Said Belkachla, Michael Bruneforth, Simon Ellis, Nadia Ghagi, Monica Githaiga, Alison Kennedy, Albert Motivans, Scott Murray, Juan Cruz Perusia, José Pessoa, Pascale Ratovondrahona, Ioulia Sementchouk, Anuja Singh, Saïd Ould Voffal, and their colleagues contributed significantly, particularly to chapters 2, 3 and 6 and the statistical tables.

Special thanks to all those who prepared background papers, notes and boxes:
Massimo Amadio, Feny de los Angeles Bautista, Caroline Arnold, Clive Belfield, Asher Ben Arieh, Paul Bennel, Tatyana A. Berezina, Jane Bertrand, Ghanem Bibi, Corinne Bitoun, A. Rae Blumberg, Mihail I. Borovkov, Roy Carr-Hill, Bidemi Carrol, Anne-Marie Chartier, Leon Derek Charles, Maysoun Chehab, Carl Corter, Anton De Grauwe, Joseph DeStefano, Tamara Dorabawila, Aline-Wendy Dunlop, Ana Patricia Elvir, Marta Encinas-Martin, Patrice Engle, Judith Evans, Hilary Fabian, Celso Luis Asensio Florez, Basma Four, Nicole Geneix, Anuradha Gupta, Youssef Hajjar, Selim Iltus, Indian National Institute of Public Cooperation and Child Development, Zeenat Janmohammed, Matthew Jukes, Haniya Kamel, Sheila B. Kamerman, Henry M. Levin, Edilberto Loaiza, Hugh McLean, Robert Myers, National Institute of Public Cooperation and Child Development, India; Yuko Nonoyama, Nina A. Notkina, Bame Nsamenang, Teresa Osicka, Steve Packer, Marina N. Polyakova, Françoise du Pouget, Fulvia Maria de Barros Mott Rosemberg, Riho Sakurai, Heather Schwartz, Roza M. Sheraizina, Maria S. Taratukhina, Mami Umayahara, Teshome Yizengaw, Asunción Valderrama, Peter Wallet, Sian Williams, Annababette Wils, Martin Woodhead, Robert Youdi, Aigli Zafeirakou and Jing Zhang.

We thank the Bernard van Leer Foundation, Save the Children USA and UNICEF New York for their support of background papers related to early childhood issues.

The background papers and a summary of discussions from Comments from the online consultation and the background papers can be viewed at www.efareport.unesco.org

The Report also benefited considerably from the advice and support of individuals, Divisions and Units within UNESCO's Education Sector, the International Institute for Educational Planning, the International Bureau of Education and the UNESCO Institute for Lifelong Learning. UNESCO's Regional Bureaux provided helpful advice on country-level activities and and on the draft outline for the thematic part of the Report, and helped facilitate commissioned studies. Soo-Hyang Choi, Yoshie Kaga and Hye-Jin Park within UNESCO's Education Sector provided strong guidance on the special theme.

We are grateful to Rosemary Bellew, Desmond Bermingham, Luc-Charles Gacougnolle and Robert Prouty in the Fast-Track Initiative secretariat, and to Julia Benn, Valérie Gaveau and Simon Scott in OECD/DAC for their continuing support and helpful advice on international cooperation and aid data, as well as to George Ingram and his colleagues in the Education Policy and Data Center at the Academy for Educational Development.

A number of individuals also contributed valuable advice and comments. These were: Frances Aboud, Carlos Aggio, Albert Kwame Akyeampong, Caroline Arnold, Kathy Bartlett, Ellen Buchwalter, Charlotte Cole, Patrice Engle, Stella Etse, Gabi Fujimoto, Deepak Grover, Joshie Kaga, Sarah Klaus, Robert Knezevic, Leslie Limage, Joan Lombardi, Lisa Long, Robert Myers, Pauline Rose, Sheldon Schaeffer, Nurper Ulkuer, Emily Vargas-Barón, Jeannette Vogelaar, Jim Wile, Diane Wroge, Minja Yang, Akemi Yonemura and Mary Eming Young.

Throughout the research and drafting process, we benefited from the expertise of the members of the Consultative Group on Early Childhood Care and Development, led by co-chairs Chanel Croker and Louise Zimanyi.

We offer thanks to Stephen Few for his help in streamlining our data-graphics and visual displays of information. Ratko Jancovic and Anais Loizillon assisted with analysis and preparation of graphs and tables.

Special thanks to Lene Buchert, Judith Evans and Steve Packer for their valuable comments on draft chapters.

The production of the Report benefited greatly from the editorial expertise of Rebecca Brite. Wenda McNevin also provided valuable support. We would also like to thank Sue Williams, Enzo Fazzino and Agnes Bardon from the Bureau of Public Information; Anne Muller, Lotfi Ben Khelifa, Fouzia Jouot-Bellami, Judith Roca and their colleagues in the UNESCO Education Documentation Centre, to Chakir Piro, and to Thierry Guednée and Eve-Marie Trastour in the Clearing House Unit for their valuable support and assistance, as well as Richard Cadiou, Fabienne Kouadio and Igor Nuk who facilitated the on-line consultation.

The EFA Global Monitoring Report Team

Director
Nicholas Burnett

Nicole Bella, Aaron Benavot, Fadila Caillaud, Vittoria Cavicchioni, Alison Clayson,
Valérie Djioze, Ana Font-Giner, Catherine Ginisty, Cynthia Guttman, Elizabeth Heen,
Keith Hinchliffe, François Leclercq, Delphine Nsengimana, Banday Nzomini,
Ulrika Peppler Barry, Paula Razquin, Isabelle Reullon, Yusuf Sayed
Alison Kennedy, (UNESCO Institute for Statistics),
Michelle J. Neuman (Special Advisor on Early Childhood Care and Education)

For more information about the Report,
please contact:
The Director
EFA Global Monitoring Report Team
c/o UNESCO
7, place de Fontenoy, 75352 Paris 07 SP, France
e-mail: efareport@unesco.org
Tel.: +33 1 45 68 21 28
Fax: +33 1 45 68 56 27
www.efareport.unesco.org

Previous EFA Global Monitoring Reports
2006. LITERACY FOR LIFE
2005. Education for All – THE QUALITY IMPERATIVE
2003/4. Gender and Education for All – THE LEAP TO EQUALITY
2002. Education for All – IS THE WORLD ON TRACK?

Contents

List of figures, tables and text boxes

Figures

Education for All Global Monitoring Report 2 0 0 7

Tables

Text boxes

Highlights of the EFA Report 2007

Time is running out to meet the EFA goals set in 2000. Despite continued overall global progress at the primary level, including for girls, too many children are not in school, drop out early or do not reach minimal learning standards. By neglecting the connections among early childhood, primary and secondary education and adult literacy, countries are missing opportunities to improve basic education across the board – and, in the process, the prospects of children, youth and adults everywhere.

Progress towards the goals

Primary education continues to expand

Primary school enrolments increased fastest between 1999 and 2004 in two of the three regions furthest from universal primary education: they grew by 27% in sub-Saharan Africa and by 19% in South and West Asia, but by only 6% in the Arab States (see Figure A). The world net enrolment ratio stands at 86%. While grade 1 enrolments rose sharply, too many children who start school still do not reach the last primary grade: fewer than 83% in half the countries of Latin America and the Caribbean with data available, fewer than two-thirds in half the countries of sub-Saharan Africa.

Out-of-school children: how many and who are they?

Progress is being made in reducing the number of primary school-age children who are not enrolled in school. Between 1999 and 2004 the number fell by around 21 million to 77 million. This is still very high, unacceptably so. Sub-Saharan Africa and South and West Asia are home to more than

three-quarters of these children, although the latter region halved its number between 1999 and 2004, mainly due to reductions in India. The global estimate, high though it is, understates the problem: data from household surveys show that many children enrolled in school do not attend regularly.

The children most likely to be out of school and to drop out live in rural areas and come from the poorest households. On average, a child whose mother has no education is twice as likely to be out of school as one whose mother has some education.

Figure A: Net enrolment ratios in primary education, 1999-2004

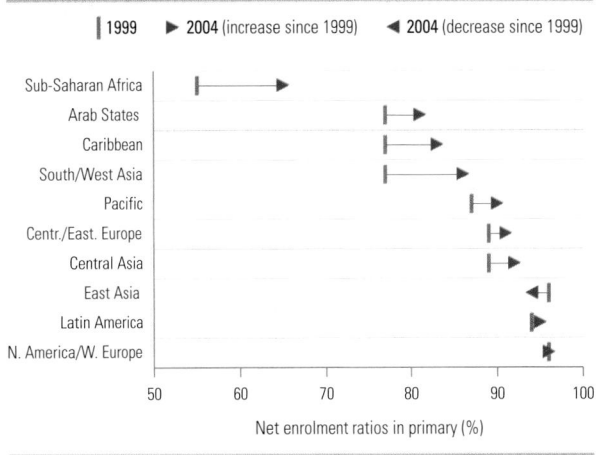

Government policies to tackle exclusion

Governments urgently need to identify the groups of children most likely never to enrol in school, in addition to those who drop out. This is the first step in implementing policies that reach out to the excluded and improve the quality, flexibility and relevance of education.

Among measures to foster inclusion: abolishing school fees, providing income support to poor and rural households to reduce reliance on child labour, teaching in children's mother tongue, offering education opportunities for disabled children and those affected by HIV/AIDS, and ensuring that youth and adults get a second chance at education.

Improving teacher recruitment, training and working conditions

There are not enough qualified and motivated teachers to reach the EFA goals. Sub-Saharan Africa needs to recruit between 2.4 million and 4 million teachers. In this region and in South and West Asia, there are too few women teachers to attract girls to school and retain them. Teacher absenteeism is also a serious problem in many developing countries.

Shorter pre-service training with more on-the-job practice and professional development, and incentives for teachers to work in remote and rural areas, are effective strategies for recruiting and retaining teachers, particularly in difficult contexts.

Secondary education: growing demand and not enough places

The pressure to expand secondary education is rising dramatically. Gross enrolment ratios rose in all developing regions but remain low in sub-Saharan Africa (30%), South and West Asia (51%) and the Arab States (66%).

Low numbers of secondary places slow the achievement of universal primary education because they reduce the incentive to complete primary school. At the same time, increasing demand for secondary education results in competition with other levels for public expenditure.

Gender parity: still not a reality

There are now 94 girls in primary school for every 100 boys, up from 92 in 1999. Of the 181 countries with 2004 data available, about two-thirds have achieved gender parity in primary education. The primary education gender gap in favour of boys has closed in only four of the twenty-six countries that had gross enrolment ratios below 90% in 2000.

Only one-third of the 177 countries with data available on secondary education have achieved parity. At this level disparities are in favour of girls as often as boys. At tertiary level, gender parity exists in only five countries out of 148 with data in 2004. Gender equality also remains an issue, with stereotypes persisting in learning materials and, too often, teachers' expectations of girls and boys differing.

Literacy: an elusive target

Some 781 million adults (one in five worldwide) lack minimum literacy skills. Two-thirds are women. Literacy rates remain low in South and West Asia (59%), sub-Saharan Africa (61%), the Arab States (66%) and the Caribbean (70%). Without concerted efforts to expand adult literacy programmes, by 2015 the global number of adult illiterates will have dropped by only 100 million. Governments must also focus on building literate environments.

Countries in conflict: often missing from the analysis

Data are unavailable for several countries, mostly in conflict or post-conflict situations, and therefore are not fully reflected in the Report's analyses. Their EFA situations remain serious and need to be remembered when considering the global EFA picture. Children living in such circumstances require custom-tailored education opportunities to restore some stability to their lives.

Finance and aid

Domestic spending

on education as a share of GNP decreased between 1999 and 2004 in 41 of the 106 countries with data, though it increased in most of the others. Public spending needs to focus on key requirements for achieving EFA: teachers, adult literacy, ECCE and inclusive policies at all levels.

School fees

were reduced or abolished in several more countries but are still far too common, a major obstacle to the enrolment and continued participation of the poor in primary school.

Total aid to basic education in low-income countries almost doubled between 2000 and 2004 (from US$1.8 billion to US$3.4 billion at 2003 prices), having previously declined. As a share of aid to the whole education sector in low-income countries, however, it remained constant at 54%. Half of all bilateral donors allocate at least half of their education aid to middle-income developing countries, and almost half allocate less than one-quarter directly to basic education.

The Fast Track Initiative provides an important coordinating mechanism for donor agencies but has not yet led to a global compact for achieving universal primary education. Since 2002, disbursements have totalled only US$96 million and so far have only reached eleven countries, though donors have increased their pledges significantly over the past year.

Funding gap: External funding requirements for EFA, including some provision for adult literacy and ECCE, are now estimated at US$11 billion a year, over three times the current level and twice what recently promised increases in overall aid are likely to bring by 2010.

Early childhood care and education

What is it?

- Formal definitions of ECCE vary. This Report adopts a holistic approach: ECCE supports children's survival, growth, development and learning – including health, nutrition and hygiene, and cognitive, social, physical and emotional development – from birth to entry into primary school in formal, informal and non-formal settings.

- ECCE programmes encompass very diverse arrangements, from parenting programmes to community-based child care, centre-based provision and formal pre-primary education, often in schools.

- Programmes typically aim at two age groups: children under 3 and those from age 3 to primary school entry (usually by age 6, always by age 8).

Why does it matter?

- ECCE is a right, recognized in the Convention on the Rights of the Child, which has won near-universal ratification.

- ECCE can improve the well-being of young children, especially in the developing world, where a child has a four in ten chance of living in extreme poverty and 10.5 million children a year die from preventable diseases before age 5.

- Early childhood is a time of remarkable brain development that lays the foundation for later learning.

- ECCE contributes to the other EFA goals (e.g. it improves performance in the first years of primary school) and to the Millennium Development Goals, especially the overarching goal of reducing poverty, as well as the education and health goals.

- It is more cost-effective to institute preventive measures and support for children early on than to compensate for disadvantage as they grow older.

- Affordable, reliable child care provides essential support for working parents, particularly mothers.

- Investment in ECCE yields very high economic returns, offsetting disadvantage and inequality, especially for children from poor families.

What is the situation?

- About 80% of developing countries have some sort of formally established maternity leave, although enforcement varies.

- The youngest children have been neglected. Almost half the world's countries have no formal programmes for children under 3.

- Enrolment in pre-primary education has tripled since 1970, though coverage remains very low in most of the developing world.

- Most OECD countries have at least two years of free pre-primary education.

- Among developing country regions, Latin America, the Caribbean and the Pacific have the highest pre-primary gross enrolment ratios; far behind come East Asia, South and West Asia, the Arab States and sub-Saharan Africa (See Figure B).

- After sharp declines in the 1990s, pre-primary enrolments in transition countries are slowly recovering in Central and Eastern Europe but still lag in Central Asia.

- Among developed and transition countries, and in Latin America, most ECCE provision is by the public sector.

- The private sector is prominent in sub-Saharan Africa, the Arab States, the Caribbean and East Asia.

- Most regions are near gender parity in pre-primary education.

- There are large disparities within countries. With a few notable exceptions, children from poorer and rural households and those socially excluded (e.g. lacking birth certificates) have significantly less access to ECCE than those from richer and urban households.

- The children most likely to benefit from ECCE programmes – those most exposed to malnutrition and preventable diseases – are the least likely to be enrolled.

- ECCE staff in developing countries typically have minimal education and pre-service training, and are often relatively poorly remunerated.

- Governments accord relatively low priority to pre-primary education in their spending. The broad mix of public and private providers and a lack of data make it difficult to calculate total national expenditure on ECCE. Countries can estimate the cost of reaching the goal by developing scenarios that differ in terms of coverage, quality and nature of provision.

- ECCE is not a priority for most donor agencies. Almost all allocate to pre-primary less than 10% of what they give for primary education, and over half allocate less than 2%.

Figure B: Gross enrolment ratios in pre-primary education, 2004

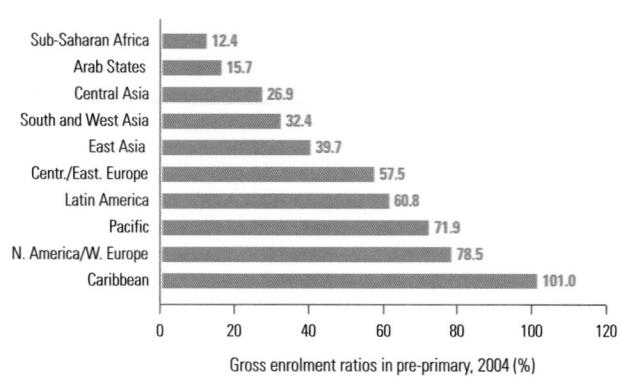

Gross enrolment ratios in pre-primary, 2004 (%)

What programmes work?

■ An approach that combines nutrition, health, care and education is more effective in improving young children's current welfare and their development than limiting interventions to one aspect.

■ Inclusive programmes build on traditional child care practices, respect children's linguistic and cultural diversity, and mainstream children with special educational needs and disabilities.

■ Mother tongue programmes are more effective than those in the official language, which remain the norm around the world.

■ Well-designed programmes can challenge gender stereotypes.

■ The single most important determinant of ECCE quality is interaction between children and staff, with a focus on the needs of the child. This requires reasonable working conditions, such as low child/staff ratios and adequate materials.

■ Continuity in staffing, curriculum and parental involvement ease the transition to primary school. Quality improvements in the early years of schooling are needed to better accommodate young children from diverse backgrounds and experiences.

What would it take to reach the ECCE goal?

■ High-level political support, an essential element.

■ A consultative process to develop a national ECCE policy for children from birth to age 8, specifying the administrative responsibilities and budgetary commitments across relevant sectors and levels of government.

■ Ongoing national and international data collection and monitoring efforts to assess needs and outcomes in meeting the EFA goals.

■ The designation of a lead ministry or agency for policy on young children and ECCE, and an interagency coordinating mechanism with decision-making power.

■ Well-enforced national quality standards covering public and private provision for all age groups.

■ Stronger and more partnerships between government and the private sector, an important ECCE stakeholder in many regions.

■ Upgrading of ECCE staff, particularly through flexible recruitment strategies, appropriate training, quality standards and remuneration that retains trained staff.

■ Increased and better-targeted public funding of ECCE, with particular attention to poor children, children living in rural areas and those with disabilities.

■ The specific inclusion of ECCE in key government resource documents, such as national budgets, sector plans and Poverty Reduction Strategy Papers.

■ More attention – and more funding – from donor agencies.

Overview

Chapter 1
Learning begins at birth

Learning begins before a child walks through the classroom door. This Report focuses on the first of the six Education for All (EFA) goal, which calls upon countries to expand and improve comprehensive early childhood care and education (ECCE), especially for the most vulnerable and disadvantaged children. It adopts a holistic approach encompassing health, nutrition, hygiene and children's cognitive development and socio-emotional well-being. Early childhood programmes are vital to offset social and economic disadvantage. ECCE is an instrument to guarantee children's rights that opens the way to all the EFA goals and contributes powerfully to reducing poverty, the overarching objective of the Millennium Development Goals.

The Report monitors progress towards all six EFA goals, giving special attention to issues of equity and inclusion. With a 2015 time horizon for achieving the goals, urgent and comprehensive action is needed, particularly to identify and enrol hard-to-reach children, make a dent in the global literacy challenge, and move ECCE up the agenda.

Chapter 2
The six goals: how are we doing?

This chapter reviews progress towards the six EFA goals since Dakar, comparing the latest available data with those for 1999. There has been considerable progress towards achieving universal primary education, with sharp enrolment increases in sub-Saharan Africa, and in South and West Asia, and more modest increases in the Arab States. Primary school progression and completion remain major concerns in those regions and, to some extent, in Latin America and the Caribbean. The number of primary school age children out of school declined by 21 million from 1999 to 2004 but remained unacceptably high at 77 million. The chapter details these children's background characteristics, notably household poverty, place of residence, gender and mother's education level. About two-thirds of countries with 2004 data have achieved gender parity in primary education, though only one-third have achieved it at the secondary level. Little progress has been made on literacy, with one in five of the world's adults still not literate.

The Education for All Development Index, calculated for 125 countries, shows improvement in many of the lowest-ranking countries. Countries lacking data – many in conflict or post-conflict situations – are not included but are likely to suffer from low levels of educational development, compounding the continuing global EFA challenge.

Chapter 3
Tackling exclusion: lessons from country experience

Education for All requires an inclusive approach. This chapter offers examples of policies and programmes that have been effective in extending education generally and, more specifically, in identifying and overcoming the barriers that deprive marginalized groups of the same learning opportunities as others. Key policies include abolishing school fees, providing financial incentives to reduce household dependence on child labour, designing specific measures for children affected by HIV/AIDS and helping schools integrate children with disabilities. Non-formal education programmes for youth and adults offer a second chance at learning and are most effective when they are community-based, flexible and relevant to learners' lives. Armed conflict – increasingly involving child soldiers – and internal displacement call for urgent interventions offering basic education services and medical and psychological care.

Countries need sound education plans to overcome exclusion and improve education quality. Adequate public spending, availability of trained and motivated teachers and the capacity to expand secondary education are three key aspects of sound plans. While the overall trend in public education spending is positive (increases of more than 30% in some twenty countries), spending as a percentage of GNP fell in forty-one countries, particularly in Latin America and the Caribbean, and in South and West Asia. Many countries are under increasing pressure to expand secondary education. The EFA goals cannot be achieved without recruiting and training new teachers, and providing incentives for those working in difficult conditions, especially in rural areas.

Chapter 4
International support: making better use of more aid

Basic education benefited from an increase in overall aid to education between 2000 and 2004. Including funds channelled as direct budget support, aid to basic education for all low-income countries increased from US$1.8 billion to US$3.4 billion. Multilateral donors allocated 11.8% of their total aid in 2003-2004 to education, with about half of this going to basic education. Donor presence remains uneven across the world's poorest countries and the relative importance donors give to education in total aid is not the same for all regions.

At US$11 billion a year, the price tag for fulfilling the EFA agenda is higher than originally expected. Even if recent promises to increase aid are met, the flows for basic education will be inadequate if its current share in total aid and its distribution across levels and income groups are maintained, and further harmonization does not occur. The share of total aid going to basic education must at least double and be focused more on low-income countries rather than on middle-income ones. The Fast Track Initiative process has become an important mechanism for donor dialogue and coordination. Greater efforts, however, will be needed internationally to persuade (a) donors to increase the volume and predictability of aid for basic education and (b) governments of low-income countries to give greater priority to basic education and to allocate to it a bigger share of the savings from debt relief.

Chapter 5
The compelling case for ECCE

Early childhood sets the foundations for life. Early childhood programmes are important, first, to guarantee the rights of young children, enshrined in the Convention on the Rights of the Child now ratified by 192 countries. Second, early childhood is a highly sensitive period marked by rapid transformations in physical, cognitive, social and emotional development. Undernutrition, deprivation of care and poor treatment are particularly damaging to young children, with repercussions often felt into the adult years.

Well-designed ECCE programmes can significantly enhance young children's well-being in these formative years and in the future, complementing the care they receive at home. Programmes that combine nutrition, health, care and education have a positive impact on cognitive outcomes. Participation in ECCE also facilitates primary school enrolment and leads to better results in the first years of school, especially for disadvantaged children. From an economic viewpoint, investment in early childhood programmes offers a high pay-off in terms of human capital, so there is a strong case for public intervention. Finally, early childhood programmes can reduce social inequality: they can compensate for vulnerability and disadvantage resulting from factors such as poverty, gender, race, ethnicity, caste or religion.

Chapter 6
Worldwide progress in early childhood care and education

This chapter first examines the changing contexts – smaller households, more working women, maternity benefits and new gender roles – in which the provision of care and education for young children has historically evolved. It then assesses countries' progress towards the ECCE goal for three groups: children under age 3, those between 3 and the primary school entry age, and vulnerable and disadvantaged children. Finally, the chapter characterizes the type, composition and professional status of the carers and educators in ECCE programmes.

Among the main findings: many countries have no programmes addressing the diverse needs (health, nutrition, care and education) of children in the first three years of life. Few countries have established national frameworks to coordinate ECCE programmes. Access to pre-primary education has expanded worldwide. ECCE enrolments fell sharply in transition countries after the breakup of the Soviet Union but are now recovering, although not to previous levels. Among developing country regions, coverage is greatest in Latin America and the Caribbean but remains low in sub-Saharan Africa and the Arab States. Children from poorer and rural households have less access to ECCE programmes than those from richer and urban ones.

In developing countries, the ECCE workforce typically possesses minimal education and pre-service training. In most industrialized countries, highly trained professionals work alongside untrained child care workers and part-time volunteers. Many countries have implemented policies to expand and upgrade their ECCE workforce, but progress is uneven and slow.

Chapter 7
The making of effective programmes

ECCE programmes are extremely diverse: there is no universal model of early childhood provision. No matter the setting, however, successful programmes offer support to parents during the child's earliest years, integrate educational activities with other services (notably health, care and nutrition) and ease the transition to primary school. Parents, or other custodial carers, are the child's first educators, and for the youngest age group the home is the prime arena for care. The past decade has seen an increase in the number of parenting programmes that aim to reach children under age 3. Home visiting programmes offer support to individual parents and can be particularly positive for at-risk families by favouring the child's development and raising parents' self-esteem. Local communities also play a key role in supporting young children and their families through home- or community-based child care.

The most common form of ECCE, particularly for the 3 to 6 age group, is centre-based provision. It is crucial to make this experience a positive one by ensuring that practices are suited to the child's age and cultural environment. Research shows that positive interactions between staff and child are the most important predictors of children's enhanced well-being. Early learning is most effective in the mother tongue yet teaching in the official language still predominates. At the same time, this first exposure to organized learning is an opportunity to challenge traditional gender roles. Finally, programmes should be inclusive and take into account circumstances of children with disabilities or in armed conflict. Because ECCE is also an important foundation for subsequent education, it is important to foster continuity between pre-primary and primary school. Several countries are integrating ECCE more closely with primary education to facilitate the transition for children.

Chapter 8
Fostering strong ECCE policies

A more favourable policy environment for ECCE is emerging, influenced by a growing body of research on its benefits and the support of strong international networks. To help build on this momentum, several key elements contribute to strengthening political will and developing national ECCE policies. High-level political endorsement can put ECCE on the agenda. In recent years, leaders in several countries have made early childhood a national priority, leading to new policies and increased resources. Broad stakeholder involvement encourages public support for ECCE. Government partnerships with international organizations or aid agencies can generate important seed money for projects that can then be taken to scale. Aligning ECCE policies with other national and sector development policies is strategic to leverage resources. Public campaigns can promote ECCE and provide information to carers.

Although national ECCE policies are country-specific, they should include guidelines on governance, quality and financing questions. ECCE involves multiple sectors, making coordination a frequent challenge. Defining a lead administrative body and setting up coordination mechanisms with real decision-making power can advance the agenda for young children. Governments need to ensure that minimum acceptable standards are met for all children, whether the provider is public or private. Expanding and improving ECCE will require additional public and private funds. In many developing countries, targeting of resources to the most disadvantaged children may be the first step of a broader national ECCE policy for all children. Finally, donor support for ECCE has been limited; increased support is essential.

Chapter 9
EFA: action now

The considerable progress made towards the EFA goals since the Dakar forum provides a measure of just how much can be accomplished when countries and the international community act together. This chapter makes nine recommendations that warrant urgent policy attention:

1. Return to the comprehensive approach of Dakar.

2. Act with urgency to enrol all children in school, expand adult literacy programmes and create opportunities for children living in conflict and post-conflict situations.

3. Emphasize equity and inclusion.

4. Increase public spending and focus it better.

5. Increase aid to basic education and allocate it where it is most needed.

6. Move ECCE up domestic and international agendas.

7. Increase public financing for ECCE and target it.

8. Upgrade the ECCE workforce, especially as regards qualifications, training and working conditions.

9. Improve the monitoring of ECCE.

Policies must address all six EFA goals and stay the course: with only nine years left to 2015, the time for comprehensive action is now.

© CARO PHOTO/SIPA

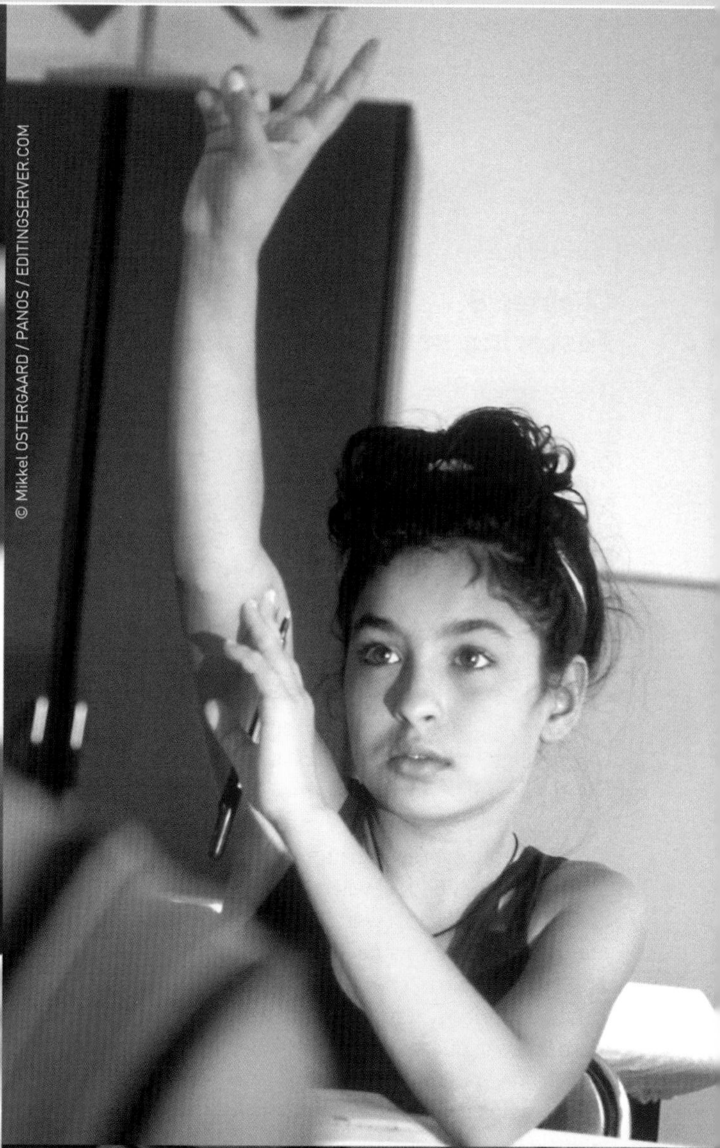

© Mikkel OSTERGAARD / PANOS / EDITINGSERVER.COM

© Zhang xinyu/IMAGINECHINA/MAXPPP / REUTERS

© AFP/Tugela Ridley

PART I. A comprehensive approach

Chapter 1

Learning begins at birth

The child's early experiences, the special focus of this year's *EFA Global Monitoring Report*, create the base for all subsequent learning. Strong early childhood foundations – including good health, nutrition and a nurturing environment – can help ensure a smooth transition to primary school, a better chance of completing basic education, and a route out of poverty and disadvantage. It is therefore no coincidence that the first EFA goal calls on countries to expand and improve early childhood care and education (ECCE), especially for the most vulnerable and disadvantaged. ECCE is an instrument to guarantee children's rights, opens the way to all the EFA goals and contributes powerfully to reducing poverty, the overarching objective of the Millennium Development Goals. It is high time to move ECCE up the policy agenda, in line with the comprehensive view of EFA as conceived in Dakar.

Learning begins at birth

Learning begins before a child walks through the classroom door. From the earliest age, children's development and learning are fostered through their interactions with caring human beings in secure, nurturing and stimulating environments. Young children's experiences in the first years of life – well before they begin school – create the foundation for subsequent learning. Although early childhood is a period of great potential for human growth and development, it is also a time when children are especially fragile and vulnerable.

Today, despite considerable progress, the status of young children remains disturbing, particularly in the poorest countries. A child born in the developing world has a four out of ten chance of living in extreme poverty, defined as living on less than US$1 a day. An estimated 10.5 million children died in 2005 before they reached age 5, most from preventable diseases and in countries that have experienced major armed conflict since 1999. AIDS has orphaned more than 15 million children under age 18, 80% of them in sub-Saharan Africa. The rights of millions of children are violated by trafficking, labour, abuse and neglect. Finally, many of the 50 million children whose births are not registered each year are unable to access basic services or schooling as a result (UNICEF, 2005b).

For all these reasons early intervention is crucial: it is far more challenging and costly to compensate for educational and social disadvantage among older children and adults than it is to provide preventive measures and support in early childhood. Good-quality early childhood care and education programmes – including immunization, parenting education, home-based activities and kindergartens, pre-schools or nurseries – provide health, nutrition, hygiene, stimulation and social interaction that support children's development and learning. Participation of young children in such programmes can lead to a more equitable society.

This edition of the *EFA Global Monitoring Report* recognizes the significance of the early years of children's lives in shaping the quality of their childhoods as well as their future education, health and economic welfare. In addition to its core function of monitoring and analysing progress on all six Education for All (EFA) goals (Box 1.1), this Report highlights the need for (a) a comprehensive approach (working toward all six goals and taking a broad view of early childhood care and education); (b) special attention to issues of equity and inclusion; and (c) urgent action in order to achieve all the EFA goals on time.

Comprehensiveness, equity and action

The EFA goals were conceived as an indivisible whole, addressing the rights of *all* children, youth and adults. Thus, the educational needs of populations in situations of conflict and crisis, or people who are marginalized through language, disability, poverty or culture, deserve special attention. The goals further call for *quality* in education for everyone, as a prerequisite for the acquisition of sustainable skills, knowledge and attitudes that enhance human capabilities and counter poverty and inequality.

In this way the EFA goals contribute directly to the Millenium Development Goals (MDGs), especially the overarching goal of eradicating poverty (Box 1.1). The EFA goals are also more ambitious than the MDGs. Cautiously phrased, the two education MDGs omit mention of 'free and compulsory' aspects of primary schooling and are restricted to seeking the elimination of gender disparities in education rather than to achieving the more ambitious gender equality espoused by the Dakar Framework. Further, literacy (EFA goal 4), early childhood care and education (EFA goal 1) and youth and adult learning needs (EFA goal 3) are not mentioned. This Report, like all its predecessors, reflects the conviction that a comprehensive approach is needed, encompassing all the EFA goals – a view also stressed at the 2005 World Summit, the 2005 EFA High-Level Group Meeting and the 2006 G8 Summit.

The EFA goals were set in 2000 with a target date of 2015. This is the fifth Report monitoring general progress and addressing a special theme: this year the theme is early childhood care and education (ECCE), the subject of the first EFA goal. Previous Reports have featured gender (2003/4), quality (2005) and adult literacy (2006). The next Report, in 2008, like the first in 2002, will not address a special theme but will review overall progress towards all six goals at the halfway mark.

Each year the information available for monitoring progress on the EFA goals improves.

Children's experiences in the first years create the foundation for subsequent learning

New monitoring features

In this 2007 Report:

- The data provided by the UNESCO Institute for Statistics (UIS) cover more countries and are more up to date, including for the school year that ended in 2004.
- A major problem with data availability for some countries persists, however, often because of recent or current armed conflict. This means the EFA situation in these countries is unlikely to be improving, but the lack of data makes it impossible to include them in the Report's statistical analyses.
- Greater use is made of other sources of data, particularly household surveys, to look in detail at educational coverage across regions, in terms of rural or urban location, household spending on education and, especially, participation in ECCE programmes and the characteristics of children who are out of school. For ECCE, UNESCO's International Bureau of Education (IBE), together with UNICEF, has established a database of country profiles especially for this Report, which may be consulted on the Report website (www.efareport.unesco.org).
- National learning assessments are examined, supplementing previous Reports' attention to regional and international ones.
- Coverage of secondary education is deepened by distinguishing for the first time between lower and upper secondary education. As countries become increasingly committed to universal basic education, they are also extending their definitions of it to include two or three years of the secondary cycle. Indeed, it is increasingly clear that the availability of lower secondary school places is an important determinant of primary completion. Secondary education is also important for EFA because in many countries it is the minimum qualification for primary teachers. Finally, as the fastest growing level in developing countries, secondary education is increasingly in direct competition with primary education for public funding.
- Analysis of aid flows for education in general and EFA in particular is extended with improved data from the OECD Development Assistance Committee (DAC) and by taking a closer look at relationships between donors and recipient governments, as well as attempting, with limited success, to review aid flows for ECCE.

Box 1.1: The Dakar EFA goals and the Millennium Development Goals

Building on two United Nations instruments, the Universal Declaration of Human Rights and the Convention on the Rights of the Child, the international community adopted the World Declaration on Education for All at Jomtien, Thailand, in 1990. At its heart is the recognition that universal education is the key to sustainable development, social justice and a brighter future.

The 2000 Dakar Framework for Action expresses the international community's commitment to a broad-based strategy for ensuring that the basic learning needs of every child, youth and adult are met within a generation and sustained thereafter. It sets the six EFA goals:

1. Expanding and improving comprehensive early childhood care and education, especially for the most vulnerable and disadvantaged children.

2. Ensuring that by 2015 all children, particularly girls, children in difficult circumstances and those belonging to ethnic minorities, have access to and complete free and compulsory primary education of good quality.

3. Ensuring that the learning needs of all young people and adults are met through equitable access to appropriate learning and life-skills programmes.

4. Achieving a 50 per cent improvement in levels of adult literacy by 2015, especially for women, and equitable access to basic and continuing education for all adults.

5. Eliminating gender disparities in primary and secondary education by 2005, and achieving gender equality in education by 2015, with a focus on ensuring girls' full and equal access to and achievement in basic education of good quality.

6. Improving all aspects of the quality of education and ensuring excellence of all so that recognized and measurable learning outcomes are achieved by all, especially in literacy, numeracy and essential life skills.

The Millennium Development Goals (MDGs), approved by world leaders at the United Nations Millennium Summit in 2000, form an agenda for reducing poverty and improving lives. For each goal, one or more targets have been set, most for 2015. The first goal cannot be achieved without education, and two other goals and two targets make explicit reference to education:

Goal 1. Eradicate extreme poverty and hunger.

Goal 2. Achieve universal primary education. (Target: ensure that by 2015 children everywhere, boys and girls, will be able to complete a full course of good quality primary schooling.)

Goal 3. Promote gender equality and empower women. (Target: eliminate gender disparity in primary and secondary education, preferably by 2005, and at all levels of education no later than 2015.)

Sources: UNESCO (2000a); United Nations (2001a).

Two aspects of EFA remain very difficult to monitor:

- Goal 3 on learning needs of youth and adults. Interpretations vary enormously, but the Report suggests how progress in this area might be monitored in future, using empirical studies of what countries are actually doing.
- National spending on education. Reporting on national expenditure remains patchy. The UIS is working to improve the data, starting with sub-Saharan Africa, but this remains the weakest element of EFA monitoring. This is unfortunate, as adequate finances and strong commitment hold the key to sustaining and extending the EFA progress achieved so far.

Addressing disadvantage and inclusion

The latest *World Development Report* from the World Bank (2005*d*) and *Human Development Report* from UNDP (2005) both highlight the inequities in opportunities that various groups face, and the setbacks these gaps can result in for children, adults and social and economic development. Educational attainment is one, if not the major, determinant of life chances and the opportunity to escape poverty. These facts are powerful reasons for reinforcing efforts to achieve the EFA goals.

Aggregate measures of education coverage hide wide variations among particular groups of children and young adults. This Report provides examples of such variations, taking a closer look at children who are not attending primary school and describing specific efforts to reduce inequities and promote inclusion. It also underlines the financial implications for governments of trying to include the hardest-to-reach children, youth and illiterate adults through such actions as fee reduction, and the hiring and training of more teachers. Access to ECCE programmes, in particular, is shown to be highly inequitable in most developing countries, yet ECCE is a particularly effective instrument for offsetting disadvantage.

The need for urgent action

With a 2015 target date for achieving the goals, very little time for action is left. A majority of countries have a six-year primary school cycle. To achieve UPE in these countries by 2015, all children of the age to complete primary school that year will have to be enrolled by 2009, less than three years away. Two steps are needed: first, identifying all hard-to-reach children and assessing their characteristics and the obstacles

With a 2015 target date for achieving the goals, very little time for action is left

to their attending school; and second, devising strategies and policies to reach them, and obtaining and allocating the financial resources, both domestic and external, needed for implementation. Addressing the first part of the gender goal, ending disparities in primary and secondary education, whose target date of 2005 has already been missed, is equally urgent. Gender issues are a recurring theme throughout the Report.

A sense of urgency about EFA is particularly necessary because many governments and donors are starting to focus more attention on economic growth and the role of the upper levels of education in fuelling the knowledge economy. The international community thus needs extra vigilance to keep the EFA goals at the forefront of international and national agendas, to maintain a comprehensive view of EFA that recognizes all six goals as interrelated parts of a whole and to ensure that the necessary financing is in place.

ECCE: a conceptual framework

The first EFA goal – expanding and improving comprehensive early childhood care and education – includes several concepts that are variously interpreted: early childhood, care, education, and vulnerable and disadvantaged children. The goal's complexity, along with its intersectoral nature and the absence of a quantitative target, makes it more difficult to monitor than some of the other EFA goals.

Understandings of and approaches to *early childhood* vary depending on local traditions, cultures, family structures and the organization of primary schooling (Dahlberg et al., 1999; Nsamenang, 2006; Woodhead, 2006). It is important to acknowledge and value this diversity. For monitoring purposes, this Report follows the increasingly recognized convention that early childhood covers the period from birth to age 8.[1] The early years are a time of remarkable brain development that lays the foundation for later learning. During this time, young children learn by manipulating objects and materials, exploring the world around them and experimenting, using trial and error. Also during the early years children receiving emotional support develop their sense of personal and physical security, and strengthen bonds with family and community. By age 8, all children around the world are expected to be in primary school.[2]

1. Although the prenatal period is often included as important for maternal and child health, it is beyond the scope of this Report.

2. Children's transition to primary school may occur as early as age 4, but nowhere is it supposed to occur later than age 8.

Guided by the Expanded Commentary on the Dakar Framework for Action on EFA goal 1 (Box 1.2), this Report focuses on both the *care* and the *education* of young children. The term 'care' generally includes attention to health, hygiene and nutrition within a nurturing and safe environment that supports children's cognitive and socio-emotional well-being. Use of the term 'education' in the early childhood years is much broader than (pre-)schooling, capturing learning through early stimulation, guidance and a range of developmental activities and opportunities. In practice, care and education cannot be separated, and good-quality provision for young children necessarily addresses both dimensions (Choi, 2002; Myers, 1995; OECD, 2001).[3] In this respect, care and education are parts of a whole: both are needed to foster holistic growth, development and learning, as the Dakar Framework states.

Defining ECCE

Drawing on this holistic approach, the Report uses the following definition:

Early childhood care and education supports children's survival growth, development and learning – including health, nutrition and hygiene, and cognitive, social, physical and emotional development – from birth to entry into primary school[4] in formal, informal and non-formal settings. Often provided by a mix of government institutions, non-governmental organizations, private providers, communities and families, ECCE represents a continuum of interconnected arrangements involving diverse actors: family, friends, neighbours; family day care for a group of children in a provider's home; centre-based programmes; classes/programmes in schools; and programmes for parents.

ECCE policies and provision vary according to the age and development of the child, and can be organized in formal, non-formal and informal arrangements (Figure 1.1). The broad, holistic scope of ECCE is captured in the policy objectives associated with it around the world:

- providing health care, immunization, feeding and nutrition;
- supporting new parents through information sharing and parenting education;
- creating a safe environment for young children to play and socialize with their peers;
- compensating for disadvantage and fostering the resilience of vulnerable children;
- promoting 'school readiness' and preparation for primary school;

Box 1.2: Comment on EFA goal 1

'All young children must be nurtured in safe and caring environments that allow them to become healthy, alert and secure and be able to learn. The past decade has provided more evidence that good quality early childhood care and education, both in families and in more structured programmes, have a positive impact on the survival, growth, development and learning potential of children. Such programmes should be comprehensive, focusing on all of the child's needs and encompassing health, nutrition and hygiene as well as cognitive and psycho-social development. They should be provided in the child's mother tongue and help to identify and enrich the care and education of children with special needs. Partnerships between governments, NGOs, communities and families can help ensure the provision of good care and education for children, especially for those most disadvantaged, through activities centred on the child, focused on the family, based within the community and supported by national, multi-sectoral policies and adequate resources.

'Governments ... have the primary responsibility of formulating early childhood care and education policies within the context of national EFA plans, mobilizing political and popular support, and promoting flexible, adaptable programmes for young children that are appropriate to their age and not mere downward extensions of formal school systems. The education of parents and other caregivers in better child care, building on traditional practices, and the systematic use of early childhood indicators, are important elements in achieving this goal.'

Source: UNESCO (2000*a*).

- providing custodial care for children of working parents and family members;
- strengthening communities and social cohesion (Kamerman 2005; UNESCO-IBE, 2006; UNICEF, 2006).

Though the various international agencies differ in the terminology they use (Choi, 2002), there is general recognition of the benefits of such a holistic approach, both within ECCE programmes and at home, as well as during the transition to primary school. This Report takes a similarly broad approach to the monitoring of ECCE. It looks at the family and community contexts, the institutions, the programmes and the policies that affect children's survival, growth, development, learning and well-being. It covers a wide variety of ECCE arrangements (Figure 1.1).

Care and education cannot be separated, and good-quality provision for young children necessarily addresses both

3. For example, many early childhood specialists argue that programmes labelled 'child care' should provide opportunities for children to grow and learn, and those labelled 'early education' should nurture children and promote their social and emotional well-being.

4. Where primary school starts at age 6, for example, ECCE programmes serve children from birth to age 5 and primary school covers the rest of early childhood (ages 6 to 8).

Figure 1.1: Schematic description of approaches to the care and education of young children

Age	Organized care and education	Informal care and child-rearing
8	C. Primary education (ISCED* level 1)	D. Informal provision of care for children aged **0 to 8**, by parents or extended family, mainly at home but sometimes in other family or community settings.
7		
6	B. ECCE policies and programmes** for ages 3 and up	
5	B1. Pre-primary education programmes designed for children at least 3 years old (ISCED 0)	
4	B2. Non-formal education programmes (age 3+)	
3		Ideally, children's health, nutrition, cognitive and psychosocial needs are addressed.
2	A. ECCE policies and programmes** for ages 0 to 2	
1	A1. Organized care and education programmes	
	A2. Non-formal care or education programmes	
0	A3. Parental leave	

Providers:
Government (national, subnational),
private (non-profit and for-profit),
international non-governmental organization,
community-based organization.

* International Standard Classification of Education, a system designed by UNESCO and the OECD as an instrument for assembling, compiling and presenting comparable indicators and statistics of education within countries and internationally.

** To be holistic, policies and programmes should address health, hygiene, nutrition, social, emotional and educational needs of children.

EFA goal 1 explicitly calls for expanding and improving ECCE for the most *vulnerable and disadvantaged children*, which makes issues of targeting potentially more important here than for other EFA goals. The benefits of good-quality ECCE are greater for the vulnerable and disadvantaged than for others. The goal's focus on these children is consistent with a rights-based perspective and with the importance of equity and inclusion to EFA more broadly. Just as early childhood arrangements vary among and within countries, so do national and local definitions of 'vulnerable and disadvantaged children'.[5] Some types of vulnerability and disadvantage are specific to certain difficult contexts (e.g. armed conflict) while others are

5. Country definitions include poor children; children with physical, emotional and learning disabilities; children in emergencies (including refugees and internally displaced children); working children in exploitative conditions; malnourished and undernourished children; abused and neglected children; street children; orphans and children in institutions; children infected and affected by HIV/AIDS; unregistered children; indigenous children; linguistic, ethnic and cultural minority children; and migrant and nomad children.

less so. Poverty is a principal source of disadvantage and it aggravates other types of vulnerability. Even in high-income countries, it is often the disadvantaged who would benefit most from early childhood programmes but who have the least access to them. This Report pays particular attention to how public policy can be designed to include the disadvantaged in ECCE and how programmes themselves can best be adapted to diverse participation.

ECCE: a right in itself

Among the EFA goals, developing country governments thus far have generally given less policy attention to early childhood (and to literacy) than to primary education and gender parity. For vulnerable and disadvantaged children, the lack of a national ECCE policy truly represents a missed opportunity. Where ECCE does get attention, it is usually geared towards ages 3 and up, and focused on the years before primary school entry, leaving opportunities for younger children overlooked.

ECCE, like EFA more generally, is both a right and a major contributor to development and poverty reduction. Fortunately, international commitment to early childhood is growing. The 1989 Convention on the Rights of the Child, signed by 192 nations, focuses on guaranteeing the rights of young children to survive, develop and be protected. The 1990 World Declaration on Education for All states that 'learning begins at birth' and encourages the development of ECCE. The World Education Forum at Dakar in 2000 reaffirmed the importance of ECCE in reaching basic education goals, as did the UN Special Session on Children in 2002. These ground-breaking legal and political commitments all recognize that children are born with the right to have their learning needs met through approaches that promote their holistic development. To date, however, these rights are far from the reality for many children.

Recent demographic, economic, social and political trends have increased the need for comprehensive ECCE policies and programmes. Urbanization and the resulting changes to household structures have reduced the role of extended family members as carers. Growing numbers of working mothers with young children have increased the demand for non-parental child care. Pressures to increase competitiveness in a world economy that is increasingly knowledge-based have led to calls for improving children's 'school readiness'. World health crises (particularly HIV/AIDS) and other emergencies (e.g. famine, natural disaster and war) require responses to protect the safety and well-being of young children. These contextual trends have influenced the types and coverage of ECCE programmes, as well as the extent to which nations have made progress towards achieving EFA goal 1.

A powerful boost to education and development

In addition to being an important goal in itself, ECCE can contribute to the realization of the other EFA goals and the MDGs. Children who participate in ECCE and have positive early learning experiences make a better transition to primary school, and are more likely to begin and complete it (EFA goal 2). By reducing dropout, repetition and special education placements, ECCE can improve the internal efficiency of primary education and decrease costs for both governments and households. Many ECCE programmes provide carers with access to parenting education and other forms of support, which in turn can improve adult learning and skills (EFA goals 3 and 4). ECCE is also an important instrument for promoting gender parity (EFA goal 5). When young children attend ECCE programmes, their older sisters or other female kin are relieved of care responsibilities, a common barrier to girls' enrolment in primary

school. Some evidence regarding primary school outcomes indicates that girls benefit more than boys from participation in ECCE. The programmes also provide an opportunity to reduce stereotypes about traditional gender roles and to foster gender equality at an age when young children are developing understandings of identity, empathy, tolerance and morality. Participation in good-quality ECCE is linked with achievement at subsequent levels of education and contributes to the quality of the education system as a whole (EFA goal 6). Moreover, when the transition to primary education is well managed, ECCE has the potential to influence the quality of pedagogy in primary school, making it more child-centred, for example.

Reaching the MDGs and reducing poverty depends on efforts to support young children's rights to health, education, protection and equality. Holistic ECCE can make a major difference in reducing poverty and hunger (MDG 1) and child mortality (MDG 4), and can help combat HIV/AIDS, malaria and other diseases (MDG 6). This role of ECCE as part of a broader anti-poverty strategy deserves far greater recognition by the international community (UNICEF, 2003).

Recognizing the benefits of good-quality ECCE to children, families and society, most OECD countries provide children with access to at least two years of free ECCE before they begin primary school, and parents receive maternal or parental leave benefits. Over the past two decades, these countries have focused on strengthening the quality and the coherence of such services (OECD, 2001). Although a growing number of policy-makers elsewhere realize the early years are a springboard for future academic and economic success, and for reducing poverty, access to good quality ECCE is still not widespread, particularly in the poorest countries. The time has come to move ECCE up the policy agenda in the developing world and among international donors in order to achieve EFA and to reduce poverty. ■

Good-quality ECCE contributes to the quality of the education system as a whole

All eyes on the alphabet outside a village primary school in Sathkira district, Bangladesh.

PART II. Monitoring
Education for All

Chapter 2

The six goals:
how are we doing?

This chapter looks at how countries have progressed since the World Education Forum in 2000, with a stronger focus on pre-primary education than in past editions (see also Chapter 6). It highlights the considerable progress towards achieving universal primary education and expresses a concern that countries trailing behind are those affected by internal conflict. Special attention is paid to children who have been left out of school. The growth of lower secondary education is emphasized and gender analysis is integrated throughout. The review of education quality focuses as always on repetition, dropout and completion, and on the supply and qualifications of teachers; new this year is reporting on the spread of national assessments of student achievement. Adult and youth literacy patterns are presented and some aspects of literate environments are discussed. The EFA Development Index, incorporating four goals, has been updated for 125 countries.

Pre-primary education: spreading, but very slowly

ISCED defines pre-primary education as all programmes that offer a structured and purposeful set of learning activities

This section focuses on pre-primary education, the education component of early childhood care and education (ECCE).[1] The International Standard Classification of Education (ISCED) defines pre-primary education (ISCED level 0) as all programmes that, in addition to providing care, offer a structured and purposeful set of learning activities, either in a formal institution or in a non-formal setting. Pre-primary programmes are usually for children aged 3 and above, and are held for the equivalent of at least two hours a day for at least one hundred days a year.

Worldwide, almost 124 million children were enrolled in pre-primary education in 2004, an increase of 10.7% over 1999 (Table 2.1).[2] Increases were particularly pronounced in sub-Saharan Africa (43.5%), the Caribbean (43.4%) and South and West Asia (40.5%). In most other regions the increases were modest, and in East Asia enrolments declined by almost 10%, mainly due to trends in China. Some 48% of the world's pre-primary enrollees were girls, a proportion unchanged since 1999 (see annex, Statistical Table 3B).

Figure 2.1 displays the pre-primary gross enrolment ratios (GER) globally and by region for 1999 and 2004.[3] The global pre-primary GER increased from 33% to 37%. Increases were rather moderate in developed and developing

1. Chapter 6 discusses the challenges involved in monitoring this goal more comprehensively.

2. In a change from previous versions of the *EFA Global Monitoring Report*, data pertain to the year in which school ended, rather than that in which the school year began.

3. Assessment of progress based solely on the GER misses important country differences in the theoretical duration of pre-primary education. For example, pre-primary education lasts four years in Romania, three in Lebanon, two in Saint Lucia and one in Ecuador – all of which have a pre-primary GER of about 75%. Other measures, such as pre-primary school life expectancy (see UIS, 2006*a*: Table 12) can provide a complementary basis for evaluating national progress (see Chapter 6).

4. Regional trends in pre-primary education are based on weighted averages of the GER. Corresponding values are not available for the net enrolment ratio due to the high number of countries with missing data (see annex, Statistical Table 3B). More detailed analyses of pre-primary enrolment ratios are discussed in Chapter 6.

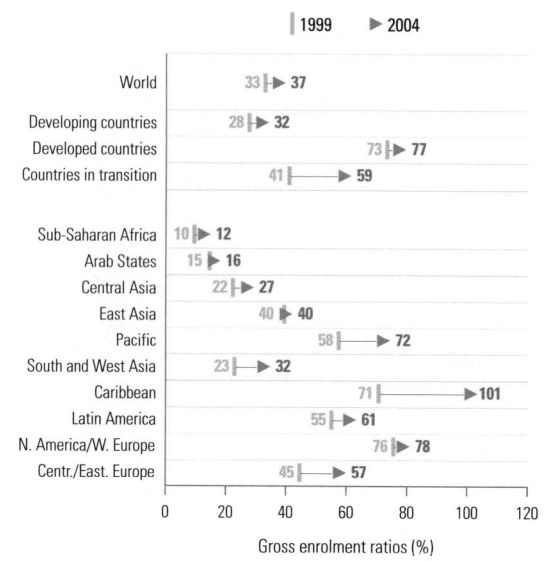

Figure 2.1: Changes in pre-primary gross enrolment ratios between 1999 and 2004, by region

1999   ► 2004

Region	1999	2004
World	33	37
Developing countries	28	32
Developed countries	73	77
Countries in transition	41	59
Sub-Saharan Africa	10	12
Arab States	15	16
Central Asia	22	27
East Asia	40	40
Pacific	58	72
South and West Asia	23	32
Caribbean	71	101
Latin America	55	61
N. America/W. Europe	76	78
Centr./East. Europe	45	57

Gross enrolment ratios (%)

Source: Annex, Statistical Table 3B.

countries (four percentage points each), but more pronounced in transition countries (eighteen percentage points). Among developing regions, there were marked increases in the Pacific and the Caribbean, and much smaller increases elsewhere; the GER for East Asia was stable.[4] A large absolute enrolment increase in sub-Saharan Africa was not matched by a similar increase in the GER because of continuing high population growth.

Most of the fifty-two countries with pre-primary GERs below 30% in 2004 are in sub-Saharan Africa and the Arab States (Figure 2.2). In general their recent progress has been slow. Among the forty-two for which the 1999 data are also available, the GERs increased in three-quarters of the countries, but typically by fewer than five percentage points. More rapid change occurred in Azerbaijan, Cameroon, Madagascar, Namibia and Tunisia. In the remaining one-quarter of the countries, pre-primary enrolment ratios declined, sometimes quite markedly, as in Bangladesh and the Palestinian Autonomous Territories, which had decreases of more than ten percentage points.

Of 104 countries with pre-primary GERs above 30% in 2004, the ratio had increased since 1999 in seventy-seven, declined in fifteen and remained almost unchanged in twelve (Table 2.2). The increase was moderate (between two and ten

Table 2.1: Pre-primary enrolment in 1999 and 2004, by region

	Total enrolment (000)		Change between 1999 and 2004 (%)
	School year ending in		
	1999	2004	
World	111 772	123 685	10.7
Developing countries	80 070	91 089	13.8
Developed countries	25 386	25 482	0.4
Countries in transition	6 316	7 115	12.6
Sub-Saharan Africa	5 129	7 359	43.5
Arab States	2 356	2 625	11.4
Central Asia	1 450	1 482	2.1
East Asia	36 152	32 831	-9.2
Pacific	416	520	25.0
South and West Asia	22 186	31 166	40.5
Caribbean	673	965	43.4
Latin America	15 720	18 154	15.5
N. America/W. Europe	19 151	19 408	1.3
Centr./East. Europe	8 538	9 176	7.5

Source: Annex, Statistical Table 3B.

Figure 2.2: Pre-primary gross enrolment ratios in 2004 and changes since 1999 in countries with GERs below 30%

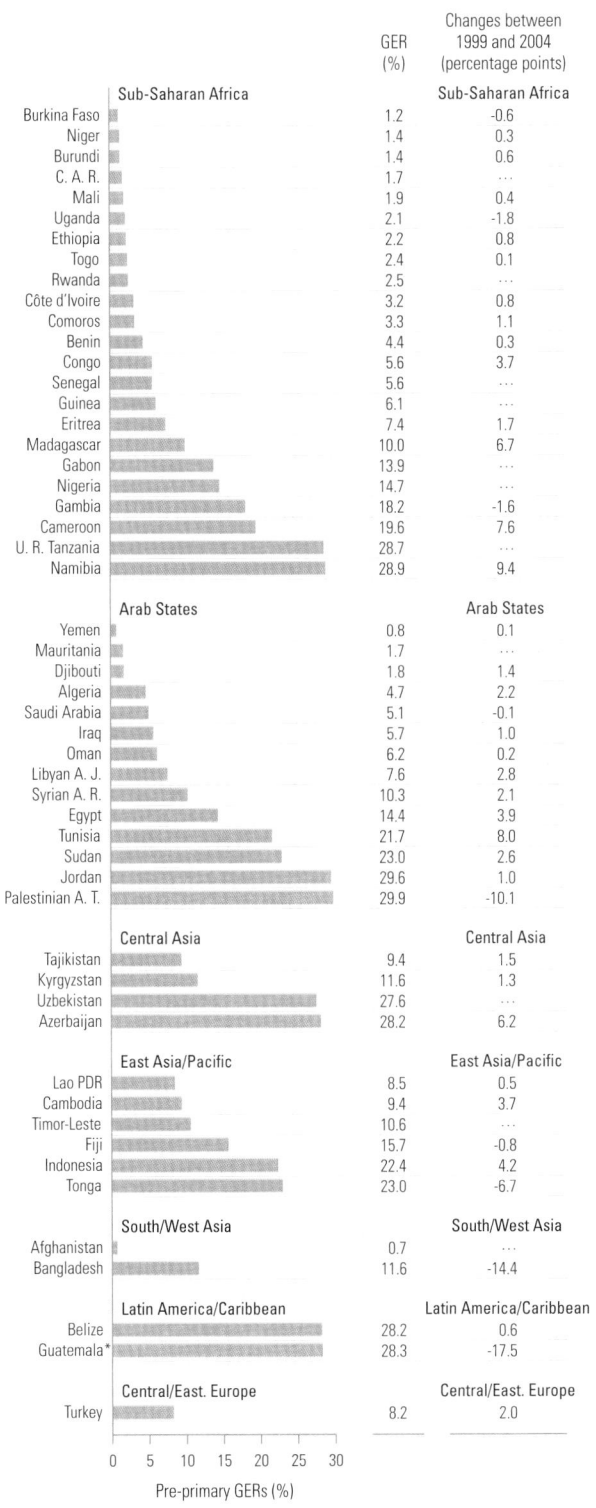

	GER (%)	Changes between 1999 and 2004 (percentage points)
Sub-Saharan Africa		**Sub-Saharan Africa**
Burkina Faso	1.2	-0.6
Niger	1.4	0.3
Burundi	1.4	0.6
C. A. R.	1.7	…
Mali	1.9	0.4
Uganda	2.1	-1.8
Ethiopia	2.2	0.8
Togo	2.4	0.1
Rwanda	2.5	…
Côte d'Ivoire	3.2	0.8
Comoros	3.3	1.1
Benin	4.4	0.3
Congo	5.6	3.7
Senegal	5.6	…
Guinea	6.1	…
Eritrea	7.4	1.7
Madagascar	10.0	6.7
Gabon	13.9	…
Nigeria	14.7	…
Gambia	18.2	-1.6
Cameroon	19.6	7.6
U. R. Tanzania	28.7	…
Namibia	28.9	9.4
Arab States		**Arab States**
Yemen	0.8	0.1
Mauritania	1.7	…
Djibouti	1.8	1.4
Algeria	4.7	2.2
Saudi Arabia	5.1	-0.1
Iraq	5.7	1.0
Oman	6.2	0.2
Libyan A. J.	7.6	2.8
Syrian A. R.	10.3	2.1
Egypt	14.4	3.9
Tunisia	21.7	8.0
Sudan	23.0	2.6
Jordan	29.6	1.0
Palestinian A. T.	29.9	-10.1
Central Asia		**Central Asia**
Tajikistan	9.4	1.5
Kyrgyzstan	11.6	1.3
Uzbekistan	27.6	…
Azerbaijan	28.2	6.2
East Asia/Pacific		**East Asia/Pacific**
Lao PDR	8.5	0.5
Cambodia	9.4	3.7
Timor-Leste	10.6	…
Fiji	15.7	-0.8
Indonesia	22.4	4.2
Tonga	23.0	-6.7
South/West Asia		**South/West Asia**
Afghanistan	0.7	…
Bangladesh	11.6	-14.4
Latin America/Caribbean		**Latin America/Caribbean**
Belize	28.2	0.6
Guatemala*	28.3	-17.5
Central/East. Europe		**Central/East. Europe**
Turkey	8.2	2.0

Pre-primary GERs (%)

* The apparent decrease in Guatemala is due to a change in the age group for which the GER is calculated, from 5-6 in 1999 to 3-6 in 2004.

Note: See source table for detailed country notes.

Source: Annex, Statistical Table 3B.

Table 2.2: Changes in pre-primary gross enrolment ratios between 1999 and 2004 in countries with GERs above 30% in 2004

	The GER has:			
	Decreased	Remained almost unchanged	Increased	
	Below -2	-2 to +2	2.1 to 10	Over 10
	(Percentage points)	(Percentage points)	(Percentage points)	(Percentage points)
Sub-Saharan Africa	Seychelles Mauritius	Ghana	Zimbabwe Lesotho Equat. Guinea Kenya	South Africa S. Tome/ Principe*
Arab States	Morocco Kuwait	United Arab Emirates	Qatar Lebanon Bahrain	
Central Asia			Armenia Mongolia	Georgia Kazakhstan
East Asia and the Pacific	Niue China Samoa	Brunei Daruss. Palau	Japan Thailand Vanuatu Macao (China) New Zealand Cook Islands Solomon Islands Malaysia Viet Nam Philippines	Rep. of Korea Papua New Guinea
South and West Asia			Maldives	India Iran, Isl. Rep. Nepal*
Latin America and the Caribbean	Chile* Costa Rica* Dominica Guyana Saint Lucia Netherlands Antilles Dominican Republic	Colombia Uruguay	Bolivia Aruba Paraguay Argentina Peru Nicaragua Barbados El Salvador Brazil	Venezuela Cuba Mexico Ecuador Jamaica Panama Bahamas Trinidad and Tobago Br. Virgin Is
North America and Western Europe	Netherlands	Greece Denmark Cyprus Canada Malta	France Switzerland United States Germany Belgium Austria Italy Sweden Portugal Israel	Finland Norway Luxembourg Spain Iceland
Central and Eastern Europe		Hungary	Poland TFYR Macedonia Albania Croatia Bulgaria Slovakia Rep. Moldova	Romania Czech Rep. Lithuania Belarus Estonia Latvia Russian Fed. Ukraine*
Number of countries (104)	15	12	46	31

* Change in the age group.

Notes: See source table for detailed country notes.
Countries are listed in order of changes in pre-primary GERs.

Sources: Annex, Statistical Table 3B.

Table 2.3: Current and target pre-primary enrolment ratios for selected countries with enrolment ratios below 30%

Country	Latest available UIS estimates*			National targets	
	Age group	GER (%)	NER (%)	Pre-primary enrolment ratios (GER or NER)	Target year
Benin	4-5	4.4	2.8	30% of 3- to 5-year-olds	2015
Bangladesh	3-5	11.6[b]	10.5[b]	All 3- to 5-year-olds attend ECCE programmes of some kind	
Burkina Faso	4-6	1.2[a]	1.2[a]	4% GER	2009
Côte d'Ivoire	3-5	3.2[c]	3.2[c]	30% of 0- to 8-year-olds	2015
D. R. Congo	3-5	...	...	50% GER	2015
Indonesia	5-6	22.4	22.4	75%	2015
Mali	3-6	1.9[b]	...	10% 15%	2008 2010
Niger	4-6	1.4	1.1	5% GER 10%	2013 2015
Senegal	4-6	5.6	3.2	30% GER	2010
Sudan	4-5	23.0	23.0	35% 100%	2007 2015
Tunisia	3-5	21.7[b]	21.7[b]	35% 41%	2006 2010
Turkey	3-5	8.2	7.9	Attain levels of EU and OECD countries	

* Unless otherwise indicated, data are for the school year ending in 2004.
a. Data are for 2002.
b. Data are for 2003.
c. Country estimates are for 2003.
Note: See source table for detailed country notes.
Sources: Annex, Statistical Table 3B; UNESCO-IIEP (2006).

percentage points) in forty-six of the seventy-seven and rapid (more than ten percentage points) in the remaining thirty-one, which included Cuba, Ecuador, Jamaica and Mexico. Especially noteworthy were the gains registered in transition countries, including Belarus, Georgia, Kazakhstan, the Russian Federation and Ukraine with increases of between twelve and thirty percentage points, and the Czech Republic, Estonia, Latvia, Lithuania and Romania, where declines observed during the 1990s were mostly reversed (see Chapter 6 for further discussion). Among the eight countries whose GERs decreased, Guyana, Mauritius, the Netherlands and Seychelles began the period with very high values. A decrease of over two percentage points occurred in China, where it was officially reported that the number of kindergarten and pre-primary classes declined by 36% between 1999 and 2003 (UNESCO, 2003*b*).

Keeping in mind that there is no quantitative target for the ECCE goal, it is instructive to compare national changes in pre-primary GERs with the targets set in national plans for 2010 or 2015. In general, these comparisons indicate unrealistically ambitious targets (see Table 2.3).[5]

---

5. The targets discussed here are contained in IIEP (2006: annex, Table 3), which summarizes recommendations and targets set forth in national development and education sector plans, national EFA action plans, Poverty Reduction Strategy Papers and Millennium Development Goal reports for forty-five countries.

Figure 2.3: Changes in gender disparities in pre-primary gross enrolment ratios between 1999 and 2004, by region

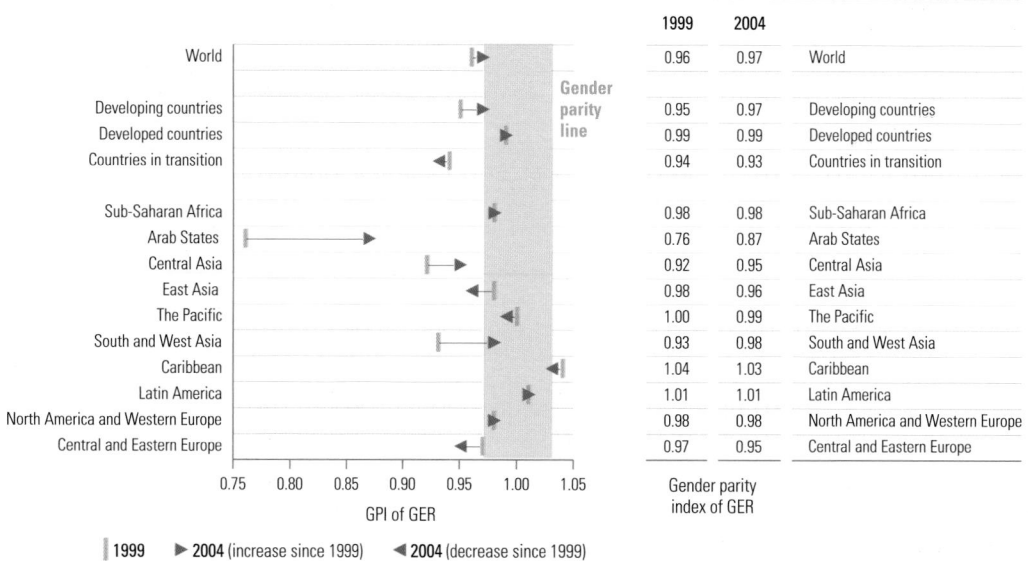

	1999	2004	
	0.96	0.97	World
	0.95	0.97	Developing countries
	0.99	0.99	Developed countries
	0.94	0.93	Countries in transition
	0.98	0.98	Sub-Saharan Africa
	0.76	0.87	Arab States
	0.92	0.95	Central Asia
	0.98	0.96	East Asia
	1.00	0.99	The Pacific
	0.93	0.98	South and West Asia
	1.04	1.03	Caribbean
	1.01	1.01	Latin America
	0.98	0.98	North America and Western Europe
	0.97	0.95	Central and Eastern Europe

Gender parity index of GER

| 1999 ► 2004 (increase since 1999) ◄ 2004 (decrease since 1999)

Source: Annex, Statistical Table 3B.

Many countries with relatively high pre-primary GERs have an objective of universal pre-school enrolment by 2015. This is the case for Chile and Mexico, whose current GERs are above 50%, but also for countries such as India, Kazakhstan and Paraguay, which have GERs below 40%. Given past growth rates, these national targets are unlikely to be achieved.

Gender disparities in pre-primary education

Figure 2.3 shows changes in gender disparities in pre-primary GERs between 1999 and 2004 globally and by region. Overall, the ratio between the female and male GERs, which provides the gender parity index (GPI), increased slightly, from 0.96 to 0.97. Indeed, it is higher at pre-primary than at primary level, probably because overall pre-primary enrolment ratios are relatively low and tend to represent mainly the more affluent, among whom gender differences are usually less pronounced than among the poor (see Chapter 6). Most regions are moving towards gender parity and considerable progress has occurred in those with high disparities. Notable improvements occurred in the Arab States, where female enrolments in 1999 were just three-quarters of male enrolments, and in South and West Asia. Among countries in the Caribbean subregion, a slight disparity in favour of girls is detectable.

In about two-thirds of the 165 countries for which pre-primary enrolment data by gender are available, the GPIs vary between 0.97 and 1.03 (see annex, Statistical Table 3B). Among the countries outside this range, the situation favours girls in thirty (GPIs above 1.03) and boys in thirty-two (GPIs below 0.97). Afghanistan, Morocco, Pakistan and Yemen have the lowest GPIs (Table 2.4). In Morocco, the GPI has improved since 1999 (from 0.52 to 0.63), but apparently because of a decrease in male enrolment rather than an increase in female enrolment. Some small progress towards gender parity has occurred in Pakistan in recent years. Of the thirty countries where the gender disparities favour girls, about half are small Pacific or Caribbean island states, and in many these disparities continue at primary and secondary level. Since the poor are much less likely to be enrolled than the relatively affluent, it cannot be assumed that these patterns and trends will necessarily continue as enrolment increases.

Table 2.4: Changes in gender disparities in pre-primary GERs between 1999 and 2004 in countries with GPIs below 0.97 or above 1.03 in 2004

Countries with disparities in favour of boys			Countries with disparities in favour of girls		
	GPI			GPI	
	1999	2004		1999	2004
Sub-Saharan Africa			**Sub-Saharan Africa**		
Eritrea	0.88	0.90	Sao Tome and Principe	1.09	1.04
Burkina Faso	1.03	0.94	Cape Verde	…	1.04
Lesotho	1.08	0.94	Central African Republic	…	1.04
Ethiopia	0.97	0.95	Congo	1.59	1.06
Comoros	1.07	0.96	Senegal	1.00	1.11
Côte d'Ivoire	0.96	0.96	Namibia	1.16	1.12
Arab States			**Arab States**		
Morocco	0.52	0.63			
Yemen	0.86	0.87			
Syrian Arab Republic	0.90	0.91			
Oman	0.88	0.91			
Jordan	0.91	0.94			
Egypt	0.95	0.95			
Palestinian A. T.	0.96	0.96			
Bahrain	0.95	0.96			
Libyan Arab Jamahiriya	0.97	0.96			
Central Asia			**Central Asia**		
Tajikistan	0.76	0.93	Mongolia	1.21	1.08
Uzbekistan	…	0.93	Georgia	1.01	1.15
			Armenia	…	1.17
East Asia and the Pacific			**East Asia and the Pacific**		
Papua N. Guinea		0.94	Philippines	1.05	1.04
			Lao PDR	1.11	1.05
			Fiji	1.02	1.06
			Indonesia	1.01	1.09
			Cook Islands	0.98	1.11
			Malaysia	1.04	1.12
			Palau	1.23	1.16
			Samoa	1.21	1.26
			Tonga	1.22	1.36
			Niue	0.93	1.58
South and West Asia			**South and West Asia**		
Afghanistan	…	0.80	Iran, Isl. Rep.	1.05	1.12
Pakistan	…	0.83			
Nepal	0.73	0.90			
Latin America and the Caribbean			**Latin America and the Caribbean**		
Cayman Is	…	0.87	El Salvador	1.01	1.04
Anguilla	…	0.90	Honduras	…	1.04
Turks/Caicos Is	…	0.90	Aruba	1.00	1.07
			Grenada	…	1.09
			Saint Lucia	0.95	1.11
			Montserrat	…	1.15
			Saint Kitts and Nevis	…	1.15
			Dominica	1.11	1.18
North America and Western Europe			**North America and Western Europe**		
United States	0.97	0.96	Malta	0.99	1.08
			Andorra	…	1.11
Central and Eastern Europe			**Central and Eastern Europe**		
Russian Federation	0.94	0.91			
Slovenia	0.91	0.95			
Turkey	0.94	0.95			
Lithuania	0.97	0.96			
Czech Republic	1.06	0.96			
Latvia	0.95	0.96			

Note: See source table for detailed country notes.
Source: Annex, Statistical Table 3B.

Primary education: advancing in enrolment

The global net enrolment ratio in primary education rose from 83% in 1999 to 86% in 2004

Progress towards universal primary education (UPE) has been made since Dakar. For the world as a whole, the global net enrolment ratio (NER) in primary education rose from 83% in 1999 to 86% in 2004 (as shown below in Table 2.7). Behind this modest global increase lie spectacular advances in those regions with the lowest coverage for primary education. The average primary NER increased from 55% to 65% in sub-Saharan Africa and from 77% to 86% in South and West Asia. These changes reflect two trends: a rapid increase in new entrants to grade 1 and continuing low survival and completion rates. Whether because they enter school late, never enter, or drop out, many primary school age children remain out of school. The quality of schooling and levels of learning achievement remain major issues everywhere, and gender parity in primary education is achieved in only four of the twenty-six countries with GERs below 90%.[6]

Access is improving rapidly in many countries

Between 1999 and 2004, the number of new entrants to grade 1 fell in some regions. This decrease mainly reflected a combination of declines in fertility rates and in the number of under- and over-age children enrolled. The number of new entrants increased by 11.5% in South and West Asia, however, and by 30.9% in sub-Saharan Africa (see annex, Statistical Table 4). In several countries, particularly in sub-Saharan Africa, the expansion was especially rapid. Over the five-year period, the number of new entrants increased by over 29% in each of the fourteen countries shown in Table 2.5, and by over 50% in seven of them. The rates of expansion in Ethiopia, Guinea, Madagascar, the Niger and the United Republic of Tanzania were particularly dramatic. In only seven of the sub-Saharan African countries for which data are available was the rate of increase less than 10%, and of these only Togo and Zimbabwe had a population of over 2 million (see annex, Statistical Tables 1 and 4). The expansion in the Arab States appears to have been far more muted, averaging just 9.1% over the period, with only Yemen demonstrating a significant increase (57%).

In all regions except the Arab States and Central and Eastern Europe, the gross intake rate

(GIR) – the total number of new entrants to grade 1 divided by the number of children who are at the official age to enter school – is over 100%. Between 1999 and 2004, the GIR increased from 118% to 131% in South and West Asia and from 88% to 105% in sub-Saharan Africa (see annex, Statistical Table 4). Regional averages mask low GIRs in many countries. The rate is below 90% in twenty countries[7] and below 65% in the Central African Republic, the Congo, Djibouti, Eritrea, Mali and the Niger. While data are not available to make the calculations for Angola, the Democratic Republic of the Congo, Guinea-Bissau, Liberia, Sierra Leone or Somalia, several of these conflict-affected countries are likely also to have low intake rates.

Most governments expect to enrol all children in grade 1 at the official age and to reach a net intake rate (NIR) of 100%. When many new entrants are under or over that age, however, the NIR does not tell much about current government efforts to expand enrolment. Out of the eighty-nine developing countries for which information is available, the over- and under-age group makes up at least half of the intake in thirty-one.[8] Twenty-two of these are in sub-Saharan Africa. For example, in Chad, Madagascar and Mozambique, between two-thirds and three-quarters of the intake are of 'incorrect' age, with the great majority being over age. As indicated

Table 2.5: Number of new entrants into grade 1 and percentage increase between 1999 and 2004 in selected countries of sub-Saharan Africa

Country	1999 (000)	2004 (000)	Increase 1999-2004 (%)	Annual increase (%)
Burundi	146	189	29.5	5.3
Cameroon	335	474	41.5	7.2
Chad	175	242	38.3	6.7
Ethiopia	1 537	3 143	104.5	15.4
Guinea	119	215	80.7	12.6
Kenya	892	1 162	30.3	5.4
Madagascar	495	897	81.2	12.6
Mali	173	254	46.8	8.0
Mozambique	536	771	43.8	7.5
Niger	133	242	82.0	12.7
Rwanda	295	456	54.6	9.1
Senegal	190	284	49.5	8.4
U. R. Tanzania	714	1 342	88.0	13.5
Zambia	252	380	50.8	8.6
Total	5 992	10 051	67.7	10.9

Note: See source table for detailed country notes.
Source: Annex, Statistical Table 4.

---

6. The twenty-six are Burkina Faso, Burundi, the Central African Republic, Chad, the Comoros, the Congo, the Cook Islands, Côte d'Ivoire, Djibouti, Eritrea, the Gambia, Ghana, Guinea, Mali, Nauru, the Niger, Niue, Oman, Pakistan, Papua New Guinea, the Republic of Moldova, Saudi Arabia, Senegal, the Sudan, the United Arab Emirates and Yemen. The Cook Islands, Nauru, Oman and the Republic of Moldova have closed the gender gap.

7. Djibouti, Oman, the Palestinian Autonomous Territories, Saudi Arabia, the Sudan and the United Arab Emirates (Arab States); the Cook Islands and Niue (Pacific); and Burkina Faso, Cape Verde, the Central African Republic, Chad, the Comoros, the Congo, Côte d'Ivoire, Equatorial Guinea, Eritrea, Mali, the Niger and Senegal (sub-Saharan Africa).

8. These data are from the UNESCO Institute for Statistics database.

in Figure 2.4, which compares GIRs and NIRs for ninety-nine developing countries, late entry is also common in Latin America and the Caribbean.

While late enrolment is better than no enrolment at all, it has serious disadvantages for children, notably a later graduation age and thus less likelihood of going on to the next level of education, and potential learning problems due to the unsuitability of the curriculum for older children. The distribution of children's ages when first enrolling in school is systematically related to several background characteristics. Table 2.6 shows, for eight sub-Saharan African countries, the share of grade 1 entrants who are at least two years over the official age and how that share varies according to gender, place of residence, household wealth and mother's education. On average, 34.5% of new entrants to first grade in these countries are at least two years over age. The likelihood of over-age enrolment is greater for particular groups, however: for instance, of the children from the poorest fifth of households in Nigeria who enrolled in grade 1, 44% were at least two years over age, compared to 17% of those from the wealthiest fifth. Similarly, while 58% of rural enrollees in Mozambique were at least two years over age, the share for urban children was 35%. In Kenya, 60% of the children with mothers lacking education were over age, compared to one-third of those whose mothers completed primary education. These patterns were common to all eight countries, and in five of the eight, boys were more likely than girls to be over age.

School participation on the rise

Enrolment in primary education worldwide has increased by 6%, from 645 million to 682 million, between 1999 and 2004 (Table 2.7). In the regions where most countries are near or at UPE, decreases in the school age population resulted in falling enrolment. The Arab States achieved some increases (6% overall), but the biggest rises occurred in South and West Asia (19%) and sub-Saharan Africa (27%).

The primary GER tends to overestimate a country's success in striving to reach UPE since it includes children who are repeating and those who are over and under age, while the NER may underestimate coverage since it represents only children of the official school age. Other measures are being developed using age-specific enrolment rates and accounting for late entrants, but the quality of data is often insufficient. Thus, this Report continues to report GERs and NERs as the

Figure 2.4: Comparison of gross and net intake rates in primary education, 2004

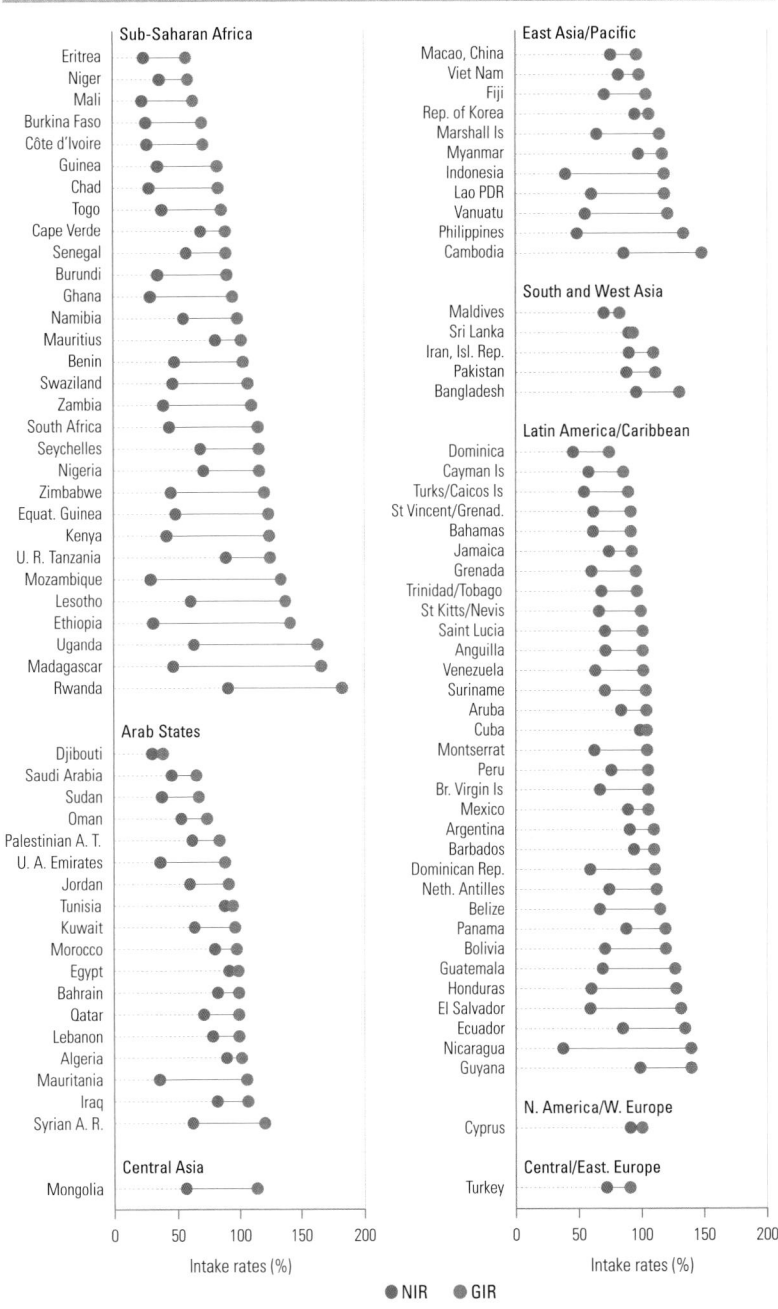

Note: Only developing countries are included. See source table for detailed country notes.
Source: Annex, Statistical Table 4.

principal indicators of participation in primary education. Figure 2.5 shows them for 100 countries for 2004.

Between 1999 and 2004, the GER increased in each developing country region except Latin America, where it fell from 121% to 118%. The ratio increased from 94% to 110% in South and

Table 2.6: Percentage of new entrants to grade 1 who are at least two years over age, by background characteristics, in eight African countries

Characteristic	Burkina Faso	Ethiopia	Ghana	Kenya	Mali	Mozambique	Namibia	Nigeria
Female	9.5	69.6	42.9	31.5	17.7	54.1	27.2	36.9
Male	17.7	69.7	48.3	42.7	16.7	49.7	31.4	31.0
Rural	17.2	74.4	47.5	39.7	22.0	58.3	31.6	36.4
Urban	5.1	41.1	41.6	22.1	7.4	35.5	20.7	27.5
Poorest 20% of households	34.3	76.4	53.7	56.3	24.4	67.9	42.8	43.6
Richest 20% of households	5.0	45.6	30.4	15.8	7.6	23.0	13.6	16.7
Mother with no education	17.2	69.0	47.9	59.9	19.5	64.6	51.1	40.1
Mother with primary education	4.1	37.7	50.5	32.7	14.5	40.1	37.9	28.6
Total	14.1	69.7	45.8	37.3	17.1	51.9	29.3	33.6

Sources: Demographic and Health Surveys 2003 for Burkina Faso, Ghana, Kenya , Mozambique and Nigeria; 2001 for Mali; 2000 for Ethiopia and Namibia.

Enrolment in primary education worldwide has increased by 6%

West Asia and from 79% to 91% in sub-Saharan Africa, a considerable achievement given persistent high population growth in both regions. The GERs are above 90% throughout Latin America and the Caribbean, East Asia and the Pacific (apart from three Pacific island nations), South and West Asia (except Pakistan), and the transition and developed countries. The situations accross the Arab States and sub-Saharan Africa are more varied. Six of the twenty Arab States have GERs below 90%, as do fourteen of the thirty-nine sub-Saharan African countries with

data available (data are missing for five conflict and post-conflict countries). The lowest GERs are found in Djibouti (39%), the Niger (45%), Burkina Faso (53%), Mali (64%) and the Central African Republic (64%).

While a higher GER does not always imply improvement (for instance, if repetition increases), it does reflect increased capacity of a system to enrol children. Between 1999 and 2004, the GERs increased by over ten percentage points in at least thirty-one countries, of which twenty were in sub-Saharan Africa. These included every

Table 2.7: Enrolment in primary education for school years ending in 1999 and 2004, by region

	Total enrolment		Gross enrolment ratios		Net enrolment ratios	
	1999	2004	1999	2004	1999	2004
	(000)	(000)	(%)	(%)	(%)	(%)
World	644 985	682 225	100.1	106.2	82.8	85.7
Developing countries	558 733	600 879	99.8	106.8	81.2	84.6
Developed countries	70 418	67 419	102.2	101.4	96.7	95.6
Countries in transition	15 834	13 926	100.0	107.3	85.0	90.7
Sub-Saharan Africa	79 772	101 424	79.0	90.9	55.0	64.9
Arab States	34 725	36 700	88.6	93.3	77.1	81.5
Central Asia	6 853	6 376	98.7	101.6	88.6	91.6
East Asia and the Pacific	217 575	206 217	111.9	113.2	96.0	93.9
East Asia	214 277	202 712	112.2	113.5	96.2	94.0
Pacific	3 298	3 505	93.9	97.9	87.4	89.6
South and West Asia	157 510	187 884	93.9	109.9	77.3	85.9
Latin America and the Caribbean	70 206	69 259	120.7	117.9	93.4	94.9
Caribbean	2 500	2 622	115.0	126.3	77.1	83.5
Latin America	67 705	66 637	121.0	117.6	94.0	95.3
North America and Western Europe	52 857	51 734	102.9	101.7	96.7	95.2
Central and Eastern Europe	25 489	22 630	99.6	101.5	89.2	90.7

Sources: Annex, Statistical Table 5.

country whose GER in 2004 was below 90%, apart from Côte d'Ivoire and the Gambia.

For all developing countries, the average NER rose from 81% in 1999 to about 85% in 2004. Regionally, NERs increased significantly in South and West Asia (from 77% to 86%) and sub-Saharan Africa (from 55% to 65%), and less spectacularly in the Arab States and in Latin America and the Caribbean. The NERs are below 80% in Nepal and Pakistan in South and West Asia, in six of the eighteen Arab States with data available, in twenty out of thirty-three sub-Saharan African countries and in one small Pacific island country (Solomon Islands). Again, however, there are many instances of significant improvement.

Figure 2.6 shows changes in NERs between 1999 and 2004. Almost all countries with ratios below 85% in 1999 improved their situation, several significantly, including Ethiopia, Lesotho, Morocco, Mozambique, Nepal, the Niger and the United Republic of Tanzania. On the other hand, several countries that were close to UPE in 1999 did not improve and some lost ground (Albania, Cape Verde, Lithuania, Malawi, Malaysia, Maldives and the Palestinian Autonomous Territories). Of the forty-five developing countries with NERs above 85% in 1999, the ratio was lower in twenty-four of them in 2004. In this group it is proving difficult to attract and retain the most marginalized out-of-school children.

Out-of-school children: mostly poor, rural and with uneducated mothers

Discussions of efforts to universalize primary education largely centre on intake and participation (enrolment) ratios, completion rates and quality. The complementary approach of this subsection is to give additional attention to those children who are not in school so as to better understand their educational experiences, if any, and their background characteristics. The closer countries are to achieving enrolment of all children in first grade and retaining them throughout primary school, the more important it becomes to identify those left out of school and prepare policies specifically for them. Much of the analysis in this subsection should be regarded as exploratory.

How many are there?

Calculating the number of children of primary school age who are not in school is not straightforward. The results – which tend to be

Figure 2.5: Comparison of gross and net enrolment ratios in primary education, 2004

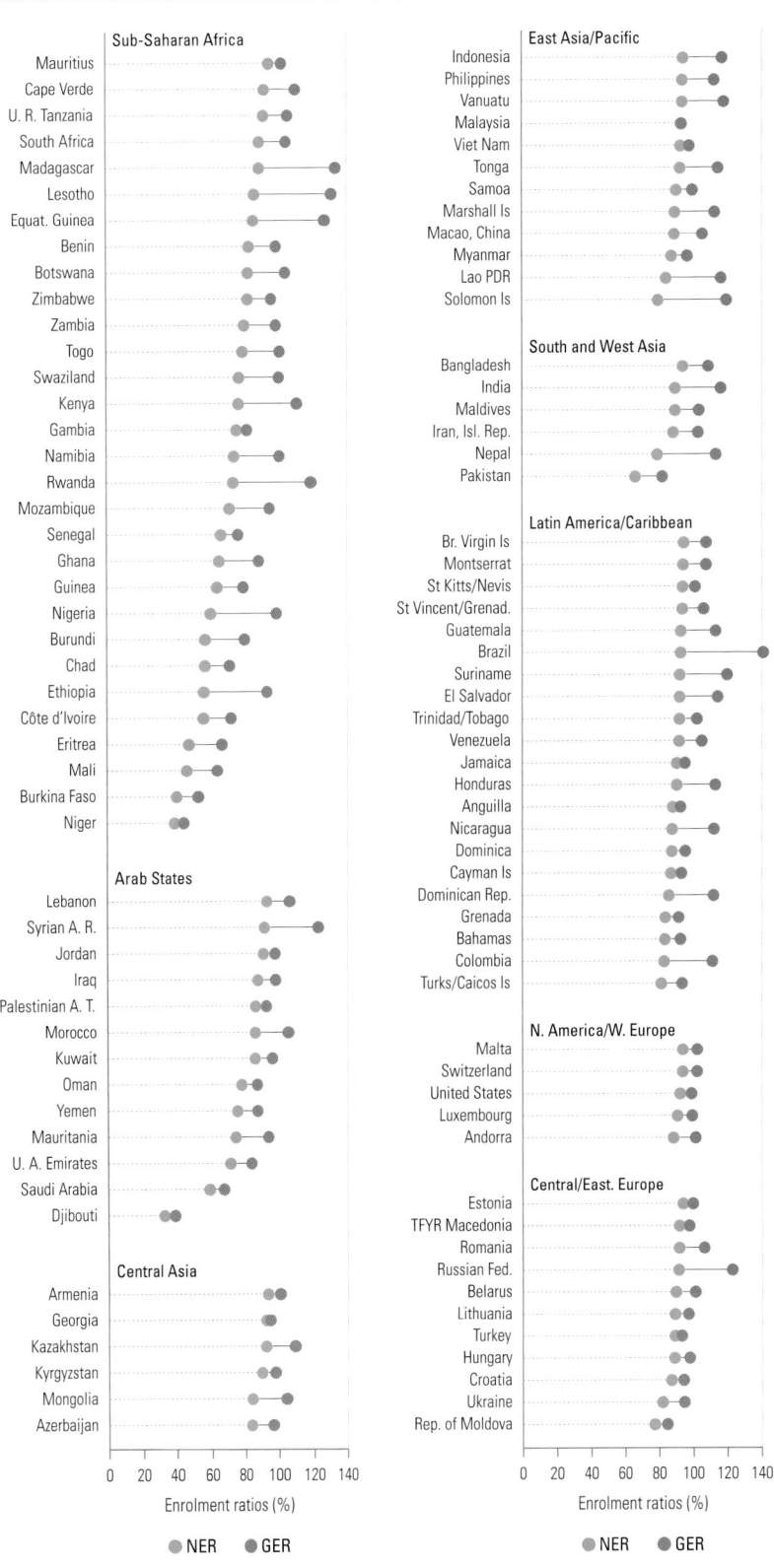

Note: Countries with NERs above 95% are not included. See source table for detailed country notes.
Source: Annex, Statistical Table 5.

Figure 2.6: Changes in primary net enrolment ratios between 1999 and 2004

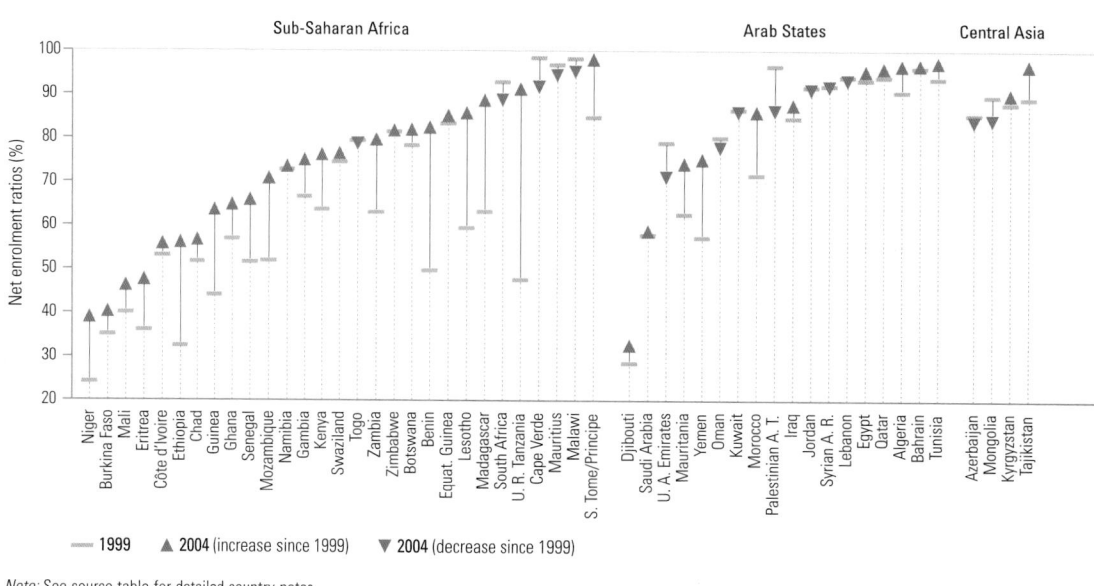

Note: See source table for detailed country notes.
Source: Annex, Statistical Table 5.

widely quoted – thus need to be considered with caution. Until recently the measure of out-of-school children used in the *EFA Global Monitoring Report* has been the number of children of primary school age who were not in primary school. The 2006 Report suggested that almost 100 million children were in this situation in 2002/03, down from almost 107 million in 1998/99. However, it also pointed out a more appropriate measure would take into account only those children of primary school age who were not enrolled in either primary or secondary school.[9] This number was estimated at 85.5 million for 2002/03. To indicate how the situation has been changing, Table 2.8 presents estimates of both measures from 1999 to 2004. Both sets show a reduction in the number of out-of-school children of around 20 million between 1999 and 2004, with a particularly large decrease between 2002 and 2004. Government reporting to the UNESCO Institute for Statistics (UIS) suggests that, in 2004, 77 million children were not enrolled in school.

9. Children of primary school age who are enrolled in pre-primary education should also be excluded from the calculation.

The UIS and UNICEF have been working to improve understanding of the experiences of out-of-school children and some of their background characteristics (UIS/UNICEF, 2005). They estimated the number of out-of-school children for the school year ending in 2002 using administrative enrolment data from governments for some countries and information from household surveys for others. For some highly populated countries, the surveys gave a more accurate picture. The resulting global estimate of children not in primary or secondary school was 115 million, whereas the estimate made solely on the basis of administrative data (shown in Table 2.8) was 94 million.

The difference lies in the nature of the data used. Administrative data are based on school records of enrolment. In household surveys, the head of each household is asked whether each member has gone to school at least one day in the past year (i.e. they record attendance, not enrolment). Both measures raise questions about the quality of data reporting pupils by age. As a result, both may underestimate the number of children who are not receiving effective schooling. For example, a recent extensive survey of primary schools and pupils across India showed that on the days that schools were visited, the average absentee rate was 30% (Pratham, 2005).

Table 2.8: Estimated numbers of children out of school, 1999–2004 (thousands)

	1999	2000	2001	2002	2003	2004
Not in primary school	110 244	107 852	105 307	107 395	101 038	91 032
Not in school	98 172	94 787	92 379	93 824	86 828	76 841

Sources: Annex, Statistical Table 5; UIS database.

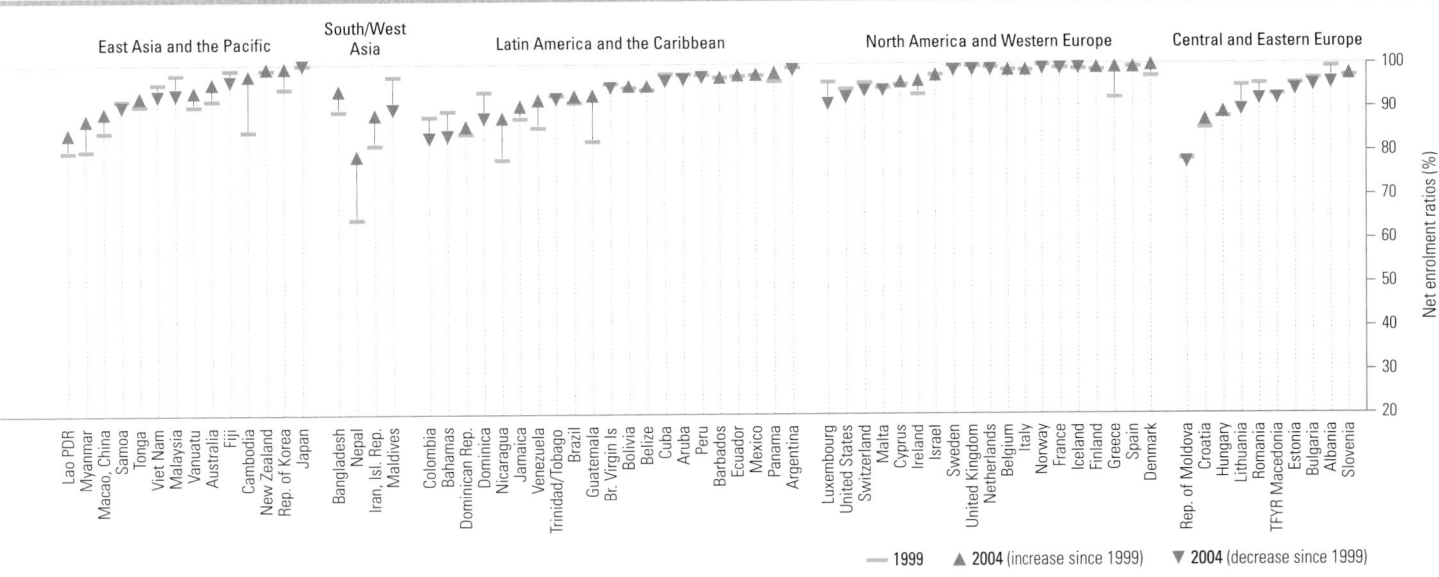

Net enrolment ratios (%)

— 1999   ▲ 2004 (increase since 1999)   ▼ 2004 (decrease since 1999)

Table 2.9: Estimated numbers of out-of-school children by gender and region, 1999 and 2004

	1999				2004			
	Total (000)	Male (000)	Female (000)	% Female	Total (000)	Male (000)	Female (000)	% Female
World	98 172	40 717	57 455	59	76 841	33 252	43 589	57
Developing countries	94 056	38 619	55 437	59	73 473	31 770	41 704	57
Developed countries	2 024	1 065	959	47	2 282	938	1 344	59
Countries in transition	2 093	1 034	1 059	51	1 086	545	541	50
Sub-Saharan Africa	43 289	20 368	22 922	53	38 020	17 914	20 106	53
Arab States	8 361	3 407	4 954	59	6 585	2 695	3 890	59
Central Asia	544	269	275	51	364	171	193	53
East Asia and the Pacific	6 827	3 381	3 446	50	9 671	4 757	4 914	51
East Asia	6 382	3 159	3 223	51	9 298	4 587	4 712	51
Pacific	445	222	222	50	373	170	203	54
South and West Asia	31 309	9 646	21 663	69	15 644	4 873	10 771	69
Latin America and the Caribbean	3 731	1 712	2 019	54	2 698	1 203	1 495	55
Caribbean	435	211	224	51	341	155	185	54
Latin America	3 296	1 501	1 795	54	2 358	1 048	1 309	56
North America and Western Europe	1 519	806	713	47	1 845	703	1 142	62
Central and Eastern Europe	2 592	1 129	1 463	56	2 014	936	1 078	54

Source: Annex, Statistical Table 5.

77 million children are not enrolled in school

Further analysis in this section focuses on the estimated 76.8 million children who in 2004 were not enrolled in either primary or secondary school, and on the global estimates broken down by region for 1999 and 2004 (Table 2.9).

Over the five-year period, the worldwide total is shown as declining very rapidly, by almost 4% a year, from roughly 98.2 million to 76.8 million. Some three-quarters of the decrease (16.7 million) occurred between 2002 and 2004 (Table 2.8). The number of out-of-

The largest numbers of out-of-school children in 2004 were in Nigeria, Pakistan, India and Ethiopia

school children fell in almost all developing country regions. The most dramatic decrease was in South and West Asia, where, the UIS database shows, the number of children out of school was halved from around 31 million in 1999 to 16 million in 2004. Much of this was due to a very large reduction in India (discussed below). A substantial, though smaller, reduction was achieved in sub-Saharan Africa between 1999 and 2004, from 43 million to 38 million, in the context of relatively high growth in the school age population.

East Asia was the only region that saw an increase in the number of out-of-school children, from 6.4 million in 1999 to 9.3 million in 2004. Driving this trend was China, the world's most populous country, where the NER in primary education dropped from 97% in 1991 (see annex, Statistical Table 12) to 94% in the school year ending in 2002 (UNESCO, 2005).

In 1999, sub-Saharan Africa and South and West Asia were home to more than three-quarters of the world's out-of-school children (with 45% and 31%, respectively). By 2004, the combined share had declined slightly, to around 69%, but with sub-Saharan Africa's share increasing to 50% while South and West Asia's share had fallen to 19%. Worldwide, 57% of all children out of school in 2004 were girls, down from 59% in 1999.

In which countries do they live?

To arrive at the global and regional totals described above, the approximate number of children out of school was estimated for countries that do not provide sufficient information for detailed calculations or whose enrolment data are inconsistent with United Nations population data. Many of these countries are in sub-Saharan Africa, including Angola, Cameroon, the Central African Republic, the Congo, the Democratic Republic of the Congo, Liberia, Sierra Leone, Somalia and Uganda. Others include Afghanistan, China and the Sudan. It is estimated that just over one-third of all out-of-school children worldwide live in countries where the data are not available or are insufficient or inconsistent. They are not included in the discussion in this subsection, which is based on country data in the statistical tables, and therefore cannot be regarded as exhaustive.

Among the 112 developing countries for which information is published, twenty-eight each had more than half a million children of primary

Figure 2.7: Developing countries with over 500,000 out-of-school children, 2004

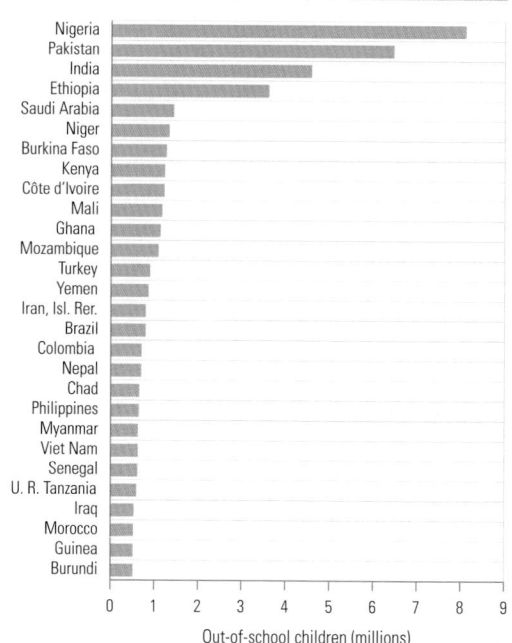

Note: These countries together account for 43.3 million out-of-school children, out of the global estimated total of 76.8 million.
See source table for detailed country notes.
Source: Annex, Statistical Table 5.

school age out of school in 2004 (Figure 2.7), and in twelve cases, the country total was over a million. Four countries alone accounted for about 23 million children out of school. Of the eight countries with 1 million to 2 million children out of school, seven are in sub-Saharan Africa. Among the sixteen countries with between half a million and a million children out of school, every EFA region except Central Asia and North America and Western Europe is represented.

Among the countries for which reliable data are available, the largest numbers of out-of-school children in 2004 were in Nigeria, Pakistan, India and Ethiopia. They were followed by Saudi Arabia, the Niger, Burkina Faso, Kenya, Côte d'Ivoire, Mali, Ghana and Mozambique.[10] Nevertheless, considerable progress has been made in some of these countries since 1999 (Table 2.10).

The largest reduction was reported to have occurred in India between 2002 and 2004, from 15.1 million to 4.6 million, although the 2004 figure is likely an underestimate, according to the results of a national survey in late 2005 (detailed below in Box 2.1). The number of out-of-school

10. The countries with the largest proportions of primary school age children out of school (over 40%) are Burundi, Burkina Faso, Chad, Côte d'Ivoire, Djibouti, Eritrea, Ethiopia, Mali, the Niger and Saudi Arabia. Six of these are also among the countries with the highest absolute number of out-of-school children.

Table 2.10: Numbers of out-of-school children in selected countries in 1999, 2002 and 2004 (thousands)

	1999	2002	2004
Mali	1 113	1 089	1 172
Côte d'Ivoire	1 253	1 144	1 223
Kenya	1 833	1 868	1 225
Burkina Faso	1 205	1 264	1 271
Niger	1 393	1 381	1 326
Ghana	1 329	1 307	1 357
Saudi Arabia	1 345	1 371	1 630
Mozambique	1 602	1 572	1 089
Ethiopia	4 961	4 633	3 615
India	…	15 136	4 583
Pakistan	…	…	6 463
Nigeria	…	…	8 110

Note: See source table for detailed country notes.
Sources: Annex, Statistical Table 5; UIS database.

children was also reported to have fallen significantly in Mozambique, and by one-third in Kenya. For Nigeria, which had the largest reported number of out-of-school children, there are no estimates prior to 2004. Although the NERs of the other seven countries in the table improved, the number of out-of-school children increased slightly in four and decreased slightly in three. This highlights the fact that when fertility rates remain high, as in most countries of sub-Saharan Africa, very large increases in the NERs are necessary if the absolute number of out-of-school children is to fall significantly.

Who are they?

To formulate effective policies to reduce the total number of children who remain out of school, it is necessary to understand better who they are. Two sets of characteristics are relevant:

■ the numbers of children who (a) were initially enrolled but dropped out, (b) are likely to be late entrants, and (c) are unlikely ever to enter school unless new efforts are made;

■ the dominant background characteristics of out-of-school children.

These issues were partially addressed in the UIS/UNICEF study (2005), whose results are reported here. New analyses based on that study are also presented.

Educational experiences. The children of primary school age who were not enrolled in school in 2004 are not homogenous with regard to schooling. Some were enrolled in primary school prior to that year, but dropped out. The challenge for governments regarding this group is to

increase opportunities and incentives for them to re-enter the education system, which often necessitates new forms of provision. A second group is children who are likely to enrol but as late entrants, like many of their older brothers and sisters. The earlier discussion of intake rates showed that, particularly in Africa, a large proportion of children who enrol in primary school are older than the official age when they do so. The children in this group are 'not yet in school' rather than 'out of school'. Of the children who do not start school at the official age, however, many never enter. While some of the initiatives that are required to entice children who have dropped out to come back to school may also be applicable to this group of children, additional measures are likely to be necessary. In Zambia in 2002, for example, 68 of every 100 primary school age children were in school. Of the 32 not in school, 8 had been enrolled and dropped out, 12 were deemed likely late entrants and the remaining 12 were characterized as unlikely ever to enrol (UIS/UNICEF, 2005).

A breakdown of out-of-school children in 2004 into the categories of dropouts, late entrants and never enrolled has been estimated by region. The analysis is dependent on age-specific enrolment data supplied to the UIS by governments and the results should be seen only as approximations. Overall, of the roughly 76.8 million who were out of school, 7.2 million had dropped out, 23.0 million were likely to enrol later and 46.6 million (roughly 61%) were unlikely ever to enrol, in the absence of additional incentives. For every two boys unlikely ever to enrol there were nearly three girls.

The distributions of children across these categories vary substantially by region (Figure 2.8). In South and West Asia, around 75% are unlikely ever to enrol and almost 14% are likely to enrol late. The proportion of those who will probably enrol late is higher in sub-Saharan Africa: almost 28%. Overall, the proportion of children not in school who are unlikely ever to enrol is greatest in the least educationally developed regions. Conversely, in Latin America and the Caribbean and in East Asia and the Pacific the share of late entrants is much higher than that of those who are not likely to enrol.

Educational experiences vary by country within regions as well as by region. Figure 2.9 shows distributions for twenty countries, mostly in sub-Saharan Africa. The contribution of late entrants varies significantly. In Kenya and Mauritania, this group appears to be the main

In Zambia 32 of 100 primary school-age children were not in school

Figure 2.8: Distribution of out-of-school children by exposure to school and by region, 2004

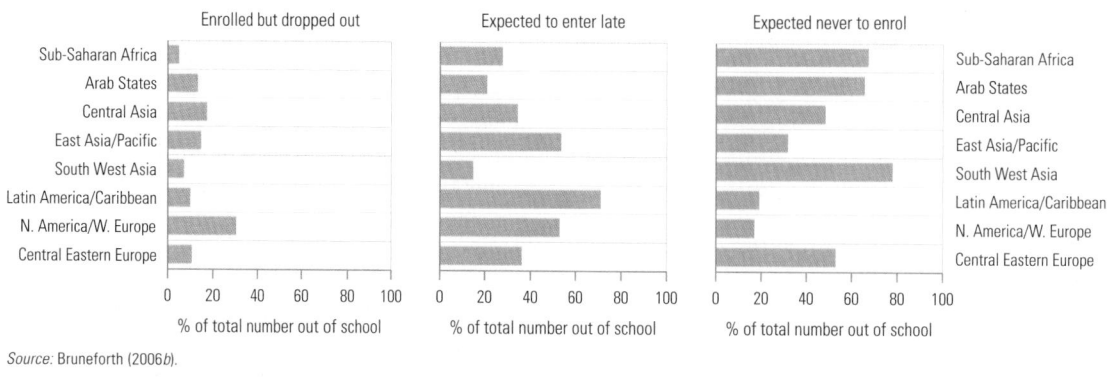

Source: Bruneforth (2006*b*).

Figure 2.9: Distribution of out-of-school children in countries facing the greatest challenges, by exposure to school, 2004

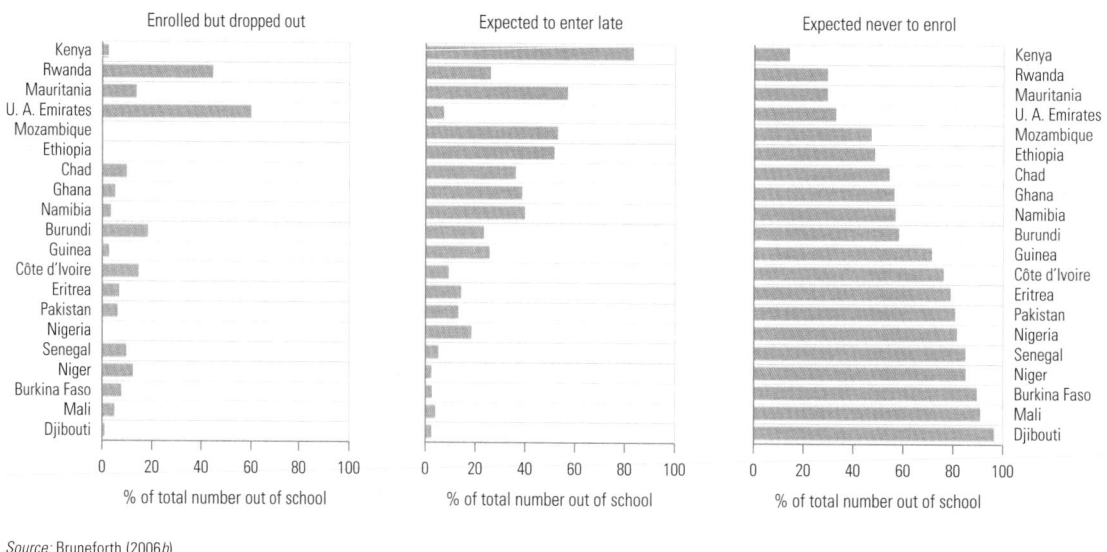

Source: Bruneforth (2006*b*).

contributor; in Ethiopia and Mozambique the numbers of late entrants and of those who never enrol are similar; in the remaining six countries late entrants are a much smaller group; and, in five of these countries, over three-quarters of those who were out of school in 2004 are unlikely ever to enrol.

Background characteristics. A disaggregation of out-of-school children on the basis of whether they have ever attended school and, if not, whether it is likely that they will enter late is useful for formulating differentiated policy responses. A better understanding of the background characteristics of these children is also useful. UIS/UNICEF (2005) used household survey data for eighty countries (for 2001/02 or

most recent) for this purpose. In these countries, 26% of all primary school age children were out of school on average, the percentage was 24% for boys and 28% for girls. The variation by gender, however, proved to be the smallest among the characteristics investigated (Figure 2.10): gender, residence, household wealth and mother's education. While 18% of primary-school age urban children were out of school, the share was 30% for rural children. Similarly, the likelihood of being out of school was strongly influenced by the wealth of the child's household. The rate was 12% for the children in the wealthiest one-fifth of households, 25% in the middle fifth and 38% in the poorest fifth. Finally, just 16% of children whose mothers had had some education were

Figure 2.10: Proportion of out-of-school among primary-school-age children in eighty countries, by category

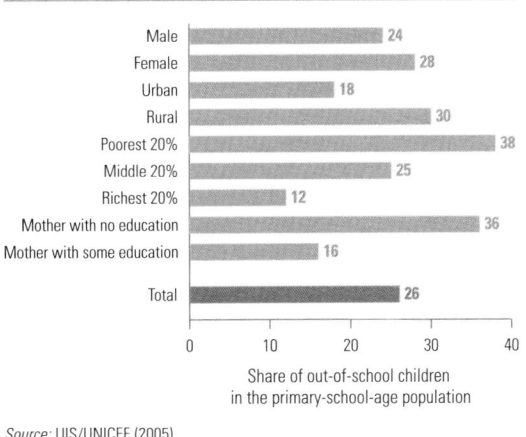

Share of out-of-school children
in the primary-school-age population

Source: UIS/UNICEF (2005).

themselves out of school, compared to 36% of those whose mothers had had no education.

Beyond these averages, the situation for each characteristic varied by region and country:

■ *Gender.* While 117 girls were not in school for every 100 boys, their exclusion was particularly marked in the Arab States (134), and South and West Asia (129), and in individual countries such as Yemen (184), Iraq (176), India (136) and Benin (136). Conversely, in Latin America and the Caribbean, for every 100 boys out of school there were 96 girls.

■ *Place of residence.* The share of children out of school was at least twice as large in rural areas as in urban areas in twenty-four of the eighty countries analysed. Burkina Faso, Eritrea, Ethiopia and Nicaragua showed the largest differences. Because of the large size of rural populations, inequalities in access result in the vast majority of out-of-school children being from rural households. Over 80% of out-of-school children in sub-Saharan Africa and South Asia live in rural areas. The share in some individual countries is even higher: Ethiopia (96%), Burkina Faso (95%), Malawi (94%), Bangladesh (84%) and India (84%).

■ *Household wealth.* Everywhere, the impact of household wealth on access to education is large for boys and girls alike: children from the poorest 20% of households are three times as likely to be out of school as children from the wealthiest 20%. The impact is particularly large in the Arab States and smallest in Central and Eastern Europe. There are countries in most regions where the gap between rich and poor

is particularly large – Nicaragua, Peru and Venezuela in Latin America; Indonesia in East Asia; Cameroon, Madagascar and Zambia in sub-Saharan Africa; Algeria and Sudan in the Arab States; and Kazakhstan in Central Asia.

■ *Mother's education.* On average a child whose mother has no education is twice as likely to be out of school as a child whose mother has some education. For South Asia and Latin America, the multiple is close to 2.5, and in twelve of the eighty countries it is 2.8 or higher. A multivariate analysis was carried out with the data for sixty-eight countries to assess the independent effect of each separate variable. Having a rural rather than an urban background was significant in thirty-one cases, being female rather than male in thirty-nine cases, having a mother with some schooling in sixty-three cases and being poor rather than rich in sixty-five cases. More detailed studies were made of India, Indonesia, Mali and Nigeria. In addition to the characteristics already mentioned, other groups found to have a higher probability of being out of school were, for India: orphans, child labourers, children of scheduled tribe households and those residing in particular states; for Indonesia, members of households with a large number of children, and those in particular regions; for Mali, child labourers and those living in certain regions; and, for Nigeria, children from male-headed households and those residing in the north.

A more recent analysis of who attends school and who does not in eight countries in sub-Saharan Africa looked at the backgrounds of children who have reached the 'official' age for *completing* primary education but have never attended, and are very unlikely ever to do so. Table 2.11 shows the results.

Except in Namibia, girls are more likely never to attend school than boys; and in all countries rural and poorer children are more likely never to attend than urban and wealthier children. While the gender differences are relatively small, those based on residence and, particularly, on household wealth are very wide. Even in countries such as Ghana, Kenya and Mozambique, where attendance rates average over 85%, the chances of a poor child not having attended school are at least eight times those of a child from the wealthiest group of households.

It is possible to move beyond the rural-urban, male-female and poorest-richest dichotomies and examine the impact of several variables at

Girls are more likely never to attend school than boys

Education for All Global Monitoring Report

2007

Table 2.11: Percentages of children who have never attended school, by background characteristics, in eight sub-Saharan African countries

	Burkina Faso	Ethiopia	Ghana	Kenya	Mali	Mozambique	Namibia	Nigeria
Female	65.7	62.1	14.9	8.9	65.9	18.7	4.7	24.9
Male	58.1	53.8	13.6	7.8	51.4	12.8	7.5	18.1
Rural	70.9	64.3	19.7	8.8	69.0	19.7	7.1	26.5
Urban	20.2	17.2	6.3	5.3	35.8	8.0	2.6	12.3
Poorest 20% of households	78.3	82.8	37.8	23.5	74.6	23.3	9.8	43.6
Richest 20% of households	26.0	35.7	3.9	3.0	32.4	2.5	1.7	1.6

Sources: Bruneforth (2006*a*); Demographic and Health Surveys 2003 for Burkina Faso, Ghana, Kenya, Mozambique and Nigeria 2001 for Mali; 2000 for Ethiopia and Namibia.

Disparities related to wealth and mother's education are stronger than those related to place of residence and gender

once. This was done for eighteen countries that have either high numbers or high proportions of children out of school (Bruneforth, 2006*c*). The results are troubling. For instance, in Guinea, an urban boy from the wealthiest quintile and with an educated mother is 126 times more likely to attend school than a rural girl from the poorest quintile with a mother who lacks education. The greatest discrepancies were found in Burkina Faso, Ethiopia, Guinea and the Niger and the lowest in Burundi, Ghana and Kenya. Overall, the disparities decrease as the net attendance rate increases, but they can still be substantial. In almost all the countries, disparities related to wealth and mother's education are stronger than those related to place of residence and gender.

In addition to the ongoing UIS/UNICEF work, the Government of India recently commissioned a survey of out-of-school children. The findings are providing new guidance for programmes to encourage more children to enrol and remain in school (Box 2.1).

Primary school progression and completion: still a concern

Increasing access to school is an important step, but ensuring that pupils progress smoothly through the grades and ultimately complete primary school is equally so. The high incidence of grade repetition and the low retention rates in many countries around the world are an indication that education systems are not functioning well.

Box 2.1: In India, an independent survey profiles out-of-school children

The Government of India commissioned a nationwide independent survey of 87,874 households, undertaken in 2005 (Social and Rural Research Institute, 2005). The objectives were to estimate (a) the numbers of out-of-school children at age 5 and in the 6-10 and 11-13 age groups in each state, classified by gender and social category (for instance, 'scheduled tribe', 'scheduled caste', 'other backward castes', 'Muslims'); (b) the distribution of enrolment by school management and grade; (c) the numbers of children with disabilities who were attending and not attending school, by disability; and (d) the number of children who had dropped out of school, by grade.

State governments had estimated that 25 million children aged 6 to 13 were out of school in 2002. The 2005 survey indicated that the number had almost been halved to 13.5 million, or 6.9% of the age group. Of these, 7.8 million were 6 to 10 years old (the official age range for primary school in a majority of states), equal to 6.1% of the age group. This total differs significantly from that of 4.6 million

out-of-school children shown for 2004 in Table 2.10. Possible reasons include differences between school attendance reported in the household survey and enrolment recorded in the school statistics reported to the UIS, and differences in school age population estimates. The 13.5 million figure for ages 6 to 13 is close to an estimate of 14.0 million out-of-school children resulting from a separate national survey organized by Pratham, a large NGO (Pratham Resource Center, 2005). Of those out of school, 32% were reported to have been enrolled but dropped out, while 68% had never enrolled.

This analysis focuses on results for the 6 to 13 age group, in line with practice by the national and state governments in India. The 6.9% rate for out-of-school children reflects rates of 6.2% for boys and 7.9% for girls. The rate in rural areas of 7.8% is significantly higher than the 4.3% in urban areas. In urban areas the rates for boys and girls are similar while in rural areas they are 6.8% for boys and 9.1% for girls. The variations by social group were much larger than those

Grade repetition

Although grade repetition rates depend partly on promotion policies,[11] the high incidence of repetition in some countries also reflects insufficient mastery of the curriculum by pupils and the low quality of education they receive. Reducing repetition should be made a policy priority.

In more than half of the 148 countries for which data are available, the share of primary school pupils who repeated a grade in 2004 was less than 5%, having decreased – often considerably – since 1999 (see annex, Statistical Table 6). In several countries, the decline resulted from initiatives to improve quality, as reflected in national targets to reduce grade repetition (Table 2.12). However, repetition remains widespread in many parts of the world, including sub-Saharan Africa, where part of the education community considers it an appropriate way to help students in difficulty (Bernard et al., 2005). In more than half the sub-Saharan African countries (particularly the French-speaking ones), the percentage of repeaters is close to or above 20%. In Equatorial Guinea it is 40%, more than three times the level in 1999. In other regions, grade repetition is much less frequent, although there are exceptions such as Brazil (21%) and Nepal (23%).

Repetition rates vary by grade. In the majority of countries, particularly those in the developing world, the highest repetition rates are usually found in grade 1. For example, in Nepal 43% of pupils repeat this grade, compared with 11% for grade 5. Grade 1 repetition rates close to 30% or more are also found in Brazil, Guatemala, the Lao People's Democratic Republic and several countries in sub-Saharan Africa.

The incidence of grade repetition partly reflects the quality of primary education, yet the high repetition rates for grade 1 in many countries also raise the issues of school transition and readiness. Indeed, for most of these countries, particularly those in sub-Saharan Africa, a link can be made between the high repetition rates, particularly in the first years of primary education, and low participation rates in pre-primary education (see Chapters 5 and 7 on the relationship between ECCE and primary school readiness).

School retention and completion

All children should remain long enough in school to master the curriculum and thus acquire at least basic literacy and numeracy skills. Several factors determine the levels of retention and, more generally, completion. Children leave school prematurely for a variety of reasons, including the costs of schooling, the need to supplement family income or take care of siblings, unfriendly school environments (particularly for girls) and poor education quality.

Grade repetition reflects the quality of primary education

11. While grade repetition is an indication of pupils' progress or even achievement, it also reflects wide variation in countries' educational approaches and sometimes cultures (Bernard et al., 2005). Some countries automatically promote pupils, while others use more stringent achievement criteria.

by gender or place of residence: the out-of-school rates were 10.0% for Muslims, 9.5% for scheduled tribes, 8.2% for scheduled castes, 6.9% for other backward castes and 3.7% for the remaining social groups. Another focus of the survey was the schooling experiences of disabled children. Around 4.3% of all out-of-school children are disabled. Of all disabled children, 38.1% are not attending school.

Variations in the rates of out-of-school children across the country are wide. They are highest in north-central and north-eastern India. Among the major states, the rates are highest in Bihar (17.0%), Jharkhand (10.9%), Assam (8.9%), West Bengal (8.7%), Madhya Pradesh (8.6%), Uttar Pradesh (8.2%) and Rajasthan (6.9%). By contrast, in the south, some states appear to have virtually achieved universal schooling for 6- to 13-year-olds: Kerala, Karnataka and Tamil Nadu record out-of-school rates between 0.5% and 2.1%. Almost half of all children out of school live in Bihar (3.2 million) and Uttar Pradesh (3.0 million), but seven other states have at least half a million each: West Bengal (1.2 million), Madhya Pradesh (1.1 million), Rajasthan (0.8 million), Jharkhand (0.6 million), and Assam, Maharashtra and Andhra Pradesh with around 0.5 million each. The situation varies not only across states but also within them. In 48 out of 598 districts nationwide, over 50,000 children are out of school. Ten states have at least one of these districts, but the majority are in Bihar (20), Uttar Pradesh (15) and West Bengal (4).

More detailed estimates of the likelihood of being out of school depending on individual background characteristics and state of residence were calculated. For instance, over 30% of rural Muslim children are out of school in Bihar, around 17% in Jharkhand, 13% in Uttar Pradesh and 11% in West Bengal. Scheduled caste children have out-of-school rates of 22% in rural Bihar and 26% in rural Jharkhand. Of the major states, West Bengal has the highest rate for scheduled tribe children: 16%. Perhaps surprisingly, the numbers of scheduled caste and Muslim boys who are out of school are higher than those for girls. This is not the case for other backward castes or scheduled tribes.

Education for All Global Monitoring Report 2 0 0 7

Table 2.12: Changes in percentage of primary school repeaters between 1999 and 2004 in relation to national targets

	Percentage of repeaters		National targets
	1999	2004	
Sub-Saharan Africa			
Benin	...	23.1	Reduce the repetition rate from 20.4% in 2001 to 10% in 2015
Burkina Faso	17.7	13.0	Reduce the share of repeaters from 17% in 1997 to 10% in 2015
Côte d'Ivoire	23.7	17.6	Reduce the repetition rate by one percentage point per year by 2015
Democratic Rep. of the Congo	...	...	Reduce the primary repetition rate from 15% to 10% in 2015
Ethiopia	11.4	7.0	
Guinea	26.2	10.5	
Mozambique	23.8	20.6	Reduce the share of repeaters from 22.5% to 11% in 2009 and 5% in 2015
South Africa	10.4	5.2	
Togo	31.2	23.8	
Arab States			
Egypt	6.0	4.0	
Morocco	12.4	13.2	Reduce the repetition rate from 13.8% to 9% in 2008, 5% in 2013 and 3% in 2015
Oman	8.0	0.8	
Saudi Arabia	5.4	4.2	Reduce the repetition rate to 5% at the elementary stage by 2015
Tunisia	18.3	7.3	
Yemen	10.6	4.3	
East Asia			
Cambodia	24.6	10.6	
Latin America and the Caribbean			
Brazil	24.0	20.6	Correct the school flow within five years by reducing the repetition and dropout rates
Costa Rica	9.2	6.9	
Haiti	...	...	Reduce the repetition rate from 25% in 1997 to 10% in 2007
Mexico	6.6	4.8	Reduce the repetition rate by one percentage point, from 7.1% to 6.1%, by the end of the 2006/07 school year
Nicaragua	4.7	10.5	Decrease the repetition rate in primary education from 10.6% in 2004 to 2% in 2015
Peru	10.2	7.6	

Note: The table shows only those countries where the percentage of repeaters was about 5% or above in 1999. See source table for detailed country notes.
Sources: Annex, Statistical Table 6; UNESCO-IIEP (2006).

Most indicators currently available to measure primary school completion are proxies that do not reveal how many children actually complete school. Many are gross rates that include all children of a cohort but do not distinguish between those who do not complete primary education because they never even enrolled and those who did enrol but did not reach or complete the last grade.

Among these proxy measures is the *gross intake rate* (GIR) to the last grade of primary education.[12] Being enrolled in the last grade is by definition the minimum prerequisite for completion. In 2004 the number of children entering the last grade of primary school as a percentage of the population at the official age for that grade was 86% worldwide, almost 99% in developed countries and 84% in developing ones.

Overall, access to the last grade of primary education is close to or well above 90% in all regions except for South and West Asia (82%), the Arab States (80%) and sub-Saharan Africa (57%)

(Figure 2.11). In Burkina Faso, Chad, Djibouti and the Niger, the GIR to the last grade is below 30% (see annex, Statistical Table 7).

Completion rates (proxied by survival rates) can also be used to assess the extent to which education systems retain children, enabling them to complete their education. This approach focuses on children who did have access to school and assesses how many of them completed the primary cycle.

In half of the 132 countries with data available for the school year ending in 2003, about 87% of a cohort of pupils who had access to primary education reached the last grade (see annex, Statistical Table 7). Survival rates to the last grade are close to 100% in developed and transition countries, where legislation on compulsory education is more strictly enforced, while the median for developing countries is below 80%. Survival rates are close to or above 90% in most Arab States for which data are available, except Mauritania (69%), Morocco (76%) and Yemen

12. The GIR to the last grade of primary is the total number of new entrants to the grade, regardless of age, expressed as a percentage of the population of theoretical entrance age for that grade.

Figure 2.11: Gross intake rates to the last grade of primary education by region, 2004

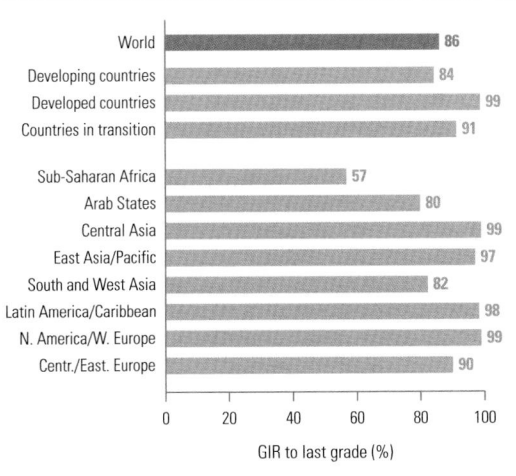

Source: Annex, Statistical Table 7.

Figure 2.12: Survival rates to last grade and primary education cohort completion rates for selected countries, 2003

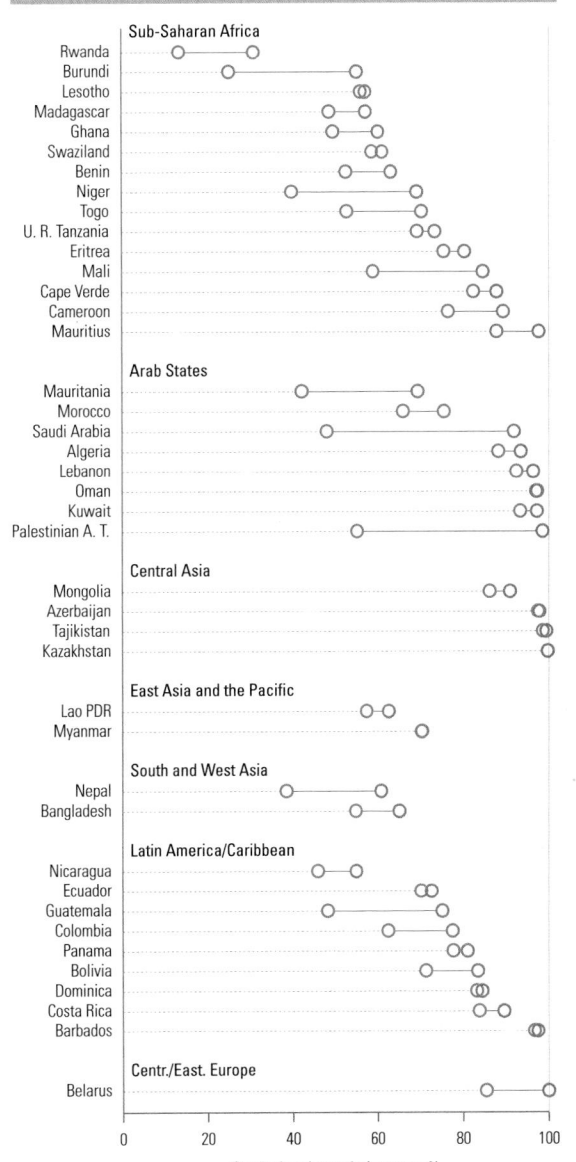

○ Cohort completion rates   ○ Survival rates to last grade

Note: See source table for detailed country notes.
Source: Annex, Statistical Table 7.

National averages often hide significant disparities among groups within countries

(67%). In Latin America and the Caribbean, despite the overall high level of access and participation in primary education, school completion remains an important UPE challenge, with survival rates less than 83% in the majority of countries. In some countries of this region, including the Dominican Republic, Guyana and Nicaragua, fewer than 60% of the children who enter primary school go on to reach the last grade.

Sub-Saharan Africa combines low levels of access to school with low completion rates: fewer than two-thirds of pupils reach the last grade in the majority of countries. In some countries, among them Chad, Equatorial Guinea, Malawi, Mozambique, Nigeria and Rwanda, more than 60% of pupils who have access to school fail to reach the last grade. While not at such levels, school retention is also low in several of the South and West Asian countries with data available; dropout rates before the last grade are over 30% in Bangladesh and Nepal, for example.

National averages often hide significant disparities among groups within countries. As Box 2.2 shows, both boys and girls who live in rural areas, are from poor families or have mothers with no education are more likely to drop out of school than other children.

How many children actually complete school?
Not all children who reach the last primary grade necessarily complete it with success according to national standards. Figure 2.12 displays both survival rates to last grade and cohort completion

rates[13] for selected countries. In most, cohort completion rates are lower than survival rates to last grade. The gap is particularly significant (above twenty percentage points) in Burundi, Guatemala, Mali, Mauritania, Nepal, the Niger, the Palestinian Autonomous Territories and Saudi Arabia. In the last two, almost all children reach the last grade but only 55% and 48%, respectively, actually complete primary education.

13. The cohort completion rate focuses on children who had access to primary education, measuring how many of them successfully completed it. It is computed as the product of the percentage of graduates from primary school (the number of graduates divided by the number of new entrants to the last grade) and the survival rate to last grade.

Recent progress
in getting
children into
school has
benefited girls
in particular

Box 2.2: Subnational disparities in school retention in Africa: who are the children who drop out of school?

In the majority of countries in sub-Saharan Africa, more than one-third of primary school pupils drop out before they reach the last grade, and thus become part of the out-of-school population. Who are these children? The UIS has examined their situation. Using data from Demographic and Health Surveys of Burkina Faso, Ethiopia, Ghana, Kenya, Mali, Mozambique, Namibia and Nigeria, and analysing the population of those aged 10 to 19 who attended school at some point and dropped out without completing their primary education, the study shows that:

- More than half of all children who left primary school in Burkina Faso, Ethiopia, Kenya, Mali and Mozambique did so without completing it. Exceptions to this pattern were Ghana and Nigeria, where more than 80% of the children who left school did so by completing it (Figure 2.13). Subnational disparities in school completion were most pronounced between children from urban and rural areas and between those from poorer and richer backgrounds. Overall, poor or rural children were ten times more likely to drop out than urban or richer children.

- In Burkina Faso, Ethiopia, Kenya, Mali and Mozambique, more than 80% of rural children who left primary school did not complete it, while the percentages were less than half for urban children. In Ethiopia, rural children were sixty times more likely to drop out than urban children.

- In Burkina Faso, Mali and Mozambique, more than 90% of the children from the poorest 40% of households (the two poorest quintiles) who left primary school did not complete it. Dropout was also frequent for the richer population (top 40%), but far less so. The differences between poor and rich children were most pronounced in Mali

Figure 2.13: Primary school dropouts by background characteristics

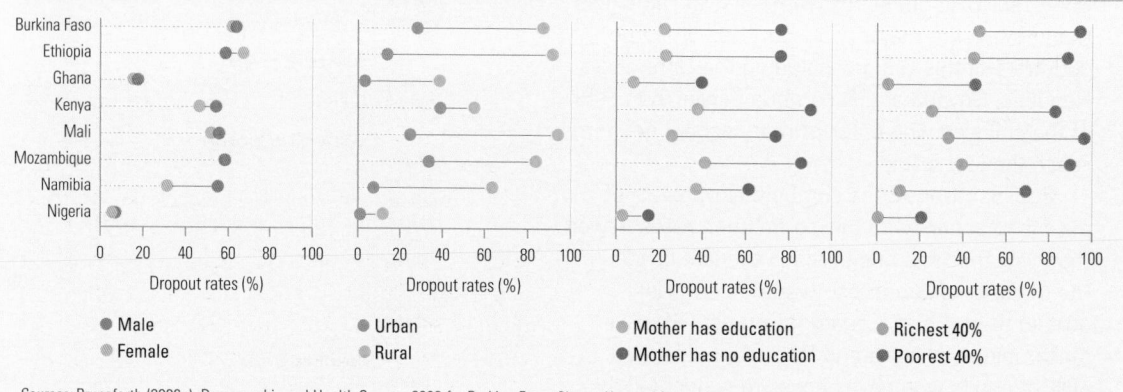

Sources: Bruneforth (2006a); Demographic and Health Surveys 2003 for Burkina Faso, Ghana, Kenya, Mozambique and Nigeria; 2001 for Mali; 2000 for Ethiopia and Namibia.

Retention and completion rates often reflect the state of learning achievement. In some countries, completion can also reflect tough selection policies due to limited availability of places at lower secondary level. To achieve UPE in such cases, it is necessary both to improve the quality of primary education and to expand access to secondary education (UNESCO, 2005).

Gender disparities in primary education

Recent progress in getting children into school has benefited girls in particular, with the global gender parity index (GPI) for the primary education GER increasing from 0.92 in 1999

to 0.94 in 2004 (Table 2.13). Rapid progress was registered in developing countries, especially in those with both low enrolment ratios and high gender disparities (Figure 2.14). This was the case in Benin, Djibouti, Equatorial Guinea, Ethiopia, the Gambia, Guinea, India, the Islamic Republic of Iran,[14] Morocco, Nepal and Yemen. Overall, about two-thirds of the 181 countries for which 2004 data were available had achieved gender parity in primary education by that year; some, including the Cook Islands, Dominica, Mauritania, Malawi, the Netherlands Antilles, Qatar and Uganda, achieved it between 1999 and 2004. On the other hand, in some countries GPIs

14. In the Islamic Republic of Iran, the sharp increase in girls' enrolment compared to 2003 is mainly due to a data reporting change: the 2004 data include adult literacy learners, who are mostly female and who were not included in 2003.

and Nigeria, where poorer children were fifty to seventy-five times more likely to leave school without completion than rich children.

- Differences between children of mothers with and without some primary education were strong, but generally less important than urban/rural or rich/poor differences. The exception was Kenya, where school-leavers without educated mothers were fourteen times more likely to have dropped out than those with educated mothers.

- Gender disparities among children who dropped out were very much smaller than the differences related to the other background characteristics, and were at a noticeable level only in Namibia.

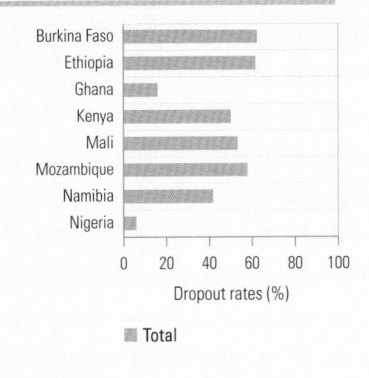

Dropout rates (%)

■ Total

decreased during the period; they include Aruba, Chile, the Dominican Republic, Kenya, Saint Lucia, Tonga and the United Republic of Tanzania.

Despite the overall positive trends, significant gender disparities remain, mostly at the expense of girls. Such gaps are now concentrated in the Arab States, South and West Asia, and sub-Saharan Africa, where overall about 90 girls are enrolled in primary school for every 100 boys (Table 2.13). In Afghanistan, Chad, the Central African Republic, the Niger, Pakistan and Yemen, the GPIs are particularly low (under 0.75). For these three regions, gender parity in education

Table 2.13: Changes in gender disparities in primary education by region between 1999 and 2004

	Gross enrolment ratios					
	1999			2004		
	Male	Female	GPI	Male	Female	GPI
	%	%	(F/M)	%	%	(F/M)
World	104.2	95.8	0.92	109.3	103.0	0.94
Developing countries	104.5	94.9	0.91	110.2	103.2	0.94
Developed countries	102.0	102.5	1.00	102.1	100.6	0.99
Countries in transition	100.7	99.4	0.99	107.9	106.8	0.99
Sub-Saharan Africa	85.4	72.5	0.85	96.3	85.4	0.89
Arab States	94.6	82.4	0.87	98.0	88.3	0.90
Central Asia	99.2	98.2	0.99	102.3	100.9	0.99
East Asia/Pacific	112.4	111.4	0.99	113.9	112.5	0.99
East Asia	112.8	111.7	0.99	114.2	112.8	0.99
Pacific	94.6	93.2	0.99	99.4	96.3	0.97
South and West Asia	102.6	84.6	0.82	114.7	104.8	0.91
Latin America/Caribbean	122.6	118.8	0.97	119.7	116.1	0.97
Caribbean	116.6	113.4	0.97	127.8	124.7	0.98
Latin America	122.9	119.0	0.97	119.4	115.8	0.97
N. America/W. Europe	102.4	103.3	1.01	102.5	100.8	0.98
Centr./East. Europe	101.6	97.5	0.96	102.8	100.1	0.97

Source: Annex, Statistical Table 5.

is part of an overall challenge involving the dismantling of gender discrimination and of the economic and political disadvantages confronting girls and women (UNICEF, 2005*a*).

Gender disparities in primary education often stem from difficulties girls face in obtaining access to school. Among these obstacles are poverty and the related issue of direct and indirect costs of education, distance to school, language and ethnicity,[15] social exclusion and the school environment.[16] In addition, girls face cultural barriers concerning their roles in the home and in society. The challenge is to implement policies tailored to overcoming

Girls face cultural barriers concerning their roles in the home and in society

15. In the **Lao People's Democratic Republic**, for example, girls from ethnic minorities are less likely to attend school (Lao PDR Ministry of Education, 2004). Ethnicity, race and language as barriers to education are particularly apparent in **Latin America and the Caribbean**, where a focus on educational disparity favouring girls can mask illiteracy and low school participation among girls from indigenous groups. **Bolivia**, for instance, reports more girls in school than boys, yet more than half of indigenous girls drop out of school before age 14 (UNICEF, 2005*a: p.*47). In **Central and Eastern Europe**, hidden within the statistics on girls' education are disparities among ethnic minorities, with minority girls being less likely to enrol in school or to attend. 'They face triple discrimination, as gender compounds the effects of bigotry and poverty' (UNICEF, 2005*a: p.*39).

16. An Oxfam study in the Philippines noted that, despite the achievement of parity, gender bias against girls and women was 'still deeply rooted in the school system', reflected in textbooks, school policies and practices, and curricula. Especially serious are school climates that 'create conditions which engender violence and sexual harassment'. Expulsion of pregnant teenage girls remains prevalent (Bernard, 2005).

Figure 2.14: Changes in gender disparities in primary education gross enrolment ratios between 1999 and 2004

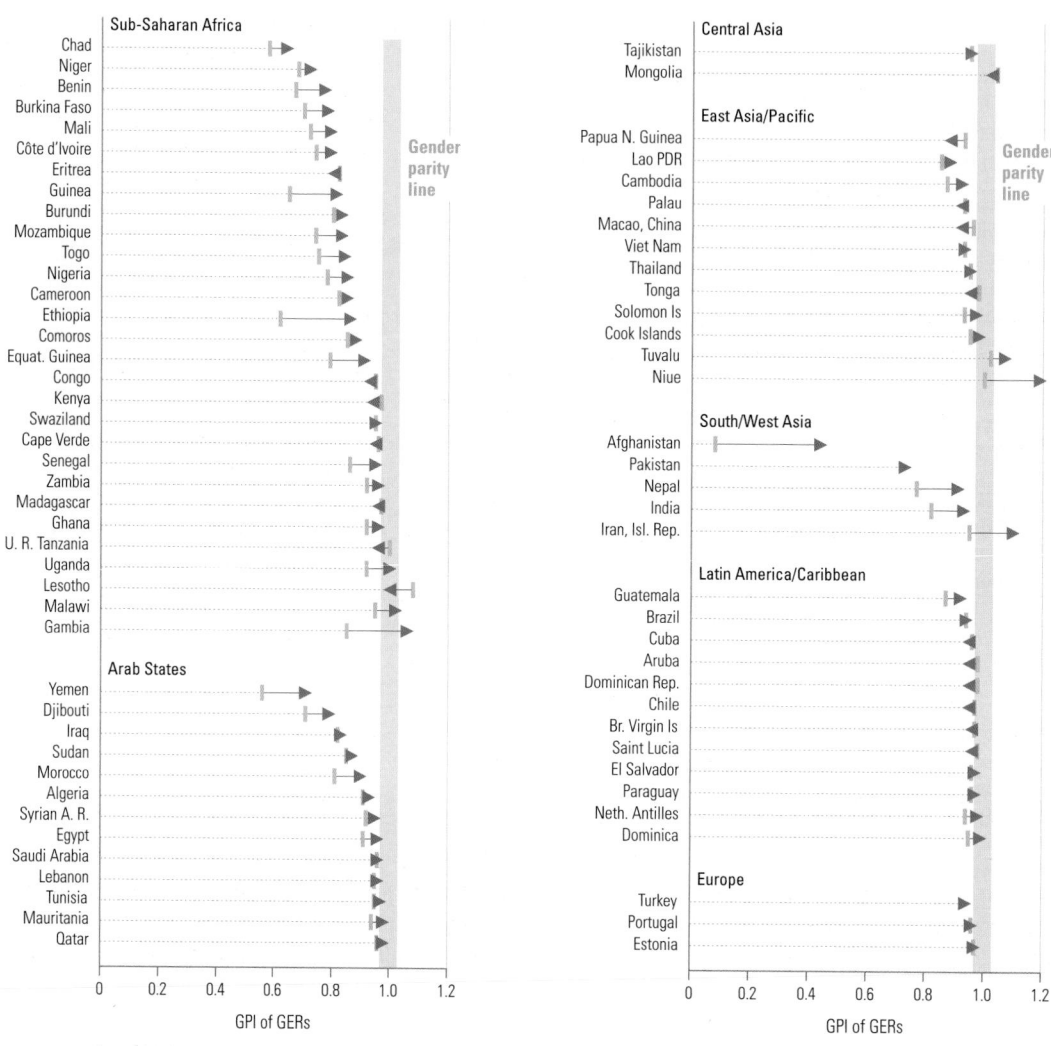

Once they
have access to
school, girls tend
to perform as
well as or better
than boys

1999 ▶ 2004 (increase since 1999) ◀ 2004 (decrease since 1999)

Note: Countries with GPIs between 0.97 and 1.03 in both 1998 and 2002 are not included. No data are available for Pakistan and Turkey in 1999.
See source table for detailed country notes.
Source: Annex, Statistical Table 5.

multiple sources of exclusion and to giving girls
the educational support and physical safety they
need to gain access to primary education and
complete it (Lewis and Lockheed, 2006). Some
countries are taking up the challenge with
success. In Guinea, for instance, the GER for
girls increased by twenty-six percentage points
between 1999 and 2004 after investment was
made to improve school sanitation (UNICEF,
2005a).

Once they have access to school, girls tend
to perform as well as or better than boys. For
the countries with data available, the median

percentage of repeaters in primary education
was less than 4% for females in 2004 while the
median for males was close to 5% (see annex,
Statistical Table 6). Almost everywhere except
sub-Saharan Africa, girls are also generally more
likely to stay in school longer than boys (see
annex, Statistical Table 7). In Latin American
and the Caribbean, for example, while school
completion is a general issue, in many countries
it is especially so for boys. In Chile, poor boys are
four times more likely to leave school early and
enter the workforce than are poor girls (UNICEF,
2005a: p.46).

Secondary education: continuing momentum

It is important to look at education beyond the primary years, for several reasons. First, secondary and tertiary education are part of the EFA goals and the Millennium Development Goals of gender parity and equality. Second, achieving UPE not only creates demand for higher levels of education but also is itself dependent on progress in secondary and tertiary education for an adequate supply of competent teachers and for sufficient secondary school places to increase the incentive to complete primary school. Finally, in a world increasingly reliant on higher levels of knowledge and training for successful social and professional integration, many governments have made the universalization of basic education,[17] rather than simply primary education, a medium-term objective.

Pressure from below

Demand for and participation in secondary education have been growing as many countries are making good progress towards achieving UPE. In 2004, some 502 million students were enrolled in secondary schools, an increase of 14% over 1999. Increases were particularly significant in the developing country regions, especially the Arab States, South and West Asia, and sub-Saharan Africa: in each, the number of secondary students rose by 20% or more during the period.

Transition to secondary education

High transition rates from the final grade of primary school to lower secondary education are common not only in developed countries and those in transition, but also in developing countries. The median rates in 2003 were close to 90% or above in all but one region (Figure 2.15): in sub-Saharan Africa the median was less than 65%. Countries with transition rates below 40% include Burkina Faso, Burundi, Côte d'Ivoire, Uganda and the United Republic of Tanzania. On the other hand, almost all those who reach the last grade of primary education go on to secondary education in Botswana, Ghana, Seychelles and South Africa.

While there are few variations in transition rates across regions, the range within them is often substantial. The greatest differences between the highest and the lowest country rates are found in Latin America and the Caribbean, sub-Saharan Africa and the Arab States region, with spreads of 87, 66 and 55 percentage points, respectively.

In spite of the relatively high average transition rates in many regions, the level of participation in secondary education tends to be much lower than at primary level. Worldwide, the average secondary GER was 65% in 2004, compared with 106% in primary education (see annex, Statistical Tables 5 and 8). The regional patterns of primary and secondary enrolment ratios are similar, though the disparities are greater for secondary

Demand for and participation in secondary education has been growing

Figure 2.15: Transition rates from primary to general secondary education, median values and regional variations, 2003

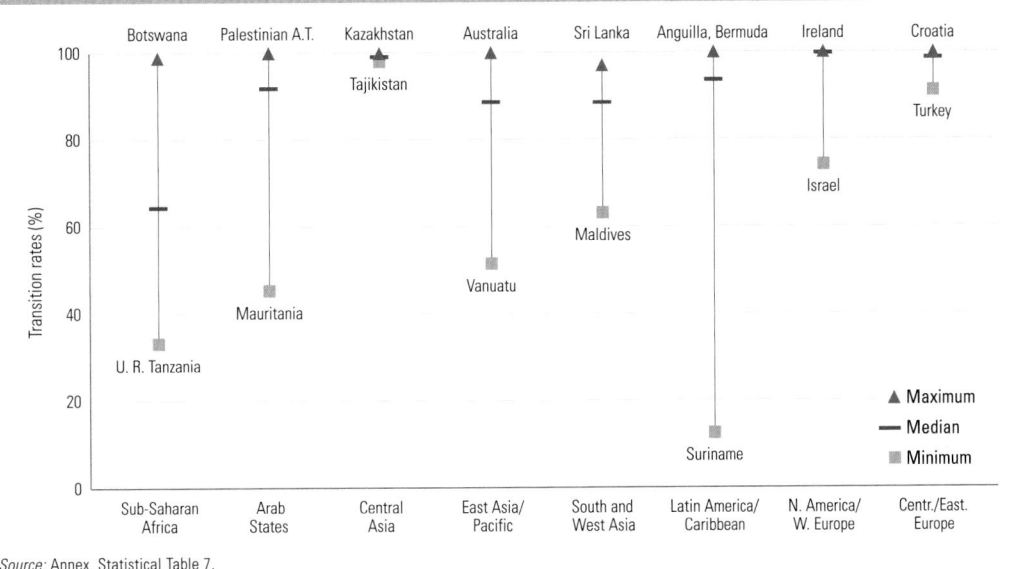

Source: Annex, Statistical Table 7.

17. The ISCED definition of basic education is primary education (first stage) plus lower secondary education (second stage).

Figure 2.16: Secondary gross enrolment ratios by level and region, 2004

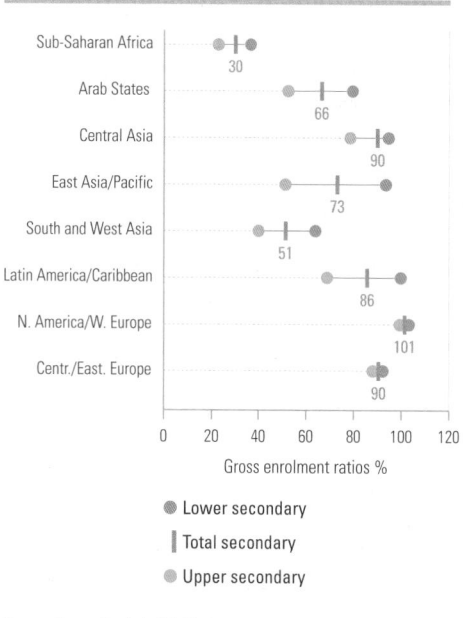

Source: Annex, Statistical Table 8.

education. North America and Western Europe have almost achieved universal secondary education, with GERs above 100% on average and NERs exceeding 90% (Figure 2.16).

High secondary GERs (about 90%) are also found in Central and Eastern Europe, Central Asia, and Latin America and the Caribbean. Participation rates in secondary education are much lower in the remaining regions, and the secondary GERs are below 30% in sub-Saharan Africa. In that region as in others, the overall levels of participation conceal significant variation among countries. Secondary education is more developed in English-speaking African countries, particularly those in the southern hemisphere, than in Central and West Africa (see annex, Statistical Table 8).

Between 1999 and 2004, secondary GERs increased in 117 of the 150 countries with data available (Figure 2.17). The increases were often noteworthy, exceeding ten percentage points in about one-third of these countries. In relative terms, increases were higher in sub-Saharan

Figure 2.17: Change in secondary gross enrolment ratios between 1999 and 2004

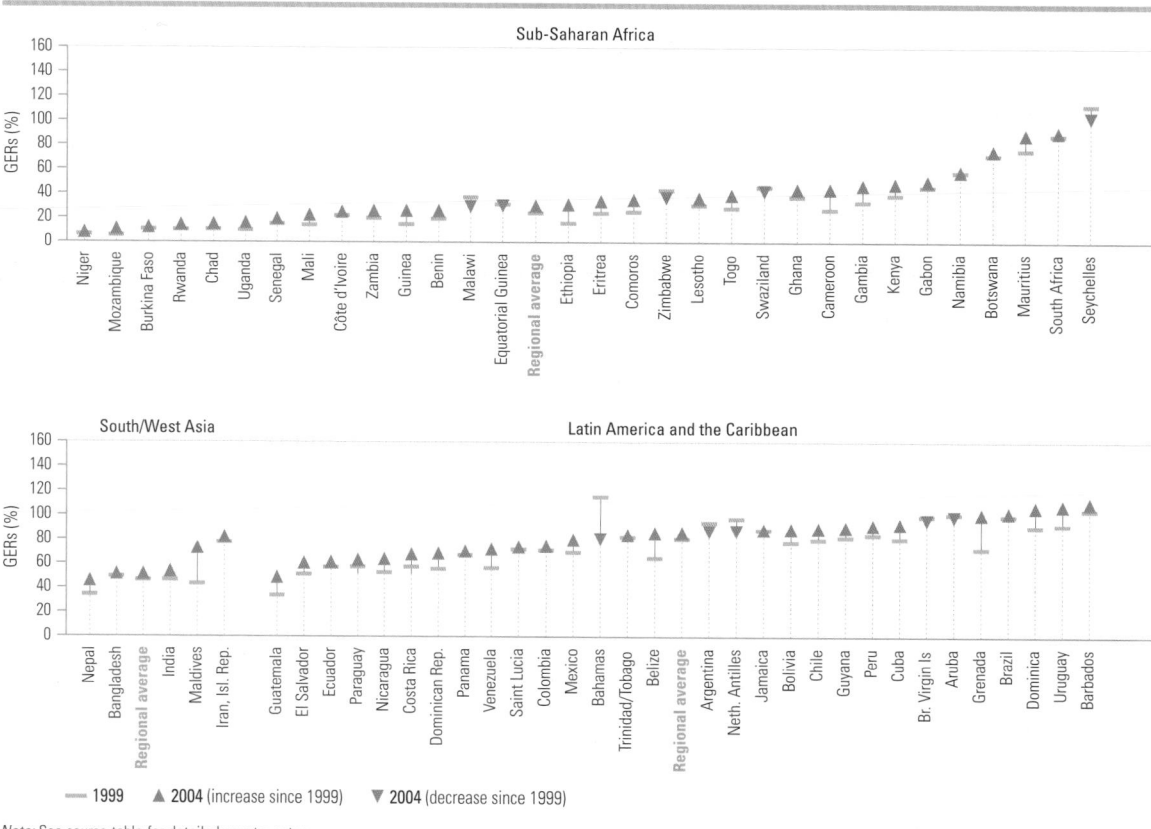

Note: See source table for detailed country notes.
Sources: Annex, Statistical Table 8; UIS database.

Africa, the Arab States, and East Asia and the Pacific, with gains of 25% in the former region and about 13% in the latter two. Secondary GERs doubled in some countries, including Ethiopia and Mozambique, albeit from low initial levels. Despite the global trend, however, some countries recorded substantial decreases, among them Malawi, the United Arab Emirates and Zimbabwe, whose GERs declined by 15% or more.

Two distinct stages

Secondary education is diverse. In addition to being subject-focused, in contrast to primary education, it consists of two levels. Lower secondary (ISCED level 2), which is usually considered the second stage of basic education, is generally designed to continue the basic programmes of the primary level, and its last year often coincides with the end of compulsory education. Upper secondary (ISCED level 3) provides a bridge between school and university or prepares students to enter the labour market (UNESCO, 1997).

In cross-national comparisons, secondary education is often considered as a whole. It is useful, however, to highlight what happens in its lower and upper stages, in terms of both level of participation and gender disparities. In a context where achieving basic education (of often nine years) for all is becoming a goal in many countries, it is increasingly important to differentiate between lower and upper secondary education and to look more closely at the lower level in particular.

The overall secondary GERs discussed above mask sometimes substantial disparities between lower and upper secondary education. The level of participation in lower secondary is much higher than in upper secondary, with worldwide average GERs of 78% and 51%, respectively, in 2004 (see annex, Statistical Table 8). As Figure 2.16 shows, this difference in participation is found in all regions except North America and Western Europe, and Central and Eastern Europe; in those two regions the levels of participation are very similar throughout

The level of participation in lower secondary is much higher than in upper secondary

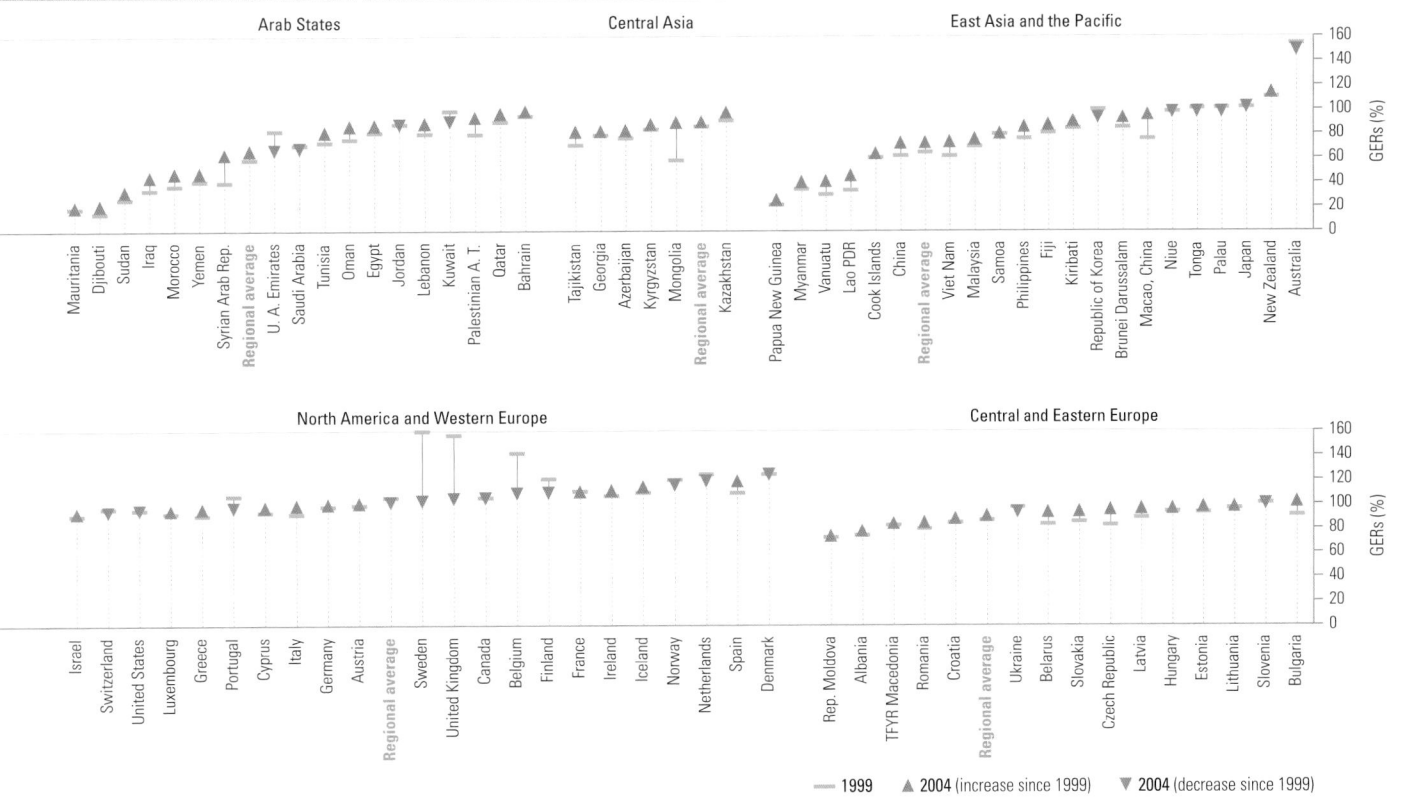

— 1999   ▲ 2004 (increase since 1999)   ▼ 2004 (decrease since 1999)

There is a gap between what is legally compulsory and what is the reality

secondary education. The participation rate differentials between the two levels are especially high in East Asia and the Pacific (forty-two percentage points) and Latin America and the Caribbean (thirty-one percentage points); by comparison, the global average is twenty-seven percentage points.

Of the 203 countries or territories covered in the statistical tables, 192 reported having laws making education compulsory. In about three-quarters of them, compulsory education includes lower secondary (see annex, Statistical Table 4), which means participation at that level is supposed to be universal. In all developed countries, all countries in transition and 80% of countries in Latin America and the Caribbean, and East Asia and the Pacific, lower secondary education is indeed compulsory and participation high, with GERs above 90% in 2004. By contrast, while three out of four Arab States make lower secondary education compulsory, actual participation averages are below 80%. In Djibouti, Mauritania, Morocco and Yemen, where lower secondary is officially compulsory, the GERs vary between 20% and 60%. This gap between what is legally compulsory and what is the reality raises two issues: whether the laws are sufficiently enforced and whether there are enough places in lower secondary school to make such enforcement feasible.

South and West Asia, and sub-Saharan Africa are the regions with the lowest levels of participation in lower secondary education, with GERs in 2004 of 64% and 36%, respectively (Figure 2.15). They are also the regions with the fewest countries making lower secondary education compulsory – fewer than 40% of the countries in each case.

Overall, while universal basic education (combining primary and lower secondary education) is increasingly becoming an objective in many countries, universal participation is still far away. This is particularly so for sub-Saharan Africa, where the average GER in basic education was 73% in 2004, compared with 90% or above in the other regions, though the ratio did increase by ten percentage points between 1999 and 2004.[18]

Technical and vocational education

Secondary education typically includes both academically oriented programmes and technical and vocational education (TVE). Of the more than 500 million students in secondary education worldwide in 2004, around 10% were enrolled in TVE (see annex, Statistical Table 8). Overall, enrolment in TVE programmes is higher in more developed countries, especially in Central and Eastern Europe, where TVE students represent about one-fifth of total secondary enrolment, compared with 8% in the developing world. However, the situation in developing regions is very diverse. TVE is well established in many Latin American and Caribbean countries, representing about 40% of total secondary enrolment in some, including Honduras, the Netherlands Antilles, Panama and Suriname. It is much less common in Central Asia, South and West Asia, and sub-Saharan Africa,[19] representing between 1% and 6% of total secondary enrolments, on average.

Gender disparities in secondary education

The higher the level of education, the greater the gender disparities. Almost invariably, gender differences in participation levels are greater in secondary than in primary education. While about two-thirds of the countries for which 2004 data are available have achieved gender parity in primary education, only one-third have reached it in secondary education (see annex, Statistical Table 8). Most of these countries are in Central and Eastern Europe, East Asia and the Pacific, Latin America and the Caribbean, and North America and Western Europe. The list also includes a few countries from other regions: Jordan, Mauritius, Qatar, Swaziland and Tunisia.

Patterns of gender disparities are more complex in secondary education than in primary. In primary education they are nearly always at the expense of girls. At secondary level, however, there are as many countries with disparities at the expense of boys as there are countries where girls are at a disadvantage. Countries with low overall secondary enrolment ratios tend to be those where disparities are at the expense of girls, while disparities at the expense of boys are observed in developed countries as well as in several Latin American and Caribbean countries. Overall, gender disparities in favour of boys tend to be more pronounced than those in favour of girls. In five countries (Afghanistan, Chad, Guinea, Togo and Yemen), fewer than 50 girls are enrolled at secondary level for every 100 boys; by contrast, in five other countries (Dominican Republic, Honduras, Kiribati, Lesotho and Suriname), roughly 120 girls are enrolled for every 100 boys.

18. These data are from the UIS database.

19. Among sub-Saharan African countries for which 2004 data are available, only in Cameroon and Rwanda does TVE represent a significant share (about one-third) of total secondary enrolment.

The average GPI for secondary education as a whole often hides substantial differences between upper and lower secondary. Figure 2.18 (see p. 48) shows that gender gaps, when they exist, are often wider in upper than lower secondary. In countries where gender disparities affect female students, most of which are in the Arab States, South and West Asia, and sub-Saharan Africa, girls' share of enrolment is lower at the upper secondary level. Similarly, gender disparities in favour of girls in developed countries and in many countries of Latin America and the Caribbean are usually more pronounced at the upper secondary level.

Gender disparities in secondary education, particularly those affecting girls, stem from disparities in primary education. In countries where girls have limited access to primary school, especially those in South and West Asia, and sub-Saharan Africa, this disadvantage persists through secondary education, even when girls do as well as, or outperform, boys, as seen earlier. Indeed, the gap tends to widen between the lower levels of schooling and upper secondary. As previous editions of the *EFA Global Monitoring Report* have indicated, factors such as puberty, pregnancy and early marriage, as well as household and societal factors, have a strong influence on gender patterns for upper secondary school participation and retention.

Gender disparities in favour of girls are linked to girls' tendency to perform better than boys, to their lower repetition rates and higher graduation rates, and to their leaving the school system later (UNESCO, 2005). This phenomenon is becoming increasingly common around the world and requires policy attention if the goal of gender parity is to be fully achieved.

Post-secondary non-tertiary education

In many countries, particularly developed ones, some graduates of secondary schools enrol in programmes that prepare them for specific occupations. These programmes, which are not part of tertiary education, are classified at ISCED level 4 and often last less than two years. In the countries where these programmes exist, enrolment is seldom more than 10% of total secondary enrolment, though in some small developing countries, such as the British Virgin Islands, Dominica, Jamaica, Seychelles, and the Turks and Caicos Islands, enrolment in ISCED level 4 programmes is equivalent to one-fifth to two-thirds of secondary enrolment. Ireland is the only developed country where a similar percentage is found (20%), at least among countries for which data are available. Women are well represented in these programmes. Their share in ISCED 4 enrolment was above 50% in the majority of countries with data available for 2004, and above 60% in one-third of them (see annex, Statistical Table 8).

Tertiary education: enrolments up but access still limited

Tertiary education is linked to the EFA goals in at least two ways: as a component of the gender equality goal and as an important provider of teachers and administrators. Worldwide, some 132 million students were enrolled in tertiary education in 2004, about 40 million more than in 1999. Three-quarters of the growth took place in developing countries, where the total number of tertiary students rose from 46 million in 1999 to 76 million in 2004 (see annex, Statistical Table 9). East Asia, led by China, accounts for about 60% (18 million) of the increase.

Figure 2.19 indicates that participation in higher education is on the rise in almost all countries for which data are available. GERs increased by more than two percentage points between 1999 and 2004 in two-thirds of the 119 countries with data. Increases of more than ten percentage points were observed in more than thirty countries, mostly developed countries and countries in transition. However, large increases were also recorded in several developing countries, including China, Macao (China) and Mauritius, all of which more than doubled their participation level during the period.

Despite the continuing expansion of tertiary education worldwide since 1999, only a small share of the relevant age group has access to this level (UIS, 2006a). The world tertiary GER was around 24% in 2004, but participation varies substantially by region. In North America and Western Europe, the average GER was around 70%; in Central and Eastern Europe and in the Pacific it was around 50%. In the Arab States, Central Asia, East Asia and the Pacific, and Latin America and the Caribbean, the participation level was between 20% and 28%. It is much lower in South and West Asia (10%) and sub-Saharan Africa (5%).

Worldwide, some 132 million students were enrolled in tertiary education in 2004, about 40 million more than in 1999. Three-quarters of the growth took place in developing countries

Gender
disparities are
more prevalent
in tertiary
education than
at lower levels

Figure 2.18: Gender disparities in secondary gross enrolment ratios by level, 2004

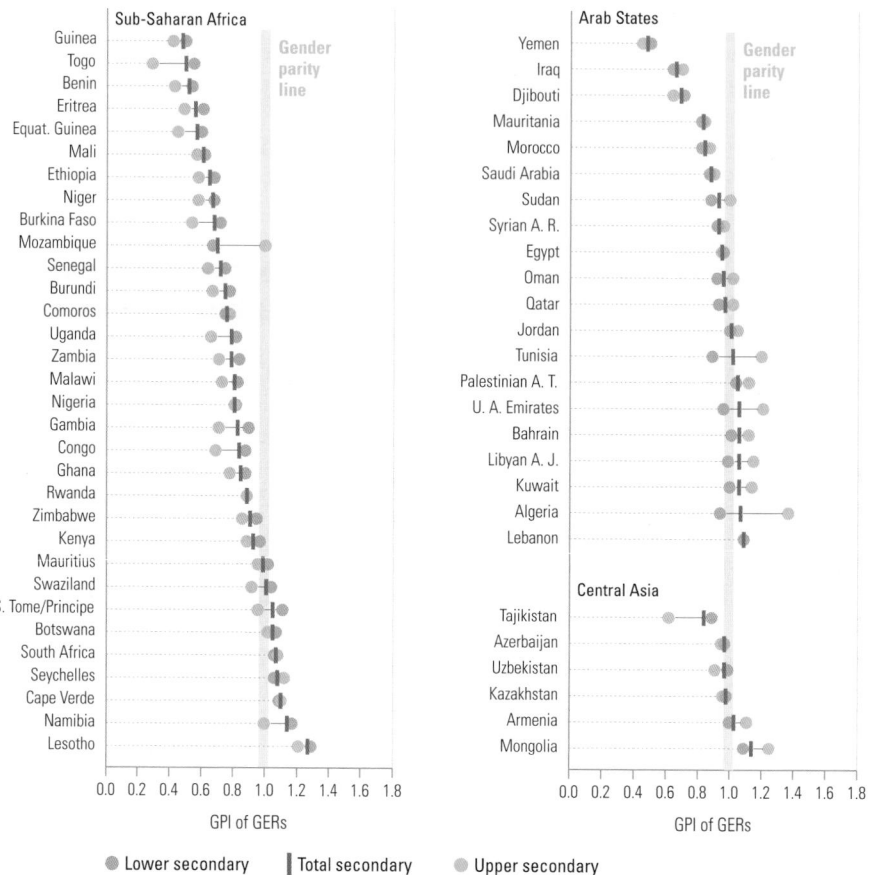

Note: Countries with GPIs between 0.97 and 1.03 at all levels are not included. See source table for detailed country notes.
Source: Annex, Statistical Table 8.

Gender disparities at tertiary level: different patterns in different regions

Gender disparities are more prevalent in tertiary education than at lower levels. Gender parity exists only in Andorra, Cyprus, Georgia, Mexico and Peru, out of the 148 countries for which 2004 data are available (see annex, Statistical Table 9). In developed and transition countries, participation in tertiary education is higher among females (the average GPI is 1.27), and the situation of males has tended to worsen since 1999. In contrast, while some improvement occurred in developing countries over the period, female participation remained below that of males in 2004: the overall GPI was 0.87, up from 0.78 in 1999. Developing-country regions display much variation, however. In general, the situation in Latin America and the Caribbean[20] and in the Pacific is close to that of developed countries, with GPIs generally well above 1. In contrast,

gender disparities favouring men are mainly observed in most countries of East Asia (average GPI: 0.88), South and West Asia (0.70) and sub-Saharan Africa (0.62). The already marginal presence of women in tertiary education in the developing world is worsening in some countries, including Burundi, the Congo, the Gambia and Macao (China). Others, however, including Ethiopia, the Lao People's Democratic Republic, Malawi, Morocco, Uganda, the United Republic of Tanzania and Yemen, are making great progress in getting more women in tertiary education.

Beyond gender parity: what about gender equality?

In much of the world, the main challenge is still to increase girls' access to education, and ensure that equal numbers of girls and boys are in school. This is gender parity. However, as the 2003/4 Report argued, gender parity in

20. Among countries of the region with data available, only in Guatemala are high gender disparities found at the expense of women (GPI of 0.72).

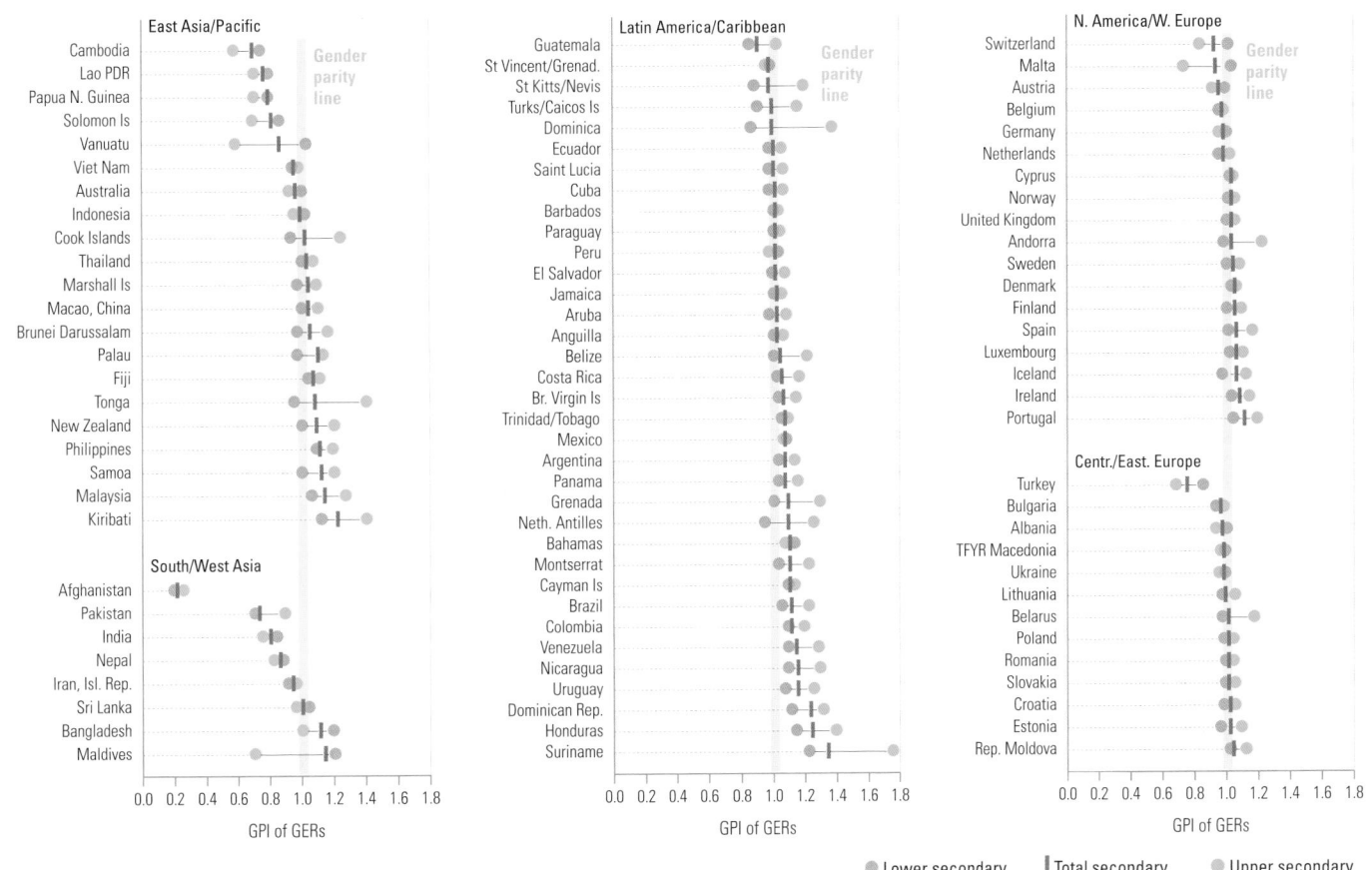

East Asia/Pacific

| Cambodia |
| Lao PDR |
| Papua N. Guinea |
| Solomon Is |
| Vanuatu |
| Viet Nam |
| Australia |
| Indonesia |
| Cook Islands |
| Thailand |
| Marshall Is |
| Macao, China |
| Brunei Darussalam |
| Palau |
| Fiji |
| Tonga |
| New Zealand |
| Philippines |
| Samoa |
| Malaysia |
| Kiribati |

South/West Asia

| Afghanistan |
| Pakistan |
| India |
| Nepal |
| Iran, Isl. Rep. |
| Sri Lanka |
| Bangladesh |
| Maldives |

Latin America/Caribbean

| Guatemala |
| St Vincent/Grenad. |
| St Kitts/Nevis |
| Turks/Caicos Is |
| Dominica |
| Ecuador |
| Saint Lucia |
| Cuba |
| Barbados |
| Paraguay |
| Peru |
| El Salvador |
| Jamaica |
| Aruba |
| Anguilla |
| Belize |
| Costa Rica |
| Br. Virgin Is |
| Trinidad/Tobago |
| Mexico |
| Argentina |
| Panama |
| Grenada |
| Neth. Antilles |
| Bahamas |
| Montserrat |
| Cayman Is |
| Brazil |
| Colombia |
| Venezuela |
| Nicaragua |
| Uruguay |
| Dominican Rep. |
| Honduras |
| Suriname |

N. America/W. Europe

| Switzerland |
| Malta |
| Austria |
| Belgium |
| Germany |
| Netherlands |
| Cyprus |
| Norway |
| United Kingdom |
| Andorra |
| Sweden |
| Denmark |
| Finland |
| Spain |
| Luxembourg |
| Iceland |
| Ireland |
| Portugal |

Centr./East. Europe

| Turkey |
| Bulgaria |
| Albania |
| TFYR Macedonia |
| Ukraine |
| Lithuania |
| Belarus |
| Poland |
| Romania |
| Slovakia |
| Croatia |
| Estonia |
| Rep. Moldova |

GPI of GERs

● Lower secondary   ▌ Total secondary   ● Upper secondary

education does not necessarily mean gender equality. There is no gender equality, for example, when women tend to be concentrated in certain tertiary disciplines, such as education, social sciences, humanities and health. Evidence shows that men's educational underachievement, where it exists, has not yet resulted in their falling behind economically and politically, and that women may need still higher qualifications than they have thus far attained in order to compete successfully for jobs, equal pay and managerial positions (UNESCO, 2003a). There is also no gender equality when sexual violence and harassment exist in schools, when teaching materials are biased and when teachers are not aware of gender issues. Public policies aimed at promoting gender equality in education thus need to go beyond initiatives that focus exclusively on enrolment ratios (UNESCO, 2005).

Education quality must accompany expansion

Because the EFA goal on the quality of education (discussed at length in the 2005 Report) involves school inputs, processes and outcomes, past editions of the *EFA Global Monitoring Report* have employed multiple indicators on education expenditure, teachers (qualifications, deployment and availability) and pupil/teacher ratios to monitor international patterns and longitudinal trends. These indicators represent key enabling factors to ensure that students learn well in school and that such learning is relevant and valuable to their lives.

A new report by the World Bank Independent Evaluation Group (2006) underscores the fact that countries have placed high priority on increasing enrolment in primary schools, but have paid far less attention to the crucial issue of whether

There is also no gender equality when sexual violence and harassment exist in schools

Figure 2.19: Changes in tertiary gross enrolment ratios between 1999 and 2004

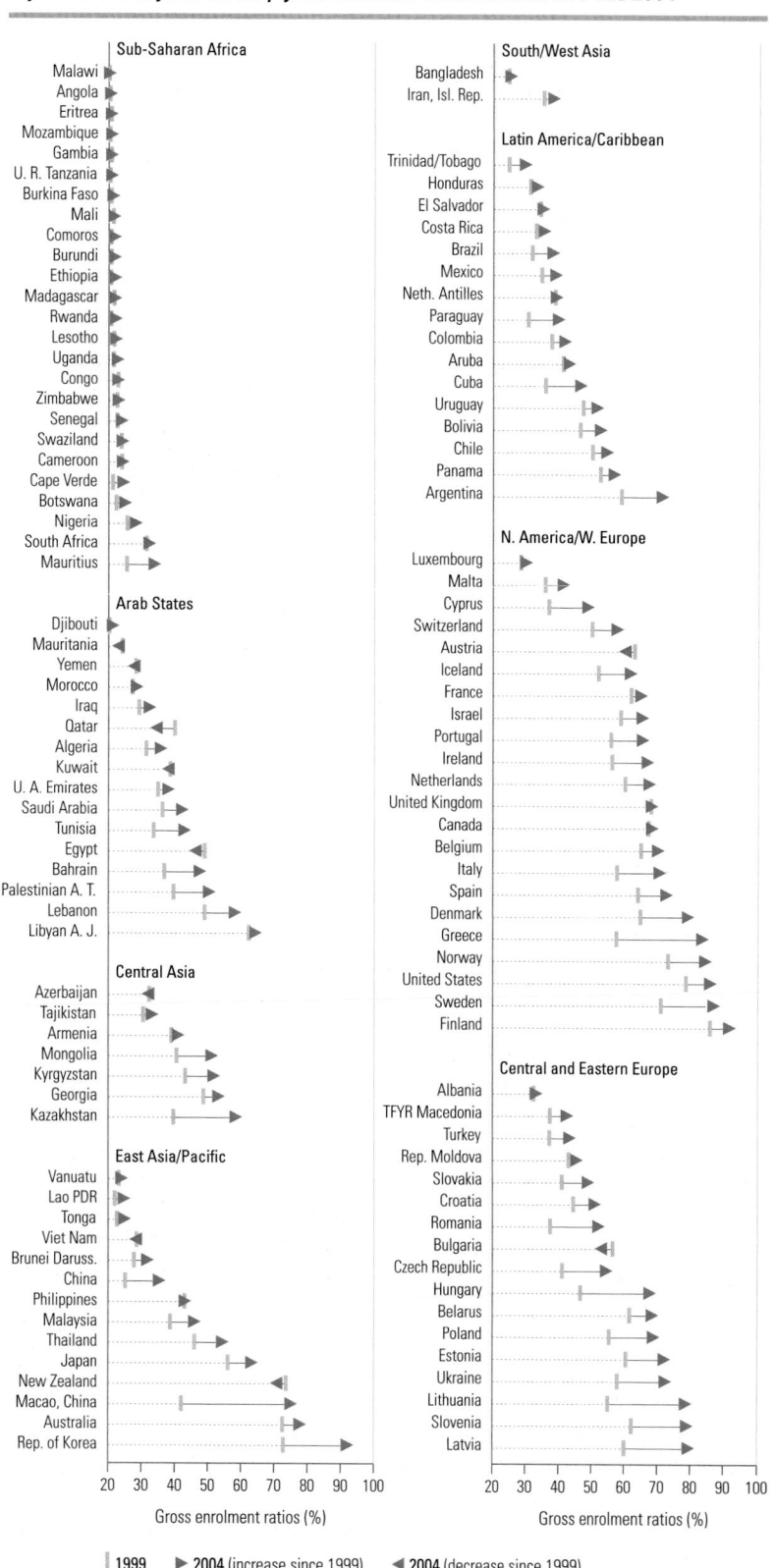

Gross enrolment ratios (%)

Gross enrolment ratios (%)

| 1999 ▶ 2004 (increase since 1999) ◀ 2004 (decrease since 1999)

Note: See source table for detailed country notes.
Source: Annex, Statistical Table 9.

children are learning adequately. It recommends that countries and development partners place the same emphasis on learning outcomes as they do on access, with the idea that current investment in primary education would thus have a far greater impact on poverty reduction and national development.

This section looks at learning outcomes (through the development of national assessments along with new findings from comparative assessments) and documents aspects of teacher deployment, training and qualifications.

Learning outcomes

Expanding access to primary schooling does not necessarily imply a trade-off with improving school quality and learning outcomes.[21] Policies can effectively enhance both access and quality – for example, by shifting more public expenditure to basic education, increasing efficiency in the allocation of resources across schools and improving pre-service and in-service teacher training.

The move towards national assessments of learning achievement

Since the 1990s, more and more governments have committed themselves to assessing student learning and gauging progress in learning outcomes over time. This monitoring takes many forms: for example, participating in comparative assessments of academic achievement or basic skills; national monitoring of the curriculum and subject-specific achievements; standards-based assessments (according to grade or age); school-based assessments of pupil progress (based on tests, performance and portfolios); and external (public) examinations at major system transition points. Learning assessments, whatever form they take, can be used not only to evaluate the strengths and weaknesses of an education system, but also to address issues of equity and to compare pupil achievements across schools, regions and systems.

Previous editions of the *EFA Global Monitoring Report* have discussed the results of comparative international and official assessments, notably those of the International Association for the Evaluation of Educational Achievement (IEA); the

21. In theory, learning outcomes include subject-based knowledge; broader skills and competencies; and attitudes, values and behaviours. In practice, however, student learning is mainly assessed in terms of the cognitive dimension.

OECD-sponsored Programme for International Student Assessment (PISA); and regional studies in Latin America (LLECE), sub-Saharan Africa (SACMEQ and PASEC) and the Pacific Islands (PILL). Region-based assessments have the advantages of providing more culturally valid tests of pupil knowledge and skills than do international assessments, and of being more adaptable to emergent policy needs (Scheerens, 2006).

With no new comparative assessments available, this Report looks at national assessments of learning outcomes, an especially significant development since the Dakar Forum (Encinas-Martin, 2006). In some countries, national assessments have developed in parallel with comparative regional or international assessments; in others, they are in lieu of them (see below).

National assessments[22] are meant to provide national stakeholders with systematic information about the status of students' learning outcomes and the extent to which students attain nationally defined standards or proficiencies. National assessments describe levels of pupil achievement, not of individual students but of a whole education system, or some clearly defined part of it (e.g. fourth grade pupils or 9-year-olds) (UNESCO-IIEP, 2001). The scientific validity of national assessments varies greatly making it difficult to compare learning achievements among countries. Nevertheless, national learning assessments are a potentially useful tool to monitor educational quality, address national policy issues and pinpoint areas for government attention and programme intervention.

The annex to this Report contains an up-to-date overview of national assessment and evaluation activities undertaken by countries in sub-Saharan Africa, the Arab States, Asia and the Pacific, and Latin America and the Caribbean. Although incomplete, this review of national assessments underscores the diversity of developing country efforts, definitions and experiences in this area. Several trends are noticeable:

■ National learning assessments in many countries have developed quite recently (mainly since 1995, especially after 2000).

■ Most countries assess student learning in the primary grades only, though some in Asia and Latin America monitor progress at both primary and secondary level.

■ Assessments are curriculum-based and subject-oriented, typically covering official

Table 2.14: Countries classified according to their experience with pupil learning assessments

	Participated in regional or international assessment	Did not participate in regional or international assessment
Conducted at least one national assessment	**A:** Argentina, Bolivia, Botswana, Brazil, Colombia, Costa Rica, Cuba, Djibouti, Dominican Rep., Ecuador, El Salvador, Guatemala, India, Jordan, Lebanon, Malawi, Mexico, Morocco, Nicaragua, Nigeria, Panama, Paraguay, Peru, Qatar, Republic of Korea, Singapore, South Africa, Uruguay, Venezuela, Zambia	**C:** Bangladesh, Gambia, Myanmar, Pakistan, Viet Nam
No evidence of having conducted a national assessment	**B:** Belize, Bahrain, China, Honduras, Iran (Isl. Rep.), Kenya, Malaysia, Mozambique, Philippines, Russian Federation, Seychelles, Syrian A. R., Thailand, Trinidad and Tobago, Tunisia, Turkey	**D:** Angola, Bahamas, Barbados, Benin, Burundi, D. R. Congo, Dominica, Grenada, Guyana, Haiti, Jamaica, Kazakhstan, Liberia, Libyan A. J., St Kitts and Nevis, St Lucia, St Vincent and the Grenadines, Sri Lanka, Sudan, Suriname, Tajikistan

Note: More complete data on national learning assessment activity would alter this classification for certain countries.
Source: Encinas-Martin (2006).

and foreign languages, mathematics and sometimes natural and social sciences, rather than assessing cross-curricular knowledge, skills or competencies as does, for instance, PISA.

■ Assessments are usually carried out by a unit in the ministry of education or by a national research institute.

The annex presents only the basic parameters of national learning assessments; information is limited regarding which stakeholders are involved, how transparent the compiled data are and whether assessments influence policy initiatives and reforms. It seems possible, however, to roughly gauge the degree of a country's commitment to assessing student learning by cross-referencing its participation in regional or international assessments, on the one hand, and national assessmentss on the other. Table 2.14 shows a sampling of countries with strong commitments to pupil learning assessments (found in category A) as well as some of those with the least experience (category D).[23]

In sum, national assessments of learning outcomes have become much more prevalent in developing countries in recent years. Despite the enormous heterogeneity of such assessments as regards target population, frequency, policy relevance, scientific rigour and other factors, they clearly indicate an important new development in national activities to monitor education quality.

22. National learning assessments are known under a variety of names, including system assessments, learning assessments and assessments of learning outcomes.

23. Table 2.14 is incomplete because in some cases there was no information on national assessments, and in others the available information was incomplete, ambiguous or both. Some countries have undertaken national assessments but no information about the studies has been published or otherwise made available. Encinas-Martin (2006) provides references for or links to all relevant preliminary or final project documents, and discusses the next steps in this research project.

New findings from comparative assessments: which factors count the most?

While no new comparative assessments have become available, new analyses of previous assessments have been published that add to the understanding of which factors contribute to successful learning.

Socio-economic background. Recent studies of pupil achievement continue to validate a core conclusion from earlier research: pupils from higher socio-economic backgrounds (those having a parent with post-secondary education or one with high occupational status, or having grown up in a home with many material possessions, especially books) tend to perform better than those from disadvantaged socio-economic backgrounds. The positive relationship between measures of socio-economic status and student achievement obtains in all countries, at all age levels, and for all subjects and competencies.

Some recent studies have paid greater attention to the influence of other family characteristics on pupil achievement, by examining immigrant status, language spoken at home, family structure and paid employment.

Immigrant or native. The OECD (2006)[24] reported that the achievements of immigrant and non-immigrant children on PISA tests of reading, mathematics and science in 2003 differed widely in many national school systems. In Austria, Belgium, Denmark, France, Germany, the Netherlands and Switzerland, learning disparities between 15-year-old immigrant students and native students of the same age were significant, and there were few disparities between first and second generation immigrants. In Australia, Canada and New Zealand however, the achievement gap between immigrants and non-immigrants was small and not considered significant (after adjustment for socio-economic status).[25] Public policy has clearly made a difference in these three countries.

Language and family structure. In eighteen of twenty high-income countries, students who spoke the test language at home had significantly higher scores in mathematics literacy than students whose home languages differed from the test language (Hampden-Thompson and Johnston, 2006).[26] There was also a significant achievement gap between students from two-parent homes and students living in other family structures in fourteen of the twenty countries.

Paid employment. After-school activities involving paid employment have been found to reduce pupil achievement in mathematics and science, especially among boys. The negative impact of after-school paid employment pertained to both high-income and middle-income countries (Post and Ling Pong, 2006).

Equity issues: how much does student achievement vary?

In addition to comparing countries according to mean achievement levels, it is equally important to examine the distribution of learning outcomes within countries. If the spread of student achievement around some mean level is extensive in a given country, that is indicative of low education equity (Scheerens and Visscher, 2004).

One way to address the equity dimension of pupil achievement is by examining socio-economic gradients of learning achievement, also known as the 'learning bar' (OECD, 2004b; Willms and Somers, 2001). Recent comparative studies have shown that the level, slope and strength of socio-economic gradients of pupil achievement vary by country and by school (Mullis et al., 2003; OECD, 2004b; Willms, 2006). For example, among non-OECD countries in the Progress in International Reading Literacy Study (PIRLS) among fourth graders, some (including Belize, the Islamic Republic of Iran, Israel, Romania and Singapore) had socio-economic gradient lines with steep slopes, indicating high inequality. Countries or territories with relatively flat slopes (i.e. low inequality) included Colombia, Hong Kong (China), Kuwait, Latvia and the Russian Federation (Willms, 2006).

Using data for fourteen sub-Saharan African countries from the second study by the Southern and Eastern Africa Consortium for Monitoring Educational Quality (SACMEQ II), Ross et al. (2005) compared national school systems according to performance (mean achievement levels) and equity (socio-economic gradients of learning achievements). As Figure 2.20 shows, Kenya, Mauritius and Seychelles were the best performers, with the highest average scores in mathematics. However, a different picture emerges when considering the equity aspect of achievement (the slope and length of the socio-economic gradient lines). On this dimension, Kenya, Mozambique and the United Republic of Tanzania were the top performers, with relatively flat gradients and above-average mathematics achievement. By contrast, Mauritius, Seychelles and South Africa showed steep socio-economic gradients, indicating more inequitable systems

24. The study focused on seventeen countries and territories with large immigrant populations: Australia, Austria, Belgium, Canada, Denmark, France, Germany, Luxembourg, the Netherlands, New Zealand, Norway, Sweden, Switzerland and the United States, among OECD countries, along with three non-OECD PISA participants: the Russian Federation, Hong Kong (China) and Macao (China).

25. The study suggested that achievement disparities between immigrant and native adolescents were more likely to be found in highly streamed education systems.

26. These findings are based on PISA 2003 and obtain after adjusting for socio-economic status.

with large gaps in mathematics achievement among pupils from different socio-economic backgrounds.[27]

Teaching staff: numbers and qualifications count

Providing an education of good quality means teachers must be recruited in adequate numbers, trained to be effective and deployed where they are needed. This subsection discusses mainly primary school teachers, but also highlights differences with secondary teachers when relevant. ECCE personnel, particularly pre-primary teachers, are discussed in Chapters 6 and 8.

Pupil/teacher ratios are improving in most countries but are still high in many

The pupil/teacher ratio (PTR)[28] measures the number of teachers in relation to the size of the pupil population, and so has implications for quality. Generally, ratios above about 40:1 make it difficult for teachers to maintain adequate quality standards. In 2004, the ratio was below 40:1 in 84% of the 174 countries with data available (Table 2.15). Most of the 28 countries that have a ratio exceeding 40:1 are in sub-Saharan Africa, although a few are in East Asia and the Pacific, and South and West Asia. Among the regions, sub-Saharan Africa has the highest median PTR (44:1), and country variations within the region are particularly striking: the Congo, Ethiopia and Malawi, for example, have ratios of 70:1 or above, while Seychelles has a ratio of 14:1. Chad, Mozambique, Afghanistan and Rwanda also have high ratios, between 62:1 and 69:1. Such high ratios impede learning.

PTRs are higher at primary level than at lower-secondary (except in East Asia, where they are similar at both), and lower-secondary PTRs tend to be higher than those at upper-secondary level, particularly in South and West Asia, and sub-Saharan Africa (see annex, Statistical Table 10A).

---

27. Ross et al. (2005) and Lee et al. (2005) discuss the complex reasons behind the large variations in student achievement.

28. PTRs discussed in this Report are based on headcounts of pupils and teachers. They are calculated by dividing the total number of pupils enrolled at a specified level of education by the number of teachers at that level. The PTR depends on an accurate count of teachers who have teaching responsibilities. In some countries, some teachers may work part-time, and figures for full-time teachers are not always available. In addition, forms of school organization such as multigrade and double shifts may not be taken into account when calculating the PTR, which is a national average. Further, data on teachers may include other education personnel, and separate data on the latter are difficult to collect in an internationally comparable way (UNESCO, 2005).

Figure 2.20: Mathematics achievement scores of grade 6 pupils in relation to socio-economic status, SACMEQ II (2000-2002)

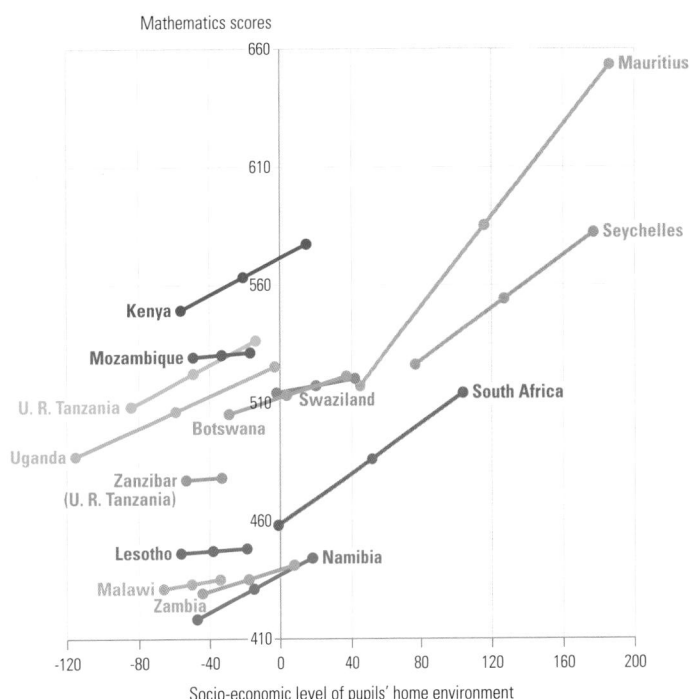

Note: The socio-economic gradient lines summarize the regression relationships between the mathematics achievement of grade 6 pupils and the socio-economic level of their home environments. The achievement scores in mathematics were transformed to an overall SACMEQ mean of 500 and standard deviation of 100. The socio-economic level of the home environment was assessed via a composite index combining information on the parents' education and characteristics such as house construction, home lighting and possessions. The index scores were transformed to an overall SACMEQ mean of zero and a standard deviation of 100. That is, the index scores were 'centred' so that a value of zero represented the socio-economic level of the home environment of an 'average SACMEQ pupil'.
Source: Ross et al. (2005).

Between 1999 and 2004, PTRs declined in most regions and countries with data available (107 out of 146 countries). The decline was most prevalent in East Asia, the Arab States, and North America and Western Europe (regions that already had PTRs below 30:1). A slight decline occurred in sub-Saharan Africa, but in the Pacific and in South and West Asia, PTRs increased, reaching a median of 40:1 in the latter. Ratios increased in more than one-fourth of the 146 countries, with the highest percentage increases in Afghanistan (80%), Bahamas (40%), United Republic of Tanzania (39%) and the Congo (35%). Countries with high ratios in 2004 also had high ratios in 1999 (see annex, Statistical Table 10A).

For particular countries, two trends are evident. First, the substantial increases in primary PTRs in Afghanistan,[29] the United Republic of Tanzania, the Congo and Kenya were accompanied by increases in the total number

29. As the 2006 Report pointed out (UNESCO, 2005), the number of teachers in Afghanistan did not grow to keep up with a large influx of new pupils, particularly girls (who were previously excluded).

Table 2.15: Distribution of countries by pupil/teacher ratios at primary level by region, 2004

Region	Below 15	15-24	25-39	40-55	55 and above
Sub-Saharan Africa (37)	Seychelles (1)	Mauritius (1)	Botswana, Cape Verde, Namibia, Swaziland, Sao Tome and Principe, Ghana, South Africa, Comoros, Gabon, Nigeria, Gambia, Zimbabwe, Kenya (13)	Côte d'Ivoire, Senegal, Lesotho, Niger, Togo, Guinea, Eritrea, Zambia, Burkina Faso, Uganda, Burundi, Benin, Mali, Madagascar, Cameroon, U. R. Tanzania (16)	Rwanda, Mozambique, Chad, Malawi, Ethiopia, Congo (6)
Arab States (18)	Qatar, Saudi Arabia, Kuwait, Lebanon (4)	U. A. Emirates, Bahrain, Syrian A. R., Oman, Jordan, Iraq, Tunisia, Egypt (8)	Algeria, Palestinian A. T., Morocco, Sudan, Djibouti (5)	Mauritania (1)	
Central Asia (7)	Azerbaijan, Georgia (2)	Kazakhstan, Tajikistan, Armenia, Kyrgyzstan (4)	Mongolia (1)		
East Asia/ Pacific (27)	Tokelau, Niue, Brunei Darussalam (3)	Cook Islands, New Zealand, Marshall Islands, Malaysia, Japan, Tuvalu, Vanuatu, Indonesia, Tonga, Thailand, China, Nauru, Viet Nam, Macao (China), Kiribati (15)	Samoa, Fiji, Republic of Korea, Myanmar, Lao PDR, Philippines, Papua New Guinea (7)	Timor-Leste (1)	Cambodia (1)
South/West Asia (9)		Maldives, Islamic Republic of Iran, Sri Lanka (3)	Pakistan, Bhutan, Nepal (3)	India, Bangladesh (2)	Afghanistan (1)
Latin America/ Caribbean (37)	Bermuda, Cuba, Turks and Caicos Islands, Cayman Islands, British Virgin Islands, Anguilla (6)	Barbados, Argentina, St Kitts/Nevis, St Vincent/Grenad., Trinidad/Tobago, Grenada, Aruba, Dominica, Suriname, Bahamas, Neth. Antilles, Uruguay, Montserrat, Brazil, Peru, Costa Rica, Saint Lucia, Ecuador, Belize, Bolivia, Panama (21)	Guyana, Chile, Jamaica, Paraguay, Colombia, Mexico, Guatemala, Dominican Republic, Honduras, Nicaragua (10)		
N. America/ W. Europe (22)	Sweden, Norway, Iceland, Italy, Greece, Luxembourg, Portugal, Belgium, Israel, Andorra, Switzerland, Austria, Spain, Germany, United States (15)	Finland, Canada, Cyprus, United Kingdom, Ireland, France, Malta (7)			
Centr./East. Europe (17)	Hungary, Poland, Latvia, Estonia, Lithuania (5)	Slovenia, Belarus, Russian Federation, Bulgaria, Romania, Slovakia, Croatia, Czech Republic, Ukraine, Republic of Moldova, TFYR Macedonia, Albania (12)			
Total: 174	36	71	39	20	8

Note: Countries are listed in ascending order of PTR. The total number of countries in each category is given in parentheses. See source table for detailed country notes.
Source: Annex, Statistical Table 10A.

Primary school teaching is predominantly a female occupation

of teachers, but these were insufficient to match increases in enrolment. Second, some countries, including Mali and the Syrian Arab Republic, did manage to decrease PTRs despite large enrolment increases.

Female teachers

In most regions, primary school teaching is predominantly a female occupation. The exceptions are South and West Asia, and sub-Saharan Africa (see annex, Statistical Table 10A). In Afghanistan, Benin, Chad and Togo, women make up one-fifth or less of the primary teacher workforce, and gender disparities persist in primary school participation (particularly in

Afghanistan, where about forty-four girls to 100 boys are enrolled in primary school). At higher levels of education, women's share of the teaching force is much lower, particularly in tertiary education, where teaching is predominantly a male occupation (Figure 2.21).

Teacher training and qualifications

Teacher training. Figures showing the proportion of trained teachers can give some indication of the likely quality of teaching staff. In about half the countries with 2004 data available (seventy-six for primary and fifty-nine for secondary), one-fifth of teachers in both primary and secondary education lacked pedagogical training. At primary

Figure 2.21: Percentage of female teachers in primary, secondary and tertiary education, regional medians, 2004

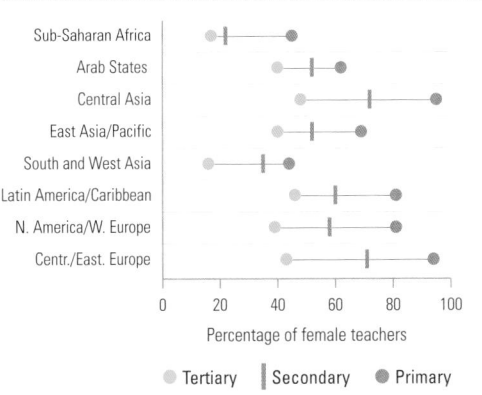

Source: Annex, Statistical Tables 10A and 10B.

Figure 2.22: Changes in the percentage of trained primary teachers between 1999 and 2004

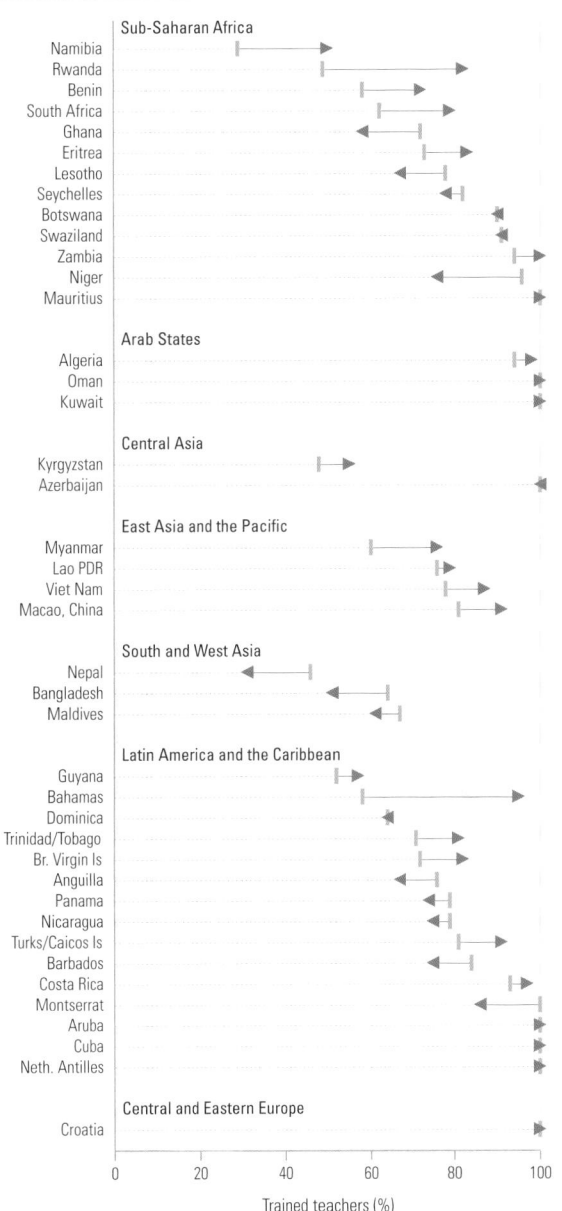

Note: Within each region, countries are listed in ascending order of the proportion of trained teachers in 1999. See source table for detailed country notes.
Source: Annex, Statistical Table 10A.

The percentage of trained primary teachers has increased slightly since 1999 in half of the countries with data

level in Lebanon, Nepal and Togo, fewer than half are trained according to national standards. In Lebanon and Nepal this is the result of an increase in the education level required for teacher training (UIS, 2006b), compounded in Lebanon with a very low PTR (14:1). Most of the eleven countries in the world where more than 50% of secondary teachers are untrained are in Latin America and the Caribbean[30] (see annex, Statistical Table 10B).

The percentage of trained primary teachers increased slightly between 1999 and 2004 in about half of the forty-one countries with data available (see annex, Statistical Table 10A). The improvement was remarkable (more than a 60% increase) in Bahamas, Namibia and Rwanda (Figure 2.22). In Namibia, this improvement was accompanied by an increased supply of teachers and hence a reduction in the PTR, although half of Namibia's teaching force still has no training. In Rwanda and Bahamas, growth in the proportion of trained teachers (by 68% and 62%, respectively) was paralleled by a decrease in absolute numbers of teachers, the latter trend leading to a deterioration in the PTR (which rose by 14% and 40%, respectively).[31]

The percentage of trained primary teachers declined in fifteen of the forty-one countries with data for the two years. The decline was particularly high in Bangladesh, Nepal and the Niger. In Nepal and the Niger (which has a policy of hiring untrained teachers – para-professionals or para-teachers – to support an increase in the enrolment ratio of more than 50%), not only did the proportion of trained teachers decline but

the PTR increased. In Bangladesh, on the other hand, the decrease in the percentage of trained teachers was accompanied by a slight decline in the PTR.

Teacher qualifications. Countries also differ in terms of their teacher qualifications (Box 2.3). The percentage of trained teachers as an

30. The eleven countries are Bangladesh, Belize, Burundi, Dominica, Grenada, Nepal, Nicaragua, Saint Kitts and Nevis, Saint Vincent and the Grenadines, Togo and the United Arab Emirates.

31. Rwanda increased the proportion of trained teachers by reorganizing teacher training institutions, opening new teacher training colleges and subsidizing two church-based teacher training institutions (UNESCO, 2005).

2007

Education for All Global Monitoring Report

Box 2.3: What does it take to be a teacher? A comparative perspective

In 2005, the UIS carried out a special survey on teachers in which it classified countries according to their minimum standards qualification for primary teaching. The results show a majority of countries requiring either a post-secondary, non-tertiary qualification or a tertiary qualification, with the necessary minimum standard qualifications ranging from six months to three years after completion of the upper-secondary level (Figure 2.23).

In sub-Saharan Africa, and East Asia and the Pacific, a few countries require lower minimum qualifications. In the Congo, Burkina Faso, Mozambique and the United Republic of Tanzania, for instance, only lower-secondary education is required. Despite this low minimum qualification, some of these countries still have high proportions of teachers who do not meet the requirement. In the Congo, for example, only 57% of teachers have completed lower-secondary education.

Sources: UIS (2006*b*: p.52).

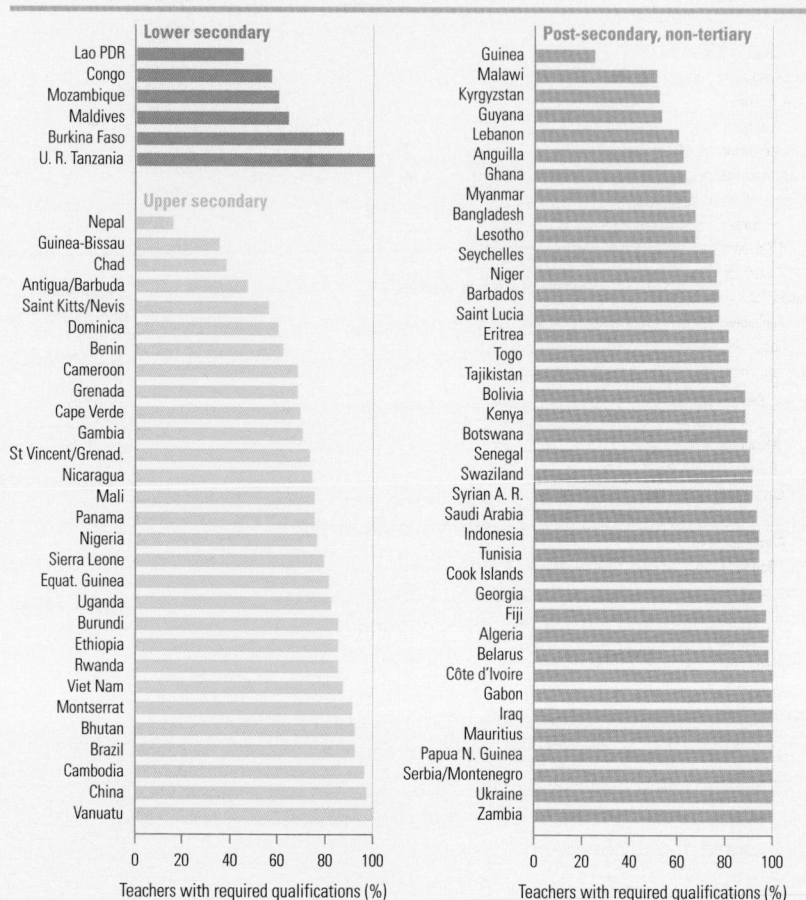

Figure 2.23: Percentage of primary teaching staff having the minimum academic qualification, 2004

indicator of teacher quality is thus of limited utility in cross-country comparisons. Moreover, as the example of Lebanon shows, changes in the percentage of trained teachers may be due to changes in the minimum teaching standards rather than in actual numbers of trained teachers.

How many teachers are needed to reach UPE in each region?

Education systems need to adapt to changing demographic patterns, which differ by regions. Although the rate of population growth has slowed worldwide since 1990, the 2004 revision of the United Nations population estimates indicates that some countries will still face increasing primary school-age populations up to 2015, especially in sub-Saharan Africa, the Arab States, and South and West Asia. In Central and Eastern

Europe, Central Asia, and East Asia and the Pacific, by contrast, sharp declines in population growth will result in decreases in the number of school-age children. In Latin America and the Caribbean, and North America and Western Europe, the primary school-age population will be more or less stable.

How will national teaching workforces need to adapt to respond to these demographic challenges and guarantee UPE by 2015? Figure 2.24 shows the percentage increase in numbers of teachers that selected countries will have to produce each year in order to achieve UPE while reducing their PTRs to 40:1. Sub-Saharan African countries will need to recruit an average of 6% more teachers each year than are currently employed, or between 2.4 million and 4.0 million teachers by 2015. Some countries,

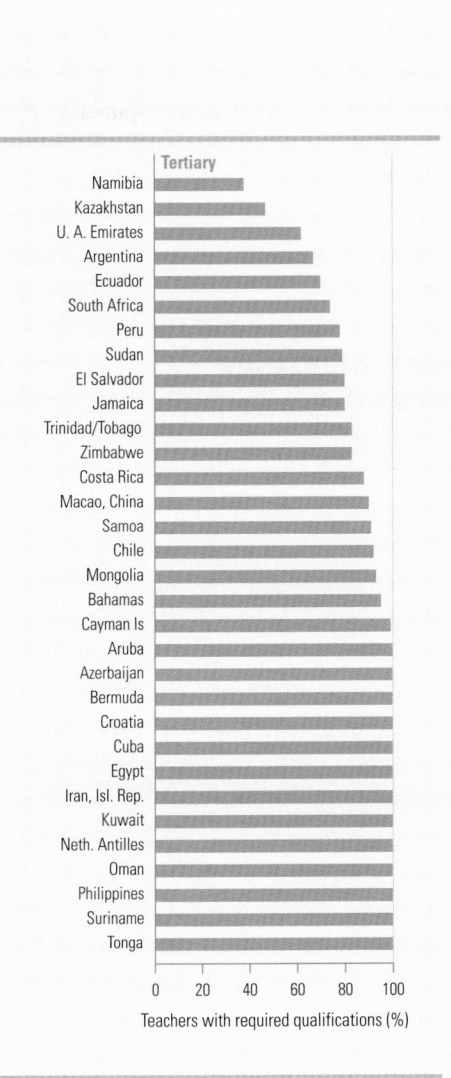

Tertiary

Teachers with required qualifications (%)

Figure 2.24: Annual percentage increase in numbers of primary teachers required to reach UPE in selected countries, 2004–2015

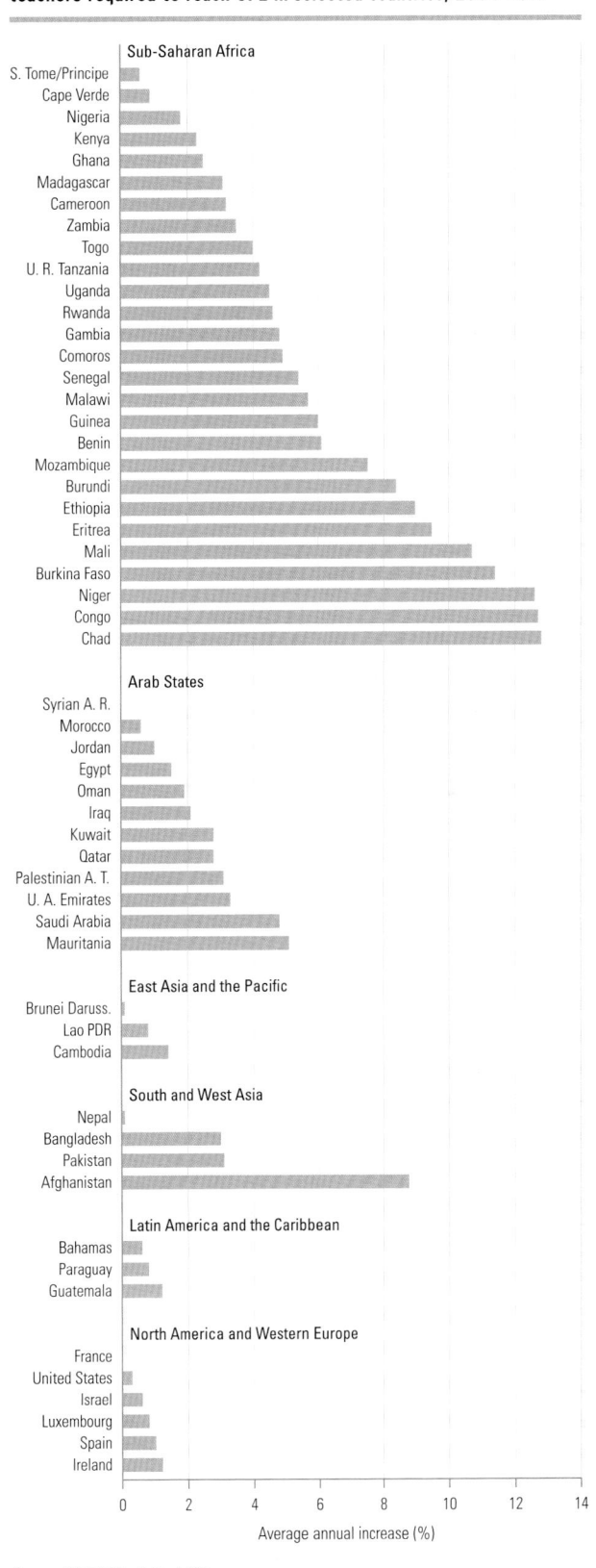

Average annual increase (%)

Source: UIS (2006*b*: Table A.2.6).

including Chad, the Congo, Burkina Faso and the Niger, will need to recruit at least 10% more teachers each year than are currently available to meet the goal by 2015. Meeting this tremendous challenge may not be feasible in all cases, raising important questions about possible alternative models of education. For other countries, the percentage increases needed may seem relatively modest, but the absolute numbers involved are very high: Bangladesh, Ethiopia, Nigeria, Pakistan and Saudi Arabia combined need more than 65,000 additional teachers per year (UIS, 2006*b*).

Although demographic patterns are important, the issue of teacher shortages goes beyond demographics and leads to the question of whether increased public spending is feasible. Opportunities in the labour market are opening up worldwide. They offer new outlets for existing and

Education for All Global Monitoring Report

2 0 0 7

potential teachers, particularly qualified ones. Salary increases may be needed to recruit and retain teachers, but financing such increases could be difficult, as teacher salaries already represent 75% or more of public expenditure on primary education in a majority of the countries that need to increase teacher numbers to achieve EFA (see annex, Statistical Table 11). An alternative would be to reduce spending on other pedagogical components, such as textbooks or materials, which would jeopardize education quality.

Some countries have teacher shortages in certain groups. Particularly serious are shortages of female teachers in countries with low enrolment of girls, and of teachers from particular ethnic and social backgrounds. In several developing countries, more and better qualified teachers are usually found in urban areas, with serious shortages of qualified teachers in rural areas (Mulkeen, 2005). In some countries, high rates of teacher absenteeism can cause schools to close and students to be sent home or to join other classes (Box 2.4). Still others face problems of teacher migration (Global Campaign For Education, 2006). In several countries, the HIV/AIDS pandemic is affecting teacher supply through increased teacher mortality, health-related absenteeism, or both (Philander, 2006).

Learning and life-skills programmes

To monitor EFA goal 3[32] and the latter part of goal 4[33] remains a challenge. Both call for 'equitable access' to learning programmes that meet the needs of youth and adults. Yet, there is no common understanding of the types of structured learning activities that come under the umbrella of 'learning and life-skills programmes'.[34] With the 2015 target year quickly approaching, it is increasingly important to examine more systematically the learning and life-skills programmes available to young people and adults, using more interpretive monitoring tools that reflect an understanding of the diversity and fragmentation of goals 3 and 4. Such an analysis also provides an opportunity to look at links between formal and non-formal education and learning.

Grasping the concept

One way to interpret goals 3 and 4 is to construct a framework for understanding them, for example through an analysis of learning needs, skills, key competencies and outcomes of learning

---

Box 2.4: Patterns of teacher absenteeism in six developing countries

In Bangladesh, Ecuador, India, Indonesia, Peru and Uganda, researchers conducted unannounced visits to about 100 randomly selected public and private primary schools per country from October 2002 to April 2003. They counted the full-time teachers who were absent but were supposed to be on duty according to the school attendance book, and excluded those who were working another shift.

On average, 19% of teachers were absent, and in most cases the absences were unauthorized. More absences were recorded among head teachers, better-educated teachers and older teachers than for their less educated and younger colleagues; and more males than females were absent. Teachers who were born in the area where they taught were less absent than those born elsewhere. Teacher absenteeism was not correlated with teacher salaries, alternative salary opportunities in the area or in-service or other recent training, or teacher inspections.

Schools with better infrastructure had lower absenteeism rates, as did schools closer to ministry of education offices. Finally, contract teachers were more likely to be absent than civil-servant teachers, and teachers in private schools were as likely to be absent as those in public schools (except in India, where private-school teachers had lower absenteeism rates than public school teachers in the same village). Interestingly, the study also found that, overall, teachers were less absent, on average, than health workers.

Source: Chaudhury et al. (2005).

---

32. 'Ensuring that the learning needs of all young people and adults are met through equitable access to appropriate learning and life-skills programmes.'

33. 'Achieving ... equitable access to basic and continuing education for all adults.'

34.
■ Under goal 3 the expanded commentary of the Dakar Framework for Action states (Paragraph 36): 'All young people should be given the opportunity for ongoing education. For those who drop out of school or complete school without acquiring the literacy, numeracy and life skills they need, there must be a range of options for continuing their learning. Such opportunities should be both meaningful and relevant to their environment and needs, help them become active agents in shaping their future and develop useful work-related skills" (UNESCO, 2000a). The 2003/4 *EFA Global Monitoring Report* opted to identify and describe learning programmes for youth and adults in a more qualitative way, combining goals 3 and 4 (UNESCO, 2003a).
■ Under goal 4 the commentary states (Paragraph 38): 'Adult and continuing education must be greatly expanded and diversified, and integrated into the mainstream of national education and poverty reduction strategies. The vital role literacy plays in lifelong learning, sustainable livelihoods, good health, active citizenship and the improved quality of life for individuals, communities and societies must be more widely recognized' (UNESCO, 2000a).

activities.[35] A second way is to deconstruct the components of the goals, using a bottom-up, more inductive approach. This involves examining the categories of learning activities that are identified by countries and regions themselves as meeting adult and youth learning needs. Previous editions of the *EFA Global Monitoring Report*, while adopting this approach, have pointed to the difficulty of arriving at an overview of who is doing what in support of the learning needs of young people and adults (UNESCO, 2002, 2003). Taking this approach should involve examining both qualitative and (where available) quantitative data at national level. More systematic monitoring at country level should document youth and adult learning from the perspective of provision, participation and access, and should pose fundamental questions, such as what the learning outcomes are and what actions countries are taking to include the excluded.

Learners may be adults or out-of-school youth re-entering basic education, or they may be young people needing basic education, life-skills[36] or livelihood skills. What characterizes the structured learning activities involved is a large diversity of provision and providers, including the public, private and civil society sectors as sole providers or in partnership. Figure 2.25 presents a conceptualization of these categories.

A first step in monitoring learning and life-skills programmes is to investigate elements of provision, participation and access to non-formal learning activities at national or subnational level. Non-formal learning in Ethiopia is an interesting example because it is integrated into the national Education Sector Development Programme (Box 2.5).

Figure 2.25: Core features of learning and life skills programmes

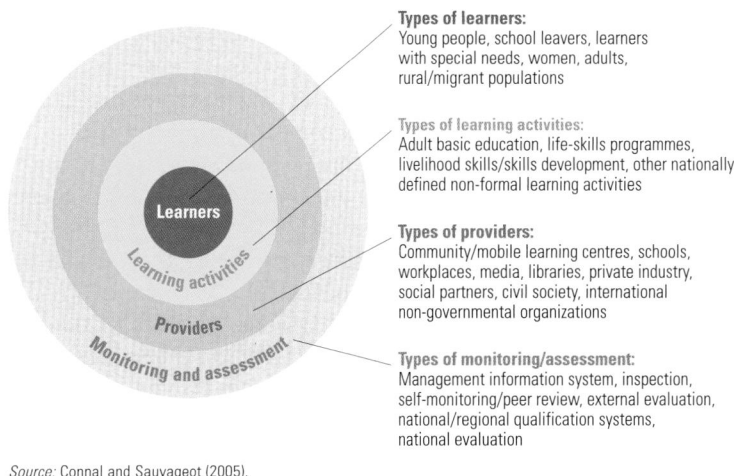

Types of learners:
Young people, school leavers, learners with special needs, women, adults, rural/migrant populations

Types of learning activities:
Adult basic education, life-skills programmes, livelihood skills/skills development, other nationally defined non-formal learning activities

Types of providers:
Community/mobile learning centres, schools, workplaces, media, libraries, private industry, social partners, civil society, international non-governmental organizations

Types of monitoring/assessment:
Management information system, inspection, self-monitoring/peer review, external evaluation, national/regional qualification systems, national evaluation

Source: Connal and Sauvageot (2005).

Box 2.5: Ethiopia's first efforts to monitor provision and participation

Ethiopia's Education Sector Development Programme (ESDP III) calls for increased access to adult and non-formal education in order to combat the problem of adult illiteracy. Ethiopia focuses on three types of activities: alternative programmes for out-of-school children aged 7 to 14; literacy programmes for people over 15; and basic skills training for youth and adults in Community Skill Training Centers (CSTCs). The youth and adult functional literacy programme aims to reach 5.2 million learners by 2011, while some 143,500 adults are to be trained in various skills in the country's 287 CSTCs. The government will formulate policy, develop curricula and set standards for quality, professional assistance and access to school buildings. Civil society is being encouraged to provide non-formal education services (Ethiopia, Ministry of Education, 2005). While ESDP III includes no key performance indicators for non-formal education, the Ministry of Education has begun collecting data on participants in the programmes.

Source: Shenkut (2006).

Instruments for monitoring learning and life-skills programmes

There are great variations among regions and countries when it comes to developing monitoring systems for non-formal learning. The European Union has made progress in identifying key competencies that can be integrated into Member States' employment policies. Competencies are closely linked to developing a European Qualifications Framework (Council of the European Union, 2006). Botswana, Cape Verde, Namibia and South Africa have education policies that build bridges between formal and non-formal

35. The Adult Literacy and Life Skills (ALL) survey and the OECD Definition and Selection of Key Competencies (DeSeCo) are examples of instruments developed to measure competencies. The ALL survey builds on foundation skills, including prose literacy, document literacy, numeracy and problem-solving. Additional skills assessed involve familiarity with the use of information and communication technology (Statistics Canada/OECD, 2005). The DeSeCo framework goes beyond assessment of skills. It defines 'competencies' as: 'abilities to meet complex demands, by drawing on and mobilizing psychosocial resources (including skills and attitudes) in a particular context'. Competencies are classified into three broad categories: using tools (e.g. language, technology) interactively; interacting in heterogeneous groups; and acting autonomously (OECD, 2005b).

36. Life skills can be described as 'a group of psychosocial competencies and interpersonal skills that help people make informed decisions, solve problems, think critically and creatively, communicate effectively, build healthy relationships, empathise with others and cope with and manage their lives in a healthy and productive manner' (WHO, 2003). The Inter-Agency Working Group on Life Skills in EFA arrived at a minimum consensus that life skills are not a domain or subject, but cross-cutting applications of knowledge, values, attitudes and skills that are important in the process of individual development and in lifelong learning (UNESCO, 2004b).

learning. The policies have facilitated the establishment of national qualification frameworks and accreditation systems that recognize learning acquired previously (Katahoire, 2006).

Overall, however, reliable and timely national and internationally comparable data on non-formal education are generally difficult to obtain. To improve this situation, a non-formal education management information system, or NFE-MIS, has been developed, and several countries are using it on a pilot basis.[37] The NFE-MIS is designed to generate reliable statistics for use by policy-makers and planners at national and subnational level. The strategy is to take an incremental approach, starting at subnational level, and provide countries with a tool to define their own conceptual frameworks for non-formal education (Connal and Sauvageot, 2005).

Two pilot projects, in the Indian states of Andra Pradesh and Madhya Pradesh, have developed, tested and implemented a set of internationally comparable monitoring and evaluation methodologies for producing national data on non-formal education. The Andhra Pradesh mapping exercise found twenty-five to thirty public and private agencies providing learning activities in NFE areas such as literacy, basic education for out-of-school children and youth (equivalency education), life skills, rural development, income generation training, non-formal higher education, religious education and leisure. A set of draft indicators was developed to measure access and participation, input, process, output, outcome and efficiency. One of the main conclusions was that India's approach to EFA was lacking in vision and policy for non-formal education. The lesson may be that it is more realistic to start small by developing NFE monitoring first at district level, where there is a great potential for using the indicators. Many agencies provide non-formal education and each has its own set of data. These flow vertically to higher levels, but virtually no horizontal data sharing takes place (Mathew and Rao, 2004). Properly collected disaggregated data at lower levels can reveal areas of inequity in access to learning and education more easily than higher-level aggregate indicators.

These examples reflect some of the complexity of monitoring learning and life-skills programmes. The 2008 *EFA Global Monitoring Report* will include a more systematic assessment of progress in meeting the learning needs of young people and adults.

781 million adults have yet to acquire minimal literacy skills

Literacy: the challenge remains

Literacy was the focus of the 2006 *EFA Global Monitoring Report*, which advocated a three-pronged strategy: UPE of good quality, greatly expanded literacy programmes for youth and adults, and more attention to literate environments. This section updates information on adult and youth literacy patterns and raises some issues about the monitoring of literate environments. As the 2006 Report emphasized, current cross-national literacy data, which are based on conventional measures, must be treated with caution since they tend to overestimate literacy levels in most countries. Until there are more direct, rather than indirect, assessments of individuals' literacy skills, this will remain a problem.

Global patterns of adult literacy

About 781 million adults worldwide, 64% of them women, have yet to acquire minimal literacy skills. The increase from the figure of 771 million given in the 2006 Report reflects the inclusion of previously unavailable data for Afghanistan and changes in population estimates.[38] The vast majority of adults denied the right to literacy live in South and West Asia, sub-Saharan Africa and East Asia. Unless national policy-makers and the international community join to make a concerted effort to significantly expand adult literacy programmes in the coming decade, by 2015 the number of adults without basic literacy skills will decline by only about 100 million worldwide, by current estimates (Table 2.16).

Between 1990 and 2004, the global adult literacy rate rose from 75% to 82%. For developing countries the literacy rate increased from 67% to 77%, mainly because of a marked reduction in the number of illiterates (by 94 million) in China, and a corresponding increase of almost thirteen percentage points in the national literacy rate. The average literacy rates improved in all regions, but remain particularly low in South and West Asia (59%), sub-Saharan Africa (61%), the Arab States (66%) and the Caribbean (70%). Despite increases in adult literacy rates of ten percentage points or more in the first two of these regions, the absolute numbers of illiterates continued to rise because of high population growth (Table 2.17).

Progress towards the literacy goal requires change in the countries with very high absolute numbers of illiterates and those with relatively

37. The NFE-MIS methodology was designed by UNESCO with assistance from the UNESCO Institute for Education (UIE, now the UNESCO Institute for Lifelong Learning (UIL)) and the UIS. Diagnostic studies have been done in Cambodia, India, Jordan and the United Republic of Tanzania.

38. The estimated number of adult illiterates in Table 2.16 is based on the 2004 revision of UN population estimates, while the data published in the 2006 Report were based on the 2002 revision.

Table 2.16: Estimated numbers of adult illiterates (age 15+) in 1990 and 2000–2004[1], and projections to 2015, by region

	1990 Total (000)	1990 % Female	2000-2004 Total (000)	2000-2004 % Female	2015 Total (000)	2015 % Female	Percentage change 1990 to 2000-2004	Percentage change 2000-2004 to 2015
World	874 019	63	780 657	64	684 160	65	-10.7	-12.4
Developing countries	857 407	63	770 255	64	674 244	65	-10.2	-12.5
Developed countries	14 855	64	9 062	63	9 318	75	-39.0	2.8
Countries in transition	1 757	78	1 340	76	599	61	-23.7	-55.3
Sub-Saharan Africa	132 597	61	143 885	61	168 007	59	8.5	16.8
Arab States	63 659	63	57 812	66	55 111	67	-9.2	-4.7
Central Asia	569	79	382	72	232	57	-32.8	-39.3
East Asia and the Pacific	232 691	69	125 359	71	80 765	71	-46.1	-35.6
East Asia	...	...	123 758	71	78 907	71	...	-36.2
Pacific	...	...	1 600	57	1 858	54	...	16.1
South and West Asia	379 849	60	399 016	63	344 529	66	5.0	-13.7
Latin America and the Caribbean	41 838	57	38 572	55	26 225	54	-7.8	-32.0
Caribbean	...	...	35 637	55	25 198	54	...	-29.3
Latin America	...	...	2 935	51	1 027	46	...	-65.0
North America and Western Europe	11 324	64	6 312	62	2 422	63	-44.3	-61.6
Central and Eastern Europe	11 494	75	9 320	79	6 871	78	-18.9	-26.3

1. Data are for the most recent year available during the period specified.
Source: Annex, Statistical Table 2.

Table 2.17: Estimated adult literacy rates (age 15+) in 1990 and 2000–2004[1], and projections to 2015, by region

	1990 Literacy rates (%) Total	1990 Male	1990 Female	1990 GPI (F/M)	2000-2004 Literacy rates (%) Total	2000-2004 Male	2000-2004 Female	2000-2004 GPI (F/M)	2015 Literacy rates (%) Total	2015 Male	2015 Female	2015 GPI (F/M)
World	75	82	69	0.84	82	87	77	0.89	87	91	84	0.92
Developing countries	67	76	58	0.76	77	83	70	0.84	84	88	79	0.89
Developed countries	98	99	98	0.99	99	99	99	0.99	99	100	99	0.99
Countries in transition	99	100	99	0.99	99	100	99	0.99	100	100	100	1.00
Sub-Saharan Africa	50	60	40	0.67	61	70	53	0.77	67	73	61	0.84
Arab States	50	64	36	0.56	66	77	55	0.72	79	86	71	0.82
Central Asia	99	99	98	0.99	99	100	99	0.99	100	100	100	1.00
East Asia and the Pacific	82	89	75	0.84	92	95	88	0.93	96	97	94	0.96
East Asia	...	...	...	...	92	95	88	0.93	96	97	94	0.96
Pacific	...	...	...	...	93	94	93	0.98	93	94	93	0.99
South and West Asia	47	60	34	0.58	59	71	46	0.66	68	78	58	0.74
Latin America and the Caribbean	85	87	83	0.96	90	91	89	0.98	94	95	94	0.99
Caribbean	...	...	...	...	70	70	70	1.00	97	96	97	1.01
Latin America	...	...	...	...	90	91	90	0.98	94	95	94	0.99
North America and Western Europe	98	98	97	0.99	99	99	99	1.00	100	100	100	1.00
Central and Eastern Europe	96	98	95	0.97	97	99	96	0.97	98	99	97	0.98

1. Data are for the most recent year available during the period specified.
Source: Annex, Statistical Table 2.

39. Absent from this list is Nigeria, for which observed data are now more than twenty years out of date. Some evidence suggests that the number of adult illiterates in Nigeria could be more than 20 million.

42. Another minor exception is North America and Western Europe, where both the illiteracy rate and the number of illiterate youth have increased slightly.

low literacy rates. Figure 2.26 examines progress in the ten countries with more than 10 million illiterates, which together account for about 70% of the world's illiterate population.[39] Literacy rates have increased in all ten countries, but population growth means that the illiterate population has declined in only the Islamic Republic of Iran, Egypt, Brazil, Indonesia and China, while it has increased in Morocco, Ethiopia, Pakistan and Bangladesh and is little changed in India.

Figure 2.26: Changes in adult literacy (age 15+) between 1990 and 2000-2004 in countries with more than 10 million illiterates

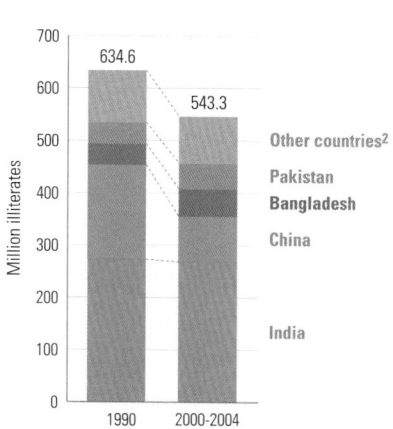

	Number of illiterates			Literacy rates		
	1990	2000-2004[1]	Change 1990 to 2000-2004	1990	2000-2004[1]	Change 1990 to 2000-2004
	(000)	(000)	(%)	(%)	(%)	(percentage points)
Morocco	9 140	10 106	10.6	38.7	52.3	13.6
Iran, Isl. Rep.	11 501	10 509	-8.6	63.2	77.0	13.8
Egypt	17 411	14 210	-18.4	47.1	71.4	24.3
Brazil	17 369	15 052	-13.3	82.0	88.6	6.6
Indonesia	23 791	15 100	-36.5	79.5	90.4	10.9
Ethiopia	19 815	23 554	18.9	28.6	45.2	16.6
Pakistan	40 817	48 818	19.6	35.4	49.9	14.5
Bangladesh	40 405	52 530	30.0	34.2	42.6	8.4
China	181 331	87 019	-52.0	78.3	90.9	12.6
India	273 066	268 426	-1.7	49.3	61.0	11.7

1. Data are for the most recent year available during the period specified. See the introduction to the statistical tables in the annex for a broader explanation of national literacy definitions, assessment methods, sources and years of data.
2. Brazil, Egypt, Ethiopia, Indonesia, Morocco, Islamic Republic of Iran.
Note: See source table for detailed country notes.
Source: Annex, Statistical Table 2.

The most recent estimates indicate that in twenty-two countries the adult literacy rate is below 60% (see annex, Statistical Table 2).[40] Fourteen are in sub-Saharan Africa (Benin, Burkina Faso, Burundi, the Central African Republic, Chad, Côte d'Ivoire, Ethiopia, Ghana, Guinea, Mali, the Niger, Senegal, Sierra Leone and Togo), four in South and West Asia (Afghanistan, Bangladesh, Nepal and Pakistan), three are Arab States (Mauritania, Morocco and Yemen) and one is in East Asia and the Pacific (Papua New Guinea). In most of these countries literacy rates have improved since 1990. If current trends continue, however, most will find it difficult to reach the EFA literacy goal by 2015 (Figure 2.27).[41]

Gender disparities in adult literacy: women are the most affected

Women account for 64% of the adults worldwide who cannot read and write with understanding a simple statement from their everyday life. This share is virtually unchanged from the 63% recorded in 1990. Globally, only 89 adult women are considered literate for every 100 literate adult men (i.e. the adult literacy GPI is 0.89). The regions with the lowest adult literacy GPIs are South and West Asia (0.66), the Arab States (0.72) and sub-Saharan Africa (0.77). The GPI in East Asia (0.93) is above the global average, while in the remaining regions gender parity has been achieved, on average. All regions have experienced increases in the GPI since 1990.

The increases are especially notable in the three regions where both illiteracy rates and gender disparities are highest: sub-Saharan Africa, South and West Asia, and the Arab States (Table 2.17).

Despite overall progress, significant disparities between adult men and women remain in some countries (see annex, Statistical Table 2). Gender disparities favouring men are especially prevalent in West and Central Africa; in Afghanistan, Bangladesh, India, Nepal and Pakistan, among countries of South and West Asia; and in Morocco and Yemen among the Arab States. In all these cases the female literacy rate is less than two-thirds the male rate. Several cases exist, however, of gender disparities favouring women; examples are Jamaica (1.16) and Lesotho (1.23). This reverse trend is growing elsewhere in the world, particularly among younger cohorts.

Youth literacy

Literacy rates among the population aged 15 to 24 tend to be higher than for the overall population aged 15 and over (Tables 2.16 and 2.18), reflecting recent developments in school expansion. Youth literacy rates have increased in all regions since 1990, resulting in a decline in the number of illiterate youth, except in sub-Saharan Africa where the population is still growing rapidly.[42]

Gender disparities in youth literacy are generally less pronounced than those in adult literacy. However, the regional patterns are the same, with South and West Asia (GPI of 0.79), the

40. Recent adult literacy rates are missing for six countries that should be added to this list: Eritrea, the Gambia, Liberia, Mozambique, Nauru and Nigeria.

41. The previous Report discussed the fact that, while early formulations of the literacy goal by the international community emphasized the need to reduce both overall adult illiteracy and the disparity between male and female illiteracy rates, the EFA goal formulated at Dakar in 2000 read: 'Achieving a 50 per cent improvement in levels of adult literacy by 2015, especially for women, and equitable access to basic and continuing education for all adults.' To better monitor national progress in improving literacy, the EFA Global Monitoring Report Team decided to measure progress in terms of a reduction in the rate of adult illiteracy in accordance with an earlier formulation of the literacy goal (i.e. halving the level of illiteracy), rather than improving levels of adult literacy by 50% (UNESCO, 2005: 66.)

Figure 2.27: Estimated adult literacy rates (age 15+) for 1990 and 2000-2004[1] and projections and targets for 2015

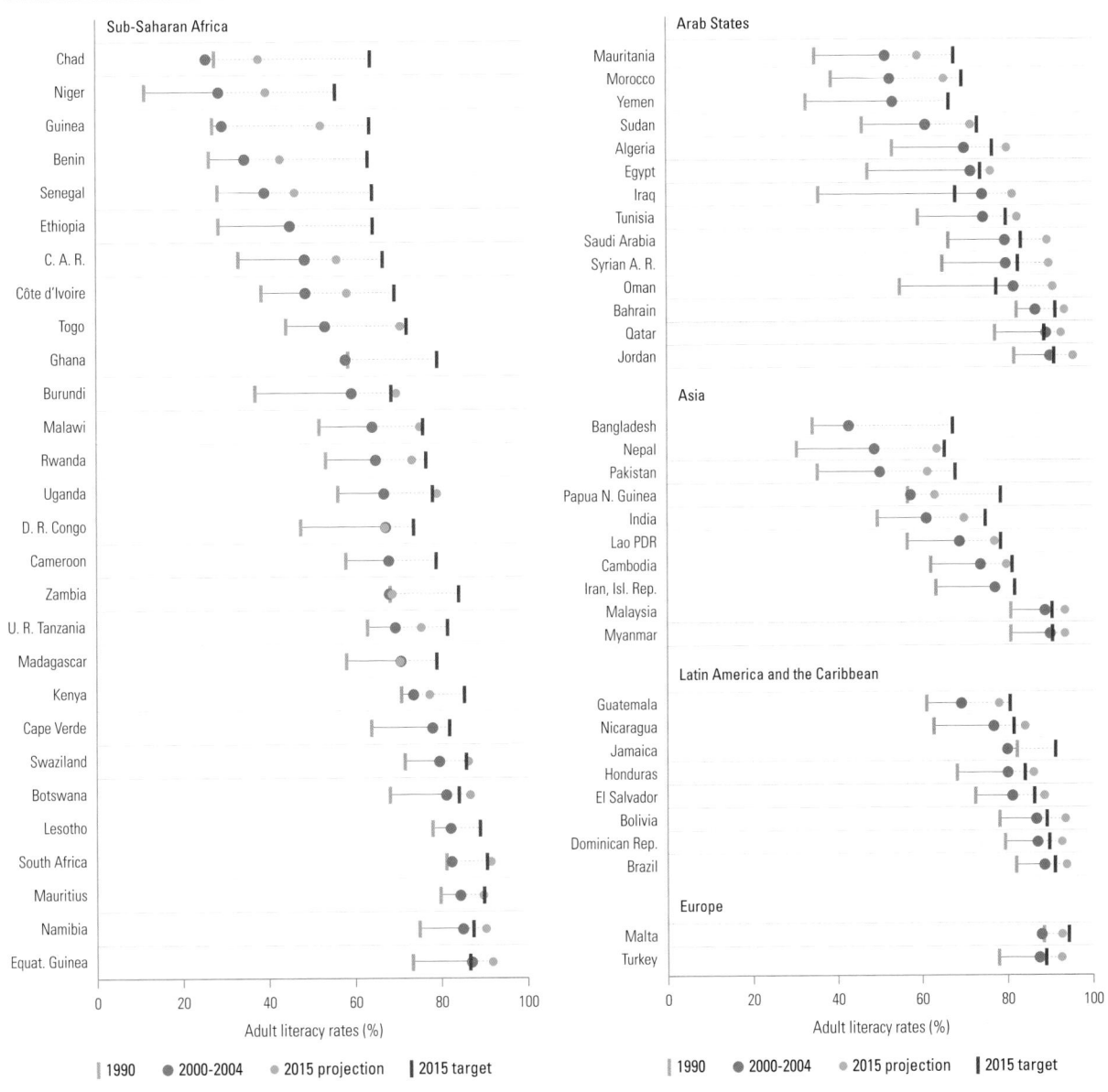

1. Data are for the most recent year available during the period specified. See the introduction to the statistical tables in the annex for a broader explanation of national literacy definitions, assessment methods, sources and years of data.

Note: Only countries with literacy rates below 90% in 2000–2004 are included; they are presented in ascending order. See source table for detailed country notes.

Source: Annex, Statistical Table 2.

Arab States (0.87) and sub-Saharan Africa being the regions with the greatest gender disparity in youth literacy (see annex, Statistical Table 2).

Literate environments: neglected but necessary

Literacy is not only about individuals, but also about literate communities and societies. Indeed, as the 2006 Report argued, the motivation and proclivity to become literate are closely related to the quality of the literate environments at home, school and work, and in the wider community. The presence of printed, written and visual materials encourages adults to adopt and integrate an array of literacy skills and activities in their everyday lives. Access to books, magazines and newspapers significantly contributes to the reading and language achievement of students.

Table 2.18: Estimated literacy rates and numbers of illiterates among young adults (aged 15-24) in 1990 and 2000-2004[1], by region

	Literacy rates ages 15-24 (%)		Number of illiterates ages 15-24 (000)		Percentage change 1990 to 2000-2004	
	1990	2000-2004	1990	2000-2004	In literacy rates	In number of illiterates
World	84.3	87.3	157 212	138 973	3.6	-11.6
Developing countries	80.9	84.8	156 410	138 083	4.8	-11.7
Developed countries	99.7	99.4	471	768	-0.2	63.1
Countries in transition	99.2	99.7	332	122	0.6	-63.2
Sub-Saharan Africa	67.5	72.9	30 468	36 894	8.0	21.1
Arab States	66.6	82.5	14 426	9 426	23.7	-34.7
Central Asia	97.7	99.7	280	47	2.0	-83.3
East Asia/Pacific	95.4	98.0	17 420	6 767	2.7	-61.2
East Asia	…	98.0	…	6 375	…	…
Pacific	…	92.1	…	392	…	…
South/West Asia	61.5	72.2	86 921	80 415	17.3	-7.5
Latin America/Caribbean	92.7	96.0	6 369	4 109	3.6	-35.5
Caribbean	…	76.8	…	745	…	…
Latin America	…	96.6	…	3 364	…	…
N. America/W. Europe	99.7	99.5	310	493	-0.2	59.0
Centr./East. Europe	98.3	98.7	1 019	823	0.4	-19.3

1. Data are for the most recent year available during the period specified.
Sources: Annex, Statistical Table 2.

Moreover, in conjunction with the United Nations Literacy Decade (2003–12), the international community has underscored the social dimension of literacy, recognizing that 'creating literate environments and societies is essential for achieving the goals of eradicating poverty, reducing child mortality, curbing population growth, achieving gender equality and ensuring sustainable development, peace and democracy' (United Nations, 2001b). This initiative should nurture dynamic literate environments, especially in schools and marginalized communities, so that literacy will be sustained beyond the Literacy Decade. Box 2.6 discusses the conceptual and measurement challenges.

Overall progress towards education for all

The earlier sections of this chapter looked at the individual EFA goals. This final section considers where the world stands with regard to EFA as a whole, including through the EFA Development Index.

Box 2.6: What is a literate environment?

Notwithstanding policy and scholarly interest in literate environments, the concept raises two formidable challenges. The first is conceptual and revolves around the question of what precisely constitutes a literate environment. The second involves issues of monitoring and assessment: how can literate environments be measured and compared across countries and over time?

An informative starting point is Easton (2006a; 2006b), who argues that literate environments are locations (spaces) that provide four interrelated types of opportunities for the application and use of literacy skills:

● access to reading material of direct interest to the neoliterate: books, brochures, newspapers, magazines, messages, letters and other practical documents, whose existence presupposes publishing facilities and the use of relevant languages to reach diverse readers;

● access to continuing education in one or both of two forms: (a) sequences of formal schooling to which the learner may accede by establishing equivalence between skills already acquired and a given level of the system – and by virtue of open

or age-neutral enrolment policies; or (b) varieties of organized non-formal education (e.g. life-skills or livelihood training, short-term professional training and trade apprenticeship) that confer other skills or elements of knowledge of interest to the learner;

● opportunities to assume new organizational roles and tasks in, for example, local governments, agricultural cooperatives or extension systems that require and exercise literate skills;

● opportunities to establish and help manage business or non-profit endeavours that require and exercise literate skills.

The combination of all four types of opportunity – in varing forms and degrees – constitutes a truly literate environment.

Government can play an important policy role with regard to all four opportunity types. For example, policy towards libraries can enhance access to reading material and to continuing education. Cost-effective strategies to expand the reach of libraries ('universities of the people') have been undertaken, with the assistance of Book Aid International, in sub-Saharan Africa. The strategies include linking school libraries

Where are we now and how far have we come?

Now that information is available for the school year ending in 2004, it is very clear that considerable – but uneven – progress has been made since Dakar:

- Pre-primary enrolments are up, but not very significantly. In some regions, pre-primary education has become the norm (e.g. North America and Western Europe, Latin America and the Caribbean); in others it is still very rare (e.g. sub-Saharan Africa). Other aspects of ECCE are discussed extensively elsewhere in this Report.
- Access to primary school is improving, a fact reflected in data on new entrants and on primary enrolments, especially in the three regions that were, and remain, farthest from the goal: sub-Saharan Africa, South and West Asia, and the Arab States. Primary school progression and completion remain major concerns, however, especially in these same regions but also to some extent in Latin America and the Caribbean. The lack of data for a number of countries, mainly in sub-

Saharan Africa, that are or have recently been affected by conflict also means the global picture is not as positive as that painted by examining only countries for which data exist.

- The number of children not in school has declined but remains much too high. Moreover, there is some evidence that countries which are getting within closing distance of UPE are finding it very difficult to succeed in the final stages of attracting the most marginalized children and retaining them through the full primary cycle.
- Considerable progress is being made towards gender parity, in particular in countries where gender differences in education are still high, but disparities remain predominant, particularly in secondary education. About two-thirds of countries with data available for 2004 have achieved gender parity in primary education; in the remainder, the disparities mainly favour boys. However, in only one-third of the countries with data available for secondary education has gender parity been reached at that level, and disparities in secondary are much more pronounced than in primary education; they can favour either girls or boys.
- No major new information is available on learning outcomes, but new analyses of past assessments, together with a new evaluation report from the World Bank, confirm that quality remains a major issue, particularly for children from poorer backgrounds. Key teacher indicators suggest the same: while pupil/teacher ratios have generally improved slightly, they remain much too high, as do the proportion of teachers who are not qualified and trained, and the rate of teacher absenteeism. The issue of quality is not confined to the three regions with the greatest enrolment challenges. It is also a concern in East Asia and the Pacific, and in Latin America and the Caribbean.
- The scope of the global literacy challenge remains much as depicted in the 2006 Report, which had literacy as its special theme: about one in five adults is still not literate (one in four adult women) and those who are not literate live mainly in South and West Asia, sub-Saharan Africa and East Asia.
- Monitoring instruments remain to be developed for the learning needs of youth and adults, and for the literate environment.

The number of children not in school has declined but remains much too high

to community libraries, rotating boxes of books by motorbike among schools, setting up reading tents, helping children produce books for young and old, setting aside special reading corners for adult women and making libraries mobile with donkey carts and camels (Makotsi, 2005). The existence of libraries and book publishing are key conditions for sustainable literate environments.

In addition to conceptual clarification, there is a need to develop clear indicators of literate environments and their multiple dimensions. For example, while government policies regarding formal education are quite explicit, official policies regarding the literate environment (e.g. on the production and publication of written texts, the housing and dissemination of information, the development of media outlets and the languages used in courts, schools and administration) are less explicit and considerably more complex to assess. Measures of the literate environment should also address the equity dimension: to what extent, and why, are some denied access to opportunities that constitute a rich literate environment?

Sources: Easton (2006*a*, 2006*b*); Makotsi (2005).

**Changes in the
EDI are positive**

The EFA Development Index

The EFA Development Index (EDI) is a composite measure of a country's situation with regard to the attainment of the EFA agenda. It was introduced in the 2003/4 *EFA Global Monitoring Report* and is updated annually. Ideally, it should include measures of all six EFA goals; currently, however, it focuses on the four most easily quantified:

- universal primary education (goal 2), proxied by the total primary net enrolment ratio;[43]
- adult literacy (goal 4), proxied by the literacy rate for those aged 15 and above;[44]
- gender parity and equality (goal 5), proxied by the gender-specific EFA index (GEI) which is an average of the GPIs for primary and secondary gross enrolment ratios and the adult literacy rate;
- quality of education (goal 6), proxied by the survival rate to grade 5.

The EDI gives equal weight to the four proxy measures of the four goals. Since each measure is expressed as a percentage, the EDI for a country ranges from 0% to 100% or, when expressed as a ratio, from 0 to 1, where 1 would represent the full achievement of EFA as summarized by the EDI. Appendix 1 to this Report gives a detailed explanation of the EDI's rationale and methodology, together with detailed values and rankings for 2004. While 125 countries are included, data limitations mean that many countries are excluded. Several of these are in conflict or post-conflict situations and are likely to suffer from low levels of educational development. They include Afghanistan, Angola, the Central African Republic, the Congo, the Democratic Republic of the Congo, Liberia, Sierra Leone, Somalia and the Sudan. The overall picture obtained from the EDI is thus informative but does not fully capture the global EFA situation.

Table 2.19 summarizes the results of EDI calculations for 2004 by region. Of the 125 countries:

- Forty-seven have an EDI score of 0.95 and above and are categorized as having achieved, or being close to achieving, the EFA goals. Most are in North America and Europe, but some are in Latin America and the Caribbean (six countries, including Barbados, Cuba and Chile) and Central Asia (four countries, including Kazakhstan and Kyrgyzstan).
- Forty-nine have an EDI value between 0.80 and 0.94. Spread across all regions, they display many combinations of the proxy measures. Sixteen of these countries have a total primary NER of at least 95%. Most of the fifteen Latin American countries in this category are there because of relatively low survival rates (the quality proxy). In the case of the Arab States, low adult literacy rates pull down the overall EDI. Most of the eight sub-Saharan African countries are in southern Africa or are small islands. From 2003 to 2004, the index increased in thirty-two countries and fell in seventeen in this category.
- Twenty-nine have an EDI score between 0.43 and 0.79. Two-thirds of these are in sub-Saharan Africa; some Arab States and countries in South and East Asia are also represented. Again, some countries have very high scores in one area (for instance, Bangladesh, Cambodia, India and Malawi have primary NERs above 95%), but in general there is a need for significant improvement on all EDI components. Burkina Faso, Chad, Guinea, Mali and the Niger, which are all in French-speaking West Africa, have scores below 0.60.

43. The total primary NER includes children of primary school age who are enrolled in either primary or in secondary education.

44. The literacy data used are based on 'conventional' assessment methods, and thus should be interpreted with caution: they are not based on any test, and may overestimate the actual literacy level.

Table 2.19: Distribution of countries by EDI values, by region, 2004

	Far from EFA: EDI below 0.80	Intermediate position EDI between 0.80 and 0.94	Close to EFA EDI between 0.95 and 0.97	EFA achieved EDI between 0.98 and 1.00	Subtotal sample	Total number of countries
Sub-Saharan Africa	19	8	1		28	45
Arab States	5	10	1		16	20
Central Asia		2	3	1	6	9
East Asia and the Pacific	2	6	2	1	11	33
South and West Asia	3	1			4	9
Latin America/Caribbean		18	3	3	24	41
N. America/W. Europe		2	1	16	19	26
Central and Eastern Europe		2	8	7	17	20
Total	29	49	19	28	125	203

Source: Annex, Appendix 1, Table 1.

Changes in the EDI between 2003 and 2004 could be assessed for 115 countries. For any given country, changes in the proxy measures are small from one year to another. Across the whole sample of countries, however, changes are in a positive direction and are greatest among those countries ranked lowest. From 2003 to 2004, on average, the index increased by 1.6% overall and by 4.3% among countries in the lowest EDI category.

There are, however, important variations within the country categories. Of the forty-four countries in the top group, the index fell in fourteen; of the forty-seven countries in the middle group, it fell in seventeen; and of the twenty-four countries in the bottom group, it fell in nine.

Apart from Zambia, all of the countries showing the greatest progress (an improvement in the EDI of 9% or more) were in the lowest group: Bangladesh, Burkina Faso, Ethiopia, Kenya, Mauritania, Mozambique and the Niger. The largest reductions were in Bahamas and the Dominican Republic. Of those countries in the lowest category, Rwanda had the largest reduction, of about 4% (Figure 2.28).

Significant increases in the proxy measures have been recorded in individual countries, although in some cases, such as adult literacy, the increases result from new surveys providing better information than the previous estimates, while in other cases they reflect real annual positive change The most important examples of actual progress are:

- Adult literacy: Niger, Burkina Faso and Egypt
- Total primary NER: Mozambique, Ethiopia, Kenya and Bangladesh
- GEI: Ethiopia and Mauritania
- Survival to grade 5: Mauritania, South Africa India, Zambia, Kenya, Ethiopia and Bangladesh.

Where we are going?

There is now huge momentum towards achieving EFA, especially the UPE goal. However even this goal is unlikely to be met by 2015 unless efforts are further accelerated. Most encouraging of all is that the greatest progress is occurring in the regions that are farthest from the goals, in part because so many countries in these regions entered the twenty-first century with a relatively shallow educational base.

No new projections have been carried out for this Report; the extra year of data it contains has not resulted in significant changes to the

Figure 2.28: The EDI in 2004 and change since 2003

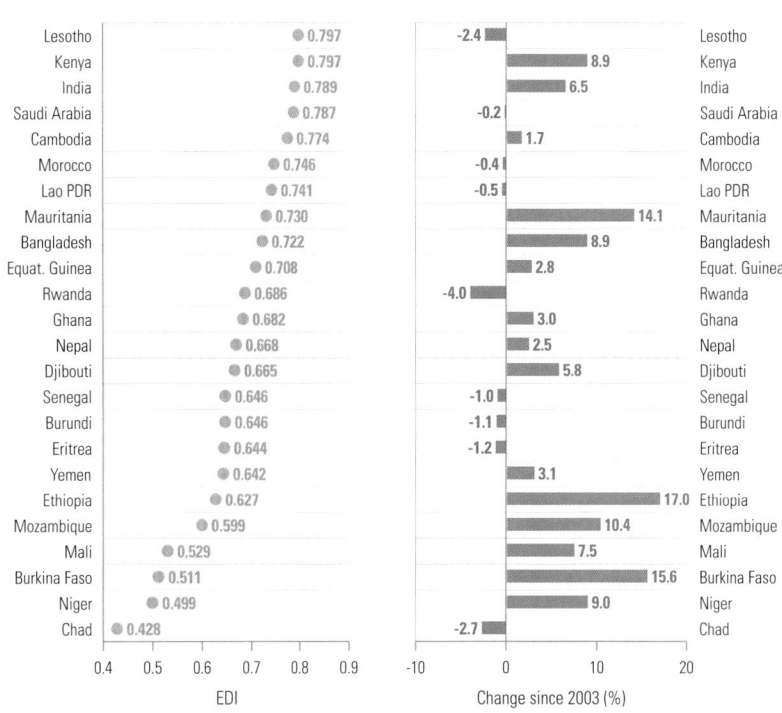

Note: Only countries with an EDI score below 0.800 are included.
Source: Annex, Appendix 1, Table 3.

projections reported in the 2006 Report. Those projections indicated that many countries were likely to achieve the EFA goals by 2015, but that a substantial group would not if trends did not accelerate. The countries most in danger of missing the goals[45] are in sub-Saharan Africa, South and West Asia, and the Arab States.

The considerable success achieved so far, particularly in these regions, demonstrates that further progress can be made. To do so requires that efforts be intensified. What is now particularly urgent is attention to:

- all the goals – those for ECCE and adult literacy continue to receive less attention than those to do with schooling, in part reflecting the Millennium Development Goals' emphasis on primary education and on gender;
- quality at all levels – now that most children in the world are enrolled in primary school, it is essential for them to acquire basic skills;
- including children and adults who are marginalized or excluded, and hence not enrolled in school or adult literacy programmes. Consideration of disadvantaged children is central to Chapter 3. ∎

45. Of eighty-seven countries that had not achieved UPE by 2002 and for which projections were made, twenty were projected to achieve it by 2015, forty-four were seen as making good progress but insufficient to reach the goal by 2015, and twenty-three were considered at risk of not achieving the goal. Of seventy-three countries with adult literacy rates below 97% for which projections were made, only twenty-three looked likely to meet the goal. Sixty-three countries out of 149 had achieved or would likely achieve gender parity at both primary and secondary education by 2015 and eighty-six were unlikely to achieve it.

PART II. Monitoring Education for All

Chapter [3] Tackling exclusion:

Side by side but worlds apart: a boy on his way to school in Phnom Penh, Cambodia, passes by a child who scavenges to earn a livelihood.

© AFP/Tang Chhin Sothy

lessons from country experience

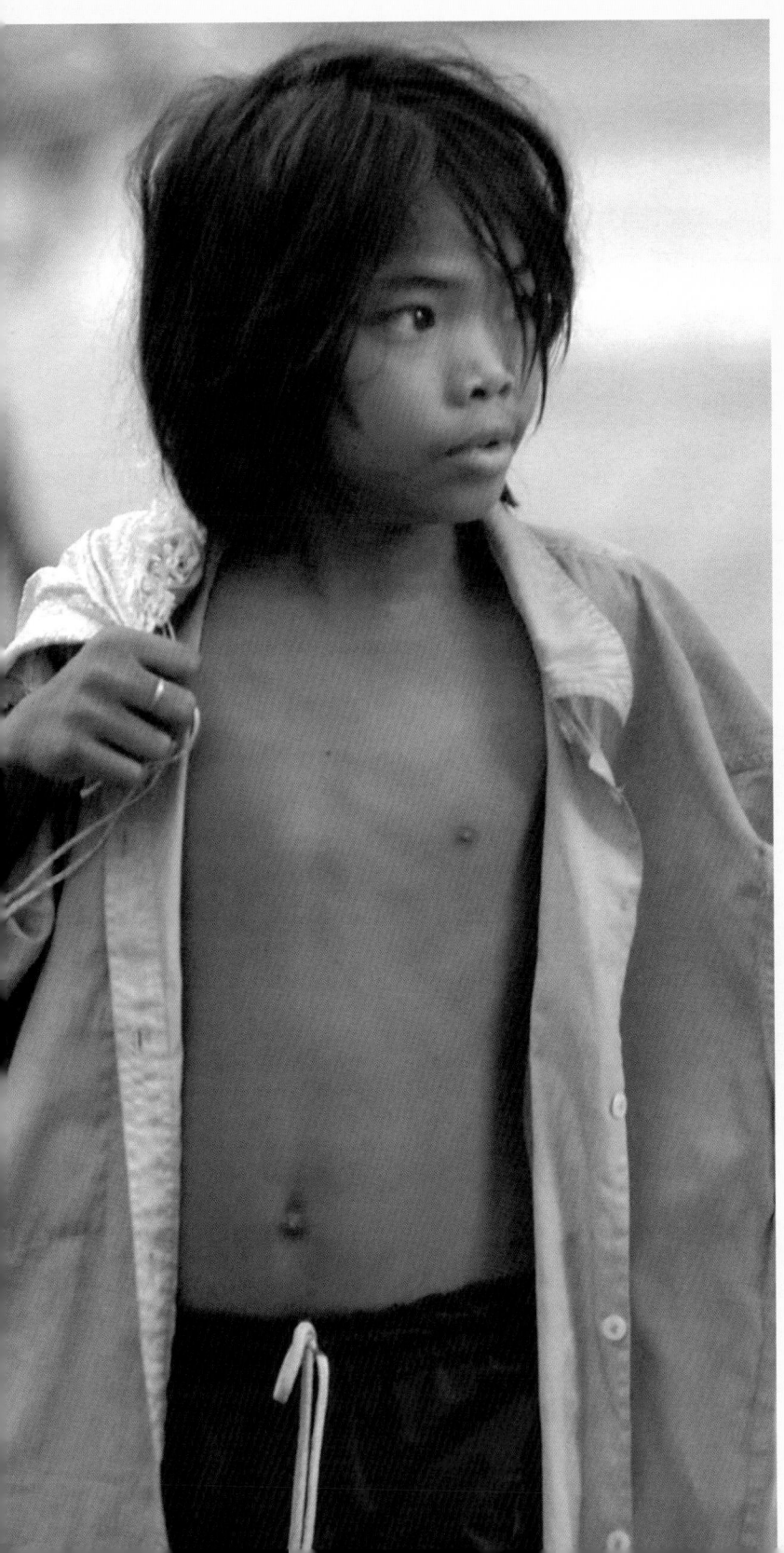

Education for All, as conceived at the 2000 World Education Forum in Dakar, requires an inclusive approach that emphasizes the need to reach groups that might not otherwise have access to education and learning. This chapter offers some examples of policies and programmes that have been effective not only in advancing education generally, but more particularly in identifying and overcoming barriers that deprive marginalized groups of the same learning opportunities as others. A sound education plan is essential for promoting inclusion. Such plans require the equitable allocation of resources, sufficient numbers of trained and motivated teachers, and a comprehensive approach encompassing all the EFA goals.

Reaching the unreached: what do government plans say?

Country plans contain many proposals to attract more children to school

National education plans of forty-five countries, including the twenty with the highest numbers of out-of-school children, were reviewed to see which categories of children and adults governments consider marginalized (UNESCO-IIEP, 2006).[1]

The groups of children and adults whom governments categorize as marginalized vary according to region. Girls and women are identified as the priority target group in sixteen sub-Saharan and four East Asian and Pacific countries. In South and West Asian countries, in the Arab States and in Turkey, governments have identified girls and women, children with special needs, working children, and migrant and nomadic families living in dispersed settlements and rural areas as target groups. In Latin America and the Caribbean, children of ethnic and linguistic minorities, and populations living in dispersed settlements or rural areas are identified as marginalized, along with some additional categories of girls, including pregnant teenagers. In a majority of countries, girls and children living in dispersed settlements in rural areas are mentioned most often as being marginalized, the former group by twenty-four countries and the latter by twenty-one. Other potential groups, such as orphans, HIV-positive children and child sex workers, are rarely singled out. Box 3.1 describes characteristics of children regarded as being particularly marginalized in Ethiopia, India, Nigeria and Pakistan.

The country plans contain many proposals to attract more children to school. One of the most common approaches (cited in twenty-two countries) is to reduce both the direct costs and the opportunity costs of education through measures such as the abolition of tuition fees and the provision of learning materials and uniforms, and the introduction of demand-enhancing measures such as free school meals and scholarships. Eighteen countries list measures to address cultural obstacles to education, notably for girls, such as increasing the number of female teachers and ensuring that schools are girl-friendly. Eight countries, mostly in Latin America and the Caribbean, intend to introduce local languages into the curriculum. Another eight plan to raise demand for education through information campaigns targeted at parents and the wider community.

National plans also discuss some of the key government strategies to overcome the many barriers faced by people living in remote areas. Fifteen plans identify increasing the number of schools accessible in remote locations as a key priority. Strategies also include building more boarding schools and local village schools, designing mobile classrooms and introducing bus services. In addition, six countries intend to introduce flexible school schedules and calendars, notably in areas where children work on farms.

Programmes for educationally excluded youth are increasingly common (cited in twenty-five countries). These provide accelerated education for older children, usually those aged 9 to 14. For example, Senegal and Guatemala plan to introduce literacy courses coupled with vocational training or income-generating activities to allow early school leavers to catch up with formal education at the lower-secondary level.

Box 3.1: Marginalized children in Ethiopia, India, Nigeria and Pakistan

Ethiopia, India, Nigeria and Pakistan account for a significant proportion of the world's out-of-school children. These countries' education plans target particular groups of children as the most marginalized.

- Ethiopia: Over-age school children; pastoralist children; school dropouts; girls; working children; children in villages with no or distant schools; poor children

- India: Working children; children who cannot afford school fees; hard-to-reach groups such as children living in small settlements or remote areas where no schooling is available; children of migrant families; children in coastal fishing communities; children with special needs; girls; scheduled caste/scheduled tribe children; urban deprived children; children from minority groups; children living below the poverty line

- Nigeria: Children of indigenous and nomadic populations; children enrolled in Koranic schools; disabled children; girls

- Pakistan: Disadvantaged children in rural and urban areas, with an emphasis on out-of-school girls and illiterate girls and women; working children

Sources:
Ethiopia: Ministry of Education (2002), Ministry of Finance and Economic Development (2002); **India:** Ministry of Human Resource Development (2003); **Nigeria:** Ministry of Education (2004); **Pakistan:** Ministry of Education (2003).

---

1. The review was conducted for this Report by the UNESCO International Institute for Educational Planning. It focused only on published government documents and did not necessarily include all planning documents, so it may not capture all government attention to the marginalized in all forty-five countries.

Legislative and constitutional barriers to education still exist in many countries. Forty-three countries have no constitutional guarantee of free and compulsory basic education, while thirty-seven limit education to citizens and legal residents, discriminating against the children of migrants, guest workers and temporary residents.[2] A birth certificate is still legally required for enrolment in many countries, denying access to those without the relevant documents (UNESCO, 2005b).[3] Girls also suffer from specific discriminatory legislation: pregnant girls are routinely expelled from school in many African countries.

Tackling exclusion:[4] promising policies and programmes

While many countries have made considerable progress in introducing policies that focus on the educational needs of marginalized children and youth, serious barriers to enrolment, retention and attainment persist. This section examines some key policies that have been used to overcome these barriers for disadvantaged groups, most notably the very poor and, in particular, girls, orphans and vulnerable children affected by AIDS, those engaged in child labour, youth who missed out on formal education, children and youth caught in armed conflict, and children with disabilities (Table 3.1). Some are universal (such as abolishing school fees) while others are targeted. Many of the examples are elaborated on elsewhere in the chapter.

Lowering the cost of education to individual households

The number of children out of school in the poorest 20% of households is more than triple that in the richest 20% (UIS/UNICEF, 2005). Direct costs to households remain a significant barrier to primary school access and attainment in more than ninety countries. Direct costs include five types of fees (for tuition, textbooks, compulsory uniforms, parent-teacher associations or community contributions, and school-based activities such as exams). A survey of ninety-four

Table 3.1: Some policies to tackle exclusion*

Policy goal	Type of intervention	Examples
Reduce the direct costs of schooling	Abolishing school fees or providing school fee waivers	Measure by the Government of Burundi abolishing primary school fees in 2005
Create financial incentives, offsetting household costs, to stimulate demand for schooling	Providing grants or scholarships for members of marginalized groups	The Gambia's Scholarship Trust Fund for Girls
	Providing financial incentives for orphans and vulnerable children	Bursary programme in Swaziland
Create incentives to overcome the need for child labour	Providing cash grants and supporting community-based efforts for child labourers	Baljyothi programme in Andra Pradesh, India, enabling children and youth to enter schools
		Bolsa Escola (merged in 2004 with other income transfer programmes) cash grant programme in Brazil, providing income support to poor families to encourage school attendance
Provide non-formal education opportunities for youths and adults who have missed out formal schooling	Providing bridging education for youths and adults	Equivalency education programmes in Indonesia giving young people and adults a second chance to obtain education
		Educatodos community school programme in Honduras, giving youths and adults who dropped out a chance to complete basic education
Provide relevant education opportunities for children and youths affected by conflict	Offering programmes to meet the needs of children and young people in post-conflict situations	Healing Classrooms Initiative in northern Ethiopia, providing support for the psychosocial and education needs of children in refugee camps
Provide appropriate education opportunities for the disabled	Offering education opportunities that respond to the needs of the disabled	Inclusive Education Fund in Uruguay, integrating the disabled into mainstream education

* The table indicates some of the main types of measures being used to lower barriers to education. They are not mutually exclusive and may be applied to other contexts or groups. For example, stipend programmes may be a viable strategy in conflict-affected contexts for demobilized children and youth.

2. The figures are taken from the report of the Special Rapporteur on Education, UN Commission on Human Rights (2002). It is important to note that the lack of constitutional guarantees does not imply that education is not provided. Nonetheless, the existence of constitutional guarantees is a significant marker of the extent to which countries consider education to be a fundamental human right that should be protected.

3. Children may lack birth certificates for many reasons, which vary by country. A certificate is often not perceived as a fundamental right, or it may require a payment not all families can afford (see UNESCO (2005b) for a detailed discussion).

4. Exclusion results from interrelated factors such as poverty and economic deprivation, gender inequality, geographic and physical location, political and legal conditions, cultural factors, disease and health constraints. Some factors relate to the availability of good schooling, its cost and the provision of learning resources. Others relate to household characteristics such as household income and parental motivation. Some causes of exclusion are general and interrelated; for example, girls who are out of school are also found in rural areas and many are infected or affected by HIV/AIDS. Other factors affect particular groups such as ethnic or linguistic minorities. See Sayed et al. (forthcoming) for a discussion of the concept of exclusion in South Africa and India.

Table 3.2: Tuition and other costs to households for education in Malawi (2002), Nigeria (2004), Uganda (2001) and Zambia (2002)

	Tuition	Parent-teacher association	School development fund	Examination fees	Boarding fees	Uniforms/ clothing	Books/ Supplies	Transport
Percentage of students whose households spent money on each item for primary education								
Malawi	1	–	57	3	0.3	69	83	1
Nigeria	14	70	29	39	0.2	88	99	5
Uganda	13	16	57	19	1	79	98	3
Zambia	73	67	–	2	0.2	81	98	2
Percentage of total annual household expenditure during primary education								
Nigeria	7	1	1	1	–	3	3	58
Uganda	9	2	3	2	4	6	5	31
Zambia	10	1	–	2	–	8	4	–

Sources: Malawi National Statistics Office and ORC Macro (2003), Nigeria National Population Commission and ORC Macro (2004), Uganda Bureau of Statistics and ORC Macro (2001) and Zambia Central Statistics Office and ORC Macro (2003).

Between 2000 and 2005 many countries abolished school fees

countries reveals that only in sixteen countries are none of these charged (World Bank, Forthcoming). Other household costs include transport and food. The relative importance of household expenses varies considerably (UNESCO, 2005b). Table 3.2 compares costs of various items in Malawi, Nigeria, Uganda and Zambia. In Nigeria and Uganda, transport is the largest cost item, while in Zambia it is food. In Viet Nam, household expenditure constitutes 44% of total public and private spending on primary education, a large proportion being for textbooks and uniforms. In India, household expenditure constitutes 43% of spending, with tuition and textbooks representing the largest share (Bentaouet-Kattan and Burnett, 2004).

Households' ability to pay may be seasonal. In Zambia, the need for educational expenditure peaks between January and March. Not only are rural incomes at their lowest at that time, but also it is necessary to buy food and anti-malaria medicine.

Between 2000 and 2005 many countries abolished school fees, including Lesotho (2000), Timor-Leste (2001), the United Republic of Tanzania (2001), Cambodia (2001), Zambia (2002), Kenya (2003), Madagascar (2003), Benin (2004), Mozambique (2004), Viet Nam (2004) and Burundi (2005). In Kenya, 1.2 million additional students entered the school system after the measure took effect. In Burundi, almost 500,000 additional primary school pupils arrived to enrol on the first day of school, double the number anticipated. Removing school fees increases enrolment but also makes it necessary to plan for the surge in order to maintain adequate

quality. To reduce the cost of education to parents and in response to the 1992 Constitutional provision of making education free and compulsory, the Ministry of Education and Sports in Ghana introduced, in 2004, a pilot capitation grants programme to forty selected deprived districts. The capitation grant was provided to schools to abolish all school levies such as charges for school-based extra-curricular activities. This programme was judged to be successful and as a result extended to all 138 districts in the country. By 2005, enrolments in basic education increased from 3.7 million to 4.3 million, an increase of about 16% (Ghana Educational Services, 2005).

Providing financial incentives can increase access for the marginalized

Many studies highlight the link between educational outcomes and poverty. For example, a longitudinal study of primary school attainment in rural areas of the Punjab and North West Frontier provinces in Pakistan concludes that economic constraints on households are a key factor in explaining high dropout rates. The sudden loss of remittances from a household member or the birth of an extra sibling both significantly increase the likelihood of dropout (Lloyd et al., 2006). Similarly, a 2002 survey of 1,000 rural and urban households in five regions of Ethiopia shows that household wealth is the major determinant of whether 8-year-olds are in school.[5] Child enrolment is also affected by household size, birth order, livestock ownership and the ability of the household to absorb economic shocks (Woldehanna et al., 2005).

5. The Young Lives study of childhood poverty in Ethiopia (Woldehanna et al., 2005) analysed data from a survey of 8-year-olds in twenty 'sentinel' sites in the Addis Ababa, Oromia, SNNP (Southern Nations, Nationalities, and People), Amhara and Tigray regions. The sentinel sites were targeted poor areas identified through criteria for the government's food insecurity designation.

Food	Private tutoring	School reports	Sport fund	Maintenance fees	Furniture, tools, etc.	Other	
					Percentage of students whose households spent money on each item for primary education		
34	4	15	–	–	–	2	Malawi
62	23	–	–	18	14	14	Nigeria
20	5	–	–	–	–	22	Uganda
24	12	–	24	10	–	4	Zambia
					Percentage of total annual household expenditure during primary education		
18	5	–	–	1	1	1	Nigeria
14	17	–	–	–	–	6	Uganda
62	13	–	1	–	–	1	Zambia

Well-targeted and -managed cash incentive programmes can be important equity-promoting measures

Providing financial incentives for enrolment by offsetting household costs is, therefore, an excellent strategy to increase access for the marginalized. Examples of such targeted incentives include direct monetary transfers as well as cash stipends and scholarships or bursaries, as in Brazil, Colombia, Kenya, Mexico, Nicaragua and Pakistan. They can be conditional on specified levels of school participation, attendance or achievement. Financial incentives can also take the form of vouchers to be exchanged for specific education or health services.

The effects on primary school enrolment and retention are greater in countries with relatively low enrolment, such as Bangladesh and Nicaragua, than in those with a higher enrolment ratio, such as Mexico. Financial incentives can also have a positive effect on secondary school enrolment, particularly for girls. Evidence of the impact of large-scale cash incentive programmes is limited mainly to Latin America (Chapman, 2006).[6] Well-targeted and -managed cash incentive programmes can be important equity-promoting measures.

Financial incentives help orphans and vulnerable children enrol

An orphan is 13% less likely to attend school than a non-orphan. In sub-Saharan Africa just under 10% of children under the age of 17 have lost at least one parent to HIV/AIDS (UNAIDS, 2006). In Kenya, children's school participation fell by 5% upon the death of a father and by 10% upon the death of a mother (Evans and Miguel, 2005). Governments and NGOs in

> **Box 3.2: Stipends and scholarships increase education access for girls**
>
> In the Gambia, the Scholarship Trust Fund for Girls is designed to increase girls' access to, retention in and performance during upper basic and secondary education. In low-income regions, the fund awards full scholarships for tuition, books and examination fees to one-third of the girls in schools with low enrolment. In less deprived regions, 10% of the girls who excel in science, technology and mathematics receive full scholarships. In 2004, more than 13,800 lower-secondary girls and more than 2,600 upper-secondary girls received scholarships. As a result of the programme, girls' enrolment in three regions rose from 32% in 1999 to 65% in 2004/05 at lower-secondary level and from 11% to 24% at upper-secondary level.
>
> *Source:* World Bank (2005b).

countries with high rates of HIV-prevalence have introduced measures that support the educational needs of orphans. Swaziland has a comprehensive bursary programme (Box 3.3). In Zambia, where more than 15% of children under 15 have lost at least one parent to HIV/AIDS (DeStefano, 2006), a programme transferring cash to the most vulnerable households (often grandparents caring for children affected by AIDS) reduced school absenteeism by 16% in nine months (Chapman, 2006). In addition to directly affecting school attendance, this type of programme has important indirect effects on education by improving young children's health, nutrition and living conditions.

6. Less rigorous evidence is available for other low-income countries, though some research on scholarship programmes has been done in the Gambia, Bangladesh, Indonesia and Malawi, among others (Chapman, 2006).

Eliminating or reducing the need for child labour can improve school attendance

Child labour[7] is directly related to widespread chronic poverty. While its incidence has declined in recent years, there are still around 218 million child labourers, three-quarters of whom are under age 15 (ILO, 2006).[8] It is estimated that almost 60% (126 million) are victims of what are deemed the worst forms of child exploitation.

Box 3.3: Bursaries for orphans and vulnerable children: the Swaziland experience

Swaziland has the world's highest prevalence of HIV and AIDS, with an overall rate of HIV infection among adults (aged 15 to 49) of 42.6% in 2004, compared to 16.1% a decade earlier. The annual growth rate in the number of orphans has doubled since 2000. The impact on education is likely to be considerably greater than in many other countries because Swaziland still levies fees for primary and secondary schooling. With the incidence of poverty at around 75% in rural areas and 50% in urban areas (in 2000/2001), school affordability is a critical issue.

Faced with these conditions, the government in 2002 began to provide bursaries for orphans and other vulnerable children attending primary and secondary schools. Total funding increased very rapidly, from US$0.22 million in 2002 to US$7.5 million in 2004.

By 2005, five out of six double orphans and three out of four paternal orphans received bursary support and enrolment and retention rates have either improved or remained stable, though it had been widely anticipated that the HIV/AIDS pandemic would result in significant declines.

Concerns remain, however, about the effectiveness and efficiency of the programme. Some eligible children have not applied because they cannot furnish their own birth certificate and the death certificate(s) of their parent(s). Also, only children already enrolled can receive bursaries, a condition originally justified because there were not enough classrooms and teachers to accommodate more children. Mismanagement and abuses of bursary funds have been widespread, including claims for non-existent children, multiple claims for the same student, double sponsors, duplication of claim vouchers, claims for non-vulnerable children of teachers, civil servants and local politicians, over-inflation of school fees by head teachers and generally very poor accounting practices. Poor selection criteria and procedures have compounded these problems. Moreover, some school administrators and teachers are not sympathetic to these children's needs. If total school charges exceed the value of the bursary, as is frequently the case, children who cannot pay the balance may be sent home.

Source: Bennell (2005).

To date, 153 countries have signed the two ILO conventions that directly address the issue of child labour: the Minimum Age Convention of 1973 and its accompanying recommendation; and the Worst Forms of Child Labour Convention of 1999. The Minimum Age Convention is significant because it compels countries to pursue national policies to abolish child labour. Moreover, it sets the minimum age at which children can work, defining it as the age at which compulsory schooling ends in any country, and stating that no child under age 15 should be working. The 1999 Convention compels all signatory countries to eliminate trafficking of children, debt bondage, child slavery and prostitution, and other illicit forms of child labour.

Many countries have introduced cash subsidy programmes to increase school enrolment and attendance by removing or reducing the need for children to work. Brazil, for example, has several programmes designed to reduce poverty and inequality by linking a minimum level of income support for poor families to compliance with key human development objectives, such as school attendance and health visits. The Bolsa Escola programme was designed to stimulate regular school attendance, reduce child labour and increase educational attainment through financial incentives to poor families. By 2002 almost all Brazilian municipalities had joined the programme, which provided assistance to the households of 5 million children (Cardoso and Portela Souza, 2003). In 2004, Bolsa Escola was merged with several other income transfer programmes to form the Bolsa Família programme.[9] Since the early 1990s child labour has declined and school attendance increased. In 2000, 92% of girls and 84% of boys aged 10 to 15 attended school and did not work, while 5% of girls and 9% of boys attended school and worked. The cash transfer programme has enabled children who previously were out of school and working to attend school (Cardoso and Portela Souza, 2003).

---

7. Child labour is defined by the 1973 ILO Convention 138 which sets the minimum age for employment at no less than the age of completion of compulsory schooling and no less than 14 years.

8. There were 246 million child labourers in 2000.

9. The Bolsa Família programme offers a single benefit to poor households that meet conditions such as school attendance. While each of the former programmes had its own emphasis (e.g. promoting schooling, health care or nutrition), all provided cash transfers to roughly the low-income group. Evaluations of the new programme are not yet available.

Community efforts that provide flexible and responsive forms of schooling are also important strategies to tackle child labour, as the example of the Baljyothi programme in India demonstrates (Box 3.4).

A second chance at learning for adults and young people

Many adolescents are not in school and do not benefit from any non-formal learning opportunities. In Bangladesh, India, Nepal and Pakistan alone, this is the case for some 250 million youngsters aged 11 to 18 (Robinson, 2004). Adults and young people need a second chance to access education. A variety of non-formal 'bridging' programmes offer equivalency education to people who were once in primary school but did not complete the cycle. For example:

■ Indonesia's 2003 Education Law provides for non-formal education to replace, complement and/or supplement formal education (Indonesia, 2003). Equivalency education offers programme packages equivalent to primary, lower-secondary and upper-secondary education. In 2005, over 500,000 persons participated. However, fewer than 25% of the participants took the national examinations that year (Indonesia Ministry of National Education, 2005; Yulaelawati, 2006).[10]

■ Uganda has a three-year programme of Basic Education for Urban Poverty Areas, offering non-formal basic education to urban out-of-school children and adolescents aged 9 to 18. It is module-based and contains adapted versions of the main subjects taught in primary schools, as well as pre-vocational training (Katahoire, 2006).

■ Since the mid-1990s India's Open Basic Education (OBE) programme has targeted neoliterates who have successfully completed literacy and post-literacy programmes. Participants may choose to learn in Hindi, English or a regional language, and there is no upper age limit. The programme offers education on three levels, each equivalent to a level of basic education in the formal school system.[11] Participants may take examinations whenever they feel prepared. The Ministry of Human Resource Development and employers recognize the OBE certificate, which may also be used to enter secondary and post-secondary education.

Box 3.4: Tackling child labour in Andra Pradesh: the Baljyothi programme

Andhra Pradesh has more working children than any other state in India. By 2000, 20% of children aged 5 to 14 in the state worked full time, and 60% of these had never attended school. Just over half were girls. The state government collaborated with an NGO, Pratyamnya, in an effort to provide education opportunities to all working children aged 10 to 14. The Baljyothi programme is the result.

Baljyothi has opened about 250 schools for working children in slum areas that lack public schools. It relies on strong community backing and uses a variety of strategies to attract children. The schools follow the government curriculum so that pupils can eventually transfer to public schools; 1,110 did so in 2000, five years into the programme. By then, over 31,000 children were enrolled in Baljyothi schools – 18,473 girls and 12,696 boys. In the slum of Borabanda, where Baljyothi started, only 200 children were out of school in 2000, down from 6,000 when the programme began.

Source: Jandhyal (2003).

■ In 1995, the government of Honduras established Educatodos, an alternative programme that targets the 540,000 out-of-school youth and adults (age 19 or above) who have not completed nine years of basic education. It operates in a variety of locations, including factories, microenterprises, NGOs, government installations, vocational centres and schools, making it easy for learners of all ages to attend. All learning is student-centred. A flexible schedule requires an average of two and a half hours of group work per day. It draws on volunteer facilitators, from varied academic and economic backgrounds, as teachers. They receive a government stipend and transport and food allowances. Educatodos has been highly successful in raising the educational profile of out-of-school youth and adults. Since its inception it has enrolled more than 500,000 students in its primary school programme (grades 1 to 6). The completion rate for this programme averaged 61% between 1996 and 2003 (Schuh-Moore, 2005).

The strength of non-formal education programmes for youth and adults is that they are adaptable to local contexts. They are effective

A variety of non-formal 'bridging' programmes offer equivalency education to people who were once in primary school but did not complete the cycle

10. The 2005 total included 7,290 'target learners' taking Package A (primary), 416,605 studying Package B (lower secondary) and 23,713 taking Package C (upper secondary).

11. OBE level A is equivalent to Classes 1-3, level B is equivalent to Classes 4-5, and level C to Classes 6-8 of the formal school system.

New forms of
war practised by
armies and
warlords alike,
target children
and youth,
seeking to turn
them into
soldiers

when they are community-based and combine
the use of local languages, relevant curriculum
and productive work. They face two challenges,
however. First, it is important to ensure that
they do not place an increased financial burden
on the poorest areas and most disadvantaged
populations (Rose, 2003). Second, non-formal
education is still often perceived as second-rate
education, with less-qualified teachers and staff,
and inadequate political and financial support.

Providing relevant education for children and youth affected by conflict

Although the number of armed conflicts[12] is in
decline worldwide, and wars cause fewer victims
today than was the case twenty years ago
(Human Security Centre, 2005), armed conflict
continues to have terrible consequences on
civilian populations: the collapse of law and
security, human rights violations, the spread
of disease, malnutrition, and an absence of
basic education and health services. Most wars
are fought in poor countries, with Africa and
Asia bearing the heaviest burden (Project
Ploughshares, 2005). At the beginning of this
century, the battle-related toll in sub-Saharan
Africa was greater than the combined deaths
and injuries in all other regions (Human Security
Centre, 2005).

While the downward trend in military conflicts
has led to a continuous reduction in the world's
refugee population, currently estimated at
19 million (UNHCR, 2006), it has not had a similar
effect on the scale of internal displacement. As
of December 2005 some 24 million people were
displaced within their own countries as a result
of conflict (Internal Displacement Monitoring
Centre, 2006).

The nature of conflict is changing. New forms
of war (Singer, 2004), practised by armies and
warlords alike, target children and youth, seeking
to turn them into soldiers (see map page 75).
As more young people are drawn into long-term
conflicts, education offers an increasingly
effective way to reduce tensions, and promote
tolerance and other values conducive to peace.

The provision of basic education services
during and after conflict must take into account
the very specific experiences of war and prepare
children and youth for peace and national
reconciliation. In Burundi, a peace education
programme aims to convey values such as
confidence, respect, tolerance and solidarity
to teachers and students alike. These values

are integrated into primary school curricula in
subjects such as the Kirundi language, art,
environmental education, music and sports,
and at the secondary level into civics education
(Rwantabagu, 2006).

Demobilized child soldiers are another
challenge. In Sierra Leone, for example, the
United Nations disarmed and demobilized some
48,000 former combatants, including nearly
7,000 children (Becker, 2004). This involved
bringing former child soldiers to a demobilization
area and immediately transferring them to
interim care centres, where they received medical
and psychological care and education while
efforts were made to reunite them with their
families. Children aged 10 to 14 took part in a
six-month Rapid Response Education Programme
that allowed them to resume their primary
education. A Community Education Investment
Programme introduced by UNICEF helped
community schools provide access. Child
protection agencies monitored the process
(Caramés et al., 2006).[13]

Significant numbers of girls are involved in
many armed conflicts, but few are included in
demobilization programmes. Perhaps girls are
overlooked because they do not serve in direct
combat, or they may be reluctant to participate
in rehabilitation because of the stigma of sexual
abuse that is a common result of conflict (Becker,
2004). Of the 6,845 child soldiers demobilized in
Sierra Leone, only 506 were girls (Caramés et al.,
2006).

Reaching the world's disabled

The estimated 600 million disabled persons in
the world are limited by both physical and social
barriers from participating fully in social and
cultural life. Some 80% of the disabled live in
developing countries. Estimates indicate that
more than one-third of out-of-school children
have a disability, and in Africa, fewer than 10%
of disabled children are in school (Balescut and
Eklindh, 2006). Only about forty-five countries in
the world have legislation aimed at assuring the
rights of people with disabilities (Schindlmayr,
2006).

Children with disabilities have the same right
to education as all children, as recognized by the
Convention on the Rights of the Child, the United
Nations Standard Rules for the Equalization of
Opportunities and the Salamanca Statement on
Special Needs Education (Balescut and Eklindh,
2006). A group is working to draft a human rights

12. An armed conflict
is defined as a political
conflict in which armed
combat involves the
armed forces of at least
one state (or one or more
armed factions seeking to
gain control of all or part
of the state), and in which
at least 1,000 people are
killed by the fighting
during the course of the
conflict (Project
Ploughshares, 2005).

13. The Disarmament,
Demobilization and
Reintegration programme
described here was
managed by UNICEF
and carried out in
collaboration with Caritas,
the International Rescue
Committee, Handicap
International and Save the
Children UK. It was
funded by Ireland, Japan,
the Netherlands, Norway,
Switzerland and UNICEF.

Map 3.1: Children and armed conflict 2003
The vast majority of armed conflicts involve the use of child combatants under 18 years of age.
In over half of the states at war in 2003 there were reports of combatants under 15.

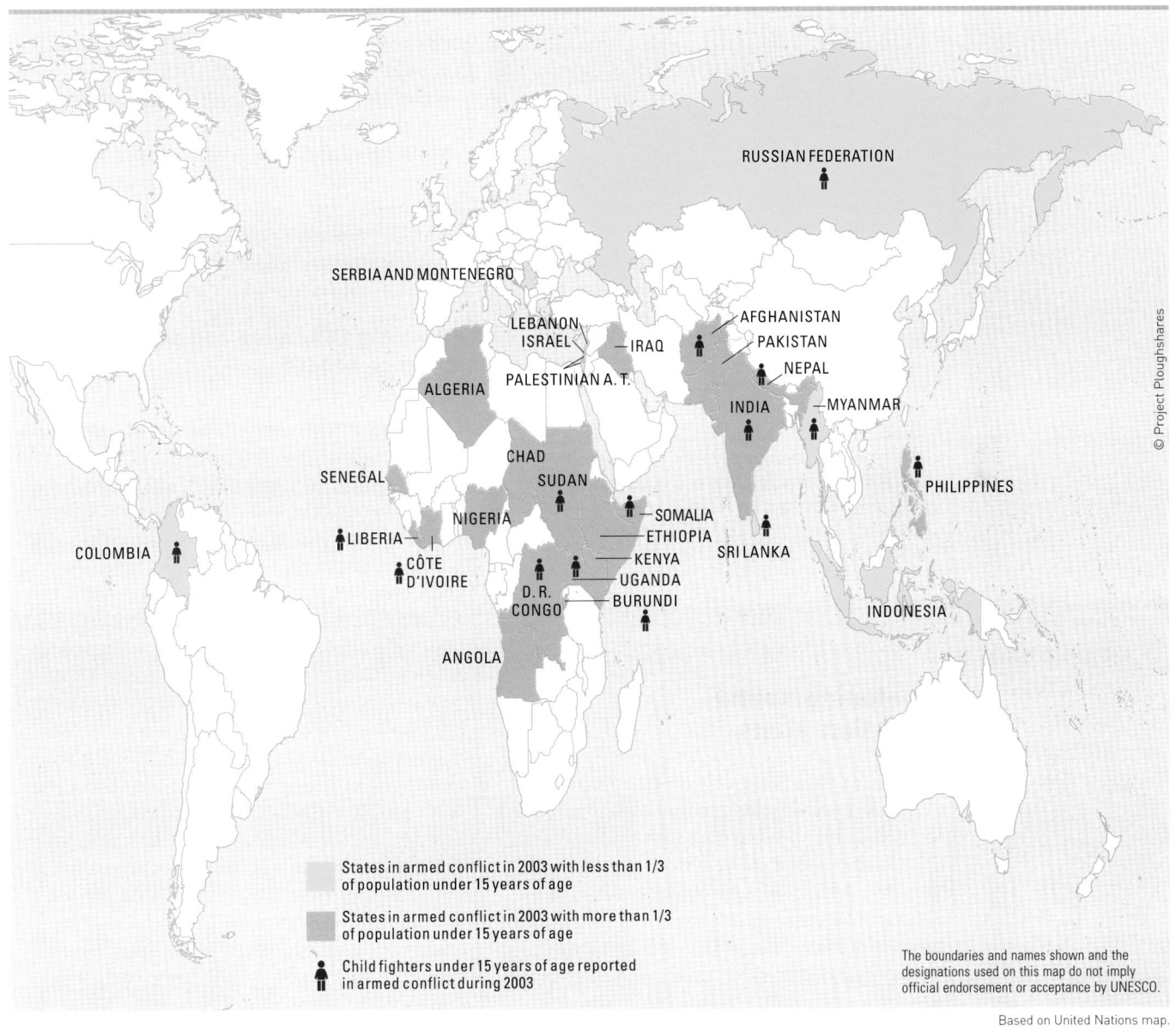

Source: Project Ploughshares (2003).

convention to promote and protect the rights and dignity of persons with disabilities, a process that was set out in UN General Assembly Resolution 56/168 of 19 December 2001. If adopted and ratified, this first human rights convention of the twenty-first century will ensure that people with disabilities enjoy the same rights as everybody else (Schindlmayr, 2006).

Views differ on how best to overcome exclusion of the disabled. Some mainstream educationists, as well as some disability organizations, argue that separate, 'specialist' services are needed. They suggest that for people with some types of disabilities (e.g. those with deafness, blindness or both), small specialized units and schools are required. Advocates of inclusive education argue that disabled children do better in mainstream settings rather than in separate ones. Uruguay is an example of a country promoting an inclusive policy (Box 3.5).

In 2004, over half the 124 developing countries for which data are available were spending less than 4.8% of GNP

Box 3.5: Mainstreaming children with disabilities: Uruguay's example

Uruguay is regarded as a pioneer in Latin America in the integration of physically impaired children into regular classrooms. It formulated its special education policy in 1985, leading to many innovative and progressive initiatives, such as the elimination of classes restricted to children with disabilities. These classes were replaced by mainstream classes offering individual support. Itinerant special education teachers have been introduced to support the learning needs of the disabled students in these classes. Through this initiative, 3,900 children with disabilities have been successfully integrated into regular schools, where they received personalized support.

Uruguay has created an Inclusive Education Fund, which promotes inclusive practices in regular schools to help them to integrate children with disabilities. The country's holistic policy aims to ensure that all children receive a good quality basic education. Despite recent economic problems, Uruguay has continued to fund its inclusive special education policy.

Source: Skipper (2005).

Developing sound education plans

The preceding section highlighted promising examples of policies and programmes to remove the barriers that prevent the world's poorest and most disadvantaged children from getting an education. Among the difficulties countries face in carrying out such programmes are the significant administrative cost required to manage them effectively, and the risk of corruption and abuse. Even more importantly, the success of such programmes depends on their being integrated within some kind of comprehensive education plan, which may entail a complete overhaul of the education system itself. To successfully meet the education needs of the marginalized requires multi-pronged strategies. For example, Bangladesh has increased access for girls through a combination of several strategies, including expansion of school availability, encouragement of pluralism in education provision both by public schools and those run by faith-based groups and NGOs, and the use of targeted interventions for girls – such as stipends – that provided incentives by alleviating

demand-side constraints such as the real and perceived high costs of education. Bangladesh has been able to expand the education of girls because its strategies are holistic, multi-pronged and coupled with a commitment to systemic education reform (UNESCO, 2005*b*).

Overcoming exclusion is not accomplished through a single intervention. Rather, it requires an integrated and comprehensive approach to education planning. What, then, are some key features of a sound education plan? An adequate financial framework and funding, the availability of effective teachers and the capacity to expand secondary education, which are discussed below.

Financing EFA: more and better-targeted spending needed

The levels of public funding for education as a whole and primary education in particular are key indicators of government commitment to the goal of education for all. While there are no clear global benchmarks, most developed countries with advanced education systems typically spend between 5% and 6% of GNP on education. In 2004, over half the 124 developing countries for which data are available were spending less than 4.8% of GNP. In fifteen of these – including several that are far from the EFA goals, such as the Niger and Pakistan – the share was below 3%, and the share was lower even than in 1999 in six of these countries (Figure 3.1). There are exceptions to this pattern. The share of education was over 7% of GNP in Cape Verde, Kenya, Kuwait, Lesotho, Malaysia, Namibia and Tunisia. The overall trend in education expenditure since 1999 has been mixed. Out of the 106 countries with comparable data for both 1999 and 2004, about two-thirds increased public spending on education as a share of GNP, some considerably (Figure 3.2). Increases of 30% or more were registered in eighteen countries.[14] On the other hand, education spending as a percentage of GNP fell in forty-one countries, particularly in Latin America (where the share fell in twelve out of the twenty-one countries with data) and South and West Asia (three out of the five with data).

The share of government expenditure devoted to education is one indicator of its importance in relation to other national priorities. The share ranges from 10% to more than 40% in the vast majority of the countries with data available for 2004 (see annex, Statistical Table 11). Education accounts for one-quarter or more of the government budget in the Comoros, Kenya,

14. Barbados, Benin, Burundi, Cambodia, Cyprus, Georgia, Kenya, the Lao People's Democratic Republic, Lebanon, Madagascar, Malawi, Malaysia, Mexico, Poland, Saint Vincent and the Grenadines, Tajikistan, Vanuatu and Zambia.

Figure 3.1: Countries spending less than 3% of GNP on education, 2004

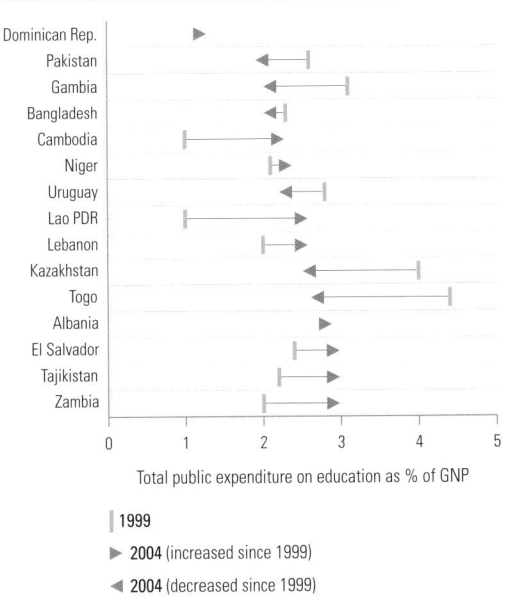

Total public expenditure on education as % of GNP

| 1999
▶ 2004 (increased since 1999)
◀ 2004 (decreased since 1999)

Source: Annex, Statistical Table 11.

Figure 3.2: Total public expenditure on education as a share of GNP

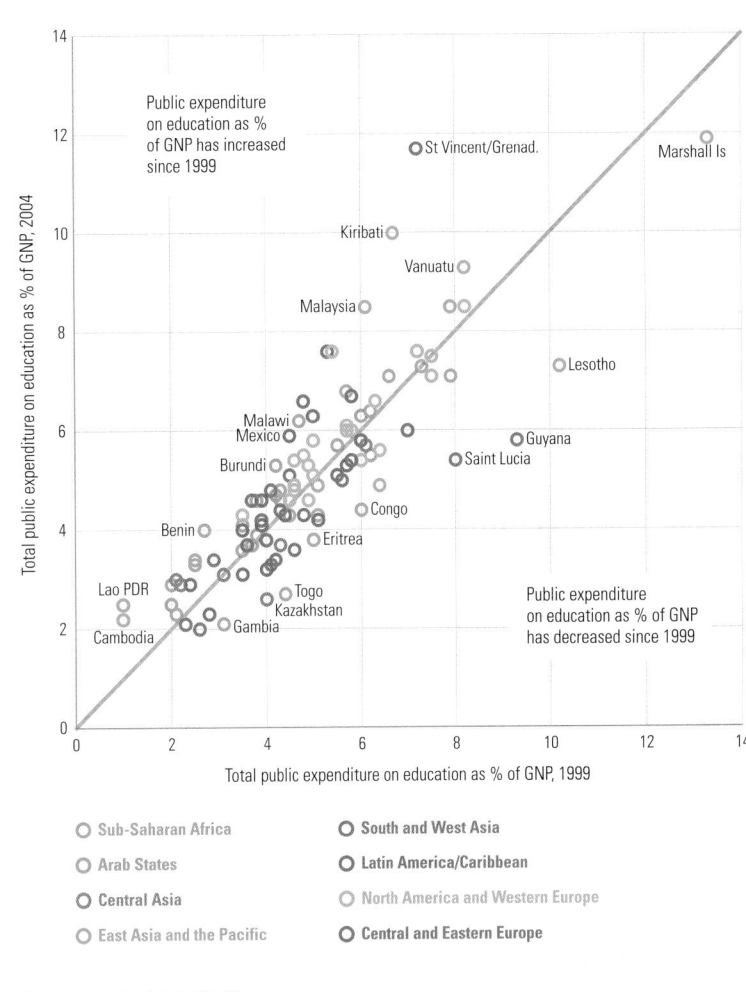

Total public expenditure on education as % of GNP, 1999

○ Sub-Saharan Africa ◉ South and West Asia
○ Arab States ◉ Latin America/Caribbean
○ Central Asia ○ North America and Western Europe
○ East Asia and the Pacific ◉ Central and Eastern Europe

Source: Annex, Statistical Table 11.

Malaysia, Morocco, Oman, Thailand and Tuvalu. At the other end of the spectrum are countries such as the Dominican Republic, the Gambia, Indonesia, Jamaica and Panama, which allocate less than 10% of central government expenditure to education.

About three-quarters of the thirty-six countries with relevant data available increased the share of education in total government expenditure between 1999 and 2004 (Figure 3.3). In Cameroon, Cuba, Georgia, Nicaragua, Tajikistan and Ukraine, the increases were about 30% or more. Substantial decreases (more than a 15% reduction in the share of education) were registered in Azerbaijan, Colombia, the Gambia, India and Peru.

In a majority of the countries that have given a relatively higher priority to education in public spending since 1999, the consequences for the education system have proved to be positive, in the form of improvement in the primary education GER. Other countries, such as India, have managed to increase coverage with no major change in the share of public spending on education and in several countries the share has increased but the GER has decreased. Thus, the efficiency of public spending is as important as the share of education in the total.

The previous section focused attention on the need for government to remove or reduce household costs of education, such as school fees. Many governments have done so. However, such initiatives can have serious implications for public finances (Box 3.6).

Balanced spending across levels and regions is needed

While the percentages of GNP and total government expenditure allocated to education are important indicators of commitment, equally significant is the distribution of education spending across the different levels of the system, and across regions and subregions.

Most of the countries for which data are available allocated less than 50% of their total education expenditure to primary education in

Figure 3.3: Change in public expenditure on education in selected countries and change in GER in primary education between 1999 and 2004

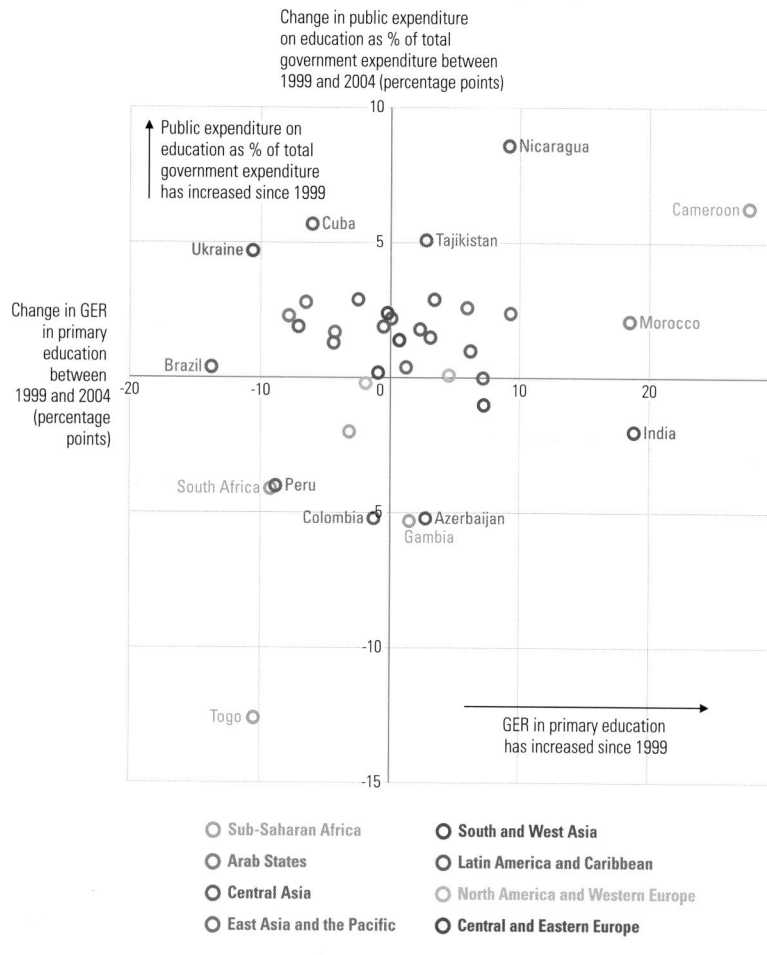

Sources: Annex, Statistical Tables 5 and 11.

2004 (Figure 3.5). This is particularly worrying for those still far from the EFA goals, such as Eritrea and Kuwait. Public spending on primary education as a percentage of GNP is below 2% in three-quarters of the ninety countries with data available – an alarming figure in those countries not on track to achieve UPE. Countries in that category spending less than 2% include Bangladesh, the Islamic Republic of Iran and Nepal in South and West Asia and sixteen countries in sub-Saharan Africa (among the countries with data).

The competition for resources between primary and secondary education in particular is likely to intensify, as the spread of UPE will require expansion at secondary level (discussed later in this chapter). This shift is already perceptible in countries that have reached or are close to reaching UPE (Figure 3.6). In some countries where primary education is not yet universal, however, such as Bangladesh and Nepal, the share of primary education has nevertheless fallen since 1999. Even if primary education is the priority in most countries, expenditure at this level worldwide still seems far from what is required to accelerate progress towards EFA.

Teachers for EFA: a crucial but undervalued resource

Chapter 2 showed that the serious shortage of trained teachers is a barrier to reaching the EFA goals, particularly in sub-Saharan Africa. Key strategies exist to enhance the motivation of teachers, particularly those working in rural areas.

Box 3.6: Education financing and the removal of school fees: the Tanzanian experience

The United Republic of Tanzania abolished school fees in 2001, resulting in a large increase in enrolment but also forcing up public spending very rapidly to offset the lost fee revenue. Public spending on education grew from 2.1% of GDP in 2000 to 4.3% in 2004 (Figure 3.4). Tanzanian spending on education as a percentage of GDP and of overall public spending shows the increasing importance of education in its national priorities particularly in light of the removal of school fees.

Figure 3.4: Priority given to education in public spending by United Republic of Tanzania, 1995/96-2004/05

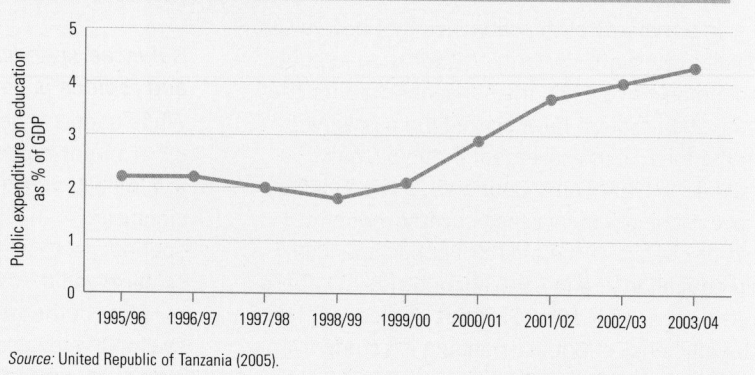

Source: United Republic of Tanzania (2005).

Figure 3.5: Basic education as a share of total spending on education in selected countries

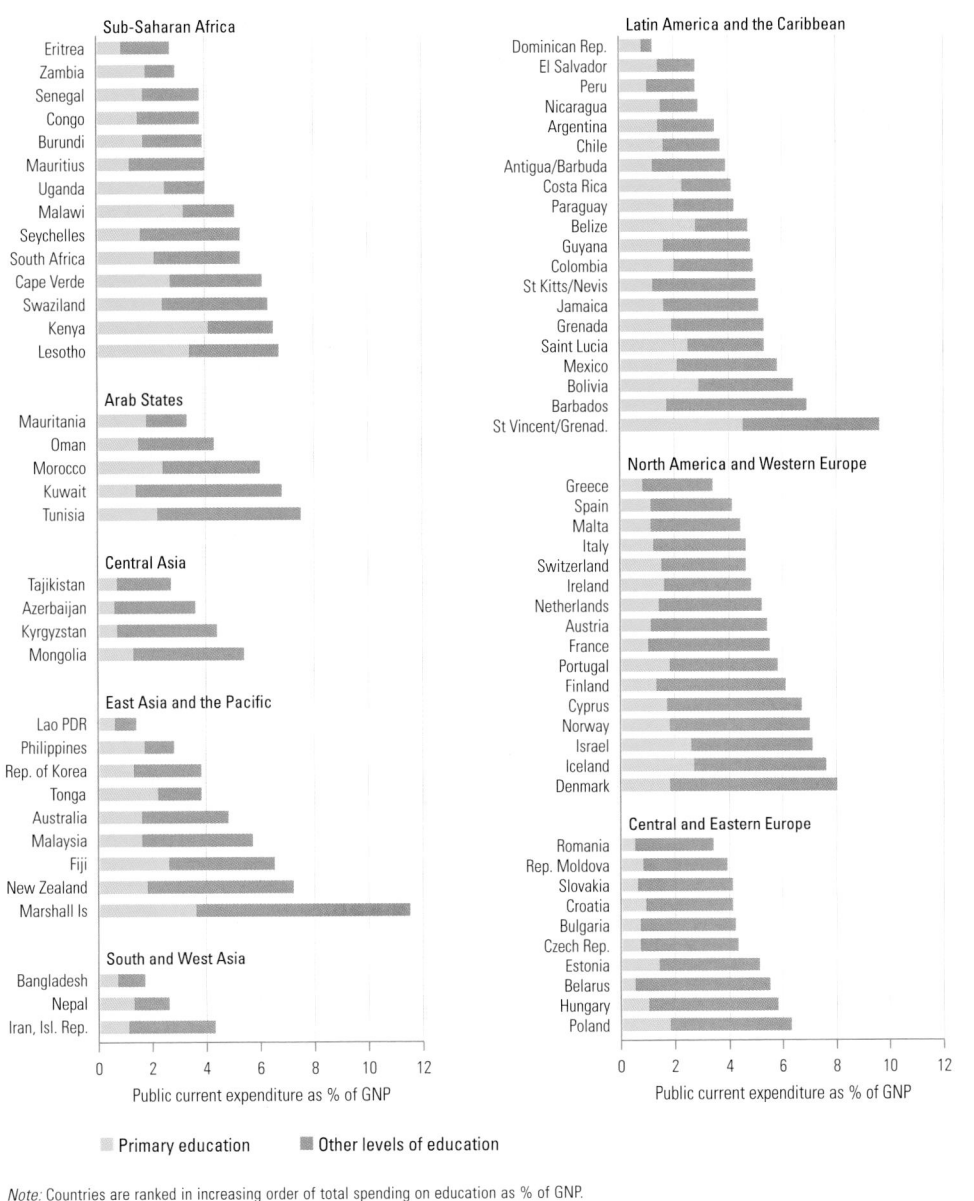

Primary education   Other levels of education

Note: Countries are ranked in increasing order of total spending on education as % of GNP.
Source: UNESCO Institute for Statistics database.

> What amounts
> to a teacher-
> motivation crisis
> has far-reaching
> consequences
> for EFA

Teacher motivation and incentives

There is growing concern that existing incentives (both monetary and non-monetary) are seriously inadequate both to recruit teachers and to keep teachers fully committed to their work in the regions with the greatest EFA challenges. That is the main finding of research in Ghana, India, Lesotho, Malawi, Sierra Leone, the United Republic of Tanzania and Zambia (Bennell and Akyeampong, 2006). In five of these countries, well over one-third of teacher respondents

indicated that teachers at their school were 'poorly' or 'very poorly' motivated. Motivation levels among primary school teachers varied considerably within each country. What amounts to a teacher-motivation crisis has far-reaching consequences for EFA. A key finding is that working in rural schools is more difficult and demotivating than teaching in urban schools, mainly because of poor living and working conditions. The unattractiveness of living and working in rural areas means most teachers

Figure 3.6: Comparison of changes in spending on primary and secondary education in selected countries since 1999

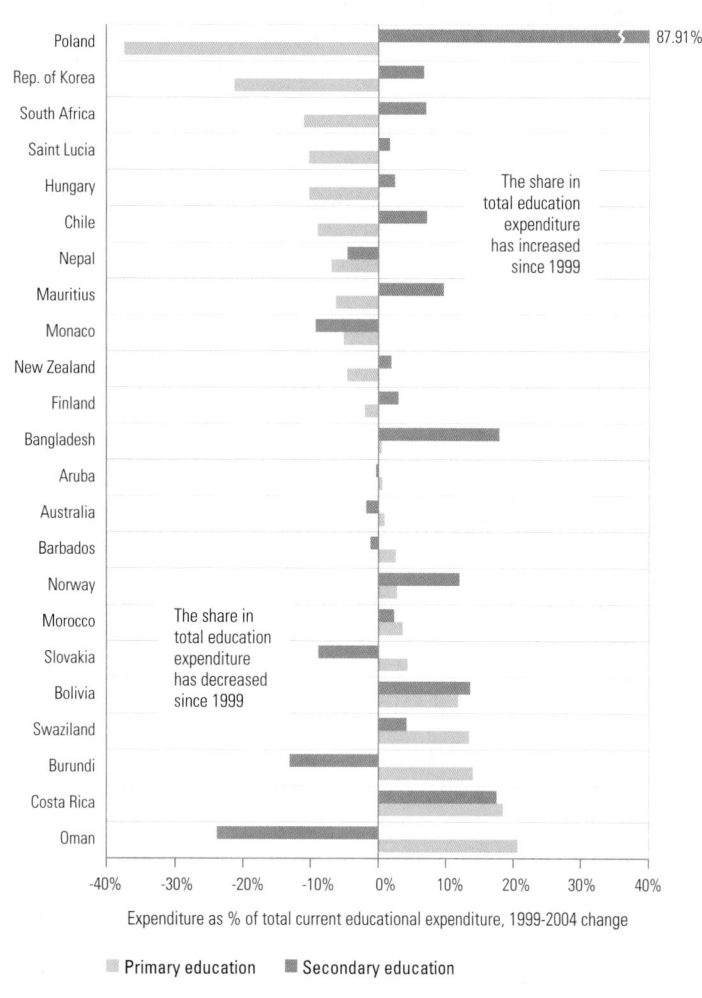

Expenditure as % of total current educational expenditure, 1999-2004 change

■ Primary education   ■ Secondary education

Source: UNESCO Institute for Statistics database.

strongly resist rural postings. Consequently, rural schools have relatively fewer qualified and experienced teachers (Table 3.3), teacher turnover is higher and, with higher vacancy rates, teachers have to work harder than their urban colleagues. Box 3.7 describes strategies to increase incentives for rural teachers.

Several Latin American countries have introduced incentive strategies to increase teacher supply and improve the performance of teachers in general, not just those in rural areas. Brazil's finance equalization reform provides funding to state and local governments for hiring, training or salary increases (Gordon and Vegas, 2005). Chile and Mexico have performance-based incentive systems (McEwan and Santibañez, 2005; Mizala and Romaguera, 2005). Decentralization and school-based management policies introduced in El Salvador and Honduras have increased teachers' participation in decision-making and improved their professional status (di Gropello and Marshall, 2005; Sawada and Ragatz, 2005). In 1996, Chile introduced a policy of monetary incentives for schools and teachers, the Sistema Nacional de Evaluación del Desempeño (National School Performance Assessment System). Preliminary evidence shows a positive effect on student performance. The teacher incentive policy was introduced after increases of about 156% in basic salaries for teachers, which resulted in more applicants of better quality for teacher education programmes. One important effect of this incentive programme is that teachers are more receptive to a performance-related pay system (Mizala and Romaguera, 2005).

Increasing the supply of teachers by reforming teacher training

A strategy to increase the supply of teachers is to reduce the length of time spent on pre-service training. More and more countries are moving towards shorter and more school-based training. In the United Kingdom, trainee teachers can now spend two-thirds of their training time in schools. In Cuba, all pre-service training is school-based (UNESCO, 2005). The integration of training with work is not straightforward, however. It requires significant resources to support those being trained, sufficient schools able to serve as training environments and enough school-based teachers who can act as mentors. The shortening of the teacher training cycle is a growing trend, particularly in sub-Saharan Africa, where countries going this route include Ghana, Guinea, Malawi, Mozambique, Uganda and the United Republic of Tanzania. In Guinea, a primary teacher education programme initiated in 1998 shortened the cycle of initial training from three years to two and delivered increased numbers of new teachers – 1,522 per year compared with 200 before the reform. The teachers trained in the new programme are as effective as those who graduated from the three-year one, and the programme is considered cost-effective in part because of a higher ratio of student teachers to teacher trainers (Dembélé, 2004).

Table 3.3: Unqualified primary school teachers by location* (percentage, rounded)

Country	Rural	Urban
Ghana	18	4
Lesotho	35	5
Malawi	77	86
Sierra Leone	43	11
U. R. Tanzania	62	29
Zambia	29	9

*As a percentage of the total number of teachers in the schools surveyed in this study.
Source: Bennell and Akyeampong (2006).

Secondary education and the EFA agenda: increasing strains

As more countries approach UPE, the pressure to expand secondary education is rising dramatically, bringing new equity issues to the fore.[15]

The mismatch between demand and supply of secondary education

Many studies have demonstrated the benefits of secondary education. It results in greater democracy (Bregman and Bryner, 2006), increases social cohesion (Lewin, 2006), helps achieve the Millennium Development Goals – especially the health-related ones (World Bank, 2005a), sustains household demand for primary education (Lewin, 2006) and contributes to countries' competitiveness in an increasingly global economy (World Bank, 2005a).

Chapter 2 described enrolment in secondary education, making the distinction between the lower-secondary and upper-secondary levels. A comparison of secondary enrolment in developed and developing countries between 1960 and 2000 reveals that the rate of enrolment growth did not keep pace with growth in demand for secondary schooling.[16] The gap between the developed and developing countries with respect to the number of 15-year-olds with at least some secondary education is increasing. South Asia and sub-Saharan Africa lag far behind; indeed, access to secondary education has increased only minimally in sub-Saharan Africa.

A shortage of secondary school places is likely to be a major problem as the number of children completing primary education grows. Projections show that in sub-Saharan Africa, the region with the lowest enrolment ratios, demand for secondary school places will rise significantly – from 0.4 million to 1.0 million in Uganda, for

Box 3.7: Incentives for rural teachers: what works

It is possible to fill posts in rural and remote areas if teachers are adequately compensated and working conditions are improved. Here are some strategies that have been shown to be effective:

● Provision of good-quality housing with running water and electricity. This is probably the most cost-effective way of attracting and retaining teachers at hard-to-staff rural schools.

● Supplementary pay, such as the 20% rural hardship allowance in Kenya and the 5% allowance in Nigeria. Pay supplements have to be sufficiently large to have an effect, however, and this can pose budgetary problems.

● More attractive career structures for primary school teachers, with regular promotions based on clearly specified and transparent performance-related criteria. Teachers who work at hard-to-staff rural schools can, for example, be given accelerated promotion and/or preferential access to professional development opportunities.

Source: Bennell and Akyeampong (2006).

instance, between 2002 and 2008, and from 0.5 million to 1.2 million in the United Republic of Tanzania, where no new fully funded government secondary schools have been built since 1980 (Lewin, 2006). The low level of provision coupled with increasing demand will place a serious strain on education systems. It is critical for governments to begin to establish policies and programmes to cope with the challenge.

Meeting the increasing demand for secondary education will likely require substantial increases in domestic and international financing to developing countries. Cost estimates vary; one study suggests that spending on secondary education will need to rise to an average of 2.3% of GNP in sub-Saharan Africa to reach a 50% transition rate from primary education (Lewin, 2004).[17]

Reducing inequity in access and coverage

Amid the growing demand, access to secondary education remains highly inequitable. Marginalized children (the poor, certain ethnic groups, the disabled and, often, girls) are mainly excluded (Bloom, 2004). In sub-Saharan Africa, the excluded are disproportionately poor, rural and female. About 50% of boys from the highest income quintile complete grade 7, but only 4% of girls from the lowest quintile. About 50% of

15. There is no single approach to the organization of secondary education. In general, countries distinguish between primary, and lower secondary and upper secondary, between basic and secondary, or between primary and secondary. The ages at which compulsory education begins and ends also differ among countries. In Africa, students are expected to stay in school until age 13, on average, compared to the age 16 in Europe. This section takes secondary education generally to be education beyond five or six years of primary schooling. Where it is necessary to distinguish between lower secondary and upper secondary, the section follows the UNESCO Institute for Statistics definitions.

16. This analysis draws on Bloom (2004), which reviews secondary school enrolments between 1960 and 2000 with projections up to 2010.

17. The author points out that the calculations involved do not take into account changes in unit cost that may arise from various reforms, such as changes to the curriculum, or from, for example, changes to the dropout and repetition rates.

urban boys complete grade 7 but only 7% of rural girls (Lewin, 2004).

Many countries have made significant efforts to expand secondary education coverage. The Republic of Korea is an example. Strong political will prioritized the expansion of all education levels, with increased government spending on education (including demand-side financing initiatives such as lotteries to support enrolling poor children in post-primary education) and encouragement of the private sector, within a clear regulatory framework (World Bank, 2005*a*).

Another example is Bangladesh, which has made significant progress over the past decade, with school enrolments doubling and the share of females in secondary enrolments increasing from 33% to 50%. This progress is attributable to government incentive policies that provide food, along with with stipends for females, for disadvantaged families. It is also the result of a public-private partnership through which 95%

of private schools receive public financing (public funds pay 90% of teachers' salaries in all recognized schools). In addition, the management structure of secondary schools is decentralized, to ensure that they respond to local needs (World Bank, 2005*a*).

South Africa has developed a different type of public-private partnership to increase access to secondary education (Box 3.8).

Conclusion

This chapter has shown that there is no single path for achieving the EFA goals. The routes are as many and diverse as the communities they serve, especially when it comes to reaching those who are marginalized. Successful programmes to tackle exclusion are those that (a) couple targeted programmes together with systemic reforms of the education system, (b) are sustainable and enduring, (c) are carefully monitored and evaluated and (d) are supported by the necessary budgetary commitments.

The examples described here illustrate the creative potential of forming alliances with local communities and civil society, and the power of financial and other incentives to overcome specific obstacles, motivating teachers to work in remote areas or making it easier for the poor, orphans, girls, women, people with disabilities and other excluded groups to gain access to good-quality education that meets their needs.

With many countries increasing primary enrolments, it is more important than ever that policies and programmes designed to provide good-quality education for all, particularly the marginalized, are monitored for equity, effectiveness and impact. Only in this way can resources be allocated to reflect national priorities, make the best use of available financing and ensure that progress towards EFA is sustainable.

Box 3.8: In South Africa, subsidies to private schools can increase access for the poor

The South African Government funds private secondary schools if they provide good-quality education and combat racism. While the public funding is limited, it is very significant for lower-cost providers that could not otherwise make ends meet. South African policy recognizes that private schools are cost-effective for the state: 'If all learners were to transfer to public schools, the cost of public education in certain provinces might increase by as much as five percent' (South Africa Department of Education, 1998: section 56). To receive a subsidy, schools must be well managed, provide a good education, serve poor communities and individuals and be run on a non-profit basis (South Africa Department of Education, 1998: section 64).

Source: Lewin and Sayed (2005).

Huddled together
in a village school
in Hà Nam province,
Viet Nam.

84

PART II. Monitoring Education for All

Chapter 4

International support: making better use of more aid

Ideally, programmes to achieve the EFA goals would be funded entirely from domestically generated resources. However, if the goals are to be met by 2015, aid is essential. About US$11 billion per year is needed right now if early childhood and adult literacy programmes are to expand and if all children are to complete primary school. Recent promises of additional aid are encouraging, but the resources have yet to materialize. Meanwhile, aid to basic education remains at less than half the amount needed annually. Moreover, there are many constraints: not enough of the aid reaches the low-income countries, nor is it sufficiently predictable; renewed attention to economic growth means increased competition from other sectors; and a lack of capacity in the education sector results in relatively low disbursement rates. At the same time, both donors and developing country governments have begun to adopt new ways of working in order to increase aid effectiveness.

Expectations and promises

In 2005 several high-profile reports and meetings raised expectations of an accelerated commitment to increase the levels and effectiveness of development aid, including through debt relief. In particular, the G8 Summit in July 2005 confirmed earlier promises by European Union members and resulted in others that would mean a US$50 billion, or 60%, annual increase in Official Development Assistance (ODA)[1] by 2010 – including a doubling of total aid for African countries – and further increases to 2015. Simultaneously, a commitment was made to write off all debts owed by a large group of the poorest countries to the International Monetary Fund, the World Bank's International Development Association and the African Development Fund.

Later in the year, the United Nations General Assembly's 'Millennium+5' summit and the annual meetings of the International Monetary Fund and the World Bank carried these initiatives forward. The decisions taken at the G8 and United Nations summits did not specify how the new aid flows would increase resources to education, though the final G8 communiqué did refer to the Fast Track Initiative, described later in this chapter, and to universal primary education.

More recently, in March 2006, the United Kingdom Government promised the equivalent of US$15 billion over the next ten years for education and called upon other governments to contribute similarly to provide the external aid required to reach the EFA goals. At their meeting in Saint Petersburg in July 2006, the G8 countries committed themselves to help 'identify the resources necessary' for countries to 'pursue their sustainable educational strategies'.

The UN summit also addressed the question of aid effectiveness. In doing so, it referred to the Paris Declaration on Aid Effectiveness, adopted by over one hundred industrialized and developing countries in March 2005. The declaration contains concrete obligations to structure and coordinate aid more closely in line with the strategies of recipient countries, reduce transaction and processing costs, untie aid and strengthen the accountability of donor and recipient governments to their citizens and parliaments. Donors agreed to these obligations in principle and participants adopted twelve targets for 2010. OECD's Development Assistance Committee (OECD-DAC) will monitor progress.

The United Kingdom promised an extra US$15 billion in aid for education

1. Explanations of many terms used here are provided in the introduction to the aid tables in the annex. This chapter examines only public official flows from OECD donor countries and multilateral organizations. Important developments in South-South aid and cooperation, and private international flows for basic education will be reviewed in the next *EFA Global Monitoring Report*.

2. Debt relief is included within ODA and accounts for around 10% of it. The effect of debt relief is to allow countries to retain domestic resources that would be used to service debt and so to increase domestic expenditure, including on basic education.

3. The OECD-DAC statistics differentiate among three groups of developing countries (and territories): fifty LDCs, twenty-two 'Other Low Income Countries' and seventy-nine middle-income countries.

Will the aid promises be met? The best news so far relates to debt relief for the poorest countries. In January 2006, the International Monetary Fund delivered US$3.4 billion of relief to nineteen countries and in March the World Bank Development Committee finalized arrangements that will result in an estimated saving of US$37 billion over forty years for seventeen countries. The amount will increase as more countries qualify.[2] In addition to this particular debt relief framework, and significant relief for Iraq and Afghanistan, the Nigerian Government and its creditors signed an agreement in late 2005. Overall, the OECD-DAC's view is that, while aid will increase over the next five years, full achievement of the aid promises 'cannot be assumed as a done deal' (OECD-DAC, 2006b: p. 18). Real ODA would need to grow 50% faster between 2004 and 2010 than the average annual growth rate from 2001 to 2004 (World Bank, 2006a). Further, the composition of any increase in aid is hard to predict. Between 2001 and 2004, debt relief, technical cooperation, and emergency and food aid represented 70% of the increase; and over half of the total increase was directed to Afghanistan and Iraq (World Bank, 2006a). Another consideration is that if increased aid is to benefit the poorest countries' efforts to reach the EFA goals, it will be needed in a form that allows not only for an increase in expenditure on education, but also for an increase in the share of aid going to the poorest countries.

What's new in aid to education since Dakar?

Total aid to developing countries is increasing

Disbursements of ODA to all developing countries fell during the early and mid-1990s, stabilized to 2000, then increased (Figure 4.1). Between 2000 and 2004 disbursements grew from US$57 billion to almost US$72 billion (2003 constant prices). In 2004, bilateral donors delivered almost three-quarters of the total and multilateral organizations one-quarter. The share of total ODA going to the seventy-two countries categorized by the OECD-DAC as low-income remained stable over 2000–2004 at around 46%, though the share for the very poorest of these, the fifty least developed countries or LDCs, increased from 26% to 32% (Figure 4.2).[3] Over half of all aid is allocated to countries in the lower- and upper-middle-income categories, a fact that underlines the political considerations in aid distribution.

Figure 4.3 shows the distribution of ODA across regions in 2000 and 2004. Sub-Saharan Africa maintained its position as the main recipient in 2004 with one-third of the total, but South and West Asia also benefited from large increases. However, the region receiving the largest increase in aid was the Arab States, mainly a result of increases for Iraq. Aid flows to all other regions were constant, and thus fell as proportions of the total. Turning to commitments, and to future flows of ODA, 32% of the increase between 2000 and 2004 was to the fifty LDCs and a further 45% to the twenty-two other low-income countries. The increase in multilateral commitments was almost entirely for these groups.

ODA is a composite of (a) financial resources that are distributed across such sectors as education, health, agriculture and roads; (b) direct budget support; (c) debt forgiveness and emergency and food aid; and (d) free-standing technical cooperation. Almost three-quarters of the total ODA in 2004 was allocated to sectors (including sector technical cooperation), though in recent years the share of sector aid has fallen as debt relief and emergency aid have increased at a faster rate (Figure 4.4).

Total aid to education – and to basic education – is also increasing

Aid commitments to education for all developing countries expanded significantly between 2000 and 2004, from US$4.6 billion to US$8.5 billion (2003 prices)[4] – an increase of 85% (Figure 4.5). Even higher growth occurred in the flows to low-income countries. These increased from US$2.5 billion to US$5.5 billion and by 2004 accounted for almost two-thirds of all education aid. The increases raised the share of aid for education among all sectors for all developing countries from 10.6% in 2000 to 13.6% in 2004 (Figure 4.6). More relevant in terms of additional support for the EFA goals is that education's share of total sector aid to the LDCs rose from 12.7% to 17.3%. These increases both in the absolute levels of aid to education and in the shares suggest that advocates have had some success in raising awareness of the importance of education in the international community.

4. All aid to education data in this chapter are in 2003 prices.

Figure 4.1: Total ODA, 1990-2004 (net disbursements in constant 2003 US$ billions)

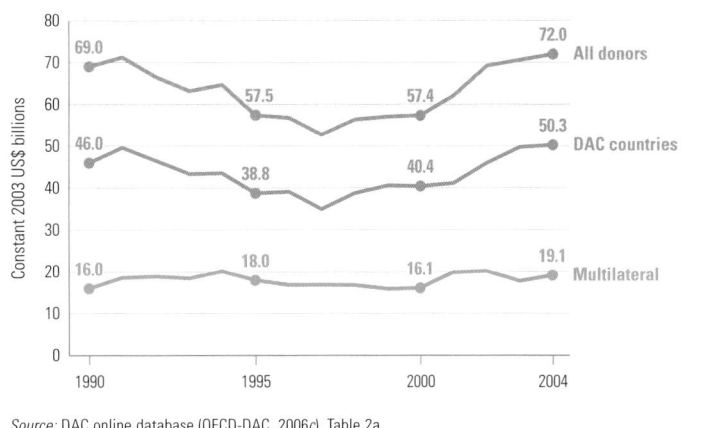

Source: DAC online database (OECD-DAC, 2006c), Table 2a.

Figure 4.2: Distribution of total ODA disbursements by income group, 1990-2004

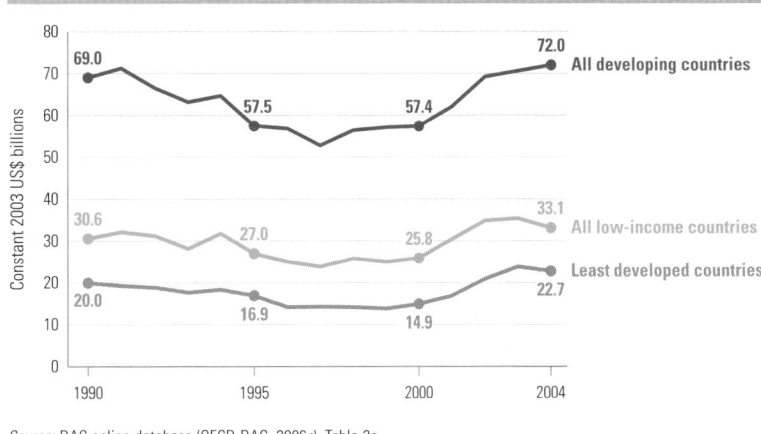

Source: DAC online database (OECD-DAC, 2006c), Table 2a.

Figure 4.3: Distribution of total ODA disbursements, selected regions, 2000 and 2004 (constant 2003 US$ billions)

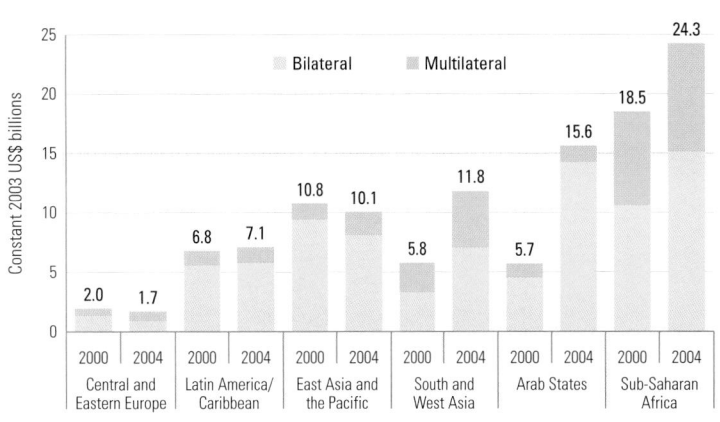

Source: DAC online database (OECD-DAC, 2006c), Table 2a.

Figure 4.4: Total ODA disbursements by type, 2000 and 2004

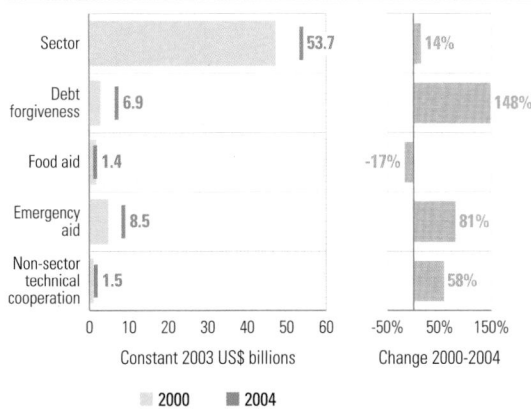

Source: DAC online database (OECD-DAC, 2006c), Table 2a.

Figure 4.5: Distribution of aid commitments to education by income group, 1999-2004

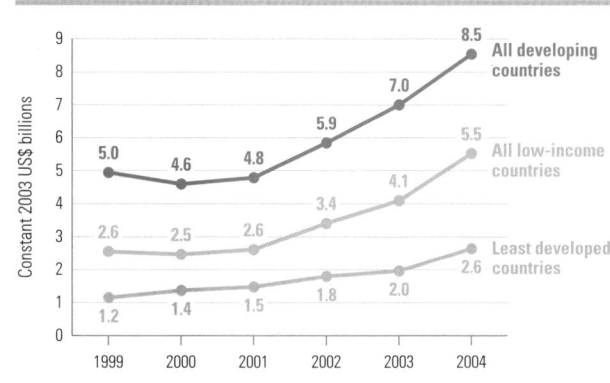

Source: CRS online database (OECD-DAC, 2006c), Table 2.

Basic education now represents 39% of direct aid to education

In the LDCs, much of the increase in aid to education has gone to basic education (Figure 4.7), commitments for which have increased from US$0.5 billion to US$1.6 billion, with most of the growth coming since 2002. A similar trend is visible across all developing countries: direct aid commitments for basic education increased at a higher rate than total aid for education, from US$1.4 billion in 2000 to US$3.3 billion in 2004. This positive trend in the past few years has resulted in basic education becoming the major recipient of direct aid to education, accounting for 39% in 2004 for all developing countries, compared with 30% in 2000.[5] The change is even greater for the LDCs, whose share of total education aid devoted to basic education increased from 37% in 2000 to 59% in 2004 (Figures 4.5 and 4.7). These shifts further underline the increased attention that donors and governments of poor countries are giving to EFA.

In addition to direct allocations to each level of education, significant amounts are included in the category 'level unspecified'. Between 2000 and 2004 these totalled between US$1 billion and US$1.5 billion annually. The category includes some support to basic education but, as last year's Report explained, the share is unknown. Here it is assumed that about half of 'level unspecified' aid is dedicated to basic education. Total aid to basic education for all developing countries would thus have been augmented by around US$0.6 billion in 2004 and for all low-income countries by some US$0.3 billion.

What about general budget support? In recent years, particularly in several sub-Saharan African countries, some project and sector programme aid has been replaced with direct budget support, over which the recipient government has greater control.[6] In 2004, direct budget support to all developing countries amounted to US$4.7 billion, including US$4.2 billion to all low-income countries. The Fast Track Initiative Secretariat estimates that 20% of general budget support goes to the education sector and that around half of that is allocated to basic education (FTI Secretariat, 2006). This would imply that direct budget support to education was about US$0.9 billion in developing countries in 2004, of which US$0.8 billion was for all low-income countries, and that half of these amounts went to basic education.

Combining all categories of aid, the amount to education for all developing countries is estimated to have increased from US$5.6 billion in 2000 to US$9.5 billion in 2004; for low-income countries the increase was from US$3.4 billion to US$6.4 billion (Table 4.1). With regard to basic education, aid to all developing countries is estimated to have increased from US$2.6 billion to US$4.4 billion, while for low-income countries the increase was from US$1.8 billion to US$3.4 billion. These amounts compare with total ODA commitments in 2004 of US$91.0 billion (OECD-DAC, 2006c: Table 3a).

While the share of technical cooperation in education ODA commitments has been falling, it is still very significant – 42% for all education and 27% for basic education in 2004 (Figure 4.8). The share is much greater for higher-income developing countries, and mainly funds scholarships and traineeships, than for low-

5. Basic education in the OECD-DAC aid statistics comprises early childhood education, primary education and basic life skills for youth and adults. Chapter 8 discusses aid to early childhood education in detail.

6. The OECD-DAC defines direct budget support as 'a method of financing a partner country's budget through a transfer of resources from an external financing agency to the partner government's national treasury. The funds thus transferred are managed in accordance with the recipient's budgetary processes' (OECD-DAC, 2005a).

Figure 4.6: Share of education in total sector-allocable aid commitments, 1999-2004

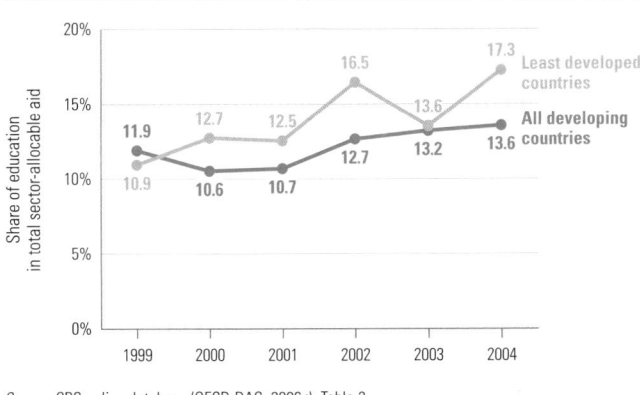

Source: CRS online database (OECD-DAC, 2006*c*), Table 2.

Figure 4.7: Distribution of aid commitments to basic education by income group, 1999-2004

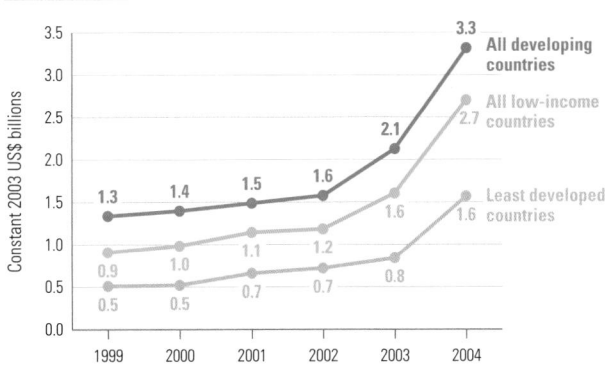

Source: CRS online database (OECD-DAC, 2006*c*), Table 2.

income ones. In sub-Saharan Africa, for example, technical cooperation represents just over 20% of total ODA, compared with over 60% in East Asia (OECD-DAC, 2006*b*).

In sum, since 2000 ODA has increased and a greater share has been allocated to the poorest countries. In addition, positive changes have occurred across the education sector. They include increases in (a) the share of education in the total amount of aid committed to sectors and (b) the share of aid to education which is directly allocated to basic education. Overall, however, the share of ODA commited directly to basic education is just 3.6% of the total – 4.8% if the wider definition is used – and one-third of this goes to middle-income developing countries.

Different donors, different priorities

Donors are not a homogenous group. Table 4.2 shows the contribution of each donor to total bilateral aid for the education sector as a whole and for basic education. In both cases, just a few donors dominate. In 2003–2004, France, Germany, Japan, the United Kingdom and the United States together contributed 72% of all bilateral aid to education. For basic education, over two-thirds was contributed by Canada, Japan, the Netherlands, the United Kingdom and the United States. If aid to basic education is to increase significantly, more donors will need to become more heavily involved, or these three major donors will need to increase their contributions, or both.

Overall, roughly one-third of all education aid goes to LDCs, one-third to other low-income countries and the remainder to middle-income

Table 4.1: Estimates of total ODA commitments for education and basic education by income group, 2000 and 2004 (constant 2003 US$ billions)

Education sector			Basic education		
	Developing countries	Low-income countries		Developing countries	Low-income countries
2000			**2000**		
Direct	4.60	2.48	Direct	1.40	0.98
			From 'level unspecified'	0.68	0.38
From budget support	1.00	0.93	From budget support	0.50	0.47
Total	**5.60**	**3.41**	Total	**2.59**	**1.83**
2004			**2004**		
Direct	8.55	5.53	Direct	3.32	2.70
			From 'level unspecified'	0.56	0.29
From budget support	0.94	0.85	From budget support	0.47	0.43
Total	**9.49**	**6.38**	Total	**4.35**	**3.42**
Change since 2000	**69.3%**	**87.2%**	Change since 2000	**68.1%**	**86.6%**

Source: CRS online database (OECD-DAC, 2006*c*), Table 2.

Figure 4.8: Share of technical cooperation in aid commitments to education and basic education, 1999-2000 and 2003-2004 averages

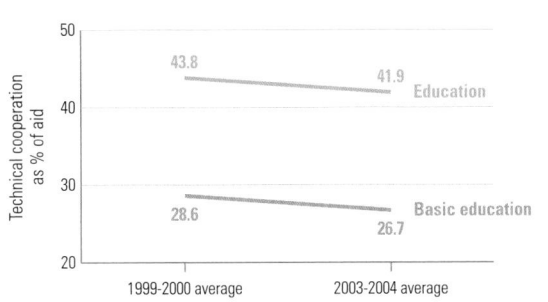

Source: CRS online database (OECD-DAC, 2006*c*), Table 2.1.

Table 4.2: Shares of donors in bilateral aid commitments to education and basic education, 2003–2004 average

Donor	Share of the country in DAC countries' aid to education	Share of the country in DAC countries' aid to basic education
Luxembourg	0.4	0.5
New Zealand	0.6	0.4
Switzerland	0.7	1.0
Ireland	0.8	1.1
Finland	0.9	0.9
Portugal	1.0	0.2
Italy	1.0	0.6
Denmark	1.1	1.7
Greece	1.3	1.9
Austria	1.3	0.2
Australia	1.7	3.2
Sweden	1.9	2.9
Belgium	2.1	0.6
Spain	2.1	1.6
Norway	2.9	5.6
Canada	3.9	7.4
Netherlands	4.1	8.0
United States	7.3	21.0
United Kingdom	8.6	26.0
Germany	16.9	5.4
Japan	19.1	6.7
France	20.3	3.3
All DAC countries	**100**	**100**

Note: DAC countries only.
Source: CRS online database (OECD-DAC, 2006c), Table 2.

Figure 4.10: Distribution by education level

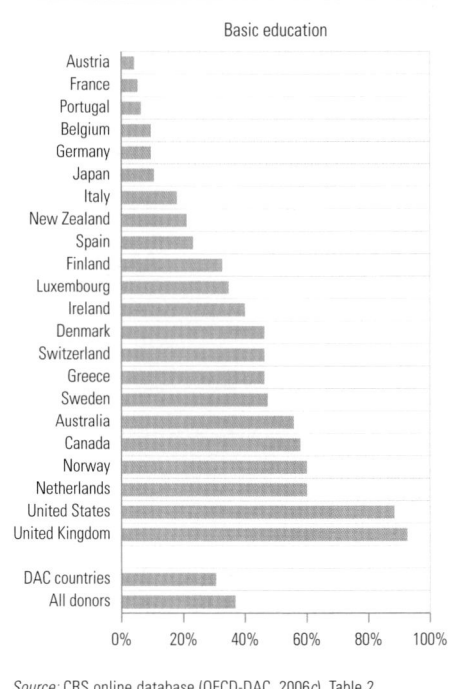

Source: CRS online database (OECD-DAC, 2006c), Table 2.

Figure 4.9: Share of education aid across income group by donor, 2003–2004 average

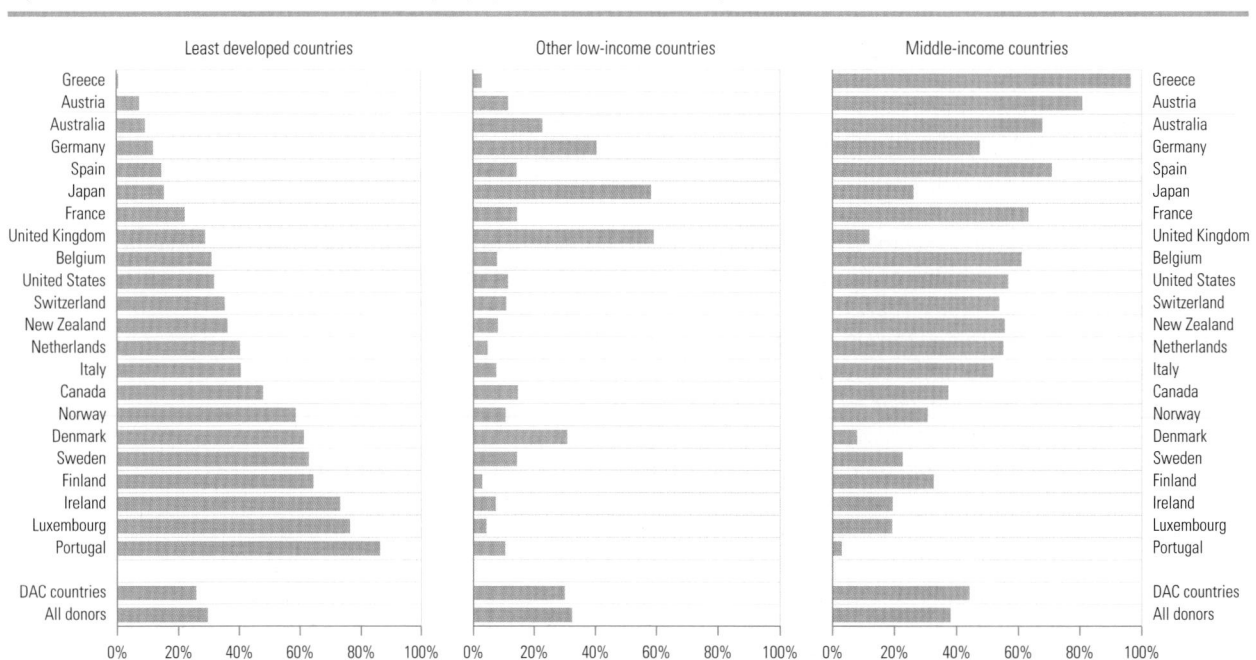

Source: CRS online database (OECD-DAC, 2006c), Table 2.

of total aid to education by donor, 2003–2004 average

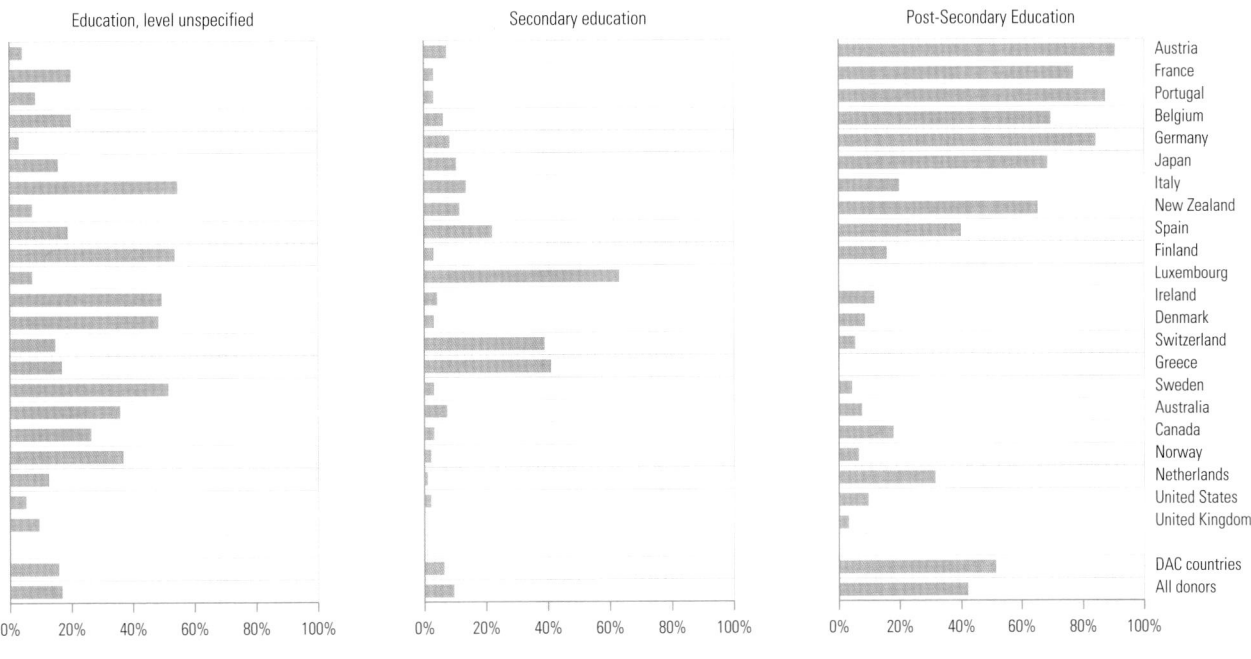

developing countries (Figure 4.5). Individual donors vary substantially in how they distribute their aid among these groups. In spite of repeated calls for a greater concentration of education aid in the poorest countries, half of the bilateral donors shown in Figure 4.9 allocate more than half of their aid for education to middle-income countries. On the other hand, eight donors allocate less than 30% to countries in this group.

Donors' priorities across education levels also vary widely, as Figure 4.10 shows. Overall, almost two-fifths of total allocable education aid is for basic education. For bilateral donors as a group the share is slightly lower, and for nine of the twenty-two DAC donors it is less than one-quarter. On the other hand, for six donors the share is over 60%. The situation is complicated by the large share of 'level unspecified' for several donors. Encouraged by DAC, donors are continually seeking to disaggregate these allocations further.

While the grants and concessional loans of the multilateral aid organizations are largely funded by the bilateral donors and as such are covered by the previous discussion of total aid, it is interesting to see what priority the multilaterals give to education in their overall aid programmes (Table 4.3). Generally, the share for education in

2003–2004 (11.8%) is similar to that of the bilateral donors and the reduction in the share of sector-allocable aid for education that occurred between 1999 and 2001 has been substantially reversed, reaching 13.5% in 2004 (see annex, Aid Table 4). The share of multilateral education aid that goes to basic education (52%) is higher than that of the bilaterals (38%).

After the International Development Association, the European Commission is the biggest multilateral donor for education. Its support is in the form of grants. Provisional 2005 data indicate that almost half of its disbursements for education were for basic education while a further 13% were for 'level unspecified'. Post-secondary education received 27%. Commitments were highest for sub-Saharan Africa (30%) and South and Central Asia (19%), with non-EU European countries receiving 13%. The largest commitments were for Bangladesh, Eritrea, India, Pakistan, Papua New Guinea and Turkey. Aid for education was almost equally divided among specific projects (37%), technical cooperation (33%) and sectorwide programmes (30%). The Commission allocates greater shares of its education aid to sub-Saharan Africa and to basic education than do donors overall.

Donors' priorities across education levels vary widely

Table 4.3: Multilateral ODA: commitments of major donors to education, 2003–2004 average

	Total ODA	Aid to education		Aid to basic education	
	Constant 2003 US$ millions	Amount (constant 2003 US$ millions)	Education as % of total ODA	Amount (constant 2003 US$ millions)	Basic education as % of total aid to education
International Development Association	9 590.4	1 023.6	14.0	676.7	66.1
European Commission	8 083.5	469.5	8.4	155.5	33.1
Asian Develoment Fund	1 629.9	243.5	16.1	94.4	38.8
African Development Fund	1 397.9	164.7	13.8	49.8	30.3
UNICEF	618.2	55.7	15.1	55.2	99.0
Inter-American Development Bank Special Fund	431.9	36.7	9.6	4.6	12.5
Total multilateral	21 751.8	1 993.6	11.8	1 036.2	52.0

Source: CRS online database (OECD-DAC, 2006c), Table 2.

Aid to education from the developing country perspective

In this section, the focus switches to the countries that receive ODA for their education sectors. Three questions are posed. First, which countries receive the largest amounts of education aid and what are their characteristics? Second, for individual countries, what is the importance of aid to the education sector and to basic education in relation to total aid receipts, and how does it vary across countries and regions? Third, how dependent on aid for the education sector are countries becoming?

Table 4.4 shows the twenty countries receiving the highest amounts of education aid commitments in 2003–2004 (the amounts are averaged for the two years). The geographical spread is wide: eight are in sub-Saharan Africa, five in South and West Asia, three each in North Africa and in East Asia, and one in Central and Eastern Europe. Seven of the twenty countries are LDCs, seven are other low-income countries and six are lower-middle-income countries, including four in the top ten. In the next highest twenty countries, half of the recipients are lower-middle-income. Thus, no very significant concentration of education aid on the poorest countries can be observed as yet. The aid tables in the annex provide more information on the education aid received annually by 148 countries between 1999 and 2004, in total and per person for 2003-2004.

Countries vary greatly in the number of bilateral donors contributing to their education sector. Table 4.5, showing this information for the seventy-two poorest countries, reveals significant differences. Thirty-six of these countries have two donors or less, twenty-five

have three to six and eleven have seven to twelve. The countries with the most bilateral donors are Ethiopia, Mali, Mozambique and the United Republic of Tanzania. Of the countries with two or fewer donors, fifteen also lack any multilateral donor presence, apart from UNICEF and/or UNESCO. This revealing distribution poses important questions about the capacity of global aid to raise education levels in a wide range of countries, an issue revisited in the final section of this chapter.

The education sector increasingly has to compete with other sectors, and with other forms of ODA, for external financial support. In 2004, education in developing countries received 10.2% of total ODA and around 13.6% of sector ODA. Roughly two-fifths was for basic education. These averages, however, are heavily influenced by the situation in a few large aid-receiving countries and hide very diverse experiences among countries and regions. Table 4.6 provides more detailed information. For a sample of seventy-nine poor and middle-income countries (here shown aggregated by region), the average share of total ODA directly allocated to the education sector in 2004 was 12.4% and education's share of all sector ODA was around 16.1%. However, for almost half of these countries (thirty-five), the share of sector-allocable ODA going to education was less than 10% while for 14 countries it was over 25%.

The relative importance given to education in total aid is not the same for all regions. Countries in South and West Asia and the Arab States in 2003–2004 received a much larger share for education (over 20% of total aid and over 30% of sector-allocable aid) than did countries in other regions. In sub-Saharan Africa, the average

Table 4.4: Twenty countries receiving the highest total amounts of aid for education, 2003–2004 average

	Aid to education (constant 2003 US$ millions)
China	826.2
Bangladesh	516.0
India	472.1
Morocco	280.2
Viet Nam	244.2
U. R. Tanzania	189.3
Pakistan	150.4
Algeria	143.2
Ghana	131.9
Tunisia	119.7
Cameroon	114.9
Nepal	114.5
Indonesia	113.6
Zambia	113.2
South Africa	110.5
Turkey	108.1
Kenya	107.0
Ethiopia	104.6
Afghanistan	104.1
Senegal	99.3

Source: CRS online database (OECD-DAC, 2006c), Table 2.

Table 4.5: Number of bilateral donors to education in the seventy-two poorest recipient countries

Number of donors	Total number of countries	Examples
12	1	U. R. Tanzania
11	2	Ethiopia, Mozambique
10	1	Mali
9	3	Bangladesh, Burkina Faso, Zambia
8	2	Pakistan, Uganda
7	2	Indonesia, Nicaragua, Senegal
6	5	Afghanistan, Benin, D. R. Congo, Rwanda, Viet Nam
5	4	Angola, Kenya, Niger, Sudan
4	8	Eritrea, Ghana, Guinea, India, Malawi, Nepal, Timor-Leste, Yemen
3	8	Bhutan, Burundi, Cambodia, Cameroon, Chad, Haiti, Lao PDR, Vanuatu
2	11	Cape Verde, Djibouti, Georgia, Lesotho, Madagascar, Mauritania, Mongolia, Nigeria, Papua New Guinea, Somalia, Togo
1	14	Central African Republic, Congo, Côte d'Ivoire, Guinea-Bissau, Guyana, Kiribati, Liberia, Myanmar, Republic of Moldova, Sao Tome and Principe, Solomon Islands, Sri Lanka, Tajikistan, Tonga
0	11	Armenia, Azerbaijan, Comoros, Gambia, Kyrgyzstan, Maldives, Sierra Leone, Saint Lucia, St Vincent/Grenad., Uzbekistan, Zimbabwe

Source: FTI Secretariat (2005).

Table 4.6: Aid for education and basic education as share of total aid and sector aid in seventy-nine countries, 2003-2004 regional averages

Regional average	Share of education in total aid	Share of education in total sector-allocable aid	Share of basic education in total aid	Share of basic education in total sector-allocable aid
Sub-Saharan Africa (22 countries)	11.0%	16.2%	2.5%	3.6%
Arab States (9 countries)	24.0%	31.8%	1.1%	1.5%
Central Asia (7 countries)	7.1%	8.9%	1.7%	2.1%
East Asia and the Pacific (8 countries)	14.2%	15.8%	1.2%	1.4%
South and West Asia (5 countries)	21.1%	31.5%	10.0%	12.4%
Latin America and the Caribbean (23 countries)	8.6%	9.8%	1.5%	1.9%
Central and Eastern Europe (5 countries)	11.0%	12.5%	1.7%	2.0%
All developing countries	**12.4%**	**16.1%**	**2.3%**	**2.9%**

Sources: CRS online database (OECD-DAC, 2006c), Table 2; annex, Statistical Table 11.

share for education across twenty-two countries was just 11% of total aid and 16% of sector-allocable aid. The distribution of aid among the different levels of education also varies by country and region. In South and West Asia, countries on average used almost 50% of education aid for basic education, compared with just over 20% in sub-Saharan Africa and in Latin America and the Caribbean. In the Arab States and in East Asia and the Pacific, the share was

lower. The very large differences between countries in the importance given to education need to be investigated further if a better understanding is to be achieved of the likely impact on the EFA goals of increased overall levels of ODA.

How important is aid to financing countries' education systems? The answer is difficult to provide, since countries vary in the ways they report aid and expenditure from domestic

Ethiopia, India and Uganda are examples of strong government ownership of education sector policies

revenue and the impact on education of direct budget support can only be approximated. However, using information on domestic education expenditure as provided to the UNESCO Institute for Statistics and on disbursements of education aid as reported by the OECD-DAC for sixty countries, some rough estimates can be made. In twenty-four of the countries, aid accounts for over 10% of total current expenditure on education, and in seven for over 20% (Figure 4.11). Some consequences of the size of these shares, particularly relating to the long-term unpredictability of aid, are returned to later in this chapter. The contribution of aid to expenditure in basic education is generally lower than for the education sector as a whole (Figure 4.12).

Streamlining aid to education

Previous editions of the *EFA Global Monitoring Report* have argued that any analysis of the effectiveness of aid in the education sector should be viewed within the wider context of international efforts to improve the quality and effectiveness of aid as a whole, as exemplified by the OECD-led Paris Declaration on Aid Effectiveness (see page 86).

Efforts to carry forward the Paris Declaration are led by the OECD-DAC's Working Party on Aid Effectiveness, established in 2003. Work on monitoring progress on twelve qualitative and quantitative indicators includes an international survey every two years from 2006 to 2010. Draft questionnaires were tested in Cambodia, Ghana, Nicaragua, Senegal, South Africa and Uganda before the survey was launched in May 2006 in all countries that indicated interest. The OECD is to publish the consolidated results in December 2006. The survey comprises a donor questionnaire, a government questionnaire and a worksheet for each participating country. In addition to the survey work, subregional consultative workshops are being held, for example in Uganda and Mali.

In March 2006, the DAC published *Managing for Development Results, Principles in Action: Sourcebook on Emerging Good Practice* (OECD-DAC, 2006d), in which examples of work at national and sector level, and in development agencies are presented. The Country Implementation Tracking Tool, another DAC initiative, looks at national efforts to streamline

policy and practice, including at sector level (OECD-DAC, 2006a), in more than sixty countries. In some of them (Ethiopia, India and Uganda are examples), where there is experience of sectorwide programmes going back as far as ten years, evidence of many of the principles in the Paris indicators already exists. These include strong government ownership of education sector policies, channelling of aid into government sector budgets, reduction of duplication of effort ('parallel project implementation units') and carrying out of joint field missions, joint analytic work and mutual progress assessments.

So far, few studies exist of the changes taking place and the lessons emerging for donors and governments in their efforts to maximize the benefits of the new procedures. Those that have been made focus mainly on direct budget support, whose flows tend to be triggered by indicators of actions or outputs in several sectors, often including education (IDD and Associates, 2006; Lawson et al., 2005; USAID, 2005). In general, the assessments are positive, but the studies say relatively little about sector experiences. One, on Mozambique, demonstrates the problems arising when all donors participate but some do not really subscribe to the harmonization agenda (Killick et al., 2005).

Before examining promising mechanisms for managing aid in the education sector more effectively, it is useful to review briefly the complex and diverse nature of current aid arrangements. Usually, external funding for education is provided directly for a discrete set of activities identified in advance – the traditional externally supported project. Alternatively, funds are added to the government budget but earmarked for a given subsector, such as primary or secondary education, and spread across a whole programme. Going one step further, they may be used to provide additional support to a comprehensive programme that affects the whole education sector. Finally, aid may not be sector-specific at all but rather transferred to the government as general budget support for distribution as the government sees fit. In some cases, all these arrangements and others exist at once: Table 4.7 presents the example of Ethiopia. Indeed, the situation of multiple forms of aid is particularly common in countries with several donors and such examples show why

Figure 4.11: Shares of aid and national spending in total expenditure on education, 2004

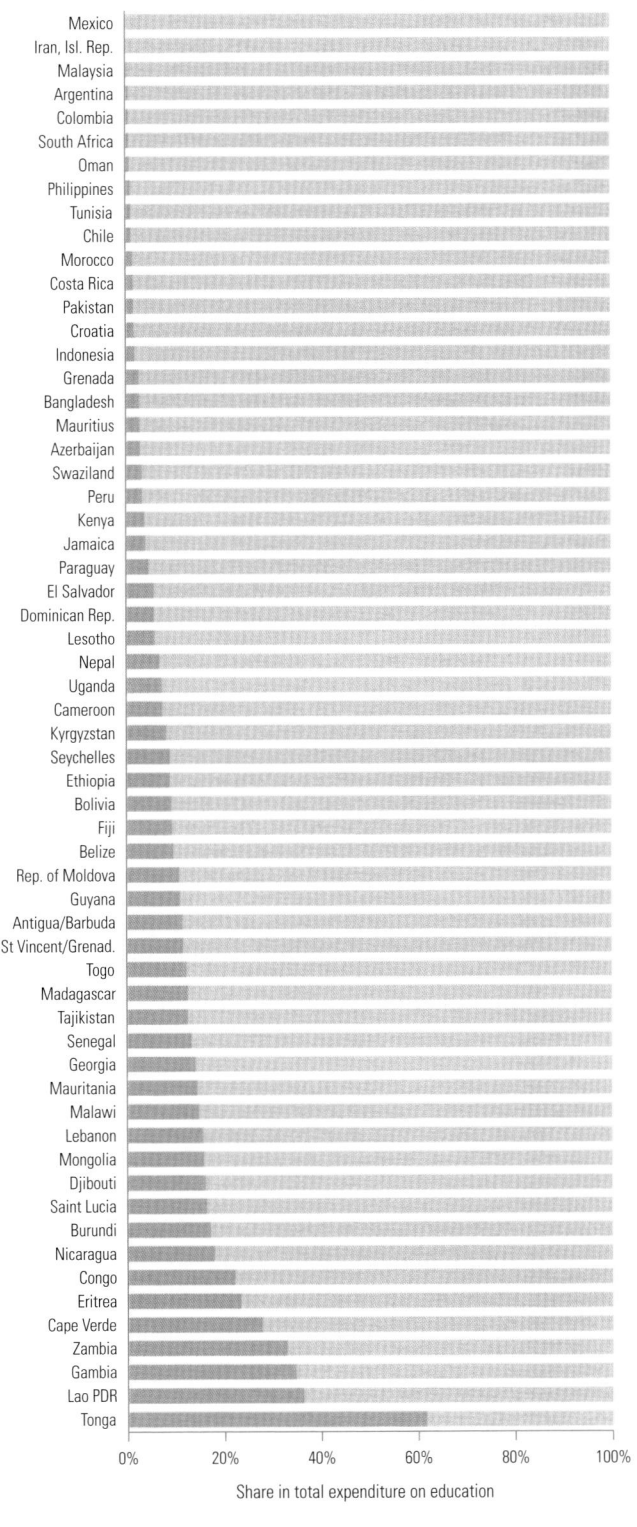

Share in total expenditure on education

■ Aid ■ National expenditure

Sources: CRS online database (OECD-DAC, 2006*c*) Table 2; annex, Statistical Table 11.

Figure 4.12: Shares of aid and national spending in total expenditure on basic education, 2004

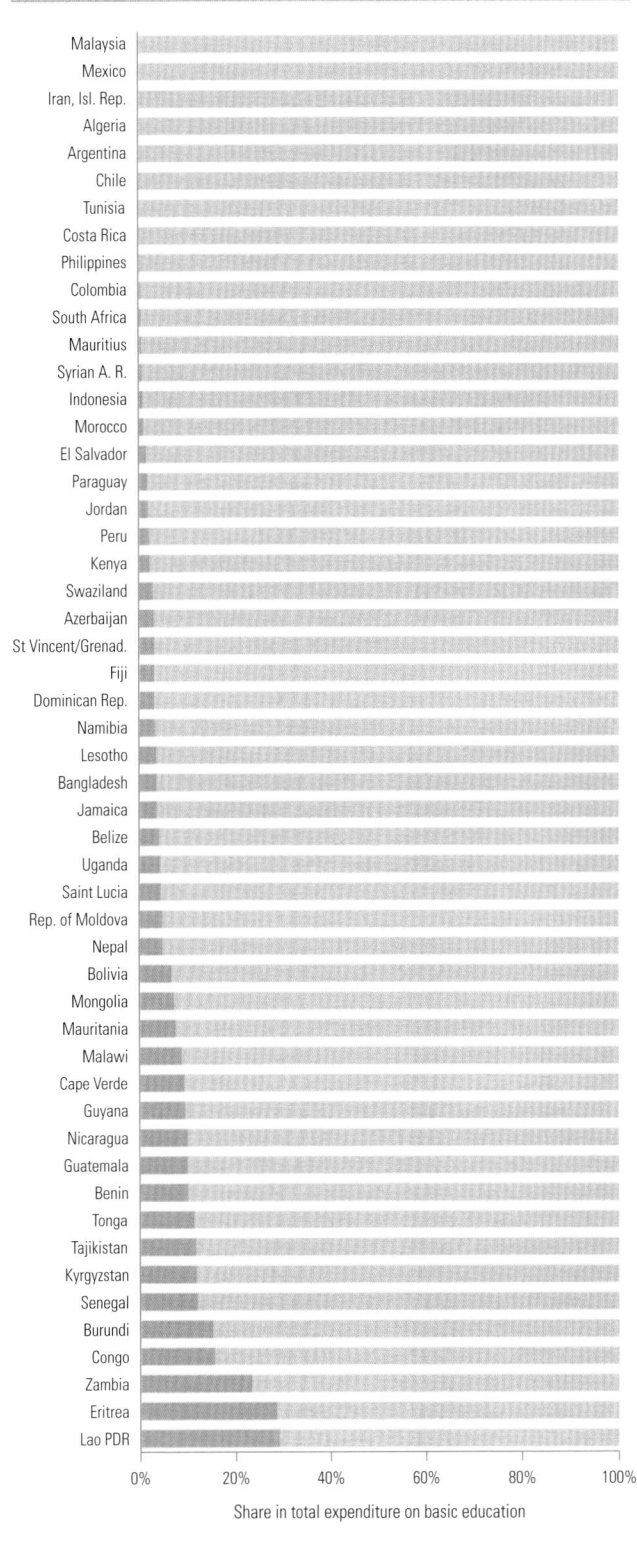

Share in total expenditure on basic education

■ Aid ■ National expenditure

Sources: CRS online database (OECD-DAC, 2006*c*) Table 2; annex, Statistical Table 11.

Table 4.7: Donors supporting the Ethiopian education system by subsector and type of aid, 2004/05 to 2009/10

	Subsector	Type of support
Belgium	Teacher training	Grant (pooled)
Finland	Teacher training Primary	Grant (pooled) Grant and technical assistance
France	Tertiary Primary Secondary	Project grant and technical assistance Grant Grant
Ireland	Teacher training Primary Multi-subsector	Grant (pooled) Grant (pooled) Grant (pooled)
Italy	Primary TVET Tertiary	Grant and project Grant and project Grant and technical assistance
Japan	Primary TVET	Project and technical assistance Technical assistance
Netherlands	Teacher training Tertiary Primary Non-formal Multi-subsector	Grant (pooled) Project Project and grant Project Grant (pooled)
Sweden	Primary Teacher training Multi-subsector	Grant (pooled) Grant (pooled) Grant
United Kingdom	Tertiary Multi-subsector Non-formal Teacher training Multi-subsector	Project Technical assistance Grant Project and grant (pooled) Grant (pooled)
United States	Teacher training Primary Non-formal	Grant Grant Grant
African Development Fund	Primary Multi-subsector	Concessional loan and technical assistance Concessional loan
European Commission	Tertiary Primary Multi-subsector	Project grant Project grant Grant (pooled)
UNDP	Multi-subsector	Grant
UNESCO	Teacher training Tertiary TVET	Technical assistance Technical assistance Technical assistance
UNICEF	Primary	Grant
World Bank (IDA)	Tertiary TVET	Concessional loan Concessional loan

Note:
'TVET' stands for 'technical and vocational education and training'.
'Multi-subsector' means a range of activities within a particular level, e.g. primary.
'Pooled grants' are mainly for the Teacher Development Fund.
'Grants' mainly support the Education Sector Development Programme and are received directly by the Ministry of Education.
'Project grants' tend to be managed by unique project implementation units.
Source: Yizengaw (2006).

there is pressure for greater harmonization. Harmonization will take time, but in the meanwhile governments need encouragement and examples of successful experiences on which to model their coordination efforts.

Joint monitoring reviews: small steps in the right direction?

A common characteristic of recent efforts to simplify aid arrangements in the education sector and to increase donors' alignment with government, and with each other, is the joint monitoring review process. Joint reviews are associated with attempts to encourage donors to combine their support around sectorwide programmes and to adopt common practices of aid management, primarily (though not exclusively) in countries with high dependence on aid. Joint reviews provide an arena for increased government-donor dialogue. They also offer a periodic assessment of the performance of the education sector (or subsector or large project) against an agreed set of objectives, targets and performance indicators. The reviews are expected to:

- increase country ownership and provide more effective support of national priorities;
- promote a more efficient division of labour among aid agencies;
- improve the efficiency and transparency of (harmonized) frameworks for monitoring and evaluation;
- improve accountability to funding sources and government partners.

Though it is not aid-dependent, India has the longest experience of joint reviews in the education sector, having held over twenty since 1995. There, the government is clearly in charge; in some other countries the process appears to be more donor-driven.

How common are joint monitoring reviews?

At least forty countries have or are expected to have education sectorwide programmes in place in 2006 (Packer, 2006). Of these, thirty are in sub-Saharan Africa. Countries with regular joint review mechanisms include Bangladesh, Benin, Burkina Faso, Cambodia, Ethiopia, Ghana, India, Kenya, Madagascar, Malawi, Mali, Mozambique, Namibia, Nepal, the Niger, Rwanda, Uganda, the United Republic of Tanzania, Viet Nam and Zambia.

What stakeholders are involved?

A sample of reviews undertaken in 2005 shows that the number of participants varies considerably. In India, with a programme supported by three donors, the government appointed ten members in 2005 and the donors a further ten. Teams of two or three people visited eight states. At the other extreme, 121 people took part in the joint monitoring review mission in Rwanda, which was held entirely in the capital, Kigali. The range of stakeholders was very broad, including members from lower administrative levels in the education system and from civil society. In Ethiopia, sixty members were divided into six groups to visit selected regions. In Malawi, of sixty-eight participants, roughly a third were from donor agencies or international NGOs. Reviews are people-intensive. Most joint reviews involve all agencies working in the education sector, whether they provide budget support, work through projects or contribute through technical assistance.

Very specific documentation is prepared for joint monitoring reviews, either because of requests made during the previous review or to enable analysis of particular themes during the current one. For example, in Ghana in 2004, a 131-page performance report was prepared, along with a 51-page progress and assessment framework that provided data on each set of activities under the major policy headings. In addition, quarterly budget summaries were provided, along with a ranking of the performance of individual districts against specific performance criteria. In the first review of a new national programme in India, in 2005, the government provided extensive documentation and reports by each of the eight states to be visited, focusing primarily on the programme's main development objectives.

Processes and issues

The reviews take different approaches. In some, the emphasis is on monitoring progress systematically against national targets; in others, it is on implementation practice and management. Reviews in Ethiopia, India and Uganda, for instance, appear to have concentrated more on targets while those in Madagascar and Rwanda have had a greater focus on implementation. Some reviews include field visits, others do not. While field visits are complex, time-consuming and relatively costly,

they make it much easier to identify inequities in levels of financing and performance across a country and to showcase good local practice.

A look at the aides-mémoires for Ethiopia, India and Rwanda gives additional insight into what issues were considered most important. The Rwandan aide-mémoire explicitly sets the review process within the wider context of poverty reduction. India's reviews are clearly structured around a small set of national, higher-order education outcomes relating to access, equity and quality in elementary education. The needs and demands of the most disadvantaged children receive considerable attention in all three cases, as do financial management and accountability. Running through the reports for the three countries is the thread of weak or severely constrained capacity for introducing reforms, improving quality and managing systems. In Ethiopia, the report states that the lack of a long-term plan for comprehensive capacity-building at regional and *woreda* (district) level constitutes a major bottleneck and that adequate resources are not provided for capacity-building. In the other two countries, capacity development is addressed more in relation to particular issues, such as teacher training.

How influential are the reviews?

It is difficult to judge to what extent joint monitoring reviews are influential and initiate change. Perhaps as a result of the reviews' comprehensive nature, the reports often fail to distil messages in a way that prioritizes needs and identifies what is possible and what is practical. Studies over time are required to test the extent to which recommendations have been accepted, put into practice and had an impact. Government participants in the Indian and Ethiopian reviews have reported that they do lead to action, and in Uganda changes in the way grants move to schools and are used by local communities resulted in part from review findings. There is less evidence that the reviews feed into wider national processes, such as those associated with poverty reduction strategies. Nor is it yet known to what extent the reviews influence donor practice. A systematic study of the review processes and outcomes could be beneficial for both governments and donors in their efforts to improve the effectiveness of aid in the education sector.

121 people took part in the joint monitoring review mission in Rwanda, which was held entirely in the capital, Kigali

Scaling up aid for education

Among the factors that will influence future levels of aid and how it is distributed across sectors will be evidence that developing country governments have the capacity to spend these funds in the ways agreed upon. Disbursement rates are relatively low in the education sector for all developing countries, even lower for basic education, and lower still for basic education in the LDCs (FTI Secretariat, 2006).

Capacity

Some institutions have argued that limitations in absorptive capacity should not be an obstacle to the scaling up of aid, provided efforts to improve capacity are undertaken simultaneously (UNDP, 2005). Others are less optimistic, pointing to the growing complexity of programmes as governments switch attention from the relatively straightforward strategy of achieving broad increases in access and start to concentrate more on the hardest-to-reach children, measures to retain all children in school and improving achievement levels. Of necessity, all these measures will have to be applied in a context of increasing demand for the expansion of secondary and tertiary education. To move forward effectively on all these fronts requires strengthening both policy-making and implementation capacity.

How can donors help? Donors can influence the capacity available to governments by increasing the quality of their own technical support and by working to revise the content and form of technical cooperation. Unfortunately, while ODA commitments for education are increasing, donors are reducing the number of their staff with sector skills. This is the case in both bilateral and multilateral agencies, and reflects the increasing shift towards programme aid and direct budget support. There are risks in this trend. Some of the benefits gained from emphasizing the maximum use of national systems and providing sectorwide support could be undermined. Moreover, providing aid in this way may reduce capacity-building efforts in countries where such efforts are not accorded national budgetary priority. Any move to downgrade capacity development efforts while augmenting broad sector support would likely be self-defeating.

> **Downgrading capacity development while augmenting sector support would be self-defeating**

Changes that could help donors minimize these potentially negative effects include (Fredriksen, 2005):
- using, retaining and strengthening existing national and regional capacity, rather than creating new capacity through long-term technical assistance and external training;
- supporting knowledge exchange so practitioners can benefit from international good practice;
- giving grants to national teams;
- improving coordination among donor agencies;
- helping address the causes of brain drain out of the education sector as well as out of the country.

Given the declining share of technical cooperation, including for capacity-building, in aid for education there is an urgent need to re-examine the ways in which the remaining resources are used.

Aid dependence

Very different issues arise from the extent and implications of aid dependence. The receipt of aid involves a trade-off: it allows an objective to be reached faster but potentially reduces governments' influence over how resources are used and introduces greater unreliability. The Government of India refused offers of substantial amounts of aid for primary education until 1993, because of concern that it would lose sovereignty over policy decisions. Even after that, aid was less than 2% of total expenditure on primary education.

In several countries donors provide over 20% of the total education budget (Figure 4.11). For the twenty country plans so far endorsed by the Fast Track Initiative, on average one-quarter of the costs will need to be covered by aid and the share goes as high as 63%. An initial attempt in 2002 by the World Bank to calculate the financing gap for reaching universal primary education by 2015 concluded that aid would need to reach an average of 42% of total expenditure on primary education and much more in some countries. Such levels of dependence underline the importance of efforts to increase alignment between donor activities and national programmes.

Predictability

Even with greater alignment, however, countries that are highly dependent on aid must still face the problem of its volatility and unpredictability. An analysis of aid flows between 1975 and 2003 in seventy-six countries showed that the aid received by developing countries was far more volatile than domestically generated revenue and that aid disbursements were only weakly related to commitments (Bulir and Hamann, 2006). Both volatility and the gap between aid commitments and disbursements appear to have increased in recent years. Between 2000 and 2003, lenders promised 50% more than was actually disbursed. More worrying, the differences tended to be larger for countries with lower per capita income.

These trends partly arise from implementation bottlenecks and constraints within recipient countries. In addition, 'donor development agencies that make aid commitments are different from those that approve aid funding (parliaments) and disburse aid (ministries of finance)' (Bulir and Hamann, 2006: p. 4). Donors need to work harder to provide guarantees of longer-term, more predictable financial aid so that countries can take the decisions necessary to increase both the demand for and the supply of education without worrying about having to reverse them if aid is reduced. It may also be prudent for developing country governments that are highly reliant on aid to assess which activities are the most important to sustain and should therefore be funded domestically.

The Fast Track Initiative: encouraging a global compact

The Fast Track Initiative (FTI) was established in 2002 to encourage a global compact that would lead to the development of 'credible' education sector plans and to greater – and more predictable – external financial support. The World Bank hosts its secretariat, and over thirty donors share its governance and costs. Last year's *EFA Global Monitoring Report* concluded that, while the political visibility of and rhetorical support for the FTI had increased substantially, no significant increases in resources for its Catalytic Fund or Education Programme Development Fund had yet resulted.[7] Nor could the FTI yet claim wider success in leveraging significant additional external funds for basic education. In addition, the 2006 Report pointed to often anecdotal evidence that agencies' in-country education advisors questioned the value added by the initiative either in bringing in extra funding or in enhancing policy dialogue, particularly in countries where the latter is well established. More positively, the Report recognized that the FTI had become an important coordinating mechanism for the donor agencies and a positive influence on donor harmonization.

Over the past year the FTI has continued to evolve. Technical support of various kinds has been provided to seventy-four countries to help them develop education sector plans; concept notes on capacity development, fragile states, HIV/AIDS and an expanded financing mechanism have been prepared; and the education plan appraisal guidelines and framework documents have been revised to provide a more holistic approach to gender issues. Sector plans have now been endorsed by local donor groups for twenty countries and the plans of a further twelve countries are expected to be endorsed by the end of 2006.[8] By the end of 2008, the secretariat estimates, the plans of fifty-nine countries may have been through this process.

In addition, the FTI has added some value by making extra resources available for improving the quality of education sector planning and programme development, and, in a few cases, by providing additional funds for endorsed plans through the Catalytic Fund. So far, however, the amounts in the Catalytic Fund remain quite small (though pledges have been accelerating recently) and a limited number of countries have benefited. As of August 2006, total donor payments into the fund were US$230 million, though with a further US$450 million pledged by a total of eleven donors by the end of 2008. Six donors had pledged over US$10 million each. Of these, the European Commission, the Netherlands and the United Kingdom were responsible for 85% of total pledges. Disbursements as of August 2006 amounted to US$96 million to eleven countries; in addition, formal commitments amounted to US$130 million. The number of donors to the Education Programme Development Fund increased from two to eight over the past year, and commitments for 2005–2007 total US$46 million, almost half from Norway.

Though there has been some growth in the resources available, it is now apparent that the Catalytic Fund, as initially conceived, is not sustainable. It was designed as a temporary source of funding for countries with few donors, the expectation being that good performance would attract additional donors. In practice, new ones have not been forthcoming and, since there is a trend among donors to reduce the number of countries they support, the problem is likely to grow. Similarly, the hoped-for solution of 'silent partnerships', in which donors with no programmes in a country would allocate funds for basic education through a donor that did have

A limited number of countries have benefited from the FTI Catalytic Fund

7. The Catalytic Fund provides up to three years of transitional support for education sector plans in countries with four or fewer bilateral donors, each contributing a minimum of US$1 million in aid. The Education Programme Development Fund finances technical assistance to help countries develop the plans.

8. The countries with endorsed plans are Burkina Faso, Djibouti, Ethiopia, the Gambia, Ghana, Guinea, Guyana, Honduras, Kenya, Lesotho, Madagascar, Mauritania, Mozambique, Nicaragua, the Niger, the Republic of Moldova, Tajikistan, Timor Leste, Viet Nam and Yemen. Those expecting endorsement by the end of 2006 are Albania, Benin, Bhutan, Burundi, Cambodia, Cameroon, Mali, Mongolia, Rwanda, Sao Tome and Principe, Senegal and Sierra Leone.

a presence, have proved more complicated than expected. To overcome the situation in which a country receiving payments from the fund suddenly faces a cut-off, donors are now considering extending the funding period. While this makes sense, it would significantly alter the nature of the fund and, without large increases in contributions, an extension for existing recipients would reduce the number of potential new ones.

While the recent increases in ODA commitments to basic education cannot be attributed solely to the influence of the FTI, they are consistent with the added international attention to basic education financing that it has stimulated. The increases begin to demonstrate the feasibility of the FTI's 'virtual fund' model, increasing overall resources for basic education through a country-by-country approach rather than through a single 'global fund' such as the one for malaria, tuberculosis and HIV/AIDS. Further, the considerable efforts that have gone into designing the FTI processes have positioned the education sector well in the event that the recent promises of additional aid are fulfilled.

The FTI's potential impact is not limited to the generation of external funding. Another expectation is that, as countries take note of the indicators and benchmarks included in the indicative framework, which provides the background for the design of education plans and their endorsement by local donors, policy-making will improve and countries will move faster towards the EFA goals. There are signs this may be occurring. Although the period is short, analysis of the experiences of the first eight FTI-endorsed countries indicates that progress has been made towards the benchmarks for teacher salaries, percentage of recurrent expenditure devoted to education, proportion of recurrent spending not devoted to salaries and average repetition rate (Umansky and Crouch, 2006). On the other hand, no progress has yet been recorded in pupil/teacher ratios and the proportion of total education expenditure devoted to primary education. A comparison of performance on several indicators between these eight countries and a control group of countries shows that gross enrolment ratios have increased more rapidly and there is some evidence of greater internal efficiency in the FTI countries.

Ultimately, however, efforts to improve the framework of the FTI and to increase its effectiveness will have a limited impact on EFA efforts unless donors undertake an aggressive,

There is evidence of greater internal efficiency in the FTI countries

high-level push to make the commitments required for FTI to become a fully global compact. Among changes this might require are (Sperling, 2006):

- commitment of funds for EFA in ways similar to those of the debt relief model, with debts automatically eliminated for countries that meet a specific set of obligations;
- more predictable and longer-term funding, including an expectation that current three- to five-year funding programmes will be rolled over if performance agreements are met;
- provision of funds, either through the FTI or bilaterally, for a quick response when governments take far-reaching steps such as abolishing fees, to ensure that the outcome is not dramatic increases in class size and decreases in quality of schooling;
- a need to embrace more consistently high-population countries such as India, Nigeria and Pakistan.

Global EFA coordination: the role of UNESCO

Each year the Report presents and comments on the activities of UNESCO in relation to its mandate to coordinate EFA. The 2006 Report suggested that the Executive Board's call for 'a concise global plan to achieve the EFA goals, including resource mobilization', through dialogue with the other convening agencies of the World Education Forum (Dakar), reflected high – and probably unrealistic – expectations (UNESCO, 2005). At the same time it pointed to opportunities to place EFA at the forefront of the international dialogue on development in the coming year: through advocacy at the 'Millennium+5' summit; by strengthening connections among UNESCO, the FTI, the E-9 countries and the High-Level Group; by exercising leadership in promoting good practices of technical cooperation and greater harmonization; and through ongoing initiatives in literacy, education for sustainable development, teacher training in sub-Saharan Africa, and HIV/AIDS and education.

Although activities are under way in each of these domains, UNESCO has yet to move into the central leadership position for EFA that was initially envisaged. The organization is generally trusted by developing country governments, yet its direct influence on the ability of countries to reach the EFA goals has been limited, including in capacity development, where one would have expected it to excel. An institutional reform programme now being implemented may reverse this situation. The reform aims to put EFA at the core of all UNESCO education activities and to strengthen UNESCO's field presence and orientation considerably by (a) decentralizing authority and resources to the field (especially the four existing regional bureaux, to which a fifth has been added in Bucharest for Europe and North America), (b) reducing overlap and providing clear accountability for topic areas and programmes, and (c) changing the internal organizational culture into one that generates openness and flexibility, in a context of clear alignment of programmes with institutional and global priorities. The outcome of the reform launched in June 2006 may determine whether UNESCO can become effective in two particular EFA-related areas in coming years: further development of a global action plan and regional EFA reviews.

The call for a global action plan by members of UNESCO's Executive Board in March 2005 emerged from a desire to increase coordination among stakeholders in the EFA movement, particularly those who convened the Dakar meeting in 2000: UNESCO, UNICEF, UNDP, UNFPA and the World Bank. In response, UNESCO initiated a consultative process aimed at harmonizing the approaches of these multilateral organizations in supporting the development and implementation of EFA national plans. To this end it has prepared an EFA Global Action Plan, which the heads of the four UN coordinating agencies for EFA, plus a World Bank representative, discussed in draft at a meeting of the United Nations Development Group Principals in July 2006. Support for the finalization of the plan was provided at the G8 submit in St Petesburg. A more fully developed version will be presented to the High-Level Group Meeting on Education for All in November 2006.

Overall, the plan is designed to achieve greater consistency at global level and provision of more effective support to EFA at national level. At its heart are the concept of 'one country, one plan'; a strategic focus on the countries having the greatest needs; a concern for the whole EFA agenda; and the intent to create a clear division of labour among international agencies in supporting national EFA plans and efforts. UNESCO's own contributions, in addition to convening the High-Level Group, the EFA Working Group, the E-9 meetings and other EFA-related gatherings, will be directed at literacy, education for work, teacher training, technology and learning outcomes. Activities will concentrate on capacity-building, monitoring and evaluation, and national planning processes. The global leadership roles for UNESCO include:

- supporting national leadership by reinforcing the role of its Education Sector as a clearinghouse of ideas and by strengthening its field operations to give better support to governments;
- promoting South-South cooperation, particularly through the E-9 countries, in the areas of teaching and learning best practices, innovative financing and innovations in information and communications technology; and through exploring potential donor support for this cooperation;
- coordinating activities to reduce national financial and capacity gaps of the countries least likely to achieve EFA;
- promoting policy analysis based on evidence and research by gathering, collating and disseminating information through headquarters staff and UNESCO institutes.

It is unclear whether the EFA Global Action Plan will result in greater interagency coordination or will mainly guide UNESCO's own future. In either case it will be important to reform the supporting international machinery as well, especially the High-Level Group, so that it becomes more action-oriented and less of a forum for general discussion whose outcomes cannot be monitored.

UNESCO has also signalled its intent to coordinate country assessments of progress towards the EFA goals halfway towards the target date of 2015. The Asia-Pacific Regional Bureau has begun monitoring country progress with a focus on 'reaching the unreached'. The Latin America and the Caribbean Regional Bureau will work within the framework of the Regional Project for Education in Latin American Countries (PRELAC), which plans to report in March 2007 on the relevance of educational services, equity and the right to education, effectiveness in achieving educational goals and management efficiency. The Caribbean is planning a regional EFA report by the end of 2007. Similarly, the Africa Regional Bureau expects to make a substantial review in 2007 focusing on the 'external efficiency of education'. These country assessments may prove very useful; however, it is not yet clear what incentives exist for countries to participate, as there has been no indication of how they might

UNESCO is preparing an EFA Global Action Plan

2007

Education for All Global Monitoring Report

benefit from the review findings. Finally, there is as yet no mechanism for bringing countries together to help set priorities at the global level, either for EFA in general or for UNESCO's programmes in particular.

$11 billion a year is needed

The most comprehensive and reliable basis for assessing the global cost of providing a quality universal primary education, and the requirements for external financial support, is the study by Bruns et al. (2003). By calculating the number of school age children to 2015, the inputs required to provide schooling for all of them and then assuming the increase in domestic resources that governments should be responsible for, the authors arrived at an estimate of US$3.7 billion per year, on average, as the additional external funding requirement for low-income countries.

An assessment of this study by the 2002 *EFA Global Monitoring Report* arrived at a significantly higher figure (UNESCO, 2002a). First, it was argued that the implicit annual growth rate of government education expenditure over the fifteen-year period used in the study was overly optimistic. In addition, extra resources would be required to (a) induce households to increase their demand for schooling for girls, and more generally for children from poorer households, by reducing the costs to them; (b) cope with the full impact of the HIV/AIDS pandemic on education systems, particularly in many sub-Saharan African countries; and (c) rehabilitate systems in countries affected by conflict, natural calamity and general instability. These considerations, the Report estimated, would require an extra US$3.1 billion a year of external finance bringing the annual total to US$6.8 billion.

The initial estimates used 2000 as the base year (UK Department for International Development, 2005). Between 2001 and 2004, additional ODA commitments to basic education in low-income countries were well below those required. To make up for this deficiency, from 2005 the annual level of external support would need to increase to around US$9 billion to 2015 (at 2003 prices). In addition, completion of a decent-quality primary education by every boy and girl does not cover all the EFA goals; allocating US$1 billion for each of the literacy and early childhood goals would result in an average annual external funding requirement of some US$11 billion.[9]

The share of basic education in total ODA for low-income countries will need to more than double

How realistic are these estimates? A partial check is provided by the education sector plans prepared for, and endorsed through, the FTI (FTI Secretariat, 2005). By 2008, the total required expenditure for primary education in the twenty plans currently endorsed is estimated at US$4.9 billion. On average, national governments expect to fund 76% of this domestically (the range is from 37% to 83%). The total external support required is estimated at US$1.2 billion annually. However, only three of these twenty countries have a population of over 20 million. The FTI expects twenty-five other countries to submit and obtain endorsement of their plans by the end of 2008. Their total annual external requirement is estimated at US$2.7 billion.

Of the twenty-seven remaining countries in the low-income category on the OECD-DAC list, several have very large populations (Bangladesh, India, Indonesia, Nigeria, Pakistan, Uganda, the United Republic of Tanzania and Zambia). Others, such as Côte d'Ivoire, Haiti, Somalia and Sudan, are in conflict or are regarded as 'fragile' in some way. The combination of several highly populated low-income countries with many whose educational infrastructure is in poor condition will translate into very large expenditure needs. These 'revised' estimates, then – at least US$9 billion a year to approach universal primary education in all countries by 2015, at least US$11 billion a year to progress towards the other EFA goals as well – appear conservative.

The share of basic education in total ODA for low-income countries will need to more than double if there is to be accelerated progress towards the goals. Such an increase will not occur automatically. As Figure 4.6 showed, education's share of total ODA that is allocated to sectors increased from 10.6% to 13.6% between 2000 and 2004. Over the same period, the share for basic education in the education sector's total allocation increased from less than one-third to about two-fifths. As a result, the amount for basic education in low-income countries in 2004 had increased significantly over previous years, but only to US$2.7 billion or about US$3.4 billion if half of all 'level unspecified' flows to the education sector and a portion of budget support are included. If, as recent international pledges suggest, the total amount of aid increases by 60% from its 2004 level by 2010, and the share to basic education remains constant, the total allocation for basic education will be US$5.4 billion, less than half of the US$11 billion estimated requirement.

9. The 2006 Report put the minimum number of illiterate adults at 771 million and estimated that making 550 million of them literate through programmes to 2015 would require around US$2 billion a year. Here we assume half of this would be financed by aid.

While the general outlook for an increased level of ODA is favourable, including the portion for supporting sector activities, the competition for it is increasing. This competition takes several forms. First, evidence in recent government poverty reduction programmes indicates that the emphasis on education, health, water and other social expenditure is increasingly accompanied by more focus on infrastructure and other activities regarded as contributing more directly to economic growth. Second, the emphasis on secondary and tertiary education is increasing. While attention has been given internationally to attainment of the EFA goals, several countries whose primary school completion levels are still low plan a major expansion of their secondary and tertiary subsectors. Almost half of bilateral aid to education is allocated to tertiary education already, though much of it is for scholarships to attend donor institutions.

The overall size of the financing gap and the increasing competition are not the only problems. While the multilateral development banks, the UN agencies and, to a lesser extent, the EC work almost exclusively with low-income countries, the bilateral donors, whose programmes constitute three-quarters of total ODA, distribute their resources very unequally. While some countries have ten or more active donors in the education sector, many more have two or fewer (Table 4.5), and the trend among bilateral donors is to reduce the number of countries in which they have programmes. Eight of the first twenty countries whose plans were endorsed by the FTI have a maximum of two donors. If bilateral donors continue directing their support to smaller numbers of countries, more resources must be channelled to the FTI Catalytic Fund, to some new mechanism with a global reach or to the multilateral agencies, if the aid that becomes available for education is to be used in the countries where the need is greatest.

The volatility and short-term nature of aid were discussed earlier. It is particularly important for governments to be able to count on the sustainability of resources to support their education sector initiatives. Countries need help to expand enrolments rapidly while at the same time providing the conditions that lead to lower dropout rates and higher learning achievement. Schools and other infrastructure need to be built *now*, teacher-training colleges need to be up and running *now*, curriculum reform and material design need to be undertaken *now*. The recent

United Kingdom commitment of US$15 billion for education over the next decade is encouraging. The gesture inspired the finance and education ministers of twenty African countries, meeting in Abuja, Nigeria, in June 2006, to develop ten-year education programmes by September 2006. Several have already been prepared for the FTI and, overall, it would probably be best to continue using the FTI rather than to develop new processes and mechanisms.

In addition to increased aid levels and more effective management of aid processes, more emphasis needs to be given to evaluating education activities and programmes supported by donors. For governments, it is in their interest to understand more systematically the nature, level and causes of changes resulting from expenditure. For donors, it is likely that their own citizens will increasingly demand evidence of results as increases in aid budgets are proposed.

Conclusion

At US$11 billion a year, the price tag for fulfilling the EFA agenda is higher than originally expected. Even if aid promises are met, the resources allocated for basic education will be inadequate if the current share of education in total aid and its distribution across levels and income groups are maintained, and further harmonization does not occur. The share of total aid going to basic education must at least double and be more focused on low-income countries rather than on middle-income ones. Aid modalities need to be further streamlined, and competition from the full Millennium Development Goals agenda and the infrastructure lobby addressed. Developing countries must demonstrate that their education sectors are capable of absorbing the aid required.

A closer alignment of donor activities with national programmes and other changes in the way aid is delivered are needed to minimize risks arising from growing aid dependence. The FTI continues to develop the frameworks to bring together credible education sector plans and additional external resources. Greater efforts will be needed internationally to convince donors to increase the volume and predictability of aid for basic education. Governments of low-income countries must be persuaded to give greater priority to education in their discussions with donors, and to allocate to it a greater share of the savings from debt relief. ∎

The price tag for the EFA agenda is US$11 billion a year

Education for All Global Monitoring Report

Nutrition makes for better learning: mealtime at a pre-school in Johannesburg, South Africa.

PART III. Early childhood care and education

Chapter 5

The compelling case for ECCE

The early childhood years set the foundations for life. Ensuring that young children have positive experiences, that their rights are guaranteed and that their needs for health, stimulation and support are met is crucial to their well-being and development. In a context where family and community structures are evolving and countries are going through rapid social and economic changes, early childhood programmes complement the roles of parents and other carers in raising children during the early years. After discussing the rights of children, this chapter reviews the evidence on the multiple benefits of early childhood programmes: easier transition to primary, better completion rates, reduced poverty, increased social equality and high economic returns. It makes the case for expanding and improving ECCE programmes in order to meet EFA goal 1.

2007

Education for All Global Monitoring Report

Early childhood in a changing world

All societies have arrangements for taking care of and educating their young children. These arrangements have evolved over time and are diverse across cultures, in keeping with differences in family and community structures, and the social and economic roles of men and women (Blumberg, 2006). However, current social and economic trends are disrupting many existing child care arrangements. In Central and Eastern Europe, and Central Asia, the transition from planned to market economies has led to the breakdown of institutions that took care of young children while their parents were at work. In developing countries, urbanization, work-driven migration and the increasing participation of women in the labour market are transforming family structures. The prevalence of nuclear families, in which fewer adults are available to take care of young children, is increasing, while extended families are declining. Armed conflict, the HIV/AIDS pandemic and environmental degradation have resulted in large numbers of orphans and, more generally, of families confronted with major difficulties in the upbringing of young children.[1]

Expanding and improving comprehensive early childhood care and education (ECCE), especially for the most vulnerable and disadvantaged children can help to meet these challenges. Early childhood programmes may include basic health and nutrition interventions, such as vaccination campaigns; parenting programmes, through which parents receive support and advice; and various centre-based activities, ranging from crèches for very young children to pre-primary schools that lay the foundations for primary schooling. They can help compensate for disruption of societal arrangements and ensure that young children's rights and interests are promoted; they can also contribute to the well-being of families and societies. Their aim should not be to substitute for the care provided by young children's primary carers – who may include parents and other family or community members – but to improve and supplement it when needed.

There is less consensus among policy-makers about the need for early childhood programmes than there is about the desirability of achieving universal primary education. Although the 738 million children aged 0 to 5 represented 11% of the world's population in 2005 (see Chapter 6),

> **Current social and economic trends are disrupting many existing child care arrangements**

early childhood programmes either are universal or cover at least two-thirds of the population in only a minority of countries, mostly developed and transition ones.[2] Moreover, some developed countries, notably the United States, do not provide for universal coverage. In many developing countries, especially those of sub-Saharan Africa, early childhood programmes are available only to a small fraction of the population, typically affluent urban families. For instance, the Democratic Republic of the Congo, with 12 million children aged 0 to 6, has only 1,200 pre-primary schools, and 60% of these are private schools located in the capital province of Kinshasa, where just 10% of the total population lives (Youdi, 2005).

This chapter makes the case for early childhood programmes. First, young children have rights, and early childhood programmes are one instrument to guarantee that these rights are respected. Second, research on human development emphasizes that young children have specific needs and that the extent to which these are satisfied affects the outcomes of their development into youth and adults. In this developmental perspective, participation in early childhood programmes is beneficial because it leads to improved outcomes, including better nutrition, health and education, in both the short and the long run. Moreover, from an economic point of view, investment in early childhood programmes offers a high pay-off in human capital and there is a strong case for public intervention. Early childhood programmes not only benefit children and families, they reduce social inequality, and benefit communities and societies at large. Most of the evidence presented in this chapter comes from programmes influenced by evolving perceptions of early childhood in Europe and North America; much more empirical research on programmes influenced by other traditions is needed.

Guaranteeing the intrinsic rights of young children

There are several human rights intruments specific to children's rights. In 1959 the United Nations General Assembly adopted the Declaration of the Rights of the Child. Although not legally binding, the Declaration affirms some of the most basic principles of children's intrinsic rights, including the provision of health care,

1. According to UNAIDS (2006), there were 15.2 million AIDS orphans aged 0 to 17 in 2005, 12 million of whom lived in sub-Saharan Africa.

2. It should be noted, though, that the regional gross enrolment ratio in pre-primary education for Latin America and the Caribbean is close to two-thirds at 62%.

housing, social security, education, and protection from neglect, cruelty and exploitation.

In 1989, the United Nations General Assembly adopted the Convention on the Rights of the Child (CRC), the most widely ratified human rights treaty in the world. As a legally binding instrument, the Convention marks the beginning of a new stage for children's rights during which new international standards need to be translated into domestic laws and practices.[3] The CRC has since served as an example for human rights documents such as the 1990 African Charter on the Rights and Welfare of the Child and the 1996 European Convention on the Exercise of Children's Rights.

The CRC rests upon four major interdependent principles:
- life, health and development (Articles 6, 24);
- non-discrimination (Article 30);
- consideration of the best interests of the child (Article 3);
- the right to be heard (Article 12).

The Convention emphasizes child well-being as well as child development and calls upon States Parties to assure that the views of children are given due weight in accordance with their age and maturity (Article 12). Children should be guided in a manner consistent with their 'evolving capacities' in the exercise of their rights (Article 5). The CRC emphasizes the right of all children to education and calls for primary education to be made compulsory and available free to all (Article 28). It also calls for parties to provide assistance to parents and legal guardians in their child-rearing responsibilities, and to make childcare services and facilities available, especially to working parents (Article 18) (OHCHR, 1989).

Providing ECCE of good quality is a powerful means of guaranteeing the rights of young children, especially those who are vulnerable and disadvantaged.

Using the Convention on the Rights of the Child to promote early childhood programmes

The CRC itself has few provisions specific to the youngest age group. Recently, however, a broader discussion has developed on how to apply child rights in early childhood. In 2005 the Committee on the Rights of the Child[4] put early childhood on its agenda, noting that young children have particular needs for nurturing, care and guidance. The working document that emerged (OHCHR,

2005) gives a clearer understanding of the human rights of all young children and the obligations of parties to fulfil them.[5] It gives a working definition of early childhood as from birth to age 8, encompassing 'all young children: at birth and throughout infancy; during the pre-school years; as well as during the transition to school'.

The committee warns in particular about discrimination against young children through such practices as inadequate feeding, selective abortion, genital mutilation and neglect. It also mentions discrimination against children with disabilities, infected or affected by HIV/AIDS, and on the basis of ethnic origin, class or caste (Paragraph 11, a and b). Parties are reminded of their obligation to develop comprehensive policies covering health, care and education for young children. The document also states that parties should provide assistance to parents and carers, including provision of parenting education, counselling and quality childcare services, backed up by monitoring systems (Paragraphs 20, 21) (OHCHR, 2005).

The working document specifies that early childhood education should be directly linked to children's right to develop their personalities, talents and mental and physical abilities from birth. Early childhood development programmes are among several activities to meet young children's right to education. These activities may be home- or community-based, or they may be pre-school programmes. They should allow for empowerment and education of parents and other carers.

The committee actively monitors national progress in children's rights, including those of early childhood (Box 5.1).

Tensions between a universal standard and culturally specific contexts

The CRC establishes a universal standard. While the CRC recognizes parents as having primary responsibility for their children, it also makes clear that parents are expected to give 'appropriate' direction to and guidance on children's active exercise of their rights. This has been interpreted by some to mean that parents are supposed to adapt their actions to reflect the rights of the child as coded in the CRC and that children's evolving capacity to exert autonomy over their lives and to exercise their rights has greater weight than the parents' right to decide what is best for the child.

The Convention on the Rights of the Child is the most widely ratified human rights treaty in the world

3. General Assembly Resolution 44/25 of 20 November 1989 adopted the convention, which entered into force on 2 September 1990, after ratification by twenty parties. Two optional protocols (on the sale of children, child prostitution and child pornography, and on the involvement of children in armed conflict) entered into force in 2004. As of May 2006, 192 countries and territories had ratified the CRC, the latest being Timor-Leste (2003).

4. The committee monitors implementation of the CRC, meeting three times a year to examine national reports. NGOs and national human rights institutions representing children's rights are encouraged to submit comments on the national reports.

5. A non-binding 'General Comment' called 'Implementing Child Rights in Early Education', it draws attention to rights and needs in early childhood and comments on the need to formulate policies, laws and practices that focus specifically on early childhood.

2007

Education for All Global Monitoring Report

Box 5.1: Monitoring progress in children's rights: Ghana's example

In 2005 and 2006, early childhood policies in Ghana were the focus of an exchange among the Government of Ghana, local NGOs and the Committee on the Rights of the Child. NGOs made a case for fundamental issues such as birth registration, data collection and effective administrative mechanisms for early childhood. The subsequent government report to the committee emphasized:

- improved data management for children's statistics, in particular through an increase in the number of assistants regularly visiting communities to register births and deaths;

- establishment of an Early Childhood Care and Development (ECCD) Policy and the formation of thirty-seven ECCD District Committees, along with a National Coordinating Committee playing an advisory role and coordinating implementation;

- inclusion of ECCD in mainstream basic education: the 2003 Strategic Plan of the Ministry of Education made pre-schools (starting from age 4) part of the Ghana Education Service and attached to every primary school.

The Ghana NGO Coalition on the Rights of the Child (2005) commented that:

- data in areas relevant to children's rights are inadequate or unavailable because systems for data collection, collation and analysis are not in place;

- an overlap in ministry mandates (e.g. both the Ministry of Women and Children's Affairs and the Ministry of Education contribute to early childhood policy-making) has the effect of delaying adoption of policy measures.

Finally, the Committee on the Rights of the Child, recommended that:

- Ghana should strengthen its system of data collection, e.g. by setting up an efficient birth registration system that covers the entire country and pays special attention to abandoned children and to asylum seeker and refugee children;

- budgetary allocations should be prioritized and increased, so that all levels of CRC implementation can be maintained;

- effective interministerial coordination of activities related to CRC implementation should be achieved (the committee noted that, at local level, capacity limitations on the part of district assemblies hamper implementation).

Sources: Committee on the Rights of the Child (2006*a*, 2006*b*, 2006*c*, 2006*d*); Ghana NGO Coalition on the Rights of the Child (2005); Republic of Ghana (2005*b*).

6. See Woodhead (2006), on which this section is based, for a critical account of the research, and Chartier and Geneix (2006) for a historical account of the development of early childhood programmes, linked to the evolution of the understanding of childhood in Europe.

The African Charter on the Rights and Welfare of the Child adds an extra dimension by imposing upon the child a duty to work 'for the cohesion of the family, to respect his parents, superiors and elders at all times and to assist them in time of need' (Organization of African Unity, 1990). A similar provision had been proposed for the CRC, but was rejected on grounds that the CRC was not an appropriate instrument through which to impose duties upon children (Alston et al., 2005).

The CRC also establishes a direct relationship between the child and the state. The state is empowered to intervene on behalf of the child if the child's best interests are at stake. Although the Convention has stressed the importance of the role of parents, some countries, including the United States, have objected to these provisions, arguing from a need to find a balance between children's and parents' rights on the one hand, and concern about public intrusion into the private domain on the other. Indeed, Somalia and the United States are the only signatory parties that have not ratified the CRC (Alston et al., 2005).

These examples reflect the difficulties of adopting a universal normative framework. Nevertheless, the near universal adoption of the CRC and its procedures of accountability through periodic monitoring by the United Nations give the CRC a status that few other international treaties can match. Despite its imperfections and its generalities, the CRC has undeniably helped shape policies to protect children's rights, including, most recently, those of early childhood.

Early childhood: a sensitive period

Children's physical and psychological development is shaped by their experiences during the first years of life. This intuitive idea has been amply confirmed by research. Indeed, there is a long history of philosophical and scientific interest in early childhood, and its impact on human development, in fields as diverse as biology, psychology, sociology, anthropology and economics, as well as in applied research on education, social policy, health, law and development studies.[6] A broad consensus has emerged among those who share this 'developmental perspective' on early childhood:

- Young children's physical, mental, social and emotional functioning differs from that of older children and adults, and comprises distinctive stages and milestones of development.

- Numerous progressive transformations occur in children's physical, mental, cognitive and socio-emotional facilities from earliest infancy to the beginning of schooling. These transformations mark the acquisition of skills and capacities, ways of relating, communicating, learning and playing.

■ Early childhood is the period when humans are most dependent on secure, responsive relationships with others (adults, siblings and peers) to assure not just their survival but also their emotional security, social integration, and cognitive skills.

■ Young children's development is especially sensitive to negative effects from early undernutrition, deprivation of care and of responsive parenting, and ill treatment.

■ If children's basic needs are not met, or they are maltreated or abused, the repercussions are often felt throughout childhood and into adulthood.

■ While early development can be summarized in terms of universal general principles, the development pathways vary and are linked to individual capacities and special needs, gender, ethnicity, and economic, social and cultural circumstances.

Neurobiology and other brain research fields have been especially influential in recent decades, as they have highlighted the role of the early years in the formation of the human brain (Center for Early Education and Development, 2002; Mustard, 2002, 2005). Brain cell connectors (synapses) form rapidly in the first few years of life: the density of synapses peaks at age 3, after which comes a plateau and then a period of elimination, when the density decreases to adult levels. Because of this pattern of synapse formation, the first three years of life are the most important for brain development. Moreover, research has shown that:

■ the overall environment (physical and emotional) within which the child is raised has an impact on brain development;

■ early exposure to toxic substances such as nicotine, alcohol and drugs can have devastating effects on the developing brain, particularly during pregnancy when the brain is being formed;

■ a negative experience or the absence of appropriate stimulation is more likely to have serious and sustained effects on a young child than on older children.

For very specific aspects of brain development, certain 'critical periods' exist before age 3, during which adequate stimulation must be received or development is impaired, in some cases permanently. For instance, the absence of a reasonable amount of light in the first weeks after birth alters the development of the visual system (e.g. development of binocularity is not possible).

Similarly, a child who never hears language, or receives extremely poor care (as in some orphanages), will likely suffer developmental deficits. Such effects have led some to envisage the first years of life as an extended critical period, a window of opportunity for development, closed by age 3.

Researchers still have much to learn, however, about the persistence of such effects and the ability of the brain to overcome them. Furthermore, the brain continues to grow and mature well into adolescence. Hence, the idea of a window of opportunity closing by age 3 is difficult to support. In general, although some critical periods do exist, the concept of 'sensitive periods' is more relevant to understanding early childhood (Bailey, 2002; Horton, 2001). Sensitive periods are times in development when the absence of some kind of stimulus results in development going awry. Sensitive periods are generally longer than critical periods and characterized by more flexibility in the timing of input or experience to the brain and in the brain's ability to learn and develop over time. Thus, it may never be too late to acquire a skill (as the notion of a critical period implies), but acquiring it early is preferable. For example, adults are certainly able to learn a second language, but it is less intuitive for them than for young children, and they typically do not learn it as well.

Early childhood programmes can enhance development

The understanding of early childhood as a time of sensitive periods leads naturally to the notion that early childhood programmes can supplement the care and education that young children receive at home, in their families and communities. Moreover, recent publications (France and Utting, 2005; Luthar, 2003; Masten, 2001) emphasize the flexibility and adaptability of humans, as well as their resilience to trauma. This implies that early childhood programmes can not only benefit all children but also compensate for young children's negative experiences as a result of conflict (within the family or society) and nutritional or emotional deprivation. To sum up, participation in comprehensive early childhood programmes of good quality can significantly alter the developmental trajectory of a child. Health, nutrition and education are areas where such benefits have been consistently identified.

The first three years of life are the most important for brain development

Good health and nutrition: building blocks for development

Young children are particularly fragile[7]. Reducing infant and child mortality has long been a key public health priority. Vaccination campaigns have reduced child mortality considerably, yet more than 10 million children aged 5 or under still die every year. More than half die from one of five transmittable diseases that can be prevented or treated: diarrhoea, pneumonia, malaria, measles and HIV/AIDS. (Box 5.2 discusses the impact of HIV/AIDS on young children.) Extending the provision of safe drinking water and proper sanitation would reduce infant and child mortality dramatically, especially when complemented by parenting programmes that facilitate improvements in breastfeeding and weaning practices. Whether formally classified as ECCE or not, measures designed to reduce mortality are certainly a first step towards establishing comprehensive early childhood programmes.

More than 10 million children aged 5 or under still die every year

The case for including health and nutrition components in early childhood programmes is broader than just assuring survival. For instance, undernutrition – severe or chronic lack of essential nutrients, resulting in height or weight below normal – impairs the development of large numbers of children. Undernutrition has a negative impact on cognitive development, including language skills, both in the short term and until adolescence or adulthood; on motor development; and on socio-emotional development.

Four types of intervention have been identified in rigorous experimental studies as having a major impact on outcomes such as attention, IQ (as variously defined) and language development. These are iron supplements, deworming, nutritional supplements and psychosocial stimulation of malnourished children. Their effects were measured in the short term and mostly in children who initially suffered from iron deficiency or undernutrition, rather than the

Box 5.2: HIV/AIDS's toll on young children

Each day 1,800 children become infected with HIV (UNAIDS, 2006). Children may contract HIV during the mother's pregnancy, labour, delivery or during breastfeeding. Other routes of infection are blood transfusion, use of contaminated syringes and needles, and sexual abuse. Children with HIV suffer from common childhood diseases more frequently than other children, with greater intensity and often with less responsiveness to drugs. Illnesses that are rarely fatal in healthy children cause high mortality in those with HIV. Without antiretroviral therapy, the disease progresses rapidly and 45% of HIV-infected children die before age 2. To reduce the impact of HIV infection, early diagnosis is required, and the child should receive good nutrition, appropriate immunizations and drug therapy for common childhood infections.

Research has documented the negative impact of HIV/AIDS on children's education:

● *Cognitive development:* research in high-income countries has demonstrated that HIV infections are associated with lower IQ and academic achievement, with weaker language skills in the late pre-school and early school-age years, and with poorer visual-motor functioning in older children. These consequences are due in part to the effects of HIV on cognitive development before children enrol in school. Studies including children from

infancy to school age find that such deficits in cognitive function can be reduced or reversed with antiretroviral therapy.

● *Socio-emotional development:* the adaptive behaviour (skills required for everyday activities) of children living with HIV improves after treatment.

● *School attendance:* evidence is increasing of the impact of the HIV/AIDS pandemic on children's schooling. Children from AIDS-afflicted families suffer from the stigma attached to the disease, with some turned away from school. Probably the greatest effect of the disease on children's education comes when one or both parents die. Few data exist on the impact of orphanhood on participation in early childhood programmes, but it is likely to be similar to that in primary school (see Box 3.3). Indeed, as user fees are more common for early childhood programmes than for primary schooling, the economic impact of parental death on school attendance may be greater.

Access to treatment is thus crucial for young children. Early childhood programmes can play a role in the fight against the pandemic through provision of treatment and through efforts aimed at including affected children and compensating for the emotional and other consequences of the disease.

Source: Jukes (2006).

7. This is based on Jukes (2006).

general child population. However, there is also evidence, from a smaller number of studies, of a long-term impact of pre-school health interventions on cognition. For example, a seminal study in Jamaica (Grantham-McGregor et al., 1991) found that the impact of psychosocial stimulation on cognitive ability could be traced until adolescence.

Nutrition and education reinforce each other

Combined nutritional and educational interventions are more likely to be successful than interventions that focus on nutrition alone. Studies in Guatemala and Viet Nam (Watanabe et al., 2005) found that nutrition packages had a much larger and longer-lasting impact on children receiving sufficient cognitive stimulation. An important implication is that, where health or nutrition problems commonly recur (for example, with seasonal variations in nutritional intake or disease transmission, or where communities are constantly exposed to diseases for which no simple preventive measures exist), educational interventions are as important as those for health.

Undernutrition has a negative impact on school participation and achievement. Studies in Pakistan (Alderman et al., 2001), the Philippines (Mendez and Adair, 1999) and the United Republic of Tanzania (Jukes, Forthcoming) have shown that stunted children (those who are short for their age) are less likely to enrol in school, and more likely to enrol later and to drop out. Poverty explains part of this correlation – children from poor families are more likely both to be undernourished and to remain out of school – but there is also a direct, causal impact of undernutrition on schooling. Parents of stunted children may consider them less mature and favour their healthier siblings instead in enrolment decisions. Stunted children may also find it more difficult to walk to school and, once there, may suffer from discrimination and stigma.

Given the links between health and nutrition, on the one hand, and education on the other, a holistic view of child development is gaining ground, with early childhood programmes designed to address both issues. For example, a programme providing iron supplementation and deworming treatment resulted in increased attendance at pre-schools in Delhi, India (Bobonis et al., Forthcoming). A pre-school feeding programme in Kenya had a similar impact (Vermeersch and Kremer, 2004).

ECCE participation improves primary school attendance and performance

The positive impact of ECCE programme participation on education at the primary level and beyond is well documented (Arnold, 2004; Bertrand and Beach, 2004; Mustard, 2005; Young, 1996, 2002)[8]. Such programmes can enhance physical well-being and motor development, social and emotional development, language development and basic cognitive skills. ECCE programmes can improve school readiness; make enrolment in the first grade of primary school more likely; reduce delayed enrolment, dropout and grade repetition; and increase completion and achievement. Effects of participation in ECCE programmes on the acquisition of both cognitive and non-cognitive skills have also been identified.

The most robust evidence comes from the evaluation of particular programmes in both developed and developing countries. Pre-school experience in the United Kingdom resulted in improved measures of intellectual development, independence, concentration and sociability during the first three years of primary schooling (Sylva et al., 2004). The benefits were higher the longer children participated in pre-school.

In a disadvantaged district of Nepal more than 95% of children attending an ECCE programme went on to primary school, compared to 75% of non-participants; the grade 1 repetition rate of participants was one-seventh that of non-participants; they had significantly higher marks on grade 1 exams (Arnold et al., 2000). The Turkish Early Enrichment Project in low-income, low-education areas of Istanbul, comprising parenting skills and pre-schooling, resulted in 86% of the children still being in school after seven years, compared with 67% for non-participants. Over the long run, participant children had higher school attainment, were more likely to attend university, began working at a later age and had higher occupational status (Kagitcibasi et al., 2001).

Participants in a Myanmar ECCE programme were more likely to enrol in primary school and had better exam results and test scores over the first three years of schooling (Lwin et al., 2004). Children who had attended pre-school in Kenya, Uganda and Zanzibar (in the United Republic of Tanzania) had better language skills than non-participants and achieved better results in school until grade 4 (Mwaura, 2005, 2006). Controlling for GDP, the higher an African country's pre-primary

A holistic view of child development is gaining ground

8. This is based on Arnold et al. (2006).

enrolment ratio, the higher its primary school completion rate and the lower its primary school repetition rate (Mingat and Jaramillo, 2003; Arnold, 2004). The impact of ECCE is stronger for children from poor families in terms of lower dropout and repetition rates than those for more advantaged children (Arnold, 2004).

The benefits of making young children ready for primary schooling through participation in early childhood programmes are further enhanced if primary schools recognize that pupils in the first two or three grades are still young children and adopt friendly teaching methods and curricula. Chapter 7 looks more closely at young children's school readiness and how primary schools can be made 'ready for children'.

Investing in early childhood pays off

ECCE programmes can thus result in improved health, nutrition and education outcomes, and these persist to some extent in the long term. From an economic perspective, therefore, it is natural to consider these programmes as

> The impact of ECCE is stronger for children from poor families

investments in human capital, and to try to compare their benefits with their costs. Are ECCE programmes profitable investments? How do they compare with other investments in human capital, notably those made at other levels of education?

Studies of the costs and benefits of specific programmes in the United States (Box 5.3) show that the returns to investment in ECCE programmes are positive. Indeed, they are higher than those of other educational interventions: the horizon over which the returns to ECCE investments are reaped is longer than for those targeting older children, youth or adults; and the skills acquired through participation in ECCE programmes are a foundation for further learning. This point has been made repeatedly in recent years by Nobel-winning economist James Heckman (2000, 2006; Heckman and Carneiro, 2003).

Comparably rigorous evaluations of early childhood programmes in developing countries are less available, but evidence has started accumulating over the past decade.[9] A pre-school health programme in Delhi increased average school participation by 7.7 percentage points

---

Box 5.3: Economic returns of ECCE programmes in the United States

Rigorous evaluation of the returns to investment in early childhood programmes requires longitudinal data (following programme participants over the long run) coupled with an intervention framework in which comparisons between participants and non-participants are not biased by selection effects. Much of the evidence cited in the literature comes from a small number of experiments conducted in the United States. The best known is the High/Scope Perry Preschool programme of 1962-67 in Ypsilanti, Michigan (Schweinhart et al., 2005). In the study, 58 of 123 low-income African-American children assessed to be at high risk of school failure were randomly assigned to a group that took part in a high-quality pre-school programme at ages 3 and 4; the remaining 65 children constituted a control group. All were assessed annually until age 11, and several times later in life, most recently at age 40. Comparisons between the programme and control groups suggest that participation in the programme led to increased IQ at age 5 (67% vs 28% above 90); enhanced success at school, including higher rates of graduation from secondary school (65% vs 45%); and higher earnings at age 40 (60% vs 40% earning more than US$20,000 a year). Detailed cost-benefit analysis suggests that the programme

cost US$15,166 per participant and yielded US$258,888 (in constant 2000 dollars) – a 17.1 : 1 benefit/cost ratio.

A major qualification is that this extremely high ratio is not representative of United States early childhood programmes in general. It pertains to a small-scale experiment conducted in the 1960s that provided very high-quality care and education to children with an especially disadvantaged social background. For example, 66% of the return consisted of 'crime savings', the costs of legal procedures and incarceration that were avoided because participants committed fewer offences than non-participants. Even excluding crime savings, however, the other public returns to the programme (education savings, welfare savings and increased taxes due to higher earnings) and the private returns were high enough to yield a 5.8 : 1 benefit/cost ratio.

Other thoroughly studied United States programmes include the Carolina Abecedarian Project (Barnett and Masse, forthcoming), the Chicago Child-Parent Centers (Temple and Reynolds, Forthcoming) and the Infant Health and Development Program (McCormick et al., 2006).

---

9. The following discussion is based on Jukes (2006).

for girls and 3.2 for boys (Bobonis et al., Forthcoming). With output per worker in India estimated at US$1,037, and the returns to each additional year of education for girls in India at 5% and boys at 9%, among other considerations, the Delhi programme would increase the net present value of lifetime wages by US$29 per child while costing only US$1.70 per child, or US$2.06 counting the US$0.36 per child for teacher wages necessitated by the additional demand for education that the health programme would entail. Thus, the return in the labour market would be US$14.07 per dollar spent.

Other developing country studies, though lacking experimental design, also suggest high returns. In Bolivia the Proyecto Integral de Desarrollo Infantil, a home-based programme of early childhood development and nutrition, had benefit/cost ratios between 2.4:1 and 3.1:1, with higher ratios for children from groups with high infant mortality, high malnutrition and low school enrolment (Van der Gaag and Tan, 1998). Other economic analyses in Colombia and Egypt find ratios of about 3:1, and the benefits in Egypt could be as high as 5.8:1 if ECCE programmes are targeted to children most at risk (Arnold, 2004).

In summary, while rigorous research (i.e. relying on experimental design and longitudinal data) on benefit/cost ratios for ECCE programmes is still limited, existing studies show high returns. United States programmes studied showed returns higher than those to other educational interventions. Evidence from developing countries also suggests strong returns but so far has been based on less rigorous analysis.

Early intervention can reduce inequalities

Even before quantitative evidence started accumulating on the impact of good quality early childhood programmes on child development, proponents of such programmes were concerned with the possibility of reducing social inequality. Their argument, now supported by research, is that intervention during the early years can compensate for vulnerability and disadvantage, regardless of underlying factors such as poverty, gender, race/ethnicity, caste or religion. Thus, the large United States public early childhood project Head Start was launched in 1964 as part of the 'War on Poverty' on the basis of theoretical work

challenging conventional class- and race-based beliefs about inherited abilities and pointing to the formative significance of the early years (Hunt, 1961). The underlying assumption was that targeted intervention could compensate for less favourable family and community background. This premise has since been empirically verified.

The High/Scope study cited in Box 5.3 is an example of a programme that helped level the playing field for disadvantaged children as they entered primary school. Other United States studies demonstrating that the benefits of early childhood programmes are higher for marginalized children include the STAR experiment in Tennessee (Krueger and Whitmore, 2001, 2002). Although most studies in developing countries have not used experimental design, research in such diverse places as Cape Verde, Egypt, Guinea, Jamaica and Nepal have consistently found that most disadvantaged children benefit from ECCE programmes.[10]

Early childhood programmes can also reduce gender inequality. In some cases, the impact of participation on health has been found to be higher for girls than for boys (Jukes, 2006); indeed, early childhood programmes can compensate for the priority that is given to boys in access to basic health care in some societies. Similarly, girls who participate in early childhood programmes are much more likely to begin school at the appropriate age and complete primary school than girls who do not (Arnold, 2004). Among Nepalese children who took part in an ECCE programme, an equal proportion of girls and boys began first grade, compared with 39% of girls and 61% of boys who did not participate (Arnold et al., 2000). Access to early childhood programmes is relatively gender-equal in a majority of countries (see Chapter 6).

It is important to preserve this equality, especially when scaling up projects that have previously reached mostly families of privileged backgrounds. Above all, the impact of early childhood programmes on gender inequality depends on how children are socialized in these programmes, and on pedagogy and curriculum (see Chapter 7).

The differential impact of ECCE programmes on the disadvantaged, whether poor children or girls, is an important argument for targeting programmes, especially when resources are constrained. Yet, targeting can be controversial. It is not always free of the patronizing idea that the poor cannot raise their children satisfactorily,

Early childhood programmes can also reduce gender inequality

10. See Arnold (2004) for a review.

or of the belief that science-based social engineering alone can solve the political issues that generate vulnerability and disadvantage. However, there is much scope for levelling the playing field through universal programmes providing the same health and nutrition services, educational experiences and socialization to all young children, whatever their social backgrounds.

Whether countries focus on targeted interventions or aim for universal ECCE coverage probably depends on political and cultural factors (see Chapter 8). Whatever the policy, there is consistent evidence that the benefits of early childhood programmes are high for vulnerable and disadvantaged children, facilitating the reduction of social inequality. Indeed, many of the studies documenting the benefits, including several mentioned above, stem from policies or experiments intended to support young children from disadvantaged backgrounds. As James Heckman observes: 'it is a rare public policy initiative that promotes fairness and social justice and at the same time promotes productivity in the economy and in society at large. Investing in disadvantaged young children is such a policy' (Heckman, 2006: p. 2).

It is time to devote increased attention to ECCE

Conclusion

This chapter has reviewed the benefits of early childhood programmes. It concludes that the case for 'expanding and improving comprehensive early childhood care and education, especially for the most vulnerable and disadvantaged children', in the words of EFA goal 1, is compelling: programmes of high quality have the potential to improve the health and nutrition of young children, to prepare them for elementary schooling, to guarantee that their rights are respected and to reduce inequality. Clearly it is time to devote increased attention to ECCE. Chapter 6 reviews its provision around the world and Chapters 7 and 8 look at the way ECCE programmes are designed, function and managed, while also examining the broader policy frameworks in place for achieving goal 1. ■

Early days in a state-run kindergarten in Budapest, Hungary, 1948.

© David Seymour / Magnum Photos

PART III. Early childhood care and education

Chapter 6

Worldwide progress in early childhood care and education

This chapter first examines the changing contexts – smaller households, more working women, maternity benefits, new gender roles – in which the provision of care and education for young children has historically evolved. It then assesses national progress towards the ECCE goal for three groups: children under age 3, those between age 3 and the primary school entry age, and vulnerable and disadvantaged children. Finally, the chapter characterizes the type, composition and professional status of the carers and educators in ECCE programmes. Among the chapter's main findings: many countries lack programmes addressing the diverse needs (health, nutrition, care, education) of children under 3; few countries have established national frameworks to coordinate ECCE programmes; access to pre-primary education has expanded worldwide, but coverage in sub-Saharan Africa and the Arab States remains low; and children from poorer and rural households enjoy fewer ECCE opportunities than those from richer and urban ones.

2 0 0 7

Education for All Global Monitoring Report

Households, children and early childhood provision

How countries provide for the care and education of young children varies greatly and cannot be neatly organized into a succinct typology. Rather, as a result of historical processes, diverse child care arrangements and education programmes have developed in each country and region. Changes in household structures, fertility levels and the social roles of women have been especially influential in shaping ECCE provision.

Changing household and family structures

Households and families are the first organizers of the care and upbringing of their young offspring. Since the 1850s, the average household size in Europe and North America has fallen by half, reaching 2.5 to 3.0 members in recent years. The numbers of both children and adults per household have decreased because of lower fertility rates and a trend away from more complex household structures towards the nuclear family. Surveys carried out in forty-three developing countries during the 1990s showed average household sizes ranging from 4.8 members in Latin America to 5.6 in the Middle East and North Africa (Bongaarts, 2001).

Changes in household size also reflect changes in their composition. The larger the household, the less likely it will be a nuclear family and, once it exceed 5.5 members, the lower will be the ratio of adults to children. As well as size and composition, a key factor is whether the adults work outside the home. When children under age 6 are raised in households where all working-age adults are employed, the availability of other household members becomes critical to the provision of early childhood care (Heymann, 2002).

Another change is the growing number of single-parent, especially mother-headed, households. In the European Union, for example, the number of single-parent families grew by 58% between 1983 and 1996, and in some countries (e.g. Ireland and United Kingdom) it doubled (Prud'homme, 2003). In every Latin American country, the incidence of female-headed households in urban areas rose during the 1990s (Chant, 2004). Throughout much of sub-Saharan Africa, surveys point to declines in marriage rates and the growing prevalence of single motherhood (Mookodi, 2000). The

nature and patterns of parent-child interactions in households headed by single mothers may differ from those in two-parent households in ways that have implications for the children's future development.

The changing demographics and regional diversity of young children

The number of young children below primary school entrance age defines the potential demand for early childhood programmes.[1] Between 1970 and 1990 the world's population aged 0 to 5 increased from 617 million to 744 million. It then slowly declined and stands now at 738 million. Another increase is projected, however, and by 2020 it is expected to reach 776 million (Table 6.1). In the developed and transition countries, as well as the East Asia and Pacific region, declines in the early childhood population were already evident in the 1970s. In Latin America and the Caribbean and, to a lesser extent, in South and West Asia, the population of young children has stabilized. By contrast, in sub-Saharan Africa and the Arab States their number continues to grow, although at a more moderate pace since 1990.

The stabilization and, in some cases, decline of the early childhood population reflect both lower fertility levels and higher mean ages at first marriage, which are influenced by growing family planning provision, women's participation in the labour force and the rise in their levels of educational attainment. UN population projections indicate that moderate growth or decline in the early childhood population will continue in coming decades, except in sub-Saharan Africa, where the number of young children is expected to increase by 35 million by 2020.

The changing demographics of early childhood can be viewed not only in absolute terms, but also as the share of the total population (Table 6.2). Worldwide, the ratio of children below age 6 to the total population has decreased from 17% in 1970 to 11% today.[2] This decrease is apparent in all regions, and notably in East Asia and the Pacific where the relative share of the early childhood population declined from 19% to 9% as fertility levels dropped sharply in urban areas of China. Less pronounced decreases occurred in all other developing regions except sub-Saharan Africa, where the share remained virtually unchanged at about one young child per five inhabitants.

Changes in the social roles of women have been influential in shaping ECCE

1. In three-quarters of 203 countries and territories the official entrance age for primary education is 6 or earlier; in one-quarter of countries children begin school at 7 (in one case, 8). Especially in poorer countries where intake rates to primary education are low and pre-school provision limited, children under 6 are the main target population of ECCE programmes. Although the *EFA Global Monitoring Report* defines 'early childhood' as spanning ages 0 to 8, this chapter focuses on the 0 to 5 group as reflecting the normative age span before entry into primary education.

2. The early childhood share of the total population is affected by increased longevity. As adults live longer, even if more children are being born, the proportion of young children in the total population may stabilize or decline.

Table 6.1: Change in population aged 0 to 5 since 1970 with projections to 2020 and regional distribution

	Population aged 0 to 5 (millions)							
						Projections		
	1970	1980	1990	2000	2005	*2010*	*2015*	*2020*
World	617	646	744	735	738	755	774	776
Developed and transition countries	108	103	105	88	87	88	88	86
Developing countries	509	543	639	646	650	667	686	690
of which:								
Sub-Saharan Africa	63	84	110	135	147	161	173	182
Arab States	26	34	42	44	47	49	51	52
East Asia and the Pacific	222	194	216	188	175	173	177	174
South and West Asia	141	173	199	205	206	214	217	215
Latin America and the Caribbean	54	62	67	68	68	68	67	66

Note: In Tables 6.1 and 6.2, data for East Asia and the Pacific refer to developing countries only; Australia, Japan and New Zealand are included in the developed country category. The total for developing countries is higher than the sum of the five regions because it also includes data for Bermuda, Cyprus, Israel, Mongolia and Turkey.
Source: UN Population Division (2005).

Table 6.2: The share of children aged 0 to 5 in the total population worldwide and by region, 1970–2020

	Population aged 0 to 5 (percentage of total population)							
						Projections		
	1970	1980	1990	2000	2005	*2010*	*2015*	*2020*
World	17	15	14	12	11	11	11	10
Developed and transition countries	10	9	9	7	7	7	7	6
Developing countries	19	16	16	13	13	12	12	11
of which:								
Sub-Saharan Africa	21	22	21	20	20	19	18	18
Arab States	21	21	19	16	15	14	13	13
East Asia and the Pacific	19	14	13	10	9	8	8	8
South and West Asia	19	18	18	15	13	13	12	11
Latin America and the Caribbean	19	17	15	13	12	11	11	10

Note: See Table 6.1.
Source: UN Population Division (2005).

Worldwide, the ratio of children below age 6 to the total population has decreased from 17% in 1970 to 11% today

Women's employment, child-rearing and child care

Most cultures have defined child-rearing and child care as women's work and belonging to the family sphere. The compatibility of woman's productive activities with child care responsibility varies by economic system (Blumberg, 2006). In many households worldwide the care of young children is organized with the help of female kin or friends. Like mother-centred child-rearing, such care arrangements are informal.

Since the 1950s a growing number of women in developing and developed countries have become economically active. In 2005 the labour force participation rates for women were over 55% in East Asia, South-East Asia and sub-Saharan Africa, and about 50% in Latin America and the Caribbean (ILO, 2004). They were considerably lower in South Asia (35%) and the Arab States (28%). Increases in women's non-agricultural employment have mainly occurred in certain labour market sectors – e.g. clerical, retail and other services – in relatively low-status, insecure jobs. In professional and managerial positions, including positions of political authority, gender discrimination continues. Thus, women are overrepresented in non- and semi-professional work and receive lower salaries than men, in both developed and developing regions. In addition, a substantial percentage of women work in the informal sector, in which steady employment, job promotions and social security are tenuous at best (ILO, 2006a).

Mothers continue to be the major direct providers of care to children

Comparative time-use surveys carried out since the mid-1990s show that, while women work more hours than men, their work tends to be in less visible, non-market activities (including child care), so the monetary value of their economic contribution to the household is less (UNDP, 2002, 2005). Moreover, in some countries (e.g. Singapore, Thailand), young women are expected to relinquish a significant portion of their wages to their parents. These patterns illustrate the complex status of economically active women whose activities are embedded in strong family networks.

Despite their increased work-related activity, mothers continue to be the major direct providers of care to children. Fathers and other men have typically had limited involvement in the care and upbringing of young children. Recently established parental leave policies (see below) seek to redress this situation and to enhance fathers' roles as carers.

In more developed countries, higher rates of female labour force participation are strongly associated with higher enrolment ratios in pre-school programmes. In developing countries, however, the association between female employment patterns and pre-primary education is weaker (O'Connor, 1988). In contexts where most mothers work in agriculture, they tend to rely on other women in the community (aunts, grandmothers, co-wives and daughters) for child care support. In response to the predominantly male migration to urban centres in some countries, women have had to increase both their farming and domestic responsibilities. This additional work rarely allows women time to explore care and education options for children who in any case may now be needed more than ever at home. In some cases the feminization of farming is associated with an increase in child labour.

Equally important to mothers' increased economic activity is the impact on early childhood of their relative control over economic resources. The greater the woman's relative economic power and the level of adult gender equality within the family, the more likely that children's welfare will be considered a priority in household decisions and that boys and girls will benefit equally from early childhood provision (Blumberg, 2006).

Overall, historical patterns suggest that mothers who work in the informal sector or who possess less economic power rely on relatives for child care or keep children with them during working hours. In such contexts, the welfare of male children often takes precedence over that of female children. Mothers with jobs in the formal sector, by contrast, are more apt to know about, and use, a wider range of options to assure their young children's welfare. They are also more likely to use structured early childhood services, where available, and to treat boys and girls equally.

Maternity and parental leave policies supporting infant care

Historically, maternal and parental leave policies have enhanced the care and well-being of infants. Laws on maternity leave, initially linked to employment provision for sick leave, were first enacted more than a century ago to protect the health of working women and their babies at the time of childbirth.[3] Supporters of maternal leave argued that relieving women of workplace pressure for a brief time before and after childbirth, while protecting their economic situation, would promote the physical well-being of both mothers and children.

Paid maternity leave was first established in Germany under Bismarck as part of a broad enactment of social insurance policies. By the First World War, thirteen countries had paid maternity leave policies and eight others had legislated unpaid maternal leave (Gauthier, 1996). By the 1970s, all major industrialized countries except Australia, Austria, Switzerland and the United States had enacted laws providing maternity leave during which all or part of the worker's wages were replaced by benefits. In some cases paid leave was supplemented by longer unpaid leave (or an extension at a lower payment level). Statutory leave was initially provided to mothers employed in certain occupations; later, coverage was extended to other occupations and, in some countries, to informal sector workers and the unemployed.[4]

The International Labour Organization (ILO) played an important role in promoting maternal leave policies (ILO, 1980, 1985). In 1919, the ILO adopted its first Maternity Protection Convention, which was significantly revised in 1952 and 2000. The first convention applied to all women working in industry and commerce,[5] and stipulated entitlement to a maternity leave of twelve weeks (six before and six after childbirth, the latter being compulsory). The convention stated that while on leave women should receive a cash benefit that

3. For more information, see Kamerman (2000*b*), Berkowitch (1999) and US Social Security Administration (2004). See Moss and Deven (1999) about developments in the European Union.

4. Maternity leave provisions resulting from collective bargaining or provided voluntarily by employers may supplement statutory provisions and raise the benefit level or extend the leave's duration, or both.

5. In 1954, the convention was extended to women working in agriculture as well.

would be at least two-thirds of their wage. The ILO reported that women had access to paid maternity leave in fifty-nine countries by 1960 and in more than a hundred countries by the 1980s (ILO, 1980, 1985). In 1999 a survey by the International Social Security Association reported that 128 countries of the 172 responding had some type of maternity leave provision (US Social Security Administration, 1999).[6] During the 1960s and 1970s, the trend in most OECD countries was towards longer and more generous maternity leaves, with benefits replacing all or most of women's wages. The current situation of maternal leaves in developing countries is examined later in this chapter.

In 1974 Sweden introduced parental leave, which enabled either the mother or the father (at the couple's discretion) to take time off from work. Other Nordic countries later followed suit. Transition countries also have paid, job-protected parental leave, as well as extended child-rearing leave with varying benefit levels. Compared to most OECD countries, the duration of these leaves is long – e.g. three years in Hungary and Slovakia, four years in the Czech Republic.

Not all leave policies were designed to meet the needs of working mothers or parents. In quite a few countries (e.g. Armenia, Georgia, Poland and Uzbekistan, and, to some extent, Austria, Finland and Germany), paid leave policies were designed to encourage low-skilled women to withdraw from the labour force during periods of high unemployment. In many cases these policies included subsidized home care of infants and toddlers by their mothers, rather than investment in more costly centre-based care (Kamerman and Kahn, 1991).

The emergence and formalization of early childhood provision

Europe and North America

Beginning in the nineteenth century European and North American countries started to organize more formal arrangements to care for, socialize and educate young children. The formalization of early childhood provision evolved in response to multiple challenges, notably:

- addressing the needs of abandoned, deprived or neglected children and the children of poor working mothers;
- providing an enriching pre-school education for middle-class children;
- providing a safe and affordable environment for the children of working women.

More recently, a fourth challenge has been added: to prepare young children for primary schooling. This objective, which necessarily implies a need for qualified professionals and state accreditation, could emerge only after the basic needs of most children (food, safety and care) were regularly met (Chartier and Geneix, 2006).

Until the eighteenth century, the only institutions involved in early childhood education were churches, which condemned infanticide and set up charitable orders to take in, baptize and raise abandoned children or orphans. Noting the marked improvement in such children's life expectancy compared with those not thus sheltered (who often died within their first year), public authorities in some European countries organized limited health care for abandoned children, and placed them with rural families, generally until about the age of 13 (Jablonka, 2006). Few, if any, institutions catered to the whole of early childhood until bottle-feeding made wet nurses unnecessary in the mid-nineteenth century. Day nurseries welcomed abandoned or sick children, whereas crèches (*nido* in Italy, *Krippe* in Germany and 'nursery' in England) offered day care to healthy children (Chartier and Geneix, 2006).

In Europe, emergent approaches to early childhood education became embodied in model institutions founded by well-known educators. Examples include J. H. Pestalozzi and the Yverdon Institute (1805-1815), Andrew Bell and Joseph Lancaster's monitorial system (1798-1810), the infant school founded by Robert Owen in Scotland (1816), Friedrich Fröbel's Kindergarten at Blankenburg (1837) and the *scuole infantili* of Father Ferrante Aporti at Cremona (1828). During the twentieth century, several exemplary institutions catering to young children – the Casa dei Bambini of Maria Montessori in Rome (1909), Ovide Decroly's École de l'Ermitage in Brussels, Roger Cousinet and Jean Piaget's Maison des petits in Geneva and A. S. Neill's famous Summerhill School – attracted educators from near and far. They focused almost exclusively on well-cared-for children above the age of 3 – that is, clean, weaned children who could walk, talk and feed themselves (Chartier and Geneix, 2006).

The development of early childhood institutions throughout the nineteenth century in different parts of Europe reflected salient historical forces: industrialization, demand for

In Europe, model institutions were founded by well-known educators

6. Sixteen weeks was the average basic paid leave, typically including six to eight weeks before and after childbirth. In almost half the countries the cash benefit replaced the full wage (or the maximum covered under social insurance). With some variation in benefit levels, this is the standard for maternity policies in the EU. In ninety-five of the countries (including all European ones), health and medical care is provided. Increasingly, in Europe, adoption is covered as well.

Maternal and parental leave policies were developed to accommodate a mother's right to care for her child

women workers, debate over ideological and political issues (e.g. custodial care vs early learning, provision for specific social classes vs all children). A great variety of early childhood institutions took root. For example, *garderies* in France, *écoles gardiennes* in Belgium, *Spielschule* in Germany, *speelscholen* in the Netherlands, 'dame schools' in Great Britain and *scuole delle maestre* in Italy provided basic care for the youngest children. Other schools, initially established by charitable, religious or philanthropic institutions, organized educational activities for young children. Examples include 'infant schools' in the United Kingdom, *salles d'asile* in France, *Kleinkinder-Bewahranstalen* in Germany, *bewaarscholen* in the Netherlands, *escuelas de párvulos* in Spain and *scuole infantili* in Italy. Many such schools were eventually taken over by government authorities. Non-religious kindergartens, supported by liberal or progressive movements, dispensed with early learning and emphasized free play, while targeting children from all social backgrounds (Chartier and Geneix, 2006).

In the United States early childhood institutions were rooted in two developments: day nurseries (equivalent to today's child care or day care centres), first established in the 1830s under voluntary auspices and designed to care for the 'unfortunate' children of working mothers; and nursery schools, developing from the early education programmes established in Massachusetts in the 1830s and the later kindergarten programmes based on the work of Fröbel. Day nurseries – custodial in nature, and providing basic child care and supervision – became more numerous in the latter part of the nineteenth century due to rapid industrialization and massive immigration. Kindergartens and nursery schools slowly became more common during the nineteenth century, and their numbers underwent a significant increase in the 1920s as demand grew for a form of enriched experience for middle-class children (Kamerman and Gatenio Gabel, 2003; Kamerman and Kahn, 1976).

During and after the Second World War, countries in Europe and North America began to reconsider the traditional role of early childhood policies and programmes (Berkovitch, 1999). In addition to providing protection for neglected children and enriching the education of middle-class children, a third focus took shape. It revolved around the growing number of women in the formal labour force who wanted decent,

affordable care for their young children. Increasingly, pre-schools were redesigned to adapt to the needs of working parents by providing basic child care during the workday and workweek (Kamerman, 2005). In some cases, governments facilitated increased female labour force participation by developing a standard public pre-school system. Maternal and parental leave policies (as noted above) were developed to accommodate a mother's right to care for her child. In Sweden, women's increased participation in the labour force drove a significant expansion of child care in the late 1970s, which in turn reduced the gender employment and wage gaps (OECD, 2005a). By the end of the twentieth century, the model of the public nursery school as a place offering education for children from all backgrounds and run by highly qualified professionals, had won the day everywhere, with allowances for national specificities (timetables, levels of state intervention and the organization of activities).

Thus, the overarching historical pattern – in Europe and North America, at least – is the movement from private charity, beginning in the nineteenth century, to public responsibility, evolving largely after the Second World War. Although the extent of public responsibility varied by country, a key distinguishing factor in most was the relative policy emphasis given to custodial care of disadvantaged children of working mothers, on the one hand, and education and socialization of all children, on the other.

Developing countries

The existence of early childhood programmes in developing countries is more recent (typically since 1970) and has involved different rationales than in Europe. As the basic needs of so many young children were not being met, many developing countries and aid agencies emphasized infant and child health, poverty reduction, safe and affordable environments for childminding, and the transition to primary schooling.

The formalization of early childhood provision shows considerable regional variation. Most African countries developed an early childhood paradigm based on age segmentation: care programmes for those under age 3 and education from 3 to compulsory school age. Centre-based provision developed for the older group (though covering only a small percentage of children) while younger children continued to be cared for by parents or kinship networks. In some post-colonial countries, pre-schools retained the structure established by the former colonial power, supplemented with national elements. In post-independence Morocco, for example, *kuttabs* (Koranic schools) survived as a source of early learning for boys aged 4 to 7 (Chartier and Geneix, 2006).

Throughout the Caribbean, services and supports for young children evolved in common ways. Health issues related to birth and immunization were considered the traditional responsibility of governments, while early childhood provision in all other areas relied upon the initiative of concerned citizens and/or organizations such as UNICEF, the Bernard van Leer Foundation and religious institutions. Except in Barbados, Grenada, and Saint Kitts and Nevis, the predominance of private or charitable initiatives is the defining feature of early childhood programmes in the subregion (Charles and Williams, 2006).

Latin America had few early childhood programmes before 1970. Governments historically took little interest in child care or pre-primary education and relied on private organizations (Myers, 1983). Pre-schools mainly served the children of urban households, and the upper and middle classes. However, beginning in the 1970s pressures to expand access to early childhood education grew steadily, with many governments initiating and expanding formal programmes for for 3- to 5-year-olds (UIS, 2001).

The Asia and Pacific region demonstrates considerable diversity. In the decades following the Second World War, early childhood programmes were relatively undeveloped. In East and South-East Asia, pre-primary education expanded slowly, mainly in urban and affluent areas, and was delivered by private providers. Children from poor and socially marginalized families were largely excluded from institutionalized ECCE (Kamerman, 2005).

What historical international surveys tell us
Three surveys sponsored by UNESCO, in 1961, 1974 and 1988, provide comparative historical information on early childhood provision. The first, synthesizing results from sixty-five countries, reported that while pre-primary education rarely sought to 'undermine or usurp' the primacy of parental or family care, new programmes to accommodate working women were multiplying. Pre-schools were expensive

to establish and operate; in some contexts, disadvantaged children received priority access. Qualified pre-primary teachers, often suffering from low status, were in short supply in all countries (UNESCO-IBE, 1961).

The 1974 survey broadened the definition of pre-schools to include day nurseries, kindergartens, residential nurseries, children's homes, educational centres, special institutions for handicapped children and religious institutions (Mialaret, 1976). More than half of the seventy-eight countries responding had pre-school programmes for 2-year-olds and nearly all had programmes for 3-year-olds. Coverage was limited and uneven in most developing countries. Many authorities, both government and non-government, were involved in pre-school education, and evidence of national coordination of programmes was limited. The survey also provided a four-category classification of pre-school education: (1) state institutions administered by ministries, typically the ministry in charge of education; (2) private institutions organized by individuals, small groups, officially recognized associations or religious organizations; (3) institutions administered by local or provincial authorities; and (4) semi-private institutions run by an individual, group or association, but under government supervision.

The 1988 survey, based on responses from eighty-eight countries, focused for the first time on ECCE programmes[7] and identified five types of institutions: kindergartens, nursery schools, ECCE institutions attached to primary schools, day care centres and others.[8] About half the countries reported having kindergartens; about 40% had institutions attached to primary schools. Half the ECCE programmes charged fees and two-thirds provided a full day's programme to meet the needs of working mothers (Fisher, 1991).

Overall, the twentieth century saw a significant expansion of early childhood programmes, many initiated and sustained by private agencies and charitable groups. Not only was there a substantial increase in the number of young children spending time in non-parental care (nurseries or child care centres), but more children participated in structured, purposeful learning activities both before and, more typically, after age 3. Programmes involving the latter age group – known as pre-school education, kindergarten or early childhood education – came to be labelled as pre-primary education corresponding to ISCED level 0 (UNESCO, 1997).[9]

The twentieth century saw a significant expansion of early childhood programmes

7. The survey defined ECCE programmes as those providing care and/or education for children from birth until age 6 or 7 (entry age for primary education) in a variety of institutions and settings, some organized by ministries, others by NGOs.

8. Crèches, *pouponnières*, pre-schools, play groups, institutions serving sick or disabled children, institutions combining health and education components, Koranic schools, India's *anganwadi* centres and so forth.

9. Pre-primary education is defined as 'programmes at the initial stage of organized instruction, primarily designed to introduce very young children, aged at least 3 years, to a school-type environment and to provide a bridge between home and school'. Variously referred to as infant education, nursery education, pre-school education, kindergarten or early childhood education, such programmes are the more formal component of ECCE. Upon completion of these programmes, children continue their education at the primary level (see glossary).

Country progress towards EFA goal 1

The data and monitoring challenge

The diversity of arrangements for organizing and funding ECCE programmes represents a formidable challenge in monitoring the ECCE goal. Box 6.1 describes recent work to compile cross-country information on early childhood provision.

It is not easy to assess national progress towards the ECCE goal:

■ The goal contains no benchmarks or quantitative targets for monitoring progress (or the lack thereof).

■ National reports on the nature and quality of early childhood provision are less standardized than those on education, since they typically involve a multiplicity of non-government actors and government authorities, and they cover children of different ages yet lack disaggregated age data.

■ Few countries compile information on 'other early childhood programmes,' even though

this category was meant to supplement data on 'pre-primary' education.[10]

■ Reporting frameworks exclude information on parental education, although this is an important element of the overall goal.

Ideally, national reports on early childhood provision should include detailed information about where and with whom young children spend their days. They also should provide information about the quality of children's care and educational experiences, assessed over time if possible. Some of this information is captured in the results of the cross-national IEA Pre-primary Project.[11] Similar studies need to be conducted more extensively.

At present, international figures on the education component of the ECCE goal remain uneven and, at times, non-comparable. More importantly, indicators of the care component of the goal (e.g. attention to health and nutrition as well as cognitive, social and emotional development) are almost completely lacking. Not surprisingly, given these reporting challenges, the *EFA Global Monitoring Report* (including Chapter 2 of this Report) has monitored progress towards the ECCE goal by relying on measures related to pre-primary institutions. Sustained efforts to augment and improve existing ECCE data are needed (see Chapter 9).

The 2000 Dakar Framework for Action (paragraphs 30 and 31) articulated several core components of early childhood programmes. They should be 'appropriate to [the children's] age and not mere downward extensions of formal school systems' and 'comprehensive, focusing on all of the child's needs and encompassing health, nutrition and hygiene as well as cognitive and psycho-social development.' The Dakar Framework also noted the importance of 'the education of parents and other caregivers in better child care, building on traditional practices, and the systematic use of early childhood indicators'.

To address these issues, this chapter expands reporting on the monitoring of the ECCE goal in three ways: by looking separately at three groups of children (those under 3, those between 3 and primary school age, and vulnerable and disadvantaged children); by expanding the number and type of indicators used to monitor progress in relation to each group of children; and by paying greater attention to the care component of early childhood provision.

10. 'Other ECCE programmes' refers to non-formal development programmes designed for children from age 3 that include organized learning activities spanning, on average, the equivalent of at least 2 hours per day and 100 days per year. This category emerged from decisions following the Dakar forum and underscored the need to develop additional measures for monitoring ECCE provision. Data on 'other ECCE programmes', which began to be compiled in 2000, are still missing for many countries.

11. See Olmsted and Montie (2001). The countries in this phase of the project were Belgium, China, Finland, Greece, Hong Kong (China), Indonesia, Ireland, Italy, Nigeria, Poland, Romania, Slovenia, Spain, Thailand and the United States.

Box 6.1: Towards a global database of national ECCE profiles

UNESCO's International Bureau of Education (IBE), in collaboration with UNICEF, has prepared draft profiles of early childhood provision in 175 non-OECD countries. The profiles, prepared for this Report, include information on ECCE legislation, official supervision and coordination of programmes, ECCE providers, personnel and training, and curriculum and pedagogy, as well as current policies and special programmes, especially those targeting vulnerable and disadvantaged children. The profiles incorporate data from the UNESCO Institute for Statistics (UIS) on official definitions of pre-primary education, entrance age and duration of ISCED level 0, enrolment ratios (GER, NER, by gender), teachers and their training, financing (average funding per child, sources) and hours per week of ECCE programmes. UNICEF added a section on parenting programmes and national systems for monitoring children's development and school readiness. The draft profiles were sent to national ministries of education and to UNICEF field offices to check, revise and supplement. By June 2006, ninety-four countries had revised their ECCE profiles.

Additional ECCE information for twenty-three OECD countries was compiled from the IBE's World Data on Education database (UNESCO-IBE, 2005) and from the OECD's Early Childhood Education and Care and Family-friendly Policy reviews. In total, then, 198 ECCE profiles were created for this Report (www.efareport.unesco.org). This database, while still uneven in completeness and detail, is an important new source of information on early childhood provision around the world.

The organization of care and education for children under 3

In developed and transition countries the demand for structured early childhood provision largely rose in line with the growth of women's employment. In developing countries, by contrast, mothers were assumed to be working at home or, if not, in agriculture or the informal sector, for instance selling or trading in the market. In rural areas children were expected to carry out household chores from an early age. With these 'realities' in mind, few governments prioritized publicly funded care or educational programmes for young children. To meet existing demand, primarily from middle class and urban families, private initiatives were encouraged.

Increasingly, working mothers are a fact of life in much of the world, and parents seek out decent and affordable care and education programmes for their children. In addition, more families are migrating to urban areas (or other countries)
in search of paid employment, often losing access to kin support networks for childrearing and child care. Thus, increased migration and female labour force participation have expanded the demand for maternal (and parental) leave benefits and early childhood provision.

Maternal and parental leave

Worldwide evidence concerning maternal or parental leave is available through comparative surveys and international compilations.[12]
In almost all OECD countries, paid and job-protected parental leave allows one or the other parent (or, in rare cases, both parents) to take off from work for a limited period, from a couple of months to a few years, to care for their babies. Policies increasingly include – and, in some countries, require – prenatal leave. Although the parameters of statutory leave (duration, extent of wage replacement and coverage for adopted children) vary in developed countries, most new parents receive some public support for caring for their children during this critical period in their development.

Among Central and Eastern European countries, which have historically provided an extensive package of child and family cash benefits, services and leaves, the transition to a market economy brought unemployment, significant reductions in social benefits and services, higher fees for services and cuts

in consumer subsidies (Kamerman, 2003; Rostgaard, 2004). By the late 1990s, however, most countries had recovered, although not always to previous levels, and the historical model of government-funded and government-provided early childhood services was reaffirmed.

Not all developing and transition countries have maternity leave policies and, where they exist, they are unevenly implemented or limited to workers in certain labour market segments. The lack of effective enforcement mechanisms is widespread. Among the 126 countries for which current information is available, approximately 80% report having established some sort of maternity leave. Such provisions are most prevalent in Latin America and the Caribbean, Central and Eastern Europe, and South and West Asia (Table 6.3). They are least available among Arab States, in East Asia and the Pacific, and in Central Asia. Three-fifths of the countries in sub-Saharan Africa have some provision, though only a small proportion of women are employed in the formal labour market and hence able to benefit. While the duration of the maternity leave varies from one week to one year, the median period is twelve weeks in most regions, with slightly higher leave provisions in Central and Eastern Europe (eighteen weeks), Central Asia (seventeen weeks) and sub-Saharan Africa (fourteen weeks). In most regions cash benefits are

Not all developing and transition countries have maternity leave policies

12. This section draws upon Kamerman (2005). Additional information can also be found in US Social Security Administration (1999) and Moss and Deven (1999).

Table 6.3: Maternity leave policies in developing and transition countries, by region, 1999–2002[1]

Region	% of countries with statutory leave	Duration of maternity leave[2] (weeks)			Mean wage replacement rate[2] (%)
		Median	Minimum	Maximum	
Sub-Saharan Africa	76	14	4	26	74
Arab States	50	12	4	14	92
Central Asia	67	17	16	20	100
East Asia and the Pacific[3]	50	12	8	20	83
South and West Asia	86	12	8	16	93
Latin America and the Caribbean	94	12	8	24	76
Central and Eastern Europe	94	18	1	52	90

1. Data are for the most recent year available during the period specified.
2. Calculations for leave duration and wage replacement included only countries with statutory leave.
In countries where various payment regimes apply, the period of maximum wage replacement was selected.
In all countries, this corresponds to the first leave period taken before and after birth, usually called maternity leave.
Several countries have other statutory leave periods (additional maternity, parental or child care leave) where wage replacement is lower or zero. These are: in Central Asia, Georgia (up to three years of unpaid leave); and in Central and Eastern Europe, Croatia (paid leave until age 1), Czech Republic (paid leave until age 4), Hungary (paid leave until age 3), Lithuania (up to a year of paid leave), Poland (up to age 3), Romania (paid leave until age 2) and Slovakia (paid leave until age 4).
3. Excludes Australia, Japan and New Zealand.
Source: Kamerman (2005).

meant to replace between 75% and 90% of the mother's wage. Moreover, in some regions (e.g. Latin America) working mothers are entitled to time off for breastfeeding (Linnecar and Yee, 2006).

National policy: few integrated frameworks

In general, few countries have established national frameworks to finance, coordinate and supervise ECCE programmes for infants and toddlers. Ministries of health or ministries associated with child welfare target health and welfare needs specific to young children, but not the broader care and educational dimensions of early childhood provision. Ministries of education tend to view the education of children under 3 as the responsibility of parents, private associations or non-government agencies. Even in cases where ministries of education have been assigned administrative responsibility for the under-3 age group (e.g. Brazil; some other countries, such as Botswana, are moving in that direction), limited information is reported about existing programmes and services.

Programmes targeting the care and education of under-3s[13]

The national profiles indicate that in just more than half (53%) of the world's countries there is at least one formal ECCE programme before pre-primary education, accepting very young children (from birth or age 1). These programmes typically provide organized custodial care and, in some cases, health services and educational activities. The most common names given to the programmes are day care services, crèches, centros infantiles, nurseries and early childhood development programmes.

To provide a basic measure of the prevalence of formal programmes targeting under-3s, Table 6.4 reports the percentage of countries in each region in which at least one programme exists. The findings show that such programmes are most prominent in North America and Western Europe, Central Asia, and Latin America and the Caribbean.

Information is limited regarding the duration (in hours per day/week) of programmes targeting under-3s. Some are full time and others accommodate children on flexible hours. For example, in Burkina Faso, the Gambia, Kazakhstan, Mozambique and the Netherlands, infants and toddlers can attend day care for as

much as ten to twelve hours per weekday. In Slovenia and Viet Nam, flexible hours in child care centres accommodate children under age 6 between four and eight-plus hours a week. In Namibia, home-based care and family visiting programmes offer services six to ten hours a week.

Belarus, Kazakhstan and Singapore, among many others, have programmes designed to accommodate part-time work schedules. In Finland and Sweden, where many mothers work part time, municipalities have a legal obligation to provide day care that meets the complex schedules of working parents. In Cambodia, Eritrea, Lebanon, Malaysia, Panama, the Syrian Arab Republic, Uruguay and Vanuatu, programmes for children below age 3 are available for four hours or less per day.

Comprehensive ECCE programmes: providing care, health and education

Of particular interest for monitoring purposes are countries in which early childhood provision for children under 3 addresses a child's overall well-being in an integrated way. A critical step in the development of comprehensive care and education for young children is the creation of national policy frameworks that cover not only custodial care, but also parent education and children's health needs, physical development and learning potential.

> **Few countries have established national frameworks to finance, coordinate and supervise ECCE programmes for infants and toddlers**

Table 6.4: Prevalence of ECCE programmes for children less than 3 years old by region, c. 2005

	Countries in region with programmes for children less than age 3 (%)[1]	Number of countries with relevant information
World	53	194
Sub-Saharan Africa	42	41
Arab States	35	20
Central Asia	89	9
East Asia and the Pacific	43	30
South and West Asia	44	9
Latin America/Caribbean	61	41
N. America/W. Europe	92	24
Central and Eastern Europe	35	20

1. Proportion of countries within a region that identify a programme targeting a population that includes children less than 3 years old (e.g. a programme for children aged 2 to 6).
Source: UNESCO-IBE (2006).

13. Information in this section is drawn from the ECCE profiles and data gathered from education officials participating in a UIS capacity-building workshop in Africa (2005).

India's 1974 National Policy on Education served as a foundation for a variety of programmes focusing on the child and the mother, notably Integrated Child Development Services (ICDS), a programme taking a life-cycle approach that was first adopted in 1975 and now reaches 23 million children.[14]

Since 1999, an African consortium, the Association for the Development of Education in Africa, has provided technical support to member countries for the development of national, cross-sectoral early childhood policy frameworks that address issues related to health, nutrition, water, sanitation, child protection and early childhood provision. Ten African countries are in various implementation stages: among them, Mauritius has drafted an integrated policy, Ghana and Namibia have ratified national ECCE policies and Eritrea is piloting a programme (Ashby, 2002; Boakye et al., 2001; Moti, 2002; Torkington, 2001).

For the most part, integrated ECCE frameworks involve national governments, with varying levels of decentralization, coupled with local operators, community leaders, teacher organizations and other stakeholders. International organizations and, in a few cases, public-private partnerships provide financial support (e.g. the Bernard van Leer Foundation in Jamaica and Colombia's Instituto Colombiano de Bienestar Familiar). The many different models of integrated care range from parental assistance programmes (Colombia and Jamaica) to community and family-focused modules (PROMESA in Colombia), teacher training (India and Mauritius), group care activities (Educa a tu Hijo in Cuba) and holistic initial education (Eritrea and Haiti). Information permitting assessment of the coverage and outcomes of integrated provision is limited and often mixed. In Dominica, Grenada, Jamaica, Saint Lucia and Saint Vincent and the Grenadines, the Roving Caregivers programme is considered an efficient means of offering critical health and care information to parents in isolated areas (Caribbean Support Initiative, 2006).

Child health, nutrition and survival

Many children in the world grow up in poor environmental conditions, have limited or no access to health services and live in impoverished households. These children are especially susceptible to waterborne disease, are more likely to have deficient diets and stunted growth, and are less likely to survive childhood and enter school (UNICEF, 2006). In most countries, ministries of health have sole responsibility for the health of children from birth to age 3. The discussion here highlights selected indicators of children's health and nutritional status, which are crucial contributors to children's well-being and their effective functioning in school.

The health and nutrition indicators in Table 6.5 are useful for assessing regional levels of children's well-being. While immunization campaigns have expanded worldwide, coverage is still unsatisfactory, particularly in the poorest regions. For example, in sub-Saharan Africa one-quarter of all 1-year-olds are not immunized against tuberculosis, one-third have never received the vaccine against diphtheria, pertussis (whooping cough) and tetanus, and two-thirds have not received the hepatitis B vaccine. In the Arab States, and East Asia and the Pacific, immunization rates against hepatitis are also quite low.

Poor diet and malnutrition are the main reasons more than one-quarter of all children under 5 in sub-Saharan Africa are moderately or severely underweight. In addition, one-third of African children in the age group suffer from moderate or severe stunting. Both problems weaken children and make them more vulnerable to illness and disease. Chronic hunger and stunting directly affect a child's ability to learn, but because coverage of early childhood provision in sub-Saharan Africa is limited, timely detection and treatment of health problems due to undernutrition are reduced. By contrast, in many developing countries, particularly in Latin America and the Caribbean, early childhood programmes have reduced the prevalence of malnutrition and stunting, and contributed to children's well-being and school readiness (see Chapter 5).

The under-5 mortality rate – the number of children per 1,000 (‰) live births who die before reaching age 5 – is generally considered the most robust indicator of childhood survival. More than the infant mortality rate (see glossary), the under-5 mortality rate captures the accumulated impact of the quality of the birthing experience, neonatal care, disabilities, breastfeeding and vaccination, as well as the effects of gender discrimination, mal- or undernutrition and inadequate health care.

Chronic hunger and stunting directly affect a child's ability to learn

---

14. See Box 8.7.

Table 6.5: Selected indicators of children's health and nutrition by region, 1996-2004[1]

	Immunization of 1-year-olds (%)			% under-5 who are:		Under-5 mortality rate (‰)
	Tuberculosis	DPT3	HepB	moderately or severely underweight	suffering from moderate or severe stunting	
	2004	2004	2004	1996-2004[1]	1996-2004[1]	2000-2005
World	84	78	49	26	31	86
Developing countries	84	76	46	27	31	95
Developed countries	...	96	63	...	...	8
Countries in transition	93	93	90	5	14	46
Sub-Saharan Africa	76	65	33	28	38	176
Arab States	88	88	77	14	21	65
Central Asia	...	...	...	...	...	79
East Asia and the Pacific	92	86	71	15	19	44
South and West Asia	...	...	...	...	...	101
Latin America and the Caribbean	96	91	83	7	16	35
North America and Western Europe	...	...	...	...	...	7
Central and Eastern Europe	...	...	...	...	...	19

1. Data are for the most recent year available during the period specified.
Note: DPT3: three doses of diphtheria, pertussis (whooping cough) and tetanus vaccine. HepB: hepatitis B vaccine.
Source: Annex, Statistical Table 3A.

In some countries, the overall situation for child survival has worsened

Statistically, this indicator captures 90% of the global mortality among children under age 18.

As Table 6.5 shows, worldwide about 86 of every 1,000 children born in recent years will not reach age 5. There are, however, significant regional differences: rates are highest in sub-Saharan Africa (176 children per 1,000) and South and West Asia (101 children per 1,000) and lowest in Europe and North America (fewer than 30). Some countries have made great strides since 1990, reducing the under-5 mortality rate by almost, or more than, half. Among them are Bangladesh, Bhutan, Bolivia, Brazil, Egypt, Guatemala, Indonesia, the Libyan Arab Jamahiriya, Nicaragua, Peru, the Syrian Arab Republic and Turkey. In some other countries, however, the overall situation for child survival has worsened. For example, in Cambodia, Cameroon, Côte d'Ivoire, Iraq, Kazakhstan, Kenya, Rwanda, Swaziland, Turkmenistan and Zimbabwe, the under-5 mortality rate has increased since 1990. According to UNICEF (2005a), of all the Millennium Development Goals, reducing child mortality remains the furthest from being achieved.[15]

Early childhood provision for children 3 and older

Government involvement

Governments play a more active role in the provision and supervision of programmes for children age 3 or older, in contrast to their limited role in programmes for those under 3. In many cases, however, this involves more than one official authority. In about 60% of the 172 countries with relevant information in their ECCE profiles, national ministries are the sole supervisors/ coordinators of programmes for children of age 3 and older; in about 30% these functions are shared by a ministry and another official body; and in the remaining 10% non-governmental organizations, subnational government entities or socio-political bodies are the sole supervisors of early childhood programmes. Examples from the third category include private organizations in the Democratic Republic of the Congo, Dominica and the Syrian Arab Republic; NGOs in Burundi, Côte d'Ivoire and the Lao People's Democratic Republic; a political organization in Viet Nam; community-based organizations in Comoros, Côte d'Ivoire and Cuba; and regional governments in Austria and Bulgaria.

In about 85% of the 154 countries with at least one ministry supervising and/or coordinating early childhood programmes, the ministry in charge of education[16] is the main one involved. In the remaining countries the most prominent ministries with oversight responsibilities are those dealing with (a) women, family, gender, children and/or youth affairs; (b) social affairs or social welfare; and (c) health. In a relatively

15. For further details on the under-5 mortality rate see World Bank (2004). Factor analyses indicate that among variables such as stunting, underweight, vitamin deficiency, breastfeeding and vaccination, the under-5 mortality rate loads strongest on an underlying factor. Millennium Development Goal 4 (United Nations, 2005) calls on countries to reduce by two-thirds the under-5 mortality rate between 1990 and 2015.

16. Variously named Ministry of Education, Ministry of Education and Youth, Ministry of Education, Sports and Culture, etc.

few cases, ministries of labour, development, planning or local government oversee early childhood programmes.

Entry age and duration of pre-primary education

All countries have one or more programmes at pre-primary level. They are most commonly called pre-school education (ninety-three countries), kindergarten (sixty-six countries), pre-primary education (fifty countries), early childhood education (thirty-four countries), nursery education (twenty-eight countries) and various combinations of the above (UNESCO-IBE, 2006).[17]

National authorities typically establish an official age at which children can enter pre-primary education. In about 85% of countries, participation in pre-primary education is not obligatory and children may enter the programmes at any age between the official entrance age and the onset of compulsory primary school attendance. Age 3 is the theoretical entrance age for pre-primary education in 70% of the world's 203 education systems (Table 6.6). In about one-quarter of countries, particularly in the Arab States, sub-Saharan Africa, and Latin America and the Caribbean, children are eligible to enrol at age 4. In a dozen countries, pre-primary education begins at age 5 or 6.[18]

Since 1998, the intended entrance age for pre-primary education has been stable. Only sixteen of the world's education systems altered their age eligibility policy: seven countries raised the official pre-primary entrance age and nine lowered it. These changes reinforced the global norm of age 3 as the start of pre-primary education.

The intended duration of pre-primary education is three years in almost half of the world's countries. Pre-primary education of shorter duration – one or two years – occurs in much of Latin America and the Caribbean, the Arab States, and East Asia and the Pacific. In a small group of countries, mainly in Central and Eastern Europe, and Central Asia, the duration is four years. As might be expected, there is an inverse relationship between the official entrance age and duration of pre-primary education: where the entrance age is higher, the duration is shorter (Table 6.7).

From a global perspective, the age groups that countries target for pre-primary education are less standardized than for primary or secondary education. Most typically, pre-primary

programmes are intended for 3- to 5-year-olds (eighty-six countries), but the target age group is 4 to 5 in thirty-one countries, 3 to 6 in thirty countries and 3 to 4 in twenty-four countries.[19]

Compulsory attendance and universal coverage in pre-primary education

Increasingly, countries are passing legislation making school attendance compulsory for children of pre-primary age (Table 6.8). While the rationales vary – for example, to underscore government commitment to early childhood provision; to expand and upgrade the quality of pre-school education; and to improve the readiness for and transition of children to primary education – the structures are quite similar. Typically, children must attend a year of pre-school, which begins at age 4 or 5 (in a few cases at age 6). Of the thirty countries with such laws, twenty-six are in Latin America and the Caribbean (ten), Central and Eastern Europe (nine), Western Europe (four) or East Asia and the Pacific (three).[20]

17. Other names include children centres (Eritrea and Greece), transition cycle (Costa Rica), preparatory education (Algeria, Macao (China) and Papua New Guinea) and initial education (Argentina, Bolivia, Dominican Republic, Panama, Peru and Venezuela).

18. Ecuador, Eritrea, Indonesia, the Islamic Republic of Iran, Malaysia, Nauru, Papua New Guinea, the Philippines, Solomon Islands, South Africa, Switzerland and the United Republic of Tanzania.

19. Other target groups include 4 to 6 (twelve countries) and 5 to 6 (four countries). In addition, some countries have one-year programmes aimed at: age 3 (one country), age 4 (five countries), age 5 (seven countries) and age 6 (two countries).

20. In addition, a Canadian province, Prince Edward Island, has made a year of pre-primary attendance compulsory for 5-year-olds.

Table 6.6: Official starting age for pre-primary education by region, 2004

| | Intended entry age for pre-primary education, 2004 | | | | |
	3	4	5	6	Total
World	142	48	11	2	203
Percentage of total	*70*	*24*	*5*	*1*	*100*
Sub-Saharan Africa	29	13	2	1	45
Arab States	9	11	0	0	20
Central Asia	9	0	0	0	9
East Asia and the Pacific	19	7	6	1	33
South and West Asia	6	2	1	0	9
Latin America and the Caribbean	28	12	1	0	41
North America and Western Europe	22	3	1	0	26
Central and Eastern Europe	20	0	0	0	20

Source: Annex, Statistical Table 3B.

Table 6.7: Duration of pre-primary education systems by official entry age, 2004

| Entry age for pre-primary education | Duration (number of countries) | | | | |
	1 year	2 years	3 years	4 years or more	Total
3	1	24	86	31	142
4	5	31	12	0	48
5 or older	9	4	0	0	13
Total	**15**	**59**	**98**	**31**	**203**

Source: Annex, Statistical Table 3B.

Table 6.8: The thirty countries with laws making pre-primary education compulsory

Regional average	Year law was enacted	Age at which compulsory education begins	Number of years of compulsory pre-primary education
Arab States			
Sudan[1]	1992	4	…
Central Asia			
Kazakhstan[2]	1999	5	1
East Asia and the Pacific			
Brunei Darussalam	1979	5	1
DPR Korea	…	5	1
Macao, China[3]	1995	5	1
South and West Asia			
Iran, Islamic Republic of	2004	5	1
Sri Lanka	1997	5	…
Latin America and Caribbean			
Argentina	1993	5	1
Colombia	1994	5	1
Costa Rica[4]	1997	4 or 5	1 or 2
Dominican Republic	1996	5	1
El Salvador	1990	4 to 6	
Mexico[5]	2002	5	1
Panama	1995	4	1
Peru[6]	2004	3	3
Uruguay	…	5	1
Venezuela	1999	4	2
North American and Western Europe			
Cyprus	2004	$4\frac{2}{3}$	1
Denmark	…	6	1
Israel	1949	3	…
Luxembourg	1963	4	2
Central and Eastern Europe			
Bulgaria	2002/2003	6	1
Hungary	1993	5	1
Latvia	2002	4	2
TFYR Macedonia	2005	6	1
Poland	2004	6	1
Republic of Moldova	…	5	1
Romania	…	6	1
Serbia and Montenegro[7]	2003	$5\frac{1}{2}$	1
Slovenia[8]	2001	6	0

1. The measure is rarely enforced.
2. The law allows pre-school education to be provided by the family, pre-school organizations or schools.
3. The ECCE profile states that by 2006 the country planned to have free pre-school education begin at age 3 (instead of 5) and last for three years. There is no mention of changing the compulsory entrance age.
4. The ECCE profile states that all pre-school is mandatory. Further research shows that only the last year of pre-school is mandatory, as of age 5.
5. Compulsory pre-primary education was to be phased in for the following ages (as of 1 September): 5 (2004/05), 4 (2005/06) and 3 (2008/09).
6. The ECCE profile states that the law requires children to attend formal or non-formal initial education programmes from age 3.
7. Data are for Serbia only.
8. Pre-primary classes, which were obligatory one year before entering school, have been discontinued and the entrance age for compulsory primary school has been lowered by one year to age 6.
Sources: UNESCO-IBE (2006); UIS database; El Salvador and Panama: Elvir and Ascensio (2006); Romania: McLean (2006).

Compulsory attendance laws tend to reflect policy intentions rather than educational realities, which depend on availability of resources and strictness of enforcement (Benavot et al., 2005). The legislation does not necessarily result in higher pre-primary enrolment. For example, the mean net enrolment ratio (NER) in pre-primary education for the ten countries in Latin America and the Caribbean with such laws is about 47%. However, for countries in this region without such legislation, the mean pre-primary NER is actually higher (58%, n=21). The corresponding results for Central and Eastern Europe are 62% (n=8) and 67% (n=7).[21] These figures raise doubts about enforcement of compulsory attendance laws and the willingness (or ability) of parents to send their children to pre-primary institutions.

In addition, compulsory attendance laws may not necessarily contribute to the development of an integrated ECCE policy targeting all children and spanning the period between birth and primary school entrance. In several Latin American countries with compulsory attendance laws (e.g. Argentina and Uruguay), policy attention and resources are focused almost exclusively on the last year of pre-primary education, to the detriment of programmes aimed at younger children and addressing their holistic development needs (Umayahara, 2005; UNESCO-OREALC, 2004). Finally, quite a few countries have achieved near universal coverage of pre-primary education (NER greater than 90%) without compulsory attendance laws (Table 6.9). Thus, while such laws may help crystallize political will and stakeholder commitment to address the needs of young children, other conditions are equally important in assuring children's actual participation in early childhood programmes and institutions.

How many hours a week do ECCE programmes last?

More than 85 countries have provided up-to-date information, incorporated in their national ECCE profiles, on the duration (weekly hours) of 118 early childhood programmes.[22] The range is

21. Incorporating the data for Turkey would bring the mean NER for countries without compulsory pre-primary in this region to 60%.

22. This section examines both pre-primary education and other ECCE programmes targeting children aged 3 and older. The 2003/4 Report reviewed national estimates of hours per week for pre-primary education alone (UNESCO, 2003a: p. 36). Among developing countries the duration ranged from as few as seven hours in Iraq, Maldives and Tajikistan to more than thirty-two hours in Cuba, Morocco, Saint Kitts and Nevis and the Syrian Arab Republic. In a majority of the countries for which data were available, the duration was twenty to twenty-five hours per week.

from five to sixty hours a week and the average about twenty-seven.[23] Figure 6.1 shows the distribution of early childhood programme duration in weekly hours, by region.[24] Most fluctuate between fifteen and forty hours. In Central and Eastern Europe, East Asia and the Pacific, Latin America and the Caribbean, and sub-Saharan Africa, some run ten hours or fewer per week. Programmes of more than forty hours are more common in Central and Eastern Europe, and North America and Western Europe.

Given the importance of early childhood programmes for working women, an alternative way to monitor programme availability is by noting the extent to which programmes operate full time (defined in this context as more than four hours per day) or part time during the week. The findings indicate that pre-primary and ECCE programmes are open most of the workweek and about half are full time. Nearly 88% of the programmes for which data are available operate five days a week. The operation of ECCE programmes can depend on who offers the programme, even within the same country and for the same age group. In Cambodia, for example, government pre-schools targeting 3- to 5-year-olds operate for five hours more per week than community pre-schools and are open thirty-eight weeks a year – between two and fourteen weeks longer than the community schools.

Table 6.9: Countries having pre-primary net enrolment ratios of at least 90% without compulsory pre-primary attendance laws

	NER of 4-year-olds[1]	Year of enrolment estimate
France	102	2002
Italy	102	2002
Spain	101	2002
Belgium	100	2002
United Kingdom	100	2002
Netherlands	99	2002
Iceland	93	2002
Malta	93	2002
Denmark	92	2002
	NER[2]	Year of enrolment estimate
Cuba	100	2004
Belarus	92	2004
Guyana	92	2004
Jamaica	91	2004
New Zealand	91	2004
Suriname	91	2004
Aruba	90	2004
Seychelles	90	2004

1. In Ireland, 4-year-olds are meant to be enrolled in primary schools (ISCED level 1). The age-specific NER for 4-year-olds in Ireland is 50%. The NERs of France, Italy and Spain are reported as exceeding 100% because they were calculated on the basis of separate data sets (population and education) derived from surveys carried out on two different dates.
2. Age groups vary by country, reflecting national definitions.
Sources: European Commission (2005); annex, Statistical Table 3B (non-European countries).

Pre-primary and ECCE programmes are open most of the workweek and about half are full time

Figure 6.1: Average hours per week of pre-primary and other ECCE programmes by region, c. 2005

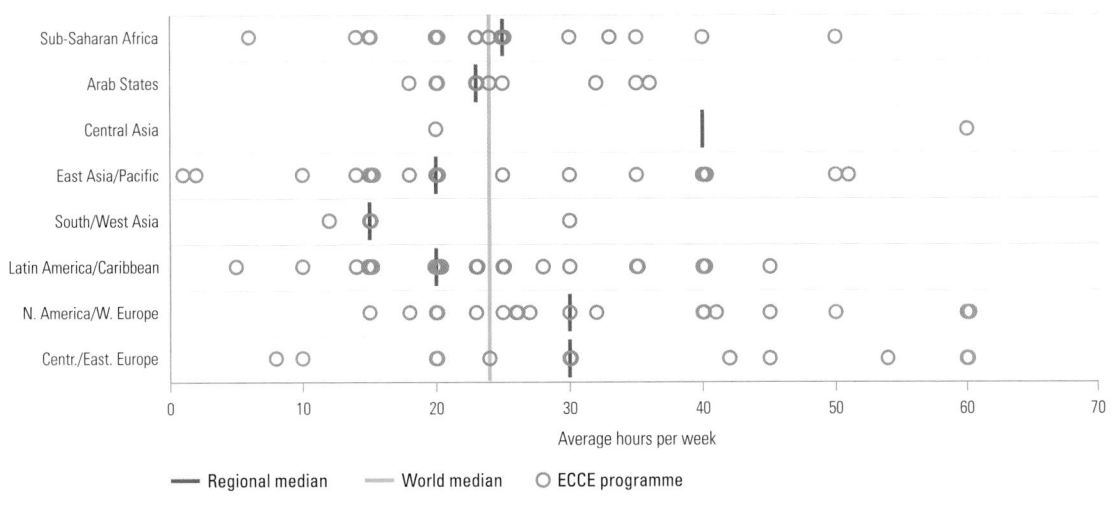

— Regional median — World median ○ ECCE programme

Note: Each point represents a programme type in a country in the specified region. Average hours are identified as programme hours during which a young child can participate. Round-the-clock programmes are not included, as children do not usually attend for the full twenty-four hours.
Source: UNESCO-IBE (2006).

23. Programmes of longer duration are not necessarily of better quality. Much of their impact depends on support provided by the home and on the quality of the programme activities.

24. In some countries, including Belarus, the Czech Republic, Finland, Latvia and Sweden, programmes can be boarding or available twenty-four hours, depending on the parents' needs. These outliers were removed from the figure.

Among developed and transition countries the trend is towards more private-sector involvement

Table 6.10: Countries classified according to the share of private pre-primary enrolment, 2004

Region	% of total enrolment in private schools		
	Low (0% to 32%)	Medium (33% - 66%)	High (more than 66%)
Sub-Saharan Africa	Cape Verde, S. Tome/Principe, U. R. Tanzania, Seychelles, South Africa, Benin, Niger, Kenya	Ghana, Equat. Guinea, Côte d'Ivoire, Togo, Burundi, Comoros, Cameroon	Gabon, Senegal, Eritrea, Congo, Mauritius, Madagascar, Guinea, Uganda, Ethiopia, Lesotho, Namibia, Rwanda
Arab States	Algeria, Iraq, Libyan A. J.	Kuwait, Egypt, Yemen, Saudi Arabia	U. A. Emirates, Syrian A. R., Sudan, Lebanon, Djibouti, Mauritania, Tunisia, Qatar, Jordan, Bahrain, Palestinian A. T., Morocco, Oman
Central Asia	Georgia, Tajikistan, Uzbekistan, Azerbaijan, Kyrgyzstan, Mongolia, Armenia, Kazakhstan		
East Asia and the Pacific	Tokelau, Tonga, Nauru, Marshall Is, Cook Islands, Thailand, Lao PDR, Cambodia	Malaysia, New Zealand, Philippines, Viet Nam, Japan	Australia, Brunei Daruss., Rep. of Korea, Macao (China), Indonesia, Fiji
South and West Asia	Iran, Isl. Rep.	Maldives, Bangladesh	Nepal
Latin America and the Caribbean	Bermuda, Montserrat, Cuba, Guyana, Mexico, Costa Rica, Nicaragua, Barbados, Panama, Venezuela, Uruguay, El Salvador, Guatemala, Peru, Honduras, Bolivia, Paraguay, Argentina, Brazil	Colombia, Dominican Rep., Suriname, Chile, Ecuador, Grenada, St Kitts/Nevis, Turks/Caicos Is	Neth. Antilles, Aruba, Bahamas, Jamaica, Cayman Is, Anguilla, Belize, Br. Virgin Is, Dominica, Saint Lucia, St Vincent/Grenad., Trinidad/Tobago
North America and Western Europe	Andorra, Greece, Israel, Luxembourg, Switzerland, Canada, Finland, Iceland, United Kingdom, France, Sweden	Spain, Malta, United States, Cyprus, Norway, Portugal, Belgium, Germany	Netherlands
Central and Eastern Europe	Belarus, TFYR Macedonia, Lithuania, Ukraine, Bulgaria, Slovakia, Rep. Moldova, Romania, Slovenia, Estonia, Czech Rep., Russian Fed., Latvia, Turkey, Hungary, Albania, Poland, Croatia		
Total countries: 155	76	34	45

Note: In each box, countries are listed in increasing order of private enrolment.
Source: Annex, Statistical Table 3B.

25. Private pre-primary institutions are defined as those 'not operated by a public authority but controlled and managed, whether for profit or not, by a private body such as a non-governmental organization, religious body, special interest group, foundation or business enterprise'. A public institution is one controlled and managed by a public education authority or agency (national/federal, state, provincial or local), whatever the origin of its financial resources.

26. The Netherlands is an exception, having a large proportion of private pre-primary enrolment.

The mix of public and private provision in pre-primary education

Table 6.10 classifies countries into three categories (low, medium and high) according to the share of total pre-primary enrolment in private institutions.[25] In about 50% of the 154 countries with data, the prevalence of private pre-primary education is less than one-third of the total. In 30% of the countries the share of private enrolment is more than 66%. In the remaining 20% of the countries the share is relatively equal. Regional variations are pronounced. In developed and transition regions (North America and Western Europe, and Central and Eastern Europe), country shares of private pre-primary enrolment are either in the low or medium categories.[26] In much of sub-Saharan Africa, the Arab States, the Caribbean and East Asia, the private sector is considerably more prominent.

Additional analyses examined the extent to which the share of private pre-primary enrolment changed between 1999 and 2004. Among developed and transition countries the trend was towards more private-sector involvement: the private share of enrolment increased by more than two percentage points in twenty-two countries and declined by more than two percentage points in only eight. Among developing countries the evidence was mixed (increases in thirty-three countries and decreases in thirty-five countries) and region-specific increases in public pre-primary education in the Arab States, decreases in East Asia and the Pacific.

Overall, the evidence suggests that public provision of pre-primary education has been an integral part of recent ECCE development in most of Europe, while in much of the developing world the private sector has played a more prominent role. In some cases, as in sub-Saharan Africa and the Arab States, private bodies established pre-primary schools that expanded modestly over time. Elsewhere, such as most Caribbean countries and the Republic of Korea, the private sector initiated more dynamic pre-primary education.

The expansion of pre-primary education
The global and regional picture
Worldwide the number of children enrolled in pre-primary education has almost tripled during the past three decades, from about 44 million in the mid-1970s to about 124 million in 2004 (Table 6.11).[27] Regional trends are especially informative. In developed and transition countries (including the former USSR), pre-primary enrolment peaked in the early 1990s and then decreased because of low birth rates as well as economic hardships in transition countries. By contrast, enrolment increases occurred in all developing regions, especially East Asia and the Pacific and South and West Asia, from the mid-1970s to the late 1990s.[28] Much of this growth reflected expansion of pre-primary education in China, where enrolment increased from 6.2 million in 1975/76 (UNESCO, 1999) to 24 million in 1998/99, before dropping to the present level of 20 million.[29]

Standardizing pre-primary enrolment by the relevant school-age population measures the coverage of pre-primary education, and can be calculated at the national, regional and global

level. Between 1975 and 2004 the global gross enrolment ratio (GER) in pre-primary education more than doubled from about 17% to 37%. In developed and transition countries about 40% of the relevant child population was enrolled in pre-primary education in 1970 and the GER had reached 73% by 2004. In developing countries the coverage of pre-primary education has been considerably less: in 1975, on average, fewer than one out of ten children were enrolled in pre-primary institutions; by 2004 the ratio had increased to about 32% or one in three.

Differences among developing country regions are especially marked (Figure 6.2). GERs have been highest in Latin America and the Caribbean and lowest in sub-Saharan Africa. Pre-primary education expanded noticeably in East Asia and the Pacific in the 1980s and 1990s, and in South and West Asia in the 1990s and 2000s. In the Arab States, by contrast, the coverage of pre-primary education, while increasing since the 1970s, has been essentially stagnant.

Differences within regions
The coverage of pre-primary education varies considerable among countries within regions.[30] In sub-Saharan Africa, half the countries have GERs below 10%, but in Mauritius and Seychelles the ratios are close to 100%. Similarly, in East Asia and the Pacific, Cambodia and the Lao People's Democratic Republic report GERs below 10% while China, the Philippines and Viet Nam have ratios between 36% and 47%, and Australia, Malaysia, New Zealand, the Republic of Korea and Thailand register near full enrolment. Three-quarters of the countries in Latin America and the

Pre-primary enrolment increased in all developing regions

27. World and regional estimates of pre-primary enrolment should be treated with caution. After the Dakar Forum and the increased emphasis on pre-primary education, some countries began reporting pre-primary enrolment more systematically than in the past. In addition, the adoption of ISCED97, which includes a more comprehensive definition of education, may have increased reporting of informal pre-primary programmes, so some enrolment increase may not reflect programme expansion. Moreover, changes in enrolment ratios can reflect both changing reporting patterns and population assessments.

28. For South and West Asia, some of the expansion involves the inclusion of enrolment in previously unreported ECCE programmes in India during the late 1990s.

29. According to the UN Population Division, China's population aged 0 to 5 also declined, from 140 million in 1990 to 103 million in 2005. Thus, the gross enrolment ratio increased from 6% of the 3 to 6 age group in 1975 to 36% of the 4 to 6 age group in 2003/04.

30. Factors that can affect the comparability of national enrolment ratios include programme duration, targeted age group, compulsory attendance legislation, eligibility restrictions and birth rates.

Table 6.11: Total enrolment in pre-primary education by region, 1970/71-2003/04 (millions)

	1970/71	1975/76	1980/81	1985/86	1990/91	1998/99	2003/04
World	...	43.7	58.4	72.5	85.4	111.8	123.7
Developed and transition countries	23.9	30.0	33.2	35.6	37.4	31.7	32.6
Developing countries	...	13.7	25.2	37.0	48.0	80.1	91.1
of which:							
Sub-Saharan Africa	0.2	0.5	1.5	1.8	2.4	5.1	7.4
Arab States	0.3	0.8	1.2	1.6	1.9	2.4	2.6
East Asia and the Pacific	...	8.1	15.2	19.7	25.9	33.3	29.9
South and West Asia	0.8	1.4	2.3	4.1	5.4	22.2	31.2
Latin America and the Caribbean	1.8	2.8	4.7	9.4	11.9	16.4	19.1

Note: During the 1970s some countries, especially in sub-Saharan Africa, did not report data on pre-primary enrolments. Thus, the regional totals probably underestimate enrolment for this period. Data for East Asia and the Pacific are for developing countries only; Australia, Japan and New Zealand are included under developed countries. The total for developing countries is higher than the sum of the five regions because it includes data for Bermuda, Cyprus, Israel, Mongolia and Turkey.
Sources: 1970/71–1990/91: UNESCO (1999); 1998/99–2003/04: UIS database.

PART III. Early childhood care and education

2 0 0 7

Education for All Global Monitoring Report

Figure 6.2: Regional trends in pre-primary gross enrolment ratios, showing a strong increase in Latin America and the Caribbean

In Belarus,
the Czech
Republic, Estonia
and Slovakia,
coverage is close
to universal

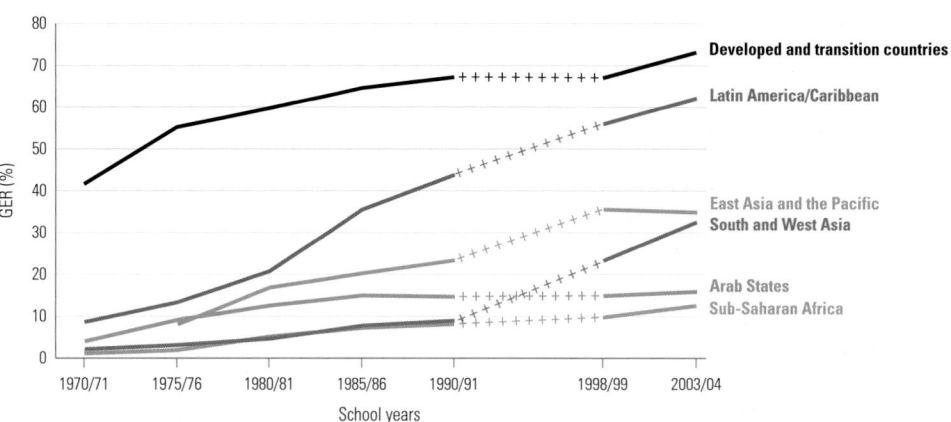

Note: Data for East Asia and the Pacific are for developing countries only; Australia, Japan and New Zealand are included under developed countries. The broken line signifies a break in the data series due to a new classification.
Sources: 1970/71, 1975/76, 1980/81: UNESCO (1991); 1985/86: UNESCO (1998); 1990/91: UNESCO (2000); 1998/99, 2003/04: UIS database.

Caribbean have GERs above 75% while the lowest ratio is 28%. In South and West Asia countries enrol between one-third and one-half of children in pre-primary education. In Central Asia, despite indications of recovery after the decline of the 1990s, no country has a GER of above 50%. In North America and Western Europe, virtually all countries have GERs above 60% and in half the ratio is 100%. In all Central and Eastern European

countries except Albania, Croatia, the Former Yugoslav Republic of Macedonia and Turkey, more than half the children are enrolled; in Belarus, the Czech Republic, Estonia and Slovakia, coverage is close to universal (See annex, Statistical Table 3B).

Country advances between 1991 and 2004

Overall, between 1991 and 2004 (Figure 6.3), four-fifths of the eighty-one countries and

Figure 6.3: Changes in pre-primary GERs between 1990/91 and 2003/04 in eighty-one countries: coverage increased in four-fifths

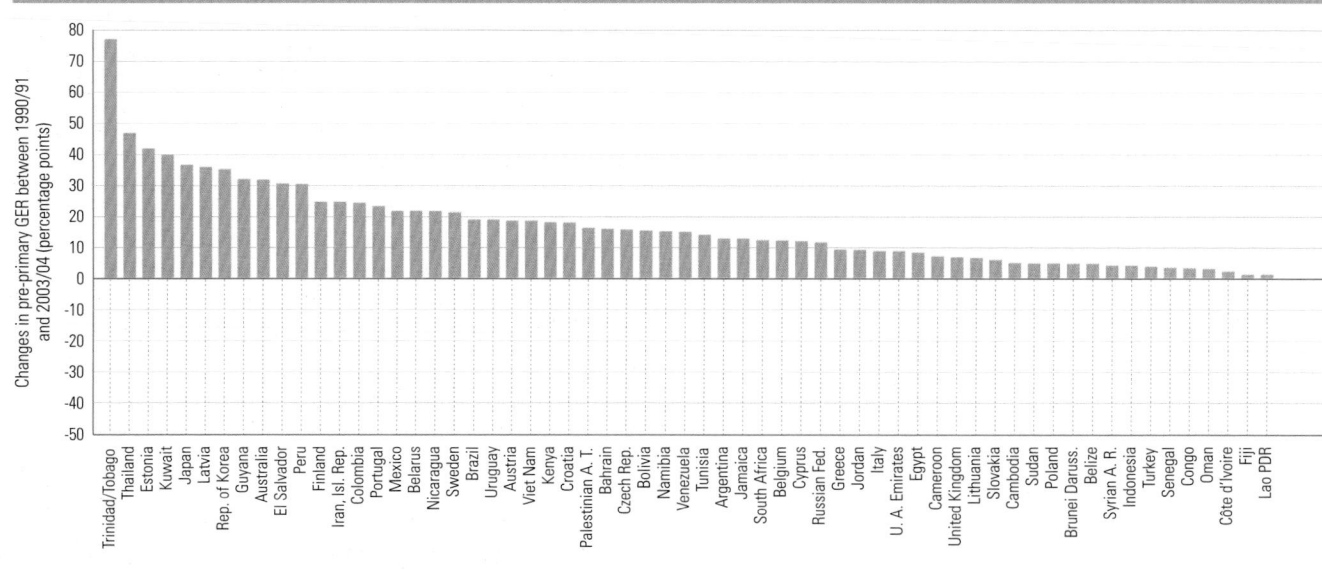

Note: Includes only those countries in which the officially targeted age group was unchanged. For Ethiopia, Republic of Korea and Thailand, the GERs are for 2004/05.
Source: Annex, Statistical Table 12.

territories with comparable data increased their coverage of pre-primary education. Among these sixty-eight countries whose GERs rose, the increase was more than twenty percentage points in nineteen countries, six to twenty percentage points in twenty-eight countries and one to five percentage points in sixteen countries.[31] On the other hand, in Albania, Armenia, Georgia, Kazakhstan, Kyrgyzstan and Tajikistan (see below), as well as in Iraq, Morocco and Togo, the GERs declined. Several countries or territories, including Fiji, Kuwait, the Palestinian Autonomous Territories and the United Kingdom, saw pre-primary coverage expand between 1991 and 1999, then contract.[32]

Cross-national analyses suggest that teacher availability is related to the expansion of pre-primary education. Specifically, the supply of pre-primary teachers in relation to the number of pupils prior to 1999 is associated with the net enrolment ratio (NER) in pre-primary education in 2004.[33] Countries with lower pupil/teacher ratios (PTRs) tended to have higher NERs (Figure 6.4).[34]

Countries in transition: recovering lost ground

While pre-primary education was expanding in much of the world, many countries in transition experienced significant declines and/or fluctuations following the break-up of the Soviet Union (see UNESCO, 2003a: pp. 37-8). Figure 6.5

Figure 6.4: The inverse relationship between the pupil/teacher ratio in 1999 and the net enrolment ratio in 2004

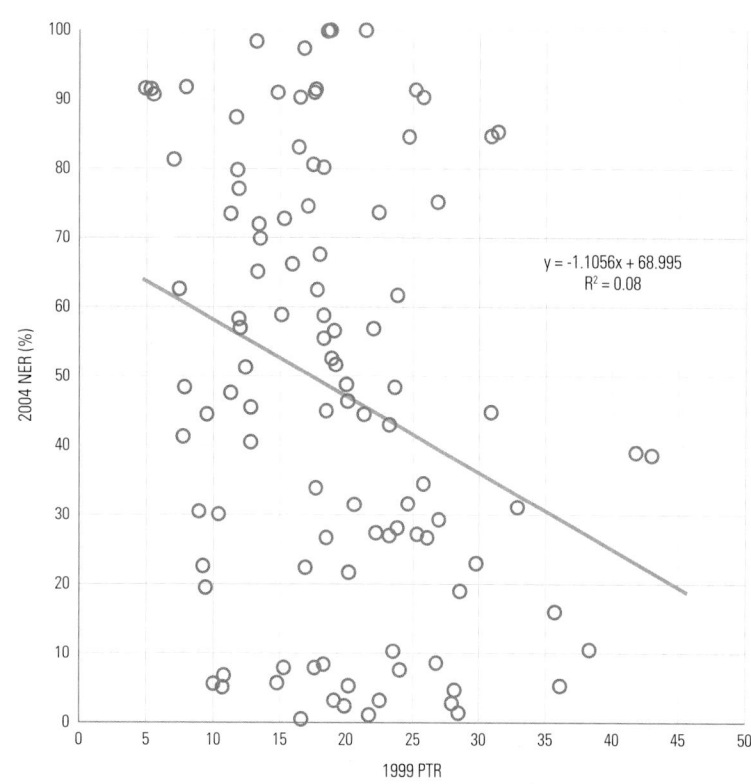

$$y = -1.1056x + 68.995$$
$$R^2 = 0.08$$

Source: Annex, Statistical Table 10A.

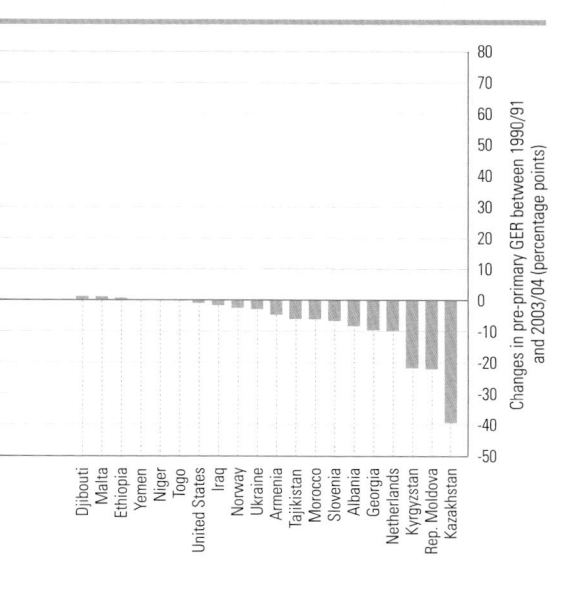

reports annual pre-primary net enrolment ratios (NERs) for children aged 3 to 6 between 1989 and 2003. In Central and Eastern Europe and the Baltic States, pre-primary enrolment levels initially dropped – sometimes precipitously – but had recovered by the end of the 1990s. In Albania, Bosnia and Herzegovina, Serbia and Montenegro and the former Yugoslav Republic of Macedonia, which had relatively low enrolment rates in the early 1990s, governments introduced various measures to increase access to kindergarten and other ECCE programmes (Albania Ministry of Finance, 2004; Zafeirakou, 2005).

Among countries belonging to the Commonwealth of Independent States (CIS), particularly in Central Asia, enrolment ratios in pre-primary education declined rapidly in the early 1990s and have yet to recover. The decrease took place despite government initiatives and policies that sought to increase the role of private providers and institutions. Kazakhstan, for instance, introduced new forms of ECCE,

31. In Australia, El Salvador, Estonia, Guyana, Japan, Kuwait, Latvia, Peru, Republic of Korea, Thailand and Trinidad and Tobago, the GER for pre-primary education increased by thirty percentage points or more.

32. Figure 6.3 does not reflect the data used for this intra-period analysis.

33. Multivariate analyses confirm the negative impact of the PTR in 1999 on growth in the pre-primary NER over 1999–2004.

34. Worldwide, the median pre-primary PTR was about 18:1 in 2004, slightly lower than the median for primary education of 21:1 (in North America and Western Europe the pre-primary median was slightly higher than the primary one; see annex, Statistical Table 10A). Cross-national variation is limited: among the 157 countries with data, the pre-primary PTR was below 25:1 in 78% of countries and above 35:1 in 9%.

Figure 6.5: Pre-primary net enrolment ratios for children aged 3 to 6 in transition countries, 1989 to 2003

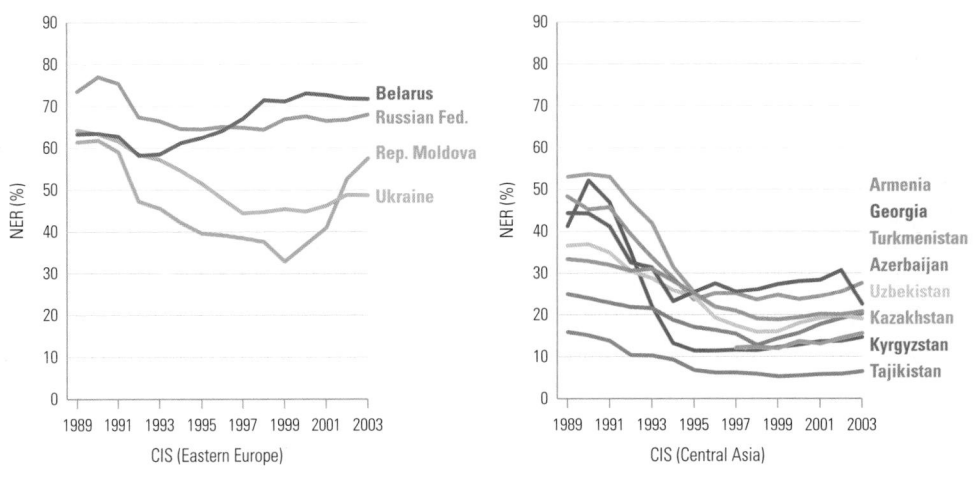

Notes:

■ Albania, Armenia, Russian Federation, Slovenia, Ukraine: GERs.

■ Belarus: 1999-2003 data are for ages 3 to 5.

■ Bosnia and Herzegovina: ages 3 to 7.

■ Czech Republic, Hungary, Slovakia: ages 3 to 5.

■ Kazakhstan: data for 1989-1995, 1997-2000 are GERs.

■ Lithuania: 1989-93 data are GERs.

■ Republic of Moldova: 1992-2003 data exclude Transdniestr.

■ Serbia and Montenegro: pupil data for 1991-98 exclude ethnic Albanians in Kosovo; 1999-2001 data exclude Kosovo.

■ Tajikistan: 1989-2001 data are GERs.

■ TFYR Macedonia: includes pre-school preparatory classes.

Source: UNICEF (2005b).

including complexes of 'kindergarten schools' as well as kindergartens and other pre-school institutions funded privately or by local government. The governments of Kyrgyzstan and Uzbekistan opened many community-based kindergartens to increase enrolment (Tabuslatova, 2006).

The challenges facing countries in transition are further compounded by the extremely large numbers of young children who live apart from their birth families in institutions or through foster care, guardianship or adoption. UNICEF (2005*b*) estimates that about 1.5 million children in transition countries live in such out-of-home care contexts. These 'social orphans' – children whose parents are living but unable or unwilling to care for them – are especially vulnerable and often have limited, if any, access to early childhood programmes.

Age-specific enrolment and participation levels in ECCE programmes

Monitoring national progress in ECCE coverage by examining gross or net enrolment ratios raises two problems. First, pre-primary enrolment data reported by education ministries may undercount children's participation in early childhood programmes funded by other ministries, private groups or local communities. The lack of consensus as to what constitutes an ECCE programme and uncertainty whether particular programmes meet international standards also contribute to the undercounting. Second, while a majority of countries define 3 to 5 or 3 to 6 as the

normative ages for enrolment in pre-primary institutions, in practice enrolment patterns vary significantly within these age spans. Thus, conventional statistics do not reveal important age-specific enrolment patterns in pre-primary education.

To address these limitations, this subsection reports age-specific participation data from three household surveys (Box 6.2) and age-specific enrolment data from a special UIS compilation. Together these new sources provide a more accurate and valid portrayal of national differences in the coverage of ECCE programmes for children aged 3 and above. They also reveal instances in which children from one age bracket may be enrolled either in pre-primary programmes or in primary schools. This 'mixed' pattern of same-aged children in pre-primary and primary education is partly determined by administrative authorities and partly by parental preferences and household decisions.[35]

Figure 6.6 reports age-specific participation rates of 3- and 4-year-old children in organized care and learning centres.[36] For 3-year-olds, participation levels varied from less than 3% in some countries (e.g. the Central African Republic, Chad, the Democratic Republic of the Congo, Egypt, Guatemala, Iraq, Rwanda and the United Republic of Tanzania) to more than 20% in others (e.g. Albania, Bahrain, Colombia, the Dominican Republic, Equatorial Guinea, Jamaica, Nicaragua, the Republic of Moldova, Trinidad and Tobago, Venezuela and Viet Nam). For 4-year-olds, participation levels were relatively high (more

35 Official eligibility requirements, for example, may determine the dates used to decide which children of what age can enrol in pre-primary or primary institutions. Not all countries rigidly enforce these requirements. In addition, in federal countries and decentralized systems, eligibility rules may not be uniform nationwide.

36. MICS survey-takers asked the mother or caretaker of 3- and 4-year-olds: 'Does [name of child] attend any organized learning or early childhood education programme, such as a private or government facility, including kindergarten or community child care?' This question includes ECCE provision that may be excluded in the formal definition of pre-primary education. Therefore, findings emerging from this question provide a more accurate depiction of the care component of the ECCE goal.

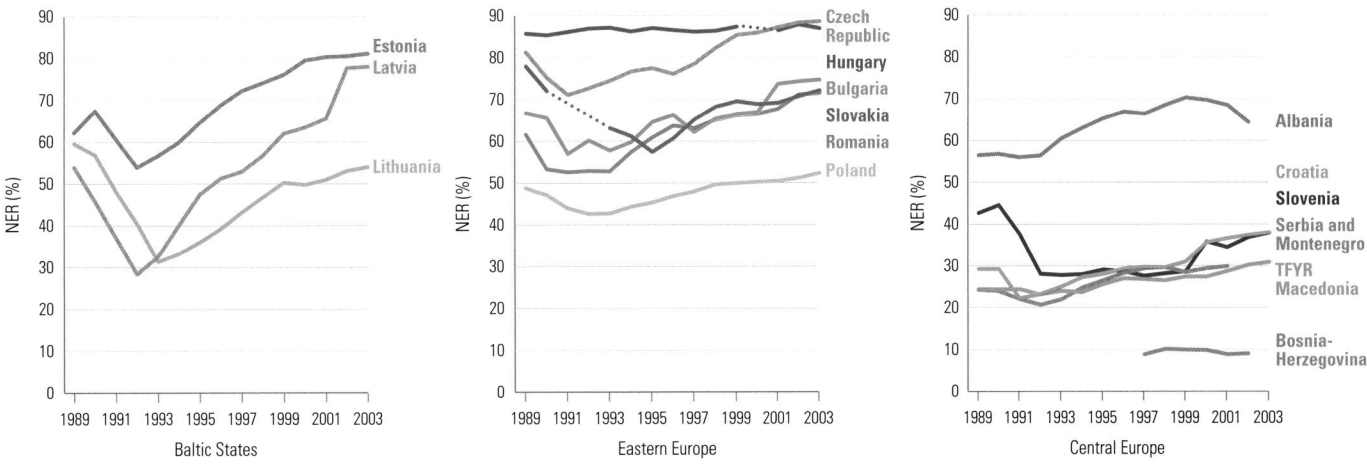

Baltic States · Eastern Europe · Central Europe

Box 6.2: Background information on the three household surveys

Much of the rest of the chapter is based on ECCE information from the second wave of the Multiple Indicator Cluster Surveys (MICS2), the Demographic and Health Surveys (DHS) and the Living Standard Measurement Surveys (LSMS). Data for MICS2[1] and DHS[2] were collected between 1999 and 2003, and those for the LSMS[3] between 1995 and 2003. All three surveys were based on nationally representative samples of households in developing countries. Researchers questioned parents or guardians of children aged 3 to 6 about their children's participation in ECCE programmes. Sixty-five countries took part in MICS2 surveys, and ECCE data are available for forty-five of them.[4] In eight DHS countries and all ten LSMS countries, the surveys obtained relevant data on ECCE.

Depending on the child's age, each household survey used different questions to gather information about participation in ECCE programmes. For example, MICS2 asked parents of 3- and 4-year-olds whether their child 'attends any organized learning or early childhood education programme, such as a private or government facility, including kindergarten or community child care', while parents of children aged 5 or older were asked whether their child attended a pre-school programme. DHS and LSMS also included age-differentiated questions about participation in ECCE programmes.[5] Strictly speaking, then, the questions asked of parents of children in the two age groups (3 to 4 and 5 to 6) are not comparable and are therefore reported separately.

Except for a few countries in the LSMS (e.g. Ecuador, Guatemala and Nicaragua), most countries in all three household surveys did not differentiate between types of pre-schools – that is, day care, kindergarten or preparatory. Despite limited variations in survey questions, the overall level of data quality is high, with relatively few non-respondents.

1. The aim of MICS2 was to assess progress towards the goals of the World Summit for Children. The methodology was developed and the surveys carried out by UNICEF in cooperation with WHO, UNESCO, the ILO, UNAIDS and the UN Statistical Division. The surveys were designed to collect data on diverse issues, such as nutrition, health, education, birth registration, family environment, child labour, and knowledge and attitudes about HIV/AIDS.

2. The DHS were designed to measure the health and nutritional status of women and children in the developing world. They provide data on standard demographic and health indicators, as well as special topics (including ECCE in the surveys of Colombia, Dominican Republic, Egypt, Haiti, Nicaragua, Uganda, the United Republic of Tanzania and Zimbabwe, to date). Survey-takers interviewed parents and guardians of children aged 2 to 6, enquiring about the children's participation in early childhood education, among other topics. Ten of these surveys had included ECCE questions as of 2004.

3. The LSMS were carried out in Albania, Bosnia, Brazil, Bulgaria, Ecuador, Guatemala, India (the states of Bihar and Uttar Pradesh), Nicaragua, Panama and Papua New Guinea. In Albania, Ecuador, Nicaragua and Panama, the relevant age group was 3 to 5 instead of 3 to 6.

4. In the other twenty countries, either the ECCE module was not included or, in a few cases, data were unavailable.

5. As with the MICS2, participants in some LSMS countries (e.g. Albania and Brazil) were asked about current pre-school attendance while for others (e.g. Papua New Guinea) the question concerned attendance in the year prior to the survey.

Sources: Nonoyama et al. (2006); Education Policy and Data Center (2006); Carr Hill (2006).

1.5 million children in transition countries live in out-of-home care contexts

Figure 6.6: Net attendance rates for ages 3 and 4 in organized care and learning programmes, showing higher participation for 4-year-olds, c. 2000

Participation
of 5- and 6-
year-olds varies
between 2% in
Burundi to 55%
in Viet Nam

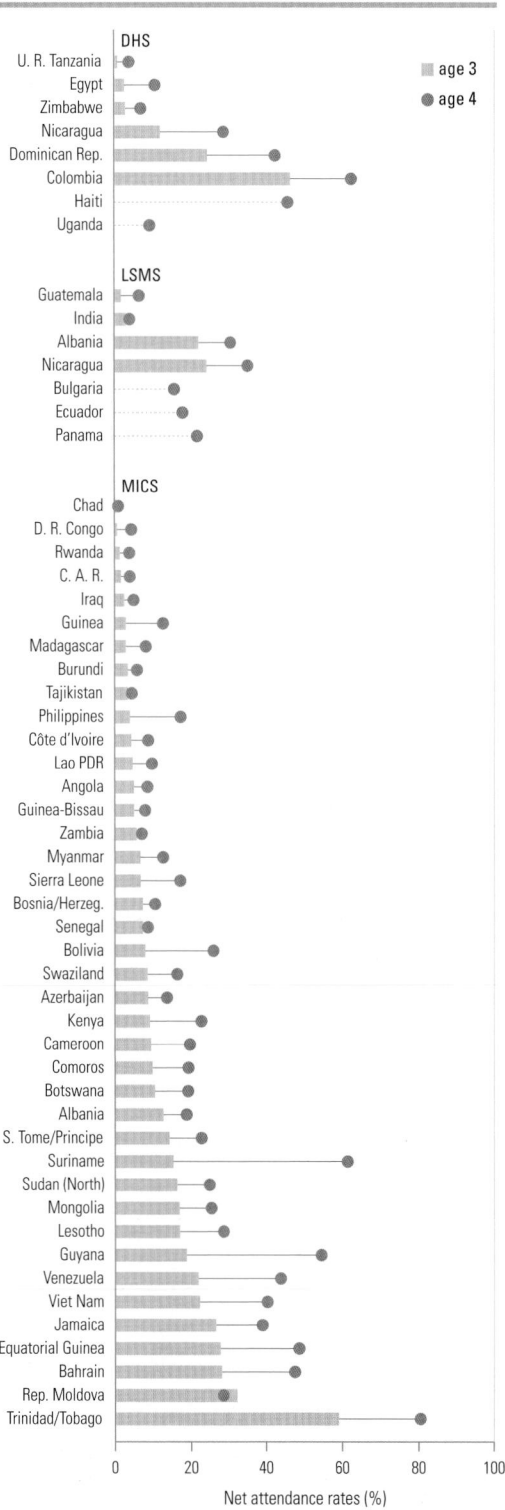

Note: Data for age 3 are unavailable for Bulgaria, Ecuador, Haiti, Panama and Uganda.
Sources: Three household surveys (Box 6.2).

than 25%) in Albania, Bahrain, Equatorial Guinea, Lesotho, Mongolia, the Republic of Moldova, Viet Nam and three-quarters of the countries in Latin America and the Caribbean. Regionally, participation rates were lower in sub-Saharan Africa and higher in Latin America and the Caribbean. Except in the Republic of Moldova, participation levels were higher for 4-year-olds than for 3-year-olds, significantly so in Bolivia, Guyana, Nicaragua, the Philippines, Suriname and Venezuela, as Figure 6.6 shows.

Figure 6.7 reports attendance rates in pre-primary institutions for 5- and 6-year-olds.[37] Among the former, cross-national variation in participation rates is considerable: from less than 2% in Burundi, the Central African Republic, Chad, Myanmar and Rwanda to more than 55% in Colombia, Ecuador, Guyana, Haiti, Nicaragua, Panama, Suriname, Venezuela and Viet Nam. Among 6-year-olds, participation levels are higher in some cases, but are similar or lower in many others. This pattern of declining coverage reflects, in large part, the onset of compulsory schooling and children's entrance into primary schools in many countries, including Bolivia, Cameroon, the Democratic Republic of the Congo, Guyana, Nicaragua, the Philippines, Suriname, Trinidad and Tobago, Viet Nam and Zimbabwe.

In sum, countries differ in two ways: the extent to which children's participation in ECCE programmes increases significantly with age or remains relatively stable, and the extent to which the transition to primary education affects participation levels in pre-primary education. To further clarify these national differences, age-specific enrolment ratios for children of ages 3 to 7 can be constructed for sixty countries (Figure 6.8).[38] The ratios are reported separately for pre-primary (dark bars) and primary (light bars). Instances of a 'mixed' transition occur at those ages with both dark and light bars – in other words, where enrolment ratios in pre-primary and primary overlap for the same age bracket.

A comparison of age-specific enrolment profiles highlights the following patterns:

■ Countries range between those in which very few children are enrolled in pre-primary education in each age category (e.g. Senegal and Yemen) to countries in which almost all children are enrolled (e.g. France and Italy).

■ In some countries enrolment ratios in pre-primary education rise quite steeply with age

37. As Nonoyama et al. (2006) point out, caution should be exercised when comparing country rates within and across household surveys for these ages.

38. Additional information on EU countries is available in European Commission (2005: pp. 128-30).

(e.g. Brazil, Cyprus and Guatemala) while in others there is little change with age (e.g. Azerbaijan and Mongolia). In the Russian Federation, enrolment levels actually decline with age.

■ In quite a few, mainly developed, countries the transition to primary occurs neatly at the official or theoretical primary entrance age, with no mixed age categories (e.g. Japan and Norway).

■ In other countries many children enter primary education earlier than the theoretical entrance age (e.g. Benin, Madagascar and Turkey).

■ Another pattern involves countries in which children of the official primary entrance age are still enrolled in pre-primary education (e.g. Mauritius and Pakistan).

■ Finally, in some countries the last two patterns coexist: children of official pre-primary age are already in primary education while others, of the official primary education age, are still in pre-primary education (e.g. Colombia and Lithuania).

Overall, careful comparisons of attendance and enrolment figures of young children in ECCE programmes are needed in order to improve assessments of programme coverage as well as progress towards the ECCE goal.

Disadvantaged and vulnerable children: limited access

Worldwide, millions of children who belong to disadvantaged groups and live in vulnerable settings are denied access to ECCE programmes, despite many studies highlighting considerable benefits accruing from their participation (see Chapter 5). This section examines which socio-demographic groups are particularly disadvantaged and which circumstances of vulnerability most impede access to ECCE programmes. It evaluates the relative importance of such socio-demographic factors as gender, place of residence, household wealth and parental education on the likelihood that a child will participate in an ECCE programme. It also considers the influence of several proxies of poverty, such as stunting and lack of a vaccination record or birth certificate. While these factors cover only selected types of disadvantage and vulnerability, they help account for major disparities in access to ECCE programmes.[39]

Do girls, children residing in rural areas or those in poorer households have significantly

Figure 6.7: Net attendance rates for ages 5 and 6 in ECCE programmes, showing significant cross-national variation, c. 2000

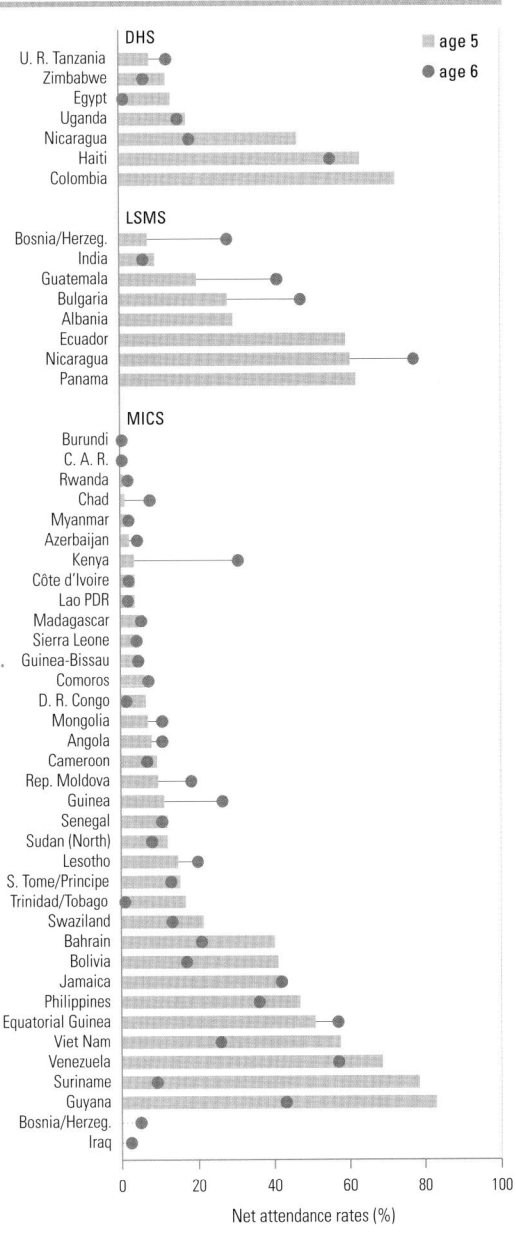

Note: Data are unavailable in some countries for children age 5 (Bosnia and Herzegovina, Iraq) or age 6 (Albania, Colombia, Ecuador, Panama).
Sources: Three household surveys (Box 6.2).

Millions of children who belong to disadvantaged groups and live in vulnerable settings are denied access to ECCE

lower participation rates in ECCE programmes than their counterparts who are male, live in urban areas or belong to richer households? Figure 6.9 shows the gender gaps and Figure 6.10 the urban-rural gaps in participation rates for care and learning programmes among 3- and 4-year-olds in countries with available

39. Children with disabilities and children living in emergency situations are discussed in Chapters 3 and 7.

Figure 6.8: Age-specific enrolment ratios for ages 3 to 7 in pre-primary and primary education, 2004

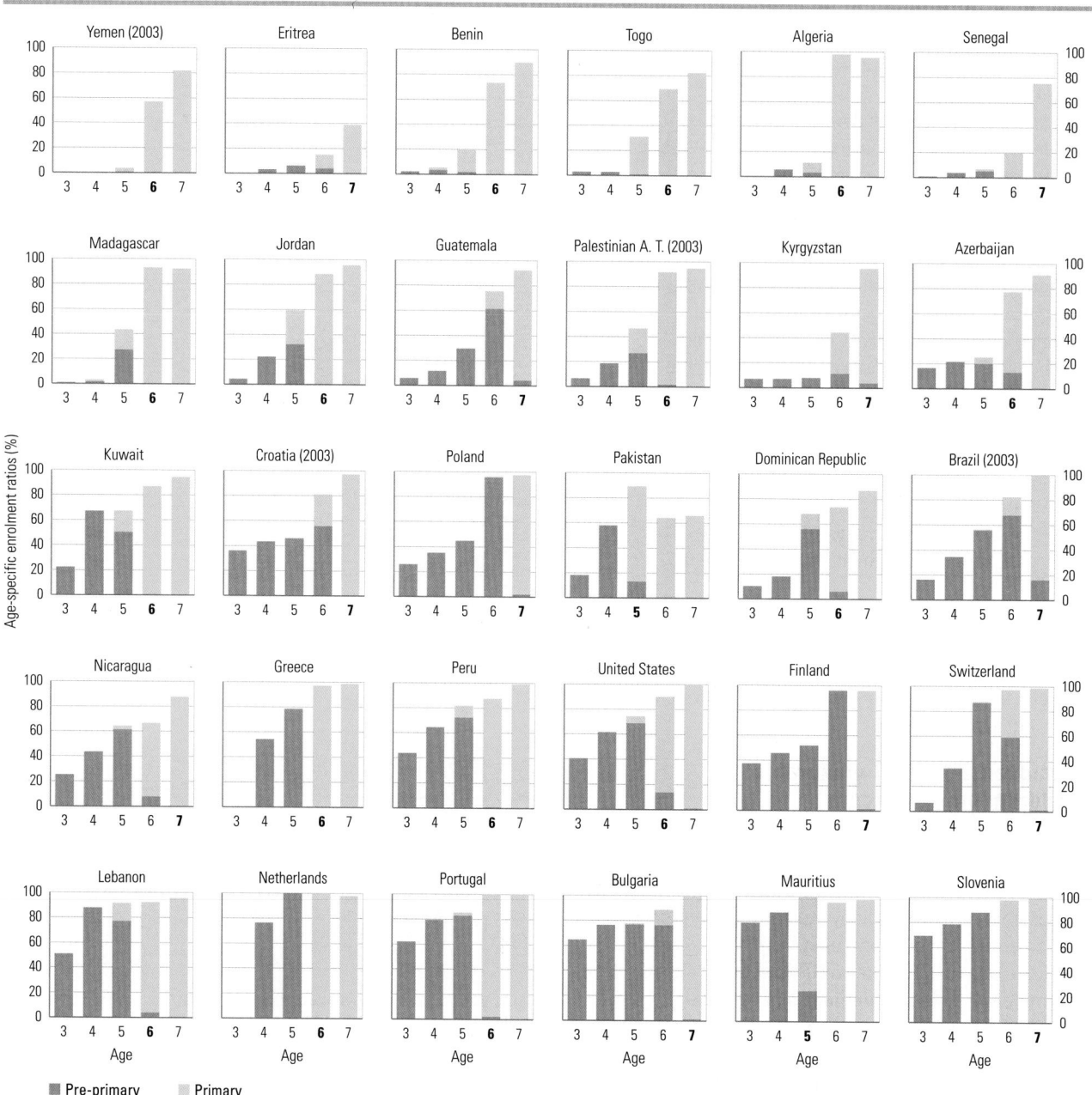

■ Pre-primary   ■ Primary

Note: Official primary school entrance age is indicated in bold for each country, except for Mongolia where it is age 8. In the following countries, compulsory education begins at an age lower than that cited as the official entrance age to primary school: Colombia, Dominican Republic, El Salvador, Guinea, Israel, Nicaragua, Republic of Moldova and Russian Federation.
Source: UIS database.

40. Nonoyama et al. (2006), Education Policy and Data Center (2006) and Carr-Hill (2006) also examine gender, urban-rural and wealth differences in attendance rates among 5- and 6-year-olds. The findings are largely similar to those reported for 3- and 4-year-olds.

data. Figure 6.11 reports household wealth disparities in participation rates, also for 3- and 4-year-olds.[40]

A comparison of boys' and girls' participation rates indicates that in most countries the gender gap is relatively small (less than 10%). In Bahrain, Colombia, Equatorial Guinea and Suriname the

gender gap favours boys, while in Bolivia, the Philippines, and Trinidad and Tobago, it favours girls (Figure 6.9). By contrast, urban-rural differences in participation rates are much larger and, except in Jamaica, always favour urban children (Figure 6.10). The proportion of rural children in early childhood programmes is often

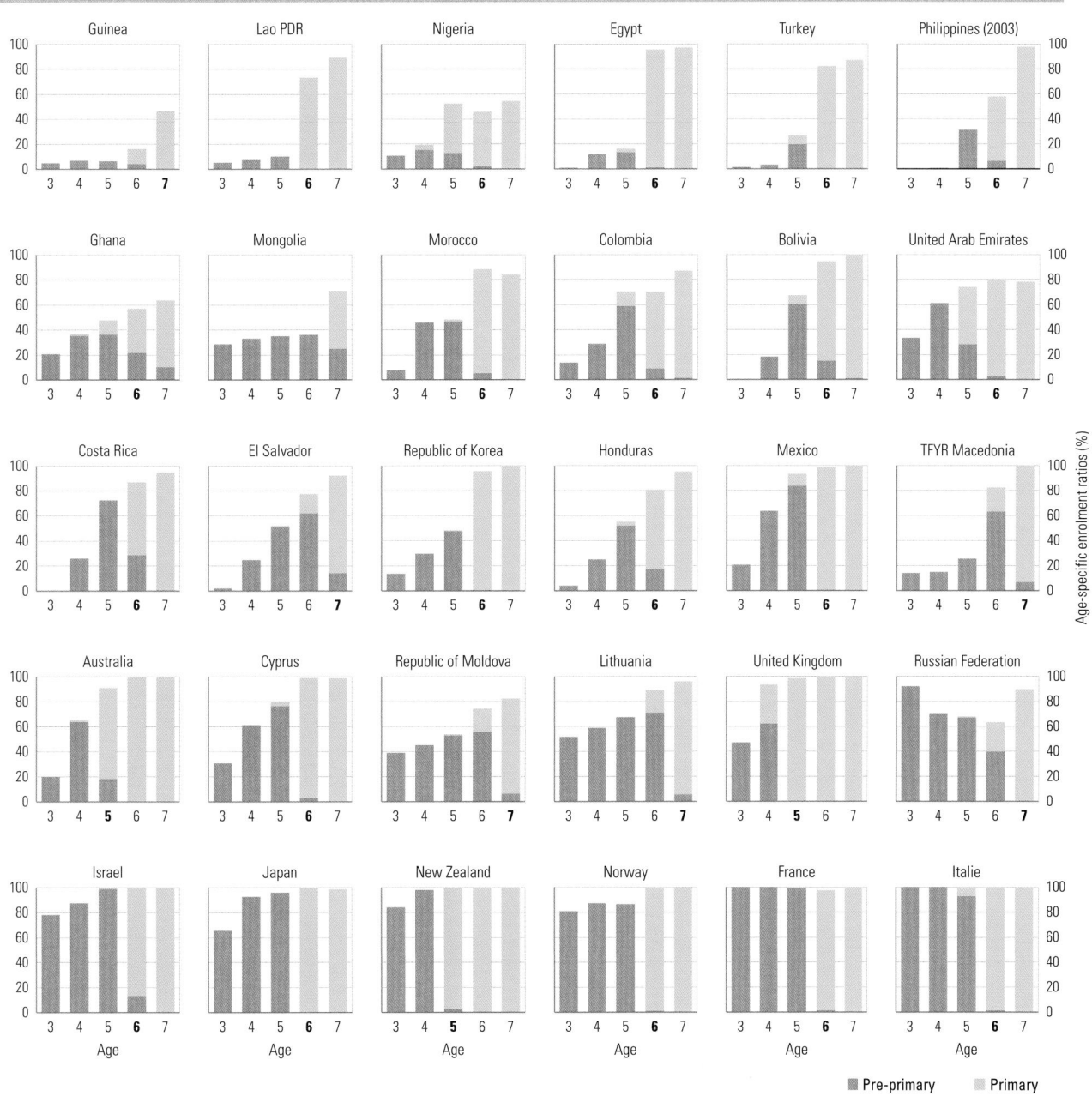

between ten and thirty percentage points lower than that of urban children. Place of residence is a more important factor than gender in accounting for participation rate disparities.

Figure 6.11 compares participation rates for the richest 40% of households with those for the poorest 40%. In general, children from poorer

households participate in ECCE programmes at considerably lower levels than do children from richer households. Poverty, like place of residence, is an important factor in access to early childhood programmes. Nevertheless, it should be noted that in Albania, Bolivia and Suriname, participation rates in poorer

Figure 6.9: Gender disparities in attendance rates for ages 3 and 4 in care and learning programmes, 1999-2003

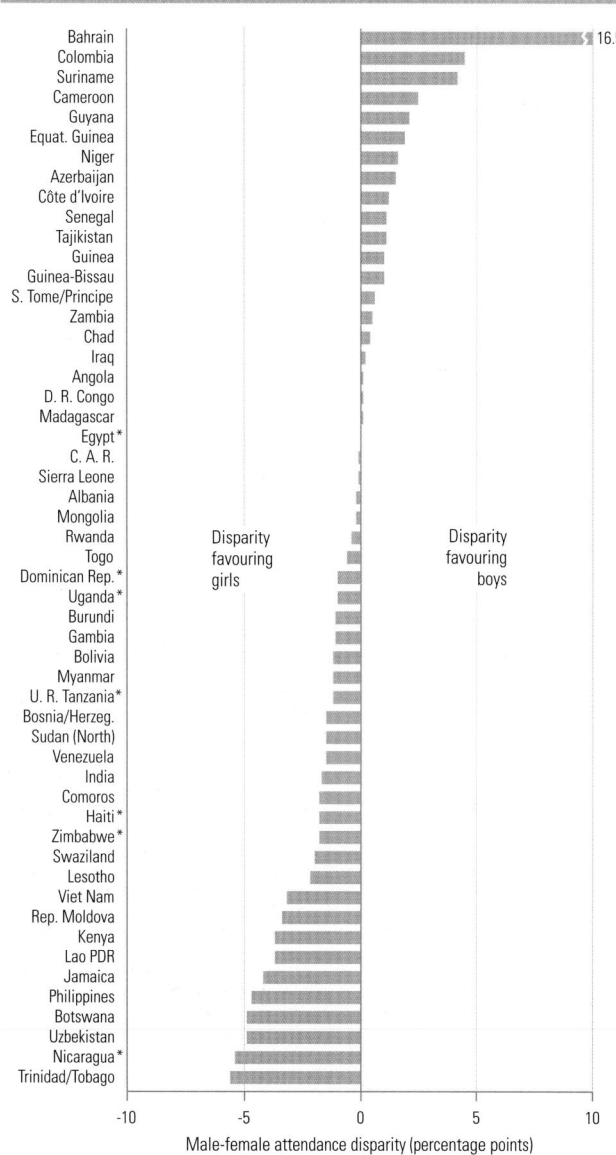

Disparity favouring girls

Disparity favouring boys

Male-female attendance disparity (percentage points)

Note: *DHS survey countries.
Sources: Three household surveys (see Box 6.2).

Figure 6.10: Urban-rural attendance disparities for ages 3 and 4 in care and learning programmes, 1999-2003

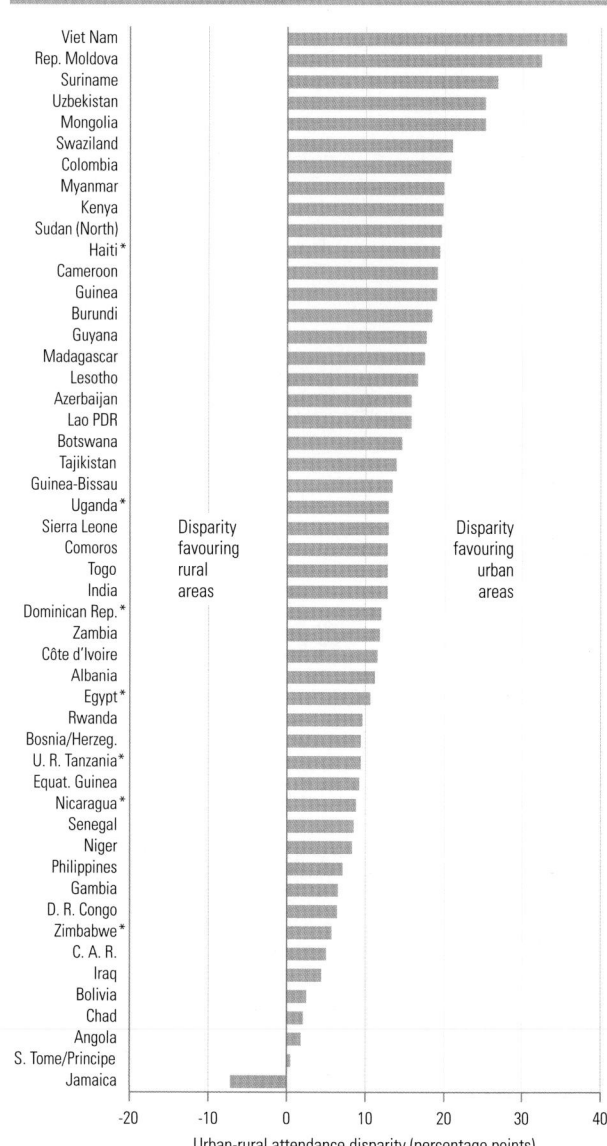

Disparity favouring rural areas

Disparity favouring urban areas

Urban-rural attendance disparity (percentage points)

Note: *DHS survey countries.
Sources: Three household surveys (see Box 6.2).

households are actually higher than in richer households, and that in some countries (e.g. Angola, Equatorial Guinea, and Trinidad and Tobago) the wealth gap is relatively small given the overall attendance rates. The evidence suggests that policy measures in these two groups of countries have successfully reached disadvantaged children.

Multivariate analyses were conducted to identify socio-demographic factors other than gender, place of residence and household wealth

41.Nonoyama et al. (2006) and Education Policy and Data Center (2006) also examined pre-primary attendance by 5- and 6-year-olds in forty-one countries.

that significantly affect the probability of a child's participating in an ECCE programme. The analyses, carried out separately in sixty-two counties with household survey data, focused once again on the participation of 3- and 4-year-olds in organized care and learning programmes.[41] They assessed the net effect of five variables – including age and mother's education in addition to gender, place of residence and household wealth – on children's ECCE participation. Table 6.12 shows the positive,

Figure 6.11: Household wealth disparities in attendance rates for ages 3 and 4 in care and learning programmes, 1999-2003

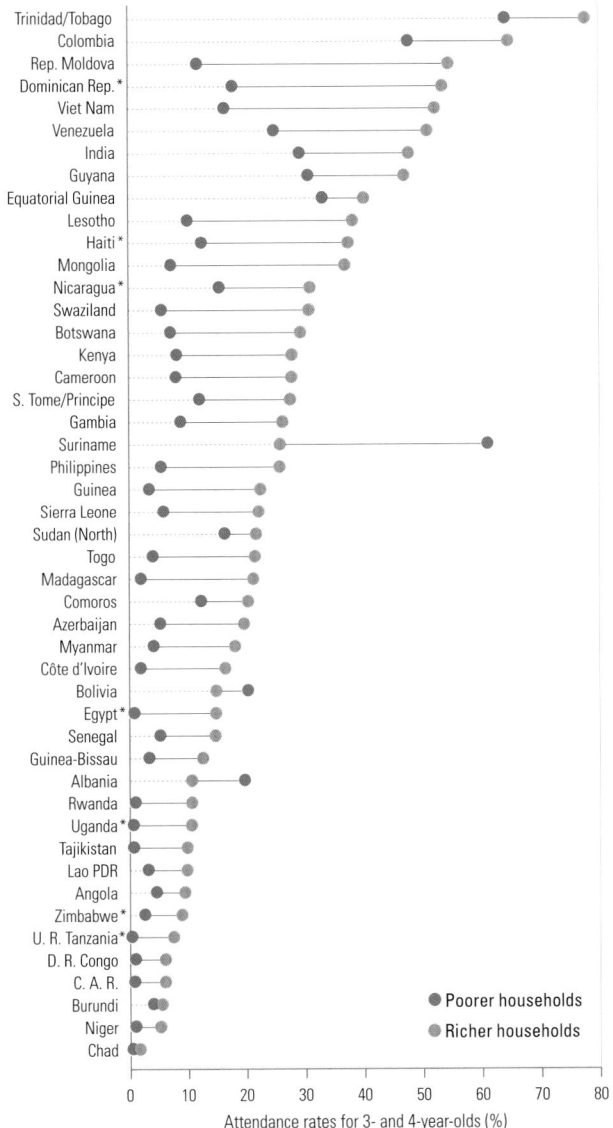

Attendance rates for 3- and 4-year-olds (%)

● Poorer households
● Richer households

Note: Richer households = top 40% by wealth; poorer households = bottom 40%.
Sources: Three household surveys (see Box 6.2)

Table 6.12: Results of multivariate analyses of ECCE participation by 3- and 4-year-olds[1]

| Variable[3] | Logit regression results (number of countries)[2] | | Not significant | Data not available |
| | Significant at p=0.05[4] | | | |
	positive	negative		
Gender				
Female	10	3	**48**	1
Age				
4	**50**	1	8	3
Place of residence				
Urban area (not standardized)	25	3	**30**	4
Mother's education				
Primary	19	1	**31**	11
Secondary or higher	**40**	0	13	9
Household wealth				
2nd quintile	8	3	**43**	8
3rd quintile	18	3	**33**	8
4th quintile	29	1	25	7
5th quintile	**37**	2	16	7
Other variables[5]				
Household size	0	5	5	0
Both parents home	0	1	7	2
Region of country	4	0	4	2
ECCE centre in village	1	0	0	9

1. This summary table gives the number of countries in which each independent variable has a significant or non-significant effect on the likelihood of participation in organized care and learning programmes. Each variable's net effect is analysed with the other variables held constant. Figures in bold indicate the main tendencies.
2. The upper part of the table deals with sixty-two of the countries involved in the household surveys discussed in Box 6.2: all forty-five of the countries in MICS2 (2000–03) with ECCE data; seven DHS countries (1999–2002); and the ten LSMS countries (1995-2003; for India, two states are used in the sample).
3. Logit regression analyses are employed when the dependent variable is dichotomous – in this case, whether a child of pre-school age has, or has not, participated in an organized early learning or pre-primary programme. The reference categories for the independent variables are (in brackets): gender (male), age (3), residence (rural), mother's education (none) and household wealth (bottom quintile).
4. Using a slightly lower significance level (i.e. p<.10), the same patterns are obtained, but with slightly more cases falling into the categories of the dominant trend.
5. The analyses reported in this section are based on the LSMS and include children aged 3 to 6. Only ten countries had variables appropriate for the multivariate analyses.
Sources: Nonoyama et al. (2006); Education Policy and Data Center (2006).

negative or non-significant relationships between each independent variable and the likelihood of ECCE programme participation.

By and large, the multivariate analyses expand and further validate the findings reported above. They demonstrate that while age is a significant factor in most countries (4-year-olds have higher participation rates than 3-year-olds), gender is not. The net effect of place of residence is mixed: in fewer than half the countries children in rural communities have lower participation rates, while

in more than half the cases this effect disappears and becomes non-significant. Both the mother's having secondary-level education and the household's relative wealth – especially in households belonging to the fourth and fifth quintiles – substantially increase the likelihood of children attending ECCE programmes in a majority of countries.

Findings on additional variables, based on a smaller sample of countries (the bottom part of Table 6.12), indicated the following:

Education for All Global Monitoring Report

2 0 0 7

■ *Household size:* In five countries children living in large households (i.e. families with three or more children) were significantly less likely to attend ECCE programmes than those in small households. The more children in a particular household, the less likely the family is to send them to ECCE programmes. In some cases household members may take care of children while others work, so parents do not deem it necessary to enrol children in child care.

■ *Two-parent households:* Having both parents at home does not appear to affect the odds of participation in ECCE programmes, after controlling for other socio-economic variables. The exception is Ecuador, where the effect is negative and significant.

■ *Subnational regions:* Brazil and Guatemala show large regional disparities in probability of ECCE attendance, even after controlling for

42. While the effect of the availability of an ECCE centre on participation levels was examined only in the Indian context, other studies provide evidence substantiating this finding.

43. Also see Carr-Hill (2006) for additional findings.

household wealth and urban residence. This may mean that certain parts of these countries are underserved in terms of ECCE centres, or it could reflect differences in culture, geography and accessibility.

■ *Availability of a centre:* In India, the supply of ECCE centres positively affects participation. Having an early learning centre in the village in which the household is located significantly increases the likelihood of attendance.[42]

The accumulation of disadvantage

Substantial evidence indicates that low birth weight, reduced breastfeeding, stunting, and iron and iodine deficiency are associated with long-term deficits in children's cognitive and motor development, and school readiness (see Chapter 5). Examining whether these factors are also related to participation in early childhood programmes suggests that the socio-economic disadvantages associated with poverty, social marginality, reduced nutrition and susceptibility to disease tend to accumulate during the first years of life and that the accumulated disadvantage significantly inhibits access to ECCE programmes for the most vulnerable children in society. The impact of these factors is further accentuated as children gain access to primary education.

To examine the influence of particular variables on participation in early learning programmes, MICS2 household surveys were analysed. The following patterns were observed:[43]

■ *Birth certificate:* In almost all the surveyed countries, children for whom a birth certificate was seen by survey takers were considerably more likely to attend organized care and learning programmes than children who had none (Figure 6.12).

■ *Vaccination:* The influence of a child having been vaccinated is similar to that of possessing a birth certificate. Children who lack vaccination records have lower ECCE participation rates than those who possess such records. Healthier children, in this case those who have been vaccinated, are more likely to attend ECCE programmes.

■ *Stunting:* In all the surveyed countries, children suffering from stunting have lower ECCE participation rates than other children. The effect is more apparent among boys than among girls.

In sum, the evidence suggests that variables such as the possession of a birth certificate and, to a lesser extent, a vaccination record are associated

Figure 6.12: Disparities in attendance rates for ages 3 and 4 in organized care and learning programmes based on possession of a birth certificate, 1999-2003

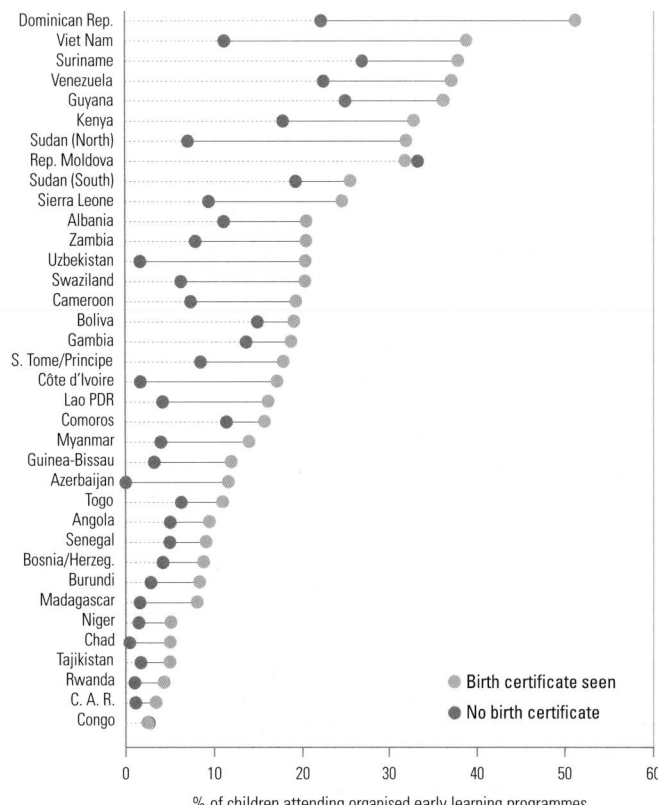

Note: The survey included a third category for which no birth certificate was in evidence (respondents stating to have the child's birth certificate, but which was not presented to the survey taker).
Sources: Three household surveys (Box 6.2).

with children's attendance in early care and learning programmes. Stunting, related to poverty, is influential in some settings and for some children but it is a less consistent predictor of ECCE participation. In other words, absolute poverty and social exclusion are important factors inhibiting ECCE participation.

Who are the child carers and pre-primary educators?

Early childhood teachers, pedagogues, nursery workers, child minders, day care staff, auxiliary nurses, volunteer helpers – these are just some of the titles used to describe the diverse workforce found in ECCE programmes and institutions. This section characterizes the type, characteristics and professional status of the heterogeneous staff working in ECCE programmes worldwide. A global and comprehensive survey remains elusive since comparable data about paid and unpaid ECCE programme staff working with infants and toddlers (under 3) are limited, especially for developing countries. As a result, this section mainly highlights teachers working in pre-primary institutions catering to older children (3 and up), about whom much more information is available.

UNESCO's 1988 survey identified three main categories of personnel working in ECCE centres: teachers (about 67% of all staff), day care workers (8%) and others (25%) (Fisher, 1991). The third category included administrators, helpers, play attendants and service staff, such as cooks, cleaners and guards.

Parents (typically mothers) may also be included in the ECCE workforce. In addition to being the first educators of their children, some parents actively assist in development, organization, management and fundraising for local ECCE programmes (Table 6.13). In developing countries and in rural areas, many ECCE programmes, especially those for disadvantaged children, would probably not be established without the collaboration of parents and community members (Fisher, 1991).

In many countries where parents have limited access to formal ECCE programmes, governments and NGOs develop parenting programmes to improve the quality of care and education that young children receive (Evans, 2006). For example, the international HIPPY (Home Instruction for Parents of Preschool

Table 6.13: Parental involvement in ECCE programmes

Type of collaboration	Countries[1]
Management/ administration of schools and centres	Benin, Bolivia, Fiji, Côte d'Ivoire, Lao PDR, Mauritius, Rwanda, San Marino, Sweden, Thailand, Yugoslavia
Parent committees and councils	Cameroon, Malawi, Nicaragua, Peru, Senegal, Syrian A. R., Ukrainian S. S. R., United Arab Emirates, USSR
Assistance in building or putting up centres	Congo, Dominica, Ghana, Grenada, Lao PDR, Mauritius, Trinidad/Tobago, Zambia
Making of toys, equipment and other materials or furnishing of centres	Albania, Belize, Benin, Fiji, Thailand, Trinidad/Tobago
Collaboration in starting, assisting or developing ECCE programmes	Cameroon, Spain, Suriname, Sweden, Thailand, Yugoslavia
Fundraising	Belize, Dominica, Fiji, Mauritius, Papua New Guinea
Collaboration with teachers and other ECCE personnel (including providing transport and supervision during field trips)	Belize, Benin, Congo, Czechoslovakia, Ghana,

1. As the survey was taken in 1988, the country names in use at the time are given.
Source: Fisher (1991).

Youngsters) programme provides parents with support and information to help them accomplish their role as first educator effectively (Westheimer, 2003). In more supportive environments, pre-schools are incorporating parental education within their learning environments. Open pre-schools in Sweden provide educational and developmental guidance to parents while their children are attending the centre (as of age 1). In Malawi, parents are trained in basic child care and pre-school activities within community-based child care groups.

What qualifications and training for pre-primary teachers?

Qualifications for pre-primary teachers vary greatly by country, as Table 6.14 shows for twenty-three developing countries for which relevant data are available. In four countries, pre-primary teachers need only a lower-secondary qualification (roughly equivalent to between nine and eleven years of formal schooling).[44] In eight countries, completion of regular upper-secondary studies is required. In the remaining

In Malawi, parents are trained in basic child care and pre-school activities within community-based child care groups

eleven countries, a post-secondary or tertiary qualification is required.

In OECD countries, tertiary education and specialized training are usually required. In France, pre-primary teachers must pass a national examination open only to holders of a three-year post-secondary diploma (OECD, 2004c). In Belgium, Denmark, Finland, Germany, Greece, Ireland, Luxembourg and Portugal, pre-primary teachers must complete at least three years of post-secondary education. A master's degree is required of pre-primary teachers in Spain (OECD/UNESCO, 2005). Sweden recently increased the university training course for pre-school teachers and 'leisure time pedagogues' from three to three-and-a-half years, making it equivalent to the requirement for primary teachers (UNESCO, 2002c).

The United States represents a special case among OECD countries. Most teachers in child care centres are not required to hold an

44. Information gathered from education officials attending a UIS capacity-building workshop in sub-Saharan Africa in August 2005 indicates that qualifications for lead and support ECCE staff may be even lower than requirements for pre-primary teachers in Burkina Faso, Lesotho, Malawi, Mauritania and Namibia.

undergraduate (bachelor's) degree (Ackerman, 2006): only fourteen states require teachers in state-funded pre-schools to have both a bachelor's degree and specialized training in early childhood (Barnett et al., 2004). Nor do teachers in private centres have to undergo any pre-service training in most states (Ackerman, 2004).

In many contexts, formal requirements are not enforced, effectively broadening the range of qualifications found among pre-primary teachers. For example, in Cuba, where enforcement is high, 100% of teachers meet formal requirements; the percentage is considerably lower in Kazakhstan (36%), the Lao People's Democratic Republic (59%) and Lebanon (52%) .

Qualification requirements also vary according to the type of ECCE professional and the nature of the tasks performed (Box 6.3). In most industrialized countries, the care and education components of early childhood provision are differentiated, leading to separate staffing policies and a 'divided workforce' (Moss, 2004). Highly trained educators or qualified pedagogues work alongside untrained child care workers, many of them part time. Some ECCE personnel work in, or are trained for, the whole spectrum of early childhood from infancy to pre-primary education; others specialize in given age brackets or in particular types of institutions, such as crèches, kindergartens or pre-schools (Moss, 2000). Researchers have identified certain categories of ECCE professionals common to many developed countries (Moss, 2000, 2004; Oberhuemer, 2000; Oberhuemer and Ulich, 1997):

- *Pedagogues*, who receive broad training in the theory and practice of pedagogy and work with children in multiple contexts from birth to compulsory school age.
- *Early childhood or pre-primary teachers*, who receive teacher training and work with children of pre-primary school age, primarily in institutional settings.
- *Child care or nursery workers*, who usually receive basic paramedical training to work in child care centres and may also be employed in early childhood services in the welfare system.
- *Qualified or trained auxiliaries* such as nurses – semi-professionals who typically work part time.
- *Family day care workers*, who have few, if any, formal qualifications or training and tend to work outside centre-based programmes; their status depends on whether they are independent providers or self-employed.

Table 6.14: Academic qualifications required of pre-primary teachers in selected countries and comparison with primary teachers, 2000-2005

Required qualification for pre-primary teachers	Country	Year	% meeting requirement	Required qualification for primary teachers[1]
Lower secondary	Burkina Faso	2002	98	same
	Chad	2003	…	higher*
	Guinea	2003	…	higher**
Lower secondary/technical	Lao PDR	2002	59	same
Upper secondary	Ecuador	2000	84	higher**
	Niger	2003	85	higher*
	Syrian A. R.	2003	87	higher*
	Cambodia	2003	93	same
	Oman	2004	…	higher**
	Bangladesh	2003	…	higher*
	Mali	2003	…	same
Upper secondary/technical	Uganda	2004	81	same
Post-secondary non-tertiary	Kazakhstan	2004	36	higher*
	Lebanon	2003	52	same
	Bolivia	2003	84	same
	Kenya	2003	…	same
	Lesotho	2003	…	same
	Senegal	2003	…	same
Tertiary	El Salvador	2003	76	same
	Cuba	2003	100	same
	Samoa	2005	…	same
	South Africa	2003	…	same
	Zimbabwe	2004	…	same

1. The number of asterisks (*) indicates how many additional ISCED levels are required to teach primary school: *= one level higher; **= two levels higher. For example in Chad, the primary teacher qualification is upper secondary, one level higher than the pre-primary teachers; in Ecuador, it is tertiary, two levels higher.
Source: UIS database.

Figure 6.13: Percentage of trained pre-primary and primary school teachers by region, 2004

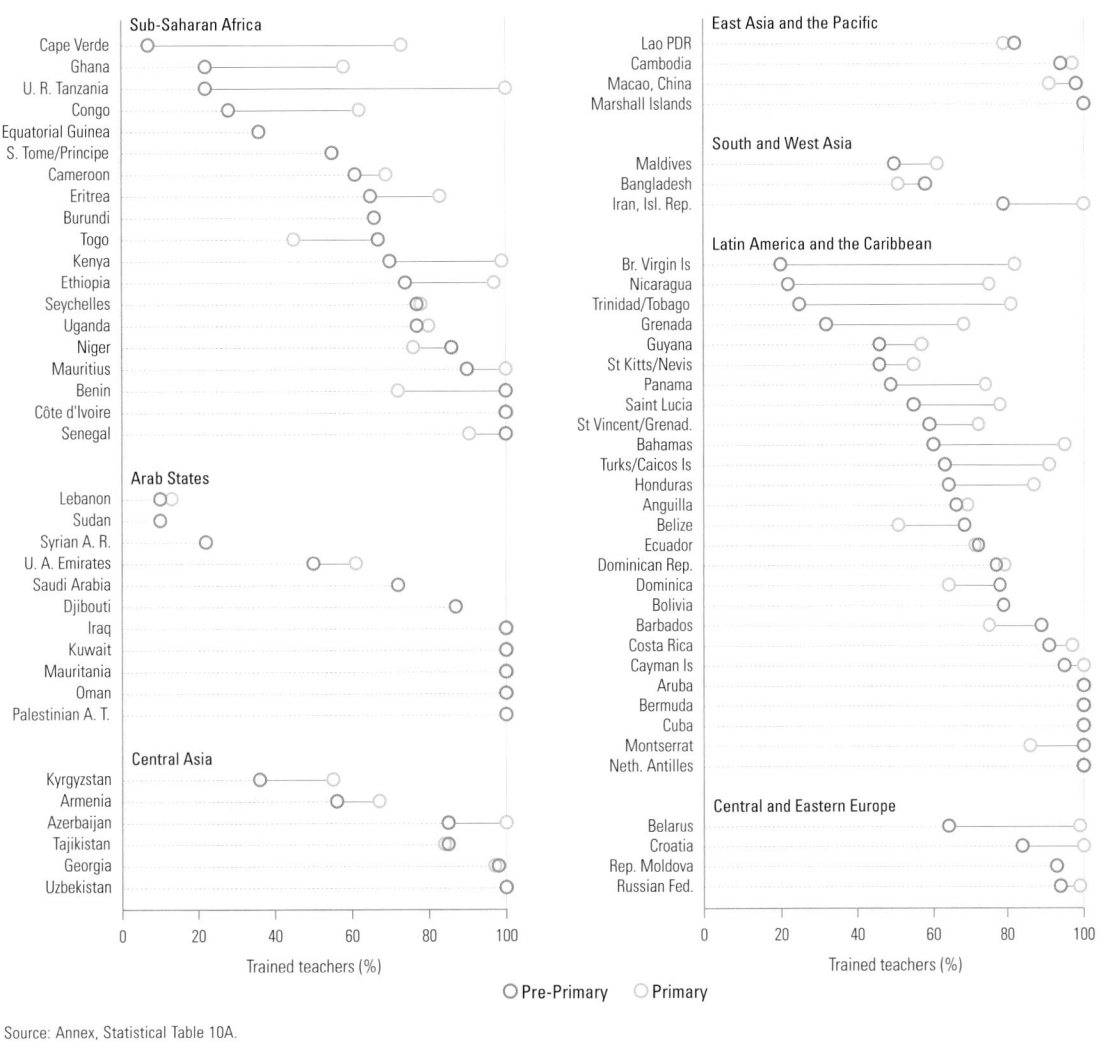

Source: Annex, Statistical Table 10A.

Almost all pre-primary school teachers are women

■ Many ECCE programmes are further staffed by *non-qualified auxiliaries* or *volunteers* such as mothers of attending children.

In general, pre-primary teachers have little pre-service training and almost always less than their primary school counterparts, as Figure 6.13 indicates. In 60% of the countries with data for 2004, more than 20% of teachers lacked any training, a percentage slightly higher than in primary education. In some countries (e.g. Bangladesh, Chad, Guinea, Oman and Syrian Arab Republic) there is no specific training programme for pre-primary teachers; only a few countries (e.g. Senegal) explicitly require teacher training. Lesotho and Uganda have recently developed training courses for pre-primary teachers: an early childhood certificate course taught at the

Lesotho College of Education and a nursery teacher certificate to be registered by Uganda's Ministry of Education (Wallet, 2006).

The age and gender composition of the ECCE workforce is related to the traditional caring roles of mothers and women. In many societies, the care and education of young children were assumed to be intuitive, maternal activities that required few formally acquired skills and little training. Thus, the prevalence of women workers in ECCE programmes represents, for many, an extension of women's traditional child care and mothering roles (Moss, 2000). Almost all pre-primary school teachers are women: the global median of women's share of the profession is 99% in contrast to 74% among primary school teachers. Among 151 countries for which data are

Box 6.3: The child care workforce in six EU countries

A recent comparative study of the child care workforce in Denmark, Hungary, Netherlands, Spain, Sweden and the United Kingdom described the characteristics of formal paid workers in child care and out-of-school care as well as residential and foster care. Informal carers and domestic workers were excluded from the study.*

The study found that the occupations and training requirements of the care workforce depended on whether the setting was domestic, group day or residential, and sometimes on the country as well. Care in domestic settings involved (a) carers in their own homes (family day care services), (b) nannies or other paid carers in the child's home or (c) foster carers. Care provided in group day settings was carried out by nursery nurses, nursing assistants and auxiliaries, and sometimes teachers. Social care workers, pedagogues and teachers were the typical occupations of those providing care to children in residential settings.

In most domestic settings carers had little or no formal training. In the United Kingdom, for example, foster carers, house parents, nannies and childminders had almost no training requirements. By contrast, most workers in group day and residential settings were required to be trained at higher levels and to have, for example, a vocational training certificate. In Spain, a medium training level was required for *canguros* ('kangaroos', nannies or other paid carers in the child's home), domestic helpers, instructors in child play centres, or those leading out-of-school or leisure activities for children. Finally, teachers, pedagogues and social care workers were required to have higher education credentials.

The study found part-time employment to be pervasive in the care occupations, partly due to the high proportions of women workers. Self-employment is very low compared to non-care occupations. Although personal carers working full time earn less annually than the total workforce on average, those on a part-time schedule earn more than the average for all part-time workers.

* This EU-funded study also examined carers for youth, disabled adults and the elderly, groups not treated in this chapter or, in the latter two cases, in this Report.

Source: van Ewijk et al. (2002).

the Republic of Korea (where fewer than 1% are 50 or older) and Japan (fewer than 6%). The age composition of pre-primary teachers has financial implications, since teachers who are more advanced in their career command higher salaries. Furthermore, when salary levels in the public sector grow more slowly than wages in other sectors or than GDP per capita, countries encounter difficulties in attracting new recruits to the profession (OECD, 2003).

In low- and middle-income countries, the more recent expansion of pre-primary education translates into a higher proportion of younger teachers than at the primary level. For instance, in Jordan some 80% of pre-primary teachers are below age 30 and in Paraguay the share is 52%. Exceptional cases include Indonesia and the Niger,[45] which have recruited large numbers of young teachers (and paraprofessionals) for primary schools to increase access and completion rates.

The importance of upgrading the ECCE workforce

Several trends are emerging regarding the expansion and upgrading of the ECCE workforce; these have implications for the development of good-quality ECCE programmes.[46] First, many countries are developing, revising or improving the training programmes through which pre-primary teachers become qualified. Some countries are expanding the availability of ECCE programme opportunities at general universities and vocational institutions. For example, in 1997 New Zealand increased the diversity and number of pre-service teacher education providers, including three-year training programmes for early childhood education, and Singapore did the same in 2001. In Egypt, universities providing education degrees have developed pre-service and in-service training programmes for non-specialized kindergarten teachers. Other countries, including Albania and the Marshall Islands, have recently developed their first programmes for pre-school teachers.

Second, many European countries (e.g. Denmark, Finland, Italy and Norway) are trying to reconcile primary and pre-primary qualifications so that teachers at both levels attain the same base qualification levels, albeit with different specializations (see Chapter 8). It should be noted that upgrading ECCE teacher qualifications does not imply that ECCE teaching methods or programmes are being usurped by the

available, male pre-primary teachers are a majority only in Nepal, Pakistan and Papua New Guinea, whereas in primary education they constitute majorities in thirty-eight countries, mostly in sub-Saharan Africa (see annex, Statistical Table 10A). The preponderance of women among pre-primary teachers also influences the design of ECCE programmes (see Chapter 7).

In OECD countries, where pre-primary education has existed for decades, the age distribution of pre-primary teachers is comparable to that of primary school teachers. In most OECD countries, more than 20% of pre-primary teachers are age 50 or older, except in

45. For details on the Niger, see L'Écuyer (2004).

46. The national ECCE profiles are the main source of information for this section.

developmentally inappropriate education components of primary school.

Third, in several developing countries, teacher training is being enhanced with research-based evidence concerning child growth and development. Following a reform in 1995, for instance, at least 30% of the training of Libyan kindergarten teachers must be devoted to educational, psychological and vocational sciences. In Mexico, the Quality Scale for Pre-school Centres, which evaluates national ECCE programmes, consists of seven research-based dimensions, including community involvement in the educational process (Myers, 2006). Singapore has adopted a national self-appraisal tool called PEAK (Pursuing Excellence at Kindergartens) to highlight problem areas in kindergartens.

Fourth, several countries are considering ways to include more men as ECCE professionals in order to strengthen the role of fathers in children's care and upbringing. In Norway, a ministerial decree aimed to increase the presence of men among kindergarten staff to 20%, but low salaries and general working conditions are considered major obstacles to reaching this goal (Box 6.4). Some other countries are considering similar policies.

Finally, many countries are strengthening in-service training or continued education as a means of improving the quality and qualifications of existing ECCE staff. In 2003, Estonia launched competence-based teacher training and in-service training requirements for pre-school teachers. Each Moroccan province has a pre-school resource centre providing continuing education and pedagogical support to teachers. The SERVOL Training Centre in Trinidad and Tobago organizes in-service training for other Caribbean islands.

In sum, the presence of knowledgeable and experienced early childhood staff – who are in short supply in most countries – helps ensure that ECCE programmes are of high quality (see Chapter 7).

The ECCE goal: slow but uneven progress

Historically, Europe and North America expanded early childhood provision earlier and more rapidly than other regions. Smaller households, changing gender roles, more working women and increased migration swelled the demand for centre-based child care programmes and pre-primary education. In developing countries, the traditional roles of women in agriculture and the informal sector meant greater reliance on kin and informal community arrangements for children's care and upbringing.

Europe and North America expanded early childhood provision earlier and more rapidly than other regions

---

Box 6.4: Salaries and teaching hours of pre-primary teachers

Improving working conditions is an important factor in increasing the overall supply of ECCE programme staff. Because of data limitations, however, it is possible here to focus only on pre-primary teachers' salaries and official hours worked for a limited number of countries.

Some data are available for eleven countries. In Argentina, Brazil, Jordan, Thailand and Uruguay, pre-primary teachers at the beginning of their careers receive lower salaries than the per capita GDP (Figure 6.14). In Argentina, Jordan and Uruguay, average salaries remain at or below the per capita GDP level at the end of the teacher's career, even after salary increments for experience or seniority have been accrued. In the rest of the countries, pre-primary teachers with the minimum required qualifications generally do better – their starting salaries are above the per capita GDP, and in some (e.g. India and Thailand) pay increases for seniority result in salaries that are more than double the

average GDP per capita. In Mexico (not included in the figure), to supplement their salaries some teachers work double shifts and others take second jobs outside education (OECD, 2004a). Additional data for the eleven countries in the figure show no evidence of major salary differences between pre-primary and primary teachers with minimum qualifications, except in Brazil (Wallet, 2006).

The number of official hours worked by pre-primary and primary school teachers in fourteen countries with available data shows no discernible relationship with salaries on a cross national basis (Figure 6.15). In countries where pre-primary teachers are paid the same salaries as primary teachers but work significantly fewer hours (e.g. India and the Philippines), unit costs are likely to be higher at the pre-primary level, since teacher salaries represent a very large share of total costs.

Figure 6.14: Average starting and ending salaries for pre-primary teachers with minimum qualifications as a factor of GDP per capita in selected countries, 2002-2003

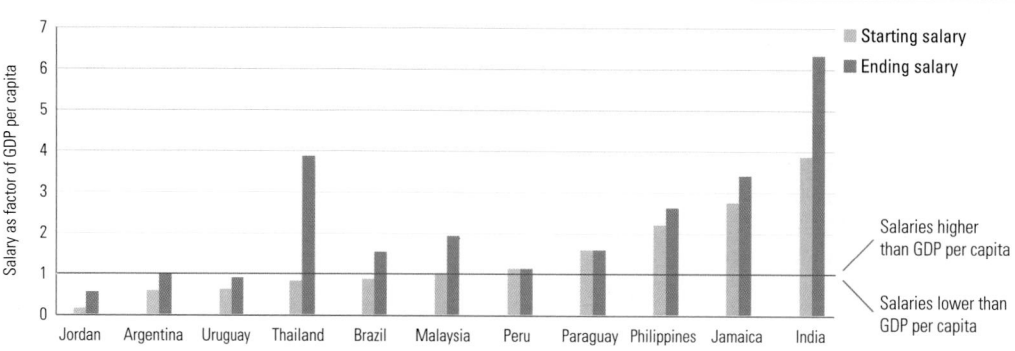

Note: Salary data for Thailand are for 2003-2004. Minimum qualifications were selected for starting and ending salaries since these categories provided the most complete data (see glossary).
Source: Wallet (2006).

Figure 6.15: Total annual number of teaching hours for pre-primary and primary teachers in selected countries, 2002-2003

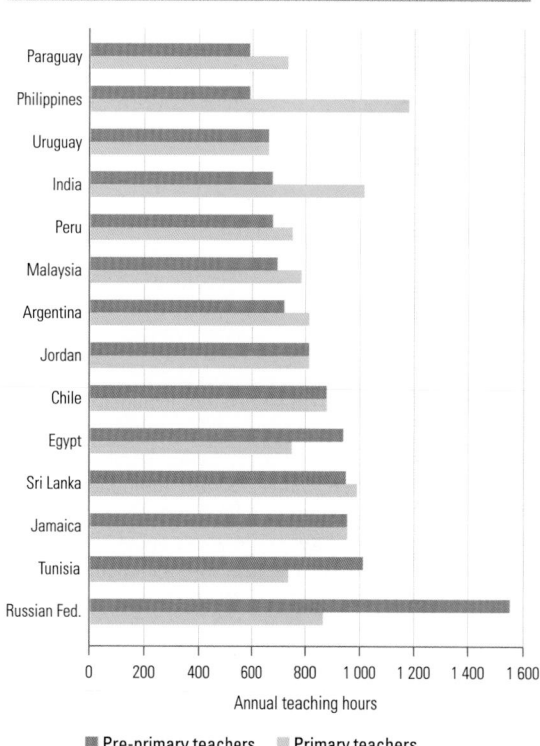

Note: Countries are listed in ascending order by pre-primary teaching hours.
Source: Wallet (2006).

This is now changing. Indeed, access to early care and pre-primary education has expanded worldwide. GERs in pre-primary education are increasing in all regions, though coverage in sub-Saharan Africa and the Arab States remains very low. After a serious decline in pre-primary education after the break-up of the Soviet Union, transition countries have regained most lost ground.

In much of the developing world, however, despite the increased coverage, children from poorer and rural households have significantly less access to early childhood programmes than those from richer and urban ones. In addition, the socio-economic disadvantages associated with poverty and social exclusion (e.g. inability to obtain a birth certificate) accumulate during the first years of life and further inhibit ECCE participation for the most vulnerable children in society.

This means government ECCE policy frameworks have the potential to make a difference for the disadvantaged, vulnerable and disabled. Yet extremely few countries have established national frameworks to coordinate or finance programmes that comprehensively address the diverse needs (health, nutrition, care, education, psychosocial development) of children in the first three years of life. For disadvantaged, vulnerable and disabled children, the lack of such national frameworks represents a truly missed opportunity. With respect to children aged 3 and older, many more official bodies – typically, but not exclusively, ministries of education – are involved in national policies and provision.

Carers and educators working in ECCE programmes and institutions, while almost uniformly female, are exceptionally diverse in terms of qualifications, training and experience. In most industrialized countries, trained staff work alongside untrained child care workers and part-time volunteers. In developing countries, the ECCE workforce, typically possesses minimal education and pre-service training. Many countries have implemented policies to expand and upgrade their ECCE workforce, but progress is uneven and slow.

Ways to improve the scope, coverage and staff of ECCE programmes so as to address the needs of all children from birth to primary school entry are examined in Chapters 7 and 8. ■

For disadvantaged, children, the lack of national frameworks represents a truly missed opportunity

A proud father with his son in Baghdad, Iraq.

Chapter $\boxed{7}$

The making of effective programmes

Early childhood programmes ensure children's holistic development by supporting and complementing efforts of parents and other carers during the early years and easing the transition to primary school. Such programmes are extremely diverse and no global model exists. However, all successful ones ensure continuity of support as the child moves from the family to a programme outside the home and eventually into primary school. One way to smooth the transition is by engaging with parents. Centre-based programmes, including pre-schools, for children from age 3 to school entry age require pedagogies and curricula that take into account the specificity of children's development and the social context within which they live. Given the relatively low participation and poor quality of many programmes in developing countries, it may be helpful to learn from and adapt others' experiences in meeting the challenge of expanding and improving early childhood care and education. This chapter offers examples from around the world.

There is no universal model of early childhood provision that can be followed globally

Learning from country experiences

There is no universal model of early childhood provision that can be followed globally. Each nation has to determine its own way forward, yet much can be learned from the experience of other countries. Good-quality ECCE builds on a nation's own experiences while drawing on and adapting lessons learned by others. For example, Western Europe's well-established and nearly universal early childhood systems, which are supported by the public sector, may not be immediately appropriate for sub-Saharan African countries where the private sector plays the key role in provision. Yet they can offer important findings relevant to curricular continuity, for example, regardless of how they are financed.

Despite the complexities of designing and implementing good-quality, holistic early childhood programmes, strong programmes share some characteristics no matter what the setting:

- focusing on and offering support to parents during children's earliest years;
- integrating educational activities with other services, notably health care, nutrition and social services;
- providing relevant educational experiences during the pre-school years and easing the transition into primary school.

This chapter examines the practices that make for continuity and a smooth transition from parental care to an early childhood programme and on to primary school.

The many meanings of early childhood

The meaning and practice of child care vary greatly within and across countries, as can be seen in the Home Observation for Measurement of the Environment (HOME) Inventory, one of the most widely used tools to measure the family environment, based on home visits in both developed and developing countries. Using observation and interviews, it assesses the quality and quantity of support and stimulation provided for children at home, as well as involvement with extended family and community that affects children. It focuses on three aspects of parent-child interactions: warmth and responsiveness, harshness and

discipline, and stimulation and teaching. Findings include the following:

- Although body contact is a near-universal form of responsiveness to very young children, differences in culture and socio-economic conditions influence how responsiveness is enacted in different countries. Belief in the 'evil eye', for instance, is strong in some societies, which has implications for face-to-face engagement as a form of responsiveness. In societies where pre-school children spend most of their time with siblings, parental responsiveness is more limited.

- Attitudes on the use of physical punishment to control children's behaviour vary widely. Generally, physical punishment seems more culturally accepted in societies where respect for elders and parental authority are highly valued, for instance in some African societies. In other cultural models, such as Mayan families in Latin America, there is more acceptance that young children's capacity to understand the consequences of their actions is limited, and parents are therefore less likely to punish their toddlers. In general, parents in societies that believe children should be deferential do not encourage them to contribute to adult conversations and respond to their emotional needs more non-verbally than verbally. Whatever the cultural context, harsh physical punishment is generally associated with negative outcomes for small children.

- Emphasis on stimulation for young children escalated in the late twentieth century, particularly in industrialized societies. Early school achievement is particularly valued in North America, Europe and parts of Asia, including Japan, the Republic of Korea and Taiwan (China). Parents in Latin America, by contrast, tend not to emphasize academic achievement early in life, as they see children as developing more slowly. In some African societies, children are expected to learn by observing rather than through direct teaching, and much emphasis is put on responsibility training.

In all societies, however, there is a strong relationship between household socio-economic status and scores on the HOME Inventory. Above and beyond cultural differences, parental income and education have a major impact on child-rearing. In all regions models of parenting are evolving, and educated parents tend to favour more stimulating and less punitive parenting. (Bradley and Corwyn, 2005).

Qualitative anthropological fieldwork underscores the fact that significant differences in parenting practices exist across and within countries. For example, young Kenyan children are often present as non-participants in situations dominated by adult interaction; they are not necessarily the focus of attention of the adults, but they are rarely if ever left alone. In contrast, young children in North America and Western Europe experience a sharp disjuncture between long periods when they are left alone and moments when they interact with their parents and receive much attention and stimulation. While young children in Kenya have few toys or other possessions that are considered their own, children in North America receive an increasing number and variety of gifts as they grow older, and are encouraged to develop individual tastes; as a result, young children in Kenya do not develop the same sense of individuality as those in North America (LeVine, 2003).

In small rural communities in Côte d'Ivoire, the care of young children is not individualized: as soon as they are able to walk (between the ages of 18 and 30 months), they are left free to wander around and it is assumed that any adult will take care of all children within sight (Gottlieb, 2004). Early learning thus takes place through experience and within groups of children who interact with most adults of the community, whether they are a given child's parents or not. Generally, young children in many sub-Saharan African societies are expected to be 'more obedient, less demanding, more helpful and more alert to and keen to meet the expectations of others; less linguistically precocious, although more likely to be bilingual; but also more independent and self-sufficient, and better able to entertain themselves' than young children in North America and Western Europe (Penn, 2006: p. 4).[1]

The emerging field of childhood studies places such observations of parenting practices in a broader perspective and emphasizes the following points:[2]

■ Young children's development is a social process. Children learn to think, feel, communicate and act by interacting with others in specific contexts. (Richards and Light, 1986; Schaffer, 1996; Woodhead et al., 1998).

■ Cultures of early childhood are also profoundly social, expressed through peer group play,

styles of dress and behaviour, patterns of consumption of commercial toys, and television and other media (Kehily and Swann, 2003).

■ Childhood contexts and practices are socially constructed. Most children today experience the world through built environments: classrooms, playgrounds, cars, buses and other forms of transport, supermarkets, etc. These are human creations that regulate children's lives. (Maybin and Woodhead, 2003; Qvortrup, 1994).

■ Childhood has been differently understood, institutionalized and regulated in different societies and periods of history. Early childhood has been reinvented and differentiated according to children's social and geographical location, their gender, ethnicity, wealth or poverty, among other factors (Cunningham, 1991; Hendrick, 1997).

■ Early childhood is also a political issue, marked by gross inequalities – in resources, access and opportunities – that are shaped by global as well as local factors (Montgomery et al., 2003; Stephens, 1995).

These perspectives draw attention to the ways early childhood is constructed and reconstructed, and how pedagogies and practices are shaped by circumstances, opportunities and constraints, and informed by multiple discourses about children's needs and nature.

Early childhood programmes should take these findings into account. Yet current programmes in most developing countries and models advocated by multilateral organizations and international NGOs are heavily influenced by developments since the nineteenth century in Europe (Chapter 6). Programmes are only rarely designed with an understanding of early childhood realities in a given country; more commonly they are driven by external ideas. The parenting practices of Western (and Westernized) middle-class families tend to be the benchmark of what is appropriate to young children's development everywhere, an assumption that can undermine the practices of other social classes and other parts of the world. When benchmarks originating in developed country institutions are used to measure what constitutes good early childhood programmes in developing countries, both the constraints and the opportunities within developing countries may be ignored.[3]

Some efforts to promote more culturally relevant programmes are highlighted in the discussion of good practice that follows.

Childhood has been differently understood in different societies and periods of history

1. See also Penn (2005).

2. The following discussion is based on Woodhead (2006).

3. For a broader discussion of these issues, see Nsamenang (2006).

Working with families and communities

The most rapid period of a child's growth occurs during the early years and it sets the foundation for later well-being. During this period it is important for children to have support in terms of protection, good health, appropriate nutrition, stimulation, language development and, most of all, interaction with and attachment to caring adults (Evans, 2000). Parents[4] or other custodial carers are children's first educators, and for the youngest group the home is the main arena of care. Carers and families can also benefit from resources in the local community that assist families in their parenting tasks.

Supporting parents

Research findings confirm that the home environment has a major impact on child development. For instance, the availability of reading materials, drawing and art supplies, and toys (especially home-made) is considered a good indicator of parental concern and sensitivity regarding play and development, and also of the quality of the home environment (Iltus, 2006).

4. As Chapter 1 points out, families may take many different forms, and a 'parent' is a main carer responsible for a young child, regardless of biological relationship.

5. Such programmes have elements that can be useful for most families, regardless of socio-economic status.

In the United States, a study of 700 first-graders found that stimulation and care in the family resulted in stronger attention and memory than did similar interactions in institutional child care environments (National Institute of Child Health and Human Development, 2005). In the Republic of Moldova, the availability of toys, and drawing and play materials in the home was a good predictor of high cognitive development scores among children aged 1 to 3, regardless of families' socio-economic status (UNICEF Moldova Country Office, 2005).

In most societies, child care is seen to be the concern of the family, immediate or extended, and not the concern of outsiders (Evans, 2000). However, as noted above, many environments affect learning and development. The best way to support the home environment is to work with the parents of very young children. Parenting programmes aiming to reach children under age 3 have proliferated in the past ten years.[5] They are most often offered through the health sector, but as ministries of education increasingly assume responsibility for education from birth onwards, they too are exploring how best to work with parents.

The two main types of parenting programme are:

- *Parent education* programmes, which provide training or learning activities for parents. They may impart actual parenting skills but can also involve livelihood skills, practical skills and others.
- *Parent support* programmes, which provide parents (or other main carers) with information on how to give children the care they require to realize their potential.

Parent support programmes, in turn, come in many different variations. They may include home visits, as in 'parents as teachers' programmes, which provide one-on-one support for individual parents. In recent years the trend has been to shift from a didactic model to a more collaborative one (Evans, 2006).

Home visiting programmes are expensive, because of the intensity of the inputs, and are thus best targeted at families at risk (Box 7.1). Visits should be weekly; less frequent visiting has not been shown to be effective. Attention must be continued for gains to be sustained. Gains achieved in programmes offered during the first two years of life are lost if the child does not continue to receive appropriate health, nutrition, care, and psycho-social stimulation. (Evans, 2000).

Box 7.1: Supporting new parents: the Community Mothers Programme in Dublin

Dublin has a support programme for first- and some second-time parents of children aged 0 to 2. It is targeted at single parents, teenagers, members of the travellers community, asylum seekers, refugees and people living in disadvantaged areas. Support and parenting advice are delivered by experienced mothers, known as Community Mothers – para-professional volunteers who are trained and supported by family development nurses. Community Mothers visit parents monthly and use a specially designed child development programme focusing on health care, nutritional improvement and overall development. In 1990 a randomized, controlled trial showed significant beneficial effects for both mothers and 1-year-olds in the programme (Johnson et al., 1993). In 1997-98 a follow-up study was carried out to find out if the benefits had been sustained (Johnson et al., 2000). About one-third of the mothers in the original intervention and control groups were located and asked for details on the child's health, the diet of mother and child, the child's development and the mother's parenting skills and feelings of self-esteem. Overall, the mothers in the intervention group demonstrated higher esteem and enthusiasm for motherhood than those not involved in the programme. This effect was evidenced by the way they interacted with their children and supported their learning and school experiences.

Source: Molloy (2002).

Parent groups are another common form of parent support. Parents with children of the same age, or with common interests and concerns, are brought together to acquire information and to share their experiences. While such groups are generally formed by professionals, it is not uncommon for parents to continue them on their own once official support has ended.

The variety of parenting programmes makes cross-national monitoring difficult. However, a review of evaluation literature on parenting support compiled in 2004[6] shows that early interventions produce better and more durable outcomes for children, and that targeted interventions (aimed at specific populations or individuals at risk for parenting difficulties) seem to work best when tackling the more complex types of parenting difficulties (Moran et al., 2004).

The many types of group-based care and support programmes for young children include home-based models (Box 7.2), community-based approaches (Box 7.3) as well as the more formal centre-based programmes discussed below.

Centre-based early childhood programmes

Centre-based care and education is the most common form of early childhood provision and government support for such programmes is increasing (Chapter 6). Centre-based programmes typically accommodate children from age 3 to the primary school entry age, offering a range of activities and learning opportunities to help young children develop the language skills, social skills and enthusiasm that are vital for their present and future well-being.

Fostering language and cognitive development

Centre-based early childhood programmes provide young children with a very different experience compared with home- and community-based arrangements. They tend to be more organized and structured, and have a stronger education component. Research in developing and developed countries has begun to identify key features of good-quality learning in centre-based programmes that have a positive

---

6. The review, by the Policy Research Bureau in the United Kingdom, is based on an analysis of over 2,000 journals, books and reports, and on evaluation of experiences with both universal and targeted parenting programmes.

Box 7.2: Hogares Comunitarios: mothers open their homes in Colombia

In the mid-1980s the Colombian Government set up a targeted programme designed to improve nutrition in poor households. Today the Hogares Comunitarios programme is one of the country's largest welfare programmes, serving more than a million children in urban and rural areas. This community nursery programme, catering for children from birth to age 6, now covers both nutrition and child care, allowing mothers to enter the labour market. Households eligible for the programme form parent associations that elect a 'community mother', who must meet minimal requirements set by the authorities. The community mother opens her home (*hogar*) to as many as fifteen children. She gives them three meals a day, constituting 70% of the recommended daily calorie intake. While earlier evaluations were inconclusive, a recent study looked at participation, anthropometric and welfare measures of children, and other outcomes such as female employment rates and hours of work. It found that the programme was reaching the poorest children and seemed well targeted. Stunting was offset: 6-year-olds who had attended Hogares since infancy were between 3.78 and 3.83 centimetres taller than those not in the programme. Children aged 13 to 17 who had attended the programme were more likely to be currently in school and less likely to have repeated a grade in the past year than those who had not.

Source: Attanasio and Vera-Hernandez (2004).

Box 7.3: ECCE in traditional societies: the Loipi programme for pastoralists in Kenya

Kenya's national policy of universal free primary education has put the pastoralist communities of the Samburu district in northern Kenya under pressure to become more settled and peri-urban. Parents need child care so they can perform daily tasks such as tending animals, finding firewood and working their gardens. *Loipi* (the Samburu word for 'shade') are enclosed places where young children are protected from danger and the sun. Grandmothers used to look after the children, passing on oral traditions and skills.

Since 1997 the Samburu, Turkana and Pokot people have pooled resources to provide care for children aged 2 to 5 through an integrated early childhood development programme. The Loipi programme is rooted in traditional approaches to child-rearing and offers access to health services, income generation and information on harmful practices such as female genital mutilation. The District Centre for Early Childhood Education and the Kenya Institute of Education provide professional guidance, while the Christian Children's Fund and the Bernard van Leer Foundation give financial and technical support.

In 2004 over 5,200 children (slightly under 50% girls) were enrolled at about seventy specially prepared enclosed sites selected by the communities. Members of the communities provided construction and play materials and built the sites. Some *loipi* also offer adult education, mother and child health services, nutritional supplements and health information. The system has improved nutrition and access to immunization and growth monitoring; also, pre-school teachers have commented on the positive influence the *loipi* have on the transition to primary school.

Source: Pennels (2005).

Education for All Global Monitoring Report

2 0 0 7

impact on young children's language and cognitive development (Bartlett and Arnold, 2006; Shonkoff and Phillips, 2000). For example, the Effective Provision of Pre-school Education Project in the United Kingdom found a strong correlation between a high-quality pre-school programme (one that provides warm interactive relationships with children and is managed by a trained teacher) and improvement in intellectual and social development (Sylva et al., 2004). A review of United States research indicated that children's development and well-being correlated strongly with programme quality. In particular, adult-child interactions were more closely associated with enhanced well-being than were structural features such as class size, staff-child ratios and staff training (Love et al., 1996). The IEA Pre-primary Project, one of the most significant cross-national studies of ECCE programmes, sought to understand whether and how experience at age 4 affected language and cognitive development at age 7 (Weikart, 2005). Seventeen countries[7] or regions varying in size, political constitution and level of development participated in the project, using jointly developed common instruments. Findings with respect to language development included:

- In all countries, children who at age 4 had been in settings where free-choice activities predominated achieved significantly or nearly significantly higher language scores at age 7 than those from settings in which pre-academic activities such as literacy and numeracy predominated.
- The amount of interaction with adults at age 4 was positively related to language performance at age 7 in countries with relatively infrequent use of directive approaches and negatively related in countries where direction was frequent.
- Teachers' level of education was positively related to children's age 7 language performance, while group size, and the quantity and variety of materials were not.
- In countries where adults often participated in children's activities, language scores at age 4 were more strongly related to the scores at age 7 than in countries with less adult participation.

With respect to cognitive development:

- Children who engaged in more whole-group activities at age 4 were more likely to have lower cognitive performance scores at age 7.

- In countries with more free-choice activities, the amount of interaction 4-year-olds had with adults was positively related to their cognitive performance at age 7, while the relationship was negative in countries with fewer free-choice activities.
- Greater availability of materials at age 4 was related to more positive cognitive performance at age 7, while teachers' education and group size were not.

ECCE: a powerful means of promoting equity

Besides their potential to enrich the lives of all young children, good early childhood programmes can compensate for disadvantage and hardship. They can also increase equity by promoting multilingual education, gender equality, and opportunities for the disabled and children in emergencies or precarious circumstances.

The overlooked advantages of multilingual education[8]

The frequency with which carers read to children and the number of books in the home help determine language development, reading outcomes and school success (Whitehurst and Lonigan, 1998). A large-scale longitudinal study of children in the United Kingdom found that the most important influence on children's success in learning to read in primary school was the extent of their direct experience with print during their pre-school years (Wells, 1985).

Poverty affects language development. By age 4 in the United States, a professional's child has heard 50 million words, a working-class family's child 30 million, and a welfare recipient's child just 12 million. At age 3, the professional's child has a larger vocabulary than the parent of the welfare child. The nature of verbal interaction also differs by socio-economic background. By age 3, the professional's child has received 700,000 encouragements, compared to 60,000 for the welfare recipient's child. School attendance later does little to attenuate these disparities (Hart and Risely, 2003). These findings clearly demonstrate the importance of exposing children – particularly those from lower socio-economic backgrounds – to language-rich environments in their early years. If difficulties with language development and communication are not addressed early in life, children are likely to face more difficulties learning and adapting to their surroundings later (Cohen, 2005).

Good early childhood programmes can compensate for disadvantage

7. Belgium (French-speaking), China, Finland,* Germany (former Federal Republic), Greece,* Hong Kong (China),* Indonesia,* Ireland,* Italy,* Nigeria, Poland,* Portugal, Romania, Slovenia, Spain,* Thailand* and the United States.* The findings summarized here refer to the ten countries marked with an asterisk, which participated in both Phase 2 and Phase 3 of the project.

8. This section draws on Arnold et al. (2006).

Children acquire languages quickly in the early years, and early childhood programmes offer them the opportunity to develop their self-esteem by using their mother tongue while acquiring a second (and sometimes a third) language (UNESCO Bangkok, 2005). Although UNESCO has encouraged mother tongue instruction[9] in early childhood and primary education since 1953, monolingualism in the official or dominant language is still the norm around the world (Arnold et al., 2006; Wolff and Ekkehard, 2000). A challenge facing most ECCE programmes is to respond to the needs of linguistically and culturally diverse children and their families.

Linguistic specialists argue that children who learn in their mother tongue for the first six to eight years (an approach known as the additive bilingual model)[10] perform better in terms of test scores and self-esteem than those who receive instruction exclusively in the official language (subtractive model) or those who make the transition too soon (before age 6 to 8) from the home language to the official language (transition model) (Thomas and Collier, 2002). It is easier to become a competent reader and communicator in the mother tongue. Once a child can read and write one language, the skills are transferable to other languages. Bilingual learning environments tend to be more comfortable for children than monolingual settings. Evidence from Bolivia, Guinea-Bissau, Mozambique and the Niger shows that parents are more likely to communicate with teachers and participate in their children's learning when local languages are used (Benson, 2002).

Mother tongue instruction is also important for promoting gender equality and social inclusion. Girls in some societies are much less likely than boys to be exposed to the official language, as they spend more time at home and with family members. Girls who are taught in their mother tongue tend to stay in school longer, perform better on achievement tests and repeat grades less than girls who do not (UNESCO Bangkok, 2005). Multilingual education also benefits other disadvantaged groups, including children from rural communities (Hovens, 2002).

Why, despite the research consensus, is multilingual education in the early years still unusual? There are many reasons. Some argue that opposition to multilingual education is a result of colonialism, where local political elites and international agencies have promoted colonial languages to the detriment of local ones.[11] The most common reasons are the views that in multilingual societies, bilingual education is generally too challenging to implement; it is too expensive; it would prevent children from learning other languages; and it would foster social and political division (Robinson, 2005). As regards the last point, however, multilingual education can, in fact, promote greater social tolerance among linguistic groups. Moreover, by facilitating the integration of different cultures and traditions into the curriculum, the use of local languages can enrich the content of education for all children (Benson, 2002).

The relationship between language and power is not easy to address, but early childhood is an important place to start. Indeed, the bilingual early childhood programmes in Cambodia, Malaysia, Myanmar, Papua New Guinea, Thailand and Viet Nam have shown promising results and have influenced language policies and practices for the first years of primary education (Kosonen, 2005). Box 7.4 gives one example.

> **The use of local languages can enrich the content of education for all children**

Box 7.4: Supporting grassroots efforts: language nests in Papua New Guinea

Grassroots efforts can lead to widespread change in language practices. In Papua New Guinea – the world's most linguistically diverse nation – a village-level, non-formal vernacular language pre-school movement led the central government to launch an ambitious effort to protect indigenous languages throughout the education system. None of the 823 living languages in Papua New Guinea is numerically or politically dominant. English had been the language of instruction since the 1950s even though it is the first language of only 1% of the country's 5.2 million people. In the 1970s, a group of parents worked with local government and NGOs to establish two-year vernacular language pre-schools, known as 'language nests'. The concept soon spread throughout the country. As part of its 1995 education reform, the government encouraged the formal school system to use vernacular language education in the first three years of primary school, followed by a gradual transition to English instruction. Today, the education system supports more than 350 languages. The Papua New Guinea experience shows that children who learn first in their mother tongues can transfer their cognitive, developmental and academic skills to English-language school environments.

Source: Wroge (2002).

---

9. The mother tongue is also referred to as the home language or local language.

10. In this model, either the mother tongue is the medium of instruction and the second language is taught as a subject by a specialist teacher, or the mother tongue is taught until about grade 5 and then the second language is gradually introduced, but is used for no more than half the day.

11. See, for instance, Alidou et al. (2005).

2 0 0 7

Education for All Global Monitoring Report

Early childhood programmes can adopt practices that value local languages, foster bilingualism and counter prejudice towards linguistic and cultural minorities. Two key examples are:

■ *Developing multilingual practices and resources.* Speaking and listening activities, especially bilingual storytelling and reading,[12] can be used in a variety of linguistic environments to give children the opportunity to develop literacy skills, which can be transferred from one language to another. Books and learning materials in other languages or dual-language books (even home-made ones) are important to promote bilingualism and tolerance of linguistic and cultural minorities as well as to raise the status of the languages spoken by children and their families.

■ *Recruit linguistically diverse staff.* To successfully implement bilingual ECCE programmes, trained, multilingual staff are needed (Benson, 2002). Not surprisingly, teachers and students communicate better when both are familiar with the languages of instruction. In primary classroom observations across Africa,[13] researchers found that the use of unfamiliar languages forced teachers to use ineffective and teacher-centred teaching methods, which undermine students' learning (Alidou et al., 2005). The best language speakers are often not trained as teachers and may need support in bilingual instruction (Johnston and Johnson, 2002). To address shortages of bilingual teachers in Western Europe (e.g. in Denmark, the Netherlands, Sweden and the United Kingdom), 'bilingual assistants' work in pre-schools with new immigrant pupils and their parents to help strengthen the mother tongue and build familiarity with the official language (OECD, 2001). In addition, there is a critical need to recruit multilingual candidates more actively for ECCE staff education and training programmes, and to train monolingual teachers in linguistic diversity. Family and community members are rich resources. They can volunteer in ECCE settings and help support language and literacy development in the home. Older children, for instance, can read to their younger siblings (Bloch and Edwards, 1999).

Curricula may emphasize gender equality; the practice is frequently different

Addressing gender stereotypes early

Gender disparities in access are much less common in early childhood programmes than at other levels, especially primary education. Pre-primary gender disparities at the expense of girls are found mostly in countries with very low gross enrolment ratios, although there are exceptions (Chapters 2 and 6). Reducing such disparities would contribute to closing the gender gap in education in general. In particular, parents whose daughters have attended early childhood programmes are more inclined to enrol them in primary school (Chapter 5).

Even where equal access exists, early childhood programmes often promote gender-specific expectations, a process that also occurs in homes and communities (Chartier and Geneix, 2006; Golombok and Fivush, 1994). Curricula may emphasize gender equality; the practice is frequently different. Teaching materials tend to promote gender-specific roles, for instance portraying male characters as powerful and active and females ones as sweet, weak, frightened and needy. Game playing can often conform to stereotype, with boys playing with blocks and girls in the 'housekeeping corner', and with girls in general having less access to the larger and more active toys and playground space (Evans, 1998). More importantly, teachers frequently do not treat boys and girls the same, which can create inequalities. Boys in pre-primary school receive more attention from their teachers than do girls, in part because teachers spend more time disciplining boys (Chartier and Geneix, 2006; Lockheed, 1982; Sadker and Sadker, 1994). Teachers also tend to call more on male volunteers and, indeed, non-volunteers. Teachers are more likely to listen and respond to boys, use more of boys' ideas in classroom discussions, ask boys more questions and give them more individual instruction, acknowledgement, praise, encouragement, corrective feedback and opportunities to answer questions correctly, in addition to engaging in social interaction more with boys. By contrast, they praise girls for being neat, following instructions exactly and raising their hands (Schau and Tittle, 1985; Vogel et al., 1991). Moreover, teachers discipline boys and girls for different kinds of misconduct, accepting aggression by boys but not by girls. In all these ways stereotypical attitudes and behaviours are inculcated in girls and boys.[14]

12. For example, the teacher or carer can read a story from beginning to end in one language, then in the other; or can alternate page by page. Monolingual teachers can engage bilingual colleagues and family members in such activities.

13. In Benin, Botswana, Burkina Faso, Ethiopia, Ghana, Guinea-Bissau, Mali, Mozambique, the Niger, South Africa, Togo and the United Republic of Tanzania.

14. Teacher behaviour also varies according to children's education and socio-economic background. Teachers tend to devote more attention to 'better' or more active pupils and to middle-class children who conform to the expectations of the school system. (Sirota, 1998).

Well-designed early childhood programmes can challenge gender stereotypes (Box 7.5). Such programmes are characterized by gender-neutral curricula. For instance, in France and Sweden, pre-primary schools have relatively gender-neutral toys and games (creative games and construction blocks). Toys that are common in homes are rare: war toys (weapons, guns, military vehicles, tanks and miniature soldiers) are not found in 90% of Swedish pre-primary schools and 70% of French ones, and the corresponding figures for fashion dolls such as Barbie are 96% and 89% (Rayna and Brougère, 2000).

Changes to the curriculum are effective only if accompanied by changes in teacher attitudes and behaviour. These in turn require changes to the teacher-training curriculum, including training in gender sensitivity and awareness, and approaches that help teachers become more reflective about their practices and the environments in which they work (Evans, 1998). They also require changes in staffing policies and practices in early childhood programmes. Women are predominant in the early childhood professions (Chapter 6). Taking care of young children has long been identified with motherhood and thus considered a female activity, associated with low pay and low status. It is often assumed that no specific training is needed to work with children. Conversely, men working with young children often evoke suspicion or prejudice, or concern that they will threaten women's sphere of power within early childhood institutions and even within the family (Murcier, 2005).

Encouraging more men to work in early childhood programmes could challenge prevailing assumptions about gender responsibilities in society more generally (Cameron and Moss, 1998).[15] Male child care workers can provide a role model of carers for boys and girls alike (Cameron, 2001). There are implications for families, too, as early childhood staff often focus on the mother as the main carer (Bloch and Buisson, 1998; Blöss and Odena, 2005). If more men worked in this field, closer relationships with fathers might develop. The impact on gender disparities would of course depend on whether men were committed to gender equality and properly trained so as to avoid perpetuating gender-unequal practices.

Despite their overall dominance among staff, women are underrepresented in administrative and leadership positions in early childhood institutions. It is important, therefore, not just to

---

Box 7.5: In Sweden, government drives the effort for gender equality in early childhood

In 2003 the minister for pre-school education formed a delegation to investigate the question of gender equality in Swedish pre-schools and to (a) promote lifelong learning that incorporates a gender perspective, (b) end stereotyped gender roles and patterns, (c) encourage debate on the promotion of gender equality in pre-schools and (d) encourage practical solutions. The delegation educates teacher trainees and politicians on these issues and distributes funds to pre-schools whose staff wish to develop methods for working with gender equality.

Source: Wetterberg (2004).

---

increase the male presence among early childhood staff, but also to improve the gender balance in management (Cameron, 2001; Sumision, 2005).

Meeting the early education needs of vulnerable groups

Chapter 3 provided a detailed review of policies and programmes to overcome exclusion in formal school settings. As EFA goal 1 makes clear, overcoming exclusion is also important even before young children enter formal schooling and, indeed, can help offset disadvantage and vulnerability. The most common form of disadvantage is poverty and many of the school-level measures described in Chapter 3 can also work in early childhood. This section focuses on programmes to provide early childhood education for two vulnerable groups that are often ignored: disabled children and those in emergency contexts.

Inclusive early childhood education for the disabled. Disabilities are common among young children in developing countries. Research in which more than 22,000 children underwent the same type of screening showed high disability prevalence rates in Bangladesh (8.2%), Jamaica (15.6%) and the city of Karachi, Pakistan (14.7%) for impairments such as seizures, cognitive, motor, vision or hearing disabilities. (Durkin et al., 1994). A study in Nigeria reported a prevalence rate for sensory-neural hearing loss of 13% among children entering school (Olusanya, 2001). Screening of 2,000 South African children under age 2 revealed a disability prevalence rate of 60/1000, including mild learning or perceptual disability, cerebral palsy, hearing loss, moderate to severe perceptual disability and epilepsy (Couper, 2002).

Changes to the curriculum are effective only if accompanied by changes in teacher attitudes and behaviour

15. Nordic countries have actively recruited men to the early childhood field. Denmark has been most successful: almost 20% of its pedagogues are male. They work with young children in kindergartens and older children in after-school programmes (OECD, 2001). Other countries have been less proactive.

Good-quality early childhood education is important for children with disabilities, as it enables early identification and remediation of impairments and for certain disabled children can aid transition into mainstream schools. Box 7.6 describes how Chile has paved the way for an inclusive approach to ECCE programmes.[16]

Sustaining children in emergencies. Provision of relevant, flexible education is critical to the support of the many young children in the world living in emergency contexts (Chapter 3). ECCE is a key part of such efforts, as it can help offset some the negative consequences of crisis and conflict. A review of experience and literature suggests the following principles are generally applicable (Kamel, 2005):

Access

- The right of access to early childhood education, recreation and related activities must be assured even in crisis situations.

16. Chile's First National Study on Disability, published in 2005, identified 129,994 pupils with disabilities in primary and secondary education. Of these, 100,521 attended special schools and 29,473 attended programmes integrated into mainstream schools (De Bonadona, 2005).

- Rapid access to education, recreation and related activities must be assured, followed by steady improvement in quality and coverage.
- ECCE should serve as a tool for child protection and harm prevention.

Resources

- ECCE programmes should use a community-based participatory approach, with emphasis on capacity-building.
- They should include a major teacher-training component and provide incentives to avoid teacher turnover.
- Crisis and recovery programmes should develop and document targets for funding that adequately meet their educational and psychosocial objectives.

Activities/curriculum

- Curriculum policy should support long-term development and encourage lasting solutions.
- ECCE programmes should be holistic, incorporating such dimensions as health and nutrition, water and sanitation.
- They should be enriched to promote tolerance, human rights and citizenship within the context of political disasters and complex emergencies.

Child Friendly Spaces, which UNICEF has established in countries including Angola, Burkina Faso, the Democratic Republic of the Congo and Liberia, are based on these principles (Box 7.7).

ECCE can ease the transition to primary schooling

ECCE of good quality is not only an end in itself; as the EFA goals recognizes, it is also an important foundation for subsequent education. This section examines how ECCE programmes can make children ready for primary school and how primary schools themselves can adapt to young children.

The two main approaches regarding the transition to primary school may be summed up as 'school readiness' and 'ready schools' (Fabian and Dunlop, 2006). The former stresses the importance of ECCE in promoting children's development and assuring their school readiness; it seeks to identify the characteristics that children should display if they are ready for school. The consensus from research is that school readiness encompasses development

---

Box 7.6: Chile's first steps towards mainstreaming children with special needs

In Chile, 5.8% of children under 16 have physical, psychological, mental or sensory disabilities. A 1994 law on integration of people with special needs, covering all social sectors, requires public and private mainstream education institutions to develop the innovations and curricular adaptations necessary to enable access for people with special needs. The Junta Nacional de Jardines Infantiles (JUNJI), or National Board of Kindergartens, established in 1970, administers ECCE provision for more than 120,500 children. Since 1995 it has been mainstreaming nursery and pre-school programmes targeting the poorest children with special needs. JUNJI centres serve children aged 3 months to 5 years with special needs (including physical, mental, visual and hearing impairments) in mainstream settings. Adapting ECCE programmes to children with special needs has involved sensitizing and training teachers through courses supported by the Special Education Department of the Ministry of Education. The National Fund for Special Education financed equipment such as wheelchairs, prostheses and hearing aids. Technical guidelines and principles were established to identify children with special needs and adapt structures to accommodate children with physical disabilities. Private organizations working with JUNJI were offered projects for sponsorship. Though coverage levels remain low, the efforts made by JUNJI and other early childhood institutions in Chile provide a good example of how to encourage practices to include children at risk of exclusion or marginalization.

Sources: Chile FONADIS (2005); Larraguibel Quiroz (1997); Umayahara (2006).

Box 7.7: Child Friendly Spaces: havens for mothers and children in emergencies

In emergency contexts, UNICEF, often working with local groups, sets up 'Child Friendly Spaces' in refugee camps, schools and other sheltered situations. They fulfil several important functions, ensuring that children have access to ECCE services and incorporating several dimensions of care, not least that of creating a sense of security for mothers and children. In Liberia, UNICEF established spaces that provided comfortable places for mothers to breastfeed; early childhood development classes with components on hygiene, nutrition, the importance of play and so on; and services related to health, nutrition, early stimulation and learning, water,

hygiene and sanitation, and protection of young children. Similar spaces were set up in the Democratic Republic of the Congo at community-based early childhood development centres. When Angola's long-running civil war ended, national and international NGOs supported the creation of Child Friendly Spaces that served over 30,000 children in seventeen war-affected provinces; with UNICEF support, two international NGOs trained trainers for the spaces who also worked with parents on child development. These trainers in turn trained over 450 volunteers from among the displaced populations to conduct child development activities.

Source: Kamel (2005).

in five distinct but interconnected domains (Arnold et al., 2006; Copple, 1997; Offord Center for Child Studies, 2005):[17]

- physical well-being and motor development (measured in terms of health, growth and disabilities),
- social and emotional development (e.g. ability to control one's own behaviour, or to play and work with other children),
- approach to learning (e.g. enthusiasm, curiosity, persistence and temperament),
- language development (e.g. vocabulary, grammar and ability to learn and communicate) and
- cognitive development and general knowledge (e.g. cognitive and problem-solving skills, such as learning to observe and to note similarities and differences).

Children vary greatly in all these areas.

The concept of 'ready schools', on the other hand, focuses on characteristics of the school environment that facilitate or hinder learning.[18] Researchers have identified several factors that can undermine readiness, among them overcrowded classes, the 'language gap' (when the language of instruction differs from the child's mother tongue), an absence of qualified and experienced first grade teachers and inadequate learning materials (Arnold et al., 2006). These factors have been particularly challenging to address in developing countries.

The relative importance of school readiness and ready schools is much debated, and transition strategies are difficult to evaluate,[19] yet it is increasingly clear that the key to effective services for young children is continuity of certain elements that characterize all good early childhood

programmes (Fabian and Dunlop, 2002; Kagan and Neuman, 1998). Strategies include the integration of ECCE with primary education, continuity of curriculum, continuity between home and school, and, for disadvantaged children who have not benefited from ECCE programmes, special activities aimed specifically at easing the entry into primary school.

Continuity through integration of ECCE with primary education

The strategy of integrating ECCE with formal primary education aims to develop a more coherent system of policy, governance, administration and monitoring for ECCE and primary schools. The trend of integration into education systems is most evident in Europe (including in Belgium, the Czech Republic, Denmark, France, Norway, Portugal, Spain, Sweden and the United Kingdom) but is observed in a few other countries, such as Brazil, Kazahkstan, South Africa and Viet Nam.

Implementing this strategy entails creating administrative structures that unite previously separate ECCE and primary education structures. To do so, countries have unified pre-primary and primary education under the governance of the public school system, fully integrating childhood services from birth through compulsory education, and sometimes even holding pre-school classes in primary school buildings. In some cases, countries have lowered the entry age for compulsory schooling to include pre-primary children (as in Argentina, Costa Rica, the Dominican Republic, Ecuador, El Salvador, Norway, Peru, Uruguay and Venezuela).

The key to effective services for young children is continuity of certain elements that characterize all good early childhood programmes

17. School readiness is influenced by the same factors as children's overall development. In addition to being positively associated with participation in pre-primary programmes and exposure to transition activities, it is affected by family income, home language, parents' education and family size. Differences between public and private pre-schools, and urban and rural residence have also been found, as have variations linked to geographical location and neighbourhood (Kohen et al., 1998; Magnuson, Meyers et al., 2004; Magnuson, Ruhm et al., 2004; Margetts, 1999; National Center for Human Resources Development, 2005; Ngaruiya, 2006). Some also found adverse effects of pre-kindergarten programmes (Magnuson, Ruhm et al., 2004).

18. This analysis is based on Arnold et al. (2006).

19. Few programmes and schools focus on the transition stage and, at those that do, transition activities are usually part of more comprehensive efforts, making it difficult to assess their impact.

While structural integration may yield benefits, it entails a risk of the education component of ECCE overshadowing the welfare, health and care components, resulting in a school-centred view of pre-primary and other ECCE services. Carried to an extreme, this can lead to undue pressure on children for academic achievement at an early age (Shaeffer, 2006; Shore, 1998).

Curriculum continuity

In most countries, ECCE programmes and the primary education system developed for different reasons, with different aims and philosophies, so the important aim of achieving continuity of curriculum is not straightforward. Examples of strategies include:

- Developing and using an integrated curriculum for pre-primary and primary school, with learning cycles organized around the development cycles of the child. This approach is taken in the Pre-Primary to Primary Transitions project in Jamaica, the Transition from Nursery School to Primary School project in Guyana and the integrated curriculum cycle used in France. Sweden has developed two curricula that are conceptually linked.
- Making an intentional connection between – or overlapping – teaching and learning styles and materials between the pre-primary and primary levels. The Releasing Confidence and Creativity programme in Pakistan provides similar instructional materials at both levels.
- Ensuring that classmates from a given pre-school classroom are transferred together to the same primary classroom, as with the Step by Step programme of transition to primary school in thirty countries of Central and Eastern Europe and Central Asia.
- Grouping learners not by age but rather by level of development. Bodh Shiksha Samiti in India and Escuela Nueva in Colombia involve multigrade classrooms using an active curriculum, methods and lesson plans that respond to differing abilities and interests (as does the Step by Step curriculum cited above).

Less integrated strategies have also contributed to pedagogical continuity and integrated learning experiences. Portugal allows children to be 'followed' over the years by the same teacher or group of teachers (a practice commonly referred as 'looping'); 'buddy programmes' in Sydney, Australia, which pair older students with those just starting, recognize the importance of early peer support (Docket and Perry, 2005).

> France uses community mediators to link schools with low-income neighbourhoods

Home-to-school continuity and parental involvement

Language and communication barriers between teachers and parents are challenging. They can be overcome, and children's transition eased, by sharing information and involving parents, taking into account their preferences and values, and respecting ethnic, cultural, linguistic, religious and other forms of diversity (Docket et al., 2000; Margetts, 1999).

Approaches include providing bilingual ECCE and primary school programmes, establishing good communication and participation networks between schools and parents, involving parents in class activities and suggesting home activities that may help prepare children for school. In the Step by Step programme in transition countries, parents and pre-school teachers review the primary school curriculum together and discuss the child's readiness. In Pakistan, parents in poor rural communities become resource people, teaching local songs and stories and demonstrating skills such as construction. The *adulte-relais* or 'resource adult' initiative in France uses community mediators to link schools with low-income neighbourhoods so as to break down communication barriers (Neuman and Peer, 2002).

In Kazakhstan, pre-primary education classes prepare 5- or 6-year-olds who have never attended pre-school (especially in rural areas) for formal schooling through a 32-week crash course in school readiness. There is some concern that such classes focus too narrowly on academic skills; it is important to focus as well on children's emotional well-being, which is vital to their adjustment to primary schooling (Choi, 2006). France's *lieux passerelles*, 'crossing places' for children with no experience of early childhood activities outside the home, are designed to foster socialization with peers and transition from home to pre-school through structured activities and free play. Parents, often from poor, immigrant backgrounds, get staff support in separating from their children, meeting other parents and taking a role in their children's education (Neuman and Peer, 2002). Though the focus is on transition from home to the *école maternelle* (pre-school) – the first contact with the school system for many immigrant families – similar activities can be adapted to transition to primary school.

Where television is widely available, either at home or community centres, television and radio programmes such as those produced through the

Sesame Workshop (Box 7.8) have proved helpful in getting children ready for school and easing the transition.

Improving transition opportunities for the disadvantaged

So far this section has been about children with access to some form of pre-school education and care. The reality for most children in the world, particularly the most disadvantaged, is that the first school experience is the start of primary school, usually around the age of 6 (see annex, Statistical Table 4). In contexts where pre-primary school is not compulsory or has low coverage, various measures can help prepare children for primary school even without formal ECCE programmes. They include visits to primary schools to familiarize children with the school environment (as in Nepal), visits by first-grade teachers to home- or centre-based ECCE settings; low pupil/teacher ratios in the early primary grades; and readiness programmes or tutorials before primary school entry or during the first few months (as in Cambodia).

In Guatemala the Centros de Aprendizaje Comunitario en Educación Preescolar (CENACEP), or Centres for Community Learning in Pre-school Education, is an accelerated thirty-five-day course of preparation for children from various ethnic backgrounds who have not had access to pre-school. Sponsored by the Ministry of Education and UNICEF, and involving community volunteers, the programme is provided to groups of thirty-five to forty children under age 6 in the three months before the beginning of the school year. Participants are better prepared socially and academically for primary school, and repetition and dropout rates have fallen in places where they were formerly a problem (Elvir and Asensio, 2006).

Conclusion

While successful ECCE programmes are extremely diverse, both within countries and around the world, certain general lessons emerge. First, early childhood programmes need to be rooted in the young children's cultural environment and care must be taken not simply to import models from abroad without appropriate adaptation. Second, parenting programmes can support positive child-rearing practices, which again need to be understood in their social and

Box 7.8: Using television to promote school readiness around the world

The Sesame Workshop illustrates the potential of the broadcast media for promoting school readiness in young children, including those without access to formal early childhood programmes. Founded in 1968, the Sesame Workshop created the legendary Sesame Street children's television series in the United States. Now in 120 countries, the Sesame Workshop partners with local writers, artists, researchers and educators to create culture-specific television and radio programmes with characters, sets and content designed to address local children's educational needs. Storybooks and other materials are distributed to children of pre-school age, and teachers and parents are trained to use the materials to support the children's learning. Examples of television and radio programmes from selected countries:

- In Egypt, *Alam Simsim* includes special emphasis on girls' education. Khokha, a female Muppet, encourages young girls to have a limitless sense of possibility.

- In South Africa, on *Takalani Sesame*, Kami, a vibrant and affectionate HIV-positive Muppet, helps children and their carers overcome the stigma of the disease.

- In Bangladesh, *Sisimpur* features the Muppet Halum, a Bangla-speaking vegetarian Bengal tiger. Once a week, flatbed cycle rickshaws carry televisions, DVD players and generators to villages with limited or no electricity so children can see the programme.

- In Israel and the Palestinian Autonomous Territories, the *Rechov Sumsum/Shara'a Simsim* promotes cross-cultural respect and understanding among Arab and Jewish pre-schoolers, countering negative stereotypes by introducing children to the everyday lives of people from different cultures.

Children around the world appreciate the Sesame characters, develop academic skills that promote their school readiness and learn from the programmes' health and social messages. Evaluations in Mexico, Portugal, the Russian Federation and Turkey have found significant differences in cognitive skills, especially literacy and mathematics, between viewers and non-viewers. Consistent though weaker findings have been found for social attitudes and behaviour.

Sources: Cole et al. (2003); Cole, Richman and McCann Brown (2001); de los Angeles-Bautista (2006); Fisch (2005).

cultural contexts. Third, good relations between pupils and ECCE teachers and staff are crucial to programme quality, and much more important than material inputs. Fourth, inclusive ECCE programmes can help offset disadvantage, whether poverty, emergency situations or special needs. They can also promote gender equality and other forms of inclusion through appropriate role models and linguistic diversity. Fifth, maintaining continuity is key in easing the transition from pre-primary to primary school and effective approaches are available even for those who have not been able to attend ECCE institutions such as pre-schools. Chapter 8 now examines policy issues raised by the expansion and improvement of ECCE as envisaged in EFA goal 1. ∎

PART III.
Early childhood care and education

Chapter 8

© EPA/NIC BOTHMA/SIPA

A kindergarten teacher holds children's attention in Toubab Dialao, Senegal, a fishing village where most inhabitants live below the poverty line.

Fostering strong ECCE policies

Although countries still face many difficulties in expanding and improving their ECCE programmes, a more favourable policy environment is emerging. Governments can help shape this enviroment by ensuring that there are adequate resources, including public funding. They also play an important role by designing strong national policies, fostering coordination among sectors and stakeholders, regulating and monitoring quality, and making a concerted effort to reach disadvantaged children and others with limited access to ECCE. This chapter draws on examples from national experience to highlight promising policy practices in the areas of governance, quality and financing. Because of competing demands on public resources, it is especially important to set clear targets and priorities.

Most plans do not take a holistic approach to ECCE

Why the need for national ECCE policies?

Existing policy and legislative action

A national ECCE policy embodies a country's commitment to young children. To date, however, national governments have accorded limited policy attention to ECCE relative to two other EFA goals: universal access to primary education and gender parity. A review of major policy documents (UNESCO-IIEP, 2006)[1] reveals that, although all education plans give some attention to early childhood, most do not take the holistic approach to ECCE promoted by the Dakar Framework for Action. UNESCO, UNICEF, the Association for the Development of Education in Africa (ADEA) and various early childhood networks have encouraged countries to develop holistic ECCE policies that address every aspect of care, education, health and nutrition for all children under 8. In practice, however, most countries focus mainly on pre-primary education, from age 3 until the start of primary school, and pay much less attention to the non-education aspects of ECCE or the needs of children under 3. While health and education sector plans and Poverty Reduction Strategy Papers (PRSPs) may cover immunization, maternal health and pre-school, they are often fragmented and tend not address the child's well-being and development as part of an integrated whole (Aidoo, 2005).

Yet, there are signs that the holistic approach is gaining ground. To create links among different policy areas affecting the lives of young children, several governments, often in partnership with UNICEF, have begun recently to elaborate national early childhood policies that cover health, nutrition, education, water, hygiene, sanitation and legal protection for young children.[2] Comprehensive early childhood policies provide governments with the authority and guidance needed to implement programmes for young children. The development of an explicit early childhood policy is not without risks: it can isolate ECCE from related sectors, including health and education; and it can result in insufficient funding or attention to implementation. An explicit ECCE policy may be ineffective, therefore, unless accompanied by a broader strategy engaging other sectors with responsibility related to early childhood. Drawing up a national vision statement of goals can help countries address the rights and needs of young children. This vision should clarify the work of the education, health and social

sectors, and require the relevant ministries or agencies to make the needed funding allocations within their current budget.[3]

Also useful is legislation that defines what must be done to enact the early childhood policies. At least eighty countries have legislation covering some aspect of ECCE. Many of these countries refer to ECCE as the first stage of the education system, thus recognizing, at least rhetorically, its place within broader education policy (UNESCO-IBE, 2006). Thirty countries have at least one year of compulsory pre-primary education; in two-thirds of these the legislation was enacted since 1990 (Table 6.8). In 2002, for example, Mexico made three years of compulsory pre-school a constitutional right, with provision to be completed by 2008 (UNESCO-IBE, 2006). Even where legislation confers entitlement to several years of ECCE, though, enrolment tends to concentrate on the year or two prior to primary education (UNESCO-OREALC, 2004b). Nine transition countries have legislated a year of free pre-primary education, usually as a means of rebuilding the extensive systems that existed during the communist era (Agranovitch, 2005). Enrolment of younger children remains low.

Many of these policies and supporting legislation are more declarations of intent than realities: national legislation enshrining provisions of international law on children is too seldom backed by strong enforcement (Vargas-Barón, 2005). Similarly, formal national commitments, made through declarations and policies, are often not matched by detailed strategies and adequate public funding. Certain conditions can facilitate or hinder successful policy development for young children, however, and these are explored below.

Building a supportive policy environment

For governments to develop strong policies for young children, the political, social and economic conditions need to be supportive. Several developments over the past ten years indicate movement in this direction:

■ *Research showing the benefits of ECCE.*
A growing body of research underlines the benefits of good-quality ECCE, especially for the disadvantaged. Although the bulk of the research comes from OECD countries, the number of studies from Asia, Africa and Latin America is increasing (see Chapter 5). This evidence has informed policy-makers' decisions and can help build the political will to support ECCE.

1. Chapter 3 describes the methodology of the review.

2. Countries with early childhood policy documents include Burkina Faso, Cambodia, Chile, Djibouti, the Gambia, Ghana, Guinea, Indonesia, Jamaica, Jordan, Malawi, Mauritania, Mongolia, Papua New Guinea, the Philippines, Senegal, Syrian Arab Republic, Thailand and Viet Nam. Cameroon, Cape Verde, Chad and the Niger are developing such documents (Diawara, 2006; Pressoir, 2006; UNESCO-IBE, 2006).

3. The issue of integrated approach vs separate focus has a parallel in early work on gender. Some countries at first created a Ministry of Gender or Women's Affairs, but without enough funding to be effective. Other sectors would drop gender issues since a separate policy and ministry were devoted to them. Gender would end up being marginalized as a government priority. The focus has now shifted to assessing gender within all the relevant sectors so as to keep the issue on the agenda.

- *Labour market trends.* The rising participation of mothers with young children in the labour force, coupled with the decline of traditional family child care (see Chapter 6), has made some governments more receptive to policies to expand and improve ECCE.
- *Emerging attention to ECCE in national development reforms.* Though the evidence is limited, attention to ECCE within instruments such as EFA plans, education and health sector plans, PRSPs and legislation appears to be on the rise.
- *International support.* Aid agencies, United Nations organizations, foundations and international NGOs have supported capacity building and funded ECCE projects that could be taken to scale. UNESCO, for instance, has supported national ECCE policy development through country reviews, policy briefs on current issues and regional, field-based capacity-building seminars.
- *Strong ECCE networks.* At grassroots level, representatives of international agencies, NGOs, researchers and providers of services for children and families have formed networks to share information and experiences within and across borders (Box 8.1).[4] These partners can use their expertise in programme development, capacity-building, training, research and evaluation to support national policy and planning efforts.

Despite these positive factors, a review of country experiences suggests that the following barriers need to be addressed to foster a policy environment to expand and improve ECCE:

- *Ambivalence about the role of government in the lives of families.* The boundaries between the public and private spheres are often unclear. Public policy tends to be limited for children under 3 except as regards extreme abuse and neglect, even though public investment has strong potential to promote long-term benefits (and cost savings).
- *Insufficient public awareness of the benefits of ECCE.* Increased public recognition of the potential contribution of ECCE to EFA and the Millennium Development Goals could foster greater national commitment to young children. Research findings need to be disseminated to key stakeholders – especially parents, who are potential advocates for increasing public policy attention to ECCE.
- *Limited financial and human resources.* Most governments allocate the bulk of their

Box 8.1: Consultative Group on Early Childhood Care and Development

Founded in 1984, the Consultative Group on Early Childhood Care and Development (CGECCD) is a global network of international agencies, foundations, researchers and service providers interested in early childhood issues in more than 100 countries. The group regularly produces the *Coordinators' Notebook,* which includes a lead article analysing key early childhood issues (e.g. quality, children and HIV/AIDS, transitions and links, children in emergencies and 0-3s) and case studies of initiatives in developing countries. The publication reaches about 3,000 individuals, networks and organizations. The CGECCD has also produced a programming manual, *Early Childhood Counts* (Evans, Myers and Ilfeld, 2000) for use by development professionals, programme planners, trainers, policy-makers and child advocates. At annual meetings, members exchange information and discuss issues related to early childhood development and children's rights. The group's secretariat maintains an active electronic mailing list and a website. The CGECCD acts as an advocate globally and locally for more attention to EFA goal 1 and serves as a resource to UNESCO and other international agencies committed to EFA.

Source: Consultative Group on Early Childhood Care and Development, www.ecdgroup.com.

education funding to compulsory schooling and most bilateral donors focus heavily on tertiary education (see Chapter 4). A lack of trained early childhood staff, linked to low pay and status, also impedes the expansion of good-quality ECCE. Even when national ECCE policies exist, successful implementation depends greatly on the capacity of local officials and partners.

- *Competing policy priorities.* In low-income countries, policy choices have immediate consequences for child survival. Much attention, understandably, is directed to HIV/AIDS, malaria and other diseases. Within education, governments face tough choices whether, for example, to expand education systems from primary down to ECCE or up towards lower-secondary education.

Supporting the policy development process

ECCE is well established in the developed countries and a more favourable policy climate is emerging in the developing world despite the many barriers. To help countries build on this

In low-income countries, policy choices have immediate consequences for child survival

4. Among the many examples are the ADEA Working Group on Early Childhood Development, the International Step by Step Association (and the related Open Society Network) and networks involving groups such as UNICEF, UNESCO, Plan International, the Aga Khan Foundation and the Bernard van Leer Foundation.

Senegal, has made early childhood a priority since the 1980s

momentum, it is useful to learn from those that have managed to generate the political will and develop national ECCE policies. Although policy strategies must necessarily be tailored to the relevant cultural, political and economic contexts, there are several key elements they seem to share:

High-level political endorsement can put ECCE on the agenda. Abdoulaye Wade, now president of Senegal, has made early childhood a priority since the 1980s, long before his election in 2000, viewing it as a lever for improving the environment and conditions in which children live as well as for developing a highly skilled and educated population (Hyde and Kabiru, 2006). As president he introduced *les cases des tous petits* – flexible, community-based centres for 0- to 6-year-olds that integrate health, education and nutrition – as an alternative to the more expensive and less culturally appropriate French pre-schools (Kamerman, 2005, Rayna, 2002). Chile, to take another example, has a long tradition of ECCE that has also benefited recently from political support at the highest level. Since her election in early 2006, President Michelle Bachelet has made a series of commitments to strengthen ECCE: to start a pre-school voucher programme for children from birth to age 3 from the poorest 40% of households, to increase enrolment in kindergarten to 60% and to expand coverage of child care centres to support women's employment (Umayahara, 2006).[5]

Broad stakeholder involvement helps promote public support. Efforts to include stakeholders increase the potential for successful implementation and bring children's issues to the fore of public debates (Addison, 2006). Engaging parents as advocates is a particularly effective way to promote sustainable programmes. Such consultations can draw out the policy development process: in Ghana, for example, it took more than ten years to develop and pass a national early childhood policy. The lengthy consultations ensured that the process of policy development was as participatory as possible.

Partnerships with international organizations or aid agencies can generate seed money for projects that can then be taken to scale, and also provide technical assistance for national planning. A decade of investment and technical support (1972-1982) from the Bernard van Leer Foundation led to Kenya's Preschool Education Project, which focused on quality issues and

community-based programmes for 3- to 5-year-olds. The World Bank has supported policy development and implementation in Egypt and Eritrea. UNICEF has formed partnerships with many countries around the world.

Aligning ECCE policies with other national and sectoral development policies is a strategic means of leveraging resources for early childhood and promoting a more holistic and intersectoral approach. Increasingly, in the poorest countries, development funding is focused on broad poverty reduction strategies and on sector-wide programmes. Ghana, Uganda and Zambia are integrating early childhood into revised PRSPs, for example (Aidoo, 2005).

Detailed action plans facilitate the implementation of ECCE policies by identifying the division of responsibilities, the allocation of resources and the time-frame for implementation. An action plan was key to assuring implementation of the national early childhood policy in Malawi. Jordan's National Plan of Action for Children (2004–13) focuses on five components: securing a healthy life; developing and strengthening capabilities of children; protecting children in difficult circumstances; expanding the role of the media; and monitoring and evaluation (UNESCO-IBE, 2006).[6] Action plans benefit from being monitored and updated as new challenges and opportunities arise.

Strategic use of public campaigns draws attention to ECCE and provides information to carers. UNICEF in the Maldives developed a fifty-two-week radio and television campaign to raise awareness about child care practices and improve the quality of child-rearing. An evaluation of the campaign found an increase in public knowledge of child development issues (e.g. the capabilities of the newborn, the importance of breastfeeding and of reading to children, and the role of fathers), and the increase was substantial where the campaign was followed by parent workshops (UNICEF, 2004). Media campaigns can also raise parental awareness of existing ECCE programmes and projects.

Components of a national ECCE policy

National policies for ECCE need to be country-specific, but all countries face similar sets of questions. These largely fall into three categories:

Governance

■ What is the starting age for compulsory schooling?

5. President Bachelet set up a technical advisory council made up of fourteen experts from various fields, along with an interministerial committee representing seven ministries, to develop a proposal for reforming Chile's ECCE policies (Chile Presidency, 2006).

6. Each component has objectives, along with activities aimed at meeting them. Each activity is linked to main and cooperating implementing partners, indicators, sources of verification for the indicators, costs and time frame.

- What ages does ECCE cover?
- What organization is responsible for policy-making, coordination and oversight of ECCE? Do separate organizations deal with 0- to 2-year-olds and 3- to 6-year-olds?
- What are the powers and responsibilities of each level of government regarding ECCE?
- What groups are authorized to provide ECCE programmes (e.g. government, public schools, private schools, parents, registered or accredited NGOs, religious groups)?
- What do activities in the programmes address (e.g. care, education, nutrition and health)? To what extent do the activities differ by age?

Quality

- Which programmes are subject to quality regulations and control?
- What are the standards regarding child/staff ratios and group sizes; physical space per child; services such as water and sanitation; feeding programmes; staff qualifications and training; and programme length?
- Are these standards set at national or local level?
- What early learning and development outcomes are expected of children?
- Is there a national curriculum framework? What themes and content does it address?
- Which pedagogical approaches are encouraged?
- Is quality assurance based on inspections or accreditation?
- What are the strategies to link ECCE and primary school?

Financing

- What are the short- and longer-term targets for expanding coverage of ECCE overall, for children under 3 and for older children?
- Which services are compulsory (e.g. vaccinations) and which are voluntary (e.g. pre-school)?
- What are the appropriate shares of public and private (household) funding?
- How will parent fees be determined?
- What is the target for the share of ECCE within total public expenditure on education?
- How is public funding allocated among government levels (block grants, categorical funding), providers (contracts, subsidies) and/or parents (vouchers, tax breaks)?
- Who is eligible for public services that are not yet universal?

- Which children are deemed vulnerable and disadvantaged?
- To what extent are children with special needs mainstreamed into regular ECCE?
- How are targeted programmes administered?
- Is international aid to be sought for ECCE programmes and, if so, within what framework?

These questions, at a minimum, need to be resolved to develop strong national policies on ECCE. Table 8.1 illustrates how six developing countries with well-developed ECCE policies approached many of the questions. The following sections discuss ECCE governance, quality and financing (including targeting the disadvantaged and the role of aid). To some extent these are the public policy dimensions of the programme characteristics discussed in Chapter 7.

Institutionalizing good governance

Governance – the allocation of responsibility within and across levels of government and between public and non-public actors – can determine whether ECCE services meet quality standards, are affordable, meet local demand, promote cost-effectiveness and achieve equity goals (Hodgkin and Newell, 1996; Kagan and Cohen, 1997). Countries tend to vary on three dimensions of governance (Kamerman, 2000*a*; Neuman, 2005):

- *administrative organization* – the agencies responsible for ECCE at national level, and the extent to which care and education are integrated;
- *decentralization* – the extent to which the authority for ECCE is vested in subnational levels of government;
- *role of private actors* – the extent to which early childhood policy-making and service delivery are shared with non-public actors.

This section discusses these dimensions, with special attention to the challenges of intersectoral and intergovernmental coordination.

Administrative organization: who should take the lead?

By definition, ECCE involves multiple sectors, programmes and actors. At national level, in most countries, ECCE policies and programmes are divided between two or more administrative departments or ministries. Most countries – but

By definition, ECCE involves multiple sectors, programmes and actors

Table 8.1: ECCE policy exemplars in six developing countries

Country	Background	Governance	Access	
Chile	■ ECCE dates from early 1970s. ■ High coverage for 4- to 6-year-olds, low coverage for under-4s. ■ 1996 education reform: pedagogical improvement, innovation through curricular reform and professional development. ■ Policies since 2001 include: 1) expanded coverage, particularly for children from the poorest households; 2) improved quality and use of work with children, families, communities and educators; 3) strengthened management system. ■ President created Technical Advisory Council in 2006 to guide early childhood policies.	■ Ministry of Education (MoE) is responsible for policy, planning, supervision, coordination and evaluation. Focuses on 4- to 6-year olds. ■ Municipalities finance and administer public and subsidized private centres. ■ National Board of Kindergartens (JUNJI), an autonomous public body responsible for kindergartens for poor children, supervises fee-charging private centres. ■ INTEGRA, a non-profit private foundation, also serves poor children (mostly under age 4). ■ In 1990, a National Commission for Early Childhood was set up to improve coordination among institutions serving children under 6.	■ About 93% of 5-year-olds; 51% of 4-year-olds, 26% of 3-year-olds and 18% of 2-year-olds participate in ECCE. ■ JUNJI has set up kindergartens in poverty-stricken areas. ■ Presidential commitments in 2006 for immediate action: pre-school vouchers for children 0 to 3 years old from the poorest 40% of households, expansion of kindergartens for 20,000 4- and 5-year-olds, and 800 new day care centres for 20,000 children.	
Ghana	■ Despite rapid expansion in ECCE and pre-school services, quality is inadequate. ■ Relatively few children benefit from ECCE. ■ ECCE policy document (2004), developed through extensive consultation, addresses access and quality. The document is now being disseminated via district multisectoral teams. ■ National policy guidelines on HIV/AIDS orphans and other vulnerable children exist since 2005.	■ Department of Social Welfare is responsible for registration and standards in crèches and other centres for children aged 0 to 2. ■ Ghana Education Service implements MoE policies for curriculum development for 3- to 5-year-olds ■ Difficulties in coordinating these two agencies have occurred. ■ The National Commission on Children, under the Ministry of Women's and Children's Affairs, is now in charge of coordinating ECCE.	■ About 40% of 5-year-olds and 35% of 4-year-olds participate in ECCE. ■ A Recent white paper on education stated that kindergarten should become part of universal, free compulsory basic education. The government's goal by the end of 2010 is to achieve 100% GER and gender equity in basic education, including kindergarten in the most deprived districts.	
Jamaica	■ ECCE dates to the 1970s, when Jamaica adopted and expanded a successful Bernard van Leer Foundation project. ■ Recent policy efforts focus on integrated approach and improved staff quality for 0- to 6-year-olds.	■ The Ministry of Education, Youth & Culture (MoEYC) assumed responsibility for the Day Care Unit (formerly part of Ministry of Health) in addition to its own Early Childhood Unit in 1998. ■ After a strategic review, the Early Childhood Commission was set up in 2002 to coordinate and monitor ECCE services.	■ About 60% of 3-year-olds and more than 95% of 4- and 5-year-olds participate in ECCE. ■ Better access needed for under 4s, those from the poorest families and those living in the most rural areas.	
Jordan	■ National team of public/private stakeholders developed the National Strategy for Early Childhood Development, from pregnancy to early elementary school. ■ The Strategy calls for the holistic development of the child and expanding the kindergarten sector. ■ The National Plan of Action for Children, includes early childhood and builds on the above strategy.	■ Ministry of Social Development is responsible for parenting education programmes and supervises centre-based child care programmes. The Ministry of Health is a partner. ■ The MoE supervises all pre-schools and provides kindergartens.	■ Goals: to increase enrolment of 4-year-olds from 28% to 35% by 2008 and to 50% by 2013; and of 5-year-olds from 47% to 52% by 2008 and to 70% by 2013. ■ MoE policy focuses on opening kindergartens in remote and disadvantaged areas. Plans call for fifty new kindergarten classes annually, and a daily meal and warm clothes for disadvantaged children.	
Thailand	■ Strong tradition of parent education, high participation and expanded access to ECCE. ■ 1997 Constitution states that government must provide basic services, including care and development, for young children and families. ■ National Policy and Strategy for Early Childhood Development 2006-2008 includes parents, carers, communities, and local and national enterprises. ■ Inadequate supply of ECCE programmes. Local communities and rural areas have limited resources to establish quality programmes. ■ Public information campaign needed on the importance of the early years.	■ In 1999, MoE transferred responsibility for pre-school to subdistrict administrative organizations and local communities. ■ Department of Local Administration supports subdistricts in extending access to quality ECCE in rural and urban settings. ■ Department of Health, Ministry of Public Health and Ministry of Social Development and Human Security are also partners. ■ Draft national policy and strategy propose a coordination committee of government and private sector stakeholders.	■ Almost 100% of 5-year-olds, about 90% of 4-year-olds and 22% of 3-year-olds participate in ECCE: pre-schools, kindergartens and child care centres. ■ Current trend is to expand one-year pre-school classes to two-year kindergartens nationwide. ■ In recent years, Office of National Primary Education Commission (ONPEC) of MoE has expanded access for children in rural areas, establishing 67,200 pre-school classes in 29,410 rural primary schools for more than 1.4 million children each year.	
Viet Nam	■ Targeted at 3- to 5-year-olds but inadequate in rural areas, among the poor and for under-3s. ■ Access and quality vary dramatically between urban and rural areas. ■ Prime Minister decided in 2002 to increase investment, expand crèches and kindergartens, give priority to the disadvantaged and disseminate child care information to families. National Project on ECCE (2006-13) builds on this earlier decision.	■ Since 1999, Ministry of Education and Training responsible for programmes for 0- to 6-year-olds. Ministry of Health and Committee of Population, Family and Children are partners. ■ 2005 Education Law defines early childhood education as part of national education system. ■ Decentralized delivery with nurseries for children aged 3 months to 3 years and kindergartens for 3- to 6-year-olds.	■ About 92% of 5-year-olds, 63% of 3- and 4-year-olds, and 16% of under-3s participate in ECCE. ■ National Project on ECCE (2006-15) prioritizes the construction of kindergartens in poor and minority areas. ■ Current policies: increase supply and coverage rate in kindergarten to between 70% and 80%, develop family day care for under 3s, and stimulate both public and private investment.	

1. Also see Chapter 6 for a review of parental leave policies in developing countries.
Sources: de los Angeles-Bautista (2004); Charles and Williams (2006); Umayahara (2006); UNESCO-IBE (2006); UNESCO-OREALC (2004*b*).

Quality	Financing	Focus on under-3s[1]
Curriculum: ■ Basic curriculum framework for 0- to 6-year-olds (2001) defines expected multidimensional learning outcomes and provides pedagogical orientation to indigenous children or those with special education needs. *Teacher training:* ■ Undergraduate and graduate courses for early childhood educators created in mid-1990s. Requires five-year university degree in education. ■ ECCE staff are gradually being trained to use the curriculum with children.	■ Government funding for ECCE is long-standing priority. ■ Total pre-primary, expenditure per student is higher than in other countries in Latin America, although much of this is private expenditure.	■ To diversify provision and reach children in poor and rural areas, MoE, JUNJI and INTEGRA support non-formal programmes. 'Know Your Child' trains mothers and other community members as educators. ■ Parent-and-Child Programme increases understanding of child development, the purpose of stimulation at each age and the importance of family.
Standards: ■ With UNICEF, government has created early development and learning standards. *Curriculum:* ■ Covers psychosocial skills, language and literacy, mathematics, environmental studies, creative activities, health, nutrition and safety. Emphasizes learning through play, encourages use of local languages. *Teacher training:* ■ National Association of Teachers offers workshops to promote the professional status of ECCE educators and improve awareness among policy-makers.	■ Government committed to supporting the expansion of kindergartens by district assemblies, NGOs, faith-based organizations and communities.	■ Birth registration has increased to 65% due to advertising and training of 1,000 health nurses from ten regions.
Curriculum: ■ Eclectic approach focusing on affective, psychomotor and cognitive domains. *Teacher training:* ■ MoEYC places one trained teacher in each basic school with enrolment of 100+. The Child Focus project and the National Council on Technical and Vocational Education and Training developed ECCE certification standards. *Assessment:* ■ Readiness Inventory of the National Assessment Programme to inform teachers about the skills of children entering grade 1.	■ Over 80% of pre-schoolers attend community-operated basic schools; about 20% are in public infant departments and private centres receiving government subsidies for teacher salaries, class materials and school meals. Parents pay fees for teachers' salaries and school maintenance.	■ Roving Caregivers provide neighbourhood and home visits to mothers with children under 4, particularly in rural areas without day care centres. Goal is to equip parents with skills to support their children's early development and learning, as well as develop a group of carers that can expand the programme.
Standards: ■ Participates in the UNICEF standards project. *Assessment:* ■ Has applied the Early Years Evaluation instrument to measure children's school readiness.	■ Government has pledged to allocate sufficient human and financial resource to achieve its objectives and seek extra funds needed. ■ Education Reform for the Knowledge Economy Project (2003-2008) helps MoE expand and improve early childhood services, in partnership with international and local funding organizations, NGOs and the private sector.	■ Recent survey revealed gaps in parents' child-rearing knowledge. Jordan developed and adopted an ECCE/parenting programme that provides parents and carers with skills and information to support the development of children aged 0 to 8. More than 200 centres reach 70,000 families.
Curriculum: ■ ONPEC has prepared the core early childhood curriculum and disseminated it to all Educational Service Area Offices to give to parents and teachers so they can work together to improve quality. ■ Demonstration kindergartens in every province are 'learning laboratories for ECCE'. ■ Continuing support is given to test and promote innovative practices. *Teacher training:* ■ MoE has organized workshops to train ECCE technical leaders.	■ ONPEC pre-primary classes are financed with US$9.41 million annual budget. ■ Government-supported public school kindergartens are more affordable and accessible than private ones for most families.	■ Department of Health runs the Parenting Education Project, the Safe Delivery Ward Project, the Nutrition and Mental Development Corner, and the Healthy Child Development Corner. ■ Parents of each newborn receive a gift box containing a guide to breastfeeding, toys, books and a colourful blanket.
Curriculum: ■ Revised national curriculum being piloted to help children develop physically, emotionally, intellectually and artistically, and prepare them for grade 1. *Teacher training* ■ Teacher income and living standards improved. More than 70% of non-formal teachers now have social welfare and health insurance. ■ Proportion of teachers and managers with at least minimum training doubled since 2000. ■ Shortage of teachers in remote areas remains a challenge.	■ Since 2002, government requires 10% of education budgets to be allocated for ECCE; only 18 out of 64 provinces and cities have done so, however; 17 provinces provide 5% to 7% and many do not finance ECCE at all. ■ Programmes are overwhelmingly public or publicly subsidized; only 1% are private. ■ Reduced fees for poor children are still too high. New effort made to increase private sector involvement.	■ Government has tried to create demand through parent education programmes and media campaigns.

Fragmented responsibility may lead to disparities in access and quality

especially in Europe and Latin America – offer one or two years of pre-primary within the education system to help prepare children for the transition to primary school. Other forms of ECCE (especially for children under age 3) fall under the auspices of ministries of health, social welfare or children and women's affairs (Kamerman, 2005).

This multisectoral distribution of responsibility is positive in that it can bring together agencies with differing areas of expertise (health, nutrition, education) and help pool resources. In other ways, however, this form of organization is problematic, as it can lead to conflict between ministries or departments.[7] On the ground, fragmented responsibility may lead to disparities in access and quality. Generally, services within education systems tend to be more universally accessible, are often free and open part of the day, whereas ECCE services within the social or health sector tend to have stricter eligibility requirements (e.g. working parents, vulnerable and disadvantaged), are less widespread and often charge fees.

If multiple ministries are involved, responsibilities need to be clearly delineated. In the United States, where nine federal agencies have responsibility at national level, overlap, duplication and inefficient allocation of resources are common (US General Accounting Office, 2000). In some countries, no one administrative body has the principal responsibility and in such cases the government may neglect ECCE. For example, when the Romanian Ministry of Health relinquished responsibility for funding and overseeing nurseries during the transition to a market economy in the 1990s, the public child care system basically collapsed (McLean, 2006).

Recognizing these challenges, a small but growing number of countries have consolidated responsibility for all forms of ECCE under one ministry to increase policy coherence. The Nordic countries pioneered this 'educare' approach in the 1970s when their systems were expanding in response to rising maternal employment. In Denmark, for example, the Ministry of Social Affairs takes the lead on ECCE for children under 6, and in Finland it is the Ministry of Social Affairs and Health. (In both countries, a pre-primary year is the responsibility of the Ministry of Education). In the Nordic countries and several others that have consolidated responsibility, quality standards such as child/staff ratios and teacher training requirements tend to be uniform throughout ECCE (OECD, 2001).

Since the late 1980s the trend has been towards designating education as the lead ministry for children from birth. Countries taking this approach include Brazil, Jamaica, Kenya, New Zealand, South Africa, Spain, Sweden and, most recently, Norway. In Viet Nam, where the Ministry of Education and Training has been responsible for early childhood since 1986, officials have found that having a single lead ministry makes it easier to develop and implement policies and monitor progress, while reducing the time spent on coordinating initiatives in different sectors (Choi, 2005). Sweden shifted responsibility for ECCE from the Ministry of Social Affairs to the Ministry of Education in 1996 to promote lifelong learning from ages 1 to 18. The government later introduced an early childhood curriculum that builds on the core principles guiding primary and secondary school, and expanded free part-time pre-school to all 4- and 5-year-olds (Lenz Taguchi and Munkammar, 2003).

Selecting education as the lead ministry tends to increase attention to children's learning as well as to the transition to primary school. As in the case of Sweden, once early education becomes part of the school system, it is more likely to be seen as a public good – which can lead to increased resources and greater access. Greater involvement of the education sector in the early childhood years carries risks, however. As it is not usually compulsory, ECCE often struggles for attention and resources within the education bureaucracy. Another concern, based on recent experiences in Belgium, France and Sweden, is that ECCE will be under pressure from primary education to become more formal and school-like (OECD, 2001; Lenz Taguchi and Munkammar, 2003).

Regardless of which agency takes the lead, coordination is needed across all institutions and sectors involved in early childhood and family issues. Experiences in several countries suggest that an interministerial body can help promote national coordination of policies and actions (Box 8.2).[8] In South Africa, for example, the Ministry of Education houses a National Coordinating Committee composed of representatives from the ministries of health, education, welfare and population development; other government departments; resource and training institutions; universities; and NGOs. The committee was instrumental in creating the pre-primary Grade R for 5- and 6-year-olds (Hyde and Kabiru, 2006).

---

7. In Ghana, for example, both the Ministry of Education and Sports and that of Manpower Development, Youth and Employment sought the national coordination responsibility for ECCE. As a compromise, the National Commission on Children, under the Ministry of Women's and Children's Affairs, was given the coordinating role, but interagency tension persists.

8. In Africa, such mechanisms exist in Kenya, Mali, Namibia, Senegal and South Africa (Hyde and Kabiru, 2006).

In general, coordinating bodies (often called councils, committees or commissions) provide a forum in which stakeholders can contribute their knowledge and perspectives to achieve a common vision – that of providing resources and developing standards, regulations, training and staffing for an integrated early childhood system. In sub-Saharan Africa, such bodies have achieved some success in coordinating pilot projects, formulating policy or conducting situational analyses. Yet, existing African structures face several challenges: they often have limited or undertrained staff, are more advisory than decision-making bodies and often fail to engage all stakeholders (Hyde and Kabiru, 2006).

In Chile, Colombia, Costa Rica, Cuba and Mexico, intersectoral coordinating bodies have improved public awareness of ECCE, increased coverage of comprehensive ECCE and developed both a shared vision of comprehensive ECCE and a collective process of policy formulation. What were the elements that made these mechanisms successful? Among them were:

- recognition of children's rights, needs and potential;
- a shared vision of comprehensive ECCE;
- sustained political will and technical leadership;
- conscious and joint national decision-making;
- full civil society participation and involvement of families and communities (UNESCO-OREALC, 2004*b*).

The effectiveness of intersectoral collaboration is also determined by which ministry takes the lead and whether the coordinating body has decision-making power. The lead ministry needs to be perceived by the others involved as having the authority to convene and to act. Other ministries and departments tend to respond when, for example, the finance ministry or prime minister's office takes the lead. The efforts of advisory-only commissions are unlikely to move the agenda for young children forward, while those with authority to make decisions about expenditure, for example, tend to have much more active and effective participation.

Decentralization – an approach to be used with caution

Decentralization of ECCE is often adopted as a strategy to increase local transparency and adapt services and resources to community needs and circumstances.[9] Yet with ECCE as with other public services, decentralization can lead to

Box 8.2: Streamlining ECCE policy in Jamaica

Jamaica's approach to creating a long-term vision for comprehensive, integrated delivery of early childhood programmes and services is instructive. First, in 1998 the Ministry of Education, Youth and Culture assumed responsibility for the Day Care Unit from the Ministry of Health in addition to its own Early Childhood Unit. An interagency group representing health, education, community development, planning, NGOs, service clubs and the University of the West Indies was formed to guide the integration process. In 2002, legislation established the Early Childhood Commission, which brings together all policies, standards and regulations pertaining to day care and early childhood development under one institutional umbrella. Comprehensive regulations now cover health, safety and nutritional requirements, and there are guidelines for fostering both children's social development and a positive learning climate. Overall, Jamaica's integrated approach maximizes limited resources by reducing duplication and fragmentation.

Source: Jamaica Ministry of Education and Youth (2003).

broader inequalities in access and quality if implementation of national policies is uneven or central governments relinquish their former responsibilities. Justifications for decentralization in transition countries, for example, often concealed cutbacks in central government spending on ECCE in general, and the financial and administrative abandonment of state responsibility for pre-schools in particular (McLean, 2006).

Indeed, during the 1990s, decentralization in transition countries led to rapid deterioration in the quality, access, supply and coverage of kindergartens and nurseries. The number of facilities decreased as some merged, others shut down and still others began operating seasonally or for shorter hours as funding and enrolment dropped (see Chapter 6). Absence of monitoring by regional authorities, loss of pedagogical assistance and shortages of teaching materials exacerbated these problems and contributed to rising numbers of children deemed unprepared for school in Armenia, Kyrgyzstan, Ukraine and other countries (McLean, 2006).

If central funds do not accompany the transfer of power to lower levels of government, poorer municipalities often cannot maintain the supply of good-quality ECCE. The loss of good teachers, inadequate in-service teacher training and lack of maintenance capacity can exacerbate the

During the 1990s, decentralization in transition countries led to rapid deterioration of kindergartens and nurseries

9. Decentralization of responsibilities such as administration, regulation, quality assurance and provision in ECCE, from higher to lower levels of government, falls on a continuum from deconcentration (low) to delegation (medium) to devolution (high). Privatization – shifting responsibility from the public to the private sector – can also be considered a form of decentralization; it is discussed in the next section.

To offset adverse effects of deregulation, Sweden introduced quality guidelines

problem. In Armenia, China, Romania, the Russian Federation and Ukraine, decentralization aggravated inequalities between wealthier urban and poorer rural communities, as well as between socio-economic classes (McLean, 2006; Corter et al., 2006; Taratukhina et al., 2006). In India, limited local capacity and uneven resources led to inefficient targeting of services and thus to geographic and socio-economic inequalities in access and quality (World Bank, 2004).

Difficulties in achieving equity within decentralized structures have led to greater central government attention to ECCE (McLean, 2006). In Slovakia, local education authorities were responsible for ECCE in 1990–96, then regional and district authorities took over (UNESCO-IBE, 2006). In Sweden, after deregulation in the 1990s led to widespread disparities in fees and quality standards, the government introduced a maximum fee for all pre-schools and a curriculum framework to establish quality guidelines (Skolverket, 2004). These examples suggest better coordination is often needed not only horizontally, among ministries, but also vertically, among levels of government.

Private actors as potential partners

Community-based organizations, NGOs, religious groups and for-profit entities – the whole range of non-public actors – can support government efforts to expand, improve and coordinate ECCE provision. As Chapter 6 showed, the private sector plays a large role in many countries. In parts of Europe, North America and Latin America, religious institutions continue to provide ECCE and often allow others to use their buildings for this purpose. The private sector is particularly prominent in sub-Saharan Africa, the Arab States, the Caribbean and East Asia. Muslim communities in the Gambia, Indonesia, Kenya, Morocco, Tunisia, Uganda and the United Republic of Tanzania have created pre-schools in recent years to ensure that children learn the national curriculum within a context that supports Islamic faith, values and practices. In some countries, religious providers contribute dramatically to the availability of ECCE. In Zanzibar (United Republic of Tanzania), the pre-school GER is 87% overall, but only 9% when Koranic schools are not included. To promote quality and sustainability of religious-

based provision, the Aga Khan Foundation has established Madrasa Resource Centres (Box 8.3) (Hyde and Kabiru, 2006; Issa, 2006).

In many countries in transition, private providers (both non-profit and for-profit) have flourished in a situation of decreased government support, financial constraints and decentralization. The diversification of providers has both encouraged innovative practices and increased inequalities in access. Whereas the government system had mostly been closed to non-professionals, some private providers encourage parent and community involvement. Families often welcome the alternatives to traditional public-sector pedagogy that non-public ECCE programmes offer. The Step by Step programme established by the Open Society Institute, for example, has influenced curricular reform throughout Central and Eastern Europe and Central Asia by encouraging a child-centred approach that can be adapted to children's diverse learning styles (see Chapter 7). At the same time, the entrance requirements and, especially, high fees imposed by many non-public providers in the transition countries have excluded many vulnerable and disadvantaged children (McLean, 2006).

The role of the for-profit sector, in particular, is somewhat controversial. As with other levels of education, proponents of for-profit ECCE argue that market-based approaches encourage competition, increase efficiency and promote parental choice. The Netherlands' 2005 child care law, for instance, transformed the previously supply-driven system to a demand-side approach. Instead of directly subsidizing providers, the government grants families subsidies to purchase market-provided services.[10] In such cases, however, if these vouchers do not cover the full cost of good-quality ECCE, low-income parents' choices can be limited to less adequate provision. In 2002, Morocco separated pre-school for 4- and 5-year-olds from the national education system and left it in the hands of the private sector, without regulating fees. The government now focuses on regulations, training and pedagogical innovations (e.g. the curriculum). Families with fewer resources are excluded from more expensive services (Choi, 2004). Another concern is the distribution of services: when demand-side approaches predominate, service gaps tend to occur in rural and low-income areas, which are less profitable and more challenging for providers (OECD, 2001).

10. For more information, see http://internationalezaken.szw.nl/index.cfm.

In sum, countries vary with regard to the extent to which the state regulates private providers, a fact with important implications for access and quality. Private providers operating outside the public system often are free to determine eligibility requirements, quality standards and fees. There is a risk of a two-track system developing, with children from more advantaged families attending more expensive and higher quality private programmes and less fortunate families resorting to low-cost, lower-quality public alternatives. To promote equity, governments should ensure that regulations exist and are applied equally to public and private settings, and, where possible, that the system does not segregate children by socio-economic background (McLean, 2006; Corter et al., 2006; Taratukhina et al., 2006).

Improving quality: regulation, accountability and staffing

The issue of quality is not explicitly noted in EFA goal 1, but the Dakar Framework for Action (Expanded Commentary, para. 30) underlines the 'positive impact' that 'good quality early childhood care and education, both in families and in more structured programmes, have .... on the survival, growth, development and learning potential of children'. A consistent research finding is that the quality of children's early experiences is related to virtually every facet of their development (OECD-CERI, 1999; Shonkoff and Phillips, 2000). Young children who receive good care, attention and stimulation in their first three years are likely to demonstrate better cognitive and language abilities, and experience more positive social interaction than children who have experienced lower-quality arrangements (National Institute of Child Health and Human Development, 2001). The benefits of well-designed, intensive forms of ECCE are less likely to 'fade out' than those of more custodial programmes (Barnett, 1995).

Some scholars reject a normative approach to defining and monitoring quality, arguing that quality is socially constructed and cannot be measured by 'objective' criteria such as standardized scales or child/staff ratios (Dahlberg et al., 1999). Although quality is relative to one's perspective, this does not mean that quality is arbitrary or that 'anything goes' (Woodhead, 1996). Rather, the critique of

Box 8.3: Resource centres enrich Madrasa pre-schools in East Africa

With support from the Aga Khan Foundation, Madrasa Resource Centres work with disadvantaged urban, peri-urban and rural Muslim communities to establish community-owned and – managed pre-schools that are culturally appropriate, affordable and sustainable. The programme supports 203 pre-schools in East Africa (66 in Kenya, 53 in Uganda and 84 in Zanzibar, United Republic of Tanzania) and has served approximately 30,000 children and trained over 4,000 community-based teachers since 1986. To date, 153 communities have pre-schools up and running; 50 more are receiving intensive support as they complete the programme.

Madrasa pre-schools perform significantly better than other pre-schools on adult-child interaction and on three-quarters of the environmental dimensions assessed by the Early Childhood Environment Rating Scale. The mean performance scores of Madrasa pre-school children were 42% higher than those of children who did not attend pre-schools. The programme has increased empowerment and self-reliance among teachers and community members. Women's participation in community life and decision-making outside the home has improved, even in the most traditional communities. The direct costs of the programme are modest – about US$15 per child per year – of which the Madrasa Resource Centres programme pays two-thirds and the community the remainder.

Sources: Issa (2006); Mwaura (2005, 2006).

normative definitions of quality has encouraged researchers and some policy-makers to favour a more participatory approach to quality assurance within early childhood settings, whereby administrators, staff, parents and sometimes children jointly determine what their goals are and how to achieve them. Indeed, Myers (2006) urges early childhood stakeholders to accommodate multiple perspectives.

Regulating programme quality

Most governments regulate ECCE programmes in order to monitor the quality of the environment and the practices that promote children's development and learning. Regulations usually focus on easy-to-measure indicators of structural quality, such as class size, child/staff ratios, availability of materials and staff training. Equally important, if not more so, are indicators of process quality, which include warm, interactive relationships between carers and children, inclusion of families, and responsiveness to cultural diversity and children with special needs. Indeed, some research indicates that interaction

Some scholars reject a normative approach to defining and monitoring quality

Given the diverse nature of ECCE programmes, international comparability is particularly difficult

11. Standardized testing to measure children's school readiness was previously common in North America and Europe, but the trend is now to use direct observation and other types of continuous assessment, which better address young children's episodic development (Neuman, 2001; Shepard et al., 1996). For a summary of readiness assessment instruments in the United States, see Mehaffie and McCall (2002).

12. The World Bank has promoted the use of first grade readiness testing in countries including India, Jordan and Turkey (National Center for Human Resources Development, 2005). The Offord Center for Child Studies (2005) in Canada has developed the Early Development Instrument, which reports on populations of children in different communities, assesses children's strengths and deficits, and predicts how they will do in elementary school. It has been used in Canada with more than 290,000 students and, on a pilot basis, in Australia, Chile, Jamaica, Kosovo and the United States. A pilot project in Colombia uses a test that measures skills and knowledge in children starting kindergarten. Viet Nam is validating early learning and developing standards for monitoring school readiness (UNESCO-IBE, 2006).

between adults and children is associated more strongly with enhanced well-being of children than are structural features (see Chapter 7) (Love et al., 1996). The importance of adult-child dynamics is an encouraging finding for those working in situations where resource constraints make many structural features hard to address (Arnold et al., 2006).

Among developing countries, five in Latin America (Chile, Colombia, Costa Rica, Ecuador and Mexico) have developed national quality standards for ECCE programmes, and seven Caribbean countries have assessed programme quality using a standardized instrument. Various quality assessment projects have also been conducted in India, Kenya, Pakistan, Singapore and Viet Nam (Myers, 2006). Many of these national instruments have been developed with the assistance of multilateral organizations, NGOs and foundations, often to provide a basis for evaluating externally funded ECCE programmes. This was the case, for instance, in Bangladesh and Viet Nam (Plan International), Kenya (Aga Khan Foundation), Pakistan (USAID and Aga Khan Foundation), Ecuador (World Bank), and parts of Latin America (Christian Children's Fund) and Eastern Europe (International Step by Step Association).

In recent years various international (Table 8.2) and national instruments have been developed to assess process quality in ECCE programmes. Their aims differ, but both often involve evaluating the quality of the environment in which child care and/or learning activities are provided, the quality of adult-child interactions and the extent of parental participation. Given the diverse nature of ECCE programmes, international comparability is particularly difficult. Nevertheless, the instruments are useful for assessing programme quality within a particular country over time.

An important policy decision is the extent to which various forms of provision are to be subject to regulation. In most countries, for instance, publicly funded services are required to follow programme quality standards, whereas informal care by family, friends and neighbours is not. As has been noted, private provision is often exempt from regulation except when publicly subsidized. The rationale for these exemptions is to limit government intervention in private spheres such as the family. From an equity perspective, however, it is harder to justify selectively monitoring the quality of some forms of ECCE but not others.

Governments need to enforce, not just develop, regulations that promote quality. Yet, many countries do not have the resources to assure sufficient inspection and monitoring. An alternative approach, accreditation, is used in some countries, including Australia, the United Kingdom, and the United States. Accreditation encourages programme staff to reflect on their practice and to address any limitations before having their work validated by an external expert. In Australia the National Childcare Accreditation Council has established a quality evaluation system for accreditation, self-evaluation and programme improvement. Public funding of programmes is contingent on their participation (Press and Hayes, 2000).

Moving towards a stronger focus on child outcomes

In a trend encouraged by some international organizations, governments increasingly have been assessing programme quality by focusing on child outcomes – agreed standards or expectations of children's performance and behaviour (Box 8.4). An outcomes approach focuses on children's learning and development rather than on the features of the early childhood programme. The process encourages stakeholders at national and subnational level to identify early learning standards in various domains, usually related to school readiness, broadly defined. These standards are based on direct observation of children.[11] They can be used to report on children's competence at a given time, and they are often used to guide pedagogy and instruction, to help families understand and support children's development, and to inform teacher training. Recently efforts have been made to align early learning standards with the curriculum and with child-focused assessments, as part of a broader strategy of holding providers accountable to policy-makers (Kagan and Britto, 2005).[12]

The standards-based approach is not without risks. One concern is that 'global' standards impose a Western view on the rest of the world and do not take cultural, linguistic and other forms of diversity into account. ECCE outcomes need to be viewed in context, especially in relation to the values set forth in national texts and curricula. Further, it is difficult to develop standards that reflect children's differing rates and approaches to learning. In addition,

Table 8.2: International instruments for assessing ECCE quality

Name of assessment tool	Major categories (number of indicators)	Purpose	Countries/regions participating
International Step by Step Association, programme and teacher standards	Programme standards: ■ Teacher-child interactions (4) ■ Family participation (9) ■ Planning a child-centred programme (5) ■ Strategies for meaningful learning (4) ■ Learning environment (3) ■ Health and safety (4) Teacher standards: ■ Individualization (4) ■ Learning environment (3) ■ Family participation (6) ■ Teaching strategies for meaningful learning (5) ■ Planning and assessment (7) ■ Professional development (4)	Planning and Improvement tool. Accreditation for Step by Step programme	**29 countries:** Albania, Armenia, Azerbaijan, Belarus, Bosnia and Herzegovina, Bulgaria, Croatia, Czech Republic, Estonia, Georgia, Haiti, Hungary, Kazakhstan, Kosovo, Kyrgyzstan, Latvia, Lithuania, TFYR Macedonia, Mongolia, Montenegro, Rep. Moldova, Romania, Russian Federation, Serbia, Slovakia, Slovenia, Tajikistan, Ukraine, Uzbekistan
Association for Childhood Education International Self-Assessment Tool	■ Environment and physical space (17) ■ Curriculum content and pedagogy (39) ■ Educators and caregivers (13) ■ Young children with special needs (24) ■ Partnership with families and communities (5)	Self-assessment by centres	**26 countries helped construct this tool, including** Botswana, Chile, China, Ecuador, Japan, Kenya, Mexico, Nigeria, United States
IEA Pre-Primary Project	Observation system focuses on process using three dimensions: ■ Management of time (e.g. time in three categories of proposed activities, group structure, pacing of activities) ■ Child activities (e.g. children's verbalization, child-child interaction, adult-child interaction, children's non-active engagement, time on task) ■ Adult behaviour (e.g. behaviour in major categories, directive teaching, degree of involvement, listening behaviour, child management)	Research	**17 countries/territories:** Belgium (French-speaking), China, Finland, Germany (former Federal Republic), Greece, Hong Kong (China), Indonesia, Ireland, Italy, Nigeria, Poland, Portugal, Romania, Slovenia, Spain, Thailand, United States
Assessment scale proposed by Save the Children, United Kingdom	■ Professional practice (clear aims, protection policy, good practice, referral, care plan, periodic review, continuum of care) (7) ■ Personal care (health and nutrition, recreation, privacy, informed choices, respect, + relationships, sense of identity, control and sanctions, voice opinions, education according to needs) (12) ■ Caregivers (4) ■ Resources (accessible/adequate; promotes health/development) (2) ■ Administration (records, confidentiality, accountability) (3)	Planning and improvement tool (staff development, assessment, monitoring) Advocacy and policy development	**7 countries:** Ethiopia, Kenya, Democratic Republic of the Congo, Rwanda, Somalia, Sudan (northen part), United Republic of Tanzania
Early Childhood Environment Rating Scale, Revised Edition, developed in United States. Similar instruments exist for infant/toddler programmes and family day care.	■ Space and furnishings (8) ■ Personal care routines (6) ■ Language-reasoning (4) ■ Activities (10) ■ Interaction (5) ■ Programme structure (4) ■ Parents and staff (6)	Research and programme improvement. Now used as qualification criteria for some programmes.	**7 Caribbean countries:** Bahamas, Dominica, Grenada, Jamaica, Montserrat, Saint Lucia, Saint Vincent and Grenadines

Note: In addition to these instruments, based on international projects and studies, some countries have developed national assessments of quality, discussed in Appendix 1 of the source document.
Source: Myers (2006), Appendix 1.

standards have the potential for misuse. While the intent is to support learning and identify any difficulties, standards might be used to stigmatize children, labelling them as 'failures'. Standards are sometimes inappropriately used to screen children to determine whether they can start school. Furthermore, 'quality' has little meaning if used to characterize an ECCE programme that achieves the desired outcomes through undesirable methods (e.g. fear or punishment) (Myers, 2006).

Promoting quality through staffing policy

Given the importance of positive staff-child interaction for early childhood experiences, several recent staffing trends and issues are notable. The first involves the move, already discussed, towards an integrated system of ECCE provision and regulation from birth to school entry. This trend, so far mostly in developed countries, has encouraged countries to restructure staff qualification requirements and training. It has also led them to bridge the divide

Box 8.4: A standards-based approach to monitoring early learning

Since 2003, the Going Global project, a partnership of UNICEF and Columbia and Yale universities, has helped countries prepare national early learning and development standards in domains including language and literacy development, social and emotional development, motor development, logic and reasoning, and approaches to learning. Table 8.3 gives an example. Going Global supports a participatory process involving countries' early childhood development experts, policy-makers, planners, parents and children in shaping early learning standards that reflect local cultural and social concepts of what children of a given age should know and be able to do. The standards are based on research and scientific knowledge on early learning, taking into consideration cultural, linguistic and socio-economic differences, as well as children with special needs. After pilot projects in Brazil, Ghana, Jordan, Paraguay, the Philippines and South Africa, Going Global is expanding to other countries in Latin America and the Caribbean, East Asia and Central Europe. Countries have used the standards to revise pre-school curricula, teacher-training models and national monitoring.

Table 8.3 A sample standard from the Going Global project: language and literacy development

Indicator	How to measure/benchmark	Preparatory learning activities
Child can follow directions that involve a two- or three-step sequence of actions.	Ask the child to get an article of clothing; put it on/wear it; and proceed to a certain location, like the entrance to the room (if outdoors, to a tree).	Give oral directions and play a game like 'carer says'. Make the children give simple directions to each other.
Child demonstrates an understanding of the message in a conversation.	Sing a nursery rhyme to the child that entails doing activities, like pointing to body parts. Ask the child to respond to your rhyme by acting/doing the activities.	Guide the child to listen for specific information in conversations with others. While listening to the radio, discuss the content with child.
Child demonstrates a gain in information by listening.	Engage the child in a conversation. See if the child is able to extend an idea expressed by you.	While telling a story or reading a book, guide the child through the development of the idea of the story.

Source: Kagan and Britto (2005).

between the education and care components. In Singapore, for example, all child care and pre-school personnel now undergo the same training and accreditation, which has increased the pool of trained staff (Choo, 2004). In the United Kingdom, where child care staff used to be paid less than early education personnel, the government introduced a national minimum wage for ECCE employment.

Second, some countries are making the entry routes into higher education and teacher training more flexible so as to attract more candidates (Oberhuemer and Ulich, 1997). For example, in Grenada, Jamaica, and Saint Vincent and the

Grenadines, credit is given for competency-based skills (Charles and Williams, 2006). In India and the Syrian Arab Republic, students can take early childhood training courses over the Internet (Faour, 2006; NIPCCD, 2006). The Early Child Development Virtual University (Box 8.5) promotes ECCE leadership development and builds capacity through both online and in-person training. In Pakistan, the Teachers Resource Centre has partnered with the Ministry of Education to expand the trained workforce by creating the Early Childhood Education Certificate Programme, the country's first teacher-training and classroom support programme for pre-primary teachers, and by offering in-service training workshops (Teachers Resource Centre Online, 2006a, 2006b).

Third, to ease children's transition from ECCE to primary schooling, several countries have implemented strategies for professional continuity. For example:

- France, Ireland, Jamaica and the United Kingdom have joint training of ECCE and primary teachers, with graduates qualified to work in pre-primary and primary schools with children aged from 2 to 12.
- China provides general child-friendly, active learning approaches to all teachers, with particular attention to those working in the first grades of primary school (Box 8.6).
- In the madrasa early childhood programme, early grade primary school teachers communicate with teachers from their feeder pre-schools. In Guyana, ECCE and primary school teachers work together in school, home visits and other after-school programmes. Such strategies encourage connections and coherence in teaching styles between two normally distinct levels.
- In Portugal, early childhood specialists are trained separately from primary school teachers but receive the same level of training, qualifications and professional status.

Despite these positive trends, around the world several areas require further attention in relation to both initial training and ongoing professional development. They include engaging parents and other carers more actively in children's development and learning; adopting inclusive practices for children with disabilities and other special education needs; working with linguistically and culturally diverse children; and meeting the needs of orphans and vulnerable children (particularly those affected by HIV/AIDS) and of children in emergency and crisis situations.

Costing and financing ECCE programmes

Previous chapters have described how ECCE programmes vary within and across countries, are offered by a broad mix of public and private providers, and are financed to varying degrees by households, governments and others. The complexity of the situation makes it difficult to calculate total national expenditure on ECCE, or even the costs of specific programmes, and harder still to make cross-national comparisons. As a result, not only is there no quantitative target for EFA goal 1, but it is not possible even to estimate the global cost of 'expanding and improving comprehensive ECCE'. This section, therefore, presents cross-country data on total public expenditure on pre-primary education, the only component of ECCE for which some comparisons are possible, and provides some country examples of programmes' unit costs. It also discusses various sources of and approaches to financing for ECCE, including the issue of targeting and the role of external donors.

Public expenditure on pre-primary education

In general, countries accord relatively low priority to pre-primary education in their public spending. Less than 10% of total public education expenditure was allocated to it in sixty-five of the seventy-nine countries with data available (Figure 8.1). Over half allocated less than 5%. Most of the fourteen countries allocating more than 10% are in Europe. As a share of GNP, public expenditure on pre-primary education was greatest in Central and Eastern Europe, at 0.5%, compared with 0.4% in North America and Western Europe and 0.2% in Latin America (see annex, Statistical Table 11). Data on these shares over time are available for only a few countries. No strong trends are observable. There is some indication that the share has fallen (from relatively high levels) in Central and Eastern Europe since 1999.

Not surprisingly, the same regional patterns hold when comparing public spending on pre-primary education with that on primary education. In Central and Eastern Europe, for the equivalent of every US$100 spent on primary education, US$67 was spent on pre-primary programmes, and some countries, including the Republic of Moldova, spent the same on each of the two levels. For North America and Western Europe,

Box 8.5: The Early Childhood Development Virtual University: work and study

The Early Childhood Development Virtual University (ECDVU) is a training and capacity-building initiative designed to help meet the need for early childhood leadership and development in Africa and the Middle East. It uses both face-to-face seminars and distance learning, allowing students to continue working in their own countries while they are studying, so that they can apply what they are learning in their daily work. Each ECDVU participant also organizes a national intersectoral network of early childhood advocates and practitioners. Students are taught by faculty from around the world and work with a mentor in each country or region. In 2004, twenty-seven out of the initial thirty students from ten countries in sub-Saharan Africa graduated with master of arts degrees from Victoria University in Canada. Five countries in the Middle East and North Africa participated in a one-year graduate programme in 2003. The ECDVU is supported by the World Bank, UNICEF and UNESCO, and by NGOs and development agencies.

Source: Early Childhood Development Virtual University (2005).

Box 8.6: Teacher education reform to strengthen progressive kindergarten practices in China

In 1989 the government of China developed a policy to build the public and political profile of ECCE and boost levels of participation. The policy promoted progressive principles for kindergartens, notably a focus on child development, active learning, attention to individual differences and group functioning, respectful relationships between staff and children, and holistic evaluation of children. These challenged traditional teaching practices, making implementation difficult. The government responded by proposing new qualification requirements especially for early childhood teachers, principals and other staff, which were adopted in 1996. In 2001, the government issued guidelines on gradually putting progressive ideas into practice, emphasizing holistic evaluation of children through interviews and direct observations, and further improvement of teacher education and training.

The country established an integrated professional training system with multiple forms and levels (e.g. pre- and in-service training, degree and non-degree, short- and long-term). Kindergarten teachers must now graduate from secondary schools and pass an examination that leads to a required early childhood teaching certificate. Pre-service training for graduates of upper-secondary schools is also offered at colleges and universities. Kindergarten principals must have, in addition, extensive work experience and in-service training in kindergarten administration.

Challenges remain despite these advances. Recent surveys in major cities such as Beijing and Shanghai show that many upper secondary graduates lack the professional knowledge and skills to observe and evaluate children as the progressive kindergarten guidelines stipulate. Faculty supervisors have limited kindergarten experience, there is insufficient access to training in rural areas and in-service training is often not aligned with the new curricular guidelines. To further enhance teacher education, the government is designing curriculum frameworks for pre-service training, preparing textbooks and encouraging local education departments to regulate teacher education institutions.

Sources: Corter et al. (2006); China Ministry of Education (2003); Wong and Pang (2002).

Figure 8.1: Share of pre-primary education in total current public spending on education, 2004

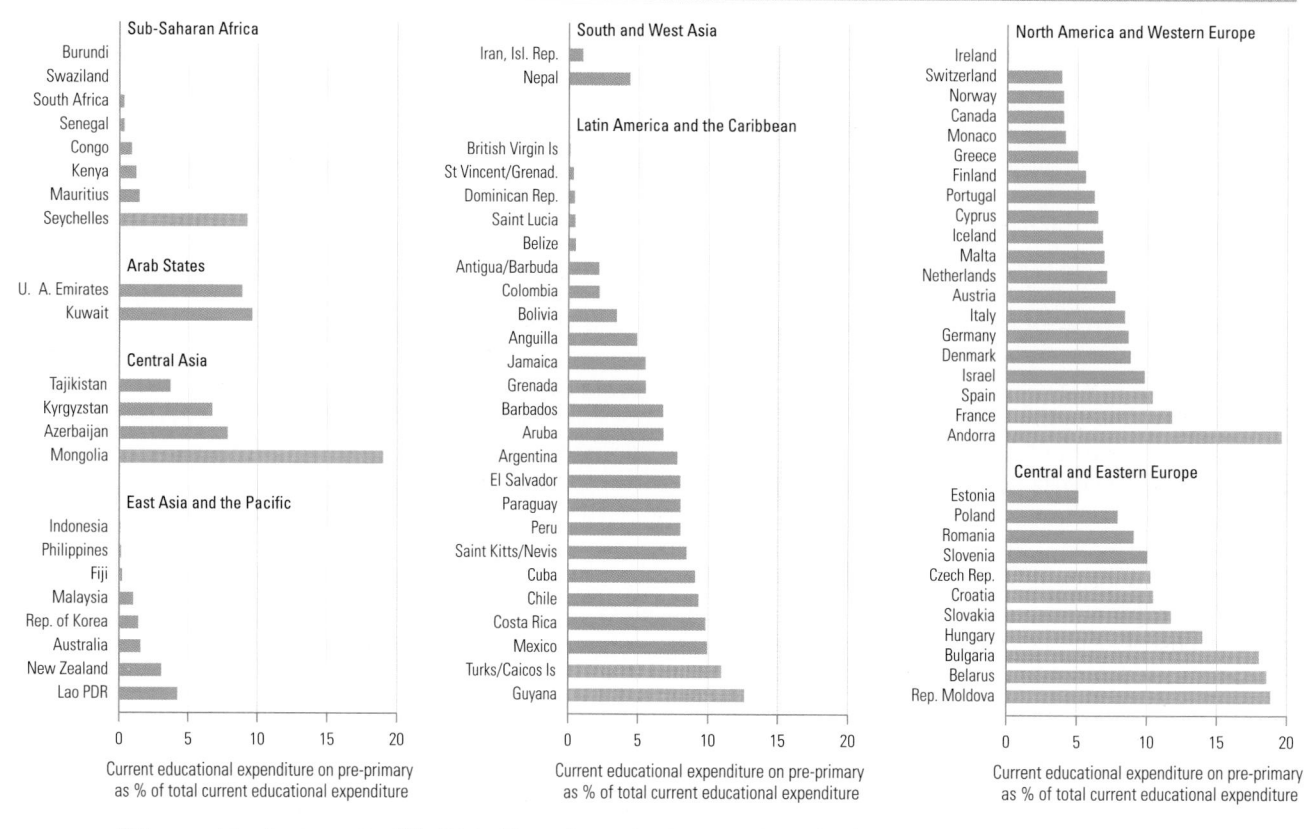

■ These countries allocate more than 10% of total public spending on education to pre-primary education.

Source: UIS database.

2007

Education for All Global Monitoring Report

The average public expenditure per pre-primary child is 85% of that at primary level

by contrast, expenditure on pre-primary programmes is equivalent to about 26% of that on primary education, though the share is as high as 60% in France and Germany. In Latin America and the Caribbean, the average expenditure on pre-primary equals 14% of that on primary, but the variation by country is wide, ranging from 1% in Bolivia to 37% in Guyana. In the few countries with data in sub-Saharan Africa, South and West Asia, and the Arab States, spending on pre-primary education is very low as a percentage of that for primary (see annex, Statistical Table 11).

The costs of ECCE programmes[13]

The small share of total public education spending allocated to pre-primary education reflects low enrolment ratios rather than low spending per child. The average public expenditure per child for all countries with data is 85% of that at primary level (see annex, Statistical Table 11). Indeed, when the state meets the full costs of pre-primary education, as tends to be the

case still in the former socialist countries of Central and Eastern Europe, unit costs are almost 25% higher in pre-primary than in primary education, mainly because of the lower pupil/staff ratios (see Chapter 6). In North America and Western Europe, and in Latin America and the Caribbean, public expenditure per child in pre-primary education averages closer to 70% of that in primary education, though the share reaches about 90% in France, Germany and Greece (see annex, Statistical Table 11).

Per-pupil expenditure in pre-primary education referred to above is arrived at by dividing total public expenditure on pre-primary by the number of children at that level in government schools.[14] Another approach to costing is to focus on the programmes themselves. In principle, this is straightforward: programmes are identified, the inputs for each listed and costed, total and unit costs estimated, and the contributions to the costs from government, households, employers and others

13. This subsection is based in part on Levin and Schwartz (2006).

separated out. In practice, however, there are several data-related problems, such as the great variety of ECCE programme types and the difficulty of obtaining information about spending on private programmes.

While it is difficult to generalize about the costs of ECCE programmes, it is possible to indicate their most important determinants and to clarify the areas where choices affecting costs can be made. Determining factors for per-pupil cost include:

- the nature and range of the service being provided (e.g. pre-school; pre-school and basic health care; pre-school, basic health care and feeding programmes);
- facilities (e.g. purpose-built structure, community building, provider's home);
- length of sessions (e.g. full day, half day, number of days per year);
- child/staff ratios;
- staff qualifications and salary levels.

The total cost depends on the number of children participating, which in turn is influenced by the demographic composition of the population, by parental demand, and by the public and private availability of programmes.

While it is not possible to provide a realistic estimate of the global cost of meeting the ECCE goal, a few country-specific exercises have been carried out, using a range of assumptions about coverage and content. For instance, the budgetary requirements for five scenarios have been estimated for Burkina Faso (Mingat, 2006), a country characterized by very low coverage of children from birth to age 6 (1.2% in 2005). Existing facilities are mainly private and concentrated in two urban centres, with parents and communities bearing most of the costs. The five alternatives differ in terms of quality and coverage. The most ambitious scenario covers 40% of children aged 0 to 6 by 2015 through parenting and centre-based programmes, and includes provision of nutritional support and educational materials. Three-quarters of the 4- to 6-year-olds are assumed to attend community-based facilities and the rest more formal pre-schools. It is estimated that the resources needed to realize this scenario exceed those expected to be available by 2015 by almost 60%. This type of exercise is useful for clarifying the financial implications of specific choices and for exploring trade-offs between, for instance, increasing coverage, reducing quality and increasing or decreasing household payments.

Key issues in financing ECCE programmes[15]

Four key issues need to be considered when financing ECCE programmes: the sources available, the channels to be used to raise and allocate funds, the extent of targeting, and ways to partner with international aid agencies and NGOs.

Public and private funding

The relative shares of public and private funding of ECCE vary considerably by country.[16] Among OECD countries, for instance, the parents' share runs as high as 60% of the total in the United States but closer to 20% in France and Sweden.[17] Among developing countries the variation is even greater. In Indonesia, ECCE is mainly regarded as a family responsibility and public funding represents no more than 5% of the total, usually as subsidies to privately operated urban child care centres. In Cuba, by contrast, the provision and funding of ECCE services are entirely up to the government. Private funding often supplements public funding to expand the level of services; for instance, families may pay for more hours or longer days than are publicly funded. Other private sources may also be available to fund ECCE programmes, including religious institutions, charities, NGOs and companies.

Public funds are often provided by more than one level of government, either directly or though subventions from one level to another. In France, the national government finances teacher salaries while local governments provide the facilities, administration and other services for the *écoles maternelles* for children from ages 3 to 5 (Neuman and Peer, 2002). For child care centres (*crèches*), public funding is shared among the national government (36%), *départements* (47%) and local governments (17%). In Sweden, public funding for ECCE is primarily the responsibility of the municipality (60%) and is funded through local income taxes. Local authorities receive block and equalization grants from the national government to cover the remainder (Gunnarsson et al., 1999). In the United States, the federal government provides around 60% of the public funding for ECCE programmes, and state and local governments contribute the rest (Belfield, 2006).

Financing mechanisms

Higher-level governments (national, regional, state) may either finance and provide ECCE

> In Indonesia, ECCE is mainly regarded as a family responsibility and public funding represents no more than 5% of the total

14. This method underestimates unit costs because households typically also pay fees and other charges, and because some of the public funds may subsidize privately provided programmes whose participants are not included in the total numbers of children.

15. This section is based largely on Belfield (2006).

16. ECCE is also supported financially in several countries by international aid agencies and NGOs, as discussed below.

17. These estimates are for fee-charging child care programmes, primarily for infants and toddlers. Part-day pre-schools for 3- to 5-year-olds in France and 4- to 6-year-olds in Sweden do not charge fees.

programmes directly or they may allocate grants to local authorities for these programmes. The contribution of matching grants may be a condition for receiving this support. In turn, local governments may raise funds directly from the local community through donations by interest groups or social clubs.

An alternative to funding the provision of ECCE programmes directly is for governments to provide resources to parents to enable them to purchase services from a variety of providers. In Taiwan (China), for instance, child care vouchers are distributed to families and can be used to pay the fees at any eligible pre-school (Ho, 2006). In the United States, states have the option of distributing federal subsidies for child care to eligible families in the form of vouchers. Families may also receive subsidies to provide home-based care (Waiser, 1999), or be compensated after purchasing private care. In France, for instance, employed parents benefit from a range of direct subsidies and tax reductions to offset the costs of centre-based and home-based forms of child care. In addition, businesses are required to finance the system through compulsory payments into the *Caisse nationale des allocations familiales* (Family Allowance Fund) (Belfield, 2006).

> In Colombia 3% of total private and public payroll is used for ECCE

18. Most countries mandate the provision of paid parental leave after childbirth, although in developing countries this may cover only employees in the formal or public sector. Paid leave allows parents to provide care themselves for their infants (see Chapter 6).

In addition to the variety of direct mechanisms for funding ECCE activities, government policies affect households' expenditure on ECCE through eligibility rules for publicly provided ECCE, through the level of fees and charges for public programmes and through the structuring of parental leave policies (Waldfogel, 2001).[18]

Corporations and other employers may contribute to the provision of ECCE, either directly by financing a company ECCE centre, or indirectly by including child care in employees' wage and benefits package and allowing parents paid leave for child care. Governments can encourage employers to contribute in this way by offering tax incentives. In Colombia, for instance, for over thirty years all private and public employers have had to deposit the equivalent of 3% of their total payroll into an earmarked account that allows the semi-autonomous Institute for Family Welfare to provide direct services and to contract with NGOs and others to provide services, including community child care, parent education, nutritional supplements, school meals and child protection. This financing strategy has given access to children's services to 21% of the population (Vargas-Barón, Forthcoming).

Other options that may be appropriate where public funds are insufficient to offer the required level of formal ECCE include microenterprise loans to child carers to establish home-based day care (Blumberg, 2006) and the bundling of day care with services such as primary schooling or health centres. Figure 8.2 summarizes the main sources and financing mechanisms for ECCE.

Targeting the disadvantaged

The ECCE goal focuses on vulnerable and disadvantaged young children. When resources are limited, how should they be allocated to those most in need? Two types of targeting are common: geographical and by income. Some governments also target particular groups such as the disabled and those in emergency situations, or they may promote inclusion by using non-financial instruments such as the provision and encouragement of multilingual education (Chapter 7).

India offers an example of geographical targeting. Its Integrated Child Development Services concentrates on urban slums, tribal areas and remote rural regions (Box 8.7). Since 2002, Viet Nam has targeted spending on disadvantaged, remote and mountainous areas, teacher training for children with special needs

Figure 8.2: Examples of funding sources and financing mechanisms for ECCE

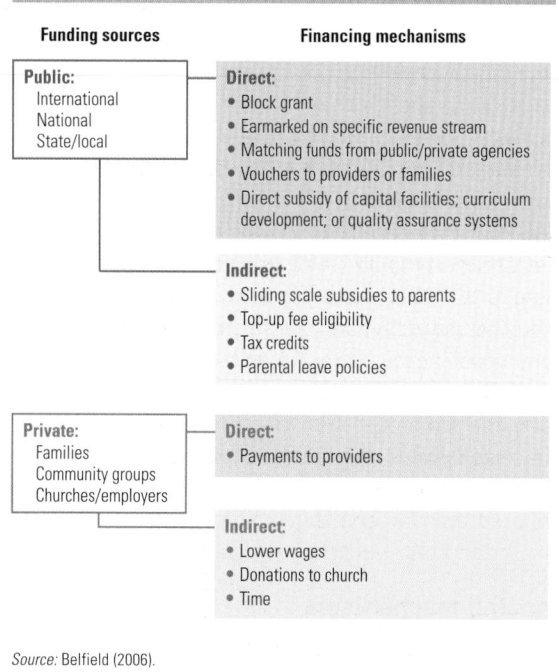

Source: Belfield (2006).

and school meal programmes, arguing that state investment is necessary for the equity issue to be efficiently addressed (Choi, 2005). Income targeting is more common and can include restricting eligibility, subsidizing the enrolment of the poor and providing vouchers.

With ECCE, as with other public services, targeting carries some risks. Targeted approaches may not attract enough political support, particularly among middle-class voters, to ensure that all eligible children are served in good-quality programmes. Targeting can segregate children, leading to a concentration of disadvantage in certain programmes, which may have a negative effect on children's learning. Finally, precise targeting is difficult.

European countries tend to combine universal coverage with additional, more intensive support to vulnerable and disadvantaged children. Belgium, France and the Netherlands, for example, fund pre-school programmes serving all children, but also provide extra resources to communities with the highest concentration of disadvantage (OECD, 2001). This approach is less applicable in many developing countries, where most children are excluded from ECCE anyway. A phase-in approach may be most feasible, whereby countries develop a national ECCE policy that is applicable to all children and settings, but begin by focusing public resources on the most disadvantaged.

International partnerships

Limits to the resources available to many developing country governments for ECCE programmes have led to partnerships with international NGOs and development agencies, which may provide both funding and technical advice (Hyde and Kabiru, 2006).[19] This support can play an important role in establishing ECCE pilot projects that can later be taken to scale, and in technical assistance and capacity-building. A survey for this Report of sixty-eight bilateral donors and multilateral agencies, to which only seventeen responded,[20] as well as analysis of aid data reported by donors to the OECD Development Assistance Committee (DAC), show, however, that ECCE is not high on the international education development agenda.

Agencies prioritize aid to centre-based preschools

The results of the donor survey suggest that few agencies have identified ECCE as a specific

Box 8.7: Packaging of services to aid India's vulnerable children

In 1975, the Government of India launched Integrated Child Development Services (ICDS) to provide a package of supplementary nutrition, immunization, health check-up and referral services, early childhood education and community participation services to vulnerable children under 6 and to pregnant and nursing mothers in city slums, tribal areas and remote rural regions. Women from the local community deliver the services through *anganwadi*, the term for informal childcare centres in the courtyards of village houses. ICDS now covers 23 million children (nearly 15% of all children of pre-school age) at an average annual cost of US$10-$22 per child, and 4.8 million expectant and nursing mothers.

The federal government has recently renewed its commitment to universalize ICDS and expand equality of opportunity to all children, in light of its positive, if uneven, impact on children's survival, growth and development. ICDS has contributed to reducing infant mortality and severe malnutrition, improving immunization rates, increasing school enrolment and reducing school drop out. In rural Tamil Nadu, Andhra Pradesh and Karnataka, for instance, ICDS has led to improved psychosocial development in both boys and girls. Indeed, even undernourished ICDS children attained higher developmental scores than well-nourished non-ICDS children.

Despite this success, the incidence of premature birth, low birth weight, neonatal and infant mortality, and maternal and child undernutrition remain of concern in the ICDS areas. Several reforms could enhance ICDS's impact: more emphasis on children under 3; better targeting (e.g., girls and children from poorer households and lower castes); more promotion of behaviour change in child care nutrition practices; and more funding for the poorest states and those with the highest levels of undernutrition.

Sources: Chandrasekhar and Ghosh (2005); Gragnolati et al.(2005); Kamerman (2005): National Institute of Public Cooperation and Child Development (2006)

component of their *overall* aid strategy (four of the respondents had done so), though seven include ECCE as a component of their *education* strategy and eight identify it within their *health* strategy.[21] As part of these broader strategies, international support for ECCE tends to be targeted for particular groups of marginalized and vulnerable children, including those with special educational needs, those most affected by hunger and poverty, those disadvantaged by gender or social status and those most affected by the HIV/AIDS pandemic.

Bilateral donors tend to give priority to centre-based ECCE programmes covering children from age 3 to primary school age. They provide less support to home-based ECCE arrangements and generally limit this to programmes serving children from age 3.

19. Between 1990 and 2005, the World Bank lending portfolio for early childhood development totalled $1.6 billion worldwide (Young, 2006).

20. More detailed discussion of the survey methodology and findings can be found at www.efareport.unesco.org.

21. Health strategies cover HIV/AIDS, reproductive health, primary health care, women's empowerment in health-related activities, orphans and other vulnerable children, young child survival and development, nutrition, micronutrient support, deworming and malaria prevention.

Figure 8.3: Aid to early childhood education, 1999-2004 annual average, by country income groups (2003 constant US$ millions)

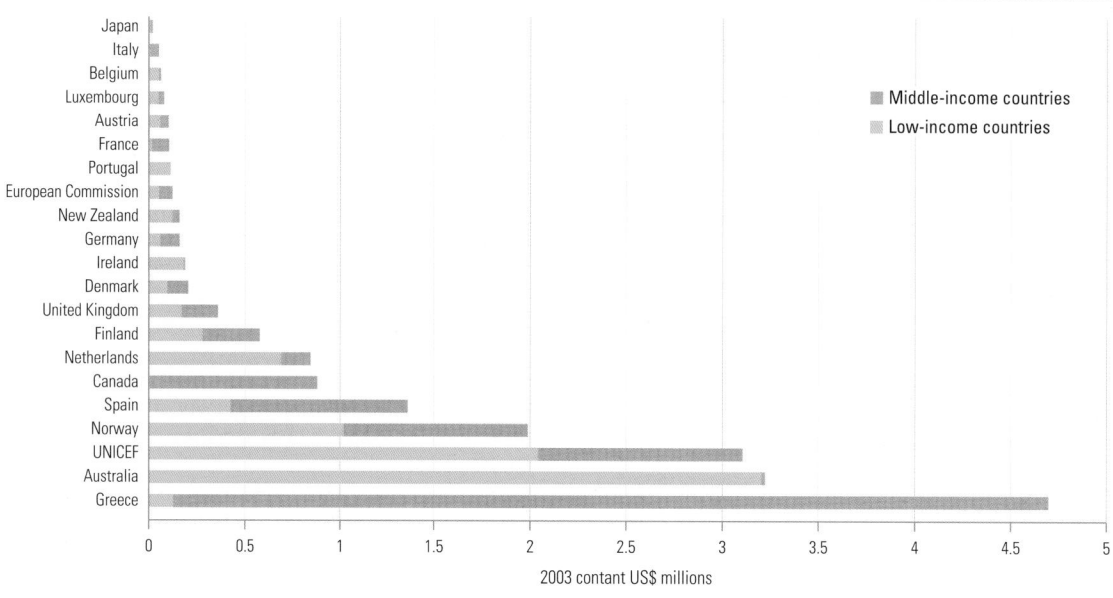

Source: CRS online database (OECD-DAC, 2006c), Table 1.

Low-income countries tend to receive less aid for ECCE than middle-income countries

Such funding priorities do not necessarily match country needs; less formal and less costly arrangements than centres can often help reach more young children of all ages, including those under 3. United Nations agencies, such as the World Food Programme, WHO, UNICEF and UNESCO, are more likely than bilateral donors to focus on children under 3 and to support informal programmes.

Much less aid for ECCE than for other levels of education

The amount of aid to ECCE is difficult to estimate from the main international aid database, the OECD-DAC's Creditor Reporting System (CRS). Not all donors report early childhood education separately from basic education. Components of ECCE may also be reported in other sectors, such as health, social security and rural affairs. The data presented in this section are limited to the education dimension of ECCE and hence seriously underestimate the total aid for ECCE. Donors have very different priorities in their allocations of education aid to early childhood education (Figure 8.3). Some, like Greece, focus support on middle-income countries, while others, such as Australia, the Netherlands and UNICEF, tend to target low-income countries.

Low-income countries tend to receive less funding for ECCE than middle-income countries. For example, of the sixty-three countries that received less than US$100,000 annually for early childhood education between 1999 and 2004, thirty-seven were low-income. Of the thirty-two countries that received more than this, fifteen were low-income and seventeen were middle-income. Since the volume of aid for early childhood education is determined partly by developing countries' demand, this is consistent with the fact that demand for early childhood education is mainly in countries that have a reasonably developed level of primary schooling (see Chapter 6).

Table 8.4 highlights the relatively low priority given to early childhood education (ECE). Nineteen of the twenty-two donors with data have allocated to pre-primary education less than 10% of what they make available for the primary level – a majority allocate less than 2%. As a share of total aid to education, the majority allocate less than 0.5%.

What next? Increasing funding and aid coordination for ECCE

What would persuade aid agencies to allocate more resources to ECCE? According to responses to the donor survey, the key would be evidence of increased commitment to ECCE by developing country governments: demonstrating financial support, making ECCE an integral part of national sector plans, developing strategies for ECCE involving all key players in the country (including the private sector and civil society) and coordinating efforts for young children across sectors. International political support from the OECD-DAC, the EFA High-Level Group and similar forums, along with more research showing the benefits of ECCE, would help increase awareness of and commitment to ECCE issues among multilateral and bilateral agencies. Aid to ECCE needs to be considered within the broader aid coordination mechanisms for education and health. To focus attention on support for young children, it may be helpful to establish country-level, thematic working groups of donors involved in ECCE.

Planning, participation, targeting and leadership

To ensure access to and participation in early childhood programmes of good quality, a favourable policy environment needs to be created. An early childhood policy or an early childhood policy framework helps to ensure that young children's rights are guaranteed and that their needs are met by the various sectors whose work has an impact on young children. A lead ministry helps create policy coherence, but it is important for ECCE not to become too narrowly affiliated with one sector. Legislation and a detailed action plan are other important supports for implementation, as is capacity-building for those charged with putting policies into practice. Involvement of a broad group of stakeholders is critical to ensuring that policy development meets diverse needs and to facilitating its implementation. Early childhood issues that are endorsed by high-level politicians or other leaders can raise the visibility of ECCE and ease policy development.

Table 8.4: Aid to early childhood education is less than aid to primary education

	Aid to early childhood education	Aid to primary education	Aid to ECE as % of aid to primary education
	1999-2004 average constant 2003 US$ millions	1999-2004 average constant 2003 US$ millions	
Japan	0.02	88.15	0.0%
European Commission	0.12	155.79	0.1%
United Kingdom	0.37	228.80	0.2%
Germany	0.16	50.00	0.3%
France	0.17	34.66	0.5%
Netherlands	1.09	160.88	0.7%
Denmark	0.20	23.66	0.9%
UNDP	0.00	0.24	1.2%
Italy	0.05	3.59	1.4%
Canada	0.88	61.34	1.4%
Ireland	0.19	10.16	1.8%
Belgium	0.06	3.14	1.9%
Luxembourg	0.08	3.82	2.0%
Portugal	0.11	3.98	2.8%
Norway	2.01	60.38	3.3%
New Zealand	0.16	2.80	5.6%
UNICEF	3.17	43.35	7.3%
Australia	3.22	38.85	8.3%
Finland	0.58	6.69	8.6%
Spain	1.39	13.15	10.6%
Austria	0.24	1.47	16.2%
Greece	4.74	6.19	76.5%

Source: CRS online database (OECD-DAC, 2006*c*), Table 1.

To promote children's healthy development, it is important to establish regulations for quality and monitoring that cover the full range of public and private settings. Governments can pursue multiple revenue sources and financing strategies, but each involves a trade-off among access, quality and equity. Equity, in particular, implies the need for more initial targeting of public ECCE resources at vulnerable and disadvantaged children, within more universal policy frameworks. Finally, international aid agencies need to accord higher priority to ECCE. Countries that align ECCE policies with education and health sector plans and poverty-reduction strategies stand a better chance of attracting additional support from donors. ∎

Favourable policy environment needs to be created

On the road in Chiapas,
Mexico.

188

PART IV.
Setting priorities

Chapter 9

EFA: action now

Chapter 1 stressed the importance of taking a comprehensive approach to EFA, of emphasizing equity and inclusion, and of taking urgent action – now. This concluding chapter summarizes progress towards the Education for All goals, only nine years before the 2015 target date and only three years before all children must be enrolled in primary school if they are to complete it by 2015. The chapter then reviews the key elements required of a national and international action agenda if the goals, including that for ECCE (this Report's special theme), are to be met on time.

The fastest progress is being made in the countries furthest from universal primary education

Where does the world stand?

The overall EFA picture is mixed. There has been significant progress since Dakar, especially on access to primary education, including for girls. The fastest progress is being made in the countries furthest from universal primary education, but it remains inadequate for the UPE and primary gender goals to be met on time. The rest of the EFA agenda is lagging, in particular with regard to improving adult literacy and to expanding programmes for children before they enter primary school. Table 9.1 summarizes progress since Dakar for EFA as a whole, for the individual goals and for related domestic and international financing. Some trends are very encouraging while others are worrying.

A nine-point agenda

To consolidate progress and to meet all the EFA goals on time, including that for ECCE, the agenda should focus on nine areas:

1. *Returning to the comprehensive approach of Dakar.* There is progress where there is commitment and prioritization – i.e. primary school enrolment, including for girls, which has captured both domestic and international attention, including that of the Fast Track Initiative. Education for All, however, is a comprehensive approach to basic education. Not all governments have taken full public responsibility for some of its most important elements, particularly adult literacy (globally, a staggering one in five adults remain without basic literacy skills) and ECCE, the special theme of this Report. It is also increasingly clear that it is necessary to expand the supply of lower secondary places as an incentive to complete primary school and hence achieve the universal primary education goal.

2. *Acting with urgency.* Time is running out. Even achieving UPE by 2015 is uncertain. In some countries, the gender parity goal, already missed in 2005, may not be met by 2015. We must act now to get all children into school and take steps to ensure that they stay there and that they learn. It is also very important to enrol disadvantaged and vulnerable children in ECCE, as they have the most to gain. Moreover, a major effort for adult literacy is seriously overdue (see the 2006 Report); the United Nations Literacy Decade has yet to take off.

Basic education increasingly faces competition for funds as governments and aid agencies turn towards sectors more commonly associated with economic growth, such as infrastructure, and towards upper secondary and higher education. Countries currently or recently in conflict have no data and so tend not to be included in this Report's analysis, but their EFA situation is unlikely to be improving. Creating education opportunities for children living in conflict and post-conflict situations should be a very high priority.

3. *Emphasizing equity and inclusion.* Despite progress, most disadvantaged children do not benefit from ECCE and far too many primary school age children are still out of school. It is more challenging and costly to compensate for disadvantage as children get older than to institute preventive measures and support early in life. A disaggregated approach is needed, focusing on particular regions and population groups within countries. In too many countries, direct and indirect household costs, including the need to have children work to supplement household income, and the payment of fees at ECCE and primary level, remain a major obstacle to poor children's early access and continued participation. For effective inclusion, which must start when children are young, there is a need also to promote the mother tongue as the initial language of instruction, to establish gender equality in staff-pupil interactions and learning materials, to ensure that children from diverse backgrounds are treated equally, to accommodate children living with disabilities, to adjust the school year to the agricultural calendar as appropriate, and to have schools and adult programmes close to where people live.

4. *Increasing public spending and focusing it better.* Many governments are not spending enough public funds on good-quality basic education, and certainly not enough on literacy and ECCE. There is a need to focus financial resources on key requirements for achieving EFA, such as increasing the supply of teachers, providing incentives to teach in rural areas, implementing policies of inclusion and expanding adult literacy and ECCE. A clear – and sustained – focus on basic education is essential to offset the increasing pressures for spending on other levels of education.

5. *Augmenting international aid and allocating it where it is most needed.* Both actual and

Table 9.1: EFA progress since Dakar

Commitments	Encouraging	Worrying
EFA as a whole	■ The EFA Development Index (EDI) increased from 2003 to 2004 in seventy-five countries.	■ The EDI fell in forty countries. ■ The lack of data for a significant number of countries, particularly those recently or currently in conflict, makes it difficult to paint the full global picture (it is unlikely that the EFA situation is improving in most conflict or post-conflict countries).
Early childhood care and education	■ Pre-primary enrolment increased sharply, particularly in sub-Saharan Africa, the Caribbean, and South and West Asia. ■ Slightly more than half the world's countries have at least one formal ECCE programme for children under 3. ■ About 80% of developing countries have some form of legally established maternity leave, although enforcement varies.	■ Despite progress, millions of children still do not have access to the basic immunization, clean water, adequate food and early stimulation they need for survival, growth and development. ■ Coverage for both under-3s and pre-primary remains considerably lower for developing countries than for developed ones. ■ Regional differences on pre-primary are striking, e.g. relatively high coverage in Latin America and the Caribbean, very low in sub-Saharan Africa and the Arab States. ■ Nearly half of all countries have no formal ECCE programmes for under-3s. ■ Variation within countries reveals large disparities in access to ECCE between rich and poor and between urban and rural. ■ Those least likely to be enrolled are the poor, rural and/or disadvantaged – those who would benefit the most from ECCE. ■ ECCE data collection is generally inadequate to monitor progress fully in developing countries.
Universal primary education	■ Enrolment ratios increased considerably, especially in the regions farthest from the goals (sub-Saharan Africa, and South and West Asia). ■ Grade 1 enrolment rose sharply, particularly in sub-Saharan Africa, and South and West Asia. ■ The number of children out of school declined.	■ Despite progress, too many children are still out of school. ■ The most marginalized are difficult to enrol and retain. ■ Attendance remains below enrolment. ■ School retention and completion is still too low in many countries.
Gender	■ About two-thirds of countries have achieved parity in primary education. ■ 94 girls per 100 boys are now enrolled in primary education, compared with 92 in 1999.	■ The 2005 target date for primary and secondary parity was missed. ■ Disparities at the expense of girls remain significant at primary level in many countries, often those with the lowest enrolment ratios. ■ Only one-third of countries have achieved parity in secondary education. ■ Gender equality is still an issue.
Quality	■ Pupil/teacher ratios improved slightly in every region except South and West Asia. ■ Developing countries' commitment to monitoring quality is rising, as evidenced by the expanding number of national learning assessments and increased participation in international and regional assessments.	■ Pupil/teacher ratios in primary education remain above 40:1 in twenty-eight countries. ■ There are too few teachers to meet UPE goal and improve pupil/teacher ratios, especially in sub-Saharan Africa. ■ High proportions of teachers are untrained and unqualified. ■ Teacher absenteeism remains a serious problem. ■ New analyses of international learning assessments confirm that students from poor households perform worse than others.
Literacy	■ Adult and youth literacy rates have improved in all regions since 1990, but very little in the past few years. ■ The absolute number of youth illiterates declined except in sub-Saharan Africa.	■ Adult literacy rates remain below 70% in South and West Asia, sub-Saharan Africa, the Arab States and the Caribbean. ■ 781 million adults, two-thirds of them women, are not literate. ■ At the current pace of improvement, the number of adults without minimal literacy skills will decrease by only 100 million by 2015. ■ The literate environment receives relatively little attention. ■ Too few countries are initiating direct assessments of literacy.
Education finance	■ Public spending on education increased as a share of GNP in about two-thirds of the countries with data. ■ Increasing numbers of countries have reduced primary school fees and other household costs.	■ The share of public spending on education in GNP declined in forty-one countries, particularly in Latin America and in South and West Asia. ■ Too many countries still charge fees.
International aid to education (constant 2003 prices)	■ Aid rose by 85% in real terms from 2000 to 2004 (but following a decline before 2000). ■ Aid to basic education in low-income countries more than doubled in real terms, to US$3.4 billion, in the same period. ■ Donor pledges will likely increase this to US$5.4 billion by 2010.	■ Aid to basic education in low-income countries falls far short of the estimated US$11 billion per year needed now to achieve EFA (even if 2010 pledges are realized). ■ Most aid is still not sufficiently long term or predictable.

ECCE requires high-level political support for early childhood policies and programmes in countries, and technical support internationally

pledged levels of aid for basic education are increasing, but they remain insufficient, given the urgency of achieving EFA. Aid to basic education in low-income countries must at least *double*; it must include aid for literacy and ECCE; it must be more predictable over a longer term; and it must be reallocated towards those countries most in need. If the Fast Track Initiative is to become a key vehicle for this endeavour, it also needs to receive much more funding, to deliver more predictable aid flows over a longer period and to broaden its focus beyond primary education to include all six EFA goals.

6. *Moving ECCE up domestic and international agendas, stressing a holistic approach.* ECCE requires high-level political support for early childhood policies and programmes in countries, and technical support internationally. Given ECCE's complexity, and its unique role in providing the individual child with strong foundations for life and learning, it is important to (a) develop a national policy framework with goals, regulations, monitoring of quality and funding commitments that span the full range of provision for children from birth to age 8; and (b) clearly designate a lead ministry or agency for ECCE that works with all related sectors. ECCE must encompass policies and programmes for children under 3, including support to parents, as well as for pre-schoolers. Although there is no one model of ECCE provision, programmes that combine nutrition, health, care and education are more effective in improving young children's current welfare and their future development than those confined to one aspect. Inclusive programmes need to build on traditional child care practices, respect children's linguistic and cultural diversity, and mainstream children with special educational needs and disabilities. The private sector plays an important role in the delivery of ECCE in many countries; the public sector must therefore both regulate it and develop effective partnerships with it, to safeguard against inequities in access and quality.

7. *Increasing public finance for ECCE and targeting it.* Although a national ECCE policy should encompass all young children, it may be appropriate initially, given resource scarcities, to target public resources to vulnerable and disadvantaged children.

To secure both domestic and international resources, and to raise the overall profile of ECCE, it is essential to include it in key documents for public resource allocation and for attracting aid, such as national budgets, sector plans and Poverty Reduction Strategy Papers. Other donors need to follow UNICEF's lead and prioritize early childhood issues.

8. *Upgrading the ECCE workforce, especially as regards qualifications, training and working conditions.* Since all the evidence demonstrates that the quality of child-staff interaction is the single most critical element in determining the quality of ECCE, nothing is more important than attracting and retaining sufficient numbers of trained and motivated staff. It is essential to overcome the common tendency to undervalue ECCE staff in terms of pay and in providing appropriate training. Quality standards are needed for all the different types of ECCE personnel. In addition, to be effective staff need reasonable working conditions as regards factors such as child/staff ratios, group sizes and the adequacy of materials.

9. *Improving the monitoring of ECCE.* As this Report shows, it is not easy to monitor progress towards the ECCE goal, especially as it relates to under-3s, given current data availability. Box 9.1 suggests options for improving data collection and provides a possible agenda for governments, the UNESCO Institute for Statistics (UIS) and the international community.

The considerable progress made towards EFA since Dakar provides a measure of just how much can be accomplished when countries and the international community join forces for concerted action. Yet EFA requires a more comprehensive approach and more sustained efforts. We must not let interest and momentum flag. EFA means education for all, not just education for some. It means all six goals, not just those related to primary school. It means paying particular attention to the early years, when effective steps to offset disadvantage can be taken at lowest cost and when strong foundations are most easily laid. Finally, it means staying the course. Failing the youngest generation today not only violates their rights, it also sows the seeds of deeper poverty and inequalities tomorrow. The challenges are clear, the agenda too. The time for action is now. ■

Box 9.1: Augmenting and improving data on ECCE

Major efforts are needed by national and international agencies to expand and improve systematic information related to the following dimensions of ECCE:

Basic health and nutrition data

● Statistics on food intake, nutrition levels, stunting and survival rates for young children are regularly collected by the WHO, the UN Population Division, UNAIDS and UNICEF. The quality and geographic coverage of such indicators are, on the whole, quite good. Donors could provide technical and financial assistance to strengthen capacity in countries needing additional support to collect such information. Reporting basic health and survival data by subnational administrative level and by household characteristics would improve their policy relevance.

ECCE programmes for infants and toddlers

● In many countries, data are unavailable on ECCE programmes (day care, crèches, nurseries, as well as nutrition and health oriented programmes). For children under 3, little is known about the organized care provided by public and private agencies and organizations. Statistics on participation in such programmes have been collected, on an ad hoc basis, in an increasing number of developing countries through household surveys such as UNICEF's Multiple Indicator Cluster Surveys and the USAID-funded Demographic and Health Surveys. Understanding differences in access to ECCE programmes among young children, especially those from disadvantaged and vulnerable backgrounds, is critical. Such surveys can complement administrative data, the collection of which needs to be improved.

● The UIS, in cooperation with other agencies, could expand the scope of its comparatively recent programme of data gathering on children under 3, which was initiated for the pre-Dakar EFA 2000 assessment exercise. Doing so will require continued and sustained exchanges with the national authorities concerned, with a view to improving the coverage and comparability of data, including more emphasis on all ECCE programmes, not just pre-primary education.

Pre-primary education

● Pre-primary education data compiled by the UIS, the OECD and Eurostat for the relevant regional groupings form the most complete set of worldwide information on the education component of ECCE. Given the considerable cross-national variations in pre-primary education, it would be useful to publish enrolment data for specific age brackets on a regular basis. Some categories of administrative data on the education component that may be too difficult or costly to collect annually could be made available less frequently, for instance every three or five years. Children's background characteristics, detailed by residence, administrative subdivision, duration and content of pre-primary programmes, could also usefully be provided periodically.

Such data could be collected jointly by the UIS and the International Bureau of Education (IBE), as has been done in the past.

Staff

● In addition to existing data on pre-primary teachers, more information is needed on the type, characteristics, employment, professional status and deployment of all categories of staff who work with young children. These data are necessary to develop policies to recruit and deploy the human resources necessary for expanding and improving opportunities for the most vulnerable and disadvantaged children.

Quality

● The need for, and usefulness of, standardized comparative data on ECCE programme quality is controversial. Yet cross-national indicators of structural quality could very usefully be compiled (e.g. teacher/pupil ratios, teachers' qualifications, expenditure and programme standards). While caution clearly is needed in interpreting and drawing conclusions from information from such a variety of contexts, it is important to recognize that a profile of quality is much more reliable than individual indicators. Once national quality assessments have been made, evidence of improvement over time should be reported to international monitoring bodies, using nationally defined baseline measures.

Expenditure

● Data on expenditure on pre-primary education are more scant than at other levels of education and are often limited to public expenditure. Cross-national data on expenditure on ECCE programmes other than pre-primary education are almost nonexistent, as are data on household spending for ECCE and on international aid for ECCE; steps need to be taken to collect all these types of data. Efforts to assess the costs of ECCE programmes are under way in various countries, mostly on an experimental basis. International organizations could build on these national case studies to guide countries in producing comparable cost information.

Qualitative data

● Qualitative data can supplement the picture of ECCE provision obtained from quantitative indicators. They should ideally include information about public policies on early childhood, the types and availability of ECCE programmes, needs assessments by parents and ECCE staff, and programme outcomes. Such data, while difficult to gather, process and summarize, can be collected through sample surveys jointly undertaken by national, regional and/or international institutions. The development of relatively standard categories and common methodologies is important to improve the availability and quality of such data.

A child hard at work in Harbin,
China, at a school mainly
for children of migrant workers.

© REUTERS

Annex

The Education for All Development Index

While each of the six EFA goals is individually important, it is also useful to have a means of indicating progress towards EFA as a whole. The EFA Development Index (EDI), a composite of relevant indicators, provides one way of doing so, at least for the four most easily quantifiable EFA goals: universal primary education (UPE), adult literacy, gender parity and the quality of education.

The two goals not yet included in the EDI are goals 1 and 3. Neither has a quantitative target for 2015. Goal 1 (early childhood care and education) is multidimensional and covers both the care and education aspects. The indicators currently available on this goal cannot easily be incorporated in the EDI because national data are insufficiently standardized and reliable, and comparable data are not available for most countries (see Chapter 6). Goal 3 (learning needs of youth and adults) has not yet been sufficiently defined for quantitative measurement (see Chapter 2).

In accordance with the principle of considering each goal to be equally important, one indicator is used as a proxy measure for each of the four EDI components,[1] and each component is assigned equal weight in the overall index. The EDI value for a particular country is thus the arithmetic mean of the observed values for each component. Since the components are all expressed as percentages, the EDI value can vary from 0 to 100% or, when expressed as a ratio, from 0 to 1. The closer a country's EDI value is to the maximum, the greater the extent of its overall EFA achievement and the nearer the country is to the EFA goal as a whole.

Choice of indicators as proxy measures of EDI components

In selecting indicators, relevance has to be balanced with data availability.

Universal primary education

The UPE goal implies both universal access to and universal completion of primary education. However, while both access and participation at this level are relatively easy to measure, there is a lack of consensus on the definition of primary school completion. Therefore, the indicator selected to measure UPE achievement (goal 2) in the EDI is the total primary net enrolment ratio (NER), which reflects the percentage of primary school age children who are enrolled in either primary or secondary school. Its value varies from 0 to 100%. A NER of 100% means all eligible children are enrolled in school in a given school year, although not all of them will necessary complete it.

Adult literacy

The adult literacy rate is used as a proxy to measure progress towards the first part of goal 4.[2] This has its limitations. First, the adult literacy indicator, being a statement about the stock of human capital, is slow to change, and thus it could be argued that it is not a good 'leading indicator' of year-by-year progress. Second, the existing data on literacy are not entirely satisfactory. Most of them are based on 'conventional' non-tested methods that usually overestimate the level of literacy among individuals.[3] New methodologies, based on tests and on the definition of literacy as a continuum of skills, are being developed and applied in some countries to improve the quality of literacy data. Providing a new data series of good quality for even a majority of countries will take many years, however. The literacy rates now used are the best currently available internationally.

Quality of education

Measures of students' learning outcomes are widely used as a proxy for the quality of education, particularly among countries at similar levels of

---

1. The EDI's gender component is itself a composite index.

2. 'Achieving a 50 per cent improvement in levels of adult literacy by 2015, especially for women'. To enable progress towards this target to be monitored for all countries, whatever their current adult literacy level, it was decided as of the 2006 *EFA Global Monitoring Report* to interpret it in terms of a reduction in the adult illiteracy rate.

3. In most countries, particularly developing countries, current literacy data are derived from methods of self-declaration or third-party reporting (e.g. a household head responding on behalf of other household members) used in censuses or household surveys. In other cases they are based on education attainment proxies. Neither method is based on any test, and both are subject to bias (overestimation of literacy), which affects the quality and accuracy of literacy data.

development. They are incomplete, as they do not include values, capacities and other non-cognitive skills that are also important aims of education, beyond cognitive skills (UNESCO, 2004*a*: pp. 43-4). They also tell nothing about the cognitive value added by schooling (as opposed to home background), or the distribution of ability among children enrolled in school.[4] Despite these drawbacks, learning outcomes would likely be the most appropriate single proxy for the average quality of education, but as comparable data are not yet available for a large number of countries, it is not yet possible to use them in the EDI.

Among the feasible proxy indicators available for a large number of countries, the survival rate to grade 5 was selected as being the best available for the quality of education component of the EDI.[5] Figure 1 shows that there is a clear positive link between such survival rates and educational achievement in sub–Saharan African countries participating in the Southern and Eastern African Consortium for Monitoring Educational Quality (SACMEQ II) assessment. The coefficient of determination is around 33%. Education systems capable of retaining a larger proportion of their pupils to grade 5 perform better, on average, on international tests.

The survival rate to grade 5 is associated even more strongly with learning outcomes in lower secondary school. Figure 2 shows that the variation in one variable explains 42% of the variation in the other one in the results of the third Trends in International Mathematics and Science Study (TIMSS) and up to 77% in the Programme for International Student Assessment (PISA) study.

Another possible proxy indicator for quality is the pupil/teacher ratio (PTR). Among SACMEQ II countries, the proportion of variation in learning outcomes explained by the PTR is 36%, which is slightly higher than that explained by survival rates to grade 5 (33%). Many other studies, however, produce much more ambiguous evidence of the relationship between the PTR and learning outcomes (UNESCO, 2004). In a multivariate context, PTRs are associated with higher learning outcomes in some studies, but not in many others. In addition, the relationship seems to vary by the level of mean test scores. For low levels of test scores, a decrease in pupils per teacher has a positive impact on learning outcomes, but for higher levels of test scores, additional teachers have only limited impact. For these reasons, the survival rate was chosen as a safer proxy for learning outcomes and hence for education quality.[6]

Figure 1: Survival rate to grade 5 and learning outcomes at primary level

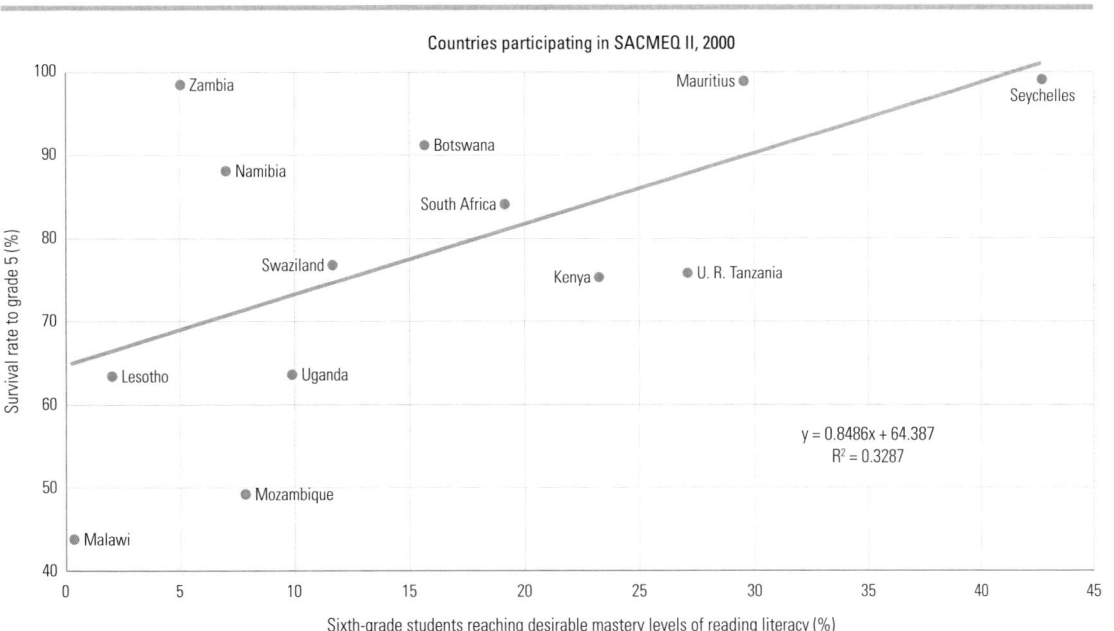

Countries participating in SACMEQ II, 2000

$y = 0.8486x + 64.387$
$R^2 = 0.3287$

Sources: UNESCO Institute for Statistics calculation, based on SACMEQ II database; annex, Statistical Table 7.

4. Strictly speaking, it would be necessary to compare average levels of cognitive achievement for pupils completing a given school grade across countries with similar levels and distributions of income and with similar levels of NER, so as to account for home background and ability cohort effects.

5. See *EFA Global Monitoring Report 2003/4*, Appendix 2, for background.

6. Another reason is that survival rates, like the other EDI components, but unlike PTRs, range from 0% to 100%. Therefore, the use of the survival rate to grade 5 in the EDI avoids a need to rescale the data.

Figure 2: Survival rate to grade 5 and learning outcomes at lower secondary level

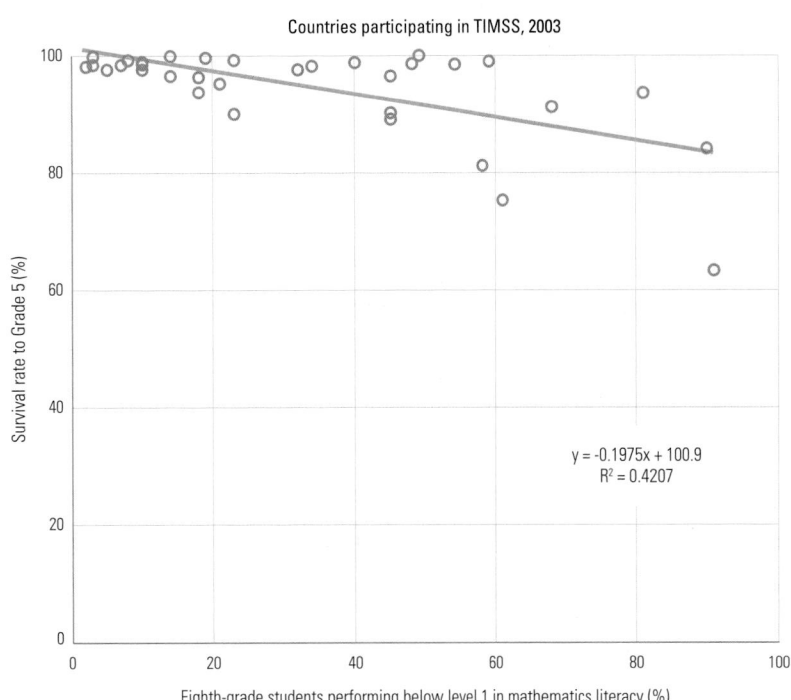

Countries participating in TIMSS, 2003

$y = -0.1975x + 100.9$
$R^2 = 0.4207$

Survival rate to Grade 5 (%)

Eighth-grade students performing below level 1 in mathematics literacy (%)

Sources: Mullis et al. (2004); annex, Statistical Table 7.

Figure 2 (continued)

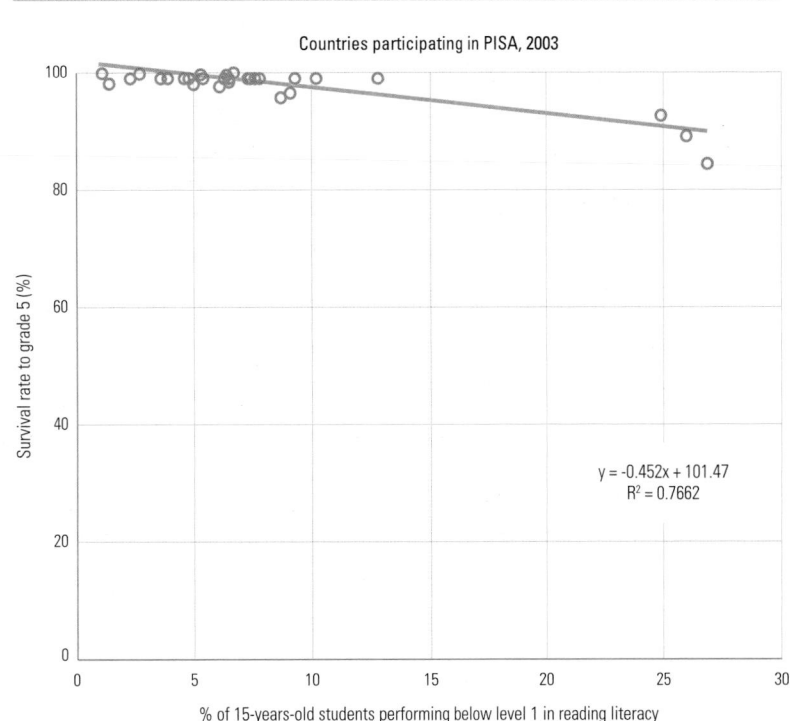

Countries participating in PISA, 2003

$y = -0.452x + 101.47$
$R^2 = 0.7662$

Survival rate to grade 5 (%)

% of 15-years-old students performing below level 1 in reading literacy

Sources: OECD (2004); annex, Statistical Table 7.

Gender

The fourth EDI component is measured by a composite index, the gender-specific EFA index (GEI). Ideally, the GEI should reflect the whole gender-related EFA goal, which calls for 'eliminating gender disparities in primary and secondary education by 2005, and achieving gender equality in education by 2015, with a focus on ensuring girls' full and equal access to and achievement in basic education of good quality'. There are thus two subgoals: gender parity (achieving equal participation of girls and boys in primary and secondary education) and gender equality (ensuring that educational equality exists between boys and girls).

The first subgoal is measured by the gender parity indexes (GPIs) for the gross enrolment ratios (GERs) at primary and secondary levels. Measuring and monitoring the broader aspects of equality in education is difficult, as the 2003/4 Report demonstrated (UNESCO, 2003a). Essentially, outcome measures, disaggregated by sex, are needed for a range of educational levels. No such measures are available on an internationally comparable basis. As a step in that direction, however, the GEI includes gender parity for adult literacy. Thus, the GEI is calculated as a simple average of three GPIs: for the GER in primary education, for the GER in secondary education and for the adult literacy rate. This means the GEI does not fully reflect the equality aspect of the EFA gender goal.

The GPI, when expressed as the ratio of females to males in enrolment ratios or the literacy rate, can exceed unity when more girls/women are enrolled or literate than boys/men. For the purposes of the index, the F/M formula is inverted to M/F in cases where the GPI is higher than 1. This solves mathematically the problem of including the GEI in the EDI (where all components have a theoretical limit of 1, or 100%) while maintaining the GEI's ability to show gender disparity. Figure 3 shows how 'transformed GPIs' are arrived at to highlight gender disparities that disadvantage males. Once all three GPI values have been calculated and converted into 'transformed GPIs' (from 0 to 1) where needed, the composite GEI is obtained by calculating a simple average of the three GPIs, with each being weighted equally.

Figure 4 illustrates the calculation for the Philippines, using data for the school year ending in 2004. The GPIs in primary education, secondary education and adult literacy were 0.985, 1.108 and 1.00, respectively, resulting in a GEI of 0.963:
GEI = 1/3 (primary GPI)
    + 1/3 (transformed secondary GPI)
    + 1/3 (adult literacy GPI)
GEI = 1/3 (0.985) + 1/3 (0.903) + 1/3 (1.00) = 0.963

Calculating the EDI

The EDI is the arithmetic mean of its four components – total primary NER, adult literacy rate, GEI and survival rate to grade 5. As a simple average, the EDI may mask important variations among its components: for example, results for goals on which a country has made less progress can offset its advances on others. Since all the EFA goals are equally important, a synthetic indicator such as the EDI is thus very useful to inform the policy debate on the prominence of all the EFA goals and to highlight the synergy among them.

Figure 5 illustrates the calculation of the EDI, again using the Philippines as an example. The total primary NER, adult literacy rate, value of the GEI and survival rate to grade 5 in 2004 were 0.944, 0.926, 0.963 and 0.753, respectively, resulting in an EDI of 0.897:
EDI = 1/4 (total primary NER)
    + 1/4 (adult literacy rate)
    + 1/4 (GEI)
    + 1/4 (survival rate to Grade 5)
EDI = 1/4 (0.944) + 1/4 (0.926) + 1/4 (0.963) + 1/4 (0.753)
    = 0.897

Data sources and country coverage

All data used to calculate the EDI for the school year ending in 2004 are from the statistical tables in this annex and the UNESCO Institute for Statistics (UIS) database, with one exception. Adult literacy data for some OECD countries that did not answer the UIS literacy survey are based on the results of the 2004 European Labour Force Survey.

Only the 125 countries with a complete set of the indicators required to calculate the EDI are included in this analysis. Many countries are thus not included in the EDI. This fact, coupled with the exclusion of goal 1 and 3, means the EDI does not yet provide a fully comprehensive global overview of overall progress towards the EFA goals.

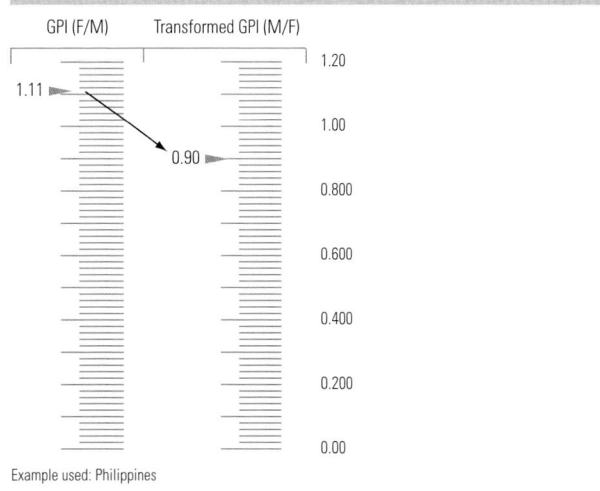

Figure 3: Calculating the 'transformed' secondary education GPI

Example used: Philippines

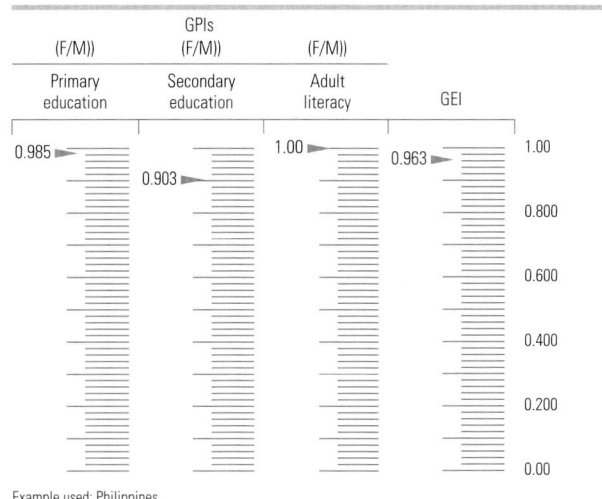

Figure 4: Calculating the GEI

Example used: Philippines

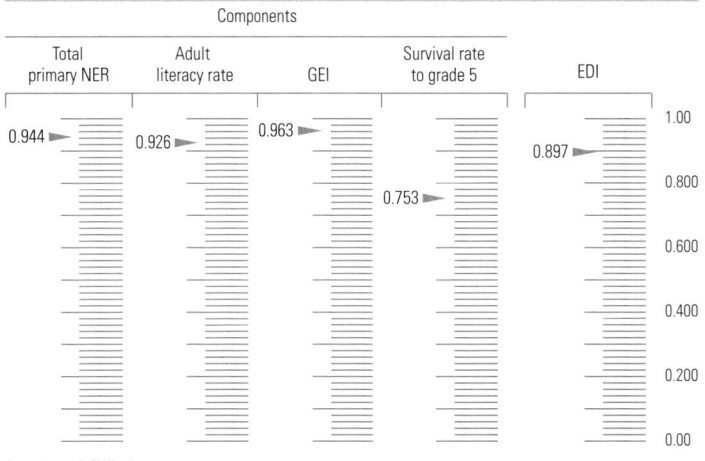

Figure 5: Calculating the EDI

Example used: Philippines

Table 1: The EFA Development Index and its components, 2004

Ranking according to level of EDI	Countries/Territories	EDI	Total primary NER[1]	Adult literacy rate	Gender-specific EFA index (GEI)	Survival rate to grade 5
High EDI						
1	United Kingdom[2]	0.994	1.000	0.998	0.990	0.990
2	Slovenia[2]	0.994	0.997	0.994	0.997	0.989
3	Finland[2]	0.994	0.995	1.000	0.982	0.999
4	Kazakhstan	0.992	0.989	0.995	0.987	0.997
5	France[2]	0.992	0.996	0.986	0.995	0.990
6	Belgium[2]	0.992	0.990	1.000	0.987	0.990
7	Germany[2, 3]	0.992	0.980	1.000	0.994	0.993
8	Norway[2]	0.991	0.989	0.989	0.990	0.996
9	Sweden[2]	0.991	0.986	1.000	0.987	0.990
10	Republic of Korea[4]	0.988	0.996	0.984	0.993	0.981
11	Latvia[3]	0.987	0.980	0.997	0.989	0.983
12	Switzerland[2]	0.986	0.982	1.000	0.971	0.990
13	Czech Republic[2, 3]	0.986	0.970	0.998	0.990	0.984
14	Poland[2]	0.986	0.975	0.981	0.990	0.997
15	Austria[2, 3]	0.986	0.970	1.000	0.982	0.990
16	Estonia	0.984	0.973	0.998	0.983	0.984
17	Barbados[4]	0.984	0.973	0.997	0.991	0.975
18	Italy	0.984	0.996	0.984	0.992	0.965
19	Israel	0.984	0.977	0.971	0.989	0.999
20	Slovakia[2, 3]	0.983	0.970	0.996	0.991	0.976
21	Hungary[2]	0.982	0.960	1.000	0.993	0.976
22	Greece	0.982	0.996	0.960	0.982	0.990
23	Ireland[2]	0.982	0.964	0.994	0.972	0.998
24	Spain[2]	0.982	0.995	0.973	0.969	0.990
25	Trinidad and Tobago	0.981	0.971	0.988	0.966	1.000
26	Cyprus	0.981	0.988	0.968	0.977	0.992
27	Cuba	0.981	0.968	0.998	0.980	0.977
28	Denmark[2]	0.980	0.999	0.952	0.980	0.990
29	Armenia	0.979	0.982	0.994	0.978	0.963
30	Lithuania	0.975	0.923	0.996	0.995	0.985
31	Kyrgyzstan	0.974	0.959	0.987	0.991	0.958
32	Croatia	0.973	0.931	0.981	0.985	0.996
33	Tajikistan	0.972	0.972	0.995	0.929	0.994
34	Belarus	0.971	0.905	0.996	0.984	1.000
35	Chile[3]	0.969	0.950	0.957	0.979	0.990
36	Fiji	0.966	0.987	0.929	0.960	0.987
37	Bulgaria	0.965	0.966	0.982	0.976	0.937
38	Romania	0.965	0.950	0.973	0.984	0.952
39	Seychelles	0.962	0.965	0.918	0.974	0.991
40	TFYR Macedonia	0.961	0.920	0.961	0.979	0.982
41	Costa Rica[3]	0.956	0.970	0.949	0.981	0.924
42	Albania	0.956	0.956	0.987	0.982	0.898
43	China	0.954	0.946	0.909	0.969	0.990
44	Luxembourg[2]	0.953	0.918	0.957	0.979	0.957
45	Bahrain	0.953	0.982	0.865	0.964	1.000
46	Ukraine	0.952	0.837	0.994	0.991	0.986
47	Netherlands Antilles	0.951	0.985	0.969	0.966	0.885
Medium EDI						
48	Mexico	0.949	0.998	0.910	0.962	0.926
49	Jordan	0.948	0.947	0.899	0.957	0.988
50	Argentina	0.946	0.995	0.972	0.976	0.843
51	Kuwait	0.946	0.911	0.933	0.969	0.972
52	Azerbaijan	0.946	0.839	0.988	0.979	0.978
53	Uruguay[3]	0.946	0.990	0.980	0.945	0.869
54	Malta	0.945	0.944	0.879	0.964	0.993
55	Portugal[2]	0.942	0.999	0.858	0.921	0.990
56	Palestinian A. T.	0.942	0.904	0.924	0.954	0.985
57	Saint Lucia[2]	0.942	0.984	0.901	0.981	0.901
58	Indonesia	0.938	0.990	0.904	0.966	0.891
59	Mauritius	0.936	0.945	0.844	0.968	0.989
60	Macao, China	0.934	0.893	0.913	0.935	0.997
61	Lebanon[4]	0.934	0.953	0.883	0.924	0.976
62	Malaysia	0.934	0.932	0.887	0.933	0.984
63	Mongolia	0.933	0.894	0.978	0.954	0.909

Table 1 (continued)

Ranking according to level of EDI	Countries/Territories	EDI	Total primary NER[1]	Adult literacy rate	Gender-specific EFA index (GEI)	Survival rate to grade 5
Medium EDI						
64	Venezuela	0.932	0.939	0.930	0.950	0.910
65	Panama	0.928	0.988	0.919	0.963	0.843
66	Republic of Moldova	0.918	0.811	0.984	0.979	0.900
67	Peru	0.916	0.996	0.877	0.953	0.836
68	Ecuador	0.914	0.994	0.910	0.989	0.763
69	Bolivia	0.911	0.968	0.867	0.944	0.864
70	Viet Nam	0.910	0.931	0.903	0.937	0.868
71	Paraguay[2,3]	0.909	0.930	0.916	0.974	0.816
72	Brazil	0.905	0.940	0.886	0.951	0.844
73	Syrian Arab Republic	0.902	0.982	0.796	0.911	0.918
74	Tunisia	0.901	0.985	0.743	0.910	0.965
75	Philippines	0.897	0.944	0.926	0.963	0.753
76	Jamaica	0.890	0.914	0.799	0.949	0.897
77	Turkey	0.889	0.893	0.874	0.841	0.946
78	South Africa	0.888	0.932	0.824	0.955	0.841
79	Egypt	0.887	0.972	0.714	0.876	0.986
80	Botswana	0.885	0.842	0.812	0.973	0.912
81	Algeria	0.880	0.990	0.699	0.872	0.962
82	Oman	0.880	0.798	0.814	0.934	0.976
83	Bahamas[4]	0.879	0.843	0.958	0.964	0.752
84	Colombia	0.879	0.849	0.928	0.963	0.775
85	Cape Verde	0.877	0.924	0.780	0.893	0.912
86	Iran, Islamic Republic of	0.864	0.887	0.770	0.897	0.902
87	El Salvador	0.861	0.941	0.811	0.965	0.728
88	Myanmar	0.860	0.876	0.899	0.963	0.703
89	Namibia	0.853	0.738	0.850	0.942	0.881
90	United Arab Emirates[4]	0.852	0.728	0.788	0.947	0.947
91	Zimbabwe[4]	0.840	0.825	0.900	0.936	0.697
92	Zambia	0.829	0.809	0.680	0.844	0.985
93	Swaziland	0.826	0.770	0.796	0.969	0.768
94	Guatemala	0.825	0.945	0.691	0.886	0.779
95	Dominican Republic	0.816	0.878	0.870	0.923	0.592
96	Nicaragua	0.811	0.942	0.767	0.949	0.588
Low EDI						
97	Lesotho	0.797	0.862	0.822	0.869	0.634
98	Kenya	0.797	0.770	0.736	0.928	0.753
99	India	0.789	0.961	0.610	0.795	0.789
100	Saudi Arabia	0.787	0.540	0.794	0.879	0.936
101	Cambodia	0.774	0.976	0.736	0.787	0.597
102	Morocco	0.746	0.867	0.523	0.781	0.812
103	Lao PDR	0.741	0.844	0.687	0.809	0.626
104	Mauritania	0.730	0.745	0.512	0.848	0.816
105	Bangladesh	0.722	0.975	0.426	0.837	0.651
106	Nigeria[4]	0.721	0.619	0.708	0.829	0.726
107	Malawi	0.719	0.961	0.641	0.834	0.438
108	Equatorial Guinea	0.708	0.857	0.870	0.780	0.326
109	Rwanda	0.686	0.735	0.649	0.904	0.458
110	Togo	0.684	0.816	0.532	0.631	0.760
111	Ghana	0.682	0.659	0.579	0.855	0.633
112	Nepal	0.668	0.802	0.486	0.776	0.608
113	Djibouti[4]	0.665	0.332	0.703	0.749	0.877
114	Senegal	0.646	0.662	0.393	0.749	0.782
115	Burundi	0.646	0.572	0.593	0.787	0.630
116	Eritrea[4]	0.644	0.483	0.605	0.686	0.803
117	Yemen[4]	0.642	0.758	0.530	0.548	0.732
118	Ethiopia	0.627	0.579	0.452	0.745	0.733
119	Benin	0.617	0.835	0.347	0.592	0.694
120	Mozambique[4]	0.599	0.710	0.504	0.691	0.492
121	Guinea	0.583	0.643	0.295	0.575	0.820
122	Mali	0.529	0.465	0.190	0.613	0.846
123	Burkina Faso	0.511	0.409	0.218	0.661	0.758
124	Niger	0.499	0.396	0.287	0.578	0.736
125	Chad	0.428	0.571	0.257	0.425	0.458

Note: Data in blue indicate that gender disparities are at the expense of boys or men, particularly at secondary level.

1. Total primary NER includes children of primary school age who are enrolled in either primary or secondary schools.

2. The adult literacy rate is a proxy measure based on educational attainment; that is, the proportion of the adult population with at least a complete primary education.

3. The NER in primary education is not published in the statistical tables as the reported number of pupils of official primary school age is believed to be underestimated. However, in order to calculate the EDI, an estimate of the total primary NER has been made. For more details, see the introduction to the statistical tables.

4. Adult literacy rates are unofficial UIS estimates generated in July 2002, using the previous UIS assessment model.

Sources: Annex, Statistical Tables 2, 5, 7 and 8; UNESCO (2005); UNESCO Institute for Statistics database; European Commission (2004) (for proxy literacy measure for European countries).

Education for All Global Monitoring Report

2007

Table 2: Countries ranked according to value of EDI and components, 2004

Countries/ Territories	EDI	Total primary NER[1]	Adult literacy rate	Gender-specific EFA index (GEI)	Survival rate to grade 5	Countries/ Territories	EDI	Total primary NER[1]	Adult literacy rate	Gender-specific EFA index (GEI)	Survival rate to grade 5
High EDI						**Medium EDI**					
United Kingdom[2]	1	1	9	14	18	Venezuela	64	69	51	72	68
Slovenia[2]	2	5	21	1	30	Panama	65	21	56	60	85
Finland[2]	3	11	1	29	4	Republic of Moldova	66	101	31	34	72
Kazakhstan	4	19	17	19	8	Peru	67	9	73	70	87
France[2]	5	8	28	2	18	Ecuador	68	14	60	17	98
Belgium[2]	6	16	1	21	18	Bolivia	69	48	77	77	81
Germany[2,3]	7	32	1	4	14	Viet Nam	70	72	64	79	80
Norway[2]	8	20	23	13	10	Paraguay[2,3]	71	74	58	44	90
Sweden[2]	9	24	1	20	18	Brazil	72	68	70	71	83
Republic of Korea[4]	10	6	30	6	43	Syrian Arab Republic	73	30	88	89	65
Latvia[3]	11	33	12	16	41	Tunisia	74	26	95	90	52
Switzerland[2]	12	29	1	47	18	Philippines	75	64	54	61	102
Czech Republic[2,3]	13	43	8	12	38	Jamaica	76	79	87	74	74
Poland[2]	14	37	34	15	7	Turkey	77	84	74	102	60
Austria[2,3]	15	44	1	28	18	South Africa	78	71	82	67	86
Estonia	16	38	11	25	39	Egypt	79	40	98	96	33
Barbados[4]	17	39	13	8	50	Botswana	80	95	85	45	66
Italy	18	10	29	7	53	Algeria	81	18	101	97	55
Israel	19	34	40	18	5	Oman	82	104	84	82	48
Slovakia[2,3]	20	45	16	10	46	Bahamas[4]	83	94	45	57	103
Hungary[2]	21	54	1	5	49	Colombia	84	92	53	63	96
Greece	22	7	44	26	18	Cape Verde	85	75	92	93	67
Ireland[2]	23	51	22	46	6	Iran, Isl. Rep.	86	86	93	92	70
Spain[2]	24	13	38	48	18	El Salvador	87	67	86	56	107
Trinidad and Tobago	25	42	25	53	1	Myanmar	88	88	68	62	109
Cyprus	26	22	42	40	15	Namibia	89	109	80	78	77
Cuba	27	47	10	32	45	U. A. Emirates[4]	90	111	91	75	59
Denmark[2]	28	2	48	33	18	Zimbabwe[4]	91	99	66	80	110
Armenia	29	28	20	39	54	Zambia	92	102	104	101	37
Lithuania	30	76	14	3	35	Swaziland	93	105	89	50	97
Kyrgyzstan	31	55	27	9	56	Guatemala	94	63	102	94	95
Croatia	32	73	33	22	11	Dominican Republic	95	87	75	87	119
Tajikistan	33	41	18	84	12	Nicaragua	96	66	94	73	120
Belarus	34	81	15	23	1						
Chile[3]	35	59	47	35	28	**Low EDI**					
Fiji	36	23	52	65	32	Lesotho	97	90	83	98	113
Bulgaria	37	49	32	41	61	Kenya	98	106	96	85	101
Romania	38	58	37	24	58	India	99	52	107	107	93
Seychelles	39	50	57	43	16	Saudi Arabia	100	120	90	95	62
TFYR Macedonia	40	77	43	38	42	Cambodia	101	35	97	108	118
Costa Rica[3]	41	46	49	30	64	Morocco	102	89	113	110	91
Albania	42	56	26	27	73	Lao PDR	103	93	103	106	116
China	43	61	62	51	17	Mauritania	104	108	114	100	89
Luxembourg[2]	44	78	46	37	57	Bangladesh	105	36	118	103	112
Bahrain	45	31	78	59	3	Nigeria[4]	106	116	99	105	108
Ukraine	46	97	19	11	34	Malawi	107	53	106	104	124
Netherlands Antilles	47	25	41	55	76	Equatorial Guinea	108	91	76	111	125
						Rwanda	109	110	105	91	122
Medium EDI						Togo	110	100	111	119	99
Mexico	48	4	61	64	63	Ghana	111	114	110	99	114
Jordan	49	60	67	66	31	Nepal	112	103	116	112	117
Argentina	50	12	39	42	84	Djibouti[4]	113	125	100	114	78
Kuwait	51	80	50	49	51	Senegal	114	113	119	113	94
Azerbaijan	52	96	24	36	44	Burundi	115	118	109	109	115
Uruguay[3]	53	17	35	76	79	Eritrea[4]	116	121	108	117	92
Malta	54	65	72	58	13	Yemen[4]	117	107	112	124	106
Portugal[2]	55	3	79	88	18	Ethiopia	118	117	117	115	105
Palestinian A. T.	56	82	55	68	36	Benin	119	98	120	121	111
Saint Lucia[2]	57	27	65	31	71	Mozambique[4]	120	112	115	116	121
Indonesia	58	15	63	54	75	Guinea	121	115	121	123	88
Mauritius	59	62	81	52	29	Mali	122	122	125	120	82
Macao, China	60	85	59	81	9	Burkina Faso	123	123	124	118	100
Lebanon[4]	61	57	71	86	47	Niger	124	124	122	122	104
Malaysia	62	70	69	83	40	Chad	125	119	123	125	123
Mongolia	63	83	36	69	69						

1. Total primary NER includes children of primary school age who are enrolled in either primary or secondary schools.

2. The adult literacy rate is a proxy measure based on educational attainment, that is, the proportion of the adult population with at least complete primary education.

3. The NER in primary education is not published in the statistical tables as the reported number of pupils of official primary school age is believed to be underestimated. However, in order to calculate the EDI, an estimate of the total primary NER has been made. For more details, see the introduction to the statistical tables.

4. Adult literacy rates are unofficial UIS estimates generated in July 2002, using the previous UIS assessment model.

Sources: Annex, Statistical Tables 2, 5, 7 and 8; UNESCO (2005); UNESCO Institute for Statistics database; European Commission (2004) (for proxy literacy measure for European countries).

Table 3: Change in EDI and its components between 2003 and 2004

Countries/ Territories	EFA Development Index		Variation 2003-2004	Change in the EDI components between 2003 and 2004 (% in relative terms)			
	2003	2004		Total primary NER[1] %	Adult literacy rate %	Gender-specific EFA index (GEI)	Survival rate to grade 5
High EDI							
United Kingdom[2]	0.980	0.994	1.5	0.0	0.1	6.2	0.0
Slovenia[2]	0.983	0.994	1.1	4.6	-0.3	0.2	0.0
Finland[2]	0.991	0.994	0.3	-0.5	0.0	1.7	0.0
Kazakhstan	0.989	0.992	0.3	0.8	0.0	-0.9	1.5
France[2]	0.992	0.992	0.0	-0.3	0.0	0.2	0.0
Belgium[2]	0.989	0.992	0.3	-1.0	0.0	2.2	0.0
Norway[2]	0.993	0.991	-0.2	-1.1	0.6	-0.3	0.0
Sweden[2]	0.982	0.991	0.9	-1.1	0.0	5.0	0.0
Republic of Korea[3]	0.990	0.988	-0.2	-0.2	0.4	0.2	-1.0
Latvia[2]	0.961	0.987	2.8	11.7	0.0	-0.1	0.5
Switzerland[2]	0.992	0.986	-0.6	-1.8	0.0	-0.6	0.0
Czech Republic[2, 4]	0.956	0.986	3.1	12.1	0.1	0.5	0.7
Poland[2]	0.983	0.986	0.3	-0.6	0.3	1.1	0.5
Estonia	0.984	0.984	0.1	-0.4	0.0	0.6	0.0
Barbados[3]	0.994	0.984	-1.0	-2.7	0.0	0.1	-1.3
Italy	0.971	0.984	1.3	-0.4	4.7	1.1	0.0
Israel	0.950	0.984	3.6	-1.6	0.2	0.5	17.3
Slovakia[2, 4]	0.956	0.983	2.9	13.4	-0.1	-0.1	-0.3
Hungary[2]	0.987	0.982	-0.4	-2.1	0.7	-0.3	0.0
Greece	0.970	0.982	1.3	-0.4	5.4	0.4	0.0
Ireland[2]	0.979	0.982	0.3	0.4	0.0	0.0	0.6
Spain[2]	0.982	0.982	0.0	-0.2	0.2	0.0	0.0
Trinidad and Tobago	0.904	0.981	8.6	1.7	0.3	0.4	40.5
Cyprus	0.983	0.981	-0.1	0.1	0.0	-0.6	-0.1
Cuba	0.976	0.981	0.5	2.3	0.0	0.1	-0.2
Denmark[2]	0.979	0.980	0.1	-0.1	0.2	0.4	0.0
Armenia	0.983	0.979	-0.3	-0.9	0.0	-0.5	0.0
Lithuania	0.976	0.975	-0.1	-1.4	0.0	0.4	0.7
Kyrgyzstan	0.965	0.974	0.9	0.7	0.0	0.7	2.5
Croatia	0.978	0.973	-0.5	-2.2	0.0	0.0	0.0
Belarus	0.978	0.971	-0.7	-4.6	0.0	0.0	1.5
Chile[4]	0.952	0.969	1.8	9.8	0.0	-0.6	-1.0
Fiji	0.944	0.966	2.3	-1.1	0.0	-0.5	11.6
Bulgaria	0.956	0.965	1.0	4.7	0.0	-0.4	-0.2
Romania	0.957	0.965	0.8	3.2	0.0	0.3	0.0
Seychelles	0.975	0.962	-1.3	-3.1	0.0	-1.9	-0.2
TFYR Macedonia	0.952	0.961	0.9	1.4	0.0	-0.1	2.4
Costa Rica[4]	0.938	0.956	2.0	7.2	-1.0	1.0	0.9
Albania	0.957	0.956	-0.1	0.7	0.0	-0.9	-0.1
China	0.954	0.954	0.0	-1.1	0.0	1.0	0.0
Luxembourg[2]	0.964	0.953	-1.2	0.5	-1.7	0.0	-3.3
Bahrain	0.930	0.953	2.4	8.0	-1.4	2.0	0.9
Ukraine	0.958	0.952	-0.6	-2.4	0.0	-0.4	0.0
Netherlands Antilles	0.927	0.951	2.6	10.8	0.3	-0.3	0.0
Medium EDI							
Mexico	0.946	0.949	0.3	0.4	0.8	0.5	-0.4
Jordan	0.946	0.948	0.2	-0.8	0.0	-0.3	1.7
Argentina	0.968	0.946	-2.2	-0.3	0.0	-0.5	-8.5
Kuwait	0.914	0.946	3.5	3.0	12.5	0.1	-0.3
Azerbaijan	0.932	0.946	1.5	5.0	0.0	0.6	1.2
Uruguay[4]	0.941	0.946	0.5	9.1	0.3	-0.7	-6.4
Malta	0.954	0.945	-0.9	-1.8	0.0	-1.9	0.0
Portugal[2]	0.938	0.942	0.4	-0.1	1.9	-0.1	0.0
Palestinian A. T.	0.950	0.942	-0.8	-4.7	0.6	0.2	0.6
Saint Lucia	0.950	0.942	-0.9	-1.5	0.0	4.9	-6.7
Indonesia	0.923	0.938	1.5	2.3	2.9	1.0	0.0
Mauritius	0.943	0.936	-0.7	-2.1	0.1	-0.5	0.0
Macao, China	0.928	0.934	0.7	2.3	0.0	0.8	0.0
Lebanon[3]	0.909	0.934	2.7	2.9	1.6	0.1	6.2
Malaysia	0.908	0.934	2.9	0.1	0.0	-1.0	13.0
Mongolia	0.916	0.933	1.9	8.7	0.0	0.9	-1.2
Venezuela	0.911	0.932	2.3	1.4	0.0	0.3	8.1
Panama	0.944	0.928	-1.7	-0.8	0.0	-0.1	-6.2
Republic of Moldova	0.910	0.918	0.9	2.6	2.3	0.2	-1.2

Education for All Global Monitoring Report 2 0 0 7

Table 3 (continued)

Countries/ Territories	EFA Development Index		Variation 2003-2004	Change in the EDI components between 2003 and 2004 (% in relative terms)			
	2003	2004		Total primary NER[1] %	Adult literacy rate %	Gender-specific EFA index (GEI)	Survival rate to grade 5
Medium EDI							
Peru	0.911	0.916	0.5	-0.2	0.0	1.9	0.0
Ecuador	0.908	0.914	0.6	-0.2	0.0	0.5	2.5
Bolivia	0.904	0.911	0.8	0.3	0.2	0.4	2.3
Viet Nam	0.910	0.910	-0.1	-1.1	0.0	1.0	-0.3
Paraguay[2, 4]	0.870	0.909	4.4	3.5	0.0	0.4	17.1
Brazil	0.905	0.905	0.0	-4.4	0.2	-0.3	5.7
Syrian Arab Republic	0.908	0.902	-0.7	-1.5	-4.0	2.1	0.3
Tunisia	0.895	0.901	0.7	0.1	0.0	2.1	0.4
Philippines	0.898	0.897	-0.2	0.2	0.0	-0.1	-0.9
Jamaica	0.923	0.890	-3.6	-4.2	-8.8	-1.4	0.0
South Africa	0.840	0.888	5.7	-0.5	0.0	0.3	29.9
Egypt	0.828	0.887	7.1	4.3	28.5	3.7	0.6
Botswana	0.859	0.885	3.0	3.8	2.9	1.5	4.1
Algeria	0.877	0.880	0.4	2.2	0.1	-0.1	-0.8
Oman	0.843	0.880	4.4	8.4	9.3	2.2	-0.4
Bahamas[3]	0.921	0.879	-4.6	-15.5	0.3	-1.6	0.0
Colombia	0.876	0.879	0.3	-5.8	-1.4	-0.6	11.6
Cape Verde	0.879	0.877	-0.2	-6.8	3.0	0.5	3.7
Iran, Isl. Rep.	0.874	0.864	-1.2	2.7	0.0	-2.3	-4.6
El Salvador	0.842	0.861	2.3	1.9	1.9	0.6	5.7
Myanmar	0.834	0.860	3.1	4.1	0.2	1.2	8.8
Namibia	0.883	0.853	-3.4	-5.9	0.0	-0.7	-6.9
United Arab Emirates[3]	0.886	0.852	-3.8	-17.9	2.0	-1.2	2.3
Zambia	0.748	0.829	10.8	15.7	0.2	-0.5	28.4
Swaziland	0.810	0.826	1.9	1.9	0.5	0.8	4.8
Guatemala	0.782	0.825	5.5	6.6	0.0	-1.6	19.6
Dominican Republic	0.865	0.816	-5.7	-8.9	-0.8	-0.6	-14.3
Nicaragua	0.817	0.811	-0.7	3.8	0.0	0.2	-9.3
Low EDI							
Lesotho	0.817	0.797	-2.4	0.0	1.0	0.9	-13.1
Kenya	0.731	0.797	8.9	13.9	0.0	0.5	27.6
India	0.741	0.789	6.5	2.5	0.0	-0.9	28.6
Saudi Arabia	0.789	0.787	-0.2	-3.5	0.0	-0.9	2.3
Cambodia	0.761	0.774	1.7	4.4	0.0	3.0	-2.0
Morocco	0.749	0.746	-0.4	-3.4	3.1	0.3	0.0
Lao PDR	0.745	0.741	-0.5	-0.7	0.1	0.9	-2.4
Mauritania	0.640	0.730	14.1	9.8	0.0	11.1	34.8
Bangladesh	0.663	0.722	8.9	11.5	3.6	1.1	20.8
Equatorial Guinea	0.689	0.708	2.8	0.8	3.3	1.3	10.6
Rwanda	0.715	0.686	-4.0	-15.6	1.5	2.4	-1.7
Ghana	0.662	0.682	3.0	3.2	7.0	2.4	0.0
Nepal	0.652	0.668	2.5	9.6	0.0	4.8	-6.4
Djibouti[3]	0.629	0.665	5.8	-3.1	5.7	6.3	9.3
Senegal	0.653	0.646	-1.0	-4.2	0.0	2.8	-2.3
Burundi	0.653	0.646	-1.1	-0.5	0.7	2.1	-6.7
Eritrea[3]	0.652	0.644	-1.2	5.9	4.9	-3.7	-6.9
Yemen[3]	0.622	0.642	3.1	4.8	8.2	5.8	-3.6
Ethiopia	0.536	0.627	17.0	20.2	8.8	12.6	24.9
Mozambique[3]	0.543	0.599	10.4	28.4	8.3	4.6	0.0
Mali	0.492	0.529	7.5	4.5	0.0	4.7	13.4
Burkina Faso	0.443	0.511	15.6	11.8	69.9	7.6	14.5
Niger	0.458	0.499	9.0	2.7	99.4	-5.3	6.4
Chad	0.439	0.428	-2.7	-9.4	0.5	-0.9	3.3

1. Total primary NER includes children of primary school age who are enrolled in either primary or secondary schools.

2. The adult literacy rate is a proxy measure based on educational attainment, that is, the proportion of the adult population with at least a complete primary education.

3. Adult literacy rates are unofficial UIS estimates generated in July 2002, using the previous UIS assessment model.

4. The NER in primary education is not published in the statistical tables as the reported number of pupils of official primary school age is believed to be underestimated. However, in order to calculate the EDI, an estimate of the total primary NER has been made. For more details, see the introduction to the statistical tables.

Sources: Annex, Statistical Tables 2, 5, 7 and 8; UNESCO (2005); UNESCO Institute for Statistics database; European Commission (2004) (for proxy literacy measure for European countries).

National learning assessments by region and country

Introduction

These tables provide an overview of assessment and evaluation activities undertaken by countries in sub-Saharan Africa, the Arab States, Asia, and Latin America and the Caribbean. Such activities aim to provide education stakeholders with systematic information about the status of students' learning outcomes and the extent to which students attain predefined standards or proficiencies. The scientific reliability and validity of national assessments vary greatly, and thus cross-country comparisons are not warranted. Nevertheless, such learning assessments represent a potentially useful tool to monitor educational quality, address national policy issues and pinpoint areas for government attention and programme intervention.

Information for the tables was compiled from an array of sources (e.g. printed material, websites, experts and contacts through UNESCO regional offices), some of which were partial and/or contradictory. Much effort has been made to verify and cross-check the reported information, but some mistakes are likely. The EFA Global Monitoring Report Team intends to continue to expand and revise this information in the coming years. For a more detailed listing of national learning assessments, see Encinas-Martin (2006).

Abbreviations used in the tables

DFID Department for International Development, United Kingdom

EU European Union

HSRC Human Sciences Research Council

ICFES Instituto Colombiano para el Fomento de la Educación Superior

IDB Inter-American Development Bank

IEA International Association for the Evaluation of Educational Achievement

IEQ Improving Educational Quality

IIEP International Institute for Educational Planning

ILI International Literacy Institute

INEE Instituto Nacional para la Evaluación de la Educación

INEP Instituto Nacional de Estudos e Pesquisas Educacionais Anísio Teixeira

MoE Ministry of Education (or equivalent national body)

NCERT National Council of Educational Research and Training

NIER National Institute for Educational Policy Research

UNICEF United Nations Children's Fund

USAID United States Agency for International Development

Education for All Global Monitoring Report 2 0 0 7

Table 1: Sub-Saharan Africa

Country	Name or description of assessment study	Organization/institution responsible for assessment	Target population	Curricular subject(s) assessed	Year(s)
Central Afr. Rep.	Quality of education	...	Grades 4, 5	French, mathematics	1997
Eritrea	Learning Achievement	MoE	Grades 1, 4	Languages, mathematics	1999
Ethiopia	Sample Baseline on Students Learning Achievement	National Organization for Examinations	Grades 4, 8	English, mathematics, environmental science, chemistry, biology	2000, 2004
Gambia	National test	MoE	Grades 2, 4, 6	English, French, mathematics (variable)	1997, 1998, 1999, 2000
Ghana	Evaluation of Implementation of Ghana's School Language Policy	USAID and IEQ	Grades 1 to 4	Languages	1999, 2000, 2001
Malawi	Primary Schools Learner Achievements Level	Annual Basic Education Statistics Census	Grades 3, 5, 7	Chicewa, English, mathematics	Annually since 2004
	Quality of Learning and Teaching in Developing Countries	DFID	4 years of schooling	English, mother tongue	1996, 1997, 1998
	Reading in English in Primary Schools	DFID	Grades 3, 4, 6	English	1993
	Reading Levels and Bilingual Literacy in Primary Schools	DFID	Grades 3, 4, 5, 6	English, local languages	1998
	Literacy Development through a Local Language in a Multilingual Setting	USAID and IEQ	Grades 2, 3, 4	Literacy skills	1999, 2000
Mauritius	Early Diagnostic Tool for Literacy and Numeracy	Mauritius Examinations Syndicate and Mauritius Institute of Education	All levels of primary school	Literacy, numeracy	Being developed
Nigeria	Universal Basic Education Programme	Universal Basic Education Commission	Grades 1, 6 (primary) and 1, 3 (secondary)	English, mathematics, sciences, social sciences	2001
South Africa	Assessment of Learning Achievement	MoE	Junior and senior secondary	English, mathematics, social studies, integrated sciences	2003
	Monitoring Education Quality	HSRC	Grade 9	English, mathematics, sciences	Annually since 1996
	Learner Assessment Results	HSRC, District Development Support Programme and USAID	Grade 3	Reading	2003
	Systemic Evaluation Study	MoE and HSRC	Grade 6	Language, mathematics, sciences	2005
Zambia	Reading Levels and Bilingual Literacy in Primary Schools	DFID	Grades 3, 4, 5, 6	English, local languages	1998
	Primary Reading Programme	Association for the Development of Education in Africa	Grades 1 to 6	Reading, writing	1999, 2002

... information not available

Table 2: Arab States

Country	Name or description of assessment study	Organization/institution responsible for assessment	Target population	Curricular subject(s) assessed	Year(s)
Algeria	Programme national d'évaluation du rendement	MoE	Grades 3, 6, 9 (primary) and 1 (secondary)	Arabic, French, mathematics	...
Djibouti	Evaluation du niveau de qualité et du rendement cognitive	Centre de Recherche, d'Information et de Production de l'Education Nationale	Primary and lower secondary	French, Arabic, mathematics	1991, 1992, 1997 – 2000
Egypt	Global Evaluation	MoE	Grades 1, 2, 3	All school subjects	Annually since 2005
Jordan	National test	MoE and DFID	Grade 10	Arabic, English, mathematics, sciences, social sciences	Annually since 2000
Lebanon	Mesure des acquis d'apprentissage	Centre de Recherche et de Développement Pédagogiques	Grade 4 + complementary year	Languages, mathematics, sciences, transversal competencies/savoir-être	1994, 1995, 1996 (variable)
Morocco	Diagnostic et appui aux apprentissages	MoE	Grades 3, 5, 8	Arabic, French, mathematics	2000
	Evaluation des pré-recquis	MoE and UNICEF	Grades 4, 6	Arabic, French, mathematics, life skills	2001
	Evaluation des acquis des élèves	MoE and EU	Grade 6	Arabic, French, mathematics, sciences	2006
Qatar	Comprehensive Educational Assessment and School Surveys	Evaluation Institute	Grades 3 to 11	Arabic, English, mathematics, sciences	Annually since 2004
Saudi Arabia	Diagnostic Test in the Public Evaluation System	MoE	Grades 1, 2, 3	Arabic, mathematics	...
United Arab Emirates	National Assessment of Student Achievement and Progress	Australian Council for Educational Research	Grades 5, 7	Literacy, numeracy	2005

... information not available

Table 3: Asia

Country	Name or description of assessment study	Organization/institution responsible for assessment	Target population	Curricular subject(s) assessed	Year(s)
Bangladesh	Assessment of the Achievement of Pupils Completion Grade 4	MoE and NCTB (National Academy for Primary Education)	Grade 4	Bangla, English, mathematics, sciences, social sciences	2000
	National Assessment	MoE	Grades 3, 5	Bangla, mathematics, sciences, social sciences, environmental studies	2001
	IDEAL Project	MoE	Grades 1 to 5	Bangla, English, mathematics, sciences, social sciences	2004
	School Based Assessment	MoE	Grade 9	Range of behaviours, activities and quantitative measures	To be decided
India	Baseline Assessment Survey	NCERT	Grades 1, 3, 4, 5, 7, 8 (variable)	Language, mathematics, environmental studies (variable)	1994, 2002, 2003, 2004 (variable)
	Mid-Term Assessment Survey	NCERT	Grades 1, 3, 4	Language, mathematics	1997
	Terminal Assessment Survey	NCERT	Grades 1, 3, 4	Language, mathematics	2001
Indonesia	Assessment of Students Learning Achievement	Educational National Standard Board	Grade 3 (primary) and senior (secondary)	Indonesian, English, mathematics	Annually since 2005
Japan	National Assessment of Learning Outcomes	NIER	Grades 5, 9, 12 (variable)	Japanese, English, mathematics, sciences, social studies, geography, history, civics	2002, 2003, 2004
	National Assessment of Student Performance	MoE and NIER	Grades 6, 9	Japanese, mathematics	2007
Lao PDR	National Literacy Survey	MoE, UNESCO and UNICEF	Age 6 and above	Reading, writing, numeracy, visual literacy	2000
Mongolia	National test	MoE	Grades 5, 9, 11	Language, mathematics	Annually since 1997
	Regional test at aigmag (district) level	State Professional Assessment Agency	Grades 5, 9, 11 (variable)	Languages, mathematics, history, physics, chemistry, biology (variable)	Every 5/6 years since 1997
Myanmar	Learning Achievement Study	MoE and UNICEF	Grades 3, 5	Myanmar language, mathematics, sciences	2005, 2006
Pakistan	National Achievement Test	MoE and National Education Assessment System	Grades 4, 8 (variable)	Languages, mathematics, sciences, social studies	2005, 2006
	Quality of Education (Learning Achievement)	Academy of Educational Planning and Management	Grade 4	Sindhi, Urdu, mathematics	2000
Republic of Korea	National Assessment of Educational Assessment	Korean Institute of Curriculum and Evaluation	Grades 6, 9, 10	Korean, English, mathematics, sciences, social studies	Annually since 2003
Singapore	Core Research Program	Centre for Research in Pedagogy and Practice	Pre-school to secondary	Languages, mathematics, sciences, ICT	2003
Viet Nam	Reading and Mathematics Assessment Study	MoE and World Bank	Grade 5	Reading, mathematics	2001

Table 4: Latin America and the Caribbean

Country	Name or description of assessment study	Organization/institution responsible for assessment	Target population	Curricular subject(s) assessed	Year(s)
Argentina	Sistema Nacional de Evaluación de la Calidad Educativa	Instituto de Calidad Educativa	Grades 3, 7 (primary) and 2, 5 (secondary)	Language, mathematics, sciences, social sciences (variable)	Annually 1993 – 2001
	Dirección Nacional de Información y Evaluación de la Calidad Educativa	MoE	Grades 3, 6, 7, 9 (primary) and 5, 6 (secondary) (variable)	Language, mathematics, sciences, social sciences (variable)	Annually 1993 – 2005
Bolivia	SIMECAL	MoE	Grades 1, 3, 6, 8 (primary) and 4 (secondary)	Language, mathematics	Annually 1996 – 2000
Brazil	National System of Evaluation of Basic Education	MoE and INEP	Grades 1, 3, 4, 5, 7, 8, 11 (variable)	Language, mathematics, sciences, social sciences (variable)	1990 – 2005 (variable)
	Exámen Nacional de Enseñanza Media	INEP	Last year of primary	Language, problem-solving,	Annually 1998 – 2005
Chile	Prueba de Evaluación del Rendimiento Escolar	MoE and Universidad Católica	Grades 4, 8	Language, mathematics, sciences, social sciences	1982, 1983, 1984
	Sistema de Medición de Calidad de la Educación	MoE	Grades 4, 8 (primary) and 2 (secondary) (variable)	Language, mathematics, sciences, social sciences, behaviour, (variable)	Annually 1988 to 2005
Colombia	Medición y Evaluación de Aprendizajes	MoE and ICFES	Grades 3, 5, 7, 9	Language, mathematics	Annually 1991 – 1994
	SABER	MoE	Grades 3, 5, 7, 9 (variable)	Language, mathematics, sciences	Annually 1997 – 2003
	Exámenes de Estado	MoE and ICFES	Grade 11	Languages, mathematics, sciences, social sciences	Annually 1980 to 2005
Costa Rica	Pruebas de Conocimientos	MoE and Universidad de Costa Rica	Grades 3, 6, 9, 11, 12 (variable)	Language, mathematics, sciences, social sciences	Annually 1986 – 1997
	Pruebas Nacionales de Bachillerato	MoE	Secondary school	Languages, mathematics, sciences, social sciences	Annually 1988 – 2003
Cuba	Pruebas de Aprendizaje	MoE, Sistema de Evaluación de la Calidad de la Educación and Instituto de Ciencias Pedagógicas	Grades 3, 4, 6, 9, 12	Language, mathematics	1975, 1996, 1997, 1998, 2000, 2002
Dominican Republic	Sistema de Pruebas Nacionales	MoE, IDB and World Bank	Grades 8 (primary) and 4 (secondary) (variable)	Language, mathematics, sciences, social sciences	Annually 1991 – 2003
Ecuador	APRENDO	MoE, World Bank and Univ. Católica	Grades 3, 7, 10	Language, mathematics	Annually 1996 – 2000
El Salvador	Sistema Nacional de Evaluación de los Aprendizajes	MoE, USAID and World Bank	Pre-school, grades 1 to 6, 9 (primary) and 2 (secondary) (variable)	Language, mathematics, sciences, social sciences, health education	Annually 1993 – 2001
	Pruebas de Aprendizaje y Aptitudes para Egresados de Educación Media	MoE	Grades 2, 3 (secondary) and technical education	Language, mathematics, sciences, social sciences	Annually 1997 – 2004
Guatemala	Sistema Nacional de Medición del Logro Académico	MoE, World Bank, and Valle de Guatemala University	Grades 3, 7 (primary) 2, 5 (secondary) (variable)	Language, mathematics, sciences, social sciences (variable)	Annually 1992 – 1996
	Programa Nacional de Evaluación del Rendimiento Escolar	MoE, World Bank and Valle de Guatemala University	Grades 1, 3, 6 (variable)	Language, mathematics	1998, 1999, 2000, 2004
	Dirección General de Educación Bilingüe Intercultural	MoE and IDB	Grades 1, 3	Language, mathematics	2003

Education for All Global Monitoring Report 2 0 0 7

Table 4 (continued)

Country	Name or description of assessment study	Organization/institution responsible for assessment	Target population	Curricular subject(s) assessed	Year(s)
Mexico	Sistema Nacional de Evaluación Educativa de la Educación Primaria	MoE	Grades 3, 4, 5, 6	Language, mathematics, sciences, social sciences	Annually 1996 – 2000
	Estándares Nacionales	MoE and INEE	Grades 2, 4, 5, 6,	Language, mathematics	Annually 1997 – 2004
	Aprovechamiento Escolar – Carrera Magistral	MoE and INEE	Grades 3 to 6 (primary) and 1 to 3 (secondary)	Language, mathematics, sciences, social sciences, foreign languages	Annually 1994 – 2005
	Instrumento para el Diagnóstico de Alumnos de Nuevo Ingreso a Secundaria	MoE	Grade 6	Reading, verbal and numerical reasoning	Annually 1995 – 2005
Nicaragua	Evaluación del Currículo Transformado	MoE	Grade 4, 5 (primary) and 3 (secondary)	Language, mathematics	1996, 1997
	Sistema Nacional de Evaluación de la Educación Básica y Media	USAID and UNESCO	Grades 3, 6	Language, mathematics	2002
Panama	Programa de Pruebas de Diagnóstico	MoE and various agencies	Grades 3, 6 (primary) and 6 (secondary) (variable)	Language, mathematics	1985, 1986, 1987, 1988, 1992
	CECE	MoE and various agencies	Grades 1 to 6 (secondary)	Language, mathematics	1995
	Sistema Nacional de Evaluación de la Calidad de la Educación	MoE and Coordinación Educativa y Cultural Centroamericana	Grades 3, 6, 9	Language, mathematics, sciences, social sciences (variable)	1999, 2000, 2001
Paraguay	Sistemas Nacionales de Evaluación del Proceso Educativo	MoE and IDB	Grades 3, 6, 9, 12	Language, mathematics, sciences, social sciences (variable)	Annually 1996 – 2001
Peru	Unidad de Medición de Calidad – UMC-CRECER	MoE	Grades 2, 4, 6 (primary) and 3 to 5 (secondary)	Language, mathematics, sciences, social sciences, citizenship (variable)	1996, 1998, 2001, 2004
Uruguay	Unidad de Medición de Resultados Educativos	Administración Nacional de Educación Pública and World Bank	Pre-school and grades 1 to 4, 6 (primary) (variable)	Language, mathematics, sciences, social sciences, behaviour, cognitive and affective development (variable)	1996, 1998, 1999, 2001, 2002
Venezuela	Sistema Nacional de Medición y Evaluación del Aprendizaje	MoE, World Bank, Univ. Católica and Centro Nacional para el Mejoramiento de la Enseñanza en Ciencia	Grade 6	Language, mathematics	1998

Statistical tables

Introduction

The most recent data on pupils, students, teachers and expenditure presented in these statistical tables are for the school year ending in 2004.[1] They are based on survey results reported to and processed by the UNESCO Institute for Statistics (UIS) before the end of May 2006. Data received after this date will be used in the next *EFA Global Monitoring Report*. A small number of countries (Ethiopia, Ghana, Mauritius, Myanmar, Nepal, the Republic of Korea, Thailand, Uganda and the United Republic of Tanzania) submitted data for the school year ending in 2005, presented in bold in the statistical tables. These statistics refer to all formal schools, both public and private, by level of education. They are supplemented by demographic and economic statistics collected or produced by other international organizations, including the United Nations Development Programme, the United Nations Population Division (UNPD) and the World Bank.

A total of 203 countries and territories are listed in the statistical tables. Most of them report their data to the UIS using standard questionnaires issued by the Institute. For some countries, however, education data are collected via surveys carried out under the auspices of the World Education Indicators (WEI) project funded by the World Bank, or are provided by the Organisation for Economic Co-operation and Development (OECD) and the Statistical Office of the European Communities (Eurostat).

Population

The indicators on access and participation in the statistical tables were calculated using the 2004 revision of population estimates produced by the UNPD. Because of possible differences between national population estimates and those of the United Nations, these indicators may differ from those published by individual countries or by other organizations.[2] The UNPD does not provide data by single year of age for countries with a total population of fewer than 80,000. Where no UNPD estimates exist, national population figures, when available, or estimates from the UIS were used to calculate enrolment ratios.

ISCED classification

Education data reported to the UIS are in conformity with the 1997 revision of the International Standard Classification of Education (ISCED). In some cases, data have been adjusted to comply with the ISCED97 classification. Data for the school year ending in 1991 may conform to the previous version of the classification, ISCED76, and therefore may not be comparable in some countries to those for years after 1997. ISCED is used to harmonize data and introduce more international comparability among national education systems. Countries may have their own definitions of education levels that do not correspond to ISCED. Therefore, some differences between nationally and internationally reported enrolment ratios may be due to the use of nationally defined education levels rather than the ISCED standard, in addition to the population issue raised above.

Adult participation in basic education

ISCED does not classify education programmes by participants' age. For example, any programme with a content equivalent to primary education, or ISCED 1, may be classed as ISCED 1 even if provided to adults. However, the guidance the UIS provides for respondents to its regular annual education survey asks countries to exclude 'data on programmes designed for people beyond regular school age'. On the other hand, the guidance for the UIS/OECD/Eurostat (UOE) and WEI questionnaires states that 'activities classified as "continuing", "adult" or "non-formal"

1. This means 2003/04 for countries with a school year that overlaps two calendar years, and 2004 for those with a calendar school year.

2. Where obvious inconsistencies exist between enrolment reported by countries and the United Nations population data, UIS may decide to not calculate or publish the enrolment ratios.

education should be included' if they 'involve studies with subject content similar to regular educational programmes' or if 'the underlying programmes lead to similar potential qualifications' as do the regular programmes. As a result of these distinctions, data from WEI countries and those for which statistics are collected via the UOE questionnaires, particularly concerning secondary education, may include programmes for older students. Despite the UIS instructions, data from countries in the regular UIS survey may also include pupils who are substantially above the official age for basic education.

Literacy data

UNESCO has long defined literacy as the ability to read and write, with understanding, a short simple statement related to one's daily life.

In many cases, the current UIS literacy statistics rely on this definition and are largely based on data sources that use a 'self-declaration' method: respondents are asked whether they are literate, as opposed to being asked a more comprehensive question or to demonstrate the skill. Some countries assume that children who complete a certain level of education are literate.[3] As definitions and methodologies used for data collection differ by country, data need to be used with caution.

Literacy data in this report cover adults of 15 years and over as well as youth of 15–24 years. They refer to 1990, 2000–2004 and 2015:

1) 1990 data represent UIS estimates used in earlier EFA reports, rebased to the 2004 UN population revision. The UIS estimation methodology can be reviewed at the UIS website (www.uis.unesco.org).

2) 2000–2004 data are from the UIS May 2006 data release, which uses directly reported national data together with UIS estimates. National literacy estimates are published in the statistical tables when available. They are obtained from national censuses or surveys taken between 1995 and 2004. The reference year and literacy definition for each country are presented after this introduction. Figures dated before 2000 will

be replaced as soon as the UIS gets more recent national estimates. For countries that did not report literacy data for the most recent year available during the 2000–2004 reference period, the tables publish UIS estimates for 2005 that are based on national data collected before 1995. All literacy figures are rebased to the 2004 UN population revision.

3) Projections to 2015 were produced using empirical information on national literate/illiterate populations provided by countries. For a description of the projection methodology, see p. 261 of the 2006 *EFA Global Monitoring Report*.

In many countries, interest in assessing the literacy skills of the population is growing. In response to this need, the UIS is developing a new methodology and data collection instrument called the Literacy Assessment and Monitoring Programme (LAMP). Following the example of the International Adult Literacy Survey (IALS), LAMP is based on actual, functional assessment of literacy skills. It aims to provide literacy data of higher quality and is based on the concept of a continuum of literacy skills rather than the common literate/illiterate dichotomy.

Estimates and missing data

Both actual and estimated data are presented throughout the statistical tables. When data are not reported to the UIS using the standard questionnaires, estimates are often necessary. Wherever possible, the UIS encourages countries to make their own estimates, which are presented as national estimates. Where this does not happen, the UIS may make its own estimates if sufficient supplementary information is available. Gaps in the tables may also arise where data submitted by a country are found to be inconsistent. The UIS makes every attempt to resolve such problems with the countries concerned, but reserves the final decision to omit data it regards as problematic.[4]

To fill the gaps in the statistical tables, data for previous school years were included when information for the school year ending in 2004 was not available. Such cases are indicated by a footnote.

---

3. For reliability and consistency reasons, the UIS has decided no longer to publish literacy data based on educational attainment proxies. Only data reported by countries based on the 'self-declaration' methods and 'household declaration' are included in the statistical tables.

---

4. For countries where the number of pupils of official primary school age is believed to be underestimated in the data reported to the UIS (Austria, Chile, Costa Rica, the Czech Republic, Germany, Latvia, Paraguay, Slovakia and Uruguay), the net enrolment ratio (NER) is not published. Nevertheless, in order to calculate the Education for All Development Index (EDI) for these countries, estimates of total primary NER were made. They were based on the national single-year enrolment ratios derived from data the countries reported, assuming that the enrolment ratios in the first year in the official age group were equal to those in the second year in the official age group. In a few cases where the national single-year enrolment ratios were not coherent, an alternative estimate was made, based on the estimated effects of the undercounting of pupils in the official age group for primary education.

Data processing timetable

The timetable for collection and publication of data used in this report was as follows.

- June 2004 (or December 2004 for some countries with a calendar school year): the final school year in the data collection period ended.

- November 2004 and May 2005: questionnaires were sent to countries whose data are collected directly either by the UIS or through the WEI and UOE questionnaires, with data submission deadlines of 31 March 2005, 1 August 2005 and 30 September 2005, respectively.

- June 2005: after sending reminders by e-mail, fax and post, the UIS began to process data and calculate indicators.

- December 2005: provisional statistical tables were produced and draft indicators sent to member states.

- February 2006: the first draft of statistical tables were produced for the *EFA Global Monitoring Report*.

- April 2006: the final statistical tables were sent to the *EFA Global Monitoring Report* team.

Regional averages

Regional figures for literacy rates, gross intake rates, gross and net enrolment ratios, and school life expectancy are weighted averages, taking into account the relative size of the relevant population of each country in each region. The averages are derived from both published data and broad estimates for countries for which no reliable publishable data are available.

The figures for the countries with larger populations thus have a proportionately greater influence on the regional aggregates. Where not enough reliable data are available to produce an overall weighted mean, a median figure is calculated for countries with available data only.

Capped figures

There are cases where an indicator theoretically should not exceed 100 (the NER, for example), but data inconsistencies may have resulted nonetheless in the indicator exceeding the theoretical limit. In these cases the indicator is 'capped' at 100 but the gender balance is maintained: the higher value, whether for male or female, is set equal to 100 and the other two values – the lower of male or female plus the figure for both sexes – are then recalculated so that the gender parity index for the capped figures is the same as that for the uncapped figures.

Footnotes to the tables, along with the glossary following the statistical tables, provide additional help in interpreting the data and information.

In this Report, two statistical tables that were included last year are not presented: one on literate environments (which has not changed significantly from what was published in the 2006 *EFA Global Monitoring Report*) and one on the distribution of tertiary-level students by field of study. These tables will be published in future Reports as appropriate.

Symbols used in the statistical tables

* National estimate

** UIS estimate

... Missing data

— Magnitude nil or negligible

. Category not applicable

./. Data included under another category

o Countries whose education data are collected through UOE questionnaires

w WEI project countries

Composition of regions

World classification

■ Countries in transition (12):
Countries of the Commonwealth of Independent
States, including 4 in Central and Eastern
Europe (Belarus, Republic of Moldova,
Russian Federation, Ukraine) and the countries
of Central Asia (minus Mongolia).

■ Developed countries (43):
North America and Western Europe (minus
Cyprus and Israel); Central and Eastern Europe
(minus Belarus, Republic of Moldova,
Russian Federation, Turkey and Ukraine);
Australia, Bermuda, Japan and New Zealand.

■ Developing countries (148):
Arab States; East Asia and the Pacific
(minus Australia, Japan and New Zealand);
Latin America and the Caribbean (minus
Bermuda); South and West Asia; sub-Saharan
Africa; Cyprus, Israel, Mongolia and Turkey.

EFA regions

■ Arab States (20 countries/territories)
Algeria, Bahrain, Djibouti, Egypt[w], Iraq, Jordan[w],
Kuwait, Lebanon, Libyan Arab Jamahiriya,
Mauritania, Morocco, Oman, Palestinian
Autonomous Territories, Qatar, Saudi Arabia,
Sudan, Syrian Arab Republic, Tunisia[w],
United Arab Emirates, Yemen.

■ Central and Eastern Europe (20 countries)
Albania[o], Belarus, Bosnia and Herzegovina[o],
Bulgaria[o], Croatia, Czech Republic[o], Estonia[o],
Hungary[o], Latvia[o], Lithuania[o], Poland[o],
Republic of Moldova, Romania[o], Russian
Federation[w], Serbia and Montenegro, Slovakia,
Slovenia[o], The former Yugoslav Republic of
Macedonia[o], Turkey[o], Ukraine.

■ Central Asia (9 countries)
Armenia, Azerbaijan, Georgia, Kazakhstan,
Kyrgyzstan, Mongolia, Tajikistan,
Turkmenistan, Uzbekistan.

■ East Asia and the Pacific
(33 countries/ territories)
Australia[o], Brunei Darussalam, Cambodia,
China[w], Cook Islands, Democratic People's
Republic of Korea, Fiji, Indonesia[w], Japan[o],
Kiribati, Lao People's Democratic Republic,
Macao (China), Malaysia[w], Marshall Islands,
Micronesia (Federated States of), Myanmar,
Nauru, New Zealand[o], Niue, Palau,
Papua New Guinea, Philippines[w], Republic
of Korea[o], Samoa, Singapore, Solomon Islands,
Thailand[w], Timor-Leste, Tokelau, Tonga,
Tuvalu, Vanuatu, Viet Nam.

■ East Asia (15 countries/territories)
Brunei Darussalam, Cambodia, China[w],
Democratic People's Republic of Korea,
Indonesia[w], Japan[o], Lao People's Democratic
Republic, Macao (China), Malaysia[w], Myanmar,
Philippines[w], Republic of Korea[o], Singapore,
Thailand[w], Viet Nam.

■ Pacific (18 countries/territories)
Australia°, Cook Islands, Fiji, Kiribati,
Marshall Islands, Micronesia (Federated
States of), Nauru, New Zealand°, Niue, Palau,
Papua New Guinea, Samoa, Solomon Islands,
Timor-Leste, Tokelau, Tonga, Tuvalu, Vanuatu.

■ Latin America and the Caribbean
(41 countries/territories)
Anguilla, Antigua and Barbuda, Argentina^w,
Aruba, Bahamas, Barbados, Belize, Bermuda,
Bolivia, Brazil^w, British Virgin Islands, Cayman
Islands, Chile^w, Colombia, Costa Rica, Cuba,
Dominica, Dominican Republic, Ecuador,
El Salvador, Grenada, Guatemala, Guyana,
Haiti, Honduras, Jamaica^w, Mexico°, Montserrat,
Netherlands Antilles, Nicaragua, Panama,
Paraguay^w, Peru^w, Saint Kitts and Nevis,
Saint Lucia, Saint Vincent and the Grenadines,
Suriname, Trinidad and Tobago, Turks and
Caicos Islands, Uruguay^w, Venezuela.

■ Caribbean (22 countries/territories)
Anguilla, Antigua and Barbuda, Aruba,
Bahamas, Barbados, Belize, Bermuda, British
Virgin Islands, Cayman Islands, Dominica,
Grenada, Guyana, Haiti, Jamaica^w, Montserrat,
Netherlands Antilles, Saint Kitts and Nevis,
Saint Lucia, Saint Vincent and the Grenadines,
Suriname, Trinidad and Tobago,
Turks and Caicos Islands.

■ Latin America (19 countries)
Argentina^w, Bolivia, Brazil^w, Chile^w, Colombia,
Costa Rica, Cuba, Dominican Republic,
Ecuador, El Salvador, Guatemala, Honduras,
Mexico°, Nicaragua, Panama, Paraguay^w, Peru^w,
Uruguay^w, Venezuela.

■ North America and Western Europe
(26 countries/territories)
Andorra, Austria°, Belgium°, Canada°, Cyprus°,
Denmark°, Finland°, France°, Germany°,
Greece°, Iceland°, Ireland°, Israel°, Italy°,
Luxembourg°, Malta°, Monaco, Netherlands°,
Norway°, Portugal°, San Marino, Spain°,
Sweden°, Switzerland°, United Kingdom°,
United States°.

■ South and West Asia (9 countries)
Afghanistan, Bangladesh, Bhutan, India^w,
Islamic Republic of Iran, Maldives, Nepal,
Pakistan, Sri Lanka^w.

■ Sub-Saharan Africa (45 countries)
Angola, Benin, Botswana, Burkina Faso,
Burundi, Cameroon, Cape Verde, Central
African Republic, Chad, Comoros, Congo,
Côte d'Ivoire, Democratic Republic of the
Congo, Equatorial Guinea, Eritrea, Ethiopia,
Gabon, Gambia, Ghana, Guinea, Guinea-Bissau,
Kenya, Lesotho, Liberia, Madagascar, Malawi,
Mali, Mauritius, Mozambique, Namibia, Niger,
Nigeria, Rwanda, Sao Tome and Principe,
Senegal, Seychelles, Sierra Leone, Somalia,
South Africa, Swaziland, Togo, Uganda, United
Republic of Tanzania, Zambia, Zimbabwe^w.

Metadata for national literacy statistics

Country or territory	Year	Data source	Literacy definition	Mode
Afghanistan	2000	MICS	Literacy is defined as the ability to read easily or with difficulty a letter or a newspaper.	Self-declaration
Albania	2001	Population Census	Literate is a person who acquires the capacities of reading and writing by himself or herself and never attended any kind of educational programme. Also considered literate is a person who acquired those capacities from schooling or literacy programmes.	Household declaration
Algeria	2002	Health Survey	The capacity to read and write.	Self-declaration
Angola	2001	MICS	Literacy is defined as the ability to read easily or with difficulty a letter or a newspaper.	Self-declaration
Argentina	2001	Population Census	A literate is a person who can read and write.	Household declaration
Armenia	2001	Population Census	Literates correspond to those individuals aged 7 years old and higher who can read and understand in any language.	Household declaration
Aruba	2000	Population Census	Person able to read a simple text and write a letter.	Household declaration
Azerbaijan	1999	Population Census	Literates are persons who can read and write, with understanding, the text. Literacy is acceptable for any language having written form.	Household declaration
Bahrain	2001	Population Census	Illiterates are persons who cannot read or write, as well as persons who can read only, for example a person who studied Qur'an.	Household declaration
Belarus	1999	Population Census	Persons aged 15+ who could neither read nor write were referred to the category of the illiterates.	Household declaration
Benin	2002	Population Census	A person is literate who can, with understanding, both read and write a short simple statement on his or her everyday life.	Household declaration
Bolivia	2001	Population Census	If the person responds that he/she knows how to read and to write, he/she is literate and if he/she does not know how to read and to write, he/she is illiterate. The survey languages were Spanish and native languages in regions of indigenous speech.	Household declaration
Bosnia and Herzegovina	2000	MICS	Literacy is defined as the ability to read easily or with difficulty a letter or a newspaper.	Self-declaration
Botswana	2003	Literacy Survey	Literacy is a responsive and context-specific multi-dimensional lifelong learning process designed to equip beneficiaries with specialized knowledge, skills, attitudes and techniques to independently engage in practices and genres involving listening, speaking, reading, writing, numeracy, technical functioning and critical thinking required in real life.	Self-declaration
Brazil	2004	Household Survey	A literate is a person who can both read and write at least a simple statement in a language he or she knows (language – Portuguese).	Self-declaration
Brunei Darussalam	2001	Population Census	Literacy is the ability of a person to read and write a simple letter or to read a newspaper column in one or two languages.	Household declaration
Bulgaria	2001	Population Census	Literates are persons who can read and write.	Household declaration
Burkina Faso	2003	Household Life Conditions Survey	Literates are persons who declare that they can read and write in any language.	Self-declaration
Burundi	2000	MICS	Literacy is defined as the ability to read easily or with difficulty a letter or a newspaper.	Self-declaration

(Continued)

Country or territory	Year	Data source	Literacy definition	Mode
Cambodia	2004	Between-census Population Survey	Literacy is the ability to read and write with understanding in any language. A person is literate when he/she can read and write a simple message in any language or dialect. A person who both cannot read and write a simple message is considered illiterate. Also to be considered illiterate is that person who is capable of reading only his/her own name or number, as well as persons who can read but not write. Children aged 0-9 were treated as illiterate by definition even if a few of them could read and write.	Self-declaration
Cameroon	2001	Deuxième Enquête auprès des Ménages – ECAMII	Literacy is the ability of people aged 15+ to read and write in French or in English.	Self-declaration
Central African Republic	2000	MICS	Literacy is defined as the ability to read easily or with difficulty a letter or a newspaper.	Self-declaration
Chad	2000	MICS	Literacy is defined as the ability to read easily or with difficulty a letter or a newspaper.	Self-declaration
Chile	2002	Population Census	A person is literate who knows how to write and to read (Spanish).	Household declaration
China	2000	Population Census	In urban areas: literate refers to a person who knows a minimum of 2000 characters. In rural areas: literate refers to a person who knows a minimum of 1500 characters.	Household declaration
Colombia	2004	Labour Force Survey	Literacy is the capacity to read and to write in one's mother tongue.	Self-declaration
Costa Rica	2000	Population Census	In the census it was asked whether the person knows how to read or write, from that we concluded literacy and illiteracy if the answer were yes or no, respectively.	Household declaration
Côte d'Ivoire	2000	MICS	Literacy is defined as the ability to read easily or with difficulty a letter or a newspaper.	Self-declaration
Croatia	2001	Population Census	A literate person is one who can read and write a simple statement on his/her everyday life; i.e. who can read and write a letter no matter what language or characters he/she uses.	Household declaration
Cuba	2002	Population Census	The people who were able to read and to write at least a simple text of facts relative to their daily life were considered literate. The people who did not fulfil that condition were regarded as illiterate.	Household declaration
Cyprus	2001	Population Census	Literates are persons who can read and write simple sentences.	Household declaration
Democratic Republic of Congo	2001	MICS	Literacy is defined as the ability to read easily or with difficulty a letter or a newspaper.	Self-declaration
Dominican Republic	2002	Population Census	Literates are all people aged 10 or older who know how to read and to write.	Household declaration
Ecuador	2001	Population Census	Literacy is the capacity to read and write.	Household declaration
Egypt	2005	Social Contract Survey	Illiterate persons are those persons who have not completed primary education and who cannot read or write	Household declaration
Equatorial Guinea	2000	MICS	Literacy is defined as the ability to read easily or with difficulty a letter or a newspaper.	Self-declaration
Estonia	2000	Population Census	'Illiterate' was recorded for a person who had not completed the level corresponding to primary education and who cannot, with understanding, both read and write a simple text on his/her everyday life at least in one language.	Household declaration
Ghana	2000	Population Census	Literacy is the ability to read and write any language with understanding. The languages in the question are English and Ghanaian languages.	Household declaration

(Continued)

Country or territory	Year	Data source	Literacy definition	Mode
Greece	2001	Population Census	Literacy is defined as the ability both to read and to write. A person, who can, with understanding, both read and write a short, simple statement on his everyday life is literate. A person who cannot, with understanding, both read and write a short, simple statement on his/her everyday life is illiterate.	Household declaration
Guatemala	2002	Population Census	Literate: a person who can read and write in a specific language. This capacity includes persons who are 7 years and over.	Household declaration
Guinea	2003	MICS	Literacy is defined as the ability to read easily or with difficulty a letter or a newspaper.	Self-declaration
Honduras	2001	Population Census	Literates refer to those who can read and write.	Household declaration
India	2001	Population Census	A literate is a person aged 7 and above who can both read and write with understanding in any language.	Household declaration
Indonesia	2004	National Socio-Economic Survey	A literate is someone who can read and write at least a simple sentence in Bahasa Indonesia.	Self-declaration
Iran, Islamic Republic of	2002	Household Employment and Unemployment Survey	A literate is an individual who can read and write a simple sentence in Farsi or any other language.	Self-declaration
Iraq	2000	MICS	Literacy is defined as the ability to read easily or with difficulty a letter or a newspaper.	Self-declaration
Israel	2004	Labour Force Survey	Illiterate are all those who declared to have never studied.	Self-declaration
Italy	2001	Population Census	Literacy is defined as the ability both to read and to write.	Household declaration
Jamaica	1999	Jamaica Adult Literacy Survey	Illiterate persons are those considered to 'have a very limited knowledge of the alphabetic system, and so may be able to identify (read) a few frequently used words but cannot understand a group of words in a phrase or a sentence. Such persons may write a few letters of the alphabet.'	Self-declaration
Jordan	2003	Household Expenditure and Income survey	Persons aged 15 years and above who can read and write in any language.	Self-declaration
Kazakhstan	1999	Population Census	na	na
Kenya	2000	MICS	Literacy is defined as the ability to read easily or with difficulty a letter or a newspaper.	Self-declaration
Kuwait	2005	Population Census	Literacy is a person's ability to read a simple statement related to his (her) every day life and understanding. It needs a series of writing and reading skills and testing that includes basic accounting skills.	Household declaration
Kyrgyzstan	1999	Population Census	Literate population is the population at the age of 6 and older which is able to read and write or only to read.	Household declaration
Lao PDR	2001	National Literacy Survey	A literate person was defined as a person who can read, write and understand simple sentences in Lao, and perform simple arithmetic calculations (numeracy). All household members aged 6 and above were asked whether they can read, write and perform simple calculations.	Self-declaration
Latvia	2000	Population Census	Illiterate is a person who cannot, with understanding, both read and write a short, simple statement or a person who can read but not write.	Household declaration
Lesotho	2001	Demographic Survey	Literates are persons who can read and write.	Self-declaration
Lithuania	2001	Population Census	A literate (no formal schooling) is a person who does not attend school but can read (with understanding) and/or write a simple sentence on topics of everyday life.	Household declaration

(Continued)

Country or territory	Year	Data source	Literacy definition	Mode
Macao, China	2001	Population Census	A person is defined as literate if he/she can, with understanding, both read and write a short, simple statement on his/her everyday life.	Household declaration
Madagascar	2000	MICS	Literacy is defined as the ability to read easily or with difficulty a letter or a newspaper.	Self-declaration
Malawi	1998	Population Census	Literates are persons able to write and read English, chichewa or another language.	Household declaration
Malaysia	2000	Population Census	Illiterates are persons aged 10 years and over who have never been to school in any language.	Household declaration
Maldives	2000	Population Census	A literate is a person who can read and write with understanding in any language: Maldivian language (Dhivehi), English, Arabic, etc.	Household declaration
Mali	1998	Population Census	Illiterate is a person who never attended school even if that person can read and write.	Household declaration
Malta	1995	Population Census	Literacy is defined as the ability both to read and to write. A person, who can, with understanding, both read and write a short, simple statement on his/her everyday life is literate. A person who cannot, with understanding, both read and write a short, simple statement on his/her everyday life is illiterate.	Household declaration
Mauritania	2000	Population Census	All persons who are able to read and write in the language specified.	Household declaration
Mauritius	2000	Population Census	A person was considered as literate if he or she was able with understanding to both read and write a simple statement in his/her everyday life.	Household declaration
Mexico	2004	National Survey on Income and Expenditure of Households	Literate persons are distinguished according to their ability to read and write a message. Message is understood as a brief and simple exposition of a daily life fact.	Self-declaration
Mongolia	2000	Population Census	Literacy is the ability to read and write simple statements in Mongolian or any other language, with understanding.	Household declaration
Morocco	2004	Population Census	na	Household declaration
Myanmar	2000	MICS	Literacy is defined as the ability to read easily or with difficulty a letter or a newspaper.	Self-declaration
Namibia	2001	Population Census	Literacy is the ability to write with understanding in any language. Persons who could read and not write were classified as non-literate. Similarly, persons who were able to write and not read were classified as non-literate.	Household declaration
Nepal	2001	Population Census	A person aged 6 years and above, who can read and write a simple letter with understanding and have simple knowledge of arithmetic is considered as literate. Language can be any.	Household declaration
Nicaragua	2001	National Survey	A literate is a person who can read and write; an illiterate is a person who can only read or who cannot read and write.	Self-declaration
Niger	2005	Survey on Basic indicators of the Wellbeing	Literate is a person who knows how to read and write in any language.	Self-declaration
Oman	2003	Population Census	A literate is an individual who is capable of both reading and writing but does not (necessarily) hold an academic qualification of any kind.	Household declaration
Pakistan	2005	Social and Living Standards Measurement Survey	A literate is one who can read a newspaper and write a simple letter in any language.	Self-declaration

(Continued)

Country or territory	Year	Data source	Literacy definition	Mode
Palestinian A. T.	2004	Labour Force Survey	A literate person is one who can both read and write a short, simple statement on his or her everyday life.	Self-declaration
Panama	2000	Population Census	Literacy is the person's aptitude to read and to write in any language.	Household declaration
Papua New Guinea	2000	Population Census	A literate is a person who could read and write with understanding at least one of English, Motu or Tokples.	Household declaration
Peru	2004	Household National Survey	Literacy is the ability to read and to write in any language. A literate is a person who knows how to read and to write in any language. The language used for the collection of the data in the survey was Spanish.	Self-declaration
Philippines	2000	Population Census	Simple literacy is the ability to read and write a simple message. A person is literate when he can both read and write a simple message in any language or dialect. A person who knows how to read and write but at the time of the census, he/she can no longer read and/or write due to some physical defects or illness, is considered literate. Disabled persons who can read and write through any means such as Braille are considered literate.	Household declaration
Qatar	2004	Population Census	na	na
Republic of Moldova	2004	Labour Force Survey	na	na
Romania	2002	Population Census	A person of 10 years old and over who graduated an educational institution, or who did not graduate from any educational institution but is attending one, or is able to read and write is considered as a literate person. A person of 10 years old and over who is not able to read and write, or is able to read or write only is an illiterate person.	Household declaration
Russian Federation	2002	Population Census	Persons having indicated some level of literacy were considered as literate. Persons who have indicated that they are unable to read and write were considered as illiterate.	Household declaration
Rwanda	2000	MICS	Literacy is defined as the ability to read easily or with difficulty a letter or a newspaper.	Self-declaration
Saudi Arabia	2000	Household Demographic Survey	A person is considered literate if he/she can read and write in any language. A blind person is considered literate if he/she can read and write the 'Braille' method.	Self-declaration
Senegal	2002	Household Survey	Literate: persons who are able to read and write in any language.	Self-declaration
Serbia and Montenegro	2003	Population Census	Literate population covers all persons who can read and write a text dealing with everyday life regardless of the language. All other persons, including also those who can only read, are considers as illiterate.	Household declaration
Seychelles	2002	Population Census	Ability to read or write a simple sentence in English, French or Creole.	Household declaration
Sierra Leone	2004	Population Census	Literacy was defined as the ability to read and write in any language.	Household declaration
Singapore	2000	Population Census	Literacy refers to a person's ability to read with understanding, e.g. a newspaper, in the language specified.	Household declaration
South Africa	1996	Population Census	na	na
Sri Lanka	2001	Population Census	The census schedule provided for recording the ability to speak, read and write Sinhalese, Tamil and English. A person was regarded as able to read and write a language only if he could both read with understanding and write a short letter or paragraph in that language. A person who is able to read and write at least one language was regarded as literate.	Household declaration

(Continued)

Country or territory	Year	Data source	Literacy definition	Mode
Sudan	2000	MICS	Literacy is defined as the ability to read easily or with difficulty a letter or a newspaper.	Self-declaration
Suriname	2004	Population Census	A person is considered literate if he/she can write a simple note or phrase.	Household declaration
Swaziland	2000	MICS	Literacy is defined as the ability to read easily or with difficulty a letter or a newspaper.	Self-declaration
Syrian Arab Republic	2004	Population Census	A literate is an individual male or female who can read and write in Arabic.	Household declaration
Tajikistan	2000	Population Census	Literates are persons who can write and read, regardless of the language.	Household declaration
Thailand	2000	Population Census	Literate persons are defined as persons aged 5 and over who are able to read and write simple statements with understanding, in any language. If a person can read but cannot write, then he/she is classified as illiterate.	Household declaration
TFYR Macedonia	2002	Population Census	Each person having completed more than three grades of primary school shall be considered literate. In addition, literate will be considered as a person without school qualification and with 1-3 grades of primary school if he/she can read and write a composition (text) in relation to everyday life (i.e. read and write a letter regardless of the language and alphabet he can read). However, if a person without education or with completed 1-3 grades of primary school can not read and write a composition (text) about everyday life, i.e. read and write a letter, he/she will be considered illiterate.	Household declaration
Togo	2000	MICS	Literacy is defined as the ability to read easily or with difficulty a letter or a newspaper.	Self-declaration
Tonga	1996	Population Census	For a person to be considered as literate in a language, that person must be able to read and write in that language.	Household declaration
Tunisia	2004	Population Census	A literate is a person who knows how to read and write at least one language.	Household declaration
Turkey	2004	Labour Force Survey	People who can write and read are accepted as literate.	Self-declaration
Turkmenistan	1995	Population Census	Literates are persons aged 7 years or more who are able to write and read.	Household declaration
Uganda	2002	Population Census	Literacy is the ability to meaningfully write or read with understanding in any language.	Household declaration
Ukraine	2001	Population Census	A person of 6 year old and older who has any level of education or can read is literate.	Household declaration
United Republic of Tanzania	2002	Population Census	Literacy is defined as the ability both to read and to write with understanding, a short, simple statement on everyday life. The ability to read and write may be in any language.	Household declaration
Vanuatu	1999	Population Census	na	na
Venezuela	2001	Population Census	na	Household declaration
Viet Nam	1999	Population Census	A literate is a person who knows how to read and write with understanding simple sentences in his/her national or ethnic language or a foreign language.	Household declaration
Zambia	1999	MICS	Literacy is defined as the ability to read easily or with difficulty a letter or a newspaper.	Self declaration

na: not available.

Education for All Global Monitoring Report 2007

Table 1
Background statistics

Country or territory	Total population (000) 2004	Average annual growth rate (%) total population 2000-2005	Average annual growth rate (%) 0-4 population 2000-2005	Life expectancy at birth (years) 2000-2005 Total	Male	Female	Total fertility rate (children per woman) 2000-2005	HIV prevalence rate (%) in adults (15-49) 2005 Total	% of women among people (age 15+) living with HIV 2005	Orphans due to AIDS (0-17) (000) 2005
Arab States										
Algeria	32 358	1.5	1.0	71.0	69.7	72.2	2.5	0.1	21.6	…
Bahrain	716	1.6	-0.3	74.2	72.9	75.8	2.5	…	…	…
Djibouti	779	2.1	0.9	52.7	51.4	53.9	5.1	3.1	60.0	6
Egypt	72 642	1.9	1.7	69.6	67.5	71.8	3.3	<0.1	…	…
Iraq	28 057	2.8	1.5	58.8	57.3	60.4	4.8	…	…	…
Jordan	5 561	2.7	-0.1	71.2	69.8	72.8	3.5	…	…	…
Kuwait	2 606	3.7	2.7	76.8	75.1	79.4	2.4	…	…	…
Lebanon	3 540	1.0	-1.9	71.9	69.7	74.0	2.3	0.1	…	…
Libyan Arab Jamahiriya	5 740	2.0	2.0	73.4	71.4	76.1	3.0	…	…	…
Mauritania	2 980	3.0	2.8	52.5	50.9	54.1	5.8	0.7	57.3	7
Morocco	31 020	1.5	1.0	69.5	67.4	71.7	2.8	0.1	21.1	…
Oman	2 534	1.0	-1.1	74.0	72.7	75.6	3.8	…	…	…
Palestinian A. T.	3 587	3.2	1.9	72.4	70.8	73.9	5.6	…	…	…
Qatar	777	5.9	2.5	72.7	71.1	75.9	3.0	…	…	…
Saudi Arabia	23 950	2.7	0.7	71.6	69.9	73.8	4.1	…	…	…
Sudan	35 523	1.9	0.8	56.3	54.9	57.9	4.4	1.6	56.3	…
Syrian Arab Republic	18 582	2.5	1.6	73.2	71.4	74.9	3.5	…	…	…
Tunisia	9 995	1.1	-0.8	73.1	71.1	75.3	2.0	0.1	22.1	…
United Arab Emirates	4 284	6.5	4.5	77.9	76.3	80.6	2.5	…	…	…
Yemen	20 329	3.1	2.2	60.3	59.1	61.7	6.2	…	…	…
Central and Eastern Europe										
Albania	3 112	0.4	-2.2	73.7	70.9	76.7	2.3	…	…	…
Belarus	9 811	-0.6	0.3	68.1	62.4	74.0	1.2	0.3	25.5	…
Bosnia and Herzegovina	3 909	0.3	-3.7	74.1	71.3	76.7	1.3	<0.1	…	…
Bulgaria	7 780	-0.7	0.5	72.1	68.8	75.6	1.2	<0.1	…	…
Croatia	4 540	0.2	-2.4	74.9	71.3	78.4	1.3	<0.1	…	…
Czech Republic	10 229	-0.1	0.2	75.5	72.2	78.7	1.2	0.1	…	…
Estonia	1 335	-0.6	1.2	71.2	65.4	76.9	1.4	1.3	24.0	…
Hungary	10 124	-0.3	-1.1	72.6	68.4	76.7	1.3	0.1	…	…
Latvia	2 318	-0.6	0.9	71.4	65.6	76.9	1.3	0.8	22.0	…
Lithuania	3 443	-0.4	-4.1	72.2	66.5	77.8	1.3	0.2	…	…
Poland	38 559	-0.1	-2.2	74.3	70.2	78.4	1.3	0.1	30.0	…
Republic of Moldova	4 218	-0.3	-3.6	67.5	63.7	71.1	1.2	1.1	57.1	…
Romania	21 790	-0.4	-0.9	71.3	67.7	75.0	1.3	<0.1	…	…
Russian Federation	143 899	-0.5	1.8	65.4	59.1	72.2	1.3	1.1	22.3	…
Serbia and Montenegro	10 510	-0.1	-0.8	73.2	70.9	75.6	1.7	0.2	20.0	…
Slovakia	5 401	0.0	-2.4	74.0	70.0	77.9	1.2	<0.1	…	…
Slovenia	1 967	0.0	-0.7	76.3	72.6	79.9	1.2	<0.1	…	…
TFYR Macedonia	2 030	0.2	-2.0	73.7	71.2	76.2	1.5	<0.1	…	…
Turkey	72 220	1.4	-0.2	68.6	66.3	70.9	2.5	…	…	…
Ukraine	46 989	-1.1	-1.9	66.1	60.1	72.5	1.1	1.4	48.8	…
Central Asia										
Armenia	3 026	-0.4	-4.0	71.4	67.9	74.6	1.3	0.1	…	…
Azerbaijan	8 355	0.6	-2.7	66.9	63.2	70.5	1.9	0.1	…	…
Georgia	4 518	-1.1	-2.1	70.5	66.5	74.3	1.5	0.2	…	…
Kazakhstan	14 839	-0.3	-1.2	63.2	57.8	68.9	2.0	0.1	56.7	…
Kyrgyzstan	5 204	1.2	0.1	66.8	62.6	71.1	2.7	0.1	…	…
Mongolia	2 614	1.2	0.1	63.9	61.9	65.9	2.4	<0.1	…	…
Tajikistan	6 430	1.1	-0.9	63.5	61.0	66.3	3.8	0.1	…	…
Turkmenistan	4 766	1.4	0.1	62.4	58.2	66.7	2.8	<0.1	…	…
Uzbekistan	26 209	1.5	0.2	66.5	63.3	69.7	2.7	0.2	13.2	…
East Asia and the Pacific										
Australia	19 942	1.1	-0.6	80.2	77.6	82.8	1.7	0.1	…	…
Brunei Darussalam	366	2.3	1.2	76.3	74.2	78.9	2.5	<0.1	…	…
Cambodia	13 798	2.0	1.4	56.0	52.1	59.6	4.1	1.6	45.4	…
China	1 307 989	0.6	-2.4	71.5	69.8	73.3	1.7	0.1	27.7	…

GNP AND POVERTY					EXTERNAL DEBT[3]					
GNP per capita[3]				Population living on less than US$2 per day (%)[4]	Total debt (US$ millions)	Total debt service (US$ millions)	Total debt as % of GNP	Public debt service as % of government current revenue	Total debt service as % of exports	
Current US$		PPP US$								
1998	2004	1998	2004	1990-2003[5]	2004	2004	2004	2002[6]	2004	Country or territory
										Arab States
1 560	2 270	4 830	6 322	15.1	21 987	5 754	7.1	21.3[x]	...	Algeria
9 610	14 370	14 120	19 673	...	...	...	...	...	...	Bahrain
790	950	1 950	2 152	...	429	18	2.5	...	...	Djibouti
1 270	1 250	3 200	4 200	43.9	30 291	2 317	2.9	...	7.6	Egypt
...	...	...	...	...	...	...	...	...	...	Iraq
1 590	2 190	3 720	4 765	7.4	8 175	700	6.0	26.0[x]	8.2	Jordan
17 390	22 470	18 960	21 610	...	...	...	...	...	...	Kuwait
3 670	6 010	4 380	5 547	...	22 177	4 350	21.0	...	...	Lebanon
...	4 400	...	...	...	...	...	...	...	...	Libyan Arab Jamahiriya
420	530	1 560	2 048	63.1	2 297	57	3.5	...	...	Mauritania
1 260	1 570	3 340	4 253	14.3	17 672	2 996	6.1	...	14.0	Morocco
6 420	9 070	11 570	14 678	...	3 872	992	4.2	14.7[x]	6.9	Oman
...	...	...	...	...	...	...	...	...	...	Palestinian A. T.
...	...	...	...	...	...	...	...	...	...	Qatar
8 120	10 140	12 280	13 811	...	...	...	...	...	...	Saudi Arabia
310	530	1 320	1 811	...	19 332	312	1.6	...	6.0	Sudan
930	1 230	3 240	3 496	...	21 521	328	1.4	...	3.5	Syrian Arab Republic
2 050	2 650	5 300	7 427	6.6	18 700	2 034	7.5	...	13.7	Tunisia
17 790	23 770	20 820	24 092	...	...	...	...	...	...	United Arab Emirates
390	550	710	809	45.2	5 488	223	1.9	...	3.5	Yemen
										Central and Eastern Europe
880	2 120	3 110	5 072	...	1 549	74	1.0	...	...	Albania
1 560	2 140	4 210	6 966	...	3 717	326	1.4	5.4[x]	2.1	Belarus
1 190	2 040	4 850	7 226	...	3 202	176	2.0	...	3.7	Bosnia and Herzegovina
1 270	2 750	5 300	7 936	...	15 661	2 456	10.4	19.1[x]	17.1	Bulgaria
4 610	6 820	8 180	11 917	...	31 548	5 294	15.8	16.9[x]	27.2	Croatia
5 490	9 130	12 470	18 423	...	45 561	8 309	8.2	9.7[x]	10.5	Czech Republic
3 750	7 080	8 730	13 631	...	10 008	1 451	13.8	2.3[x]	15.7	Estonia
4 380	8 370	10 410	15 801	...	63 159	17 156	18.1	...	25.2	Hungary
2 650	5 580	6 570	11 816	...	12 661	1 375	10.0	4.9[x]	21.1	Latvia
2 760	5 740	7 980	12 693	...	9 475	1 760	8.2	11.1[x]	14.3	Lithuania
4 210	6 100	8 770	12 730	...	99 190	34 551	14.5	11.4[x]	34.6	Poland
400	720	1 320	1 953	...	1 868	248	8.5	29.4	12.1	Republic of Moldova
1 520	2 960	5 490	8 329	...	30 034	4 725	6.6	16.4[x]	17.2	Romania
2 140	3 400	5 760	9 684	...	197 335	21 181	3.7	12.0[x]	9.8	Russian Federation
...	2 680	...	...	...	15 882	981	4.1	...	...	Serbia and Montenegro
4 030	6 480	10 480	14 477	...	22 068	5 052	12.4	14.0[x]	...	Slovakia
9 740	14 770	14 730	20 828	...	...	...	...	...	...	Slovenia
1 920	2 420	5 790	6 562	...	2 044	244	4.6	...	10.5	TFYR Macedonia
3 060	3 750	6 150	7 724	10.3	161 595	33 940	11.3	26.0[x]	35.9	Turkey
850	1 270	3 580	6 330	...	21 652	4 301	6.7	8.2[x]	10.7	Ukraine
										Central Asia
570	1 060	2 150	4 156	...	1 224	107	3.4	...	8.0	Armenia
510	940	2 000	3 811	...	1 986	236	3.0	...	5.2	Azerbaijan
700	1 060	1 780	2 895	...	2 082	218	4.1	18.0	11.2	Georgia
1 350	2 250	3 570	6 933	...	32 310	8 774	23.1	18.6[x]	38.0	Kazakhstan
350	400	1 320	1 856	...	2 100	161	7.6	...	14.2	Kyrgyzstan
460	600	1 510	2 042	74.9	1 517	41	2.6	11.6[x]	2.9	Mongolia
170	280	660	1 155	...	896	101	5.1	25.5[x]	6.8	Tajikistan
550	...	2 490	...	...	...	...	...	...	...	Turkmenistan
620	450	1 360	1 862	...	5 007	848	7.1	...	...	Uzbekistan
										East Asia and the Pacific
21 240	27 070	23 700	29 339	...	...	...	...	...	...	Australia
...	...	...	...	...	...	...	...	...	...	Brunei Darussalam
270	350	1 440	2 311	77.7	3 377	27	0.6	...	0.8	Cambodia
740	1 500	3 200	5 885	46.7	248 934	23 656	1.2	...	3.5	China

Table 1 (continued)

Country or territory	DEMOGRAPHY[1] Total population (000) 2004	Average annual growth rate (%) total population 2000-2005	Average annual growth rate (%) 0-4 population 2000-2005	Life expectancy at birth (years) 2000-2005 Total	Male	Female	Total fertility rate (children per woman) 2000-2005	HIV/AIDS[2] HIV prevalence rate (%) in adults (15-49) 2005 Total	% of women among people (age 15+) living with HIV 2005	Orphans due to AIDS (0-17) (000) 2005
Cook Islands	18	-1.0	…	…	…	…	…	…	…	…
DPR Korea	22 384	0.6	-2.1	63.0	60.1	66.1	2.0	…	…	…
Fiji	841	0.9	-0.8	67.8	65.7	70.0	2.9	0.1	…	…
Indonesia	220 077	1.3	0.6	66.5	64.6	68.6	2.4	0.1	17.1	…
Japan	127 923	0.2	-0.6	81.9	78.3	85.3	1.3	<0.1	58.2	…
Kiribati	97	2.1	…	…	…	…	…	…	…	…
Lao PDR	5 792	2.3	1.4	54.5	53.3	55.8	4.8	0.1	…	…
Macao, China	457	0.7	-6.9	80.0	77.8	82.0	0.8	…	…	…
Malaysia	24 894	1.9	0.0	73.0	70.8	75.5	2.9	0.5	25.4	…
Marshall Islands	60	3.5	…	…	…	…	…	…	…	…
Micronesia	110	0.6	1.1	67.5	66.9	68.2	4.4	…	…	…
Myanmar	50 004	1.1	-1.4	60.1	57.4	62.9	2.5	1.3	31.4	…
Nauru	13	2.2	…	…	…	…	…	…	…	…
New Zealand	3 989	1.1	-0.5	79.0	76.7	81.3	2.0	0.1	…	…
Niue	1	-2.2	…	…	…	…	…	…	…	…
Palau	20	0.7	…	…	…	…	…	…	…	…
Papua New Guinea	5 772	2.1	-0.3	55.1	54.7	55.8	4.1	1.8	59.6	…
Philippines	81 617	1.8	0.0	70.2	68.1	72.4	3.2	<0.1	28.3	…
Republic of Korea	47 645	0.4	-4.7	76.8	73.2	80.5	1.2	<0.1	56.9	…
Samoa	184	0.8	-1.3	70.0	67.1	73.5	4.4	…	…	…
Singapore	4 273	1.5	-4.7	78.6	76.7	80.5	1.4	0.3	27.3	…
Solomon Islands	466	2.6	1.5	62.2	61.6	62.9	4.3	…	…	…
Thailand	63 694	0.9	-0.1	69.7	66.0	73.7	1.9	1.4	39.3	…
Timor-Leste	887	5.4	12.3	55.1	54.1	56.3	7.8	…	…	…
Tokelau	1	-0.3	…	…	…	…	…	…	…	…
Tonga	102	0.4	-1.6	72.1	70.9	73.4	3.5	…	…	…
Tuvalu	10	0.5	…	…	…	…	…	…	…	…
Vanuatu	207	2.0	0.6	68.4	66.8	70.4	4.2	…	…	…
Viet Nam	83 123	1.4	0.4	70.4	68.4	72.4	2.3	0.5	33.6	…
Latin America and the Caribbean										
Anguilla	12	1.7	…	…	…	…	…	…	…	…
Antigua and Barbuda	81	1.3	…	…	…	…	…	…	…	…
Argentina	38 372	1.0	-0.7	74.3	70.6	78.1	2.4	0.6	27.7	…
Aruba	98	1.5	…	…	…	…	…	…	…	…
Bahamas	319	1.4	0.0	69.5	66.2	72.7	2.3	3.3	58.5	…
Barbados	269	0.3	-0.8	74.9	71.1	78.3	1.5	1.5	…	…
Belize	264	2.1	0.1	71.9	69.5	74.5	3.2	2.5	27.8	…
Bermuda	64	0.4	…	…	…	…	…	…	…	…
Bolivia	9 009	2.0	0.8	63.9	61.8	66.0	4.0	0.1	27.9	…
Brazil	183 913	1.4	0.7	70.3	66.4	74.4	2.3	0.5	36.1	…
British Virgin Islands	22	1.4	…	…	…	…	…	…	…	…
Cayman Islands	44	2.5	…	…	…	…	…	…	…	…
Chile	16 124	1.1	-1.4	77.9	74.8	80.8	2.0	0.3	27.1	…
Colombia	44 915	1.6	-0.1	72.2	69.2	75.3	2.6	0.6	28.1	…
Costa Rica	4 253	1.9	-0.2	78.1	75.8	80.6	2.3	0.3	27.4	…
Cuba	11 245	0.3	-0.8	77.2	75.3	79.1	1.6	0.1	55.3	…
Dominica	79	0.3	…	…	…	…	…	…	…	…
Dominican Republic	8 768	1.5	0.6	67.1	63.7	70.9	2.7	1.1	50.0	…
Ecuador	13 040	1.4	-0.2	74.2	71.3	77.2	2.8	0.3	54.5	…
El Salvador	6 762	1.8	0.2	70.7	67.7	73.7	2.9	0.9	28.3	…
Grenada	102	0.3	…	…	…	…	…	…	…	…
Guatemala	12 295	2.4	1.7	67.1	63.4	70.8	4.6	0.9	27.1	…
Guyana	750	0.2	-1.3	62.8	59.8	65.9	2.3	2.4	60.0	…
Haiti	8 407	1.4	0.8	51.5	50.6	52.3	4.0	3.8	53.3	…
Honduras	7 048	2.3	0.3	67.6	65.6	69.7	3.7	1.5	26.2	…
Jamaica	2 639	0.5	-1.9	70.7	68.9	72.5	2.4	1.5	27.6	…
Mexico	105 699	1.3	-0.7	74.9	72.4	77.4	2.4	0.3	23.3	…
Montserrat	4	2.8	…	…	…	…	…	…	…	…
Netherlands Antilles	181	0.8	-0.1	76.1	72.9	79.1	2.1	…	…	…
Nicaragua	5 376	2.0	0.0	69.5	67.2	71.9	3.3	0.2	23.6	…

GNP AND POVERTY					EXTERNAL DEBT[3]					
GNP per capita[3]				Population living on less than US$2 per day (%)[4]	Total debt (US$ millions)	Total debt service (US$ millions)	Total debt as % of GNP	Public debt service as % of government current revenue	Total debt service as % of exports	
Current US$		PPP US$								
1998	2004	1998	2004	1990-2003[5]	2004	2004	2004	2002[6]	2004	Country or territory
...	...	...	...	...	...	...	...	...	...	Cook Islands
...	...	...	...	<2.0	...	...	...	...	...	DPR Korea
2 370	2 720	4 540	5 747	...	202	15	0.6	...	...	Fiji
670	1 140	2 650	3 485	52.4	140 649	20 464	8.2	22.4[x]	22.1	Indonesia
33 660	37 050	24 750	29 814	...	...	...	...	...	...	Japan
1 150	970	...	...	...	...	...	...	...	...	Kiribati
310	390	1 340	1 878	73.2	2 056	53	2.2	...	...	Lao PDR
15 220	...	18 420	...	...	...	...	...	...	...	Macao, China
3 630	4 520	7 180	9 715	9.3	52 145	9 187	8.2	...	...	Malaysia
...	2 320	...	...	...	...	...	...	...	...	Marshall Islands
1 900	2 300	...	...	...	...	...	...	...	...	Micronesia
...	...	...	...	...	7 239	125	...	...	3.8	Myanmar
...	...	...	...	...	...	...	...	...	...	Nauru
15 340	19 990	17 000	22 257	...	...	...	...	...	...	New Zealand
...	...	...	...	...	...	...	...	...	...	Niue
...	6 870	...	...	...	...	...	...	...	...	Palau
850	560	2 190	2 277	...	2 149	474	13.6	...	...	Papua New Guinea
1 080	1 170	3 830	4 946	46.4	60 550	11 570	12.8	49.4[x]	20.9	Philippines
9 200	14 000	12 490	20 526	...	...	...	...	...	...	Republic of Korea
1 390	1 840	4 540	5 605	...	562	21	5.6	...	...	Samoa
23 500	24 760	20 110	27 372	...	...	...	...	...	...	Singapore
880	560	2 240	1 798	...	176	17	6.5	...	...	Solomon Islands
2 110	2 490	5 600	7 933	32.5	51 307	12 376	7.8	24.3[x]	10.6	Thailand
...	550	...	...	...	...	...	...	...	...	Timor-Leste
...	...	...	...	...	...	...	...	...	...	Tokelau
1 720	1 860	5 640	7 855	...	81	3	1.4	...	...	Tonga
...	...	...	...	...	...	...	...	...	...	Tuvalu
1 240	1 390	2 990	2 945	...	118	3	1.1	...	...	Vanuatu
350	540	1 760	2 702	...	17 825	780	1.8	16.1	...	Viet Nam
										Latin America and the Caribbean
...	...	...	...	...	...	...	...	...	...	Anguilla
8 090	9 480	8 690	11 098	...	...	...	...	...	...	Antigua and Barbuda
8 230	3 580	12 230	12 526	14.3	169 247	12 377	8.6	43.6[x]	28.5	Argentina
...	...	...	...	...	...	...	...	...	...	Aruba
12 940	...	14 580	...	...	...	...	...	...	...	Bahamas
8 220	...	13 720	...	...	702	88	3.3	...	5.2	Barbados
2 710	3 940	4 540	6 554	...	959	332	31.3	...	62.5	Belize
...	...	...	...	...	...	...	...	...	...	Bermuda
1 000	960	2 280	2 600	34.3	6 096	513	6.1	17.4[x]	18.6	Bolivia
4 610	3 000	6 720	7 935	22.4	222 026	53 710	9.2	...	46.8	Brazil
...	...	...	...	...	...	...	...	...	...	British Virgin Islands
...	...	...	...	...	...	...	...	...	...	Cayman Islands
4 880	5 220	8 490	10 608	9.6	44 058	9 566	10.4	8.0[x]	24.2	Chile
2 410	2 020	6 030	6 945	22.6	37 732	7 688	8.2	...	33.0	Colombia
3 590	4 470	7 480	9 216	9.5	5 700	686	3.8	16.9[x]	7.3	Costa Rica
...	...	...	...	...	...	...	...	...	...	Cuba
3 280	3 670	4 940	5 291	...	226	19	7.3	...	...	Dominica
1 850	2 100	5 010	6 863	<2.0	6 965	750	4.4	...	6.4	Dominican Republic
1 800	2 210	3 160	3 768	40.8	16 868	3 731	13.0	...	36.0	Ecuador
1 870	2 320	4 350	4 894	58.0	7 250	617	4.0	...	8.8	El Salvador
3 020	3 750	5 730	7 047	...	433	29	7.6	...	...	Grenada
1 660	2 190	3 700	4 263	37.4	5 532	546	2.0	...	7.4	Guatemala
860	1 020	3 590	4 244	...	1 331	49	6.5	...	5.8	Guyana
440	...	1 700	...	...	1 225	133	3.7	...	...	Haiti
740	1 040	2 400	2 760	44.0	6 332	333	4.7	...	7.8	Honduras
2 650	3 300	3 370	3 950	13.3	6 399	835	9.9	21.6[x]	14.8	Jamaica
4 020	6 790	7 800	9 645	26.3	138 689	51 292	7.7	...	22.9	Mexico
...	...	...	...	...	...	...	...	...	...	Montserrat
...	...	...	...	...	...	...	...	...	...	Netherlands Antilles
690	830	2 780	3 481	79.9	5 145	126	2.9	...	5.8	Nicaragua

Table 1 (continued)

Country or territory	Total population (000) 2004	Average annual growth rate (%) total population 2000-2005	Average annual growth rate (%) 0-4 population 2000-2005	Life expectancy at birth (years) 2000-2005 Total	Life expectancy at birth (years) 2000-2005 Male	Life expectancy at birth (years) 2000-2005 Female	Total fertility rate (children per woman) 2000-2005	HIV prevalence rate (%) in adults (15-49) 2005 Total	% of women among people (age 15+) living with HIV 2005	Orphans due to AIDS (0-17) (000) 2005
Panama	3 175	1.8	0.7	74.7	72.3	77.4	2.7	0.9	25.3	...
Paraguay	6 017	2.4	1.4	70.9	68.6	73.1	3.9	0.4	26.9	...
Peru	27 562	1.5	-0.6	69.8	67.3	72.4	2.9	0.6	28.6	...
Saint Kitts and Nevis	42	1.1	...	...	...	...	...	...	...	...
Saint Lucia	159	0.8	0.3	72.3	70.8	73.9	2.2	...	...	...
St Vincent/Grenad.	118	0.5	0.4	71.0	68.2	73.8	2.3	...	...	...
Suriname	446	0.7	-1.4	69.0	65.8	72.5	2.6	1.9	27.5	...
Trinidad and Tobago	1 301	0.3	0.5	69.9	66.9	73.0	1.6	2.6	57.7	...
Turks and Caicos Islands	25	6.1	...	...	...	...	...	...	...	...
Uruguay	3 439	0.7	-0.1	75.3	71.6	78.9	2.3	0.5	55.8	...
Venezuela	26 282	1.8	0.6	72.8	69.9	75.8	2.7	0.7	28.2	...
North America and Western Europe										
Andorra	67	0.4	...	...	...	...	...	...	...	...
Austria	8 171	0.23	-1.2	78.9	75.9	81.7	1.4	0.3	19.2	...
Belgium	10 400	0.2	-0.3	78.8	75.7	81.9	1.7	0.3	38.6	...
Canada	31 958	1.0	-0.7	79.9	77.3	82.4	1.5	0.3	16.3	...
Cyprus	826	1.2	-1.5	78.5	76.0	81.0	1.6	...	...	...
Denmark	5 414	0.3	-0.8	77.1	74.8	79.4	1.8	0.2	23.6	...
Finland	5 235	0.3	-1.1	78.4	75.0	81.7	1.7	0.1	...	...
France	60 257	0.4	0.4	79.4	75.8	83.0	1.9	0.4	34.6	...
Germany	82 645	0.1	-2.0	78.6	75.6	81.4	1.3	0.1	30.6	...
Greece	11 098	0.3	-0.4	78.2	75.6	80.8	1.3	0.2	21.5	...
Iceland	292	0.9	-0.6	80.6	78.7	82.5	2.0	0.2	...	...
Ireland	4 080	1.7	2.7	77.7	75.1	80.3	1.9	0.2	36.0	...
Israel	6 601	2.0	1.4	79.6	77.5	81.6	2.9	...	...	...
Italy	58 033	0.1	0.1	80.0	76.8	83.0	1.3	0.5	33.3	...
Luxembourg	459	1.3	0.5	78.4	75.1	81.4	1.7	0.2	...	...
Malta	400	0.5	-3.1	78.3	75.8	80.7	1.5	0.1	...	...
Monaco	35	1.1	...	...	...	...	...	...	...	...
Netherlands	16 226	0.5	0.1	78.3	75.6	81.0	1.7	0.2	34.7	...
Norway	4 598	0.5	-1.2	79.3	76.7	81.8	1.8	0.1	...	...
Portugal	10 441	0.5	0.2	77.2	73.8	80.5	1.5	0.4	4.1	...
San Marino	28	0.9	...	...	...	...	...	...	...	...
Spain	42 646	1.1	3.0	79.4	75.8	83.1	1.3	0.6	22.9	...
Sweden	9 008	0.4	1.1	80.1	77.8	82.3	1.6	0.2	31.3	...
Switzerland	7 240	0.2	-2.3	80.4	77.6	83.1	1.4	0.4	36.9	...
United Kingdom	59 479	0.3	-1.0	78.3	75.9	80.6	1.7	0.2	31.3	...
United States	295 410	1.0	0.6	77.3	74.6	80.0	2.0	0.6	25.0	...
South and West Asia										
Afghanistan	28 574	4.6	3.9	46.0	45.8	46.3	7.5	<0.1	...	...
Bangladesh	139 215	1.9	0.6	62.6	61.8	63.4	3.2	<0.1	12.7	...
Bhutan	2 116	2.2	1.1	62.7	61.5	63.9	4.4	<0.1	...	...
India	1 087 124	1.6	-0.1	63.1	61.7	64.7	3.1	0.9	28.6	...
Iran, Islamic Republic of	68 803	0.9	0.2	70.2	68.8	71.7	2.1	0.2	16.7	...
Maldives	321	2.5	0.4	66.3	66.9	65.8	4.3	...	...	...
Nepal	26 591	2.1	0.0	61.4	60.9	61.7	3.7	0.5	21.6	...
Pakistan	154 794	2.0	0.6	62.9	62.7	63.1	4.3	0.1	16.7	...
Sri Lanka	20 570	0.9	-0.2	73.9	71.3	76.7	2.0	<0.1	...	...
Sub-Saharan Africa										
Angola	15 490	2.8	2.9	40.7	39.2	42.2	6.8	3.7	60.7	160
Benin	8 177	3.2	2.5	53.8	53.0	54.5	5.9	1.8	58.4	62
Botswana	1 769	0.1	-1.3	36.6	36.0	37.1	3.2	24.1	53.8	120
Burkina Faso	12 822	3.2	2.7	47.4	46.7	48.1	6.7	2.0	57.1	120
Burundi	7 282	3.0	2.9	43.5	42.5	44.4	6.8	3.3	60.8	120
Cameroon	16 038	1.9	1.0	45.8	45.1	46.5	4.6	5.4	61.7	240
Cape Verde	495	2.4	2.0	70.2	66.8	73.0	3.8	...	...	...
Central African Republic	3 986	1.3	0.6	39.4	38.5	40.3	5.0	10.7	56.5	140
Chad	9 448	3.4	3.6	43.6	42.5	44.8	6.7	3.5	56.3	57

GNP AND POVERTY					EXTERNAL DEBT[3]					
GNP per capita[3]				Population living on less than US$2 per day (%)[4]	Total debt (US$ millions)	Total debt service (US$ millions)	Total debt as % of GNP	Public debt service as % of government current revenue	Total debt service as % of exports	
Current US$		PPP US$								
1998	2004	1998	2004	1990-2003[5]	2004	2004	2004	2002[6]	2004	Country or territory
3 650	4 210	5 520	6 726	17.6	9 469	1 401	11.0	…	14.3	Panama
1 810	1 140	4 650	4 817	33.2	3 433	501	6.8	22.7[x]	13.5	Paraguay
2 210	2 360	4 410	5 395	37.7	31 296	2 732	4.2	20.5[x]	17.1	Peru
6 020	…	10 030	…	…	316	47	13.4	…	…	Saint Kitts and Nevis
3 690	4 180	5 060	5 595	…	413	26	3.9	…	…	Saint Lucia
2 610	3 400	4 720	6 026	…	257	21	5.5	…	…	St Vincent/Grenad.
2 320	2 230	…	…	…	…	…	…	…	…	Suriname
4 490	8 730	7 260	11 431	39.0	2 926	401	3.4	…	…	Trinidad and Tobago
…	…	…	…	…	…	…	…	…	…	Turks and Caicos Islands
6 620	3 900	8 860	9 026	3.9	12 376	1 543	12.2	26.3[x]	34.9	Uruguay
3 490	4 030	5 760	5 829	32.0	35 570	6 632	6.2	23.1[x]	16.0	Venezuela

North America and Western Europe

…	…	…	…	…	…	…	…	…	…	Andorra
27 040	32 280	25 160	31 803	…	…	…	…	…	…	Austria
25 580	31 280	24 410	31 535	…	…	…	…	…	…	Belgium
20 000	28 310	23 980	30 757	…	…	…	…	…	…	Canada
12 110	16 510	15 140	22 234	…	…	…	…	…	…	Cyprus
32 770	40 750	26 450	31 768	…	…	…	…	…	…	Denmark
24 750	32 880	22 120	29 804	…	…	…	…	…	…	Finland
24 770	30 370	23 180	29 456	…	…	…	…	…	…	France
26 630	30 690	23 900	28 168	…	…	…	…	…	…	Germany
11 780	16 730	15 170	22 229	…	…	…	…	…	…	Greece
27 460	37 920	25 140	32 370	…	…	…	…	…	…	Iceland
20 610	34 310	21 010	32 926	…	…	…	…	…	…	Ireland
16 730	17 360	17 940	23 775	…	…	…	…	…	…	Israel
20 560	26 280	22 820	28 019	…	…	…	…	…	…	Italy
44 700	56 380	42 910	61 610	…	…	…	…	…	…	Luxembourg
8 790	12 050	15 290	18 589	…	…	…	…	…	…	Malta
…	…	…	…	…	…	…	…	…	…	Monaco
25 170	32 130	24 860	31 362	…	…	…	…	…	…	Netherlands
35 240	51 810	32 380	38 680	…	…	…	…	…	…	Norway
10 960	14 220	15 370	19 241	…	…	…	…	…	…	Portugal
…	…	…	…	…	…	…	…	…	…	San Marino
14 830	21 530	17 830	24 750	…	…	…	…	…	…	Spain
28 700	35 840	21 570	29 881	…	…	…	…	…	…	Sweden
41 560	49 600	28 680	35 661	…	…	…	…	…	…	Switzerland
22 830	33 630	22 570	31 431	…	…	…	…	…	…	United Kingdom
30 620	41 440	31 600	39 824	…	…	…	…	…	…	United States

South and West Asia

…	…	…	…	…	…	…	…	…	…	Afghanistan
360	440	1 440	1 969	82.8	20 344	675	1.1	…	5.2	Bangladesh
450	760	…	…	…	593	12	1.8	6.1	…	Bhutan
420	620	2 150	3 116	79.9	122 723	19 094	2.8	13.1[x]	…	India
1 710	2 320	5 420	7 533	7.3	13 622	1 938	1.2	…	…	Iran, Islamic Republic of
1 950	2 410	…	…	…	345	32	4.5	10.1	4.6	Maldives
220	250	1 210	1 485	82.5	3 354	114	1.7	14.9	5.5	Nepal
470	600	1 760	2 174	65.6	35 687	4 285	4.6	19.6	21.2	Pakistan
850	1 010	3 050	4 208	50.7	10 887	766	4.0	19.5[x]	8.5	Sri Lanka

Sub-Saharan Africa

520	930	1 510	1 930	…	9 521	2 050	11.9	…	14.8	Angola
390	450	890	1 085	…	1 916	64	1.6	…	…	Benin
3 290	4 360	6 200	9 581	50.1	524	49	0.6	…	…	Botswana
250	350	950	1 168	81.0	1 967	59	1.2	…	…	Burkina Faso
140	90	600	662	89.2	1 385	88	13.7	…	…	Burundi
600	810	1 620	2 117	50.6	9 496	645	4.6	…	…	Cameroon
1 300	1 720	4 040	5 662	…	517	26	2.7	…	…	Cape Verde
290	310	1 070	1 103	84.0	1 078	18	1.4	…	…	Central African Republic
220	250	860	1 337	…	1 701	46	1.7	…	…	Chad

Table 1 (continued)

Country or territory	Total population (000) 2004	Average annual growth rate (%) total population 2000-2005	Average annual growth rate (%) 0-4 population 2000-2005	Life expectancy at birth (years) 2000-2005 Total	Male	Female	Total fertility rate (children per woman) 2000-2005	HIV prevalence rate (%) in adults (15-49) 2005 Total	% of women among people (age 15+) living with HIV 2005	Orphans due to AIDS (0-17) (000) 2005
Comoros	777	2.6	1.9	63.0	60.9	65.1	4.9	<0.1	…	…
Congo	3 883	3.0	3.2	51.9	50.6	53.1	6.3	5.3	61.0	110
Côte d'Ivoire	17 872	1.6	0.9	46.0	45.2	46.8	5.1	7.1	58.8	450
D. R. Congo	55 853	2.8	3.3	43.1	42.1	44.1	6.7	3.2	58.4	680
Equatorial Guinea	492	2.3	2.5	43.5	42.8	44.2	5.9	3.2	58.8	5
Eritrea	4 232	4.3	4.1	53.5	51.5	55.4	5.5	2.4	58.5	36
Ethiopia	75 600	2.4	1.6	47.6	46.5	48.6	5.9	…	…	…
Gabon	1 362	1.7	0.3	54.6	53.8	55.4	4.0	7.9	58.9	20
Gambia	1 478	2.8	1.9	55.5	54.0	56.9	4.7	2.4	57.9	4
Ghana	21 664	2.1	1.2	56.7	56.2	57.2	4.4	2.3	60.0	170
Guinea	9 202	2.2	1.9	53.6	53.2	54.0	5.9	1.5	67.9	28
Guinea-Bissau	1 540	3.0	3.2	44.6	43.1	46.2	7.1	3.8	58.6	11
Kenya	33 467	2.2	3.0	47.0	47.9	46.2	5.0	6.1	61.7	1 100
Lesotho	1 798	0.1	-0.6	36.7	34.9	38.1	3.6	23.2	60.0	97
Liberia	3 241	1.4	1.7	42.5	41.4	43.5	6.8	…	…	…
Madagascar	18 113	2.8	1.5	55.3	54.0	56.7	5.4	0.5	27.7	13
Malawi	12 608	2.3	1.2	39.6	39.7	39.6	6.1	14.1	58.8	550
Mali	13 124	3.0	2.5	47.8	47.1	48.4	6.9	1.7	60.0	94
Mauritius	1 233	1.0	-0.3	72.1	68.7	75.6	2.0	0.6	…	…
Mozambique	19 424	2.0	1.3	41.9	41.0	42.8	5.5	16.1	60.0	510
Namibia	2 009	1.4	-1.7	48.6	47.7	49.4	4.0	19.6	61.9	85
Niger	13 499	3.4	3.0	44.3	44.2	44.3	7.9	1.1	59.2	46
Nigeria	128 709	2.2	1.6	43.3	43.1	43.5	5.8	3.9	61.5	930
Rwanda	8 882	2.4	2.0	43.6	41.9	45.3	5.7	3.1	56.9	210
Sao Tome and Principe	153	2.3	1.9	62.9	61.9	63.8	4.1	…	…	…
Senegal	11 386	2.4	1.5	55.6	54.4	56.8	5.0	0.9	58.9	25
Seychelles	80	0.9	…	…	…	…	…	…	…	…
Sierra Leone	5 336	4.1	4.3	40.6	39.3	42.0	6.5	1.6	60.5	31
Somalia	7 964	3.2	2.8	46.2	45.0	47.3	6.4	0.9	57.5	23
South Africa	47 208	0.8	-0.1	49.0	47.1	51.0	2.8	18.8	58.5	1 200
Swaziland	1 034	0.2	-1.5	32.9	32.5	33.4	4.0	33.4	57.1	63
Togo	5 988	2.7	2.1	54.2	52.3	56.2	5.4	3.2	61.0	88
Uganda	27 821	3.4	3.7	46.8	46.5	47.1	7.1	6.7	57.8	1 000
United Republic of Tanzania	37 627	2.0	1.1	46.0	45.6	46.4	5.0	6.5	54.6	1 100
Zambia	11 479	1.7	1.2	37.4	37.9	36.9	5.7	17.0	57.0	710
Zimbabwe	12 936	0.6	-0.5	37.2	37.5	36.9	3.6	20.1	59.3	1 100

	Sum	Weighted average						Weighted average		
World	6 374 924	1.2	0.1	67.0	64.9	69.2	2.7	1.0	47.7	15 200
Countries in transition	278 263	-0.3	0.2	65.8	62.0	69.8	1.6	…	…	…
Developed countries	1 002 588	0.5	-0.1	78.3	75.4	81.2	1.6	…	…	…
Developing countries	5 094 073	1.4	0.1	64.9	63.2	66.6	3.1	…	…	…
Arab States	305 562	2.2	1.3	67.3	65.6	69.0	3.6	…	…	…
Central and Eastern Europe	404 186	-0.01	0.1	68.6	64.0	73.6	1.5	…	…	…
Central Asia	75 961	0.7	-0.6	65.7	62.0	69.6	2.4	…	…	…
East Asia and the Pacific	2 086 758	0.8	-1.4	71.2	69.1	73.3	2.2	…	…	…
East Asia	2 054 036	0.8	-1.5	71.1	69.1	73.3	1.9	…	…	…
Pacific	32 721	1.4	0.1	74.2	71.9	76.5	4.6	…	…	…
Latin America/Caribbean	548 723	1.4	0.1	71.5	68.3	74.9	2.6	…	…	…
Caribbean	15 428	1.1	0.2	…	…	…	…	…	…	…
Latin America	533 295	1.4	0.1	72.1	68.9	75.4	2.5	…	…	…
N. America/W. Europe	731 046	0.7	0.2	78.4	75.4	81.2	1.7	…	…	…
South and West Asia	1 528 108	1.7	0.2	63.2	61.9	64.5	3.2	…	…	…
Sub-Saharan Africa	694 581	2.3	1.9	46.0	45.3	46.7	46.6	5.5	…	…

1. United Nations Population Division statistics, 2004 revision, medium variant, UN Population Division (2005).
2. UNAIDS (2006).
3. World Bank (2006c).
4. UNDP (2005).
5. Data are for the most recent year available during the period specified.
6. World Bank (2005c).

GNP AND POVERTY					EXTERNAL DEBT[3]					
GNP per capita[3]				Population living on less than US$2 per day (%)[4]	Total debt (US$ millions)	Total debt service (US$ millions)	Total debt as % of GNP	Public debt service as % of government current revenue	Total debt service as % of exports	
Current US$		PPP US$								
1998	2004	1998	2004	1990-2003[5]	2004	2004	2004	2002[6]	2004	Country or territory
410	560	1 640	1 932	...	306	3	0.9	...	...	Comoros
530	760	670	739	...	5 829	350	10.7	9.2x	...	Congo
780	760	1 510	1 474	38.4	11 739	543	3.7	16.6x	6.9	Côte d'Ivoire
110	110	710	675	...	11 841	121	1.9	...	...	D. R. Congo
1 060	...	3 570	7 579	...	291	5	...	...	...	Equatorial Guinea
220	190	1 070	962	...	681	19	2.1	...	...	Eritrea
100	110	600	750	80.7	6 574	97	1.2	...	5.3	Ethiopia
3 870	4 080	5 570	5 699	...	4 150	223	3.6	...	...	Gabon
320	280	1 500	1 885	82.9	674	34	8.6	...	...	Gambia
380	380	1 760	2 221	78.5	7 035	240	2.7	...	6.6	Ghana
520	410	1 810	2 158	...	3 538	172	4.5	...	19.9	Guinea
140	160	660	694	...	765	45	16.7	...	...	Guinea-Bissau
360	480	990	1 130	58.3	6 826	364	2.3	...	8.6	Kenya
690	730	2 640	3 254	56.1	764	53	3.2	...	4.5	Lesotho
110	120	...	...	...	2 706	1	0.2	...	...	Liberia
260	290	760	843	85.1	3 462	81	1.9	...	...	Madagascar
220	160	560	631	76.1	3 418	60	3.3	...	...	Malawi
250	330	720	953	90.6	3 316	103	2.2	...	...	Mali
3 760	4 640	8 610	11 955	...	2 294	260	4.3	15.8x	7.4	Mauritius
200	270	760	1 168	78.4	4 651	83	1.4	...	4.5	Mozambique
2 050	2 380	5 890	7 515	55.8	...	...	...	...	...	Namibia
200	210	780	776	85.3	1 950	51	1.7	...	...	Niger
260	430	760	966	90.8	35 890	2 412	4.0	...	8.2	Nigeria
250	210	980	1 241	83.7	1 656	24	1.3	...	11.2	Rwanda
270	390	...	...	...	362	10	16.2	...	...	Sao Tome and Principe
510	630	1 330	1 662	67.8	3 938	335	4.4	20.0x	...	Senegal
7 320	8 190	...	15 883	...	615	52	7.7	...	8.1	Seychelles
150	210	470	547	74.5	1 723	27	2.5	...	10.9	Sierra Leone
...	...	...	...	...	2 849	...	...	...	...	Somalia
3 290	3 630	8 820	10 964	34.1	28 500	3 825	1.8	8.1x	6.4	South Africa
1 400	1 660	4 340	5 650	...	470	44	1.8	...	1.7	Swaziland
350	310	1 580	1 508	...	1 812	21	1.0	...	...	Togo
290	250	1 110	1 448	...	4 822	103	1.5	4.9x	6.9	Uganda
230	320	470	671	59.7	7 799	119	1.1	...	5.3	United Republic of Tanzania
330	400	700	890	87.4	7 279	424	8.3	...	...	Zambia
560	620	2 640	2 041	83.0	4 797	93	2.0	...	...	Zimbabwe
Weighted average					Weighted average					
...	6 329	...	8 844	...	...	...	...	...	...	World
...	...	...	...	...	...	...	...	...	...	Countries in transition
...	...	...	...	...	...	...	...	...	...	Developed countries
...	...	...	...	...	...	...	...	...	...	Developing countries
...	...	...	...	...	...	...	...	...	...	Arab States
...	...	...	...	...	...	...	...	...	...	Central and Eastern Europe
...	...	...	...	...	...	...	...	...	...	Central Asia
...	1 416	...	5 332	...	588 888	78 813	3.0	...	6.8	East Asia and the Pacific
...	...	...	...	...	...	...	...	...	...	East Asia
...	...	...	...	...	...	...	...	...	...	Pacific
...	3 576	...	7 661	...	778 970	156 724	8.1	...	26.4	Latin America/Caribbean
...	...	...	...	...	...	...	...	...	...	Caribbean
...	...	...	...	...	...	...	...	...	...	Latin America
...	...	...	...	...	...	...	...	...	...	N. America/W. Europe
...	...	...	...	...	...	...	...	...	...	South and West Asia
...	601	...	1 842	...	235 056	13 808	2.9	...	7.9	Sub-Saharan Africa

(x) Data are for 2001.

Table 2
Adult and youth literacy

Country or territory	ADULT LITERACY RATE (15 and over) (%)									ADULT ILLITERATES (15 and over)					
	1990			2000-2004[1]			Projected 2015			1990		2000-2004[1]		Projected 2015	
	Total	Male	Female	Total	Male	Female	Total	Male	Female	Total (000)	% Female	Total (000)	% Female	Total (000)	% Female
Arab States															
Algeria	53	64	41	70*	80*	60*	80	87	72	6 804	62	6 423	66	5 638	69
Bahrain	82	87	75	87*	89*	84*	93	96	90	61	55	66	49	45	61
Djibouti	53	67	40	…	…	…	…	…	…	146	65	…	…	…	…
Egypt	47	60	34	71*	83*	59*	76	85	67	17 411	63	14 210	71	14 526	70
Iraq	36	51	20	74*	84*	64*	81	88	74	6 607	62	3 707	69	4 371	67
Jordan	82	90	72	90*	95*	85*	95	98	92	320	72	330	74	228	77
Kuwait	77	79	73	93*	94*	91*	96	96	95	317	47	139	49	110	43
Lebanon	80	88	73	…	…	…	…	…	…	349	72	…	…	…	…
Libyan Arab Jamahiriya	68	83	51	…	…	…	…	…	…	780	71	…	…	…	…
Mauritania	35	46	24	51*	60*	43*	59	66	52	743	60	732	60	955	59
Morocco	39	53	25	52*	66*	40*	65	77	54	9 140	62	10 106	65	9 022	68
Oman	55	67	38	81*	87*	74*	91	93	87	458	56	300	57	208	60
Palestinian Autonomous Territories	…	…	…	92*	97*	88*	97	99	96	…	…	153	78	82	75
Qatar	77	77	76	89*	89*	89*	92	92	93	78	28	67	29	58	28
Saudi Arabia	66	76	50	79*	87*	69*	89	94	84	3 288	59	2 681	65	2 253	68
Sudan[2]	46	60	32	61*	71*	52*	71	79	63	8 021	63	7 557	63	8 143	64
Syrian Arab Republic	65	82	48	80*	86*	74*	90	95	84	2 365	75	2 348	65	1 653	77
Tunisia	59	72	47	74*	83*	65*	82	90	75	2 086	65	1 878	68	1 549	71
United Arab Emirates	71	71	71	…	…	…	…	…	…	379	29	…	…	…	…
Yemen	33	55	13	53	72	33	…	…	…	3 852	66	5 288	70	…	…
Central and Eastern Europe															
Albania	77	87	67	99*	99*	98*	99	99	99	509	71	28	69	17	59
Belarus	99	100	99	100*	100*	99*	100	100	100	42	76	33	77	16	54
Bosnia and Herzegovina	…	…	…	97*	99*	94*	97	99	96	…	…	106	86	90	85
Bulgaria	97	98	96	98*	99*	98*	98	99	98	195	70	121	66	99	62
Croatia	97	99	95	98*	99*	97*	99	100	99	113	85	69	83	38	73
Czech Republic	…	…	…	…	…	…	…	…	…	…	…	…	…	…	…
Estonia	100	100	100	100*	100*	100*	100	100	100	3	53	3	57	2	55
Hungary	99	99	99	…	…	…	…	…	…	78	63	…	…	…	…
Latvia	…	…	…	100*	100*	100*	100	100	100	…	…	5	64	4	55
Lithuania	99	100	99	100*	100*	100*	100	100	100	20	67	10	54	8	54
Poland	…	…	…	…	…	…	…	…	…	…	…	…	…	…	…
Republic of Moldova	97	99	96	98*	99*	98*	100	100	100	80	83	56	75	15	54
Romania	97	99	96	97*	98*	96*	98	98	97	519	77	491	71	411	63
Russian Federation	99	100	99	99*	100*	99*	100	100	100	858	76	676	75	343	55
Serbia and Montenegro[2]	…	…	…	96*	99*	94*	98	99	98	…	…	246	85	139	79
Slovakia	…	…	…	…	…	…	…	…	…	…	…	…	…	…	…
Slovenia	100	100	100	100	100	100	…	…	…	7	58	6	56	…	…
TFYR Macedonia	…	…	…	96*	98*	94*	98	99	97	…	…	62	77	41	74
Turkey	78	89	66	87*	95*	80*	92	97	88	8 147	75	6 389	81	4 607	82
Ukraine	99	100	99	99*	100*	99*	100	100	100	237	77	229	80	72	84
Central Asia															
Armenia	97	99	96	99*	100*	99*	100	100	100	63	80	14	76	4	71
Azerbaijan	…	…	…	99*	99*	98*	100	100	100	…	…	67	79	21	88
Georgia	…	…	…	…	…	…	…	…	…	…	…	…	…	…	…
Kazakhstan	99	99	98	100*	100*	99*	100	100	100	133	79	53	77	23	53
Kyrgyzstan	…	…	…	99*	99*	98*	100	100	99	…	…	41	74	17	77
Mongolia	…	…	…	98*	98*	98*	98	97	98	…	..	36	56	53	40
Tajikistan	98	99	97	99*	100*	99*	100	100	100	55	77	19	71	5	51
Turkmenistan	…	…	…	99*	99*	98*	100	100	100	…	…	31	73	12	65
Uzbekistan	99	99	98	…	…	…	…	…	…	164	80	…	…	…	…
East Asia and the Pacific															
Australia	…	…	…	…	…	…	…	…	…	…	…	…	…	…	…
Brunei Darussalam	86	91	79	93*	95*	90*	96	97	94	24	66	17	65	14	67
Cambodia	62	78	49	74*	85*	64*	80	87	72	2 061	74	2 262	73	2 295	71
China	78	87	69	91*	95*	87*	96	98	93	181 331	70	87 019	73	48 790	75
Cook Islands	…	…	…	…	…	…	…	…	…	…	…	…	…	…	…
Democratic People's Republic of Korea	…	…	…	…	…	…	…	…	…	…	…	…	…	…	…

YOUTH LITERACY RATE (15-24) (%)									YOUTH ILLITERATES (15-24)						
1990			2000-2004[1]			Projected 2015			1990		2000-2004[1]		Projected 2015		Country or territory
Total	Male	Female	Total	Male	Female	Total	Male	Female	Total (000)	% Female	Total (000)	% Female	Total (000)	% Female	
															Arab States
77	86	68	90*	94*	86*	94	94	94	1 174	69	705	69	381	51	Algeria
96	96	95	97*	97*	97*	100	100	100	3.5	54	3	43	0.14	48	Bahrain
73	82	64	...	...	...	...	...	...	30	67	...	...	...	...	Djibouti
61	71	51	85*	90*	79*	88	91	86	3 975	62	2 382	67	1 810	60	Egypt
41	56	25	85*	89*	80*	84	87	82	2 260	62	765	63	1 159	57	Iraq
97	98	95	99*	99*	99*	100	100	100	23	66	10	61	6	37	Jordan
88	88	87	100*	100*	100*	100	100	100	46	51	1	38	0.07	44	Kuwait
92	95	89	...	...	...	...	...	...	43	72	...	...	...	...	Lebanon
91	99	83	...	...	...	...	...	...	78	94	...	...	...	...	Libyan Arab Jamahiriya
46	56	36	61*	68*	55*	66	70	63	214	59	199	58	258	56	Mauritania
55	68	42	70*	81*	60*	82	89	74	2 265	64	1 888	67	1 147	69	Morocco
86	95	75	97*	98*	97*	99	100	99	43	82	14	59	3	66	Oman
...	...	...	99*	99*	99*	99	99	100	...	...	7	57	7	29	Palestinian Autonomous Territories
90	88	93	96*	95*	98*	100	100	99	5.7	29	4	24	1	55	Qatar
85	91	79	96*	98*	94*	100	100	100	446	68	157	75	12	49	Saudi Arabia
65	76	54	77*	85*	71*	82	85	78	1 804	65	1 468	64	1 622	59	Sudan[2]
80	92	67	92*	94*	90*	97	98	97	523	81	333	62	121	58	Syrian Arab Republic
84	93	75	94*	96*	92*	98	98	98	263	77	118	67	40	53	Tunisia
85	82	89	...	...	...	...	...	...	43	28	...	...	...	...	United Arab Emirates
50	74	25	72	86	58	...	...	...	1 148	73	1 242	74	...	...	Yemen
															Central and Eastern Europe
95	97	92	99*	99*	99*	99	99	99	34	75	3	46	3	42	Albania
100	100	100	100*	100*	100*	100	100	100	2.7	50	3	40	2	49	Belarus
...	...	...	100*	100*	100*	100	100	100	...	...	1	38	0.46	49	Bosnia and Herzegovina
99	100	99	98*	98*	98*	97	98	97	7.1	59	20	52	19	53	Bulgaria
100	100	100	100*	100*	100*	100	100	100	2.3	52	2	48	2	37	Croatia
...	...	...	...	...	...	...	...	...	...	...	...	...	...	...	Czech Republic
100	100	100	100*	100*	100*	100	100	100	0.5	42	0.5	40	0.27	49	Estonia
100	100	100	...	...	...	...	...	...	3.9	56	...	...	...	...	Hungary
...	...	...	100*	100*	100*	100	100	100	...	...	1	43	1	33	Latvia
100	100	100	100*	100*	100*	100	100	100	1.2	46	1	43	1	49	Lithuania
...	...	...	...	...	...	...	...	...	...	...	...	...	...	...	Poland
100	100	100	100*	99*	100*	100	99	100	1.3	48	4	47	2	0	Republic of Moldova
99	99	99	98*	98*	98*	97	97	97	28	54	77	49	64	45	Romania
100	100	100	100*	100*	100*	100	100	100	42	47	67	41	44	33	Russian Federation
...	...	...	99*	99*	99*	99	99	99	...	...	7	52	8	48	Serbia and Montenegro[2]
...	...	...	...	...	...	...	...	...	...	...	...	...	...	...	Slovakia
100	100	100	100	100	100	...	...	...	0.7	44	1	49	...	...	Slovenia
...	...	...	99*	99*	98*	99	99	99	...	...	4	59	4	56	TFYR Macedonia
93	97	88	96*	98*	93*	96	98	95	843	79	583	77	519	71	Turkey
100	100	100	100*	100*	100*	100	100	100	11	43	14	42	10	49	Ukraine
															Central Asia
100	100	99	100*	100*	100*	100	100	100	2.6	63	1	37	0.45	48	Armenia
...	...	...	100*	100*	100*	100	100	100	...	...	2	43	2	49	Azerbaijan
...	...	...	...	...	...	...	...	...	...	...	...	...	...	...	Georgia
100	100	100	100*	100*	100*	100	100	100	5.9	45	4	40	4	49	Kazakhstan
...	...	...	100*	100*	100*	100	100	100	...	...	3	42	4	49	Kyrgyzstan
...	...	...	98*	97*	98*	96	95	98	...	...	12	34	19	30	Mongolia
100	100	100	100*	100*	100*	100	100	100	2.2	55	2	49	2	49	Tajikistan
...	...	...	100*	100*	100*	100	100	100	...	...	2	49	1.8	46	Turkmenistan
100	100	100	...	...	...	...	...	...	14	57	...	...	...	...	Uzbekistan
															East Asia and the Pacific
...	...	...	...	...	...	...	...	...	...	...	...	...	...	...	Australia
98	98	98	99*	99*	99*	100	100	100	1.0	43	1	49	0.08	97	Brunei Darussalam
73	81	66	83*	88*	79*	90	93	88	479	66	543	63	323	62	Cambodia
95	97	93	99*	99*	99*	100	100	100	11 709	72	2 260	63	980	47	China
...	...	...	...	...	...	...	...	...	...	...	...	...	...	...	Cook Islands
...	...	...	...	...	...	...	...	...	...	...	...	...	...	...	Democratic People's Republic of Korea

Table 2 (continued)

Country or territory	ADULT LITERACY RATE [15 and over] (%) 1990 Total	Male	Female	2000-2004[1] Total	Male	Female	Projected 2015 Total	Male	Female	ADULT ILLITERATES [15 and over] 1990 Total (000)	% Female	2000-2004[1] Total (000)	% Female	Projected 2015 Total (000)	% Female
Fiji	89	92	85	...	...	...	...	...	...	51	63	...	...	...	...
Indonesia	80	87	73	90*	94*	87*	95	97	93	23 791	68	15 100	69	8 805	70
Japan	...	...	...	...	...	...	...	...	...	...	...	...	...	...	...
Kiribati	...	...	...	...	...	...	...	...	...	...	...	...	...	...	...
Lao People's Democratic Republic	57	70	43	69*	77*	61*	77	82	72	1 017	67	970	64	1 066	62
Macao, China	91	95	87	91*	95*	88*	95	97	93	26	73	31	74	21	74
Malaysia	81	87	74	89*	92*	85*	93	95	91	2 190	66	1 722	64	1 441	64
Marshall Islands	...	...	...	...	...	...	...	...	...	...	...	...	...	...	...
Micronesia (Federated States of)	...	...	...	...	...	...	...	...	...	...	...	...	...	...	...
Myanmar	81	87	74	90*	94*	86*	93	95	92	4 922	68	3 201	70	2 812	63
Nauru	30	47	14	...	...	...	...	...	...	...	...	...	...	...	...
New Zealand	...	...	...	...	...	...	...	...	...	...	...	...	...	...	...
Niue	...	...	...	...	...	...	...	...	...	...	...	...	...	...	...
Palau	...	...	...	...	...	...	...	...	...	...	...	...	...	...	...
Papua New Guinea	57	64	48	57*	63*	51*	63	66	60	1 046	57	1 321	56	1 718	53
Philippines	92	92	91	93*	93*	93*	94	94	95	2 986	53	3 503	50	3 929	47
Republic of Korea	...	...	...	...	...	...	...	...	...	...	...	...	...	...	...
Samoa	98	99	97	99	99	99	...	...	...	1.9	61	1	57	...	...
Singapore	89	94	83	93*	97*	89*	96	98	95	265	75	232	77	151	74
Solomon Islands	...	...	...	...	...	...	...	...	...	...	...	...	...	...	...
Thailand	...	...	...	93*	95*	91*	96	97	95	...	...	3 354	66	2 341	66
Timor-Leste	...	...	...	...	...	...	...	...	...	...	...	...	...	...	...
Tokelau	...	...	...	...	...	...	...	...	...	...	...	...	...	...	...
Tonga	...	...	...	99*	99*	99*	99	99	100	...	...	1	47	0.37	47
Tuvalu	...	...	...	...	...	...	...	...	...	...	...	...	...	...	...
Vanuatu	...	...	...	74*	...	...	...	...	...	...	...	28	...	...	...
Viet Nam	...	...	...	90*	94*	87*	94	95	93	...	...	4 909	69	4 419	58
Latin America and the Caribbean															
Anguilla	...	...	...	...	...	...	...	...	...	...	...	...	...	...	...
Antigua and Barbuda	...	...	...	...	...	...	...	...	...	...	...	...	...	...	...
Argentina	96	96	96	97*	97*	97*	98	98	98	965	54	756	52	617	49
Aruba	...	...	...	97*	98*	97*	...	...	...	...	...	2	57	...	...
Bahamas	94	94	95	...	...	...	...	...	...	10	44	...	...	...	...
Barbados	99	99	99	...	...	...	...	...	...	1.2	57	...	...	...	...
Belize	...	...	...	...	...	...	...	...	...	...	...	...	...	...	...
Bermuda	...	...	...	...	...	...	...	...	...	...	...	...	...	...	...
Bolivia	78	87	70	87*	93*	81*	93	97	90	862	71	683	74	476	77
Brazil	82	83	81	89*	88*	89*	94	93	94	17 369	53	15 052	50	9 837	47
British Virgin Islands	...	...	...	...	...	...	...	...	...	...	...	...	...	...	...
Cayman Islands	...	...	...	...	...	...	...	...	...	...	...	...	...	...	...
Chile	94	94	94	96*	96*	96*	97	97	97	555	55	495	52	397	51
Colombia	88	89	88	93*	93*	93*	96	96	97	2 584	53	2 217	52	1 379	48
Costa Rica	94	94	94	95*	95*	95*	96	96	97	121	50	138	47	134	46
Cuba	95	95	95	100*	100*	100*	100	100	100	395	51	18	52	9.5	50
Dominica	...	...	...	...	...	...	...	...	...	...	...	...	...	...	...
Dominican Republic	79	80	79	87*	87*	87*	93	92	93	891	50	731	49	528	45
Ecuador	88	90	85	91*	92*	90*	94	95	93	775	60	741	57	643	56
El Salvador	72	76	69	81	84	79	89	90	87	835	59	857	58	647	59
Grenada	...	...	...	...	...	...	...	...	...	...	...	...	...	...	...
Guatemala	61	69	53	69*	75*	63*	78	83	73	1 895	60	2 035	62	2 116	65
Guyana	97	98	96	...	...	...	...	...	...	13	66	...	...	...	...
Haiti	40	43	37	...	...	...	...	...	...	2 305	55	...	...	...	...
Honduras	68	69	67	80*	80*	80*	86	85	87	851	51	773	49	814	46
Jamaica	82	78	86	80*	74*	86*	...	...	...	274	40	340	37	...	...
Mexico	87	91	84	91*	92*	90*	96	96	95	6 501	64	6 521	60	3 975	62
Montserrat	...	...	...	...	...	...	...	...	...	...	...	...	...	...	...
Netherlands Antilles	96	96	96	97	97	97	...	...	...	6.1	52	4	53	...	...
Nicaragua	63	63	63	77*	77*	77*	84	83	85	787	51	691	51	708	46
Panama	89	90	88	92*	93*	91*	94	95	94	171	53	163	54	156	55
Paraguay	90	92	88	...	...	...	...	...	...	237	60	...	...	...	...
Peru	...	...	...	88*	93*	82*	92	96	89	...	...	2 271	73	1 762	73
Saint Kitts and Nevis	...	...	...	...	...	...	...	...	...	...	...	...	...	...	...

YOUTH LITERACY RATE (15-24) (%)									YOUTH ILLITERATES (15-24)						Country or territory
1990			2000-2004[1]			Projected 2015			1990		2000-2004[1]		Projected 2015		
Total	Male	Female	Total	Male	Female	Total	Male	Female	Total (000)	% Female	Total (000)	% Female	Total (000)	% Female	
98	98	98	...	...	...	...	...	...	2.9	54	...	...	...	...	Fiji
95	97	93	99*	99*	99*	99	99	99	1 872	65	549	56	322	38	Indonesia
...	...	...	...	...	...	...	...	...	...	...	...	...	...	...	Japan
...	...	...	...	...	...	...	...	...	...	...	...	...	...	...	Kiribati
70	79	61	78*	83*	75*	84	87	81	235	66	225	59	238	59	Lao People's Democratic Republic
97	99	96	100*	99*	100*	100	100	100	1.6	88	0.25	26	0	50	Macao, China
95	95	94	97*	97*	97*	99	99	99	179	55	120	48	66	45	Malaysia
...	...	...	...	...	...	...	...	...	...	...	...	...	...	...	Marshall Islands
...	...	...	...	...	...	...	...	...	...	...	...	...	...	...	Micronesia (Federated States of)
88	90	86	95*	96*	93*	97	96	97	973	58	524	60	333	41	Myanmar
47	67	27	...	...	...	...	...	...	...	...	...	...	...	...	Nauru
...	...	...	...	...	...	...	...	...	...	...	...	...	...	...	New Zealand
...	...	...	...	...	...	...	...	...	...	...	...	...	...	...	Niue
...	...	...	...	...	...	...	...	...	...	...	...	...	...	...	Palau
69	74	62	67*	69*	64*	68	66	69	277	60	342	52	496	46	Papua New Guinea
97	97	97	95*	94*	96*	95	94	96	342	46	759	43	947	40	Philippines
...	...	...	...	...	...	...	...	...	...	...	...	...	...	...	Republic of Korea
99	99	99	100	99	100	...	...	...	0.3	49	0.2	39	...	...	Samoa
99	99	99	100*	99*	100*	100	99	100	5.6	39	2	38	2	16	Singapore
...	...	...	...	...	...	...	...	...	...	...	...	...	...	...	Solomon Islands
...	...	...	98*	98*	98*	99	99	99	...	...	223	53	143	50	Thailand
...	...	...	...	...	...	...	...	...	...	...	...	...	...	...	Timor-Leste
...	...	...	...	...	...	...	...	...	...	...	...	...	...	...	Tokelau
...	...	...	99*	99*	99*	100	100	100	...	...	0.13	46	0.02	72	Tonga
...	...	...	...	...	...	...	...	...	...	...	...	...	...	...	Tuvalu
...	...	...	...	...	...	...	...	...	...	...	...	...	...	...	Vanuatu
94	94	94	94*	94*	94*	96	95	96	802	54	956	52	734	44	Viet Nam
															Latin America and the Caribbean
...	...	...	...	...	...	...	...	...	...	...	...	...	...	...	Anguilla
...	...	...	...	...	...	...	...	...	...	...	...	...	...	...	Antigua and Barbuda
98	98	98	99*	99*	99*	99	99	99	97	44	71	40	55	43	Argentina
...	...	...	99*	99*	99*	...	...	...	...	...	0.11	43	...	...	Aruba
96	95	98	...	...	...	...	...	...	1.9	34	...	...	...	...	Bahamas
100	100	100	...	...	...	...	...	...	0.1	49	...	...	...	...	Barbados
...	...	...	...	...	...	...	...	...	...	...	...	...	...	...	Belize
...	...	...	...	...	...	...	...	...	...	...	...	...	...	...	Bermuda
93	96	89	97*	99*	96*	99	99	99	98	74	43	72	22	49	Bolivia
92	91	93	97*	96*	98*	99	98	100	2 363	42.0	1 123	33	309	17	Brazil
...	...	...	...	...	...	...	...	...	...	...	...	...	...	...	British Virgin Islands
...	...	...	...	...	...	...	...	...	...	...	...	...	...	...	Cayman Islands
98	98	98	99*	99*	99*	99	99	99	48	44	26	40	20	42	Chile
95	94	96	98*	98*	98*	99	98	100	369	44	167	39	106	19	Colombia
97	97	98	98*	97*	98*	98	98	98	15	43	18	40	16	41	Costa Rica
99	99	99	100*	100*	100*	100	100	100	17	51	1	51	0	0	Cuba
...	...	...	...	...	...	...	...	...	...	...	...	...	...	...	Dominica
87	87	88	94*	93*	95*	96	94	98	190	47	102	39	76	24	Dominican Republic
95	96	95	96*	96*	96*	97	96	97	95	56	88	49	91	43	Ecuador
84	85	83	90	91	89	96	95	96	172	55	132	53	64	44	El Salvador
...	...	...	...	...	...	...	...	...	...	...	...	...	...	...	Grenada
73	80	66	82*	86*	78*	87	89	85	461	63	421	62	425	60	Guatemala
100	100	100	...	...	...	...	...	...	0.3	51	...	...	...	...	Guyana
55	56	54	...	...	...	...	...	...	578	51	...	...	...	...	Haiti
80	78	81	89*	87*	91*	91	88	94	201	47	152	40	159	32	Honduras
91	87	95	...	...	...	...	...	...	42	28	...	...	...	...	Jamaica
95	96	94	98*	98*	98*	99	98	99	897	59	492	49	284	40	Mexico
...	...	...	...	...	...	...	...	...	...	...	...	...	...	...	Montserrat
97	97	98	98	98	99	...	...	...	0.7	46	0.4	44	...	...	Netherlands Antilles
68	68	69	86*	84*	89*	91	87	95	254	49	154	40	124	28	Nicaragua
95	96	95	96*	97*	96*	96	97	96	24	54	21	55	23	52	Panama
96	96	95	...	...	...	...	...	...	36	53	...	...	...	...	Paraguay
94	97	92	97*	98*	96*	98	98	98	243	71	174	66	124	49	Peru
...	...	...	...	...	...	...	...	...	...	...	...	...	...	...	Saint Kitts and Nevis

Table 2 (continued)

Country or territory	ADULT LITERACY RATE (15 and over) (%) 1990 Total	Male	Female	2000-2004[1] Total	Male	Female	Projected 2015 Total	Male	Female	ADULT ILLITERATES (15 and over) 1990 Total (000)	% Female	2000-2004[1] Total (000)	% Female	Projected 2015 Total (000)	% Female
Saint Lucia	...	...	...	...	...	...	...	...	...	...	...	...	...	...	...
Saint Vincent and the Grenadines	...	...	...	...	...	...	...	...	...	...	...	...	...	...	...
Suriname	...	...	...	90*	92*	87*	93	95	92	...	...	32	62	23	62
Trinidad and Tobago	97	98	96	99	99	98	...	...	...	26	70	13	69	...	...
Turks and Caicos Islands	...	...	...	...	...	...	...	...	...	...	...	...	...	...	...
Uruguay	97	96	97	98	98	98	...	...	...	80	46	53	42	...	...
Venezuela	89	90	88	93*	93*	93*	96	95	96	1 358	55	1 166	52	973	47
North America and Western Europe															
Andorra	...	...	...	...	...	...	...	...	...	...	...	...	...	...	...
Austria	...	...	...	...	...	...	...	...	...	...	...	...	...	...	...
Belgium	...	...	...	...	...	...	...	...	...	...	...	...	...	...	...
Canada	...	...	...	...	...	...	...	...	...	...	...	...	...	...	...
Cyprus	94	98	91	97*	99*	95*	99	99	98	29	80	18	79	10.7	74
Denmark	...	...	...	...	...	...	...	...	...	...	...	...	...	...	...
Finland	...	...	...	...	...	...	...	...	...	...	...	...	...	...	...
France	...	...	...	...	...	...	...	...	...	...	...	...	...	...	...
Germany	...	...	...	...	...	...	...	...	...	...	...	...	...	...	...
Greece	95	98	92	96*	98*	94*	98	99	97	419	77	375	73	231.8	69
Iceland	...	...	...	...	...	...	...	...	...	...	...	...	...	...	...
Ireland	...	...	...	...	...	...	...	...	...	...	...	...	...	...	...
Israel	91	95	88	97*	98*	96*	99	99	98	267	71	136	74	81	77
Italy	...	...	...	98*	99*	98*	99	99	99	...	...	785	64	427	64
Luxembourg	...	...	...	...	...	...	...	...	...	...	...	...	...	...	...
Malta	88	88	89	88*	86*	89*	93	91	94	32	49	36	45	26	39
Monaco	...	...	...	...	...	...	...	...	...	...	...	...	...	...	...
Netherlands	...	...	...	...	...	...	...	...	...	...	...	...	...	...	...
Norway	...	...	...	...	...	...	...	...	...	...	...	...	...	...	...
Portugal	...	...	...	...	...	...	...	...	...	...	...	...	...	...	...
San Marino	...	...	...	...	...	...	...	...	...	...	...	...	...	...	...
Spain	...	...	...	...	...	...	...	...	...	...	...	...	...	...	...
Sweden	...	...	...	...	...	...	...	...	...	...	...	...	...	...	...
Switzerland	...	...	...	...	...	...	...	...	...	...	...	...	...	...	...
United Kingdom	...	...	...	...	...	...	...	...	...	...	...	...	...	...	...
United States	...	...	...	...	...	...	...	...	...	...	...	...	...	...	...
South and West Asia															
Afghanistan	...	...	...	28*	43*	13*	36	52	19	...	...	9 048	59	14 585	61
Bangladesh	34	44	24	43	52	33	...	...	...	40 405	56	52 530	57	...	...
Bhutan	...	...	...	...	...	...	...	...	...	...	...	...	...	...	...
India	49	62	36	61*	73*	48*	70	80	60	273 066	61	268 426	65	274 871	66
Iran, Islamic Republic of	63	72	54	77*	84*	70*	...	...	...	11 501	61	10 509	64	...	...
Maldives	95	95	95	96*	96*	96*	98	97	98	6.0	50	6	47	6.7	45
Nepal	30	47	14	49*	63*	35*	63	76	52	7 718	62	7 661	65	7 923	68
Pakistan	35	49	20	50*	63*	36*	61	72	50	40 817	60	48 818	62	49 413	63
Sri Lanka[2]	89	93	85	91*	92*	89*	93	94	92	1 342	67	1 380	57	1 262	54
Sub-Saharan Africa															
Angola	...	...	...	67*	83*	54*	70	81	60	...	...	2 401	74	3 403	69
Benin	26	38	15	35*	48*	23*	43	56	30	2 014	59	2 718	60	3 718	61
Botswana	68	66	70	81*	80*	82*	87	86	88	249	49	206	50	146	46
Burkina Faso	...	...	...	22*	29*	15*	32	37	27	...	...	5 052	55	6 554	53
Burundi	37	48	27	59*	67*	52*	70	74	66	1 950	61	1 373	62	1 724	58
Cameroon	58	69	48	68*	77*	60*	...	...	...	2 699	64	2 764	64	...	...
Cape Verde	64	76	54	78	87	71	...	...	...	67	71	68	71	...	...
Central African Republic	33	47	21	49*	65*	33*	56	69	44	1 132	63	1 107	67	1 218	66
Chad	28	37	19	26*	41*	13*	38	54	22	2 375	58	3 206	61	4 166	64
Comoros	54	61	46	...	...	...	...	...	...	129	59	...	...	...	...
Congo	67	77	58	...	...	...	...	...	...	440	66	...	...	...	...
Côte d'Ivoire	39	51	26	49*	61*	39*	58	67	49	4 151	57	4 733	59	5 567	60
D. R. Congo	47	61	34	67*	81*	54*	67	76	58	10 519	64	8 901	71	13 353	64
Equatorial Guinea	73	86	61	87*	93*	80*	92	94	90	55	74	33	76	28	63

YOUTH LITERACY RATE (15-24) (%)									YOUTH ILLITERATES (15-24)						Country or territory
1990			2000-2004[1]			Projected 2015			1990		2000-2004[1]		Projected 2015		
Total	Male	Female	Total	Male	Female	Total	Male	Female	Total (000)	% Female	Total (000)	% Female	Total (000)	% Female	
...	...	...	...	...	...	...	...	...	...	...	...	...	...	...	Saint Lucia
...	...	...	...	...	...	...	...	...	...	...	...	...	...	...	Saint Vincent and the Grenadines
...	...	...	95*	96*	94*	96	97	95	...	...	5	57	3	58	Suriname
100	100	100	100	100	100	...	...	...	0.8	51	1	50	...	...	Trinidad and Tobago
...	...	...	...	...	...	...	...	...	...	...	...	...	...	...	Turks and Caicos Islands
99	98	99	99	99	100	...	...	...	6	34	4	32	...	...	Uruguay
96	95	97	97*	96*	98*	98	97	99	155	42	137	34	120	27	Venezuela
															North America and Western Europe
...	...	...	...	...	...	...	...	...	...	...	...	...	...	...	Andorra
...	...	...	...	...	...	...	...	...	...	...	...	...	...	...	Austria
...	...	...	...	...	...	...	...	...	...	...	...	...	...	...	Belgium
...	...	...	...	...	...	...	...	...	...	...	...	...	...	...	Canada
100	100	100	100*	100*	100*	100	100	100	0.3	29	0.25	40	0.12	49	Cyprus
...	...	...	...	...	...	...	...	...	...	...	...	...	...	...	Denmark
...	...	...	...	...	...	...	...	...	...	...	...	...	...	...	Finland
...	...	...	...	...	...	...	...	...	...	...	...	...	...	...	France
...	...	...	...	...	...	...	...	...	...	...	...	...	...	...	Germany
100	99	100	99*	99*	99*	100	100	100	7	37	16	45	5	57	Greece
...	...	...	...	...	...	...	...	...	...	...	...	...	...	...	Iceland
...	...	...	...	...	...	...	...	...	...	...	...	...	...	...	Ireland
99	99	98	100*	100*	100*	100	100	100	10	61	2	100	.	.	Israel
...	...	...	100*	100*	100*	100	100	100	...	...	12	47	7	57	Italy
...	...	...	...	...	...	...	...	...	...	...	...	...	...	...	Luxembourg
98	96	99	96*	94*	98*	97	96	99	1.3	18	2	27	1.3	20	Malta
...	...	...	...	...	...	...	...	...	...	...	...	...	...	...	Monaco
...	...	...	...	...	...	...	...	...	...	...	...	...	...	...	Netherlands
...	...	...	...	...	...	...	...	...	...	...	...	...	...	...	Norway
...	...	...	...	...	...	...	...	...	...	...	...	...	...	...	Portugal
...	...	...	...	...	...	...	...	...	...	...	...	...	...	...	San Marino
...	...	...	...	...	...	...	...	...	...	...	...	...	...	...	Spain
...	...	...	...	...	...	...	...	...	...	...	...	...	...	...	Sweden
...	...	...	...	...	...	...	...	...	...	...	...	...	...	...	Switzerland
...	...	...	...	...	...	...	...	...	...	...	...	...	...	...	United Kingdom
...	...	...	...	...	...	...	...	...	...	...	...	...	...	...	United States
															South and West Asia
...	...	...	34*	51*	18*	49	66	30	...	...	2 889	61	4 259	66	Afghanistan
42	51	33	51	59	43	...	...	...	12 240	56	13 941	57	...	...	Bangladesh
...	...	...	...	...	...	...	...	...	...	...	...	...	...	...	Bhutan
64	73	54	76*	84*	68*	84	88	79	59 032	61	46 290	66	37 689	62	India
86	92	81	...	...	...	...	...	...	1 424	68	...	...	...	...	Iran, Islamic Republic of
98	98	98	98*	98*	98*	98	98	99	0.7	48	1	46	1	41	Maldives
47	67	27	70*	81*	60*	83	88	77	1 921	68	1 437	66	1 193	65	Nepal
47	63	31	65*	76*	55*	74	80	68	10 787	63	11 612	64	10 039	60	Pakistan
95	96	94	96*	95*	96*	97	97	98	171	57	168	43	99	39	Sri Lanka[2]
															Sub-Saharan Africa
...	...	...	72*	84*	63*	70	77	64	...	...	749	70	1 256	61	Angola
40	57	25	45*	59*	33*	53	65	40	569	63	828	61	1 065	62	Benin
83	79	87	94*	92*	96*	97	95	100	50	38	26	36	11	2	Botswana
...	...	...	31*	38*	25*	40	41	39	...	...	1 725	54	2 199	50	Burkina Faso
52	58	45	73*	77*	70*	78	78	78	517	57	348	57	440	49	Burundi
81	86	76	...	...	...	...	...	...	414	64	...	...	...	...	Cameroon
81	87	76	91	93	88	...	...	...	13	65	11	62	...	...	Cape Verde
52	66	39	59*	70*	47*	62	70	54	262	65	315	65	397	62	Central African Republic
48	58	38	38*	56*	23*	46	61	31	592	60	955	64	1 375	65	Chad
57	64	50	...	...	...	...	...	...	45	58	...	...	...	...	Comoros
93	95	90	...	...	...	...	...	...	36	66	...	...	...	...	Congo
53	65	40	61*	71*	52*	66	72	59	1 052	62	1 349	62	1 611	59	Côte d'Ivoire
69	80	58	70*	78*	63*	67	71	62	2 226	68	3 013	63	5 091	57	D. R. Congo
93	97	89	95*	95*	95*	95	93	97	4.7	77	4	49	7	33	Equatorial Guinea

Table 2 (continued)

Country or territory	ADULT LITERACY RATE (15 and over) (%)									ADULT ILLITERATES (15 and over)					
	1990			2000-2004[1]			Projected 2015			1990		2000-2004[1]		Projected 2015	
	Total	Male	Female	Total	Male	Female	Total	Male	Female	Total (000)	% Female	Total (000)	% Female	Total (000)	% Female
Eritrea	46	58	35	...	...	...	...	...	...	874	64	...	...	...	...
Ethiopia	29	37	20	45	52	38	...	...	...	19 815	57	23 554	57	...	...
Gabon	...	...	...	...	...	...	...	...	...	...	...	...	...	...	...
Gambia	26	32	20	...	...	...	...	...	...	397	55	...	...	...	...
Ghana	58	70	47	58*	66*	50*	58	64	51	3 546	64	4 894	60	7 306	57
Guinea	27	42	13	29*	43*	18*	52	63	40	2 545	59	3 507	58	3 293	61
Guinea-Bissau	...	...	...	...	...	...	...	...	...	...	...	...	...	...	...
Kenya	71	81	61	74*	78*	70*	77	78	77	3 508	68	4 480	58	5 755	51
Lesotho	78	65	89	82*	74*	90*	...	...	...	183	29	182	32	...	...
Liberia	39	55	23	...	...	...	...	...	...	690	64	...	...	...	...
Madagascar	58	66	50	71*	77*	65*	71	74	68	2 780	60	2 609	60	4 150	55
Malawi	52	69	36	64*	75*	54*	75	81	69	2 429	69	2 133	69	2 190	62
Mali	...	...	...	19*	27*	12*	26	34	18	...	...	4 601	56	7 131	56
Mauritius	80	85	75	84*	88*	81*	90	91	88	150	62	138	63	109	59
Mozambique	33	49	18	...	...	...	...	...	...	4 850	65	...	...	...	...
Namibia	75	77	72	85*	87*	83*	90	90	91	197	56	163	57	142	48
Niger	11	18	5	29*	43*	15*	40	52	26	3 821	53	5 033	59	6 061	60
Nigeria	49	59	38	...	...	...	...	...	...	25 081	61	...	...	...	...
Rwanda	53	63	44	65*	71*	60*	73	76	71	1 661	62	1 471	61	1 757	57
Sao Tome and Principe	...	...	...	...	...	...	...	...	...	...	...	...	...	...	...
Senegal	28	38	19	39*	51*	29*	46	56	37	3 058	59	3 672	61	4 780	61
Seychelles	...	...	...	92*	91*	92*	...	...	...	...	...	5	50	...	...
Sierra Leone	...	...	...	35*	47*	24*	33	44	22	...	...	1 972	60	2 656	59
Somalia	...	...	...	...	...	...	...	...	...	...	...	...	...	...	...
South Africa	81	82	80	82*	84*	81*	92	92	91	4 252	54	4 867	56	2 839	51
Swaziland	72	74	70	80*	81*	78*	86	86	87	130	59	118	57	85	49
Togo	44	60	29	53*	69*	38*	71	81	61	1 183	65	1 391	67	1 379	67
Uganda	56	69	43	67*	77*	58*	79	85	74	3 987	65	4 230	65	4 318	63
United Republic of Tanzania	63	76	51	69*	78*	62*	75	80	71	5 277	68	6 194	63	6 858	59
Zambia	68	79	59	68*	76*	60*	69	73	64	1 413	67	1 797	63	2 441	57
Zimbabwe	81	87	75	...	...	...	...	...	...	1 101	66	...	...	...	...

	Weighted average									Sum	%F	Sum	%F	Sum	%F
World	75	82	69	82	87	77	87	91	84	874 019	63	780 657	64	684 160	65
Countries in transition	99	100	99	99	100	99	100	100	100	1 757	78	1 340	76	599	61
Developed countries	98	99	98	99	99	99	99	100	99	14 855	64	9 062	63	9 318	75
Developing countries	67	76	58	77	83	70	84	88	79	857 407	63	770 255	64	674 244	65
Arab States	50	64	36	66	77	55	79	86	71	63 659	63	57 812	66	55 111	67
Central and Eastern Europe	96	98	95	97	99	96	98	99	97	11 494	75	9 320	79	6 871	78
Central Asia	99	99	98	99	100	99	100	100	100	569	79	382	72	232	57
East Asia and the Pacific	82	89	75	92	95	88	96	97	94	232 691	69	125 359	71	80 765	71
East Asia	...	...	...	92	95	88	96	97	94	...	...	123 758	71	78 907	71
Pacific	...	...	...	93	94	93	93	94	93	...	...	1 600	57	1 858	54
Latin America and the Caribbean	85	87	83	90	91	89	94	95	94	41 838	57	38 572	55	26 225	54
Caribbean	...	...	...	70	70	70	97	96	97	...	...	2 935	51	1 027	46
Latin America	...	...	...	90	91	90	94	95	94	...	...	35 637	55	25 198	54
North America and Western Europe	98	98	97	99	99	99	100	100	100	11 324	64	6 312	62	2 422	63
South and West Asia	47	60	34	59	71	46	68	78	58	379 849	60	399 016	63	344 529	66
Sub-Saharan Africa	50	60	40	61	70	53	67	73	61	132 597	61	143 885	61	168 007	59

Note: For countries indicated with (*), national observed literacy data are used. For all others, UIS literacy estimates are used. The estimates were generated in July 2002, using the previous UIS assessment model. They are based on observed data for years between 1990 and 1994.

The population used to generate the number of illiterates is from the United Nations Population Division 2004 estimates (2005). For countries with national observed literacy data, the population corresponding to the year of the census or survey was used. For countries with UIS estimates, the population used was that of 2005.

YOUTH LITERACY RATE (15-24) (%)   YOUTH ILLITERATES (15-24)

1990 Total	1990 Male	1990 Female	2000-2004[1] Total	2000-2004[1] Male	2000-2004[1] Female	Projected 2015 Total	Projected 2015 Male	Projected 2015 Female	1990 Total (000)	1990 % Female	2000-2004[1] Total (000)	2000-2004[1] % Female	Projected 2015 Total (000)	Projected 2015 % Female	Country or territory
61	73	49	...	...	...	...	...	...	234	65	...	...	...	...	Eritrea
43	52	34	61	66	56	...	...	...	5 587	58	6 098	56	...	...	Ethiopia
...	...	...	...	...	...	...	...	...	...	...	...	...	...	...	Gabon
42	50	34	...	...	...	...	...	...	95	58	...	...	...	...	Gambia
82	88	75	71*	76*	65*	70	73	67	537	67	1 200	58	1 590	54	Ghana
44	62	26	47*	59*	34*	65	75	55	647	65	908	60	834	63	Guinea
...	...	...	...	...	...	...	...	...	...	...	...	...	...	...	Guinea-Bissau
90	93	87	80*	80*	81*	77	74	80	477	65	1 349	49	1 966	43	Kenya
87	77	97	...	...	...	...	...	...	38	12	...	...	...	...	Lesotho
57	75	39	...	...	...	...	...	...	176	71	...	...	...	...	Liberia
72	78	67	70*	73*	68*	69	69	68	645	60	923	54	1 555	51	Madagascar
63	76	51	76*	82*	71*	84	85	83	655	68	525	62	573	52	Malawi
...	...	...	24*	32*	17*	32	39	24	...	...	1 692	54	2 565	54	Mali
91	91	91	95*	94*	95*	97	95	98	18	49	12	42	7	29	Mauritius
49	66	32	...	...	...	...	...	...	1 358	68	...	...	...	...	Mozambique
87	86	89	92*	91*	93*	93	91	95	36	44	29	42	39	37	Namibia
17	25	9	37*	52*	23*	48	58	39	1 350	53	1 667	60	1 980	58	Niger
74	81	66	...	...	...	...	...	...	4 445	63	...	...	...	...	Nigeria
73	78	67	78*	79*	77*	78	78	79	362	60	382	53	495	50	Rwanda
...	...	...	...	...	...	...	...	...	...	...	...	...	...	...	Sao Tome and Principe
40	50	30	49*	58*	41*	53	60	46	912	58	1 142	59	1 421	57	Senegal
...	...	...	99*	99*	99*	...	...	...	...	...	0.13	35	...	...	Seychelles
...	...	...	48*	59*	37*	48	58	39	...	...	522	61	691	59	Sierra Leone
...	...	...	...	...	...	...	...	...	...	...	...	...	...	...	Somalia
88	89	88	94*	93*	94*	97	96	98	865	51	531	47	299	33	South Africa
85	85	85	88*	87*	90*	89	87	91	26	52	26	45	30	42	Swaziland
63	79	48	74*	84*	64*	84	87	80	275	72	288	69	265	60	Togo
70	80	60	77*	83*	71*	88	89	86	1 034	66	1 216	62	998	55	Uganda
83	89	77	78*	81*	76*	78	78	78	853	68	1 628	55	2 170	49	United Republic of Tanzania
81	86	76	69*	73*	66*	67	68	65	315	64	663	55	1 042	52	Zambia
94	97	91	...	...	...	...	...	...	130	72	...	...	...	...	Zimbabwe

Weighted average Total	Male	Female	Total	Male	Female	Total	Male	Female	Sum	%F	Sum	%F	Sum	%F	
84	88	80	87	90	84	90	92	89	157 212	62	138 973	62	114 256	58	World
99	99	99	100	100	100	100	100	100	332	49	122	45	88	38	Countries in transition
100	100	100	99	99	99	99	100	99	471	51	768	50	770	61	Developed countries
81	86	76	85	89	81	89	91	87	156 410	62	138 083	62	113 399	58	Developing countries
67	77	55	82	88	77	89	92	87	14 426	65	9 426	67	7 508	60	Arab States
98	99	97	99	99	98	98	99	98	1 019	75	823	68	777	64	Central and Eastern Europe
98	98	98	100	100	100	100	100	100	280	50	47	48	59	38	Central Asia
95	97	94	98	98	98	99	99	99	17 420	68	6 767	57	4 756	46	East Asia and the Pacific
...	...	...	98	98	98	99	99	99	...	...	6 375	57	4 234	46	East Asia
...	...	...	92	93	92	90	90	90	...	...	392	52	522	46	Pacific
93	93	93	96	96	96	98	98	98	6 369	50	4 109	45	2 129	38	Latin America and the Caribbean
...	...	...	77	76	78	98	97	99	...	...	745	47	164	25	Caribbean
...	...	...	97	96	97	98	98	98	...	...	3 364	44	1 965	39	Latin America
100	100	100	99	100	99	100	100	100	310	48	493	50	118	46	North America and Western Europe
61	71	51	72	80	63	82	86	76	86 921	61	80 415	63	46 697	64	South and West Asia
67	75	60	73	78	68	72	74	69	30 468	61	36 894	59	52 212	55	Sub-Saharan Africa

1. Data are for the most recent year available during the period specified.
See the introduction to the statistical tables for a broader explanation of national
literacy definitions, assessment methods, sources and years of data.
2. Literacy data for the most recent year do not include some geographic regions.

Table 3A
Early childhood care and education (ECCE): care

	CHILD SURVIVAL[1]		CHILD WELL-BEING[2]					
				% of children under age 5 suffering from:				
	Infant mortality rate	Under-5 mortality rate	Infants with low birth weight	Underweight		Wasting	Stunting	Vitamin A supplementation coverage rate (%)
				moderate and severe	severe	moderate and severe	moderate and severe	
Country or territory	(‰) 2000-2005	(‰) 2000-2005	(%) 1998-2004[3]	1996-2004[3]	1996-2004[3]	1996-2004[3]	1996-2004[3]	(6-59 months) 2003
Arab States								
Algeria	37	41	7	10	3	8	19	…
Bahrain	14	17	8	9	2	5	10	…
Djibouti	93	140	…	18	6	13	26	75
Egypt	37	43	12	9	1	4	16	…
Iraq	94	124	15	16	2	6	22	…
Jordan	23	27	10	4	1	2	9	…
Kuwait	10	12	7	10	3	11	24	…
Lebanon	22	26	6	3	0	3	12	…
Libyan Arab Jamahiriya	19	21	7	5	1	3	15	…
Mauritania	97	156	…	32	10	13	35	…
Morocco	38	46	11	9	2	4	24	…
Oman	16	18	8	24	4	13	23	…
Palestinian A. T.	21	24	9	4	1	3	9	…
Qatar	12	14	10	6	…	2	8	…
Saudi Arabia	23	27	11	14	3	11	20	…
Sudan[2]	72	119	31	17	7	…	…	34
Syrian Arab Republic	18	21	6	7	1	4	18	…
Tunisia	22	25	7	4	1	2	12	…
United Arab Emirates	9	10	15	14	3	15	17	…
Yemen	69	95	32	46	15	12	53	36
Central and Eastern Europe								
Albania	25	34	3	14	1	11	34	…
Belarus	15	18	5	…	…	…	…	…
Bosnia and Herzegovina	14	16	4	4	1	6	10	…
Bulgaria	13	17	10	…	…	…	…	…
Croatia	7	8	6	1	…	1	1	…
Czech Republic	6	6	7	1	0	2	2	…
Estonia	10	12	4	…	…	…	…	…
Hungary	8	11	9	2	0	2	3	…
Latvia	10	14	5	…	…	…	…	…
Lithuania	9	12	4	…	…	…	…	…
Poland	9	10	6	…	…	…	…	…
Republic of Moldova	26	31	5	3	…	3	10	…
Romania	18	22	9	6	1	3	8	…
Russian Federation	17	22	6	3	1	4	13	…
Serbia and Montenegro	13	15	4	2	0	4	5	…
Slovakia	8	10	7	…	…	…	…	…
Slovenia	5	7	6	…	…	…	…	…
TFYR Macedonia	16	18	6	6	1	4	7	…
Turkey	42	49	16	4	1	1	12	…
Ukraine	16	18	5	1	0	0	3	…
Central Asia								
Armenia	30	35	7	3	0	2	13	…
Azerbaijan	76	91	11	7	1	2	13	…
Georgia	40	43	7	3	0	2	12	…
Kazakhstan	61	77	8	4	0	2	10	…
Kyrgyzstan	55	66	7	11	2	3	25	…
Mongolia	58	85	7	13	3	6	25	87
Tajikistan	89	116	15	…	…	5	36	…
Turkmenistan	78	99	6	12	2	6	22	…
Uzbekistan	58	70	7	8	2	7	21	93
East Asia and the Pacific								
Australia	5	6	7	…	…	…	…	…
Brunei Darussalam	6	7	10	…	…	…	…	…
Cambodia	95	140	11	45	13	15	45	47
China	35	41	4	8	…	…	14	…

CHILD WELL-BEING[2]

% of children who are			1-year-old children immunized against (%)							
Exclusively breastfed (<6 months)	Breastfed with complementary food (6-9 months)	Still breastfeeding (20-23 month)	Tuberculosis	Diphtheria Pertussis Tetanus		Polio	Measles	Hepatitis B	Haemophilus influenzae type b	
				Corresponding vaccines:						
			BCG	DPT1†	DPT3†	Polio3	Measles	HepB3	Hib3	Country or territory
1996-2004[3]	1996-2004[3]	1996-2004[3]	2004	2004	2004	2004	2004	2004	2004	

										Arab States
13	38	22	98	93	86	86	81	81	…	Algeria
34	65	41	70	97	98	98	99	98	98	Bahrain
…	…	…	78	81	64	64	60	…	…	Djibouti
30	72	31	98	98	97	97	97	97	…	Egypt
12	51	27	93	93	81	87	90	70	…	Iraq
27	70	12	58	96	95	95	99	95	95	Jordan
12	26	9	…	99	98	98	97	94	98	Kuwait
27	35	11	…	98	92	92	96	88	92	Lebanon
…	…	23	99	99	97	97	99	99	…	Libyan Arab Jamahiriya
20	78	57	86	83	70	68	64	…	…	Mauritania
31	66	15	95	99	97	97	95	95	10	Morocco
…	92	73	99	99	99	99	98	99	99	Oman
29	78	11	98	97	96	96	96	96	…	Palestinian A. T.
12	48	21	99	99	96	95	99	97	96	Qatar
31	60	30	95	96	96	96	97	96	96	Saudi Arabia
16	47	40	51	79	55	55	59	…	…	Sudan
81	50	6	99	99	99	99	98	99	99	Syrian Arab Republic
47	…	22	97	97	97	97	95	96	97	Tunisia
34	52	29	98	96	94	94	94	92	94	United Arab Emirates
12	76	…	63	92	78	78	76	49	…	Yemen
										Central and Eastern Europe
6	24	6	97	98	97	98	96	99	…	Albania
…	…	…	99	99	99	99	99	99	…	Belarus
6	…	…	95	93	84	87	88	81	79	Bosnia and Herzegovina
…	…	…	98	95	95	94	95	94	…	Bulgaria
23	…	…	98	96	96	98	96	…	93	Croatia
…	…	…	99	98	98	96	97	98	98	Czech Republic
…	…	…	99	98	94	95	96	90	27	Estonia
…	…	…	99	99	99	99	99	…	99	Hungary
…	…	…	99	99	98	97	99	99	95	Latvia
…	…	…	99	94	94	90	98	94	35	Lithuania
…	…	…	94	99	99	98	97	98	…	Poland
…	…	…	96	99	98	98	96	99	…	Republic of Moldova
…	…	…	99	98	97	97	97	99	…	Romania
…	…	…	96	98	97	98	98	96	…	Russian Federation
11	33	11	97	96	97	96	96	89	…	Serbia and Montenegro
…	…	…	98	99	99	99	98	99	99	Slovakia
…	…	…	98	97	92	93	94	…	93	Slovenia
37	8	10	94	96	94	95	96	…	…	TFYR Macedonia
21	38	24	88	86	85	85	81	77	…	Turkey
22	…	…	98	96	99	99	99	98	…	Ukraine
										Central Asia
30	51	13	96	97	91	93	92	91	…	Armenia
7	39	16	99	98	96	97	98	97	…	Azerbaijan
18	12	12	91	88	78	66	86	64	…	Georgia
36	73	17	65	85	82	99	99	99	…	Kazakhstan
24	77	21	98	99	99	98	99	99	…	Kyrgyzstan
51	55	57	95	99	99	95	96	95	…	Mongolia
50	…	…	97	87	82	84	89	81	…	Tajikistan
13	71	27	99	98	97	98	97	96	…	Turkmenistan
19	49	45	99	99	99	99	98	99	…	Uzbekistan
										East Asia and the Pacific
…	…	…	…	97	92	92	93	95	95	Australia
…	…	…	99	99	92	92	99	99	92	Brunei Darussalam
12	72	59	95	92	85	86	80	…	…	Cambodia
51	32	15	94	97	91	92	84	72	…	China

Table 3A (continued)

	CHILD SURVIVAL[1]		CHILD WELL-BEING[2]					
				% of children under age 5 suffering from:				
	Infant mortality rate	Under-5 mortality rate	Infants with low birth weight	Underweight		Wasting	Stunting	Vitamin A supplementation coverage rate (%)
				moderate and severe	severe	moderate and severe	moderate and severe	
	(‰)	(‰)	(%)					(6-59 months)
Country or territory	2000-2005	2000-2005	1998-2004[3]	1996-2004[3]	1996-2004[3]	1996-2004[3]	1996-2004[3]	2003
Cook Islands	...	...	3	...	...	...	...	...
DPR Korea	46	59	7	23	8	7	37	95
Fiji	22	27	10	8	1	8	3	...
Indonesia	43	54	9	28	9	...	...	62
Japan	3	4	8	...	...	...	...	...
Kiribati	...	...	5	13	...	11	28	45
Lao PDR	88	141	14	40	13	15	42	64
Macao, China	8	8	...	...	...	...	...	...
Malaysia	10	13	9	11	1	...	...	...
Marshall Islands	...	...	12	...	...	...	...	23
Micronesia (Federated States of)	38	48	18	...	...	...	...	95
Myanmar	75	112	15	32	7	9	32	87
Nauru	...	...	...	...	...	...	...	...
New Zealand	5	7	6	...	...	...	...	...
Niue	...	...	0	...	...	...	...	...
Palau	...	...	9	...	...	...	...	...
Papua New Guinea	71	98	11	35	...	...	...	1
Philippines	28	34	20	28	...	6	30	76
Republic of Korea	4	5	4	...	...	...	...	...
Samoa	26	31	4	...	...	...	...	...
Singapore	3	4	8	14	...	4	11	...
Solomon Islands	34	58	13	21	4	7	27	...
Thailand	20	25	9	19	...	6	16	...
Timor-Leste	94	134	12	46	15	12	49	95
Tokelau	...	...	...	...	...	...	...	...
Tonga	21	25	0	...	...	...	...	...
Tuvalu	...	...	5	...	...	...	...	...
Vanuatu	34	42	6	20	...	...	19	...
Viet Nam	30	39	9	28	4	7	32	99
Latin America and the Caribbean								
Anguilla	...	...	...	...	...	...	...	...
Antigua and Barbuda	...	...	8	10	4	10	7	...
Argentina	15	17	8	5	1	3	12	...
Aruba	...	...	...	...	...	...	...	...
Bahamas	14	16	7	...	...	...	...	...
Barbados	11	12	10	6	1	5	7	...
Belize	31	41	6	6	1	...	...	...
Bermuda	...	...	...	...	...	...	...	...
Bolivia	56	72	7	8	1	1	27	38
Brazil	27	35	10	6	1	2	11	...
British Virgin Islands	...	...	...	...	...	...	...	...
Cayman Islands	...	...	...	...	...	...	...	...
Chile	8	10	5	1	...	0	2	...
Colombia	26	33	9	7	1	1	14	...
Costa Rica	10	12	7	5	0	2	6	...
Cuba	6	8	6	4	0	2	5	...
Dominica	...	...	10	5	0	2	6	...
Dominican Republic	35	51	11	5	1	2	9	40
Ecuador	25	30	16	12	...	...	26	...
El Salvador	26	35	7	10	1	1	19	...
Grenada	...	...	9	...	...	...	...	...
Guatemala	39	52	12	23	4	2	49	...
Guyana	49	68	12	14	3	11	11	...
Haiti	62	110	21	17	4	5	23	25
Honduras	32	48	14	17	...	1	29	35
Jamaica	15	21	10	4	...	2	5	...
Mexico	21	25	8	8	1	2	18	...
Montserrat	...	...	...	...	...	...	...	...
Netherlands Antilles	13	15	...	...	...	...	...	...

CHILD WELL-BEING[2]

% of children who are			1-year-old children immunized against (%)							
Exclusively breastfed	Breastfed with complementary food	Still breastfeeding	Tuberculosis	Diphtheria Pertussis Tetanus		Polio	Measles	Hepatitis B	Haemophilus influenzae type b	
				Corresponding vaccines:						
(<6 months)	(6-9 months)	(20-23 month)	BCG	DPT1†	DPT3†	Polio3	Measles	HepB3	Hib3	Country or territory
1996-2004[3]	1996-2004[3]	1996-2004[3]	2004	2004	2004	2004	2004	2004	2004	
19	…	…	99	99	99	99	99	99	…	Cook Islands
65	31	37	95	75	72	99	95	98	…	DPR Korea
47	…	…	93	75	71	76	62	73	71	Fiji
40	75	59	82	88	70	70	72	75	…	Indonesia
…	…	…	…	99	99	97	99	…	…	Japan
80	…	…	94	75	62	61	56	67	…	Kiribati
23	10	47	60	66	45	46	36	45	…	Lao PDR
…	…	…	…	…	…	…	…	…	…	Macao, China
29	…	12	99	99	99	95	95	95	99	Malaysia
63	…	…	91	71	64	68	70	72	46	Marshall Islands
60	…	…	62	83	78	82	85	80	65	Micronesia (Federated States of)
15	66	67	85	86	82	82	78	54	…	Myanmar
…	…	…	95	93	80	59	40	75	…	Nauru
…	…	…	…	96	90	82	85	90	90	New Zealand
…	…	…	96	99	99	99	99	99	99	Niue
59	…	…	…	99	98	98	99	98	98	Palau
59	74	66	54	60	46	36	44	45	…	Papua New Guinea
34	58	32	91	90	79	80	80	40	…	Philippines
…	…	…	93	95	88	90	99	92	…	Republic of Korea
…	…	…	93	90	68	41	25	70	…	Samoa
…	…	…	99	95	94	94	94	93	…	Singapore
65	…	…	84	82	80	75	72	72	…	Solomon Islands
4	71	27	99	99	98	98	96	96	…	Thailand
31	82	35	72	65	57	57	55	…	…	Timor-Leste
…	…	…	…	…	…	…	…	…	…	Tokelau
62	…	…	99	99	99	99	99	99	…	Tonga
…	…	…	99	99	98	98	98	98	…	Tuvalu
50	…	…	63	73	49	53	48	56	…	Vanuatu
15	…	26	96	92	96	96	97	94	…	Viet Nam

Latin America and the Caribbean

% of children who are			1-year-old children immunized against (%)							
…	…	…	…	…	…	…	…	…	…	Anguilla
…	…	…	…	91	97	97	97	97	97	Antigua and Barbuda
…	…	…	99	95	90	95	95	88	90	Argentina
…	…	…	…	…	…	…	…	…	…	Aruba
…	…	…	…	99	93	92	89	93	93	Bahamas
…	…	…	…	97	93	93	98	93	93	Barbados
24	54	23	99	99	95	95	95	96	96	Belize
…	…	…	…	…	…	…	…	…	…	Bermuda
54	74	46	93	94	81	79	64	84	81	Bolivia
…	30	17	99	96	96	98	99	90	96	Brazil
…	…	…	…	…	…	…	…	…	…	British Virgin Islands
…	…	…	…	…	…	…	…	…	…	Cayman Islands
63	47	…	96	94	94	94	95	…	94	Chile
26	58	25	92	95	89	89	92	89	89	Colombia
35	47	12	90	89	90	90	88	89	90	Costa Rica
41	42	9	99	89	88	98	99	99	99	Cuba
…	…	…	99	99	99	99	99	…	…	Dominica
10	41	16	97	88	71	57	79	71	71	Dominican Republic
35	70	25	99	99	90	93	99	90	90	Ecuador
24	76	43	94	90	90	90	93	83	83	El Salvador
39	…	…	…	87	83	84	74	83	83	Grenada
51	67	47	98	94	84	84	75	…	…	Guatemala
11	42	31	94	90	91	91	88	91	91	Guyana
24	73	30	71	76	43	43	54	…	…	Haiti
35	61	34	93	96	89	90	92	89	89	Honduras
…	…	…	85	86	77	71	80	77	77	Jamaica
38	36	21	99	99	98	98	96	98	98	Mexico
…	…	…	…	…	…	…	…	…	…	Montserrat
…	…	…	…	…	…	…	…	…	…	Netherlands Antilles

Table 3A (continued)

Country or territory	CHILD SURVIVAL[1]		CHILD WELL-BEING[2]						
				% of children under age 5 suffering from:					
	Infant mortality rate	Under-5 mortality rate	Infants with low birth weight	Underweight		Wasting	Stunting		Vitamin A supplementation coverage rate (%)
	(‰)	(‰)	(%)	moderate and severe	severe	moderate and severe	moderate and severe		(6-59 months)
	2000-2005	2000-2005	1998-2004[3]	1996-2004[3]	1996-2004[3]	1996-2004[3]	1996-2004[3]		2003
Nicaragua	30	40	12	10	2	2	20		91
Panama	21	27	10	7	...	1	14		...
Paraguay	37	45	9	5	...	1	14		...
Peru	33	52	11	7	1	1	25		...
Saint Kitts and Nevis	...	...	9	...	...	...	...		...
Saint Lucia	15	20	8	14	...	6	11		...
Saint Vincent and the Grenadines	26	31	10	...	...	...	...		...
Suriname	26	31	13	13	2	7	10		...
Trinidad and Tobago	14	19	23	7	0	4	5		...
Turks and Caicos Islands	...	...	...	...	...	...	...		...
Uruguay	13	15	8	5	1	1	8		...
Venezuela	18	29	9	4	1	3	13		...
North America and Western Europe									
Andorra	...	...	...	...	...	...	...		...
Austria	5	6	7	...	...	...	...		...
Belgium	4	6	8	...	...	...	...		...
Canada	5	6	6	...	...	...	...		...
Cyprus	6	7	...	...	...	...	...		...
Denmark	5	6	5	...	...	...	...		...
Finland	4	5	4	...	...	...	...		...
France	4	5	7	...	...	...	...		...
Germany	4	6	7	...	...	...	...		...
Greece	6	8	8	...	...	...	...		...
Iceland	3	4	4	...	...	...	...		...
Ireland	5	7	6	...	...	...	...		...
Israel	5	6	8	...	...	...	...		...
Italy	5	6	6	...	...	...	...		...
Luxembourg	5	7	8	...	...	...	...		...
Malta	7	8	6	...	...	...	...		...
Monaco	...	...	...	...	...	...	...		...
Netherlands	5	6	...	...	...	...	...		...
Norway	4	5	5	...	...	...	...		...
Portugal	6	7	8	...	...	...	...		...
San Marino	...	...	...	...	...	...	...		...
Spain	5	6	6	...	...	...	...		...
Sweden	3	4	4	...	...	...	...		...
Switzerland	4	6	6	...	...	...	...		...
United Kingdom	5	6	8	...	...	...	...		...
United States	7	8	8	1	0	1	2		...
South and West Asia									
Afghanistan	149	252	...	39	12	7	54		86
Bangladesh	59	79	36	48	13	13	43		87
Bhutan	56	84	15	19	3	3	40		...
India	68	99	30	47	18	16	46		45
Iran, Islamic Republic of	34	39	7	11	2	5	15		...
Maldives	43	55	22	30	7	13	25		...
Nepal	64	88	21	48	13	10	51		96
Pakistan	79	114	19	38	12	13	37		95
Sri Lanka	17	20	22	29	...	14	14		...
Sub-Saharan Africa									
Angola	139	245	12	31	8	6	45		68
Benin	105	161	16	23	5	8	31		98
Botswana	51	106	10	13	2	5	23		...
Burkina Faso	121	196	19	38	14	19	39		95
Burundi	106	187	16	45	13	8	57		95
Cameroon	94	163	11	18	4	5	32		86
Cape Verde	30	36	13	14	2	6	16		...

CHILD WELL-BEING[2]

% of children who are			1-year-old children immunized against (%)							
Exclusively breastfed	Breastfed with complementary food	Still breastfeeding	Tuberculosis	Diphtheria	Pertussis Tetanus	Polio	Measles	Hepatitis B	Haemophilus influenzae type b	
					Corresponding vaccines:					
(<6 months)	(6-9 months)	(20-23 month)	BCG	DPT1†	DPT3†	Polio3	Measles	HepB3	Hib3	
1996-2004[3]	1996-2004[3]	1996-2004[3]	2004	2004	2004	2004	2004	2004	2004	Country or territory
31	68	39	88	92	79	80	84	79	79	Nicaragua
25	38	21	99	99	99	99	99	99	99	Panama
22	60	...	82	91	76	75	89	76	76	Paraguay
67	76	49	91	95	87	87	89	87	91	Peru
56	...	...	89	87	96	96	98	96	95	Saint Kitts and Nevis
...	...	...	99	99	91	91	95	91	91	Saint Lucia
...	...	...	99	99	99	99	99	99	99	Saint Vincent and the Grenadines
9	25	11	...	92	85	84	86	...	...	Suriname
2	19	10	...	91	94	94	95	94	94	Trinidad and Tobago
...	...	...	...	...	...	...	...	...	...	Turks and Caicos Islands
...	...	...	99	98	95	95	95	94	94	Uruguay
7	50	31	97	99	86	83	80	82	61	Venezuela
										North America and Western Europe
...	...	...	...	99	99	99	98	54	95	Andorra
...	...	...	...	97	83	83	74	83	83	Austria
...	...	...	...	97	95	96	82	65	95	Belgium
...	...	...	...	97	91	88	95	...	83	Canada
...	...	...	...	99	98	98	86	88	58	Cyprus
...	...	...	...	95	95	95	96	...	95	Denmark
...	...	...	98	98	98	96	97	...	96	Finland
...	...	...	85	98	97	97	86	28	86	France
...	...	...	...	98	97	94	92	81	90	Germany
...	...	...	88	96	88	87	88	88	88	Greece
...	...	...	...	99	99	99	93	...	99	Iceland
...	...	...	90	96	89	89	81	...	89	Ireland
...	...	...	...	98	96	92	96	98	96	Israel
...	...	...	...	98	96	97	84	95	90	Italy
...	...	...	...	98	98	98	91	49	86	Luxembourg
...	...	...	...	76	55	55	87	8	55	Malta
...	...	...	90	99	99	99	99	99	99	Monaco
...	...	...	...	98	98	98	96	...	97	Netherlands
...	...	...	...	91	91	91	88	...	93	Norway
...	...	...	83	98	95	95	95	94	95	Portugal
...	...	...	...	95	98	98	98	97	98	San Marino
...	...	...	...	98	96	97	97	97	96	Spain
...	...	...	16	99	99	99	94	1	98	Sweden
...	...	...	...	98	95	95	82	...	91	Switzerland
...	...	...	...	96	90	91	81	...	91	United Kingdom
...	...	...	...	99	96	92	93	92	94	United States
										South and West Asia
...	29	54	78	80	66	66	61	...	...	Afghanistan
36	69	94	95	95	85†	85	77	...	...	Bangladesh
...	...	...	92	93	89	90	87	89	...	Bhutan
37	44	66	73	71	64	70	56	...	...	India
44	...	0	99	99	99	98	96	95	...	Iran, Islamic Republic of
10	85	...	98	98	96	96	97	97	...	Maldives
68	66	92	85	88	80	80	73	87	...	Nepal
16	31	56	80	75	65	65	67	65	...	Pakistan
84	...	73	99	98	97	97	96	85	...	Sri Lanka
										Sub-Saharan Africa
11	77	37	72	75	59	57	64	...	...	Angola
38	66	62	99	99	83	89	85	89	...	Benin
34	57	11	99	98	97	97	90	79	...	Botswana
19	38	81	99	99	88	83	78	...	...	Burkina Faso
62	46	85	84	86	74	69	75	83	83	Burundi
21	80	29	83	80	73	72	64	...	...	Cameroon
57	64	13	79	78	75	76	69	68	...	Cape Verde

Table 3A (continued)

Country or territory	CHILD SURVIVAL[1] Infant mortality rate (‰) 2000-2005	CHILD SURVIVAL[1] Under-5 mortality rate (‰) 2000-2005	Infants with low birth weight (%) 1998-2004[3]	CHILD WELL-BEING[2] % of children under age 5 suffering from: Underweight moderate and severe 1996-2004[3]	Underweight severe 1996-2004[3]	Wasting moderate and severe 1996-2004[3]	Stunting moderate and severe 1996-2004[3]	Vitamin A supplementation coverage rate (%) (6-59 months) 2003
Central African Republic	98	176	14	24	6	9	39	84
Chad	116	203	10	28	9	11	29	...
Comoros	58	77	25	25	9	12	42	...
Congo	72	108	...	14	3	4	19	89
Côte d'Ivoire	118	189	17	17	5	7	21	...
D. R. Congo	119	212	12	31	9	13	38	80
Equatorial Guinea	102	181	13	19	4	7	39	...
Eritrea	65	94	21	40	12	13	38	52
Ethiopia	100	172	15	47	16	11	52	65
Gabon	58	95	14	12	2	3	21	30
Gambia	77	129	17	17	4	9	19	91
Ghana	62	102	16	22	5	7	30	78
Guinea	106	166	16	21	...	11	33	98
Guinea-Bissau	120	211	22	25	7	10	30	...
Kenya	68	118	10	20	4	6	30	33
Lesotho	67	123	14	18	4	5	46	75
Liberia	142	224	...	26	8	6	39	...
Madagascar	79	131	17	42	11	13	48	91
Malawi	111	184	16	22	...	5	45	92
Mali	133	220	23	33	11	11	38	61
Mauritius	15	18	14	15	2	14	10	...
Mozambique	101	182	15	24	6	4	41	50
Namibia	44	78	14	24	5	9	24	93
Niger	153	264	13	40	14	14	40	95
Nigeria	114	200	14	29	9	9	38	27
Rwanda	116	190	9	27	7	6	41	86
Sao Tome and Principe	82	112	20	13	2	4	29	...
Senegal	83	133	18	23	6	8	25	...
Seychelles	...	...	...	6	0	2	5	...
Sierra Leone	165	290	23	27	9	10	34	84
Somalia	126	211	...	26	7	17	23	...
South Africa	43	74	15	12	2	3	25	...
Swaziland	73	143	9	10	2	1	30	80
Togo	93	137	18	25	7	12	22	84
Uganda	81	139	12	23	5	4	39	...
United Republic of Tanzania	104	164	13	22	4	3	38	91
Zambia	95	173	12	23	...	5	49	73
Zimbabwe	62	117	11	13	2	6	27	46

	Weighted average	Weighted average		Weighted average				
World	57	86	16	26	10	10	31	61
Countries in transition	37	46	9	5	1	3	14	...
Developed countries	6	8	7	...	...	...	...	...
Developing countries	63	95	17	27	10	10	31	61
Arab States	49	65	15	14	3	6	21	...
Central and Eastern Europe	15	19	...	...	...	...	...	...
Central Asia	64	79	...	...	...	...	...	...
East Asia and the Pacific	35	44	7	15	...	...	19	73
East Asia	35	44	...	...	...	...	...	...
Pacific	34	47	...	...	...	...	...	...
Latin America/Caribbean	26	35	9	7	1	2	16	...
Caribbean	...	...	...	...	...	...	...	...
Latin America	25	33	...	...	...	...	...	...
N. America/W. Europe	6	7	...	...	...	...	...	...
South and West Asia	69	101	...	...	...	...	...	...
Sub-Saharan Africa	103	176	14	28	8	9	38	64

1. United Nations Population Division statistics, 2004 revision, medium variant, UN Population Division (2005).
2. UNICEF (2005).
3. Data are for the most recent year available during the period specified.

CHILD WELL-BEING²

% of children who are			1-year-old children immunized against (%)							Country or territory
			Tuberculosis	Diphtheria Pertussis Tetanus		Polio	Measles	Hepatitis B	Haemophilus influenzae type b	
Exclusively breastfed	Breastfed with complementary food	Still breastfeeding	Corresponding vaccines:							
(<6 months)	(6-9 months)	(20-23 month)	BCG	DPT1†	DPT3†	Polio3	Measles	HepB3	Hib3	
1996-2004³	1996-2004³	1996-2004³	2004	2004	2004	2004	2004	2004	2004	
17	77	53	70	65	40	40	35	…	…	Central African Republic
2	77	66	38	68	50	47	56	…	…	Chad
21	34	45	79	85	76	73	73	77	…	Comoros
4	94	13	85	67	67	67	65	…	…	Congo
5	73	38	51	63	50	50	49	50	…	Côte d'Ivoire
24	79	52	78	76	64	63	64	…	…	D. R. Congo
24	…	…	73	65	33	39	51	…	…	Equatorial Guinea
52	43	62	91	91	83	83	84	83	…	Eritrea
55	43	77	82	93	80	80	71	…	…	Ethiopia
6	62	9	89	69	38	31	55	…	…	Gabon
26	37	54	95	95	92	90	90	90	90	Gambia
53	62	67	92	88	80	81	83	80	80	Ghana
23	43	73	71	75	69	68	73	…	…	Guinea
37	36	67	80	86	80	80	80	…	…	Guinea-Bissau
13	84	57	87	72	73	73	73	73	73	Kenya
15	51	58	83	83	78	78	70	67	…	Lesotho
35	70	45	60	48	31	33	42	…	…	Liberia
67	78	64	72	71	61	63	59	61	…	Madagascar
44	93	77	97	99	89	94	80	89	89	Malawi
25	32	69	75	99	76	72	75	73	…	Mali
21	…	…	99	98	98	98	98	98	…	Mauritius
30	80	65	87	88	72	70	77	72	…	Mozambique
19	57	37	71	88	81	81	70	…	…	Namibia
1	56	61	72	75	62	62	74	…	…	Niger
17	64	34	48	43	25	39	35	…	…	Nigeria
84	79	71	86	94	89	89	84	89	89	Rwanda
56	53	42	99	99	99	99	91	99	…	Sao Tome and Principe
24	64	49	95	95	87	87	57	54	…	Senegal
…	…	…	99	99	99	99	99	99	…	Seychelles
4	51	53	83	77	61	61	64	…	…	Sierra Leone
9	13	8	50	50	30	30	40	…	…	Somalia
7	67	30	97	99	93	94	81	92	92	South Africa
24	60	25	84	94	83	82	70	78	…	Swaziland
18	65	65	91	83	71	71	70	…	…	Togo
63	75	50	99	99	87	86	91	87	87	Uganda
41	91	55	91	99	95	95	94	95	…	United Republic of Tanzania
40	87	58	94	94	80	80	84	…	80	Zambia
33	90	35	95	90	85	85	80	85	…	Zimbabwe

Weighted average			Weighted average							
36	51	46	84	86	78	80	76	49	…	World
22	45	26	93	94	93	94	93	90	…	Countries in transition
…	…	…	…	98	96	94	92	63	92	Developed countries
36	51	46	84	84	76	79	74	46	…	Developing countries
29	60	23	88	94	88	89	89	77	…	Arab States
…	…	…	…	…	…	…	…	…	…	Central and Eastern Europe
…	…	…	…	…	…	…	…	…	…	Central Asia
43	44	27	92	94	86	87	83	71	…	East Asia and the Pacific
…	…	…	…	…	…	…	…	…	…	East Asia
…	…	…	…	…	…	…	…	…	…	Pacific
…	45	26	96	96	91	92	92	83	91	Latin America/Caribbean
…	…	…	…	…	…	…	…	…	…	Caribbean
…	…	…	…	…	…	…	…	…	…	Latin America
…	…	…	…	…	…	…	…	…	…	N. America/W. Europe
…	…	…	…	…	…	…	…	…	…	South and West Asia
30	67	53	76	77	65	68	66	33	…	Sub-Saharan Africa

† This was the first year that DPT1 coverage was estimated. Coverage for DPT1 should be at least as high as DPT3.
Discrepancies where DPT1 coverage is lower than DPT3 reflect deficiencies in the data collection and reporting process.
UNICEF and WHO are working with national and territorial systems to eliminate these discrepancies.

Table 3B
Early childhood care and education (ECCE): education

Country or territory	Age group 2004	ENROLMENT IN PRE-PRIMARY EDUCATION				Enrolment in private institutions as % of total enrolment		GROSS ENROLMENT RATIO (GER) IN PRE-PRIMARY EDUCATION (%)							
		School year ending in				School year ending in		School year ending in							
		1999		2004		1999	2004	1999				2004			
		Total (000)	% F	Total (000)	% F			Total	Male	Female	GPI (F/M)	Total	Male	Female	GPI (F/M)
Arab States															
1 Algeria	4-5	36	49	57	48	.	.	3	3	3	1.00	5	5	5	0.97
2 Bahrain	3-5	14	48	18	48	100	99	35	36	34	0.95	45	46	44	0.96
3 Djibouti	4-5	0.2	60	0.8	49	100	77	0.4	0.3	0.5	1.50	2	2	2	0.99
4 Egypt	4-5	328	48	470	48	54	37	11	11	10	0.95	14	15	14	0.95
5 Iraq	4-5	68	48	91	49	.	.	5	5	5	0.98	6	6	6	1.00
6 Jordan	4-5	74	46	88	47	100	95	29	30	27	0.91	30	30	29	0.94
7 Kuwait	4-5	57	49	62	49	24	33	79	78	80	1.02	71	71	70	0.98
8 Lebanon	3-5	143	48	154	49	78	76	67	68	66	0.97	74	75	74	0.98
9 Libyan Arab Jamahiriya	4-5	10	48**	17**,z	48**,z	.	15**,z	5	5**	5**	0.97**	8**,z	8**,z	7**,z	0.96**,z
10 Mauritania	3-5	...	...	5	...	...	78	...	...	...	...	2	...	...	...
11 Morocco	4-5	805	34	685	38	100	100	62	81	43	0.52	53	65	41	0.63
12 Oman	4-5	7	45	7	46	100	100	6	6	6	0.88	6	6	6	0.91
13 Palestinian A. T.	4-5	77	48	70	48	100	100	40	41	39	0.96	30	31	29	0.96
14 Qatar	3-5	8	48	12	49	100	93	25	26	25	0.97	32	33	32	0.99
15 Saudi Arabia	3-5	93	46	96	...	50	46	5	5	5	0.90	5	...	...	...
16 Sudan	4-5	366	...	446	50	90**	74	20	...	...	...	23	23	23	1.03
17 Syrian Arab Republic	3-5	108	46	146	46	67	73	8	9	8	0.90	10	11	10	0.91
18 Tunisia	3-5	78	47	109**,z	48**,z	88	86y	14	14	13	0.95	22**,z	22**,z	22**,z	0.99**,z
19 United Arab Emirates	4-5	64	48	78	48	68	72	63	64	62	0.97	64	64	63	0.99
20 Yemen	3-5	12	45	15	46	37	45	0.7	0.8	0.6	0.86	0.8	0.8	0.7	0.87
Central and Eastern Europe															
21 Albania	3-5	82	50	81z	49z	.	6z	44	42	45	1.07	49z	48z	50z	1.03z
22 Belarus	3-5	263	47*	267	48	–	–	80	82*	77*	0.95*	104	105	103	0.98
23 Bosnia and Herzegovina	3-5	...	...	...	...	...	...	...	...	...	...	...	...	...	...
24 Bulgaria	3-6	219	48	201	48	0.1	0.3	69	69	68	0.99	78	78	77	0.99
25 Croatia	3-6	81	48	87z	48z	5	8z	40	40	39	0.98	47z	47z	46z	0.98z
26 Czech Republic	3-5	312	50	289	48	2	1	94	91	97	1.06	107	110	105	0.96
27 Estonia	3-6	55	48	54	48	0.7	1.4	90	90	89	0.99	114	115	113	0.98
28 Hungary	3-6	376	48	328	48	3	4	80	80	79	0.98	81	82	80	0.98
29 Latvia	3-6	58	48	61	48	1	2	53	54	52	0.95	79	81	78	0.96
30 Lithuania	3-6	94	48	88	48	0.3	0.2	51	51	50	0.97	64	66	63	0.96
31 Poland	3-6	958	49	832	49	3	7	50	50	50	1.01	53	52	53	1.01
32 Republic of Moldova	3-6	103	48	95	48*	...	0.8	41	42	40	0.96	50	51*	50*	0.97*
33 Romania	3-6	625	49	637	49	0.6	1	63	63	64	1.02	76	75	76	1.02
34 Russian Federation	3-6	3 471	47**	4 385	46	7**	1	55	57**	53**	0.94**	85	89	81	0.91
35 Serbia and Montenegro[1]	3-6	166	48	...	...	.	...	44	44	44	0.99	...	...	...	...
36 Slovakia	3-5	169	...	154	48	0.4	0.7	83	...	...	...	92	93	91	0.97
37 Slovenia	3-6	59	46	41	47	1	1	75	79	72	0.91	59	60	57	0.95
38 TFYR Macedonia	3-6	33	49	33	48	.	.	28	28	28	1.01	32	32	32	1.00
39 Turkey	3-5	261	47	358	48	6	4	6	6	6	0.94	8	8	8	0.95
40 Ukraine	3-5	1 103	48	977	48	0.04	0.3	48	49	48	0.98	82	83	80	0.97
Central Asia															
41 Armenia	3-6	57	...	47	50	–	2	26	...	...	...	31	29	34	1.17
42 Azerbaijan	3-5	111	46	109	48	–	0.1	22	23	21	0.89	28	28	28	1.01
43 Georgia	3-5	74	48	74	51	0.1	–	38	37	38	1.01	49	45	52	1.15
44 Kazakhstan	3-6	165	48	269	48	10	5	15	16	15	0.95	31	32	31	0.97
45 Kyrgyzstan	3-6	48	43	49	49	1	0.8	10	11	9	0.80	12	12	12	0.99
46 Mongolia	3-7	74	54	90	51	4	0.8	25	23	28	1.21	35	34	36	1.08
47 Tajikistan	3-6	56	42	63	47	.	.	8	9	7	0.76	9	10	9	0.93
48 Turkmenistan	3-6	...	...	...	...	...	...	...	...	...	...	...	...	...	...
49 Uzbekistan	3-6	...	...	615**	47**	...	...	...	...	...	...	28**	29**	27**	0.93**
East Asia and the Pacific															
50 Australia	4-4	...	...	262	49	...	66	...	...	...	...	102	102	102	1.00
51 Brunei Darussalam	3-5	11	49	12	48	66	67	51	50	52	1.04	52	52	52	1.00
52 Cambodia	3-5	58**	50**	95	49	22**	24	6**	6**	6**	1.03**	9	9	9	0.99
53 China	4-6	24 030	46	20 039	45**	...	...	38	39	37	0.97	36	37**	35**	0.92**

NET ENROLMENT RATIO (NER) IN PRE-PRIMARY EDUCATION (%) — School year ending in 2004				GROSS ENROLMENT RATIO (GER) IN PRE-PRIMARY AND OTHER ECCE PROGRAMMES (%) — School year ending in 1999				2004				PRE-PRIMARY SCHOOL LIFE EXPECTANCY (expected number of years of pre-primary schooling) — School year ending in 2004			NEW ENTRANTS TO THE FIRST GRADE OF PRIMARY EDUCATION WITH ECCE EXPERIENCE (%) — School year ending in 2004			
Total	Male	Female	GPI (F/M)	Total	Male	Female	GPI (F/M)	Total	Male	Female	GPI (F/M)	Total	Male	Female	Total	Male	Female	
																		Arab States
5	5	5	0.97	...	...	...	...	...	...	...	...	0.1	0.1	0.1	3	3	3	1
44	45	44	0.96	...	...	...	...	47	48	46	0.96	1.3	1.4	1.3	73	75	72	2
1	1	1	0.98	0.4	0.3	0.5	1.50	2	2	2	0.99	0.04	0.04	0.04	...	...	...	3
8	8	7	0.95	11	11	10	0.95	14	15	14	0.95	0.3	0.3	0.3	...	...	...	4
6	6	6	1.00	5	5	5	0.98	6	6	6	1.00	0.1	0.1	0.1	...	...	...	5
27	28	27	0.95	29	30	27	0.91	30	30	29	0.94	0.6	0.6	0.6	49	...	...	6
59**	59**	58**	0.98**	79	78	80	1.02	71	71	70	0.98	1.4	1.4	1.4	84^z	84^z	84^z	7
72	73	71	0.98	67	68	66	0.97	74	75	74	0.98	2.2	2.3	2.2	93	93	94	8
...	...	...	...	...	...	...	...	...	...	...	...	0.2**,z	0.2**,z	0.1**,z	...	...	...	9
...	...	...	...	...	...	...	...	4	...	...	...	0.1**	...	...	25	25	24	10
46	56	36	0.65	63	83	44	0.53	...	...	...	...	1.1	1.3	0.8	...	...	...	11
5	6	5	0.89	6	6	6	0.88	6	6	6	0.91	0.1	0.1	0.1	...	...	...	12
19	19	19	0.96	40	41	39	0.96	30	31	29	0.96	0.6	0.6	0.6	...	...	...	13
31	32	31	0.98	25	26	25	0.97	32	33	32	0.99	1.0	1.0	1.0	...	...	...	14
5	...	...	...	5	5	5	0.90	5	...	...	...	0.2	...	...	...	...	...	15
23	23	23	1.03	20	...	...	...	23	23	23	1.03	0.5	0.5	0.5	49	52	44	16
10	11	10	0.91	8	9	8	0.90	10	11	10	0.91	0.3	0.3	0.3	30	29	30	17
22**,z	22**,z	22**,z	0.99**,z	14	14	13	0.95	22**,z	22**,z	22**,z	0.99**,z	0.6**,z	0.7**,z	0.6**,z	...	...	...	18
45	45	45	0.98	63	64	62	0.97	64	64	63	0.99	1.3	1.3	1.3	82	81	83	19
0.5**,z	0.5**,z	0.5**,z	0.94**,z	...	...	...	...	...	...	...	...	0.02**	0.02**	0.02**	...	...	...	20
																		Central and Eastern Europe
49^z	48^z	50^z	1.03^z	44	42	45	1.07	49^z	48^z	50^z	1.03^z	1.5^z	1.4^z	1.5^z	...	...	...	21
92	92	91	0.99	...	...	...	...	121	122	119	0.98	3.1	3.1	3.1	...	...	...	22
...	...	...	...	...	...	...	...	...	...	...	...	...	...	...	...	...	...	23
74	74	73	0.99	69	69	68	0.99	78	78	77	0.99	3.1	3.1	3.1	...	...	...	24
46^z	46^z	45^z	0.97^z	46	46	45	0.99	53^z	54^z	53^z	0.98^z	1.9^z	1.9^z	1.8^z	98*,z	98*,z	98*,z	25
...	...	...	...	94	91	97	1.06	107	110	105	0.96	3.2	3.2	3.1	...	...	...	26
92	93	91	0.98	90	90	89	0.99	114	115	113	0.98	4.5	4.6	4.5	...	...	...	27
80	81	79	0.98	...	...	...	...	81	82	80	0.98	3.2	3.3	3.2	...	...	...	28
...	...	...	...	53	54	52	0.95	79	81	78	0.96	3.2	3.2	3.1	...	...	...	29
63	64	61	0.97	56	57	55	0.97	64	66	63	0.96	2.6	2.6	2.5	...	...	...	30
51	51	52	1.01	50	50	50	1.01	53	52	53	1.01	2.1	2.1	2.1	...	...	...	31
48	49*	48*	0.97*	41	42	40	0.96	50	51*	50*	0.97*	2.0	2.0*	2.0*	...	...	...	32
75	74	76	1.03	63	63	64	1.02	76	75	76	1.02	3.0	3.0	3.1	...	...	...	33
...	...	...	...	...	...	...	...	85	89	81	0.91	3.3	3.5	3.2	...	...	...	34
...	...	...	...	...	...	...	...	...	...	...	...	...	...	...	...	...	...	35
...	...	...	...	83	...	...	...	92	93	91	0.97	2.7	2.8	2.7	...	...	...	36
59	60	57	0.95	87	91	83	0.92	59	60	57	0.95	2.4	2.4	2.3	...	...	...	37
30	30	30	1.01	31	31	32	1.01	36	35	36	1.00	1.3	1.3	1.3	...	...	...	38
8	8	8	0.95	...	...	...	...	...	...	...	...	0.2	0.3	0.2	...	...	...	39
41	42	41	0.98	48	49	48	0.98	82	83	80	0.97	2.4	2.4	2.3	46^y	...	...	40
																		Central Asia
...	...	...	...	26	...	...	...	31	29	34	1.17	1.3**	1.2**	1.4**	...	...	...	41
19	19	20	1.04	22	24	21	0.89	29	28	29	1.01	0.8	0.8	0.8	6	6	6	42
41	38	43	1.14	38	37	38	1.01	49	45	52	1.15	1.4	1.4	1.5	2	2	2	43
30	31	30	0.97	15	16	15	0.95	31	32	31	0.97	1.2	1.3	1.2	...	...	...	44
8	8	8	0.99	10	11	9	0.80	12	12	12	0.99	0.5	0.5	0.5	14	14	14	45
32	...	...	...	...	...	...	...	...	...	...	...	1.7	1.7**	1.8**	...	...	...	46
7	7	7	0.94	...	...	...	...	...	...	...	...	0.4	0.4	0.4	...	...	...	47
...	...	...	...	...	...	...	...	...	...	...	...	...	...	...	...	...	...	48
21^z	...	...	...	...	...	...	...	...	...	...	...	1.1**	1.1**	1.1**	...	...	...	49
																		East Asia and the Pacific
64	64	64	1.00	...	...	...	...	102	102	102	1.00	1.0	1.0	1.0	...	...	...	50
...	...	...	...	51	50	52	1.04	52	52	52	1.00	1.6**	1.6**	1.6**	88^y	88^y	88^y	51
9	9	9	1.00	6**	6**	6**	1.03**	9	9	9	0.99	0.3	0.3	0.3	12	11	13	52
...	...	...	...	38	39	37	0.97	36	37**	35**	0.92**	1.1	1.1**	1.0**	...	...	...	53

Table 3B (continued)

		Age group	ENROLMENT IN PRE-PRIMARY EDUCATION				Enrolment in private institutions as % of total enrolment		GROSS ENROLMENT RATIO (GER) IN PRE-PRIMARY EDUCATION (%)							
			School year ending in				School year ending in		School year ending in							
			1999		2004		1999	2004	1999				2004			
	Country or territory	2004	Total (000)	% F	Total (000)	% F			Total	Male	Female	GPI (F/M)	Total	Male	Female	GPI (F/M)
54	Cook Islands[1]	4-4	0.4	47	0.5z	50z	25	22z	86	87	85	0.98	91**,z	87**,z	97**,z	1.11**,z
55	DPR Korea	4-5	...	...	...	...	...	...	...	...	...	...	...	...	...	...
56	Fiji	3-5	9	49	9	50	...	100	17	16	17	1.02	16	15	16	1.06
57	Indonesia	5-6	1526**	49**	1850	51	99**	98	18**	18**	18**	1.01**	22	21	23	1.09
58	Japan	3-5	2962	49**	3060	...	65	66	82	82**	83**	1.02**	85	...	...	...
59	Kiribati[1]	3-5	...	...	5**	...	...	...	...	...	...	...	68**	...	...	...
60	Lao PDR	3-5	37	52	42	50	18	24	8	8	8	1.11	8	8	9	1.05
61	Macao, China	3-5	17	47	12	48	94	94	89	91	86	0.95	92	93	91	0.98
62	Malaysia	5-5	572	50	603z	52z	49	40z	102	100	104	1.04	108z	101z	114z	1.12z
63	Marshall Islands	4-5	1.6	50	1.5**,z	49**,z	19	18y	...	...	...	...	50**,z	49**,z	50**,z	1.02**,z
64	Micronesia	3-5	3	...	...	...	...	...	37	...	...	...	...	...	...	...
65	Myanmar	3-4	41	...	...	...	90	...	2	...	...	...	...	...	...	...
66	Nauru	3-5	...	...	0.6z	48z	...	17y	...	...	...	...	71**,z	71**,z	72**,z	1.02**,z
67	New Zealand	3-4	101	49	103	49	24	44	88	88	89	1.00	92	92	93	1.01
68	Niue[1]	4-4	0.1	44	0.0	61	.	...	154	159	147	0.93	97	75	119	1.58
69	Palau[1]	3-5	0.7	54	0.6	52	24	...	63	56	69	1.23	64**	59**	68**	1.16**
70	Papua New Guinea	6-6	54	47	96**,z	47**,z	1	...	35	36	35	0.96	59**,z	61**,z	57**,z	0.94**,z
71	Philippines	5-5	593	50	783	50	47	45	31	30	31	1.05	40	39	41	1.04
72	Republic of Korea	5-5	535	47	**543**	**48**	75	**77**	80	80	80	1.00	**91**	**91**	**91**	**1.00**
73	Samoa	3-4	5**	53**	5**	54**	100**	...	51**	47**	56**	1.21**	49**	44**	55**	1.26**
74	Singapore	3-5	...	...	...	...	...	...	...	...	...	...	...	...	...	...
75	Solomon Islands	3-5	13**	48**	16**,z	48**,z	...	...	35**	35**	35**	1.01**	41**,z	41**,z	41**,z	0.99**,z
76	Thailand	3-5	2745	49	**2712****	**49****	19	22**,z	88	89	87	0.98	**90**	**91**	**89**	**0.97**
77	Timor-Leste	4-5	...	...	4y	...	...	...	...	...	...	...	11y	...	...	...
78	Tokelau[2]	3-4	...	...	0.1z	45z	...	.z	...	...	...	...	...	...	...	...
79	Tonga	3-4	1.6	53	1.1	56	...	12	30	27	33	1.22	23	20	27	1.36
80	Tuvalu[1]	3-5	...	...	0.7	50**	...	...	...	...	...	...	99	98**	100**	1.02**
81	Vanuatu	3-5	8	50	9**,y	49**,y	...	...	49	47	51	1.08	52**,y	52**,y	52**,y	1.01**,y
82	Viet Nam	3-5	2179	48	2175	48	49	60z	41	42	40	0.94	47	47	46	0.98
	Latin America and the Caribbean															
83	Anguilla	3-4	0.5	52	0.5	50	100	100	...	...	...	...	116**	123**	110**	0.90**
84	Antigua and Barbuda	3-4	...	...	...	...	...	...	...	...	...	...	...	...	...	...
85	Argentina	3-5	1191	50	1266z	49z	28	28z	57	56	57	1.02	62z	62z	62z	1.01z
86	Aruba[1]	4-5	3	49	3	50	83	79	97	97	97	1.00	100	97	104	1.07
87	Bahamas	3-4	1.4	51	4**,z	49**,z	...	79**,z	12	11	12	1.09	31**,z	31**,z	31**,z	0.99**,z
88	Barbados	3-4	6	49	6	49	...	17	82	83	82	0.98	89	89	90	1.01
89	Belize	3-4	4	50	4	50	...	100	28	27	28	1.03	28	28	28	1.01
90	Bermuda[1]	4-4	...	...	0.4y	51y	...	.y	...	...	...	...	52y	...	...	...
91	Bolivia	4-5	208	49	226**	49**	9	23**	45	45	45	1.01	48**	47**	48**	1.01**
92	Brazil	4-6	5733	49	6992z	49z	28	29z	58	58	58	1.00	68z	68z	68z	1.00z
93	British Virgin Islands[1]	3-4	0.5	53	0.7	49	100	100	62	57	66	1.16	93	92	93	1.01
94	Cayman Islands	3-4	0.5	46	0.6	46	88	92	...	...	...	...	44**	48**	41**	0.87**
95	Chile	3-5	450	49	394	49	45	47	77	78	77	0.99	52	52	52	0.99
96	Colombia	3-5	1034	50	1066	50	45	37	36	36	37	1.02	38	37	38	1.01
97	Costa Rica	4-5	70	49	102	49	10	11	84	84	85	1.01	64	64	65	1.01
98	Cuba	3-5	484	50	484	48	.	.	105	104	107	1.03	116	117	116	0.98
99	Dominica[1]	3-4	3	52	1.8	52	100	100	80	76	85	1.11	65	60	70	1.18
100	Dominican Republic	3-5	195	49	184	49	45	43	34	34	34	1.01	32	31	32	1.01
101	Ecuador	5-5	181	50	221	49	39	47	64	63	66	1.04	77	76	77	1.01
102	El Salvador	4-6	194	49	246	50	22**	18**	42	42	43	1.01	51	50	53	1.04
103	Grenada[1]	3-4	...	...	3	52	...	58z	...	...	...	...	81	77	84	1.09
104	Guatemala	3-6	308	49	426	50	22	19	46	46	45	0.97	28	28	28	1.01
105	Guyana	4-5	37	49	33**	49**	1	1z	122	122	121	0.99	108**	109**	107**	0.99**
106	Haiti	3-5	...	...	...	...	...	...	...	...	...	...	...	...	...	...
107	Honduras	3-5	...	...	190	50	...	23	...	...	...	...	33	32	34	1.04
108	Jamaica	3-5	138	51	153	50	88	90	78	75	81	1.08	92	91	94	1.03
109	Mexico	4-5	3361	50	3743	50	9	11	73	72	73	1.01	84	84	85	1.01
110	Montserrat[1]	3-4	0.1	52	0.1	49	.	–	...	...	...	...	93	87	100	1.15
111	Netherlands Antilles	4-5	7	50	6**,z	49**,z	75	75**,z	120	120	120	1.00	113**,z	115**,z	111**,z	0.97**,z
112	Nicaragua	3-6	161	50	199	50	17	16	28	28	29	1.04	35	34	35	1.03

NET ENROLMENT RATIO (NER) IN PRE-PRIMARY EDUCATION (%)				GROSS ENROLMENT RATIO (GER) IN PRE-PRIMARY AND OTHER ECCE PROGRAMMES (%)								PRE-PRIMARY SCHOOL LIFE EXPECTANCY (expected number of years of pre-primary schooling)			NEW ENTRANTS TO THE FIRST GRADE OF PRIMARY EDUCATION WITH ECCE EXPERIENCE (%)			
School year ending in 2004				School year ending in 1999				School year ending in 2004				School year ending in 2004			School year ending in 2004			
Total	Male	Female	GPI (F/M)	Total	Male	Female	GPI (F/M)	Total	Male	Female	GPI (F/M)	Total	Male	Female	Total	Male	Female	
...	...	...	...	86	87	85	0.98	91**,z	87**,z	97**,z	1.11**,z	0.9**,z	0.9**,z	1.0**,z	...	...	...	54
...	...	...	...	...	...	...	...	...	...	...	...	...	...	...	...	...	...	55
14	14	15	1.06	17	16	17	1.02	16	15	16	1.06	0.5	0.5	0.5	...	...	...	56
22	21	23	1.09	...	...	...	...	...	...	...	...	0.4	0.4	0.5	37	38	37	57
85	...	...	...	...	...	...	...	99	...	...	...	2.5	...	...	...	...	...	58
...	...	...	...	...	...	...	...	68**	...	...	...	2.0**	...	...	...	...	...	59
8	8	8	1.06	8	8	8	1.11	8	8	9	1.05	0.3	0.2	0.3	8	8	9	60
85	86	85	0.98	89	91	86	0.95	92	93	91	0.98	2.7	2.8	2.7	96	96	96	61
75z	72z	79z	1.10z	102	100	104	1.04	108z	101z	114z	1.12z	1.1z	1.0z	1.1z	78z	76z	81z	62
48**,y	47**,y	48**,y	1.02**,y	...	...	...	...	50**,z	49**,z	50**,z	1.02**,z	1.0**,z	1.0**,z	1.0**,z	...	...	...	63
...	...	...	...	37	...	...	...	...	...	...	...	...	...	...	...	...	...	64
...	...	...	...	2	...	...	...	...	...	...	...	...	...	...	...	...	...	65
...	...	...	...	...	...	...	...	71**,z	71**,z	72**,z	1.02**,z	2.1**,z	2.1**,z	2.2**,z	...	...	...	66
91	91	92	1.01	151	151	151	1.00	...	...	...	...	1.8	1.8	1.9	...	...	...	67
...	...	...	...	154	159	147	0.93	97	75	119	1.58	1.0**	0.8**	1.2**	...	...	...	68
...	...	...	...	63	56	69	1.23	64**	59**	68**	1.16**	1.9**	1.8**	2.0**	...	...	...	69
...	...	...	...	35	36	35	0.96	59**,z	61**,z	57**,z	0.94**,z	0.6**,z	0.6**,z	0.6**,z	...	...	...	70
31**,z	32**,z	31**,z	0.97**,z	31	30	31	1.05	40	39	41	1.04	0.4	0.4	0.4	59	59	60	71
48	**48**	**48**	**1.00**	80	80	80	1.00	**91**	**91**	**91**	**1.00**	**1.0**	**1.0**	**0.9**	...	...	...	72
...	...	...	...	51**	47**	56**	1.21**	49**	44**	55**	1.26**	1.0**	0.9**	1.1**	...	...	...	73
...	...	...	...	...	...	...	...	...	...	...	...	...	...	...	...	...	...	74
...	...	...	...	35**	35**	35**	1.01**	41**,z	41**,z	41**,z	0.99**,z	1.2**,z	1.2**,z	1.2**,z	...	...	...	75
85**	86**	83**	0.97**	...	...	...	...	...	...	...	...	2.7	2.7	2.7	...	...	...	76
...	...	...	...	...	...	...	...	...	...	...	...	0.2y	...	...	...	...	...	77
...	...	...	...	...	...	...	...	...	...	...	...	...	...	...	...	...	...	78
...	...	...	...	30	27	33	1.22	23	20	27	1.36	0.5	0.4	0.5	...	...	...	79
...	...	...	...	...	...	...	...	99	98**	100**	1.02**	3.0**	3.0**	3.0**	...	...	...	80
...	...	...	...	49	47	51	1.08	52**,y	52**,y	52**,y	1.01	1.6**,y	1.5**,y	1.6**,y	...	...	...	81
43y	...	...	...	41	42	40	0.94	47	47	46	0.98	1.4**	1.4**	1.4**	...	...	...	82

Latin America and the Caribbean

Total	Male	Female	GPI (F/M)	Total	Male	Female	GPI (F/M)	Total	Male	Female	GPI (F/M)	Total	Male	Female	Total	Male	Female	
91**,z	97**,z	85**,z	0.87**,z	...	...	...	...	116**	123**	110**	0.90**	2.3**	2.5**	2.2**	100**	100**	100**	83
...	...	...	...	...	...	...	...	...	...	...	...	...	...	...	...	...	...	84
62z	61z	62z	1.01z	58	58	59	1.02	...	...	...	...	1.9z	1.8z	1.9z	90z	90z	91z	85
90	88	93	1.07	97	97	97	1.00	100	97	104	1.07	2.0	1.9	2.1	88	89	87	86
23y	23y	22y	0.99y	12	11	12	1.09	31**,z	31**,z	31**,z	0.99**,z	0.6**,z	0.6**,z	0.6**,z	...	...	...	87
81	82	79	0.96	82	83	82	0.98	89	89	90	1.01	1.8	1.8	1.8	100	100	100	88
27	27	26	0.95	28	27	28	1.03	31	31	32	1.02	0.6	0.6	0.6	...	...	...	89
37**,y	...	...	...	...	...	...	...	52y	...	...	...	0.5y	...	...	...	...	...	90
39**	39**	39**	1.01**	45	45	45	1.01	48**	47**	48**	1.01**	1.0**	1.0**	1.0**	63z	62z	63z	91
53z	57z	47z	0.83z	...	...	...	...	68z	68z	68z	1.00z	2.0z	2.0z	2.0z	...	...	...	92
81	79	83	1.05	...	...	...	...	142	141	143	1.01	1.8	1.8	1.9	98	98	98	93
44**	48**	41**	0.87**	...	...	...	...	78**	83**	74**	0.89**	0.9**	1.0**	0.8**	90	90	90	94
...	...	...	...	77	78	77	0.99	52	52	52	0.99	1.5	1.5	1.5	...	...	...	95
34	34	34	1.01	36	36	37	1.02	38	37	38	1.01	1.1	1.1	1.1	...	...	...	96
...	...	...	...	94	94	95	1.01	67	67	67	1.01	1.3	1.3	1.3	81	79	83	97
100z	...	...	...	189	184	193	1.05	209	208	210	1.01	3.5	3.5	3.5	98	99	98	98
56**,z	56**,z	55**,z	0.97**,z	80	76	85	1.11	65	60	70	1.18	1.3**	1.2**	1.4**	100	100	100	99
28	28	28	1.03	34	34	34	1.01	32	31	32	1.01	1.0	0.9	1.0	...	...	...	100
62	62	63	1.01	94	92	95	1.03	158	158	159	1.01	0.8	0.8	0.8	55	54	56	101
46**	45**	47**	1.05**	42	42	43	1.01	51	50	53	1.04	1.5	1.5	1.6	...	...	...	102
80z	...	...	...	...	...	...	...	81	77	84	1.09	1.6**	1.5**	1.7**	...	...	...	103
27	27	27	1.01	46	46	45	0.97	28	28	28	1.01	1.2	1.2	1.2	80y	78y	82y	104
91z	92z	91z	1.00z	122	122	121	0.99	108**	109**	107**	0.99**	2.2**	2.2**	2.1**	100z	100z	100z	105
...	...	...	...	...	...	...	...	...	...	...	...	...	...	...	...	...	...	106
27	26	27	1.04	...	...	...	...	...	...	...	...	1.0	1.0	1.0	...	...	...	107
91	90	93	1.04	78	75	81	1.08	92	91	94	1.03	2.8	2.7	2.8	...	...	...	108
74	73	74	1.00	73	72	73	1.01	84	84	85	1.01	1.7	1.7	1.7	...	...	...	109
77	75	80	1.07	...	...	...	...	93	87	100	1.15	1.9	1.8	2.0	100	100	100	110
100**,z	...	...	...	...	...	...	...	...	...	...	...	2.3**,z	2.3**,z	2.2**,z	...	...	...	111
35	34	35	1.03	...	...	...	...	43	44	42	1.03	1.4	1.4	1.4	43	41	44	112

Table 3B (continued)

		Age group	ENROLMENT IN PRE-PRIMARY EDUCATION				Enrolment in private institutions as % of total enrolment		GROSS ENROLMENT RATIO (GER) IN PRE-PRIMARY EDUCATION (%)							
			School year ending in				School year ending in		School year ending in							
			1999		2004		1999	2004	1999				2004			
	Country or territory	2004	Total (000)	% F	Total (000)	% F			Total	Male	Female	GPI (F/M)	Total	Male	Female	GPI (F/M)
113	Panama	4-5	49	49	73	49	23	17	39	39	39	1.01	55	54	55	1.02
114	Paraguay	3-5	123	50	148**	49**	29	28**	27	27	28	1.03	31**	31**	32**	1.01**
115	Peru	3-5	1 017	50	1 090	49	15	20	55	55	56	1.02	60	60	61	1.01
116	Saint Kitts and Nevis[1]	3-4	...	...	1.9	51	...	61**	...	...	...	...	101	94	109	1.15
117	Saint Lucia	3-4	6	48	4	52	100	100	84	86	82	0.95	71	67	74	1.11
118	St Vincent/Grenad.	3-4	...	...	4	49	...	100	...	...	...	...	86	87	84	0.97
119	Suriname	4-5	...	...	17**,z	49**,z	...	46**,z	...	...	...	...	90**,z	90**,z	91**,z	1.01**,z
120	Trinidad and Tobago	3-4	23**	50**	30	49	100**	100	60**	60**	61**	1.01**	86	87	86	1.00
121	Turks and Caicos Islands[1]	4-5	0.8	54	0.9	50	47	63	...	...	...	...	106	112	100	0.90
122	Uruguay	3-5	100	49	104**	49**	...	17**	59	59	60	1.02	61**	61**	61**	1.01**
123	Venezuela	3-5	738	50	915	49	20	17	45	44	45	1.03	55	55	55	1.01
	North America and Western Europe															
124	Andorra[1]	3-5	...	...	3	49	...	2	...	...	...	...	127**	121**	134**	1.11**
125	Austria	3-5	225	49	217	48	25	27	83	83	82	0.99	89	90	89	0.99
126	Belgium	3-5	399	49	399	49	56	54	110	111	110	0.98	116	117	116	1.00
127	Canada	4-5	529	49	512**,y	49**,y	5	8**,y	67	66	67	1.01	68**,y	68**,y	67**,y	1.00**,y
128	Cyprus[1]	3-5	19	49	16	49	54	41	60	59	60	1.02	61	61	61	1.01
129	Denmark	3-6	251	49	250	49	27	...	91	91	91	1.00	91	91	91	1.00
130	Finland	3-6	125	49	139	49	10	8	49	49	48	0.99	59	59	58	0.99
131	France	3-5	2 393	49	2 499	49	13	13	111	111	111	1.00	114	113	114	1.00
132	Germany	3-5	2 333	48	2 238	48	54	59	93	94	93	0.98	97	97	96	0.99
133	Greece	4-5	143	49	140	49	3	3	68	67	68	1.01	66	66	67	1.02
134	Iceland	3-5	15	48	16**	49**	5	8**	109	110	108	0.98	126**	126**	126**	1.00**
135	Ireland	3-3	...	...	...	...	...	...	...	...	...	...	...	...	...	...
136	Israel	3-5	355	48	429	48	7	4	104	105	103	0.99	112	112	112	0.99
137	Italy	3-5	1 578	48	1 644	48	30	28	96	97	95	0.98	103	103	102	0.99
138	Luxembourg	3-5	12	48	14	49	5	6	72	73	72	0.99	83	83	84	1.02
139	Malta	3-4	10	48	9	50	37	39	102	103	102	0.99	104	100	108	1.08
140	Monaco[2]	3-5	0.9	52	...	...	26	...	...	...	...	...	...	...	...	...
141	Netherlands	4-5	390	49	350	48	69	70	98	99	98	0.99	89	90	88	0.98
142	Norway	3-5	139	50	154	...	40	41	75	73	77	1.06	85	...	...	...
143	Portugal	3-5	220	49	254	49	52	47	68	68	68	1.00	76	75	77	1.03
144	San Marino	3-5	...	...	...	...	...	...	...	...	...	...	...	...	...	...
145	Spain	3-5	1 131	49	1 356	49	32	35	100	101	100	0.99	111	112	111	1.00
146	Sweden	3-6	360	49	329	48	10	14	78	78	78	1.01	85	85	85	0.99
147	Switzerland	5-6	158	48	154	49	6	7	92	92	92	1.00	95	95	94	0.99
148	United Kingdom[3]	3-4	1 155	49	822	49	6	9	79	78	79	1.00	59	59	59	1.00
149	United States	3-5	7 183	48	7 436	48	34	40	59	60	58	0.97	62	63	61	0.96
	South and West Asia															
150	Afghanistan	3-6	...	...	25**	43**	...	...	...	...	...	...	0.7**	0.7**	0.6**	0.80**
151	Bangladesh	3-5	2 585	52	1 165z	49z	...	49z	26	25	27	1.12	12z	11z	12z	1.01z
152	Bhutan[4]	4-5	0.3	48	...	...	100	...	...	...	...	...	...	...	...	...
153	India	3-5	13 869	48	25 497	49	...	...	20	20	19	0.99	36	36	36	1.00
154	Iran, Islamic Republic of	5-5	220	50	436	52	...	8	13	13	14	1.05	37	35	39	1.12
155	Maldives	3-5	12	48	13	49	30	39z	46	46	46	1.00	48	47	49	1.03
156	Nepal	3-4	238**	41**	**512**	**46**	...	80z	11**	13**	10**	0.73**	**36**	**38**	**34**	**0.90**
157	Pakistan	3-4	...	...	3 574	44	...	...	...	...	...	...	45	48	40	0.83
158	Sri Lanka	4-4	...	...	...	...	...	...	...	...	...	...	...	...	...	...
	Sub-Saharan Africa															
159	Angola	3-5	...	...	...	...	...	...	...	...	...	...	...	...	...	...
160	Benin	4-5	18	48	22	49	20	27	4	4	4	0.97	4	4	4	1.00
161	Botswana	3-5	...	...	...	...	...	...	...	...	...	...	...	...	...	...
162	Burkina Faso	4-6	20	50	14**,y	48**,y	34	...	2	2	2	1.03	1**,y	1**,y	1**,y	0.94**,y
163	Burundi	4-6	5	50	9	49	49	60	0.8	0.8	0.8	1.01	1	1	1	0.97
164	Cameroon	4-5	104	48	176	50	57	64	12	12	12	0.95	20	20	20	0.99
165	Cape Verde	3-5	...	...	21	51	...	—	...	...	...	...	53	52	54	1.04
166	Central African Republic	3-5	...	...	6**	51**	...	...	...	...	...	...	2**	2**	2**	1.04**
167	Chad	3-5	...	...	...	...	...	...	...	...	...	...	...	...	...	...

NER in Pre-Primary Education (%) 2004 Total	Male	Female	GPI (F/M)	GER 1999 Total	Male	Female	GPI (F/M)	GER 2004 Total	Male	Female	GPI (F/M)	Pre-Primary SLE 2004 Total	Male	Female	New Entrants w/ ECCE 2004 Total	Male	Female	
52	51	52	1.02	42	41	42	1.01	59	59	60	1.02	1.1	1.1	1.1	64	63	65	113
...	...	...	...	27	27	28	1.03	...	...	...	...	0.9**	0.9**	0.9**	76ᶻ	75ᶻ	76ᶻ	114
60	60	61	1.01	57	57	58	1.02	60	60	61	1.01	1.8	1.8	1.8	...	...	...	115
83**,z	77**,z	90**,z	1.16**,z	...	...	...	...	143	134	153	1.15	2.0**	1.9**	2.2**	...	...	...	116
57	53	61	1.14	...	...	...	...	94	90	98	1.09	1.4	1.3	1.5	100ʸ	100ʸ	100ʸ	117
...	...	...	...	...	...	...	...	86	87	84	0.97	1.7**	1.7**	1.7**	100	100	100	118
90**,z	90**,z	91**,z	1.01**,z	...	...	...	...	...	...	...	...	1.8**,z	1.8**,z	1.8**,z	...	...	...	119
70	70	70	1.00	60**	60**	61**	1.01**	86	87	86	1.00	1.7	1.7	1.7	81*	80*	82*	120
65	67	64	0.96	...	...	...	...	106	112	100	0.90	2.1	2.2	1.9	100	100	100	121
...	...	...	...	59	59	60	1.02	...	...	...	...	1.8**	1.8**	1.8**	95ᶻ	95ᶻ	95ᶻ	122
49	49	50	1.02	54	53	54	1.02	59	59	59	1.01	1.7	1.6	1.7	...	...	...	123

North America and Western Europe

100ʸ	...	...	...	...	...	...	...	127**	121**	134**	1.11**	3.8	3.6**	4.0**	...	...	...	124
...	...	...	...	...	...	...	...	89	90	89	0.99	2.6	2.7	2.6	...	...	...	125
100	100	100	1.00	110	111	110	0.98	116	117	116	1.00	3.5	3.5	3.5	...	...	...	126
68**,y	68**,y	67**,y	1.00**,y	...	...	...	...	...	...	...	...	1.3**,y	1.3**,y	1.3**,y	...	...	...	127
57	56	57	1.02	87	87	86	0.99	61	61	61	1.01	1.8	1.8	1.8	...	...	...	128
91	91	91	1.00	...	...	...	...	91	91	91	1.00	3.6	3.6	3.6	...	...	...	129
58	58	58	1.00	49	49	48	0.99	59	59	58	0.99	2.3	2.3	2.3	...	...	...	130
100	100	100	1.00	111	111	111	1.00	114	113	114	1.00	3.4	3.4	3.4	...	...	...	131
...	...	...	...	93	94	93	0.98	97	97	96	0.99	2.9	2.9	2.9	...	...	...	132
66	66	67	1.02	68	67	68	1.01	66	66	67	1.02	1.3	1.3	1.3	...	...	...	133
91**	91**	92**	1.00**	109	110	108	0.98	126**	126**	126**	1.00**	3.8**	3.8**	3.8**	...	...	...	134
...	...	...	...	...	...	...	...	...	...	...	...	...	...	...	...	...	...	135
88	88	89	1.01	104	105	103	0.99	112	112	112	0.99	3.4	3.4	3.3	...	...	...	136
98	99	98	0.99	96	97	95	0.98	103	103	102	0.99	3.1	3.1	3.1	...	...	...	137
72	71	73	1.02	72	73	72	0.99	...	...	...	...	2.5	2.5	2.5	...	...	...	138
87	85	89	1.05	102	103	102	0.99	104	100	108	1.08	2.1	2.0	2.1	...	...	...	139
...	...	...	...	...	...	...	...	...	...	...	...	...	...	...	...	...	...	140
89	90	88	0.98	...	...	...	...	89	90	88	0.98	1.8	1.8	1.8	...	...	...	141
85	...	...	...	75	73	77	1.06	85	...	...	...	2.6	...	...	...	...	...	142
75	74	76	1.03	68	68	68	1.00	76	75	77	1.03	2.3	2.2	2.3	...	...	...	143
...	...	...	...	...	...	...	...	...	...	...	...	...	...	...	...	...	...	144
97	97	97	1.00	100	101	100	0.99	111	112	111	1.00	3.3	3.3	3.3	...	...	...	145
85	85	84	0.99	78	78	78	1.01	85	85	85	0.99	3.4	3.4	3.4	...	...	...	146
73	73	72	0.99	92	92	92	1.00	95	95	94	1.00	1.9	1.9	1.9	...	...	...	147
55	55	55	1.00	...	...	...	...	59	59	59	1.00	1.2	1.2	1.2	...	...	...	148
57	...	...	...	59	60	58	0.97	62	63	61	0.96	1.9	2.0	1.7	...	...	...	149

South and West Asia

...	...	...	...	...	...	...	...	0.7**	0.7**	0.6**	0.80**	0.03**	0.03**	0.02**	...	...	...	150
11ᶻ	10ᶻ	11ᶻ	1.01ᶻ	...	...	...	...	...	...	...	...	0.3ᶻ	0.3ᶻ	0.4ᶻ	23ʸ	24ʸ	22ʸ	151
...	...	...	...	...	...	...	...	...	...	...	...	...	...	...	...	...	...	152
...	...	...	...	...	...	...	...	36	36	36	1.00	1.1**	1.1**	1.1**	...	...	...	153
27ᶻ	25ᶻ	29ᶻ	1.13ᶻ	13	13	14	1.05	37	35	39	1.12	0.4**	0.3**	0.4**	26	27	26	154
45ʸ	44ʸ	45ʸ	1.02ʸ	46	46	46	1.00	48	47	49	1.03	1.4**	1.4**	1.5**	68ᶻ	68ᶻ	69ᶻ	155
...	...	...	...	11**	13**	10**	0.73**	36	38	34	0.90	0.7**	0.8	0.7	19	19	18	156
38*	42*	34*	0.81*	...	...	...	...	...	...	...	...	0.9	1.0	0.8	...	...	...	157
...	...	...	...	...	...	...	...	...	...	...	...	...	...	...	...	...	...	158

Sub-Saharan Africa

...	...	...	...	...	...	...	...	...	...	...	...	...	...	...	...	...	...	159
3	3	3	1.01	4	4	4	0.97	...	...	...	...	0.1	0.1	0.1	...	...	...	160
...	...	...	...	...	...	...	...	...	...	...	...	...	...	...	...	...	...	161
1**,y	1**,y	1**,y	0.94**,y	...	...	...	...	1**,y	1**,y	1**,y	0.94**,y	0.04**,y	0.04**,y	0.03**,y	3	3	3	162
...	...	...	...	0.8	0.8	0.8	1.01	1	1	1	0.97	0.04**	0.04**	0.04**	4	3	4	163
...	...	...	...	12	12	12	0.95	20	20	20	0.99	0.4**	0.4**	0.4**	...	...	...	164
51	50	51	1.04	...	...	...	...	53	52	54	1.04	1.6	1.6	1.6	78	77	79	165
2**	2**	2**	1.04**	...	...	...	...	2**	2**	2**	1.04**	0.1**	0.1**	0.1**	...	...	...	166
...	...	...	...	...	...	...	...	...	...	...	...	...	...	...	...	...	...	167

Table 3B (continued)

	Country or territory	Age group 2004	ENROLMENT IN PRE-PRIMARY EDUCATION School year ending in 1999 Total (000)	%F	2004 Total (000)	%F	Enrolment in private institutions as % of total enrolment School year ending in 1999	2004	GROSS ENROLMENT RATIO (GER) IN PRE-PRIMARY EDUCATION (%) School year ending in 1999 Total	Male	Female	GPI (F/M)	2004 Total	Male	Female	GPI (F/M)
168	Comoros	3-5	1.3	51	2	48	100	62	2	2	2	1.07	3	3	3	0.96
169	Congo	3-5	6	61	22	51	85	79	2	1	2	1.59	6	5	6	1.06
170	Côte d'Ivoire	3-5	36	49	49*,z	49*,z	46	46**,z	2	2	2	0.96	3*,z	3*,z	3*,z	0.96*,z
171	D. R. Congo	3-5	...	...	...	...	...	...	...	...	...	...	...	...	...	...
172	Equatorial Guinea	3-6	17	51	24z	...	37	37**,y	31	31	32	1.04	40z	...	...	...
173	Eritrea	5-6	12	47	19	47	97	76	6	6	5	0.88	7	8	7	0.90
174	Ethiopia	4-6	90	49	**153**	**49**	100	**100**	1	1	1	0.97	**2**	**2**	**2**	**0.95**
175	Gabon	3-5	...	...	16**,y	...	...	73**,y	...	...	...	...	14**,y	...	...	...
176	Gambia	3-6	29	47	30**	50**	...	...	20	21	19	0.91	18**	18**	19**	1.03**
177	Ghana	3-5	667**	49**	**731**	**50**	33**	**34**	40**	40**	40**	1.02**	**42**	**41**	**42**	**1.03**
178	Guinea	3-6	...	...	68	49	...	91	...	...	...	...	6	6	6	1.03
179	Guinea-Bissau	4-6	4**	51**	...	...	62**	...	3**	3**	3**	1.05**	...	...	...	...
180	Kenya	3-5	1 188	50	1 628	49	10	32z	44	44	44	1.00	53	54	53	0.99
181	Lesotho	3-5	33**	52**	41**	48**	100**	100**	23**	23**	24**	1.08**	31**	32**	30**	0.94**
182	Liberia	3-5	112	42	...	...	39	...	41	47	35	0.74	...	...	...	...
183	Madagascar	3-5	50**	51**	171**	...	93**	90z	3**	3**	3**	1.02**	10**	...	...	...
184	Malawi	3-5	...	...	...	...	...	...	...	...	...	...	...	...	...	...
185	Mali	3-6	21	51	32**,z	49**,z	...	...	1	1	1	1.09	2**,z	2**,z	2**,z	1.01**,z
186	Mauritius	3-4	42	50	**37**	**49**	85	**83**	100	99	101	1.02	**95**	**95**	**96**	**1.01**
187	Mozambique	3-5	...	...	...	...	...	...	...	...	...	...	...	...	...	...
188	Namibia	3-5	35	53	49**,z	52**,z	100	100**,z	19	18	21	1.16	29**,z	27**,z	30**,z	1.12**,z
189	Niger	4-6	12	50	18	49	33	30	1	1	1	1.05	1	1	1	1.01
190	Nigeria	3-5	...	...	1 753	49	...	...	...	...	...	...	15	15	15	1.00
191	Rwanda	4-6	...	...	19**,y	50**,y	...	100**,y	...	...	...	...	3**,y	3**,y	2**,y	0.98**,y
192	Sao Tome and Principe	4-6	4**	51**	5	50	–**	–	27**	26**	28**	1.09**	42	42	43	1.04
193	Senegal	4-6	24	50	55	52	68	74	3	3	3	1.00	6	5	6	1.11
194	Seychelles[1]	4-5	3	49	3	49	5	5z	109	107	111	1.04	102	103	100	0.98
195	Sierra Leone	3-5	...	...	...	...	...	...	...	...	...	...	...	...	...	...
196	Somalia	3-5	...	...	...	...	...	...	...	...	...	...	...	...	...	...
197	South Africa	6-6	207	50	345z	50z	26	8z	20	20	20	1.01	33z	33z	34z	1.03z
198	Swaziland	3-5	...	...	...	...	...	...	...	...	...	...	...	...	...	...
199	Togo	3-5	11	50	13**	50**	53	59**	2	2	2	0.99	2**	2**	2**	0.98**
200	Uganda	4-5	66**	50**	42	49	100**	99y	4**	4**	4**	1.00**	2	2	2	0.99
201	United Republic of Tanzania	5-6	...	...	**639**	**50**	...	**2**	...	...	...	...	**29**	**29**	**29**	**1.02**
202	Zambia	3-6	...	...	...	...	...	...	...	...	...	...	...	...	...	...
203	Zimbabwe	3-5	439**	51**	448z	45z	...	...	41**	40**	41**	1.03**	43z	...	...	...

			Sum	%F	Sum	%F	Median		Weighted average							
I	World	...	111 772	48	123 685	48	36	39	33	34	32	0.96	37	38	37	0.97
II	Countries in transition	...	6 316	47	7 115	47	1	0.8	41	42	40	0.94	59	61	57	0.93
III	Developed countries	...	25 386	49	25 482	47	8	8	73	74	73	0.99	77	77	77	0.99
IV	Developing countries	...	80 070	47	91 089	48	49	54	28	28	27	0.95	32	32	31	0.97
V	Arab States	...	2 356	42	2 625	46	89	76	15	17	13	0.76	16	17	15	0.87
VI	Central and Eastern Europe	...	8 538	48	9 176	47	1	1	45	45	44	0.97	57	59	56	0.95
VII	Central Asia	...	1 450	47	1 482	48	2	0.8	22	23	22	0.92	27	28	26	0.95
VIII	East Asia and the Pacific	...	36 568	47	33 352	47	48	45	40	40	39	0.98	40	41	39	0.96
IX	East Asia	...	36 152	47	32 831	47	57	60	40	40	39	0.98	40	40	39	0.96
X	Pacific	...	416	49	520	48	...	...	58	58	58	1.00	72	72	72	0.99
XI	Latin America/Caribbean	...	16 392	49	19 119	49	39	44	56	55	56	1.01	62	62	62	1.01
XII	Caribbean	...	673	50	965	50	88	85	71	69	72	1.04	101	99	103	1.03
XIII	Latin America	...	15 720	49	18 154	49	23	21	55	55	56	1.01	61	61	61	1.01
XIV	N. America/W. Europe	...	19 151	48	19 408	47	26	20	76	76	75	0.98	78	79	78	0.98
XV	South and West Asia	...	22 186	47	31 166	48	...	44	23	24	22	0.93	32	33	32	0.98
XVI	Sub-Saharan Africa	...	5 129	49	7 359	49	55	64	10	10	9	0.98	12	13	12	0.98

1. National population data were used to calculate enrolment ratios.
2. Enrolment ratios were not calculated due to lack of United Nations population data by age.

3. The decline in enrolment is essentially due to a re-classification of programmes. From 2004, it was decided to include children categorized as being aged '4 rising 5' in primary education enrolment rather than pre-primary enrolment even if they started the school year at this education level. These are children who are under 5 but over 4.5 and typically (although not always) will start primary school reception classes in the second or third term of the school year. Note that the fall of 261,182 in the ISCED 0 enrolment is boradly offset by an increase of 197,571 in ISCCED 1 enrolment.

NER Total	NER Male	NER Female	NER GPI (F/M)	GER 1999 Total	GER 1999 Male	GER 1999 Female	GER 1999 GPI (F/M)	GER 2004 Total	GER 2004 Male	GER 2004 Female	GER 2004 GPI (F/M)	SLE Total	SLE Male	SLE Female	Entrants Total	Entrants Male	Entrants Female	
...	...	...	...	...	...	...	...	...	...	...	...	0.1**	0.1**	0.1**	...	...	...	168
6	5	6	1.06	2	1	2	1.59	6	5	6	1.06	0.2	0.2	0.2	10	10	11	169
3*,z	3*,z	3*,z	0.96*,z	2	2	2	0.96	3*,z	3*,z	3*,z	0.96*,z	0.1*,z	0.1*,z	0.1*,z	...	...	...	170
...	...	...	...	...	...	...	...	...	...	...	...	...	...	...	...	...	...	171
39z	...	...	...	31	31	32	1.04	40z	...	...	...	1.6z	...	...	...	...	...	172
5	5	5	0.95	6	6	5	0.88	7	8	7	0.90	0.1	0.2	0.1	...	...	...	173
...	...	...	...	1	1	1	0.97	**2**	**2**	**2**	**0.95**	**0.1****	**0.1****	**0.1****	...	...	...	174
...	...	...	...	...	...	...	...	...	...	...	...	0.4**,y	...	...	...	...	...	175
...	...	...	...	...	...	...	...	22**	22**	22**	1.01**	0.7**	0.7**	0.7**	...	...	...	176
27	**26**	**28**	**1.06**	40**	40**	40**	1.02**	**42**	**41**	**42**	**1.03**	**1.3**	**1.3**	**1.3**	...	...	...	177
6	6	6	1.03	...	...	...	...	6	6	6	1.03	0.2	0.2	0.2	17	17	18	178
...	...	...	...	3**	3**	3**	1.05**	...	...	...	...	...	...	...	...	...	...	179
29	29	30	1.03	44	44	44	1.00	53	54	53	0.99	1.7	1.7	1.7	...	...	...	180
...	...	...	...	23**	23**	24**	1.08**	31**	32**	30**	0.94**	0.9**	0.9**	0.9**	...	...	...	181
...	...	...	...	...	...	...	...	...	...	...	...	...	...	...	...	...	...	182
10**	...	...	...	3**	3**	3**	1.02**	10**	...	...	...	0.3**	...	...	...	...	...	183
...	...	...	...	...	...	...	...	...	...	...	...	...	...	...	...	...	...	184
...	...	...	...	1	1	1	1.09	2**,z	2**,z	2**,z	1.01**,z	0.1**,z	0.1**,z	0.1**,z	7	7	8	185
83	83	83	1.00	100	99	101	1.02	**95**	**95**	**96**	**1.01**	**1.9****	**1.9****	**1.9****	100	100	100	186
...	...	...	...	...	...	...	...	...	...	...	...	...	...	...	...	...	...	187
...	...	...	...	...	...	...	...	...	...	...	...	0.9**,z	0.8**,z	0.9**,z	...	...	...	188
1	1	1	1.00	1	1	1	1.05	1	1	1	1.01	0.04	0.04	0.04	19z	19z	19z	189
11	11	11	0.97	...	...	...	...	...	...	...	...	0.4	0.4	0.4	...	...	...	190
...	...	...	...	...	...	...	...	3**,y	3**,y	2**,y	0.98**,y	0.1**,y	0.1**,y	0.1**,y	...	...	...	191
30	30	31	1.04	...	...	...	...	48	47	49	1.04	1.2	1.2	1.3	...	...	...	192
3	3	3	1.12	...	...	...	...	...	...	...	...	0.2	0.2	0.2	4	4	5	193
90	91	90	1.0	109	107	111	1.04	102	103	100	0.98	2.1	2.1	2.1	100	100	100	194
...	...	...	...	...	...	...	...	...	...	...	...	...	...	...	...	...	...	195
...	...	...	...	...	...	...	...	...	...	...	...	...	...	...	...	...	...	196
16z	16z	16z	1.02z	...	...	...	...	53z	52z	54z	1.03z	0.3z	0.3z	0.3z	...	...	...	197
...	...	...	...	...	...	...	...	...	...	...	...	...	...	...	...	...	...	198
2**	2**	2**	0.98**	2	2	2	0.99	2**	2**	2**	0.98**	0.1**	0.1**	0.1**	...	...	...	199
...	...	...	...	...	...	...	...	...	...	...	...	0.0**	0.0**	0.0**	...	...	...	200
29	**29**	**29**	**1.02**	...	...	...	...	...	...	...	...	**0.6**	**0.6**	**0.6**	...	...	...	201
...	...	...	...	...	...	...	...	...	...	...	...	...	...	...	16	16	16	202
...	...	...	...	41**	40**	41**	1.03**	43z	47z	39z	0.82z	1.3**,z	1.4**,z	1.2**,z	...	...	...	203

Median				Median								Weighted average			Median			
...	...	...	...	46	46	45	0.98	56	56	56	0.99	1.0	1.0	1.0	...	...	...	I
...	...	...	...	26	...	...	...	49	45	52	1.15	2.2	2.3	2.1	...	...	...	II
...	...	...	...	76	75	78	1.03	85	...	...	...	2.2	2.3	2.2	...	...	...	III
...	...	...	...	40	41	39	0.96	48	47	48	1.02	0.9	0.9	0.8	...	...	...	IV
...	...	...	...	20	...	...	...	22	22	22	1.01	0.4	0.4	0.3	...	...	...	V
...	...	...	...	55	56	54	0.96	78	78	77	0.99	2.0	2.1	2.0	...	...	...	VI
...	...	...	...	22	24	21	0.89	31	29	34	1.17	1.0	1.1	1.0	...	...	...	VII
...	...	...	...	41	42	40	0.94	55	56	54	0.96	1.0	1.1	1.0	...	...	...	VIII
...	...	...	...	39	40	38	0.95	49	50	49	0.99	1.0	1.1	1.0	...	...	...	IX
...	...	...	...	49	47	51	1.08	61	60	63	1.04	0.9	0.9	0.9	...	...	...	X
...	...	...	...	59	58	59	1.02	79	80	79	0.99	1.7	1.7	1.7	...	...	...	XI
...	...	...	...	...	...	...	...	91	90	92	1.02	2.9	2.8	2.9	...	...	...	XII
...	...	...	...	55	55	56	1.02	59	59	60	1.02	1.7	1.7	1.7	...	...	...	XIII
...	...	...	...	92	92	92	1.00	91	91	91	1.00	2.2	2.3	2.1	...	...	...	XIV
...	...	...	...	...	...	...	...	36	36	36	1.00	0.9	0.9	0.9	...	...	...	XV
...	...	...	...	...	...	...	...	10	...	...	...	0.4	0.4	0.3	...	...	...	XVI

Column group headings:
- NET ENROLMENT RATIO (NER) IN PRE-PRIMARY EDUCATION (%) — School year ending in 2004 — Total, Male, Female, GPI (F/M)
- GROSS ENROLMENT RATIO (GER) IN PRE-PRIMARY AND OTHER ECCE PROGRAMMES (%) — School year ending in 1999 and 2004 — Total, Male, Female, GPI (F/M)
- PRE-PRIMARY SCHOOL LIFE EXPECTANCY (expected number of years of pre-primary schooling) — School year ending in 2004 — Total, Male, Female
- NEW ENTRANTS TO THE FIRST GRADE OF PRIMARY EDUCATION WITH ECCE EXPERIENCE (%) — School year ending in 2004 — Total, Male, Female

4. Enrolment ratios were not calculated due to inconsistencies between enrolment and the United Nations population data.

Data in bold are for the school year ending in 2005.
(z) Data are for the school year ending in 2003.
(y) Data are for the school year ending in 2002.

Table 4
Access to primary education

Country or territory	Compulsory education (age group)	Legal guarantee of free education[1]	New entrants (000) School year ending in 1999	New entrants (000) School year ending in 2004	GIR 1999 Total	GIR 1999 Male	GIR 1999 Female	GIR 1999 GPI (F/M)	GIR 2004 Total	GIR 2004 Male	GIR 2004 Female	GIR 2004 GPI (F/M)
Arab States												
1 Algeria[2]	6-16	Yes	745	628	101	102	100	0.98	102	103	100	0.98
2 Bahrain	…	Yes	13	13	101	99	103	1.04	100	100	99	0.99
3 Djibouti	6-15	No	6	8	30	34	25	0.74	39	42	35	0.83
4 Egypt[3]	6-13	Yes	1 451**	1 577**	92**	94**	90**	0.96**	99**	99**	99**	0.99**
5 Iraq	6-11	Yes	709**	826	102**	109**	95**	0.88**	107	110	103	0.94
6 Jordan[2]	6-16	Yes	126	133	102	101	102	1.00	92	91	92	1.01
7 Kuwait[2]	6-14	Yes	35	41**	97	97	98	1.01	97**	96**	97**	1.01**
8 Lebanon[2, 3]	6-12	Yes	71	71	102	106	98	0.92	100	100	99	0.99
9 Libyan Arab Jamahiriya[2]	6-15	Yes	…	…	…	…	…	…	…	…	…	…
10 Mauritania[3]	6-14	Yes	…	89	…	…	…	…	106	106	105	0.99
11 Morocco[3]	6-14	Yes	731	623	112	115	109	0.94	98	100	96	0.96
12 Oman	…	Yes	52	44	86	86	86	1.00	74	74	75	1.02
13 Palestinian A. T.	6-15	…	95	93	105	104	106	1.01	84	85	84	0.99
14 Qatar[3]	6-14	Yes	11**	11**	111**	112**	109**	0.98**	100**	100**	100**	1.00**
15 Saudi Arabia[3]	6-11	Yes	379	402	66	66	65	0.99	66	66	66	1.00
16 Sudan[3]	6-13	Yes	…	637	…	…	…	…	68	73	62	0.85
17 Syrian Arab Republic[2]	6-12	Yes	466	543	107	110	103	0.94	120	122	118	0.97
18 Tunisia	6-16	Yes	204	162	101	101	100	1.00	95	94	96	1.02
19 United Arab Emirates[3]	6-15	Yes	47	54	91	93	90	0.97	89	89	88	0.99
20 Yemen[3]	6-14	Yes	440	691**	78	91	65	0.71	110**	122**	97**	0.80**
Central and Eastern Europe												
21 Albania	6-13	Yes	67**	60[z]	102**	103**	102**	0.99**	102[z]	103[z]	102[z]	0.99[z]
22 Belarus[3]	6-16	Yes	173	91	131	132	130	0.99	102	103	102	0.99
23 Bosnia and Herzegovina[3]	…	Yes	…	…	…	…	…	…	…	…	…	…
24 Bulgaria[2, 3]	7-16	Yes	93	72.4	101	102	100	0.98	106	107	104	0.98
25 Croatia	7-15	Yes	50	49[z]	94	95	93	0.98	98[z]	99[z]	97[z]	0.98[z]
26 Czech Republic	6-15	Yes	124	92	101	102	100	0.98	97	97	96	0.99
27 Estonia	7-15	Yes	18	13	100	100	99	0.98	101	101	101	1.00
28 Hungary	7-16	Yes	127	104	102	104	100	0.97	95	96	94	0.98
29 Latvia[3]	7-15	Yes	32	19	96	96**	96**	0.99**	90	90	89	0.99
30 Lithuania[2]	7-16	Yes	54	40	105	105	104	0.99	101	101	102	1.01
31 Poland[2, 4]	7-18	Yes	535	422	101	…	…	…	97	97**	97**	1.00**
32 Republic of Moldova[3]	6-16	Yes	62	48	85	85**	85**	1.00**	88	89	88	0.99
33 Romania[3]	7-14	Yes	269	276	94	94	94	0.99	126	126	126	1.00
34 Russian Federation[3]	6-15	Yes	1 659	1 313	86	…	…	…	97	98**	97**	0.99**
35 Serbia and Montenegro[5]	7-14	…	…	…	…	…	…	…	…	…	…	…
36 Slovakia[2]	6-16	Yes	75	58	102	102	101	0.99	96	97	96	0.99
37 Slovenia[2]	7-15	Yes	21	26	99	99	99	0.99	142	142	141	0.99
38 TFYR Macedonia[2, 3]	7-15	Yes	32	27	102	102	102	1.00	98	98	97	0.99
39 Turkey[3]	6-14	Yes	…	1 311	…	…	…	…	91	93	88	0.95
40 Ukraine[3]	6-17	Yes	623	457	93	94	93	0.99	105	105*	105*	1.00*
Central Asia												
41 Armenia[3]	7-15	Yes	…	44	…	…	…	…	99	96	101	1.06
42 Azerbaijan[3]	6-17	Yes	175	137	94	94	95	1.01	95	96	93	0.97
43 Georgia[3]	6-14	Yes	74	58	99	99**	100**	1.02**	106	107	105	0.98
44 Kazakhstan	7-17	Yes	…	241	…	…	…	…	105	106	105	0.99
45 Kyrgyzstan[3]	7-15	Yes	120*	108	99*	99*	100*	1.02*	98	99	97	0.98
46 Mongolia	8-16	No	70	61	111	111	111	1.00	114	113	115	1.02
47 Tajikistan[3]	7-15	Yes	177	164	99	101	96	0.95	96	98**	94**	0.96**
48 Turkmenistan	7-15	Yes	…	…	…	…	…	…	…	…	…	…
49 Uzbekistan[3]	7-16	Yes	…	596**	…	…	…	…	102**	102**	102**	1.00**
East Asia and the Pacific												
50 Australia	5-15	Yes	…	271	…	…	…	…	104	105	104	0.99
51 Brunei Darussalam	5-16	No	8	7	107	107	106	0.99	101	103	100	0.93
52 Cambodia[3]	…	Yes	404**	495	117**	120**	114**	0.95**	148	154	143	0.93
53 China[3, 6]	6-14	Yes	…	18 339	…	…	…	…	94	95	93	0.98
54 Cook Islands[5]	5-15	…	1	0.4[z]	131	…	…	…	80**,[z]	81**,[z]	78**,[z]	0.96**,[z]

NET INTAKE RATE (NIR) IN PRIMARY EDUCATION (%)								SCHOOL LIFE EXPECTANCY (expected number of years of formal schooling from primary to tertiary education)						
School year ending in								School year ending in						
1999				2004				1999			2004			
Total	Male	Female	GPI (F/M)	Total	Male	Female	GPI (F/M)	Total	Male	Female	Total	Male	Female	
Arab States														
77	79	76	0.97	90	91	89	0.98	...	...	...	12.5**	12.6**	12.5**	1
86	83	88	1.06	83	83	82	0.98	13.1**	12.6**	13.7**	14.2**	13.7**	14.8**	2
22	25	19	0.75	30	34	27	0.80	3.2**	...	...	4.0**	4.6**	3.4**	3
68**	67**	69**	1.02**	92**	92**	91**	0.99**	12.5**	...	...	12.0**	...	...	4
79**	83**	75**	0.90**	82	86	79	0.92	8.2**	9.4**	7.0**	9.6**	10.9**	8.2**	5
...	...	...	...	60	60	60	1.00	...	...	...	13.1**	12.9**	13.2**	6
62	63	61	0.97	64**	63**	66**	1.04**	13.7**	13.0**	14.4**	12.5**	11.7**	13.3**	7
75**	77**	74**	0.95**	79	79	78	0.99	13.2**	13.0**	13.3**	14.1**	13.9**	14.4**	8
...	...	...	...	...	...	...	...	...	...	...	16.2**,z	15.7**,z	16.8**,z	9
...	...	...	...	36**	37**	35**	0.95**	6.9**	...	...	7.5**	7.8**	7.2**	10
51	53	49	0.93	80	82	79	0.96	8.0**	8.9**	7.1**	9.9**	10.5**	9.2**	11
70	69	70	1.01	53	53	54	1.02	...	...	...	11.5**	11.6**	11.3**	12
...	...	...	...	62	63	61	0.96	12.0	11.9	12.0	13.4	13.2	13.6	13
...	...	...	...	72**	74**	70**	0.95**	12.9**	12.2**	13.8**	12.7**	12.4**	13.4**	14
40	48	32	0.68	45**	47**	44**	0.95**	9.9**	10.1**	9.7**	9.9**	10.0**	9.7**	15
...	...	...	...	38	41	35	0.84	4.7**	...	...	...	...	...	16
60	61	60	0.98	63	63	62	0.98	...	...	...	...	...	...	17
...	...	...	...	88	88	89	1.02	12.9**	13.0**	12.7**	13.7**	...	...	18
48	48	47	0.99	37	38	35	0.93	11.2**	10.7**	12.0**	10.3**,z	9.7**,z	11.2**,z	19
26	31	21	0.68	...	...	...	...	7.7**	10.4**	4.8**	8.8**	11.0**	6.5**	20
Central and Eastern Europe														
...	...	...	...	...	...	...	...	11.1**	11.1**	11.0**	11.3z	11.2z	11.3z	21
76	77	76	0.99	85*	86*	85*	0.99*	13.5**	13.3**	13.8**	14.4	14.1	14.7	22
...	...	...	...	...	...	...	...	...	...	...	...	...	...	23
...	...	...	...	87y	87y	87y	1.01y	13.0	12.6	13.3	13.3	13.3	13.2	24
68	69	66	0.97	71z	73z	70z	0.95z	12.0	11.9	12.2	12.9z	12.7z	13.1z	25
...	...	...	...	...	...	...	...	13.5**	13.4**	13.5**	14.7	14.6	14.9	26
...	...	...	...	...	...	...	...	14.5	14.0	15.0	15.8	14.8	16.8	27
...	...	...	...	65**	67**	63**	0.94**	13.8**	13.6**	14.1**	15.0	14.6	15.4	28
...	...	...	...	...	...	...	...	13.7	12.9	14.4	15.4	14.4	16.3	29
...	...	...	...	...	...	...	...	14.1	13.6	14.6	15.6	14.9	16.4	30
...	...	...	...	...	...	...	...	...	...	...	15.0	14.4	15.6	31
...	...	...	...	...	...	...	...	9.8**	9.6**	10.0**	10.3	9.9	10.6	32
...	...	...	...	78y	78y	77y	0.99y	11.9	11.7	12.0	13.3	13.0	13.6	33
...	...	...	...	...	...	...	...	...	...	...	13.4**	12.8**	13.9**	34
...	...	...	...	...	...	...	...	13.3	13.3	13.4	...	...	...	35
...	...	...	...	...	...	...	...	13.1**	13.0**	13.3**	14.1	13.9	14.4	36
...	...	...	...	...	...	...	...	14.8**	14.4**	15.3**	16.6**	16.1**	17.2**	37
...	...	...	...	75y	76y	74y	0.98y	11.9	11.9	11.9	12.1	11.9	12.3	38
...	...	...	...	72**	74**	71**	0.96**	...	...	...	11.1	12.0	10.1	39
66	...	...	...	78*	78*	78*	1.00*	12.6**	12.4**	12.8**	13.7	13.5*	14.0*	40
Central Asia														
...	...	...	...	88	85	91	1.07	...	...	...	11.3	10.9	11.7	41
...	...	...	...	63	64	62	0.97	10.1	10.2	10.0	10.8	11.0	10.7	42
69	68**	69**	1.02**	90	90	90	1.00	11.6**	11.5**	11.6**	12.3	12.2	12.4	43
...	...	...	...	67	69	65	0.95	12.0	11.8	12.2	14.7	14.3	15.1	44
58*	59*	58*	0.99*	60	61	59	0.95	11.5	11.4	11.7	12.4	12.1	12.7	45
83	83	82	1.00	57	58	55	0.95	8.7**	7.8**	9.6**	11.6	10.8	12.5	46
66	68	65	0.95	...	...	...	...	9.7**	10.5**	8.8**	10.7	11.7	9.7	47
...	...	...	...	...	...	...	...	...	...	...	...	...	...	48
...	...	...	...	85z	85**,z	85**,z	1.0**,z	...	...	...	11.4**	11.6**	11.2**	49
East Asia and the Pacific														
...	...	...	...	71	69	74	1.07	20.0**	19.8**	20.3**	20.3	20.2	20.4	50
...	...	...	...	...	...	...	...	13.4**	13.1**	13.7**	13.8**	13.5**	14.2**	51
69**	70**	68**	0.97**	86	88	85	0.96	...	...	...	9.7**,z	10.5**,z	8.9**,z	52
...	...	...	...	...	...	...	...	...	...	...	11.2**	11.3**	11.1**	53
...	...	...	...	...	...	...	...	10.6**	10.5**	10.6**	10.0**,z	10.0**,z	10.0**,z	54

Table 4 (continued)

	Country or territory	Compulsory education (age group)	Legal guarantee of free education[1]	New entrants (000) School year ending in 1999	2004	GIR 1999 Total	Male	Female	GPI (F/M)	GIR 2004 Total	Male	Female	GPI (F/M)
55	DPR Korea	6-15	Yes	…	…	…	…	…	…	…	…	…	…
56	Fiji	6-15	No	…	19	…	…	…	…	104	105	103	0.98
57	Indonesia	7-15	No	…	4 877	…	…	…	…	118	121	116	0.96
58	Japan[4]	6-15	Yes	…	1 182**	…	…	…	…	98**	98**	98**	1.00**
59	Kiribati[5]	6-15	No	3	3	109	106	113	1.06	126	124	127	1.02
60	Lao PDR	6-10	No	180	186	121	128	114	0.89	118	123	114	0.93
61	Macao, China	5-14	…	6	5	88	88	89	1.01	96	102	91	0.89
62	Malaysia	…	No	…	525[z]	…	…	…	…	94[z]	94[z]	94[z]	1.00[z]
63	Marshall Islands[2]	6-14	No	1	2**,[z]	…	…	…	…	115**,[z]	116**,[z]	113**,[z]	0.98**,[z]
64	Micronesia	6-13	No	…	…	…	…	…	…	…	…	…	…
65	Myanmar	5-9	No	1 226	**1 158****	112	111	113	1.02	**117****	**117****	**116****	**0.99****
66	Nauru[5]	6-16	No	…	0.3[y]	…	…	…	…	97[y]	99[y]	95[y]	0.97[y]
67	New Zealand[4]	5-16	Yes	…	56**	…	…	…	…	100**	100**	99**	0.99**
68	Niue[5]	5-16	…	0.05	0.02	105	79	137	1.73	70	47	100	2.11
69	Palau[2, 5]	6-17	Yes	0.4**	…	118**	120**	115**	0.96**	…	…	…	…
70	Papua New Guinea	6-14	No	154	152**,[z]	105	109	100	0.92	95**,[z]	101**,[z]	90**,[z]	0.89**,[z]
71	Philippines[3]	6-12	Yes	2 551	2 615	133	137	130	0.95	134	138	129	0.93
72	Republic of Korea[2, 4]	6-15	Yes	711	**658**	106	105	107	1.02	**106**	**105**	**107**	**1.02**
73	Samoa	5-14	No	5	6**	105	106	104	0.98	101**	101**	101**	1.00**
74	Singapore	6-16	No	…	…	…	…	…	…	…	…	…	…
75	Solomon Islands	…	No	…	…	…	…	…	…	…	…	…	…
76	Thailand	6-14	No	1 037**	…	97**	101**	94**	0.93**	…	…	…	…
77	Timor-Leste	7-15	…	…	…	…	…	…	…	…	…	…	…
78	Tokelau[7]	…	…	…	0.03[z]	…	…	…	…	…	…	…	…
79	Tonga	6-14	No	3	3	107	109	104	0.95	119	127	112	0.88
80	Tuvalu[5]	7-14	No	0.2**	0.2**	89**	94**	83**	0.89**	93**	91**	96**	1.05**
81	Vanuatu	6-12	No	6**	7	109**	109**	109**	1.00**	121	124	118	0.96
82	Viet Nam[3]	6-14	Yes	2 035	1 569	107	111	103	0.93	98	101	95	0.95
	Latin America and the Caribbean												
83	Anguilla	5-17	…	0.2	0.2	…	…	…	…	101**	78**	134**	1.72**
84	Antigua and Barbuda	5-16	Yes	…	…	…	…	…	…	…	…	…	…
85	Argentina[2, 3]	5-15	Yes	781	762[z]	112	111	112	1.00	110[z]	110[z]	110[z]	1.00[z]
86	Aruba[5]	6-16	…	1	2	106	109	103	0.94	104	106	102	0.96
87	Bahamas	5-16	No	7	6	117	122	111	0.91	92	94	89	0.95
88	Barbados	4-16	Yes	4	4	110	110	109	0.99	110	111	109	0.97
89	Belize	5-14	Yes	8	8	129	130	127	0.98	115	115	115	1.00
90	Bermuda	5-16	…	…	0.8[y]	…	…	…	…	101[y]	…	…	…
91	Bolivia[3]	6-13	Yes	282	278**	124	124	125	1.01	120**	119**	120**	1.01**
92	Brazil[3]	7-14	Yes	…	3 964[z]	…	…	…	…	117[z]	…	…	…
93	British Virgin Islands[5]	5-16	…	0.4	0.4	106	109	103	0.95	105	113	98	0.87
94	Cayman Islands	5-16	…	0.6	1	…	…	…	…	86**	88**	83**	0.94**
95	Chile[2]	6-14	Yes	284	260	95	95	94	0.99	98	99	97	0.98
96	Colombia[2, 3]	5-15	No	1 267	1 168	134	137	131	0.96	123	126	120	0.95
97	Costa Rica[3]	6-15	Yes	87	87	104	104	105	1.01	107	108	107	0.99
98	Cuba	6-14	Yes	164	147	100	103	97	0.95	104	105	103	0.98
99	Dominica[5]	5-16	No	2	1	111	118	104	0.88	74	75	74	0.98
100	Dominican Republic[3]	5-13	Yes	267	212	138	143	133	0.93	111	118	104	0.88
101	Ecuador[3]	5-14	Yes	374	388	134	134	134	1.00	135	136	134	0.99
102	El Salvador[3]	4-15	Yes	196**	207	132**	136**	128**	0.94**	132	134	129	0.96
103	Grenada[5]	5-16	No	2	2[z]	117	119	115	0.97	96[z]	97[z]	94[z]	0.97[z]
104	Guatemala	7-15	Yes	425	452	132	136	128	0.94	127	129	125	0.97
105	Guyana[3]	6-15	Yes	18	21**	123	120	126	1.05	140**	140**	140**	1.00**
106	Haiti	6-11	No	…	…	…	…	…	…	…	…	…	…
107	Honduras[2, 3]	6-13	Yes	…	243	…	…	…	…	128	129	127	0.99
108	Jamaica	6-11	No	…	53	…	…	…	…	92	93	92	0.99
109	Mexico[3]	6-15	Yes	2 509	2 362	109	109	109	0.99	106	106	105	0.99
110	Montserrat[5]	5-14	…	0.1	0.1	…	…	…	…	104	95	117	1.23
111	Netherlands Antilles	6-15	…	4**	3**,[z]	116**	114**	119**	1.05**	112**,[z]	109**,[z]	115**,[z]	1.06**,[z]
112	Nicaragua[3]	6-16	Yes	203	200	147	150	143	0.95	140	144	135	0.94
113	Panama[3]	6-11	Yes	69	79	112	113	111	0.99	119	121	118	0.97

Table 4

	NET INTAKE RATE (NIR) IN PRIMARY EDUCATION (%)								SCHOOL LIFE EXPECTANCY (expected number of years of formal schooling from primary to tertiary education)						
	School year ending in								School year ending in						
	1999				2004				1999			2004			
	Total	Male	Female	GPI (F/M)	Total	Male	Female	GPI (F/M)	Total	Male	Female	Total	Male	Female	
	...	...	...	...	...	...	...	...	...	...	...	...	...	...	55
	...	...	...	...	71	71	71	0.99	...	...	...	13.3**	13.1**	13.5**	56
	...	...	...	...	40	41	39	0.94	...	...	...	11.7	11.9	11.5	57
	...	...	...	...	...	...	...	...	14.4**	14.6**	14.3**	14.8**	15.0**	14.7**	58
	...	...	...	...	...	...	...	...	11.7	11.2	12.2	12.6*	12.0*	13.2*	59
	55	56	54	0.96	61	61	61	1.00	8.4**	9.4**	7.4**	9.3**	10.2**	8.3**	60
	63	60	65	1.07	76	79	72	0.91	12.1**	12.4**	11.9**	15.3	16.4	14.4	61
	...	...	...	...	...	...	...	...	12.3**	12.1**	12.4**	12.9[z]	12.3[z]	13.5[z]	62
	...	...	...	...	65**,[y]	62**,[y]	67**,[y]	1.08**,[y]	...	...	...	13.0**,[z]	13.0**,[z]	12.9**,[z]	63
	...	...	...	...	...	...	...	...	...	...	...	...	...	...	64
	77**	...	...	...	98[z]	97[z]	98[z]	1.01[z]	...	...	...	7.3**,[y]	...	...	65
	...	...	...	...	...	...	...	...	...	...	...	7.9**,[z]	7.8**,[z]	8.0**,[z]	66
	...	...	...	...	...	...	...	...	17.7**	16.9**	18.5**	18.2	17.3	19.0	67
	...	...	...	...	...	...	...	...	11.9	11.5	12.4	11.1	10.8	11.6	68
	...	...	...	...	...	...	...	...	...	...	...	...	...	...	69
	...	...	...	...	...	...	...	...	6.0**	6.3**	5.6**	...	...	...	70
	47**	48**	45**	0.95**	49	47	52	1.11	11.6**	11.4**	11.9**	12.0**	11.7**	12.4**	71
	99	98	100	1.02	95**	94**	96**	1.03**	15.0**	15.8**	14.1**	16.2	17.2	15.2	72
	77	77	77	1.00	...	...	...	...	12.3**	12.1**	12.5**	...	...	...	73
	...	...	...	...	...	...	...	...	...	...	...	...	...	...	74
	...	...	...	...	...	...	...	...	7.1	7.5	6.6	8.0**,[z]	8.4**,[z]	7.5**,[z]	75
	...	...	...	...	...	...	...	...	...	...	...	12.4**	12.3**	12.4**	76
	...	...	...	...	...	...	...	...	...	...	...	11.2**,[y]	...	...	77
	...	...	...	...	...	...	...	...	...	...	...	...	...	...	78
	50	51	49	0.95	...	...	...	...	13.3**	13.0**	13.5**	13.4**	13.3**	13.6**	79
	...	...	...	...	...	...	...	...	...	...	...	...	...	...	80
	...	...	...	...	56	57	55	0.97	9.1**	...	...	10.5**	10.9**	10.1**	81
	80	...	...	...	82**,[y]	...	...	...	10.3**	10.7**	9.8**	10.5**	10.9**	10.1**	82

Latin America and the Caribbean

	Total	Male	Female	GPI (F/M)	Total	Male	Female	GPI (F/M)	Total	Male	Female	Total	Male	Female	
	...	...	...	...	72**	57**	93**	1.63**	...	...	...	11.9**	11.8**	12.3**	83
	...	...	...	...	...	...	...	...	...	...	...	...	...	...	84
	...	...	...	...	91[z]	91[z]	91[z]	1.00[z]	15.1**	14.4**	15.9**	15.4[z]	14.5[z]	16.2[z]	85
	88	89	86	0.98	84	86	81	0.94	13.3**	13.2**	13.4**	13.4	13.3	13.5	86
	84	85	83	0.97	62	62	61	0.99	13.3	13.5	13.0	11.0	10.9	11.2	87
	85**	86**	85**	0.99**	94	94	94	1.00	14.0**	13.4**	14.6**	...	...	...	88
	79**	80**	77**	0.96**	67	68	66	0.97	...	...	...	13.3**	13.3**	13.3**	89
	...	...	...	...	...	...	...	...	...	...	...	15.3**,[y]	...	...	90
	69**	68**	69**	1.03**	71**	71**	71**	1.01**	13.5**	...	...	14.3**	...	...	91
	...	...	...	...	...	...	...	...	14.2**	13.9**	14.4**	14.0[z]	13.6[z]	14.3[z]	92
	73**	70**	76**	1.09**	67**	70**	64**	0.92**	15.8**	15.0**	16.7**	15.9**	14.6**	17.1**	93
	...	...	...	...	58	60	56	0.94	...	...	...	...	...	...	94
	...	...	...	...	...	...	...	...	12.8**	12.9**	12.7**	13.7**	13.9**	13.5**	95
	58**	60**	57**	0.96**	...	...	...	...	11.1**	10.8**	11.4**	11.5**	11.3**	11.8**	96
	...	...	...	...	...	...	...	...	10.3**	10.2**	10.4**	10.7**,[z]	...	...	97
	97**	100**	95**	0.95**	99	100	98	0.98	12.3**	12.1**	12.4**	14.4**	14.4**	14.3**	98
	80	83	78	0.94	46	46	46	1.01	12.3**	11.7**	13.0**	13.4**	13.2**	13.6**	99
	60	60	60	1.00	59**,[z]	62**,[z]	57**,[z]	0.9**,[z]	...	...	...	12.5**	11.9**	13.2**	100
	84	83	84	1.01	85	85	85	1.01	...	...	...	...	...	...	101
	...	...	...	...	59**	59**	59**	1.00**	10.7**	10.9**	10.6**	11.5**	11.6**	11.5**	102
	74**	74**	74**	1.00**	61**,[z]	60**,[z]	61**,[z]	1.00**,[z]	...	...	...	12.1**	11.8**	12.3**	103
	57	59	54	0.92	69	70	68	0.97	...	...	...	9.3**,[z]	9.9**,[z]	8.8**,[z]	104
	90**	88**	91**	1.04**	99**,[z]	100**,[z]	98**,[z]	0.98**,[z]	...	...	...	12.5**,[z]	...	...	105
	...	...	...	...	...	...	...	...	...	...	...	...	...	...	106
	...	...	...	...	60	59	61	1.03	...	...	...	11.0**	10.5**	11.5**	107
	...	...	...	...	74**	73**	76**	1.04**	...	...	...	11.5**,[z]	11.0**,[z]	12.0**,[z]	108
	87	87	87	1.00	89[z]	89[z]	89[z]	1.00[z]	11.6**	11.7**	11.5**	12.6	12.5	12.7	109
	...	...	...	...	63	54	73	1.36	...	...	...	13.6	13.5	13.7	110
	80**	75**	84**	1.12**	75**,[y]	67**,[y]	82**,[y]	1.22**,[y]	15.3**	15.0**	15.6**	14.3[y]	13.8[y]	14.7[y]	111
	41	42	40	0.95	38	39	36	0.93	...	...	...	10.8**,[z]	10.6**,[z]	11.0**,[z]	112
	84**	84**	84**	1.00**	88**	87**	89**	1.02**	12.6**	12.1**	13.1**	13.4**	12.8**	14.0**	113

Table 4 (continued)

	Country or territory	Compulsory education (age group)	Legal guarantee of free education[1]	New entrants (000) School year ending in 1999	New entrants (000) School year ending in 2004	GIR 1999 Total	GIR 1999 Male	GIR 1999 Female	GIR 1999 GPI (F/M)	GIR 2004 Total	GIR 2004 Male	GIR 2004 Female	GIR 2004 GPI (F/M)
114	Paraguay[3]	6-14	Yes	179**	164**	122**	125**	120**	0.96**	107**	109**	106**	0.97**
115	Peru[3]	6-16	Yes	676	639	111	111	111	1.00	105	105	106	1.01
116	Saint Kitts and Nevis[5]	5-16	No	…	1	…	…	…	…	100	99	101	1.02
117	Saint Lucia	5-16	No	4**	3	98**	99**	96**	0.97**	101	103	98	0.95
118	St Vincent/Grenad.	5-15	No	…	2	…	…	…	…	92	94	89	0.94
119	Suriname[3]	6-11	Yes	…	10**,z	…	…	…	…	104**,z	109**,z	98**,z	0.90**,z
120	Trinidad and Tobago[2, 3]	5-12	Yes	20	17*	98	99	97	0.98	96*	97*	96*	0.98*
121	Turks and Caicos Islands[5]	4-16	…	0.3**	0.3	…	…	…	…	89	86	93	1.09
122	Uruguay[3]	6-15	Yes	60	60**	107	107	107	1.00	106**	106**	106**	1.00**
123	Venezuela[3]	6-15	Yes	537	556	98	99	97	0.98	101	103	100	0.97
	North America and Western Europe												
124	Andorra[2]	6-16	…	…	1	…	…	…	…	110**	108**	112**	1.04**
125	Austria[2, 4]	6-15	Yes	100	89**	106	107	104	0.98	105**	105**	105**	1.00**
126	Belgium[4]	6-18	Yes	…	120**	…	…	…	…	103**	103**	104**	1.01**
127	Canada	6-16	Yes	…	387**,y	…	…	…	…	97**,y	97**,y	96**,y	0.99**,y
128	Cyprus[2, 5]	6-15	Yes	…	10	…	…	…	…	100	100	101	1.01
129	Denmark	7-16	Yes	66	69	100	100	100	1.00	98	98	99	1.01
130	Finland	7-16	Yes	65	61	100	101	100	1.00	98	98	97	0.99
131	France	6-16	Yes	736	…	102	103**	101**	0.98**	…	…	…	…
132	Germany	6-18	Yes	869	844	100	101	100	1.00	105	105	105	1.00
133	Greece[2]	6-15	Yes	…	109**	…	…	…	…	102**	103**	102**	0.99**
134	Iceland	6-16	Yes	4	4**	99	101	97	0.96	99**	102**	96**	0.94**
135	Ireland	6-15	Yes	51	56	99	100	98	0.98	101	102	101	0.99
136	Israel[3]	5-15	Yes	…	123	…	…	…	…	101	99	102	1.03
137	Italy[2]	6-16	Yes	558	557	100	101	99	0.99	103	103	103	1.00
138	Luxembourg	6-15	Yes	5	6	97	…	…	…	101	101	101	1.00
139	Malta[2]	5-16	Yes	5	5	102	102	101	0.99	97	96	98	1.01
140	Monaco[2]	6-16	No	…	…	…	…	…	…	…	…	…	…
141	Netherlands[2, 4]	6-17	Yes	199	197	100	101	99	0.99	100	100	99	0.99
142	Norway	6-16	Yes	61	61	99	100	99	0.98	98	98	98	1.00
143	Portugal[2]	6-15	Yes	…	107**	…	…	…	…	97**	97**	97**	1.01**
144	San Marino[2]	6-16	No	…	…	…	…	…	…	…	…	…	…
145	Spain	6-16	Yes	403**	391**	106**	106**	105**	0.99**	100**	101**	100**	0.99**
146	Sweden	7-16	Yes	127	97**	104	105	103	0.98	93**	92**	93**	1.01**
147	Switzerland	7-15	Yes	82	77	96	94	98	1.04	91	89	94	1.05
148	United Kingdom	5-16	Yes	…	…	…	…	…	…	…	…	…	…
149	United States	6-17	No	4 235	4 010**	102	105	100	0.95	99**	100**	99**	0.99**
	South and West Asia												
150	Afghanistan	7-12	…	…	1 563	…	…	…	…	180	226	131	0.58
151	Bangladesh	6-10	Yes	4 005	4 318	121	122	119	0.98	130	129	131	1.02
152	Bhutan[3, 8]	6-16	Yes	12	…	…	…	…	…	…	…	…	…
153	India[3]	6-14	Yes	29 639	31 813	127	138	115	0.83	135	139	130	0.94
154	Iran, Islamic Republic of	6-10	Yes	1 563	1 374	90	91	90	0.99	110	102	118	1.15
155	Maldives	6-12	No	8	7**	93	93	94	1.01	83**	83**	83**	1.00**
156	Nepal	6-10	Yes	…	**794**	…	…	…	…	**110**	**115**	**105**	**0.91**
157	Pakistan	5-9	No	…	4 422*	…	…	…	…	111*	126*	95*	0.76*
158	Sri Lanka[2]	5-14	Yes	…	303**	…	…	…	…	93**	90**	96**	1.06**
	Sub-Saharan Africa												
159	Angola[2, 3]	6-14	Yes	…	…	…	…	…	…	…	…	…	…
160	Benin	6-11	No	…	247	…	…	…	…	103	112	94	0.84
161	Botswana	6-15	Yes	50	47	111	112	110	0.99	105	108	102	0.94
162	Burkina Faso	6-15	No	154	272	45	53	38	0.72	71	76	66	0.87
163	Burundi	7-12	No	146**	189	72**	79**	65**	0.83**	91	95	86	0.91
164	Cameroon	6-11	No	335**	474	79**	87**	71**	0.81**	108	115	100	0.87
165	Cape Verde[2]	6-16	No	13**	11	101**	102**	100**	0.98**	90	90	89	0.99
166	Central African Republic	6-15	No	…	71*,y	…	…	…	…	64*,y	75*,y	52*,y	0.69*,y
167	Chad[2, 3]	6-14	Yes	175	242**	72	84	59	0.70	84**	98**	70**	0.71**
168	Comoros[2]	6-14	No	13	15	70	76	64	0.84	70	74	66	0.89

Table 4

NET INTAKE RATE (NIR) IN PRIMARY EDUCATION (%)								SCHOOL LIFE EXPECTANCY (expected number of years of formal schooling from primary to tertiary education)						
School year ending in								School year ending in						
1999				2004				1999			2004			
Total	Male	Female	GPI (F/M)	Total	Male	Female	GPI (F/M)	Total	Male	Female	Total	Male	Female	
...	...	...	...	...	...	...	...	11.1**	11.1**	11.1**	11.5**,z	11.4**,z	11.6**,z	114
79	79	80	1.00	76	76	76	1.01	...	...	...	13.7**	13.5**	14.0**	115
...	...	...	...	66**	66**	67**	1.00**	...	...	...	13.4**	13.2**	13.7**	116
69**	69**	68**	0.99**	71**,z	72**,z	70**,z	0.97**,z	...	...	...	12.9**	12.2**	13.6**	117
...	...	...	...	62**,z	62**,z	62**,z	1.00**,z	...	...	...	11.7**	11.8**	11.6**	118
...	...	...	...	71**,z	71**,z	71**,z	1.00**,z	...	...	...	12.2**,y	11.3**,y	13.2**,y	119
69	69	70	1.01	68*	68*	68*	1.00*	11.9**	11.7**	12.1**	12.3**	12.1**	12.5**	120
...	...	...	...	55	50	59	1.17	...	...	...	12.4**	11.4**	13.3**	121
...	...	...	...	...	...	...	...	13.9**	13.1**	14.8**	15.2**,z	13.9**,z	16.2**,z	122
60**	60**	61**	1.01**	63	63	64	1.00	...	...	...	11.7**,z	11.5**,z	12.0**,z	123
											North America and Western Europe			
...	...	...	...	54**	53**	56**	1.05**	...	...	...	11.3**	11.3**	11.3**	124
...	...	...	...	...	...	...	...	15.2**	15.3**	15.2**	15.3	15.2	15.5	125
...	...	...	...	...	...	...	...	17.8**	17.4**	18.2**	16.0**	15.8**	16.2**	126
...	...	...	...	...	...	...	...	16.0**	15.7**	16.3**	15.7**,y	15.3**,y	16.2**,y	127
...	...	...	...	91y	90y	92y	1.02y	12.5	12.4	12.7	13.6	13.5	13.6	128
...	...	...	...	...	...	...	...	16.1**	15.6**	16.6**	16.7	16.0	17.3	129
...	...	...	...	93**	92**	93**	1.01**	17.4**	16.7**	18.2**	17.0	16.5	17.6	130
...	...	...	...	...	...	...	...	15.7**	15.4**	16.0**	15.8	15.4	16.1	131
...	...	...	...	...	...	...	...	16.1**	16.2**	15.9**	...	...	...	132
...	...	...	...	96**	96**	96**	1.00**	13.8**	13.5**	14.1**	15.8	15.5	16.2	133
...	...	...	...	97**	100**	94**	0.94**	16.7**	16.1**	17.3**	18.3**	17.3**	19.3**	134
...	...	...	...	...	...	...	...	16.4**	15.9**	16.8**	17.8	17.6	18.1	135
...	...	...	...	...	...	...	...	15.0**	14.6**	15.4**	15.4	15.0	15.8	136
...	...	...	...	95z	96z	95z	1.00z	14.9**	14.6**	15.1**	15.9	15.6	16.3	137
...	...	...	...	...	...	...	...	13.1**	13.1**	13.2**	13.5**	13.4**	13.7**	138
...	...	...	...	...	...	...	...	...	...	...	14.8	14.9	14.7	139
...	...	...	...	...	...	...	...	...	...	...	...	...	...	140
...	...	...	...	98z	98z	97z	0.98z	16.5**	16.8**	16.3**	16.5	16.6	16.4	141
...	...	...	...	...	...	...	...	17.5**	16.9**	16.9**	17.7	16.9	18.4	142
...	...	...	...	...	...	...	...	15.7**	15.4**	16.1**	15.2	14.7	15.7	143
...	...	...	...	...	...	...	...	...	...	...	...	...	...	144
...	...	...	...	...	...	...	...	15.9	15.5	16.2	16.2	15.8	16.7	145
...	...	...	...	...	...	...	...	19.1**	17.5**	20.7**	16.0	15.1	16.9	146
...	...	...	...	55z	55z	56z	1.01z	15.1**	15.7**	14.5**	15.2	15.6	14.8	147
...	...	...	...	...	...	...	...	20.0**	19.3**	20.7**	16.6	16.1	17.1	148
...	...	...	...	70**	68**	72**	1.05**	15.9**	...	...	15.8**	15.2**	16.5**	149
											South and West Asia			
...	...	...	...	...	...	...	...	...	...	...	6.7**	9.4**	3.8**	150
91	91	91	1.00	96**,z	96**,z	97**,z	1.01**,z	9.2**	9.3**	9.1**	9.2z	9.0z	9.3z	151
...	...	...	...	...	...	...	...	...	...	...	...	...	...	152
...	...	...	...	...	...	...	...	...	...	...	10.1**	10.9**	9.4**	153
44**	44**	43**	0.97**	90	90	90	0.99	11.5**	12.1**	10.9**	12.5**	12.7**	12.2**	154
80**	79**	80**	1.01**	70y	70y	70y	1.00y	11.8**	11.7**	11.9**	11.2**	11.1**	11.4**	155
...	...	...	...	...	...	...	...	...	...	...	8.9**,z	9.8**,z	8.0**,z	156
...	...	...	...	88*	100*	76*	0.76*	...	...	...	6.2**	7.1**	5.2**	157
...	...	...	...	90**	87**	92**	1.06**	...	...	...	**6.5**	**7.3**	**5.6**	158
											Sub-Saharan Africa			
...	...	...	...	...	...	...	...	3.7**	4.0**	3.4**	...	...	...	159
...	...	...	...	48	52	44	0.84	6.3**	7.9**	4.8**	...	...	...	160
22	20	24	1.20	...	...	...	...	11.2**	11.1**	11.3**	11.9**	11.6**	12.2**	161
19	23	16	0.71	26	29	24	0.85	3.5**	4.2**	2.8**	4.1**	4.7**	3.5**	162
...	...	...	...	35	37	34	0.91	...	...	...	5.9**	6.6**	5.3**	163
...	...	...	...	...	...	...	...	7.7**	...	...	10.6**	11.9**	9.4**	164
65**	64**	66**	1.03**	70	69	70	1.01	...	...	...	11.0**	11.0**	11.0**	165
...	...	...	...	...	...	...	...	...	...	...	...	...	...	166
22	25	18	0.71	29y	33y	24y	0.73y	...	...	...	...	...	...	167
16	18**	13**	0.70**	...	...	...	...	6.5**	7.1**	5.9**	8.0**	8.7**	7.3**	168

Education for All Global Monitoring Report

2007

Table 4 (continued)

	Country or territory	Compulsory education (age group)	Legal guarantee of free education[1]	New entrants (000) School year ending in 1999	New entrants (000) School year ending in 2004	GIR 1999 Total	GIR 1999 Male	GIR 1999 Female	GIR 1999 GPI (F/M)	GIR 2004 Total	GIR 2004 Male	GIR 2004 Female	GIR 2004 GPI (F/M)
169	Congo[3]	6-15	Yes	...	78	...	...	...	...	65	66	63	0.95
170	Côte d'Ivoire	6-15	No	309	354*,z	65	72	58	0.80	72*,z	75*,z	68*,z	0.91*,z
171	D. R. Congo[3]	6-13	Yes	767	...	51	49	52	1.07	...	...	...	...
172	Equatorial Guinea	7-11	Yes	33	16y	269	313	225	0.72	123y	137y	110y	0.80y
173	Eritrea	7-13	No	57	69	59	65	52	0.81	58	63	52	0.82
174	Ethiopia	7-12	No	1537	**3143**	78	93	63	0.69	**141**	**148**	**135**	**0.91**
175	Gabon	6-16	No	...	35**,z	...	...	...	...	94**,z	94**,z	94**,z	1.00**,z
176	Gambia	...	Yes	28	31	83	85	80	0.94	81	79	83	1.04
177	Ghana[2,3]	6-15	Yes	469	**538**	86	88	84	0.96	**95**	**94**	**96**	**1.02**
178	Guinea	6-12	No	119	215	51	55	45	0.82	83	87	79	0.92
179	Guinea-Bissau[3]	7-12	Yes	36**	...	93**	110**	76**	0.69**	...	...	...	...
180	Kenya[3]	6-13	Yes	892	1169*	103	105	102	0.97	124*	127*	121*	0.95*
181	Lesotho	6-12	No	51	62	106	106	107	1.01	137	144	131	0.91
182	Liberia[2]	6-16	No	50	...	59	72	46	0.63	...	...	...	...
183	Madagascar[3]	6-14	Yes	495	897	107	108	106	0.98	166	168	164	0.97
184	Malawi	6-13	Yes	616	712	177	176	178	1.01	171	164	178	1.08
185	Mali[3]	7-15	Yes	173**	254	51**	58**	44**	0.77**	64	69	58	0.85
186	Mauritius[3]	...	Yes	22	**20**	98	96	99	1.04	**102**	**102**	**102**	**1.00**
187	Mozambique	6-12	No	536	771	102	110	93	0.85	134	138	129	0.94
188	Namibia[3]	6-15	Yes	54	58**,z	92	90	93	1.03	99**,z	99**,z	99**,z	0.99**,z
189	Niger[3]	7-12	Yes	133	242	40	46	33	0.71	59	68	51	0.75
190	Nigeria[3]	6-11	Yes	...	4210**	...	...	...	...	112**	120**	103**	0.86**
191	Rwanda[3]	6-12	Yes	295	456	134	119	148	1.25	183	183	183	1.00
192	Sao Tome and Principe	7-12	Yes	4	5	109	110	108	0.98	116	116	117	1.01
193	Senegal	7-12	Yes	190	284	64	66**	63**	0.96**	90	89	91	1.03
194	Seychelles[5]	6-15	Yes	2	1	117	116	118	1.02	116	119	113	0.94
195	Sierra Leone	...	No	...	...	...	...	...	...	...	...	...	...
196	Somalia	6-13	...	...	...	...	...	...	...	...	...	...	...
197	South Africa	7-15	No	1157	1188z	114	115	112	0.98	115z	118z	112z	0.94z
198	Swaziland	6-12	No	31	31z	100	102	98	0.96	107z	110z	104z	0.94z
199	Togo	6-15	No	139	149	91	97	86	0.88	86	90	82	0.91
200	Uganda	...	No	...	1550	...	...	...	...	163	164	163	1.00
201	United Republic of Tanzania[3]	7-13	Yes	714	**1342**	72	72	72	0.99	**125**	**125**	**124**	**0.99**
202	Zambia	7-13	No	252	380	78	77	78	1.01	110	110	110	1.00
203	Zimbabwe	6-12	No	398	417z	110	111	108	0.97	120z	122z	118z	0.97z

				Sum	Sum	Weighted average							
I	World	...	...	130129	134132	106	110	101	0.92	111	115	108	0.94
II	Countries in transition	...	...	4232	3376	94	94	94	0.99	100	101	100	0.99
III	Developed countries	...	...	12288	11622	101	103	100	0.98	101	101	101	1.00
IV	Developing countries	...	...	113609	119134	107	112	101	0.91	113	116	109	0.94
V	Arab States	...	...	6186	6747	89	92	85	0.92	94	97	92	0.94
VI	Central and Eastern Europe	...	...	5479	4612	94	96	93	0.97	98	99	97	0.98
VII	Central Asia	...	...	1785	1529	101	101	100	1.00	102	103	102	0.99
VIII	East Asia and the Pacific	...	...	38021	33761	105	105	104	0.99	102	103	101	0.98
IX	East Asia	...	...	37460	33179	105	106	105	0.99	102	103	101	0.98
X	Pacific	...	...	561	582	102	103	101	0.98	106**	108	104	0.96
XI	Latin America/Caribbean	...	...	13159	12813	119	122	116	0.95	115**	118	113	0.96
XII	Caribbean	...	...	565	548	164	162	166	1.02	162**	161	164	1.02
XIII	Latin America	...	...	12595	12265	117	121	114	0.94	114**	116	111	0.96
XIV	N. America/W. Europe	...	...	9243	8852	102	104	101	0.97	101	101	101	0.99
XV	South and West Asia	...	...	40273	44892	118	128	107	0.84	131	138	125	0.90
XVI	Sub-Saharan Africa	...	...	15982	20924	88	94	82	0.88	105	109	101	0.92

1. *Source:* Tomasevsky (2003).
2. Information on compulsory education comes from the Reports under the United Nations Human Rights Treaties.

3. Some primary school fees continue to be charged despite the legal guarantee of free education (World Bank, 2002; Bentaouet-Kattan, 2005).

4. No tuition fees are charged but some direct costs have been reported (World Bank, 2002; Bentaouet-Kattan, 2005).

5. National population data were used to calculate enrolment ratios.
6. Children can enter primary school at age 6 or 7.

NET INTAKE RATE (NIR) IN PRIMARY EDUCATION (%)

SCHOOL LIFE EXPECTANCY
(expected number of years of formal schooling from primary to tertiary education)

Total	Male	Female	GPI (F/M)	Total	Male	Female	GPI (F/M)	Total	Male	Female	Total	Male	Female	
											7.7**,z	8.5**,z	7.0**,z	169
27	30	24	0.79	27*,z	28*,z	26*,z	0.94*,z	6.2**	7.4**	4.9**	...	...	...	170
23	22	24	1.09	...	...	...	...	4.3**	...	...	...	...	...	171
...	...	...	...	49y	62y	36y	0.58y	...	...	...	...	...	...	172
19	20	17	0.89	25	26	23	0.87	4.5**	5.1**	3.9**	5.6**	6.7**	4.5**	173
20	23	18	0.80	31	33	30	0.92	3.8**	4.8**	2.9**	5.6**	6.6**	4.6**	174
...	...	...	...	...	...	...	...	11.9**	12.3**	11.5**	...	...	...	175
48**	49**	47**	0.96**	...	...	...	...	7.0**	7.8**	6.1**	7.8**	8.0**	7.7**	176
29**	29**	29**	1.00**	**29****	**29****	**30****	**1.03****	...	...	...	**8.3****	**8.7****	**7.9****	177
19	20	18	0.89	35	36	35	0.97	...	...	...	6.9	8.1	5.6	178
...	...	...	...	...	...	...	...	...	...	...	...	...	...	179
30**	29**	31**	1.05**	42**,z	41**,z	43**,z	1.05**,z	...	...	...	9.9**	10.2**	9.5**	180
28	27	29	1.06	61**	61**	62**	1.01**	9.3	8.8	9.8	10.9**,z	10.6**,z	11.2**,z	181
...	...	...	...	...	...	...	...	8.1**	9.6**	6.5**	...	...	...	182
...	...	...	...	47**,z	46**,z	48**,z	1.05**,z	6.1**	6.2**	5.9**	...	...	...	183
...	...	...	...	...	...	...	...	11.1**	11.8**	10.4**	9.6**	9.8**	9.5**	184
...	...	...	...	23	26	21	0.82	4.0**	...	...	5.4**	6.3**	4.5**	185
72	71	74	1.03	81	81	81	1.00	12.1**	12.2**	12.0**	13.5**	13.6**	13.3**	186
18	18	17	0.93	30**	29**	30**	1.01**	5.4**	...	...	7.6**	8.4**	6.8**	187
52**	51**	54**	1.07**	55**,z	54**,z	57**,z	1.06**,z	...	...	...	10.9**,z	10.8**,z	11.1**,z	188
25	30	20	0.68	37	43	31	0.72	...	...	...	3.2**	3.8**	2.6**	189
...	...	...	...	69**	74**	64**	0.86**	...	...	...	8.8**	9.7**	7.9**	190
...	...	...	...	91**	90**	92**	1.03**	6.8**	...	...	8.2**	8.3**	8.2**	191
...	...	...	...	...	...	...	...	7.6**	8.4**	6.9**	10.1	10.2	10.1	192
36	36**	35**	0.96**	58	57	59	1.02	5.0**	...	...	6.2**	...	...	193
75	74	77	1.03	69z	67z	72z	1.06z	14.0	13.9	14.2	12.8**	12.4**	13.2**	194
...	...	...	...	...	...	...	...	...	...	...	...	...	...	195
...	...	...	...	...	...	...	...	...	...	...	...	...	...	196
43	44	42	0.96	44z	45z	43z	0.97z	13.3**	13.1**	13.5**	13.0**,z	12.7**,z	13.0**,z	197
42	41	44	1.06	47z	46z	47z	1.01z	9.8**	10.1**	9.5**	9.4**,z	9.6**,z	9.2**,z	198
37	40	35	0.87	39	41	37	0.90	9.1**	11.1**	7.1**	...	...	...	199
...	...	...	...	64	63	65	1.03	10.1**	10.8**	9.5**	10.4**	10.7**	10.2**	200
14	13	15	1.16	**90**	**89**	**90**	**1.02**	5.1**	5.2**	5.1**	...	...	...	201
35	33	36	1.07	39	38	41	1.06	6.5**	6.9**	6.1**	...	...	...	202
...	...	...	...	45z	45z	46z	1.03z	9.7**	...	...	9.1**,z	9.3**,z	8.9**,z	203

			Median							Weighted average				
...	...	...	...	67	70	64	0.92	9.9	10.3	9.4	10.7	11.0	10.4	I
...	...	...	...	81	81	81	1.00	11.9	11.8	12.0	12.7	12.5	12.9	II
...	...	...	...	...	...	...	...	15.8	15.5	16.1	15.7	15.4	16.1	III
...	...	...	...	64	63	65	1.03	9.1	9.7	8.5	10.1	10.5	9.7	IV
62	63	61	0.97	63	63	64	1.01	9.6	10.3	8.9	10.3	10.8	9.7	V
...	...	...	...	...	...	...	...	12.1	12.1	12.0	12.9	12.9	12.8	VI
...	...	...	...	67	69	65	0.95	10.9	11.1	10.8	11.7	11.8	11.6	VII
...	...	...	...	...	...	...	...	10.5	10.6	10.3	11.5	11.6	11.5	VIII
...	...	...	...	...	...	...	...	10.4	10.6	10.2	11.5	11.6	11.4	IX
...	...	...	...	...	...	...	...	14.5	14.4	14.6	14.7	14.7	14.7	X
79	80	78	0.98	69	69	68	0.98	12.5	12.4	12.6	13.0	12.8	13.2	XI
80	75	84	1.12	67	70	64	0.92	11.0	11.1	10.9	11.9	11.9	11.9	XII
69	68	69	1.03	71	71	71	1.01	12.6	12.4	12.7	13.0	12.8	13.2	XIII
...	...	...	...	...	...	...	...	16.2	15.8	16.6	15.9	15.5	16.4	XIV
...	...	...	...	90	87	92	1.06	8.3	9.3	7.2	9.6	10.3	8.8	XV
28	27	29	1.06	45	45	45	1.00	6.5	7.2	5.8	7.6	8.3	6.9	XVI

7. Enrolment ratios were not calculated due to lack of United Nations population data by age.
8. Enrolment ratios were not calculated due to inconsistencies between enrolment and the United Nations population data.

Data in bold are for the school year ending in 2005.
(z) Data are for the school year ending in 2003.
(y) Data are for the school year ending in 2002.

Table 5
Participation in primary education

Country or territory	Age group 2004	School-age population[1] (000) 2003	ENROLMENT IN PRIMARY EDUCATION				Enrolment in private institutions as % of total enrolment		GROSS ENROLMENT RATIO (GER) IN PRIMARY EDUCATION (%)			
			School year ending in 1999		School year ending in 2004		School year ending in 1999	2004	School year ending in 1999			
			Total (000)	% F	Total (000)	% F			Total	Male	Female	GPI (F/M)
Arab States												
1 Algeria	6-11	4 035	4 779	47	4 508	47	.	.	105	110	100	0.91
2 Bahrain	6-11	80	76	49	83	49	19	23	105	105	105	1.01
3 Djibouti	6-11	124	38	41	49	44	9	15	35	40	29	0.71
4 Egypt	6-10	7 873	8 086**	47**	7 928**	48**	…	8**	101**	106**	97**	0.91**
5 Iraq	6-11	4 402	3 604	44	4 335	44	.	.	92	101	83	0.82
6 Jordan	6-11	815	706	49	800	49	29	30	99	99	99	1.00
7 Kuwait	6-9	164	140	49	158	49	32	32	100	99	101	1.01
8 Lebanon	6-11	425	395	48	454	48	66	65	115	117	112	0.95
9 Libyan Arab Jamahiriya	6-11	662	822	48	744**,z	49**,z	.	3**,z	114	115	113	0.98
10 Mauritania	6-11	461	346	48	434	49	2	7	87	89	84	0.94
11 Morocco	6-11	3 843	3 462	44	4 070	46	4	5	87	96	78	0.81
12 Oman	6-11	351	316	48	306	49	5	4	91	92	89	0.97
13 Palestinian A. T.	6-9	418	368	49	389	49	9	8	106	106	107	1.01
14 Qatar	6-11	64	61	48	65	48	37	42	105	107	103	0.96
15 Saudi Arabia	6-11	3 544	2 260	48	2 386	48	6	7	70	71	69	0.96
16 Sudan	6-11	5 337	2 513**	45**	3 208	46	2**	4	51**	55**	47**	0.85**
17 Syrian Arab Republic	6-9	1 784	2 738	47	2 193	48	4	4	102	107	98	0.92
18 Tunisia	6-11	1 118	1 443	47	1 228	48	1	1	114	117	111	0.95
19 United Arab Emirates	6-10	304	270	48	255	48	44	58	90	91	89	0.97
20 Yemen	6-11	3 552	2 303	35	3 108	40	1	2	73	93	52	0.56
Central and Eastern Europe												
21 Albania	6-9	237	292	48	253z	48z	.	2z	110	111	109	0.98
22 Belarus	6-9	399	632	48	404	48	0.1	0.1	109	110	108	0.98
23 Bosnia and Herzegovina	6-9	186	…	…	…	…	…	…	…	…	…	…
24 Bulgaria	7-10	300	412	48	314.2	48.3	0.3	0.4	106	107	104	0.97
25 Croatia	7-10	202	203	49	192z	49z	0.1	0.2z	92	93	92	0.98
26 Czech Republic	6-10	525	655	49	534	48	1	1	104	104	103	0.99
27 Estonia	7-12	92	127	48	92	48	1	2	102	104	100	0.97
28 Hungary	7-10	456	503	48	447	48	5	6	102	102	101	0.98
29 Latvia	7-10	100	141	48	92	48	1	1	99	100	98	0.98
30 Lithuania	7-10	175	220	48	170	49	0.4	0.4	103	104	102	0.98
31 Poland	7-12	2 888	3 434	48	2 856	49	…	1	98	99	97	0.98
32 Republic of Moldova	7-10	237	262	49	202	49	…	1	84	84	85	1.00
33 Romania	7-10	944	1 285	49	1 006	48	.	0.2	105	105	104	0.98
34 Russian Federation[3]	7-9	4 335	6 138	49	5 330	49	0.3	0.5	100	100	99	0.99
35 Serbia and Montenegro[4]	7-10	…	418	49	…	…	.	…	104	105	103	0.99
36 Slovakia	6-9	257	317	49	255	48	4	4	103	103	102	0.99
37 Slovenia	7-10	76	92	48	93	49	0.1	0.1	101	102	100	0.99
38 TFYR Macedonia	7-10	116	130	48	113	48	.	.	101	102	100	0.98
39 Turkey	6-11	8 437	…	…	7 873	48	.	2	…	…	…	…
40 Ukraine	6-9	1 953	2 200	49	1 851	49	0.3	0.5	105	106	105	0.99
Central Asia												
41 Armenia	7-9	143	…	…	145	48	…	1	…	…	…	…
42 Azerbaijan	6-9	627	707	49	607	48	–	0.1	94	94	94	1.00
43 Georgia	6-11	381	302	49	363	48	0.5	3	98	98	98	1.00
44 Kazakhstan	7-10	989	1 249	49	1 080	49	1	1	98	98	98	1.00
45 Kyrgyzstan	7-10	453	470	49	444	49	0.2	0.3	98	98	97	0.99
46 Mongolia	8-11	226	251	50	236	49	0.5	3	98	97	100	1.04
47 Tajikistan	7-10	691	690	48	690	48	.	.	97	100	95	0.95
48 Turkmenistan	7-9	317	…	…	…	…	…	…	…	…	…	…
49 Uzbekistan	7-10	2 446	…	…	2 441**	49**	…	.z	…	…	…	…
East Asia and the Pacific												
50 Australia	5-11	1 881	1 885	49	1 935	49	27	29	98	98	98	1.00
51 Brunei Darussalam	6-11	42	46	47	46.4	47.9	36	36	114	115	112	0.97
52 Cambodia	6-11	2 023	2 127	46	2 763	47	2	0.6	99	106	92	0.87
53 China[5]	7-11	102 869	…	…	120 999	47	…	…	…	…	…	…

GROSS ENROLMENT RATIO (GER) IN PRIMARY EDUCATION (%)				NET ENROLMENT RATIO (NER) IN PRIMARY EDUCATION (%)								OUT-OF-SCHOOL CHILDREN (000)[2]						
School year ending in 2004				School year ending in 1999				2004				School year ending in 1999			2004			
Total	Male	Female	GPI (F/M)	Total	Male	Female	GPI (F/M)	Total	Male	Female	GPI (F/M)	Total	Male	Female	Total	Male	Female	
Arab States																		
112	116	107	0.93	91	93	89	0.96	97	98	95	0.98	362	141	221	41	–	41	1
104	104	104	1.00	96	95	97	1.02	97	96	97	1.01	0.9	0.9	0.1	1.5	1.0	0.5	2
39	44	35	0.79	28	33	24	0.73	33	36	29	0.81	79	37	42	83	40	44	3
101**	103**	98**	0.96**	93**	97**	90**	0.93**	95**	97**	94**	0.97**	320**	28**	293**	220**	58**	161**	4
98	108	89	0.83	85	91	78	0.85	88	94	81	0.86	603	175	428	540	129	411	5
98	98	99	1.01	92	91	92	1.01	91	90	92	1.02	33	18	15	43	26	17	6
96	96	97	1.00	87	86	87	1.01	86**	85**	87**	1.03**	10	5	5	15**	9**	6**	7
107	109	105	0.96	94**	96**	92**	0.96**	93	94	93	0.99	13**	4**	9**	20	10	10	8
112**,z	113**,z	112**,z	1.00**,z	...	...	...	...	...	...	...	...	...	...	...	...	...	...	9
94	95	93	0.98	63	65	61	0.94	74	75	74	0.99	150	71	78	117	58	60	10
106	111	100	0.90	72	77	66	0.86	86	89	83	0.94	1114	456	659	528	218	310	11
87	88	87	1.00	80	80	80	1.00	78	77	79	1.02	63	32	30	71	38	33	12
93	93	93	1.00	97	96	97	1.01	86	86	86	1.00	4	3	1	40	22	19	13
102	102	101	0.98	94	94	94	1.01	96	97	95	0.99	0.6	0.4	0.3	0.6	0.1	0.5	14
67	69	66	0.96	58	60	56	0.93	59**	62**	56**	0.91**	1345	651	694	1425**	682**	743**	15
60	64	56	0.87	...	...	...	...	...	...	...	...	...	...	...	...	...	...	16
123	126	120	0.95	92**	95**	88**	0.93**	92	94	90	0.96	137**	22**	115**	32	–	32	17
110	112	108	0.97	94	95	92	0.98	97	97	98	1.00	72	30	42	17	11	6	18
84	85	82	0.97	79	79	79	0.99	71	72	70	0.97	56	28	28	83	41	42	19
87	102	72	0.71	57	72	42	0.59	75**	87**	63**	0.73**	1334	449	885	861**	229**	632**	20
Central and Eastern Europe																		
104z	105z	104z	0.99z	99**	100**	99**	0.99**	96z	96z	95z	0.99z	1.6**	–**	1.6**	11z	5z	6z	21
101	103	99	0.97	...	...	...	...	90	91**	88**	0.97**	...	...	...	38	16**	21**	22
...	...	...	...	...	...	...	...	...	...	...	...	...	...	...	...	...	...	23
105	106	104	0.98	97	98	96	0.98	95	96	95	0.99	5	1	4	10	5	5	24
94z	95z	94z	0.99z	85	86	85	0.98	87z	88z	87z	0.99z	18	9	9	14z	7z	7z	25
102	103	101	0.99	...	...	...	...	...	...	...	...	...	...	...	...	...	...	26
100	101	98	0.97	96**	96**	95**	0.98**	94	94	94	1.00	0.2**	0.0**	0.2**	3.2	1.9	1.3	27
98	99	97	0.99	88	88	88	0.99	89	90	88	0.99	15	8	7	18.3	9.7	8.6	28
93	94	91	0.97	...	...	...	...	...	...	...	...	...	...	...	14	7	7	29
97	98	97	0.99	95	96	95	0.99	89	90	89	1.00	4	2	2	13.5	7.1	6.4	30
99	99	99	0.99	...	...	...	...	97	97	98	1.00	...	...	...	73.2	40.6	32.6	31
85	85	85	0.99	78**	...	...	...	78	78	77	0.99	58**	...	...	45	23	22	32
107	107	106	0.98	96	96	95	0.99	92	92	92	0.99	1.6	–	1.6	47	23	24	33
123	123	123	1.00	...	...	...	...	91**	91**	92**	1.01**	...	...	...	369**	198**	171**	34
...	...	...	...	...	...	...	...	...	...	...	...	...	...	...	...	...	...	35
99	100	98	0.99z	...	...	...	...	...	...	...	...	...	...	...	...	...	...	36
123	123	122	0.99z	97	98	97	0.99	98	98	98	1.00	0.5	0.1	0.4	0.2	0.2	–	37
98	98	98	1.00z	93	94	92	0.98	92	92	92	1.00	1.4	0.1	1.3	2.9	1.6	1.3	38
93	96	90	0.94	...	...	...	...	89**	92**	87**	0.95**	...	...	...	900**	354**	546**	39
95	95	95	1.00	...	...	...	...	82	82*	82*	1.00*	...	...	...	317	162*	155*	40
Central Asia																		
101	99	103	1.03	...	...	...	...	94	92	95	1.04	...	...	...	3	3	–	41
97	98	96	0.98	85	85	86	1.01	84	85	83	0.98	110	58	52	101	50	51	42
95	95	95	1.00	...	...	...	...	93	93	92	0.99	...	...	...	26	13	13	43
109	110	109	0.99	...	...	...	...	93	93	92	0.99	...	...	...	11	4	6	44
98	98	98	1.00	88*	89*	87*	0.99*	90	90	90	0.99	35*	17*	18*	18	10	9	45
104	104	105	1.02	90	88	91	1.04	84	84	84	1.01	20	13	7	24	13	11	46
100	102	97	0.95	89	92	86	0.94	97	99	94	0.96	78	30	48	20	3	17	47
...	...	...	...	...	...	...	...	...	...	...	...	...	...	...	...	...	...	48
100**	100**	99**	0.99**	...	...	...	...	...	...	...	...	...	...	...	...	...	...	49
East Asia and the Pacific																		
103	103	103	1.00	92	92	92	1.01	96	96	96	1.00	154	82	72	77	42	35	50
109	109	109	1.00	...	...	...	...	...	...	...	...	...	...	...	...	...	...	51
137	142	131	0.92	85**	89**	81**	0.91**	98	100	96	0.96	321	119	201	48	4	44	52
118	118	117	1.00	...	...	...	...	...	...	...	...	...	...	...	...	...	...	53

Table 5 (continued)

	Country or territory	Age group 2004	School-age population[1] (000) 2003	ENROLMENT IN PRIMARY EDUCATION School year ending in 1999 Total (000)	1999 % F	2004 Total (000)	2004 % F	Enrolment in private institutions as % of total enrolment School year ending in 1999	2004	GROSS ENROLMENT RATIO (GER) IN PRIMARY EDUCATION (%) School year ending in 1999 Total	Male	Female	GPI (F/M)
54	Cook Islands[4]	5-10	…	3	46	2[z]	47[z]	15	19[z]	96	99	94	0.95
55	DPR Korea	6-9	1 580	…	…	…	…	…	…	…	…	…	…
56	Fiji	6-11	107	116	48	113	48	…	99	110	111	110	0.99
57	Indonesia	7-12	24 917	…	…	29 142	49	…	16	…	…	…	…
58	Japan	6-11	7 228	7 692	49	7 257	49	1	0.9	101	101	101	1.00
59	Kiribati[4]	6-11	…	14	49	16	50	…	…	104	104	105	1.01
60	Lao PDR	6-10	760	828	45	885	46	2	2	117	126	107	0.85
61	Macao, China	6-11	38	47	47	40	47	95**	95	100	102	97	0.96
62	Malaysia	6-11	3 299	3 040	48	3 056[z]	49[z]	6	1[z]	100	101	99	0.98
63	Marshall Islands	6-11	…	8	48	9**,[z]	47**,[z]	25	24[y]	…	…	…	…
64	Micronesia	6-11	16	…	…	…	…	…	…	…	…	…	…
65	Myanmar	5-9	5 112	4 733	49	**4 948**	**50**	.	.	88	88	87	0.99
66	Nauru	6-11	…	…	…	1[z]	47[z]	…	21[y]	…	…	…	…
67	New Zealand	5-10	347	361	49	353	48	2	2	102	102	103	1.01
68	Niue[4]	5-10	…	0.3	46	0.2	51	.	…	99	99	98	1.00
69	Palau[4]	6-10	…	2	47	2**	48**	18	…	114	118	109	0.93
70	Papua New Guinea	7-12	926	623	45	681**,[z]	45**,[z]	2	…	78	81	75	0.93
71	Philippines	6-11	11 586	12 503	49	13 018	49	8	7	113	113	113	1.00
72	Republic of Korea	6-11	3 983	3 845	47	**4 125**	**47**	2	**1**	95	95	96	1.01
73	Samoa	5-10	31	27	48	31	48	16	17	99	99	98	0.98
74	Singapore	6-11	381	…	…	…	…	…	…	…	…	…	…
75	Solomon Islands	6-11	73	58	46	88	47	…	…	88	91	85	0.93
76	Thailand	6-11	6 205	6 120	48	**5 975**	**48**	13	**16**	94	97	92	0.95
77	Timor-Leste	6-11	120	…	…	184[y]	…	…	…	…	…	…	…
78	Tokelau[6]	5-10	…	…	…	0.2[z]	50[z]	…	.[z]	…	…	…	…
79	Tonga	5-10	15	17	46	17	47	7	9	112	113	110	0.98
80	Tuvalu[4]	6-11	…	1	48	1	50	…	…	98	97	99	1.02
81	Vanuatu	6-11	33	34	48	39	48	…	…	110	111	109	0.98
82	Viet Nam	6-10	8 523	10 250	47	8 350	47	0.3	0.3[z]	108	112	104	0.93
	Latin America and the Caribbean												
83	Anguilla	5-11	…	2	50	1	50	5	11	…	…	…	…
84	Antigua and Barbuda	5-11	…	…	…	…	…	…	…	…	…	…	…
85	Argentina	6-11	4 156	4 821	49	4 675[z]	49[z]	20	21[z]	117	116	117	1.00
86	Aruba[4]	6-11	…	9	49	10	48	83	80	112	114	111	0.98
87	Bahamas	5-10	37	34	49	34	49	…	20	95	96	94	0.98
88	Barbados	5-10	21	25	49	22	49	…	11	108	108	107	0.98
89	Belize	5-10	39	44	48	49	49	…	82	118	120	116	0.97
90	Bermuda[4]	5-10	…	…	…	4.9[y]	50.3[y]	…	35[y]	…	…	…	…
91	Bolivia	6-11	1 362	1 445	49	1 546**	49**	8	20**,[z]	113	114	112	0.98
92	Brazil	7-10	13 509	20 939	48	18 919[z]	48[z]	8	9[z]	155	159	150	0.94
93	British Virgin Islands[4]	5-11	…	3	49	3	48	13	19	112	113	110	0.97
94	Cayman Islands	5-10	…	3	47	3	49	36	33	…	…	…	…
95	Chile	6-11	1 694	1 805	48	1 756	48	45	50	101	102	99	0.97
96	Colombia	6-10	4 727	5 162	49	5 259	49	20	17	113	113	112	1.00
97	Costa Rica	6-11	499	552	48	558	48	7	7	108	109	107	0.98
98	Cuba	6-11	903	1 074	48	906	48	.	.	106	109	104	0.96
99	Dominica[4]	5-11	…	12	48	10	48	24	30	104	107	102	0.95
100	Dominican Republic	6-11	1 145	1 315	49	1 282	48	14**	15**	113	114	112	0.98
101	Ecuador	6-11	1 702	1 899	49	1 990	49	21	28	114	114	114	1.00
102	El Salvador	7-12	914	940	48	1 045	48	11**	10**	111	113	109	0.96
103	Grenada[4]	5-11	…	…	…	16	49	…	76[z]	…	…	…	…
104	Guatemala	7-12	2 015	1 824	46	2 281	47	15	11	101	108	94	0.87
105	Guyana	6-11	88	107	49	111**	49**	1	1[z]	119	120	118	0.98
106	Haiti	6-11	1 230	…	…	…	…	…	…	…	…	…	…
107	Honduras	6-11	1 113	…	…	1 257	49	…	…	…	…	…	…
108	Jamaica	6-11	348	316**	49**	331	49	4**	8	93**	93**	93**	1.00**
109	Mexico	6-11	13 540	14 698	49	14 781	49	7	8	109	110	107	0.97
110	Montserrat[4]	5-11	…	0.4	44	0.5	45	38	37	…	…	…	…
111	Netherlands Antilles	6-11	18	25	48	23**,[z]	49**,[z]	74	73**,[z]	134	139	130	0.94

	GROSS ENROLMENT RATIO (GER) IN PRIMARY EDUCATION (%)				NET ENROLMENT RATIO (NER) IN PRIMARY EDUCATION (%)								OUT-OF-SCHOOL CHILDREN (000)[2]						
	School year ending in 2004				School year ending in								School year ending in						
					1999				2004				1999			2004			
	Total	Male	Female	GPI (F/M)	Total	Male	Female	GPI (F/M)	Total	Male	Female	GPI (F/M)	Total	Male	Female	Total	Male	Female	
	82**,z	83**,z	81**,z	0.98**,z	85	87	83	0.96	...	...	...	...	0.4	0.2	0.2	...	...	...	54
	...	...	...	...	...	...	...	...					...	...	...	...	...	...	55
	106	107	105	0.98	99	99	99	1.01	96	97	96	0.99	1.1	0.8	0.4	1.4	0.6	0.9	56
	117	118	116	0.98	...	...	...	...	94	95	93	0.98	...	...	...	242	–	242	57
	100	100	101	1.00	100	100	100	1.00	100	100	100	1.00	3	–	3	7	7	–	58
	115	113	116	1.03	88**	88**	88**	1.00**	...	...	...	...	1.3**	0.7**	0.6**	...	...	...	59
	116	124	109	0.88	80	84	77	0.92	84	87	82	0.94	141	59	82	119	50	68	60
	106	110	101	0.92	85	84	85	1.01	89	91	88	0.97	7	4	3	4	2	2	61
	93z	94z	93z	1.00z	98	99	97	0.98	93z	93z	93z	1.00z	67	20	46	222z	112z	110z	62
	113**,z	116**,z	109**,z	0.94**,z	...	...	...	...	90**,z	90**,z	89**,z	0.99**,z	...	...	...	0.7**,z	0.3**,z	0.3**,z	63
																			64
	97	**96**	**98**	**1.02**	80**	81**	80**	0.99**	**88**	**87**	**88**	**1.02**	1 051**	521**	530**	**634**	**340**	**293**	65
	84**,z	84**,z	83**,z	0.99**,z															66
	102	102	102	1.00	99	98	99	1.01	99	99	99	1.00	3.1	2.4	0.7	1.9	0.8	1.1	67
	87	80	95	1.19	99	99	98	1.00	...	...	...	...	0.004	0.002	0.002	...	...	...	68
	114**,z	119**,z	109**,z	0.92**,z	97**	99**	94**	0.94**	...	...	...	...	0.05**	0.0**	0.05**	...	...	...	69
	75**,z	80**,z	70**,z	0.88**,z	...	...	...	...					...	...	...				70
	112	113	111	0.99	...	...	...	...	94	93	95	1.02	...	...	...	646.4	391.6	254.9	71
	105	**105**	**104**	**0.99**	94	94	95	1.01	**99**	**100**	**99**	**1.00**	214	121	93	**14**	**4**	**10**	72
	100	100	100	1.00	92	92	91	0.99	90**	90**	91**	1.00**	2	0.8	0.8	0.3**	0.3**	–**	73
																			74
	119	121	117	0.97	...	...	...	...	80	80	79	0.99	...	...	...	15	8	7	75
	97	**100**	**95**	**0.95**															76
	140y	...	...	...															77
					...				...				...			...			78
	115	118	112	0.95	91	92	89	0.97	93	95	91	0.96	1.4	0.6	0.7	0.7	0.2	0.5	79
	99	95	102	1.07	...	...	...	...					...	...	...				80
	118	120	116	0.97	91	91	90	0.99	94	95	93	0.98	2.8	1.4	1.4	2	0.7	0.9	81
	98	101	94	0.93	96	...	...	...	93**,y	...	...	...	393	...	...	634**,y			82

Latin America and the Caribbean

	Total	Male	Female	GPI (F/M)	Total	Male	Female	GPI (F/M)	Total	Male	Female	GPI (F/M)	Total	Male	Female	Total	Male	Female	
	93**	91**	94**	1.03**	...	...	...	...	88**	87**	89**	1.02**	...	...	...	0.1**	0.1**	0.0**	83
	...	...	...	...	...	...	...	...					...	...	...	...	...	...	84
	112z	113z	112z	0.99z	99*	99*	99*	1.00*	99z	99z	98z	0.99z	10*	5*	5*	22z	3z	19z	85
	114	117	111	0.95	98	97	98	1.01	97	97	96	0.99	0.2	0.1	0.1	0.3	0.1	0.2	86
	93	93	93	1.00	89	90	89	0.99	84	83	85	1.02	4	1.8	1.8	6	3	3	87
	107	108	106	0.99	97**	97**	97**	0.99**	97	98	97	0.99	0.7**	0.3**	0.4**	0.6	0.2	0.3	88
	124	126	123	0.98	94**	94**	94**	1.00**	95	95	96	1.01	2**	0.9**	0.8**	0.6	0.5	0.1	89
	102y	...	...	...												...	...	...	90
	113**	114**	113**	0.99**	95	95	95	1.00	95**	95**	96**	1.01**	52	26	26	44**	25**	18**	91
	141z	145z	137z	0.94z	91	...	...	...	93z	...	...	...	1 032	...	...	800z	...	...	92
	108	110	105	0.96	96**	95**	97**	1.02**	95**	95**	95**	1.00**	0.04**	0.03**	0.02**	0.1**	0.1**	0.1**	93
	93**	96**	91**	0.95**	...	...	...	...	87**	89**	85**	0.95**	...	...	...	0.4**	0.1**	0.2**	94
	104	106	101	0.95	...	...	...	...	...	...	...	...	...	...	...	...	...	...	95
	111	112	111	0.99	88	88**	89**	1.01**	83	83	84	1.01	431	232**	200**	713	379	334	96
	112	112	111	0.99	...	...	...	...					...	...	...				97
	100	103	98	0.95	98	98	98	1.00	96	98	95	1.00	4	4	–	29	9	20	98
	95	96	95	0.99	94**	95**	93**	0.98**	88	87	88	1.01	0.4**	0.1**	0.2**	0.7	0.4	0.3	99
	112	115	109	0.95	84	84	85	1.01	86	85	87	1.02	167	90	78	140	77	63	100
	117	117	117	1.00	97	97	98	1.01	98**	97**	98**	1.01**	17	14	3	11**	11**	–**	101
	114	116	112	0.97	...	...	...	...	92**	92**	92**	1.00**	...	...	...	54**	29**	25**	102
	92	94	90	0.96	...	...	...	...	84	84	84	0.99	0.01	–	0.01	2	1.1	1.1	103
	113	118	108	0.92	82	86	79	0.91	93	95	91	0.95	292	114	178	112	32	80	104
	126**	127**	125**	0.99**	...	...	...	...					...	...	...	...	...	...	105
																			106
	113	113	113	1.00	...	...	...	...	91	90	92	1.02	...	...	...	70	43	27	107
	95	95	95	1.00	88**	88**	88**	1.00**	91	90	91	1.01	38**	19**	18**	30	16	14	108
	109	110	108	0.98	98	98	97	1.00	98	98	98	1.00	25	16	9	29.6	22.3	7.3	109
	108	109	106	0.97	...	...	...	...	94	96	92	0.96	...	...	...	0.0	–	0.0	110
	126**,z	127**,z	124**,z	0.98**,z	...	...	...	...	...	...	...	...	...	...	...	...	...	...	111

Table 5 (continued)

	Country or territory	Age group 2004	School-age population[1] (000) 2003	Enrolment in primary education — 1999 Total (000)	% F	2004 Total (000)	% F	Enrolment in private institutions as % of total enrolment — 1999	2004	GER in primary education (%) — 1999 Total	Male	Female	GPI (F/M)
112	Nicaragua	7-12	840	830	49	942	49	16	15	103	103	103	1.01
113	Panama	6-11	383	393	48	430	48	10	10	108	110	106	0.97
114	Paraguay	6-11	893.6	951**	48**	946**	48**	15**	16**	113**	115**	111**	0.96**
115	Peru	6-11	3 629.6	4 350	49	4 133	49	13	15	123	123	122	0.99
116	Saint Kitts and Nevis[4]	5-11	...	...	...	6	50	...	16	...	...	...	...
117	Saint Lucia	5-11	23	26	49	24	48	2**	3	103	104	102	0.98
118	Saint Vincent and the Grenadines	5-11	17	...	...	18	48	...	3	...	...	...	...
119	Suriname	6-11	54	...	...	65**,z	49**,z	...	48**,z	...	...	...	...
120	Trinidad and Tobago	5-11	134	172	49	137*	49*	72**	72*	102	102	101	0.99
121	Turks and Caicos Islands[4]	6-11	...	2	49	2	51	18	24	...	...	...	...
122	Uruguay	6-11	336	366	49	366**	48**	...	12**	112	113	111	0.99
123	Venezuela	6-11	3 287	3 261	49	3 453	48	15	14	100	101	99	0.98
	North America and Western Europe												
124	Andorra	6-11	...	...	...	4	47	...	1	...	...	...	...
125	Austria	6-9	352	389	48	373	49	4	5	102	103	102	0.99
126	Belgium	6-11	719	763	49	747	49	55	55	104	104	103	0.99
127	Canada	6-11	2 401	2 404	49	2 461**,y	49**,y	5	7**,y	98	98	98	1.00
128	Cyprus[4]	6-11	...	64	48	62	49	4	6	97	98	97	1.00
129	Denmark	7-12	416	372	48	420	49	11	12	102	102	102	1.00
130	Finland	7-12	386	383	49	388	49	1	1	99	99	99	1.00
131	France	6-10	3 610	3 944	49	3 783	49	15	15	107	107	106	0.99
132	Germany	6-9	3 300	3 767	49	3 305	49	2	3	106	106	105	0.99
133	Greece	6-11	647	646	48	657	48	7	7	94	94	95	1.00
134	Iceland	6-12	31	30	48	31**	49**	1	1**	99	100	98	0.98
135	Ireland	4-11	423	457	49	450	48	1	1	103	104	103	0.99
136	Israel	6-11	703	722	49	775	49	...	–	112	113	112	0.99
137	Italy	6-10	2 731	2 876	48	2 768	48	7	7	103	103	102	0.99
138	Luxembourg	6-11	34.8	31	49	35	49	7	7	100	99	100	1.01
139	Malta	5-10	30	35	49	31	48	36	38	106	106	106	1.01
140	Monaco[6]	6-10	...	2	50	...	...	31	...	...	...	...	...
141	Netherlands	6-11	1 194	1 268	48	1 283	48	68	69	108	109	107	0.98
142	Norway	6-12	437	412	49	432	49	1	2	100	100	100	1.00
143	Portugal	6-11	653	815	48	758	48	9	10	124	127	121	0.96
144	San Marino	6-10	...	...	...	...	...	...	...	...	...	...	...
145	Spain	6-11	2 318.9	2 580	48	2 498	48	33	33	107	108	106	0.98
146	Sweden	7-12	697.2	763	49	691	49	3	6	110	108	111	1.03
147	Switzerland	7-12	519.6	530	49	532	49	3	4	104	104	104	0.99
148	United Kingdom	5-10	4 398	4 661	49	4 686	49	5	5	102	102	102	1.01
149	United States	6-11	24 813	24 938	49	24 559	...	12	10	101	100	103	1.03
	South and West Asia												
150	Afghanistan	7-12	4 771	957	7	4 430	29	...	...	25	46	4	0.08
151	Bangladesh	6-10	16 480	17 622	49	17 953	50	37	39z	110	110	109	0.99
152	Bhutan[7]	6-12	...	81	46	91**,y	47**,y	2	...	...	...	...	...
153	India	6-10	117 206	110 986	43	136 194**	47**	...	...	97	107	87	0.82
154	Iran, Islamic Republic of	6-10	7 093	8 667	47	7 307	51	...	4	96	98	93	0.95
155	Maldives	6-12	61	74	49	63	48	3	2z	130	130	131	1.01
156	Nepal	5-9	3 534	3 588	42	**4 030**	**46**	...	15z	114	128	98	0.77
157	Pakistan	5-9	19 748	...	...	16 207	41	...	...	...	...	...	...
158	Sri Lanka	5-9	1 650	...	...	1 612.3**	...	...	–	...	...	...	...
	Sub-Saharan Africa												
159	Angola	6-9	1 806	1 057**	46**	...	...	5**	...	64**	69**	59**	0.86**
160	Benin	6-11	1 335	872	39	1 320	43	7	11	74	89	59	0.67
161	Botswana	6-12	314	322	50	329	49	5	5z	102	101	102	1.00
162	Burkina Faso	7-12	2 150	816	40	1 140	43	11	13	44	52	36	0.70
163	Burundi	7-12	1 212	702**	44**	968	45	1**	2	61**	68**	54**	0.80**
164	Cameroon	6-11	2 552	2 134	45	2 979	46	28	23**	89	98	80	0.82
165	Cape Verde	6-11	77	92	49	85	49	–	–	119	122	116	0.96

GROSS ENROLMENT RATIO (GER) IN PRIMARY EDUCATION (%)				NET ENROLMENT RATIO (NER) IN PRIMARY EDUCATION (%)								OUT-OF-SCHOOL CHILDREN (000)[2]						
School year ending in 2004				School year ending in 1999				School year ending in 2004				School year ending in 1999			School year ending in 2004			
Total	Male	Female	GPI (F/M)	Total	Male	Female	GPI (F/M)	Total	Male	Female	GPI (F/M)	Total	Male	Female	Total	Male	Female	
112	113	111	0.98	78	78	79	1.01	88	89	87	0.99	145	76	69	49	25	23	112
112	114	111	0.97	96	96	96	0.99	98	98	98	1.00	11	5	6	5	2	3	113
106**	108**	104**	0.97**	...	...	...	...	...	...	...	...	...	...	...	...	...	...	114
114	114	114	0.99	98**	98**	98**	1.00**	97	97	97	1.00	2**	–**	2**	14.6	12.3	2.3	115
101	98	105	1.07	...	...	...	...	94	91	98	1.08	...	...	...	0.2	0.2	–	116
106	108	103	0.96	91**	91**	91**	0.99**	98	99	96	0.97	2**	1.0**	1.0**	0.4	0.1	0.3	117
106	109	103	0.95	...	...	...	...	94**	95**	92**	0.97**	...	...	...	0.6**	0.3**	0.4**	118
120**,z	118**,z	121**,z	1.02**,z	...	...	...	...	92**,z	90**,z	96**,z	1.07**,z	...	...	...	3.3**,z	2.7**,z	0.6**,z	119
102*	104*	101*	0.97*	93	93	93	1.00	92*	92*	92*	0.99*	5	3	2	4*	2*	2*	120
94	92	95	1.03	...	...	...	...	81	78	85	1.08	...	...	...	0.4	0.2	0.1	121
109**	110**	108**	0.98**	...	...	...	...	...	...	...	...	...	...	...	...	...	...	122
105	106	104	0.98	86	85	86	1.01	92	92	92	1.01	423	226	197	199	110	90	123

North America and Western Europe

101**	102**	100**	0.98**	...	...	...	...	89**	90**	87**	0.97**	...	...	...	0.5**	0.2**	0.3**	124
106	106	106	1.00	...	...	...	...	...	...	...	...	...	...	...	...	...	...	125
104	104	104	0.99	99	99	99	1.00	99	99	99	1.00	8	4	4	7	4	3	126
100**,y	100**,y	100**,y	1.00**,y	97	97	97	1.00	...	...	...	...	70	36	34	...	...	...	127
98	98	97	1.00	95	95	95	1.00	96	96	96	1.00	1.3	0.7	0.7	0.8	0.4	0.4	128
101	101	101	1.00	97	97	97	1.00	100	100	100	1.00	8	4	3	0.4	0.4	–	129
101	101	100	0.99	99	99	98	1.00	99	99	99	1.00	5	2	3	2	0.9	1.0	130
105	105	104	0.99	99	99	99	1.00	99	99	99	1.00	9	6	3	14	11	4	131
100	100	100	1.00	...	...	...	...	...	...	...	...	...	...	...	...	...	...	132
102	102	101	0.99	92	92	93	1.01	99	100	99	0.99	31	17	14	3	–	3	133
101**	102**	100**	0.98**	99	100	98	0.98	99**	100**	98**	0.98**	0.3	–	0.3	0.3**	–**	0.3**	134
106	107	106	0.99	93	93	93	1.01	96	96	96	1.00	31	16	14	15	8	7	135
110	110	111	1.01	98	98	98	1.00	98	97	98	1.01	15	7	8	16	9	7	136
101	102	101	1.00	99	99	98	0.99	99	99	99	1.00	9	–	9	11	4	7	137
99	100	99	1.00	96	95	97	1.02	91	91	91	1.00	0.9	0.6	0.3	2.9	1.5	1.4	138
102	103	102	0.99	95	94	96	1.02	94	94	94	1.00	2	1.0	0.7	1.8	0.9	0.9	139
...	...	...	...	...	...	...	...	...	...	...	...	...	...	...	...	...	...	140
107	109	106	0.97	99	100	99	0.99	99	99	98	0.99	6	0.1	6	14	3	11	141
99	99	99	1.00	100	100	100	1.00	99	99	99	1.00	0.7	0.3	0.5	4.8	2.4	2.4	142
116	119	114	0.96	...	...	...	...	99	99	99	0.99	...	...	...	0.8	–	0.8	143
...	...	...	...	...	...	...	...	...	...	...	...	...	...	...	...	...	...	144
108	109	107	0.98	99	...	...	...	99	100	99	0.99	13	...	...	13	3	10	145
99	99	99	1.00	100	100	99	0.99	99	99	98	1.00	2	–	2	9.5	4.4	5.2	146
102	103	102	0.99	96	96	95	0.99	94	94	94	1.00	2	1.3	1.1	9	5	4	147
107	107	107	1.00	100	99	100	1.01	99	99	99	1.00	20	20	0.5	0.9	0.8	0.2	148
99	...	...	...	94	94	94	1.00	92	...	...	...	1 154	622	532	1 626	...	...	149

South and West Asia

93	127	56	0.44	...	...	...	...	...	...	...	...	...	...	...	...	...	...	150
109	107	111	1.03	89*	89*	89*	1.00*	94*	93*	96*	1.03*	1 151	610	541	404	354	51	151
...	...	...	...	...	...	...	...	...	...	...	...	...	...	...	...	...	...	152
116**	120**	112**	0.93**	...	...	...	...	90**	92**	87**	0.94**	...	...	...	4 583**	654**	3 929**	153
103	98	108	1.10	82**	83**	80**	0.97**	89	89	88	0.99	1 666**	799**	868**	803	400	402	154
104	105	102	0.97	97	97	98	1.01	90y	89y	90y	1.01y	1.3	0.8	0.6	6y	3y	3y	155
113	**118**	**108**	**0.91**	65*	72*	57*	0.79*	79**	84**	74**	0.87**	1 046	413	633	**698****	**264****	**434****	156
82	95	69	0.73	...	...	...	...	66*	76*	56*	0.73*	...	...	...	6 463*	2 259*	4 204*	157
98**	...	...	...	...	...	...	...	98**	...	...	...	...	...	...	47**	...	...	158

Sub-Saharan Africa

...	...	...	...	...	...	...	...	...	...	...	...	...	...	...	...	...	...	159
99	111	86	0.77	50*	59*	40*	0.68*	83	93	72	0.78	585	241	344	220.0	43.7	176.3	160
105	105	104	0.99	78	77	80	1.04	82**	81**	83**	1.03**	63	35	28	50**	28**	22**	161
53	59	47	0.78	35	41	29	0.69	40	46	35	0.77	1 205	551	655	1 271	590	681	162
80	87	73	0.83	...	...	...	...	57	60	54	0.89	...	...	...	518	240	278	163
117	126	107	0.85	...	...	...	...	...	...	...	...	...	...	...	...	...	...	164
111	113	108	0.95	99**	99**	98**	0.98**	92	92	91	0.99	0.8**	0.1**	0.7**	6	3	3	165

Table 5 (continued)

	Country or territory	Age group 2004	School-age population[1] (000) 2003	ENROLMENT IN PRIMARY EDUCATION School year ending in 1999 Total (000)	%F	2004 Total (000)	%F	Enrolment in private institutions as % of total enrolment School year ending in 1999	2004	GROSS ENROLMENT RATIO (GER) IN PRIMARY EDUCATION (%) School year ending in 1999 Total	Male	Female	GPI (F/M)
166	Central African Republic	6-11	654	...	...	421**	41**	...	...	...	...	...	...
167	Chad	6-11	1585	840	37	1125**	39**	25	34ʸ	64	81	47	0.58
168	Comoros	6-11	121	83	45	104	46	12	10	76	82	69	0.85
169	Congo	6-11	659	276	49	584	48	10	25	50	51	48	0.95
170	Côte d'Ivoire	6-11	2877	1911	43	2046*,ᶻ	44*,ᶻ	12	11**,ᶻ	70	80	60	0.74
171	D. R. Congo	6-11	9304	4022	47	...	...	19	...	48	51	46	0.90
172	Equatorial Guinea	7-11	65	75	44	78ʸ	48ʸ	33	...	132	148	116	0.79
173	Eritrea	7-11	564	262	45	375	44	11	8	57	62	51	0.82
174	Ethiopia	7-10	8430	4368	38	**8019**	**46**	...	**5****	59	72	45	0.62
175	Gabon	6-11	217	265	50	281**	49**	17	29**	132	132	132	1.00
176	Gambia	7-12	215	150	46	175	51	3**	...	80	86	74	0.85
177	Ghana	6-11	3291	2377	47	**2930**	**48**	13	**21**	76	79	72	0.92
178	Guinea	7-12	1451	727	38	1147	43	15	21	57	68	45	0.65
179	Guinea-Bissau	7-12	247	145**	40**	...	...	19**	...	70**	84**	56**	0.67**
180	Kenya	6-11	5325	4782	49	5926	48	...	...	93	94	92	0.97
181	Lesotho	6-12	326	365	52	427	50	...	0.3	105	101	110	1.08
182	Liberia	6-11	552	396	42	...	...	38	...	85	97	72	0.74
183	Madagascar	6-10	2521	2012	49	3366	49	22	19	94	95	92	0.97
184	Malawi	6-11	2274	2582	49	2842	50	...	...	139	143	136	0.95
185	Mali	7-12	2191	959	41	1397	43	22	35	51	59	43	0.72
186	Mauritius	5-10	123	133	49	**124**	**49**	24	25	105	105	106	1.00
187	Mozambique	6-12	3761	2302	43	3569	45	...	...	69	79	59	0.74
188	Namibia	6-12	408	383	50	409ᶻ	50ᶻ	4	4ᶻ	104	103	105	1.02
189	Niger	7-12	2194	530	39	980	40	4	4	29	34	23	0.68
190	Nigeria	6-11	21277	16869**	43**	21111	45	5**	...	88**	98**	77**	0.78**
191	Rwanda	7-12	1470	1289	50	1753	51	...	1	99	100	98	0.98
192	Sao Tome and Principe	7-12	22	24	49	30	49	–	–	106	108	105	0.98
193	Senegal	7-12	1819	1034	46**	1383	48	12	11	61	66**	57**	0.86**
194	Seychelles[4]	6-11	...	10	49	9	49	5	5ᶻ	116	117	116	0.99
195	Sierra Leone	6-11	798	...	...	...	...	...	...	...	...	...	...
196	Somalia	6-12	1407	...	...	...	...	...	...	...	...	...	...
197	South Africa	7-13	7153	7935	49	7470ᶻ	49ᶻ	2	2ᶻ	114	116	113	0.98
198	Swaziland	6-12	204	213	49	208ᶻ	48ᶻ	–	–ᶻ	100	102	98	0.95
199	Togo	6-11	974	954	43	985	46	36	40	112	127	96	0.75
200	Uganda	6-12	5883	6288	47	**7152**	**50**	...	9	126	132	120	0.92
201	United Republic of Tanzania	7-13	7023	4190	50	**7541**	**49**	0.2	**1**	64	64	64	1.00
202	Zambia	7-13	2278	1556	48	2251	49	...	2	75	78	72	0.92
203	Zimbabwe	6-12	2433	2460	49	2362ᶻ	49ᶻ	88	87ᶻ	98	100	97	0.97

			Sum	Sum	%F	Sum	%F	Median		Weighted average			
I	World	...	642092	644985	47	682225	47	7	8	100	104	96	0.92
II	Countries in transition	...	12949	15834	49	13926	49	0.3	0.6	100	101	99	0.99
III	Developed countries	...	66509	70418	49	67419	48	4	4	102	102	102	1.00
IV	Developing countries	...	562634	558733	46	600879	47	11	11	100	105	95	0.91
V	Arab States	...	39355	34725	46	36700	46	7	7	89	95	82	0.87
VI	Central and Eastern Europe	...	22273	25489	48	22630	48	0.4	1.0	100	102	97	0.96
VII	Central Asia	...	6274	6853	49	6376	49	0.5	0.8	99	99	98	0.99
VIII	East Asia and the Pacific	...	182126	217575	48	206217	48	7	16	112	112	111	0.99
IX	East Asia	...	178546	214277	48	202712	48	4	2	112	113	112	0.99
X	Pacific	...	3581	3298	48	3505	48	16	21	94	95	93	0.99
XI	Latin America/Caribbean	...	58710	70206	48	69259	48	15	16	121	123	119	0.97
XII	Caribbean	...	2062	2500	49	2622	49	21	27	115	117	113	0.97
XIII	Latin America	...	56649	67705	48	66637	48	15	15	121	123	119	0.97
XIV	N. America/W. Europe	...	50883	52857	49	51734	48	7	6	103	102	103	1.01
XV	South and West Asia	...	170919	157510	44	187884	46	...	4	94	103	85	0.82
XVI	Sub-Saharan Africa	...	111551	79772	45	101424	47	11	10	79	85	72	0.85

1. Data are for 2003 except for countries with a calendar school year, in which case data are for 2004.

2. Data reflect the actual number of children not enrolled at all, derived from the total primary NER, which measures the proportion of primary school age children who are enrolled either in primary or in secondary schools.

3. In countries where two or more education structures exist, indicators were calculated on the basis of the most common or widespread structure. In the Russian Federation this is three grades of primary education starting at age 7. However, a four-grade structure also exists, in which about one-third of primary pupils are enrolled. Gross enrolment ratios may be overestimated.

GROSS ENROLMENT RATIO (GER) IN PRIMARY EDUCATION (%) — 2004				NET ENROLMENT RATIO (NER) IN PRIMARY EDUCATION (%) — 1999				NER 2004				OUT-OF-SCHOOL CHILDREN (000)[2] — 1999			OUT-OF-SCHOOL CHILDREN (000)[2] — 2004			
Total	Male	Female	GPI (F/M)	Total	Male	Female	GPI (F/M)	Total	Male	Female	GPI (F/M)	Total	Male	Female	Total	Male	Female	
64**	76**	52**	0.69**	…	…	…	…	…	…	…	…	…	…	…	…	…	…	166
71**	86**	56**	0.64**	52	64	40	0.62	57**,z	68**,z	46**,z	0.68**,z	636	236	400	657**,z	243**,z	413**,z	167
85	91	80	0.88	49	54	45	0.85	…	…	…	…	53	24	28	…	…	…	168
89	92	85	0.93	…	…	…	…	…	…	…	…	…	…	…	…	…	…	169
72*,z	80*,z	63*,z	0.79*,z	53	61	46	0.75	56*,z	62*,z	50*,z	0.80*,z	1 254	523	731	1 223*,z	519*,z	705*,z	170
…	…	…	…	…	…	…	…	…	…	…	…	…	…	…	…	…	…	171
127y	133y	121y	0.91y	83	93	73	0.79	85y	92y	78y	0.85y	9	2	7	9y	2y	6y	172
66	74	59	0.80	36	39	34	0.86	48	52	44	0.85	293	140	153	291	135	156	173
93	**101**	**86**	**0.86**	33	38	28	0.74	**56****	**58****	**55****	**0.94****	4 962	2 297	2 665	**3 615****	**1 734****	**1 880****	174
130**	130**	129**	0.99**	…	…	…	…	…	…	…	…	…	…	…	…	…	…	175
81	79	84	1.06	67	71	62	0.88	75**	73**	77**	1.06**	61	26	35	52**	28**	24**	176
88	**90**	**87**	**0.96**	57**	58**	56**	0.96**	**65**	**65**	**65**	**0.99**	1 330**	659**	670**	**1 129**	**572**	**557**	177
79	87	71	0.81	44	51	36	0.71	64	69	58	0.84	709	317	392	519	228	291	178
…	…	…	…	45**	53**	37**	0.71**	…	…	…	…	114**	49**	65**	…	…	…	179
111	114	108	0.94	64	63	64	1.01	76	76	77	1.00	1 834	934	899	1 226	618	607	180
131	131	131	1.00	60	56	63	1.13	86	83	88	1.06	139	76	63	45	27	18	181
…	…	…	…	41	47	36	0.77	…	…	…	…	271	123	148	…	…	…	182
134	136	131	0.96	63	63	63	1.01	89	89	89	1.00	785	396	389	272	136	136	183
125	123	126	1.02	98	99	97	0.98	95	93	98	1.05	23	–	23	89	71	19	184
64	71	56	0.79	40**	46**	34**	0.73**	46	50	43	0.85	1 113**	507**	606**	1 172	557	615	185
102	**102**	**102**	**1.00**	97	96	97	1.01	**95**	**94**	**95**	**1.02**	4	2	2	**7**	**4**	**3**	186
95	104	86	0.83	52	58	46	0.80	71	75	67	0.90	1 602	703	899	1 089	475	614	187
101z	100z	102z	1.01z	73	70	76	1.08	74z	71z	76z	1.08z	100	56	44	106z	59z	47z	188
45	52	37	0.72	24	29	20	0.68	39	46	32	0.71	1 393	674	718	1 326	609	717	189
99	107	91	0.85	…	…	…	…	60**	64**	57**	0.89**	…	…	…	8 109.6**	3 786**	4 323**	190
119	118	120	1.02	…	…	…	…	73	72	75	1.04	…	…	…	390	205	185	191
133	134	132	0.98	85	85	84	0.99	98	98	98	1.00	3	2	2	0.01	–	0.01	192
76	78	74	0.95	52	55**	48**	0.88**	66	68	64	0.95	808	379**	429**	616	296	320	193
110	109	110	1.00	…	…	…	…	96	96	97	1.01	…	…	…	0.3	0.2	0.1	194
…	…	…	…	…	…	…	…	…	…	…	…	…	…	…	…	…	…	195
…	…	…	…	…	…	…	…	…	…	…	…	…	…	…	…	…	…	196
105z	107z	103z	0.97z	93	92	94	1.02	89z	88z	89z	1.01z	171	139	32	487z	287z	200z	197
101z	103z	98z	0.95z	75	74	75	1.02	77z	76z	77z	1.01z	53	28	25	48z	24z	23z	198
101	110	92	0.84	79	89	70	0.79	79	85	72	0.85	147.6	28.6	119.0	180	55	125	199
118	**118**	**117**	**1.00**	…	…	…	…	…	…	…	…	…	…	…	…	…	…	200
106	**108**	**104**	**0.96**	48	47	49	1.04	**91**	**92**	**91**	**0.98**	3 405	1 736	1 669	**604**	**273**	**331**	201
99	101	97	0.96	63	64	62	0.96	80	80	80	1.00	760	370	391	435	221	214	202
96z	97z	95z	0.98z	81	81	82	1.01	82z	81z	82z	1.01z	449	230	219	429z	224z	206z	203

Weighted average				Weighted average				Weighted average				Sum			Sum			
106	109	103	0.94	83	86	80	0.93	86	88	84	0.96	98 172	40 717	57 455	76 841	33 252	43 589	I
107	108	107	0.99	85	85	84	0.99	91	91	90	0.99	2 093	1 034	1 059	1 086	545	541	II
101	102	101	0.99	96	96	96	1.00	96	96	95	0.99	2 024	1 065	959	2 282	938	1 344	III
107	110	103	0.94	81	84	78	0.92	85	87	82	0.95	94 056	38 619	55 437	73 473	31 770	41 704	IV
93	98	88	0.90	77	81	73	0.89	81	85	78	0.92	8 361	3 407	4 954	6 585	2 695	3 890	V
101	103	100	0.97	89	91	88	0.97	91	92	90	0.98	2 592	1 129	1 463	2 014	936	1 078	VI
102	102	101	0.99	89	89	88	0.99	92	92	91	0.98	544	269	275	364	171	193	VII
113	114	112	0.99	96	96	96	1.00	94	94	94	0.99	6 827	3 381	3 446	9 671	4 757	4 914	VIII
114	114	113	0.99	96	96	96	1.00	94	94	94	0.99	6 382	3 159	3 223	9 298	4 587	4 712	IX
98	99	96	0.97	87	88	87	0.99	90	91	88	0.97	445	222	222	373	170	203	X
118	120	116	0.97	93	94	93	0.98	95	96	94	0.99	3 731	1 712	2 019	2 698	1 203	1 495	XI
126	128	125	0.98	77	79	76	0.96	83	85	82	0.96	435	211	224	341	155	185	XII
118	119	116	0.97	94	95	93	0.98	95	96	95	0.99	3 296	1 501	1 795	2 358	1 048	1 309	XIII
102	103	101	0.98	96	96	96	1.00	96	97	95	0.98	1 519	806	713	1 845	703	1 142	XIV
110	115	105	0.91	77	84	70	0.83	86	89	82	0.92	31 309	9 646	21 663	15 644	4 873	10 771	XV
91	96	85	0.89	55	58	52	0.89	65	67	63	0.93	43 289	20 368	22 922	38 020	17 914	20 106	XVI

4. National population data were used to calculate enrolment ratios.

5. Children enter primary school at age 6 or 7. Since 7 is the most common entrance age, enrolment ratios were calculated using the 7-11 age group for both enrolment and population. NER is not published due to inconsistencies between enrolment and the United Nations population data by age.

6. Enrolment ratios were not calculated due to lack of United Nations population data by age.

7. Enrolment ratios were not calculated due to inconsistencies between enrolment and the United Nations population data.

Data in bold are for the school year ending in 2005.

(z) Data are for the school year ending in 2003.

(y) Data are for the school year ending in 2002.

Table 6
Internal efficiency: repetition in primary education

Country or territory	Duration[1] of primary education 2004	Grade 1 Total	Grade 1 Male	Grade 1 Female	Grade 2 Total	Grade 2 Male	Grade 2 Female	Grade 3 Total	Grade 3 Male	Grade 3 Female	Grade 4 Total	Grade 4 Male	Grade 4 Female
Arab States													
1 Algeria	6	10.5	12.1	8.8	9.3	11.3	7.1	10.2	12.7	7.3	11.0	13.8	7.9
2 Bahrain	6	2.8	2.4	3.1	5.3	5.2	5.3	3.2	3.8	2.5	3.1	3.6	2.5
3 Djibouti	6	2.6**	2.8**	2.3**	16.7**	16.0**	17.5**	20.0**	18.7**	21.6**	19.7**	18.3**	21.5**
4 Egypt	5	–**	–**	–**	2.9**	3.5**	2.1**	3.6**	4.5**	2.5**	5.3**	6.6**	3.8**
5 Iraq	6	…	…	…	…	…	…	…	…	…	…	…	…
6 Jordan	6	0.3	0.3	0.3	0.3	0.2	0.3	0.3	0.3	0.3	1.3	1.1	1.4
7 Kuwait	4	3.7**	3.9**	3.5**	1.9**	1.9**	1.9**	3.1**	3.6**	2.6**	1.5**	1.8**	1.2**
8 Lebanon	6	5.4	6.5	4.3	7.2	8.6	5.6	7.4	9.1	5.5	19.6	22.1	16.7
9 Libyan Arab Jamahiriya	6	…	…	…	…	…	…	…	…	…	…	…	…
10 Mauritania	6	15.1	14.8	15.3	13.8	13.8	13.8	15.3	14.9	15.7	15.0	14.3	15.8
11 Morocco	6	17.2[y]	18.2[y]	16.1[y]	14.9[y]	16.6[y]	12.9[y]	15.4[y]	17.7[y]	12.8[y]	12.4[y]	14.8[y]	9.4[y]
12 Oman	6	0.2	0.1	0.3	0.1	0.1	0.1	0.0	0.1	0.0	1.7	2.0	1.3
13 Palestinian A. T.	4	–	–	–	–	–	–	–	–	–	0.6	0.7	0.6
14 Qatar	6	3.0**,[y]	3.4**,[y]	2.5**,[y]	…	…	…	…	…	…	…	…	…
15 Saudi Arabia	6	8.2	8.9	7.3	3.4	4.3	2.4	4.2	6.0	2.3	4.0	5.0	3.0
16 Sudan	6	1.7	0.4	3.1	2.1	0.6	3.8	2.4	0.8	4.4	2.6	1.1	4.5
17 Syrian Arab Republic	4	11.9	12.8	10.9	7.7	8.8	6.5	5.6	6.4	4.8	4.2	4.7	3.6
18 Tunisia	6	0.6	0.6	0.5	10.4	11.8	8.8	1.8	2.2	1.4	8.8	10.8	6.6
19 United Arab Emirates	5	3.0	2.8	3.3	1.9	2.0	1.8	1.8	2.0	1.7	2.4	3.6	1.1
20 Yemen	6	3.6**	3.7**	3.4**	4.1**	4.2**	3.9**	4.9**	5.2**	4.4**	5.5**	6.1**	4.4**
Central and Eastern Europe													
21 Albania	4	3.9**,[y]	4.5**,[y]	3.2**,[y]	2.7**,[y]	3.0**,[y]	2.2**,[y]	2.0**,[y]	2.3**,[y]	1.8**,[y]	2.2**,[y]	2.5**,[y]	2.0**,[y]
22 Belarus	4	0.3	0.3	0.3	0.1	…	…	0.02	…	…	0.02	…	…
23 Bosnia and Herzegovina	4	…	…	…	…	…	…	…	…	…	…	…	…
24 Bulgaria	4	0.8	0.9	0.7	2.8	3.3	2.2	2.3	2.7	1.8	2.7	3.1	2.2
25 Croatia	4	0.9[y]	1.0[y]	0.8[y]	0.3[y]	0.3[y]	0.2[y]	0.2[y]	0.2[y]	0.1[y]	0.1[y]	0.1[y]	0.1[y]
26 Czech Republic	5	1.6	1.7	1.5	1.0	1.1	0.9	0.9	1.0	0.7	0.9	1.1	0.7
27 Estonia	6	1.4[y]	1.6[y]	1.2[y]	0.9[y]	1.3[y]	0.6[y]	1.7[y]	2.3[y]	1.0[y]	2.0[y]	2.7[y]	1.1[y]
28 Hungary	4	4.2	4.8	3.6	1.7	2.0	1.4	1.2	1.6	0.9	1.2	1.5	0.9
29 Latvia	4	4.9	6.7	3.0	1.8	2.5	1.1	1.6	2.2	0.9	1.8	2.4	1.0
30 Lithuania	4	1.3	1.7	0.9	0.4	0.5	0.3	0.3	0.4	0.2	0.4	0.6	0.2
31 Poland	6	0.7	…	…	0.3	…	…	0.4	…	…	0.8	…	…
32 Republic of Moldova	4	0.6	0.6	0.6	0.3	0.3	0.3	0.2	0.2	0.2	0.3	0.3	0.3
33 Romania	4	4.8	5.5	4.1	1.9	2.3	1.5	1.5	1.8	1.1	1.7	2.0	1.4
34 Russian Federation	3	0.9	…	…	…	…	…	…	…	…	.	.	.
35 Serbia and Montenegro	4	…	…	…	…	…	…	…	…	…	…	…	…
36 Slovakia	4	5.0	5.2	4.9	2.1	2.3	1.9	1.5	1.7	1.3	1.5	1.6	1.3
37 Slovenia	4	0.6	0.7	0.5	0.6	0.7	0.5	0.6	0.7	0.4	0.4	0.5	0.3
38 TFYR Macedonia	4	0.2	0.2	0.2	0.2	0.2	0.1	0.1	0.2	0.1	0.1	0.1	0.1
39 Turkey	6	4.7**	4.9**	4.6**	2.2**	2.1**	2.4**	2.3**	1.9**	2.8**	2.7**	2.0**	3.5**
40 Ukraine	4	0.3	0.3**	0.2**	0.1	0.1**	0.1**	0.05	0.03**	0.06**	…	…	…
Central Asia													
41 Armenia	3	–	–	–	0.2	0.2	0.2	0.2	0.2	0.2	.	.	.
42 Azerbaijan	4	0.3	0.3	0.3	0.3	0.2	0.3	0.2	0.2	0.2	0.3	0.3	0.3
43 Georgia	6	0.2	0.2	0.2	0.2	0.2	0.2	0.2	0.3	0.1	0.3	0.4	0.1
44 Kazakhstan	4	0.1	0.1	0.0	0.2	0.2	0.1	0.1	0.2	0.1	0.1	0.1	0.1
45 Kyrgyzstan	4	0.1	0.1	0.1	0.1	0.1	0.1	0.1	0.1	0.1	0.1	0.1	0.1
46 Mongolia	4	1.3	1.4	1.2	0.5	0.6	0.5	0.3	0.3	0.2	0.2	0.2	0.2
47 Tajikistan	4	0.2	0.2**	0.2**	0.2	0.2**	0.2**	0.2	0.2**	0.2**	0.3	0.3**	0.3**
48 Turkmenistan	3	…	…	…	…	…	…	…	…	…	.	.	.
49 Uzbekistan	4	–**,[y]	–**,[y]	–**,[y]	–**,[y]	–**,[y]	–**,[y]	–**,[y]	–**,[y]	–**,[y]	–**,[y]	–**,[y]	–**,[y]
East Asia and the Pacific													
50 Australia	7	–**	–**	–**	–**	–**	–**	–**	–**	–**	–**	–**	–**
51 Brunei Darussalam	6	0.9**	1.4**	0.3**	1.1**	1.6**	0.5**	0.9**	1.4**	0.4**	2.0**	2.8**	1.1**
52 Cambodia	6	19.3	20.3	18.1	11.8	12.9	10.5	9.2	10.3	7.8	6.4	7.5	5.2
53 China	5	1.4[y]	1.6**,[y]	1.3**,[y]	0.2[y]	0.2**,[y]	0.1**,[y]	0.1[y]	0.2**,[y]	0.1**,[y]	0.1[y]	0.1**,[y]	0.1**,[y]
54 Cook Islands	6	–[y]	–[y]	–[y]	…	…	…	…	…	…	…	…	…
55 DPR Korea	4	…	…	…	…	…	…	…	…	…	…	…	…
56 Fiji	6	4.6	5.7	3.4	2.2	2.7	1.6	2.1	2.7	1.5	1.5	2.2	0.8

REPETITION RATES BY GRADE IN PRIMARY EDUCATION (%) | REPEATERS, ALL GRADES (%)

| | School year ending in 2003 | | | | | | | | | | School year ending in | | | | | |
| | Grade 5 | | | Grade 6 | | | Grade 7 | | | 1999 | | | 2004 | | | |
Total	Male	Female	Total	Male	Female	Total	Male	Female	Total	Male	Female	Total	Male	Female	
— **Arab States**															
11.5	14.5	8.2	16.0	19.1	12.4	.	.	.	11.9	14.6	8.7	11.8	14.3	8.9	1
2.8	3.5	2.1	2.0	3.1	0.7	.	.	.	3.8	4.6	3.1	3.2	3.6	2.7	2
22.1**	20.6**	24.0**	33.1**	32.5**	33.9**	.	.	.	16.6	16.7**	16.4**	18.0	17.4	18.7	3
8.1**	10.0**	5.9**	.	.	.	.	.	.	6.0**	7.1**	4.6**	4.0**	5.0**	2.9**	4
...	...	...	...	...	...	.	.	.	10.0	10.7	9.2	8.0	9.1	6.5	5
2.1	1.9	2.2	2.3	2.3	2.2	.	.	.	0.7	0.7	0.7	1.0	1.0	1.1	6
.	.	.	.	.	.	.	.	.	3.3	3.4	3.1	2.5**	2.8**	2.3**	7
12.3	13.9	10.6	10.8	12.3	9.2	.	.	.	9.1	10.5	7.7	10.6	12.3	8.7	8
...	...	...	...	...	...	.	.	.	...	...	...				9
15.8	15.3	16.4	23.3	22.4	24.3	.	.	.	...	...	...	14.4	14.1	14.6	10
10.6y	13.0y	7.6y	9.4y	11.5y	6.7y	.	.	.	12.4	14.1	10.2	13.2	15.2	11.0	11
1.6	2.0	1.1	0.9	1.2	0.7	.	.	.	8.0	9.5	6.4	0.8	0.9	0.6	12
.	.	.	.	.	.	.	.	.	2.1	2.2	2.0	0.2	0.2	0.2	13
...	...	...	4.6**,y	7.0**,y	2.0**,y	.	.	.	2.7**	3.5**	1.9**	...	...	...	14
3.4	3.7	3.2	1.4	1.4	1.3	.	.	.	5.4	6.6	4.2	4.2	5.0	3.3	15
2.7	1.3	4.4	2.7	1.2	4.6	.	.	.	...	...	...	2.2	0.8	3.8	16
.	.	.	.	.	.	.	.	.	6.5	7.2	5.6	7.5	8.3	6.6	17
11.6	13.7	9.2	7.5	9.1	5.7	.	.	.	18.3	20.0	16.4	7.3	8.7	5.7	18
2.2	3.1	1.1	.	.	.	.	.	.	3.5	4.4	2.5	2.2	2.6	1.8	19
5.5**	6.1**	4.4**	4.5**	5.1**	3.3**	.	.	.	10.6	11.7*	8.7*	4.3**	4.8**	3.7**	20
— **Central and Eastern Europe**															
.	.	.	.	.	.	.	.	.	3.9**	4.6**	3.2**	2.8z	3.2z	2.4z	21
.	.	.	.	.	.	.	.	.	0.5	0.5	0.5	0.1	0.1	0.1	22
.	.	.	.	.	.	.	.	.	...	...	...	...	...	...	23
.	.	.	.	.	.	.	.	.	3.2	3.7	2.7	2.3	2.7	1.8	24
.	.	.	.	.	.	.	.	.	0.4	0.5	0.3	0.4z	0.4z	0.3z	25
0.8	1.0	0.6	.	.	.	.	.	.	1.2	1.5	1.0	1.1	1.2	0.9	26
2.3y	3.6y	1.0y	3.5y	5.4y	1.3y	.	.	.	2.5	3.5	1.4	2.0	3.0	1.0	27
.	.	.	.	.	.	.	.	.	2.2	2.1	2.2	2.2	2.6	1.7	28
.	.	.	.	.	.	.	.	.	2.1	2.7**	1.3**	2.7	3.7	1.6	29
.	.	.	.	.	.	.	.	.	0.9	1.3	0.5	0.6	0.8	0.4	30
0.8	...	...	0.5	...	...	.	.	.	1.2	...	...	0.6	0.9	0.2	31
.	.	.	.	.	.	.	.	.	0.9	0.9**	0.9**	0.4	0.4	0.4	32
.	.	.	.	.	.	.	.	.	3.4	4.1	2.6	2.4	2.9	2.0	33
.	.	.	.	.	.	.	.	.	1.2	...	...	0.7	...	...	34
.	.	.	.	.	.	.	.	.	...	...	...	...	...	...	35
.	.	.	.	.	.	.	.	.	2.3	2.6	2.0	2.6	2.8	2.4	36
.	.	.	.	.	.	.	.	.	1.0	1.3	0.7	0.5	0.6	0.4	37
.	.	.	.	.	.	.	.	.	0.0	0.1	0.0	0.2	0.2	0.1	38
2.6**	1.8**	3.5**	4.7**	3.6**	6.0**	.	.	.	...	...	...	3.2	2.7	3.8	39
.	.	.	.	.	.	.	.	.	0.8	...	...	0.1	0.1	0.1	40
— **Central Asia**															
.	.	.	.	.	.	.	.	.	...	...	...	0.1	0.1	0.1	41
.	.	.	.	.	.	.	.	.	0.4	0.4	0.4	0.3	0.3	0.3	42
...	...	...	...	...	...	.	.	.	0.3	0.5**	0.2**	0.3	0.4	0.2	43
.	.	.	.	.	.	.	.	.	0.3	...	...	0.1	0.2	0.1	44
.	.	.	.	.	.	.	.	.	0.3	0.4	0.2	0.1	0.1	0.1	45
.	.	.	.	.	.	.	.	.	0.9	1.0	0.8	0.6	0.7	0.6	46
.	.	.	.	.	.	.	.	.	0.5	0.5**	0.6**	0.2	0.2**	0.2**	47
.	.	.	.	.	.	.	.	.	...	...	...	...	...	...	48
.	.	.	.	.	.	.	.	.	...	...	...	–**	–**	–**	49
— **East Asia and the Pacific**															
–**	–**	–**	–**	–**	–**	–**	–**	–**	...	...	...	–	–	–	50
1.6**	2.5**	0.6**	8.7**	11.5**	5.5**	.	.	.	.	.	.	2.6	3.6	1.4	51
4.2	4.9	3.4	2.1	2.4	1.8	.	.	.	24.6**	25.4**	23.5**	10.6	11.6	9.4	52
0.1y	0.1**,y	0.1**,y	.	.	.	.	.	.	...	...	...	0.3	0.3	0.3	53
...	...	...	.	.	.	.	.	.	2.6	...	...	...	...	...	54
...	...	...	.	.	.	.	.	.	...	...	...	...	...	...	55
2.0	2.5	1.6	0.4	0.5	0.2	.	.	.	...	...	...	2.2	2.7	1.5	56

Table 6 (continued)

	Country or territory	Duration[1] of primary education 2004	REPETITION RATES BY GRADE IN PRIMARY EDUCATION (%) School year ending in 2003 Grade 1			Grade 2			Grade 3			Grade 4		
			Total	Male	Female	Total	Male	Female	Total	Male	Female	Total	Male	Female
57	Indonesia	6	6.0	6.1	6.0	3.5	3.4	3.6	3.0	2.9	3.0	2.3	2.3	2.3
58	Japan	6	…	…	…	…	…	…	…	…	…	…	…	…
59	Kiribati	6	.	.	.	.	.	.	.	.	.	.	.	.
60	Lao PDR	5	34.8	35.3	34.2	19.7	21.0	18.1	13.0	14.6	11.2	8.3	9.9	6.3
61	Macao, China	6	2.4	2.8	2.0	3.2	4.4	1.9	5.0	6.7	3.2	6.9	8.5	5.1
62	Malaysia	6	.	.	.	.	.	.	.	.	.	.	.	.
63	Marshall Islands	6	.ʸ	.ʸ	.ʸ	…	…	…	…	…	…	…	…	…ʸ
64	Micronesia	6	…	…		…			…			…		
65	Myanmar	5	**1.3****	**1.3****	**1.3****	**0.6****	**0.6****	**0.6****	**0.6****	**0.6****	**0.6****	**0.5****	**0.5****	**0.5****
66	Nauru	6	−ʸ	−ʸ	−ʸ	−ʸ	−ʸ	−ʸ	−ʸ	−ʸ	−ʸ	−ʸ	−ʸ	−ʸ
67	New Zealand	6	…	…		…			…			…		
68	Niue	6	.ʸ	.ʸ	.ʸ	…			…			…		
69	Palau	5	…	…		…			…			…		
70	Papua New Guinea	6	−ʸ	−ʸ	−ʸ	−ʸ	−ʸ	−ʸ	−ʸ	−ʸ	−ʸ	−ʸ	−ʸ	−ʸ
71	Philippines	6	4.8	5.6	3.8	2.5	3.3	1.7	1.8	2.4	1.1	1.2	1.7	0.7
72	Republic of Korea	6	0.0	0.0	0.0	**0.01**	**0.00**	**0.01**	0.0	0.0	0.0	**0.01**	**0.00**	**0.01**
73	Samoa	6	5.3ˣ	6.1**,ˣ	4.4**,ˣ	1.8ˣ	…	…	1.4ˣ	…	…	1.7ˣ	…	…
74	Singapore	6	…	…		…			…			…		
75	Solomon Islands	6	…	…		…			…			…		
76	Thailand	6	…	…		…			…			…		
77	Timor-Leste	6	…	…		…			…			…		
78	Tokelau	6	.ʸ	.ʸ	.ʸ	.ʸ	.ʸ	.ʸ	.ʸ	.ʸ	.ʸ	.ʸ	.ʸ	.ʸ
79	Tonga	6	.ˣ	.ˣ	.ˣ	.ˣ	.ˣ	.ˣ	.ˣ	.ˣ	.ˣ	.ˣ	.ˣ	.ˣ
80	Tuvalu	6	.	.		.			.			.		
81	Vanuatu	6	13.2**	13.4**	13.0**	…	…	…	…	…	…	…	…	…
82	Viet Nam	5	5.4**,ʸ	6.2**,ʸ	4.4**,ʸ	2.6**,ʸ	3.0**,ʸ	2.1**,ʸ	1.7**,ʸ	2.0**,ʸ	1.3**,ʸ	1.6**,ʸ	1.9**,ʸ	1.2**,ʸ
	Latin America and the Caribbean													
83	Anguilla	7	2.4	2.1	2.7	19.4	22.6	16.2	26.8	22.5	32.5	19.0	28.6	10.3
84	Antigua and Barbuda	7	…	…		…			…			…		
85	Argentina	6	9.9ˣ	11.4ˣ	8.4ˣ	7.1ˣ	8.3ˣ	5.8ˣ	6.2ˣ	7.3ˣ	5.0ˣ	5.2ˣ	6.3ˣ	4.1ˣ
86	Aruba[4]	6	14.1	15.6	12.4	12.4	15.1	9.6	9.3	11.3	7.1	7.5	8.6	6.5
87	Bahamas	6	.	.	.	…								
88	Barbados	6	.	.	.	.	.	.	.	.	.	.	.	.
89	Belize	6	16.6	18.2	15.0	10.8	12.7	8.7	10.7	12.8	8.6	9.7	11.4	8.0
90	Bermuda	6	.ˣ	.ˣ	.ˣ	.ˣ	.ˣ	.ˣ	.ˣ	.ˣ	.ˣ	.ˣ	.ˣ	.ˣ
91	Bolivia	6	1.4**	1.5**	1.4**	1.3**	1.4**	1.2**	1.6**	1.7**	1.5**	1.5**	1.6**	1.3**
92	Brazil	4	29.3ˣ	29.3**,ˣ	29.3**,ˣ	19.7ˣ	…	…	15.4ˣ	…	…	13.5ˣ	…	…
93	British Virgin Islands	7	7.8	9.6	5.6	7.1	9.7	4.6	4.9	6.4	2.8	2.6	3.6	1.5
94	Cayman Islands	6	−ʸ	−ʸ	−ʸ	…			…			…		
95	Chile	6	2.3	2.6	2.0	3.1	3.6	2.6	1.7	2.0	1.3ʸ	2.3	2.9	1.7
96	Colombia	5	7.4**	8.0**	6.7**	4.3**	4.7**	3.9**	3.5**	3.8**	3.1**	2.6**	3.0**	2.2**
97	Costa Rica	6	13.6**	15.3**	11.7**	8.1**	9.2**	6.9**	6.3**	7.5**	5.0**	7.9**	9.0**	6.6**
98	Cuba	6	−	−	−	1.7	2.3	1.0	−	−	−	1.1	1.6	0.6
99	Dominica	7	7.2	9.1	5.1	5.1	6.7	3.4	2.6	3.4	1.9	2.9	3.8	2.0
100	Dominican Republic	6	3.4	3.9**	2.8**	5.4	6.4**	4.4**	12.6	15.6**	9.4**	7.8	9.5**	6.0**
101	Ecuador	6	3.9**	4.2**	3.6**	2.8**	3.1**	2.4**	1.8**	2.1**	1.5**	1.4**	1.6**	1.2**
102	El Salvador	6	15.5**	17.0**	13.9**	5.7**	6.5**	4.8**	4.3**	5.0**	3.7**	4.1**	4.8**	3.3**
103	Grenada	7	4.2ʸ	5.6ʸ	2.7ʸ	2.0ʸ	2.1ʸ	1.9ʸ	2.2ʸ	3.1ʸ	1.4ʸ	1.9ʸ	2.6ʸ	1.2ʸ
104	Guatemala	6	26.9**	28.2**	25.5**	14.4**	15.1**	13.7**	11.3**	12.0**	10.4**	7.7**	8.3**	6.9**
105	Guyana	6	1.6**,ʸ	1.9**,ʸ	1.2**,ʸ	1.4**,ʸ	1.8**,ʸ	1.1**,ʸ	2.4**,ʸ	2.8**,ʸ	2.0**,ʸ	1.5**,ʸ	1.8**,ʸ	1.2**,ʸ
106	Haiti	6	…	…		…			…			…		
107	Honduras	6	…	…		…			…			…		
108	Jamaica	6	4.1	5.3	2.7	1.1	1.5	0.8	0.9	1.1	0.6	4.0	5.5	2.3
109	Mexico	6	7.6	8.8	6.3	7.5	8.8	6.1	5.1	6.2	3.9	4.3	5.3	3.3
110	Montserrat	7	3.9**	8.1**	−**	2.8**	2.4**	3.2**	6.8**	8.7**	3.6**	…	…	…
111	Netherlands Antilles	6	18.9**,ʸ	24.8**,ʸ	12.4**,ʸ	13.6**,ʸ	15.7**,ʸ	11.2**,ʸ	11.4**,ʸ	14.4**,ʸ	8.5**,ʸ	12.2**,ʸ	14.4**,ʸ	10.0**,ʸ
112	Nicaragua	6	17.7**	18.9**	16.4**	10.7**	11.9**	9.3**	10.5**	11.8**	9.1**	8.1**	9.2**	6.9**
113	Panama	6	8.5**	9.2**	7.7**	8.4**	9.7**	7.0**	6.2**	7.2**	5.1**	4.2**	5.3**	3.0**
114	Paraguay	6	13.7ʸ	15.2ʸ	12.0ʸ	9.8ʸ	11.4ʸ	8.1ʸ	7.3ʸ	8.6ʸ	5.9ʸ	5.3ʸ	6.4ʸ	4.1ʸ
115	Peru	6	5.2ˣ	5.4ˣ	5.0ˣ	16.6ˣ	17.0ˣ	16.2ˣ	13.5ˣ	13.8ˣ	13.2ˣ	9.6ˣ	9.8ˣ	9.4ˣ
116	Saint Kitts and Nevis	7	.	.	.	.	.	.	.	.	.	.	.	.
117	Saint Lucia	7	5.8	6.8	4.7	1.5	1.7	1.3	1.5	2.1	0.9	0.8	0.8	0.7

REPETITION RATES BY GRADE IN PRIMARY EDUCATION (%) — REPEATERS, ALL GRADES (%)

Grade 5 (2003) Total	Male	Female	Grade 6 (2003) Total	Male	Female	Grade 7 (2003) Total	Male	Female	1999 Total	Male	Female	2004 Total	Male	Female	
1.6	1.6	1.6	0.2	0.3	0.2	.	.	.	...	...	...	2.9	2.9	2.9	57
...	...	...	...	...	...	.	.	.	...	...	...	...	...	...	58
.	.	.	.	.	.	.	.	.	.	.	.	.	.	.	59
5.3	6.4	3.9	.	.	.	.	.	.	20.9	22.4	19.1	19.9	21.1	18.5	60
8.0	10.2	5.4	7.1	8.9	5.1	.	.	.	6.3	7.3	5.1	5.9	7.5	4.1	61
.	.	.	.	.	.	.	.	.	.	.	.	.z	.z	.z	62
.y	.y	.y	.y	.y	.y	.	.	.	.	.	.	.z	.z	.z	63
...	...	...	...	...	...	.	.	.	...	...	...	...	...	...	64
0.3**	**0.3****	**0.3****	.	.	.	.	.	.	1.7	1.7**	1.7**	**0.7****	**0.7****	**0.7****	65
−y	−y	−y	−y	−y	−y	.	.	.	−	−	−	−z	−z	−z	66
...	...	...				.	.	.	...	...	...				67
...	...	...	.y	.y	.y	.	.	.	.	.	.	.	.	.	68
...	...	...	.	.	.	.	.	.	−			...	...	...	69
−y	−y	−y	−y	−y	−y	.	.	.	−	−	−	−**,z	−**,z	−**,z	70
1.0	1.4	0.6	0.4	0.5	0.2	.	.	.	1.9	2.4	1.4	2.1	2.8	1.5	71
0.0	**0.0**	**0.0**	**0.0**	**0.0**	**0.0**	.	.	.	−	−	−	**0.01**	**0.00**	**0.01**	72
1.5x	...	...	1.1x	1.4**,x	0.8**,x	.	.	.	1.0	1.1	0.9	0.9**	1.1**	0.7**	73
...	...	...	...	...	...	.	.	.	...	...	...	...	...	...	74
...	...	...	...	...	...	.	.	.	...	...	...	...	...	...	75
...	...	...	...	...	...	.	.	.	3.5	3.4	3.5	...	...	...	76
...	...	...	...	...	...	.	.	.	...	...	...				77
.y	.y	.y	.y	.y	.y	.	.	.	.	.	.	.z	.z	.z	78
.x	.x	.x	29.2**,x	31.3**,x	26.8**,x	.	.	.	8.8	8.5	9.2	6.2**,y	6.9**,y	5.5**,y	79
.	.	.	13.5**	13.5**	13.5**	.	.	.	10.6**	11.1**	9.9**	10.7	11.5**	9.7**	81
...	...	...													80
0.2**,y	0.2**,y	0.2**,y	.	.	.	.	.	.	3.8	4.2	3.2	2.4**,z	2.8**,z	1.9**,z	82

Latin America and the Caribbean

Grade 5 Total	Male	Female	Grade 6 Total	Male	Female	Grade 7 Total	Male	Female	1999 Total	Male	Female	2004 Total	Male	Female	
30.4	28.8	32.0	28.9	24.5	33.7	25.5	26.2	24.8	0.3	0.4	0.3	21.8	22.8	20.8	83
...	...	...	...	...	...	...	...	...	...	...	...	...	...	...	84
4.3x	5.2x	3.3x	3.6x	4.5x	2.7x	.	.	.	6.1	7.1	5.0	6.4z	7.5z	5.2z	85
6.0	5.8	6.2	3.8	4.1	3.4	.	.	.	7.7	9.5	5.9	8.5	9.6	7.3	86
...	...	...	...	...	...	.	.	.	.	.	.	.	.	.	87
.	.	.	.	.	.	.	.	.	.	.	.	.	.	.	88
9.5	11.4	7.4	8.8	10.2	7.4	.	.	.	9.7	10.8	8.4	10.8	12.5	9.0	89
.x	.x	.x	.x	.x	.x	.	.	.	.	.	.	.y	.y	.y	90
1.4**	1.6**	1.3**	2.9**	3.3**	2.5**	.	.	.	2.4	2.6	2.3	1.6**	1.7**	1.5**	91
.	.	.	.	.	.	.	.	.	24.0	24.0	24.0	20.6y	...	...	92
3.4	4.4	2.3	...	...	...	0.5	1.1	−	3.8**	4.1**	3.6**	4.1	5.6	2.5	93
...	...	...	...	...	...	.	.	.	0.2**	0.2**	0.1**	−	−	−	94
2.8	3.8	1.8	2.7	3.6	1.8	.	.	.	2.4	2.9	1.9	2.4	3.0	1.9	95
2.2**	2.4**	1.9**	.	.	.	.	.	.	5.2	5.8	4.6	4.3	4.7	3.8	96
5.7**	6.8**	4.6**	0.5**	0.5**	0.4**	.	.	.	9.2	10.4	7.9	6.9	8.0	5.8	97
0.5	0.8	0.3	0.2	0.3	0.1	.	.	.	1.9	2.6	1.1	0.7	0.9	0.4	98
3.2	5.5	0.9	2.3	3.5	0.9	5.7	6.0	5.4	3.6	3.8	3.5	4.3	5.7	2.9	99
6.2	7.9**	4.5**	5.0	6.5**	3.6**	.	.	.	4.1	4.5	3.7	7.3	8.8	5.5	100
0.9**	1.0**	0.8**	0.5**	0.6**	0.4**	.	.	.	2.7	3.0	2.4	2.0**	2.3**	1.8**	101
3.5**	4.2**	2.7**	3.2**	4.0**	2.5**	.	.	.	7.1**	7.7**	6.4**	6.7**	7.6**	5.7**	102
1.4y	1.5y	1.3y	2.1y	...	...	4.0y	3.5y	4.5y	2.7**	3.3**	2.0**	3.4	4.6	2.1	103
4.9**	5.3**	4.5**	1.8**	1.9**	1.7**	.	.	.	14.9	15.8	13.8	13.3	14.0	12.5	104
0.9**,y	1.2**,y	0.6**,y	0.8**,y	0.9**,y	0.8**,y	.	.	.	3.1	3.6	2.5	1.5**	1.7**	1.1**	105
...	...	...	...	...	...	.	.	.	...	...	...				106
...	...	...	...	...	...	.	.	.	...	...	...	8.5	9.4	7.5	107
1.0	1.1	0.9	6.2	5.6	6.7	.	.	.	...	...	...	2.8	3.3	2.3	108
2.9	3.7	2.1	0.5	0.7	0.4	.	.	.	6.6	7.6	5.5	4.8	5.8	3.8	109
−**	−**	−**	4.6**	7.9**	−**	6.3**	8.7**	4.0**	0.5	0.5	0.6	3.4	5.0	1.4	110
11.2**,y	12.5**,y	9.8**,y	6.6**,y	8.4**,y	5.0**,y	.	.	.	12.0**	14.5**	9.3**	12.6**,z	15.5**,z	9.6**,z	111
6.2**	7.3**	5.1**	3.3**	4.0**	2.6**	.	.	.	4.7	5.3	4.1	10.5	11.8	9.2	112
2.9**	3.7**	2.0**	1.2**	1.5**	0.9**	.	.	.	6.4	7.4	5.2	5.5	6.4	4.5	113
3.2y	3.9y	2.4y	1.5y	1.9y	1.0y	.	.	.	7.8	8.8	6.7	7.3**	8.5**	6.0**	114
8.1x	8.4x	7.8x	3.9x	4.1x	3.8x	.	.	.	10.2	10.5	9.9	7.6	7.8	7.4	115
.	.	.	.	.	.	.	.	.	.	.	.	.	.	.	116
1.2	1.3	1.0	1.2	1.3	1.0	4.0	3.5	4.5	2.4**	2.8**	2.0**	2.3	2.6	2.1	117

Table 6 (continued)

	Country or territory	Duration[1] of primary education 2004	REPETITION RATES BY GRADE IN PRIMARY EDUCATION (%) School year ending in 2003 Grade 1 Total	Grade 1 Male	Grade 1 Female	Grade 2 Total	Grade 2 Male	Grade 2 Female	Grade 3 Total	Grade 3 Male	Grade 3 Female	Grade 4 Total	Grade 4 Male	Grade 4 Female
118	St Vincent/Grenad.	7	5.6	6.9	4.1	4.7	5.4	3.8	5.2	6.5	3.7	7.4	9.8	4.8
119	Suriname	6	…	…	…	…	…	…	…	…	…	…	…	…
120	Trinidad and Tobago	7	11.0*	13.0*	8.9*	5.3*	6.3*	4.1*	4.1*	4.8*	3.3*	3.6*	4.3*	2.8*
121	Turks and Caicos Islands	6	0.9	1.8	–	10.5	13.0	8.5	3.6	3.9	3.3	2.9	4.1	1.6
122	Uruguay	6	16.7**	19.0**	14.1**	10.5**	11.8**	9.1**	7.7**	9.1**	6.3**	6.2**	7.5**	4.8**
123	Venezuela	6	11.7	13.6	9.6	9.2	11.0	7.2	8.6	10.6	6.6	6.5	8.0	4.9
	North America and Western Europe													
124	Andorra	6	–	–	–	–	–	–	–	–	–	–	–	–
125	Austria	4	…	…	…	…	…	…	…	…	…	…	…	…
126	Belgium	6	…	…	…	…	…	…	…	…	…	…	…	…
127	Canada	6	…	…	…	…	…	…	…	…	…	…	…	…
128	Cyprus	6	1.3	1.5	1.2	0.1	0.1	0.1	0.03	0.1	–	0.04	0.02	0.1
129	Denmark	6	.y	.y	.y	.y	.y	.y	.y	.y	.y	.y	.y	.y
130	Finland	6	0.8	1.0	0.6	0.9	1.1	0.7	0.4	0.5	0.3	0.2	0.2	0.1
131	France	5	…	…	…	…	…	…	…	…	…	…	…	…
132	Germany	4	1.5	1.6	1.4	1.9	2.0	1.9	1.5	1.6	1.3	0.9	1.0	0.8
133	Greece	6	…	…	…	…	…	…	…	…	…	…	…	…
134	Iceland	7	–	–	–	–	–	–	–	–	–	–	–	–
135	Ireland	8	2.5	2.8	2.1	1.6	1.8	1.3	0.9	1.0	0.8	0.6	0.6	0.5
136	Israel	6	2.2	2.9	1.3	1.1	1.4	0.8	1.1	1.4	0.7	1.3	1.6	0.9
137	Italy	5	0.4	0.5	0.3	0.3	0.4	0.2	0.2	0.3	0.2	0.2	0.3	0.1
138	Luxembourg	6	5.7	6.3	5.1	4.5	4.3	4.8	6.1	6.9	5.1	4.5	5.7	3.2
139	Malta	6	0.8y	0.8y	0.8y	0.7y	0.9y	0.5y	0.7y	0.6y	0.7y	0.8y	0.9y	0.6y
140	Monaco	5	…	…	…	…	…	…	…	…	…	…	…	…
141	Netherlands	6	.y	.y	.y	.y	.y	.y	.y	.y	.y	.y	.y	.y
142	Norway	7	–	–	–	–	–	–	–	–	–	–	–	–
143	Portugal	6	…	…	…	…	…	…	…	…	…	…	…	…
144	San Marino	5	…	…	…	…	…	…	…	…	…	…	…	…
145	Spain	6	…	…	…	…	…	…	…	…	…	…	…	…
146	Sweden	6	…	…	…	…	…	…	…	…	…	…	…	…
147	Switzerland	6	1.1	1.3	1.0	2.6	2.6	2.5	1.9	1.9	1.8	1.6	1.7	1.4
148	United Kingdom	6	…	…	…	…	…	…	…	…	…	…	…	…
149	United States	6	…	…	…	…	…	…	…	…	…	…	…	…
	South and West Asia													
150	Afghanistan	6	…	…	…	…	…	…	…	…	…	…	…	…
151	Bangladesh	5	7.1	6.8	7.4	6.7	6.6	6.7	9.2	9.4	8.9	7.7	8.2	7.3
152	Bhutan	7	…	…	…	…	…	…	…	…	…	…	…	…
153	India	5	3.5	3.6	3.4	2.7	2.7	2.7	3.8	3.8	3.8	4.0	4.2	3.8
154	Iran, Islamic Republic of	5	4.2	4.9	3.5	2.6	3.4	1.9	1.7	2.3	1.0	1.8	2.5	1.1
155	Maldives	7	5.8y	6.5y	5.2y	.y	.y	.y	.y	.y	.y	.y	.y	.y
156	Nepal	5	43.0**	42.6**	43.5**	16.6**	15.6**	17.8**	12.4**	12.1**	12.7**	12.9**	12.5**	13.4**
157	Pakistan	5	…	…	…	…	…	…	…	…	…	…	…	…
158	Sri Lanka	5	…	…	…	…	…	…	…	…	…	…	…	…
	Sub-Saharan Africa													
159	Angola	4	…	…	…	…	…	…	…	…	…	…	…	…
160	Benin	6	22.4	22.3	22.4	20.6	20.2	21.2	25.8	25.1	26.8	22.7	21.6	24.2
161	Botswana	7	10.1	10.1	10.0	4.5**	5.6**	3.4**	4.3**	5.5**	3.1**	10.3**	13.1**	7.5**
162	Burkina Faso	6	7.6	7.7	7.4	10.7	10.8	10.6	13.5	13.9	12.9	14.6	14.5	14.8
163	Burundi	6	29.8	28.8	30.9	29.6	28.2	31.3	27.9	26.6	29.6	26.9	25.1	29.1
164	Cameroon	6	32.9	33.5	32.2	23.0	23.5	22.3	21.2	21.5	20.8	36.4	36.8	35.8
165	Cape Verde	6	1.0	1.2	0.8	26.2	29.8	22.0	0.5	0.7	0.4	22.6	25.5	19.4
166	Central African Republic	6	…	…	…	…	…	…	…	…	…	…	…	…
167	Chad	6	27.2**	27.2**	27.2**	24.3**	24.0**	24.9**	25.4**	25.0**	25.9**	23.4**	22.7**	24.4**
168	Comoros	6	30.2	31.3	28.8	28.1	…	…	27.7	…	…	23.5	…	…
169	Congo	6	33.4	34.4	32.3	23.8	24.2	23.4	35.2	36.0	34.2	30.0	30.8	29.1
170	Côte d'Ivoire	6	13.3**,y	14.0**,y	12.5**,y	…	…	…	…	…	…	…	…	…
171	D. R. Congo	6	…	…	…	…	…	…	…	…	…	…	…	…
172	Equatorial Guinea	5	48.1**,x	44.6**,x	51.7**,x	40.2**,x	38.1**,x	42.2**,x	33.6**,x	32.8**,x	34.4**,x	32.5**,x	33.0**,x	32.0**,x
173	Eritrea	5	29.7	29.4	30.2	19.6	19.2	20.1	19.9	19.5	20.4	22.0	20.7	23.7
174	Ethiopia	4	9.1	9.7	8.5	7.6	8.1	7.0	7.5	8.1	6.6	10.2	10.5	9.7

REPETITION RATES BY GRADE IN PRIMARY EDUCATION (%) | REPEATERS, ALL GRADES (%)

| | School year ending in 2003 | | | | | | | | | | School year ending in | | | | | |
| | Grade 5 | | | Grade 6 | | | Grade 7 | | | 1999 | | | 2004 | | | |
Total	Male	Female	Total	Male	Female	Total	Male	Female	Total	Male	Female	Total	Male	Female	
6.6	7.6	5.6	5.0	5.9	4.2	9.5	9.6	9.4	...	...	...	6.4	7.4	5.2	118
...	...	...	...	...	...	...	...	...							119
4.4*	5.5*	3.3*	4.4*	5.1*	3.7*	3.1*	3.3*	2.9*	4.7	4.9	4.4	5.2*	6.1*	4.2*	120
7.1	7.3	6.9	12.2	14.0	9.9				...	...	...	5.5	6.7	4.3	121
4.9**	6.0**	3.7**	2.3**	2.9**	1.7**	.	.	.	7.9	9.3	6.5	8.3**	9.7**	6.9**	122
4.5	5.6	3.4	1.9	2.3	1.4	.	.	.	7.0**	8.5**	5.5**	7.3	8.9	5.7	123

North America and Western Europe

−	−	−	−	.	−	.	.	.	...	...	...	−	−	−	124
...	...	...	.	.	.	.	.	.	1.5	1.8	1.3	...	...	...	125
...	...	...	...	...	...	.	.	.	...	...	...	...	...	...	126
...	...	...	...	...	...	.	.	.	...	...	...	...	...	...	127
0.03	0.02	0.04	0.1	0.2	0.1	.	.	.	0.4	0.5	0.3	0.3	0.3	0.2	128
.y	.y	.y	.y	.y	.y	.	.	.	.	.	.	.	.	.	129
0.2	0.2	0.1	0.2	0.2	0.1	.	.	.	0.4	0.6	0.3	0.4	0.5	0.3	130
...	...	...	.	.	.	.	.	.	4.2	4.2**	4.2**	...	...	...	131
...	...	...	.	.	.	.	.	.	1.7	1.9	1.5	1.5	1.6	1.3	132
									...	...	...				133
−	−	−	−	−	−	−	−	−	−	−	−	−**	−**	−**	134
0.7	0.6	0.7	0.6	0.6	0.6	0.8	0.8	0.7	1.8	2.1	1.6	1.0	1.1	0.9	135
1.2	1.6	0.8	1.0	1.3	0.7	.	.	.	...	...	...	1.6	2.0	1.1	136
0.4	0.4	0.3	.	.	.	.	.	.	0.4	0.5	0.3	0.3	0.4	0.2	137
3.7	4.0	3.4	1.0	1.4	0.7	.	.	.	...	...	...	4.3	4.8	3.8	138
0.7y	0.8y	0.5y	9.0y	9.9y	7.9y	.	.	.	2.1	2.4	1.8	2.0	2.4	1.6	139
...	...	...	.	.	.	.	.	.	−	−	−	...	...		140
.y	.y	.y	.y	.y	.y	.	.	.	.	.	.	.	.	.	141
−	−	−	−	−	−	−	−	−	.	.	.	−	−	−	142
...	...	...	.	.	.	.	.	.	...	...	...	...	...	...	143
...	...	...	.	.	.	.	.	.	...	...	...	...	...	...	144
...	...	...	...	...	...	.	.	.	...	...	...	...	...	...	145
...	...	...	...	...	...	.	.	.	...	...	...	...	...	...	146
1.6	1.9	1.3	1.0	1.3	0.8	.	.	.	1.8	1.9	1.6	1.6	1.7	1.4	147
...	...	...	...	...	...	.	.	.	.	.	.	...	...	...	148
...	...	...	...	...	...	.	.	.	...	...	...	...	...	...	149

South and West Asia

...	...	...	...	...	...	.	.	.	...	...	...	...	...	...	150
5.1	5.5	4.7	.	.	.	.	.	.	6.5	6.8	6.2	7.0	7.2	6.9	151
...	...	...	...	...	...	...	...	...	12.1	12.5	11.7	12.9**,y	13.5**,y	12.3**,y	152
3.9	4.1	3.7	...	...	...	.	.	.	4.0	4.0	4.1	3.2**	3.3**	3.1**	153
0.8	1.2	0.5	.	.	.	.	.	.	...	...	...	2.3	3.0	1.6	154
.y	.y	.y	.y	.y	.y	...	...	...	8.4**	7.6**	9.2**	11.3**	11.6**	10.9**	155
10.8**	**10.7****	**11.0****	.	.	.	.	.	.	22.9	22.2	23.8	**23.1****	**22.9****	**23.3****	156
...	...	...	.	.	.	.	.	.	...	...	...	...	...	...	157
...	...	...	.	.	.	.	.	.	...	...	...	...	...	...	158

Sub-Saharan Africa

.	.	.	.	.	.	.	.	.	29.0**	29.0**	29.0**	...	...	...	159
30.8	29.8	32.2	31.4	30.8	32.4	.	.	.	...	...	...	23.1	23.0	23.2	160
2.8**	3.5**	2.2**	2.4**	2.9**	2.0**	0.2**	0.2**	0.2**	3.3	3.9	2.7	5.2**	6.2**	4.2**	161
15.7	15.2	16.4	33.1	32.2	34.5	.	.	.	17.7	17.5	18.0	13.0	13.2	12.8	162
37.1	33.7	41.5	43.6	39.8	48.4	.	.	.	20.3**	20.3**	20.4**	29.1	27.8	30.6	163
24.3	24.9	23.6	22.1	23.1	20.9	.	.	.	26.7**	26.8**	26.5**	25.1	25.6	24.5	164
0.6	0.6	0.6	16.2	18.0	14.3	.	.	.	11.6**	12.8**	10.3**	13.0	15.0	10.8	165
...	...	...	...	...	...	.	.	.	...	...	...	...	...	...	166
22.3**	21.5**	23.8**	24.7**	24.6**	25.1**	.	.	.	25.9	25.7	26.3	24.2**	23.8**	24.7**	167
22.7	...	...	27.2	...	...	.	.	.	26.0	26.4	25.5	27.1	28.2	25.9	168
25.4	26.4	24.4	10.8	10.4	11.3	.	.	.	...	...	...	24.5	25.1	23.9	169
...	...	...	...	...	...	.	.	.	23.7	22.8**	24.9**	17.6*,z	17.5*,z	17.7*,z	170
...	...	...	...	...	...	.	.	.	...	...	...	...	...	...	171
33.5**,x	32.0**,x	35.0**,x	.	.	.	.	.	.	11.8	9.3	14.9	40.5y	38.1y	43.0y	172
14.5	14.0	15.3	.	.	.	.	.	.	19.4	18.2	20.8	21.3	20.6	22.2	173
.	.	.	.	.	.	.	.	.	11.4	10.7	12.5	**7.0**	**7.6**	**6.3**	174

Table 6 (continued)

REPETITION RATES BY GRADE IN PRIMARY EDUCATION (%)

School year ending in 2003

	Country or territory	Duration[1] of primary education 2004	Grade 1 Total	Male	Female	Grade 2 Total	Male	Female	Grade 3 Total	Male	Female	Grade 4 Total	Male	Female
175	Gabon	6	48.1**,y	49.1**,y	47.0**,y	33.2**,y	33.7**,y	32.6**,y	37.0**,y	38.3**,y	35.6**,y	24.8**,y	25.1**,y	24.5**,y
176	Gambia	6	13.0**	8.6**	17.2**	…	…	…	…	…	…	…	…	…
177	Ghana	6	**9.7**	**10.1**	**9.3**	**6.4**	**6.5**	**6.3**	**5.9**	**6.0**	**5.8**	**5.3**	**5.4**	**5.3**
178	Guinea	6	6.6	6.6	6.7	13.6	13.1	14.3	7.8	7.1	8.7	14.8	13.7	16.5
179	Guinea-Bissau	6	…	…	…	…	…	…	…	…	…	…	…	…
180	Kenya	6	6.2*	6.5*	6.0*	6.6*	6.8*	6.3*	5.6*	5.9*	5.2*	5.9*	6.2*	5.6*
181	Lesotho	7	23.1	25.6	20.2	21.5	24.2	18.4	17.4	20.2	14.5	16.2	19.2	13.4
182	Liberia	6	…	…	…	…	…	…	…	…	…	…	…	…
183	Madagascar	5	42.4	43.4	41.4	30.9	32.7	29.1	33.7	34.8	32.5	26.8	27.5	26.2
184	Malawi	6	17.5x	17.9x	17.0x	17.0x	17.3x	16.7x	16.7x	17.0x	16.5x	14.3x	14.5x	14.1x
185	Mali	6	13.4	13.1	13.8	12.9	12.7	13.3	20.3	19.6	21.2	24.5	23.6	25.7
186	Mauritius	6	.	.	.	.	.	.	.	.	.	.	.	.
187	Mozambique	7	25.8x	25.4x	26.1x	25.0x	24.7x	25.4x	25.2x	24.5x	26.2x	22.0x	21.1x	23.3x
188	Namibia	7	14.9**,y	15.6**,y	14.2**,y	11.6**,y	13.7**,y	9.4**,y	11.3**,y	13.7**,y	9.0**,y	12.6**,y	15.0**,y	10.3**,y
189	Niger	6	0.1	0.1	0.1	3.6	3.4	4.0	5.5	5.3	5.8	6.8	6.5	7.3
190	Nigeria	6	4.0**	3.8**	4.2**	3.2**	3.1**	3.4**	2.8**	2.7**	2.9**	2.5**	2.4**	2.6**
191	Rwanda	6	21.9	21.9	21.9	17.8	18.0	17.5	19.1	18.8	19.3	20.7	20.0	21.3
192	Sao Tome and Principe	6	31.3	32.1	30.5	25.7	28.0	23.1	24.4	25.3	23.3	18.2	18.8	17.5
193	Senegal	6	9.6	9.5	9.6	11.2	11.2	11.3	12.7	12.9	12.5	12.2	12.1	12.3
194	Seychelles	6	.	.	.	.	.	.	.	.	.	.	.	.
195	Sierra Leone	6	…	…	…	…	…	…	…	…	…	…	…	…
196	Somalia	7	…	…	…	…	…	…	…	…	…	…	…	…
197	South Africa	7	7.0y	6.8y	7.1y	5.2y	6.0y	4.3y	5.5y	6.4y	4.5y	5.9y	6.9y	4.8y
198	Swaziland	7	18.6y	21.0y	15.9y	16.1y	19.2y	12.7y	19.9y	24.7y	14.4y	16.6y	19.0y	14.1y
199	Togo	6	28.6	29.0	28.2	23.9	24.0	23.8	26.1	25.6	26.7	21.9	21.1	22.8
200	Uganda	7	13.8x	14.1x	13.4x	10.0x	10.3x	9.8x	10.8x	10.9x	10.6x	10.6x	10.7x	10.5x
201	United Republic of Tanzania	7	**0.5**	**0.5**	**0.4**	**5.9**	**6.0**	**5.8**	**5.0**	**4.6**	**5.4**	**14.6**	**14.0**	**15.3**
202	Zambia	7	5.4x	5.5x	5.3x	6.7x	6.9x	6.5x	6.9x	7.1x	6.6x	7.9x	8.3x	7.5x
203	Zimbabwe	7	.y	.y	.y	.y	.y	.y	.y	.y	.y	.y	.y	.y

			Grade 1 Total	Male	Female	Grade 2 Total	Male	Female	Grade 3 Total	Male	Female	Grade 4 Total	Male	Female
I	World[2]	…	4.7	5.3	4.0	3.6	3.4	3.8	3.5	4.2	2.8	4.0	5.5	2.3
II	Countries in transition	…	0.2	0.2	0.2	0.2	0.2	0.2	0.1	0.2	0.1	0.2	0.3	0.1
III	Developed countries	…	1.0	1.2	0.9	0.9	1.2	0.7	0.8	0.8	0.7	0.8	…	…
IV	Developing countries	…	7.0	6.8	7.1	6.9	7.6	6.1	5.6	6.1	5.0	6.4	7.5	5.2
V	Arab States	…	3.0	3.1	2.9	4.1	4.2	3.9	3.6	4.5	2.5	4.2	4.7	3.6
VI	Central and Eastern Europe	…	1.1	…	…	0.9	1.3	0.6	0.9	1.0	0.7	1.0	1.3	0.8
VII	Central Asia	…	0.1	0.2	0.1	0.2	0.2	0.1	0.2	0.2	0.1	0.2	0.2	0.2
VIII	East Asia and the Pacific	…	2.4	2.8	2.0	1.8	…	…	1.4	…	…	1.5	2.2	0.8
IX	East Asia	…	3.6	4.2	2.9	2.6	3.2	1.9	1.7	2.2	1.2	1.8	2.4	1.2
X	Pacific	…	–	–	–	–	–	–	–	–	–	.	.	.
XI	Latin America/Caribbean	…	7.4	8.0	6.7	7.1	9.0	5.2	5.7	6.9	4.4	4.3	5.3	3.3
XII	Caribbean	…	5.6	6.9	4.1	5.2	6.5	3.8	4.5	5.6	3.1	3.6	4.3	2.8
XIII	Latin America	…	9.2	10.3	8.1	7.8	9.0	6.5	6.2	7.3	5.0	4.6	5.5	3.7
XIV	N. America/W. Europe	…	1.0	1.0	0.9	0.8	1.0	0.6	0.5	0.5	0.5	0.4	0.4	0.3
XV	South and West Asia	…	5.8	6.5	5.2	6.7	6.6	6.7	9.2	9.4	8.9	5.9	6.2	5.5
XVI	Sub-Saharan Africa	…	14.9	15.6	14.2	17.0	17.3	16.7	17.4	20.2	14.5	16.6	19.0	14.1

1. Duration in this table is defined according to ISCED97 and may differ from that reported nationally.
2. All values shown are medians.

Data in bold are for the school year ending in 2004 for repetition rates by grade, and the school year ending in 2005 for percentage of repeaters (all grades).

(z) Data are for the school year ending in 2003.
(y) Data are for the school year ending in 2002.
(x) Data are for the school year ending in 2001.

REPETITION RATES BY GRADE IN PRIMARY EDUCATION (%) | REPEATERS, ALL GRADES (%)

| | School year ending in 2003 | | | | | | | | | School year ending in | | | | | | |
| | Grade 5 | | | Grade 6 | | | Grade 7 | | | 1999 | | | 2004 | | | |
Total	Male	Female	Total	Male	Female	Total	Male	Female	Total	Male	Female	Total	Male	Female	
27.7**,y	27.4**,y	28.0**,y	19.3**,y	18.9**,y	19.6**,y	.	.	.	...	...	...	34.4**,z	35.1**,z	33.7**,z	175
...	...	...	...	...	...	.	.	.	12.2	12.1	12.3	...	...	...	176
4.6	**4.6**	**4.6**	**5.1**	**5.2**	**5.0**	.	.	.	4.2	4.3	4.1	**5.8**	**6.0**	5.7	177
9.1	8.3	10.2	18.7	17.5	20.6	.	.	.	26.2	25.5	27.4	10.5	10.1	11.0	178
...	...	...	...	...	...	.	.	.	24.0**	23.6**	24.5**	...	...	...	179
5.7*	5.6*	5.7*	5.5*	5.8*	5.3*	12.6**	12.9**	12.3**	...	...	...	5.8*	6.0*	5.6*	180
16.0	18.7	13.6	10.9	12.5	9.7	14.9	15.0	14.8	20.3	22.9	17.9	18.2	20.7	15.6	181
...	...	...	...	...	...	.	.	.	...	...	...	...	...	...	182
27.7	28.0	27.5	.	.	.	.	.	.	28.3**	29.2**	27.4**	30.0	30.9	29.0	183
10.7x	10.0x	11.6x	11.4x	11.2x	11.5x	.	.	.	14.4	14.4	14.4	18.0	18.4	17.6	184
29.5	28.4	31.1	28.2	27.4	29.5	.	.	.	17.4	17.2	17.7	19.0	18.7	19.3	185
.	.	.	21.8**	24.8**	18.6**	.	.	.	3.8	4.1	3.5	**4.8****	**5.6****	**4.0****	186
21.3x	20.1x	23.2x	23.8x	22.6x	25.5x	28.0x	26.4x	30.5x	23.8	23.2	24.7	20.6	20.6	20.5	187
19.5**,y	21.5**,y	17.4**,y	10.8**,y	11.5**,y	10.1**,y	10.6**,y	10.6**,y	10.5**,y	12.3	13.9	10.7	13.1**,z	14.6**,z	11.6**,z	188
9.7	9.2	10.5	21.8	21.3	22.4	.	.	.	12.2	12.4	11.8	5.3	5.1	5.5	189
2.4**	2.4**	2.5**	1.8**	1.8**	1.8**	.	.	.	...	...	...	3.0**	3.0**	3.1**	190
22.6	21.7	23.5	17.7	17.2	18.2	.	.	.	29.1	29.2	29.0	18.8	18.7	18.9	191
18.0	17.1	18.8	29.0	27.0	31.0	.	.	.	30.7	32.6	28.7	24.6	25.4	23.8	192
16.1	15.7	16.6	26.7	25.8	27.8	.	.	.	14.4	14.5**	14.2**	12.9	13.1	12.8	193
.	.	.	.	.	.	.	.	.	.	.	.	.	.	.	194
...	...	...	...	...	...	.	.	.	...	...	...	...	...	...	195
...	...	...	...	...	...	...	...	...	...	...	...	...	...	...	196
4.8y	5.6y	3.9y	4.5y	5.3y	3.8y	3.2y	3.6y	2.8y	10.4	11.6	9.2	5.2z	6.0z	4.4z	197
15.3y	15.3y	15.3y	15.2y	16.4y	14.0y	9.0y	9.9y	8.3y	17.1	19.5	14.5	16.3z	18.9z	13.7z	198
22.0	21.4	22.7	18.4	17.6	19.5	.	.	.	31.2	30.9	31.6	23.8	23.6	24.1	199
10.5x	10.4x	10.7x	11.0x	10.8x	11.1x	8.9x	9.7x	7.8x	...	...	...	13.7	13.8	13.7	200
0.3	**0.3**	**0.3**	**0.1**	**0.1**	**0.1**	**0.01**	**0.01**	**0.01**	3.2	3.1	3.2	**4.3**	**4.2**	**4.4**	201
7.9x	8.2x	7.4x	9.0x	9.6x	8.4x	15.2x	16.4x	13.6x	6.1**	6.4**	5.8**	6.9	7.1	6.8	202
.y	.y	.y	.y	.y	.y	.y	.y	.y	.	.	.	.z	.z	.z	203

Total	Male	Female	Total	Male	Female	Total	Male	Female	Total	Male	Female	Total	Male	Female	
4.2	4.9	3.4	4.4	5.1	3.5	.	.	.	4.1	4.3	4.0	4.3	4.8	3.8	I
.	.	.	.	.	.	.	.	.	0.5	0.5	0.5	0.1	0.1	0.1	II
.	.	.	0.5	...	...	.	.	.	1.6	1.8	1.4	1.0	1.2	0.9	III
4.9	5.7	4.1	4.7	3.6	6.0	.	.	.	7.7	9.5	5.9	6.7	7.6	5.7	IV
6.8	8.1	5.1	4.6	7.0	2.0	.	.	.	6.5	7.2	5.6	4.3	4.9	3.5	V
.	.	.	.	.	.	.	.	.	1.2	...	...	0.9	...	...	VI
.	.	.	.	.	.	.	.	.	0.4	0.5	0.3	0.2	0.2	0.2	VII
1.0	1.4	0.6	0.4	0.5	0.2	.	.	.	2.6	...	...	2.2	2.7	1.5	VIII
1.3	2.0	0.6	1.3	1.5	1.0	.	.	.	3.6	3.8	3.4	2.5	3.2	1.7	IX
.	.	.	0.4	0.5	0.2	.	.	.	...	...	...	...	...	...	X
3.5	4.2	2.7	2.9	3.3	2.5	.	.	.	5.0	5.5	4.4	5.9	7.0	4.8	XI
3.9	4.9	2.8	4.6	7.9	–	.	.	.	3.4	3.7	3.0	4.3	5.7	2.9	XII
3.5	4.2	2.7	2.1	2.6	1.6	.	.	.	6.5	7.5	5.4	6.9	8.0	5.8	XIII
0.4	0.4	0.3	0.4	0.4	0.4	.	.	.	1.0	1.2	0.8	0.4	0.5	0.3	XIV
4.5	4.8	4.2	.	.	.	.	.	.	8.4	7.6	9.2	9.2	9.4	8.9	XV
16.1	17.2	15.1	18.1	17.4	18.9	.	.	.	17.6	17.4	17.8	17.6	17.5	17.7	XVI

Education for All Global Monitoring Report 2007

Table 7
Internal efficiency: primary education dropout and completion rates

	Country or territory	Duration[1] of primary education 2004	DROPOUT RATES BY GRADE IN PRIMARY EDUCATION (%) School year ending in 2003															
			Grade 1			Grade 2			Grade 3			Grade 4			Grade 5		
			Total	Male	Female	Total	Male	Female	Total	Male	Female	Total	Male	Female	Total	Male	Female
	Arab States																
1	Algeria	6	0.9	1.6	0.2	0.7	0.8	0.6	0.6	0.6	0.5	1.3	1.4	1.1	2.5	3.1	1.9
2	Bahrain	6	–	–	–	0.1	0.3	–	–	–	–	–	–	–	0.5	0.3	0.6
3	Djibouti	6	2.3ˣ	2.7ˣ	1.9ˣ	3.5ˣ	3.9ˣ	2.8ˣ	1.9ˣ	0.8ˣ	3.4ˣ	4.2**,ˣ	2.6**,ˣ	6.4**,ˣ	…	…	…
4	Egypt	5	0.2**	0.3**	0.1**	0.4**	0.5**	0.4**	0.3**	0.3**	0.2**	0.4**	0.5**	0.3**			
5	Iraq	6	…	…	…	…	…	…	…	…	…	…	…	…	…	…	…
6	Jordan	6	0.7	1.2	0.3	–	–	–	–	–	–	0.9	0.3	1.5	1.0	0.8	1.2
7	Kuwait	4	0.8**	0.5**	1.1**	0.9**	0.8**	1.1**	1.0**	0.9**	1.1**	…	…	…	.	.	.
8	Lebanon	6	–	–	–							2.0	3.1	0.8	2.2	3.2	1.1
9	Libyan Arab Jamahiriya	6	…	…	…	…	…	…									
10	Mauritania	6	–	–	–	3.8	3.2	4.4	6.1	6.1	6.0	7.7	8.7	6.7	12.5	12.5	12.5
11	Morocco	6	6.3ʸ	6.1ʸ	6.6ʸ	2.9ʸ	2.4ʸ	3.5ʸ	3.5ʸ	3.3ʸ	3.7ʸ	4.4ʸ	4.2ʸ	4.6ʸ	6.3ʸ	6.3ʸ	6.3ʸ
12	Oman	6	1.2	1.4	1.0	0.3	0.3	0.2	0.1	0.1	0.2	0.8	0.8	0.7	0.6	0.3	0.9
13	Palestinian A. T.	4	0.4	0.7	0.1	–	–	–	1.5	1.6	1.4	…	…	…	.	.	.
14	Qatar	6	…	…	…	…	…	…	…	…	…	…	…	…	…	…	…
15	Saudi Arabia	6	1.2	1.2	1.2	1.6	2.4	0.8	3.0	2.9	3.1	0.4	–	1.8	1.9	1.8	2.0
16	Sudan	6	1.6	1.3	2.0	0.9	0.7	1.2	1.2	1.4	1.1	4.3	4.8	3.8	4.2	4.3	4.1
17	Syrian Arab Republic	4	3.3	3.4	3.3	2.8	2.9	2.6	1.6	1.5	1.7	…	…	…	.	.	.
18	Tunisia	6	–	–	–	0.9	0.8	1.0	0.8	0.9	0.6	1.6	1.6	1.5	2.9	3.2	2.6
19	United Arab Emirates	5	4.2	4.3	4.1	–	–	–	0.6	1.0	0.2	0.6	0.6	0.7			
20	Yemen	6	11.3**	10.2**	12.7**	5.2**	4.1**	6.6**	4.9**	3.3**	7.2**	7.2**	5.4**	10.1**	7.6**	6.6**	9.4**
	Central and Eastern Europe																
21	Albania	4	1.7**,ʸ	3.0**,ʸ	0.3**,ʸ	4.2**,ʸ	4.9**,ʸ	3.4**,ʸ	4.3**,ʸ	3.7**,ʸ	4.9**,ʸ	…	…	…	.	.	.
22	Belarus	4	–	–	–	–	–	–	–	–	–	…	…	…	.	.	.
23	Bosnia and Herzegovina	4	…	…	…	…	…	…	…	…	…	…	…	…	.	.	.
24	Bulgaria	4	3.3	3.6	2.9	1.8	2.1	1.5	1.3	1.2	1.4	…	…	…	.	.	.
25	Croatia	4	–ʸ	–ʸ	–ʸ	–ʸ	–ʸ	–ʸ	–ʸ	–ʸ	–ʸ	…	…	…	.	.	.
26	Czech Republic	5	0.9	1.1	0.7	0.3	0.3	0.4	0.2	0.3	0.1	0.2	0.0	0.3	…	…	…
27	Estonia	6	–ʸ	–ʸ	–ʸ	0.7ʸ	0.7ʸ	0.6ʸ	0.7ʸ	0.7ʸ	0.6ʸ	0.3ʸ	0.7ʸ	–ʸ	0.7ʸ	0.6ʸ	0.8ʸ
28	Hungary	4	2.1	2.3	1.9	0.2	0.1	0.2	0.0	–	0.1	…	…	…	.	.	.
29	Latvia	4	1.2	0.9	1.5	0.2	0.3	0.1	0.2	–	0.5	…	…	…	.	.	.
30	Lithuania	4	0.7	0.7	0.8	0.3	0.4	0.1	0.5	0.7	0.3	…	…	…	.	.	.
31	Poland	6	0.2	…	…	–	–	–	–	–	–	…	…	…	–	–	–
32	Republic of Moldova	4	6.9	7.7	6.0	1.6	0.9	2.3	1.8	2.0	1.5	…	…	…	.	.	.
33	Romania	4	2.1	2.5	1.8	1.4	1.5	1.2	1.2	1.2	1.1	…	…	…	.	.	.
34	Russian Federation	3	…	…	…	…	…	…	…	…	…						
35	Serbia and Montenegro	4	…	…	…	…	…	…	…	…	…	…	…	…	.	.	.
36	Slovakia	4	1.7	1.8	1.6	0.4	0.4	0.4	0.2	0.3	0.2	…	…	…	.	.	.
37	Slovenia	4	0.6ʸ	0.7ʸ	0.4ʸ	0.1ʸ	0.3ʸ	–ʸ	0.4ʸ	0.5ʸ	0.3ʸ	…	…	…	.	.	.
38	TFYR Macedonia	4	0.8	1.0	0.6	0.5	0.4	0.5	0.5	0.6	0.5	…	…	…	.	.	.
39	Turkey	6	–**	–**	–**	1.9**	1.8**	2.0**	2.3**	1.9**	2.7**	2.3**	1.9**	2.8**	3.1**	1.5**	4.8**
40	Ukraine	4	0.5ˣ	–**,ˣ	1.3**,ˣ	0.9ˣ	1.3**,ˣ	0.5**,ˣ	…	…	…	…	…	…	.	.	.
	Central Asia																
41	Armenia	3	2.6ʸ	2.7ʸ	2.4ʸ	1.2ʸ	1.1ʸ	1.2ʸ	…	…	…	.	.	.	.	.	.
42	Azerbaijan	4	0.1	0.8	–	0.8	1.3	0.1	0.6	1.3	–	…	…	…	.	.	.
43	Georgia	6	0.3ʸ	–ʸ	1.1ʸ	0.6ʸ	0.9ʸ	0.3ʸ	1.0ʸ	0.3ʸ	1.6ʸ	…	…	…	…	…	…
44	Kazakhstan	4	–	–	–	–	–	–	–	–	–	…	…	…	.	.	.
45	Kyrgyzstan	4	1.3	2.4	0.2	1.3	1.5	1.1	1.6	2.1	1.2	…	…	…	.	.	.
46	Mongolia	4	5.6	5.5	5.7	2.0	1.9	2.0	1.7	2.2	1.2	…	…	…	.	.	.
47	Tajikistan	4	–	–**	–**	0.5	–**	1.1**	0.7	0.8**	0.6**	…	…	…	.	.	.
48	Turkmenistan	3	…	…	…	…	…	…	…	…	…	.	.	.	.	.	.
49	Uzbekistan	4	1.2**,ʸ	0.1**,ʸ	2.3**,ʸ	2.4**,ʸ	3.1**,ʸ	1.6**,ʸ	0.4**,ʸ	0.4**,ʸ	0.4**,ʸ	…	…	…	.	.	.
	East Asia and the Pacific																
50	Australia	7	5.3**	6.0**	4.6**	3.4**	3.8**	3.1**	3.3**	3.5**	3.0**	3.0**	3.3**	2.7**	2.9**	3.1**	2.7**
51	Brunei Darussalam	6	–**	–**	–**	–**	–**	–**	–**	–**	–**	–**	–**	–**	–**	–**	–**
52	Cambodia	6	12.0	11.6	12.5	11.8	12.4	11.1	9.5	10.3	8.5	9.0	9.4	8.5	9.9	9.5	10.4
53	China	5	–ʸ	–**,ʸ	–**,ʸ	–ʸ	–**,ʸ	–**,ʸ	0.2ʸ	0.0**,ʸ	0.4**,ʸ	1.3ʸ	1.3**,ʸ	1.3**,ʸ	…	…	…

DROPOUT RATES BY GRADE IN PRIMARY EDUCATION (%) School year ending in 2003 Grade 6			DROPOUTS ALL GRADES (%) School year ending in 2003			PRIMARY EDUCATION COMPLETION												
						SURVIVAL RATE TO GRADE 5 (%) School year ending in 2003			SURVIVAL RATE TO LAST GRADE (%) School year ending in 2003			GROSS INTAKE RATE TO LAST GRADE (%) School year ending in 2003			PRIMARY COHORT COMPLETION RATE (%) School year ending in 2003			
Total	Male	Female	Total	Male	Female	Total	Male	Female	Total	Male	Female	Total	Male	Female	Total	Male	Female	
Arab States																		
…	…	…	6.6	8.4	4.6	96.2	95.0	97.4	93.4	91.6	95.4	94.3	94.0	94.5	88.2	86.1	90.5	1
…	…	…	0.03	0.04		…	…	…	100.0	100.0	100.0	101.6	99.9	103.3	…	…	…	2
…	…	…				87.7**,x	89.6**,x	85.2**,x	…	…	…	29.1	33.1	25.0	…	…	…	3
…	…	…	1.4**	1.7**	1.0**	98.6**	98.3**	99.0**	98.6**	98.3**	99.0**	94.6**	96.4**	92.8**	…	…	…	4
…	…	…				…	…	…	…	…	…	74.1	85.0	62.7	…	…	…	5
…	…	…	2.2	2.0	2.4	98.8	98.7	98.8	97.8	98.0	97.6	96.7	97.0	96.3	…	…	…	6
·	·	·	2.8**	2.2**	3.4**	·	·	·	97.2**	97.8**	96.6**	91.3**	90.8**	91.8**	93.3**	93.8**	92.7**	7
…	…	…	3.7	7.1	–	97.6	95.4	100.0	96.3	92.9	100.0	94.1	91.9	96.5	92.4	88.8	96.3	8
																		9
…	…	…	30.6	31.3	29.8	81.6	80.7	82.7	69.4	68.7	70.2	43.1	45.1	41.0	42.2	43.7	40.4	10
…	…	…	24.5y	24.0y	25.1y	81.2y	82.0y	80.4y	75.5y	76.0y	74.9y	75.4	78.7	72.0	66.0y	67.2y	64.7y	11
…	…	…	3.0	3.0	3.0	97.6	97.3	97.9	97.0	97.0	97.0	91.3	92.9	89.6	97.3	97.6	97.0	12
·	·	·	1.5	1.8	1.2	·	·	·	98.5	98.2	98.8	98.1	97.5	98.7	55.0	51.9	58.3	13
…	…	…	…	…	…	…	…	…	…	…	…	92.1**,z	93.1**,z	91.0**,z	…	…	…	14
…	…	…	8.2	7.6	8.8	93.6	94.1	93.1	91.8	92.4	91.2	61.8	62.4	61.1	47.9			15
…	…	…	12.1	12.0	12.1	91.9	92.0	91.8	87.9	88.0	87.9	48.8	53.1	44.5	…	…	…	16
·	·	·	8.2	8.4	8.0	…	…	…	91.8	91.6	92.0	106.6	108.7	104.3	…	…	…	17
…	…	…	6.7	7.2	6.1	96.5	96.4	96.7	93.3	92.8	93.9	97.1	96.7	97.5	…	…	…	18
…	…	…	5.3	6.0	4.6	94.7	94.0	95.4	94.7	94.0	95.4	75.4	77.1	73.6	…	…	…	19
…	…	…	32.7**	27.7**	39.7**	73.2**	77.8**	66.9**	67.3**	72.3**	60.3**	62.3**	78.3**	45.6**	…	…	…	20
Central and Eastern Europe																		
·	·	·	10.2**,y	11.5**,y	8.6**,y	·	·	·	89.8**,y	88.5**,y	91.4**,y	99.0z	98.9z	99.2z	…	…	…	21
·	·	·	–	–	–	·	·	·	100.0	…	…	100.7	102.6	98.7	85.4	…	…	22
·	·	·	…	…	…	·	·	·	…	…	…	…	…	…	…	…	…	23
·	·	·	6.3	6.9	5.7	·	·	·	93.7	93.1	94.3	98.2	99.0	97.4	…	…	…	24
·	·	·	0.4y	0.9y	–y	·	·	·	99.6y	99.1y	100.0y	91.4z	91.9z	90.8z	…	…	…	25
…	…	…	1.6	1.7	1.4	98.4	98.3	98.6	98.4	98.3	98.6	103.8	103.6	104.0	…	…	…	26
…	…	…	2.3y	2.9y	1.6y	98.4y	97.6y	99.2y	97.7y	97.1y	98.4y	101.5	102.7	100.2	…	…	…	27
·	·	·	2.4	2.5	2.3	·	·	·	97.6	97.5	97.7	95.7	95.4	96.0	…	…	…	28
·	·	·	1.7	1.2	2.1	·	·	·	98.3	98.8	97.9	92.3	92.6	92.0	…	…	…	29
·	·	·	1.5	1.7	1.2	·	·	·	98.5	98.3	98.8	97.9	98.6	97.2	…	…	…	30
·	·	·	0.3	…	…	99.7	…	…	99.7	…	…	100.3	…	…	…	…	…	31
·	·	·	10.0	10.4	9.6	·	·	·	90.0	89.6	90.4	82.5	82.3	82.8	…	…	…	32
·	·	·	4.8	5.3	4.2	·	·	·	95.2	94.7	95.8	93.3	93.8	92.8	…	…	…	33
·	·	·	…	…	…	·	·	·	…	…	…	…	…	…	…	…	…	34
			…	…	…				…	…	…	…	…	…	…	…	…	35
·	·	·	2.4	2.5	2.2	·	·	·	97.6	97.5	97.8	99.4	99.3	99.6	…	…	…	36
…	…	…	1.1y	1.6y	0.7y	…	…	…	98.9y	98.4y	99.3y	102.4z	102.9z	101.9z	…	…	…	37
·	·	·	1.8	2.0	1.6	·	·	·	98.2	98.0	98.4	96.4	95.6	97.3	…	…	…	38
…	…	…	8.4**	6.6**	10.4**	94.6**	94.9**	94.3**	91.6**	93.4**	89.6**	87.8	93.1	82.3	…	…	…	39
·	·	·	1.4x	1.1**,x	1.8**,x	·	·	·	98.6x	98.9**,x	98.2**,x	…	…	…	…	…	…	40
Central Asia																		
·	·	·	3.7y	3.8y	3.6y	·	·	·	96.3y	96.2y	96.4y	106.6	105.6	107.6	…	…	…	41
·	·	·	2.2	4.1	–	·	·	·	97.8	95.9	100.0	96.1	97.0	95.2	97.5	…	…	42
…	…	…	1.8y	0.8y	2.9y	…	…	…	98.2y	99.2y	97.1y	85.6	83.8	87.5	…	…	…	43
·	·	·	0.3	–	0.7	·	·	·	99.7	100.0	99.3	110.0	110.4	109.5	99.8	100.0	99.5	44
·	·	·	4.2	5.8	2.4	·	·	·	95.8	94.2	97.6	93.1	92.7	93.4	…	…	…	45
·	·	·	9.1	9.5	8.7	·	·	·	90.9	90.5	91.3	95.5	94.7	96.3	86.2	…	…	46
·	·	·	0.6	–**	1.3**	·	·	·	99.4	100.0**	98.7**	91.9	94.2**	89.6**	98.6	99.5**	97.7**	47
·	·	·				·	·	·										48
·	·	·	3.9**,y	3.7**,y	4.2**,y	·	·	·	96.1**,y	96.3**,y	95.8**,y	98.1z	98.4z	97.9z	…	…	…	49
East Asia and the Pacific																		
3.0**	3.3**	2.7**	19.2**	21.0**	17.3**	85.8**	84.3**	87.4**	80.8**	79.0**	82.7**	98.2	97.4	99.0	…	…	…	50
…	…	…	…	…	…	…	…	…	…	…	…	111.9	111.7	112.1	…	…	…	51
…	…	…	46.5	47.6	45.3	59.7	58.2	61.3	53.5	52.4	54.7	81.7	85.4	77.8	…	…	…	52
…	…	…	1.0y	–**,y	2.0**,y	99.0y	100.0**,y	98.0**,y	99.0y	100.0**,y	98.0**,y	99.5z	99.4z	99.6z	…	…	…	53

Table 7 (continued)

	Country or territory	Duration[1] of primary education 2004	Grade 1 Total	Grade 1 Male	Grade 1 Female	Grade 2 Total	Grade 2 Male	Grade 2 Female	Grade 3 Total	Grade 3 Male	Grade 3 Female	Grade 4 Total	Grade 4 Male	Grade 4 Female	Grade 5 Total	Grade 5 Male	Grade 5 Female
			DROPOUT RATES BY GRADE IN PRIMARY EDUCATION (%) — School year ending in 2003														
54	Cook Islands	6	…	…	…	…	…	…	…	…	…	…	…	…	…	…	…
55	DPR Korea	4	…	…	…	…	…	…	…	…	…	…	…	…	.		.
56	Fiji	6	2.1	2.3	2.0	0.5	0.3	0.6	–	–	–	–	–	–	3.3	3.3	3.2
57	Indonesia	6	3.9y	3.7y	4.1y	1.8y	1.3y	2.3y	1.3y	2.4y	0.2y	3.8y	4.3y	3.3y	3.0y	2.9y	3.1y
58	Japan	6	…	…	…	…	…	…	…	…	…	…	…	…	…	…	…
59	Kiribati[2]	6	12.0	11.4	12.5	2.9	4.2	1.6	0.8	1.6	0.1	3.3	8.7	–	0.6	1.5	–
60	Lao PDR	5	13.2	13.6	12.7	7.3	7.6	7.0	6.3	6.1	6.6	5.9	5.2	6.8	…	…	…
61	Macao, China	6	–	–	–	–	–	–	–	–	–	…	…	…	…	…	…
62	Malaysia	6	1.7y	1.7y	1.6y	–y	–y	–y	–y	–y	–y	0.3y	0.1y	0.5y	0.7y	0.7y	0.7y
63	Marshall Islands	6	6.7**,x	4.3**,x	9.2**,x	…	…	…	…	…	…	…	…	…	…	…	…
64	Micronesia	6	…	…	…	…	…	…	…	…	…	…	…	…	…	…	…
65	Myanmar	5	**13.2****	**13.4****	**13.1****	**5.6****	**5.5****	**5.6****	**7.1****	**8.4****	**5.7****	**7.3****	**8.6****	**6.0****	…	…	…
66	Nauru[2]	6	28.8x	32.6x	24.3x	8.8x	6.0x	11.9x	38.2x	58.0x	13.5x	23.3x	2.1x	37.0x	17.3x	17.4x	17.3x
67	New Zealand	6	…	…	…	…	…	…	…	…	…	…	…	…	…	…	…
68	Niue[2]	6	…	…	…	…	…	…	…	…	…	…	…	…	…	…	…
69	Palau	5	…	…	…	…	…	…	…	…	…	…	…	…	…	…	…
70	Papua New Guinea	6	7.2**,y	6.8**,y	7.8**,y	13.7**,y	13.1**,y	14.3**,y	9.4**,y	9.8**,y	9.0**,y	6.5**,y	6.9**,y	6.0**,y	14.2**,y	14.0**,y	14.4**,y
71	Philippines	6	14.4	16.0	12.5	4.6	5.4	3.7	3.5	4.6	2.4	3.4	4.3	2.4	4.1	5.4	2.9
72	Republic of Korea	6	–	–	–	**0.7**	**0.7**	**0.6**	**0.7**	**0.7**	**0.6**	**0.6**	**0.6**	**0.6**	**0.7**	**0.7**	**0.8**
73	Samoa	6	4.8y	…	…	…	…	…	…	…	…	…	…	…	…	…	…
74	Singapore	6	…	…	…	…	…	…	…	…	…	…	…	…	…	…	…
75	Solomon Islands	6	…	…	…	…	…	…	…	…	…	…	…	…	…	…	…
76	Thailand	6	…	…	…	…	…	…	…	…	…	…	…	…	…	…	…
77	Timor-Leste	6	…	…	…	…	…	…	…	…	…	…	…	…	…	…	…
78	Tokelau	6	…	…	…	…	…	…	…	…	…	…	…	…	…	…	…
79	Tonga	6	…	…	…	…	…	…	…	…	…	…	…	…	…	…	…
80	Tuvalu[2]	6	15.9x	25.6x	4.5x	2.8x	…	…	10.4x	…	…	4.5x	…	…	10.4x	…	…
81	Vanuatu	6	9.5**	10.1**	8.8**	…	…	…	…	…	…	…	…	…	…	…	…
82	Viet Nam	5	5.5**,y	5.3**,y	5.8**,y	0.9**,y	1.6**,y	0.05**,y	8.2**,y	7.5**,y	9.0**,y	–**,y	–**,y	–**,y	…	…	…

Latin America and the Caribbean

	Country or territory	Duration[1] of primary education 2004	Grade 1 Total	Grade 1 Male	Grade 1 Female	Grade 2 Total	Grade 2 Male	Grade 2 Female	Grade 3 Total	Grade 3 Male	Grade 3 Female	Grade 4 Total	Grade 4 Male	Grade 4 Female	Grade 5 Total	Grade 5 Male	Grade 5 Female
83	Anguilla	7	20.5	16.5	23.9	6.0	–	12.6	…	…	…	…	…	…	…	…	…
84	Antigua and Barbuda	7	…	…	…	…	…	…	…	…	…	…	…	…	…	…	…
85	Argentina	6	5.1y	5.3y	4.9y	3.3y	3.4y	3.2y	3.3y	3.3y	3.2y	3.8y	4.0y	3.6y	3.9y	4.4y	3.4y
86	Aruba[2]	6	1.9	2.2	1.4	0.7	1.6	–	–	–	–	0.8	0.5	1.0	…	…	…
87	Bahamas	6	3.9**	6.6**	1.1**	…	…	…	…	…	…	…	…	…	…	…	…
88	Barbados	6	1.1	1.6	0.5	1.2	0.8	1.6	0.4	0.6	0.2	0.6	1.7	–	–	–	–
89	Belize	6	–	–	–	…	…	…	…	…	…	…	…	…	…	…	…
90	Bermuda[2]	6	0.1x	…	…	1.5x	…	…	2.5x	…	…	–x	…	…	1.2x	…	…
91	Bolivia	6	5.3**	5.5**	5.1**	1.8**	1.8**	1.7**	4.6**	4.2**	5.0**	2.4**	1.8**	3.1**	3.4**	1.8**	5.1**
92	Brazil	4	6.8x	…	…	1.3x	…	…	4.1x	…	…	.		.			
93	British Virgin Islands[2]	7	1.1	2.1	…	…	…	…	…	…	…	…	…	…	…	…	…
94	Cayman Islands	6	…	…	…	…	…	…	…	…	…	…	…	…	…	…	…
95	Chile	6	0.4	0.4	0.5	1.3	1.5	1.1	–	–	–	–	–	–	0.5	0.7	0.3
96	Colombia	5	18.8**	19.9**	17.5**	2.4**	2.8**	2.0**	0.9**	1.4**	0.3**	–**	–**	–**	…	…	…
97	Costa Rica	6	3.8**	3.8**	3.7**	–**	–**	–**	1.3**	0.3**	2.4**	3.0**	3.6**	2.4**	3.0**	3.1**	3.0**
98	Cuba	6	1.4	1.6	1.1	1.1	1.0	1.1	–	–	–	0.1	0.1	0.1	0.4	0.3	0.4
99	Dominica[2]	7	9.5	10.1	8.8	3.5	2.6	4.5	0.5	–	1.9	2.0	1.0	3.0	–	–	–
100	Dominican Republic	6	14.9	16.8**	12.8**	12.4	17.0**	7.1**	7.3	5.9**	8.9**	11.0	12.1**	9.9**	8.5	9.3**	7.8**
101	Ecuador	6	12.9**	13.0**	12.8**	2.9**	3.1**	2.7**	3.7**	4.0**	3.4**	5.5**	6.1**	4.9**	4.8**	4.3**	5.3**
102	El Salvador	6	9.0**	9.6**	8.3**	8.3**	7.9**	8.7**	4.2**	5.1**	3.3**	6.3**	7.3**	5.2**	4.2**	3.9**	4.5**
103	Grenada[2]	7	13.4y	13.3y	13.4y	1.2y	4.0y	–y	5.9y	10.1y	1.6y	1.1y	1.1y	1.1y	–y	…	…
104	Guatemala	6	8.3**	7.8**	8.8**	6.0**	5.9**	6.1**	2.8**	2.3**	3.4**	2.1**	1.5**	2.7**	3.4**	3.6**	3.1**
105	Guyana	6	22.4**,x	23.4**,x	21.3**,x	5.2**,x	5.4**,x	5.1**,x	4.8**,x	3.7**,x	5.9**,x	7.5**,x	8.0**,x	6.9**,x	8.3**,x	2.3**,x	14.4**,x
106	Haiti	6	…	…	…	…	…	…	…	…	…	…	…	…	…	…	…
107	Honduras	6	…	…	…	…	…	…	…	…	…	…	…	…	…	…	…
108	Jamaica	6	–y	–**,y	–**,y	1.2y	…	…	1.0y	…	…	8.1y	…	…	5.3y	…	…
109	Mexico	6	2.7	3.0	2.5	1.3	1.4	1.1	1.8	1.9	1.6	1.3	1.5	1.1	2.4	2.7	2.1
110	Montserrat[2]	7	3.9**	…	…	19.4**	…	…	…	…	…	…	…	…	…	…	…
111	Netherlands Antilles	6	4.9x	1.8x	8.4x	2.8x	4.8x	0.9x	2.0x	…	…	0.3x	…	…	5.4x	…	…
112	Nicaragua	6	15.6**	16.4**	14.8**	6.8**	7.9**	5.7**	8.2**	8.8**	7.5**	12.4**	13.9**	10.9**	6.3**	6.4**	6.1**

Education for All Global Monitoring Report 2007

Dropout rates by grade in primary education (%) Grade 6			Dropouts all grades (%)			Survival rate to grade 5 (%)			Survival rate to last grade (%)			Gross intake rate to last grade (%)			Primary cohort completion rate (%)			
School year ending in 2003			School year ending in 2003			School year ending in 2003			School year ending in 2003			School year ending in 2003			School year ending in 2003			
Total	Male	Female	Total	Male	Female	Total	Male	Female	Total	Male	Female	Total	Male	Female	Total	Male	Female	
...	...	...	...	...	...	...	...	...	...	...	...	...	...	...	...	...	...	54
•	•	•	...	...	...	•	•	•	...	...	...	...	...	...	...	...	...	55
...	...	...	4.2	3.0	5.4	98.7	100.0	97.4	95.8	97.0	94.6	104.9	104.7	105.1	...	...	...	56
...	...	...	13.6[y]	14.3[y]	12.9[y]	89.1[y]	88.3[y]	89.9[y]	86.4[y]	85.7[y]	87.1[y]	100.6[z]	100.6[z]	100.5[z]	...	...	...	57
...	...	...	...	...	...	...	...	...	...	...	...	...	...	...	...	...	...	58
...	...	...	18.6	25.0	11.2	81.9	76.2	88.4	81.4	75.0	88.8	118.1	116.1	120.3	...	...	...	59
•	•	•	37.4	37.9	36.9	62.6	62.1	63.1	62.6	62.1	63.1	74.0	78.3	69.6	57.3	56.9	57.8	60
...	...	...	...	...	...	99.7	99.4	100.0	...	...	...	102.1	102.3	101.8	...	...	...	61
...	...	...	2.3[y]	2.0[y]	2.7[y]	98.4[y]	98.7[y]	98.0[y]	97.7[y]	98.0[y]	97.3[y]	91.0[z]	90.8[z]	91.1[z]	...	...	...	62
...	...	...	...	...	...	...	...	...	...	...	...	125.0**[z]	122.6**[z]	127.5**[z]	...	...	...	63
...	...	...	...	...	...	...	...	...	...	...	...	...	...	...	...	...	...	64
•	•	•	29.7**	31.8**	27.5**	70.3**	68.2**	72.5**	70.3**	68.2**	72.5**	77.7**	76.4**	79.1**	70.4**	69.0**	71.8**	65
...	...	...	74.6[x]	78.5[x]	69.9[x]	30.8[x]	26.1[x]	36.3[x]	25.4[x]	21.5[x]	30.1[x]	74.1[y]	70.9[y]	77.8[y]	...	...	...	66
...	...	...	...	...	...	...	...	...	...	...	...	...	...	...	...	...	...	67
...	...	...	...	...	...	...	...	...	...	...	...	81.1	88.9	73.7	...	...	...	68
•	•	•	...	...	...	...	...	...	...	...	...	...	...	...	...	...	...	69
...	...	...	41.8**[y]	41.5**[y]	42.1**[y]	67.8**[y]	68.1**[y]	67.6**[y]	58.2**[y]	58.5**[y]	57.9**[y]	53.9**[z]	57.9**[z]	49.5**[z]	...	...	...	70
...	...	...	27.8	32.4	22.7	75.3	71.5	79.6	72.2	67.6	77.3	96.6	93.4	99.9	...	...	...	71
...	...	...	2.6	2.7	2.5	98.1	97.9	98.3	97.4	97.3	97.5	104.1	104.1	104.1	...	...	...	72
...	...	...	...	...	...	...	...	...	...	...	...	96.1**	94.2**	98.2**	...	...	...	73
...	...	...	...	...	...	...	...	...	...	...	...	...	...	...	...	...	...	74
...	...	...	...	...	...	...	...	...	...	...	...	...	...	...	...	...	...	75
...	...	...	...	...	...	...	...	...	...	...	...	...	...	...	...	...	...	76
...	...	...	...	...	...	...	...	...	...	...	...	...	...	...	...	...	...	77
...	...	...	...	...	...	...	...	...	...	...	...	...	...	...	...	...	...	78
...	...	...	...	...	...	...	...	...	...	...	...	106.9**[y]	108.0**[y]	105.5**[y]	...	...	...	79
...	...	...	37.4[x]	...	...	69.9[x]	...	...	62.6[x]	...	...	103.1**	94.3**	113.3**	...	...	...	80
...	...	...	...	...	...	...	...	...	...	...	...	87.2	88.2**	86.2**	...	...	...	81
•	•	•	13.2**[y]	12.8**[y]	13.5**[y]	86.8**[y]	87.2**[y]	86.5**[y]	86.8**[y]	87.2**[y]	86.5**[y]	100.8**[z]	103.9**[z]	97.6**[z]	...	...	...	82

Latin America and the Caribbean

Dropout rates by grade in primary education (%) Grade 6			Dropouts all grades (%)			Survival rate to grade 5 (%)			Survival rate to last grade (%)			Gross intake rate to last grade (%)			Primary cohort completion rate (%)			
Total	Male	Female	Total	Male	Female	Total	Male	Female	Total	Male	Female	Total	Male	Female	Total	Male	Female	
...	...	...	...	...	...	...	...	...	...	...	...	53.7**	54.8**	52.7**	...	...	...	83
...	...	...	...	...	...	...	...	...	...	...	...	...	...	...	...	...	...	84
...	...	...	19.1[y]	20.3[y]	17.9[y]	84.3[y]	83.6[y]	85.1[y]	80.9[y]	79.7[y]	82.1[y]	100.5[z]	98.0[z]	103.1[z]	...	...	...	85
...	...	...	2.9	3.7	2.1	...	...	...	97.1	96.3	97.9	93.6	94.8	92.4	...	...	...	86
...	...	...	...	...	...	...	...	...	...	...	...	96.3	96.0	96.7	...	...	...	87
...	...	...	2.5	4.3	0.5	...	...	...	97.5	95.7	99.5	108.0	110.0	105.8	96.7	94.0	99.6	88
...	...	...	...	...	...	...	...	...	...	...	...	103.3	102.8	103.8	...	...	...	89
...	...	...	5.5[x]	...	...	96.3[x]	...	...	95.2[x]	...	...	110.1[y]	...	...	...	...	...	90
...	...	...	16.6**	14.4**	18.8**	86.4**	87.2**	85.6**	83.4**	85.6**	81.2**	100.2**	102.4**	97.9**	71.3[y]	71.7[y]	70.8[y]	91
•	•	•	15.6[x]	...	...	•	•	•	84.4[x]	...	...	126.0[z]	...	...	...	...	...	92
...	...	...	...	...	...	...	...	...	...	...	...	104.3	102.7	105.9	...	...	...	93
...	...	...	...	...	...	...	...	...	...	...	...	102.0**	105.5**	98.5**	...	...	...	94
...	...	...	1.6	1.5	1.6	99.0	99.2	98.7	98.4	98.5	98.4	95.4	96.2	94.6	...	...	...	95
•	•	•	22.5**	25.1**	19.8**	77.5**	74.9**	80.2**	77.5**	74.9**	80.2**	94.3	92.3	96.4	62.5[x]	59.4[x]	65.9[x]	96
...	...	...	10.5**	10.8**	10.2**	92.4**	92.2**	92.7**	89.5**	89.2**	89.8**	92.3	91.2	93.5	83.8**	83.0**	84.7**	97
...	...	...	2.6	2.3	3.0	97.7	98.0	97.4	97.4	97.7	97.0	92.6	93.1	92.1	...	...	...	98
1.6	1.6	1.7	15.6	14.3	17.0	84.3	86.3	82.3	84.4	85.7	83.0	107.4	111.4	103.5	83.2	83.4	83.0	99
...	...	...	46.1	51.0**	40.4**	59.2	54.5**	64.9**	53.9	49.0**	59.6**	90.8	88.2	93.4	...	...	...	100
...	...	...	27.4**	28.0**	26.8**	76.3**	75.3**	77.3**	72.6**	72.0**	73.2**	100.6**	100.0**	101.1**	70.2**	69.6**	70.9**	101
...	...	...	30.4**	32.1**	28.4**	72.8**	70.8**	75.0**	69.6**	67.9**	71.6**	85.7**	85.2**	86.2**	...	...	...	102
—[y]	...	...	17.4[y]	...	...	79.0[y]	73.0[y]	85.4[y]	84.9[y]	...	...	90.2[z]	90.4[z]	89.9[z]	...	...	...	103
...	...	...	24.9**	23.7**	26.1**	77.9**	79.4**	76.4**	75.1**	76.3**	73.9**	70.2	74.9	65.4	48.1**[y]	50.6**[y]	45.4**[y]	104
...	...	...	41.2**[x]	38.0**[x]	44.4**[x]	64.3**[x]	63.5**[x]	65.0**[x]	58.8**[x]	62.0**[x]	55.6**[x]	95.3**	99.1**	91.5**	...	...	...	105
...	...	...	...	...	...	...	...	...	...	...	...	...	...	...	...	...	...	106
...	...	...	...	...	...	...	...	...	...	...	...	79.4	77.1	81.8	...	...	...	107
...	...	...	15.1[y]	...	...	89.7[y]	...	...	84.9[y]	...	...	84.4	83.1	85.7	...	...	...	108
...	...	...	9.6	10.7	8.5	92.6	91.8	93.5	90.4	89.3	91.5	98.9	98.1	99.6	...	...	...	109
...	...	...	...	...	...	...	...	...	...	...	...	59.3	53.6	65.4	...	...	...	110
...	...	...	16.9[x]	...	...	88.5[x]	...	...	83.1[x]	...	...	100.9**[z]	94.5**[z]	107.4**[z]	...	...	...	111
...	...	...	45.2**	48.5**	41.5**	58.8**	55.3**	62.5**	54.8**	51.5**	58.5**	73.5	70.0	77.0	45.8**[y]	42.1**[y]	49.7**[y]	112

Table 7 (continued)

Country or territory	Duration[1] of primary education 2004	Grade 1 Total	Grade 1 Male	Grade 1 Female	Grade 2 Total	Grade 2 Male	Grade 2 Female	Grade 3 Total	Grade 3 Male	Grade 3 Female	Grade 4 Total	Grade 4 Male	Grade 4 Female	Grade 5 Total	Grade 5 Male	Grade 5 Female
113 Panama	6	6.0**	7.1**	4.8**	3.6**	4.0**	3.1**	2.6**	2.9**	2.3**	3.3**	3.8**	2.8**	3.8**	3.6**	3.9**
114 Paraguay	6	5.6[y]	5.8[y]	5.3[y]	3.6[y]	3.9[y]	3.3[y]	3.8[y]	4.1[y]	3.4[y]	5.0[y]	5.3[y]	4.6[y]	5.9[y]	6.4[y]	5.3[y]
115 Peru	6	6.4[x]	6.7[x]	6.0[x]	3.1[x]	2.9[x]	3.4[x]	3.5[x]	2.8[x]	4.3[x]	2.6[x]	2.3[x]	2.8[x]	6.1[x]	5.5[x]	6.6[x]
116 Saint Kitts and Nevis[2]	7	0.4	0.4	0.4	4.1	8.9	–	...	...	...	...	...	...	...	...	...
117 Saint Lucia	7	0.3	1.2	–	2.9	3.5	2.4	0.9	0.5	1.5	5.9	5.5	6.2	–	–	–
118 St Vincent/Grenad.	7	–	–	–	3.0**,[y]	...	...	3.5[y]	...	...	4.2[y]	...		4.2[y]	...	...
119 Suriname	6	...	...	...	...	...	...	...	...	...	...	...	...	...	...	...
120 Trinidad and Tobago	7	–*	...	...	0.3*	...	...	1.4*	...	...	–*	...	...	0.3*	...	...
121 Turks and Caicos Islands[2]	6	...	...	...	20.2[y]	10.8[y]	27.8[y]	8.5[y]	9.4[y]	7.5[y]	12.9[y]	20.1[y]	2.9[y]	2.2[y]	–[y]	6.5[y]
122 Uruguay	6	3.1**	3.1**	3.2**	3.1**	3.7**	2.5**	2.5**	2.9**	1.9**	3.6**	2.7**	4.6**	1.3**	2.6**	–**
123 Venezuela	6	2.9	3.2	2.5	1.1	1.6	0.6	1.8	2.3	1.2	2.6	3.5	1.7	2.3	2.9	1.7
North America and Western Europe																
124 Andorra	6	...	...	...	...	...	...	...	...	...	...	...	...	...	...	...
125 Austria	4	...	...	...	...	...	...	...	...	...	...	...	...	.	.	.
126 Belgium	6	...	...	...	...	...	...	...	...	...	...	...	...	...	...	...
127 Canada	6	...	...	...	...	...	...	...	...	...	...	...	...	...	...	...
128 Cyprus[2]	6	–	–	–	–	–	–	...	...	...	...	...	...	...	...	...
129 Denmark	6	...	...	...	...	...	...	...	...	...	...	...	...	...	...	...
130 Finland	6	–	–	–	0.0	0.1	–	–	–	–	...	...	...	...	...	...
131 France	5	...	...	...	...	...	...	...	...	...	...	...	...			
132 Germany	4	0.1	0.4	–	0.5	0.5	0.4	0.2	0.2	0.2	...	...	...	.	.	.
133 Greece	6	...	...	...	...	...	...	...	...	...	...	...	...	...	...	...
134 Iceland	7	–[y]	–[y]	–[y]	0.3[y]	0.9[y]	–[y]	–[y]	–[y]	–[y]	–[y]	–[y]	–[y]	–[y]	–[y]	–[y]
135 Ireland	8	–	–	–	–	–	–	–	–	–	–	–	–			
136 Israel	6	–	–	–	–	–	–	–	–	–	–	–	–	0.4	0.6	0.3
137 Italy	5	–[x]	–[x]	–[x]	1.0[x]	0.9[x]	1.1[x]	1.6[x]	1.6[x]	1.5[x]	1.1[x]	1.0[x]	1.1[x]			
138 Luxembourg	6	–			–			4.2	3.4	5.1	2.9	6.0		...	...	...
139 Malta	6	0.9[y]	0.5[y]	1.2[y]	–[y]	–[y]	–[y]	–[y]	–[y]	–[y]	0.3[y]	0.8[y]	–[y]	0.3[y]	0.2[y]	0.4[y]
140 Monaco	5	...	...	...	...	...	...	...	...	...	...	...	...	...	...	...
141 Netherlands	6	–[y]	–[y]	–[y]	–[y]	–[y]	–[y]	–[y]	–[y]	–[y]	–[y]	–[y]	–[y]	1.9**,[y]	1.3**,[y]	2.6**,[y]
142 Norway	7	–	–	–	–	–	–	–	–	–	–	–	–	–	–	–
143 Portugal	6	...	...	...	...	...	...	...	...	...	...	...	...	...	...	...
144 San Marino	5	...	...	...	...	...	...	...	...	...	...	...	...			
145 Spain	6	...	...	...	...	...	...	...	...	...	...	...	...	...	...	...
146 Sweden	6	...	...	...	...	...	...	...	...	...	...	...	...	...	...	...
147 Switzerland	6	...	...	...	...	...	...	...	...	...	...	...	...	...	...	...
148 United Kingdom	6	...	...	...	...	...	...	...	...	...	...	...	...	...	...	...
149 United States	6	...	...	...	...	...	...	...	...	...	...	...	...	...	...	...
South and West Asia																
150 Afghanistan	6	...	...	...	...	...	...	...	...	...	...	...	...	...	...	...
151 Bangladesh	5	14.6	17.6	11.2	9.9	11.4	8.3	5.8	5.2	6.4	7.2	5.5	8.9	...	...	...
152 Bhutan	7	...	...	...	...	...	...	...	...	...	...	...	...	...	...	...
153 India	5	14.4	14.0	14.9	4.4	3.6	5.2	4.4	4.0	4.9	–	–	–	...	...	...
154 Iran, Islamic Republic of	5	0.8	1.9	–	3.2	2.7	3.6	2.7	2.0	3.4	3.2	2.6	3.7	...	...	...
155 Maldives	7	...	...	...	...	...	...	...	...	...	...	...	...	...	...	...
156 Nepal	5	**9.4**	**10.5**	**8.1**	**9.8**	**12.0**	**7.2**	**7.9**	**8.5**	**7.2**	**7.1**	**8.2**	**5.7**	...	...	...
157 Pakistan	5	...	...	...	...	...	...	...	...	...	...	...	...	...	...	...
158 Sri Lanka	5	...	...	...	...	...	...	...	...	...	...	...	...	...	...	...
Sub-Saharan Africa																
159 Angola	4	...	...	...	...	...	...	...	...	...	...	...	...	.	.	.
160 Benin	6	8.7	8.9	8.3	6.9	6.8	7.0	3.1	3.6	2.5	7.9	7.4	8.6	5.5	5.1	6.1
161 Botswana	7	2.3**	3.1**	1.3**	–**	–**	–**	5.8**	7.1**	4.5**	0.5**	0.9**	0.1**	2.7**	2.0**	3.3**
162 Burkina Faso	6	6.8	6.8	6.7	3.8	3.8	3.7	7.0	7.5	6.4	6.0	6.9	4.6	7.4	7.6	7.1
163 Burundi	6	10.8	10.3	11.2	5.8	6.0	5.5	7.0	7.2	6.8	6.2	6.0	6.4	6.2	7.1	5.1
164 Cameroon	6	...	...	...	...	...	...	...	...	...	...	...	...	...	...	...
165 Cape Verde	6	–	–	–	2.1	2.9	1.2	0.7	0.9	0.4	4.3	5.8	2.7	3.8	2.0	5.5
166 Central African Republic	6	...	...	...	...	...	...	...	...	...	...	...	...	...	...	...
167 Chad	6	17.1**	15.9**	18.8**	8.4**	8.1**	8.9**	11.9**	10.3**	14.3**	14.6**	11.3**	19.8**	15.0**	11.6**	21.1**

DROPOUT RATES BY GRADE IN PRIMARY EDUCATION (%) School year ending in 2003 Grade 6			DROPOUTS ALL GRADES (%) School year ending in 2003			PRIMARY EDUCATION COMPLETION SURVIVAL RATE TO GRADE 5 (%) School year ending in 2003			SURVIVAL RATE TO LAST GRADE (%) School year ending in 2003			GROSS INTAKE RATE TO LAST GRADE (%) School year ending in 2003			PRIMARY COHORT COMPLETION RATE (%) School year ending in 2003			
Total	Male	Female	Total	Male	Female	Total	Male	Female	Total	Male	Female	Total	Male	Female	Total	Male	Female	
...	...	...	19.0**	21.1**	16.7**	84.3**	82.0**	86.8**	81.0**	78.9**	83.3**	96.6	96.4	96.9	77.7**,y	76.2**,y	79.3**,y	113
...	...	...	23.3y	25.1y	21.4y	81.6y	80.2y	83.1y	76.7y	74.9y	78.6y	90.2**	89.7**	90.7**	...	...	...	114
...	...	...	21.9x	20.6x	23.3x	83.6x	84.5x	82.7x	78.1x	79.4x	76.7x	99.5	100.1	98.9	...	...	...	115
...	...	...	...	...	...	...	...	...	...	...	...	114.3	112.9	115.7	...	...	...	116
...	...	...	...	...	...	90.1	89.4	90.8	...	...	...	101.6	104.3	98.9	...	...	...	117
4.8y	...	...	20.9**,y	...	...	88.0**,y	...	...	79.1**,y	...	...	92.9	83.0	102.8	...	...	...	118
																		119
3.3*	...	...	3.8*	...	...	100.0*	...	...	96.2*	...	...	94.2*	93.1*	95.3*	...	...	...	120
			55.2y	...	...	45.9y	41.8y	51.4y	44.8y	...	...	96.3	100.5	91.9	...	...	...	121
...	...	...	14.3**	15.8**	12.6**	86.9**	86.5**	87.4**	85.7**	84.2**	87.4**	90.8**	89.0**	92.7**	...	...	...	122
...	...	...	11.1	14.1	8.0	91.0	88.6	93.6	88.9	85.9	92.0	89.4	87.0	92.0	...	...	...	123

North America and Western Europe

Total	Male	Female	Total	Male	Female	Total	Male	Female	Total	Male	Female	Total	Male	Female	Total	Male	Female	
...	...	...	...	...	...	...	...	...	...	...	...	102.7**	104.2**	101.1**	...	...	...	124
...	...	...	...	...	...	.	.	.	...	...	...	...	...	...	...	...	...	125
...	...	...	...	...	...	...	...	...	...	...	...	...	...	...	...	...	...	126
...	...	...	...	...	...	...	...	...	...	...	...	...	...	...	...	...	...	127
...	...	...	1.3	–	2.7	99.2	100.0	98.3	98.7	100.0	97.3	87.6	88.1	87.0	...	...	...	128
...	...	...	...	...	...	...	...	...	...	...	...	99.4	99.2	99.6z	...	...	...	129
...	...	...	0.2	0.5	–	99.9	99.9	100.0	99.8	99.5	100.0	99.6	99.4	99.8z	...	...	...	130
.	.	.	...	...	...	...	...	...	...	...	...	...	...	...	...	...	...	131
.	.	.	0.7	1.1	0.4	.	.	.	99.3	98.9	99.6	95.8	96.0	95.6	...	...	...	132
.	.	.																133
–y	–y	–y	0.4y	...	...	99.7y	100.0y	99.4y	99.6y	...	...	106.1**	105.6**	106.6**	...	...	...	134
–	–	–	...	...	...	99.8	99.6	100.0	...	...	...	101.0	99.7	102.3	...	...	...	135
...	...	...	0.1	...	...	99.9	100.0	99.9	99.9	...	...	104.6	104.1	105.1	...	...	...	136
.	.	.	3.5x	4.0x	3.0x	96.5x	96.0x	97.0x	96.5x	96.0x	97.0x	101.3	101.5	101.2	...	...	...	137
...	...	...	...	...	...	95.7	93.3	98.1	...	...	...	80.2	79.5	80.9	...	...	...	138
...	...	...	1.0y	1.4y	0.5y	99.3y	98.8y	99.9y	99.0y	98.6y	99.5y	100.3	100.1	100.5	...	...	...	139
.	.	.																140
...	...	...	1.7**,y	1.2**,y	2.2**,y	99.8y	99.7y	100.0y	98.3**,y	98.8**,y	97.8**,y	99.9**,z	100.9**,z	98.9**,z	...	...	...	141
–	–	–	0.6	1.2	–	99.6	99.2	100.0	99.4	98.8	100.0	101.4	101.4	101.4	...	...	...	142
...	...	...	...	...	...	...	...	...	...	...	...	...	...	...	...	...	...	143
...	...	...	...	...	...	...	...	...	...	...	...	...	...	...	...	...	...	144
...	...	...	...	...	...	...	...	...	...	...	...	...	...	...	...	...	...	145
...	...	...	...	...	...	...	...	...	...	...	...	...	...	...	...	...	...	146
...	...	...	...	...	...	...	...	...	...	...	...	96.9	95.8	98.1	...	...	...	147
...	...	...	...	...	...	...	...	...	...	...	...	...	...	...	...	...	...	148
...	...	...	...	...	...	...	...	...	...	...	...	...	...	...	...	...	...	149

South and West Asia

Total	Male	Female	Total	Male	Female	Total	Male	Female	Total	Male	Female	Total	Male	Female	Total	Male	Female	
...	...	...	...	...	...	...	...	...	...	...	...	...	...	...	...	...	...	150
.	.	.	34.9	36.9	32.7	65.1	63.1	67.3	65.1	63.1	67.3	76.4	74.1	78.8	54.7	51.8	58.0	151
...	...	...	...	...	...	...	...	...	...	...	...	...	...	...	...	...	...	152
.	.	.	21.1	18.8	23.7	78.9	81.2	76.3	78.9	81.2	76.3	88.5	92.9	83.9	...	...	...	153
...	...	...	9.8	9.3	10.2	90.2	90.7	89.8	90.2	90.7	89.8	94.6	92.3	96.9	...	...	...	154
...	...	...	...	...	...	...	...	...	...	...	...	99.7**	97.8**	101.7**	...	...	...	155
.	.	.	39.2**	43.4**	33.9**	60.8**	56.6**	66.1**	60.8**	56.6**	66.1**	74.7**	79.6**	69.5**	38.6**	35.4**	42.8**	156
.	.	.	...	...	...	...	...	...	...	...	...	...	...	...	...	...	...	157
			...	...	...	...	...	...				...	...	...	...	...	...	158

Sub-Saharan Africa

Total	Male	Female	Total	Male	Female	Total	Male	Female	Total	Male	Female	Total	Male	Female	Total	Male	Female	
.	.	.	...	...	...	.	.	.	...	...	...	...	...	...	...	...	...	159
...	...	...	36.9	36.2	38.1	69.4	69.5	69.1	63.1	63.8	61.9	48.8	59.0	38.3	52.4	52.4	52.5	160
3.9**	3.9**	3.9**	14.8**	17.3**	12.3**	91.2**	88.1**	94.6**	85.2**	82.7**	87.7**	92.0**	89.9**	94.1**	...	...	...	161
...	...	...	30.8	32.3	28.7	75.8	74.4	77.9	69.2	67.7	71.3	29.5	33.5	25.3	...	...	...	162
...	...	...	45.1	44.2	46.4	63.0	64.0	61.7	54.9	55.8	53.6	33.1	39.3	26.9	25.1	25.2	24.9	163
...	...	...	10.7	11.0	10.4	98.0	96.3	100.0	89.3	89.0	89.6	63.3	68.9	57.6	76.5	76.2	76.9	164
...	...	...	12.2	14.0	10.4	91.2	87.8	94.8	87.8	86.0	89.6	95.4	95.6	95.3	82.4	74.2	90.7	165
...	...	...	...	...	...	...	...	...	...	...	...	...	...	...	...	...	...	166
...	...	...	63.3**	56.9**	72.4**	45.8**	50.9**	38.5**	36.7**	43.1**	27.6**	29.5**	40.6**	18.4**	...	...	...	167

Table 7 (continued)

DROPOUT RATES BY GRADE IN PRIMARY EDUCATION (%)
School year ending in 2003

	Country or territory	Duration[1] of primary education 2004	Grade 1 Total	Grade 1 Male	Grade 1 Female	Grade 2 Total	Grade 2 Male	Grade 2 Female	Grade 3 Total	Grade 3 Male	Grade 3 Female	Grade 4 Total	Grade 4 Male	Grade 4 Female	Grade 5 Total	Grade 5 Male	Grade 5 Female
168	Comoros	6	10.6	12.1	8.7	4.7	…	…	6.0	…	…	9.4	…	…	7.6	…	…
169	Congo	6	6.3y	5.8y	6.8y	1.2y	1.4y	0.9y	9.6y	9.9y	9.3y	8.2y	8.6y	7.7y	10.9y	9.9y	11.9y
170	Côte d'Ivoire	6	…	…	…	…	…	…	…	…	…	…	…	…	…	…	…
171	D. R. Congo	6	…	…	…	…	…	…	…	…	…	…	…	…	…	…	…
172	Equatorial Guinea	5	23.3**,x	26.8**,x	19.6**,x	3.1**,x	0.5**,x	5.5**,x	10.2**,x	7.9**,x	12.5**,x	12.8**,x	12.9**,x	12.6**,x	…	…	…
173	Eritrea	5	5.9	5.7	6.1	2.2	1.1	3.6	2.2	0.9	3.9	5.2	2.6	8.7	…	…	…
174	Ethiopia	4	**15.5**	**15.5**	**15.6**	**6.4**	**7.0**	**5.7**	**4.5**	**5.2**	**3.8**	.	.	.	.	.	.
175	Gabon	6	3.6**,y	3.6**,y	3.6**,y	–**,y	–**,y	–**,y	6.7**,y	6.4**,y	7.0**,y	9.0**,y	8.9**,y	9.1**,y	12.5**,y	13.2**,y	11.8**,y
176	Gambia	6	…	…	…	…	…	…	…	…	…	…	…	…	…	…	…
177	Ghana	6	10.4y	9.5y	11.4y	11.3y	14.9y	7.3y	8.0y	7.4y	8.6y	10.8y	10.3y	11.3y	5.0y	10.1y	–y
178	Guinea	6	1.2	–	3.7	1.6	0.2	3.3	8.1	7.4	9.0	6.1	5.2	7.4	6.0	5.2	7.2
179	Guinea-Bissau	6	…	…	…	…	…	…	…	…	…	…	…	…	…	…	…
180	Kenya	6	11.6*	11.8*	11.4*	4.5*	4.4*	4.7*	2.1*	2.4*	1.7*	7.2*	5.2*	9.3*	3.2*	3.2*	3.3*
181	Lesotho	7	12.4	12.6	12.2	5.5	5.8	5.2	5.6	6.7	4.3	10.5	13.8	7.3	3.7	5.3	2.3
182	Liberia	6	…	…	…	…	…	…	…	…	…	…	…	…	…	…	…
183	Madagascar	5	10.3	10.2	10.4	3.3	3.4	3.2	8.7	8.6	8.8	8.8	8.7	8.8	…	…	…
184	Malawi	6	24.4x	23.7x	25.1x	9.5x	8.5x	10.4x	15.4x	14.6x	16.3x	11.8x	4.7x	19.3x	22.5x	27.3x	16.6x
185	Mali	6	17.9	29.5	3.8	0.7	–	2.2	2.0	0.6	3.9	–	–	–	–	–	–
186	Mauritius	6	…	…	…	0.0x	0.6x	–x	0.4x	0.4x	0.5x	0.8x	0.2x	1.4x	1.3x	2.1x	0.4x
187	Mozambique	7	14.9x	13.5x	16.5x	9.9x	9.1x	10.8x	12.1x	11.4x	12.9x	11.5x	10.4x	13.2x	20.2x	21.3x	18.5x
188	Namibia	7	6.3**,y	7.7**,y	4.8**,y	2.9**,y	3.0**,y	2.7**,y	1.1**,y	1.5**,y	0.8**,y	0.3**,y	–**,y	1.1**,y	3.0**,y	3.4**,y	2.5**,y
189	Niger	6	5.8	5.1	6.7	8.0	7.4	9.0	7.4	7.2	7.6	7.1	7.0	7.2	5.4	5.8	4.9
190	Nigeria	6	8.7**	9.1**	8.3**	2.7**	3.0**	2.3**	7.1**	7.4**	6.7**	11.1**	12.0**	9.9**	13.5**	13.3**	13.7**
191	Rwanda	6	21.0	21.4	20.5	11.7	11.7	11.7	10.8	13.4	8.3	12.4	13.8	11.0	24.9	23.9	25.9
192	Sao Tome and Principe	6	5.3	4.3	6.4	4.7	5.9	3.3	4.9	4.3	5.5	13.8	14.5	13.1	7.2	9.7	4.8
193	Senegal	6	9.7	9.3	10.1	4.5	4.4	4.7	4.1	4.1	4.0	2.8	2.5	3.1	6.4	6.4	6.4
194	Seychelles[2]	6	–y	–y	–y	–y	–y	–y	0.4y	0.4y	0.4y	0.6y	1.5y	–y	–y	–y	–y
195	Sierra Leone	6	…	…	…	…	…	…	…	…	…	…	…	…	…	…	…
196	Somalia	7	…	…	…	…	…	…	…	…	…	…	…	…	…	…	…
197	South Africa	7	10.7y	12.2y	9.1y	1.0y	1.1y	0.8y	0.8y	0.8y	0.8y	2.9y	3.7y	2.1y	3.0y	3.8y	2.1y
198	Swaziland	7	6.1y	6.5y	5.7y	3.3y	5.3y	1.0y	5.1y	4.5y	5.9y	6.3y	6.7y	5.8y	8.1y	15.1y	0.1y
199	Togo	6	7.7	7.6	7.9	2.3	1.8	2.9	4.7	4.2	5.4	4.0	2.7	5.6	5.2	3.2	7.9
200	Uganda	7	22.4x	22.1x	22.8x	0.3x	1.0x	–x	4.0x	4.7x	3.3x	8.7x	8.7x	8.7x	13.4x	13.2x	13.7x
201	United Republic of Tanzania	7	**10.6**	**10.8**	**10.3**	**3.0**	**2.4**	**3.7**	**5.2**	**5.4**	**4.8**	**6.3**	**6.6**	**6.0**	**1.6**	**1.2**	**1.9**
202	Zambia	7	0.2x	–x	1.5x	–x	…	…	0.3x	…	…	2.7x	…	…	3.9x	…	…
203	Zimbabwe	7	15.3**,y	15.6**,y	14.9**,y	11.1**,y	11.8**,y	10.4**,y	6.0**,y	6.4**,y	5.5**,y	1.7**,y	2.1**,y	1.2**,y	2.3**,y	2.0**,y	2.7**,y

Median

		Duration 2004	Grade 1 Total	Grade 1 Male	Grade 1 Female	Grade 2 Total	Grade 2 Male	Grade 2 Female	Grade 3 Total	Grade 3 Male	Grade 3 Female	Grade 4 Total	Grade 4 Male	Grade 4 Female	Grade 5 Total	Grade 5 Male	Grade 5 Female
I	World	…	3.3	3.6	2.9	1.6	1.6	1.6	1.8	2.3	1.2	3.0	3.5	2.5	…	…	…
II	Countries in transition	…	0.4	–	1.2	0.8	1.3	0.3	0.6	1.1	0.3	…	…	…	.	.	.
III	Developed countries	…	0.6	0.7	0.4	0.3	0.6	0.2	0.2	0.1	0.4	…	…	…	.	.	.
IV	Developing countries	…	5.6	5.7	5.5	2.9	…	…	3.1	3.6	2.5	3.8	4.3	3.3	3.8	3.6	3.9
V	Arab States	…	0.9	1.6	0.2	0.9	0.8	1.0	1.0	0.9	1.1	1.6	1.6	1.5	2.5	3.1	1.9
VI	Central and Eastern Europe	…	0.8	1.0	0.6	0.4	0.4	0.4	0.5	0.6	0.3	…	…	…	.	.	.
VII	Central Asia	…	0.7	0.1	1.7	1.0	1.2	0.7	0.7	0.8	0.6	…	…	…	.	.	.
VIII	East Asia and the Pacific	…	6.1	4.8	7.5	2.8	…	…	3.3	3.5	3.0	3.3	8.7	–	…	…	…
IX	East Asia	…	3.9	3.7	4.1	0.9	1.6	0.05	1.3	2.4	0.2	1.3	1.3	1.3	…	…	…
X	Pacific	…	7.2	6.8	7.8	…	…	…	…	…	…	…	…	…	…	…	…
XI	Latin America/Caribbean	…	3.9	…	…	2.9	3.5	2.4	2.6	…	…	2.6	3.5	1.7	3.2	2.4	4.0
XII	Caribbean	…	1.1	2.1	–	2.9	3.5	2.4	1.4	…	…	1.5	1.1	2.0	0.7	…	…
XIII	Latin America	…	5.8	6.5	5.1	3.0	3.4	2.6	3.0	2.8	3.3	3.0	3.6	2.4	3.6	3.6	3.5
XIV	N. America/W. Europe	…	…	…	…	…	…	…	…	…	…	…	…	…	…	…	…
XV	South and West Asia	…	…	…	…	…	…	…	…	…	…	…	…	…	…	…	…
XVI	Sub-Saharan Africa	…	10.0	9.7	10.2	3.3	5.3	1.0	5.6	6.7	4.3	6.7	6.9	6.5	5.5	5.1	6.1

1. Duration in this table is defined according to ISCED97 and may differ from that reported nationally.
2. National population data were used to calculate the gross intake rate to the last grade.

Data in bold are for the school year ending in 2004 for dropout, survival and primary cohort graduation rates, and the school year ending in 2005 for gross intake rate to last grade.

DROPOUT RATES BY GRADE IN PRIMARY EDUCATION (%) School year ending in 2003 Grade 6			DROPOUTS ALL GRADES (%) School year ending in 2003			PRIMARY EDUCATION COMPLETION												
						SURVIVAL RATE TO GRADE 5 (%) School year ending in 2003			SURVIVAL RATE TO LAST GRADE (%) School year ending in 2003			GROSS INTAKE RATE TO LAST GRADE (%) School year ending in 2003			PRIMARY COHORT COMPLETION RATE (%) School year ending in 2003			
Total	Male	Female	Total	Male	Female	Total	Male	Female	Total	Male	Female	Total	Male	Female	Total	Male	Female	
...	...	...	44.1	...	...	62.7	...	...	55.9	...	...	50.4	51.7	49.0	...	...	...	168
...	...	...	44.6y	44.7y	44.6y	66.3y	65.4y	67.2y	55.4y	55.3y	55.4y	66.4	69.6	63.2	...	...	...	169
...	...	...	...	...	...	...	...	...	...	...	...	...	...	...	...	...	...	170
...	...	...	...	...	...	...	...	...	...	...	...	...	...	...	...	...	...	171
.	.	.	67.4**,x	66.2**,x	68.7**,x	32.6**,x	33.8**,x	31.3**,x	32.6**,x	33.8**,x	31.3**,x	50.4y	53.8y	47.0y	...	...	...	172
.	.	.	19.7	13.7	27.2	80.3	86.3	72.8	80.3	86.3	72.8	44.3	52.9	35.5	75.5	81.8	67.8	173
.	.	.	**26.7**	**27.7**	**25.3**	.	.	.	**73.3**	**72.3**	**74.7**	**55.0**	**61.1**	**48.8**	...	...	...	174
...	...	...	44.5**,y	46.3**,y	42.6**,y	69.3**,y	67.9**,y	70.7**,y	55.5**,y	53.7**,y	57.4**,y	66.2**,z	64.8**,z	67.6**,z	...	...	...	175
...	...	...	...	...	...	...	...	...	...	...	...	...	...	...	...	...	...	176
...	...	...	40.0y	44.7y	34.7y	63.3y	61.8y	64.7y	60.0y	55.3y	65.3y	**72.1**	**75.2**	**68.7**	49.4y	46.1y	53.1y	177
...	...	...	23.4	17.8	30.2	82.0	87.1	75.8	76.6	82.2	69.8	48.5	57.6	38.8	...	...	...	178
...	...	...	...	...	...	...	...	...	...	...	...	...	...	...	...	...	...	179
...	...	...	27.2*	26.0*	28.6*	75.3*	76.6*	74.0*	72.8*	74.0*	71.4*	91.8*	93.2*	90.3*	...	...	...	180
5.2	7.6	3.2	43.1	50.9	35.4	63.4	58.0	68.9	56.9	49.1	64.6	71.0	60.0	82.0	55.8	...	...	181
...	...	...	...	...	...	...	...	...	...	...	...	...	...	...	...	...	...	182
.	.	.	43.0	43.9	42.2	57.0	56.1	57.8	57.0	56.1	57.8	45.3	44.6	46.0	48.5	...	...	183
...	...	...	67.2x	65.4x	69.1x	43.8x	49.7x	38.1x	32.8x	34.6x	30.9x	58.5	59.8	57.2	...	...	...	184
...	...	...	15.4	13.1	27.3	...	...	...	84.6	86.9	72.7	44.0	57.9	29.6	58.8	62.4	47.9	185
...	...	...	2.4x	3.8x	0.9x	98.9x	98.2x	99.5x	97.6x	96.2x	99.1x	99.7	97.8	101.7	87.8x	81.0x	94.8x	186
10.8x	11.3x	10.2x	69.2x	67.5x	71.3x	49.2x	52.7x	44.9x	30.8x	32.5x	28.7x	29.0	34.7	23.4	...	...	...	187
3.5**,y	5.1**,y	1.9**,y	18.5**,y	22.1**,y	15.0**,y	88.1**,y	86.6**,y	89.6**,y	81.5**,y	77.9**,y	85.0**,y	80.7**,z	76.3**,z	85.3**,z	...	...	...	188
...	...	...	30.8	29.9	32.2	73.6	74.9	71.7	69.2	70.1	67.8	25.0	29.8	20.0	39.9	40.9	38.6	189
...	...	...	37.4**	38.6**	35.9**	72.6**	71.1**	74.6**	62.6**	61.4**	64.1**	75.6**	82.4**	68.4**	...	...	...	190
...	...	...	69.1	70.3	68.0	45.8	42.9	48.7	30.9	32.9	32.0	37.4	38.0	36.8	13.4	14.8	11.8	191
...	...	...	39.7	42.3	37.0	66.5	65.7	67.2	60.3	57.7	63.0	74.9	72.7	77.0	...	...	...	192
...	...	...	27.8	27.1	28.6	78.2	79.0	77.4	72.2	72.9	71.4	45.2	48.7	41.7	...	...	...	193
...	...	...	0.9y	1.7y	—y	...	...	...	99.1y	98.3y	100.0y	115.7z	114.0z	117.6z	...	...	...	194
...	...	...	...	...	...	...	...	...	...	...	...	...	...	...	...	...	...	195
...	...	...	...	...	...	...	...	...	...	...	...	...	...	...	...	...	...	196
3.3y	3.7y	2.9y	21.3y	24.7y	17.7y	84.1y	81.7y	86.7y	78.7y	75.3y	82.3y	95.6z	93.8z	97.5z	...	...	...	197
10.0y	10.5y	9.6y	39.0y	47.4y	29.2y	76.8y	73.7y	79.9y	61.0y	52.6y	70.8y	61.3z	58.3z	64.2z	58.5y	49.8y	68.7y	198
...	...	...	29.7	25.1	35.2	76.0	72.8		70.3	74.9	64.8	66.3	77.6	55.0	52.6y	59.5y	44.4y	199
22.0x	20.3x	23.8x	59.3x	58.6x	60.1x	63.6x	62.9x	64.4x	40.7x	41.4x	39.9x	57.1	60.9	53.3	...	...	...	200
1.6	**1.3**	**1.9**	**26.6**	**26.2**	**26.9**	**75.8**	**75.6**	**76.0**	**73.4**	**73.8**	**73.1**	**54.2**	**55.3**	**53.1**	69.3**,y	74.4**,y	64.6**,y	201
6.6x	...	...	12.5x	...	...	98.5x	...	...	87.5x	...	...	66.2	70.9	61.5	...	...	...	202
8.8**,y	7.9**,y	9.7**,y	37.9**,y	38.4**,y	37.5**,y	69.7**,y	68.2**,y	71.2**,y	62.1**,y	61.6**,y	62.5**,y	80.2**,z	81.8**,z	78.6**,z	...	...	...	203

			Median						Weighted averages						Median			
...	...	...	13.4	13.6	13.2	...	...	...	86.6	86.4	86.8	86.1	88.4	83.6	...	...	...	I
.	.	.	2.0	2.5	1.5	.	.	.	98.0	97.5	98.5	91.4	91.8	91.0	...	...	...	II
.	.	.	1.7	1.2	2.2	.	.	.	98.3	98.8	97.8	98.8	99.4	98.2	...	...	...	III
...	...	...	20.3	...	...	81.6	80.4	82.9	79.7	...	...	84.4	87.0	81.6	...	...	...	IV
...	...	...	5.9	7.2	4.6	94.7	94.0	95.4	94.1	92.8	95.4	80.0	83.8	76.1	...	...	...	V
.	.	.	1.7	1.6	1.8	.	.	.	98.3	98.4	98.2	90.1	91.6	88.5	...	...	...	VI
.	.	.	2.9	3.9	1.8	.	.	.	97.1	96.1	98.2	99.0	99.6	98.5	...	...	...	VII
...	...	...	...	...	...	...	...	...	...	...	...	97.1	97.3	96.8	...	...	...	VIII
...	...	...	13.6	14.3	12.9	88.0	87.7	88.2	86.4	85.7	87.1	97.3	97.5	97.1	...	...	...	IX
...	...	...	...	...	...	...	...	...	...	...	...	84.1	84.8	83.4	...	...	...	X
...	...	...	16.9	...	...	84.3	83.6	85.1	83.1	...	...	98.3	97.9	98.8	...	...	...	XI
...	...	...	15.6	14.3	17.0	...	...	...	84.4	85.7	83.0	68.3	68.3	68.4	...	...	...	XII
...	...	...	19.1	20.7	17.3	84.3	82.0	86.8	80.9	79.3	82.7	99.3	98.8	99.7	...	...	...	XIII
...	...	...	...	...	...	...	...	...	...	...	...	99.0	99.7	98.2	...	...	...	XIV
...	...	...	...	...	...	...	...	...	...	...	...	82.3	86.5	77.9	...	...	...	XV
...	...	...	33.9	33.0	35.2	72.6	71.1	74.6	66.1	67.0	64.8	56.8	61.5	52.1	...	...	...	XVI

(z) Data are for the school year ending in 2003.
(y) Data are for the school year ending in 2002.
(x) Data are for the school year ending in 2001.

Table 8
Participation in secondary[1] and post-secondary non-tertiary[2] education

Country or territory	TRANSITION FROM PRIMARY TO SECONDARY GENERAL EDUCATION (%) School year ending in 2003 — Total	Male	Female	Age group 2004	School-age population (000) 2003[3]	ENROLMENT IN SECONDARY EDUCATION Total enrolment School year ending in 2004 — Total (000)	% F	Enrolment in private institutions as % of total enrolment School year ending in 2004	Enrolment in technical and vocational education School year ending in 2004 — Total (000)	% F	GROSS ENROLMENT RATIO (GER) IN SECONDARY EDUCATION (%) Lower secondary School year ending in 2004 — Total	Male	Female	GPI (F/M)
Arab States														
1 Algeria	79	76	83	12-17	4 558	3 677	51	.	422	39	105	108	102	0.94
2 Bahrain	97	96	99	12-17	70	70	50	16	15	39	102	102	103	1.01
3 Djibouti	59**	60**	57**	12-18	123	27	40	21	2	49	26	30	21	0.71
4 Egypt	86**	83**	89**	11-16	9 566	8 330**	48**	5**	2 525**	46**	98**	100**	96**	0.96**
5 Iraq	...	...	...	12-17	3 810	1 706	39	.	135	32	57	69	44	0.64
6 Jordan	97	97	97	12-17	704	616	49	17	36	37	93	93	93	1.00
7 Kuwait	95**	95**	95**	10-17	297	267	50	28	16	47	90	90	90	1.00
8 Lebanon	86	83	89	12-17	405	359	51	52	48	40	100	96	105	1.09
9 Libyan Arab Jamahiriya	...	...	...	12-17	740	798**,z	50**,z	3**,z	178**,z	53**,z	122**,z	122**,z	122**,z	0.99**,z
10 Mauritania	45	47	44	12-18	440	89	45	10	3	42	20	22	18	0.82
11 Morocco	79**	79**	80**	12-17	3 950	1 879	45	5	115	39	61	67	55	0.82
12 Oman	99	99	99	12-17	331	286	48	1.1	.	.	93	97	89	0.92
13 Palestinian A. T.	100	100	100	10-17	671	628	50	4	5	29	102	100	104	1.04
14 Qatar	...	...	...	12-17	56	54	49	32	0.5	.	101	105	98	0.93
15 Saudi Arabia	97	100	93	12-17	3 005	2 037	46	8	66	9	69	74	65	0.87
16 Sudan	90	88	92	12-16	3 940	1 293	47	10	28	34	47	50	44	0.88
17 Syrian Arab Republic	94	93	95	10-17	3 557	2 249	47	4	128	44	84	87	80	0.92
18 Tunisia	88	86	90	12-18	1 488	1 210	49	4	...	...	102	108	96	0.89
19 United Arab Emirates	96	96	96	11-17	421	279	49	41	1.6	.	72	73	70	0.96
20 Yemen	...	...	...	12-17	3 029	1 446	31	2	9	5	54	71	35	0.50
Central and Eastern Europe														
21 Albania	99**,y	98**,y	100**,y	10-17	509	396z	48z	3z	20z	49z	102z	102z	102z	1.00z
22 Belarus	99	100	97	10-16	1 037	970	49	0.1	5	33	107	108	105	0.97
23 Bosnia and Herzegovina	...	...	...	10-17	414	...	...	...	...	...	...	...	...	...
24 Bulgaria	96	96	96	11-17	690	705	48	0.8	209	38	88	91	85	0.93
25 Croatia	100y	100y	100y	11-18	447	400z	49z	1.0z	146z	46z	94z	95z	93z	0.98z
26 Czech Republic	99	99	99	11-18	1 027	982	49	7	382	46	99	99	99	1.01
27 Estonia	96y	93y	98y	13-18	127	124	49	2	17	33	110	112	108	0.96
28 Hungary	99**	98**	99**	11-18	998	963	49	9	130	38	99	99	98	0.99
29 Latvia	98	97	99	11-18	285	275	49	1	41	38	99	100	98	0.98
30 Lithuania	99	99	99	11-18	439	431	49	0.4	38	35	100	101	98	0.97
31 Poland	100	...	...	13-18	3 599	3 480	49	2	877	40	98	99	97	0.98
32 Republic of Moldova	98	97	99	11-17	543	400	50	1	23	38	79	78	79	1.02
33 Romania	98	98	98	11-18	2 532	2 155	49	0.6	673	44	96	97	95	0.99
34 Russian Federation	...	...	...	10-16	14 588	13 559	49	0.5	2 033	37	89	89	89	1.01
35 Serbia and Montenegro	...	...	...	11-18	...	...	...	...	...	...	...	...	...	...
36 Slovakia	98	98	99	10-18	715	674	49	6	227	47	97	98	97	0.99
37 Slovenia	99**,y	100**,y	99**,y	11-18	188	188	49	1.1	64	43	99	100	98	0.98
38 TFYR Macedonia	98	99	98	11-18	257	216	48	0.5	58	43	94	95	94	0.99
39 Turkey	91**	93**	89**	12-16	6 728	5 331	42	2	1 321	31	85	92	78	0.85
40 Ukraine	99x	99**,x	100**,x	10-16	4 787	4 446	48*	0.4	320	33*	93	94*	93*	0.99*
Central Asia														
41 Armenia	99**	98**	100**	10-16	429	393	50	0.6	2	30	97	97	97	1.00
42 Azerbaijan	99	99	99	10-16	1 306	1 086	48	0.3	3	31	87	88	86	0.97
43 Georgia	98y	98y	99y	12-16	388	320	49	3	9	31	92	93	92	0.99
44 Kazakhstan	100	100	100	11-17	2 130	2 090	49	0.8	98	35	100	101	99	0.98
45 Kyrgyzstan	99	98	100	11-17	833	733	50	0.5	28	35	90	90	91	1.01
46 Mongolia	99	99	99	12-17	372	333	53	3	21	49	95	91	99	1.09
47 Tajikistan	98	98**	97**	11-17	1 191	974	45	.	24	28	93	98	88	0.89
48 Turkmenistan	...	...	...	10-16	809	...	...	...	...	...	...	...	...	...
49 Uzbekistan	100**,y	100**,y	99**,y	11-17	4 475	4 235**	49**	.	378**	44**	98**	98**	97**	0.99**
East Asia and the Pacific														
50 Australia[4]	100**,y	100**,y	100**,y	12-17	1 678	2 492	48	30	1 044	45	112	113	112	1.00
51 Brunei Darussalam	89**	87**	93**	12-18	45	42	49	13	3	40	115	116	113	0.97
52 Cambodia	83	85	80	12-17	2 150	632**	40**	0.4**	15**	34**	44	50	37	0.74
53 China	97	97	97	12-17	136 167	98 763	47	...	12 852**	51**	101	101	101	1.00

GROSS ENROLMENT RATIO (GER) IN SECONDARY EDUCATION (%)								NET ENROLMENT RATIO (NER) IN SECONDARY EDUCATION (%)				INTERNAL EFFICIENCY			POST-SECONDARY NON-TERTIARY EDUCATION		
Upper secondary				Total secondary				Total secondary				Repeaters in secondary general education (%)			Total enrolment		
School year ending in 2004				School year ending in 2004				School year ending in 2004				School year ending in 2004			School year ending in 2004		
Total	Male	Female	GPI (F/M)	Total	Male	Female	GPI (F/M)	Total	Male	Female	GPI (F/M)	Total	Male	Female	Total (000)	% F	
57	48	66	1.37	81	78	84	1.07	66**	65**	68**	1.05**	...	...	...	64	50	1
95	90	101	1.12	99	96	102	1.06	90	87	93	1.07	5.8	7.9	4.0	3	29	2
15	18	12	0.64	22	25	18	0.69	19**	22**	15**	0.70**	6.0**,y	6.1**,y	5.8**,y	0.3	24	3
76**	78**	75**	0.95**	87**	89**	85**	0.95**	79**,y	81**,y	77**,y	0.94**,y	7.3**	8.5**	6.1**	224	49	4
31	37	26	0.70	45	54	36	0.66	38	44	31	0.71	8.5	9.7	6.5	49	36	5
75	74	77	1.05	87	87	88	1.01	81	80	82	1.02	2.7	2.7	2.6	·	·	6
90	84	96	1.14	90	87	93	1.06	78**,y	76**,y	80**,y	1.05**,y	7.8**	9.1**	6.4**	10	60	7
77	74	80	1.09	89	85	93	1.09	...	...	...	...	11.7	12.5	11.1	·	·	8
88**,z	82**,z	94**,z	1.15**,z	104**,z	101**,z	107**,z	1.06**,z	...	...	...	...	...	...	...	...	...	9
21	22	19	0.84	20	22	18	0.83	14**	16**	13**	0.82**	13.1	12.4	14.0	1.4	63	10
34	37	32	0.87	48	52	43	0.84	35**,z	38**,z	32**,z	0.86**,z	16.4z	18.6z	13.7z	83	45	11
79	79	80	1.02	86	88	85	0.96	75	74	75	1.01	6.5	8.1	4.7	...	...	12
65	62	69	1.12	94	91	96	1.05	89	87	92	1.05	2.0	2.2	1.7	·	·	13
92	91	93	1.02	97	98	95	0.97	87	88	86	0.98	...	...	...	·	·	14
66	69	62	0.90	68	72	64	0.88	52**	54**	51**	0.96**	6.6	6.9	6.3	54	...	15
23	23	23	1.00	33	34	32	0.93	...	...	...	...	...	...	...	·	·	16
30	31	29	0.96	63	65	61	0.93	58	60	56	0.93	7.8	9.2	6.3	41	55	17
66	60	72	1.20	81	80	82	1.02	64z	61z	67z	1.11z	14.6	17.5	12.0	5	27	18
59	54	66	1.21	66	65	68	1.06	62	61	64	1.06	4.5	6.0	2.9	·	·	19
41	57	25	0.45	48	64	31	0.48	...	...	...	...	...	...	...	27**	21**	20

Arab States

Total	Male	Female	GPI (F/M)	Total	Male	Female	GPI (F/M)	Total	Male	Female	GPI (F/M)	Total	Male	Female	Total (000)	% F	
53z	55z	51z	0.93z	78z	79z	77z	0.97z	74z	75z	73z	0.98z	4.2z	4.5z	3.8z	.z	.z	21
66	61	71	1.17	93	93	94	1.01	87	87**	88**	1.01**	0.1	0.1	0.1	121	36	22
...	...	...	...	...	...	...	...	...	...	...	...	...	...	...	·	·	23
119	120	118	0.98	102	104	100	0.96	88	90	87	0.98	1.7	2.3	1.2	3	38	24
83z	81z	85z	1.05z	88z	87z	89z	1.02z	85z	84z	86z	1.02z	0.5z	0.8z	0.3z	.z	.z	25
93	92	94	1.02	96	95	96	1.01	90	89	91	1.02	1.0	1.3	0.7	22	38	26
88	84	92	1.09	98	97	99	1.02	90	89	91	1.03	3.6	4.9	2.5	11	62	27
94	94	95	1.00	97	97	96	0.99	91**	91**	90**	0.99**	2.8**	3.4**	2.1**	59	46	28
93	92	95	1.03	96	97	96	1.00	89	88	89	1.01	2.4	3.4	1.3	6	71	29
93	91	96	1.05	98	99	98	0.99	93	93	93	1.01	1.1	1.5	0.6	9	58	30
96	94	98	1.04	97	96	97	1.01	90	89	92	1.03	1.7	2.9	0.5	76	63	31
63	59	66	1.12	74	72	75	1.04	69	67	70	1.05	0.3	0.3	0.3	·	·	32
76	74	77	1.04	85	85	86	1.01	81	80	82	1.03	2.0	2.9	1.2	55	62	33
101	102	99	0.97	93	93	93	0.99	76**	73**	78**	1.07**	0.7	...	...	221	57	34
...	...	...	...	...	...	...	...	...	...	...	...	...	...	...	...	...	35
91	89	93	1.05	94	94	95	1.01	90	89	91	1.02	1.5	1.8	1.1	3	49	36
100	100	101	1.00	100	100	100	1.00	95	94	95	1.00	1.3	2.4	0.3	1.5	68	37
74	76	73	0.96	84	85	83	0.98	81**,y	82**,y	80**,y	1.0**,y	0.5	0.6	0.4	–	–	38
75	89	60	0.68	79	90	68	0.75	...	...	...	...	0.5	0.6	0.3	·	·	39
92	94*	89*	0.95*	93	94*	92*	0.98*	84	83*	84*	1.00*	0.04	0.04**	0.04**	173	52*	40

Central and Eastern Europe

Total	Male	Female	GPI (F/M)	Total	Male	Female	GPI (F/M)	Total	Male	Female	GPI (F/M)	Total	Male	Female	Total (000)	% F	
79	75	83	1.11	91	90	93	1.03	89	88	90	1.03	0.2**	0.3**	0.1**	31	70	41
73	74	71	0.95	83	84	82	0.97	77	78	76	0.98	0.6	0.7	0.5	73	59	42
68	68	68	1.00	82	83	82	0.99	81	81	81	1.00	0.3	0.4	0.1	26	65	43
94	95	92	0.96	98	99	97	0.98	92	93	92	0.99	0.2	0.2	0.1	251	54	44
82	81	83	1.02	88	88	88	1.01	...	...	...	...	0.1	0.2	0.1	27	64	45
78	70	87	1.25	90	84	95	1.14	82	77	88	1.14	0.1	0.1	0.1	1	48	46
52	64	40	0.62	82	89	75	0.84	79	86	73	0.85	0.4	0.4**	0.4**	29	53	47
...	...	...	...	...	...	...	...	...	...	...	...	...	...	...	...	...	48
87**	91**	83**	0.91**	95**	96**	93**	0.97**	...	...	...	...	–z	–z	–z	...	...	49

Central Asia

Total	Male	Female	GPI (F/M)	Total	Male	Female	GPI (F/M)	Total	Male	Female	GPI (F/M)	Total	Male	Female	Total (000)	% F	
221	230	212	0.92	149	152	145	0.96	85**	85**	86**	1.01**	–z	–z	–z	171	53	50
77	72	83	1.16	94	91	96	1.05	...	...	...	...	8.8	10.2	7.3	0.1y	60y	51
15**	20**	11**	0.57**	29**	35**	24**	0.69**	26**	30**	22**	0.73**	4.4	5.6	2.7	9z	32z	52
45	45	45	1.00	73	73	73	1.00	...	...	...	...	0.3**	0.4**	0.2**	611	52	53

East Asia and the Pacific

Table 8 (continued)

		TRANSITION FROM PRIMARY TO SECONDARY GENERAL EDUCATION (%) School year ending in 2003			Age group	School-age population (000)	ENROLMENT IN SECONDARY EDUCATION Total enrolment School year ending in 2004		Enrolment in private institutions as % of total enrolment School year ending in 2004	Enrolment in technical and vocational education School year ending in 2004		GROSS ENROLMENT RATIO (GER) IN SECONDARY EDUCATION (%) Lower secondary School year ending in 2004			
	Country or territory	Total	Male	Female	2004	2003[3]	Total (000)	% F		Total (000)	% F	Total	Male	Female	GPI (F/M)
54	Cook Islands	…	…	…	11-18	…	2[z]	49[z]	19[z]	.	.	85**,[z]	88**,[z]	81**,[z]	0.93**,[z]
55	DPR Korea	…	…	…	10-15	2346	…	…		.	.	…	…	…	…
56	Fiji	99	100	99	12-18	116	102	50	92	3	28	100	98	102	1.04
57	Indonesia	84	84	84	13-18	25506	16354	49	43	2198	43	80	79	81	1.02
58	Japan	…	…	…	12-17	7771	7894	49	19	1015	43	101	101	101	1.00
59	Kiribati[5]	94	89	100	12-17		12	53	…	-	-	111	105	118	1.12
60	Lao PDR	78	80	76	11-16	827	380	42	1.1	5	35	56	62	49	0.79
61	Macao, China	92	89	95	12-17	49	47	50	94	3	48	116	116	116	1.00
62	Malaysia	…	…	…	12-18	3383	2519[z]	52[z]	5[z]	139[z]	42[z]	98[z]	96[z]	101[z]	1.06[z]
63	Marshall Islands	99**,[y]			12-17		6**,[z]	50**,[z]	34[y]	.	.	126**,[z]	128**,[z]	124**,[z]	0.97**,[z]
64	Micronesia				12-17	16	…	…	…	…	…	…	…	…	…
65	Myanmar	**72****	**72****	**71****	10-15	6363	**2589**	**49**	.	–	–	**45**	**46**	**45**	**0.98**
66	Nauru	82[x]	75[x]	89[x]	12-17		0.6[z]	50[z]	19[y]	.[z]	.[z]	…	…	…	…
67	New Zealand	…	…	…	11-17	427	489	51	12	55	57	109	109	109	1.00
68	Niue[5]	…	…	…	11-16		0.2	51	…	.	.	…	…	…	…
69	Palau	…	…	…	11-17		2**	50**	…	.	.	104**	105**	103**	0.97**
70	Papua New Guinea	77**,[y]	77**,[y]	77**,[y]	13-18	758	190**,[z]	41**,[z]	…	17**,[z]	27**,[z]	35**,[z]	38**,[z]	30**,[z]	0.79**,[z]
71	Philippines	97	97	96	12-15	7348	6309	52	20	.	.	91	87	95	1.09
72	Republic of Korea	**99**	**99**	**98**	12-17	4011	**3693**	**47**	**34**	**515**	**47**	**95**	**95**	**96**	**1.00**
73	Samoa	96**	95**	97**	11-17	30	24	51	32	.	.	100	100	100	1.00
74	Singapore	…	…	…	12-16	316	…	…	…	…	…	…	…	…	…
75	Solomon Islands	70**,[y]	71**,[y]	68**,[y]	12-18	75	22**,[z]	43**,[z]	…	.	.	49**,[z]	52**,[z]	45**,[z]	0.86**,[z]
76	Thailand	…	…	…	12-17	6478	**4718**	**50**	**13**	**871**	**44**	**86**	**86**	**86**	**1.00**
77	Timor-Leste	…	…	…	12-17	143	47[y]	…	…	–[y]	–[y]	41[y]	…	…	…
78	Tokelau[6]	88[y]	92[y]	82[y]	11-16		0.2[z]	48[z]	.[z]	.[z]	.[z]	…	…	…	…
79	Tonga	76**	75**	79**	11-16	14	14	49**	…	1.1	32**	93**	95**	91**	0.95**
80	Tuvalu[6]	69[x]	85[x]	53[x]	12-17		0.9	…	…	…	…	…	…	…	…
81	Vanuatu	51**	49**	53**	12-18	33	14	45	…	3	30	47**	47**	48**	1.03**
82	Viet Nam	100**,[y]	99**,[y]	100**,[y]	11-17	13054	9589	48	11**,[z]	360	52	87	89	84	0.94

Latin America and the Caribbean

		Total	Male	Female	2004	2003[3]	Total (000)	% F		Total (000)	% F	Total	Male	Female	GPI (F/M)
83	Anguilla	100	…	…	12-16		1.2	52	.**,[z]	0.1**	60**	89**	90**	89**	1.00**
84	Antigua and Barbuda	…	…	…	12-16		…	…	…	…	…	…	…	…	…
85	Argentina	93[y]	92[y]	94[y]	12-17	4087	3499[z]	51[z]	27[z]	1286[z]	52[z]	100[z]	98[z]	101[z]	1.03[z]
86	Aruba[5]	99	98	100	12-16		7	51	92	1.2	40	114	116	113	0.97
87	Bahamas	95**	96**	94**	11-16	35	28	52	24	.	.	83	78	88	1.13
88	Barbados	98	96	100	11-15	19	21	50	5	0.1	14	113	113	113	1.00
89	Belize	87	85	89	11-16	37	31	50	74**,[z]	3	43	96	96	95	1.00
90	Bermuda[5]	100[x]	…	…	11-17		5[y]	51[y]	41[y]	.[y]	.[y]	101[y]	…	…	…
91	Bolivia	91**	92**	91**	12-17	1214	1075**	48**	28**,[y]	…	…	…	…	…	…
92	Brazil	…	…	…	11-17	23781	24593[z]	52[z]	11[z]	452[z]	73[z]	115[z]	113[z]	118[z]	1.05[z]
93	British Virgin Islands[5]	69**,[x]	62**,[x]	76**,[x]	12-16		1.7	52	4	0.2	37	114	113	116	1.03
94	Cayman Islands	91[x]	89[x]	93[x]	11-16		3	51	28	.	.	110**	106**	115**	1.09**
95	Chile	97	95	98	12-17	1789	1595	49	51	384	46	100	101	99	0.98
96	Colombia	100**	100**	100**	11-16	5435	4051	52	22	318	55	82	78	85	1.09
97	Costa Rica	92**	93**	90**	12-16	439	297	50	12**	58	50	84	83	84	1.02
98	Cuba	98	98	99	12-17	1008	932	49	.	260	43	103	104	101	0.97
99	Dominica[5]	94[y]	94[y]	94[y]	12-16		7	50	33	0.3	62	125	134	115	0.86
100	Dominican Republic	87**	85**	90**	12-17	1144	783	54	25**	31	59	81	76	85	1.11
101	Ecuador	74	76	71	12-17	1632	997	49	33	223	52	69	71	68	0.97
102	El Salvador	94**	94**	94**	13-18	822	496**	50**	20**,[z]	…	…	77**	78**	77**	0.99**
103	Grenada[5]	…	…	…	12-16		14	51	60[z]	0.8	46	107	107	107	1.00
104	Guatemala	96**	97**	95**	13-17	1437	699	47	74	202	52	53	58	49	0.85
105	Guyana	…	…	…	12-16	71	64**	60**	2[z]	5**	52**	118[z]	…	…	…
106	Haiti	…	…	…	12-18	1483	…	…	…	…	…	…	…	…	…
107	Honduras	…	…	…	12-16	847	555	55	…	207	55	60	56	64	1.14
108	Jamaica	97[y]	…	…	12-16	279	246	50	6	–	–	96	96	96	1.00
109	Mexico	94	95	92	12-17	13052	10404	51	15	1540	57	104	100	108	1.08
110	Montserrat[5]	…	…	…	12-16		0.3	49	.**,[z]	.	.	119	118	121	1.03
111	Netherlands Antilles	…	…	…	12-17	18	15**,[z]	52**,[z]	81**,[z]	6**,[z]	54**,[z]	116**,[z]	120**,[z]	112**,[z]	0.94**,[z]
112	Nicaragua	…	…	…	13-17	654	416	53	28	22	54	73	70	76	1.09

GROSS ENROLMENT RATIO (GER) IN SECONDARY EDUCATION (%)								NET ENROLMENT RATIO (NER) IN SECONDARY EDUCATION (%)				INTERNAL EFFICIENCY			POST-SECONDARY NON-TERTIARY EDUCATION		
Upper secondary				Total secondary				Total secondary				Repeaters in secondary general education (%)			Total enrolment		
School year ending in 2004				School year ending in 2004				School year ending in 2004				School year ending in 2004			School year ending in 2004		
Total	Male	Female	GPI (F/M)	Total	Male	Female	GPI (F/M)	Total	Male	Female	GPI (F/M)	Total	Male	Female	Total (000)	% F	
41**,z	37**,z	46**,z	1.24**,z	64**,z	63**,z	65**,z	1.02**,z	...	...	...	...	...	...	...	...	...	54
...	...	...	...	...	...	...	...	...	...	...	...	...	...	...	...	...	55
70	67	74	1.11	88	85	91	1.07	83**	80**	85**	1.06**	2.7	2.7	2.8	1.0z	54z	56
48	50	47	0.95	64	64	64	0.99	57	57	57	0.99	0.4	0.6	0.2	.	.	57
102	102	102	1.00	102	101	102	1.00	100**	...	...	...	...	...	...	15	62	58
70	59	82	1.40	91	82	100	1.22	70	65	76	1.18	...	...	...	...	...	59
35	41	29	0.70	46	52	39	0.76	37	40	34	0.85	2.5	3.3	1.3	21	45	60
76	73	80	1.10	96	94	98	1.04	77	74	80	1.08	10.2	12.2	8.2	.	.	61
57z	50z	64z	1.27z	76z	71z	81z	1.14z	76z	71z	81z	1.14z	...	...	...	170z	46z	62
67**,z	65**,z	70**,z	1.09**,z	87**,z	85**,z	88**,z	1.04**,z	74**,z	72**,z	77**,z	1.06**,z	3.1**,y	3.1**,y	3.2**,y	...	...	63
...	...	...	...	...	...	...	...	...	...	...	...	...	...	...	...	...	64
31	**31**	**32**	**1.02**	**41**	**41**	**40**	**0.99**	**38**	**38**	**37**	**0.98**	**2.2****	**2.2****	**2.3****	.	.	65
...	...	...	...	48**,z	46**,z	50**,z	1.07**,z	...	...	...	...	.z	.z	.z	.	.	66
121	111	132	1.20	114	110	119	1.09	95	93	96	1.03	...	...	...	38	55	67
...	...	...	...	98	100	95	0.95	...	...	...	...	.	.	.	.	.	68
93**	88**	99**	1.13**	98**	95**	101**	1.1**	...	...	...	...	...	...	...	.	.	69
6**,z	7**,z	5**,z	0.70**,z	26**,z	29**,z	23**,z	0.79**,z	...	...	...	...	–**,z	–**,z	–**,z	.z	.z	70
69	63	76	1.19	86	82	90	1.11	61	56	67	1.20	1.9	2.9	0.9	543	65	71
90	**90**	**90**	**1.00**	**93**	**93**	**93**	**1.00**	**90**	**90**	**91**	**1.00**	**0.02****	**0.02****	**0.02****	.	.	72
72	65	79	1.20	80	76	85	1.12	66**	62**	70**	1.14**	3.4**	3.4**	3.4**	.	.	73
...	...	...	...	...	...	...	...	...	...	...	...	...	...	...	.	.	74
15**,z	17**,z	12**,z	0.69**,z	30**,z	33**,z	26**,z	0.81**,z	26**,z	28**,z	24**,z	0.86**,z	–**,z	–**,z	–**,z	.	.	75
61	**58**	63	**1.07**	**73**	**72**	74	**1.03**	**64**	**64**	**65**	**1.02**	...	...	...	**18****	**53****	76
26y	...	...	...	34y	...	...	...	...	...	...	...	...	...	...	.y	.y	77
...	...	...	...	...	...	...	...	.z	.z	.z	.z	.z					78
108**	91**	127**	1.4**	98	94**	102**	1.08**	68**	61**	75**	1.2**	11.0	10.8	11.1	0.2	54	79
...	...	...	...	...	...	...	...	...	...	...	...	...	...	...	...	...	80
32**	41**	24**	0.58**	41	44	38	0.86	39**	42**	36**	0.86**	.	.	.	.	.	81
55	55	54	0.98	73	75	72	0.95	65**,y	...	...	...	1.3**,z	1.9**,z	0.7**,z	.	.	82

Latin America and the Caribbean

119**	116**	123**	1.06**	100**	99**	102**	1.02**	93**	93**	93**	1.00**	–	–	–	0.1	72	83
...	...	...	...	...	...	...	...	...	...	...	...	...	...	...	...	...	84
73z	69z	77z	1.13z	86z	84z	89z	1.07z	79z	76z	82z	1.07z	11.5z	13.7z	9.4z	.z	.z	85
87	84	90	1.08	98	97	100	1.02	74	73	75	1.02	17.5	18.2	16.9	.	.	86
78	75	80	1.07	80	76	84	1.10	74	70	78	1.12	.	.	.	.	.	87
106	104	107	1.03	110	109	111	1.01	95	93	98	1.05	.	.	.	4	48	88
63	57	69	1.21	85	84	87	1.04	71**	70**	73**	1.05**	6.3	7.3	5.3	3	42	89
74y	...	...	...	86y	...	...	...	...	...	...	...	.y	.y	.y	.y	.y	90
79**	81**	77**	0.94**	89**	90**	87**	0.97**	74**	74**	73**	0.99**	3.4**	4.0**	2.7**	...	...	91
85z	77z	94z	1.22z	102z	97z	107z	1.11z	76z	73z	78z	1.07z	17.4y	...	...	.	.	92
66	62	71	1.14	96	93	98	1.06	80	75	84	1.11	9.5**	12.4**	7.0**	1.1	69	93
84**	79**	89**	1.13**	97**	93**	102**	1.10**	91**	87**	96**	1.10**	–	–	–	0.1	61	94
84	82	85	1.03	89	89	90	1.01	78	77	79	1.02	2.7	3.3	2.2	.	.	95
59	54	65	1.19	75	71	78	1.11	55**	52**	58**	1.11**	2.6**	3.2**	2.1**	.	.	96
44	41	48	1.16	68	66	69	1.05	50	48	52	1.07	10.2	11.7	8.6	.	.	97
83	80	85	1.06	93	92	93	1.01	87	86	87	1.02	1.0	1.4	0.7	20	77	98
80	68	93	1.37	107	107	106	0.99	90**	89**	92**	1.03**	8.1	10.2	6.0	1.9	60	99
62	54	71	1.31	68	61	76	1.23	49**	45**	54**	1.21**	3.1**	4.0**	2.4**	.	.	100
52	51	54	1.05	61	61	61	1.00	52	52	53	1.01	3.9	4.6	3.2	.	.	101
43**	41**	44**	1.07**	60**	60**	61**	1.01**	48**,z	47**,z	49**,z	1.03**,z	3.2**,z	4.0**,z	2.3**,z	.	.	102
91	80	103	1.29	101	96	105	1.09	78**	75**	82**	1.10**	7.8**	9.6**	6.1**	1.1**	66**	103
41	41	42	1.02	49	51	46	0.90	34**	35**	32**	0.92**	3.1**	3.5**	2.5**	.	.	104
49z	...	...	...	90z	...	...	...	...	...	...	...	...	...	...	2**	28**	105
...	...	...	...	...	...	...	...	...	...	...	...	...	...	...	...	...	106
75	63	87	1.39	65	58	73	1.24	...	...	...	...	...	...	...	.	.	107
76	74	78	1.05	88	87	89	1.02	79	78	81	1.03	1.5	1.9	1.0	48	45	108
53	52	55	1.06	80	77	82	1.07	64	63	65	1.03	2.1	2.7	1.5	.	.	109
106	96	118	1.22	114	109	120	1.10	100	...	...	...	–			0.02	59	110
71**,z	63**,z	79**,z	1.25**,z	87**,z	83**,z	90**,z	1.09**,z	77**,z	73**,z	81**,z	1.10**,z	...	...	...	0.4**,z	84**,z	111
49	43	56	1.29	64	59	68	1.15	41	38	43	1.13	6.7	8.0	5.5	.	.	112

Table 8 (continued)

| | | TRANSITION FROM PRIMARY TO SECONDARY GENERAL EDUCATION (%) | | | ENROLMENT IN SECONDARY EDUCATION | | | | | | | GROSS ENROLMENT RATIO (GER) IN SECONDARY EDUCATION (%) | | | |
| | | School year ending in 2003 | | | Age group | School-age population (000) | Total enrolment School year ending in 2004 | | Enrolment in private institutions as % of total enrolment School year ending in 2004 | Enrolment in technical and vocational education School year ending in 2004 | | Lower secondary School year ending in 2004 | | | |
	Country or territory	Total	Male	Female	2004	2003[3]	Total (000)	% F		Total (000)	% F	Total	Male	Female	GPI (F/M)
113	Panama	64**	63**	65**	12-17	362	254	51	15	102	50	85	84	86	1.03
114	Paraguay	91[y]	91[y]	91[y]	12-17	825	519**	50**	20**	47**	47**	75**	75**	74**	1.00**
115	Peru	94[x]	96[x]	92[x]	12-16	2905	2662	50	22	279	62	103	101	105	1.03
116	Saint Kitts and Nevis[5]	...	...	...	12-16	...	5	50	3	.	.	125	133	117	0.88
117	Saint Lucia	69**	62**	76**	12-16	17	13	50	5**	0.6	31	78	79	77	0.97
118	St Vincent/Grenad.	74	68	78	12-16	13	10	49	32**,[y]	1.8	32	95	96	94	0.98
119	Suriname	12**,[y]	15**,[y]	10**,[y]	12-17	54	41**,[z]	56**,[z]	21**,[z]	18**,[z]	52**,[z]	82**,[z]	74**,[z]	90**,[z]	1.22**,[z]
120	Trinidad and Tobago	97*	96*	99*	12-16	126	105*	51*	27*	0.9	28	84*	83*	86	1.05*
121	Turks and Caicos Islands[5]	72[y]	72[y]	71[y]	12-16	...	1.5	49	13	0.1**	50**	87	92	82	0.90
122	Uruguay	85**	78**	92**	12-17	322	348**	52**	10**	31**	43**	113**	109**	117**	1.07**
123	Venezuela	98	97	100	12-16	2712	1954	52	24	68	51	85	81	88	1.09
	North America and Western Europe														
124	Andorra	96	95	96	12-17	...	3	50	5	0.2	48	91**	92**	89**	0.98**
125	Austria	...	...	...	10-17	763	770	47	9	292	43	105	106	104	0.99
126	Belgium	...	...	...	12-17	740	806	48	68	326	43	116	119	113	0.95
127	Canada	...	...	...	12-17	2557	2622**,[y]	49**,[y]	6**,[y]	102**,[y]	36**,[y]	97**,[y]	98**,[y]	97**,[y]	0.99**,[y]
128	Cyprus[5]	100	100	100	12-17	...	65	49	13	4	18	101	101	102	1.02*
129	Denmark	100[y]	100[y]	99[y]	13-18	362	450	50	13	123	45	119	118	121	1.03
130	Finland	100	100	100	13-18	389	426	50	7	120	46	100	100	100	1.00
131	France	...	...	...	11-17	5269	5827	49	25	1528	44	110	111	109	0.99
132	Germany	99	99	99	10-18	8357	8361	48	8	1791	42	103	103	103	1.00
133	Greece	...	...	...	12-17	723	696	48	6	125	39	96	97	95	0.98
134	Iceland	100[y]	99[y]	100[y]	13-19	30	35**	50**	4**	7**	38**	102**	103**	100**	0.97**
135	Ireland	100[y]	...	...	12-16	287	321	51	0.6	50	55	105	103	107	1.03
136	Israel	74	74	74	12-17	655	607	49	–	125	42	77	77	77	1.01
137	Italy	100	100	99	11-18	4549	4506	48	5	1696	43	107	108	105	0.97
138	Luxembourg	...	...	...	12-18	37	35	50	18	11	48	102	101	103	1.02
139	Malta	91[y]	90[y]	92[y]	11-17	40	42	47	28	7	27	106	104	107	1.03
140	Monaco	...	...	...	11-17	...	...	...	...	...	...	...	...	...	...
141	Netherlands	98**	96**	100**	12-17	1176	1397	48	83	725	47	130	133	127	0.95
142	Norway	100	100	100	13-18	346	400	49	7	132	46	102	101	102	1.01
143	Portugal	...	...	...	12-17	688	665	51	15	94	43	109	107	111	1.04
144	San Marino	...	...	...	11-18	...	...	...	...	...	...	...	...	...	...
145	Spain	...	...	...	12-17	2560	3048	50	29	423	48	120	120	120	1.01
146	Sweden	...	...	...	13-18	694	712	49	8	193	54	104	104	104	1.00
147	Switzerland	100	100	100	13-19	603	564	47	7	176	40	111	110	112	1.01
148	United Kingdom	...	...	...	11-17	5453	5700	49	29	1298	49	100	100	100	1.00
149	United States	...	...	...	12-17	25544	24217	49.4	9	.	.	102	101	104	1.03
	South and West Asia														
150	Afghanistan	...	...	...	13-18	3819	594	16	...	3	4	21	34	7	0.19
151	Bangladesh	95[y]	92[y]	99[y]	11-17	21877	11051[z]	51[z]	96[z]	127[z]	26[z]	69[z]	63[z]	75[z]	1.19[z]
152	Bhutan[7]	...	...	...	13-16	...	29**,[y]	45**,[y]	...	0.5**,[y]	39**,[y]	...	...	...	...
153	India	85	87	82	11-17	156704	83858	43	...	727**	15**	71	77	65	0.84
154	Iran, Islamic Republic of	92	95	88	11-17	12598	10313	47	7	872	37	89	93	85	0.91
155	Maldives	63**,[y]	58**,[y]	68**,[y]	13-17	40	29**	52**	9[z]	1.1**	30**	108	98	118	1.20
156	Nepal	**76****	**78****	**73****	10-16	4385	**2054**	**45****	28[z]	**22****	**22****	**71**	**76**	**66**	**0.88**
157	Pakistan	...	...	...	10-16	26734	7272	41	23	131	17	32	37	26	0.70
158	Sri Lanka	97**,[y]	96**,[y]	98**,[y]	10-17	2827	2332**	49**	-	...	...	95**	94**	97**	1.04**
	Sub-Saharan Africa														
159	Angola	...	...	...	10-16	2753	...	...	...	...	...	...	...	...	...
160	Benin	51[y]	51[y]	51[y]	12-18	1305	338**	33**	18**	31	42	34**	44**	24**	0.54**
161	Botswana	99**	100**	98**	13-17	226	170**	51**	4**	11**	38**	87	84	89	1.07
162	Burkina Faso	40**	42**	37**	13-19	2030	246**	40**	34**,[y]	19**	50**	16**	19**	14**	0.72**
163	Burundi	34	35	33	13-19	1254	152	43	9	12	49	16	18	14	0.78
164	Cameroon	48	47	49	12-18	2652	1161	41*	43	399	30*	...	...	...	...
165	Cape Verde	72	69	76	12-17	76	50	52	–	2	40	93	89	97	1.09
166	Central African Republic	...	...	...	12-18	653	72**,[y]	...	...	...	...	14**,[y]	...	...	...
167	Chad	56**	60**	46**	12-18	1468	222**	24**	17[y]	...	...	19**	28**	9**	0.33**

GROSS ENROLMENT RATIO (GER) IN SECONDARY EDUCATION (%)								NET ENROLMENT RATIO (NER) IN SECONDARY EDUCATION (%)				INTERNAL EFFICIENCY			POST-SECONDARY NON-TERTIARY EDUCATION		
Upper secondary				Total secondary				Total secondary				Repeaters in secondary general education (%)			Total enrolment		
School year ending in 2004				School year ending in 2004				School year ending in 2004				School year ending in 2004			School year ending in 2004		
Total	Male	Female	GPI (F/M)	Total	Male	Female	GPI (F/M)	Total	Male	Female	GPI (F/M)	Total	Male	Female	Total (000)	% F	
55	51	59	1.15	70	68	73	1.07	64	61	67	1.10	4.8	6.0	3.7	7	61	113
51**	50**	52**	1.04**	63**	62**	63**	1.01**	52**	51**	54**	1.06**	1.1**	1.4**	0.7**	2^z		114
74	75	73	0.97	92	91	92	1.01	69	69	69	1.00	4.6	5.6	3.6		...	115
88	80	95	1.19	110	111	108	0.97	98	100	97	1.0	2.7	2.5	2.8	0.8	59	116
66	64	68	1.06	74	74	74	1.00	63**	63**	62**	1.00**	0.2**	0.2**	0.2**	2	65	117
52	53	50	0.95	78	79	76	0.97	62	62	63	1.02	9.6	10.8	8.5	1.2	65	118
57**,z	41**,z	72**,z	1.75**,z	73**,z	63**,z	84**,z	1.34**,z	63**,z	53**,z	74**,z	1.38**,z	—**,z	—**,z	—**,z	.^z	.^z	119
83*	79*	87*	1.09*	84*	81*	86*	1.07*	72**	70**	74**	1.05**	0.9*	1.1*	0.7*	9	62	120
97	91	104	1.15	91	91	90	0.99	78**	78**	78**	1.00**	1.9^z	2.2^z	1.6^z	0.6	73	121
102**	91**	114**	1.25**	108**	100**	116**	1.15**	69**	66**	72**	1.10**	10.1**	11.8**	8.7**	4^z	38^z	122
53	47	60	1.28	72	67	77	1.14	61	57	66	1.15	8.4	10.4	6.5	.	.	123

North America and Western Europe

Total	Male	Female	GPI (F/M)	Total	Male	Female	GPI (F/M)	Total	Male	Female	GPI (F/M)	Total	Male	Female	Total (000)	% F	
61**	55**	67**	1.22**	81**	80**	83**	1.03**	71**	71**	72**	1.01**	—	—	—	.	.	124
97	102	92	0.91	101	104	98	0.95	90	91	89	0.98	...	...	...	71	61	125
105	107	104	0.98	109	111	107	0.97	97**,z	96**,z	97**,z	1.01**,z	...	...	...	26	60	126
113**,y	113**,y	112**,y	1.00**,y	105**,y	105**,y	105**,y	0.99**,y	...	...	...	...	...	...	...	298**,y	42**,y	127
94	92	96	1.04	98	96	99	1.03	93	92	95	1.03	1.7	2.5	1.1	.^z	.^z	128
130	126	134	1.06	124	122	127	1.05	92	91	94	1.03	.	.	.	1.0	22	129
119	113	124	1.09	109	107	112	1.05	94	94	94	1.01	0.3	0.4	0.3	—	—	130
111	110	113	1.03	111	110	111	1.01	96	95	97	1.02				28	65	131
95	97	92	0.95	100	101	99	0.98	...	...	...	...	3.1	3.6	2.6	458	48	132
97	96	98	1.03	96	96	97	1.01	87	85	88	1.04	...	...	...	33	54	133
125**	118**	132**	1.12**	115**	111**	118**	1.06**	86**	85**	88**	1.04**	—**	—**	—**	0.6^z	40^z	134
121	113	129	1.14	112	108	116	1.08	87	84	89	1.06	2.0**	1.9**	2.1**	62	36	135
109	109	108	0.99	93	93	93	1.00	89	89	89	1.00	2.1	3.1	1.0	14	49	136
94	94	95	1.00	99	100	98	0.99	92	92	93	1.02	3.2	4.3	2.3	52	55	137
89	85	93	1.10	95	92	98	1.06	79	77	82	1.07	.^z	.^z	.^z	1.0	22	138
105	120	88	0.73	105	109	102	0.93	88	85	90	1.06	1.4	1.6	1.2	0.4	45	139
...	...	...	...	...	...	...	...	...	...	...	...	...	...	...	.^z	.^z	140
107	106	108	1.02	119	120	118	0.98	89	89	90	1.01	4.5	5.0	4.0	6.6	22.8	141
130	127	133	1.05	116	114	117	1.03	96	96	97	1.01	...	...	...	6.0	17.8	142
85	78	93	1.19	97	92	102	1.11	82^z	78^z	87^z	1.11^z	...	...	...	1.8	32.0	143
...	...	...	...	...	...	...	...	...	...	...	...	...	...	...	...	...	144
118	109	127	1.16	119	116	123	1.06	97	95	99	1.04	...	...	...	.	.	145
101	97	105	1.08	103	101	105	1.04	98	97	100	1.03	...	...	...	5.3	42.3	146
80	87	72	0.83	93	97	89	0.92	83	86	80	0.93	2.3	2.5	2.1	29	70	147
108	105	110	1.05	105	103	106	1.03	95	93	97	1.03	...	...	...	...	...	148
87	88	87	0.99	95	94	95	1.01	90	89	91	1.02	...	...	...	429	69	149

South and West Asia

Total	Male	Female	GPI (F/M)	Total	Male	Female	GPI (F/M)	Total	Male	Female	GPI (F/M)	Total	Male	Female	Total (000)	% F	
10	15	4	0.25	16	25	5	0.21	...	...	...	...	...	...	...	4	63	150
37^z	37^z	37^z	1.00^z	51^z	49^z	54^z	1.11^z	48^z	45^z	51^z	1.11^z	5.6^z	5.9^z	5.2^z	25^z	40^z	151
...	...	...	...	...	...	...	...	...	...	...	...	...	...	...	—	—	152
40	45	34	0.75	54	59	47	0.80	49**	54**	43**	0.80**	4.7	5.1	4.2	481	29	153
77	78	75	0.96	82	84	79	0.94	78	80	76	0.9	...	...	...	881**,z	16**,z	154
18**	21**	15**	0.70**	73**	68**	78**	1.14**	51**,y	48**,y	55**,y	1.15**,y	...	...	...	0.7^z	64^z	155
25	**27****	**22****	**0.82****	**46**	**49****	**42****	**0.86****	...	...	...	...	**11.7**,z**	**10.8**,z**	**12.9**,z**	.	.	156
16	17	15	0.89	27	31	23	0.73	...	...	...	...	...	...	...	132	17	157
70**	72**	69**	0.96**	83**	82**	83**	1.00**	...	...	...	...	...	...	...	.	.	158

Sub-Saharan Africa

Total	Male	Female	GPI (F/M)	Total	Male	Female	GPI (F/M)	Total	Male	Female	GPI (F/M)	Total	Male	Female	Total (000)	% F	
...	...	...	...	...	...	...	...	...	...	...	...	...	...	...	.	.	159
14**	20**	9**	0.43**	26**	34**	18**	0.52**	...	...	...	...	23.1**	22.8**	23.8**	...	...	160
58**	57**	58**	1.02**	75**	73**	77**	1.05**	61**	58**	64**	1.10**	0.6**	0.4**	0.8**	16**,z	52**,z	161
6**	7**	4**	0.54**	12**	14**	10**	0.68**	10**	11**	8**	0.68**	27.6**	26.5**	29.2**	...	...	162
7	8	6	0.67	12	14	10	0.75	...	...	...	...	20.3	18.7	22.4	.	.	163
...	...	...	...	44	51*	36*	0.70*	...	...	...	...	10.2	9.9	10.5	...	...	164
52	49	54	1.10	66	63	69	1.10	55	52	58	1.12	20.1	20.9	19.3	1.1	66	165
8**,y	...	...	...	12**,y	...	...	...	...	...	...	...	...	...	...			166
...	...	...	...	15**	23**	7**	0.32**	11**,z	16**,z	5**,z	0.3**,z	21.1**	20.7**	22.3**	.	.	167

Table 8 (continued)

Country or territory	TRANSITION FROM PRIMARY TO SECONDARY GENERAL EDUCATION (%) School year ending in 2003 Total	Male	Female	Age group 2004	School-age population (000) 2003[3]	ENROLMENT IN SECONDARY EDUCATION Total enrolment School year ending in 2004 Total (000)	% F	Enrolment in private institutions as % of total enrolment School year ending in 2004	Enrolment in technical and vocational education School year ending in 2004 Total (000)	% F	GROSS ENROLMENT RATIO (GER) IN SECONDARY EDUCATION (%) Lower secondary School year ending in 2004 Total	Male	Female	GPI (F/M)
168 Comoros	67	72	61	12-18	122	43	43	41	0.2	7	41	47	35	0.75
169 Congo	78	78	78	12-18	609	235**	46**	22**	43**	48**	50	53	47	0.88
170 Côte d'Ivoire	40x	42x	36x	12-18	3046	737**,y	36**,y	...	...	...	31**,y	39**,y	23**,y	0.59**,y
171 D. R. Congo	...	...	...	12-17	7690	...	...	...	...	...	...	...	...	...
172 Equatorial Guinea	...	...	...	12-18	76	21**,y	36**,y	...	1.4y	20y	41**,y	51**,y	31**,y	0.60**,y
173 Eritrea	81	85	76	12-17	575	194	36	6	1.8	28	61	75	46	0.61
174 Ethiopia	**85**	**84**	**85**	11-18	14097	**4506**	**39**	**6****	**106**	**51**	**44**	**53**	**36**	**0.68**
175 Gabon	...	...	...	12-18	221	105**,y	...	30**,y	8y	34y	62**,y	...	...	...
176 Gambia	...	...	...	13-18	182	85**	45**	...	0.6**	77**	59	63	56	0.90
177 Ghana	**97****	**95****	**100****	12-17	3057	**1350****	**45****	**14****	21	14	**64**	**68**	**59**	**0.88**
178 Guinea	68	73	60	13-19	1349	349	31	10**	8**	46**	32	43	21	0.50
179 Guinea-Bissau	...	...	...	13-17	166	...	...	...	...	...	...	...	...	...
180 Kenya	95**	94**	97**	12-17	5041	2420**	48**	...	15**	46**	87	89	86	0.97
181 Lesotho	63	64	62	13-17	246	89	56	1.5	1.3	56	45	40	51	1.29
182 Liberia	...	...	...	12-17	461	...	...	...	...	...	...	...	...	...
183 Madagascar	55	56	55	11-17	2870	...	...	...	...	...	25**	25**	25**	0.98**
184 Malawi	76x	78x	73x	12-17	1751	505	45	...	.	.	41	44	37	0.83
185 Mali	60	62	57	13-18	1781	398	37**	22	49	42**	30	37	23	0.62
186 Mauritius	**67****	**61****	**72****	11-17	143	**128****	**49****	73y	**18****	**31****	99	98	100	1.02
187 Mozambique	45x	43x	46x	13-17	2261	243	41	...	24	28	16	19	13	0.67
188 Namibia	88**,y	87**,y	88**,y	13-17	253	141z	53z	4y	.z	.z	74z	68z	80z	1.17z
189 Niger	49	51	48	13-19	2013	158	39	12	3	43	11	13	9	0.68
190 Nigeria	...	...	...	12-17	18250	6316	44	...	...	...	37	41	33	0.82
191 Rwanda	...	...	...	13-18	1420	204	48	44z	72	48	18	19	17	0.89
192 Sao Tome and Principe	55	57	53	13-17	18	7	50	–	0.1	23	63	59	66	1.11
193 Senegal	47	49	45	13-19	1859	360	42	26	4	40	25	29	21	0.75
194 Seychelles[5]	95	93	97	12-16	...	7	51	4z	.	.	109	106	112*	1.06
195 Sierra Leone	...	...	...	12-17	682	...	...	...	...	...	...	...	...	...
196 Somalia	...	...	...	13-17	825	...	...	...	...	...	...	...	...	...
197 South Africa	95y	94y	96y	14-18	4918	4447z	51z	3z	260z	40z	95z	92z	97z	1.06z
198 Swaziland	77y	76y	78y	13-17	150	62z	50z	–z	0.7z	26z	50z	49z	51z	1.04z
199 Togo	64	67	61	12-18	964	375	33	26	20	18	54	69	38	0.55
200 Uganda	36**	36**	36**	13-18	3944	**651****	**44****	45	**32****	**32****	**19****	**21****	**17****	**0.82****
201 United Republic of Tanzania	33**	34**	33**	13-19	5289	...	...	...	...	...	...	...	...	...
202 Zambia	54**,x	52**,x	57**,x	14-18	1411	364	44	4	7	8	40	43	36	0.84
203 Zimbabwe	70**,y	69**,y	70**,y	13-18	2099	758z	48z	71y	.z	.z	55z	56z	53z	0.95z

		Median			Sum	Sum	% F	Median	Sum	% F	Weighted average			
I	World	94	94	94	...	772990	502560	47	12	49224	46	78	80	76	0.94
II	Countries in transition	99	98	100	...	32516	29770	49	0.5	2937	37	92	93	92	0.99
III	Developed countries	99	99	99	...	84125	85067	49	7	15291	44	103	103	103	1.00
IV	Developing countries	87	84	89	...	656350	387723	47	17	30996	48	74	77	71	0.93
V	Arab States	92	90	93	...	41163	27272	47	9	3814	43	79	84	74	0.88
VI	Central and Eastern Europe	99	98	99	...	40760	36880	48	1	6959	39	92	93	91	0.98
VII	Central Asia	99	98	100	...	11933	10729	48	1	577	41	95	96	93	0.98
VIII	East Asia and the Pacific	88	89	87	...	219134	159785	48	19	18904	49	93	94	93	1.00
IX	East Asia	91	88	94	...	215814	156337	48	13	17778	50	93	94	93	1.00
X	Pacific	85	84	86	...	3320	3449	48	...	1126	45	88	89	88	0.99
XI	Latin America/Caribbean	94	94	94	...	66657	57109	51	24	5710	55	100	97	102	1.05
XII	Caribbean	94	94	94	...	2191	1270	50	26	40	49	75	73	76	1.04
XIII	Latin America	93	93	93	...	64466	55838	51	22	5670	55	100	98	103	1.05
XIV	N. America/W. Europe	100	100	99	...	61893	62685	49	9	10047	45	103	103	104	1.01
XV	South and West Asia	88	91	85	...	229189	117524	44	16	1359	36	64	69	59	0.86
XVI	Sub-Saharan Africa	64	67	61	...	102261	30576	43	14	1854	36	36	41	32	0.78

1. Refers to lower and upper secondary education (ISCED levels 2 and 3).
2. Corresponds to ISCED level 4. Like secondary education, it includes general as well as technical and vocational programmes.
3. Data are for 2003 except for countries with a calendar school year, in which case data are for 2004.
4. Enrolment data for upper secondary education include adult education, which explains the high level of GER.
5. National population data were used to calculate enrolment ratios.

GROSS ENROLMENT RATIO (GER) IN SECONDARY EDUCATION (%)								NET ENROLMENT RATIO (NER) IN SECONDARY EDUCATION (%)				INTERNAL EFFICIENCY			POST-SECONDARY NON-TERTIARY EDUCATION		
Upper secondary				Total secondary				Total secondary				Repeaters in secondary general education (%)			Total enrolment		
School year ending in 2004				School year ending in 2004				School year ending in 2004				School year ending in 2004			School year ending in 2004		
Total	Male	Female	GPI (F/M)	Total	Male	Female	GPI (F/M)	Total	Male	Female	GPI (F/M)	Total	Male	Female	Total (000)	% F	
27	30	24	0.78	35	40	30	0.76	...	...	...	...	16.4	15.4	17.7	0.7**	46**	168
21**	25**	17**	0.69**	39**	42**	35**	0.84**	...	...	...	...	24.2	23.5**	25.0**	6	68	169
...	...	...	...	25**,y	32**,y	18**,y	0.55**,y	20**,y	26**,y	15**,y	0.57**,y	15.8y	15.8y	15.8y	...	...	170
...	...	...	...	...	...	...	...	...	...	...	...	...	...	...	.	.	171
13y	17y	8y	0.45y	30**,y	38**,y	22**,y	0.57**,y	...	...	...	...	...	...	...	.	.	172
19	26	13	0.49	34	43	24	0.56	24	28	19	0.66	17.0	16.4	18.3	1.1**	8**	173
16	**20**	**11**	**0.58**	**31**	**37**	**25**	**0.65**	**28****	**34****	**22****	**0.65****	9.3z	7.8z	12.0z	**30****	**39****	174
32**,y	...	...	...	50**,y	...	...	...	...	...	...	...	21.7**,y	...	...			175
33**	39**	28**	0.71**	47**	51**	42**	0.83**	45**	49**	41**	0.83**	...	...	...	1.7z	71z	176
23**	**25****	**20****	**0.78****	**44****	**47****	**40****	**0.85****	**37****	**39****	**35****	**0.90****	2.4**,z	2.4**,z	2.5**,z	19**,z	29**,z	177
16**	22**	9**	0.42**	26	34	17	0.48	21**	28**	14**	0.51**	11.8	10.6	14.5	.	.	178
...	...	...	...	...	...	...	...	...	...	...	...	...	...	...			179
29**	30**	27**	0.89**	48**	50**	46**	0.93**	40**	40**	40**	1.01**	...	...	...	10**	82**	180
23	21	25	1.21	36	32	41	1.27	23	18	28	1.54	9.2	9.3	9.0	0.6**	50**	181
...	...	...	...	...	...	...	...	...	...	...	...	...	...	...	.	.	182
...	...	...	...	...	...	...	...	...	...	...	...	14.3	14.5	14.2	17**,y	34**,y	183
16	18	13	0.73	29	32	26	0.81	25	27	23	0.86	...	...	...	...	...	184
14	18**	10**	0.57**	22	28**	17**	0.61**	...	...	...	...	...	...	...	.	.	185
80**	**81****	**78****	**0.96****	**88****	**89****	**88****	**0.99****	**82****	**82****	**83****	**1.01****	12.3	13.7	11.1	9	22	186
3	3	3	1.00	11	13	9	0.70	4	5	4	0.78	22.3	21.8	22.9	.	.	187
30z	30z	30z	1.00z	58z	54z	62z	1.14z	37z	32z	43z	1.35z	7.8**,z	6.8**,z	8.6**,z	3z	31z	188
3	4	2	0.58	8	9	6	0.67	7	8	5	0.68	7.3	6.7	8.1	0.4	46	189
32	35	28	0.81	35	38	31	0.81	27**	30**	25**	0.82**	...	...	...	...	...	190
10	11	10	0.89	14	15	14	0.89	...	...	...	...	...	...	...	.	.	191
26	26	25	0.96	40	39	41	1.05	26	25	27	1.07	32.4	30.8	34.0	0.4	41	192
11	13	9	0.64	19	22	16	0.72	15	18	13	0.72	12.3	12.2	12.6	...	...	193
92	87	98	1.12	102	98	106	1.08	93	90	96	1.07	.z	.z	.z	1.7	59	194
...	...	...	...	...	...	...	...	...	...	...	...	...	...	...	.z	.z	195
...	...	...	...	...	...	...	...	...	...	...	...	...	...	...	.z	.z	196
88z	84z	91z	1.08z	90z	87z	94z	1.07z	...	...	...	...	10.9z	11.4z	10.4z	171z	40z	197
29z	30z	28z	0.92z	42z	42z	42z	1.01z	29z	26z	32z	1.24z	12.0z	12.3z	11.7z	.z	.z	198
17	27	8	0.29	39	52	26	0.50	...	...	...	...	22.6	22.8	22.3	...	...	199
9**	**11****	**7****	**0.66****	**16****	**18****	**14****	**0.79****	**13****	**14****	**12****	**0.87****	1.9	1.9	1.9	.	.	200
...	...	...	...	...	...	...	...	...	...	...	...	**3.2****	**2.5****	**4.1****	−y	−y	201
16	18	13	0.71	26	29	23	0.79	24**	27**	21**	0.78**	5.1	5.0	5.2	.	.	202
27z	29z	25z	0.86z	36z	38z	35z	0.91z	34z	35z	33z	0.93z	.z	.z	.z	0.9z	11z	203
Weighted average				Weighted average				Weighted average				Median			Sum	% F	
51	53	50	0.94	65	67	63	0.94	58	59	56	0.95	3.2	4.2	2.3	...	...	I
90	93	88	0.95	92	93	91	0.98	84	84	84	0.99	0.2	0.3	0.1	...	...	II
99	99	100	1.01	101	101	101	1.01	91	90	92	1.02	1.7	2.9	0.5	...	...	III
44	46	42	0.92	59	61	57	0.92	52	54	50	0.93	6.1	6.7	5.5	...	...	IV
52	53	51	0.96	66	69	63	0.91	56	58	54	0.93	7.3	8.5	6.1	...	...	V
88	91	85	0.93	90	92	88	0.96	82	83	81	0.98	1.2	1.9	0.5	...	...	VI
78	82	75	0.92	90	92	88	0.96	85	86	84	0.97	0.2	0.3	0.1	...	...	VII
51	51	51	1.00	73	73	73	1.00	69	69	69	1.00	2.2	2.2	2.3	...	...	VIII
50	50	50	1.00	72	72	72	1.00	69	69	69	1.00	2.1	2.6	1.6	...	...	IX
131	132	130	0.98	104	105	103	0.98	68	68	69	1.01	...	...	...	...	...	X
69	64	73	1.14	86	82	89	1.08	67	65	69	1.06	3.2	4.0	2.3	...	...	XI
42	41	43	1.04	58	56	59	1.04	41	39	43	1.10	1.9	2.2	1.6	...	...	XII
70	65	75	1.14	87	83	90	1.08	67	66	69	1.06	3.7	4.3	3.0	...	...	XIII
99	99	100	1.01	101	101	102	1.01	91	90	92	1.02	2.1	3.1	1.0	...	...	XIV
40	44	35	0.80	51	56	46	0.83	45	49	41	0.83	...	...	...	...	...	XV
23	25	20	0.78	30	34	26	0.78	24	26	21	0.81	12.3	12.2	12.6	...	...	XVI

6. Enrolment ratios were not calculated due to lack of United Nations population data by age.
7. Enrolment ratios were not calculated due to inconsistencies between enrolment and the United Nations population data.

Data in bold are for the school year ending in 2005.

(z) Data are for the school year ending in 2003.
(y) Data are for the school year ending in 2002.
(x) Data are for school year ending in 2001.

Table 9
Participation in tertiary education

	ENROLMENT IN TERTIARY EDUCATION													
	Total students enrolled (000)						Gross enrolment ratio (GER) (%)							
	School year ending in						School year ending in							
	1999			2004			1999				2004			
Country or territory	Total	Male	Female	Total	Male	Female	Total	Male	Female	GPI (F/M)	Total	Male	Female	GPI (F/M)
Arab States														
Algeria	456**	...	...	716	351	365	14**	...	...	...	20	19	20	1.08
Bahrain	11	4**	7**	19**	7**	12**	21	16**	27**	1.76**	34**	25**	45**	1.84**
Djibouti	0.2	...	...	1.1	0.6	0.5	0.3	...	...	...	2	2	1	0.82
Egypt	2 447**	...	...	2 512**	...	...	36**	...	...	...	33**	...	...	...
Iraq	272	179	93	413	263	149	11	15	8	0.54	15	19	11	0.59
Jordan	...	...	...	214	104	110	...	...	...	...	39	37	41	1.10
Kuwait	32**	10**	22**	42**	12**	30**	23**	14**	34**	2.39**	22**	12**	33**	2.72**
Lebanon	113	56	57	155	74	81	36	36	37	1.04	48	45	50	1.12
Libyan Arab Jamahiriya	308	158**	150**	359ʸ	175ʸ	185ʸ	53	53**	52**	0.98**	55ʸ	53ʸ	58ʸ	1.09ʸ
Mauritania	13	...	...	9	7	2	5	...	...	...	3	5	2	0.31
Morocco	273	159	114	344	187	157	9	10	8	0.74	11	11	10	0.87
Oman	...	...	...	34	15	19	...	...	...	...	13	11	15	1.37
Palestinian A. T.	66	36	30	122	62	60	25	26	23	0.89	38	37	39	1.04
Qatar	9**	3**	6**	9**	3**	6**	25**	13**	41**	3.23**	18**	10**	30**	3.05**
Saudi Arabia	350	150	199	574	237	337	20	17	24	1.38	28	22	33	1.50
Sudan	201	106	95	...	...	...	6	6	6	0.92	...	...	...	...
Syrian Arab Republic	...	...	...	...	...	...	...	...	...	...	...	...	...	...
Tunisia	157**	81**	76**	292	127	165	17**	17**	17**	0.97**	29	24	33	1.36
United Arab Emirates	40**	13**	27**	68**,ᶻ	23**,ᶻ	45**,ᶻ	19**	10**	31**	3.03**	22**,ᶻ	12**,ᶻ	39**,ᶻ	3.24**,ᶻ
Yemen	164	130	34	192	142	50	10	16	4	0.28	9	14	5	0.38
Central and Eastern Europe														
Albania	39	15	23	44ᶻ	16ᶻ	27ᶻ	16	13	18	1.40	16ᶻ	13ᶻ	20ᶻ	1.56ᶻ
Belarus	387	171	216	507	218	290	52	45	59	1.32	61	51	71	1.39
Bosnia and Herzegovina	...	...	...	...	...	...	...	...	...	...	...	...	...	...
Bulgaria	270	109	161	228	109	120	46	36	56	1.54	41	38	44	1.16
Croatia	96	45	51	122ᶻ	57ᶻ	65ᶻ	31	28	33	1.16	39ᶻ	35ᶻ	42ᶻ	1.19ᶻ
Czech Republic	231	116	115	319	155	163	26	26	27	1.03	43	41	45	1.10
Estonia	49	21	28	66	25	41	51	42	60	1.42	65	49	82	1.68
Hungary	279	128	151	422	180	242	33	30	37	1.24	60	50	70	1.40
Latvia	82	32	51	128	48	79	50	38	62	1.64	74	55	94	1.72
Lithuania	107	43	64	183	73	110	44	35	53	1.52	73	57	89	1.56
Poland	1 399	601	798	2 044	868	1 177	44	37	52	1.38	61	51	72	1.41
Republic of Moldova	104	46	58	127	54	72	29	25	32	1.28	32	27	37	1.37
Romania	408	200	208	686	310	376	22	21	23	1.09	40	36	45	1.26
Russian Federation	...	...	...	8 622**	3 708**	4 915**	...	...	...	...	68**	58**	79**	1.36**
Serbia and Montenegro[2]	197	92	106	...	...	...	34	31	37	1.19	...	...	...	...
Slovakia	123	59	64	165	76	89	26	25	28	1.11	36	33	40	1.23
Slovenia	79	35	44	104	45	59	53	45	61	1.36	74	62	86	1.38
TFYR Macedonia	35	16	19	47	20	27	22	19	24	1.28	28	23	33	1.39
Turkey	1 465	884	581	1 973	1 156	817	22	25	17	0.68	29	34	24	0.73
Ukraine	1 737	821	916	2 465	1 136*	1 329*	47	44	51	1.14	66	60*	71*	1.19*
Central Asia														
Armenia	61	28	33	79	35	44	24	22	25	1.11	26	24	29	1.21
Azerbaijan	108	66	42	123	66	56	15	19	12	0.64	15	16	14	0.87
Georgia	130	63	68	155	77	78	36	35	37	1.07	41	41	42	1.03
Kazakhstan	324	151	173	664	283	382	25	23	26	1.16	48	40	56	1.38
Kyrgyzstan	131	65	67	205	94	111	29	28	30	1.04	40	36	43	1.19
Mongolia	65	23	42	109	42	67	26	18	34	1.88	39	29	48	1.64
Tajikistan	76	57	19	108	82	27	13	19	7	0.35	16	25	8	0.33
Turkmenistan	...	...	...	...	...	...	...	...	...	...	...	...	...	...
Uzbekistan	...	...	...	408**	229**	179**	...	...	...	...	15**	17**	14**	0.80**
East Asia and the Pacific														
Australia	846	388	458	1 003	460	543	66	59	72	1.22	72	65	80	1.23
Brunei Darussalam	3	1	2	**4.9**	**1.7**	**3.2**	10	7	13	1.87	**15**	**10**	**20**	**1.98**
Cambodia	...	...	...	45	31	14	...	...	...	...	3	4	2	0.46
China	6 366	...	...	19 417	10 905**	8 512**	6	...	...	...	19	21**	17**	0.85**
Cook Islands	.	.	.	.	.	.	.	.	.	.	.	.	.	.

Table 9

DISTRIBUTION OF STUDENTS BY ISCED LEVEL (%) / FOREIGN STUDENTS (000)

Total students School year ending in 2004			Percentage of females at each level School year ending in 2004			School year ending in 1999			2004			Country or territory
Level 5A	Level 5B	Level 6	Level 5A	Level 5B	Level 6	Total	Male	Female	Total	Male	Female	
												Arab States
77	19	4	57	26	43	...	...	...	4.7	...	...	Algeria
82**	18**	0.0**	65**	55**	50**	...	...	...	1.3z	0.9z	0.4z	Bahrain
62	38	.	42	49	.	–	–	–	–y	–y	–y	Djibouti
89**	...	0.7**	...	...	...	...	...	...	...	...	...	Egypt
78	17	5	39	22	35	...	...	...	3.6	2.9	0.7	Iraq
84	11	5	51	61	34	...	...	...	23.2	15.8	7.4	Jordan
...	...	...	...	...	...	...	...	...	...	...	...	Kuwait
85	14	1	54	45	35	15.6	...	...	13.9	7.0	7.0	Lebanon
72y	26y	2y	52y	50y	38y	...	...	...	...	...	...	Libyan Arab Jamahiriya
94**	5**	0.9**	24**	20**	6**	...	...	...	0.2**	...	...	Mauritania
82	13	5	46	46	33	4.2	3.5	0.7	6.4	4.8	1.6	Morocco
99	.	1	56	.	22	...	...	...	...	...	...	Oman
90	10	.	49	49	.	2.8	2.0	0.8	–	–	–	Palestinian A. T.
98**	1**	0.2**	67**	76**	21**	...	...	...	1.6z	0.7z	1.0z	Qatar
84	14	2	66	18	35	6.1	4.5	1.5	12.2	8.4	3.8	Saudi Arabia
...	...	...	...	...	...	...	...	...	...	...	...	Sudan
...	...	...	...	...	...	...	...	...	...	...	...	Syrian Arab Republic
70	23	7	...	...	...	2.7j	...	...	2.3	...	...	Tunisia
...	...	...	...	...	...	...	...	...	...	...	...	United Arab Emirates
...	...	...	...	...	...	...	...	...	...	...	...	Yemen
												Central and Eastern Europe
99z	1z	./.1,z	62z	81z	./.1,z	0.8	0.6	0.2	0.5z	0.4z	0.1z	Albania
67	32	1	58	56	52	2.7	...	...	2.4	...	...	Belarus
...	...	...	...	...	...	...	...	...	...	...	...	Bosnia and Herzegovina
91	7	2	52	57	51	8.4	4.9	3.5	8.3	4.9	3.4	Bulgaria
66z	34z	0.2z	55z	50z	36z	0.5j	...	...	2.8z	1.5z	1.3z	Croatia
82	10	7	51	66	36	4.6	2.7	1.9**	14.9	7.5	7.4	Czech Republic
60	37	3	61	63	54	0.8	0.3	0.5	0.8	0.4	0.4	Estonia
93	5	2	57	62	42	8.9j	4.1	4.8	12.9	6.0	6.9	Hungary
87	12	1	63	55	58	1.8j	...	...	1.3	...	...	Latvia
70	29	1	59	62	56	0.5	0.4	0.1	0.7	0.4	0.3	Lithuania
97	1	2	57	81	48	5.7j	3.0	2.7	8.1	3.6	4.5	Poland
84	15	2	57	56	60	1.7	...	...	2.5	1.6	0.9	Republic of Moldova
91	7	3	55	57	51	13.3	8.0	5.3	10.5	...	...	Romania
75**	23**	...	58	55	...	41.2	...	...	75.8	...	...	Russian Federation
...	...	...	...	...	...	1.3	0.8	0.5	...	...	...	Serbia and Montenegro[2]
91	3	6	54	78	41	...	...	...	1.5	0.9	0.6z	Slovakia
50	50	–	60	53	–	0.7	0.4	0.3	0.9	0.4	0.5z	Slovenia
94	6	–	58	48	–	0.3	0.2	0.1	0.1	0.1	0.1z	TFYR Macedonia
70	29	1	43	39	39	18.3v	13.1	5.2	15.3	10.5	4.8z	Turkey
75	24	1	54*	53*	50	18.3	...	...	15.6	...	...	Ukraine
												Central Asia
98	.	2	56	.	35	...	...	...	3.3	2.5	0.8	Armenia
99	.	1	46	.	27	1.7	1.1	0.6	2.0	1.6	0.4	Azerbaijan
99	.	1	50	.	64	0.3	...	...	1.1	...	...	Georgia
99	.	1	57	.	52	7.5	...	...	8.7	...	...	Kazakhstan
99	.	1	54	.	64	1.1	0.5**	0.6**	16.2	7.5*	8.8*	Kyrgyzstan
93	6	1	62	61	59	0.3	0.1	0.1	0.4	0.2	0.2	Mongolia
99	.	1	25	.	31	5.0	3.7**	1.3**	2.2	1.8	0.4	Tajikistan
...	...	...	...	...	...	...	...	...	...	...	...	Turkmenistan
59**	40**	1**	39**	51**	39**	...	...	...	...	...	...	Uzbekistan
												East Asia and the Pacific
80	16	4	55	51	49	117.5	60.0	57.5	167.0	91.6	75.4	Australia
62	**38**	**0.3**	**68**	**64**	**15**	0.1	0.05	0.05	**0.2**	**0.1**	**0.1**	Brunei Darussalam
99	.	1	31	.	27	0.02	0.02	0.01	0.04	0.03	0.01	Cambodia
51.6	47.7	0.7	44**	44**	28**	...	...	...	...	...	...	China
.	.	.	.	.	.	.	.	.	.	.	.	Cook Islands

Table 9 (continued)

Country or territory	ENROLMENT IN TERTIARY EDUCATION													
	Total students enrolled (000)						Gross enrolment ratio (GER) (%)							
	School year ending in						School year ending in							
	1999			2004			1999				2004			
	Total	Male	Female	Total	Male	Female	Total	Male	Female	GPI (F/M)	Total	Male	Female	GPI (F/M)
DPR Korea	…	…	…	…	…	…	…	…	…	…	…	…	…	…
Fiji	…	…	…	13	6	7	…	…	…	…	15	14	17	1.20
Indonesia	…	…	…	3 551	1 995	1 556	…	…	…	…	17	19	15	0.79
Japan	3 941	2 180	1 760	4 032	2 183	1 848	45	49	41	0.85	54	57	51	0.89
Kiribati	.	.	.	.	.	.	.	.	.	.	.	.	.	.
Lao PDR	12	8	4	34	21	13	2	3	2	0.49	6	7	5	0.63
Macao, China	7	4	3	25	15	10	27	31	24	0.77	69	84	54	0.65
Malaysia	473	237	237	726[z]	310[z]	415[z]	23	23	24	1.04	32[z]	27[z]	38[z]	1.41[z]
Marshall Islands	…	…	…	0.9**[z]	0.4**[z]	0.5**[z]	…	…	…	…	17**[z]	15**[z]	19**[z]	1.30**[z]
Micronesia	2	…	…	…	…	…	14	…	…	…	…	…	…	…
Myanmar	…	…	…	555**[y]	…	…	…	…	…	…	11**[y]	…	…	…
Nauru	.	.	.	.	.	.	.	.	.	.	.	.	.	.
New Zealand	167	69	99	179	77	103	67	55	79	1.45	63	53	74	1.40
Niue	.	.	.	.	.	.	.	.	.	.	.	.	.	.
Palau	…	…	…	0.5**[y]	0.2**[y]	0.3**[y]	…	…	…	…	40**[y]	27**[y]	57**[y]	2.15**[y]
Papua New Guinea	…	…	…	.	.	.	.	.	.	.	.	.	.	.
Philippines	2 209	995	1 213	2 421	1 085	1 336	29	25	32	1.26	29	25	32	1.28
Republic of Korea	2 636	1 713	923	**3 225**	**2 037**	**1 188**	66	83	47	0.57	**90**	**110**	**69**	**0.62**
Samoa	1.9	1.0	0.9	…	…	…	12	11	12	1.04	…	…	…	…
Singapore	…	…	…	…	…	…	.	.	.	.	.	.	.	.
Solomon Islands	.	.	.	.	.	.	.	.	.	.	.	.	.	.
Thailand	1 814	846	969	**2 359**	**1 123**	**1 236**	32	30	35	1.16	**43**	**41**	**45**	**1.11**
Timor-Leste	…	…	…	6*[y]	3*[y]	3*[y]	…	…	…	…	10*[y]	8*[y]	12*[y]	1.48*[y]
Tokelau	.	.	.	.	.	.	.	.	.	.	.	.	.	.
Tonga	0.4	0.2	0.2	0.7[z]	0.3[z]	0.4[z]	3	3	4	1.27	6[z]	5[z]	8[z]	1.68[z]
Tuvalu	.	.	.	.	.	.	.	.	.	.	.	.	.	.
Vanuatu	0.6**	…	…	0.96**	0.61**	0.35**	4**	…	…	…	5**	6**	4**	0.58**
Viet Nam	810	462	348	845**	482**	363**	11	12	9	0.76	10**	11**	9**	0.77**
Latin America and the Caribbean														
Anguilla	.	.	.	.	.	.	.	.	.	.	.	.	.	.
Antigua and Barbuda	.	.	.	.	.	.	.	.	.	.	.	.	.	.
Argentina	1 601	614	987	2 101[z]	848[z]	1 254[z]	49	37	60	1.63	64[z]	51[z]	77[z]	1.51[z]
Aruba[2]	1.4	0.7	0.8	1.7	0.7	1.0	26	24	28	1.16	29	23	34	1.51
Bahamas	.	.	.	.	.	.	.	.	.	.	.	.	.	.
Barbados	7	2	5	…	…	…	32	20	45	2.29	…	…	…	…
Belize	…	…	…	0.7	0.2	0.5	…	…	…	…	3	2	4	2.43
Bermuda[2]	…	…	…	2.0**[y]	0.9**[y]	1.1**[y]	…	…	…	…	62**[y]	…	…	…
Bolivia	253	…	…	346**	…	…	33	…	…	…	41**	…	…	…
Brazil	2 457	1 092	1 365	3 994[z]	1 740[z]	2 254[z]	14	13	16	1.26	22[z]	19[z]	25[z]	1.32[z]
British Virgin Islands	.	.	.	.	.	.	.	.	.	.	.	.	.	.
Cayman Islands[3]	0.4**	0.1**	0.3**	…	…	…	…	…	…	…	…	…	…	…
Chile	451	239	212	581	302	279	38	39	36	0.91	43	44	42	0.95
Colombia	878	420	458	1 113	542	571	22	21	23	1.11	27	26	28	1.09
Costa Rica	59	28	31	79**[z]	38**[z]	42**[z]	16	15	17	1.17	19**[z]	18**[z]	20**[z]	1.16**[z]
Cuba	153	72	82	236[z]	103[z]	133[z]	20	18	21	1.18	33[z]	28[z]	38[z]	1.34[z]
Dominica	.	.	.	.	.	.	.	.	.	.	.	.	.	.
Dominican Republic	…	…	…	294**	114**	180**	…	…	…	…	33**	25**	41**	1.64**
Ecuador	…	…	…	…	…	…	.	.	.	.	.	.	.	.
El Salvador	118	53	65	120	55	65	18	16	19	1.25	19	17	20	1.22
Grenada	.	.	.	.	.	.	.	.	.	.	.	.	.	.
Guatemala	…	…	…	115**[z]	65**[z]	49**[z]	…	…	…	…	10**[z]	11**[z]	8**[z]	0.72**[z]
Guyana	…	…	…	7	2	5	…	…	…	…	9	6	12	1.91
Haiti	…	…	…	…	…	…	.	.	.	.	.	.	.	.
Honduras	85**	38**	47**	123**	51**	72**	14**	12**	16**	1.29**	16**	13**	20**	1.46**
Jamaica	…	…	…	46**[z]	14**[z]	32**[z]	…	…	…	…	19**[z]	12**[z]	26**[z]	2.29**[z]
Mexico	1 838	950	888	2 323	1 162	1 160	18	19	17	0.92	23	24	23	0.98
Montserrat	.	.	.	.	.	.	.	.	.	.	.	.	.	.
Netherlands Antilles	2	1	1	2.3[y]	0.9[y]	1.4[y]	23	22	25	1.13	24[y]	19[y]	28[y]	1.49[y]
Nicaragua	…	…	…	104**[z]	50**[z]	54**[z]	…	…	…	…	18**[z]	17**[z]	19**[z]	1.11**[z]
Panama	109	43	66	130	51	79	41	31	50	1.59	46	35	57	1.59
Paraguay	66	28	38	149**	64**	85**	13	11	15	1.38	24**	21**	28**	1.37**

DISTRIBUTION OF STUDENTS BY ISCED LEVEL (%) / FOREIGN STUDENTS (000)

Total students — Level 5A	Level 5B	Level 6	% females — Level 5A	Level 5B	Level 6	1999 Total	Male	Female	2004 Total	Male	Female	Country or territory
...	...	...	...	...	...	...	...	...	...	...	...	DPR Korea
86	12	1	52	63	43	...	...	...	4.2	2.0**	2.2**	Fiji
73	26	2	42	49	35	0.3	...	...	0.4	...	...	Indonesia
74	24	2	41	63	29	56.6	32.0	24.5	117.9	60.8	57.1	Japan
.	.	.	.	.	.	...	...	...	...	...	...	Kiribati
41	59	.	40	37	.	0.08	0.07	0.01	0.22	0.15	0.06	Lao PDR
87	12	1	37	63	27	...	...	...	14.6	10.5	4.1	Macao, China
48z	50z	1z	58z	57z	40z	3.5	...	...	28y	...	...	Malaysia
14**,z	86**,z	—**,z	57**,z	56**,z	—**,z	...	...	...	...	...	...	Marshall Islands
...	...	...	...	...	...	...	...	...	...	...	...	Micronesia
99.3**,y	0.5**,y	0.2**,y	...	33**,y	...	...	...	...	...	...	...	Myanmar
.	.	.	.	.	.	.	.	.	.	.	.	Nauru
73	25	2	57	57	51	6.9	3.4	3.5	37.4	19.6**	17.9**	New Zealand
.	.	.	.	.	.	.	.	.	.	.	.	Niue
100**,y	.	.	63**,y	.	.	...	...	...	...	...	...	Palau
...	...	...	...	...	...	...	...	...	...	...	...	Papua New Guinea
90	10	0.4	55	53	63	3.5	...	...	2.2	...	...	Philippines
60	**39**	**1**	**37**	**37**	**31**	...	...	...	**10.8**	**5.8**	**5.0**	Republic of Korea
...	...	...	...	...	...	0.1	0.06	0.04	...	...	...	Samoa
...	...	...	...	...	...	...	...	...	...	...	...	Singapore
.	.	.	.	.	.	...	...	...	...	...	...	Solomon Islands
84	**16**	**0.3**	**53**	**47**	**51**	1.9j	...	...	4.1j,q,y	...	...	Thailand
...	...	...	...	...	...	...	...	...	...	...	...	Timor-Leste
.	.	.	.	.	.	.	.	.	.	.	.	Tokelau
30**,z	42**,z	28**,z	34**,z	97**,z	34**,z	...	...	...	...	...	...	Tonga
.	.	.	.	.	.	.	.	.	.	.	.	Tuvalu
...	...	...	...	...	...	...	...	...	...	...	...	Vanuatu
69**	28**	3**	52**	21**	37**	0.5	0.4	0.1	1.0z	0.9z	0.2z	Viet Nam
												Latin America and the Caribbean
.	.	.	.	.	.	.	.	.	.	.	.	Anguilla
.	.	.	.	.	.	.	.	.	.	.	.	Antigua and Barbuda
73z	26z	0.3z	56z	70z	57z	...	...	...	3y	...	...	Argentina
23	77	.	76	55	.	...	...	...	0.09z	0.08**,z	0.01**,z	Aruba 2
.	.	.	.	.	.	...	...	...	...	...	...	Bahamas
...	...	...	...	...	...	...	...	...	...	...	...	Barbados
100	.	.	70	.	.	...	...	...	—	—	—	Belize
.y	100**,y	.y	.y	55**,y	.y	...	...	...	...	...	...	Bermuda 2
...	...	...	...	...	...	...	...	...	...	...	...	Bolivia
...	...	3z	...	...	57z	...	...	...	1.2z	...	...	Brazil
.	.	.	.	.	.	.	.	.	.	.	.	British Virgin Islands
...	...	...	...	...	...	...	...	...	...	...	...	Cayman Islands 3
73.6	26.1	0.3	50	42	40	1.5	...	...	5z	...	...	Chile
81.8	18.1	0.1	52	46	35	...	...	...	...	...	...	Colombia
85.2**,z	14.6**,z	0.1**,z	54**,z	43**,z	53**,z	...	...	...	1.6	...	...	Costa Rica
99z	.z	1z	56z	.	37z	...	...	...	13.7	...	...	Cuba
.	.	.	.	.	.	...	...	...	...	...	.	Dominica
91**	8**	0.6**	65**	25**	40**	...	...	...	...	...	...	Dominican Republic
...	...	...	...	...	...	...	...	...	...	...	...	Ecuador
89**	11**	0.0**	54**	56**	9**	...	...	...	0.5z	0.2z	0.3z	El Salvador
.	.	.	.	.	.	...	...	...	...	...	.	Grenada
95**,z	5**,z	.**,z	42**,z	66**,z	.**,z	...	...	...	...	...	...	Guatemala
72	28	.	62	75	.	...	...	...	.	.	.	Guyana
...	...	...	...	...	...	...	...	...	...	...	...	Haiti
91**	9**	0.0**	58**	67**	33**	...	...	...	0.8z	0.5z	0.3z	Honduras
37**,z	56**,z	7**,z	73**,z	68**,z	71**,z	0.6	...	...	...	...	...	Jamaica
96	3	1	50	41	39	2.3	...	...	1.9y	...	...	Mexico
.	.	.	.	.	.	.	.	.	.	.	.	Montserrat
15y	64y	21y	44y	59y	73y	...	...	...	...	...	...	Netherlands Antilles
95**,z	5**,z	.**,z	52**,z	59**,z	.**,z	...	...	...	...	...	...	Nicaragua
87.0	12.9	0.1	62	53	59	...	...	...	...	...	...	Panama
81**	18**	...	55**	68**	...	...	...	...	...	...	...	Paraguay

Table 9 (continued)

	ENROLMENT IN TERTIARY EDUCATION														
	Total students enrolled (000)						Gross enrolment ratio (GER) (%)								
	School year ending in						School year ending in								
	1999			2004			1999				2004					
Country or territory	Total	Male	Female	Total	Male	Female	Total	Male	Female	GPI (F/M)	Total	Male	Female	GPI (F/M)		
Peru	…	…	…	897**	449**	448**	…	…	…	…	33**	33**	34**	1.03**		
Saint Kitts and Nevis	.	.	.	.	.	.	.	.	.	.	.	.	.	.		
Saint Lucia	…	…	…	2	1	2	…	…	…	…	14	6	22	3.46		
St Vincent/Grenad.	.	.	.	.	.	.	.	.	.	.	.	.	.	.		
Suriname	…	…	…	5ʸ	2ʸ	3ʸ	…	…	…	…	12ʸ	9ʸ	15ʸ	1.62ʸ		
Trinidad and Tobago	7.6	3.2	4.3	17	7	9	6	5	7	1.38	12	11	13	1.26		
Turks and Caicos Islands[2]	0.03	–	0.03	0.01	–	0.01	…	…	…	…	0.4	–	0.8	.		
Uruguay	91**	34**	57**	101**,ᶻ	34**,ᶻ	67**,ᶻ	34**	25**	44**	1.76**	39**,ᶻ	26**,ᶻ	53**,ᶻ	2.04**,ᶻ		
Venezuela	…	…	…	983**,ᶻ	482**,ᶻ	502**,ᶻ	…	…	…	…	39**,ᶻ	38**,ᶻ	41**,ᶻ	1.08**,ᶻ		
North America and Western Europe																
Andorra	…	…	…	0.3	0.2	0.2	…	…	…	…	9**	9**	9**	1.00**		
Austria	253	126	127	239	111	127	54	52	55	1.04	50	46	54	1.19		
Belgium	352	166	185	386	178	208	56	52	60	1.15	63	57	69	1.21		
Canada	1 193	529	664	1 255ʸ	547ʸ	708ʸ	59	51	67	1.32	60ʸ	51ʸ	70ʸ	1.36ʸ		
Cyprus[2]	11	5	6	21	11	10	21	19	23	1.25	36	36	35	0.98		
Denmark	190	83	107	217	92	126	56	48	64	1.33	74	61	87	1.42		
Finland	263	121	142	300	140	160	82	74	91	1.22	90	82	98	1.20		
France	2 012	917	1 095	2 160	971	1 189	52	47	58	1.24	56	49	63	1.28		
Germany	…	…	…	…	…	…	…	…	…	…	…	…	…	…		
Greece	388	193	195	597	288	309	47	45	49	1.11	79	73	86	1.17		
Iceland	8	3	5	11**	4**	7**	40	30	50	1.68	52**	38**	67**	1.78**		
Ireland	151	70	81	188	84	104	45	41	49	1.20	59	51	66	1.28		
Israel	247	105	142	301	133	168	48	40	57	1.44	56	49	65	1.33		
Italy	1 797	806	991	1 986	870	1 117	47	41	53	1.28	63	54	72	1.34		
Luxembourg	2.7	1.3	1.4	3**	1**	2**	11	10	11	1.09	12**	11**	13**	1.18**		
Malta	6	3	3	8	3	4	20	18	21	1.13	26	23	30	1.34		
Monaco	.	.	.	.	.	.	.	.	.	.	.	.	.	.		
Netherlands	470	238	232	543	267	277	50	50	50	1.01	59	57	62	1.08		
Norway	187	80	108	214	86	127	66	56	78	1.40	80	64	98	1.54		
Portugal	357	157	199	395	174	221	45	39	51	1.30	57	49	65	1.32		
San Marino	…	…	…	…	…	…	…	…	…	…	…	…	…	…		
Spain	1 787	839	948	1 840	850	990	55	50	60	1.18	66	59	72	1.22		
Sweden	335	142	193	430	174	256	64	53	75	1.41	84	66	102	1.55		
Switzerland	156	91	65	196	108	88	38	44	31	0.70	47	52	42	0.80		
United Kingdom	2 081	974	1 107	2 247	965	1 282	60	56	64	1.15	60	51	70	1.37		
United States	13 769	6 106**	7 663**	16 900	7 256	9 645	73	63**	83**	1.31**	82	69	96	1.39		
South and West Asia																
Afghanistan	…	…	…	28	22	6	…	…	…	…	1	2	0.5	0.28		
Bangladesh	709	480	229	877ᶻ	596ᶻ	281ᶻ	6	8	4	0.51	7ᶻ	9ᶻ	4ᶻ	0.50ᶻ		
Bhutan[4]	1.5**	0.9**	0.5**	…	…	…	…	…	…	…	…	…	…	…		
India	…	…	…	11 853	7 325	4 528	…	…	…	…	12	14	9	0.66		
Iran, Islamic Republic of	1 308	740	568	1 955	951	1 004	19	21	17	0.80	22	21	24	1.11		
Maldives	.	.	.	0.07ᶻ	0.02ᶻ	0.05ᶻ	.	.	.	.	0.2ᶻ	0.1ᶻ	0.3ᶻ	2.37ᶻ		
Nepal	…	…	…	147	107	41	…	…	…	…	6	8	3	0.40		
Pakistan	…	…	…	521	298	222	…	…	…	…	3	4	3	0.80		
Sri Lanka	…	…	…	…	…	…	…	…	…	…	…	…	…	…		
Sub-Saharan Africa																
Angola	8	5	3	13**,ᶻ	8**,ᶻ	5**,ᶻ	0.6	0.7	0.5	0.63	0.8**,ᶻ	1.0**,ᶻ	0.7**,ᶻ	0.66**,ᶻ		
Benin	16	13	3	…	…	…	3	4	1	0.26	…	…	…	…		
Botswana	5.5	3.1	2.4	13	7	6	3	3	3	0.79	6	7	6	0.85		
Burkina Faso	10	8	2	19**	15**	4**	1	2	0.5	0.30	2**	3**	0.8**	0.29**		
Burundi	5	4	1	16	11	4	1.0	1.4	0.6	0.41	2	3	1	0.37		
Cameroon	67	…	…	84*	51**	33**	5	…	…	…	5*	6**	4**	0.64**		
Cape Verde	0.7	…	…	3.0	1.4	1.6	2	…	…	…	6	5	6	1.10		
Central African Republic	6	5	1	…	…	…	1.8	3.1	0.6	0.18	…	…	…	…		
Chad	…	…	…	…	…	…	…	…	…	…	…	…	…	…		
Comoros	0.6	0.4	0.3	1.8**	1.0**	0.8**	1	1	0.9	0.75	2**	3**	2**	0.77**		
Congo	11	8	2	12**,ᶻ	10**,ᶻ	2**,ᶻ	4	6	1	0.26	4**,ᶻ	6**,ᶻ	1**,ᶻ	0.19**,ᶻ		

DISTRIBUTION OF STUDENTS BY ISCED LEVEL (%) · FOREIGN STUDENTS (000)

Total students School year ending in 2004			Percentage of females at each level School year ending in 2004			1999			2004			Country or territory
Level 5A	Level 5B	Level 6	Level 5A	Level 5B	Level 6	Total	Male	Female	Total	Male	Female	
56**	44**	...	45	56	...	...	...	...	...	...	...	Peru
.	.	.	.	.	.	...	.	.	.	.	.	Saint Kitts and Nevis
86	14	.	79	71	.	...	.	.	.	.	.	Saint Lucia
.	.	.	.	.	.	...	.	.	.	.	.	St Vincent/Grenad.
63**,y	37**,y	.y	49**,y	84**,y	.y	...	...	...	...	...	...	Suriname
52	34	15	60	48	57	1.0	0.5	0.5	1.0	0.4**	0.5**	Trinidad and Tobago
.	100	.	.	100	.	.	.	.	—	—		Turks and Caicos Islands[2]
74**,z	26**,z	...	60z	85z	...	0.9	...	...	...	...	...	Uruguay
62**,z	34**,z	4**,z	47**,z	58**,z	...	...	...	...	2.5	...	...	Venezuela
												North America and Western Europe
28	72	.	60	44	.	...	...	...	0.03**,z	...	...	Andorra
83	11	7	52	66	46	29.8	15.2	14.6	33.7	16.0	17.7	Austria
46	52	2	51	57	39	36.1	18.9	17.2	26.2	...	...	Belgium
73y	25y	2y	58y	52y	46y	35.5j	20.0	15.6	87.6y	46.2y	41.5y	Canada
19	80	1	75	41	50	1.9	1.1	0.7	6.7	5.2	1.5	Cyprus[2]
85	13	2	60	48	43	12.3	4.8	7.5	9.9	3.8	6.1	Denmark
93	0	7	54	45	51	4.8	2.8	2.0	10.3	5.8	4.5	Finland
71	24	5	55	56	47	131.0±	...	...	237.6	...	...	France
...	...	...	...	...	...	178.2	96.2	82.0	260.3	130.8	129.5	Germany
63	34	3	54	49	42	...	...	...	12z	...	...	Greece
94.1**	5.6**	0.3**	64**	51**	53**	0.2	0.1	0.1	0.6z	0.2z	0.4z	Iceland
64	34	2	57	52	46	7.2eo	...	...	12.7	6.3	6.4	Ireland
80	17	3	57	51	53	...	...	...	...	...	...	Israel
97	1	2	56	66	51	23.5	11.7	11.8	40.6	17.5	23.2	Italy
59.6**	39.5**	0.9**	54**	52**	52**	0.7j	...	...	...	...	...	Luxembourg
85	15	0.2	55	60	24	0.3j	0.1	0.2	0.4	0.2	0.2	Malta
.	.	.	.	.	.	.	.	.	.	.	.	Monaco
99	.	1	51	.	41	13.6	7.4	6.3	26.2	12.0	14.1	Netherlands
96	2	2	60	55	43	9.0	4.2	4.8	9.7	4.2	5.5	Norway
94	1	4	56	54	54	...	...	...	16.2	8.2	7.9	Portugal
...	...	...	...	...	...	...	...	...	...	...	...	San Marino
82	14	4	54	51	51	33.0	16.2	16.7	15.1	7.3	7.7	Spain
91	4	5	61	48	47	24.4	13.5	11.0	17.3	8.6	8.7	Sweden
72	20	8	47	41	39	25.3	14.2	11.1	35.7	19.6	16.1	Switzerland
73	23	4	55	67	44	232.5	124.2	108.3	300.1	157.7	142.4	United Kingdom
77	21	2	56	60	51	451.9	262.6	189.4	572.5	...	...	United States
												South and West Asia
...	...	...	...	...	...	...	...	...	...	...	...	Afghanistan
90.7z	9.1z	0.2z	34z	14z	28z	...	...	...	0.4z	...	...	Bangladesh
...	...	...	...	...	...	...	...	...	...	...	...	Bhutan[4]
99	.	0.6	38	.	39	...	...	...	7.6	...	...	India
74	25	0.8	55	42	25	...	...	...	1.8	1.0	0.7	Iran, Islamic Republic of
.z	100z	.z	.**	70**	.**	.	.	.	—z	—z	—z	Maldives
99**	.**	0.6**	28**	.**	23**	...	...	...	...	...	...	Nepal
96	3	2	43	29	28	...	...	...	0.4z	...	...	Pakistan
...	...	...	...	...	...	...	...	...	—z	—z	—z	Sri Lanka
												Sub-Saharan Africa
100**,z	.z	—**,z	40**,z	.z	—**,z	...	...	...	...	...	...	Angola
...	...	...	...	...	...	...	...	...	...	...	...	Benin
67	19	14	45	47	44	...	...	...	...	...	...	Botswana
...	...	...	...	...	...	...	...	...	...	...	...	Burkina Faso
32.5	67.1	0.4	25	29	19	0.1	...	...	0.5y	...	...	Burundi
...	...	...	...	...	...	...	...	...	1.5	...	...	Cameroon
99.7	.	0.3	53	.	63	...	...	...	...	...	...	Cape Verde
...	...	...	...	...	...	...	...	...	...	...	...	Central African Republic
...	...	...	...	...	...	...	...	...	...	...	...	Chad
68**	32**	.**	39**	52**	.	.	.	.	...	...	...	Comoros
84.4**,z	15.0**,z	0.6**,z	16**,z	13**,z	31**,z	...	...	...	0.1	...	...	Congo

Table 9 (continued)

Country or territory	ENROLMENT IN TERTIARY EDUCATION													
	Total students enrolled (000)						Gross enrolment ratio (GER) (%)							
	School year ending in						School year ending in							
	1999			2004			1999				2004			
	Total	Male	Female	Total	Male	Female	Total	Male	Female	GPI (F/M)	Total	Male	Female	GPI (F/M)
Côte d'Ivoire	97	71	25	…	…	…	6	10	3	0.36	…	…	…	…
D. R. Congo	60**	…	…	…	…	…	1**	…	…	…	…	…	…	…
Equatorial Guinea	…	…	…	…	…	…	…	…	…	…	…	…	…	…
Eritrea	4	3	1	5	4	1	1	2	0.3	0.15	1.1	1.9	0.3	0.15
Ethiopia	52	43	10	172	129	43	0.9	1.4	0.3	0.23	2	4	1	0.34
Gabon	7.5	4.8	2.7	…	…	…	7	9	5	0.54	…	…	…	…
Gambia	1	1	0.3	1.5	1.2	0.3	1.1	1.7	0.5	0.29	1.2	1.9	0.5	0.23
Ghana	…	…	…	70	48	22	…	…	…	…	3	4	2	0.48
Guinea	…	…	…	17	15	3	…	…	…	…	2.2	3.6	0.7	0.20
Guinea-Bissau	0.5**	0.4**	0.1**	…	…	…	0.4**	0.7**	0.1**	0.18**	…	…	…	…
Kenya	…	…	…	108	68	41	…	…	…	…	3	4	2	0.60
Lesotho	4	1	3	6ᶻ	2ᶻ	4ᶻ	2	2	3	1.64	3ᶻ	2ᶻ	3ᶻ	1.51ᶻ
Liberia	21	17	4	…	…	…	8	13	3	0.24	…	…	…	…
Madagascar	31	17	14	42	22	20	2	2	2	0.84	3	3	2	0.90
Malawi	3.2	2.3	0.9	5.1	3.3	1.8	0.3	0.4	0.2	0.38	0.4	0.5	0.3	0.54
Mali	19	…	…	26	18	8	2	…	…	…	2	3	1	0.47
Mauritius	7.6	4.1	3.5	18	8	10	7	7	6	0.88	17	14	20	1.39
Mozambique	10	…	…	22	15	7	0.6	…	…	…	1.2	1.6	0.7	0.46
Namibia	…	…	…	12ᶻ	6ᶻ	6ᶻ	…	…	…	…	6ᶻ	6ᶻ	7ᶻ	1.15ᶻ
Niger	…	…	…	9	6	2	…	…	…	…	0.8	1.1	0.4	0.40
Nigeria	744**	…	…	1 290	844	446	7**	…	…	…	10	13	7	0.55
Rwanda	6	…	…	25	15	10	0.9	…	…	…	3	3	2	0.62
Sao Tome and Principe	…	…	…	.	.	.	…	…	…	…	.	.	.	.
Senegal	29	…	…	52	…	…	3	…	…	…	5	…	…	…
Seychelles	.	.	.	.	.	.	.	.	.	.	.	.	.	.
Sierra Leone	…	…	…	9**,ʸ	6**,ʸ	3**,ʸ	…	…	…	…	2**,ʸ	3**,ʸ	1**,ʸ	0.40**,ʸ
Somalia	…	…	…	…	…	…	…	…	…	…	…	…	…	…
South Africa	633	292	341	718ᶻ	332ᶻ	386ᶻ	14	13	15	1.17	15ᶻ	14ᶻ	17ᶻ	1.17ᶻ
Swaziland	5	3	2	7	3	3	5	5	4	0.86	5	5	5	1.07
Togo	15	12	3	…	…	…	3	5	1	0.21	…	…	…	…
Uganda	41	27**	14**	88	54	34	2	2**	1**	0.53**	3	4	3	0.62
United Republic of Tanzania	19	15	4	43	30	13	0.6	1.0	0.3	0.27	1.2	1.7	0.7	0.41
Zambia	23**	16**	7**	…	…	…	2**	3**	1**	0.46**	…	…	…	…
Zimbabwe	43**	…	…	56**,ᶻ	34**,ᶻ	22**,ᶻ	3**	…	…	…	4**,ᶻ	5**,ᶻ	3**,ᶻ	0.63**,ᶻ

	Sum			Sum			Weighted average				Weighted average			
World	91 963	47 791	44 173	131 813	66 548	65 265	18	18	18	0.97	24	23	24	1.03
Countries in transition	9 272	4 258	5 014	13 496	6 002	7 495	41	37	45	1.20	54	48	61	1.28
Developed countries	36 337	16 982	19 355	42 574	19 234	23 339	55	50	60	1.19	65	57	73	1.27
Developing countries	46 354	26 550	19 804	75 743	41 312	34 431	11	12	9	0.78	16	17	15	0.87
Arab States	5 151	3 008	2 144	6 517	3 410	3 107	19	22	16	0.74	21	21	20	0.95
Central and Eastern Europe	12 960	6 030	6 930	18 509	8 377	10 132	39	36	43	1.19	54	48	60	1.25
Central Asia	1 279	669	610	1 884	928	956	19	20	18	0.92	25	24	26	1.05
East Asia and the Pacific	22 073	12 772	9 301	38 696	21 099	17 597	13	15	11	0.77	23	24	21	0.89
East Asia	21 034	12 300	8 734	37 475	20 543	16 932	13	15	11	0.75	22	24	21	0.88
Pacific	1 039	472	567	1 220	556	664	46	41	51	1.24	49	43	55	1.27
Latin America/Caribbean	10 652	5 045	5 607	14 576	6 785	7 790	21	20	23	1.12	28	26	30	1.17
Caribbean	69	36	33	102	38	64	5	5	5	0.91	6	5	8	1.70
Latin America	10 583	5 009	5 574	14 474	6 748	7 726	22	21	23	1.12	29	27	31	1.16
N. America/W. Europe	28 202	12 920	15 282	32 866	14 554	18 313	61	55	68	1.23	70	60	79	1.32
South and West Asia	9 496	5 997	3 499	15 465	9 345	6 120	7	9	6	0.63	11	12	9	0.70
Sub-Saharan Africa	2 150	1 350	800	3 300	2 050	1 250	4	5	3	0.59	5	6	4	0.62

1. Data are included in ISCED level 5A.
2. National population data were used to calculate enrolment ratios.
3. Enrolment ratios were not calculated due to lack of United Nations population data by age.
4. Enrolment ratios were not calculated due to inconsistencies between enrolment and the United Nations population data.

(eo) Full-time only.
(j) Data refer to ISCED levels 5A and 6 only.
(l) Data refer to ISCED level 5B only.

DISTRIBUTION OF STUDENTS BY ISCED LEVEL (%) — FOREIGN STUDENTS (000)

Total students — School year ending in 2004			Percentage of females at each level — School year ending in 2004			Foreign students — 1999			Foreign students — 2004			Country or territory
Level 5A	Level 5B	Level 6	Level 5A	Level 5B	Level 6	Total	Male	Female	Total	Male	Female	
...	...	...	...	...	...	...	...	...	...	...	...	Côte d'Ivoire
...	...	...	...	...	...	...	...	...	...	...	...	D. R. Congo
...	...	...	...	...	...	...	...	...	...	...	...	Equatorial Guinea
77	23	.	12	16	.	0.1	0.08	0.02	–	–	–	Eritrea
100	.	0.0	25	.	–	...	...	...	...	...	...	Ethiopia
...	...	...	...	...	...	0.4	...	...	...	...	...	Gabon
100	.	.	19	.	.	...	...	...	–	–	–	Gambia
86.7	13.0	0.3	32	26	17	...	...	...	...	...	...	Ghana
...	...	...	...	...	.	...	...	...	0.4	0.3	0.1	Guinea
...	...	...	...	...	...	...	...	...	...	...	...	Guinea-Bissau
62	33	5	35	43	36	...	...	...	...	...	...	Kenya
51z	49z	.z	53z	70z	.z	1.0	0.5	0.5	0.1z	0.06z	0.05z	Lesotho
...	...	...	...	...	...	...	...	...	...	...	...	Liberia
80	18	2	47	47	44	1.1	...	...	1.2	0.9	0.3	Madagascar
100	.	.	35	.	.	...	...	...	...	...	...	Malawi
95	5	.	31	51	.	1.2	...	...	...	...	...	Mali
42	57	0.9	48	65	38	...	...	...	0.1	0.0	0.0	Mauritius
100	.	.	32	.	.	...	...	...	...	...	...	Mozambique
60.5z	39.4z	0.1z	55z	51z	44z	...	...	...	1.0z	...	...	Namibia
...	...	...	...	...	...	...	...	...	0.1	0.1	0.0	Niger
58**	41	1**	26**	46	39**	...	...	...	...	...	...	Nigeria
65	35	.	41	36	.	0.07	...	...	...	...	...	Rwanda
.	.	.	.	.	.	...	...	...	.	.	.	Sao Tome and Principe
...	...	...	...	...	...	1.3	...	...	...	...	...	Senegal
.	.	.	.	.	.	.	.	.	.	.	.	Seychelles
44**,y	56**,y	.	16**,y	39**,y	.	...	...	...	...	...	...	Sierra Leone
...	...	...	...	...	...	...	...	...	...	...	...	Somalia
87z	12z	1z	53z	64z	39z	...	...	...	50.0z	23.0z	27.0z	South Africa
100	.	.	52	.	.	0.1	...	...	0.1y	...	...	Swaziland
...	...	...	...	...	...	0.5	0.4	0.2	...	...	...	Togo
62	36	2	41	35	37	...	...	...	...	...	...	Uganda
74	20	6	30	28	27	...	...	...	0.3	0.2	0.1	United Republic of Tanzania
...	...	...	...	...	...	...	...	...	...	...	...	Zambia
38**,z	59**,z	...	32z	44z	...	...	...	...	...	...	...	Zimbabwe

Median			Median			Sum			Sum			
82	15	3	54	52	40	...	...	...	...	...	...	World
98	.	2	54	.	51	...	...	...	...	...	...	Countries in transition
82	10	7	56	55	46	...	...	...	...	...	...	Developed countries
82	18	...	50	49	...	...	...	...	...	...	...	Developing countries
84	11	5	52	47	35	...	...	...	...	...	...	Arab States
83	13	4	57	57	49	...	...	...	...	...	...	Central and Eastern Europe
99	.	1	52	.	45	...	...	...	...	...	...	Central Asia
73	26	2	52	53	...	...	...	...	...	...	...	East Asia and the Pacific
74	24	2	43	48	35	...	...	...	...	...	...	East Asia
...	...	...	...	...	...	...	...	...	...	...	...	Pacific
82	18	...	55	58	.	...	...	...	...	...	...	Latin America/Caribbean
.	.	.	.	.	.	...	...	...	...	...	...	Caribbean
86	14	0.1	54	56	40	...	...	...	...	...	...	Latin America
80	17	3	56	52	47	...	...	...	...	...	...	N. America/W. Europe
96	3	2	38	...	28	...	...	...	...	...	...	South and West Asia
75	22	...	35	...	...	...	...	...	...	...	...	Sub-Saharan Africa

(v) Data do not include ISCED level 6.
(q) Data cover only 80% of students.
± Partial data.

Data in bold are for the school year ending in 2005.
(z) Data are for the school year ending in 2003.
(y) Data are for the school year ending in 2002.

Table 10A
Teaching staff in pre-primary and primary education

	PRE-PRIMARY EDUCATION											
	Teaching staff				Trained teachers (%)[1]						Pupil/teacher ratio[2]	
	School year ending in				School year ending in						School year ending in	
	1999		2004		1999			2004			1999	2004
Country or territory	Total (000)	% F	Total (000)	% F	Total	Male	Female	Total	Male	Female		
Arab States												
Algeria	1	93	2	81	…	…	…	…	…	…	28	26
Bahrain	0.7	100	1**	100**	18	.	18	…	…	…	21	22**
Djibouti	0.01	100	0.04	77	…	…	…	87	67	93	29	21
Egypt	14**	99**	19	99	…	…	…	…	…	…	24**	24
Iraq	5	100	6	100	…	…	…	100	.	100	15	16
Jordan	3	100	4z	98z	…	…	…	…	…	…	22	20z
Kuwait	4	100	5	100	100	100	100	100	.	100	15	13
Lebanon	11	95	9	99	…	…	…	10	18	10	13	16
Libyan Arab Jamahiriya	1	100	1.8**,z	99**,z	…	…	…	…	…	…	8	10**,z
Mauritania	…	…	0.2	100	…	…	…	100	.	100	…	19
Morocco	40	40	39	52	…	…	…	…	…	…	20	17
Oman	0.4	100	0.3	100	93	.	93	100	.	100	20	21
Palestinian A. T.	3	100	3	100	…	…	…	100	100	100	29	27
Qatar	0.4**	96**	1	99	…	…	…	…	…	…	21**	15
Saudi Arabia	9	100	10	100	…	…	…	72y	−y	72y	11	10
Sudan	12**	84**	14	96	…	…	…	10	21	10	30**	33
Syrian Arab Republic	5	96	7	98	87	84	87	22	10	22	24	22
Tunisia	4	95	6**,z	95**,z	…	…	…	…	…	…	20	19**,z
United Arab Emirates	3	100	4	100	59	71	59	50	14	50	19	18
Yemen	0.8	93	1.0	97	…	…	…	…	…	…	17	15
Central and Eastern Europe												
Albania	4	100	4z	100z	…	…	…	…	…	…	20	21z
Belarus	53	…	44	99	…	…	…	64	65	64	5	6
Bosnia and Herzegovina	…	…	…	…	…	…	…	…	…	…	…	…
Bulgaria	19	100**	17	100	…	…	…	…	…	…	11	11
Croatia	6	100	7z	100z	76	86	76	84z	100z	84z	13	12z
Czech Republic	17	100**	22	100**	…	…	…	…	…	…	18	13
Estonia	7	100	7	100	…	…	…	…	…	…	8	8
Hungary	32	100	31	100	…	…	…	…	…	…	12	10
Latvia	1	100	6	100	…	…	…	…	…	…	46	11
Lithuania	13	99	11	100	…	…	…	…	…	…	7	8
Poland	77**	…	53**	98**	…	…	…	…	…	…	12**	16**
Republic of Moldova	13	100	10	100	92**	.**	92**	93z	.z	93z	8	10
Romania	37	100	35	100	…	…	…	…	…	…	17	18
Russian Federation	508**	…	611	…	…	…	…	94**,z	…	…	7**	7
Serbia and Montenegro	12	100	…	…	96	−	96	…	…	…	14	…
Slovakia	16	100	12	100	…	…	…	…	…	…	10	13
Slovenia	3	99**	3	100	…	…	…	…	…	…	18	16
TFYR Macedonia	3	99	3	99	…	…	…	…	…	…	10	11
Turkey	17	99**	19	95	…	…	…	…	…	…	15	19
Ukraine	143	100	118	99	…	…	…	…	…	…	8	8
Central Asia												
Armenia	7.8	…	5	100	…	…	…	56	20	56	7	9
Azerbaijan	12	100	11	100	78	.	78	85	.	85	9	10
Georgia	6	100	7z	100z	…	…	…	98z	.z	98z	13	10z
Kazakhstan	19	…	25	99	…	…	…	…	…	…	9	11
Kyrgyzstan	3	100	2z	100z	32	−	32	36z	33z	36z	18	21z
Mongolia	3	100	3	96	99	75	99	…	…	…	25	28
Tajikistan	5	100	5	100	…	…	…	85z	.z	85z	11	14
Turkmenistan	…	…	…	…	…	…	…	…	…	…	…	…
Uzbekistan	…	…	64**	95**	…	…	…	100z	100z	100z	…	10**
East Asia and the Pacific												
Australia	…	…	…	…	…	…	…	…	…	…	…	…
Brunei Darussalam	0.6*	83*	0.5**	86**	…	…	…	…	…	…	20*	23**
Cambodia	2**	99**	3	99	…	…	…	94y	…	…	27**	30
China	875	94	…	…	…	…	…	…	…	…	27	…
Cook Islands	0.03	100	0.03z	100z	…	…	…	…	…	…	14	18z

PRIMARY EDUCATION

Teaching staff				Trained teachers (%)[1]						Pupil/teacher ratio[2]		
School year ending in				School year ending in						School year ending in		
1999		2004		1999			2004			1999	2004	
Total (000)	% F	Total (000)	% F	Total	Male	Female	Total	Male	Female			Country or territory

Arab States

Total (000)	% F	Total (000)	% F	Total	Male	Female	Total	Male	Female	1999	2004	Country or territory
170	46	170	50	94	92	96	98	98	99	28	27	Algeria
...	...	5**,y	76**,y	...	...	...	...	...	...	...	16**,y	Bahrain
1.0	28	1.3**,y	30**,y	...	...	...	...	...	...	40	34**,y	Djibouti
346**	52**	363**	55**	...	...	...	...	...	...	23**	22**	Egypt
141	72	211	72	...	...	...	100	100	100	25	21	Iraq
...	...	39**,z	64**,z	...	...	...	...	...	...	...	20**,z	Jordan
10	73	12	86	100	100	100	100	100	100	13	13	Kuwait
28	82	32	84	...	...	...	13	15	13	14	14	Lebanon
...	...	...	...	...	...	...	...	...	...	...	...	Libyan Arab Jamahiriya
7	26	10	28	...	...	...	100	100	100	47	45	Mauritania
123	39	148	45	...	...	...	...	...	...	28	28	Morocco
12	52	16**	62**	100	100	99	100**,y	100**,y	100**,y	25	19**	Oman
...	...	14	61	...	...	...	...	...	...	...	27	Palestinian A. T.
5	75	7	85	...	...	...	...	...	...	13	9	Qatar
185	54	204	52	...	...	...	...	...	...	12	12	Saudi Arabia
...	...	105**,z	62**,z	...	...	...	...	...	...	...	29**,z	Sudan
111**	68**	125**	62**	...	...	...	...	...	...	25**	18**	Syrian Arab Republic
60	50	60	51	...	...	...	...	...	...	24	21	Tunisia
17	73	17	83	...	...	...	61	70	59	16	15	United Arab Emirates
77**	21**	...	...	...	...	...	...	...	...	30**	...	Yemen

Central and Eastern Europe

Total (000)	% F	Total (000)	% F	Total	Male	Female	Total	Male	Female	1999	2004	Country or territory
13**	75**	12z	76z	...	...	...	...	...	...	23**	21z	Albania
32	99	26	99	...	...	...	99	98	99	20	15	Belarus
...	...	...	...	...	...	...	...	...	...	...	...	Bosnia and Herzegovina
23	91**	19	93	...	...	...	...	...	...	18	17	Bulgaria
11	89	11z	90z	100	100	100	100z	100z	100z	19	18z	Croatia
36	85**	30	84**	...	...	...	...	...	...	18	18	Czech Republic
8	86**	8**,y	...	...	...	...	...	...	...	16	14**,y	Estonia
47	85	43	96	...	...	...	...	...	...	11	10	Hungary
9	97	7	97	...	...	...	...	...	...	15	13	Latvia
13	98	12	98	...	...	...	...	...	...	17	15	Lithuania
...	...	226**	85**	...	...	...	...	...	...	...	13**	Poland
12	96	10	98	...	...	...	...	...	...	21	19	Republic of Moldova
69	86	58	87	...	...	...	...	...	...	19	17	Romania
349**	98**	320**	99**	...	...	...	99**,z	...	...	18**	17**	Russian Federation
21**	82**	...	...	100**	100**	100**	...	...	...	20**	...	Serbia and Montenegro
17	93	14	92	...	...	...	...	...	...	19	18	Slovakia
6	96	6	97	...	...	...	...	...	...	14	15	Slovenia
6	66	6	69	...	...	...	...	...	...	22	20	TFYR Macedonia
...	...	...	...	...	...	...	...	...	...	...	...	Turkey
107	98	100	98	...	...	...	99.7	...	...	20	19	Ukraine

Central Asia

Total (000)	% F	Total (000)	% F	Total	Male	Female	Total	Male	Female	1999	2004	Country or territory
...	...	7	99	...	...	...	67	84	66	...	22	Armenia
37	83	43	85	100	100	100	100	100	100	19	14	Azerbaijan
17	92	17z	95z	...	...	...	97z	...	...	17	14z	Georgia
...	...	60	98	...	...	...	...	...	...	...	18	Kazakhstan
19	95	18	96	48	49	48	55	55	55	24	24	Kyrgyzstan
8	93	7	94	...	...	...	...	...	...	32	33	Mongolia
31	56	32	64	...	...	...	84	...	...	22	22	Tajikistan
...	...	...	...	...	...	...	...	...	...	...	...	Turkmenistan
...	...	...	...	...	...	...	...	...	...	...	...	Uzbekistan

East Asia and the Pacific

Total (000)	% F	Total (000)	% F	Total	Male	Female	Total	Male	Female	1999	2004	Country or territory
...	...	...	...	...	...	...	...	...	...	...	...	Australia
3*	66*	4**	74**	...	...	...	...	...	...	14*	13**	Brunei Darussalam
45**	37**	50	41	...	...	...	97	...	...	48**	55	Cambodia
6 752	50**	5 747**	53**	...	...	...	97**,y	...	...	...	21**	China
0.1	86	0.1z	...	...	...	...	...	...	...	18	16z	Cook Islands

Table 10A (continued)

Country or territory	Teaching staff 1999 Total (000)	% F	2004 Total (000)	% F	Trained teachers (%)[1] 1999 Total	Male	Female	2004 Total	Male	Female	Pupil/teacher ratio[2] 1999	2004
DPR Korea	...	...	...	...	...	...	...	...	...	...	...	...
Fiji	...	...	0.4	99	...	...	...	...	...	...	...	21
Indonesia	91**	98**	139	98	...	...	...	...	...	...	17**	13
Japan	96	...	104	...	...	...	...	...	...	...	31	30
Kiribati	...	...	...	...	...	...	...	...	...	...	...	...
Lao PDR	2	100	3	99	86	100	86	82ᶻ	100ᶻ	82ᶻ	18	17
Macao, China	0.5	100	0.5	99	93	–	93	98	100	98	31	26
Malaysia	21	100	28ᶻ	99ᶻ	...	...	...	...	...	...	27	21ᶻ
Marshall Islands	0.1	...	0.1**,ᶻ	60**,ᶻ	...	...	...	100ʸ	100ʸ	100ʸ	11	12**,ᶻ
Micronesia	...	...	...	...	...	...	...	...	...	...	...	...
Myanmar	2	...	...	...	...	...	...	...	...	...	22	...
Nauru	...	...	0.04ᶻ	100ᶻ	...	...	...	...	...	...	...	13ᶻ
New Zealand	6.8	98	7	99	...	...	...	...	...	...	15	14
Niue	0.01	100	...	...	...	...	...	...	...	...	11	...
Palau	...	...	...	...	...	...	...	...	...	...	...	...
Papua New Guinea	2	41	3**,ᶻ	37**,ᶻ	...	...	...	...	...	...	30	35**,ᶻ
Philippines	18	...	25	96	100**	...	...	...	...	...	33	31
Republic of Korea	23	100	**26**	**99**	...	...	...	...	...	...	24	**21**
Samoa	...	...	0.1**	94**	...	...	...	...	...	...	...	42**
Singapore	...	...	...	...	...	...	...	...	...	...	...	...
Solomon Islands	...	...	...	...	...	...	...	...	...	...	...	...
Thailand	111	79	...	...	...	...	...	...	...	...	25	...
Timor-Leste	...	...	...	...	...	...	...	...	...	...	...	...
Tokelau	...	...	0.01ᶻ	100ᶻ	...	...	...	...	...	...	...	15ᶻ
Tonga	0.1	100	...	...	...	...	...	...	...	...	18	...
Tuvalu	...	...	0.1ʸ	...	...	...	...	...	...	...	...	9ʸ
Vanuatu	...	...	0.8**,ʸ	99**,ʸ	...	...	...	...	...	...	...	10**,ʸ
Viet Nam	94	100	107	100**,ᶻ	44	.	44	...	...	...	23	20
Latin America and the Caribbean												
Anguilla	0.03	100	0.04	100	38	.	38	66**	.**	66**	18	13
Antigua and Barbuda	...	...	...	...	...	...	...	...	...	...	...	...
Argentina	50	96	53**,ᶻ	97**,ᶻ	...	...	...	...	...	...	24	24ʸ
Aruba	0.1	100	0.1	99	100	–	100	100	100	100	26	20
Bahamas	0.2	97	0.3**,ᶻ	100**,ᶻ	53	50**	53**	60ʸ	.ʸ	60ʸ	9	11**,ᶻ
Barbados	0.3**	99**	0.4**	98**	84**	–**	85**	89**	25**	90**	17**	16**
Belize	0.2	98	0.2	99	...	...	...	68.2**,ᶻ	50.0**,ᶻ	68.4**,ᶻ	19	17
Bermuda	...	...	0.1ʸ	100ʸ	...	...	...	100ʸ	.ʸ	100ʸ	...	7ʸ
Bolivia	5	93	6**	92**	...	...	...	79ᶻ	32ᶻ	82ᶻ	42	41**
Brazil	304	98	364ᶻ	94ᶻ	...	...	...	...	...	...	19	19ᶻ
British Virgin Islands	0.1	98	0.05	100	15	.	16	20**	.**	20**	7	14
Cayman Islands	0.1	96	0.04	100	...	...	...	95	.	95	9	13
Chile	...	...	18	98	...	...	...	...	...	...	...	21
Colombia	59	94	50	96	...	...	...	...	...	...	18	21
Costa Rica	4	97	6	95	92	.	...	91	...	...	19	16
Cuba	26	98	27	100	98	.	100	100	.	100	19	18
Dominica	0.1	100	0.1	100	75	.	75	78**	.**	78**	18	13
Dominican Republic	8	95	9	96	...	...	...	77	72	78	24	21
Ecuador	10	90	13	87	...	...	...	72	60	73	18	17
El Salvador	...	...	...	...	...	...	...	...	...	...	...	...
Grenada	0.2	96	0.2	99	...	...	...	32ᶻ	–ᶻ	33ᶻ	18	15
Guatemala	12	...	17	...	...	...	...	...	...	...	26	25
Guyana	2	99	2**	99**	38	41	38	46ᶻ	18ᶻ	46ᶻ	18	15**
Haiti	...	...	...	...	...	...	...	...	...	...	...	...
Honduras	...	...	10	94	...	...	...	64	53	65	...	20
Jamaica	5	...	7	98**	...	...	...	...	...	...	25	22
Mexico	150	94	132	95	...	...	...	...	...	...	22	28
Montserrat	0.01	100	0.01	100	100	.	100	100	.	100	12	14
Netherlands Antilles	0.3	99	0.3**,ᶻ	100**,ᶻ	100	100	100	100ʸ	100ʸ	100ʸ	21	19**,ᶻ
Nicaragua	6	97	9	97	32	19	33	22	35	22	26	22
Panama	3	98	4	96	36	35	36	49	15	51	19	18

PRIMARY EDUCATION

Teaching staff				Trained teachers (%)[1]						Pupil/teacher ratio[2]		Country or territory
School year ending in				School year ending in						School year ending in		
1999		2004		1999			2004			1999	2004	
Total (000)	% F	Total (000)	% F	Total	Male	Female	Total	Male	Female			
…	…	…	…	…	…	…	…	…	…	…	…	DPR Korea
…	…	4	57	…	…	…	…	…	…	…	28	Fiji
…	…	1 448	52	…	…	…	…	…	…	…	20	Indonesia
367	…	379	…	…	…	…	…	…	…	21	19	Japan
0.6	62	0.6	73	…	…	…	…	…	…	25	25	Kiribati
27	43	28	45	76	69	85	79	73	87	31	31	Lao PDR
1.5	87	1.6	89	81	62	84	91	77	93	31	24	Macao, China
143	66	175z	66z	…	…	…	…	…	…	21	18z	Malaysia
0.6	…	0.5**,z	34**,z	…	…	…	…	…	…	15	17**,z	Marshall Islands
…	…	…	…	…	…	…	…	…	…	…	…	Micronesia
155	73	**160**	**81**	60	60	60	**76**	**80**	**75**	31	**31**	Myanmar
…	…	0.1z	95z	…	…	…	…	…	…	…	22z	Nauru
20	82	22	83	…	…	…	…	…	…	18	16	New Zealand
0.02	100	0.02	100	…	…	…	…	…	…	16	12	Niue
0.1	82	…	…	…	…	…	…	…	…	15	…	Palau
17	39	19**,z	39**,z	…	…	…	…	…	…	36	35**,z	Papua New Guinea
360	87	377	89	100**	…	…	…	…	…	35	35	Philippines
124	64	**142**	**74**	…	…	…	…	…	…	31	**29**	Republic of Korea
1.1**	71**	1.2**	73**	…	…	…	…	…	…	24**	25**	Samoa
…	…	…	…	…	…	…	…	…	…	…	…	Singapore
3	41	…	…	…	…	…	…	…	…	19	…	Solomon Islands
298	63	298**,z	58**,z	…	…	…	…	…	…	21	21**,z	Thailand
…	…	4y	30y	…	…	…	…	…	…	…	51y	Timor-Leste
…	…	0.04z	69z	…	…	…	…	…	…	…	6z	Tokelau
0.8	67	0.8	63	…	…	…	…	…	…	21	20	Tonga
0.1	…	0.1	80**,z	…	…	…	…	…	…	19	19	Tuvalu
1.4	49	1.9	54	…	…	…	…	…	…	24	20	Vanuatu
337	78	363	78	78	75	78	87y	87y	87y	30	23	Viet Nam

Latin America and the Caribbean

Teaching staff				Trained teachers (%)						Pupil/teacher ratio		Country or territory
0.07	87	0.1	90	76	78	76	67	40	70	22	14	Anguilla
…	…	…	…	…	…	…	…	…	…	…	…	Antigua and Barbuda
221	88	270**,z	86**,z	…	…	…	…	…	…	22	17**,z	Argentina
0.5	78	0.6	81	100	100	100	100	100	100	19	18	Aruba
2	63	1.7	97	58	57**	59**	95	82	95	14	20	Bahamas
1.4**	75**	1.4**	76**	84**	76**	87**	75**	82**	72**	18**	16**	Barbados
1.9**	64**	2**	72**	…	…	…	51**	51**	52**	24**	23**	Belize
…	…	0.5y	88y	…	…	…	100y	100y	100y	…	9y	Bermuda
58**	61**	65**	61**	…	…	…	…	…	…	25**	24**	Bolivia
807	93	861z	90z	…	…	…	…	…	…	26	22z	Brazil
0.2	86	0.2	94	72	55	75	82**	100**	81**	18	14	British Virgin Islands
0.2	89	0.3	81	…	…	…	100	98	100	15	13	Cayman Islands
56	77	64	78	…	…	…	…	…	…	32	27	Chile
215	77	188	77	…	…	…	…	…	…	24	28	Colombia
20	80	25	79	93	…	…	97	…	…	27	22	Costa Rica
91	79	88	77	100	100	100	100	100	100	12	10	Cuba
0.6	75	0.5	83	64	46	70	64	42	68	20	19	Dominica
42**	75**	42**,z	82**,z	…	…	…	79y	…	…	31**	33**z	Dominican Republic
71	68	86	70	…	…	…	71	71	71	27	23	Ecuador
…	…	…	…	…	…	…	…	…	…	…	…	El Salvador
1.0	73	0.9	76	…	…	…	68z	66z	68z	20	18	Grenada
48	…	74	…	…	…	…	…	…	…	38	31	Guatemala
4	86	4**	86**	52	52	52	57z	57**,z	57**,z	27	27**	Guyana
…	…	…	…	…	…	…	…	…	…	…	…	Haiti
…	…	38	75	…	…	…	87	86	88	…	33	Honduras
…	…	12	89**	…	…	…	…	…	…	…	28	Jamaica
540	62	519	66	…	…	…	…	…	…	27	28	Mexico
0.02	84	0.02	100	100	100	100	86	–	86	21	21	Montserrat
1.3	86	1.1**,z	86**,z	100	100	100	100y	100y	100y	20	20**,z	Netherlands Antilles
24	83	27	79	79	63	82	75	53	81	34	35	Nicaragua
15	75	18	76	79	86	77	74	80	72	26	24	Panama

Table 10A (continued)

Country or territory	Teaching staff 1999 Total (000)	Teaching staff 1999 % F	Teaching staff 2004 Total (000)	Teaching staff 2004 % F	Trained teachers (%)[1] 1999 Total	1999 Male	1999 Female	Trained teachers (%)[1] 2004 Total	2004 Male	2004 Female	Pupil/teacher ratio[2] 1999	2004
PRE-PRIMARY EDUCATION												
Paraguay	...	...	6**	88**	...	...	...	...	...	...	...	26**
Peru	...	...	46	97	...	...	...	...	...	...	...	24
Saint Kitts and Nevis	...	...	0.3	100	...	...	...	46**	.**	46**	...	7
Saint Lucia	0.5	100	0.3	100	...	...	...	55	.	55	12	12
Saint Vincent and the Grenadines	...	...	0.3	100	...	...	...	59**	.**	59**	...	11
Suriname	...	...	0.7**,z	99**,z	...	...	...	...	...	...	...	24**,z
Trinidad and Tobago	2**	100**	2	100	20**	—**	20**	25**	.**	25**	13**	13
Turks and Caicos Islands	0.1**	92**	0.1**	100**	61**	40**	63**	63**	.**	63**	13**	12**
Uruguay	3	98**	4**	...	...	...	...	...	...	...	31	28**
Venezuela	...	...	...	...	...	...	...	...	...	...	...	...
North America and Western Europe												
Andorra	...	...	0.2	92	...	...	...	...	...	...	...	15
Austria	14	99	15	99	...	...	...	...	...	...	16	15
Belgium	...	...	29	98	...	...	...	...	...	...	...	14
Canada	29	68**	28**,y	68**,y	...	...	...	...	...	...	18	18**,y
Cyprus	1	99	0.9	99	...	...	...	...	...	...	19	18
Denmark	45	92	...	...	...	...	...	...	...	...	6	...
Finland	10	96	11	97	...	...	...	...	...	...	12	12
France	128	78	139	81	...	...	...	...	...	...	19	18
Germany	...	...	190	98	...	...	...	...	...	...	...	12
Greece	9	...	11	99	...	...	...	...	...	...	16	13
Iceland	3	98	4	97	...	...	...	...	...	...	5	4**
Ireland	...	...	...	...	...	...	...	...	...	...	...	...
Israel	...	...	...	...	...	...	...	...	...	...	...	...
Italy	119	99	132	100	...	...	...	...	...	...	13	12
Luxembourg	...	...	1.1	98	...	...	...	...	...	...	...	13
Malta	0.9	99	0.2	99	...	...	...	...	...	...	12	54
Monaco	0.1**	100**	...	...	...	...	...	...	...	...	18**	...
Netherlands	...	...	...	...	...	...	...	...	...	...	...	...
Norway	...	...	...	...	...	...	...	...	...	...	...	...
Portugal	...	...	14	98	...	...	...	...	...	...	...	18
San Marino	...	...	...	...	...	...	...	...	...	...	...	...
Spain	68	93	101	91	...	...	...	...	...	...	17	13
Sweden	...	...	34	96	...	...	...	...	...	...	...	10
Switzerland	10**	99**	11	98	...	...	...	...	...	...	15**	15
United Kingdom	...	...	43	97	...	...	...	...	...	...	...	19
United States	327	95	403	91	...	...	...	...	...	...	22	18
South and West Asia												
Afghanistan	...	...	4**	100**	...	...	...	...	...	...	...	7**
Bangladesh	68	33	32z	88z	...	...	...	58z	...	...	38	36z
Bhutan	0.01	31	...	...	100	100	100	...	...	...	22	...
India	...	...	630	72	...	...	...	...	...	...	...	41
Iran, Islamic Republic of	9	98	25	89	...	...	...	79**,z	...	...	23	18
Maldives	0.4	90	0.5z	96z	47	46	47	50z	32z	51z	31	22z
Nepal	10**	31**	12**,z	41**,z	—**	—**	—**	—**,z	—**,z	—**,z	24**	20**,z
Pakistan	...	...	86**	45**	...	...	...	...	...	...	...	41**
Sri Lanka	...	...	...	...	...	...	...	...	...	...	...	...
Sub-Saharan Africa												
Angola	...	...	...	...	...	...	...	...	...	...	...	...
Benin	0.6	61	0.6	66	100	100	100	100	100	100	28	36
Botswana	...	...	...	...	...	...	...	...	...	...	...	...
Burkina Faso	...	...	0.5**,y	66**,y	...	...	...	...	...	...	...	29**,y
Burundi	0.2**	99**	0.3	92	...	...	...	66	25	69	28**	28
Cameroon	4	97	9	97	...	...	...	61	...	...	23	20
Cape Verde	...	...	1.0	100	...	...	...	7	.	7	...	22
Central African Republic	...	...	...	...	...	...	...	...	...	...	...	...
Chad	...	...	...	...	...	...	...	...	...	...	...	...
Comoros	0.1**	94**	0.5	...	...	...	...	...	...	...	26**	...

PRIMARY EDUCATION

Teaching staff				Trained teachers (%)[1]						Pupil/teacher ratio[2]		Country or territory
School year ending in				School year ending in						School year ending in		
1999		2004		1999			2004			1999	2004	
Total (000)	% F	Total (000)	% F	Total	Male	Female	Total	Male	Female			
...	...	34**	72**	...	...	...	...	...	...	...	28**	Paraguay
...	...	186	63	...	...	...	...	...	...	...	22	Peru
...	...	0.4	85	...	...	...	55	56**	55**	...	17	Saint Kitts and Nevis
1.2	84**	1.1	86	...	...	...	78	74	78	22	23	Saint Lucia
...	...	1.0**	73**	...	...	...	72**	66**	75**	...	17**	Saint Vincent and the Grenadines
...	...	3.3**,z	85**,z	...	...	...	...	...	...	...	19**,z	Suriname
8	76	8*	73*	71	74	71	81*	72*	84*	21	18*	Trinidad and Tobago
0.1**	92**	0.2	90	81**	63**	82**	91**	100**	90**	18**	11	Turks and Caicos Islands
18	92**	18**	...	...	...	...	...	...	...	20	21**	Uruguay
...	...	...	...	...	...	...	...	...	...	...	...	Venezuela
												North America and Western Europe
...	...	0.3	77	...	...	...	...	...	...	...	13	Andorra
29	89	28	91	...	...	...	...	...	...	13	13	Austria
...	...	65	78	...	...	...	...	...	...	...	12	Belgium
134	...	143**,y	68**,y	...	...	...	...	...	...	18	17**,y	Canada
4	67	4	83	...	...	...	...	...	...	18	18	Cyprus
37	63	...	...	...	...	...	...	...	...	10	...	Denmark
22	71	24	76	...	...	...	...	...	...	17	16	Finland
209	78	203	81	...	...	...	...	...	...	19	19	France
221	82	233	83	...	...	...	...	...	...	17	14	Germany
48	...	58	62	...	...	...	...	...	...	14	11	Greece
3**	76**	3**	78**	...	...	...	...	...	...	11**	11**	Iceland
21	85	25	83	...	...	...	...	...	...	22	18	Ireland
54	...	62	85	...	...	...	...	...	...	13	12	Israel
254	95	261	95	...	...	...	...	...	...	11	11	Italy
...	...	3	71	...	...	...	...	...	...	...	12	Luxembourg
1.8	87	1.7	87	...	...	...	...	...	...	20	19	Malta
0.1**	87**	...	...	...	...	...	...	...	...	16**	...	Monaco
...	...	...	...	...	...	...	...	...	...	...	...	Netherlands
...	...	41**	73**	...	...	...	...	...	...	...	11**	Norway
...	...	66	82	...	...	...	...	...	...	...	12	Portugal
...	...	...	...	...	...	...	...	...	...	...	...	San Marino
172	68	179	69	...	...	...	...	...	...	15	14	Spain
62	80	68	81	...	...	...	...	...	...	12	10	Sweden
41**	72**	41	78	...	...	...	...	...	...	13**	13	Switzerland
244	76	259	81	...	...	...	...	...	...	19	18	United Kingdom
1 618	86	1 652	88	...	...	...	...	...	...	15	15	United States
												South and West Asia
26	–	68	22	...	...	...	...	...	...	36	65	Afghanistan
312	33	327	39	64	64	64	51z	55z	45z	56	55	Bangladesh
1.9	32	2**,y	36**,y	100	100	100	...	...	...	42	38**,y	Bhutan
3 135*	33*	3 454	44	...	...	...	...	...	...	35*	40	India
327	53	365	58	...	...	...	100	100	100	27	20	Iran, Islamic Republic of
3	60	4z	64z	67	70	65	61z	60z	61z	24	18z	Maldives
92	23	**101**	**30**	46	50	35	**31**	**32**	**27**	39	**40**	Nepal
...	...	432	45	...	...	...	...	...	...	...	37	Pakistan
...	...	70	79**	...	...	...	...	...	...	...	22	Sri Lanka
												Sub-Saharan Africa
...	...	...	...	...	...	...	...	...	...	...	...	Angola
16	23	26	19	58	52	77	72	70	82	53	52	Benin
12	81	13	79	90	81	92	90z	86z	91z	27	26	Botswana
17	25	23	28	...	...	...	89	89	92	49	49	Burkina Faso
12**	54**	19	54	...	...	...	...	...	...	57**	51	Burundi
41	36	55	40	...	...	...	69	68	69	52	54	Cameroon
3**	62**	3	67	...	...	...	73	65	77	29**	27	Cape Verde
...	...	...	...	...	...	...	...	...	...	...	...	Central African Republic
12	9	16**	10**	...	...	...	...	...	...	68	69**	Chad
2	26	3	33	...	...	...	...	...	...	35	35	Comoros

Table 10A (continued)

Country or territory	PRE-PRIMARY EDUCATION Teaching staff School year ending in 1999 Total (000)	% F	2004 Total (000)	% F	Trained teachers (%)[1] School year ending in 1999 Total	Male	Female	2004 Total	Male	Female	Pupil/teacher ratio[2] School year ending in 1999	2004
Congo	0.6	100	1.1	86	...	...	...	28	–	33	10	19
Côte d'Ivoire	2	96	2*,z	80*,z	...	...	...	100*,z	100*,z	100*,z	23	22*,z
D. R. Congo	...	...	...	...	...	...	...	...	...	...	...	...
Equatorial Guinea	0.4	36	0.6z	80z	...	...	...	36z	46z	33z	43	39z
Eritrea	0.3	97	0.5	96	65	22	66	65	57	65	36	38
Ethiopia	2	93	5**	90**	63	37	65	74	60	75	36	32**
Gabon	...	...	0.5**,y	98**,y	...	...	...	...	...	...	...	30**,y
Gambia	...	...	0.8**	56**	...	...	...	...	...	...	...	38**
Ghana	26.4**	91**	29	91	24**	14**	25**	22	25	22	25**	25
Guinea	...	...	1.9	...	...	...	...	...	...	...	...	36
Guinea-Bissau	0.2**	73**	...	...	...	...	...	...	...	...	21**	...
Kenya	44.0	55	70	87	...	...	...	70	54	72	27	23
Lesotho	...	...	2**	99**	...	...	...	–y	–**,y	–**,y	...	20**
Liberia	6.2	19	...	...	...	...	...	...	...	...	18	...
Madagascar	...	...	4**	91**	...	...	...	...	...	...	...	48**
Malawi	...	...	...	...	...	...	...	...	...	...	...	...
Mali	...	...	2**,z	73**,z	...	...	...	...	...	...	...	21**,z
Mauritius	2.5	100	3	100	100	.	100	90	.	90	16	15
Mozambique	...	...	...	...	...	...	...	...	...	...	...	...
Namibia	1.3	88	...	...	77	12	86	...	...	...	27	...
Niger	0.5	98	0.8	99	100	100	100	86	64	86	22	24
Nigeria	...	...	...	...	...	...	...	...	...	...	...	...
Rwanda	...	...	0.6**,y	86**,y	...	...	...	...	...	...	...	35**,y
Sao Tome and Principe	...	...	0.2**,z	94**,z	...	...	...	55y	75y	53y	...	25**,z
Senegal	1.3	78	2.0	80	...	...	...	100	100	100	19	28
Seychelles	0.2	100	0.2**	100**	86	.	86	77z	.z	77z	16	15**
Sierra Leone	...	...	...	...	...	...	...	...	...	...	...	...
Somalia	...	...	...	...	...	...	...	...	...	...	...	...
South Africa	5.8**	80**	...	...	...	...	...	...	...	...	36**	...
Swaziland	...	...	...	...	...	...	...	...	...	...	...	...
Togo	0.6	97	0.7**	91**	...	...	...	67z	70z	67z	20	18**
Uganda	2.7**	70**	3**,z	83**,z	...	...	...	77y	56y	81y	25**	25**,z
United Republic of Tanzania	...	...	11	58	...	...	...	22	16	27	...	57
Zambia	...	...	...	...	...	...	...	...	...	...	...	...
Zimbabwe	...	...	20z	100z	...	...	...	...	...	...	...	23z
World[3]	...	98	...	99	...	...	...	...	...	...	19	18
Countries in transition	...	100	...	100	...	...	...	85	.	85	8	10
Developed countries	...	99	...	99	...	...	...	...	...	...	15	13
Developing countries	...	98	...	98	...	...	...	...	...	...	22	21
Arab States	...	100	...	99	...	...	...	87	67	93	20	19
Central and Eastern Europe	...	100	...	100	...	...	...	...	...	...	12	11
Central Asia	...	100	...	100	...	...	...	85	.	85	11	10
East Asia and the Pacific	...	...	...	99	...	...	...	...	...	...	23	21
East Asia	...	99	...	99	...	...	...	...	...	...	25	22
Pacific	...	...	...	99	...	...	...	...	...	...	...	14
Latin America and the Caribbean	...	98	...	99	...	...	...	67	.	67	19	18
Caribbean	...	99	...	100	...	...	...	64	.	64	18	13
Latin America	...	96	...	96	...	...	...	...	...	...	22	21
N. America/W. Europe	...	98	...	98	...	...	...	...	...	...	16	15
South and West Asia	...	33	...	88	...	...	...	...	...	...	24	22
Sub-Saharan Africa	...	...	...	91	...	...	...	...	...	...	...	25

1. Data on trained teachers (defined according to national standards) are not collected for countries whose education statistics are gathered through the OECD, Eurostat or the World Education Indicators questionnaires.
2. Based on headcounts of pupils and teachers.
3. All regional values shown are medians.

PRIMARY EDUCATION

Teaching staff				Trained teachers (%)[1]						Pupil/teacher ratio[2]		Country or territory
School year ending in				School year ending in						School year ending in		
1999		2004		1999			2004			1999	2004	
Total (000)	% F	Total (000)	% F	Total	Male	Female	Total	Male	Female			
5	42	7	45	...	...	...	62	57	68	61	83	Congo
45	20	48*,z	24*,z	...	...	...	100*,z	100*,z	100*,z	43	42*,z	Côte d'Ivoire
155	21	...	...	...	...	...	...	...	...	26	...	D. R. Congo
1.3	28	...	...	...	...	...	...	...	...	57	...	Equatorial Guinea
6	35	8	36	73	75	69	83	91	70	47	47	Eritrea
69**	37**	**111**	**45**	...	...	...	**97**	**96**	**98**	64**	**72**	Ethiopia
6	42	8**	45**	...	...	...	100z	100z	100z	44	36**	Gabon
5	29	5	31	72	72**	72**	...	...	...	33	37	Gambia
80	32	**89**	**31**	72	64	89	**58**	**49**	**78**	30	**33**	Ghana
16	25	25	24	...	...	...	...	...	...	47	45	Guinea
3**	20**	...	...	...	...	...	...	...	...	44**	...	Guinea-Bissau
148	42	150	44	...	...	...	99	98	99	32	40	Kenya
8	80	10	80	78	68	81	67	...	...	44	44	Lesotho
10	19	...	...	...	...	...	...	...	...	39	...	Liberia
43	58	64	60**	...	...	...	...	...	...	47	52	Madagascar
41**	40**	41**	46**	...	...	...	...	...	...	63**	70**	Malawi
15*	23*	27	28	...	...	...	...	...	...	62*	52	Mali
5	54	**5**	**63**	100	100	100	100	100	100	26	**23**	Mauritius
37	25	55	30	...	...	...	...	...	...	61	65	Mozambique
12	67	14**,z	61**,z	29	27	30	50**,y	50**,y	49**,y	32	28**,z	Namibia
13	31	22	36	98	98	98	76	78	72	41	44	Niger
440**	47**	580	51	...	...	...	51	39	62	38**	36	Nigeria
24	55	28	51	49	52	46	82	79	85	54	62	Rwanda
0.7	...	0.9	56	...	...	...	...	...	...	36	32	Sao Tome and Principe
21	23**	32	24	...	...	...	91y	96y	72y	49	43	Senegal
0.7	85	0.7**	85**	82	76	83	78z	67z	80z	15	14**	Seychelles
...	...	...	...	...	...	...	...	...	...	...	...	Sierra Leone
...	...	...	...	...	...	...	...	...	...	...	...	Somalia
227	78	221z	74z	62	65	61	79z	77z	79z	35	34z	South Africa
6	75	7z	75z	91	89	92	91z	91z	91z	33	31z	Swaziland
23	13	22	13	...	...	...	45	44	52	41	44	Togo
113**	33**	**143**	**39**	...	...	...	80	79	83	56**	**50**	Uganda
104	45	**135**	**48**	...	...	...	**100**	**100**	**100**	40	**56**	United Republic of Tanzania
33	49	46**	48**	94	93	95	100y	100y	100y	47	49**	Zambia
60	47	61z	51z	...	...	...	...	...	...	41	39z	Zimbabwe
...	71	...	74	...	...	...	...	...	...	24	21	World[3]
...	97	...	98	...	...	...	98	...	...	20	18	Countries in transition
...	85	...	83	...	...	...	...	...	...	17	14	Developed countries
...	62	...	64	...	...	...	...	...	...	28	27	Developing countries
...	52	...	62	...	...	...	...	...	...	25	20	Arab States
...	91	...	94	...	...	...	...	...	...	19	17	Central and Eastern Europe
...	92	...	95	...	...	...	84	...	...	22	22	Central Asia
...	66	...	69	...	...	...	...	...	...	21	21	East Asia and the Pacific
...	66	...	70	...	...	...	...	...	...	31	23	East Asia
...	67	...	66	...	...	...	...	...	...	19	20	Pacific
...	78	...	81	...	...	...	79	...	...	22	21	Latin America and the Caribbean
...	84	...	86	76	78	76	79	73	81	20	18	Caribbean
...	77	...	77	...	...	...	...	...	...	26	24	Latin America
...	79	...	81	...	...	...	...	...	...	15	13	N. America/W. Europe
...	33	...	44	...	...	...	...	...	...	36	38	South and West Asia
...	36	...	45	...	...	...	81	79	84	44	44	Sub-Saharan Africa

Data in bold are for the school year ending in 2005.   (z) Data are for the school year ending in 2003.   (y) Data are for the school year ending in 2002.

Table 10B
Teaching staff in secondary and tertiary education, school year ending in 2004

Country or territory	SECONDARY EDUCATION												TERTIARY EDUCATION	
	Teaching staff						Trained teachers (%)[1]			Pupil/teacher ratio[2]			Teaching staff	
	Lower secondary		Upper secondary		Total secondary		Total secondary			Lower secondary	Upper secondary	Total secondary		
	Total (000)	% F	Total (000)	% F	Total (000)	% F	Total	Male	Female				Total (000)	% F
Arab States														
Algeria	113**	51**	64**	46**	176**	49**	...	...	...	21**	20**	21**	26	32
Bahrain	3**,y	55**,y	3**,y	53**,y	5**,y	54**,y	...	...	...	14**,y	11**,y	12**,y	0.8**	36**
Djibouti	0.4**,y	23**,y	0.3**,y	22**,y	0.7**,y	23**,y	...	...	...	34**,y	19**,y	28**,y	0.1	19
Egypt	231**	45**	257**	38**	488**	41**	...	...	...	20**	14**	17**	81**	...
Iraq	60	59	31	56	91	58	100	100	100	19	19	19	19	35
Jordan	22**,z	62**,z	12z	49z	34**,z	58**,z	...	...	...	20**,z	14z	18**,z	8**	20**
Kuwait	12	55	13	53	25	54	100	100	100	11	10	11	1.6**	23**
Lebanon	...	...	...	...	43	52	...	...	...	...	...	8	20	37
Libyan Arab Jamahiriya	...												16**,z	...
Mauritania	...	...	...	...	3	12	100	100	100	...	...	28	0.3	5
Morocco	60**	36**	40**	29**	100**	33**	...	...	...	20**	16**	18**	19	23
Oman	10**	51**	8**	56**	18**	54**	100**,y	100**,y	100**,y	16**	16**	16**	1.1	25
Palestinian A. T.	19	50	4	47	23	50	...	...	...	28	23	27	4	15
Qatar	3	56	3	54	5	55	...	...	...	11	9	10	0.7**	31**
Saudi Arabia	103	50	79	50	181	50	...	...	...	11	12	11	25	34
Sudan	26**	66**	27	53	53**	59**	...	...	...	29**	20	25**	...	...
Syrian Arab Republic	...	...	43	43	...	...	...	...	...	...	10	...	...	...
Tunisia	35	49	34	39	69	44	...	...	...	19	16	18	15	40z
United Arab Emirates	11	56	10	54	21	55	47	47	47	16	11	13	3**,y	...
Yemen	...	...	...	...	...	...	...	...	...	...	...	...	...	...
Central and Eastern Europe														
Albania	16z	57z	6z	55z	22z	56z	...	...	...	16z	21z	18z	1.7z	41z
Belarus	...	...	...	...	105	79	...	...	...	...	...	9	43	55
Bosnia and Herzegovina	...													
Bulgaria	26	80	32	75	58	77	...	...	...	13	12	12	21	45
Croatia	17z	69z	20z	65z	37z	67z	100z	100z	100z	12z	10z	11z	8z	37z
Czech Republic	37	82**	39	55**	76	68**	...	...	...	14	12	13	25**	39**
Estonia	6**,y	...	6**,y	...	12**,y	...	...	...	...	10**,y	10**,y	10**,y	7	49
Hungary	51**	78**	47	64	98**	71**	...	...	...	10**	10	10**	25	39
Latvia	15	85	10	78	25	82	...	...	...	11	11	11	6	55
Lithuania	...	...	...	...	42	81	...	...	...	...	...	10	13	53
Poland	127**	74**	115**	65**	242**	70**	...	...	...	13**	16**	14**	90**	...
Republic of Moldova	23	77	8	71	31	76	...	...	...	13	13	13	8	55
Romania	93	68	65	63	158	66	...	...	...	12	16	14	30	42
Russian Federation	...	...	...	...	1 322**	...	93**,z	...	...	...	...	10**	601**	54**
Serbia and Montenegro	...													
Slovakia	28	76	24	77	52	77	...	...	...	13	13	13	13	40
Slovenia	8	78	9	64	16	71	...	...	...	11	12	11	4	33
TFYR Macedonia	8	50	6	55	14	52	...	...	...	14	16	15	3	44
Turkey	...	...	160	41	...	...	...	...	...	...	19	...	79	38
Ukraine	...	...	...	...	361	79	...	...	...	...	...	12	187	...
Central Asia														
Armenia	29	80	11	84	40	81	67	54	70	10	9	10	12	46
Azerbaijan	...	...	...	...	127	65	100z	100z	100z	...	...	9	14	44
Georgia	...	...	...	...	49z	82z	...	...	...	...	...	9z	14	49
Kazakhstan	...	...	...	...	185	85	...	...	...	...	...	11	41	60
Kyrgyzstan	...	...	...	...	53	72	73	72	74	...	...	14	12	50
Mongolia	10	73	5	70	15	72	...	...	...	24	20	23	5z	53z
Tajikistan	...	...	...	...	62	45	92	...	...	...	...	16	7	33
Turkmenistan	...													
Uzbekistan	...	...	...	...	...	...	...	...	...	...	...	...	25**	38**
East Asia and the Pacific														
Australia	...	...	...	...	...	...	...	...	...	...	...	...	10	...
Brunei Darussalam	...	...	...	...	4	57	...	...	...	...	...	10	**0.6**	**36**
Cambodia	19	33	6**	26**	25**	31**	99y	99**,y	99**,y	25	26**	25**	4	16
China	3 449**	45**	1 866**	41**	5 314**	43**	...	...	...	20**	17**	19**	850**,z	45**,z
Cook Islands	...	...	...	...	0.1z	...	...	...	...	...	...	15z	.	...

Table 10B (continued)

	SECONDARY EDUCATION												TERTIARY EDUCATION	
	Teaching staff						Trained teachers (%)[1]			Pupil/teacher ratio[2]			Teaching staff	
	Lower secondary		Upper secondary		Total secondary		Total secondary			Lower secondary	Upper secondary	Total secondary		
Country or territory	Total (000)	% F	Total (000)	% F	Total (000)	% F	Total	Male	Female				Total (000)	% F
DPR Korea	...	...	...	...	...	...	...	...	...	...	...	...	...	...
Fiji	3	50	1.5**	50**	5**	50**	...	...	...	22	22**	22**	...	...
Indonesia	683	41	469	38	1 152	40	...	...	...	15	13	14	272	39ᶻ
Japan	259		353		613		...	...	...	15	12	13	496	...
Kiribati	0.3	55	0.3	45	0.6	50	...	...	...	23	14	19	...	...
Lao PDR	9	42	5	42	14	42	97	96	98	27	26	27	1.9	34
Macao, China	1.1	61	0.9	51	2	57	64	51	73	24	22	23	1.2	32
Malaysia	84**,ᶻ	64**,ᶻ	58**,ᶻ	62**,ᶻ	142**,ᶻ	63**,ᶻ	...	...	...	18**,ᶻ	18**,ᶻ	18**,ᶻ	45**,ᶻ	47**,ᶻ
Marshall Islands	0.2**,ᶻ	35**,ᶻ	0.2**,ᶻ	42**,ᶻ	0.4**,ᶻ	39**,ᶻ	...	...	...	17**,ᶻ	17**,ᶻ	17**,ᶻ	0.05**,ᶻ	51**,ᶻ
Micronesia	...	...	...	...	...	...	...	...	...	...	...	...	...	...
Myanmar	**58**	**84**	**20**	**78**	**78**	**82**	**84**	**84**	**84**	**33**	**33**	**33**	...	...
Nauru	...	...	...	...	0.03ᶻ	53ᶻ	...	...	...	...	...	19ᶻ	...	...
New Zealand	17	65	21	55	38	60	...	...	...	16	11	13	16	47
Niue	...	...	...	...	0.03	68	...	...	...	...	...	8	.	.
Palau	...	...	...	...	...	...	...	...	...	...	...	...	0.05**,ʸ	46**,ʸ
Papua New Guinea	...	...	...	...	8**,ᶻ	37**,ᶻ	...	...	...	...	...	23**,ᶻ	...	...
Philippines	135	76	33	75	168	76	...	...	...	38	37	38	114	56
Republic of Korea	**96**	**64**	**112**	**38**	**208**	**50**	...	...	...	**20**	**16**	**18**	**176**	**29**
Samoa	0.4**	74**	0.8**	53**	1.1**	60**	...	...	...	25**	19**	21**	...	...
Singapore	...	...	...	...	...	...	...	...	...	...	...	...	...	...
Solomon Islands	...	...	...	...	...	...	...	...	...	...	...	...	.	.
Thailand	127**,ᶻ	57**,ᶻ	89**,ᶻ	50**,ᶻ	216**,ᶻ	54**,ᶻ	...	...	...	24**,ᶻ	26**,ᶻ	25**,ᶻ	66**,ᶻ	47**,ᶻ
Timor-Leste	1.1ʸ	...	0.6ʸ	...	1.6ʸ	...	...	...	...	28ʸ	29ʸ	28ʸ	0.1*,ʸ	9*,ʸ
Tokelau	...	...	...	...	0.02ʸ	40ʸ	...	...	...	...	...	13ʸ	.	.
Tonga	...	...	...	...	1.0ʸ	52ʸ	...	...	...	...	...	14ʸ	...	...
Tuvalu	...	...	...	...	...	...	...	...	...	...	...	...	.	.
Vanuatu	...	...	...	...	0.9**,ʸ	36**,ʸ	...	...	...	...	...	14**,ʸ	0.04**,ʸ	...
Viet Nam	281	68	110	57	391	65	92**,ʸ	91**,ʸ	92**,ʸ	24	27	25	39**	40**
Latin America and the Caribbean														
Anguilla	0.04**	71**	0.03**	71**	0.07	71	60	71	55	16**	16**	16	.	.
Antigua and Barbuda	...	...	...	...	...	...	...	...	...	...	...	...	.	.
Argentina	110**,ᶻ	67**,ᶻ	92**,ᶻ	64**,ᶻ	202**,ᶻ	66**,ᶻ	...	...	...	19**,ᶻ	16**,ᶻ	17**,ᶻ	131**,ᶻ	50**,ᶻ
Aruba	0.2**	50**	0.2**	51**	0.5	51	95	95	95	15**	15**	15	0.2	47
Bahamas	0.9	73	0.8	71	1.7	72	97	96**	98**	17	16	17	.	.
Barbados	0.8**	57**	0.5**	56**	1.3**	57**	63**	60**	65**	17**	17**	17**	...	...
Belize	1.3**	64**	0.4**	64**	1.6**	64**	43**	25**	53**	19**	19**	19**	0.1	49**
Bermuda	0.3ʸ	67ʸ	0.3ʸ	67ʸ	0.7ʸ	67ʸ	100ʸ	100ʸ	100ʸ	7ʸ	7ʸ	7ʸ	0.1**,ʸ	55**,ʸ
Bolivia	19**	61**	26**	47**	45**	53**	...	...	...	...	24**	24**	18**	...
Brazil	918ᶻ	89ᶻ	549ᶻ	69ᶻ	1 468ᶻ	82ᶻ	...	...	...	17ᶻ	17ᶻ	17ᶻ	300ᶻ	46ᶻ
British Virgin Islands	0.1	62	0.1	79	0.2	68	69**	71**	68**	11	7	9	.	.
Cayman Islands	0.1	60	0.1**	48**	0.2**	54**	100**	99**	100**	15	9**	11**	...	...
Chile	23	78	41	54	63	63	...	...	...	27	24	25	...	...
Colombia	122**	52**	42**	50**	164	52	...	...	...	25**	24**	25	88*	33*
Costa Rica	12	52	5	56	17	53	89	...	...	18	16	18	4**,ᶻ	...
Cuba	44	65	41	46	84	56	79	79	78	12	10	11	45ᶻ	37ᶻ
Dominica	0.3	65	0.1	66	0.4	65	36	32	38	17	17	17	...	...
Dominican Republic	9	76	17	51	26	59	82	73	88	35	28	30	11**	41**
Ecuador	44*	50*	31*	48*	75*	49*	69*	63*	76*	13*	14*	13*	...	...
El Salvador	...	...	...	...	...	...	...	...	...	...	...	...	8	32
Grenada	0.5**,ᶻ	64**,ᶻ	0.2**,ᶻ	61**,ᶻ	0.7ᶻ	63ᶻ	31**,ᶻ	34**,ᶻ	29**,ᶻ	19**,ᶻ	22**,ᶻ	20ᶻ	.	.
Guatemala	28	...	17	...	45	...	...	...	...	17	13	15	4**,ᶻ	...
Guyana	...	...	...	...	4**	61**	57**,ᶻ	54**,ᶻ	59**,ᶻ	...	...	16**	0.3	46
Haiti	...	...	...	...	...	...	...	...	...	...	...	...	...	...
Honduras	11	56	5	52	17	55	64	59	69	28	45	33	7**	38**
Jamaica	...	...	...	...	13	67**	...	...	...	...	...	19	2**,ᶻ	60**,ᶻ
Mexico	349	49	231	42	580	46	...	...	...	20	15	18	241	...
Montserrat	0.02**	58**	0.01**	64**	0.03	60	70	50	83	9**	10**	9	.	.
Netherlands Antilles	0.8**,ᶻ	58**,ᶻ	0.4**,ᶻ	49**,ᶻ	1.2**,ᶻ	55**,ᶻ	100ʸ	100ʸ	100ʸ	9**,ᶻ	19**,ᶻ	13**,ᶻ	0.3**,ʸ	44**,ʸ
Nicaragua	9	55	4	57	13	55	46	38	52	33	31	32	7**,ᶻ	46**,ᶻ
Panama	9	60	7	53	16	57	83	79	87	16	15	16	10	44
Paraguay	21**	64**	23**	61**	44**	62**	...	...	...	15**	9**	12**	...	...

Table 10B (continued)

Country or territory	SECONDARY EDUCATION												TERTIARY EDUCATION	
	Teaching staff						Trained teachers (%)[1]			Pupil/teacher ratio[2]			Teaching staff	
	Lower secondary		Upper secondary		Total secondary		Total secondary			Lower secondary	Upper secondary	Total secondary		
	Total (000)	% F	Total (000)	% F	Total (000)	% F	Total	Male	Female				Total (000)	% F
Peru	...	...	...	...	161	43	...	...	...	...	...	17	56ʸ	...
Saint Kitts and Nevis	0.3**	59**	0.1**	60**	0.4	59	35	36**	35**	11**	11**	11	.	.
Saint Lucia	0.5**	66**	0.3**	65**	0.8**	65**	60**	58**	62**	16**	16**	16**	0.2	76
St Vincent/Grenad.	0.4**	57**	0.1**	58**	0.5**	57**	42**	49**	37**	20**	20**	20**	.	.
Suriname	1.9**,ᶻ	61**,ᶻ	0.8**,ᶻ	61**,ᶻ	3**,ᶻ	61**,ᶻ	...	...	...	15**,ᶻ	14**,ᶻ	15**,ᶻ	0.6**,ʸ	48**,ʸ
Trinidad and Tobago	3**	62**	2**	62**	5**	62**	56**	58**	54**	19**	19**	19**	1.7	34**
Turks and Caicos Islands	0.1**	60**	0.1**	60**	0.2**	60**	100**	100**	100**	10**	10**	10**	0.0**	33**
Uruguay	18**	...	6**	...	24**	...	...	...	...	11**	27**	15**	13**	...
Venezuela	...	...	...	...	...	...	...	...	...	...	...	...	...	...
North America and Western Europe														
Andorra	0.4**	58**	0.1**	59**	0.5	58	...	...	...	7**	8**	7	0.1	48
Austria	43	68	29	50	72	61	...	...	...	9	13	11	30**	29**
Belgium	37	59	83	57	120	58	...	...	...	8	6	7	26	40
Canada	...	...	...	...	...	...	...	...	...	...	...	...	132**,ʸ	43**,ʸ
Cyprus	3	67	3	53	6	60	...	...	...	12	11	11	1.5	42
Denmark	...	...	...	...	...	...	...	...	...	...	...	...	...	...
Finland	21	72	...	...	...	...	...	...	...	10	...	...	19	45
France	245	65	267	53	511	59	...	...	...	13	10	11	136	39
Germany	425	59	172	46	598	56	...	...	...	13	16	14	290	34
Greece	40	64	43	48	84	56	...	...	...	8	8	8	26	36
Iceland	1.3**	78**	1.6**	50**	3**	62**	...	...	...	11**	14**	12**	1.7	44
Ireland	...	...	...	...	...	...	...	...	...	...	...	...	14	39
Israel	22	78	39	67	61	71	...	...	...	11	9	10	...	...
Italy	179	76	238	59	417	66	...	...	...	10	11	11	92	33
Luxembourg	...	...	...	...	3	44	...	...	...	...	...	10	...	...
Malta	3	59	0.8	33	4	53	...	...	...	10	15	11	0.6	23ᶻ
Monaco	...	...	...	...	...	...	...	...	...	...	...	...	.	.
Netherlands	...	...	...	...	110	44	...	...	...	...	...	13	45	34
Norway	20**	73**	26**	47**	46**	58**	...	...	...	9**	8**	9**	18**	37**
Portugal	37	71	49	68	86	69	...	...	...	10	6	8	36	42
San Marino	...	...	...	...	...	...	...	...	...	...	...	...	...	...
Spain	155	...	122	...	277	55	...	...	...	13	9	11	141	38
Sweden	38	63	37	51	75	57	...	...	...	10	9	9	38	42
Switzerland	32	47	...	...	...	...	...	...	...	9	...	...	26	27
United Kingdom	147	60	346	60	493	60	...	...	...	16	10	12	112	38
United States	881	65	744	55	1625	60	...	...	...	15	15	15	1175	43
South and West Asia														
Afghanistan	26	32	...	...	...	...	...	...	...	16	...	...	1.8	12
Bangladesh	183ᶻ	15ᶻ	173ᶻ	17ᶻ	356ᶻ	16ᶻ	31ᶻ	30ᶻ	35ᶻ	36ᶻ	26ᶻ	31ᶻ	61ᶻ	15ᶻ
Bhutan	...	...	...	...	...	...	...	...	...	...	...	...	...	...
India	1312	37	1274	31	2586	34	...	...	...	37	28	32	539	40
Iran, Islamic Republic of	243	49	283	46	526	47	100	100	100	19	20	20	103	16
Maldives	1.8ᶻ	34ᶻ	0.3ᶻ	39ᶻ	2ᶻ	35ᶻ	81ʸ	79ʸ	86ʸ	15ᶻ	8ᶻ	14ᶻ	0.04ᶻ	67ᶻ
Nepal	**26**	**16**	**22**	**9**	**48****	**13****	28ʸ	29ʸ	21ʸ	**56****	**28****	**43****	...	...
Pakistan	162*	54*	36*	35*	197*	51*	...	...	...	38*	32*	37*	61	13
Sri Lanka	66	64**	51	62**	117	63**	...	...	...	20	19	20	...	...
Sub-Saharan Africa														
Angola	...	...	...	...	...	...	...	...	...	...	...	...	1.3**,ʸ	20**,ʸ
Benin	9**	10**	3**	16**	12**	12**	...	...	...	30**	22**	28**	...	...
Botswana	...	...	...	...	12**	47**	93ᶻ	94ᶻ	93ᶻ	...	...	14**	...	...
Burkina Faso	...	...	...	...	8**	11**	...	...	...	...	...	31**	0.6**	...
Burundi	...	...	...	...	8**	21**	37ᶻ	39ᶻ	28ᶻ	...	...	19**	0.7	14
Cameroon	...	...	...	...	36*	36**	...	...	...	...	...	33*	3*	...
Cape Verde	1.1	39	1.1	39	2	39	61	59	64	23	23	23	0.4	46
Central African Republic	...	...	...	...	...	...	...	...	...	...	...	...	...	...
Chad	...	...	...	...	...	...	...	...	...	...	...	...	...	...
Comoros	1.8	16	1.3	9	3	13	51ᶻ	...	...	16	11	14	0.1**	15**
Congo	4	15	3**	11**	7**	13**	...	...	...	45	18**	34**	0.9**,ᶻ	...

Table 10B (continued)

Country or territory	SECONDARY EDUCATION												TERTIARY EDUCATION	
	Teaching staff						Trained teachers (%)[1]			Pupil/teacher ratio[2]			Teaching staff	
	Lower secondary		Upper secondary		Total secondary		Total secondary			Lower secondary	Upper secondary	Total secondary		
	Total (000)	% F	Total (000)	% F	Total (000)	% F	Total	Male	Female				Total (000)	% F
Côte d'Ivoire	…	…	…	…	…	…	…	…	…	…	…	…	…	…
D. R. Congo	…	…	…	…	…	…	…	…	…	…	…	…	…	…
Equatorial Guinea	…	…	…	…	…	…	…	…	…	…	…	…	…	…
Eritrea	2	10	1.8	13	4	11	50	48	64	55	39	48	0.4	14
Ethiopia	**60**	**19**	**23**	**10**	**83**	**17**	…	…	…	**57**	**47**	**54**	5	9
Gabon	3**,y	17**,y	…	…	…	…	…	…	…	31**,y	…	…	…	…
Gambia	1.1	16	0.9	12	2	14	…	…	…	51	31**	42**	0.1	16
Ghana	**56**	**20**	**16****	**14****	**72****	**18****	…	…	…	**18**	**22****	**19****	4	14
Guinea	…	…	…	…	10**	6**	…	…	…	…	…	33**	1.1	5
Guinea-Bissau	…	…	…	…	…	…	…	…	…	…	…	…	…	…
Kenya	28	44	48**	34**	77**	38**	…	…	…	52	20**	32**	…	…
Lesotho	…	…	…	…	3	56	85	83	86	…	…	26	0.5z	50**,z
Liberia	…	…	…	…	…	…	…	…	…	…	…	…	…	…
Madagascar	…	…	…	…	…	…	…	…	…	…	…	…	1.6	27
Malawi	8**,y	25**,y	4**,y	21**,y	11y	24y	…	…	…	51**,y	34**,y	46**,y	0.4	32
Mali	7	15	…	…	…	…	…	…	…	41	…	…	1.0	…
Mauritius	…	…	…	…	**7**	**55**	…	…	…	…	…	**17**	…	…
Mozambique	…	…	…	…	…	…	…	…	…	…	…	…	3	22
Namibia	5**,z	54**,z	1.3**,z	47**,z	6**,z	52**,z	…	…	…	24**,z	22**,z	24**,z	0.9z	27z
Niger	3	21	2	14	5	19	100	100	100	44	11	31	…	…
Nigeria	…	…	…	…	148	36	76	71	86	…	…	43	37	17
Rwanda	…	…	…	…	8	20	…	…	…	…	…	26	1.7	12
Sao Tome and Principe	0.2	14	…	…	…	…	…	…	…	23	…	…	.	.
Senegal	10	14	3	14	14	14	51	50	55	27	25	26	…	…
Seychelles	…	…	…	…	0.5**	54**	91z	90z	93z	…	…	14**	.	.
Sierra Leone	…	…	…	…	…	…	…	…	…	…	…	…	1.2**,y	15**,y
Somalia	…	…	…	…	…	…	…	…	…	…	…	…	…	…
South Africa	67**,z	49**,z	82**,z	51**,z	149z	50z	89y	88y	90y	28**,z	31**,z	30z	43z	50z
Swaziland	2**,z	47**,z	1.3**,z	45**,z	4z	46z	92z	91z	93z	19**,z	13**,z	17z	0.3	24
Togo	…	…	…	…	11	7	47	47	39	…	…	34	…	…
Uganda	…	…	…	…	**34****	**22****	82	81	86	…	…	**19****	4	19
United Republic of Tanzania	…	…	…	…	…	…	…	…	…	…	…	…	3	16
Zambia	6**	26**	5**	28**	11**	27**	…	…	…	38**	28**	34**	…	…
Zimbabwe	…	…	…	…	34z	40z	…	…	…	…	…	22z	…	…

	SECONDARY EDUCATION												TERTIARY EDUCATION	
World[3]	…	56	…	54	…	55	…	…	…	17	16	17	…	38
Countries in transition	…	…	…	…	…	79	…	…	…	…	…	11	…	50
Developed countries	…	65	…	55	…	60	…	…	…	10	15	11	…	40
Developing countries	…	…	…	…	…	52	…	…	…	…	…	19	…	33
Arab States	…	…	…	…	…	52	…	…	…	19	16	18	…	40
Central and Eastern Europe	…	78	…	64	…	71	…	…	…	13	12	12	…	43
Central Asia	…	…	…	…	…	72	…	…	…	…	…	11	…	48
East Asia and the Pacific	…	…	…	…	…	52	…	…	…	21	15	19	…	40
East Asia	…	59	…	51	…	56	…	…	…	24	22	23	…	39
Pacific	…	…	…	…	…	50	…	…	…	17	17	17	…	…
Latin America/Caribbean	…	58	…	64	…	60	69	71	68	17	16	17	…	46
Caribbean	…	…	…	…	…	62	62	59	63	…	…	16	…	47
Latin America	…	55	…	57	…	55	…	…	…	19	16	17	…	…
N. America/W. Europe	…	58	…	59	…	58	…	…	…	10	11	11	…	39
South and West Asia	…	34	…	39	…	35	…	…	…	36	26	31	…	16
Sub-Saharan Africa	…	…	…	…	…	22	…	…	…	30	22	28	…	17

1. Data on trained teachers (defined according to national standards) are not collected for countries whose education statistics are gathered through the OECD, Eurostat or the World Education Indicators questionnaires.

2. Based on headcounts of pupils and teachers.
3. All regional values shown are medians.

Data in bold are for the school year ending in 2005.
(z) Data are for the school year ending in 2003.
(y) Data are for the school year ending in 2002.

Table 11
Education finance

Country or territory	Total public expenditure on education as % of GNP		Total public expenditure on education as % of total government expenditure		Public current expenditure on education as % of total public expenditure on education		Public current expenditure on pre-primary education per pupil (unit cost) in constant 2003 US$		Public current expenditure on pre-primary education per pupil (unit cost) at PPP in constant 2003 US$		Public current expenditure on pre-primary education as % of GNP	
	1999	2004	1999	2004	1999	2004	1999	2004	1999	2004	1999	2004
Arab States												
1 Algeria	...	...	...	...	...	...	...	...	...	...	...	...
2 Bahrain	...	...	...	...	...	...	...	–ʸ	...	–ʸ	...	–ʸ
3 Djibouti	...	5.6	...	20.5	...	97.1	...	...	...	...	...	...
4 Egypt	...	...	...	...	...	...	...	...	...	...	...	...
5 Iraq	...	...	...	...	81.7	...	...	...	...	...	...	...
6 Jordan	5.0	...	20.6	...	...	...	...	7ʸ	...	17ʸ	...	0.01ʸ
7 Kuwait	...	7.6	...	17.4	...	90.8	...	...	...	...	...	0.7
8 Lebanon	2.0	2.5	10.4	12.7	...	94.1	...	...	...	...	...	...
9 Libyan Arab Jamahiriya	...	...	...	...	68.4	...	...	...	...	...	...	...
10 Mauritania	3.7**	3.7**	...	...	...	86.7**	...	...	...	...	...	...
11 Morocco	6.2	6.4	25.7	27.8	90.8	94.1	.	.	.	.	.	.
12 Oman	4.3**	4.8**,ʸ	...	26.1**	90.1**	88.1**	.	.	.	.	.	.ʸ
13 Palestinian Autonomous Territories	...	...	...	...	...	...	...	...	...	...	...	...
14 Qatar	...	...	...	...	...	88.4**	...	...	...	...	...	...
15 Saudi Arabia	...	...	...	...	...	...	...	...	...	...	...	...
16 Sudan	...	...	...	...	...	...	...	...	...	...	...	...
17 Syrian Arab Republic	...	...	...	...	...	...	...	...	...	...	...	...
18 Tunisia	7.9**	8.5ᶻ	17.7**	...	...	88.4ʸ	...	...	...	...	...	...
19 United Arab Emirates	...	...	...	22.5**,ʸ	...	93.2**,ʸ	...	1 106ᶻ	...	...	...	...
20 Yemen	...	...	...	...	...	...	...	...	...	...	...	...
Central and Eastern Europe												
21 Albania	...	2.8**,ʸ	...	...	...	...	...	...	...	...	...	...
22 Belarus	6.0	5.8	...	13.0	...	95.2	...	666	...	1 975	...	1.0
23 Bosnia and Herzegovina	...	...	...	...	...	...	...	...	...	...	...	...
24 Bulgaria	...	4.4ᶻ	...	...	...	96.0**,ʸ	...	589**,ʸ	...	2 139**,ʸ	...	0.6**,ʸ
25 Croatia	...	4.6ʸ	...	10.0ʸ	...	90.2ʸ	...	1 342ʸ	...	2 674ʸ	...	0.4ʸ
26 Czech Republic	4.1	4.8ᶻ	9.7	...	90.9**	89.8ʸ	1 088**	1 239ʸ	2 487**	2 676ʸ	0.4**	0.4ʸ
27 Estonia	7.0	6.0ʸ	...	...	...	86.1ʸ	...	421ʸ	...	1 005ʸ	...	0.3ʸ
28 Hungary	5.0	6.3ᶻ	12.8	...	91.4**	92.7**,ᶻ	1 281**	1 927**,ᶻ	3 155**	3 439**,ᶻ	0.7**	0.8**,ᶻ
29 Latvia	5.8	5.4ᶻ	...	...	...	...	...	...	...	...	...	...
30 Lithuania	...	5.4ᶻ	...	...	...	95.9ʸ	...	...	...	...	...	...
31 Poland	4.8	6.6ᶻ	11.4	12.8ʸ	93.0**	95.9**,ᶻ	815**	1 223**,ᶻ	1 787**	2 537**,ᶻ	0.4**	0.5**,ᶻ
32 Republic of Moldova	3.9**	4.2**,ᶻ	...	21.4ʸ	...	92.7ʸ	...	194ʸ	...	735ʸ	...	0.8ʸ
33 Romania	3.6**	3.7ᶻ	...	...	...	90.9**,ʸ	...	255**,ʸ	...	819**,ʸ	...	0.3**,ʸ
34 Russian Federation	...	3.8ᶻ	...	12.3ᶻ	...	...	...	...	...	...	...	...
35 Serbia and Montenegro	4.3**	...	...	...	...	...	...	...	...	...	...	...
36 Slovakia	4.3	4.4ᶻ	13.8	...	95.8**	92.9**,ᶻ	823**	1 016**,ᶻ	2 381**	2 272**,ᶻ	0.5**	0.5**,ᶻ
37 Slovenia	...	6.1ʸ	...	...	...	92.0**,ʸ	...	2 818**,ʸ	...	4 683**,ʸ	...	0.6**,ʸ
38 TFYR Macedonia	4.2**	3.4ᶻ	...	...	...	...	...	...	...	...	...	...
39 Turkey	4.0	3.8ᶻ	...	...	...	...	...	...	...	...	...	...
40 Ukraine	3.7	4.6	13.6	18.3	...	...	...	...	...	...	...	...
Central Asia												
41 Armenia	3.1**	3.1**,ʸ	...	...	...	...	...	...	...	...	...	...
42 Azerbaijan	4.3	3.7**	24.4	19.2ᶻ	99.2	98.0ᶻ	...	167ᶻ	...	698ᶻ	...	0.3ᶻ
43 Georgia	2.1	3.0	10.3	13.1	...	97.3	...	...	...	...	...	...
44 Kazakhstan	4.0	2.6	14.4	...	...	...	...	...	...	...	...	...
45 Kyrgyzstan	3.7	4.6**,ᶻ	...	...	99.3	95.4ʸ	...	110ʸ	...	557ʸ	...	0.3ʸ
46 Mongolia	6.1	5.7	...	...	...	94.5	...	158	...	532	...	1.0
47 Tajikistan	2.2	2.9	11.8	16.9	90.0	91.7	...	26**	...	95**	...	0.1**
48 Turkmenistan	...	...	...	...	...	...	...	...	...	...	...	...
49 Uzbekistan	...	...	...	...	...	...	...	...	...	...	...	...
East Asia and the Pacific												
50 Australia	5.1	4.9ᶻ	...	...	96.1**	96.3**,ᶻ	...	1 435ᶻ	...	1 619ᶻ	0.1**	0.1ᶻ
51 Brunei Darussalam	...	...	9.3**	...	96.6	...	...	...	...	...	...	...
52 Cambodia	1.0	2.2	8.7	...	...	...	...	...	...	...	...	...
53 China	2.1	...	13.0	...	93.2**	...	12**	...	55**	...	0.03**	...
54 Cook Islands	0.4	...	13.1**	...	98.6	...	...	...	...	...	0.03	...
55 DPR Korea	...	...	...	...	...	...	...	...	...	...	...	...

	Public current expenditure on pre-primary education per pupil as % of GNP per capita		Public current expenditure on primary education per pupil (unit cost) in constant 2003 US$		Public current expenditure on primary education per pupil (unit cost) at PPP in constant 2003 US$		Public current expenditure on primary education as % of GNP		Public current expenditure on primary education per pupil as % of GNP per capita		Public current expenditure on primary education as % of public current expenditure on education		Primary teachers' compensation as % of public current expenditure on primary education		Teachers' compensation as % of public current expenditure on education		
	1999	2004	1999	2004	1999	2004	1999	2004	1999	2004	1999	2004	1999	2004	1999	2004	
Arab States																	
...	...	...	...	225**,z	...	657**,z	...	1.6**,z	...	11.0**,z	...	...	...	...	...	...	1
...	...	–y	...	...	...	...	...	1.9**,y	...	16.3**,y	...	...	...	...	...	...	2
...	...	...	...	...	...	...	...	...	...	...	...	...	...	...	...	...	3
...	...	...	...	...	...	...	...	...	...	...	...	...	...	...	...	...	4
...	...	...	...	...	...	...	...	...	...	...	...	...	...	...	...	...	5
...	...	0.4y	221	247y	496	575y	1.9	1.9y	13.0	13.3y	...	...	77.8	94.6	...	...	6
...	...	26.8	...	...	...	...	...	1.4	...	22.8	...	20.8	...	78.6	...	...	7
...	...	...	...	...	...	...	...	...	...	...	...	...	...	...	...	...	8
...	...	...	...	...	...	...	...	...	...	...	12.1**	...	...	...	...	...	9
...	...	...	...	49z	...	227z	...	1.8	...	12.0	...	54.3	...	...	...	...	10
...	.	.	233	296	641	680	2.2	2.4	18.4	18.6	39.1	40.5	...	...	...	...	11
...	.	.y	...	...	...	...	1.4	1.5**,y	10.6	11.6**,y	35.9**	43.4**	...	90.7	...	...	12
...	...	...	...	...	...	...	...	...	...	...	...	...	...	...	...	...	13
...	...	...	...	...	...	...	...	...	...	...	...	...	...	...	...	...	14
...	...	...	...	...	...	...	...	...	...	...	...	...	...	...	...	...	15
...	...	...	...	...	...	...	...	...	...	...	...	...	...	...	...	...	16
...	...	...	117	142y	...	...	1.7	2.1y	10.2	12.6y	...	...	...	...	...	...	17
...	...	...	...	370**,y	...	1164**,y	...	2.2**,y	...	16.0**,y	...	36.7**,y	...	...	...	...	18
...	...	...	...	...	...	...	...	...	...	...	...	36.4**,y	...	82.8z	...	...	19
...	...	...	...	...	...	...	...	...	...	...	...	...	...	...	...	...	20
Central and Eastern Europe																	
...	...	...	...	...	...	...	...	...	...	...	...	...	...	...	...	...	21
...	...	37.5	...	232**	...	687**	...	0.5**	...	13.0**	...	9.7**	...	...	...	...	22
...	...	...	...	...	...	...	...	...	...	...	...	...	...	...	...	...	23
...	...	24.8**,y	...	377**,y	...	1368**,y	...	0.7**,y	...	15.9**,y	...	20.2**,y	...	60.7z	...	53.1z	24
...	...	22.4y	...	1275**,y	...	2540**,y	...	0.9**,y	...	21.3**,y	...	22.0**,y	...	...	...	...	25
...	14.2**	15.3y	805**	900y	1838**	1944y	0.7**	0.7y	10.5**	11.1y	17.8**	15.8y	45.0	50.1z	42.1	44.5z	26
...	...	6.9y	...	1056y	...	2524y	...	1.4y	...	17.3y	...	27.1y	...	...	...	...	27
...	19.7**	24.9**,z	1174**	1727**,z	2891**	3081**,z	0.9**	1.0**,z	18.0**	22.3**,z	19.5**	17.5**,z	...	...	...	...	28
...	...	...	...	...	...	...	...	...	...	...	...	...	...	...	...	...	29
...	...	...	...	...	...	...	...	...	...	...	...	...	...	...	...	...	30
...	16.7**	22.9**,z	1104**	1242**,z	2419**	2575**,z	2.0**	1.8**,z	22.6**	23.2**,z	45.3**	31.6**,z	...	...	...	...	31
...	...	40.8y	...	69**,y	...	260**,y	...	0.8**,y	...	14.4**,y	...	18.6**,y	...	...	...	...	32
...	...	10.4**,y	...	240**,y	...	771**,y	...	0.5**,y	...	9.8**,y	...	14.2**,y	...	...	...	...	33
...	...	...	...	...	...	...	...	...	...	...	...	...	...	...	...	...	34
...	...	...	...	...	...	...	...	...	...	...	...	...	...	...	...	...	35
...	16.0**	16.9**,z	519**	744**,z	1501**	1663**,z	0.6**	0.6**,z	10.1**	12.3**,z	14.5**	15.1**,z	62.1	49.1z	56.4	46.6z	36
...	...	...	...	...	...	...	...	...	...	...	...	...	...	...	...	...	37
...	...	20.6**,y	...	...	...	...	...	...	...	...	...	...	...	...	...	...	38
...	...	...	...	...	...	...	...	...	...	...	...	...	...	...	...	...	39
...	...	...	...	...	...	...	...	...	...	...	...	...	...	...	...	...	40
Central Asia																	
...	...	...	...	...	...	...	...	...	...	...	...	...	...	...	...	69.9y	41
...	...	20.7z	...	64**,z	...	269**,z	...	0.6**,z	...	8.0**,z	...	17.5**,z	...	...	...	...	42
...	...	...	...	...	...	...	...	...	...	...	...	...	...	...	...	...	43
...	...	...	...	...	...	...	...	...	...	...	...	...	...	...	...	...	44
...	...	32.2y	...	27**,y	...	136**,y	...	0.7**,y	...	7.8**,y	...	15.9**,y	47.5**	...	37.3	...	45
...	...	29.6	...	78	...	261	...	1.3	...	14.5	...	24.3	...	...	...	...	46
...	...	10.0**	...	16**	...	61**	...	0.7**	...	6.4**	...	25.8**	...	...	...	...	47
...	...	...	...	...	...	...	...	...	...	...	...	...	...	...	...	...	48
...	...	...	...	...	...	...	...	...	...	...	...	...	...	...	...	...	49
East Asia and the Pacific																	
...	...	5.6z	3816**	4152**,z	4553**	4682**,z	1.6**	1.6**,z	16.0**	16.1**,z	32.9**	33.2**,z	59.6	61.6z	49.2	49.5y	50
...	...	...	...	...	...	...	...	...	...	...	...	...	...	...	...	...	51
...	...	...	...	...	...	...	...	...	...	...	...	...	...	...	...	...	52
...	1.5**	...	...	...	...	...	0.7**	...	...	...	34.3**	...	...	...	...	...	53
...	1.3*	...	...	...	...	...	0.2	...	1.6*	...	53.0	...	...	...	...	...	54
...	...	...	...	...	...	...	...	...	...	...	...	...	...	...	...	...	55

Table 11 (continued)

Country or territory	Total public expenditure on education as % of GNP		Total public expenditure on education as % of total government expenditure		Public current expenditure on education as % of total public expenditure on education		Public current expenditure on pre-primary education per pupil (unit cost) in constant 2003 US$		Public current expenditure on pre-primary education per pupil (unit cost) at PPP in constant 2003 US$		Public current expenditure on pre-primary education as % of GNP	
	1999	2004	1999	2004	1999	2004	1999	2004	1999	2004	1999	2004
56 Fiji	5.7	6.8	18.3	20.0y	...	97.4	...	28	...	56	...	0.01
57 Indonesia	...	1.0z	...	9.0**,y	...	87.9**,z	...	0.7**,z	...	2**,z	...	0.00**,z
58 Japan	3.5	3.6z	9.3	...	...	...	...	...	...	...	...	...
59 Kiribati	8.2	9.3**,y	...	...	...	...	...	...	...	...	...	...
60 Lao People's Democratic Republic	1.0	2.5	...	11.0**,z	...	58.2	...	27y	...	138y	...	0.05y
61 Macao, China	3.6	...	13.5	16.1y	...	89.0z	...	...	...	...	...	...
62 Malaysia	6.1	8.5z	25.2	28.0z	...	68.3**,z	...	94**,z	...	213**,z	...	0.1**,z
63 Marshall Islands	13.3	11.9**	...	15.8z	...	97.2y	...	...	...	...	...	...
64 Micronesia (Federated States of)	6.5	...	...	...	...	...	...	...	...	...	...	...
65 Myanmar	0.6	...	8.1	...	63.8	...	...	...	...	...	−	...
66 Nauru	...	...	...	...	...	...	...	...	...	...	...	...
67 New Zealand	7.3	7.3	...	15.1z	95.1**	99.7**,z	1512**	1230**,z	1934**	1399**,z	0.2**	0.2**,z
68 Niue	...	...	...	10.1y	99.7	97.3y	...	...	...	...	...	...
69 Palau	...	9.7**,y	...	...	...	...	...	...	...	...	...	...
70 Papua New Guinea	...	...	...	...	...	...	...	...	...	...	...	...
71 Philippines	...	3.0z	...	17.2z	...	94.0**,z	...	4**,z	...	17**,z	...	0.00**,z
72 Republic of Korea	3.8	4.6z	13.1	15.5y	80.3**	80.7**,z	262**	569**,z	382**	810**,z	0.03**	0.1**,z
73 Samoa	4.5	4.3**,y	13.3	13.7**,y	98.9	...	.	.	.	.	.	.
74 Singapore	...	...	...	...	...	...	...	...	...	...	−	...
75 Solomon Islands	3.3**	...	...	...	...	...	...	...	...	...	...	...
76 Thailand	5.1	4.3	...	**40.0**	...	...	...	...	...	...	...	...
77 Timor-Leste	...	...	...	...	...	...	...	...	...	...	...	...
78 Tokelau	...	...	...	14.5z	...	...	...	...	...	...	...	...
79 Tonga	6.4**	4.9	...	13.5z	...	77.5y	...	...	...	...	...	−y
80 Tuvalu	...	...	...	44.0y	67.9	...	...	...	...	...	...	...
81 Vanuatu	6.7	10.0z	17.4	...	83.7	...	−	...	−	...	−	...
82 Viet Nam	...	...	...	...	...	...	...	...	...	...	...	...
Latin America and the Caribbean												
83 Anguilla	...	...	...	...	...	41.0z	...	...	...	...	...	...
84 Antigua and Barbuda	3.5	4.0y	18.9**	...	100.0	96.2y	...	...	...	...	...	0.1y
85 Argentina	4.6	3.6z	13.3	14.6z	94.0	99.4**,y	...	292**,y	...	1158**,y	...	0.3**,y
86 Aruba	...	...	13.8	15.6y	89.5	85.8	...	...	...	...	...	...
87 Bahamas	...	...	...	...	...	...	...	...	...	...	...	...
88 Barbados	5.3	7.6	15.4	17.3z	91.6	91.5	439	2013**,z	690	3241**,z	0.1	0.5**,z
89 Belize	5.7**	5.3	17.1**	18.1z	...	90.9z	...	57z	...	109z	...	0.03z
90 Bermuda	...	...	...	...	...	...	...	...	...	...	...	...
91 Bolivia	5.8	6.7**	15.8	18.1z	84.3	95.5z	52	75z	120	217z	0.2	0.2z
92 Brazil	4.4	4.3y	10.4	10.9y	95.1**	...	294**	...	647**	...	0.4**	...
93 British Virgin Islands	...	...	...	17.8	...	70.9	...	...	...	...	...	...
94 Cayman Islands	...	...	...	...	...	...	...	...	...	...	...	...
95 Chile	3.9	4.1	17.0	18.5	87.6	90.3z	...	640z	...	1432z	...	0.4z
96 Colombia	4.5	5.1	16.9	11.7	...	95.5	...	80	...	264	...	0.1
97 Costa Rica	5.5	5.1	...	18.5	99.6	79.4	606	682	1302	1476	0.3	0.4
98 Cuba	7.7	...	13.7	19.4	...	86.0	...	...	...	...	...	...
99 Dominica	5.5**	...	...	...	...	...	...	...	...	...	...	...
100 Dominican Republic	...	1.2	...	6.3	...	96.6	...	4	...	15	...	0.00
101 Ecuador	2.0	...	9.7	...	92.7*	...	...	...	...	...	...	...
102 El Salvador	2.4**	2.9**	17.1**	20.0y	...	97.4z	...	137z	...	288z	...	0.2z
103 Grenada	...	6.0z	...	12.9z	...	87.1**,z	...	302**,z	...	573**,z	...	0.3**,z
104 Guatemala	...	...	...	...	...	...	...	82	...	158	...	0.1
105 Guyana	9.3**	5.8	18.4**	18.4y	...	83.2	...	132**	...	556**	...	0.6
106 Haiti	...	...	...	...	...	...	...	...	...	...	...	...
107 Honduras	...	...	...	...	...	...	...	...	...	...	...	...
108 Jamaica	...	5.3	...	9.5z	...	96.0**	...	122**	...	160**	...	0.3**
109 Mexico	4.5	5.9z	22.6	...	95.0	97.3y	...	920y	...	1288y	...	0.5y
110 Montserrat	...	...	10.7**	...	47.3	65.0	...	...	...	...	...	...
111 Netherlands Antilles	...	...	14.0	...	93.8	...	...	...	...	...	...	...
112 Nicaragua	4.0	3.2**,z	6.4	15.0y	...	90.8y	...	5	...	22	...	0.02
113 Panama	5.1	4.2**	...	8.9**	...	...	307	...	459	...	0.1	...
114 Paraguay	4.8	4.3z	8.8	10.8z	87.9	95.7y	...	144y	...	652y	...	0.3y
115 Peru	3.5	3.1y	21.1	17.1y	87.9	93.8y	...	123y	...	293y	...	0.2y
116 Saint Kitts and Nevis	5.6**	5.0**	13.3**	12.7z	...	99.7y	...	419y	...	669y	...	0.3y

Public current expenditure on pre-primary education per pupil as % of GNP per capita		Public current expenditure on primary education per pupil (unit cost) in constant 2003 US$		Public current expenditure on primary education per pupil (unit cost) at PPP in constant 2003 US$		Public current expenditure on primary education as % of GNP		Public current expenditure on primary education per pupil as % of GNP per capita		Public current expenditure on primary education as % of public current expenditure on education		Primary teachers' compensation as % of public current expenditure on primary education		Teachers' compensation as % of public current expenditure on education		
1999	2004	1999	2004	1999	2004	1999	2004	1999	2004	1999	2004	1999	2004	1999	2004	
...	1.3	...	437	...	859	...	2.6	...	19.6	...	40.1	...	...	...	...	56
...	0.1**,z	...	27**,z	...	92**,z	...	0.3**,z	...	2.5**,z	...	39.2**,z	...	78.3z	...	80.6z	57
...	...	...	...	...	...	...	...	...	...	...	...	...	...	...	...	58
...	...	...	...	...	...	...	...	...	...	...	...	...	...	...	...	59
...	7.3y	...	15y	...	76y	...	0.6y	...	4.0y	...	54.3y	...	...	...	...	60
...	...	...	...	...	...	...	...	...	...	...	...	...	...	...	...	61
...	2.3**,z	...	522**,z	...	1187**,z	...	1.6**,z	...	13.1**,z	...	28.3**,z	69.6	69.2z	60.2	55.9z	62
...	...	...	...	...	...	...	3.6y	...	22.2**,y	...	45.0y	...	68.6y	...	59.6y	63
...	...	...	...	...	...	...	...	...	...	...	...	...	...	...	...	64
—	...	...	...	...	...	...	...	...	...	...	...	...	...	...	...	65
...	...	...	...	...	...	...	...	...	...	...	...	...	...	...	...	66
9.0**	8.5**,z	3212**	2827**,z	4107**	3215**,z	1.8**	1.8**,z	19.1**	19.5**,z	26.7**	25.5**,z	...	...	...	...	67
...	...	...	...	...	...	...	...	...	...	31.9	29.1y	...	...	...	...	68
...	...	...	...	...	...	...	...	...	...	...	...	...	...	...	...	69
...	...	...	...	...	...	...	...	...	...	...	...	...	...	...	...	70
...	0.4**,z	...	110**,z	...	480**,z	...	1.7**,z	...	10.3**,z	...	59.4**,z	...	90.2z	...	82.0z	71
2.5**	4.4**,z	1625**	1857**,z	2369**	2642**,z	1.3**	1.3**,z	15.7**	14.5**,z	43.5**	34.2**,z	...	63.4z	...	54.1z	72
·	·	112**	...	387**	...	1.4**	...	9.1**	...	32.4**	...	...	...	...	...	73
...	...	...	...	...	...	...	...	...	...	...	...	...	...	...	...	74
...	...	...	...	...	...	...	...	...	...	...	...	...	...	...	...	75
...	...	...	...	...	...	...	...	...	...	...	...	...	...	...	...	76
...	...	...	...	...	...	...	...	...	...	...	...	...	...	...	...	77
...	...	...	...	...	...	...	...	...	...	...	...	...	...	...	...	78
...	...	...	194y	...	968y	...	2.2y	...	12.9y	...	59.1y	...	...	...	...	79
...	...	...	...	...	...	...	...	...	...	...	...	...	...	...	...	80
—	...	185	...	446	...	2.2	...	12.0	...	38.9	...	94.3	...	90.4	...	81
...	...	...	...	...	...	...	...	...	...	...	...	...	...	...	...	82
														Latin America and the Caribbean		
...	...	...	...	...	...	...	...	...	...	...	47.7z	...	...	...	...	83
...	...	...	...	...	...	...	1.2y	...	...	...	29.7y	66.4	90.1y	56.1	69.5y	84
...	9.4**,y	456	342**,y	697	1357**,y	1.6	1.4**,y	12.1	11.1**,y	36.7	35.4**,y	...	66.5z	...	72.2z	85
...	...	...	...	...	...	...	...	...	...	29.9	30.1	...	...	...	...	86
...	...	...	...	...	...	...	...	...	...	...	...	...	...	...	...	87
4.7	22.0**,z	1186	1967**,z	1865	3167**	1.2	1.7**	12.6	21.0**	24.4	25.0**	...	...	...	...	88
...	1.7z	...	513z	...	987z	...	2.8z	...	15.3z	...	54.8z	...	...	...	...	89
...	...	...	...	...	...	...	...	...	...	...	...	...	...	...	...	90
6.1	8.5z	97**	147z	223**	427z	2.0**	2.9z	11.3**	16.7z	41.0**	45.8z	...	...	...	...	91
11.3**	...	298**	...	656**	...	1.4**	...	11.4**	...	33.3**	...	...	...	...	...	92
...	...	...	...	...	...	...	...	...	...	...	28.7	...	...	...	...	93
...	...	...	...	...	...	...	...	...	...	...	...	...	...	...	...	94
...	14.8z	530	640z	940	1433z	1.5	1.6z	13.0	14.8z	44.5	40.5z	...	...	...	...	95
...	4.6	...	292	...	966	...	2.0	...	16.7	...	40.0	91.0*	76.5	91.0*	...	96
17.0	16.4	641	716	1376	1550	2.6	2.3	18.0	17.2	47.2	56.0	...	...	...	...	97
...	...	...	...	...	...	...	...	...	...	...	32.0	...	...	...	...	98
...	...	...	...	...	...	...	...	...	...	...	...	...	...	...	...	99
...	0.2	...	97	...	337	...	0.8	...	5.4	...	66.0	...	82.9	...	75.1	100
...	...	...	...	...	...	...	...	...	...	...	...	...	...	...	...	101
...	6.3z	...	207**,z	...	434**,z	...	1.4**,z	...	9.5**,z	...	52.0**,z	...	...	...	...	102
...	8.9**,z	...	393**,z	...	745**,z	...	1.9**,z	...	11.6**,z	...	35.3**,z	...	93.5z	...	79.6z	103
...	4.0	...	96	...	186	...	0.9	...	4.7	...	...	...	...	...	...	104
...	13.6**	...	108**	...	454**	...	1.6	...	11.1**	...	34.1	...	...	...	...	105
...	...	...	...	...	...	...	...	...	...	...	...	...	...	...	...	106
...	...	...	...	...	...	...	...	...	...	...	...	...	...	...	...	107
...	4.8**	...	323**	...	422**	...	1.6**	...	12.6**	...	31.4**	...	83.3	...	76.3	108
...	15.6y	671	845y	1121	1183y	1.8	2.1y	11.8	14.3y	40.8	39.3y	86.3	85.7z	81.1	77.8z	109
...	...	...	...	...	...	...	...	...	...	...	...	...	...	...	...	110
...	...	...	...	...	...	...	...	...	...	...	...	...	...	...	...	111
...	0.7	...	66	...	286	...	1.5	...	8.5	...	...	...	97.6	...	94.6	112
8.1	...	520	...	778	...	1.9	...	13.7	...	...	...	...	...	...	...	113
...	13.9y	...	121y	...	547y	...	2.0y	...	11.7y	...	46.6y	...	74.5z	...	75.3z	114
...	5.8y	148	138y	335	327y	1.2	1.0y	7.2	6.5y	40.4	36.1y	...	...	...	...	115
...	5.8*,y	...	581y	...	928y	...	1.2y	...	8.0*,y	...	33.7y	...	...	...	...	116

Table 11 (continued)

Country or territory	Total public expenditure on education as % of GNP		Total public expenditure on education as % of total government expenditure		Public current expenditure on education as % of total public expenditure on education		Public current expenditure on pre-primary education per pupil (unit cost) in constant 2003 US$		Public current expenditure on pre-primary education per pupil (unit cost) at PPP in constant 2003 US$		Public current expenditure on pre-primary education as % of GNP	
	1999	2004	1999	2004	1999	2004	1999	2004	1999	2004	1999	2004
117 Saint Lucia	8.0	5.4	21.3	...	78.5	99.3	34**	41	43**	55	0.03**	0.02
118 Saint Vincent and the Grenadines	7.2**	11.7	...	20.3y	...	82.2	...	...	...	...	...	0.03y
119 Suriname	...	...	...	...	...	...	...	...	...	...	...	...
120 Trinidad and Tobago	3.9	4.6**,y	16.4**	...	96.0	...	85**	...	130**	...	0.03	...
121 Turks and Caicos Islands	...	...	17.4	16.5y	72.8	95.9z	...	...	...	...	...	...
122 Uruguay	2.8	2.3z	...	7.9z	92.3	...	...	...	...	...	...	...
123 Venezuela	...	...	...	...	...	...	...	...	...	...	...	...
North America and Western Europe												
124 Andorra	...	...	...	...	...	97.2	...	...	...	...	...	...
125 Austria	6.4	5.6z	12.4	...	94.1**	96.2y	4331**	4796y	4379**	5524y	0.4**	0.4y
126 Belgium	5.7	6.1z	11.6	...	...	...	...	...	...	...	...	...
127 Canada	6.0	5.4y	...	...	98.4**	97.2**,y	3107**	3246**,y	3838**	4194**,y	0.2**	0.2**,y
128 Cyprus	5.4	7.6z	...	...	86.2	88.4y	989	2299y	1285	...	0.2	0.4y
129 Denmark	8.2	8.5z	14.9	...	...	93.6y	5638**	5901y	4793**	5686y	0.7**	0.7y
130 Finland	6.3	6.6z	12.5	...	93.7**	92.1**,z	3724**	3914**,z	3536**	3481**,z	0.3**	0.3**,z
131 France	5.8	6.0z	11.5	...	91.4**	91.6y	4239**	4321y	4118**	4852y	0.6**	0.6y
132 Germany	4.6	4.8y	9.5	...	...	...	3277**	3919**,y	3177**	4424**,y	0.3**	0.4**,y
133 Greece	3.5	4.3z	7.0	...	78.0**	78.6y	1664**	1787**,y	2359**	2775**,y	0.2**	0.2**,y
134 Iceland	...	8.2z	...	...	...	92.7**,z	...	3236**,z	...	2779**,z	...	0.5**,z
135 Ireland	4.9	5.3y	13.2	...	91.2**	89.7**,y	...	...	...	...	0.00**	0.00**,y
136 Israel	7.5	7.5z	13.9	13.7y	93.7**	94.2y	1728**	1959y	1926**	2445y	0.6**	0.7y
137 Italy	4.6	4.9z	9.5	...	94.6**	93.4y	3688**	3399y	4262**	4374y	0.4**	0.4y
138 Luxembourg	3.6**	...	8.5**	...	...	...	...	...	...	...	...	...
139 Malta	4.9**	4.6y	...	...	...	95.6y	...	1543y	...	2699y	...	0.3y
140 Monaco	...	...	5.1	...	91.9	91.2	...	...	...	...	...	...
141 Netherlands	4.8	5.5z	10.4	...	96.2**	94.6y	4170**	4533y	4300**	5078y	0.3**	0.3y
142 Norway	7.2	7.6z	15.6	...	89.6	91.5**,z	10905**	4131**,z	10380**	3215**,z	0.7**	0.3**,z
143 Portugal	5.7**	6.0z	12.8**	...	92.6**	95.5y	1825**	2115y	2641**	3265y	0.3**	0.3y
144 San Marino	...	...	...	...	...	...	...	...	...	...	...	...
145 Spain	4.5	4.6z	11.3	...	91.1**	91.4y	2100**	2838y	2647**	3828y	0.3**	0.4y
146 Sweden	7.5	7.1z	13.6	...	...	...	...	...	...	...	...	...
147 Switzerland	5.0	5.1z	15.2	...	90.2	91.0y	3746	4196y	2765	3384y	0.2	0.2y
148 United Kingdom	4.6	5.4z	11.4	11.5**,y	...	...	...	...	...	...	...	...
149 United States	5.0	5.8z	...	...	...	...	...	...	...	...	...	...
South and West Asia												
150 Afghanistan	...	...	...	...	...	...	...	...	...	...	...	...
151 Bangladesh	2.3	2.1	15.3	15.5z	63.7	79.5	18**	...	74**	...	0.1**	...
152 Bhutan	...	...	...	...	...	...	.	...	.	...	.	...
153 India	4.1	3.3z	12.7	10.7z	98.0**	...	11**	...	55**	...	0.04**	...
154 Iran, Islamic Republic of	4.6	4.8	18.7	17.7z	90.9	89.9z	...	126z	...	426z	...	0.04z
155 Maldives	...	8.6**	...	...	...	80.6z	...	...	...	...	...	...
156 Nepal	2.9**	3.4z	12.5**	14.9z	73.6**	76.8z	–**	25**,z	–**	145**,z	–	0.1**,z
157 Pakistan	2.6	2.0	...	...	88.9	80.3	...	...	...	...	...	...
158 Sri Lanka	...	...	...	...	...	...	...	...	...	...	...	...
Sub-Saharan Africa												
159 Angola	3.0**	...	...	...	88.7**	...	...	...	...	...	...	...
160 Benin	2.5**	3.3**,y	...	...	93.8**	...	...	56**,y	...	145**,y	...	0.04**,y
161 Botswana	...	...	...	...	...	...	...	...	...	...	...	...
162 Burkina Faso	...	...	...	...	...	...	...	...	...	...	...	...
163 Burundi	4.2	5.3	...	13.0y	88.2	73.4	10	0.6	57	5	0.01	0.00
164 Cameroon	2.7**	4.0	10.9**	17.2	...	80.1	...	...	...	...	...	...
165 Cape Verde	...	7.4	...	20.7	...	81.8	...	...	...	...	...	...
166 Central African Republic	...	...	...	...	...	...	...	...	...	...	...	...
167 Chad	2.0**	...	...	...	...	...	...	...	...	...	...	...
168 Comoros	3.8**	3.9y	...	24.1y	...	...	...	...	...	...	...	...
169 Congo	6.0	4.4**,y	22.0	...	92.9	85.9**,y	32	55**,y	41	65**,y	0.01	0.03**,y
170 Côte d'Ivoire	5.6	...	25.5**	...	74.0	...	7	...	14	...	0.00	...
171 D. R. Congo	...	...	...	...	...	...	...	...	...	...	...	...
172 Equatorial Guinea	...	...	...	...	...	90.5**,z	...	...	...	...	...	...

Public current expenditure on pre-primary education per pupil as % of GNP per capita		Public current expenditure on primary education per pupil (unit cost) in constant 2003 US$		Public current expenditure on primary education per pupil (unit cost) at PPP in constant 2003 US$		Public current expenditure on primary education as % of GNP		Public current expenditure on primary education per pupil as % of GNP per capita		Public current expenditure on primary education as % of public current expenditure on education		Primary teachers' compensation as % of public current expenditure on primary education		Teachers' compensation as % of public current expenditure on education		
1999	2004	1999	2004	1999	2004	1999	2004	1999	2004	1999	2004	1999	2004	1999	2004	
0.8**	1.0	858**	717	1 093**	965	3.3**	2.5	19.8**	17.1	52.7**	47.3	87.6	…	88.4	…	117
…	…	…	932	…	1 651	…	4.5	…	30.5	…	47.1	…	93.7y	…	48.7y	118
…	…	…	…	…	…	…	…	…	…	…	…	…	…	…	…	119
1.4**	…	670	…	1 026	…	1.5	…	11.1	…	39.8	…	77.5	…	77.1	…	120
…	…	…	…	…	…	…	…	…	…	29.7	21.8**,z	63.5**	67.9**,y	56.6	76.0y	121
…	…	292	…	408	…	0.8	…	7.6	…	32.4	…	71.3	45.0z	70.9	46.5z	122
…	…	…	…	…	…	…	…	…	…	…	…	…	…	…	…	123
														North America and Western Europe		
…	…	…	…	…	…	…	…	…	…	…	29.1	…	92.6y	…	79.2y	124
15.0**	15.7y	6 920**	7 072y	6 997**	8 144y	1.1**	1.1y	23.9**	23.1y	19.0**	19.7y	71.5	69.6z	63.9	60.6z	125
…	…	…	…	…	…	…	…	…	…	…	…	…	64.7z	…	64.8z	126
13.7**	12.7**,y	…	…	…	…	…	…	…	…	…	…	…	…	54.0	50.3y	127
6.9*	15.2*,y	2 419	2 895y	3 144	…	1.6	1.7y	17.0*	19.1*,y	33.9	30.3y	…	79.9z	…	80.1z	128
15.1**	15.3y	8 796**	8 793y	7 479**	8 474y	1.6**	1.8y	23.6**	22.8y	…	21.7y	48.9	51.2z	48.2	50.1z	129
13.4**	12.7**,y	4 692**	5 123**,z	4 455**	4 556**,z	1.2**	1.3**,z	16.8**	16.6**,z	21.1**	20.7**,z	…	57.5z	…	48.7z	130
15.2**	14.8y	4 457**	4 781y	4 329**	5 368y	1.1**	1.0y	16.0**	16.3y	20.2**	20.2y	…	54.1z	…	55.9z	131
11.7**	13.4**,y	3 897**	4 442**,y	3 778**	5 015**,y	0.6**	0.6**,y	13.9**	15.2**,y	15.2**	14.0**,y	…	…	…	…	132
12.3**	11.9**,y	1 604**	2 017**,y	2 273**	3 131**,y	0.7**	0.8**,y	11.8**	13.5**,y	25.2**	25.4**,y	…	…	…	…	133
…	9.1**,z	…	8 742**,z	…	7 508**,z	…	2.7**,z	…	24.6**,z	…	35.1**,z	…	…	…	…	134
…	…	3 268**	4 187y	3 479**	4 968**,y	1.5**	1.6**,y	11.9**	13.7**,y	32.2**	32.5**,y	83.4	79.8y	69.4	68.2y	135
10.4**	11.8y	3 280**	3 593y	3 655**	4 485y	2.4**	2.6y	19.8**	21.6y	34.1**	35.4y	…	…	…	…	136
15.4**	13.5y	4 795**	6 080y	5 541**	7 824y	1.0**	1.2y	20.0**	24.2y	23.1**	26.1y	…	63.2z	…	61.4z	137
…	…	…	…	…	…	…	…	…	…	…	…	…	71.7**,z	…	…	138
…	12.5y	…	1 629y	…	2 851y	…	1.1y	…	13.2y	…	24.7y	…	60.5y	…	59.9y	139
…	…	…	…	…	…	…	…	…	…	17.7	16.8	…	…	…	…	140
13.4**	14.4y	4 551**	5 357y	4 693**	6 001y	1.2**	1.4y	14.6**	17.0y	25.5**	27.8y	…	…	…	…	141
24.1**	8.5**,z	7 900**	9 116**,z	7 520**	7 093**,z	1.6**	1.8**,z	17.4**	18.8**,z	24.7**	25.4**,z	…	…	…	…	142
13.3**	14.9y	2 794**	3 415y	4 043**	5 272y	1.6**	1.8y	20.4**	24.1y	31.0**	31.8y	…	82.4z	…	…	143
…	…	…	…	…	…	…	…	…	…	…	…	…	…	…	…	144
11.5**	14.6y	3 331**	3 630y	4 199**	4 897y	1.2**	1.1y	18.2**	18.7y	28.1**	27.1y	78.3	75.8z	74.7	72.0z	145
…	…	…	…	…	…	…	…	…	…	…	…	49.8	57.0z	32.3	…	146
8.1	8.9y	8 834	9 685y	6 521	7 810y	1.4	1.5y	19.2	20.6y	31.6	30.5y	72.4	72.2z	68.6	68.3z	147
…	…	…	…	…	…	…	…	…	…	…	…	52.4	50.4z	50.5	53.8z	148
…	…	…	…	…	…	…	…	…	…	…	…	55.9	55.4z	51.5	46.3z	149
														South and West Asia		
…	…	…	…	…	…	…	…	…	…	…	…	…	…	…	…	150
5.4**	…	13	19	54	91	0.6	0.7	3.9	5.2	38.9	39.0	…	…	…	…	151
…	…	…	…	…	…	…	…	…	…	…	…	…	…	…	…	152
2.2**	…	51**	…	262**	…	1.2**	…	10.5**	…	29.9**	…	…	80.5z	…	84.9z	153
…	7.5z	…	164z	…	556z	…	1.1z	…	9.7z	…	25.0z	…	…	…	…	154
…	…	…	…	…	…	…	…	…	…	…	…	…	…	…	…	155
−**	11.6**,z	14**	18**,z	81**	103**,z	1.1**	1.3**,z	7.3**	8.3**,z	52.7**	49.1**,z	…	…	…	…	156
…	…	…	…	…	…	…	…	…	…	…	…	…	…	…	…	157
…	…	…	…	…	…	…	…	…	…	…	…	…	…	…	…	158
														Sub-Saharan Africa		
…	…	…	…	…	…	…	…	…	…	…	…	…	…	…	…	159
…	13.0**,y	…	47**,y	…	124**,y	…	1.7**,y	…	11.1**,y	…	…	…	…	…	…	160
…	…	…	…	…	…	…	…	…	…	…	…	…	…	…	…	161
…	…	…	…	…	…	…	…	…	…	…	…	…	…	…	…	162
11.7	0.7	11**	11	64**	83	1.4	1.7	13.0**	13.1	38.9	44.4	…	…	…	…	163
…	…	53	…	158	…	1.2	…	7.9	…	…	…	…	…	…	…	164
…	…	…	261	…	756	…	2.7	…	15.5	…	44.2	…	96.0	…	…	165
…	…	…	…	…	…	…	…	…	…	…	…	…	…	…	…	166
…	…	…	…	…	…	…	…	…	…	…	…	…	…	…	…	167
…	…	…	…	…	…	…	…	…	…	…	…	…	…	…	…	168
5.1	7.9**,y	151	73**,y	195	87**,y	2.0	1.5**,y	24.1	10.6**,y	35.9	40.2**,y	…	…	…	…	169
0.8	…	131	…	262	…	1.8	…	15.5	…	43.4	…	…	…	…	…	170
…	…	…	…	…	…	…	…	…	…	…	…	…	…	…	…	171
…	…	…	…	…	…	…	…	…	…	…	…	…	…	…	…	172

Table 11 (continued)

	Country or territory	Total public expenditure on education as % of GNP		Total public expenditure on education as % of total government expenditure		Public current expenditure on education as % of total public expenditure on education		Public current expenditure on pre-primary education per pupil (unit cost) in constant 2003 US$		Public current expenditure on pre-primary education per pupil (unit cost) at PPP in constant 2003 US$		Public current expenditure on pre-primary education as % of GNP	
		1999	2004	1999	2004	1999	2004	1999	2004	1999	2004	1999	2004
173	Eritrea	5.0	3.8	...	...	69.5**	70.9	...	–	...	–	...	–
174	Ethiopia	4.3**	4.6**,y	...	...	...	63.9**,y	...	...	...	...	...	...
175	Gabon	3.8**	...	...	...	87.3**	...	...	...	...	...	...	...
176	Gambia	3.1	2.1**	14.2	8.9y	86.8	86.4**,z	...	...	...	...	...	...
177	Ghana	4.2**	...	...	...	...	**85.6**	...	...	...	...	...	...
178	Guinea	2.1**	...	...	...	...	...	...	...	...	...	...	...
179	Guinea-Bissau	2.3	...	4.8	...	...	...	...	...	...	...	...	...
180	Kenya	6.6	7.1	...	29.2	95.5	92.2	0.1**	7	0.2**	14	0.00**	0.1
181	Lesotho	10.2	7.3**,y	25.5	...	74.1	91.3**,y	–	...	–	...	...	...
182	Liberia	...	...	...	...	...	...	...	...	...	...	...	...
183	Madagascar	2.5**	3.4	...	18.2	...	75.6	...	...	...	...	...	...
184	Malawi	4.7	6.2z	24.6	...	81.8	81.8z	...	...	...	...	...	–z
185	Mali	3.0**	...	...	...	89.6**	...	45**	...	144**	...	0.03**	...
186	Mauritius	4.2	4.7	17.7	15.7	91.1	83.9	56	70	145	171	0.1	0.1
187	Mozambique	2.5**	...	...	...	...	...	...	...	...	...	...	...
188	Namibia	7.9	7.1z	...	...	93.9	...	–**	...	–**	...	–	...
189	Niger	2.1**	2.3	...	...	...	...	...	...	...	...	...	...
190	Nigeria	...	...	...	...	...	...	...	...	...	...	...	...
191	Rwanda	...	...	...	...	...	...	...	...	...	...	...	...
192	Sao Tome and Principe	...	...	...	...	...	...	...	...	...	...	...	...
193	Senegal	3.5**	4.1	...	...	...	91.2	...	15	...	36	...	0.01
194	Seychelles	5.5	5.7**	...	...	...	93.5**	...	1 237**	...	...	...	0.5**
195	Sierra Leone	...	...	...	...	...	...	...	...	...	...	...	...
196	Somalia	...	...	...	...	...	...	...	...	...	...	...	...
197	South Africa	6.2	5.5	22.2	18.1	98.1	95.8	2*	64	6*	154	0.00	0.02
198	Swaziland	6.0	6.3	...	...	100.0	100.0	...	...	...	...	0.00	0.00
199	Togo	4.4	2.7y	26.2	13.6y	96.7	95.2y	...	...	...	...	...	...
200	Uganda	...	5.3**	...	18.3**	...	75.0**	...	.	.	.	...	.
201	United Republic of Tanzania	2.2**	...	...	...	...	...	...	.	...	...	...	.
202	Zambia	2.0	2.9	...	14.8	...	99.1	...	...	...	...	...	.
203	Zimbabwe	...	...	...	...	...	...	...	...	...	...	...	...
I	World[1]	4.5	4.8	...	...	...	91.5	...	...	...	...	...	...
II	Countries in transition	3.7	3.7	...	16.9	...	93.5	...	...	...	...	...	...
III	Developed countries	5.0	5.4	11.5	...	...	92.7	...	2 466	...	3 240	...	0.4
IV	Developing countries	4.3	4.7	...	...	...	90.1	...	...	...	...	...	...
V	Arab States	...	...	...	...	...	...	...	...	...	...	...	...
VI	Central and Eastern Europe	4.3	4.6	...	...	...	92.7	...	1 016	...	2 272	...	0.5
VII	Central Asia	3.7	3.1	...	...	...	95.4	...	...	...	...	...	...
VIII	East Asia and the Pacific	4.8	4.9	...	...	...	...	...	...	...	...	...	...
IX	East Asia	3.5	3.3	11.1	...	...	...	...	...	...	...	...	...
X	Pacific	6.4	7.3	...	...	...	...	...	...	...	...	...	...
XI	Latin America and the Caribbean	4.7	4.8	15.8	16.1	...	92.6	...	...	...	...	...	0.2
XII	Caribbean	...	...	16.4	...	...	89.0	...	...	...	...	...	...
XIII	Latin America	4.5	4.1	14.7	14.8	92.5	95.5	...	130	...	293	...	0.2
XIV	North America and Western Europe	5.2	5.7	11.6	...	91.9	92.7	3 688	3 399	3 536	3 654	0.3	0.4
XV	South and West Asia	2.9	3.3	...	...	88.9	80.3	...	...	...	...	...	...
XVI	Sub-Saharan Africa	3.8	4.6	...	...	...	...	...	...	...	...	...	...

1. All regional values shown are medians.   Data in bold are for 2005.   (z) Data are for 2003.   (y) Data are for 2002.

Public current expenditure on pre-primary education per pupil as % of GNP per capita		Public current expenditure on primary education per pupil (unit cost) in constant 2003 US$		Public current expenditure on primary education per pupil (unit cost) at PPP in constant 2003 US$		Public current expenditure on primary education as % of GNP		Public current expenditure on primary education per pupil as % of GNP per capita		Public current expenditure on primary education as % of public current expenditure on education		Primary teachers' compensation as % of public current expenditure on primary education		Teachers' compensation as % of public current expenditure on education		
1999	2004	1999	2004	1999	2004	1999	2004	1999	2004	1999	2004	1999	2004	1999	2004	
...	−	...	18	...	92	...	0.9	...	10.0	...	32.5	...	...	...	...	173
...	...	...	...	...	...	...	...	...	...	...	...	...	...	...	...	174
...	...	...	...	...	...	...	...	...	...	...	...	...	...	...	...	175
...	...	47	...	226	...	2.2	...	18.3	...	80.3	...	...	74.8	...	...	176
...	...	...	...	...	...	...	...	...	...	...	**34.4**	...	...	...	...	177
...	...	...	...	...	...	...	...	...	...	...	...	...	...	...	...	178
...	...	...	...	...	...	...	...	...	...	...	...	...	...	...	...	179
0.01**	1.6	...	95	...	211	...	4.1	...	23.3	...	62.9	...	...	...	...	180
−	...	111	115**,y	441	676**,y	3.2	3.4**,y	15.3	14.7**,y	42.8	50.8**,y	84.5	...	57.3	...	181
...	...	...	...	...	...	...	...	...	...	...	...	...	...	...	...	182
...	...	...	...	...	...	...	...	...	...	...	...	...	...	...	...	183
...	...	...	20^z	...	78^z	...	3.2^z	...	13.4^z	...	62.7^z	...	...	...	...	184
15.4**	...	46**	...	147**	...	1.3**	...	15.7**	...	48.9**	...	...	...	...	...	185
1.6	1.8	383	438	999	1 071	1.2	1.2	11.0	11.1	31.9	29.9	...	...	...	...	186
...	...	...	...	...	...	...	...	...	...	...	...	...	...	...	...	187
−**	...	447	301^z	1 459	876^z	4.4	4.0^z	20.7	19.4^z	59.4	...	...	...	...	...	188
...	...	...	...	...	...	...	...	...	...	...	...	...	...	...	...	189
...	...	...	...	...	...	...	...	...	...	...	...	...	...	...	...	190
...	...	...	...	...	...	...	...	...	...	...	...	...	...	...	...	191
...	...	...	...	...	...	...	...	...	...	...	...	...	...	...	...	192
...	2.5	...	81	...	193	...	1.7	...	13.6	...	44.3	...	...	...	...	193
...	15.4**	...	1 169**	...	...	...	1.6**	...	14.5**	...	30.6**	...	62.1^z	...	50.9^z	194
...	...	...	...	...	...	...	...	...	...	...	...	...	...	...	...	195
...	...	...	...	...	...	...	...	...	...	...	...	...	...	...	...	196
0.1*	2.3	488*	374	1 461*	897	2.7	2.1	15.2*	13.4	45.2	40.2	...	87.6	...	...	197
...	...	153	166**	489	382**	2.0	2.4**	9.4	11.7**	33.2	37.7**	...	...	...	...	198
...	...	30**	...	139**	...	1.8**	...	9.9**	...	43.0**	...	79.4	...	...	...	199
.	.	...	17.4**	...	96**	...	2.5**	...	8.7**	...	61.9**	...	...	...	...	200
...	...	...	...	...	...	...	...	...	...	...	...	...	...	...	...	201
...	...	...	36	...	65	...	1.8	...	9.4	...	63.5	...	92.8	...	72.6	202
...	...	...	...	...	...	...	...	...	...	...	...	...	...	...	...	203
...	...	...	...	...	...	...	...	...	...	...	...	...	...	...	...	I
...	...	...	...	...	...	...	...	...	...	...	...	...	...	...	...	II
...	14.0	...	3 630	...	4 682	...	1.2	...	17.3	...	25.4	...	...	...	...	III
...	...	...	...	...	...	...	...	...	...	...	...	...	...	...	...	IV
...	...	...	...	...	...	...	...	...	...	...	...	...	...	...	...	V
...	22.4	...	822	...	1 804	...	0.7	...	15.2	...	18.0	...	...	...	...	VI
...	...	...	...	...	...	...	...	...	...	...	...	...	...	...	...	VII
...	...	...	...	...	...	...	...	...	...	...	...	...	...	...	...	VIII
...	...	...	...	...	...	...	...	...	...	...	...	...	...	...	...	IX
...	...	...	...	...	...	...	...	...	...	...	...	...	...	...	...	X
...	...	...	...	...	...	...	1.6	...	...	...	37.7	...	...	...	...	XI
...	...	...	...	...	...	...	...	...	...	...	33.7	...	...	...	...	XII
...	7.4	...	177	...	490	...	1.5	...	11.4	...	40.5	...	...	...	...	XIII
13.4	13.4	4 457	4 781	4 329	5 320	1.2	1.4	17.4	18.8	25.2	26.1	...	64.7	...	60.6	XIV
...	...	...	...	...	...	...	...	...	...	...	...	...	...	...	...	XV
...	...	...	...	...	...	...	...	...	...	...	...	...	...	...	...	XVI

Table 12
Trends in basic or proxy indicators to measure EFA goals 1, 2, 3, 4 and 5

	GOAL 1						GOAL 2					
	Early childhood care and education						Universal primary education					
	GROSS ENROLMENT RATIO (GER) IN PRE-PRIMARY EDUCATION						NET ENROLMENT RATIO (NER) IN PRIMARY EDUCATION					
	School year ending in						School year ending in					
	1991		1999		2004		1991		1999		2004	
Country or territory	Total (%)	GPI (F/M)	Total (%)	GPI (F/M)	Total (%)	GPI (F/M)	Total (%)	GPI (F/M)	Total (%)	GPI (F/M)	Total (%)	GPI (F/M)
Arab States												
1 Algeria	...	...	3	1.00	5	0.97	89	0.88	91	0.96	97	0.98
2 Bahrain	29	1.03	35	0.95	45	0.96	99	1.00	96	1.02	97	1.01
3 Djibouti	0.6	1.46	0.4	1.50	2	0.99	29	0.72**	28	0.73	33	0.81
4 Egypt	6	0.99	11	0.95	14	0.95	84**	0.84**	93**	0.93**	95**	0.97**
5 Iraq	7	0.95	5	0.98	6	1.00	94**	0.88**	85	0.85	88	0.86
6 Jordan	20	0.89	29	0.91	30	0.94	94	1.01	92	1.01	91	1.02
7 Kuwait	31	1.01	79	1.02	71	0.98	49**	0.93**	87	1.01	86**	1.03**
8 Lebanon	...	...	67	0.97	74	0.98	73**	0.97**	94**	0.96**	93	0.99
9 Libyan Arab Jamahiriya	...	...	5	0.97**	8**,z	0.96**,z	96**	0.96**	...	...	...	...
10 Mauritania	...	...	...	...	2	...	35**	0.74**	63	0.94	74	0.99
11 Morocco	60	0.46	62	0.52	53	0.63	56	0.70	72	0.86	86	0.94
12 Oman	3	0.89	6	0.88	6	0.91	69	0.95	80	1.00	78	1.02
13 Palestinian Autonomous Territories	14	...	40	0.96	30	0.96	...	...	97	1.01	86	1.00
14 Qatar	28	0.93	25	0.97	32	0.99	89	0.98	94	1.01	96	0.99
15 Saudi Arabia	7	0.87	5	0.90	5	...	59	0.81	58	0.93	59**	0.91**
16 Sudan[2]	18	0.57	20	...	23	1.03	40**	0.75**	...	...	...	...
17 Syrian Arab Republic	6	0.88	8	0.90	10	0.91	91	0.91	92**	0.93**	92	0.96
18 Tunisia	8	...	14	0.95	22**,z	0.99**,z	94	0.92	94	0.98	97	1.00
19 United Arab Emirates	55	0.96	63	0.97	64	0.99	103	0.98	79	0.99	71	0.97
20 Yemen	0.7	0.94	0.7	0.86	0.8	0.87	51**	0.38**	57	0.59	75**	0.73**
Central and Eastern Europe												
21 Albania	57	...	44	1.07	49z	1.03z	95**	1.01**	99**	0.99**	96z	0.99z
22 Belarus	82	...	80	0.95*	104	0.98	86**	0.95**	...	...	90	0.97**
23 Bosnia and Herzegovina	...	...	...	...	...	...	...	...	...	...	...	...
24 Bulgaria	90	1.00	69	0.99	78	0.99	86	0.99	97	0.98	95	0.99
25 Croatia	28	0.98	40	0.98	47z	0.98z	79	1.00	85	0.98	87z	0.99z
26 Czech Republic	92	0.97	94	1.06	107	0.96	87**	1.00**	...	...	...	...
27 Estonia	72	0.98	90	0.99	114	0.98	100**	0.99**	96**	0.98**	94	1.00
28 Hungary	109	0.97	80	0.98	81	0.98	91	1.01	88	0.99	89	0.99
29 Latvia	43	1.00	53	0.95	79	0.96	92**	0.99**	...	...	...	...
30 Lithuania	58	1.00	51	0.97	64	0.96	...	...	95	0.99	89	1.00
31 Poland	48	...	50	1.01	53	1.01	97	1.00	...	...	97	1.00
32 Republic of Moldova	72	0.95	41	0.96	50	0.97*	89**	0.99**	78**	...	78	0.99
33 Romania	71	1.04	63	1.02	76	1.02	81**	1.00**	96	0.99	92	0.99
34 Russian Federation[3]	73	...	55	0.94**	85	0.91	99**	1.00**	...	...	91**	1.01**
35 Serbia and Montenegro[2,4]	...	...	44	0.99	...	...	...	...	...	...	...	...
36 Slovakia	86	...	83	...	92	0.97	...	...	...	...	...	...
37 Slovenia	65	0.94	75	0.91	59	0.95	96**	1.01**	97	0.99	98	1.00
38 TFYR Macedonia	...	...	28	1.01	32	1.00	94	0.99	93	0.98	92	1.00
39 Turkey	4	0.92	6	0.94	8	0.95	89	0.92**	...	...	89**	0.95**
40 Ukraine	85	0.92	48	0.98	82	0.97	80**	1.00**	...	...	82	1.00*
Central Asia												
41 Armenia	36	...	26	...	31	1.17	...	...	...	...	94	1.04
42 Azerbaijan	18	0.84	22	0.89	28	1.01	89	0.99	85	1.01	84	0.98
43 Georgia	58	...	38	1.01	49	1.15	97**	1.00**	...	...	93	0.99
44 Kazakhstan	71	...	15	0.95	31	0.97	89**	0.99**	...	...	93	0.99
45 Kyrgyzstan	34	1.02	10	0.80	12	0.99	92**	1.00**	88*	0.99*	90	0.99
46 Mongolia	38	1.23	25	1.21	35	1.08	90**	1.02**	90	1.04	84	1.01
47 Tajikistan	16	...	8	0.76	9	0.93	77**	0.98**	89	0.94	97	0.96
48 Turkmenistan	...	...	...	...	...	...	...	...	...	...	...	...
49 Uzbekistan	73	...	...	...	28**	0.93**	78**	0.99**	...	...	...	...
East Asia and the Pacific												
50 Australia	71	0.99	...	...	102	1.00	99	1.00	92	1.01	96	1.00
51 Brunei Darussalam	47	0.98	51	1.04	52	1.00	92	0.98	...	...	...	...
52 Cambodia	4	0.91	6**	1.03**	9	0.99	69**	0.84**	85**	0.91**	98	0.96
53 China[5]	22	1.00	38	0.97	36	0.92**	97	0.96	...	...	...	...
54 Cook Islands[4]	...	...	86	0.98	91**,z	1.11**,z	...	...	85	0.96	...	...

	GOAL 3				GOAL 4				GOAL 5											
	Learning needs of all youth and adults				Improving levels of adult literacy				Gender parity in primary education						Gender parity in secondary education						
	YOUTH LITERACY RATE (15-24)				ADULT LITERACY RATE (15 and over)				GROSS ENROLMENT RATIO (GER)						GROSS ENROLMENT RATIO (GER)						
									School year ending in						School year ending in						
	1990		2000-2004[1]		1990		2000-2004[1]		1991		1999		2004		1991		1999		2004		
	Total (%)	GPI (F/M)	Total (%)	GPI (F/M)	Total (%)	GPI (F/M)	Total (%)	GPI (F/M)	Total (%)	GPI (F/M)	Total (%)	GPI (F/M)	Total (%)	GPI (F/M)	Total (%)	GPI (F/M)	Total (%)	GPI (F/M)	Total (%)	GPI (F/M)	
Arab States																					
	77	0.79	90*	0.92*	53	0.64	70*	0.76*	96	0.85	105	0.91	112	0.93	60	0.79	…	…	81	1.07	1
	96	0.99	97*	1.00*	82	0.86	87*	0.94*	110	1.00	105	1.01	104	1.00	100	1.04	94	1.08	99	1.06	2
	73	0.78	…	…	53	0.59	…	…	35	0.72	35	0.71	39	0.79	11	0.66	15	0.72	22	0.69	3
	61	0.72	85*	0.88*	47	0.56	71*	0.71*	92	0.83	101**	0.91**	101**	0.96**	71	0.79	81**	0.91**	87**	0.95**	4
	41	0.44	85*	0.91*	36	0.38	74*	0.76*	108	0.83	92	0.82	98	0.83	44	0.63	34	0.63	45	0.66	5
	97	0.97	99*	1.00*	82	0.80	90*	0.89*	101	1.01	99	1.00	98	1.01	63	1.04	88	1.03	87	1.01	6
	88	0.99	100*	1.00*	77	0.91	93*	0.96*	60	0.95	100	1.01	96	1.00	43	0.98	99**	1.02**	90	1.06	7
	92	0.93	…	…	80	0.83	…	…	106**	0.97**	115	0.95	107	0.96	…	…	80	1.10	89	1.09	8
	91	0.84	…	…	68	0.62	…	…	104	0.94	114	0.98	112**,z	1.00**,z	86	…	…	…	104**,z	1.06**,z	9
	46	0.65	61*	0.82*	35	0.52	51*	0.73*	50	0.73	87	0.94	94	0.98	13	0.46	19**	0.73**	20	0.83	10
	55	0.62	70*	0.75*	39	0.47	52*	0.60*	64	0.69	87	0.81	106	0.90	35	0.72	37	0.79	48	0.84	11
	86	0.79	97*	0.99*	55	0.57	81*	0.85*	85	0.92	91	0.97	87	1.00	45	0.81	75	0.99	86	0.96	12
	…	…	99*	1.00*	…	…	92*	0.91*	…	…	106	1.01	93	1.00	…	…	79	1.04	94	1.05	13
	90	1.05	96*	1.03*	77	0.98	89*	0.99*	101	0.93	105	0.96	102	0.98	84	1.06	90	1.07	97	0.97	14
	85	0.86	96*	0.96*	66	0.66	79*	0.80*	73	0.86	70	0.96	67	0.96	44	0.79	71	0.87	68	0.88	15
	65	0.71	77*	0.84*	46	0.53	61*	0.73*	48	0.77	51**	0.85**	60	0.87	21	0.79	26**	…	33	0.93	16
	80	0.73	92*	0.96*	65	0.58	80*	0.86*	101	0.90	102	0.92	123	0.95	48	0.73	40	0.91	63	0.93	17
	84	0.81	94*	0.96*	59	0.65	74*	0.78*	114	0.89	114	0.95	110	0.97	45	0.79	73	1.02	81	1.02	18
	85	1.08	…	…	71	0.99	…	…	115	0.97	90	0.97	84	0.97	68	1.16	82	1.08	66	1.06	19
	50	0.34	72	0.67	33	0.23	53	0.46	64**	0.35**	73	0.56	87	0.71	…	…	41	0.37	48	0.48	20
Central and Eastern Europe																					
	95	0.94	99*	1.00*	77	0.77	99*	0.99*	100	1.00	110	0.98	104z	0.99z	78	0.86	74	0.95	78z	0.97z	21
	100	1.00	100*	1.00*	99	1.00	100*	1.00*	96	0.96	109	0.98	101	0.97	95	…	83	1.06	93	1.01	22
	…	…	100*	1.00*	…	…	97*	0.95*	…	…	…	…	…	…	…	…	…	…	23
	99	1.00	98*	1.00*	97	0.98	98*	0.99*	98	0.97	106	0.97	105	0.98	75	1.04	91	0.98	102	0.96	24
	100	1.00	100*	1.00*	97	0.96	98*	0.98*	85	0.99	92	0.98	94z	0.99z	76	1.10	84	1.02	88z	1.02z	25
	…	…	…	…	…	…	…	…	96	1.00	104	0.99	102	0.99	91	0.97	83	1.04	96	1.01	26
	100	1.00	100*	1.00*	100	1.00	100*	1.00*	111	0.97	102	0.97	100	0.97	98	1.11	93	1.04	98	1.02	27
	100	1.00	…	…	99	1.00	…	…	95	1.00	102	0.98	98	0.99	79	1.01	94	1.02	97	0.99	28
	…	…	100*	1.00*	…	…	100*	1.00*	97	0.99	99	0.98	93	0.97	91	1.00	89	1.04	96	1.00	29
	100	1.00	100*	1.00*	99	1.00	100*	1.00*	92	0.95	103	0.98	97	0.99	92	…	96	1.01	98	0.99	30
	…	…	…	…	…	…	…	…	98	0.99	98	0.98	99	0.99	81	1.05	…	…	97	1.01	31
	100	1.00	100*	1.00*	97	0.97	98*	0.99*	93	1.00	84	1.00	85	0.99	80	1.09	72	1.01	74	1.04	32
	99	1.00	98*	1.00*	97	0.97	97*	0.98*	91	1.00	105	0.98	107	0.98	92	0.99	79	1.01	85	1.00	33
	100	1.00	100*	1.00*	99	0.99	99*	1.00*	109	1.00	100	0.99	123	1.00	93	1.06	…	…	93	0.99	34
	…	…	99*	1.00*	…	…	96*	0.95*	…	…	104	0.99	…	…	…	…	92	1.01	…	…	35
	…	…	…	…	…	…	…	…	…	…	103	0.99	99	0.99z	…	…	85	1.02	94	1.01	36
	100	1.00	100	1.00	100	1.00	100	1.00	100	…	101	0.99	123	0.99z	89	…	101	1.02	100	1.00	37
	…	…	99*	0.99*	…	…	96*	0.96*	99	0.98	101	0.98	98	1.00z	56	0.99	82	0.97	84	0.98	38
	93	0.91	96*	0.95*	78	0.74	87*	0.84*	99	0.92	…	…	93	0.94	48	0.63	…	…	79	0.75	39
	100	1.00	100*	1.00*	99	0.99	99*	0.99*	89	1.00	105	0.99	95	1.00	93	…	97	1.02*	93	0.98*	40
Central Asia																					
	100	1.00	100*	1.00*	97	0.97	99*	0.99*	…	…	…	…	101	1.03	…	…	…	…	91	1.03	41
	…	…	100*	1.00*	…	…	99*	0.99*	111**	0.99**	94	1.00	97	0.98	88	1.01	76	1.00	83	0.97	42
	…	…	…	…	…	…	97*	0.95*	97	1.00	98	1.00	95	1.00	95	0.97	79	0.98	82	0.99	43
	100	1.00	100*	1.00*	99	0.99	100*	1.00*	90	0.99	98	1.00	109	0.99	99	1.04	91	0.99	98	0.98	44
	…	…	100*	1.00*	…	…	99*	0.99*	…	…	98	0.99	98	1.00	100	1.02	84	1.02	88	1.01	45
	…	…	98*	1.01*	…	…	98*	1.00*	97	1.02	98	1.04	104	1.02	82	1.14	58	1.27	90	1.14	46
	100	1.00	100*	1.00*	98	0.98	99*	1.00*	91	0.98	97	0.95	100	0.95	102	…	71	0.86	82	0.84	47
	…	…	100*	1.00*	…	…	99*	0.99*	…	…	…	…	…	…	…	…	…	…	48
	100	1.00	…	…	99	0.98	…	…	81	0.98	…	…	100**	0.99**	99	0.91	…	…	95**	0.97**	49
East Asia and the Pacific																					
	…	…	…	…	…	…	…	…	108	0.99	98	1.00	103	1.00	83	1.03	154	1.00	149	0.96	50
	98	1.01	99*	1.00*	86	0.87	93*	0.95*	114	0.94	114	0.97	109	1.00	77	1.09	85	1.09	94	1.05	51
	73	0.81	83*	0.90*	62	0.63	74*	0.76*	87	0.81	99	0.87	137	0.92	29	0.43	16**	0.53**	29**	0.69**	52
	95	0.95	99*	0.99*	78	0.79	91*	0.91*	125	0.93	…	…	118	1.00	49	0.75	62	…	73	1.00	53
	…	…	…	…	…	…	…	…	…	…	96	0.95	82**,z	0.98**,z	…	…	60	1.08	64**,z	1.02**,z	54

Table 12 (continued)

	Country or territory	GOAL 1 Early childhood care and education GROSS ENROLMENT RATIO (GER) IN PRE-PRIMARY EDUCATION School year ending in						GOAL 2 Universal primary education NET ENROLMENT RATIO (NER) IN PRIMARY EDUCATION School year ending in					
		1991		1999		2004		1991		1999		2004	
		Total (%)	GPI (F/M)	Total (%)	GPI (F/M)	Total (%)	GPI (F/M)	Total (%)	GPI (F/M)	Total (%)	GPI (F/M)	Total (%)	GPI (F/M)
55	Democratic People's Republic of Korea	…	…	…	…	…	…	…	…	…	…	…	…
56	Fiji	14	1.07	17	1.02	16	1.06	…	…	99	1.01	96	0.99
57	Indonesia	18	…	18**	1.01**	22	1.09	97	0.96	…	…	94	0.98
58	Japan	48	1.02	82	1.02**	85	…	100	1.00	100	1.00	100	1.00
59	Kiribati[4]	…	…	…	…	68**	…	…	…	88**	1.00**	…	…
60	Lao People's Democratic Republic	7	0.87	8	1.11	8	1.05	63**	0.85**	80	0.92	84	0.94
61	Macao, China	88	1.00	89	0.95	92	0.98	81**	0.98**	85	1.01	89	0.97
62	Malaysia	42	1.03	102	1.04	108z	1.12z	…	…	98	0.98	93z	1.00z
63	Marshall Islands	…	…	…	…	50**,z	1.02**,z	…	…	…	…	90**,z	0.99**,z
64	Micronesia (Federated States of)	…	…	37	…	…	…	…	…	…	…	…	…
65	Myanmar	…	…	2	…	…	…	98**	0.97**	80**	0.99**	**88**	**1.02**
66	Nauru	…	…	…	…	71**,z	1.02**,z	…	…	…	…	…	…
67	New Zealand	76	0.98	88	1.00	92	1.01	98	1.00	99	1.01	99	1.00
68	Niue[4]	…	…	154	0.93	97	1.58	…	…	99	1.00	…	…
69	Palau[4]	…	…	63	1.23	64**	1.16**	…	…	97**	0.94**	…	…
70	Papua New Guinea	0.3	1.02	35	0.96	59**,z	0.94**,z	…	…	…	…	…	…
71	Philippines	12	…	31	1.05	40	1.04	96**	0.99**	…	…	94	1.02
72	Republic of Korea	55	0.98	80	1.00	**91**	**1.00**	104	1.01	94	1.01	**99**	**1.00**
73	Samoa	…	…	51**	1.21**	49**	1.26**	…	…	92	0.99	90**	1.00**
74	Singapore	…	…	…	…	…	…	…	…	…	…	…	…
75	Solomon Islands	35	0.96	35**	1.01**	41**,z	0.99**,z	…	…	…	…	80	0.99
76	Thailand	43	0.99	88	0.98	**90**	**0.97**	76**	0.97**	…	…	…	…
77	Timor-Leste	…	…	…	…	11y	…	…	…	…	…	…	…
78	Tokelau[6]	…	…	…	…	…	…	…	…	…	…	…	…
79	Tonga	…	…	30	1.22	23	1.36	…	…	91	0.97	93	0.96
80	Tuvalu[4]	…	…	…	…	99	1.02**	…	…	…	…	…	…
81	Vanuatu	…	…	49	1.08	52**,y	1.01**,y	…	…	91	0.99	94	0.98
82	Viet Nam	28	…	41	0.94	47	0.98	90**	0.92**	96	…	93**,y	…
	Latin America and the Caribbean												
83	Anguilla	…	…	…	…	116**	0.90**	…	…	…	…	88**	1.02**
84	Antigua and Barbuda	…	…	…	…	…	…	…	…	…	…	…	…
85	Argentina	49	…	57	1.02	62z	1.01z	…	…	99*	1.00*	99z	0.99z
86	Aruba[4]	…	…	97	1.00	100	1.07	…	…	98	1.01	97	0.99
87	Bahamas	…	…	12	1.09	31**,z	0.99**,z	90**	1.03**	89	0.99	84	1.02
88	Barbados	…	…	82	0.98	89	1.01	80**	0.99**	97**	0.99**	97	0.99
89	Belize	23	1.14	28	1.03	28	1.01	94**	0.99**	94**	1.00**	95	1.01
90	Bermuda[4]	…	…	…	…	52y	…	…	…	…	…	…	…
91	Bolivia	32	0.99	45	1.01	48**	1.01**	…	…	95	1.00	95**	1.01**
92	Brazil	48	…	58	1.00	68z	1.00z	85	…	91	…	93z	…
93	British Virgin Islands[4]	…	…	62	1.16	93	1.01	…	…	96**	1.02**	95**	1.00**
94	Cayman Islands	…	…	…	…	44**	0.87**	…	…	…	…	87**	0.95**
95	Chile	72	1.01	77	0.99	52	0.99	89	0.98	…	…	…	…
96	Colombia	13	…	36	1.02	38	1.01	69	…	88	1.01**	83	1.01
97	Costa Rica	65	1.02	84	1.01	64	1.01	87	1.01	…	…	…	…
98	Cuba	102	0.82	105	1.03	116	0.98	93	1.01	98	1.00	96	1.00
99	Dominica[4]	…	…	80	1.11	65	1.18	…	…	94**	0.98**	88	1.01
100	Dominican Republic	…	…	34	1.01	32	1.01	57**	2.18**	84	1.01	86	1.02
101	Ecuador	42	…	64	1.04	77	1.01	98**	1.01**	97	1.01	98**	1.01**
102	El Salvador	21	1.08	42	1.01	51	1.04	…	…	…	…	92**	1.00**
103	Grenada[4]	…	…	…	…	81	1.09	…	…	…	…	84	0.99
104	Guatemala	25	0.97	46	0.97	28	1.01	…	…	82	0.91	93	0.95
105	Guyana	76	1.03	122	0.99	108**	0.99**	89	1.00	…	…	…	…
106	Haiti	34	0.95	…	…	…	…	22	1.05	…	…	…	…
107	Honduras	13	1.06	…	…	33	1.04	89	1.02	…	…	91	1.02
108	Jamaica	80	1.02	78	1.08	92	1.03	96	1.00	88**	1.00**	91	1.01
109	Mexico	63	1.02	73	1.01	84	1.01	98	0.97**	98	1.00	98	1.00
110	Montserrat[4]	…	…	…	…	93	1.15	…	…	…	…	94	0.96
111	Netherlands Antilles	…	…	120	1.00	113**,z	0.97**,z	…	…	…	…	…	…
112	Nicaragua	13	1.08	28	1.04	35	1.03	73	1.03	78	1.01	88	0.99
113	Panama	57	…	39	1.01	55	1.02	…	…	96	0.99	98	1.00

	GOAL 3				GOAL 4				GOAL 5						GOAL 5						
	Learning needs of all youth and adults				Improving levels of adult literacy				Gender parity in primary education						Gender parity in secondary education						
	YOUTH LITERACY RATE (15-24)				ADULT LITERACY RATE (15 and over)				GROSS ENROLMENT RATIO (GER)						GROSS ENROLMENT RATIO (GER)						
									School year ending in						School year ending in						
	1990		2000-2004[1]		1990		2000-2004[1]		1991		1999		2004		1991		1999		2004		
	Total (%)	GPI (F/M)	Total (%)	GPI (F/M)	Total (%)	GPI (F/M)	Total (%)	GPI (F/M)	Total (%)	GPI (F/M)	Total (%)	GPI (F/M)	Total (%)	GPI (F/M)	Total (%)	GPI (F/M)	Total (%)	GPI (F/M)	Total (%)	GPI (F/M)	
...	...	...	...	...	...	...	...	...	...	...	...	...	...	...	...	...	...	...	...	...	55
98	1.00	...	...	89	0.93	...	...	133	1.00	110	0.99	106	0.98	64	0.95	81	1.11	88	1.07	56
95	0.97	99*	1.00*	80	0.84	90*	0.92*	114	0.98	...	...	117	0.98	46	0.83	...	...	64	0.99	57
...	...	...	...	...	...	...	...	100	1.00	101	1.00	100	1.00	97	1.02	102	1.01	102	1.00	58
...	...	...	...	...	...	...	...	...	...	104	1.01	115	1.03	...	...	84	1.18	91	1.22	59
70	0.76	78*	0.90*	57	0.61	69*	0.79*	103	0.79	117	0.85	116	0.88	24*	0.62*	33	0.69	46	0.76	60
97	0.97	100*	1.00*	91	0.92	91*	0.92*	99	0.96	100	0.96	106	0.92	65*	1.11*	76	1.08	96	1.04	61
95	0.99	97z	1.00*	81	0.86	89*	0.93*	95	1.00	100	0.98	93z	1.00z	57	1.05	69	1.10	76z	1.14z	62
...	...	...	...	...	...	...	...	...	...	...	...	113**,z	0.94**,z	...	...	...	...	87**,z	1.04**,z	63
...	...	...	...	...	...	...	...	...	...	...	...	...	...	...	...	...	...	...	...	64
88	0.96	95*	0.98*	81	0.85	90*	0.92*	107	0.96	88	0.99	**97**	**1.02**	22	0.98	34	1.00	**41**	**0.99**	65
47	0.41	...	...	30	0.30	...	...	...	...	...	...	84**,z	0.99**,z	...	...	...	...	48**,z	1.07**,z	66
...	...	...	...	...	...	...	...	101	0.99	102	1.01	102	1.00	90	1.02	110	1.06	114	1.09	67
...	...	...	...	...	...	...	...	...	...	99	1.00	87	1.19	...	...	98	1.10	98	0.95	68
...	...	...	...	...	...	...	...	...	...	114	0.93	114**,z	0.92**,z	...	...	101	1.07	98**	1.1**	69
69	0.84	67*	0.93*	57	0.75	57*	0.80*	66	0.88	78	0.93	75**,z	0.88**,z	12	0.61	22	0.76	26**,z	0.79**,z	70
97	1.00	95*	1.01*	92	0.99	93*	1.00*	109	0.99	113	0.99	112	0.99	71	1.04	76	1.09	86	1.11	71
...	...	...	...	...	...	...	...	105	1.01	95	1.01	**105**	**0.99**	90	0.97	100	1.00	**93**	**1.00**	72
99	1.00	100	1.00	98	0.99	99	1.00	124	1.02	99	0.98	100	1.00	33	1.96	80	1.10	80	1.12	73
99	1.00	100*	1.00*	89	0.88	93*	0.92*	103	0.97	...	...	...	...	67	0.93	...	...	...	...	74
...	...	...	...	...	...	...	...	86	0.86	88	0.93	119	0.97	15	0.61	24	0.75	30**,z	0.81**,z	75
...	...	98*	1.00*	...	...	93*	0.95*	98	0.96	94	0.95	**97**	**0.95**	31	0.94	...	...	**73**	**1.03**	76
...	...	...	...	...	...	...	...	...	...	...	...	140y		...	...	34y		...	...	77
...	...	...	...	...	...	...	...	...	...	...	...	...	...	...	...	...	...	...	...	78
...	...	99*	1.00*	...	...	99*	1.00*	112	0.97	112	0.98	115	0.95	99	1.03	101	1.11	98	1.08**	79
...	...	...	...	...	...	...	...	...	...	98	1.02	99	1.07	...	...	...	...	...	...	80
...	...	...	...	...	...	74*	...	95	0.96	110	0.98	118	0.97	18	0.80	30	0.88	41	0.86	81
94	0.99	94*	0.99*	...	...	90*	0.93*	107	0.93	108	0.93	98	0.93	32	...	62	0.90	73	0.95	82

Latin America and the Caribbean

	Total (%)	GPI (F/M)	Total (%)	GPI (F/M)	Total (%)	GPI (F/M)	Total (%)	GPI (F/M)	Total (%)	GPI (F/M)	Total (%)	GPI (F/M)	Total (%)	GPI (F/M)	Total (%)	GPI (F/M)	Total (%)	GPI (F/M)	Total (%)	GPI (F/M)	
...	...	...	...	...	...	...	...	...	...	...	...	93**	1.03**	...	...	...	...	100**	1.02**	83
...	...	...	...	...	...	...	...	...	...	...	...	...	...	...	...	...	...	...	...	84
98	1.00	99*	1.00*	96	1.00	97*	1.00*	108	...	117	1.00	112z	0.99z	72	...	94	1.07	86z	1.07z	85
...	...	99*	1.00*	...	...	97*	1.00*	...	...	112	0.98	114	0.95	...	...	101	1.05	98	1.02	86
96	1.02	...	...	94	1.02	...	...	96	1.03	95	0.98	93	1.00	...	...	115	0.96	80	1.10	87
100	1.00	...	...	99	1.00	...	...	93	1.00	108	0.98	107	0.99	...	...	104	1.05	110	1.01	88
...	...	...	...	...	...	...	...	112	0.98	118	0.97	124	0.98	44	1.15	64	1.08	85	1.04	89
...	...	...	...	...	...	...	...	...	...	...	...	102*,y	...	...	...	...	...	86y		90
93	0.93	97*	0.98*	78	0.80	87*	0.87*	97	0.92	113	0.98	113**	0.99**	...	...	78	0.93	89**	0.97**	91
92	1.03	97*	1.02*	82	0.98	89*	1.00*	104	...	155	0.94	141z	0.94z	40	...	99	1.11	102z	1.11z	92
...	...	...	...	...	...	...	...	...	...	112	0.97	108	0.96	...	...	99	0.91	96	1.06	93
...	...	...	...	...	...	...	...	...	...	...	...	93**	0.95**	...	...	...	...	97**	1.10**	94
98	1.00	99*	1.00[1]	94	0.99	96*	1.00[1]	101	0.98	101	0.97	104	0.95	73	1.07	79	1.04	89	1.01	95
95	1.01	98*	1.01*	88	0.99	93*	1.00*	103	1.02	113	1.00	111	0.99	50	1.19	71	1.11	75	1.11	96
97	1.01	98*	1.01*	94	1.00	95*	1.00*	103	0.99	108	0.98	112	0.99	45	1.06	57	1.09	68	1.05	97
99	1.00	100*	1.00*	95	1.00	100*	1.00*	99	0.97	106	0.96	100	0.95	90	1.14	80	1.06	93	1.01	98
...	...	...	...	...	...	...	...	...	...	104	0.95	95	0.99	...	...	90	1.35	107	0.99	99
87	1.02	94*	1.03*	79	0.99	87*	1.00*	94**	1.01**	113	0.98	112	0.95	...	...	55	1.27	68	1.23	100
95	0.99	96*	1.00*	88	0.94	91*	0.97*	116	0.99	114	1.00	117	1.00	55*	...	57	1.03	61	1.00	101
84	0.97	90	0.99	72	0.91	81	0.94	81	1.01	111	0.96	114	0.97	25	1.22	51	0.98	60**	1.01**	102
...	...	...	...	...	...	...	...	...	...	...	...	92	0.96	...	...	72**	1.26**	101	1.09	103
73	0.82	82*	0.91*	61	0.77	69*	0.84*	81	0.87	101	0.87	113	0.92	23	...	33	0.84	49	0.90	104
100	1.00	...	...	97	0.98	...	...	94	0.98	119	0.98	126**	0.99**	79	1.06	81	1.02	90z		105
55	0.96	...	...	40	0.87	...	...	48	0.94	...	...	...	...	21*	0.96*	...	...	...	...	106
80	1.03	89*	1.05*	68	0.98	80*	1.01*	108	1.04	...	...	113	1.00	33	1.25	...	...	65	1.24	107
91	1.09	...	...	82	1.10	80*	1.16*	101	0.99	93**	1.00**	95	1.00	65	1.06	88**	1.02**	88	1.02	108
95	0.98	98*	1.00*	87	0.93	91*	0.97*	111	0.97	109	0.97	109	0.98	52	1.00	69	1.02	80	1.07	109
...	...	...	...	...	...	...	...	...	...	...	...	108	0.97	...	...	...	...	114	1.10	110
97	1.00	98	1.00	96	1.00	97	1.00	...	...	134	0.94	126**,z	0.98**,z	93	1.19	97	1.16	87**,z	1.09**,z	111
68	1.01	86*	1.06*	63	1.00	77*	1.00*	94	1.06	103	1.01	112	0.98	45	1.22	52**	1.19**	64	1.15	112
95	0.99	96*	0.99*	89	0.98	92*	0.99*	105	...	108	0.97	112	0.97	62	...	67	1.07	70	1.07	113

Table 12 (continued)

		GOAL 1						GOAL 2					
		Early childhood care and education						Universal primary education					
		GROSS ENROLMENT RATIO (GER) IN PRE-PRIMARY EDUCATION						NET ENROLMENT RATIO (NER) IN PRIMARY EDUCATION					
		School year ending in						School year ending in					
		1991		1999		2004		1991		1999		2004	
	Country or territory	Total (%)	GPI (F/M)	Total (%)	GPI (F/M)	Total (%)	GPI (F/M)	Total (%)	GPI (F/M)	Total (%)	GPI (F/M)	Total (%)	GPI (F/M)
114	Paraguay	30	1.05	27	1.03	31**	1.01**	94	0.99	...	...	...	...
115	Peru	30	1.03	55	1.02	60	1.01	...	...	98**	1.00**	97	1.00
116	Saint Kitts and Nevis[4]	...	...	...	...	101	1.15	...	...	...	...	94	1.08
117	Saint Lucia	52	...	84	0.95	71	1.11	95**	0.97**	91**	0.99**	98	0.97
118	Saint Vincent and the Grenadines	44	1.10	...	...	86	0.97	...	...	...	...	94**	0.97**
119	Suriname	82	1.01	...	...	90**,z	1.01**,z	81**	1.06**	...	...	92**,z	1.07**,z
120	Trinidad and Tobago	9	1.01	60**	1.01**	86	1.00	91	0.99	93	1.00	92*	0.99*
121	Turks and Caicos Islands[4]	...	...	...	...	106	0.90	...	...	...	...	81	1.08
122	Uruguay	42	1.02	59	1.02	61**	1.01**	91	1.01	...	...	...	...
123	Venezuela	40	1.02	45	1.03	55	1.01	87	1.03	86	1.01	92	1.01
	North America and Western Europe												
124	Andorra	...	...	...	...	127**	1.11**	...	...	...	...	89**	0.97**
125	Austria	71	0.99	83	0.99	89	0.99	88**	1.02**	...	...	...	...
126	Belgium	104	1.00	110	0.98	116	1.00	96	1.02	99	1.00	99	1.00
127	Canada	61	1.00	67	1.01	68**,y	1.00**,y	98	1.00	97	1.00	...	...
128	Cyprus[4]	49	0.99	60	1.02	61	1.01	87	1.00	95	1.00	96	1.00
129	Denmark	99	1.00	91	1.00	91	1.00	98	1.00	97	1.00	100	1.00
130	Finland	34	...	49	0.99	59	0.99	98**	1.00**	99	1.00	99	1.00
131	France	84	0.99	111	1.00	114	1.00	101	1.00	99	1.00	99	1.00
132	Germany	...	...	93	0.98	97	0.99	...	...	...	...	...	...
133	Greece	57	1.00	68	1.01	66	1.02	95	0.99	92	1.01	99	0.99
134	Iceland	...	...	109	0.98	126**	1.00**	101**	0.99**	99	0.98	99**	0.98**
135	Ireland	103	0.98	...	...	...	...	90	1.02	93	1.01	96	1.00
136	Israel	85	...	104	0.99	112	0.99	92**	1.03**	98	1.00	98	1.01
137	Italy	94	1.01	96	0.98	103	0.99	103**	1.00**	99	0.99	99	1.00
138	Luxembourg	92	...	72	0.99	83	1.02	...	...	96	1.02	91	1.00
139	Malta	103	0.95	102	0.99	104	1.08	97	0.99	95	1.02	94	1.00
140	Monaco[6]	...	...	...	...	...	...	...	...	...	...	...	...
141	Netherlands	99	1.01	98	0.99	89	0.98	95	1.04	99	0.99	99	0.99
142	Norway	88	...	75	1.06	85	...	100	1.00	100	1.00	99	1.00
143	Portugal	52	0.99	68	1.00	76	1.03	98	1.00	...	...	99	0.99
144	San Marino	...	...	...	...	...	...	...	...	...	...	...	...
145	Spain	59	1.03	100	0.99	111	1.00	103	1.00	99	1.00	99	0.99
146	Sweden	64	...	78	1.01	85	0.99	100	1.00	100	0.99	99	1.00
147	Switzerland	60	1.00	92	1.00	95	1.00	84	1.02	96	0.99	94	1.00
148	United Kingdom	52	1.02	79	1.00	59	1.00	100	0.97	100	1.01	99	1.00
149	United States	63	0.97	59	0.97	62	0.96	97	1.00	94	1.00	92	...
	South and West Asia												
150	Afghanistan	...	...	...	...	0.7**	0.80**	...	...	...	...	...	...
151	Bangladesh	...	...	26	1.12	12z	1.01z	...	...	89*	1.00*	94*	1.03*
152	Bhutan[7]	...	...	...	...	...	...	...	...	...	...	...	...
153	India	3	0.89	20	0.99	36	1.00	...	...	...	...	90**	0.94**
154	Iran, Islamic Republic of	12	0.95	13	1.05	37	1.12	92**	0.92**	82**	0.97**	89	0.99
155	Maldives	...	...	46	1.00	48	1.03	...	...	97	1.01	90y	1.01y
156	Nepal	...	...	11**	0.73**	**36**	**0.90**	...	...	65*	0.79*	79**	0.87**
157	Pakistan	...	...	...	...	45	0.83	33**	...	...	...	66*	0.73*
158	Sri Lanka[2]	...	...	...	...	...	...	...	...	...	...	98**	...
	Sub-Saharan Africa												
159	Angola	47	0.51	...	...	...	...	50**	0.95**	...	...	...	...
160	Benin	2	0.85	4	0.97	4	1.00	41**	0.54**	50*	0.68*	83	0.78
161	Botswana	...	...	...	...	...	...	83	1.09	78	1.04	82**	1.03**
162	Burkina Faso	0.8	1.03	2	1.03	1**,y	0.94**,y	29	0.64	35	0.69	40	0.77
163	Burundi	...	...	0.8	1.01	1	0.97	53**	0.85**	...	...	57	0.89
164	Cameroon	13	1.01	12	0.95	20	0.99	74**	0.87**	...	...	...	...
165	Cape Verde	...	...	...	...	53	1.04	91**	0.95**	99**	0.98**	92	0.99
166	Central African Republic	6	...	...	...	2**	1.04**	52	0.66	...	...	...	...
167	Chad	...	...	...	...	...	...	35**	0.45**	52	0.62	57**,z	0.68**,z
168	Comoros	...	...	2	1.07	3	0.96	57**	0.73**	49	0.85		

				GOAL 3					GOAL 4							GOAL 5								
				Learning needs of all youth and adults					Improving levels of adult literacy						Gender parity in primary education						Gender parity in secondary education			
				YOUTH LITERACY RATE (15-24)					ADULT LITERACY RATE (15 and over)						GROSS ENROLMENT RATIO (GER)						GROSS ENROLMENT RATIO (GER)			
				1990		2000-2004[1]			1990		2000-2004[1]			School year ending in						School year ending in				
														1991		1999		2004		1991		1999		2004	
Total (%)	GPI (F/M)	Total (%)	GPI (F/M)	Total (%)	GPI (F/M)	Total (%)	GPI (F/M)	Total (%)	GPI (F/M)	Total (%)	GPI (F/M)	Total (%)	GPI (F/M)	Total (%)	GPI (F/M)	Total (%)	GPI (F/M)	Total (%)	GPI (F/M)	Total (%)	GPI (F/M)	Total (%)	GPI (F/M)	
96	0.99	...	...	90	0.96	...	...	106	0.97	113**	0.96**	106**	0.97**	31	1.06	57	1.04	63**	1.01**	114
94	0.95	97*	0.98*	...	...	88*	0.88*	118	0.97	123	0.99	114	0.99	67	0.94	83	0.94	92	1.01	115
...	...	...	...	...	...	...	...	119	1.02	...	...	101	1.07	85	1.11	...	...	110	0.97	116
...	...	...	...	...	...	...	...	139	0.94	103	0.98	106	0.96	53	1.45	72	1.28	74	1.00	117
...	...	...	...	...	...	...	...	112	0.98	...	...	106	0.95	58	1.24	...	...	78	0.97	118
...	...	95*	0.98*	...	...	90*	0.95*	104	1.03	...	...	120**,z	1.02**,z	58	1.16	...	...	73**,z	1.34**,z	119
100	1.00	100	1.00	97	0.98	99	0.99	97	0.99	102	0.99	102*	0.97*	80	1.05	82	1.08	84**	1.07**	120
...	...	...	...	...	...	...	...	...	...	...	...	94	1.03	...	...	...	...	91	0.99	121
99	1.01	99	1.01	97	1.01	98	1.01	108	0.99	112	0.99	109**	0.98**	84	...	92	1.17	108**	1.15**	122
96	1.01	97*	1.02*	89	0.97	93*	0.99*	95	1.03	100	0.98	105	0.98	34	1.38	56	1.23	72	1.14	123

North America and Western Europe

Total (%)	GPI (F/M)	Total (%)	GPI (F/M)	Total (%)	GPI (F/M)	Total (%)	GPI (F/M)	Total (%)	GPI (F/M)	Total (%)	GPI (F/M)	Total (%)	GPI (F/M)	Total (%)	GPI (F/M)	Total (%)	GPI (F/M)	Total (%)	GPI (F/M)	Total (%)	GPI (F/M)	Total (%)	GPI (F/M)	
...	...	...	...	...	...	...	...	...	...	...	...	101**	0.98**	...	...	...	...	81**	1.03**	124
...	...	...	...	...	...	...	...	101	1.00	102	0.99	106	1.00	102	0.93	99	0.96	101	0.95	125
...	...	...	...	...	...	...	...	100	1.01	104	0.99	104	0.99	102	1.01	142	1.08	109	0.97	126
...	...	...	...	...	...	...	...	104	0.98	98	1.00	100**,y	1.00**,y	101	1.00	105	0.99	105**,y	0.99**,y	127
100	1.00	100*	1.00*	94	0.93	97*	0.96*	90	1.00	97	1.00	98	1.00	72	1.02	93	1.03	98	1.03	128
...	...	...	...	...	...	...	...	98	1.00	102	1.00	101	1.00	109	1.01	124	1.06	124	1.05	129
...	...	...	...	...	...	...	...	99	0.99	99	1.00	101	0.99	116	1.19	121	1.09	109	1.05	130
...	...	...	...	...	...	...	...	108	0.99	107	0.99	105	0.99	98	1.05	110	1.00	111	1.01	131
...	...	...	...	...	...	...	...	101	1.01	106	0.99	100	1.00	...	...	98	0.98	100	0.98	132
100	1.00	99*	1.00*	95	0.95	96*	0.96*	98	0.99	94	1.00	102	0.99	94	0.98	90	1.04	96	1.01	133
...	...	...	...	...	...	...	...	101	0.99	99	0.98	101**	0.98**	100	0.96	109	1.05	115**	1.06**	134
...	...	...	...	...	...	...	...	102	1.00	103	0.99	106	0.99	100	1.09	107	1.06	112	1.08	135
99	0.99	100*	1.00*	91	0.93	97*	0.97*	98	1.03	112	0.99	110	1.01	88	1.08	90	1.04	93	1.00	136
...	...	100*	1.00*	...	...	98*	0.99*	104	1.00	103	0.99	101	1.00	83	1.00	92	0.99	99	0.99	137
...	...	...	...	...	...	...	...	90	1.09	100	1.01	99	1.00	76	...	92	1.03	95	1.06	138
98	1.03	96*	1.04*	88	1.01	88*	1.03*	108	0.96	106	1.01	102	0.99	83	0.94	...	...	105	0.93	139
...	...	...	...	...	...	...	...	...	...	...	...	...	...	...	...	...	...	...	...	140
...	...	...	...	...	...	...	...	102	1.03	108	0.98	107	0.97	120	0.92	124	0.96	119	0.98	141
...	...	...	...	...	...	...	...	100	1.00	100	1.00	99	1.00	103	1.03	120	1.02	116	1.03	142
...	...	...	...	...	...	...	...	119	0.95	124	0.96	116	0.96	66	1.16	106	1.08	97	1.11	143
...	...	...	...	...	...	...	...	...	...	...	...	...	...	...	...	...	...	...	...	144
...	...	...	...	...	...	...	...	109	0.99	107	0.98	108	0.98	104	1.07	109	1.07	119	1.06	145
...	...	...	...	...	...	...	...	100	1.00	110	1.03	99	1.00	90	1.05	160	1.28	103	1.04	146
...	...	...	...	...	...	...	...	90	1.01	104	0.99	102	0.99	99	0.95	96	0.90	93	0.92	147
...	...	...	...	...	...	...	...	107	0.97	102	1.01	107	1.00	88	1.00	157	1.12	105	1.03	148
...	...	...	...	...	...	...	...	103	0.98	101	1.03	99	...	92	1.01	95	...	95	1.01	149

South and West Asia

Total (%)	GPI (F/M)	Total (%)	GPI (F/M)	Total (%)	GPI (F/M)	Total (%)	GPI (F/M)	Total (%)	GPI (F/M)	Total (%)	GPI (F/M)	Total (%)	GPI (F/M)	Total (%)	GPI (F/M)	Total (%)	GPI (F/M)	Total (%)	GPI (F/M)	Total (%)	GPI (F/M)	Total (%)	GPI (F/M)	
...	...	34*	0.36*	...	...	28*	0.29*	25	0.55	25	0.08	93	0.44	14	0.51	...	...	16	0.21	150
42	0.65	51	0.73	34	0.53	43	0.64	...	...	110	0.99	109	1.03	...	...	49	1.01	51z	1.11z	151
...	...	...	...	...	...	...	...	...	...	...	...	...	...	...	...	...	...	...	...	152
64	0.74	76*	0.80*	49	0.58	61*	0.65*	98	0.76	97	0.82	116**	0.93**	44	0.60	46	0.69	54	0.80	153
86	0.88	...	...	63	0.75	77*	0.84*	109	0.90	96	0.95	103	1.10	57	0.75	77	0.93	82	0.94	154
98	1.00	98*	1.00*	95	1.00	96*	1.00*	...	...	130	1.01	104	0.97	...	...	43	1.07	73**	1.14**	155
47	0.41	70*	0.75*	30	0.30	49*	0.56*	110	0.63	114	0.77	**113**	**0.91**	34	0.46	34	0.70	**46**	**0.86****	156
47	0.49	65*	0.72*	35	0.41	50*	0.57*	...	...	...	...	82	0.73	25	0.48	...	...	27	0.73	157
95	0.98	96*	1.01*	89	0.91	91*	0.97*	107	0.95	...	...	98**	...	71	1.08	...	...	83**	1.00**	158

Sub-Saharan Africa

Total (%)	GPI (F/M)	Total (%)	GPI (F/M)	Total (%)	GPI (F/M)	Total (%)	GPI (F/M)	Total (%)	GPI (F/M)	Total (%)	GPI (F/M)	Total (%)	GPI (F/M)	Total (%)	GPI (F/M)	Total (%)	GPI (F/M)	Total (%)	GPI (F/M)	Total (%)	GPI (F/M)	Total (%)	GPI (F/M)	
...	...	72*	0.75*	...	...	67*	0.65*	80	0.92	64**	0.86**	...	...	11	...	13	0.83**	...	...	159
40	0.44	45*	0.56*	26	0.41	35*	0.49*	54	0.51	74	0.67	99	0.77	10	0.42	19	0.47	26**	0.52**	160
83	1.10	94*	1.04*	68	1.07	81*	1.02*	101	1.07	102	1.00	105	0.99	44	1.18	72	1.10	75**	1.05**	161
...	...	31*	0.65*	...	...	22*	0.52*	36	0.64	44	0.70	53	0.78	7	0.53	10	0.61	12**	0.68**	162
52	0.77	73*	0.92*	37	0.55	59*	0.78*	71	0.84	61**	0.80**	80	0.83	5	0.58	...	...	12	0.75	163
81	0.88	...	...	58	0.69	68*	0.78*	99	0.86	89	0.82	117	0.85	27	0.71	27**	0.83**	44	0.70*	164
81	0.87	91	0.95	64	0.71	78	0.82	111	0.94	119	0.96	111	0.95	21*	...	...	...	66	1.10	165
52	0.60	59*	0.67*	33	0.44	49*	0.52*	64	0.64	...	...	64**	0.69**	11	0.40	...	...	12**,y	...	166
48	0.65	38*	0.42*	28	0.51	26*	0.31*	52	0.45	64	0.58	71**	0.64**	7	0.20	10	0.26	15**	0.32**	167
57	0.78	...	...	54	0.76	...	...	75	0.73	76	0.85	85	0.88	18*	0.65*	25	0.81	35	0.76	168

Education for All Global Monitoring Report 2 0 0 7

Table 12 (continued)

		GOAL 1						GOAL 2					
		Early childhood care and education						Universal primary education					
		GROSS ENROLMENT RATIO (GER) IN PRE-PRIMARY EDUCATION						NET ENROLMENT RATIO (NER) IN PRIMARY EDUCATION					
		School year ending in						School year ending in					
		1991		1999		2004		1991		1999		2004	
	Country or territory	Total (%)	GPI (F/M)	Total (%)	GPI (F/M)	Total (%)	GPI (F/M)	Total (%)	GPI (F/M)	Total (%)	GPI (F/M)	Total (%)	GPI (F/M)
169	Congo	2	0.99	2	1.59	6	1.06	79**	0.93**	...	...	...	...
170	Côte d'Ivoire	0.9	0.94	2	0.96	3*,z	0.96*,z	45	0.71**	53	0.75	56*,z	0.80*,z
171	D. R. Congo	...	...	...	...	...	...	54	0.78	...	...	...	...
172	Equatorial Guinea	...	...	31	1.04	40z	...	91**	0.97**	83	0.79	85y	0.85y
173	Eritrea	...	...	6	0.88	7	0.90	16**	0.98**	36	0.86	48	0.85
174	Ethiopia	2	1.01	1	0.97	**2**	**0.95**	22**	0.75**	33	0.74	**56****	**0.94****
175	Gabon	...	...	...	...	14**,y	...	85**	1.00**	...	...	...	...
176	Gambia	...	...	20	0.91	18**	1.03**	48**	0.71**	67	0.88	75**	1.06**
177	Ghana	...	...	40**	1.02**	**42**	**1.03**	54**	0.89**	57**	0.96**	65	**0.99**
178	Guinea	...	...	...	...	6	1.03	27**	0.53**	44	0.71	64	0.84
179	Guinea-Bissau	...	...	3**	1.05**	...	...	38**	0.56**	45**	0.71**	...	...
180	Kenya	35	...	44	1.00	53	0.99	...	...	64	1.01	76	1.00
181	Lesotho	...	...	23**	1.08**	31**	0.94**	71	1.24	60	1.13	86	1.06
182	Liberia	...	...	41	0.74	...	...	...	...	41	0.77	...	...
183	Madagascar	...	...	3**	1.02**	10**	...	64**	1.00**	63	1.01	89	1.00
184	Malawi	...	...	...	...	...	...	48	0.93	98	0.98	95	1.05
185	Mali	...	...	1	1.09	2**,z	1.01**,z	21	0.61	40**	0.73**	46	0.85
186	Mauritius	...	...	100	1.02	**95**	**1.01**	91	1.00	97	1.01	**95**	**1.02**
187	Mozambique	...	...	...	...	...	...	43	0.79	52	0.80	71	0.90
188	Namibia	14	1.01	19	1.16	29**,z	1.12**,z	...	...	73	1.08	74z	1.08z
189	Niger	1	0.97	1	1.05	1	1.01	22	0.60	24	0.68	39	0.71
190	Nigeria	...	...	...	...	15	1.00	...	...	...	...	60**	0.89**
191	Rwanda	...	...	...	...	3**,y	0.98**,y	66	0.99	...	...	73	1.04
192	Sao Tome and Principe	...	...	27**	1.09**	42	1.04	...	...	85	0.99	98	1.00
193	Senegal	2	1.03	3	1.00	6	1.11	43**	0.75**	52	0.88**	66	0.95
194	Seychelles[4]	...	...	109	1.04	102	0.98	...	...	...	...	96	1.01
195	Sierra Leone	...	...	...	...	...	...	43**	0.73**	...	...	...	...
196	Somalia	...	...	...	...	...	...	9**	0.55**	...	...	...	...
197	South Africa	21	1.01	20	1.01	33z	1.03z	90	1.03	93	1.02	89z	1.01z
198	Swaziland	...	...	...	...	...	...	75	1.05	75	1.02	77z	1.01z
199	Togo	3	0.97	2	0.99	2**	0.98**	64	0.71	79	0.79	79	0.85
200	Uganda	...	...	4**	1.00**	2	0.99	...	...	...	...	...	...
201	United Republic of Tanzania	...	...	...	...	**29**	**1.02**	49	1.01	48	1.04	**91**	**0.98**
202	Zambia	...	...	...	...	...	...	...	...	63	0.96	80	1.00
203	Zimbabwe	...	...	41**	1.03**	43z	...	...	...	81	1.01	82z	1.01z

		Median		Weighted average				Weighted average					
I	World	...	...	33	0.96	37	0.97	81	0.88	83	0.93	86	0.96
II	Countries in transition	...	...	41	0.94	59	0.93	89	0.99	85	0.99	91	0.99
III	Developed countries	...	...	73	0.99	77	0.99	96	1.00	96	1.00	96	0.99
IV	Developing countries	...	...	28	0.95	32	0.97	79	0.86	81	0.92	85	0.95
V	Arab States	...	...	15	0.76	16	0.87	73	0.81	77	0.89	81	0.92
VI	Central and Eastern Europe	...	...	45	0.97	57	0.95	90	0.98	89	0.97	91	0.98
VII	Central Asia	...	...	22	0.92	27	0.95	84	0.99	89	0.99	92	0.98
VIII	East Asia and the Pacific	...	...	40	0.98	40	0.96	96	0.96	96	1.00	94	0.99
IX	East Asia	...	...	40	0.98	40	0.96	96	0.96	96	1.00	94	0.99
X	Pacific	...	...	58	1.00	72	0.99	91	0.98	87	0.99	90	0.97
XI	Latin America and the Caribbean	...	...	56	1.01	62	1.01	86	0.99	93	0.98	95	0.99
XII	Caribbean	...	...	71	1.04	101	1.03	52	1.01	77	0.96	83	0.96
XIII	Latin America	...	...	55	1.01	61	1.01	87	0.99	94	0.98	95	0.99
XIV	North America and Western Europe	...	...	76	0.98	78	0.98	97	1.00	96	1.00	96	0.98
XV	South and West Asia	...	...	23	0.93	32	0.98	72	0.66	77	0.83	86	0.92
XVI	Sub-Saharan Africa	...	...	10	0.98	12	0.98	54	0.87	55	0.89	65	0.93

1. Data are for the most recent year available during the period specified. See the introduction to the statistical tables for a broader explanation of national literacy definitions, assessment methods, and sources and years of data. For countries indicated with (*), national observed literacy data are used. For all others, UIS literacy estimates are used. The estimates were generated in July 2002, using the previous UIS assessment model. They are based on observed data for years between 1990 and 1994.
2. Literacy data for the most recent year do not include some geographic regions.

3. In countries where two or more education structures exist, indicators were calculated on the basis of the most common or widespread structure. In the Russian Federation this is three grades of primary education starting at age 7. However, a four-grade structure also exists, in which about one-third of primary pupils are enrolled. Gross enrolment ratios may be overestimated.
4. National population data were used to calculate enrolment ratios.

GOAL 3				GOAL 4				GOAL 5												
Learning needs of all youth and adults				Improving levels of adult literacy				Gender parity in primary education						Gender parity in secondary education						
YOUTH LITERACY RATE (15-24)				ADULT LITERACY RATE (15 and over)				GROSS ENROLMENT RATIO (GER)						GROSS ENROLMENT RATIO (GER)						
								School year ending in						School year ending in						
1990		2000-2004¹		1990		2000-2004¹		1991		1999		2004		1991		1999		2004		
Total (%)	GPI (F/M)	Total (%)	GPI (F/M)	Total (%)	GPI (F/M)	Total (%)	GPI (F/M)	Total (%)	GPI (F/M)	Total (%)	GPI (F/M)	Total (%)	GPI (F/M)	Total (%)	GPI (F/M)	Total (%)	GPI (F/M)	Total (%)	GPI (F/M)	
93	0.95	...	...	67	0.75	...	...	117	0.90	50	0.95	89	0.93	46	0.73	...	...	39**	0.84**	169
53	0.62	61*	0.74*	39	0.51	49*	0.63*	64	0.71	70	0.74	72*,z	0.79*,z	21	0.48	22**	0.54**	25**,y	0.55**,y	170
69	0.72	70*	0.81*	47	0.56	67*	0.67*	70	0.75	48	0.90	...	...	...	...	18	0.52	...	...	171
93	0.92	95*	1.00*	73	0.71	87*	0.86*	163**	0.96**	132	0.79	127y	0.91y	...	...	31	0.37	30**,y	0.57**,y	172
61	0.68	...	...	46	0.59	...	...	21	0.94	57	0.82	66	0.80	...	...	24	0.68	34	0.56	173
43	0.66	61	0.86	29	0.53	45	0.73	30	0.66	59	0.62	**93**	**0.86**	13	0.75	15	0.62	**31**	**0.65**	174
...	...	...	...	...	...	...	...	141**	0.98**	132	1.00	130**	0.99**	...	...	45	0.86	50**,y	...	175
42	0.68	...	...	26	0.62	...	...	61	0.68	80	0.85	81	1.06	18	0.49	33	0.65	47**	0.83**	176
82	0.86	71*	0.86*	58	0.67	58*	0.75*	74	0.85	76	0.92	**88**	**0.96**	35	0.65	37	0.80	**44****	**0.85****	177
44	0.43	47*	0.57*	27	0.30	29*	0.43*	36	0.49	57	0.65	79	0.81	9	0.34	15**	0.37**	26	0.48	178
...	...	...	...	...	...	...	...	50**	0.55**	70**	0.67**	...	...	...	...	...	...	...	...	179
90	0.93	80*	1.01*	71	0.75	74*	0.90*	94	0.96	93	0.97	111	0.94	28	0.77	38	0.96	48**	0.93**	180
87	1.26	...	...	78	1.37	82*	1.23*	109	1.22	105	1.08	131	1.00	24	1.42	30	1.35	36	1.27	181
57	0.51	...	...	39	0.41	...	...	...	...	85	0.74	...	...	...	...	29	0.65	...	...	182
72	0.86	70*	0.94*	58	0.75	71*	0.85*	93	0.98	94	0.97	134	0.96	17	0.97	14**	0.96**	...	...	183
63	0.68	76*	0.86*	52	0.53	64*	0.72*	66	0.84	139	0.95	125	1.02	8	0.46	37	0.70	29	0.81	184
...	...	24*	0.52*	...	...	19*	0.44*	26	0.60	51	0.72	64	0.79	7	0.52	14	0.54	22	0.61**	185
91	1.00	95*	1.02*	80	0.88	84*	0.91*	109	1.00	105	1.00	**102**	**1.00**	55	1.04	76	0.98	**88****	**0.99****	186
49	0.48	...	...	33	0.37	...	...	61	0.75	69	0.74	95	0.83	7	0.57	5	0.69	11	0.70	187
87	1.04	92*	1.03*	75	0.94	85*	0.96*	132	1.05	104	1.02	101z	1.01z	45	1.24	57	1.13	58z	1.14z	188
17	0.37	37*	0.44*	11	0.28	29*	0.35*	26	0.60	29	0.68	45	0.72	6	0.44	6	0.65	8	0.67	189
74	0.82	...	...	49	0.65	...	...	87	0.81	88**	0.78**	99	0.85	25	0.74	24	0.91	35	0.81	190
73	0.86	78*	0.98*	53	0.70	65*	0.84*	70	0.97	99	0.98	119	1.02	8	0.75	10	1.00	14	0.89	191
...	...	...	...	...	...	...	...	...	...	106	0.98	133	0.98	...	...	...	...	40	1.05	192
40	0.60	49*	0.70*	28	0.49	39*	0.57*	53	0.73	61	0.86**	76	0.95	15	0.53	15	0.64	19	0.72	193
...	...	99*	1.01*	...	...	92*	1.01*	...	...	116	0.99	110	1.00	...	...	113	1.04	102	1.08	194
...	...	48*	0.63*	...	...	35*	0.52*	53	0.70	...	...	...	...	18	0.57	...	...	...	...	195
...	...	...	...	...	...	...	...	...	...	...	...	...	...	...	...	...	...	...	...	196
88	1.00	94*	1.01*	81	0.98	82*	0.96*	109	0.99	114	0.98	105z	0.97z	69	1.18	88	1.13	90z	1.07z	197
85	1.01	88*	1.03*	72	0.95	80*	0.97*	94	0.99	100	0.95	101z	0.95z	42	0.96	45	1.00	42z	1.01z	198
63	0.60	74*	0.76*	44	0.47	53*	0.56*	94	0.65	112	0.75	101	0.84	20	0.34	28	0.40	39	0.50	199
70	0.76	77*	0.86*	56	0.63	67*	0.75*	70	0.85	126	0.92	**118**	**1.00**	11	0.59	10**	0.66**	16**	0.79**	200
83	0.87	78*	0.94*	63	0.68	69*	0.80*	68	0.98	64	1.00	**106**	**0.96**	5	0.77	6**	0.82**	...	...	201
81	0.88	69*	0.91*	68	0.75	68*	0.78*	93	...	75	0.92	99	0.96	21	...	20	0.77**	26	0.79	202
94	0.95	...	...	81	0.87	...	...	107	0.97	98	0.97	96z	0.98z	48	0.78	43	0.88	36z	0.91z	203
Weighted average				Weighted average				Weighted average						Weighted average						
84	0.91	87	0.93	75	0.84	82	0.89	99	0.89	100	0.92	106	0.94	52	0.83	60	0.92	65	0.94	I
99	1.00	100	1.00	99	0.99	99	0.99	97	0.99	100	0.99	107	0.99	95	1.0	89	1.03	92	0.98	II
100	1.00	99	1.00	98	0.99	99	0.99	102	0.99	102	1.00	101	0.99	93	1.0	103	1.01	101	1.01	III
81	0.88	85	0.91	67	0.76	77	0.84	98	0.87	100	0.91	107	0.94	42	0.7	53	0.88	59	0.92	IV
67	0.71	82	0.87	50	0.56	66	0.72	84	0.80	89	0.87	93	0.90	51	0.8	59	0.88	66	0.91	V
98	0.98	99	0.99	96	0.97	97	0.97	98	0.98	100	0.96	101	0.97	81	1.0	86	1.00	90	0.96	VI
98	1.00	100	1.00	99	0.99	99	0.99	90	0.99	99	0.99	102	0.99	98	0.99	86	0.97	90	0.96	VII
95	0.96	98	0.99	82	0.84	92	0.93	117	0.94	112	0.99	113	0.99	50	0.83	64	0.96	73	1.00	VIII
...	...	98	0.99	...	...	92	0.93	117	0.94	112	0.99	114	0.99	50	0.83	64	0.96	72	1.00	IX
...	...	92	0.99	...	...	93	0.98	99	0.98	94	0.99	98	0.97	66	1.00	107	1.01	104	0.98	X
93	1.00	96	1.01	85	0.96	90	0.98	104	0.97	121	0.97	118	0.97	51	1.09	80	1.07	86	1.08	XI
...	...	77	1.04	...	...	70	1.00	71	0.97	115	0.97	126	0.98	43	1.04	55	1.03	58	1.04	XII
...	...	97	1.01	...	...	90	0.98	104	0.97	121	0.97	118	0.97	51	1.09	81	1.07	87	1.08	XIII
100	1.00	99	1.00	98	0.99	99	1.00	104	0.99	103	1.01	102	0.98	94	1.01	105	1.01	101	1.01	XIV
61	0.72	72	0.79	47	0.58	59	0.66	92	0.76	94	0.82	110	0.91	41	0.60	46	0.74	51	0.83	XV
67	0.80	73	0.88	50	0.67	61	0.77	72	0.84	79	0.85	91	0.89	22	0.75	24	0.80	30	0.78	XVI

5. Children enter primary school at age 6 or 7. Since 7 is the most common entrance age, enrolment ratios were calculated using the 7-11 age group for both enrolment and population. NER is not published for more recent years due to inconsistencies between enrolment and the United Nations population data by age.

6. Enrolment ratios were not calculated due to lack of United Nations population data by age.

7. Enrolment ratios were not calculated due to inconsistencies between enrolment and the United Nations population data.

Data in bold are for the school year ending in 2005.

(z) Data are for the school year ending in 2003.

(y) Data are for the school year ending in 2002.

Table 13
Trends in basic or proxy indicators to measure EFA goal 6

		GOAL 6 Educational quality													
		SCHOOL LIFE EXPECTANCY (expected number of years of formal schooling from primary to tertiary education)									SURVIVAL RATE TO GRADE 5				
		1991			School year ending in 1999			2004			1991		School year ending in 1999		2003	
	Country or territory	Total	Male	Female	Total	Male	Female	Total	Male	Female	Total (%)	GPI (F/M)	Total (%)	GPI (F/M)	Total (%)	GPI (F/M)
	Arab States															
1	Algeria	10.0	11.1	8.8	…	…	…	12.5**	12.6**	12.5**	94.5	0.99	95.0	1.02	96.2	1.02
2	Bahrain	13.6	13.4	13.9	13.1**	12.6**	13.7**	14.2**	13.7**	14.8**	89.2	1.01	97.4**	1.01**	…	…
3	Djibouti	…	…	…	3.2**	…	…	4.0**	4.6**	3.4**	87.3	1.81	76.7	1.19	87.7**,x	0.95**,x
4	Egypt	9.6	10.8	8.4	12.5**	…	…	12.0**	…	…	…	…	99.1**	1.01**	98.6**	1.01**
5	Iraq	9.8	11.1	8.4	8.2**	9.4**	7.0**	9.6**	10.9**	8.2**	…	…	65.6**	0.94**	…	…
6	Jordan	12.5	12.3	12.6	…	…	…	13.1**	12.9**	13.2**	…	…	97.7	0.99	98.8	1.00
7	Kuwait	…	…	…	13.7**	13.0**	14.4**	12.5**	11.7**	13.3**	…	…	…	…	.	.
8	Lebanon	11.9	12.0	11.8	13.2**	13.0**	13.3**	14.1**	13.9**	14.4**	…	…	91.3	1.07	97.6	1.05
9	Libyan Arab Jamahiriya	12.9	13.5	12.4	…	…	…	16.2**,z	15.7**,z	16.8**,z	…	…	…	…	.	.
10	Mauritania	4.1	5.0	3.2	6.9**	…	…	7.5**	7.8**	7.2**	75.3	0.99	67.9**	0.94**	81.6	1.02
11	Morocco	6.5	7.7	5.3	8.0**	8.9**	7.1**	9.9**	10.5**	9.2**	75.1	1.02	81.9	1.00	81.2y	0.98y
12	Oman	8.2	8.7	7.6	…	…	…	11.5**	11.6**	11.3**	96.9	0.99	93.7	1.00	97.6	1.01
13	Palestinian A. T.	…	…	…	12.0	11.9	12.0	13.4	13.2	13.6	…	…	…	…	.	.
14	Qatar	12.4	11.9	13.2	12.9**	12.2**	13.8**	12.7**	12.4**	13.4**	64.1	1.02	…	…	.	.
15	Saudi Arabia	7.8	8.4	7.2	9.9**	10.1**	9.7**	9.9**	10.0**	9.7**	82.9	1.03	95.3	1.00	93.6	0.99
16	Sudan	4.1	4.6	3.6	4.7**	…	…	…	…	…	93.8	1.09	84.1**	1.10**	91.9	1.00
17	Syrian Arab Republic	9.8	10.8	8.8	…	…	…	…	…	…	96.0	0.98	91.8	0.99	.	.
18	Tunisia	10.5	11.3	9.6	12.9**	13.0**	12.7**	13.7**	…	…	86.4	0.83	92.1	1.02	96.5	1.00
19	United Arab Emirates	11.4	11.0	12.0	11.2**	10.7**	12.0**	10.3**,z	9.7**,z	11.2**,z	80.0	0.99	92.4	0.99	94.7	1.02
20	Yemen	5.1	7.6	2.6	7.7**	10.4**	4.8**	8.8**	11.0**	6.5**	…	…	…	…	73.2**	0.86**
	Central and Eastern Europe															
21	Albania	11.5	11.7	11.3	11.1**	11.1**	11.0**	11.3z	11.2z	11.3z	…	…	…	…	.	.
22	Belarus	13.1	12.9	13.2	13.5**	13.3**	13.8**	14.4	14.1	14.7	…	…	…	…	.	.
23	Bosnia and Herzegovina	8.7	8.7	8.8	…	…	…	…	…	…	…	…	…	…	.	.
24	Bulgaria	12.3	12.3	12.4	13.0	12.6	13.3	13.3	13.3	13.2	90.6	0.99	…	…	.	.
25	Croatia	11.0	11.0	11.1	12.0	11.9	12.2	12.9z	12.7z	13.1z	…	…	…	…	.	.
26	Czech Republic	11.9	12.1	11.7	13.5**	13.4**	13.5**	14.7	14.6	14.9	…	…	98.3	1.01	98.4	1.00
27	Estonia	12.8	12.5	13.0	14.5	14.0	15.0	15.8	14.8	16.8	…	…	99.1	1.01	98.4y	1.02y
28	Hungary	11.4	11.4	11.4	13.8**	13.6**	14.1**	15.0	14.6	15.4	97.6	1.26	…	…	.	.
29	Latvia	12.4	12.2	12.6	13.7	12.9	14.4	15.4	14.4	16.3	…	…	…	…	.	.
30	Lithuania	12.7	12.6	12.8	14.1	13.6	14.6	15.6	14.9	16.4	…	…	…	…	.	.
31	Poland	12.2	12.1	12.4	…	…	…	15.0	14.4	15.6	97.8	1.08	98.6	…	99.7	.
32	Republic of Moldova	11.9	11.7	12.1	9.8**	9.6**	10.0**	10.3	9.9	10.6	…	…	…	…	.	.
33	Romania	11.5	11.5	11.4	11.9	11.7	12.0	13.3	13.0	13.6	…	…	…	…	.	.
34	Russian Federation	12.4	11.9	12.9	…	…	…	13.4**	12.8**	13.9**	…	…	…	…	.	.
35	Serbia and Montenegro	8.8	8.7	9.0	13.3	13.3	13.4	…	…	…	…	…	…	…	.	.
36	Slovakia	12.0	12.1	11.9	13.1**	13.0**	13.3**	14.1	13.9	14.4	…	…	…	…	.	.
37	Slovenia	12.3	12.0	12.6	14.8**	14.4**	15.3**	16.6**	16.1**	17.2**	…	…	…	…	.	.
38	TFYR Macedonia	11.0	11.0	11.0	11.9	11.9	11.9	12.1	11.9	12.3	…	…	…	…	.	.
39	Turkey	8.5	9.5	7.4	…	…	…	11.1	12.0	10.1	97.6	0.99	…	…	94.6**	0.99**
40	Ukraine	12.2	12.1	12.3	12.6**	12.4**	12.8**	13.7	13.5*	14.0*	97.7	…	…	…	.	.
	Central Asia															
41	Armenia	10.4	10.0	10.8	…	…	…	11.3	10.9	11.7	…	…	…	…	.	.
42	Azerbaijan	10.6	10.8	10.4	10.1	10.2	10.0	10.8	11.0	10.7	…	…	…	…	.	.
43	Georgia	12.4	12.3	12.4	11.6**	11.5**	11.6**	12.3	12.2	12.4	…	…	…	…	.	.
44	Kazakhstan	12.6	12.3	12.9	12.0	11.8	12.2	14.7	14.3	15.1	…	…	…	…	.	.
45	Kyrgyzstan	10.4	10.3	10.5	11.5	11.4	11.7	12.4	12.1	12.7	…	…	…	…	.	.
46	Mongolia	9.4	8.8	10.0	8.7**	7.8**	9.6**	11.6	10.8	12.5	…	…	…	…	.	.
47	Tajikistan	11.7	12.0	11.4	9.7**	10.5**	8.8**	10.7	11.7	9.7	…	…	…	…	.	.
48	Turkmenistan	12.1	12.0	12.3	…	…	…	…	…	…	…	…	…	…	.	.
49	Uzbekistan	11.6	11.8	11.3	…	…	…	11.4**	11.6**	11.2**	…	…	…	…	.	.
	East Asia and the Pacific															
50	Australia	13.4	13.2	13.7	20.0**	19.8**	20.3**	20.3	20.2	20.4	98.8	1.01	…	…	85.8**	1.0**
51	Brunei Darussalam	12.5	12.5	12.6	13.4**	13.1**	13.7**	13.8**	13.5**	14.2**	…	…	91.8	1.00	…	…
52	Cambodia	7.2	8.6	5.8	…	…	…	9.7**,z	10.5**,z	8.9**	…	…	56.3**	0.93**	59.7	1.05
53	China	9.3	10.0	8.6	…	…	…	11.2**	11.3**	11.1**	86.0	1.36	97.3	1.00	99.0y	0.98**,y

GOAL 6

Educational quality

PUPIL/TEACHER RATIO IN PRIMARY EDUCATION[1]			% FEMALE TEACHERS IN PRIMARY EDUCATION			TRAINED PRIMARY SCHOOL TEACHERS[2] as % of total		PUBLIC CURRENT EXPENDITURE ON PRIMARY EDUCATION AS % GNP			PUBLIC CURRENT EXPENDITURE ON PRIMARY EDUCATION PER PUPIL (unit cost) in constant 2003 US$			PUBLIC CURRENT EXPENDITURE ON PRIMARY EDUCATION PER PUPIL (unit cost) at PPP in constant 2003 US$			
1991	1999	2004	1991	1999	2004	1999	2004	1991	1999	2004	1991	1999	2004	1991	1999	2004	
																	Arab States
28	28	27	39	46	50	94	98	4.5	...	1.6**,z	498	...	225**,z	1261	...	657**,z	1
19*	...	16**,y	54*	...	76**,y	...	...	...	...	1.9**,y	...	...	...	...	...	...	2
43	40	34**,y	37	28	30**,y	...	...	...	...	...	383	...	...	...	...	...	3
24	23**	22**	52	52**	55**	...	...	...	...	...	...	...	...	...	...	...	4
25	25	21	70	72	72	...	100	...	...	...	...	...	...	...	...	...	5
25	...	20**,z	62	...	64**,z	...	...	...	1.9	1.9y	...	221	247y	...	496	575y	6
18	13	13	61	73	86	100	100	1.5	...	1.4	...	...	...	...	...	...	7
...	14	14	...	82	84	...	13	...	...	...	...	...	...	...	...	...	8
14	...	...	...	...	...	...	...	...	...	...	...	...	...	...	...	...	9
45	47	45	18	26	28	...	100	...	...	1.8	...	...	49z	...	...	227z	10
27	28	28	37	39	45	...	...	1.6	2.2	2.4	203	233	296	534	641	680	11
28	25	19**	47	52	62**	100	100**,y	1.6	1.4	1.5**,y	...	...	...	...	...	...	12
...	...	27	...	...	61	...	...	...	...	...	...	...	...	...	...	...	13
11	13	9	72	75	85	...	...	...	...	...	...	...	...	...	...	...	14
16	12	12	48	54	52	...	...	...	...	...	...	...	...	...	...	...	15
34	...	29**,z	51	...	62**,z	...	...	...	...	...	...	...	...	...	...	...	16
25	25**	18**	64	68**	62**	...	...	...	1.7	2.1y	...	117	142y	...	83	95y	17
28	24	21	45	50	51	...	...	...	...	2.2**,y	...	...	370**,y	...	...	1164**,y	18
18	16	15	64	73	83	...	61	...	...	...	...	...	...	...	...	...	19
...	30**	...	...	21**	...	...	...	...	...	...	...	...	...	...	...	...	20
																	Central and Eastern Europe
19	23**	21z	55	75**	76z	...	...	...	...	...	...	...	...	...	...	...	21
...	20	15	...	99	99	...	99	1.8	...	0.5**	...	...	232**	...	...	687**	22
...	...	...	...	...	...	...	...	...	...	...	...	...	...	...	...	...	23
15	18	17	77	91**	93	...	...	2.8	...	0.7**,y	...	...	377**,y	...	...	1368**,y	24
19	19	18z	75	89	90z	100	100z	...	...	0.9**,y	...	...	1275**,y	...	...	2540**,y	25
23	18	18	...	85**	84**	...	...	...	0.7**	0.7y	...	805**	900y	...	1838**	1944y	26
...	16	14**,y	...	86**	...	...	...	...	...	1.4y	...	...	1056y	...	...	2524y	27
12	11	10	84	85	96	...	...	2.4	0.9**	1.0**,z	1244	1174**	1727**,z	3195	2891**	3081**,z	28
15	15	13	...	97	97	...	...	...	...	...	...	...	...	...	...	...	29
18	17	15	94	98	98	...	...	...	...	...	...	...	...	...	...	...	30
16	...	13**	...	...	85**	...	...	1.8	2.0**	1.8**,z	434	1104**	1242**,z	1231	2419**	2575**,z	31
23	21	19	97	96	98	...	...	...	...	0.8**,y	...	...	69**,y	...	...	260**,y	32
22	19	17	84	86	87	...	...	...	...	0.5**,y	...	...	240**,y	...	...	771**,y	33
22	18**	17**	99	98**	99**	...	99**,z	...	...	...	...	...	...	...	...	...	34
...	20**	...	...	82**	...	100**	...	...	...	...	...	...	...	...	...	...	35
...	19	18	...	93	92	...	...	...	0.6**	0.6**,z	...	519**	744**,z	...	1501**	1663**,z	36
...	14	15	...	96	97	...	...	1.0	...	...	1694	...	...	2877	...	...	37
21	22	20	...	66	69	...	...	...	...	...	...	...	...	...	...	...	38
30	...	...	43	...	...	...	...	1.3	...	...	301	...	...	504	...	...	39
22	20	19	98	98	98	...	99.7	...	...	...	...	...	...	...	...	...	40
																	Central Asia
...	...	22	...	...	99	...	67	...	...	...	...	...	...	...	...	...	41
...	19	14	...	83	85	100	100	...	...	0.6**,z	...	...	64**,z	...	...	269**,z	42
17	17	14z	92	92	95z	...	97z	...	...	...	...	...	...	...	...	...	43
21	...	18	96	...	98	...	...	...	...	...	...	...	...	...	...	...	44
...	24	24	81	95	96	48	55	...	...	0.7**,y	...	...	27**,y	...	...	136**,y	45
28	32	33	90	93	94	...	...	...	...	1.3	...	...	78	...	...	261	46
21	22	22	49	56	64	...	84	...	...	0.7**	...	...	16**	...	...	61**	47
...	...	...	...	...	...	...	...	...	...	...	...	...	...	...	...	...	48
24	...	...	79	...	...	...	...	...	...	...	...	...	...	...	...	...	49
																	East Asia and the Pacific
17	...	...	72	...	...	...	...	...	1.6**	1.6**,z	...	3816**	4152**,z	...	4553**	4682**,z	50
15	14*	13**	57	66*	74**	...	...	0.5	...	...	...	...	...	...	...	...	51
33	48**	55	31	37**	41	...	97	...	...	...	...	...	...	...	...	...	52
22	...	21**	43	50**	53**	...	97**,y	...	0.7**	...	...	...	...	...	...	...	53

Table 13 (continued)

		SCHOOL LIFE EXPECTANCY (expected number of years of formal schooling from primary to tertiary education)									SURVIVAL RATE TO GRADE 5					
		1991			School year ending in 1999			2004			1991		School year ending in 1999		2003	
	Country or territory	Total	Male	Female	Total	Male	Female	Total	Male	Female	Total (%)	GPI (F/M)	Total (%)	GPI (F/M)	Total (%)	GPI (F/M)
54	Cook Islands	...	...	...	10.6**	10.5**	10.6**	10.0**,z	10.0**,z	10.0**,z	...	...	...	...	...	...
55	DPR Korea	...	...	...	...	...	...	...	...	...	...	...	...	...	.	.
56	Fiji	8.6	8.8	8.5	...	...	...	13.3**	13.1**	13.5**	87.0	0.97	87.4	0.96	98.7	0.97
57	Indonesia	10.0	10.6	9.5	...	...	...	11.7	11.9	11.5	83.6	...	...	...	89.1y	1.02y
58	Japan	13.3	13.5	13.0	14.4**	14.6**	14.3**	14.8**	15.0**	14.7**	100.0	1.00	...	...	...	...
59	Kiribati	...	...	...	11.7	11.2	12.2	12.6*	12.0*	13.2*	92.0	...	...	...	81.9	1.16
60	Lao PDR	7.0	8.1	6.0	8.4**	9.4**	7.4**	9.3**	10.2**	8.3**	...	...	54.3	0.98	62.6	1.02
61	Macao, China	11.5	12.0	11.2	12.1**	12.4**	11.9**	15.3	16.4	14.4	...	...	...	...	99.7y	1.01y
62	Malaysia	10.1	10.1	10.2	12.3**	12.1**	12.4**	12.9z	12.3z	13.5z	97.3	1.00	...	...	98.4y	0.99y
63	Marshall Islands	...	...	...	...	...	...	13.0**,z	13.0**,z	12.9**,z	...	...	...	...	...	...
64	Micronesia	...	...	...	...	...	...	...	...	...	...	...	...	...	...	...
65	Myanmar	6.8	6.9	6.7	...	...	...	7.3**,y	...	...	...	...	...	...	**70.3****	**1.06****
66	Nauru	...	...	...	...	...	...	7.9**,z	7.8**,z	8.0**,z	...	...	...	...	30.8x	1.39x
67	New Zealand	14.7	14.5	14.8	17.7**	16.9**	18.5**	18.2	17.3	19.0	...	...	...	...	...	...
68	Niue	...	...	...	11.9	11.5	12.4	11.1	10.8	11.6	...	...	...	...	...	...
69	Palau	...	...	...	...	...	...	...	...	...	...	...	...	...	...	...
70	Papua New Guinea	4.8	5.3	4.3	6.0**	6.3**	5.6**	...	...	...	69.3	0.97	64.8	0.92	67.8**,y	0.99**,y
71	Philippines	10.8	10.6	11.1	11.6**	11.4**	11.9**	12.0**	11.7**	12.4**	...	...	...	...	75.3	1.11
72	Republic of Korea	13.6	14.3	12.9	15.0**	15.8**	14.1**	**16.2**	**17.2**	**15.2**	99.5	1.00	99.9	1.00	**98.1**	**1.00**
73	Samoa	11.3	10.5	12.2	12.3**	12.1**	12.5**	...	...	...	...	...	93.5	1.05*	...	...
74	Singapore	11.9	12.4	11.5	...	...	...	...	...	...	...	...	...	...	...	...
75	Solomon Islands	...	...	...	7.1	7.5	6.6	8.0**,z	8.4**,z	7.5**,z	87.8	1.28	...	...	...	...
76	Thailand	8.7	8.9	8.5	...	...	...	**12.4****	**12.3****	**12.4****	...	...	...	...	...	...
77	Timor-Leste	...	...	...	...	...	...	11.2**,y	...	...	...	...	...	...	...	...
78	Tokelau	...	...	...	...	...	...	...	...	...	...	...	...	...	...	...
79	Tonga	14.0	14.0	14.1	13.3**	13.0**	13.5**	13.4**	13.3**	13.6**	...	...	...	...	...	...
80	Tuvalu	...	...	...	...	...	...	...	...	...	...	...	...	...	69.9x	...
81	Vanuatu	...	...	...	9.1**	...	...	10.5**	10.9**	10.1**	...	...	...	...	...	...
82	Viet Nam	7.5	7.9	7.2	10.3**	10.7**	9.8**	10.5**	10.9**	10.1**	...	...	82.8	1.08	86.8**,y	0.99**,y
	Latin America and the Caribbean															
83	Anguilla	...	...	...	...	...	...	11.9**	11.8**	12.3**	...	...	...	...	...	...
84	Antigua and Barbuda	...	...	...	...	...	...	...	...	...	...	...	...	...	...	...
85	Argentina	13.1	12.8	13.3	15.1**	14.4**	15.9**	15.4z	14.5z	16.2z	...	...	90.3	1.00	84.3y	1.02y
86	Aruba	...	...	...	13.3**	13.2**	13.4**	13.4	13.3	13.5	...	...	96.8	0.99	...	...
87	Bahamas	12.2	11.7	12.8	13.3	13.5	13.0	11.0	10.9	11.2	83.9	...	...	...	...	...
88	Barbados	7.8	7.7	8.0	14.0**	13.4**	14.6**	...	...	...	...	...	93.2	0.97	...	...
89	Belize	10.9	10.9	11.0	...	...	...	13.3**	13.3**	13.3**	67.4	0.96	77.8	1.04	...	...
90	Bermuda	...	...	...	...	...	...	15.3**,y	...	...	...	...	...	...	96.3x	...
91	Bolivia	10.4	11.1	9.7	13.5**	...	...	14.3**	...	...	...	...	82.2	0.97	86.4**	0.98**
92	Brazil	10.3	10.1	10.0	14.2**	13.9**	14.4**	14.0z	13.6z	14.3z	72.7	...	...	...	.	.
93	British Virgin Islands	...	...	...	15.8**	15.0**	16.7**	15.9**	14.6**	17.1**	...	...	...	...	...	...
94	Cayman Islands	...	...	...	...	...	...	...	...	...	...	...	93.4**	...	...	...
95	Chile	12.2	12.2	12.1	12.8**	12.9**	12.7**	13.7**	13.9**	13.5**	92.3	0.97	99.9	1.00	99.0	**1.00**
96	Colombia	9.0	8.5	9.2	11.1**	10.8**	11.4**	11.5**	11.3**	11.8**	76.3	...	66.6	1.08	77.5**	1.07**
97	Costa Rica	10.0	10.1	9.9	10.3**	10.2**	10.4**	10.7**,z	...	...	84.1	1.02	91.0	1.03	92.4**	1.00**
98	Cuba	12.3	11.8	12.7	12.3**	12.1**	12.4**	14.4**	14.4**	14.3**	91.6	...	93.7	1.00	97.7	0.99
99	Dominica	...	...	...	12.3**	11.7**	13.0**	13.4**	13.2**	13.6**	75.4	...	91.3**	...	84.3	0.95
100	Dominican Republic	8.1	8.2	7.9	...	...	...	12.5**	11.9**	13.2**	...	...	75.1	1.11	59.2	1.19**
101	Ecuador	11.4	11.6	11.2	...	...	...	...	...	...	...	...	77.0	1.01	76.3**	1.03**
102	El Salvador	8.8	8.9	8.8	10.7**	10.9**	10.6**	11.5**	11.6**	11.5**	58.0	1.08	65.4**	1.01**	72.8**	1.06**
103	Grenada	...	...	...	...	...	...	12.1**	11.8**	12.3**	...	...	49.4**	0.89**	79.0y	1.17y
104	Guatemala	6.7	7.3	6.0	...	...	...	9.3**,z	9.9**,z	8.8**,z	...	...	56.0	1.06	77.9**	0.96**
105	Guyana	9.9	9.8	9.9	...	...	...	12.5**,z	...	...	...	...	97.4	...	64.3**,x	1.02**,x
106	Haiti	4.6	4.8	4.4	...	...	...	...	...	...	...	...	...	...	...	...
107	Honduras	8.7	8.3	8.9	...	...	...	11.0**	10.5**	11.5**	...	...	...	...	...	...
108	Jamaica	11.0	10.9	11.0	...	...	...	11.5**,z	11.0**,z	12.0**,z	...	...	...	...	89.7y	...
109	Mexico	10.6	10.7	10.3	11.6**	11.7**	11.5**	12.6	12.5	12.7	79.5	2.06	89.0	1.02	92.6	1.02
110	Montserrat	...	...	...	...	...	...	13.6	13.5	13.7	...	...	...	...	...	...
111	Netherlands Antilles	...	...	...	15.3**	15.0**	15.6**	14.3y	13.8y	14.7y	...	...	84.2**	1.10**	88.5x	...

GOAL 6
Educational quality

PUPIL/TEACHER RATIO IN PRIMARY EDUCATION[1]			% FEMALE TEACHERS IN PRIMARY EDUCATION			TRAINED PRIMARY SCHOOL TEACHERS[2] as % of total		PUBLIC CURRENT EXPENDITURE ON PRIMARY EDUCATION AS % GNP			PUBLIC CURRENT EXPENDITURE ON PRIMARY EDUCATION PER PUPIL (unit cost) in constant 2003 US$			PUBLIC CURRENT EXPENDITURE ON PRIMARY EDUCATION PER PUPIL (unit cost) at PPP in constant 2003 US$			
School year ending in			School year ending in			School year ending in		School year ending in			School year ending in			School year ending in			
1991	1999	2004	1991	1999	2004	1999	2004	1991	1999	2004	1991	1999	2004	1991	1999	2004	
...	18	16^z	...	86	...	...	...	...	0.2	...	...	...	...	...	...	...	54
...	...	...	...	...	...	...	...	...	...	...	...	...	...	...	...	...	55
31	...	28	57	...	57	...	...	...	...	2.6	...	...	437	...	...	859	56
23	...	20	51	...	52	...	...	...	...	0.3**,^{z}	...	...	27**,^{z}	...	...	92**,^{z}	57
21	21	19	58	...	...	...	...	...	...	...	...	...	...	...	...	...	58
29	25	25	58	62	73	...	...	...	...	...	...	...	...	...	...	...	59
27	31	31	38	43	45	76	79	...	...	0.6^y	...	...	15^y	...	...	76^y	60
...	31	24	...	87	89	81	91	...	...	...	...	...	...	...	...	...	61
20	21	18^z	57	66	66^z	...	...	1.5	...	1.6**,^{z}	285	...	522**,^{z}	543	...	1 187**,^{z}	62
...	15	17**,^{z}	...	...	34**,^{z}	...	...	...	...	3.6^y	...	...	...	...	...	...	63
...	...	...	...	...	...	...	...	...	...	...	...	...	...	...	...	...	64
48	31	**31**	62	73	**81**	60	**76**	...	...	...	...	...	...	...	...	...	65
...	...	22^z	...	...	95^z	...	...	...	...	...	...	...	...	...	...	...	66
17	18	16	80	82	83	...	...	1.7	1.8**	1.8**,^{z}	2 637	3 212**	2 827**,^{z}	3 061	4 107**	3 215**,^{z}	67
20	16	12	...	100	100	...	...	...	...	...	...	...	...	...	...	...	68
...	15	...	...	82	...	...	...	...	...	...	...	...	...	...	...	...	69
31	36	35**,^{z}	34	39	39**,^{z}	...	...	...	...	...	...	...	...	...	...	...	70
33	35	35	...	87	89	100**	...	...	...	1.7**,^{z}	...	...	110**,^{z}	...	...	480**,^{z}	71
36	31	**29**	50	64	**74**	...	...	1.3	1.3**	1.3**,^{z}	855	1 625**	1 857**,^{z}	1 012	2 369**	2 642**,^{z}	72
26	24**	25**	72	71**	73**	...	...	...	1.4**	...	...	112**	...	...	387**	...	73
26	...	...	...	...	...	...	...	...	...	...	...	...	...	...	...	...	74
21	19	...	...	41	...	...	...	2.2	...	...	104	...	...	270	...	...	75
22	21	21**,^{z}	...	63	58**,^{z}	...	...	1.5	...	...	181	...	...	422	...	...	76
...	...	51^y	...	...	30^y	...	...	...	...	...	...	...	...	...	...	...	77
...	...	6^z	...	...	69^z	...	...	...	...	...	...	...	...	...	...	...	78
23	21	20	67	67	63	...	...	...	...	2.2^y	...	...	194^y	...	...	968^y	79
...	19	19	...	...	80**,^{z}	...	...	...	...	...	...	...	...	...	...	...	80
29	24	20	40	49	54	...	...	...	2.2	...	...	185	...	...	446	...	81
35	30	23	...	78	78	78	87^y	...	...	...	...	...	...	...	...	...	82

Latin America and the Caribbean

...	22	14	...	87	90	76	67	...	...	...	...	...	...	...	...	...	83
...	...	...	...	...	...	...	...	...	...	1.2^y	...	...	...	...	...	...	84
...	22	17**,^{z}	...	88	86**,^{z}	...	...	...	1.6	1.4**,^{y}	...	456	342**,^{y}	...	697	1 357**,^{y}	85
...	19	18	...	78	81	100	100	...	...	...	...	...	...	...	...	...	86
...	14	20	...	63	97	58	95	...	...	...	...	...	...	...	...	...	87
18	18**	16**	72	75**	76**	84**	75**	...	1.2	1.7**	...	1 186	1 967**,^{z}	...	1 865	3 167**	88
26	24**	23**	70	64**	72**	...	51**	2.7	...	2.8^z	273	...	513^z	453	...	987^z	89
...	...	9^y	...	...	88^y	...	100^y	1.1	...	...	...	...	...	...	...	...	90
24	25**	24**	59	61**	61**	...	...	...	2.0**	2.9^z	...	97**	147^z	...	223**	427^z	91
23	26	22^z	...	93	90^z	...	...	...	1.4**	...	...	298**	...	...	656**	...	92
19	18	14	...	86	94	72	82**	...	...	...	...	...	...	...	...	...	93
...	15	13	...	89	81	...	100	...	...	...	...	...	...	...	...	...	94
25	32	27	73	77	78	...	...	...	1.5	1.6^z	...	530	640^z	...	940	1 433^z	95
30	24	28	...	77	77	...	...	...	...	2.0	...	...	292	...	...	966	96
32	27	22	80	80	79	93	97	1.2	2.6	2.3	241	641	716	566	1 376	1 550	97
13	12	10	79	79	77	100	100	...	...	...	...	...	...	...	...	...	98
29	20	19	81	75	83	64	64	...	...	...	...	...	...	...	...	...	99
...	31**	33**,^{z}	...	75**	82**,^{z}	...	79^y	...	...	0.8	...	...	97	...	...	337	100
30	27	23	...	68	70	...	71	...	...	...	...	...	...	...	...	...	101
...	...	...	...	...	...	...	...	...	...	1.4**,^{z}	...	...	207**,^{z}	...	...	434**,^{z}	102
...	20	18	...	73	76	...	68^z	...	...	1.9**,^{z}	...	...	393**,^{z}	...	...	745**,^{z}	103
34	38	31	...	...	...	...	...	...	...	0.9	...	...	96	...	...	186	104
30	27	27**	76	86	86**	52	57^z	...	...	1.6	...	...	108**	...	...	454**	105
23	...	...	45	...	...	...	...	0.7	...	...	39	...	...	213	...	...	106
38	...	33	74	...	75	...	87	...	...	...	...	...	...	...	...	...	107
34	...	28	...	...	89**	...	...	1.5	...	1.6**	335	...	323**	641	...	422**	108
31	27	28	...	62	66	...	...	0.8	1.8	2.1^y	260	671	845^y	453	1 121	1 183^y	109
...	21	21	...	84	100	100	86	...	...	...	...	...	...	...	...	...	110
...	20	20**,^{z}	...	86	86**,^{z}	100	100^y	...	...	...	...	...	...	...	...	...	111

Table 13 (continued)

		GOAL 6														
		Educational quality														
		SCHOOL LIFE EXPECTANCY (expected number of years of formal schooling from primary to tertiary education)									SURVIVAL RATE TO GRADE 5					
		School year ending in									School year ending in					
		1991			1999			2004			1991		1999		2003	
	Country or territory	Total	Male	Female	Total	Male	Female	Total	Male	Female	Total (%)	GPI (F/M)	Total (%)	GPI (F/M)	Total (%)	GPI (F/M)
112	Nicaragua	8.4	8.0	8.8	...	...	...	10.8**,z	10.6**,z	11.0**,z	44.1	3.33	48.4	1.19	58.8**	1.13**
113	Panama	11.2	11.0	11.3	12.6**	12.1**	13.1**	13.4**	12.8**	14.0**	...	...	91.9	1.01	84.3**	1.06**
114	Paraguay	8.7	8.8	8.6	11.1**	11.1**	11.1**	11.5**,z	11.4**,z	11.6**,z	74.0	1.02	78.1**	1.05**	81.6y	1.04y
115	Peru	12.0	12.2	11.8	...	...	...	13.7**	13.5**	14.0**	...	...	87.4	0.98	83.6x	0.98x
116	Saint Kitts and Nevis	13.7	13.4	14.1	...	...	...	13.4**	13.2**	13.7**	...	...	...	...	...	...
117	Saint Lucia	12.9	12.6	13.1	...	...	...	12.9**	12.2**	13.6**	96.1	1.02	90.1**	...	90.1	1.02
118	St Vincent/Grenad.	12.3	11.8	12.8	...	...	...	11.7**	11.8**	11.6**	...	...	...	...	88.0**,y	...
119	Suriname	11.1	10.7	11.4	...	...	...	12.2**,y	11.3**,y	13.2**,y	...	...	...	...	...	...
120	Trinidad and Tobago	11.1	11.1	11.2	11.9**	11.7**	12.1**	12.3**	12.1**	12.5**	...	...	100.0	...	100.0*	...
121	Turks and Caicos Islands	...	...	...	...	...	...	12.4**	11.4**	13.3**	...	...	...	...	45.9y	1.23y
122	Uruguay	12.9	12.2	13.7	13.9**	13.1**	14.8**	15.2**,z	13.9**,z	16.2**,z	96.9	1.03	...	...	86.9**	1.01**
123	Venezuela	10.8	10.6	10.9	...	...	...	11.7**,z	11.5**,z	12.0**,z	86.0	1.09	90.8	1.08	91.0	1.06
North America and Western Europe																
124	Andorra	...	...	...	...	...	...	11.3**	11.3**	11.3**	...	...	...	...	...	...
125	Austria	13.9	14.3	13.5	15.2**	15.3**	15.2**	15.3	15.2	15.5	...	...	...	...	.	
126	Belgium	14.0	13.9	14.0	17.8**	17.4**	18.2**	16.0**	15.8**	16.2**	90.9	1.02	...	...	...	...
127	Canada	16.9	16.5	17.4	16.0**	15.7**	16.3**	15.7**,y	15.3**,y	16.2**,y	96.7	1.04	...	...	...	...
128	Cyprus	10.3	10.3	10.4	12.5	12.4	12.7	13.6	13.5	13.6	99.9	1.00	96.1	1.03	99.2	0.98
129	Denmark	14.2	14.0	14.3	16.1**	15.6**	16.6**	16.7	16.0	17.3	94.2	1.00	100.0	1.00	...	...
130	Finland	15.2	14.5	15.9	17.4**	16.7**	18.2**	17.0	16.5	17.6	99.8	1.00	99.8	1.00	99.9	1.00
131	France	14.3	14.0	14.6	15.7**	15.4**	16.0**	15.8	15.4	16.1	96.4	1.37	98.0	0.99	...	...
132	Germany	14.6	15.0	14.2	16.1**	16.2**	15.9**	...	...	...	...	...	...	...	.	.
133	Greece	13.4	13.5	13.3	13.8**	13.5**	14.1**	15.8	15.5	16.2	99.7	1.00	...	...	...	...
134	Iceland	15.3	15.3	15.4	16.7**	16.1**	17.3**	18.3**	17.3**	19.3**	...	...	99.8	1.00	99.7y	0.99y
135	Ireland	12.7	12.6	12.9	16.4**	15.9**	16.8**	17.8	17.6	18.1	99.5	1.01	95.1	1.03	99.8	1.00
136	Israel	13.1	12.8	13.4	15.0**	14.6**	15.4**	15.4	15.0	15.8	...	...	...	...	99.9	1.00
137	Italy	13.5	13.5	13.4	14.9**	14.6**	15.1**	15.9	15.6	16.3	...	...	96.6	...	96.5x	1.01x
138	Luxembourg	11.1	10.9	11.3	13.1**	13.1**	13.2**	13.5**	13.4**	13.7**	...	...	96.3**	1.08**	95.7	1.05
139	Malta	12.9	13.3	12.5	...	...	...	14.8	14.9	14.7	99.3	1.01	99.4	0.99	99.3y	1.01y
140	Monaco	...	...	...	...	...	...	...	...	...	82.9	0.81	...	...	...	...
141	Netherlands	14.9	15.1	14.6	16.5**	16.8**	16.3**	16.5	16.6	16.4	...	...	99.9	1.00	99.8y	1.00y
142	Norway	14.3	14.0	14.5	17.5**	16.9**	16.9**	17.7	16.9	18.4	99.6	1.01	...	...	99.6	1.01
143	Portugal	12.2	11.9	12.5	15.7**	15.4**	16.1**	15.2	14.7	15.7	...	...	...	...	...	...
144	San Marino	...	...	...	...	...	...	...	...	...	...	...	...	...	...	...
145	Spain	14.5	14.2	14.8	15.9	15.5	16.2	16.2	15.8	16.7	...	...	...	...	...	...
146	Sweden	13.0	12.7	13.3	19.1**	17.5**	20.7**	16.0	15.1	16.9	99.8	1.00	...	...	...	...
147	Switzerland	13.6	14.0	13.1	15.1**	15.7**	14.5**	15.2	15.6	14.8	...	...	...	...	...	...
148	United Kingdom	14.1	14.4	13.9	20.0**	19.3**	20.7**	16.6	16.1	17.1	...	...	...	...	...	...
149	United States	15.3	14.9	15.7	15.9**	...	...	15.8**	15.2**	16.5**	...	...	...	...	...	...
South and West Asia																
150	Afghanistan	2.5	3.2	1.7	...	...	...	6.7**	9.4**	3.8**	...	...	...	...	...	...
151	Bangladesh	6.1	7.1	5.1	9.2**	9.3**	9.1**	9.2z	9.0z	9.3z	...	...	64.9	1.16	65.1	1.07
152	Bhutan	1.5	1.8	1.2	...	...	...	...	...	...	...	...	90.4	1.04	...	...
153	India	8.1	9.5	6.5	...	...	...	10.1**	10.9**	9.4**	...	...	62.0	0.95	78.9	0.94
154	Iran, Islamic Republic of	9.6	10.6	8.6	11.5**	12.1**	10.9**	12.5**	12.7**	12.2**	89.9	0.98	...	...	90.2	0.99
155	Maldives	...	...	...	11.8**	11.7**	11.9**	11.2**	11.1**	11.4**	...	...	...	...	...	...
156	Nepal	7.5	9.4	5.4	...	...	...	8.9**,z	9.8**,z	8.0**,z	51.3	0.99	58.0	1.10	**60.8**	1.17**
157	Pakistan	4.5	5.9	3.1	...	...	...	6.2**	7.1**	5.2**	...	...	...	...	...	...
158	Sri Lanka	11.2	11.2	11.3	...	...	...	**6.5**	**7.3**	**5.6**	92.2	1.01	...	...	...	...
Sub-Saharan Africa																
159	Angola	4.0	4.4	3.7	3.7**	4.0**	3.4**	...	...	...	...	...	...	...	.	.
160	Benin	3.8	5.1	2.4	6.3**	7.9**	4.8**	...	...	...	54.8	1.02	...	...	69.4	0.99
161	Botswana	9.6	9.3	10.0	11.2**	11.1**	11.3**	11.9**	11.6**	12.2**	84.0	1.06	86.6	1.06	91.2**	1.07**
162	Burkina Faso	2.7	3.4	2.1	3.5**	4.2**	2.8**	4.1**	4.7**	3.5**	69.7	0.96	68.3	1.05	75.8	1.05
163	Burundi	4.9	5.4	4.4	...	...	...	5.9**	6.6**	5.3**	61.7	0.89	...	...	63.0	0.96
164	Cameroon	8.3	9.2	7.4	7.7**	...	...	10.6**	11.9**	9.4**	...	...	80.7**	...	98.0	1.04
165	Cape Verde	...	...	...	...	...	...	11.0**	11.0**	11.0**	...	...	...	...	91.2	1.08

GOAL 6

Educational quality

PUPIL/TEACHER RATIO IN PRIMARY EDUCATION[1]			% FEMALE TEACHERS IN PRIMARY EDUCATION			TRAINED PRIMARY SCHOOL TEACHERS[2] as % of total		PUBLIC CURRENT EXPENDITURE ON PRIMARY EDUCATION AS % GNP			PUBLIC CURRENT EXPENDITURE ON PRIMARY EDUCATION PER PUPIL (unit cost) in constant 2003 US$			PUBLIC CURRENT EXPENDITURE ON PRIMARY EDUCATION PER PUPIL (unit cost) at PPP in constant 2003 US$			
School year ending in			School year ending in			School year ending in		School year ending in			School year ending in			School year ending in			
1991	1999	2004	1991	1999	2004	1999	2004	1991	1999	2004	1991	1999	2004	1991	1999	2004	
36	34	35	86	83	79	79	75	...	...	1.5	...	...	66	...	...	286	112
...	26	24	...	75	76	79	74	1.7	1.9	...	369	520	...	645	778	...	113
25	...	28**	...	...	72**	...	...	...	...	2.0y	...	...	121y	...	...	547y	114
29	...	22	...	...	63	...	...	...	1.2	1.0y	...	148	138y	...	335	327y	115
22	...	17	74	...	85	...	55	1.1	...	1.2y	...	...	581y	...	...	928y	116
29	22	23	83	84**	86	...	78	2.5	3.3**	2.5	385	858**	717	529	1 093**	965	117
20	...	17**	67	...	73**	...	72**	3.0	...	4.5	374	...	932	737	...	1 651	118
22	...	19**,z	84	...	85**,z	...	...	...	...	...	...	...	...	...	...	...	119
26	21	18*	70	76	73*	71	81*	...	1.5	...	...	670	...	...	1 026	...	120
...	18**	11	...	92**	90	81**	91**	...	...	...	...	...	...	...	...	...	121
22	20	21**	...	92**	...	...	...	0.9	0.8	...	244	292	...	420	408	...	122
23	...	...	74	...	...	...	...	...	...	...	...	...	...	...	...	...	123

North America and Western Europe

PUPIL/TEACHER RATIO			% FEMALE TEACHERS			TRAINED		AS % GNP			unit cost US$			at PPP US$			
...	...	13	...	...	77	...	...	...	...	...	...	...	...	...	...	...	124
11	13	13	82	89	91	...	...	0.9	1.1**	1.1y	4 790	6 920**	7 072y	4 359	6 997**	8 144y	125
...	...	12	...	...	78	...	...	1.2	...	...	3 939	...	...	3 723	...	...	126
15	18	17**,y	69	...	68**,y	...	...	...	...	...	...	...	...	...	...	...	127
21	18	18	60	67	83	...	...	1.2	1.6	1.7y	1 317	2 419	2 895y	1 647	3 144	...	128
...	10	...	...	63	...	...	...	...	1.6**	1.8y	...	8 796**	8 793y	...	7 479**	8 474y	129
...	17	16	...	71	76	...	...	1.8	1.2**	1.3**,z	5 213	4 692**	5 123**,z	3 696	4 455**	4 556**,z	130
...	19	19	...	78	81	...	...	0.9	1.1**	1.0y	2 987	4 457**	4 781y	2 624	4 329**	5 368y	131
...	17	14	...	82	83	...	...	...	0.6**	0.6**,y	...	3 897**	4 442**,y	...	3 778**	5 015**,y	132
19	14	11	52	...	62	...	...	0.6	0.7**	0.8**,y	932	1 604**	2 017**,y	1 272	2 273**	3 131**,y	133
...	11**	11**	...	76**	78**	...	...	...	...	2.7**,z	...	...	8 742**,z	...	...	7 508**,z	134
27	22	18	77	85	83	...	...	1.5	1.5**	1.6**,y	2 185	3 268**	4 187**,y	2 102	3 479**	4 968**,y	135
15	13	12	82	...	85	...	...	1.9	2.4**	2.6y	1 775	3 280**	3 593y	2 005	3 655**	4 485y	136
12	11	11	91	95	95	...	...	0.8	1.0**	1.2y	3 348	4 795**	6 080y	3 060	5 541**	7 824y	137
13	...	12	51	...	71	...	...	...	...	...	...	...	...	...	...	...	138
21	20	19	79	87	87	...	...	0.9	...	1.1y	825	...	1 629y	1 158	...	2 851y	139
...	16**	...	...	87**	...	...	...	...	...	...	...	...	...	...	...	...	140
17	...	...	53	...	...	...	...	0.9	1.2**	1.4y	3 276	4 551**	5 357y	3 072	4 693**	6 001y	141
...	...	11**	...	...	73**	...	...	2.5	1.6**	1.8**,z	11 666	7 900**	9 116**,z	9 637	7 520**	7 093**,z	142
14	...	12	81	...	82	...	...	1.8	1.6**	1.8y	2 010	2 794**	3 415y	2 912	4 043**	5 272y	143
6	...	...	89	...	...	...	...	...	...	...	...	...	...	...	...	...	144
22	15	14	73	68	69	...	...	0.8	1.2**	1.1y	1 826	3 331**	3 630y	1 781	4 199**	4 897y	145
10	12	10	77	80	81	...	...	3.2	...	...	11 973	...	...	7 185	...	...	146
...	13**	13	...	72**	78	...	...	2.1	1.4	1.5y	15 072	8 834	9 685y	10 208	6 521	7 810y	147
20	19	18	78	76	81	...	...	1.2	...	...	3 294	...	...	3 100	...	...	148
...	15	15	...	86	88	...	...	...	...	...	...	...	...	...	...	...	149

South and West Asia

PUPIL/TEACHER RATIO			% FEMALE TEACHERS			TRAINED		AS % GNP			unit cost US$			at PPP US$			
...	36	65	...	–	22	...	...	...	...	...	...	...	...	...	...	...	150
...	56	55	...	33	39	64	51z	...	0.6	0.7	...	13	19	...	54	91	151
...	42	38**,y	...	32	36**,y	100	...	...	...	...	...	...	...	...	...	...	152
47	35*	40	28	33*	44	...	...	...	1.2**	...	...	51**	...	...	262**	...	153
31	27	20	53	53	58	...	100	...	...	1.1z	...	...	164z	...	...	556z	154
...	24	18z	...	60	64z	67	61z	...	...	...	...	...	...	...	...	...	155
39	39	**40**	14	23	**30**	46	**31**	...	1.1**	1.3**,z	...	14**	18**,z	...	81**	103**,z	156
...	...	37	27	...	45	...	...	...	...	...	...	...	...	...	...	...	157
31	...	22	...	...	79**	...	...	...	...	...	...	...	...	...	...	...	158

Sub-Saharan Africa

PUPIL/TEACHER RATIO			% FEMALE TEACHERS			TRAINED		AS % GNP			unit cost US$			at PPP US$			
32	...	...	...	...	...	...	...	...	...	...	...	...	...	...	...	...	159
36	53	52	25	23	19	58	72	...	...	1.7**,y	...	...	47**,y	...	...	124**,y	160
30	27	26	78	81	79	90	90z	...	...	...	...	...	...	...	...	...	161
57	49	49	27	25	28	...	89	...	...	...	...	...	...	...	...	...	162
67	57**	51	46	54**	54	...	...	1.5	1.4	1.7	16	11**	11	59	64**	83	163
51	52	54	30	36	40	...	69	...	1.2	...	...	53	...	...	158	...	164
...	29**	27	...	62**	67	...	73	...	...	2.7	...	...	261	...	...	756	165

Table 13 (continued)

		GOAL 6 Educational quality															
		SCHOOL LIFE EXPECTANCY (expected number of years of formal schooling from primary to tertiary education)									SURVIVAL RATE TO GRADE 5						
		School year ending in									School year ending in						
		1991			1999			2004			1991		1999		2003		
	Country or territory	Total	Male	Female	Total	Male	Female	Total	Male	Female	Total (%)	GPI (F/M)	Total (%)	GPI (F/M)	Total (%)	GPI (F/M)	
166	Central African Republic	4.8	6.0	3.5	…	…	…	…	…	…	23.0	0.90	…	…	…	…	
167	Chad	3.4	4.9	2.0	…	…	…	…	…	…	50.5	0.74	55.1	0.86	45.8**	0.76**	
168	Comoros	5.8	6.8	4.8	6.5**	7.1**	5.9**	8.0**	8.7**	7.3**	…	…	…	…	62.7	…	
169	Congo	11.0	12.1	9.9	…	…	…	7.7**,z	8.5**,z	7.0**,z	60.1	1.16	…	…	66.3y	1.03y	
170	Côte d'Ivoire	5.8	7.2	4.5	6.2**	7.4**	4.9**	…	…	…	72.5	0.93	69.1	0.89	…	…	
171	D. R. Congo	5.7	6.9	4.6	4.3**	…	…	…	…	…	54.7	0.86	…	…	…	…	
172	Equatorial Guinea	10.8	11.9	9.8	…	…	…	…	…	…	…	…	…	…	32.6**,x	0.93**,x	
173	Eritrea	…	…	…	4.5**	5.1**	3.9**	5.6**	6.7**	4.5**	…	…	95.3	0.95	80.3	0.84	
174	Ethiopia	2.7	3.2	2.2	3.8**	4.8**	2.9**	5.6**	6.6**	4.6**	18.3	1.47	…	…	.	.	
175	Gabon	10.8	10.8	10.8	11.9**	12.3**	11.5**	…	…	…	…	…	…	…	69.3**,y	1.04**,y	
176	Gambia	…	…	…	7.0**	7.8**	6.1**	7.8**	8.0**	7.7**	…	…	…	…	…	…	
177	Ghana	6.6	7.5	5.8	…	…	…	**8.3**	**8.7**	**7.9**	80.5	0.98	…	…	63.3y	1.05y	
178	Guinea	2.9	4.0	1.8	…	…	…	6.9	8.1	5.6	58.6	0.76	…	…	82.0	0.87	
179	Guinea-Bissau	3.5	4.6	2.4	…	…	…	…	…	…	…	…	…	…	…	…	
180	Kenya	9.3	9.7	8.9	…	…	…	9.9**	10.2**	9.5**	76.7	1.04	…	…	75.3*	0.97*	
181	Lesotho	9.5	8.6	10.4	9.3	8.8	9.8	10.9**,z	10.6**,z	11.2**,z	65.9	1.26	74.0	1.20	63.4	1.19	
182	Liberia	3.2	4.1	2.3	8.1**	9.6**	6.5**	…	…	…	…	…	…	…	…	…	
183	Madagascar	6.2	6.3	6.1	6.1**	6.2**	5.9**	…	…	…	21.1	0.96	51.1	1.02	57.0	1.03	
184	Malawi	6.0	6.7	5.3	11.1**	11.8**	10.4**	9.6**	9.8**	9.5**	64.4	0.80	49.0	0.77	43.8x	0.77x	
185	Mali	2.0	2.6	1.5	4.0**	…	…	5.4**	6.3**	4.5**	69.7	0.95	78.3**	0.97**	…	…	
186	Mauritius	10.4	10.4	10.5	12.1**	12.2**	12.0**	13.5**	13.6**	13.3**	97.4	1.01	99.5	0.99	98.9x	1.01x	
187	Mozambique	3.7	4.3	3.0	5.4**	…	…	7.6**	8.4**	6.8**	34.2	0.87	42.7	0.79	49.2x	0.85x	
188	Namibia	11.6	11.1	12.2	…	…	…	10.9**,z	10.8**,z	11.1**,z	62.3	1.08	92.2	1.02	88.1**,y	1.03**,y	
189	Niger	2.0	2.6	1.4	…	…	…	3.2**	3.8**	2.6**	62.4	1.06	…	…	73.6	0.96	
190	Nigeria	6.7	7.5	5.8	…	…	…	8.8**	9.7**	7.9**	89.1	…	…	…	72.6**	1.05**	
191	Rwanda	6.1	6.2	5.9	6.8**	…	…	8.2**	8.3**	8.2**	59.9	0.97	45.4	…	45.8	1.13	
192	Sao Tome and Principe	…	…	…	7.6**	8.4**	6.9**	10.1	10.2	10.1	…	…	…	…	66.5	1.02	
193	Senegal	4.5	5.4	3.5	5.0**	…	…	6.2**	…	…	84.5	…	…	…	78.2	0.98	
194	Seychelles	…	…	…	14.0	13.9	14.2	12.8**	12.4**	13.2**	92.7	1.03	99.2	1.02	…	…	
195	Sierra Leone	5.1	6.2	4.0	…	…	…	…	…	…	…	…	…	…	…	…	
196	Somalia	1.2	1.7	0.8	…	…	…	…	…	…	…	…	…	…	…	…	
197	South Africa	11.9	11.7	12.1	13.3**	13.1**	13.5**	13.0**,z	12.7**,z	13.0**,z	…	…	64.8	0.99	84.1y	1.06y	
198	Swaziland	9.3	9.5	9.0	9.8**	10.1**	9.5**	9.4**,z	9.6**,z	9.2**,z	77.0	1.09	79.9	1.22	76.8y	1.08y	
199	Togo	7.6	9.8	5.4	9.1**	11.1**	7.1**	…	…	…	48.0	0.80	…	…	76.0	0.93	
200	Uganda	5.6	6.2	5.0	10.1**	10.8**	9.5**	10.4**	10.7**	10.2**	36.0	…	…	…	63.6x	1.02x	
201	United Republic of Tanzania	5.4	5.6	5.3	5.1**	5.2**	5.1**	…	…	…	81.3	1.02	…	…	**75.8**	**1.00**	
202	Zambia	7.7	8.3	7.1	6.5**	6.9**	6.1**	…	…	…	…	…	80.6	0.94	98.5x	…	
203	Zimbabwe	10.6	11.2	10.0	9.7**	…	…	9.1**,z	9.3**,z	8.9**,z	76.1	1.12	…	…	69.7**,y	**1.04**,y	

		Weighted average									Median						
I	World	9.1	9.7	8.4	9.9	10.3	9.4	10.7	11.0	10.4	…	…	…	…	…	…	
II	Countries in transition	12.1	11.9	12.4	11.9	11.8	12.0	12.7	12.5	12.9	…	…	…	…	.	.	
III	Developed countries	14.1	14.0	14.2	15.8	15.5	16.1	15.7	15.4	16.1	…	…	…	…	.	.	
IV	Developing countries	8.3	9.1	7.4	9.1	9.7	8.5	10.1	10.5	9.7	…	…	…	…	81.6	1.03	
V	Arab States	8.4	9.4	7.3	9.6	10.3	8.9	10.3	10.8	9.7	86.9	1.00	92.1	1.02	94.7	1.02	
VI	Central and Eastern Europe	11.3	11.3	11.3	12.1	12.1	12.0	12.9	12.9	12.8	…	…	…	…	.	.	
VII	Central Asia	11.6	11.6	11.5	10.9	11.1	10.8	11.7	11.8	11.6	…	…	…	…	.	.	
VIII	East Asia and the Pacific	9.5	10.1	9.0	10.5	10.6	10.3	11.5	11.6	11.5	…	…	…	…	…	…	
IX	East Asia	9.5	10.1	9.0	10.4	10.6	10.2	11.5	11.6	11.4	…	…	…	…	88.0	1.01	
X	Pacific	11.1	11.0	11.2	14.5	14.4	14.6	14.7	14.7	14.7	…	…	…	…	…	…	
XI	Latin America/Caribbean	10.3	10.3	10.2	12.5	12.4	12.6	13.0	12.8	13.2	…	…	89.6	…	84.3	1.02	
XII	Caribbean	7.1	7.1	7.0	11.0	11.1	10.9	11.9	11.9	11.9	…	…	…	…	…	…	
XIII	Latin America	10.4	10.4	10.3	12.6	12.4	12.7	13.0	12.8	13.2	79.5	…	84.8	0.98	84.3	1.06	
XIV	N. America/W. Europe	14.7	14.6	14.9	16.2	15.8	16.6	15.9	15.5	16.4	…	…	…	…	.	.	
XV	South and West Asia	7.5	8.9	6.1	8.3	9.3	7.2	9.6	10.3	8.8	…	…	…	…	.	.	
XVI	Sub-Saharan Africa	6.0	6.7	5.4	6.5	7.2	5.8	7.6	8.3	6.9	63.4	0.93	…	…	72.6	1.05	

1. Based on headcounts of pupils and teachers.

2. Data on trained teachers (defined according to national standards) are not collected for countries whose education statistics are gathered through the OECD, Eurostat or the World Education Indicators questionnaires.

Data in bold are for the school year ending in 2005.

GOAL 6
Educational quality

PUPIL/TEACHER RATIO IN PRIMARY EDUCATION[1]			% FEMALE TEACHERS IN PRIMARY EDUCATION			TRAINED PRIMARY SCHOOL TEACHERS[2] as % of total		PUBLIC CURRENT EXPENDITURE ON PRIMARY EDUCATION AS % GNP			PUBLIC CURRENT EXPENDITURE ON PRIMARY EDUCATION PER PUPIL (unit cost) in constant 2003 US$			PUBLIC CURRENT EXPENDITURE ON PRIMARY EDUCATION PER PUPIL (unit cost) at PPP in constant 2003 US$			
School year ending in			School year ending in			School year ending in		School year ending in			School year ending in			School year ending in			
1991	1999	2004	1991	1999	2004	1999	2004	1991	1999	2004	1991	1999	2004	1991	1999	2004	
77	...	...	25	...	...	...	...	1.2	...	...	42	...	...	92	...	...	166
66	68	69**	6	9	10**	...	...	0.7	...	...	22	...	...	58	...	...	167
37	35	35	...	26	33	...	...	...	...	...	...	...	...	...	...	...	168
65	61	83	32	42	45	...	62	...	2.0	1.5**,y	...	151	73**,y	...	195	87**,y	169
37	43	42*,z	18	20	24*,z	...	100*,z	...	1.8	...	...	131	...	...	262	...	170
40	26	...	24	21	...	...	...	...	...	...	...	...	...	...	...	...	171
...	57	...	...	28	...	...	...	...	...	...	...	...	...	...	...	...	172
38	47	47	45	35	36	73	83	...	...	0.9	...	...	18	...	...	92	173
36	64**	**72**	24	37**	**45**	...	**97**	1.5	...	...	23	...	...	61	...	...	174
...	44	36**	...	42	45**	...	100z	...	...	...	...	...	...	...	...	...	175
31	33	37	31	29	31	72	...	1.3	2.2	...	38	47	...	169	226	...	176
29	30	**33**	36	32	**31**	72	**58**	...	...	...	...	...	...	...	...	...	177
40	47	45	22	25	24	...	...	...	...	...	...	...	...	...	...	...	178
...	44**	...	...	20**	...	...	...	...	...	...	...	...	...	...	...	...	179
32	32	40	38	42	44	...	99	3.2	...	4.1	69	...	95	196	...	211	180
54	44	44	80	80	80	78	67	...	3.2	3.4**,y	...	111	115**,y	...	441	676**,y	181
...	39	...	...	19	...	...	...	...	...	...	...	...	...	...	...	...	182
40	47	52	...	58	60**	...	...	...	...	...	...	...	...	...	...	...	183
61	63**	70**	31	40**	46**	...	...	1.1	...	3.2z	...	...	20z	...	...	78z	184
47	62*	52	25	23*	28	...	...	...	1.3**	...	...	46**	...	...	147**	...	185
21	26	**23**	45	54	**63**	100	100	1.3	1.2	1.2	246	383	438	557	999	1 071	186
55	61	65	23	25	30	...	...	...	...	...	...	...	...	...	...	...	187
...	32	28**,z	...	67	61**,z	29	50**,y	...	4.4	4.0z	...	447	301z	...	1 459	876z	188
42	41	44	33	31	36	98	76	...	...	...	...	...	...	...	...	...	189
39	38**	36	43	47**	51	...	51	...	...	...	...	...	...	...	...	...	190
57	54	62	46	55	51	49	82	...	...	...	...	...	...	...	...	...	191
...	36	32	...	...	56	...	...	...	...	...	...	...	...	...	...	...	192
53	49	43	27	23**	24	...	91y	1.7	...	1.7	100	...	81	157	...	193	193
...	15	14**	...	85	85**	82	78z	...	...	1.6**	...	...	1 169**	...	...	...	194
35	...	...	...	...	...	...	...	...	...	...	...	...	...	...	...	...	195
...	...	...	...	...	...	...	...	...	...	...	...	...	...	...	...	...	196
27	35	34z	58	78	74z	62	79z	4.1	2.7	2.1	632	488*	374	1 537	1 461*	897	197
32	33	31z	78	75	75z	91	91z	1.4	2.0	2.4**	110	153	166**	369	489	382**	198
58	41	44	19	13	13	...	45	...	1.8**	...	...	30**	...	...	139**	...	199
33	56**	**50**	...	33**	**39**	...	80	...	...	2.5**	...	...	17.4**	...	...	96**	200
36	40	**56**	40	45	**48**	...	**100**	...	...	...	...	...	...	...	...	...	201
...	47	49**	...	49	48**	94	100y	...	...	1.8	...	...	36	...	...	65	202
39	41	39z	40	47	51z	...	...	4.3	...	...	...	...	...	...	...	...	203

Median			Median			Median		Median			Median			Median			
27	24	21	58	71	74	...	...	...	...	...	...	...	...	...	...	...	I
22	20	18	94	97	98	...	97	...	...	...	...	...	...	...	...	...	II
17	17	14	...	85	83	...	...	...	...	1.2	...	...	3 630	...	...	4 682	III
30	28	27	48	62	64	...	...	...	...	...	...	...	...	...	...	...	IV
25	25	20	51	52	62	...	...	...	...	...	...	...	...	...	...	...	V
20	19	17	84	91	94	...	...	...	...	0.7	...	...	822	...	...	1 804	VI
21	22	22	85	92	95	...	84	...	...	...	...	...	...	...	...	...	VII
26	21	21	57	66	69	...	...	...	...	...	...	...	...	...	...	...	VIII
...	31	23	...	66	70	...	...	...	...	...	...	...	...	...	...	...	IX
...	19	20	...	67	66	...	...	...	...	...	...	...	...	...	...	...	X
26	22	21	...	78	81	...	79	...	...	1.6	...	...	...	...	...	...	XI
25	20	18	...	84	86	76	79	...	...	...	...	...	...	...	...	...	XII
30	26	24	...	77	77	...	...	...	...	1.5	...	...	177	...	...	490	XIII
15	15	13	77	79	81	...	...	1.2	1.2	1.4	3 276	4 457	4 781	3 060	4 329	5 320	XIV
...	36	38	...	33	44	...	...	...	...	...	...	...	...	...	...	...	XV
39	44	44	32	36	45	...	81	...	...	...	...	...	...	...	...	...	XVI

(z) Data are for the school year ending in 2003.   (y) Data are for the school year ending in 2002.   (x) Data are for the school year ending in 2001.

Aid tables

Introduction

Most of the data on aid used in this Report are derived from the OECD's International Development Statistics (IDS) database, which records information provided annually by all member countries of the OECD Development Assistance Committee (DAC). The IDS comprises the DAC database, which provides aggregate data, and the Creditor Reporting System, which provides project- and activity-level data. The IDS is available online at www.oecd.org/dac/stats/idsonline. It is updated frequently. The data presented in this Report were downloaded between May and June 2006.

The focus of this section of the annex on aid data is Official Development Assistance. This term and others used in describing aid data are explained below to help in understanding the tables in this section and the data presented in Chapter 4. Private funds are not included.

Aid recipients and donors

Official Development Assistance (ODA) is public funds provided to developing countries to promote their economic and social development. It is concessional: that is, it takes the form either of a grant or of a loan carrying a lower rate of interest than is available in the market and, usually, a longer than normal repayment period. ODA may be provided directly by a government (bilateral ODA) or through an international agency (multilateral ODA). ODA includes technical cooperation (see below).

Developing countries are those in Part I of the DAC List of Aid Recipients, which essentially comprises all low- and middle-income countries. Twelve central and eastern European countries, including new independent states of the former Soviet Union, plus a set of more advanced developing countries are in Part II of the list, and aid to them is referred to as Official Aid (OA). The data presented in this Report do not include OA unless indicated.

Bilateral donors are countries that provide development assistance directly to recipient countries. The majority (Australia, Austria, Belgium, Canada, Denmark, Finland, France, Germany, Greece, Ireland, Italy, Japan, Luxembourg, the Netherlands, New Zealand, Norway, Portugal, Spain, Sweden, Switzerland, the United Kingdom and the United States) are members of the DAC, a forum of major bilateral donors established to promote the volume and effectiveness of aid. Non-DAC bilateral donors include the Republic of Korea and some Arab states. Bilateral donors also contribute substantially to the financing of multilateral donors through contributions recorded as multilateral ODA. The financial flows from multilateral donors to recipient countries are also recorded as ODA receipts.

Multilateral donors are international institutions with government membership that conduct all or a significant part of their activities in favour of developing countries. They include multilateral development banks (e.g. the World Bank and the Inter-American Development Bank), United Nations agencies (e.g. UNDP and UNICEF) and regional groupings (e.g. the European Commission and Arab agencies). The development banks also make non-concessional loans to several middle- and higher-income countries, and these are not counted as part of ODA.

Types of aid

Unallocated aid: some contributions are not susceptible to allocation by sector and are reported as non-sector-allocable aid. Examples are aid for general development purposes (direct budget support), balance-of-payments support, action relating to debt (including debt relief) and emergency assistance.

Basic education: the definition of basic education varies by agency. The DAC defines it as covering primary education, basic life skills for youth and adults, and early childhood education.

Education, level unspecified: the aid to education reported in the DAC database includes basic, secondary and post-secondary education, and a subcategory called 'education, level unspecified'. This subcategory covers aid related to any activity that cannot be attributed solely to the development of a single level of education.

Sector budget funding: funds contributed directly to the budget of a ministry of education are often reported by donors in this subcategory. Although this aid will in practice mainly be used for specific levels of education, such information is not available in the DAC database. This reduces accuracy in assessing the amount of resources made available for each specific level of education.

Technical cooperation (sometimes referred to as technical assistance): according to the DAC Directives, technical cooperation is the provision of know-how in the form of personnel, training, research and associated costs. It includes (a) grants to nationals of aid recipient countries receiving education or training at home or abroad; and (b) payments to consultants, advisers and similar personnel as well as teachers and administrators serving in recipient countries (including the cost of associated equipment). Where such assistance is related specifically to a capital project, it is included with project and programme expenditure and not separately reported as technical cooperation. The aid activities reported in this category vary by donor, as interpretations of the definition are broad.

Debt relief: this includes debt forgiveness, i.e. the extinction of a loan by agreement between the creditor (donor) and the debtor (aid recipient), and other action on debt, including debt swaps, buy-backs and refinancing. In the DAC database, debt forgiveness is reported as a grant. It raises gross ODA but not necessarily net ODA (see below).

Aid data

Commitments and disbursements: a commitment is a firm obligation by a donor, expressed in writing and backed by the necessary funds, to provide specified assistance to a country or multilateral organization. The amount specified is recorded as a commitment. Disbursement is the release of funds to, or purchase of goods or services for, a recipient; in other words, the amount spent. Disbursements record the actual

international transfer of financial resources or of goods or services valued by the donor. As the aid committed in a given year can be disbursed later, sometimes over several years, the annual aid figures based on commitments differ from those based on disbursements.

Gross and net disbursements: gross disbursements are the total aid extended. Net disbursements are the total aid extended minus amounts of loan principal repaid by recipients or cancelled through debt forgiveness.

Current and constant prices: aid figures in the DAC database are expressed in US$. When other currencies are converted into dollars at the exchange rates prevailing at the time, the resulting amounts are at current prices and exchange rates. When comparing aid figures between different years, adjustment is required to compensate for inflation and changes in exchange rates. Such adjustments result in aid being expressed in constant dollars, i.e. in dollars fixed at the value they held in a given reference year, including their external value in terms of other currencies. Thus, amounts of aid for any year and in any currency expressed in 2003 constant dollars reflect the value of that aid in terms of the purchasing power of dollars in 2003. In this Report, most aid data are presented in 2003 constant dollars. The indices used for adjusting currencies and years (called deflators) are derived from Table 36 of the statistical annex of the 2005 DAC annual report (OECD-DAC, 2006). Figures in previous editions of the *EFA Global Monitoring Report* were based on the constant prices of different years (the 2006 Report was based on 2002 constant prices), so figures for a given country for a given year in these editions differ from the figures presented in this Report for the same year.

For more detailed and precise definitions of terms used in the DAC database, see the DAC Directives, available at www.oecd.org/dac/stats/dac/directives

Source: OECD-DAC (2000, 2006c).

Table 1: Bilateral ODA from DAC countries: total ODA, aid to education, aid to basic education, level unspecified (commitments), 1999-2004

Donor	Total ODA (constant 2003 US$ millions)						Per capita ODA (constant 2003 US$)	Total aid to education (constant 2003 US$ millions)					
	1999	2000	2001	2002	2003	2004	2003-04 average	1999	2000	2001	2002	2003	2004
Australia	834.7	926.1	875.0	949.2	974.6	1 013.7	50.1	161.9	166.0	101.1	77.9	75.4	72.7
Austria	720.5	484.5	535.2	558.2	276.8	343.0	38.0	142.8	71.8	75.2	83.9	75.6	73.3
Belgium	528.5	645.3	682.0	905.8	1 502.1	884.1	114.9	68.6	83.6	85.7	109.9	100.1	123.6
Canada	1 363.3	1 578.3	1 423.7	1 992.5	1 875.3	2 158.9	63.4	110.7	156.8	137.1	244.6	316.6	203.4
Denmark	900.1	1 225.2	1 213.1	1 034.9	845.3	1 466.8	213.8	11.1	98.1	25.5	92.8	36.9	103.5
Finland	299.1	255.1	357.9	373.6	388.9	326.8	68.5	22.0	23.2	31.3	40.2	41.3	34.7
France	5 650.9	4 419.4	4 233.6	5 768.2	7 203.6	6 247.1	111.9	1 688.7	978.9	1 017.4	1 125.9	1 268.7	1 362.7
Germany	4 852.0	3 784.4	4 523.6	5 572.1	5 647.4	5 509.9	67.5	812.7	705.3	743.0	839.2	982.3	993.3
Greece	92.2	133.5	112.0	132.7	228.3	268.3	22.4	5.8	7.7	11.1	10.4	80.5	73.6
Ireland	185.5	211.7	246.9	325.5	351.8	360.0	88.0	29.5	40.7	49.9	63.1	50.7	45.7
Italy	726.3	973.2	858.9	1 488.4	1 298.0	877.3	18.8	42.3	29.5	81.5	73.0	24.5	73.3
Japan	12 470.9	12 227.4	11 720.7	9 844.6	15 205.6	12 397.1	108.0	1 081.8	647.3	796.6	982.3	988.9	1 215.6
Luxembourg	102.8	120.0	...	...	...	152.3	...	19.3	28.3	...	...	...	22.0
Netherlands	2 258.6	3 880.7	3 202.5	5 500.3	3 201.1	2 532.2	177.1	186.9	225.7	280.8	389.2	226.5	348.5
New Zealand	122.4	116.6	120.1	117.5	129.2	135.3	33.3	43.0	37.4	40.0	33.6	30.8	31.7
Norway	1 501.2	1 005.4	1 386.8	1 271.5	1 468.9	1 389.8	311.7	155.4	61.7	97.5	144.2	133.0	138.0
Portugal	347.5	437.9	247.4	228.3	184.3	784.0	46.4	25.2	34.7	42.1	44.1	63.1	48.6
Spain	811.6	1 267.7	1 733.8	1 443.6	1 406.8	1 452.4	33.7	97.9	200.0	190.9	187.0	156.1	109.2
Sweden	1 256.3	1 312.7	1 418.2	1 554.9	1 779.4	1 868.0	202.9	73.3	54.2	53.4	96.2	83.9	103.4
Switzerland	836.1	816.1	836.3	897.5	950.0	1 094.2	141.3	30.3	36.8	34.9	40.0	39.4	38.3
United Kingdom	2 499.9	3 234.8	3 304.6	4 050.9	4 030.4	4 904.0	75.2	239.8	203.0	233.4	139.4	348.4	393.0
United States	10 981.8	10 631.5	9 937.0	12 347.7	20 936.0	23 049.6	74.8	356.4	270.3	330.5	288.3	277.6	570.2
All DAC countries	49 342.1	49 687.7	48 969.3	56 358.2	69 883.4	69 214.8	79.8	5 405.3	4 160.7	4 458.9	5 105.1	5 400.2	6 178.3

Sources: Total ODA, aid to education and aid to basic education: DAC online database (OECD-DAC, 2006c), Table 5.
Population data: United Nations Population Division statistics, 2004 revision, medium variant.

Table 2: Bilateral aid from DAC countries: total ODA, aid to education and basic education as percentage of gross national income (commitments), 1999-2004

Donor	Total ODA as % of GNI						Total aid to education as % of GNI					
	1999	2000	2001	2002	2003	2004	1999	2000	2001	2002	2003	2004
Australia	0.191	0.205	0.191	0.200	0.198	0.200	0.037	0.037	0.022	0.016	0.015	0.014
Austria	0.308	0.201	0.222	0.225	0.111	0.132	0.061	0.030	0.031	0.034	0.030	0.028
Belgium	0.186	0.217	0.221	0.299	0.488	0.278	0.024	0.028	0.028	0.036	0.033	0.039
Canada	0.190	0.206	0.175	0.240	0.220	0.248	0.015	0.020	0.017	0.029	0.037	0.023
Denmark	0.452	0.599	0.582	0.495	0.405	0.683	0.006	0.048	0.012	0.044	0.018	0.048
Finland	0.209	0.168	0.234	0.237	0.242	0.195	0.015	0.015	0.020	0.026	0.026	0.021
France	0.339	0.253	0.238	0.324	0.400	0.340	0.101	0.056	0.057	0.063	0.071	0.074
Germany	0.211	0.159	0.190	0.231	0.236	0.224	0.035	0.030	0.031	0.035	0.041	0.040
Greece	0.063	0.088	0.070	0.080	0.132	0.149	0.004	0.005	0.007	0.006	0.047	0.041
Ireland	0.189	0.194	0.213	0.270	0.276	0.262	0.030	0.037	0.043	0.052	0.040	0.033
Italy	0.053	0.068	0.059	0.103	0.089	0.059	0.003	0.002	0.006	0.005	0.002	0.005
Japan	0.299	0.288	0.273	0.230	0.348	0.273	0.026	0.015	0.019	0.023	0.023	0.027
Luxembourg	0.492	0.538	...	...	...	0.606	0.092	0.127	...	...	...	0.087
Netherlands	0.463	0.757	0.620	1.082	0.641	0.490	0.038	0.044	0.054	0.077	0.045	0.067
New Zealand	0.203	0.189	0.193	0.167	0.176	0.175	0.071	0.060	0.064	0.048	0.042	0.041
Norway	0.740	0.481	0.643	0.577	0.661	0.613	0.077	0.029	0.045	0.065	0.060	0.061
Portugal	0.263	0.308	0.171	0.157	0.127	0.534	0.019	0.024	0.029	0.030	0.043	0.033
Spain	0.110	0.165	0.220	0.178	0.168	0.162	0.013	0.026	0.024	0.023	0.019	0.012
Sweden	0.491	0.487	0.491	0.526	0.589	0.593	0.029	0.020	0.019	0.033	0.028	0.033
Switzerland	0.259	0.244	0.243	0.259	0.282	0.318	0.009	0.011	0.010	0.012	0.012	0.011
United Kingdom	0.155	0.195	0.192	0.227	0.220	0.258	0.015	0.012	0.014	0.008	0.019	0.021
United States	0.109	0.101	0.094	0.116	0.191	0.202	0.004	0.003	0.003	0.003	0.003	0.005
All DAC countries	0.194	0.186	0.177	0.201	0.251	0.241	0.021	0.015	0.015	0.018	0.019	0.022

Notes:
■ (···) indicates that data are not available.
■ Aid to basic education as % of GNI excludes the part of 'education, level unspecified' that is allocated to basic education.

Sources: Total ODA, aid to education and aid to basic education: DAC online database (OECD-DAC, 2006c), Table 5. Data on GNI: DAC online database (OECD-DAC, 2006c), Table 1.

Aid to basic education (constant 2003 US$ millions)						Education, level unspecified (constant 2003 US$ millions)						Donor
1999	2000	2001	2002	2003	2004	1999	2000	2001	2002	2003	2004	
26.7	39.1	39.4	32.8	32.1	31.8	3.5	5.1	10.0	8.8	12.3	15.9	Australia
3.8	2.2	0.7	1.5	3.4	2.7	2.2	4.6	4.1	4.3	2.8	2.7	Austria
2.6	5.3	9.5	9.1	6.3	18.5	15.9	17.6	13.2	14.3	21.7	22.0	Belgium
11.5	18.0	50.7	79.6	130.2	110.4	30.0	47.2	18.8	62.4	104.0	18.0	Canada
0.9	58.4	8.1	27.7	11.5	45.6	4.0	14.4	3.4	62.6	20.1	47.0	Denmark
0.5	0.5	6.8	8.2	3.2	2.7	18.0	15.7	21.5	26.9	27.1	22.8	Finland
14.6	146.3	186.6	195.9	209.6	240.1	805.1	60.2	227.8	35.8	53.6	58.1	France
91.1	78.1	56.0	88.2	86.5	95.7	37.1	40.2	36.8	55.1	30.9	32.0	Germany
...	0.0	...	...	32.7	32.0	2.0	1.8	4.1	4.4	12.0	12.8	Greece
...	...	...	...	...	26.8	...	40.7	49.9	63.1	...	10.6	Ireland
0.4	0.3	0.1	0.4	0.1	17.8	30.2	10.6	50.4	60.0	8.9	28.3	Italy
48.0	39.5	81.2	106.6	57.8	34.3	239.9	44.6	171.9	112.9	209.2	344.3	Japan
3.3	9.7	...	...	...	3.9	9.1	10.6	...	...	...	12.1	Luxembourg
88.9	133.9	223.2	264.2	153.7	226.1	48.5	59.1	26.1	46.5	27.0	10.5	Netherlands
2.2	2.0	3.0	3.2	3.5	9.9	0.8	0.5	1.1	2.3	2.7	1.5	New Zealand
97.2	17.9	19.7	70.2	70.7	68.2	26.5	10.9	9.1	24.3	29.5	39.9	Norway
0.1	4.4	4.8	5.7	4.1	2.0	8.0	7.6	13.0	10.5	3.2	5.9	Portugal
18.1	14.9	21.6	31.6	29.4	25.6	22.8	123.1	85.0	45.3	23.6	22.5	Spain
36.8	31.8	7.3	21.8	26.9	32.0	17.0	18.8	24.4	49.1	42.3	54.9	Sweden
10.4	9.6	10.8	14.3	13.7	14.4	13.5	10.8	9.2	6.2	5.4	7.7	Switzerland
75.1	82.9	81.4	76.6	233.3	280.2	147.5	104.4	136.2	50.6	105.4	109.9	United Kingdom
129.9	200.8	212.4	222.2	224.8	486.6	29.8	...	3.5	13.6	6.2	36.3	United States
662.1	895.7	1 023.4	1 259.9	1 333.6	1 807.4	1 511.4	648.6	919.4	758.9	748.0	915.7	All DAC countries

Notes:

■ (···) indicates that data are not available.

■ Data for some donors for some years represent disbursements and others represent commitments.

■ Totals do not include countries where data are not available.

■ Aid to education does not count the part of general budget support that recipient countries may allocate to education.

■ Aid to basic education does not count the part of education sector budget support (most of which is reported as 'level unspecified') that may benefit basic education.

Aid to basic education as % of GNI						Donor
1999	2000	2001	2002	2003	2004	
0.006	0.009	0.009	0.007	0.007	0.006	Australia
0.002	0.001	0.000	0.001	0.001	0.001	Austria
0.001	0.002	0.003	0.003	0.002	0.006	Belgium
0.002	0.002	0.006	0.010	0.015	0.013	Canada
0.000	0.029	0.004	0.013	0.006	0.021	Denmark
0.000	0.000	0.004	0.005	0.002	0.002	Finland
0.001	0.008	0.010	0.011	0.012	0.013	France
0.004	0.003	0.002	0.004	0.004	0.004	Germany
...	0.000	...	...	0.019	0.018	Greece
...	...	...	...	...	0.020	Ireland
0.000	0.000	0.000	0.000	0.000	0.001	Italy
0.001	0.001	0.002	0.002	0.001	0.001	Japan
0.016	0.044	...	...	...	0.016	Luxembourg
0.018	0.026	0.043	0.052	0.031	0.044	Netherlands
0.004	0.003	0.005	0.005	0.005	0.013	New Zealand
0.048	0.009	0.009	0.032	0.032	0.030	Norway
0.000	0.003	0.003	0.004	0.003	0.001	Portugal
0.002	0.002	0.003	0.004	0.004	0.003	Spain
0.014	0.012	0.003	0.007	0.009	0.010	Sweden
0.003	0.003	0.003	0.004	0.004	0.004	Switzerland
0.005	0.005	0.005	0.004	0.013	0.015	United Kingdom
0.001	0.002	0.002	0.002	0.002	0.004	United States
0.002	0.003	0.004	0.004	0.005	0.006	All DAC countries

Education for All Global Monitoring Report 2007

Table 3: ODA from multilateral donors: total ODA, total aid to education and aid to basic education (commitments), 2003-04 average

Donor	Total ODA (constant 2003 US$ millions)	Education (constant 2003 US$ millions)	Education as % of total sector-allocable ODA
African Development Fund	1 397.9	164.7	13.8
Asian Development Fund	1 629.9	243.5	16.1
European Commission	8 083.5	469.5	8.4
International Development Association	9 590.4	1 023.6	14.0
Inter-American Development Bank Special Fund	431.9	36.7	9.6
UNICEF	618.2	55.7	15.1
Total	21 751.8	1 993.6	11.8

Note:
(···) indicates that data are not available.

Source: CRS online database (OECD-DAC, 2006c), Table 2.

Table 4: ODA from multilateral donors by level of education (commitments), 1999-2004

Donor	Total ODA (constant 2003 US$ millions)						Total aid to education (constant 2003 US$ millions)					
	1999	2000	2001	2002	2003	2004	1999	2000	2001	2002	2003	2004
African Development Fund	583.4	976.4	1 452.4	1 005.4	1 484.4	1 311.4	79.4	52.0	77.1	92.6	214.1	115.3
Asian Development Fund	1 276.3	1 144.7	1 597.0	1 181.0	1 850.4	1 409.4	150.3	91.8	40.1	271.3	215.3	271.7
European Commission	7 169.6	8 047.4	7 225.2	8 151.8	8 045.1	8 121.9	351.2	531.6	265.5	274.5	563.2	375.8
International Development Association	6 183.9	6 739.5	8 199.9	9 211.0	8 214.4	10 966.4	730.5	453.0	621.3	687.8	593.4	1 453.8
Inter-American Development Bank Special Fund	276.0	388.8	539.4	454.9	562.9	300.8	10.2	···	38.9	34.1	36.0	37.3
UNDP	524.4	···	···	···	···	···	12.5	···	···	···	···	···
UNICEF	···	388.9	446.2	642.2	631.0	605.4	···	55.9	66.2	54.5	58.0	53.5
Total	16 013.6	17 685.7	19 460.1	20 646.3	20 788.2	22 715.3	1 334.1	1 184.3	1 109.0	1 414.7	1 679.9	2 307.3

Donor	Share of education in total sector-allocable ODA (%)						Share of 'education, level unspecified' in total aid to education (%)					
	1999	2000	2001	2002	2003	2004	1999	2000	2001	2002	2003	2004
African Development Fund	14.8	7.0	6.5	10.9	16.6	10.4	78.5	64.3	78.2	19.0	17.6	51.6
Asian Development Fund	11.8	8.8	2.6	23.1	12.7	20.3	0.0	38.0	0.0	24.6	21.5	0.0
European Commission	7.6	10.6	5.5	5.3	10.5	6.4	8.9	4.7	28.5	8.3	23.4	24.2
International Development Association	14.2	8.4	9.6	13.5	9.2	17.7	53.6	63.2	46.4	2.5	14.5	11.6
Inter-American Development Bank Special Fund	3.7	0.0	7.4	7.5	7.3	13.8	100.0	···	70.0	0.0	100.0	75.4
UNDP	2.9	···	···	···	···	···	65.8	···	···	···	···	···
UNICEF	···	16.4	15.8	14.1	15.3	14.8	···	0.0	0.0	0.0	0.0	0.0
Total	10.9	9.2	7.3	10.5	10.5	13.5	37.7	32.0	40.7	8.8	20.1	15.0

Notes:
■ (···) indicates that data are not available.
■ Totals do not include countries where data are not available.

Source: CRS online database (OECD-DAC, 2006c), Table 2.

Basic education (constant 2003 US$ millions)	Basic education as % of total aid to education	Donor
49.8	30.3	African Development Fund
94.4	38.8	Asian Development Fund
155.5	33.1	European Commission
676.7	66.1	International Development Association
9.2	25.1	Inter-American Development Bank Special Fund
55.2	99.0	UNICEF
1 036.2	52.0	Total

Basic education (constant 2003 US$ millions)						Secondary education (constant 2003 US$ millions)						Post-secondary education (constant 2003 US$ millions)					
1999	2000	2001	2002	2003	2004	1999	2000	2001	2002	2003	2004	1999	2000	2001	2002	2003	2004
17.1	18.6	14.5	75.0	98.3	1.4	...	...	...		43.2	54.5	...	...	2.3	...	35.0	...
...	...	16.3	114.0	79.0	109.8	143.3	56.9	23.7	15.9	31.8	161.9	7.0	...	...	74.7	58.3	...
262.2	320.9	61.5	62.4	221.8	89.2	11.6	92.9	91.0	97.8	61.7	53.2	46.2	92.8	37.5	91.4	147.6	142.7
207.7	67.8	332.9	163.1	429.6	923.8	77.1	25.6	...	428.2	37.7	283.1	54.3	73.6	...	79.5	40.3	78.7
...	...	...	34.1	...	9.2	...	...	...	...	...	...	...	...	11.6	...	...	...
2.0	...	...	...	...	...	1.7	...	...	...	...	...	0.6	...	...	...	...	...
...	55.9	66.2	54.4	57.3	53.1	...	...	...	0.0	0.6	0.4	...	...	0.0	0.1	0.1	0.1
489.0	463.1	491.4	503.0	886.0	1 186.4	233.7	175.4	114.7	541.8	175.0	553.1	108.1	166.4	51.4	245.7	281.3	221.4

Share of basic education in total aid to education (%)						Share of secondary education in total aid to education (%)						Share of post-secondary education in total aid to education (%)					
1999	2000	2001	2002	2003	2004	1999	2000	2001	2002	2003	2004	1999	2000	2001	2002	2003	2004
21.5	35.7	18.8	81.0	45.9	1.2	...	...	...	...	20.2	47.3	...	...	2.9	...	16.4	...
...	...	40.7	42.0	36.7	40.4	95.4	62.0	59.3	5.9	14.8	59.6	4.6	...	...	27.6	27.1	...
74.6	60.4	23.1	22.7	39.4	23.7	3.3	17.5	34.3	35.6	11.0	14.2	13.1	17.5	14.1	33.3	26.2	38.0
28.4	15.0	53.6	23.7	72.4	63.5	10.6	5.7	...	62.2	6.4	19.5	7.4	16.2	...	11.6	6.8	5.4
...	...	...	100.0	...	24.6	...	...	...	...	...	...	...	...	30.0	...	...	...
15.9	...	...	...	...	...	13.3	...	...	...	...	...	4.9	...	...	...	...	...
...	100.0	100.0	99.9	98.8	99.2	...	...	...	0.0	1.1	0.7	...	...	0.0	0.1	0.1	0.1
36.7	39.1	44.3	35.6	52.7	51.4	17.5	14.8	10.3	38.3	10.4	24.0	8.1	14.0	4.6	17.4	16.7	9.6

Table 5: ODA to education and basic education by recipient country, total amounts and per capita/per primary school-age child (commitments)

Country	Aid to education (constant 2003 US$ millions)							Aid to education per capita (constant 2003 US$)	Aid to basic education (constant 2003 US$ millions)							Aid to basic education per primary-school-age child (constant 2003 US$)
	1999	2000	2001	2002	2003	2004	2003-2004 average	annual average 2003-2004	1999	2000	2001	2002	2003	2004	2003-2004 average	annual average 2003-2004
Arab States	624.8	779.1	836.5	797.7	889.0	1218.4	1053.7	3.6	53.2	201.9	75.1	126.1	155.3	395.0	275.1	7.1
Algeria	81.9	79.3	153.8	90.2	122.4	163.9	143.2	4.5	0.0	0.2	1.8	0.2	1.5	19.3	10.4	2.6
Bahrain	0.1	0.2	0.2	0.2	0.4	0.4	0.4	0.5	...	...	...	...	...	...	...	0.0
Djibouti	22.0	27.0	15.9	18.3	22.9	21.7	22.3	28.9	5.2	0.2	0.1	3.2	7.2	0.1	3.7	29.9
Egypt	155.4	89.6	127.7	155.2	120.7	66.9	93.8	1.3	15.6	44.9	24.7	92.6	81.1	35.2	58.1	7.4
Iraq	4.3	6.1	6.4	6.5	10.1	169.1	89.6	3.2	...	0.4	0.4	0.2	1.8	144.5	73.1	16.6
Jordan	20.2	16.2	54.7	18.7	24.4	43.0	33.7	6.1	0.0	0.2	0.3	4.0	0.1	25.4	12.7	15.6
Lebanon	25.2	29.6	31.6	28.4	36.1	45.8	41.0	11.6	1.5	0.5	0.9	0.3	1.9	0.5	1.2	2.7
Libyan Arab Jamahiriya	2.7	0.0	0.0	0.0	0.0	0.0	0.0	0.0	0.0	0.0	0.0	0.0	0.0	0.0	0.0	0.0
Mauritania	21.9	12.8	87.9	12.2	13.7	26.0	19.8	6.7	0.1	2.2	0.5	2.3	0.7	0.9	0.8	1.7
Morocco	152.4	167.7	195.7	300.1	240.0	320.5	280.2	9.1	4.3	4.1	4.2	8.3	6.6	4.6	5.6	1.5
Oman	0.1	0.5	0.2	0.4	0.4	0.7	0.5	0.2	0.0	0.1	0.1	0.0	0.0	0.0	0.0	0.1
Palestinian A. T.	52.8	55.1	31.9	41.9	61.1	24.3	42.7	12.2	25.3	20.6	9.5	4.7	27.4	2.2	14.8	36.9
Saudi Arabia	1.2	1.1	1.2	1.2	3.3	3.8	3.5	0.1	0.0	0.0	0.0	0.0	0.0	0.0	0.0	0.0
Sudan	10.2	11.0	16.7	14.6	14.9	30.6	22.8	0.6	0.5	1.8	7.0	2.3	5.8	17.1	11.5	2.2
Syrian Arab Republic	20.4	38.2	22.9	27.6	33.0	59.8	46.4	2.5	0.0	0.4	0.2	0.1	1.1	0.6	0.8	0.5
Tunisia	49.3	130.5	58.8	64.4	160.6	78.7	119.7	12.1	0.0	48.9	0.6	2.3	0.3	0.2	0.3	0.3
Yemen	4.9	114.5	30.9	17.8	25.0	163.1	94.1	4.6	0.6	77.7	24.8	5.7	19.9	144.6	82.3	23.2
Central and Eastern Europe	293.2	278.4	201.1	221.2	315.8	336.1	326.0	3.2	125.0	16.4	17.0	33.2	42.2	45.9	44.1	4.6
Albania	10.8	30.3	15.5	14.4	85.0	83.6	84.3	27.2	0.1	3.4	2.8	0.6	30.7	29.5	30.1	125.5
Bosnia and Herzegovina	18.6	29.5	31.3	35.0	25.9	35.1	30.5	7.8	1.1	2.6	2.7	12.4	0.4	1.8	1.1	5.9
Croatia	16.8	16.7	12.9	13.7	21.1	18.1	19.6	4.3	0.0	0.0	1.9	0.0	0.0	3.3	1.7	8.3
Republic of Moldova	2.1	2.6	3.2	5.3	10.6	10.5	10.5	2.5	0.0	0.2	0.2	0.1	0.3	4.0	2.2	9.1
Serbia and Montenegro	27.4	38.2	43.0	68.1	58.6	44.2	51.4	4.9	0.0	0.9	3.7	17.4	6.0	4.7	5.4	...
Slovenia	4.8	4.7	4.6	4.1	0.0	0.0	0.0	0.0	0.0	0.0	0.0	0.0	0.0	0.0	0.0	0.0
TFYR Macedonia	6.9	15.4	21.7	10.1	28.4	14.7	21.6	10.6	0.7	6.4	3.6	1.1	3.0	0.5	1.7	14.5
Turkey	206.0	141.0	68.8	70.6	86.1	130.0	108.1	1.5	123.1	2.8	2.1	1.6	1.8	2.1	1.9	0.2
Central Asia	92.2	57.3	147.7	77.1	150.2	178.2	164.2	2.2	8.0	16.6	21.5	10.3	53.8	35.2	44.5	7.0
Armenia	6.9	6.9	6.7	4.5	8.3	26.7	17.5	5.8	0.0	0.3	0.2	0.2	2.6	7.9	5.2	35.9
Azerbaijan	6.9	2.8	2.4	4.1	22.3	5.8	14.0	1.7	0.0	0.4	0.4	0.4	18.4	0.3	9.4	14.1
Georgia	12.3	9.8	38.9	14.1	25.8	23.6	24.7	5.4	0.1	0.7	0.2	0.2	1.6	1.2	1.4	4.7
Kazakhstan	20.6	7.0	6.5	4.2	7.2	15.1	11.1	0.8	0.0	2.9	2.9	0.1	0.3	0.2	0.2	0.2
Kyrgyzstan	2.0	3.3	8.5	2.5	6.0	24.0	15.0	2.9	0.0	0.5	5.0	0.4	0.2	6.5	3.4	7.4
Mongolia	13.1	17.4	16.5	36.3	34.7	37.7	36.2	13.9	7.9	7.1	6.8	7.8	8.6	10.0	9.3	40.6
Tajikistan	10.7	2.9	2.9	2.6	24.7	15.5	20.1	3.1	0.0	2.6	2.4	0.5	21.2	8.1	14.6	21.1
Turkmenistan	5.1	0.8	1.3	0.8	0.8	2.9	1.9	0.4	0.0	0.6	1.0	0.2	0.2	0.3	0.2	0.7
Uzbekistan	14.7	6.5	63.9	8.1	20.5	27.0	23.7	0.9	0.0	1.7	2.7	0.6	0.6	0.7	0.7	0.3
East Asia and the Pacific	1079.7	529.4	564.6	1002.3	1540.8	1503.0	1521.9	0.8	147.1	133.0	146.2	252.2	429.2	152.5	290.9	1.7
Cambodia	26.7	14.6	18.6	102.4	20.4	37.1	28.7	2.1	10.3	2.4	1.3	28.0	2.2	9.6	5.9	2.9
China	169.8	106.0	166.5	469.3	821.7	830.8	826.2	0.6	22.6	5.6	3.4	6.1	99.2	6.5	52.8	0.5
Cook Islands	0.1	0.0	0.0	1.5	1.4	2.8	2.1	116.7	0.0	0.0	0.0	0.0	0.1	0.1	0.1	...
DPR Korea	42.7	0.0	0.0	0.0	0.0	0.0	0.0	0.0	0.0	0.0	0.0	0.0	0.0	0.0	0.0	0.0
Fiji	5.0	3.3	0.8	9.1	21.7	27.0	24.4	29.1	0.0	1.4	0.3	4.0	0.9	0.2	0.5	5.1
Indonesia	196.9	109.9	161.0	217.9	87.2	139.9	113.6	0.5	59.0	49.1	86.8	159.5	20.2	49.7	35.0	1.4
Kiribati	2.7	7.6	9.9	2.5	1.8	2.3	2.0	21.2	0.0	0.0	0.0	0.0	0.4	0.1	0.2	...
Lao PDR	11.1	28.3	38.8	34.4	15.3	40.0	27.6	4.8	0.7	2.0	1.5	24.7	4.6	11.1	7.8	10.3
Malaysia	307.2	6.3	3.8	15.2	22.9	33.5	28.2	1.1	0.0	0.1	0.2	0.0	0.1	0.1	0.1	0.0
Marshall Islands	0.6	0.0	8.0	0.2	1.1	11.9	6.5	108.5	0.0	0.0	8.0	0.0	0.2	0.3	0.3	...
Micronesia	1.2	0.0	0.0	0.2	1.2	27.0	14.1	128.4	0.0	0.0	0.0	0.2	0.3	0.2	0.3	15.3
Myanmar	3.0	2.1	4.0	7.1	12.9	15.0	13.9	0.3	0.9	1.5	2.6	2.2	6.5	2.4	4.5	0.9
Nauru	0.1	0.0	0.0	0.0	0.0	0.1	0.1	4.9	0.0	0.0	0.0	0.0	0.0	0.0	0.0	...
Niue	0.5	0.0	0.0	0.6	0.5	0.3	0.4	260.2	0.0	0.0	0.0	0.1	0.0	0.0	0.0	...
Palau	0.4	0.0	0.3	0.2	1.0	0.9	1.0	49.5	0.0	0.0	0.0	0.0	0.5	0.4	0.4	...
Papua New Guinea	51.0	94.9	16.1	10.3	70.8	14.6	42.7	7.5	37.7	51.4	7.3	6.4	56.6	0.2	28.4	31.5
Philippines	104.2	19.8	18.4	38.5	32.3	72.6	52.4	0.6	12.9	1.4	4.6	1.8	10.4	38.6	24.5	2.1
Republic of Korea	1.0	1.0	0.9	1.7	1.9	1.3	1.6	0.0	0.0	0.0	0.1	0.1	0.3	0.1	0.2	0.1

Table 5 (continued)

Country	Aid to education (constant 2003 US$ millions) 1999	2000	2001	2002	2003	2004	2003-2004 average	Aid to education per capita (constant 2003 US$) annual average 2003-2004	Aid to basic education (constant 2003 US$ millions) 1999	2000	2001	2002	2003	2004	2003-2004 average	Aid to basic education per primary-school-age child (constant 2003 US$) annual average 2003-2004
Samoa	2.8	9.6	0.1	5.9	6.6	13.6	10.1	55.1	1.7	0.3	0.0	0.0	0.0	0.4	0.2	6.6
Solomon Islands	5.1	5.4	0.8	0.8	5.3	6.4	5.8	12.7	0.0	0.1	0.1	0.0	3.8	5.1	4.4	60.8
Thailand	21.8	12.0	15.1	11.0	41.4	43.1	42.3	0.7	0.1	0.1	0.1	0.0	1.6	1.4	1.5	0.2
Timor-Leste	2.8	9.0	12.5	13.2	13.5	13.7	13.6	15.9	1.1	1.1	0.4	0.6	7.1	5.5	6.3	51.2
Tokelau	0.2	0.0	0.0	0.1	0.2	0.3	0.2	178.0	0.0	0.0	0.0	0.0	0.1	0.0	0.0	…
Tonga	2.0	1.1	0.3	1.9	6.3	4.1	5.2	51.1	0.0	0.4	0.0	0.0	0.4	0.1	0.3	18.3
Tuvalu	0.7	1.0	0.0	1.2	5.1	3.3	4.2	404.6	0.0	0.0	0.0	0.0	0.0	0.0	0.0	…
Vanuatu	6.9	4.9	7.0	4.1	16.4	5.0	10.7	52.5	0.0	0.1	0.2	0.0	0.5	0.4	0.4	13.1
Viet Nam	113.4	92.6	81.7	52.9	332.0	156.4	244.2	3.0	0.2	16.2	29.4	18.6	213.3	20.1	116.7	13.2
Latin America/Caribbean	**452.7**	**360.7**	**454.4**	**414.3**	**506.5**	**530.6**	**518.5**	**1.0**	**189.2**	**116.0**	**136.0**	**133.0**	**114.6**	**176.7**	**145.6**	**2.5**
Anguilla	4.8	0.3	0.0	0.6	0.1	0.0	0.0	3.4	0.0	0.2	0.0	0.0	0.0	0.0	0.0	…
Antigua and Barbuda	2.3	0.6	0.8	0.0	5.6	0.0	2.8	35.1	0.0	0.0	0.0	0.0	0.0	0.0	0.0	…
Argentina	12.2	11.4	12.0	17.3	16.3	16.7	16.5	0.4	0.4	0.2	0.1	0.7	0.5	0.6	0.5	0.1
Barbados	0.1	0.1	4.7	0.1	0.1	0.1	0.1	0.3	0.0	0.0	0.0	0.0	0.0	0.0	0.0	0.0
Belize	0.1	1.5	0.0	0.3	0.4	0.5	0.5	1.7	0.0	1.1	0.0	0.1	0.2	0.2	0.2	5.1
Bolivia	35.7	36.1	37.6	30.1	66.9	104.9	85.9	9.6	25.3	27.2	18.7	16.9	14.7	82.6	48.7	35.8
Brazil	29.5	38.4	35.5	37.0	45.9	42.6	44.2	0.2	4.8	4.1	1.8	1.3	3.7	1.4	2.5	0.2
Chile	14.5	11.7	8.6	9.8	12.1	11.1	11.6	0.7	0.5	0.6	0.2	0.1	0.0	0.2	0.1	0.1
Colombia	32.6	20.2	21.5	26.0	28.7	26.1	27.4	0.6	5.7	0.6	1.1	1.2	1.8	2.5	2.2	0.5
Costa Rica	3.2	2.7	16.2	2.8	3.5	4.6	4.1	1.0	0.4	0.0	0.1	0.4	0.0	2.0	1.0	2.1
Cuba	4.7	8.0	11.3	7.5	7.5	10.1	8.8	0.8	0.0	0.2	2.2	0.9	1.4	2.3	1.9	2.0
Dominica	0.3	0.2	0.3	0.3	0.3	0.3	0.3	3.9	0.0	0.0	0.0	0.0	0.0	0.0	0.0	…
Dominican Republic	14.0	23.7	13.8	12.3	7.4	11.5	9.4	1.1	10.9	0.3	9.7	7.9	1.9	7.1	4.5	3.9
Ecuador	8.9	7.1	11.9	29.4	16.7	24.3	20.5	1.6	1.1	0.3	2.3	1.6	2.3	2.6	2.5	1.4
El Salvador	16.1	10.0	15.9	18.8	8.7	8.6	8.6	1.3	6.5	4.5	10.1	11.8	4.6	3.8	4.2	4.6
Grenada	0.0	0.1	0.0	0.1	4.9	0.0	2.5	24.2	0.0	0.0	0.0	0.0	0.0	0.0	0.0	…
Guatemala	31.5	20.9	26.7	26.4	19.2	15.2	17.2	1.4	21.4	9.4	7.5	12.0	10.5	6.4	8.5	4.3
Guyana	6.7	3.0	0.9	35.0	29.4	1.4	15.4	20.6	0.0	0.2	0.2	34.2	27.3	0.2	13.7	156.2
Haiti	16.3	22.6	49.3	19.3	13.5	15.4	14.4	1.7	4.3	11.5	9.9	12.9	6.5	6.9	6.7	5.4
Honduras	28.1	9.7	90.9	31.1	62.2	60.0	61.1	8.8	3.4	5.4	54.6	12.5	8.7	22.0	15.4	13.8
Jamaica	10.3	15.7	3.5	4.0	5.6	5.5	5.6	2.1	9.2	15.1	3.1	3.8	4.9	4.8	4.8	13.9
Mexico	13.7	14.0	15.9	24.7	27.8	24.3	26.0	0.2	1.0	1.1	1.0	1.0	0.1	0.9	0.5	0.0
Montserrat	0.0	0.6	0.3	0.7	1.6	0.3	0.9	239.2	0.0	0.4	0.0	0.4	0.0	0.0	0.0	…
Nicaragua	107.9	37.1	24.9	16.0	41.1	84.8	63.0	11.8	82.6	27.2	5.8	2.9	7.1	16.7	11.9	14.2
Panama	18.3	4.0	11.0	3.6	8.0	2.4	5.2	1.7	0.3	1.2	0.3	0.3	0.0	0.1	0.0	0.1
Paraguay	3.3	3.6	5.2	3.3	7.4	6.8	7.1	1.2	1.0	1.5	1.5	1.3	2.1	2.0	2.0	2.3
Peru	23.3	23.2	23.0	24.0	33.9	37.2	35.5	1.3	7.3	3.1	4.6	6.1	8.7	9.6	9.1	2.5
Saint Kitts and Nevis	0.0	0.0	0.0	0.0	3.6	0.0	1.8	43.7	0.0	0.0	0.0	0.0	0.0	0.0	0.0	…
Saint Lucia	0.7	0.2	0.2	7.1	1.5	0.4	1.0	6.0	0.5	0.0	0.0	0.0	0.4	0.2	0.3	11.7
St Vincent/Grenad.	0.0	1.1	0.0	1.8	14.2	3.0	8.6	73.0	0.0	0.0	0.0	0.0	6.4	0.3	3.3	196.3
Suriname	0.9	1.0	0.9	3.2	1.5	1.6	1.5	3.5	0.0	0.0	0.0	2.4	0.0	0.4	0.2	3.8
Trinidad and Tobago	0.4	0.4	0.6	0.4	1.1	0.6	0.8	0.6	0.0	0.0	0.0	0.0	0.0	0.0	0.0	0.0
Turks and Caicos Islands	2.7	0.0	…	0.1	…	0.1	0.1	1.6	2.7	0.0	…	0.1	…	0.1	0.1	…
Uruguay	3.2	3.9	3.5	2.0	2.7	3.2	3.0	0.9	0.0	0.1	1.3	0.0	0.5	0.7	0.6	1.8
Venezuela	6.6	27.6	7.7	19.3	7.4	7.1	7.3	0.3	0.0	0.7	0.0	0.4	0.4	0.2	0.3	0.1
N. America/West. Europe	**0.4**	**0.4**	**0.6**	**1.7**	**0.0**	**0.0**	**0.0**	**0.0**	**0.0**	**0.0**	**0.0**	**0.0**	**0.0**	**0.0**	**0.0**	**0.0**
Malta	0.4	0.4	0.6	1.7	0.0	0.0	0.0	0.0	0.0	0.0	0.0	0.0	0.0	0.0	0.0	0.0
South and West Asia	**772.1**	**657.1**	**594.9**	**815.3**	**762.1**	**2 279.2**	**1 520.7**	**1.0**	**237.4**	**349.8**	**318.2**	**100.2**	**410.7**	**1 735.0**	**1 072.8**	**6.3**
Afghanistan	6.2	6.0	9.6	50.3	34.3	173.9	104.1	3.7	0.5	1.6	4.3	7.0	23.5	129.6	76.6	16.2
Bangladesh	160.0	69.7	131.5	255.5	245.6	786.4	516.0	3.7	81.1	49.8	49.2	14.0	226.4	590.9	408.7	24.8
Bhutan	5.2	3.9	9.5	6.5	51.9	3.3	27.6	13.3	0.0	0.4	8.7	0.4	4.3	1.2	2.7	…
India	381.8	388.4	358.7	338.5	77.3	867.0	472.1	0.4	65.4	280.4	240.5	14.4	25.6	808.9	417.3	3.6
Iran, Islamic Republic of	76.1	55.1	49.3	44.8	51.4	51.0	51.2	0.7	0.0	0.5	0.4	0.4	0.5	0.5	0.5	0.1
Maldives	7.1	21.9	0.3	5.0	1.3	14.4	7.9	24.5	0.0	0.2	0.3	4.9	0.4	0.4	0.4	6.7
Nepal	86.5	17.1	12.8	31.7	59.4	169.5	114.5	4.3	78.0	8.7	8.0	1.1	9.2	158.8	84.0	23.8
Pakistan	7.9	33.9	14.6	73.6	138.2	162.6	150.4	1.0	0.7	7.6	4.5	56.4	119.9	41.9	80.9	4.1
Sri Lanka	41.4	61.0	8.4	9.4	102.7	51.3	77.0	3.8	11.7	0.6	2.3	1.7	0.8	2.8	1.8	1.1

Education for All Global Monitoring Report

Table 5 (continued)

Country	Aid to education (constant 2003 US$ millions)							Aid to education per capita (constant 2003 US$)	Aid to basic education (constant 2003 US$ millions)							Aid to basic education per primary-school-age child (constant 2003 US$)
	1999	2000	2001	2002	2003	2004	2003-2004 average	annual average 2003-2004	1999	2000	2001	2002	2003	2004	2003-2004 average	annual average 2003-2004
Sub-Saharan Africa	1 233.3	1 418.9	1 405.3	1 674.5	2 093.1	1 679.7	1 886.4	2.8	519.1	481.9	672.2	827.0	816.8	629.3	723.0	6.5
Angola	13.7	22.1	35.4	26.6	77.5	13.8	45.6	3.0	2.1	3.3	24.8	13.7	8.9	2.2	5.5	3.1
Benin	20.3	27.7	24.9	42.6	38.6	40.2	39.4	4.9	9.0	6.6	7.6	8.6	19.2	21.8	20.5	15.5
Botswana	21.4	1.4	1.1	3.3	4.9	0.8	2.9	1.6	0.3	0.1	0.1	0.2	0.2	0.2	0.2	0.7
Burkina Faso	48.2	19.6	26.7	84.9	53.5	54.5	54.0	4.3	32.3	5.7	12.0	71.6	36.2	41.2	38.7	18.2
Burundi	2.5	2.1	2.3	3.6	18.2	4.4	11.3	1.6	0.0	0.8	0.5	1.4	0.7	1.3	1.0	0.8
Cameroon	73.0	63.2	76.5	83.1	114.9	114.9	114.9	7.2	8.7	1.8	9.8	10.0	13.6	12.8	13.2	5.2
Cape Verde	24.0	12.4	13.9	21.7	48.7	29.5	39.1	80.1	2.8	0.3	1.3	0.5	0.8	2.1	1.5	18.8
Central African Republic	6.0	7.9	6.6	13.4	7.1	6.8	7.0	1.8	0.1	0.8	0.1	6.2	0.3	0.6	0.4	0.7
Chad	9.2	7.7	16.5	9.9	49.8	15.7	32.8	3.6	2.3	2.8	1.6	4.4	44.4	7.0	25.7	16.7
Comoros	4.9	5.8	6.0	6.7	6.3	8.2	7.2	9.4	0.0	0.3	0.2	0.2	0.1	0.2	0.1	1.2
Congo	14.0	15.0	15.4	22.0	18.2	36.3	27.3	7.1	0.0	0.3	1.6	0.4	0.9	8.0	4.4	6.7
Côte d'Ivoire	78.0	41.5	27.5	73.2	31.2	31.2	31.2	1.8	19.9	4.6	3.4	39.7	2.2	1.8	2.0	0.7
Democratic Rep. of the Congo	9.4	16.0	15.6	26.3	22.2	69.4	45.8	0.8	0.7	5.4	4.2	5.2	3.6	44.4	24.0	2.6
Equatorial Guinea	7.0	8.5	6.5	6.3	7.2	7.3	7.3	14.9	2.4	2.2	0.9	2.9	0.9	2.6	1.8	27.2
Eritrea	7.1	51.2	5.6	4.9	58.4	1.8	30.1	7.4	0.3	43.2	1.1	0.1	45.8	0.9	23.3	43.2
Ethiopia	31.4	55.4	66.7	57.1	103.0	106.2	104.6	1.4	14.5	19.8	13.9	17.0	25.0	39.7	32.4	3.9
Gabon	20.1	21.3	26.3	20.8	21.1	23.3	22.2	16.4	4.1	2.1	7.8	1.8	1.9	3.0	2.4	11.3
Gambia	8.2	10.4	1.3	15.8	1.2	5.7	3.4	2.3	6.4	8.9	0.5	15.0	0.4	4.9	2.6	12.3
Ghana	136.9	18.2	16.9	17.5	133.4	130.4	131.9	6.2	116.9	8.7	9.1	8.2	68.1	39.5	53.8	16.4
Guinea	26.3	34.7	97.2	33.4	22.7	17.5	20.1	2.2	13.9	17.6	90.8	21.5	14.1	7.6	10.8	7.6
Guinea-Bissau	5.4	6.5	5.0	4.6	14.1	4.0	9.1	6.0	2.5	0.6	0.4	0.4	10.4	0.8	5.6	23.4
Kenya	16.1	40.6	24.7	13.8	141.6	72.4	107.0	3.2	8.2	30.3	1.4	5.8	122.1	12.8	67.4	12.8
Lesotho	23.5	5.5	7.8	3.0	25.5	12.2	18.8	10.5	0.2	2.1	1.0	1.8	23.6	9.8	16.7	50.8
Liberia	1.6	1.6	1.3	1.5	2.3	3.5	2.9	0.9	0.3	1.0	0.5	0.5	1.8	2.9	2.3	4.2
Madagascar	20.9	24.7	19.2	22.1	36.4	50.7	43.5	2.4	0.0	0.8	0.6	1.0	11.9	11.4	11.7	4.7
Malawi	15.0	164.4	41.6	43.8	30.1	24.0	27.0	2.2	0.4	117.2	14.1	40.4	9.3	10.7	10.0	4.5
Mali	28.9	86.3	45.6	100.6	73.8	63.5	68.7	5.3	16.6	18.7	35.8	56.5	34.3	47.9	41.1	19.0
Mauritius	9.6	11.5	11.3	12.1	12.9	13.9	13.4	10.9	0.0	0.1	0.2	0.3	0.2	0.0	0.1	0.7
Mozambique	114.7	76.3	77.4	176.9	76.2	48.1	62.2	3.2	14.8	41.1	31.3	32.1	27.6	29.3	28.4	7.6
Namibia	12.1	29.7	16.2	11.7	44.1	5.8	25.0	12.6	5.7	19.5	12.9	7.5	40.3	4.0	22.2	54.7
Niger	14.7	11.2	23.0	13.1	73.4	28.0	50.7	3.9	0.5	4.8	3.7	8.5	50.3	21.0	35.7	16.7
Nigeria	12.1	89.8	22.2	132.5	17.1	55.9	36.5	0.3	3.3	16.6	14.1	115.1	1.1	46.4	23.8	1.1
Rwanda	16.8	55.1	37.4	14.7	12.3	12.0	12.1	1.4	3.5	4.1	1.3	2.0	3.3	1.7	2.5	1.7
Sao Tome and Principe	2.3	4.0	4.9	4.4	4.7	7.0	5.9	38.7	0.4	0.5	0.6	0.7	0.6	0.5	0.6	24.7
Senegal	53.0	112.0	46.1	108.8	114.8	83.9	99.3	8.8	18.0	11.6	6.4	52.1	15.6	14.6	15.1	8.4
Seychelles	0.7	1.9	0.8	0.8	0.9	0.7	0.8	10.2	0.0	0.0	0.0	0.0	0.0	0.0	0.0	…
Sierra Leone	1.1	1.7	7.3	27.7	59.7	8.1	33.9	6.6	0.1	0.8	4.5	26.0	57.9	6.0	32.0	41.8
Somalia	7.0	1.7	18.1	4.2	3.5	16.0	9.7	1.2	0.1	0.8	1.0	3.4	1.4	4.5	2.9	2.1
South Africa	61.5	81.4	122.5	67.5	150.3	70.8	110.5	2.4	29.7	38.6	64.9	20.4	42.6	4.6	23.6	3.3
Swaziland	1.8	0.6	0.2	0.4	0.8	0.4	0.6	0.6	0.1	0.0	0.1	0.2	0.1	0.4	0.2	1.2
Togo	10.9	10.0	10.4	10.5	20.0	12.7	16.3	2.8	1.7	1.1	0.8	0.2	7.2	0.3	3.7	3.9
Uganda	76.9	98.6	74.9	53.6	49.7	42.6	46.1	1.7	71.2	13.3	54.1	26.5	30.8	29.2	30.0	5.2
United Republic of Tanzania	20.8	33.9	233.6	187.9	140.0	238.6	189.3	5.1	11.9	15.6	211.5	158.1	33.8	84.1	58.9	8.4
Zambia	120.3	13.5	56.9	75.1	144.8	81.5	113.2	10.0	93.0	5.5	18.9	35.4	2.3	43.6	23.0	10.1
Zimbabwe	24.3	14.3	8.4	10.4	6.3	5.6	6.0	0.5	0.3	2.1	1.0	3.6	1.0	1.4	1.2	0.5
Total	4 548.4	4 081.2	4 205.0	5 004.0	6 257.4	7 725.1	6 991.2	1.4	1 279.0	1 315.6	1 386.1	1 482.0	2 022.6	3 169.5	2 596.0	4.6
Total of 'country unspecified'	402.5	522.5	591.7	846.9	755.0	821.4	788.2	…	63.3	88.5	105.0	95.4	112.3	147.7	130.0	…
Total all countries	4 950.9	4 603.8	4 796.7	5 850.9	7 012.4	8 546.6	7 779.5	…	1 342.2	1 404.1	1 491.0	1 577.4	2 134.8	3 317.2	2 726.0	…

Notes:
- (…) indicates that data are not available.
- 'Country unspecified' aid includes aid to a region, without specification of countries, or to an area (e.g. West Indies, countries of former Yugoslavia).

Sources: Aid commitments to basic education from all DAC countries: CRS online database (OECD-DAC, 2006*c*), Table 2. Population: Annex, Statistical Table 1 and UIS database.
School-age population: Annex, Statistical Table 5 and UIS database.

Glossary

Accreditation. Recognition and approval of the academic standards of an educational institution by some external, impartial body of high public esteem.

Achievement. Performance on standardized tests or examinations that measure knowledge or competence in a specific subject area. The term is sometimes used as an indication of education quality within an education system or when comparing a group of schools.

Adult education. Educational activities, offered through formal, non-formal or informal frameworks, targeted at adults and aimed at advancing, or substituting for, initial education and training. The purpose may be to (a) complete a given level of formal education or professional qualification; (b) acquire knowledge and skills in a new field (not necessarily for a qualification); and/or (c) refresh or update knowledge and skills. See also **Basic education** and **Continuing education**.

Adult literacy rate. Number of literate persons aged 15 and above, expressed as a percentage of the total population in that age group. Different ways of defining and assessing literacy yield different results regarding the number of persons designated as literate.

Age-specific enrolment ratio (ASER). Enrolment of a given age or age-group, regardless of the level of education in which pupils or students are enrolled, expressed as a percentage of the population of the same age or age group.

Basic education. The whole range of educational activities taking place in various settings (formal, non formal and informal), that aim to meet **basic learning needs**. According to the **International Standard Classification of Education** (see **ISCED** below), basic education comprises primary education (first stage of basic education) and lower secondary education (second stage).

Basic learning needs. Defined in the World Declaration on Education for All (Jomtien, Thailand, 1990) as essential tools for learning (e.g. literacy, oral expression, numeracy, problem solving) as well as basic learning content (e.g. knowledge, skills, values and attitudes) that individuals should acquire in order to survive, develop personal capacities, live and work in dignity, participate in development, improve quality of life, make informed decisions and continue the learning process. The scope of basic learning needs, and how they should be met, varies by country and culture, and changes over time.

Child, or under-5, mortality rate. Probability of dying between birth and exactly 5 years of age expressed per 1,000 live births.

Cognitive development. The development of the mental action or process of acquiring knowledge through thought, experience and senses.

Compulsory education or attendance. Educational programmes that children and young people are legally obliged to attend, usually defined in terms of a number of grades or an age range, or both.

Constant prices. A way to express financial values in real terms, which enables comparisons over time. To measure changes in real national income or product, economists calculate the value of total production in each year at constant prices using a set of prices that applied in a chosen base year.

Continuing (or **further**) **education**. A general term referring to a wide range of educational activities designed to meet the basic learning needs of adults. See also **Adult education** and **Lifelong learning**.

Disability. A physical or mental condition which may be temporary or permanent, and which limits a person's opportunities to take part in the community on an equal level with others.

Dropout rate by grade. Percentage of pupils or students who drop out from a given grade in a given school year. It is the difference between 100% and the sum of the promotion and repetition rates.

Early childhood. The period of a child's life from birth to age 8.

Early childhood care and education (ECCE). Programmes that, in addition to providing children with care, offer a structured and purposeful set of learning activities either in a formal institution (pre-primary or ISCED 0) or as part of a non-formal child development programme. ECCE programmes are normally designed for children from age 3 and include organized learning activities that constitute, on average, the equivalent of at least 2 hours per day and 100 days per year.

Education for All Development Index (EDI). Composite index aimed at measuring overall progress towards EFA. At present, the EDI incorporates four of the most easily quantifiable EFA goals – universal primary education as measured by the net enrolment ratio, adult literacy as measured by the adult literacy rate, gender parity as measured by the **gender-specific EFA index**, and quality of education as measured by the survival rate to grade 5. Its value is the arithmetical mean of the observed values of these four indicators.

Elementary education. See **Primary education**.

Enrolment. Number of pupils or students enrolled at a given level of education, regardless of age. See also **gross enrolment ratio** and **net enrolment ratio**.

Entrance age (official). Age at which pupils or students would enter a given programme or level of education – assuming they had started at the official entrance age for the lowest level, studied full-time throughout and progressed through the system without repeating or skipping a grade. The theoretical entrance age to a given programme or level may be very different from the actual or even the most common entrance age.

Equity: In education, the extent to which access and opportunities for children and adults are just and fair. This implies reduction in disparities based on gender, poverty, residence, ethnicity, language or other characteristics.

Fields of study in tertiary or higher education.

Education: teacher training and education science.

Humanities and arts: humanities, religion and theology, fine and applied arts.

Social sciences, business and law: social and behavioural sciences, journalism and information, business and administration, law.

Science: life and physical sciences, mathematics, statistics and computer sciences.

Engineering, manufacturing and construction: engineering and engineering trades, manufacturing and processing, architecture and building.

Agriculture: agriculture, forestry and fishery, veterinary studies.

Health and welfare: medical sciences and health related sciences, social services.

Services: personal services, transport services, environmental protection, security services.

Foreign students. Students enrolled in an education programme in a country of which they are not permanent residents.

Gender parity index (GPI). Ratio of female to male values (or male to female, in certain cases) of a given indicator. A GPI of 1 indicates parity between sexes; a GPI above or below 1 indicates a disparity in favour of one sex over the other.

Gender-specific EFA index (GEI). Composite index measuring relative achievement of gender parity in total participation in primary and secondary education as well as gender parity in adult literacy. The GEI is calculated as an arithmetical mean of the gender parity indices of the primary and secondary gross enrolment ratios and of the adult literacy rate.

General education. Programmes designed to lead students to a deeper understanding of a subject or group of subjects, especially, but not necessarily, with a view to preparing them for further education at the same or a higher level. These programmes are typically school-based and may or may not contain vocational elements. Their successful completion may or may not provide students with a labour-market-relevant qualification.

Grade. Stage of instruction usually equivalent to one complete school year.

Graduate. A person who has successfully completed the final year of a level or sub-level of education. In some countries completion occurs as a result of passing an examination or a series of examinations. In other countries it occurs after a requisite number of course hours have been accumulated. Sometimes both types of completion occur within a country.

Gross enrolment ratio (GER). Total enrolment in a specific level of education, regardless of age, expressed as a percentage of the population in the official age group corresponding to this level of education. For the tertiary level, the population used is that of the five-year age group following on from the secondary school leaving age. The GER can exceed 100% due to early or late entry and/or grade repetition.

Gross intake rate (GIR). Total number of new entrants to a given grade of primary education, regardless of age, expressed as a percentage of the population at the official school entrance age for that grade.

Gross domestic product (GDP). The value of all final goods and services produced in a country in one year (see also **Gross national product**). GDP can be measured by adding up all of an economy's (a) income (wages, interest, profits and rents) or (b) expenditure (consumption, investment, government purchases) plus net exports (exports minus imports). Both results should be the same because one person's expenditure is always another person's income, so the sum of all incomes must equal the sum of all expenditures.

Gross national product (GNP). The value of all final goods and services produced in a country in one year (**gross domestic product**) plus income that residents have received from abroad, minus income claimed by non residents. GNP may be much less than GDP if much of the income from a country's production flows to foreign persons or firms. But if the people or firms of a country hold large amounts of the stocks and bonds of firms or governments of other countries, and receive income from them, GNP may be greater than GDP.

Gross national product per capita. GNP divided by the total population at mid-year.

HIV/AIDS orphan. A child up to the age of 17 who has lost one or both parents due to HIV/AIDS.

HIV prevalence rate. Estimated number of people of a given age group living with HIV/AIDS at the end of a given year, expressed as a percentage of the total population of the corresponding age group.

Illiterate (see **Literate**)

Inclusive education. Education that addresses the learning needs of all children, youth and adults with a specific focus on those who are vulnerable to marginalization and exclusion.

Indigenous language. A language that originated in a specified territory or community and was not brought in from elsewhere. See **mother tongue language** and **vernacular language**.

Infant mortality rate. Probability of dying between birth and exactly 1 year of age, expressed per 1,000 live births.

Informal education. Learning that takes place in daily life without clearly stated objectives. The term refers to a lifelong process whereby every individual acquires attitudes, values, skills and knowledge from daily experiences and the educative influences and resources in his/her environment – e.g. family and neighbours, work and play, the marketplace, the library, mass media.

International Standard Classification of Education (ISCED). Classification system designed to serve as an instrument for assembling, compiling and presenting comparable indicators and statistics of education both within countries and internationally. The system, introduced in 1976, was revised in 1997 (ISCED97).

Labour force participation rate. Expresses the share of employed plus unemployed people in comparison with the working age population.

Language (or **medium**) **of instruction**. Language(s) used for teaching and learning in formal or non formal educational settings.

Least developed countries (LDCs). Low-income countries which, according to the United Nations, have human resource weaknesses and are economically vulnerable. A category used to guide donors and countries in allocating foreign assistance.

Life expectancy at birth. Theoretical number of years a newborn infant would live if prevailing patterns of age-specific mortality rates in the year of birth were to stay the same throughout the child's life.

Lifelong learning. The concept of learning as a process that continues throughout life to address an individual's learning needs. The term is used widely in adult education to refer to learning processes in many forms and at many levels. See also **adult education** and **continuing education**.

Literacy. According to UNESCO's 1958 definition, the term refers to the ability of an individual to read and write with understanding a simple short statement related to his/her everyday life. The concept of literacy has since evolved to embrace multiple skill domains, each conceived on a scale of different mastery levels and serving different purposes. Many today view literacy as the ability to identify, interpret, create, communicate and compute, using printed and written materials in various contexts. Literacy is a process of learning that enables individuals to achieve personal goals, develop their knowledge and potential, and participate fully in the community and wider society.

Literate/Illiterate. As used in the statistical tables, the term refers to a person who can/cannot read and write with understanding a simple statement related to her/his everyday life.

Literate environment. The term can have at least two meanings: (a) the availability of written, printed and visual materials in learners' surrounding environment, enabling them to make use of their basic reading and writing skills; and/or (b) the prevalence of literacy in households and communities, enhancing the prospects of successful literacy acquisition by learners.

Literate society. A social setting within which (a) the vast majority of the population acquires and uses basic literacy skills; (b) major social, political and economic institutions (e.g. offices, courts, libraries, banks) contain an abundance of printed matter, written records and visual materials, and emphasize the reading and writing of texts; and (c) the exchange of text-based information is facilitated and lifelong learning opportunities are provided.

Mother tongue language. Main language spoken in the home environment and acquired as a first language. Sometimes known as a home language. See **indigenous language** and **vernacular language**.

National language. Language spoken by a large part of the population of a country, which may or may not be designated an **official language** (i.e., a language designated by law to be employed in the public domain).

Net attendance rate (NAR). Number of pupils in the official age group for a given level of education who attend school in that level, expressed as a percentage of the population in that age group.

Net enrolment ratio (NER). Enrolment of the official age group for a given level of education, expressed as a percentage of the population in that age group.

Net intake rate (NIR). **New entrants** to the first grade of primary education who are of the official primary-school entrance age, expressed as a percentage of the population of that age.

New entrants. Pupils entering a given level of education for the first time; the difference between enrolment and repeaters in the first grade of the level.

New entrants to the first grade of primary education with ECCE experience. Number of new entrants to the first grade of primary school who have attended the equivalent of at least 200 hours of organized ECCE programmes, expressed as a percentage of the total number of new entrants to the first grade.

Non-formal education. Learning activities typically organized outside the formal education system. The term is generally contrasted with formal and **informal education**. In different contexts, non-formal education covers educational activities aimed at imparting adult literacy, basic education for out-of-school children and youth, life skills, work skills and general culture. Such activities usually have clear learning objectives, but vary by duration, in conferring certification for acquired learning, and in organizational structure.

Opportunity cost. Refers to the benefit foregone by using a scarce resource for one purpose instead of its next best alternative use.

Out-of-school children. Children in the official primary school age range who are not enrolled in either primary or secondary schools.

Pedagogue. Person trained in teaching skills. In early childhood professions a pedagogue works with the theory and pratice of **pedagogy**, with emphasis on a relational and holistic approach. The distinction between pedagogue and teacher differs accross countries.

Pedagogy. The profession, science or theory of teaching.

Post-secondary non-tertiary education (ISCED level 4). Programmes that lie between the upper secondary and tertiary levels from an international point of view, even though they might clearly be considered upper secondary or tertiary programmes in a national context. They are often not significantly more advanced than programmes at ISCED 3 (upper secondary) but they serve to broaden the knowledge of students who have completed a programme at that level. The students are usually older than those at ISCED level 3. ISCED 4 programmes typically last between six months and two years.

Pre-primary education (ISCED level 0). Programmes at the initial stage of organized instruction, primarily designed to introduce very young children, aged at least 3 years, to a school-type environment and provide a bridge between home and school. Variously referred to as infant education, nursery education, pre-school education, kindergarten or early childhood education, such programmes are the more formal component of ECCE. Upon completion of these programmes, children continue their education at ISCED 1 (primary education).

Primary cohort completion rate. The number of pupils who complete the final year of primary school expressed as a percentage of the number who entered the first year.

Primary education (ISCED level 1). Programmes normally designed on a unit or project basis to give pupils a sound basic education in reading, writing and mathematics, and an elementary understanding of subjects such as history, geography, natural sciences, social sciences, art and music. Religious instruction may also be featured. These subjects serve to develop pupils' ability to obtain and use information they need about their home, community or country. Also known as elementary education.

Private enrolment. Number of pupils/students enrolled in institutions that are not operated by public authorities but controlled and managed, whether for profit or not, by private bodies such as non-governmental organizations, religious bodies, special interest groups, foundations or business enterprises.

Process quality (of ECCE). Indicators of ECCE programme quality that focus on the nature of the relationships between carers and children, the inclusion of families, and the responsiveness to cultural diversity and to children with special needs.

Public enrolment. Number of students enrolled in institutions that are controlled and managed by public authorities or agencies (national/federal, state/provincial or local), whatever the origins of their financial resources.

Public expenditure on education. Total current and capital expenditure on education by local, regional and national governments, including municipalities. Household contributions are excluded. It covers public expenditure for both public and private institutions. Current expenditure includes expenditure for goods and services that are consumed within a given year and have to be renewed the following year, such as staff salaries and benefits; contracted or purchased services; other resources, including books and teaching materials; welfare services and items such as furniture and equipment, minor repairs, fuel, telecommunications, travel, insurance and rent. Capital expenditure includes expenditure for construction, renovation and major repairs of buildings and the purchase of heavy equipment or vehicles.

Pupil. A child enrolled in pre-primary or primary education. Youth and adults enrolled at more advanced levels are often referred to as students.

Pupil/teacher ratio (PTR). Average number of pupils per teacher at a specific level of education, based on headcounts for both pupils and teachers.

Purchasing power parity (PPP). An exchange rate that accounts for price differences among countries, allowing international comparisons of real output and incomes.

Quintile. In statistics, each of five equal groups into which a population can be divided according to the distribution of values of a variable.

Repetition rate by grade. Number of repeaters in a given grade in a given school year, expressed as a percentage of enrolment in that grade the previous school year.

Repeaters. Number of pupils enrolled in the same grade or level as the previous year, expressed as a percentage of the total enrolment in that grade or level.

School life expectancy (SLE). Number of years a child of school entrance age is expected to spend at school or university, including years spent on repetition. It is the sum of the age-specific enrolment ratios for primary, secondary, post-secondary non-tertiary and tertiary education.

School-age population. Population of the age group officially corresponding to a given level of education, whether enrolled in school or not.

School readiness. Children's development in several interconnected domains relevant to starting school, including physical well-being and motor development, social and emotional development, approach to learning, language development, and cognitive development and general knowledge.

Secondary education. Programmes at ISCED levels 2 and 3. Lower secondary education (ISCED 2) is generally designed to continue the basic programmes of the primary level but the teaching is typically more subject-focused, requiring more specialized teachers for each subject area. The end of this level often coincides with the end of compulsory education. In upper secondary education (ISCED 3), the final stage of secondary education in most countries, instruction is often organized even more along subject lines and teachers typically need a higher or more subject-specific qualification than at ISCED level 2.

Structural quality (of ECCE). Indicators of ECCE programme quality, often used by governments for regulatory purposes, which focus on class size, staff-child ratios, availability of materials and staff training.

Stunting. Proportion of under-5s falling below minus 2 and minus 3 standard deviations from the median height-for-age of the reference population. Low height for age is a basic indicator of malnutrition.

Survival rate by grade. Percentage of a cohort of students who are enrolled in the first grade of an education cycle in a given school year and are expected to reach a specified grade, regardless of repetition.

Teachers or teaching staff. Number of persons employed full time or part time in an official capacity to guide and direct the learning experience of pupils and students, irrespective of their qualifications or the delivery mechanism, i.e. face-to-face and/or at a distance. Excludes educational personnel who have no active teaching duties (e.g. headmasters, headmistresses or principals who do not teach) and persons who work occasionally or in a voluntary capacity.

Teacher compensation consists of a teacher's base salary and all bonuses. Base salary refers to the minimum scheduled gross annual salary for a full-time teacher with the minimum training necessary to be qualified at the beginning of his or her teaching career. Reported base salaries are defined as the total sum of money paid by the employer for the labour supplied minus the employers' contribution to social security and pension funding. Bonuses that are a regular part of the annual salary, like a thirteenth month or holiday bonus, are normally included in the base salary.

Technical and vocational education. Programmes designed mainly to prepare students for direct entry into a particular occupation or trade (or class of occupations or trades). Successful completion of such programmes normally leads to a labour-market relevant vocational qualification recognized by the competent authorities (ministry of education, employers' associations) in the country in which it is obtained.

Tertiary or higher education. Programmes with an educational content more advanced than what is offered at ISCED levels 3 and 4. The first stage of tertiary education, ISCED level 5, includes level 5A, composed of largely theoretically based programmes intended to provide sufficient qualifications for gaining entry to advanced research programmes and professions with high skill requirements; and level 5B, where programmes are generally more practical, technical and/or occupationally specific. The second stage of tertiary education, ISCED level 6, comprises programmes devoted to advanced study and original research, and leading to the award of an advanced research qualification.

Total debt service. Sum of principal repayments and interest paid in foreign currency, goods or services on long-term debt, or interest paid on short-term debt, as well as repayments (repurchases and charges) to the International Monetary Fund.

Total fertility rate. Average number of children that would be born to a woman if she were to live to the end of her childbearing years (15 to 49) and bear children at each age in accordance with prevailing age-specific fertility rates.

Trained teacher. Teacher who has received the minimum organized teacher training normally required for teaching at the relevant level in a given country.

Transition rate to secondary education. New entrants to the first grade of secondary education in a given year, expressed as a percentage of the number of pupils enrolled in the final grade of primary education in the previous year.

Undernourished population. People whose food and nutritional intake is chronically insufficient to meet their minimum energy requirements.

Vernacular language. A language spoken by the people of a country or a region, as distinguished from official standards or global languages.

Youth literacy rate. Number of literate persons aged 15 to 24, expressed as a percentage of the total population in that age group.

References*

Ackerman, D. J. 2004. States' efforts in improving the qualifications of early care and education teachers. *Educational Policy*, Vol. 18, No. 2, pp. 311-37.

— 2006. The costs of being a child care teacher: revisiting the problem of low wages. *Educational Policy*, Vol. 20, No. 1, p. 85.

Addison, R. 2006. *ECD Policy Development and Implementation: Ghana's Experience*. Accra, Ghana National Commission on Children.

Agranovitch, M. 2005. Toward EFA goals achievement: regional overviews of Armenia, Azerbaijan, Belarus, Georgia, Moldova and the Russian Federation. Background paper for *EFA Global Monitoring Report 2006*.

Aidoo, A. A. 2005. *Ensuring a Supportive Policy Environment*. Working paper presented at the 3rd Conference on Early Childhood Development in Africa, Accra, 30 May–3 June.

Albania Ministry of Finance. 2004. *Progress Report on Implementation of the National Strategy for Socio-economic Development during 2003: Objectives and Long Term Vision, Priority Action Plan 2004-2007*. Tirana, Ministry of Finance.

Alderman, H., Behrman, J. R., Lavy, V. and Menon, R. 2001. Child health and school enrollment: a longitudinal analysis. *Journal of Human Resources*, Vol. 36, No. 1, pp. 185-205.

Alidou, H., Boly, A., Brock-Utne, B., Diallo, Y. S., Heugh, K. and Wolff, H. E. 2005. *Optimizing Learning and Education in Africa– the Language Factor: A Stock-Taking Research on Mother Tongue and Bilingual Education in sub-Saharan Africa*. Paper presented at the Conference on Bilingual Education and the Use of Local Languages, Windhoek, 3–5 August.

Alston, P., Tobin, J. and Darrow, M. 2005. *Laying the Foundations for Children's Rights, An Independent Study of Some Key Legal and Institutional Aspects of the Impact of the Convention on the Rights of the Child*. Florence, UNICEF.

Arnold, C. 2004. Positioning ECCD in the 21st Century. *Coordinators' Notebook: An International Resource for Early Childhood Development*, Toronto, Ont., Vol. 28.

Arnold, C., Bartlett, K., Gowani, S. and Merali, R. 2006. Is everybody ready? Readiness, transition and continuity: reflections and moving forward. Background paper for *EFA Global Monitoring Report 2007*.

Arnold, C., Bartlett, S., Hill, J., Katiwada, C. and Sapkota, P. 2000. *Bringing up Children in a Changing World: Who's Right? Whose Rights?* Kathmandu, UNICEF/Save the Children.

Ashby, A. 2002. Namibia: moving towards equity, access and quality. *ADEA Newsletter*, ADEA, Vol. 14, No. 2, pp. 12-4. http://www.adeanet.org/newsletter/latest/V14N2-eng_coul.pdf (Accessed 29 August 2006.)

Attanasio, O. and Vera-Hernandez, M. 2004. *Medium and Long Run Effects of Nutrition and Child Care: Evaluation of a Community Nursery Programme in Rural Colombia*. London, Institute for Fiscal Studies.

Bailey, D. B. J. 2002. Are critical periods critical for early childhood education? The role of timing in early childhood pedagogy. *Early Childhood Research Quarterly*, Vol. 17, pp. 281-94.

Balescut, J. and Eklindh, K. 2006. Historical perspective on education for persons with disabilities. Background paper for *EFA Global Monitoring Report 2006*.

Barnett, W. S. 1995. Long-term effects of early childhood programs on cognitive and school outcomes. *The Future of Children*, Vol. 5, No. 3, pp. 25-50.

Barnett, W. S., Hustedt, J. T., Robin, K. B. and Schulman, K. L. 2004. *The State of Preschool. 2004 State Preschool Yearbook*. New Brunswick, N.J., National Institute for Early Childhood Research, Rutgers University.

Barnett, S. W. and Masse, L. N. Forthcoming. Comparative benefit-cost analysis of the Abecedarian Program and its policy implications. *Economics of Education Review*.

Bartlett, K. and Arnold, C. 2006. Is Everybody Ready? Readiness, transition and continuity: reflections and moving forward. Background paper for *EFA Global Monitoring Report* 2007.

Becker, J. 2004. *Children as Weapons of War*, Human Rights Watch. http://hrw.org/wr2k4/11.htm (Accessed 2 August 2006.)

Belfield, C. 2006. Financing early childhood care and education: an international review. Background paper for *EFA Global Monitoring Report* 2007.

Benavot, A., Resnik, J. and Corrales, J. 2005. *Global Educational Expansion: Historical Legacies and Political Obstacles*, Cambridge, Mass., American Academy of Arts and Sciences. http://www.amacad.org/publications/ubase_GlobalExpansion.aspx (Accessed 4 September 2006.)

Bennell, P. 2005. *Countering the Impact of the AIDS Epidemic on the Education Sector in Swaziland.* Brighton, UK, Knowledge and Skills for Development.

Bennell, P. and Akyeampong, K. 2006. *Is There a Teacher Motivation Crisis in sub-Saharan Africa and South Asia? Key Findings and Recommendations of an International Research Project, Knowledge and Skills for Development.* Brighton, UK, Knowledge and Skills for Development.

Benson, C. J. 2002. Real and potential benefits of bilingual programmes in developing countries. *International Journal of Bilingual Education and Bilingualism,* Vol. 5, No. 6, pp. 303-17.

Bentaouet-Kattan, R. 2005. Primary school fees: an update. Background paper for *EFA Global Monitoring Report* 2006.

Bentaouet-Kattan, R. and Burnett, N. 2004. *User Fees in Primary Education.* Washington, DC, World Bank. (Education for All Working Papers, Departmental Working Paper, 30108.)

Berkovitch, N. 1999. *From Motherhood to Citizenship: Women's Rights and International Organizations.* Baltimore, Md., Johns Hopkins University Press.

Bernard, A. 2005. Global monitoring report: East Asia regional analysis. Background paper for *EFA Global Monitoring Report* 2006.

Bernard, J. M., Simon, O. and Vianou, K. 2005. *Le Redoublement: Mirage de L'école Africaine?* [Repetition: a mirage for African schools?] Dakar, CONFEMEN.

Bertrand, J. and Beach, J. 2004. *A Guide to International Early Childhood Education. Critical Success Factors Report. Conducted for the Egypt Program, American and Middle East Branch.* Gatineau, Que., Canadian International Development Agency.

Bloch, C. and Edwards, V. 1999. Young children's literacy in multilingual classrooms: comparing developments in South Africa and the UK. Limage, L. (ed.), *Comparative Perspectives on Language and Literacy: Selected Papers from the Work of the Language and Literacy Commission of the 10th World Congress of Comparative Education Societies.* Dakar, UNESCO/BREDA.

Bloch, F. and Buisson, M. 1998. *La Garde des Enfants, Une Histoire de Femmes: Entre Don, Equité et Rémunération* [Child Care, A Woman's Story: Between Gift, Equity and Remuneration]. Paris, L'Harmattan.

Bloom, D. E. 2004. *Beyond the Basics: Patterns, Trends, and Issues in Secondary Education in Developing Countries.* Cambridge, Mass., Harvard University, Harvard School of Public Health.

Blöss, T. and Odena, S. 2005. Idéologies et pratiques sexuées des rôles parentaux [Gender-related ideologies and practices in parental roles]. *Recherches et Prévisions,* Vol. 80, June, pp. 77-91.

Blumberg, R. L. 2006. How mother's economic activities and empowerment affect Early Childhood Care and Education (ECCE) for boys and girls: a theory-guided exploration across history, cultures and societies. Background paper for *EFA Global Monitoring Report* 2007.

Boakye, J. K. A., Adamu-Issah, M. and Etse, S. 2001. *Elaboration de la Politique de Développement de la Petite Enfance au Ghana: Etude de Cas* [Policy-Making on Early Childhood Development in Ghana: Case Study]. http://www.adeanet.org/publications/docs/wgecd_doc/ECD%20GHANA.doc (Accessed 29 August 2006.)

Bobonis, G., Miguel, E. and Sharma, C. Forthcoming. Iron deficiency anemia and school performance. *Journal of Human Resources.*

Bongaarts, J. 2001. *Household Size and Composition in the Developing World*. New York, Population Council. (Policy Research Division, Working Paper, 144.)

Bradley, R. H. and Corwyn, R. F. 2005. Caring for children around the world: a view from HOME. *International Journal of Behavioral Development*, Vol. 29, No. 6, pp. 468-78.

Bregman, J. and Bryner, K. 2006. Quality of secondary education in Africa (SEIA), *ADEA Biennial Meeting 2003*. Grand Baie, Mauritius, ADEA.

Bruneforth, M. 2006a. Characteristics of children who drop out of school and comments on the drop-out population compared to the population of out-of-school children. Background paper for *EFA Global Monitoring Report* 2007.

— 2006b. Interpreting the distribution of out-of-school children by past and expected future school enrolment. Background paper for *EFA Global Monitoring Report* 2007.

— 2006c. Results from multivariate analysis on school attendance and out-of-school children. Background paper for *EFA Global Monitoring Report* 2007.

Bruns, B., Mingat, A. and Rakoomala, R. 2003. *Achieving Universal Primary Education by 2015: A Chance for Every Child*. Washington, DC, World Bank.

Bulir, A. and Hamann, A. 2006. *Volatility of Development Aid: From the Frying Pan into the Fire?* Washington, DC, International Monetary Fund. (Working Paper.)

Cameron, C. 2001. Promise or problem? A review of the literature on men working in early childhood services. *Gender, Work and Organization*, Vol. 8, No. 4, pp. 430-53.

Cameron, C. and Moss, P. 1998. Men as carers for children: an introduction. Owen, Moss, P. and Cameron, C. (eds), *Men as Workers in Services for Young Children*. London, Institute of Education, University of London.

Caramés, A., Fisas, V. and Luz, D. 2006. *Analysis of Disarmament, Demobilisation and Reintegration (DDR) Programmes Existing in the World During 2005*. Madrid/Barcelona, Ministerio de Asuntos Exteriores y de Cooperación, Agencia Española de Cooperación Internacional/Escola de Cultura de Pau.

Cardoso, E. and Portela Souza, A. 2003. *The Impact of Cash Transfers on Child Labor and School Attendance in Brazil*. Nashville, Tenn., Vanderbilt University Department of Economics. (Working Paper, 0407.)

Caribbean Support Initiative. 2006. *Update on Saint Lucia Chapter Roving Caregivers Program, January*, Bridgetown, Caribbean Support Initiative. http://www.csinews.org/QUARTERLY%20REPORT%20RCP%20SLU.pdf (Accessed May 24 2006.)

Carr-Hill, R. 2006. Assessment of international early childhood education data. Background paper for *EFA Global Monitoring Report* 2007.

Center for Early Education and Development. 2002. *Talking Reasonably and Responsibly About Early Brain Development*. Minneapolis, Minn., University of Minnesota.

Chandrasekhar, C. P. and Ghosh, J. 2005. Integrated Child Development Services scheme—the unfulfilled potential. *The Hindu Business Line*, Opinion–Social welfare, 22 March. http://www.blonnet.com/2005/03/22/stories/2005032202430900.htm (Accessed 29 August 2006.)

Chant, S. 2004. *Female Headship and the «Feminisation of Poverty»*. Brasilia, UNDP, International Poverty Center. (In Focus: The Challenge of Poverty.)

Chapman, K. 2006. *Using Social Transfers to Scale Up Equitable Access to Education and Health Services*. London, DFID Policy Division, Scaling up Services team.

Charles, L. and Williams, S. 2006. ECCE in the Caribbean. Background paper for *EFA Global Monitoring Report* 2007.

Chartier, A.-M. and Geneix, N. 2006. Pedagogical approaches to early childhood education. Background paper for *EFA Global Monitoring Report* 2007.

Chaudhury, N., Hammer, J., Kremer, M., Maralidharan, K. and Rogers, F. H. 2005. Missing in action: teacher and health worker absence in developing countries. *The Journal of Economic Perspectives*, Vol. 20, No. 1, pp. 91-116.

Chile FONADIS. 2005. *Primer Estudio Nacional de la Discapacidad en Chile* [First National Study on Disability in Chile]. Santiago, Gobierno de Chile, Fondo Nacional de la Discapacidad.

Chile Presidency. 2006. *Newsroom*, 30 March. http://www.presidencyofchile.cl/view/viewArticulo.asp?idArticulo=5723&tipo=Sitio%20Presidencia&seccion=Sitio%20Presi dencia (Accessed 12 September 2006.)

China Ministry of Education. 2003. *Let more Chinese Children Have Access to Early Childhood Care and Education*. Paper presented at the Fifth E-9 Ministerial Review Meeting in Egypt, Cairo, 19–21 December.

Choi, S.-H. 2002. *Early childhood care? Development? Education?* Paris, UNESCO. (UNESCO Policy Brief on Early Childhood, 1.)

— 2004. *Encourage Private Sector: Pre-school Education Reform in Morocco*. Paris, UNESCO. (UNESCO Policy Brief on Early Childhood, 20.)

— 2005. *Supporting the Poorest: Vietnam's Early Childhood Policy*. Paris, UNESCO. (UNESCO Policy Brief on Early Childhood, 29.)

— 2006. *Ensuring Equitable Access to Preschool Education: Kazakhstan's Experience*. Paris, UNESCO. (UNESCO Policy Brief on Early Childhood, 33.)

Choo, K. K. 2004. *Inter-ministerial Collaboration in Early Childhood Training in Singapore*. Singapore, UNESCO. (UNESCO Policy Brief on Early Childhood, 24.)

Cohen, N. 2005. The impact of language development on the psychosocial and emotional development of young children. Tremblay, R. E., Barr, R. G. and Peters, R. D. (eds), *Encyclopaedia on Early Childhood Development*. Montreal, Que., Centre for Early Childhood Development, pp. 1-7.

Cole, C. F., Arafat, C., Tidhar, C., Zidan Tafesh, W., Fox, N. A., Killen, M., Ardila-Rey, A., Leavitt, L. A., Lesser, G., Richman, B. A. and Yung, F. 2003. The educational impact of Rechov Sumsum/Shara'a Simsim: a Sesame Street television series to promote respect and understanding among children living in Israel, the West Bank, and Gaza. *International Journal of Behavioral Development,* Vol. 27, No. 5, pp. 409–22.

Cole, C. F., Richman, B. A. and McCann Brown, S. A. 2001. The world of Sesame Street research. Fisch, S. M. and Truglio, R. T. (eds), *«G» is for Growing*. Mahwah, N.J., Erlbaum, pp. 147-79.

Committee on the Rights of the Child. 2006a. *Concluding Observations: Ghana*. Geneva. (Committee on the Rights of the Child, forty-first session, 9-27 January.)

— 2006b. *Consideration of Reports Submitted by States Parties Under Article 44 of the Convention Concluding Observations of the Committee on the Rights of the Child: Ghana*. Geneva. (Committee on the Rights of the Child, forty-first session, 9-27 January.)

— 2006c. *Summary Record of the 1091st Meeting (Chamber A) Consideration of Reports by States Parties (continued) (a)*. Geneva. (Committee on the Rights of the Child, forty-first session, 9-27 January.)

— 2006d. *Summary Record of the 1093rd Meeting (Chamber A) Consideration of Reports of States Parties (continued) (b) Second periodic report of Ghana (continued)*. Geneva. (Committee on the Rights of the Child, forty-first session, 9-27 January.)

Connal, C. and Sauvageot, C. 2005. *NFE-MIS Handbook. Developing a Sub-National Non-Formal Education Management Information System*. Paris, UNESCO. (UN Literacy Decade Publication.)

Consultative Group on Early Childhood Care and Development. *Early Childhood Counts: Rights from the Start*, Toronto, Ont., CGECCD. http://www.ecdgroup.com/ (Accessed 12 September 2006.)

Copple, C. 1997. *Getting a Good Start in School*, Washington, DC, National Education Goals Panel, Goal 1 Early Childhood Assessments Resource Group. http://govinfo.library.unt.edu/negp/Reports/good-sta.htm (Accessed 10 March 2006.)

Corsaro, W. 1997. *The Sociology of Childhood*. Thousand Oaks, Calif., Pine Forge Press.

Corter, C., Janmohammed, Z., Zhang, J. and Bertrand, J. 2006. Selected issues concerning early childhood care and education in China. Background paper for *EFA Global Monitoring Report* 2007.

Council of the European Union. 2006. *Modernising Education and Training: A Vital Contribution to Prosperity and Social Cohesion in Europe*. Brussels, Council of the European Union. (2006 Joint progress report on implementation of the «Education & Training 2010 work programme», 7022/06.)

Couper, J. 2002. Prevalence of childhood disability in rural KwaZulu-Natal. *South Africa Medical Journal,* Vol. 92, No. 7, pp. 549-52.

Cunningham, H. 1991. *The Children of The Poor: Representations of Childhood Since The Seventeenth Century*. Oxford, UK, Blackwell.

Dahlberg, G., Moss, P. and Pence, A. 1999. *Beyond Quality in Early Childhood Education and Care: Postmodern Perspectives*. London, Falmer Press.

De Bonadona, M. 2005. *Special Report: Education and Disability*. Santiago, Instituto Libertad Ideas para Chile.

de los Angeles-Bautista, F. 2004. *Early Childhood Care and Education in South-East Asia: Working for Access, Quality and Inclusion in Thailand, the Philippines, and Viet Nam*. Bangkok, UNESCO Bangkok.

— 2006. From birth to eight: play and learn in a digital world. Media in the lives of young children and their caregivers and teachers. Background paper prepared for *EFA Global Monitoring Report* 2007.

Dembélé, M. 2004. Competent teachers for African classrooms: looking ahead. *IIEP Newsletter,* Paris, Vol. XXII, No. 1, pp. 5-6.

DeStefano, J. 2006. *Meeting EFA: Zambia - Community Schools*. Washington, DC, Academy for Educational Development. (Educational Quality Improvement Program 2.)

di Gropello, E. and Marshall, J. H. 2005. Teacher effort and schooling outcomes in rural Honduras. Vegas, E. (ed.), *Incentives to Improve Teaching: Lessons from Latin America*. Washington, DC, World Bank, pp. 307-57.

Diawara, R. F. 2006. *Une Année D'éducation Pré-primaire Obligatoire Pour Tous Les Enfants* [A Year of Compulsory Pre-primary Education for All Children]. Paper presented at the ADEA Biennale on Education in Africa, Libreville, 27-31 March.

Docket, S. and Perry, B. 2005. «A buddy doesn't let kids get hurt in the playground»: starting school with buddies. *International Journal of Transitions in Childhood,* Vol. 1, pp. 22-34.

Docket, S., Perry, B., Howard, P. and Meckley, A. 2000. *What Do Early Childhood Educators and Parents Think Is Important about Children's Transition to School? A Comparison between Data from the City and the Bush*. Paper presented at the Australian Association for Research in Education Annual Conference, Melbourne, Australia, 1999.

Durkin, M., Davidson, L. L., Desai, P., Hasan, M., Shrout, P. O., Thorburn, M. J., Wang, W. and Zaman, S. S. 1994. Validity of the ten questions screen for childhood disability: results from population based studies in Bangladesh, Jamaica and Pakistan. *Epidemiology,* Vol. 5, No. 2, pp. 283-9.

Early Childhood Development Virtual University. 2005. *ECDVU: An Overview*, Victoria, ECDVU. http://www.ecdvu.org/home.asp (Accessed 21 April 2006.)

Easton, P. B. 2006a. *Creating a Literate Environment: Hidden Dimensions and Implications for Policy*. Paper presented at the ADEA Biennale on Education in Africa, Libreville, 27-31 March.

— 2006b. *Investing in Literacy: Where, Why and How*. Paper presented at the ADEA Biennale on Education in Africa, Libreville, 27-31 March.

Education Policy and Data Center. 2006. Early Childhood Care and Education (ECCE) national profiles for selected countries. Background paper for *EFA Global Monitoring Report* 2007.

Elvir, A. P. and Asensio, C. L. 2006. Early childhood care and education in Central America: challenges and prospects. Background paper for *EFA Global Monitoring Report* 2007.

Encinas-Martin, M. 2006. A global survey of educational evaluation: international, regional and national assessments of student learning. Background paper for *EFA Global Monitoring Report* 2007.

Ethiopia Ministry of Education. 2002. *The Ethiopia Education Sector Development Program 2002/05*. Addis Ababa, Ministry of Education.

— 2005. *Education Sector Development Program III (ESDP-III). 2005/2006 - 2010/2011 (1998 EFY - 2002 EFY). Program Action Plan (PAP)*. Addis Ababa, Ministry of Education. (Final Draft.)

Ethiopia Ministry of Finance and Economic Development. 2002. *Ethiopia: Sustainable Development and Poverty Reduction Program*. Addis Ababa, Ministry of Finance and Economic Development.

European Commission. 2004. *EUROSTAT. European Labor Force Survey 2004 Microdata*. http://epp.eurostat.ec.europa.eu/portal/page?_pageid=1913,47567825,1913_47568351&_dad=portal&_schema=PORTAL#B (Accessed 15 September 2006.)

— 2005. *Key Data on Education in Europe 2005*. Brussels/Luxembourg, Eurydice/Eurostat, Office for Official Publications of the European Communities.

Evans, D. and Miguel, E. A. 2005. *Orphans and Schooling in Africa: A Longitudinal Analysis*, Institute of Business and Economic Research, Center for International and Development Economics Research, University of California, Berkeley. (C05-143.)

Evans, J. 2000. Parents and ECD programmes. *Early Childhood Matters: The Bulletin of the Bernard van Leer Foundation*, The Hague, June, No. 95, pp. 3-5.

— 2006. Parenting programmes: an important ECD intervention strategy. Background paper for *EFA Global Monitoring Report* 2007.

Evans, J. L., Myers, R. G. and Ilfeld, E. M. 2000. *Early Childhood Counts: A Programming Guide on Early Childhood Care for Development*. Washington, DC, World Bank.

Evans, K. S. 1998. Combating gender disparity in education: guidelines for early childhood educators. *Early Childhood Education Journal*, Vol. 26, No. 2, pp. 83-7.

Fabian, H. and Dunlop, A.-W. 2006. Outcomes of good practice in transition processes for children entering primary school. Background paper for *EFA Global Monitoring Report* 2007.

— (eds). 2002. *Transitions in the Early Years: Debating Continuity and Progression for Children in Early Education*. London, Routledge Falmer.

Faour, B. 2006. Early childhood care and education in four Arab countries. Background paper *EFA Global Monitoring Report* 2007.

Fisch, S. 2005. Children's learning from television. *TeleviZIon*, Vol. 18, pp. 10-4.

Fisher, E. A. 1991. *Early Childhood Care and Education (ECCE): A World Survey*. Paris, UNESCO. (The Young Child and the Family Environment Project, 1990-1995, SHS/91/WS/12.)

France, A. and Utting, D. 2005. The paradigm of 'risk and protection-focused prevention' and its impact on services for children and families. *Children & Society*, No. 19, pp. 77-90.

Fredriksen, B. 2005. *Building Capacity in the Education Sector in Africa: The Need to Strengthen External Agencies' Capacity to help*. Paper presented at the seminar on 'Building Capacity for the Education Sector in Africa, Oslo, 13-14 October.

FTI Secretariat. 2005. *Education For All Fast Track Initiative, Progress Report, 2005*. Washington, DC, Fast Track Initiative.

— 2006. *Education For All Fast Track Initiative, Analysis of Official Development Assistance*. Washington, DC, Fast Track Initiative. (Prepared for the FTI Technical Meeting in Moscow, March 2006.)

Gauthier, A. H. 1996. *The State and the Family: A Comparative Analysis of Family Policies in Industrialized Countries*. Oxford, UK, Oxford University Press.

Ghana Education Service. 2005. *Evaluation Report on Capitation Grant*. Accra, GES.

Ghana NGO Coalition on the Rights of the Child. 2005. *The Ghana NGO Report to the UN Committee on the Rights of the Child on Implementation of the Convention of the Rights of the Child by the Republic of Ghana*. Accra, Ghana NGO Coalition on the Rights of the Child.

Global Campaign for Education. 2006. *Teachers For All: What Governments and Donors Should Do.* Johannesburg, South Africa, Global Campaign for Education. (Policy briefing.)

Golombok, S. and Fivush, R. 1994. *Gender Development.* New York, Cambridge University Press.

Gordon, N. and Vegas, E. 2005. Educational finance equalization, spending, teacher quality, and student outcomes: the case of Brazil's FUNDEF. Vegas, E. (ed.), *Incentives to Improve Teaching: Lessons from Latin America.* Washington, DC, World Bank, pp. 151-86.

Gottlieb, A. 2004. *The After-Life is Where we Come From: The Culture of Infancy in West Africa.* Chicago, IL, Chicago University Press.

Gragnolati, M., Shekar, M. and Das Gupta, M. 2005. *India's Undernourished Children: A Call for Reform and Action.* Washington, DC, World Bank, Health, Nutrition and Population. (Discussion paper, 34638.)

Grantham-McGregor, S. M., Powell, C. A., Walker, S. P. and Himes, J. H. 1991. Nutritional supplementation, psychosocial stimulation, and mental-development of stunted children - the Jamaican study. *The Lancet,* Vol. 338, No. 8758, pp. 1-5.

Gunnarsson, L., Martin Korpi, B. and Nordenstam, U. 1999. *Early Childhood Education and Care Policy in Sweden.* Stockholm, Ministry of Education and Science. (Background report prepared for the OECD thematic review of early childhood education and care policy.)

Hampden-Thompson, G. and Johnston, J. S. 2006. *Variation in the Relationship Between Non-school Factors and Student Achievement on International Assessments.* Washington, DC, US Department of Education, Institute of Education Science, National Center for Education Statistics. (Statistics in Brief, NCES 2006014.)

Hart, B. and Risely, T. R. 2003. *Meaningful Differences in the Everyday Experiences of Young American Children.* Baltimore, Md., Paul H. Brookes Publishing.

Heckman, J. J. 2000. Policies to foster human capital. *Research in Economics,* Vol. 54, No. 1, pp. 3-56.

— 2006. *Investing in Disadvantaged Young Children is an Economically Efficient Policy.* Paper presented at the Committee for Economic Development/PEW Charitable Trusts/PNC Financial Services Group forum on 'Building the Economic Case for Investments in Preschool, New York, 10 January.

Heckman, J. J. and Carneiro, P. 2003. Human capital policy. Heckman, J. and Krueger, A. (eds), *Inequality in America: What Role for Human Capital Policy?* Cambridge, Mass., MIT Press.

Hendrick, H. 1997. *Children, Childhood and English Society 1880-1990.* Cambridge, UK, Cambridge University Press.

Heymann, J. 2002. *Social Transformations and Their Implications for the Global Demand for ECCE.* Paris, UNESCO. (UNESCO Policy Brief on Early Childhood, 8.)

Ho, M.-S. 2006. The politics of preschool education vouchers in Taiwan. *Comparative Education Review,* Vol. 50, No. 1, pp. 66-89.

Hodgkin, R. and Newell, P. 1996. *Effective Government Structures for Children: Report of a Gulbenkian Foundation Inquiry.* London, Gulbenkian Foundation.

Horton, J. C. 2001. Critical periods in the development of the visual system. Bailey, D. B. J., Bruer, J. T., Symons, F. J. and Lichtman, J. W. (eds), *Critical Thinking about Critical Periods.* Baltimore, Md., Paul H. Brookes Publishing, pp. 27-44.

Hovens, M. 2002. Bilingual education in West Africa: does it work? *International Journal of Bilingual Education and Bilingualism,* Vol. 5, No. 5, pp. 249-66.

Human Security Centre. 2005. *Human Security Report 2005: War and Peace in the 21st Century.* New York/Oxford, University of British Columbia, Canada/Oxford University Press.

Hunt, J. M. V. 1961. *Intelligence and Experience.* New York, Ronald Press.

Hyde, K. A. L. and Kabiru, M. N. 2006. *Early Childhood Development as an Important Strategy to Improve Learning Outcomes.* Paris, ADEA, Working Group on Early Childhood Development.

IDD and Associates. 2006. *Executive Summary. Joint Evaluation of General Budget Support 1994-2004: Burkina Faso, Malawi, Mozambique, Nicaragua, Rwanda, Uganda, Vietnam*. Birmingham, UK, International Development Department, University of Birmingham.

ILO. 1980. *Equal Opportunities and Equal Treatment for Men and Women in Employment*. Geneva, ILO. (Report of the Director-General, International Labour Conference, 66th session, Report VI.)

— 1985. *Equal Opportunities and Equal Treatment for Men and Women in Employment*. Geneva, ILO. (Report of the Director-General, International Labour Conference, 71st session, Report VII.)

—2004. *Global Employment Trends for Women*. Geneva, ILO.

— 2006*a. Changing Patterns in the World of Work*. Geneva, ILO. (Report of the Director-General, International Labour Conference, 95th Session 2006, Report I [C].)

— 2006*b. The End of Child Labor: Within Reach. Global Report Under the Follow-up to the ILO Declaration on Fundamental Principles and Rights at Work*. Paper presented at the International Labor Conference. 95th Session 2006, Geneva. (Report I [B].)

Iltus, S. 2006. Significance of home environments as proxy indicators for early childhood care and education. Background paper for *EFA Global Monitoring Report* 2007.

India Ministry of Human Resource Development. 2003. *Education for All: National Plan of Action*. New Delhi, Ministry of Human Resource Development, Department of Elementary Education and Literacy.

Indonesia Ministry of National Education. 2005. *Annual Work Plan Year 2005*. Jakarta, Ministry of National Education.

Internal Displacement Monitoring Centre. 2006. *Internal Displacement: Global Overview of Trends and Developments in 2005*. Geneva, Norwegian Refugee Council.

Issa, S. 2006. *A costing model of the Madrasa Early Childhood Development Program in East Africa*. Paper presented at the ADEA Biennale on Education in Africa, Libreville, 27-31 March. (Working paper.)

Jablonka, I. 2006. *Sans Père ni Mère: Histoire des Enfants de l'Assistance Publique 1874-1939* [Without Father and Mother: Story of the Children on Public Assistance, 1874-1939]. Paris, Seuil.

Jamaica Ministry of Education Youth and Culture. 2003. *Implementation*, Kingston, Ministry of Education, Youth and Culture; Early Childhood Unit. http://www.moec.gov.jm/divisions/ed/earlychildhood/index.htm (Accessed 12 September 2006.)

Jandhyal, K. 2003. Baljyothi: bringing child labour into schools. Ramchandran, V. (ed.), *Getting Children Back to School: Case Studies in Primary Education*. New Delhi, Sage.

Johnson, Z., Howell, F. and Molloy, B. 1993. Community mothers' programme: randomised controlled trial of non-professional intervention in parenting. *British Medical Journal*, 1993, p. 306. http://www.ncbi.nlm.nih.gov/entrez/query.fcgi?cmd=Retrieve&db=PubMed&list_uids=8518642&dopt=Abstract (Accessed 29 May 2006.)

Johnson, Z., Molloy, B., Scallan, E., Fitzpatrick, P., Rooney, B., Keegan, T. and Bryne, P. 2000. Community mothers programme: seven year follow-up of a randomized controlled trial of non-professional intervention in parenting. *Journal of Public Health Medicine,* Vol. 22, No. 3, pp. 337-42.

Johnston, B. and Johnson, K. A. 2002. Preschool immersion education for indigenous languages: a survey of resources. *Canadian Journal of Native Education*, Vol. 26, No. 2, pp. 107-23.

Jukes, M. 2006. Early childhood health, nutrition and education. Background paper for *EFA Global Monitoring Report* 2007.

— Forthcoming. *Associations between Nutritional Status and Practical Activities of School Age Children in Tanzania*.

Kagan, S. L. and Britto, P. R. 2005. *Going Global with Early Learning and Development Standards: Final report to UNICEF*. New York, National Center for Children and Families, Teachers College, Columbia University.

Kagan, S. L. and Cohen, N. E. 1997. *Not by Chance: Creating an Early Care and Education System for America's Children*. New Haven, Conn., Yale University, Bush Center.

Kagan, S. L. and Neuman, M. J. 1998. Lessons from three decades of transition research. *Elementary School Journal*, Vol. 98, No. 4, pp. 365-79.

Kagitcibasi, C., Unar, D. and Bekman, S. 2001. Long term effects of early intervention: Turkish low-income mothers and children. *Applied Developmental Psychology*, Vol. 22, pp. 333-61.

Kamel, H. 2005. Early childhood care and education in emergency situations. Background paper for *EFA Global Monitoring Report* 2007.

Kamerman, S. B. 2000*a*. Early childhood education and care: an overview of developments in the OECD countries. *International Journal of Educational Research*, Vol. 33, No. 1, pp. 7-30.

— 2000*b*. Parental leaves: an essential ingredient in early childhood care and education. *Social Policy Report*, Vol. 14, No. 2, pp. 3-15. http://www.childpolicy.org/SocialPolicyReport-2000_v14n2.pdf

— 2003. Welfare states, family policies, early childhood education, care, and family support, *Consultation Meeting on Family Support Policy in Central and Eastern Europe*. Budapest, UNESCO/Council of Europe.

— 2005. A global history of early childhood education and care (ECEC). Background paper for *EFA Global Monitoring Report* 2007.

Kamerman, S. B. and Gatenio Gabel, S. 2003. Overview of the current policy context. Cryer, D. and Clifford, R. M. (eds), *Early Childhood Education & Care in the USA*. Baltimore, Md., Paul H. Brookes Publishing.

Kamerman, S. B. and Kahn, A. J. 1976. *Social Services in the United States*. Philadelphia, Pa., Temple University Press.

— (eds). 1991. *Childcare, Parental Leave and the Under 3s: Policy Innovation in Europe*. Westport, Conn., Greenwood Publishing.

Katahoire, A. R. 2006. *Selected Cases of Fruitful Interactions Between Formal and Non-formal Education in Africa*. Paper presented at the ADEA Biennale on Education in Africa, Libreville, 27-31 March. (Working Group on Non-Formal Education.)

Kehily, M. J. and Swann, J. (eds). 2003. *Children's Cultural Worlds*, Vol. 3. Chichester, UK, Wiley/Open University.

Killick, A., Castel-Branco, C. and Gerster, R. 2005. *Perfect Partners? The Performance of Aid Partners to Mozambique, 2004*, Commissioned by the Programme Aid Partners and Financed by the Swiss State Secretariat for Economic Affairs and the UK's Department for International Development.

Kohen, D. E., Hertzman, C. and Brooks-Gunn, J. 1998. *Neighbourhood Influences on Children's School Readiness*. Hull, Que., Applied Research Branch, Strategic Policy, Human Resources Development Canada. (Working Papers Series, W-98-15E.)

Kosonen, K. 2005. Education in local languages: policy and practice in Southeast Asia. *First Languages First: Community-Based Literacy Programmes for Minority Language Contexts in Asia*. Bangkok, UNESCO Bangkok.

Krueger, A. B. and Whitmore, D. M. 2001. The effect of attending a small class in the early grades on college-test taking and middle school test results: evidence from project STAR. *Economic Journal*, Vol. 111, January, pp. 1-28.

— 2002. Would smaller classes help close the black-white achievement gap? Chubb, J. and Loveless, T. (eds), *Bridging the Achievement Gap*. Washington, DC, Brookings Institution Press.

L'Ecuyer, F. 2004. *Education Rights: Education Conflict Reaches New Depths in Niger*. http://spip.red.m2014.net/article.php3?id_article=24 (Accessed 28 July 2006.)

Lao PDR Ministry of Education. 2004. *EFA National Plan of Action: Situation Analysis*, Vientiane, Ministry of Education.

Larraguibel Quiroz, E. 1997. *Special Education Needs in Early Childhood Care and Education in the JUNJI (Junta Nacional de Jardines Infantiles) of Chile*. Paris, UNESCO. (First Steps Stories on Inclusion in Early Childhood Education.)

Lawson, A., Gerster, R. and Hoole, D. 2005. *Learning from Experience with Performance Assessment Frameworks for General Budget Support. Synthesis Report*, Commissioned and financed by the Swiss State Secretariat for Economic Affairs.

Lee, V. E., Zuze, T. L. and Ross, K. N. 2005. *School Effectiveness in 14 sub-Saharan African Countries: Links with 6th Graders' Reading Achievement*. Paper presented at the American Education Research Association Annual Meeting, Montreal, Que., 11–15 April.

Lenz Taguchi, H. and Munkammar, I. 2003. *Consolidating Governmental Early Childhood Education and Care Services Under the Ministry of Education and Sciences: A Swedish Case Study*. Paris, UNESCO. (UNESCO Early Childhood and Family Policy Series, 6.)

Levin, H. M. and Schwartz, H. L. 2006. Costs of early childhood care and education programs. Background paper for *EFA Global Monitoring Report* 2007.

LeVine, R. 2003. *Childhood Socialization: Comparative Studies of Parenting, Learning and Educational Change*. Hong Kong, China, Comparative Education Research Centre.

Lewin, K. 2004. Education for all: planning and financing secondary education in Africa (SEIA), *Donor Conference on SEIA*. Vrije, Netherlands, University of Amsterdam.

— 2006. *Why Some Millennium Development Goals Will Not Be Met: Access To Education in Sub-Saharan Africa and South Asia*. Paper presented at the Comparative and International Education Society Annual Meeting, Honolulu, Hawaii, 14-18 March.

Lewin, K. and Sayed, Y. 2005. *Private or Public Secondary Schooling in Africa? Exploring the Evidence in South Africa and Malawi*. London, DFID.

Lewis, M. and Lockheed, M. 2006. *Who's Out-of-School? Excluded Girls in a Globalizing World*. Washington, DC, Center for Global Development.

Linnecar, A. and Yee, V. 2006. *WABA Activity Sheet 6: Maternity Legislation: Protecting Women's Eight to Breastfeed*, Penang, Malaysia, World Alliance for Breastfeeding Action. http://www.waba.org.my/activitysheet/acsh6.htm (Accessed June 20 2006.)

Lloyd, C. B., Mete, C. and Grant, M. J. 2006. *The Implications of Changing Educational and Family Circumstances for Children's Grade Progression in Rural Pakistan: 1997-2004*. New York, Population Council. (Policy Research Division Working Papers, 209.)

Lockheed, M. 1982. *Sex Equity in Classroom Interaction Research: An Analysis of Behavior Chains*. Paper presented at the Annual Meeting of the American Educational Research Association, New York.

Love, J., Schochet, P. and Meckstroth, A. 1996. *Are They in Any Real Danger: What Research Does—and Doesn't—Tell Us About Child Care Quality and Children's Well Being*. Princeton, N.J., Mathematica Policy Research, Inc.

Luthar, S. S. 2003. *Resilience and Vulnerability: Adaptation in the Context of Childhood Adversities*. Cambridge, UK, Cambridge University Press.

Lwin, T., K., Oo, N. and Arnold, C. 2004. *Myanmar ECD Impact Study*. Westport, Conn., Save the Children USA.

Magnuson, K. A., Meyers, M. K., Ruhm, C. and Waldfogel, J. 2004. Inequality in pre-school education and school readiness, *American Educational Research Journal*, Vol. 41, No. 1, pp. 115–57.

Magnuson, K. A., Ruhm, C. and Waldfogel, J. 2004. *Does Prekindergarten Improve School Preparation and Performance?* Madison, Wis., University of Wisconsin-Madison. (Revised.)

Makotsi, R. 2005. *Sharing Resources - How Library Networks Can Help Reach Education Goals*. London, Book Aid International. (Research paper.)

Malawi National Statistics Office and ORC Macro. 2003. *Malawi DHS EdData Survey 2002: Education Data for Decision-making*. Calverton, Md., Malawi National Statistics Office and ORC Macro.

Margetts, K. 1999. Transition to school: looking forward, *Australian Early Childhood Association National Conference*. Darwin, Australia, 14-17 July.

Masten, A. S. 2001. Ordinary magic: resilience processes in development. *American Psychologist,* Vol. 56, No. 3, pp. 227-33.

Mathew, A. and Rao, C. K. M. 2004. *Indicators of Non-Formal Education. A Study*. Paris, UNESCO.

Maybin, J. and Woodhead, M. 2003. Socializing children. Maybin, J. and Woodhead, M. (eds), *Childhoods In Context*. Chichester, UK, Wiley.

McCormick, M. C., Brooks-Gunn, J., Buka, S. L., Goldman, J., Yu, J., Salganik, M., Scott, D. T., Bennett, F. C., Kay, L. L., Bernbaum, J. C., Bauer, C. R., Martin, C., Woods, I. R., Martin, A. and Casey, P. H. 2006. Early intervention in low birth weight premature infants: results at 18 years of age for the infant health and development program. *Pediatrics,* Vol. 117, No. 3, pp. 771-80.

McEwan, P. J. and Santibañez, L. 2005. Teacher and principal incentives in Mexico. Vegas, E. (ed.), *Incentives to Improve Teaching: Lessons from Latin America.* Washington, DC, World Bank, pp. 213-53.

McLean, H. 2006. Reflections on changes in legislation and national policy frameworks: ECCE in Armenia, Kyrgyzstan, Romania and Ukraine. Background paper for *EFA Global Monitoring Report* 2007.

Mehaffie, K. E. and McCall, R. B. 2002. *Kindergarten Readiness: An Overview of Issues and Assessments.* Pittsburgh, Pa., University of Pittsburgh. (Office of Child Development, Special Report.)

Mendez, M. A. and Adair, L. S. 1999. Severity and timing of stunting in the first two years of life affect performance on cognitive tests in late childhood. *Journal of Nutrition,* Vol. 129, No. 8, pp. 1555-62.

Mialaret, G. 1976. *World Survey of Pre-School Education.* Paris, UNESCO.

Mingat, A. 2006. *Evaluating the Costs of Scaling up ECD Interventions: The World Bank Costing Model with Burkina Faso and the Gambia.* Working paper presented at the ADEA Biennale on Education in Africa, Libreville, 27-31 March.

Mingat, A. and Jaramillo, A. 2003. *Early Childhood Care and Education in Sub-Saharan Africa: What Would it Take to Meet the Millennium Development Goals?* Washington, DC, World Bank.

Mizala, A. and Romaguera, P. 2005. Teachers' salary structures and incentives in Chile. Vegas, E. (ed.), *Incentives to Improve Teaching: Lessons from Latin America.* Washington, DC, World Bank, pp. 103-50.

Molloy, B. 2002. *Still Going Strong: A Tracer Study of the Community Mothers Programme, Dublin, Ireland.* The Hague, Bernard van Leer Foundation.

Montgomery, H., Burr, R. and Woodhead, M. 2003. *Changing Childhoods: Local and Global.* Chichester, UK, Wiley/Open University.

Mookodi, G. 2000. The complexities of female household headship in Botswana. *Pula: Botswana Journal of African Studies,* Vol. 14, No. 2, pp. 148-64.

Moran, P., Ghate, D. and van der Merwe, A. 2004. *What Works in Parenting Support? A Review of the International Evidence.* London, Policy Research Bureau. (Research Report, RR574.)

Moss, P. 2000. *Workforce Issues in Early Childhood Education and Care.* Paper presented at the Consultative Meeting on International Developments in Early Childhood Education and Care, New York, 11-12 May.

— 2004. *The Early Childhood Workforce Structure in "Developed" Countries: Basic Structures and Education.* Paris, UNESCO. (UNESCO Policy Brief on Early Childhood, 27.)

Moss, P. and Deven, F. 1999. *Parental Leaves: Progress or Pitfall?* Brussels/The Hague, NIDI/CBGS Publications. (Research and Policy Issues in Europe, 35.)

Moti, M. 2002. ECD in Mauritius: an evolving vision of ECD. *ADEA Newsletter,* ADEA, Vol. 14, No. 2, pp. 15-7. http://www.adeanet.org/newsletter/latest/V14N2-eng_coul.pdf (Accessed 29 August 2006.)

Mulkeen, A. 2005. *Teachers for Rural Schools: A Challenge for Africa.* Paper presented at the Ministerial Seminar on Education for Rural People in Africa: Policy Lessons, Options and Priorities, Addis Ababa, 7-9 September.

Mullis, I. V. S., Martin, M. O., Gonzalez, E. J. and Chrostowski, S. J. 2004. *TIMSS 2003 International Mathematics Report: Findings From IEA's Trends in International Mathematics and Science Study at the Fourth and Eighth Grades.* Chestnut Hill, Mass., TIMSS & PIRLS International Study Center, Boston College.

Mullis, I. V. S., Martin, M. O., Gonzalez, E. J. and Kennedy, A. M. 2003. *PIRLS International Report: IEA's Study of Reading Literacy Achievement in Primary Schools in 35 Countries.* Chestnut Hill, Mass., TIMSS & PIRLS International Study Center, Boston College.

Murcier, N. 2005. Le loup dans la bergerie: prime éducation et rapports sociaux de sexe [The wolf in the sheepfold: primary education and sociosexual relationships]. *Recherches et Prévisions,* No. 80, pp. 67-75.

Mustard, J. F. 2002. Development and the brain: the base for health, learning, and behavior throughout life. Young, M. E. (ed.), *From Early Child Development to Human Development: Investing in Our Children's Future.* Washington, DC, World Bank, Human Development Network.

— 2005. *Behavior (Affect), Literacy, and Early Child Development.* Paper presented at The Founders' Network, Early Childhood, Monterrey, Mexico, 25 May.

Mwaura, P. 2005. *Preschool Impact on Children's Readiness, Continuity, and Cognitive Progress at Preschool and Beyond: A Case for Madrasa Resource Centre Programme in East Africa.* Geneva, Aga Khan Foundation. (Unpublished Report.)

— 2006. *Madrasa Resource Centre Early Childhood Development Programme: Making a Difference.* Nairobi, Aga Khan Foundation.

Myers, R. G. 1983. *Early Childhood in Latin America.* Paper presented at Preventing School Failure: The Relationship Between Preschool and Primary Education. Workshop on Preschool Research held in Bogota, Colombia, 26-29 May 1981.

— 1995. *The Twelve Who Survive: Strengthening Programmes of Early Childhood Development in the Third World.* Ypsilanti, Mich., High/Scope Press.

— 2006. Quality in programmes of early childhood care and education (ECCE). Background paper for *EFA Global Monitoring Report* 2007.

National Center for Human Resources Development. 2005. Learning readiness. Education Reform for Knowledge Economy (ERFKE) Project, Phase III of the Learning Readiness Assessment (National Level), Early Childhood Education (ECD). Background paper for *EFA Global Monitoring* Report 2007.

National Institute of Child Health and Human Development. 2001. Non-maternal care and family factors in early development: an overview of the NICHD Study of Early Child Care. *Journal of Applied Developmental Psychology,* Vol. 22, pp. 457-92.

— 2005. Predicting individual differences in attention, memory, and planning in first graders from experiences at home, child care and school. *Developmental Psychology,* Vol. 41, No. 1, pp. 99-114.

National Institute of Public Cooperation and Child Development. 2006. Select issues concerning ECCE in India: a case study. Background paper for *EFA Global Monitoring Report* 2007.

Netherlands Ministry of Social Affairs and Employment. 2006. *Work/Family Arrangements,* Netherlands Ministry of Social Affairs and Employment. http://internationalezaken.szw.nl/index.cfm?fuseaction=dsp_rubriek&rubriek_id=13039#3038310 (Accessed 13 September 2006.)

Neuman, M. J. 2001. Hand in hand: improving the links between ECEC and schools in OECD countries. Kamerman, Sheila B. (ed.), *Early Childhood and Care: International Perspectives.* New York, Institute for Child and Family Policy, Columbia University.

— 2005. Governance of early childhood education and care: recent developments in OECD countries. *Early Years: An International Journal of Research and Development,* Vol. 25, No. 2, pp. 127-39.

Neuman, M. J. and Peer, S. 2002. *Equal From the Start: Promoting Educational Opportunity for All Pre-School Children – Learning From the French Experience.* New York, French-American Foundation.

Ngaruiya, S. 2006. *Pre-school Education and School Readiness: the Kenya Experience,* Paper presented at the ADEA Biennale on Education in Africa, Libreville, 27-31 March.

Nigeria Ministry of Education. 2004. *National Policy on Education.* Lagos, Federal Ministry of Education.

Nigeria National Population Commission and ORC Macro. 2004. *Nigeria DHS EdData Survey 2004: Education Data for Decision-Making.* Calverton, Md., Nigeria National Population Commission and ORC Macro.

Nonoyama, Y., Loaiza, E. and Engle, P. 2006. Participation in organized early learning centers: findings from household surveys. Background paper for *EFA Global Monitoring Report* 2007.

Nsamenang, A. B. 2006. Cultures in early childhood care and education. Background paper for *EFA Global Monitoring Report* 2007.

O'Connor, S. M. 1988. Women's labour force participation and preschool enrollment: a cross-national perspective, 1965-1980. *Sociology of Education,* Vol. 61, No. 1, pp. 15-28.

Oberhuemer, P. 2000. Conceptualizing the professional role in early childhood centres: emerging profiles in four European countries. *Early Childhood Research and Practice,* Germany, Vol. 2, No. 2.

Oberhuemer, P. and Ulich, M. 1997. *Working with Young Children in Europe: Provision and Staff Training.* London, Paul Chapman Publisher.

OECD. 2001. *Starting Strong: Early Childhood Education and Care.* Paris, OECD.

— 2003. *Education at a Glance: OECD Indicators - 2003.* Paris, OECD.

— 2004a. *Early Childhood Education and Care Policy: Country Note for Mexico.* Paris, OECD.

— 2004b. *Learning for Tomorrow's World: First Results from PISA 2003.* Paris, OECD, Programme for International Student Assessment.

— 2004c. *OECD Country Note: Early Childhood Education and Care Policy in France.* Paris, OECD.

— 2005a. *Babies and Bosses: Reconciling Work and Family Life. Canada, Finland, Sweden and the United Kingdom* Vol. 4. Paris, OECD. (4 vols)

— 2005b. *The Definition and Selection of Key Competencies: Executive Summary.* Paris, OECD.

— 2006. *Where Immigrants Succeed: A Comparative Review of Performance and Engagement in PISA 2003.* Paris, OECD.

OECD-CERI. 1999. *Education Policy Analysis, 1999.* Paris, OECD.

OECD-DAC. 2000. *DAC Statistical Reporting Directives.* (DCD/DAC [2000] 10.)

— 2005a. *Harmonising Donor Practices for Effective Aid Delivery. Vol. 2.* Paris, OECD. (DAC Guidelines and Reference Series.)

— 2005b. *Paris Declaration on Aid Effectiveness: Harmonization, Alignment, Results and Mutual Accountability. High Level Forum on Aid Effectiveness,* Paris, 28 February–2 March.

— 2006a. *Aid Harmonisation and Alignment Directory.* Paris, OECD.

— 2006b. *Development Cooperation Report 2005.* Paris, OECD. (OECD Journal on Development.)

— 2006c. *International Development Statistics, Online Databases on Aid and Other Resource Flows.* www.oecd.org/dac/stats/idsonline (Accessed 13 September 2006.)

— 2006d. *Managing for Development Results. Principles in Action: Sourcebook on Emerging Good Practice.* Paris, OECD.

OECD/UNESCO. 2005. *Policy Review Report: Early Childhood Care and Education in Brazil.* Paris, OECD/UNESCO.

OHCHR. 1989. *Convention on the Rights of the Child. Adopted and Opened for Signature, Ratification and Accession by General Assembly Resolution 44/25 of 20 November 1989. Entry into Force 2 September 1990, in Accordance With Article 49.* Geneva, Office of the High Commissioner on Human Rights. http://www.unhchr.ch/html/menu3/b/k2crc.htm (Accessed 2 August 2006.)

— 2005. *General Comment No. 7 (2005) Implementing Child Rights in Early Education.* Geneva, Office of the High Commissioner on Human Rights. http://www.unhchr.ch/tbs/doc.nsf/898586b1dc7b4043c1256a450044f331/dde31f35ffa9a51cc125712a0037d577/$FILE/G05 44829.pdf

Offord Center for Child Studies. 2005. *School Readiness to Learn (SRL) Project. EDI Factsheet,* Hamilton, Ont. http://www.offordcentre.com/readiness/EDI_factsheet.html (Accessed 29 March 2006.)

Olmsted, P. P. and Montie, J. (eds). 2001. *Early Childhood Settings in 15 Countries: What Are Their Structural Characteristics? The IEA Pre-primary Project, Phase 2.* Ypsilanti, Mich., High/Scope Press.

Olusanya, B. 2001. Early detection of hearing impairment in a developing country: what options? *Audiology,* Vol. 40, pp. 141-7.

Organization of African Unity. 1990. *African Charter on the Rights and Welfare of the Child, OAU.* (Doc CAB/LEG/24.9/49.)

Packer, S. 2006. Joint Monitoring Review missions in the education sector: an introductory note. Background paper for *EFA Global Monitoring Report* 2007.

Pakistan Ministry of Education. 2003. *National Plan of Action on Education for All (2001-2015)*. Karachi, Ministry of Education.

Penn, H. 2005. *Unequal Childhoods: Young Children's Lives in Poor Countries*. London and New York, Routledge. (Contesting Early Childhood Series.)

— 2006. *Contesting Early Childhood: Unequal Childhoods*. Paper presented at Contesting Early Childhood... and Opening for Change Conference, London, Institute of Education, University of London, 11-12 May.

Pennels, J. 2005. *The Loipi Programme in Samburu District, Kenya*, International Extension College. (Revised draft.)

Philander, F. 2006. AIDs cuts teacher numbers. *New Era*, 6 April. http://allafrica.com/stories/printable/200604060279.html (Accessed 3 May 2006.)

Post, D. and Ling Pong, S. 2006. Where and why does economic activity conflict with academic achievement? An update based on the TIMSS study. Paper presented to the EFA Global Monitoring Report team. Paris.

Pratham Resource Center. 2005. *Annual Status Report of Education (Rural) 2005*. Mumbai, India, Pratham Resource Center.

Press, F. and Hayes, A. 2000. *Early Childhood Education and Care Policy in Australia*. Sydney, Institute of Early Childhood, Macquarie University. (Background report prepared for the OECD Thematic Review of Early Childhood Education and Care Policy.)

Pressoir, E. 2006. *Coordination du Développement et de la Mise en Oeuvre des Politiques* [Coordination of Policy Development and Implementation]. Paper presented at the ADEA Biennale on Education in Africa, Libreville, 27-31 March.

Project Ploughshares. 2003. *Children and Armed Conflicts 2003*, Waterloo, Ont., Project Ploughshares. http://www.ploughshares.ca/imagesarticles/ACRO4/Child_Soldiers_Map.pdf (Accessed 17 September 2006.)

— 2005. *Armed Conflicts Report 2005*, Waterloo, Ont., Project Ploughshares. http://www.ploughshares.ca/libraries/ACRText/ACR-TitlePageRev.htm (Accessed 2 August 2006.)

Prud'homme, N. 2003. Social protection for single-parent families, *International Social Security Association Conference, Towards Sustainable Social Security Systems*. Limassol, Cyprus, International Social Security Association.

Qvortrup, J. 1994. *Childhood Matters*. Avebury, UK, Aldershot.

Rayna, S. 2002. *La Mise en Oeuvre de la Politique Integrée de la Petite Enfance au Sénégal* [Implementation of the Integrated Policy on Early childhood in Senegal]. Paris, UNESCO. (UNESCO Early Childhood and Family Policy Series, 2.)

Rayna, S. and Brougère, G. 2000. *Traditions et Innovations Dans l'Education Préscolaire, Perspectives Internationales* [Traditions and Innovations in Pre-school Education: International Perspectives]. Paris, Institut National de Recherche Pédagogique.

Republic of Ghana. 2005a. *Consideration of Reports Submitted by States Parties under Article 44 of the Convention. Second Periodic Reports of States Parties Due in 1997*. Geneva. (Committee on the Rights of the Child, forty-first session, 9-17 January.)

— 2005b. *The Republic of Ghana Report to the UN Committee on the Convention on the Rights of the Child. Supplementary Report*. Geneva. (Committee on the Rights of the Child, Document CRC/C/GHA/Q/2/Add.1.)

Richards, M. and Light, P. (eds). 1986. *Children of Social Worlds*. Cambridge, Mass., Polity Press.

Robinson, C. 2004. *Out-of-School Adolescents in South Asia: A Cross-National Study*. Paris, UNESCO.

— 2005. Languages and literacies. Background paper for *EFA Global Monitoring Report* 2006.

Rose, P. 2003. Communities, gender and education: evidence from sub-Saharan Africa. Background paper for *EFA Global Monitoring Report* 2003/4.

Ross, K., Zuze, L. and Ratsatsi, D. 2005. *The Use of Socioeconomic Gradient Lines to Judge the Performance of School Systems*. Paper presented at the SACMEQ Research Conference, Paris, 28 September-2 October.

Rostgaard, T. 2004. *Family Support Policy in Central and Eastern Europe: A Decade and a Half of Transition*. Paris, UNESCO. (UNESCO Early Childhood and Family Policy Series, 8.)

Rwantabagu, P. H. 2006. L'éducation à la paix en situation post-conflit: cas du Burundi [Peace education in a post-conflict situation: the case of Burundi], *Colloque International Sur la Paix, Violences, Conflits et Perspectives de Paix en Afrique*. Yaoundé, 6-10 mars.

Sadker, D. and Sadker, M. 1994. *Failing at Fairness: How Our Schools Cheat Girls*. New York, Touchstone.

Sawada, Y. and Ragatz, A. 2005. Decentralization of education, teacher behavior, and outcomes: the case of El Salvador's EDUCO program. Vegas, E. (ed.), *Incentives to Improve Teaching: Lessons from Latin America*. Washington, DC, World Bank, pp. 255-306.

Sayed, Y., Subrahmanian, R., Soudien, C., Balagopalan, S. and Carrim, N. Forthcoming. *Education Exclusion and Inclusion: Policy and Implementation in India and South Africa*. London, DFID.

Schaffer, H. R. 1996. *Social Development*. Oxford, UK, Blackwell.

Schau, C. G. and Tittle, C. K. 1985. Educational equity and sex role development. Klein, S. S. (ed.), *Handbook for Achieving Sex Equity through Education*. Baltimore, Md., Johns Hopkins University Press, pp. 78-90.

Scheerens, J. 2006. *The Use of International Comparative Assessment Studies to Answer Questions about Educational Productivity and Effectiveness*. Paper presented at the conference on Liberal Education - International Perspectives, organized by The Liberal Institute of the Friedrich Naumann Foundation, Potsdam, 2-4 September, 2005. (Published as Occasional Paper, 12.)

Scheerens, J. and Visscher, A. J. 2004. *School Factors Related to Quality and Equity*. Paris, OECD. (PISA thematic report.)

Schindlmayr, T. 2006. We need a global treaty for the disabled. *International Herald Tribune*, 17 August 2006.

Schuh-Moore, A. 2005. *Meeting EFA: Honduras-Educatodos*. Washington, DC, Academy for Educational Development. (Educational Quality Improvement Program 2.)

Schweinhart, L. J., Montie, J., Xiang, J., Barnett, W. S., Belfield, C. R. and Nores, N. 2005. *Lifetime Effects: The High/Scope Perry Preschool Study through Age 40*. Ypsilanti, Mich., High/Scope Press.

Shaeffer, S. 2006. Formalize the informal or «informalize» the formal: the transition from pre-school to primary. *IIEP Newsletter*, Paris, Vol. XXIV, No. 1.

Shenkut, M. K. 2006. Ethiopia: where and who are the world's illiterates? Background paper for *EFA Global Monitoring Report 2007*.

Shepard, L. A., Taylor, G. A. and Kagan, S. 1996. *Trends in Early Childhood Assessment Policies and Practices*. Los Angeles, Calif., Center for Research on Evaluation Standards and Student Testing.

Shonkoff, J. P. and Phillips, D. (eds) 2000. *From Neurons to Neighborhoods: The Science of Early Childhood Development*. Washington, DC, National Academy Press.

Shore, R. 1998. *Ready Schools: A Report of the Goal 1 Ready Schools Resource Group*. Washington, DC, National Education Goals Panel.

Singer, P. W. 2004. *Children at War*. Washington, DC, Brookings Institution Press.

Sirota, R. 1998. *L'école Primaire au Quotidien* [Primary School Every Day]. Paris, Presses Universitaires de France.

Skipper, S. 2005. *Education for All: Uruguay's Integrated Approach to Include Children with Disabilities and Improve the Quality of Basic Education*. Paper presented at Comparative and International Education Society Conference "Beyond Dichotomies". Palo Alto, Calif., 22-26 March

Skolverket. 2004. *Pre-School in Transition: A National Evaluation of the Swedish Pre-School*. Stockholm, Skolverket [Swedish National Agency for Education]. (Summary of Report, 239.)

Social and Rural Research Institute. 2005. *All India Survey of Out-Of-School Children in the 6-13 Years Age Group*, SRI (A specialist unit of IMRB International). (Submitted to the Department of Elementary Education and Literacy, Ministry of Human Resource Development, Government of India/Educational Consultants India Ltd.)

South Africa Department of Education. 1998. National norms and standards for school funding, *Government Gazette*, Vol. 400. No. 19347, South Africa Department of Education.

Sperling, G. 2006. *Filling the Glass: Moving the FTI Towards a True Global Compact on Education, Testimony to Council on Foreign Relations.* Washington DC.

Statistics Canada/OECD. 2005. *Learning a Living: First Results of the Adult Literacy and Life Skills Survey.* Ottawa/Paris, Canada Minister of Industry/OECD.

Stephens, S. 1995. *Children and the Politics of Culture.* Princeton, N.J., Princeton University Press.

Sumision, J. 2005. Male teachers in early childhood education: issues and case study. *Early Childhood Research Quarterly*, Vol. 20, pp. 111-23.

Sylva, K., Melhuish, E. C., Sammons, P., Siraj-Blatchford, I. and Taggart, B. 2004. *The Effective Provision of Pre-school Education (EPPE) Project: Final Report. A Longitudinal Study Funded by the DfES 1997–2004.* London, DfES/Institute of Education, University of London.

Tabuslatova, S. 2006. Central Asia and Kazakhstan: regional overview of progress towards the EFA situation since Dakar. Background paper for *EFA Global Monitoring Report* 2006.

Taratukhina, M. S., Polyakova, M. N., Berezina, T. A., Notkina, N. A., Sheraizina, R. M. and Borovkov, M. I. 2006. Early childhood care and education in the Russian Federation. Background paper for *EFA Global Monitoring Report* 2007.

Teachers Resource Center Online. 2006*a*. *ECE Certificate Program*, Karachi, TRC. http://www.trconline.org/ECE-CP/ (Accessed 26 July 2006.)

— 2006*b*. *Our Services: Workshops at TRC*, Karachi, TRC. http://www.trconline.org/trcweb/trc/services_workshops.asp (Accessed 26 July 2006.)

Temple, J. A. and Reynolds, A. J. Forthcoming. Benefits and costs of investments in preschool education: evidence from the child-parent centers and related programs. *Economics of Education Review.*

Thomas, W. P. and Collier, V. P. 2002. *A National Study of School Effectiveness for Language Minority Students' Long-Term Academic Achievement.* Santa Cruz, Calif., Center for Research on Education, Diversity and Excellence. (Final report.)

Tomasevsky, K. 2003. School fees as hindrance to universalizing primary education. Background paper for *EFA Global Monitoring Report* 2003/4.

Torkington, K. 2001. *Working Group on Early Childhood Development Policy Project: A Synthesis Report*, Paris, ADEA.

Uganda Bureau of Statistics and ORC Macro. 2001. *Uganda DHS EdData Survey 2001: Education Data for Decision-making.* Calverton, Md., Uganda Bureau of Statistics and ORC Macro.

UIS. 2001. *Latin America and the Caribbean Regional Report.* Montreal, Que., UNESCO Institute for Statistics.

— 2006*a*. *Global Education Digest 2006: Comparing Education Statistics across the World.* Montreal, Que., UNESCO Institute for Statistics.

— 2006*b*. *Teachers and Educational Quality: Monitoring Global Needs for 2015.* Montreal, Que., UNESCO Institute for Statistics.

UIS/UNICEF. 2005. *Children Out of School: Measuring Exclusion from Primary Education.* Montreal/New York, UNESCO Institute for Statistics/UNICEF.

UK Department for International Development. 2005. *From Commitment to Action: Education.* London, UK DFID.

Umansky, I. and Crouch, L. 2006. *Fast Track Initiative: Initial Evidence of Impact.* Research Triangle Park, N.C., RTI International. (Prepared for the World Bank.)

Umayahara, M. 2005. Regional overview of progress toward EFA since Dakar: Latin America. Background paper for *EFA Global Monitoring Report* 2006.

— 2006. Early childhood education policies in Chile: from pre-Jomtien to post-Dakar. Background paper for *EFA Global Monitoring Report* 2007.

UN Population Division. 2005. *UN Population Prospects: The 2004 Revision Population Database*. New York, United Nations.

UNAIDS. 2006. *2006 Report on the Global AIDS Epidemic. A UNAIDS 10th Anniversary Special Edition*. Geneva, UNAIDS.

UNCHR. 2002. *Report of the Special Rapporteur, Katarina Tomasevski, Submitted Pursuant to Commission on Human Rights Resolution 2002/23*. (Advanced Edited Version, E/CN.4/2003/913.)

UNDP. 2002. *Human Development Report 2002: Deepening Democracy in a Fragmented World*. New York, UNDP.

— 2005. *Human Development Report 2005. International Cooperation at a Crossroads: Aid, Trade and Security in an Unequal World*. New York, UNDP.

UNESCO. 1990. *World Declaration on Education for All. Adopted by the World Conference on Education for All Meeting Basic Learning Needs*. Jomtien, Published by UNESCO for the Secretariat of the International Consultative Forum on Education for All.

— 1991. *World Education Report*. Paris, UNESCO.

— 1997. *International Standard Classification of Education (ISCED) 1997*. Paris, UNESCO. (BPE.98/WS/1.)

— 1998. *World Education Report*. Paris, UNESCO.

— 1999. *Statistical Yearbook 1999*. Paris, UNESCO.

— 2000a. *The Dakar Framework for Action: Education for All - Meeting our Collective Commitments*. World Education Forum, Dakar, UNESCO.

— 2000b. *World Education Report*. Paris, UNESCO.

— 2002a. *EFA Global Monitoring Report 2002. Education for All: Is the World on Track?* Paris, UNESCO.

— 2002b. *Integrating Early Childhood into Education: The Case of Sweden*. Paris, UNESCO. (UNESCO Policy Brief on Early Childhood, 3.)

— 2003a. *EFA Global Monitoring Report 2003/4. Gender and Education for All: The Leap to Equality*. Paris, UNESCO.

— 2003b. *A National Case Study of Services Provided for Children: Early Childhood Care and Education in China*. Beijing, UNESCO. (ECE case studies.)

— 2004a. *EFA Global Monitoring Report 2005. Education for All: The Quality Imperative*. Paris, UNESCO.

— 2004b. *Report of the Inter-Agency Working Group on Life Skills in EFA*. Paper presented at the Inter-Agency Working Group on Life Skills in EFA, Paris, 29–31 March.

— 2005. *EFA Global Monitoring Report 2006. Education for All: Literacy for Life*. Paris, UNESCO.

UNESCO Bangkok. 2005. *Advocacy Brief on Mother Tongue-Based Teaching and Education for Girls*. Bangkok, UNESCO Bangkok.

UNESCO-IBE. 1961. *Organization of Pre-Primary Education, 1961 Survey*. Geneva and Paris, UNESCO International Bureau of Education.

— 2005. *World Data on Education*, Geneva, UNESCO International Bureau of Education. http://www.ibe.unesco.org/countries/WDE/WorldDataE.htm (Accessed August 31 2006.)

— 2006. *Cross-National Compilation of National ECCE Profiles*. Geneva, UNESCO International Bureau of Education.

UNESCO-IIEP. 2001. *Using Assessment to Improve the Quality of Education*. Paris, UNESCO International Institute of Educational Planning.

— 2006. EFA GMR 07 - IIEP synthesis paper. Background paper for *EFA Global Monitoring Report* 2007.

UNESCO-OREALC. 2004a. *Education for All in Latin America: A Goal within Our Reach. Regional EFA Monitoring Report 2003*. Santiago, UNESCO Regional Bureau for Education in Latin America and the Caribbean.

— 2004b. *Inter-sectoral Co-ordination in Early Childhood Policies and Programmes: A synthesis of Experiences in Latin America*. Santiago, UNESCO Regional Bureau for Education in Latin America and the Caribbean.

UNHCR. 2006. *The State of the World's Refugees: Human Displacement in the New Millennium*. New York, Oxford University Press.

UNICEF. 2003. *The Millennium Development Goals: They are about Children*. New York, UNICEF.

— 2004. *First Steps. Maldives. Evaluation of ECCD Media Campaign*. Malé, UNICEF Maldives.

— 2005a. *Gender Achievement and Prospects in Education. The GAP Report*. New York, UNICEF.

— 2005b. *The State of the World's Children 2005: Childhood under Threat*. New York, UNICEF.

— 2005c. *TransMonee 2005: Data Indicators and Features on the State of Children in CEE/CIS and Baltic States*. Florence, Italy, UNICEF Innocenti Research Centre.

— 2006. *The State of the World's Children 2006*. New York, UNICEF.

UNICEF Moldova Country Office. 2005. *Influence of Parental and Family Factors on Child Development: Secondary Analysis of Data from the National Baseline Study on Family KAP (Knowledge, Attitude and Practices) in the Area of Early Childhood Care and Development (ECCD)*. Chisinau, UNICEF Moldova Country Office.

United Nations. 2001a. *General Assembly Resolution. Road Map towards the Implementation of the United Nations Millennium Declaration. Fifty-sixth Session. Item 40 of the Provisional Agenda. Follow-up to the Outcome of the Millennium Summit*. New York. (Report of the Secretary-General, A/56/326.)

— 2001b. *Resolution on Literacy Decade*. (Adopted by the General Assembly [on the Report of the Third Committee (A/56/572)], 88th plenary meeting.)

— 2005. *UN Millennium Development Goals*, New York, United Nations. http://www.un.org/millenniumgoals/ (Accessed 2 September 2006.)

United Republic of Tanzania Ministry of Education and Vocational Training. 2005. *Basic Education Statistics*, Dar es Salaam, Ministry of Education and Vocational Training. www.moe.go.tz/statistics.html (Accessed 29 August 2006.)

US General Accounting Office. 2000. *Early Education and Care: Overlap Indicates Need to Assess Crosscutting Programs*. Washington, DC, Government Printing Office. (GAO/HEHS-00-78.)

US Social Security Administration. 1999. *Social Security Programs throughout the World - 1999*. Washington, DC, Government Printing Office.

— 2004. *Social Security Programs throughout the World*. Washington, DC, Government Printing Office.

USAID. 2005. *General Budget Support: Key Findings of Five USAID Studies*. USAID, Washington, DC. (PPC Evaluation Paper, 7.)

Van der Gaag, J. and Tan, J.-P. 1998. *The Benefits of Early Child Development Programs: An Economic Analysis*. Washington, DC, World Bank.

van Ewijk, H., Hens, H. and Lammersen, H. 2002. *Mapping of Care Services and the Care Workforce*. London, Institute of Education, University of London, Thomas Coram Research Unit. (Care Work in Europe: Current Understandings and Future Directions, Consolidated report, WP3.)

Vargas-Barón, E. 2005. *Planning Policies for Early Childhood Development: Guidelines for Action*. Paris, UNESCO.

— Forthcoming. *Payroll Taxes for Child Development: Lessons from Colombia*. Paris, UNESCO. (UNESCO Policy Brief on Early Childhood.)

Vermeersch, C. and Kremer, M. 2004. *School Meals, Educational Achievement, and School Competition: Evidence from a Randomized Evaluation*. Washington, DC, World Bank.

Vogel, D. A., Lake, M. A., Evans, S. and Karraker, K. H. 1991. Children's and adult's sex-stereotyped perceptions of infants. *Sex Roles*, Vol. 24, No. 9/10, pp. 605-16.

Waiser, M. 1999. *Early Childhood Care and Development Programs in Latin America: How Much Do They Cost?* Washington, DC, World Bank.

Waldfogel, J. 2001. International policies toward parental leave and childcare. *Future of Children,* Vol. 11, pp. 122-43.

Wallet, P. 2006. Pre-primary teachers: a global comparison of quantity and quality. Background paper for *EFA Global Monitoring Report* 2007.

Watanabe, K., Flores, R., Fujiwara, J. and Lien, T. H. T. 2005. Early childhood development interventions and cognitive development of young children in rural Vietnam. *Journal of Nutrition,* Vol. 135, No. 8, pp. 1918-25.

Weikart, D. P. 2005. *A Brief History of the IEA Preprimary Project.* Ypsilanti, Mich., High/Scope Educational Research Foundation. (The IEA Preprimary Project Final Report: Cognitive and language performance at age 7, Draft Manuscript.)

Wells, G. 1985. Preschool literacy-related activities and success in school. Olson, D. R., Torrance, N. and Hildyard, A. (eds), *Language, Literacy and Learning.* New York, Cambridge University Press, pp. 229-55.

Westheimer, M. (ed.). 2003. *Parents Making a Difference: International Research on the Home Instruction for Parents of Preschool Youngsters (HIPPY) Program.* Jerusalem, The Hebrew University Magnes Press.

Wetterberg, T. 2004. *Gender Equality: Starting Young.* Swedish Institute.

Whitehurst, J. and Lonigan, C. 1998. Child development and emergent literacy. *Child Development,* Vol. 69, No. 3, pp. 848-72.

WHO. 2003. *Skills for Health. Skills-Based Health Education Including Life Skills: An Important Component of a Child-Friendly/Health-Promoting School.* Geneva, World Health Organization. (Information Series on School Health, 9.)

Willms, J. D. 2006. *Learning Divides: Ten Key Policy Questions About the Performance and Equity of Schools and Schooling Systems.* (Report prepared for UNESCO Institute for Statistics.)

Willms, J. D. and Somers, M.-A. 2001. Family, classrooms, and school effects on children's educational outcomes in Latin America. *School Effectiveness and School Improvement,* Vol. 12, No. 4, pp. 409-45.

Woldehanna, T., Mekonnen, A., Jones, N., Tefera, B., Seager, J., Aleumu, T. and Asgedom, G. 2005. *Education Choices in Ethiopia: What Determines Whether Poor Households Send Their Children to School?* London, Save the Children. (Young Lives, Working Paper, 15.)

Wolff, H. and Ekkehard. 2000. *Pre-school Child Multilingualism and Its Educational Implications in the African Context.* Cape Town, PRAESA. (Occasional Papers, 4.)

Wong, M. N. C. and Pang, L. 2002. Early childhood education in China: issues and development. Chan, L. K. S. and Mellor, E. J. (eds), *International Developments in Early Childhood Services.* New York, Peter Lang. (Rethinking Childhood.)

Woodhead, M. 1996. *In Search of the Rainbow: Pathways to Quality in Large Scale Programmes for Young Disadvantaged Children.* The Hague, Bernard van Leer Foundation.

— 2006. Early childhood care and education. Changing perspectives on early childhood: theory, research and policy. Background paper for *EFA Global Monitoring Report* 2007.

Woodhead, M., Faulkner, D. and Littleton, K. (eds). 1998. *Cultural Worlds of Early Childhood.* London, Routledge.

Woodhead, M. and Montgomery, H. 2003. *Understanding Childhood: An Interdisciplinary Approach.* Chichester, UK, Wiley.

World Bank. 2002. *User Fees in Primary Education.* Washington, DC, World Bank. (Mimeograph, review draft.)

— 2004a. *Millennium Development Goals: Under-Five Mortality Rate,* Washington, DC, World Bank. http://ddp-ext.worldbank.org/ext/GMIS/gdmis.do?siteId=2&contentId=Content_t13&menuId=LNAVO1HOME1 (Accessed July 13, 2006.)

— 2004b. *Reaching Out to the Child: An Integrated Approach to Child Development.* New Delhi, Oxford University Press.

— 2005a. *Expanding Opportunities and Building Competencies for Young People: A New Agenda for Secondary Education.* Washington, DC, World Bank.

— 2005b. *Implementation Completion Report on a Credit in the Amount of SDR 15.0 million (US 20 million Equivalent) to the Republic of The Gambia for a Third Education Sector Project.* Washington, DC, World Bank.

— 2005c. *World Development Indicators*. Washington, DC, World Bank.

— 2005d. *World Development Report 2006: Equity and Development*, Washington, DC/New York, World Bank/Oxford University Press. (32204.)

— 2006a. *Global Monitoring Report 2006*. Washington DC, World Bank.

— 2006b. *Swaziland. Achieving Education for All: Challenges and Policy Directions*. Washington, DC, World Bank, Africa Region Human Development Network. (Working Paper, 109.)

— 2006c. *World Development Indicators*. Washington, DC, World Bank.

— Forthcoming. *Implementing Free Primary Education: Achievement and Challenges*. Washington, DC, World Bank. (Education Sector Human Development Network Report.)

World Bank Independent Evaluation Group. 2006. *From Schooling Access to Learning Outcomes: An Unfinished Agenda. An Evaluation of World Bank Support to Primary Education*. Washington, DC, World Bank. (Conference edition.)

Wroge, D. 2002. *Papua New Guinea's Vernacular Language Preschool Programme*. Paris, UNESCO. (UNESCO Policy Brief on Early Childhood, 7.)

Yizengaw, T. 2006. Government-donor relations in the preparations and implementation of the education sector development programs of Ethiopia. Background paper for *EFA Global Monitoring Report* 2007.

Youdi, R. V. 2005. Protection et éducation de la petite enfance (PEPE) en République Démocratique du Congo (RDC) [Protection and education in early childhood in the Democratic Republic of the Congo]. Background paper for *EFA Global Monitoring Report* 2007.

Young, M. E. 1996. Progress for children. *Early Child Development: Investing in the Future*. Washington, DC, World Bank.

— 2006. *Measuring ECD*. Paper presented at the Colloquium on Measuring Early Childhood Development, Vaudreuil-Dorion, Que., 26-28 April.

— (ed.). 2002. *From Early Child Development to Human Development: Investing in Our Children's Future*. Washington, DC, World Bank.

Yulaelawati, E. 2006. *Report of National Examination of Equivalency Education*. Jakarta, Directorate of Equivalency Education, Directorate General of Out School.

Zafeirakou, A. 2005. How to provide education and care to all young children 0 to 7? Early childhood care and education in South East Europe: progress challenges, new orientations. Background paper for *EFA Global Monitoring Report* 2007.

Zambia Central Statistics Office and ORC Macro. 2003. *Zambia DHS EdData Survey 2002: Education Data for Decision-Making*. Calverton, Md. Zambia Central Statistics Office and ORC Macro.

Abbrevations

ACEI	Association for Childhood Education International
ADEA	Association for the Development of Education in Africa
AIDS	Acquired immune deficiency syndrome
AKF	Aga Khan Foundation
ALL	Adult Literacy and Lifeskills Survey
CENACEP	Centros de Aprendizaje Comunitario en Educación Preescolar
CERI	Centre for Educational Research and Innovation (OECD)
CGECCD	Consultative Group on Early Childhood Care and Development
CIS	Commonwealth of Independent States
CONFENEM	Conférence des Ministres de l'Education des pays ayant le français en partage
CRC	Convention on the Rights of the Child
CRS	Creditor Reporting System
CSTC	Community Skills Training Center (Ethiopia)
DAC	Development Assistance Committee (OECD)
DeSeCo	Definition and Selection of Key Competencies
DFID	Department for International Development, United Kingdom
DHS	Demographic and Health Surveys
DVD	Digital versatile disc
E-9	Nine high-population countries (Bangladesh, Brazil, China, Egypt, India, Indonesia, Mexico, Nigeria, Pakistan)
EC	European Commission
ECCD	Early childhood care and development
ECCE	Early childhood care and education
ECD	Early childhood development
ECDVU	The Early Child Development Virtual University
ECE	Early childhood education
ECERS	Early Childhood Environment Rating Scale
EDI	Education for All Development Index
EFA	Education for All
ESD	Education for Sustainable Development
ESDP III	Education Sector Development Programme III (Ethiopia)
EU	European Union
EUROSTAT	Statistical Office of the European Communities
FRESH	Focusing Resources on Effective School Health
FTI	Fast Track Initiative
G8	Group of Eight (Canada, France, Germany, Italy, Japan, Russian Federation, United Kingdom and United States, plus EU representatives)
GDP	Gross domestic product
GEI	Gender-specific EFA Index
GER	Gross enrolment ratio

GIR Gross intake rate

GNI Gross national income

GNP Gross national product

GPI Gender parity index

HIPPY Home Instruction for Parents of Pre-School Youngsters

HIV/AIDS Human immuno-deficiency virus/acquired immune deficiency syndrome

HOME Home Observation for Measurement of the Environment

HSRC Human Sciences Research Council

IALS International Adult Literacy Survey

IBE International Bureau of Education (UNESCO)

ICCPR International Covenant on Civil and Political Rights

ICDS Integrated Child Development Services

ICFES Instituto Colombiano para el Fomento de la Educación Superior

ICT Information and communication technology

IDB Inter-American Development Bank

IDS International Development Statistics (OECD-DAC)

IEA International Association for the Evaluation of Educational Achievement

IEA/PPP IEA Pre-Primary Project

IEQ Improving Educational Quality

IIEP International Institute for Educational Planning (UNESCO)

ILI International Literacy Institute

ILO International Labour Office/Organization

IMF International Monetary Fund

INEE Instituto Nacional para la Evaluación de la Educación

INEP Instituto Nacional de Estudos e Pesquisas Educacionais Anísio Teixeira

I-PRSP Interim Poverty Reduction Strategy Paper

IQ Intelligence Quotient

ISCED International Standard Classification of Education

JUNJI Junta Nacional de Jardines Infantiles (National Board of Kindergartens, Chile)

LAMP Literacy Assessment and Monitoring Programme

LDCs Least developed countries

LLECE Laboratorio Latinamericano de Evaluación de la Calidad de la Educación
(Latin American Laboratory for the Assessment of Quality in Education)

LSMS Living Standard Measurement Surveys

MDG Millennium Development Goal

MICS Multiple Indicator Cluster Surveys (UNICEF)

MoE Ministry of Education (or equivalent national body)

NCERT National Council of Educational Research and Training

NER Net enrolment ratio

NFE Non-formal education

NFE-MIS Non-Formal Education Management Information System

NGO Non-governmental organization

NICHD National Institute of Child Health and Human Development

NIER	National Institute for Educational Policy Research
NIPCCD	National Institute of Public Cooperation and Child Development
NIR	Net intake rate
OA	Official Aid
OBE	Open Basic Education
ODA	Official Development Assistance
OECD	Organisation for Economic Co-operation and Development
OHCHR	Office of the United Nations High Commissioner for Human Rights
OREALC	UNESCO Regional Bureau for Education in Latin America and the Caribbean
OVC	Orphans and vulnerable children
PASEC	Programme d'analyse des systèmes éducatifs de la CONFEMEN (Programme of Analysis of Education Systems for Francophone countries)
PEAK	Pursuing Excellence at Kindergartens
PIDI	Proyecto Integral de Desarrollo Infantil (Integrated Child Development Project, Bolivia)
PILL	Pacific Islands Literacy Level
PIRLS	Progress in Reading Literacy Study
PISA	Programme for International Student Assessment
PROMESA	Proyecto de Mejoramiento Educativo, de Salud y del Ambiente (Programme for the healthy physical, emotional and intellectual development of young children, Colombia).
PRSP	Poverty Reduction Strategy Paper
PTR	Pupil/teacher ratio
SACMEQ	Southern and Eastern Africa Consortium on Monitoring Educational Quality
SERVOL	Service Volunteered for All (Trinidad and Tobago)
SNNP	Southern Nations, Nationalities and People (Ethiopia)
STAR	Programme Student–Teacher Achievement Ratio Programme
TIMSS	Trends in International Mathematics and Science Study
TVE	Technical and Vocational Education
UIE	UNESCO Institute for Education (now UNESCO Institute for Lifelong Learning, UIL)
UIL	UNESCO Institute for Lifelong Learning
UIS	UNESCO Institute for Statistics
UNAIDS	Joint United Nations Programme on HIV/AIDS
UNDP	United Nations Development Programme
UNESCO	United Nations Educational, Scientific and Cultural Organization
UNFPA	United Nations Population Fund
UNGEI	United Nations Girls' Education Initiative
UNICEF	United Nations Children's Fund
UOE	UIS/OECD/Eurostat
UPC	Universal primary completion
UPE	Universal primary education
USAID	United States Agency for International Development
USSR	Union of Soviet Socialist Republics
WEI	World Education Indicators
WHO	World Health Organization

Index

This index is in word-by-word order. Page numbers in *italics* indicate figures and tables; those in **bold** refer to material in boxes. The letter 'n' following a page number indicates information in a note at the side of the page. The term 'ECCE' in subheadings refers to early childhood care and education. Definitions of terms can be found in the glossary, and additional information on countries can be found in the statistical annex.

2072

Education for All Global Monitoring Report

EFA Global Monitoring Report Questionnaire

Feedback please!

The **Education for All Global Monitoring Report** *is an independent report published annually by UNESCO. Please take a few minutes to respond to our questions and tell us who you are. We welcome your comments and suggestions.*

The questionnaire can be mailed or faxed (see address below); or you may fill it out electronically on the GMR website at ***www.efareport.unesco.org***

PERSONAL/PROFESSIONAL INFORMATION

Name:

Affiliation:

Address:

City: Country:

E-mail:

What is your main professional sector/activity?

EFA GLOBAL MONITORING REPORT

How did you find out about the GMR?

Have you seen previous editions?

Do you consult the print edition of the full Report?   the Summary Report?

Do you consult the web edition of the full Report?   the Summary Report?

Do you consult the CD edition of the full Report?   the Summary Report?

Explain how you use the Report:

YOUR OPINION

How could the Report be improved?

Statistical tables currently represent nearly half of the Global Monitoring Report.

Would it alter your appreciation of the Report if these were produced separately?

Comments or suggestions

GMR REGIONAL OVERVIEWS

Are you familiar with the regional overviews produced from each year's GMR?

Have you ever consulted a GMR regional overview?

If yes, was it the print edition?   The web edition?   Both?

Which region(s)?

Describe how you use the regional overview(s):

Comments or suggestions:

GMR WEBSITE

Have you ever visited the GMR website?

What were you looking for, and did you find it?

Have you ever consulted the background papers on the website?

Do you use the statistical tool to build your own tables?

How could the website be improved?

GMR NEWS ALERTS

Would you like to receive occasional Global Monitoring Report news alerts by e-mail?

If yes, please indicate your email address here:

(You are free to unsubscribe at any time)

ANY OTHER COMMENTS OR SUGGESTIONS

Thank you.

The EFA Global Monitoring Report Team
Paris, France

Mailing address and fax

EFA Global Monitoring Report Team
Attn: GMR Feedback
UNESCO,
7, Place de Fontenoy,
75352 Paris 07, France

Fax: +33 (0) 1 45 68 56 41
www.efareport.unesco.org
email: efareport@unesco.org